Forty-Two Lives in Treatment

The Guilford Psychoanalysis Series
Robert S. Wallerstein, Editor

Associate Editors
Leonard Shengold
Neil J. Smelser
Albert J. Solnit
Edward Weinshel

Forty-Two Lives in Treatment
Robert S. Wallerstein

In Preparation
Psychoanalytic Education: Selected Papers of Joan Fleming
Stanley Weiss, Editor

Object Relations Approach to Child Psychoanalysis
Paulina F. Kernberg

Forty-Two Lives
in Treatment

A *Study of*
Psychoanalysis and Psychotherapy

ROBERT S. WALLERSTEIN, M.D.

The Report of the Psychotherapy Research Project
of The Menninger Foundation, 1954–1982

THE GUILFORD PRESS
New York   London

Library of Congress Cataloging in Publication Data

Wallerstein, Robert S.
    Forty-two lives in treatment.

    (The Guilford psychoanalysis series)
    "The report of the Psychotherapy Research Project of
the Menninger Foundation, 1954–1982."
    Bibliography: p.
    Includes index.
    1. Psychotherapy—Case studies. 2. Psychoanalysis—
Case studies. I. Menninger Foundation. Psychotherapy
Research Project. II. Title. III. Series. [DNLM:
1. Mental Disorders—therapy—case studies. 2.. Psychoanalysis—case studies. 3. Psychotherapy—case studies.
WM 40 W198f]

    RC465.W35 1986   616.89'14'0926   84-22409
    ISBN 0-89862-325-1

To the therapists and the patients of The Menninger Foundation, whose work together provided the substance of this book,

and to

Judy, Michael, Nina, and Amy, whose care and commitment nourished and inspired it.

Preface

Like the 42 individuals whose stories it tells, this book has turned out to have many facets. It is the final clinical accounting of the Psychotherapy Research Project (PRP) of The Menninger Foundation, chronicling, over now a 30-year span, the treatment careers and the subsequent life careers of a cohort of 42 patients, half treated in psychoanalysis and half in equally long-term expressive and supportive psychoanalytic psychotherapies. The book is a combined process–outcome study of these intensive treatments. They have been examined from several perspectives (those of the patient, of the therapy and the therapist, and of the interacting external life situation) and over several points in time (focused as an Initial Study before treatment, a Termination Study after treatment, and a Follow-Up Study several years later); PRP is probably unique in the world of psychotherapy research in having obtained 100% follow-up information, which in a significant segment of the cohort has extended over the full 30-year span of observation. In this, and in other senses that will emerge in the reading of the book, PRP has probably been the most comprehensive as well as most ambitious psychotherapy research program ever conceived and carried out. Its theoretical framework has been psychoanalysis, and its theoretical goal has been to amplify, revise, and extend the theory of psychoanalytic therapy.

For reasons that will also become clear in the reading, however important the project may thus be for its contributions to the field of psychoanalytic psychotherapy research (and for the directions it may point toward for successor studies), it may also well turn out to have been a unique creature of its particular time within the historic development of the field and its particular place within the (probably unmatched) enabling ecology of The Menninger Foundation. For one thing, there have been advances in the substantive technology of psychotherapy research over the several decades since the creation of this project, with today's state of the art coercing toward different kinds of research designs. Other considerations that require accommodation are as varied as the precipitously escalated financing costs of team research; the changed social and economic context of the psychotherapeutic enterprise; the altered parameters of the mental health delivery system (with the need to rethink the rationale of the treatment sanatorium in the new world of "deinstitutionalized" mental health care); and the evolving new guidelines of the propriety and ethics of research with human subjects. All these factors together would make it well-nigh impossible to carry out this kind of psychotherapy research program with this precise design within any therapeutic setting or under any institutional auspices in today's world. Certain kinds of learning opportunities may thus turn out to have been unique and no longer available in the same way.

In addition, this book has also evolved into a casebook of psychoanalysis and psychotherapy. It describes 42 lives in treatment, and also before treatment and after treatment; each of the 42 cases, though referred to in a variety of places in different contexts throughout the book, is also described as a story in itself at one particular place in the book, and in a fullness that has unhappily become all too rare in contemporary clinical literature. Each case description has been written with the intent to enable the reader to grasp the nature of the patient and the illness, of the treatment plan and its execution, and of the treatment outcome over the short term and the long term. Most importantly, each is designed to illustrate the basis on which I believe the discerned changes came about or were brought about—through what operative mechanisms or interacting factors in the patient, the therapist and the treatment, and the evolving life situation. And, from this perspective, the book has also become a detailed specification of my conceptualization of the various change mechanisms operative in the expressive psychotherapies (preeminently psychoanalysis) and in the supportive psychotherapies. About the expressive psychotherapies, which are devoted to the interpretive uncovering and working through of intrapsychic conflicts, there is of course a vast network of psychoanalytic literature; about the supportive psychotherapies, devoted to repairing the ego's damaged or faltering adaptive and coping capacities, there has been a remarkable paucity of psychodynamic literature. As a collection, then, of comprehensively studied and described cases, and particularly in its illumination of the mechanisms of supportive psychotherapy, this book has turned out to have heuristic and conceptual values for our educational enterprise and for theoretical clarification and advancement—contributions that were not necessarily part of the original consciously elaborated project intent.

Accomplishing such multiply interlocking aims must clearly have involved the dedicated labor of many coworkers. Undertaking to credit their contributions here becomes far more than the dutiful listing of all the people whom authors usually ritualistically acknowledge in a book's preface as having played some helpful role in the evolution of the final creative product. PRP, because of the breadth and complexity of its design, was truly, from its start in 1954, the result of the collaborative activities of a committed and devoted band of clinicians and researchers, drawn together in this shared endeavor and working together as enduring colleagues and friends. Many observers have marveled at the organization of a project that made possible the study of an entire cohort of 42 patients over so long a time span without any attrition in the research population being followed. More impressive, however, to those of us within the project was the cohesion of the research group itself over its many-year span of data gathering—with essentially no losses. That may be a tribute to the group selection and composition, or to the special élan that came to imbue it, or to the intrinsic excitement of the shared intellectual adventure. It is probably a tribute to all of these.

The initial planning group and emerging steering committee for PRP consisted of Lewis Robbins and myself as cochairs and principal investigators, together with Gerald Ehrenreich, Bernard Hall, Lester Luborsky, Gardner Murphy, and Helen Sargent. A large group was recruited early to join with the planning group and to undertake the various research project tasks. Joining Gerald Ehrenreich in the psychological testing team were Irwin Rosen and Richard Siegal, and later Stephen Appelbaum. It subsequently fell to Stephen Appelbaum to write the 1977 book on the study of the psychological testing data that came from the project. Joining Bernard Hall and Lester Luborsky on the Termination Study and Follow-Up Study teams were Michalina Fabian, Ernst Ticho, and Gertrude Ticho, and later William Tarnower and Otto Kernberg. A group formed to study specifically the Situational Variables included Herbert Modlin and Mildred Faris, and then Harold Voth and Marjorie Orth. Harold Voth and Marjorie Orth later wrote the 1973 book on the role of situational or environmental factors in relation to change in psychotherapy. Helen Sargent was joined in the Prediction Study by Leonard Horwitz and Ann Appelbaum, and Leonard Horwitz then wrote the 1974 book on the longitudinal study of clinical predictions in psychotherapy. Helen Sargent was also joined by Lolafaye Coyne, the statistician for the project, in the semiquantitative aspects of the project study; this group was later joined by Otto Kernberg and Esther Burstein as well. Otto Kernberg, in turn, subsequently led the group of six coauthors who wrote the 1972 monograph reporting the statistical quantitative data and the mathematical facet theory results of the project. Martin Mayman joined the project to pursue his special psychological projective test interests, geared to the study of object representations and object relations. Rudolf Ekstein, Karl Menninger, and Ishak Ramzy all served as valued in-house senior advisors and consultants. Lastly, during the final data-gathering and data-analyzing years of the project, another new and large group of collaborators was recruited—David Beale, Francis Broucek, Donald Colson, Siebolt Frieswyk, Helene Gerall, Gerard Haigh, T. W. Mathews, Rowe Mortimer, David Rosenstein, and Sydney Smith. In all, 37 staff members of The Menninger Foundation participated in PRP over its 15-year active working span, with time allocations ranging from a few hours per week (for many) to major time or full time (for a few).

In addition, the project had 10 different official consultants over its life span—Karl Menninger, plus 9 others from outside The Menninger Foundation. Of these, John Benjamin consistently played the most important role, as regular visitor, as persistent methodological critic, as gadfly, as advisor, and as exhorter. Many of the design questions of the project took their shape in the crucible of the ongoing dialogues with him. Of almost comparable importance were the equally frequent visits of Wayne Holtzman, who inspired, helped forge, and gave conceptual warrant to the statistical techniques evolved to deal with the quantification possibilities of our clinical and subjectivistic data. For the particular foray into the application of facet theory and multidimensional scalogram analysis to our potentially mathematical data, we drew on Louis Guttman (in Jerusalem) and James Lingoes. Other consultants played more circumscribed but equally valued roles: David Bakan on issues of overall method and design; Merton Gill and Maxwell Gitelson on issues of clinical relevance and validity; Robert Holt on issues of research–clinical interactions; and Arnold Pfeffer on issues of follow-up assessment and meaning. The project would not have been what it was without the important participation of all these consultants, on the occasion of their many visits to Topeka; in one instance, a group from Topeka went to work with our data for several months in Jerusalem.

All of this took considerable sums of money. We were fortunate to obtain grant support from the Foundations' Fund for Research in Psychiatry; from the

Ford Foundation, during the brief window of opportunity during which that foundation was actively supporting mental health research; and from the National Institute of Mental Health (Research Grant No. MH-8308). Of course, we also had the constant support—financial, administrative, and moral—of The Menninger Foundation itself. The project was an official Menninger Foundation activity; in addition to the time allocated by it for the researchers' participation, the entire professional staff of The Foundation was enjoined to cooperate with the project in the study of those of their patients who were selected by the project as research subjects. In all, 37 investigators, 10 consultants, and over $1 million (in 1954 dollars and at 1954 salary levels) were brought together to make the project's work possible over its span of operation from its inception in 1954 until the completion of its active data gathering in the late 1960s.

The writing of this book was in its turn an equally large project, involving many people and the aid of much helpful circumstance. It was made possible primarily by the fortunate opportunity of two Fellowship years that I spent at the Center for Advanced Study in the Behavioral Sciences at Stanford, California. The first year, partially supported by a grant to the Center from the Foundations' Fund for Research in Psychotherapy, was in 1964–1965 when I was on leave from my position as Director of Research at The Menninger Foundation (and Principal Investigator of PRP). Though the data gathering on the patients' treatment and official follow-up careers was not complete in all instances, I spent the year basically in studying the several hundred pages of accumulated clinical and research data on each patient and summarizing these data into a clinical accounting on each one, ranging from 50 to 70 typescript pages for each—a documentation of that patient, that treatment, that course and outcome, and my conceptualization of what had changed and how those changes had come about. The rare second Fellowship year, partially supported by a grant to the Center from the John D. and Catherine T. MacArthur Foundation, came in 1981–1982, which was for me a sabbatical year away from my position as Professor and Chairman of the Department of Psychiatry of the University of California at San Francisco School of Medicine. The 17-year interval did provide the useful occasion to search out follow-up data on our research sample at almost the 30-year mark—actually an unparalleled research opportunity, which was pursued surprisingly successfully. This second Fellowship year was spent in creating the manuscript of this book from the write-ups that I had done in the earlier period on the individual cases.

In this writing task, I had very important, even indispensable, help. Margaret Amara, librarian at the Center for Advanced Study, and her assistant, Bruce Harley, were able to provide all the library and bibliographic help and resources that I required with unfailing promptness, accuracy, and friendliness. Irwin Rosen, still at The Menninger Foundation, and a member of the original PRP core group, was a constantly willing liaison in ferreting out current follow-up data on many of the patients. This involved search of the institution's clinical records, as well as personal contacts and inquiries within the network of The Menninger Foundation therapeutic community (staff, ex-patients, current patients, etc.). Sarah Heil Hunt and Mary Patton were the two PRP secretaries in Topeka who maintained the secretarial and archival work of the project and typed the original clinical case write-ups in 1964–1965. Kira Tiedgens, my present secretary, typed and corrected the entire manuscript of this book. She accomplished this with a combination of steady, punctual accuracy and willing cheerfulness that lightened enormously the otherwise often thankless drudgery of the undertaking. Robert Mnookin, Professor of Law at Stanford University, and friend and colleague during my second fellowship year at the Center, helped shape the legal and ethical considerations regarding the publication today, and in terms of today's research guidelines, of research data gathered two to three decades ago under different research rules.

Publication, too, has had its indispensable helpers. I owe the title of the book to Merton Gill, who from the time he was a site visitor for the original Ford Foundation grant application in the early 1950s has been a warm friend and friendly critic to me and to the project. It was he who was convinced and convinced me, back then, that I would bring this project and this book to successful completion and final publication now. James Blight, then an editor at The Guilford Press, was inspired by the conception and the execution of the book and vigorously promoted the happy marriage between my manuscript and publication by Guilford. Paul Friedman—lawyer and psychoanalytic student in Washington, D.C., and an expert in this area of publication ethics and legal liability—guided both my publisher and myself to a proper consideration of issues of disguising confidential personal material without distorting the clinical meanings and implications. To Marie Sprayberry's meticulous copy editing, I owe much of the linguistic clarity and directness that I think the book has; yet all of it has been accomplished in a way fully congruent, not just with my material and my contents, but also with my writing style and idiosyncratic idiom. Lastly, my publisher, Seymour Weingarten, in the process of publication has become a friend and colleague not just in this, but in other shared ventures.

And as is usual, but also correct, I need to say that with all these proper credits to so many colleagues and helpers—both in the carrying out of PRP at The Meninger Foundation, and in the writing of this book, which brings that project to its final closure—all the shortcomings of conception and of execution, must remain my own responsibility.

Robert S. Wallerstein, M.D.
San Francisco, California
March 1985

Contents

Section V. The Treatment Course: The Processes of Psychoanalysis and Expressive Psychotherapy

Section VI. The Treatment Course: The Processes of Expressive–Supportive Psychotherapy

Section VII. The Treatment Courses and Outcomes: Overviews

Section VIII. The Follow-Up Courses and Outcomes: Overviews

Section IX. What Have We Learned from These Cases?

Appendices

I

Preview and Rationale

So far, I have tried to indicate that essentially there are two kinds of research approaches to the psychotherapeutic process: the clinical, used preponderantly by practicing analysts and therapists; and the experimental, exemplified chiefly by clinical research psychologists. While changes are gradually taking place, it appears that clinical penetration and scientific rigor have varied inversely. Furthermore, the two approaches undoubtedly reflect the temperaments of the proponents. If the advances of psychoanalysis as a therapeutic technique are compared with the experimental research contributions, there can be little argument as to which has more profoundly enriched theory and practice of psychotherapy. To make the point more boldly, I believe that, up to the present, research contributions have had exceedingly little influence on the practical procedures of psychotherapy. This, in view of the advocacy of more and more research, the expansion of facilities and the greater availability of federal and private financial support, is a deeply disquieting state of affairs requiring closer scrutiny. Why is this so? Why have research contributions had so little impact? Is it that they have nothing to teach the practicing therapist? Are therapists so impervious to scientific findings that they are unable to profit from them? Is our knowledge of the subject matter so rudimentary that at this stage research cannot possibly be expected to have left its mark on clinical practices? I raise these questions, not as a therapeutic nihilist but as a researcher who feels that important answers should come from research. But, I must confess that I am not fully convinced that they will. A closer look at the contemporary scene may not enable one to discern trends to forecast the future, but it may help to clarify the schism that divides practicing therapists and investigators doing research on the therapeutic process. (Strupp, 1960, p. 63)

This book is the story of the Psychotherapy Research Project (PRP) of The Menninger Foundation, an effort at a comprehensive natural history of (as well as formal research study of) psychoanalysis and psychoanalytically based psychotherapies. It is one attempt to respond positively to the lament — and the challenge — posed so thoughtfully by Hans Strupp, himself a distinguished member of that devoted band of pioneers in systematic and formal psychotherapy research. The volume is, at the same time, but one paradigm (see Wallerstein, 1977b) for such research study of psychotherapy as a human helping enterprise.

3

The Conception and Purpose of This Volume

HISTORY OF THE PROJECT

PRP was formally organized under the cochairmanship of Lewis L. Robbins and myself in 1954. Its stated purpose was to learn more about the nature and effectiveness of the everyday clinical work of the large, prominent clinical community gathered into the group private practice of psychotherapy and psychoanalysis, in conjunction with a psychoanalytic sanatorium (The C. F. Menninger Hospital), the varieties of intermediate care, and the outpatient facilities that together constitute The Menninger Foundation clinical community. Simply put, we wanted to learn more about *what* changes take place in psychoanalysis and in the range of psychoanalytically oriented psychotherapies (the outcome question in formal research design); we also wanted to learn *how* those changes come about, through the interaction of what constellation of factors or variables in the patient, in the therapy and the therapist, and in the patient's ongoing life situation (the process question).

Actually, a forerunner to the formally organized PRP was a proposal made by Paul Bergman in 1948, in which he, together with a group of like-minded Menninger staff colleagues, fashioned one of the conceptions of PRP—that of opening "windows" of access to the events of psychotherapy. That group also devised the first instrument of the later PRP, the 100-point anchored Health–Sickness Rating Scale (HSRS) during those precursor years (Watterson, 1954). Over the course of the first 4 years of formal project operation (1954–1958), very comprehensive "Initial Studies" were done on patients entering psychoanalysis and (psychoanalytically oriented) psychotherapy at The Menninger Foundation at the rate of one per month (other than during summer vacation), with the investment of about 40 hours each per month by the two collaborators in this aspect of PRP's work (Robbins and myself). For reasons to be detailed later, having to do with the design of the quantitative aspects of the project, the total sample size had to be a multiple of 6; when Robbins left Topeka in 1958, a total sample of 42 had had Initial Studies and were launched into their ongoing treatment course. In view of the tremendous time investments involved (or projected) for every aspect of PRP's endeavors, it was felt that this sample size of 42 was the maximum that could be properly encompassed within our overall project design. Though a very small number indeed for statistical studies of group-averaged similarities and dif-

5

ferences, it is a very large number for the comprehensive clinical study of each
patient that was built into the project design.

In keeping with PRP's commitment to a perfectly *naturalistic* research study
and project design (the various dimensions that comprise this "naturalistic" commitment are specified in Section II in detail), the treatments of the patients were
on a course of indeterminate, though expectedly long-term, duration, whether
they were specifically psychoanalysis or some less intensive (fewer sessions per
week) expressive or supportive psychotherapy. Patients who were designedly projected for *brief* psychotherapeutic approaches were among those excluded from
project participation; however, some of the patients terminated or disrupted their
treatments "prematurely" (in terms of our initial expectations and predictions),
and so we ended with a range of treatment durations from a minimum of only
7 months to a maximum of over 10 years before we could undertake "Termination Studies." Even so, in view of the funding and time constraints of even this
very long-range and seemingly unending project, a few Termination Studies had
to be done on a "cutoff" basis; that is, we had to assess these cases at a point of
a presumed stabilized plateau in a treatment seemingly going on indefinitely, with
the ongoing quasi-permanent nature of the continued psychotherapeutic support
being encompassed as one aspect of (and presumably an essential bulwark to?)
the degree of stabilized psychic functioning achieved by those patients to that point.

Following the Termination Studies, done at the point of actual or "cutoff"
termination (up to 1964), the patients entered the follow-up phase. In keeping
with the customs in cancer follow-up study, we would ideally have planned our
"Follow-Up Studies" at 5 years posttermination. Again, however, funding and
time exigencies pushed us to a compromised 2- to 3-year follow-up interval, at
which time we invited each ex-patient (and the significant relative, spouse, or other)
back to Topeka at our expense for a comprehensive Follow-Up Study, as much
comparable to our Initial Study as we could make it. The last formal follow-up
data gathering took place in 1966. However, in selected instances—through the
various happenstances of ex-PRP patients contacting their former therapists still
in Topeka, other Menninger Foundation staff members, or friends in the professional or the patient community—we have had more extended (though of course
less systematic) follow-up accountings, up to a maximum of 23½ years after treatment termination.[1]

---

1. In addition, for the purposes of writing this book, I have at this time (spring 1982) systematically contacted all the available ex-therapists of former PRP patients in order to inquire whether they have had any
post-Follow-Up contact with their former patients (beyond what was already in our PRP files through the
various routes already mentioned), in any official manner (therapeutic or consulting) or unofficially (through
social visit, mail, or phone call). From all sources combined, the following overall spans of information
have become available for use in this book: With 28 patients (two-thirds of the sample), there has been
enough contact with, or news of, the ex-patient for some assessment of subsequent life functioning. Four
are now still in ongoing treatment (a class we call "therapeutic lifers"); two of these are still at The Menninger Foundation, one of them is still in Topeka but no longer at The Menninger Foundation, and one
of them is with his original therapist but in a distant part of the country. It is now between 25 and 30
years since the onsets of those treatments. With 12 more patients, we have follow-up knowledge of various
kinds and in varying depth for periods ranging from 12 to 24 years posttreatment, averaging over 17 years;
this group includes 2 who have died of physical illness, 15 and 12 years after their treatment terminations,
respectively. And with 12 more patients, we have information over a shorter time span—from 4 to 7 years
posttreatment—including 2 persons followed to their death from mental-illness-related causes, in each in-

Carrying out this massive research undertaking enlisted the energies and time commitments (ranging from a few hours a week up to full time) of 37 investigators, almost all of them clinician–investigators; 23 of these carried major project responsibilities, sustained in many instances over the almost two decades of the project's formal data collecting and data analysis. The 37 all mentioned in the preface to this volume were first listed and given credit for their unstinting contribution of time, energy, and inspiration by Smith (in the introduction to Kernberg, Burstein, Coyne, Appelbaum, Horwitz, & Voth, 1972, pp. v–vi). I conclude the present chapter with a special tribute to two of the investigators (now deceased), Helen D. Sargent and Richard S. Siegal. Mention was also made in the introduction to Kernberg *et al.* (as well as in the preface here) of the 10 distinguished colleague consultants who helped guide our project through its shaping, its operating, and its data analyzing over its lifespan; the contributions of one of them (the late John D. Benjamin) are especially evident in the conceptualizing throughout the initial organizational sections of this book.

The project labors of this group of dedicated collaborators have to this point resulted in 68 publications, listed in chronological order as Appendix 4 to this book. Four of those publications are concluding books or monographs on various aspects of the outcomes of the project endeavors. In order of appearance, they are as follows:

1. The monograph by Kernberg *et al.* (1972) on the statistical and mathematical data of the project (titled somewhat misleadingly "Final Report," since it is the final report only of the quantitative aspects of the project work).

2. The book by Voth and Orth (1973) on the specific role of the Situational (or environmental) Variables in affecting the course and outcome of psychotherapeutic processes.

3. The book by Horwitz (1974) on the assessment of the predictions made at the point of Initial Study about the course and outcome of the projected therapy. Though there were only 42 patients in the study, the outcomes of about 1700 individual predictions (about 40 per patient) on the interacting effects of about 70 variables in three classes—Patient; Treatment and Therapist; and Situational—were encompassed in the Prediction Study.

4. The book by S. A. Appelbaum (1977) on the comparative study of the comprehensive psychological projective test battery devised by Rapaport,[2] as administered to the project patients, at the three cross-sectional points in time (Initial, Termination, and Follow-Up).

---

stance 7 years after the treatment termination. With the other 14 patients (one-third of our sample), our knowledge stops at the point of official Follow-Up Study. Of those 14, 4 died of mental-illness-related causes within our span of official observation; 6 had no further contact with either The Menninger Foundation or their former therapist after our official Follow-Up Study; and with 4 who had no further Menninger Foundation contact, the former therapist is unavailable, either having died (3 of them) or being gravely ill (1 person). The details and the specifications in all these cases are spelled out over the entire course of this book.

2. This battery includes the Wechsler–Bellevue Form I, the Rorschach Test, the Word Association Test, the BRL Object Sorting Test, the Thematic Apperception Test (TAT), and the Babcock Story Recall.

Two of these manuscripts were preceded by a number of years by multiple-authored monographs, with Sargent in each instance the senior author (Sargent, Coyne, Wallerstein, & Holtzman, 1967; Sargent, Horwitz, Wallerstein, & Appelbaum, 1968). The first of these was the statement of the plan, design, and sample handling of data for the quantitative studies; the second was the comparable statement for the Prediction Study.

All told, this project represents the very considerable work and output of a large group of investigators, held together by shared commitment over a very long span of time invested in what I think is the most intensively studied and systematically documented large collection (large in terms of intensive clinical study) of psychotherapy cases extant. It should be added that out of the hundreds of pages of records from the treatments and from the research studies made at the three designated points in time on each of the project patients, a summary document called a "Case Study" has been drawn up for each patient. Each Case Study begins by describing the nature of that patient, his or her life history, character structure, and unfolding illness picture, followed by the dynamic case formulation, treatment planning, and treatment prognostication. An accounting is then given of the treatment course and outcome through the treatment and follow-up periods (for however long they are documented). The Case Study ends with an overall synthesizing statement trying to account for what has changed and what has not (the outcome questions), and how things have changed, through what kinds of interactions among our three sets of variables — Patient; Treatment and Therapist; and Situational (the process questions). These Case Studies, all written by me, run between 50 and 70 double-spaced typewritten pages each; they are the resource data from which the accounts of the treatment and follow-up careers of the 42 patients that are given in this book are condensed.[3]

THE FOCUS ON THE CLINICAL ACCOUNTING

Given all this prior work and prior published output, what does remain that merits scientific presentation in this volume? What has not been written in this plethora of scientific reports from PRP is an overall statement of what we have learned *clinically* from the variety of cases studied, from each individually, and from the whole number in whatever logical subgroupings, about what happens in psychotherapy — and more, a statement of what we have learned from what has happened or not happened that could beneficially alter our technique and practice. In effect, the purpose of this volume is to responsibly address the questions posed in the quotation from Strupp (1960) placed as the opening statement of this section. It is a matter of taking the 42 detailed Case Studies that I prepared — summaries of all the data gathered by all the research investigators in the project at the several points in time (Initial, Termination, and Follow-Up) and from the standpoint of

---

3. The complete file of these Case Studies exists in three copies. One is in my own files at Langley Porter Institute, Department of Psychiatry, University of California at San Francisco School of Medicine. Another copy is in the files of PRP at The Menninger Foundation, Topeka, Kansas. We are planning to make the third copy available through the American Documentation Institute. Qualified scholars in psychotherapy research who desire access to this material can arrange it through contact with me at Langley Porter Institute, 401 Parnassus Avenue, San Francisco, California 94143.

the several sets of variables (Patient, Treatment and Therapist, and Situational) —and out of them fashioning a coherent clinical accounting of what we have learned about psychoanalysis and psychoanalytic psychotherapy as treatment modalities for the amelioration of psychiatric illness.

My *perspective* for this undertaking, in addition to the 42 overall case summaries that I constructed, derives from my ongoing central role in the planning, guidance, and execution of this project over its lifespan. As noted earlier, I served as cochairman and co-principal investigator of PRP with Lewis Robbins from 1954 to 1958. After Robbins's departure, I served as chairman and principal investigator from 1958 to 1966, when I in turn left Topeka (for San Francisco); I continued to act as senior investigator and consultant to the PRP group in Topeka through the years 1966 to 1972, during which period Otto Kernberg was chairman and principal investigator. My *warrant* for this undertaking derives from the central value accorded the *clinical* enterprise in our shared conceptualization, not just as the vehicle or the substance of the therapeutic activity, but also as the vital data base and data instrument of the research activity.

It was Helen Sargent who, more than any other individual, was the architect of PRP's overall method and design. In her major theoretical statement, "Intrapsychic Change: Methodological Problems in Psychotherapy Research" (Sargent, 1961)—embedded in considerations of philosophy of science and with comparative illustrations drawn from the developments of modern-day quantum physics— Sargent squarely placed the *clinical judgments* of informed and knowledgeable clinician–observers as the central *primary* data of clinical psychotherapy research. And such clinical judgments or clinical inferences, she averred, can be subjected to the selfsame rigorous scientific scrutiny as any other so-called "harder" direct observational or behavioral data; that is, interjudge reliability can be appropriately assessed, testable (and refutable) predictions can be based on them, and so forth. The reader is referred to Sargent's article for the justification, both in conceptualization and in the history and the philosophy of science, of this principled positioning of clinical judgments both as the primary data base and as a central avenue of access to research inference and research conclusion. This same issue is also discussed in detail, but from a different perspective, in a later article (Wallerstein & Sampson, 1971), where there is (among other considerations) explicated reference to Erikson's (1958) concept of "disciplined subjectivity" and Waelder's (1962) defense of the role of "introspection or empathy" in the handling of evidence and inference. Those arguments are not repeated here.[4]

---

4. I do want, however, to call attention here to Allport's (1937) comparable statement of an unswervingly clinical rendering to be made in his pioneering comprehensive accounting of psychological personality theory. He said,

> Similar is the case of the currently popular statistical methodologies. Many believe these are indispensable in supplying the factual ground for the science of personality. Sometimes they are useful; but many times they are not. In any event, mere arrays of statistics are never capable of self-interpretation. It is for this reason that I have preferred in most cases to state the results of research as clearly as possible in words, proceeding at once with the interpretation of the results. If the argument is sound, statistics can do no more than symbolize the fact; if the argument is unsound, statistical elaboration can never make it sound and may even increase the confusion. So, at a time when in many quarters mathematical symbolizing enjoys exaggerated favor, I prefer for clarity's sake to stick to the verbal method of exposition and argument, especially since it seems to me the only one wherewith to co-ordinate the field as a whole. (p. viii)

John Benjamin, in consultations with PRP in 1956 and 1957, [5] pointed to the particular strengths of PRP's design in relation to such a resolutely clinical approach to data evaluation. To begin with, in addition to our own explicit project focus on the study of the process and outcome aspects of psychotherapy, he pointed to another powerful, implicit, and even prior aim: to set out in detail systematic and well-documented accounts of the natural history of psychiatric illness and its psychotherapeutic treatment. Benjamin felt that to do this as systematically and as comprehensively as this on the scale planned by PRP, using well-trained (seasoned and experienced) and at the same time relatively impartial clinician–observers, would be in itself a singular contribution to the field of psychotherapy research, and one not to be slighted because of its obviousness. He felt this to be the only study he knew that provided such thorough evaluation by experienced clinicians at the several points in time, Initial, Termination, and Follow-Up. The strengths of PRP he pointed to in this regard were as follows:

1. We were using highly experienced clinicians as judges of the treatment processes and outcomes.

2. We were providing the research judges with a wide assortment of materials, including interview observations and judgments from several different people (the therapists, the supervisors, the patients, and the others as already mentioned), as well as the other kinds of material already mentioned (psychological tests, clinical records, etc.). All this would make it possible for the research judges to note consistencies and discrepancies among observers and observations in coming to their own assessments about the accuracy and the adequacy of the information going into their judgment matrix.

3. We were providing for interjudge checks of agreement at several points. These checks would allow us to state how well these experienced judges could agree with one another, and also (since we had verbatim primary data in the form of many recorded interviews) how well other judges brought in at a later point in time could agree with the present judges.

By contrast with this PRP organization, Benjamin felt the psychotherapy research literature to that point to be characteristically very limited in scope, usually only behavioral in data orientation, often untheoretical, and even, too often, essentially unclinical.

This statement of intent and of plan at this point, which some might consider uncompromisingly clinical, is not meant to diminish the values to be drawn from other, and even quantitative, approaches to psychotherapy research data where such approaches are appropriate. Lee Cronbach, in consultation to our project in 1962, discussed what he called three uses of statistics or quantifications in science. These are (1) heuristic, to help one organize one's data or to explore it as economically as possible and to learn as much from it as possible; (2) demonstrative, or communicative, to inform others concerning the nature of one's data; and (3) probative, or evidential, to establish that certain relationships exist beyond what is possible by chance. (Too often people think of statistics only in the "proving" sense, either trying to use statistics to prove things that cannot yet be proved

---

5. Detailed notes are available on these project consultations with each of our listed consultants.

in a quantitative way, or falsely assuming that if statistics cannot be used to amass proof, they have no place at all.)

I think that my statement as preface to the monograph on the quantitative aspects of PRP by Kernbert *et al.* (1972) states amply my convictions concerning the extent to which that book—in its write-up of the factor-analytic studies derived from the intercorrelational matrices based on the rank orderings at the different points in time of the different sets of variables, as well as in its discussion of the applications of Guttman's facet theory to our quantitative data using multidimensional scalogram analysis—has succeeded in carrying reasonably far the three kinds of uses of quantification described by Cronbach in our project conclusions. The reader is referred to Kernberg *et al.* to make his or her own assessment of how well PRP has been able to implement our design architect's (Helen Sargent's) "deeply held conviction that clinical operations can be subjected to quantifying techniques without doing violence to either the clinical concepts or the clinical data. [It was in accord with this conviction] that this whole search for, and development of, what we hope will be compelling ways of stating and demonstrating the findings of clinical research in mathematical form has taken place" (preface by Wallerstein to monograph by Sargent *et al.*, 1967, p. 243).

But at the same time there are sharp limitations, certainly within the extent of present-day knowledge, on the meanings that can be read into statistically derived emergents from our clinical research data. S. A. Appelbaum (1977) has addressed these issues directly in his book on the comparative study of the project's psychological test data. In Chapter 5, "Profile of Change: Factor Analytic Study of Patient Variables," he prefaces the presentation of his findings and discussion with an introduction in which he talks of "the innumerable combinations of intrapsychic variables which make up personalities, variables as dissimilar from one another as are their owner's thumbprints," He goes on to say,

> These combinations do exist in real life. Yet a factor analytic study of such data in no way confirms that the *post hoc* explanations for the factors which we offer are reflected in real life. They could be made to sound plausible whether they existed in the particular instances or not. This is simply another manifestation of the problem we encountered throughout the Project which stemmed from our ambitious objective of treating clinical data, in part, statistically. The reader may judge the plausibility of the clinical thinking which explicates the various factors recorded in the following section. (p. 221)

In the following chapter, in presenting 34 profiles of change clustered by using Ward's (1963) hierarchical grouping method, Appelbaum makes his point even more tersely: "As with the factor analytic study, clinical thinking which elaborates the statistical results may be plausible but not necessarily definitive or a guarantee that groupings are other than chance or artifacts. We do believe, however, that plausibility counts" (p. 227).

So much for the sketchiest statement of the place of numbers, pro and con. As has, I trust, been made quite clear, the present book, which is a clinical accounting, is essentially without numbers—and for that matter, without (experimental) manipulation of conditions or of data. I discuss this in more detail later, in the description in Section II of the premises of our naturalistic design. I want only at this point to call attention to the pertinence of two statements made by

Rapaport in his monograph, "The Structure of Psychoanalytic Theory: A Systematizing Attempt" (1960). The first occurs in his discussion of the "intrinsic validity" of Freud's reasoning and descriptive writing, which "often had to serve him as that indicator of validity which in older sciences is usually provided by quantitative measures" (p. 14). In footnoted reference to the phrase "intrinsic validity," Rapaport states: "By intrinsic validity I mean what literary criticism means when it speaks of a 'valid statement': the great writer achieves a form which makes the expression of his observations, feelings, and thoughts a 'valid statement'. But even in everyday life, some of us convey an experience so that it is clear, convincing, and pregnant with meaning, while the reports of others are pale, pointless, and diffuse, as if they were third-hand" (footnote, p. 14). It is this kind of "intrinsic validity" toward which the clinical accounting of this book strives.[6]

Rapaport's other statement critical to this discussion is a repetition of the often-made observation concerning the amenability of observation to direct manipulation as a requirement for scientific study. Of this, he says: "But manipulability is not an indispensable criterion; it may be replaced by observation (as in astronomy), or by seeking out 'nature's experiments' (as in evolution theory)" (p. 72). Of course, the extent to which psychotherapy can be considered a true "scientific experiment" and subject to the rigorous control and scrutiny that this term implies, rather than being more akin to "nature's experiment" and subject only to properly disciplined natural observation, has itself been the subject of some contention in the literature. That argument has been discussed elsewhere[7]; it is not germane in this context, where the claim to credibility necessarily rests on clinical and not on experimental *or* on statistical grounds.

SPECIAL MENTION:
HELEN D. SARGENT AND RICHARD S. SIEGAL

At the beginning of this chapter, I have spoken of the large number of investigators (37) as well as significant consultants (10) whose collective labors over a two-decade span comprised the activity and the productivity of PRP. I have also mentioned the succession of leadership over that same span. By way of concluding this chapter, I feel it highly appropriate to give very special mention to two individuals—Helen D. Sargent and Richard S. Siegal—who played central and indispensable roles in the fashioning of PRP, and whose labors in it were cut short by their untimely deaths before they could see the successful fulfillment of the undertakings that they had each, in different ways, so lovingly helped bring into being.

Helen Sargent, who died on her 55th birthday on Christmas Day, 1959, was (as already stated) more than any other single individual the architect of the design, the methods, and the instruments of the project. Because of her death at a very early stage in PRP's long history, she contributed, as sole or shared author, only eight of the project's large array of publications. Of those, only four appeared

---

6. See an extended development of these same issues in Wallerstein and Sampson (1971, pp. 18 ff).

7. See Wallerstein and Sampson (1971, pp. 13–14).

in her lifetime, three in the first collection of five papers in 1956 (Luborsky & Sargent, 1956; Sargent, 1956a, 1956b) and one in the second collection of three papers in 1958 (Sargent *et al.*, 1958). Her most important papers were posthumous. Two of these she finished herself (Sargent, 1960, 1961); one of them (1961) is the paper already referred to earlier in this chapter as the path-breaking paper for the whole field of this kind of clinical psychotherapy research.

Even more complexly majestic were Sargent's contributions to our two major formalized areas of research design. Her first contribution was in fashioning, from the usual elements of clinical judgments and prognostication that characterize the clinical enterprise, a formal, logical Prediction Study. This Prediction Study met all the criteria of generating testable, discretely defined individual predictions that could be confirmed or refuted via predetermined evidence set down in advance, in ways that avoided circularity, post hoc rationalization, or contamination of the judgmental process by knowledge of the predicted event, and in ways that (depending on the outcome of the prediction) could be circled back into strengthening or weakening the theoretical assumptions concerning the theory of psychoanalytic therapy that the predictions were designed to test. Sargent's second major contribution was in fashioning—out of the clinically congenial judgments of comparing two patients, two treatments, or two situations in terms of which has more than the other of any particular attribute or aspect at issue (her adaptation of the Fechnerian method of paired comparisons)—a structure of quantifying endeavors that could lead to profiles facilitating interpatient comparisons (singly and in groups), as well as rank orderings with (ultimately) quasi-cardinal properties, intercorrelational matrices, and factor analyses. And all of Sargent's work in both these areas—the formal, logical Prediction Study and the quantitative studies— originated in operations that were clinically congenial to and willingly undertaken by psychoanalytic clinicians.

These two major areas of contribution each eventuated in a monograph setting forth the conception and the design (Sargent *et al.*, 1967, 1968). In both cases the ideas and the plan were hers, but at the time of her death there were extant only bare sketches for manuscripts that were to be published. In both cases the monographs were finished for her; the way in which this was done in each case is detailed in the prefaces that I, as a coauthor with her in each of these undertakings, wrote for the two monographs. I ended one of those prefaces with the sentence: "We trust that these are all faithful to the common understanding that existed when Dr. Sargent was with us and are as she would have approved; if not necessarily just as she would have written" (Sargent *et al.*, 1967, p. 244). It took others—Horwitz (1974) with the Prediction Study, and Kernberg *et al.* (1972) with the quantitative studies—to present the project results in these areas and to complete the labors that Sargent started.

The third report from PRP in 1960, a collection of three papers, contains a fuller scientific appreciation of Helen Sargent and her role in our project (Wallerstein, 1960). Another paper, devoted more broadly to her overall position in the field of psychology, appeared in a professional journal elsewhere (Mayman & Sells, 1960). Every study that comes from the project, this book included, owes much to her.

The other special mention I wish to make is of Richard S. Siegal, who died in April 1967 when only 39, at an even earlier point in his career. Though not the originator of the project's psychological test studies, he was the clinical psychologist who most clearly grasped the great potential of the projective psychological test battery—administered repetitively before long-term treatments, at their conclusion, and once again at a several-year-later follow-up point. Siegal clearly saw the repetitive use of the battery as an unparalleled means by which to explore the tests as an instrument not only for assessing personality structure and functioning, but also for determining treatment-related change in structure and functioning, and thereby simultaneously for learning more about the tests and more about how treatment works. Siegal undertook to gather clinical psychologist collaborators (Rosen and S. A. Appelbaum) for this task, and, when stricken fatally ill, continued to the end of his active working capacity at the study of the tests and the work on the book that S. A. Appelbaum ultimately wrote for him (1977). That book is dedicated "To Richard S. Siegal. A small but significant cruelty of his lot was not to have been able to finish this book." Again, all the understandings that have come from the project, those in this book included, owe much to him.

The Congruence of Observation and Conclusion: Comments on Earlier Publications

The four concluding books or monographs already published on outcomes or results in various aspects of the project endeavors—the study of life situation and environment; the study of (repeated) psychological testing; the formal Prediction Study; and the study of the quantitative (statistical and mathematical) aspects— have already been mentioned. Each work, of course, represents the perceptions of its particular author(s); however, coming out of a vast pool of shared data and (varyingly) shared outlook, each work to some extent must also represent the project as a whole. I have, of course, been closely familiar with each publication in its creation as well as in its final shaping, and have the advantage of this overview (and of hindsight) in writing *this* book after all the other works and in the light of their contributions. At the same time it should be clear, given the particular data base used in each work and the particular focus and bias reflected in those who labored in that area of the total project design, that inevitably perspectives and conclusions might be reached within one framework and advanced in one book that might be at some variance with the perspectives and conclusions reached within another framework and advanced in another book.

It seems appropriate, therefore, that for orienting purposes, I briefly sketch out in advance at this point how I see this book and its focus in relation to those other books, outlining my perspectives both of general agreement and of disagreement. I return to all of these issues in more detail in the final section of this book, where I present my own overall conclusions in the light of the kinds of documentation that I am able to marshal in the body of my text.

THE ROLE OF THE ENVIRONMENT:
VOTH AND ORTH'S BOOK

I begin with the book by Voth and Orth (1973) on the role of the environment (or the patient's evolving life situation) in relation to assessed change over the course of therapy. I see their detailed presentation of the role of environment or situational vicissitudes as making two major contributions to the study of psychotherapy and its results. The first is a much-needed balance and corrective in the field. It is the proper fulfillment of Sargent's vision (Sargent, Modlin, Faris, & Voth, 1958) that the usual focus in psychotherapy research on the contributions of the interacting dyad of patient and therapist tends to overlook the often significant role played by the evolving and interacting environment or external life situation of the patient in either facilitating or limiting the conditions and possibilities for change. The entire book by Voth and Orth can be viewed as a filling-in of the vital importance of this often-overlooked dimension. I very briefly quote some of Voth and Orth's general or contextual remarks on this issue: "[R]esearch in psychotherapy has had difficulty incorporating the patient–environment dimension" (p. 2), and yet "psychiatric illness rarely, if ever, develops 'spontaneously' and . . . while unconscious forces are clearly the ultimate cause or source of the illness, the nature of the individual's interaction, that is, involvement, with his environment provides a clearer understanding of the illness and why it developed at a particular time" (p. 15). This, they say, is in one sense no more than a (documented) call "that clinicians might profitably renew their interest in the time-honored psychiatric concept referred to as the 'precipitating event'" (p. 25). Those who read Voth and Orth's book will all agree, I think, that they do make out a compelling case for their assertion that "When health is to be assessed one must ask the corollary question, under what environmental conditions?" (p. 87). Fewer, however, may agree with their perspective that the psychotherapists (and their supervisors) under study in PRP were as derelict as the wider therapeutic community in not giving proper attention and conceptual place to the role of the patient–environment interaction, both in providing understanding of treatment-induced changes and in exerting positive or negative leverage in regard to the reach and the limitation of those changes.

The second major area of contribution of the Voth and Orth book to which I wish to draw special attention is the strong documentation that often enough, or perhaps for the most part,

> patients in therapy or analysis should be treated when living in their usual life circumstances . . . the phrase generally refers to the commitments and responsibilities of the patient, particularly prior to and including the time he became ill. . . . Being in one's usual life circumstances provides a context for treatment and increases the patient's opportunities for better working through those conflicts which treatment exposes. This rule does not overlook the other clinical fact that if regression is severe, good treatment planning should include the removal of the patient from the circumstances which have overwhelmed him. (p. 84)

Clearly, this has often been a very salient treatment issue in the particular treatment situation at The Menninger Foundation: Many patients come to Topeka for treatment that is either not at all available in their home communities or not available there with the hospital and backup resources deemed necessary in their particular instances. Their treatment then gets carried out with separations (often prolonged) between the patients in Topeka and the families in the home communities (often distant). The point is real, and clearly psychiatric treatment carried out far from home in this way is inherently more problematic, especially "when the patient is living more or less in an environmental vacuum" (p. 85). Specific instances in which this particular issue raised by Voth and Orth has posed a major treatment problem are detailed in the present book, but so will instances of the opposite phenomenon—that is, cases where the treatment could be best carried out *only* with removal from the pathogenic environment and its illness-provoking and illness-maintaining pressures (see Wallerstein, 1973, pp. 13–14, for elaboration of that conceptualization). I do feel that in this regard the Voth and Orth book (despite the specific disclaimer quoted above) has been too one-sidedly focused on the dangers from the one direction, at the cost of blurring the (equal) risks from the other direction.

It is this very one-sidedness of emphasis that to me is at the root of the counterpart problem for advancement of knowledge in this field that is posed by the Voth and Orth book. There is, to be sure, a further disclaimer represented in the statement that theirs may be "an oversimplified view of psychogenesis. One can all too easily hold the environment directly or solely responsible for both the patient's illness and for his improvement or failure to improve during treatment or, conversely, fail to recognize the vital role the environment may have played in the patient's life" (p. 2). However, the central thesis of their book is that since "core-neurotic conflicts" were not thoroughly resolved in the overwhelming majority (perhaps in hardly any) of the patients in treatment with psychoanalysis and/or other psychoanalytic psychotherapy, then the improvements that did occur in a substantial number of the patients must have been due to the removal of "conflict triggers"[1] (i.e., situational factors). This conception is linked in turn to their (again one-sided) emphasis on the overwhelmingly central role of the dynamic interaction of "conflict triggers" with "core-neurotic conflicts" in both the pathogenesis of, and the mechanism of recovery from, psychiatric disorder.

Voth and Orth state their thesis as follows: "The process of decreasing the level or intensity of environmental commitment [either by 'shedding' of life responsibilities through illness, or through coming to Topeka, or as a consequence of treatment in some other way] appears to us to be the primary basis for the symptomatic improvements of many of the patients. This is not to say that other factors did not contribute to the symptomatic improvements" (p. 86). As I see it, this much-overstated emphasis on the role of one kind of witting or unwitting change mechanism—the "manipulation" of the patient–environment interaction through separation or disengagement of the conflicted individual from particular "conflict-triggering" circumstances or interactions—stems from the overly easy dichotomization of perceived change as being due only to "conflict resolution" *or* to removal of "conflict triggers." Many of the presentations of course and out-

---

1. "Degree to Which the Situational Factor Is Conflict-Triggering" is one of the Situational Variables, to be listed later. It is discussed in detail in Sargent *et al.* (1958, pp. 153–154).

come of psychotherapy in the present book illustrate numerous other mechanisms of change beyond those adumbrated by Voth and Orth.

This same point of the multiplicity of operating change mechanisms has been made, by each in somewhat differing ways, in the book by Horwitz (1974) on the Prediction Study and in the monograph by Kernberg *et al.* (1972) on the quantitative studies. In fact, Kernberg *et al.* take a quite opposite position on the role of specific environmental pressures and on the (beneficial) consequences attendant upon their mitigation, in a number of statistically backed statements. For instance, they assert that the initial levels of the Situational Variables have *no* predictive value for therapy outcomes (p. 50); in a statement from the mathematical facet theory study, they claim that no relationship can be demonstrated between outcome and all the environmental variables (p. 142). Their overall conclusion is that the role of the Situational Variables as codeterminants of outcomes can not be empirically demonstrated, and that this finding seems to reflect a variety of factors: (1) that the Situational Variables were theoretically less soundly based, since they were clinical conceptualizations that were originated *de novo* within PRP and had no history of either established clinical consensus and usage or of prior empirical testing; (2) that their relationships to the observable clinical data were less clearly understood; and (3) that they were found to discriminate poorly one patient from the other, particularly at the point of the Initial Studies (pp. 68–69). Kernberg *et al.* conclude from this that "the Situational Variables as conceptualized in this study did not provide sufficient basis to draw a final conclusion about their relevance to the study of the process and outcome of treatments conducted within the framework of psychoanalytic theory" (p. 69).

It should perhaps be reiterated that Voth and Orth do allow for some caveat to their thesis of the dichotomized either–or basis of treatment-related change when they say that such change may not have to reflect thorough conflict resolution: "Through supportive treatment the ego may have been strengthened so as to adequately contain the patient's unconscious forces when greater commitments are made. Therefore, assessments of the patient, using other methods, must be made alongside those which determine whether or not the environment continues to be conflict-triggering" (p. 69). But these assessments invoking "other methods" are no better specified by these authors than by such phrases as "spontaneous resolution of unconscious conflicts . . . within the protective bounds of hospitalization and long-term supportive treatment," or "managed to become more manly," or "emerged from an acute decompensation," or "picked an entirely different kind of man," or "surprised the research team by his capacity to marry and father children" (these are descriptions of five different patients, mentioned on pp. 73 and 74), or "Some internal changes had apparently occurred during this supportive treatment" (p. 78). Again, much of the present book is devoted to the effort to specify and delineate those "other methods" or mechanisms. To put it another way, I try to demonstrate the various ways in which a central thesis such as that of Voth and Orth serves to seriously underestimate the role, the values, and the multiple potentials for effecting desired change that reside in the so-called more "supportive" psychotherapeutic approach. As a necessary corollary to this whole point, it should of course be added that to whatever extent a patient's disengaging geographically and/or psychologically from pathologically conflict-triggering situations or relationships did take place and served to operate beneficially upon the patient's psychic status, there would of course still be the relevant distinction between the extent to which this favorable occurrence was just a fortuitous life happenstance or the logical consequence of a treatment-induced capacity to effect favorable changes in life circumstance.

I should mention one additional facet to this underestimation of the role and value of other factors than conflict resolution (i.e., underestimation of all the varieties of supportive psychotherapeutic mechanisms) as vital factors in producing change in treatment. Implicit in this underestimation is a value-loaded (verging on moralistic) and oversimplified equating of the concepts of what is "conflict-triggering" with what is "need-congruent,"[2] so that "need congruence," as defined by Voth and Orth in terms of the "need to mature" and to take an "appropriate" (i.e., responsible and committed) adult working or homemaking role and a heterosexual gender identity, becomes identical with what invariably turns out to be "conflict-triggering" to the mentally ill. And, *pari passu*, disengagement from these "conflict-triggering" forces in the patients who fail of conflict resolution in their treatments becomes seen as the vehicle to relieve the play of "need-congruent" forces that evoke their symptoms and their character and behavior disturbances. Here, too, I trust that the present book offers an alternate, broader conception of environmental need congruence (and need incongruence)—one that makes need congruence not just a statement of fit with an idealized, simplified, and value-loaded traditional conceptualization of "appropriate" masculine and feminine societal roles, but rather a broader conceptualization of the fit between the array of environmental pressures and opportunities on the one hand, and the array of the patient's maladaptive (neurotic) and adaptive (healthy) strivings (and their inhibition) on the other hand.

THE PSYCHOLOGICAL TEST DATA:
S. A. APPLEBAUM'S BOOK

Like the Voth and Orth book, the book by S. A. Applebaum (1977) on the comparative study of the projective psychological test batteries on the PRP patients at the three points in time (Initial, Termination, and Follow-Up), for the purpose of elucidating the role of specified Patient Variables as predictors of change, as determinants of change, and as criteria of change, has also made signal contributions—not just to its defined arena, but to the overall purpose and scope of the PRP as well. As is appropriate to the nature of its primary data source and the way of thinking about its data (in the so-called "Rapaport tradition"; cf. Rapaport, 1945, 1946), I see the major contribution of Appelbaum's book in the way that it, more than any of the other publications from the project, has self-consciously addressed issues of fundamental conceptualization (and, where necessary, of reconceptualization) of the variables that have been our clinical as well as our investigative working tools. It should be added that this task of conceptualization is equally vital to every other such program of systematic study of psycho-

---

2. "Congruence of Situations with Needs, Interests, Capacities, etc." is another of the Situational Variables, to be listed later. It is also discussed in detail in Sargent *et al.* (1958, p. 155).

logical phenomena and psychological change, whatever the theoretical perspectives adhered to by those who carry it out.

Illustrative of Appelbaum's approach is the fact that Chapter 3 (of the book's 10) — a chapter that assesses discerned change in each of the Patient Variables between the Initial and the Termination Studies, and that in each instance sets this change within the context of how that variable has been conceptualized within our project — occupies almost 50% of the entire book's text. An excellent illustrative example within this chapter of this (re)conceptualization of a Patient Variable is the discussion on p. 189 of "Extent of Desired Change," where Appelbaum starts with the original conception of the variable (set down in the initial presentation from PRP in the professional literature; see Wallerstein & Robbins, 1956) and then develops the need to rethink this formulation in the light of data and of considerations stemming from the perspectives that arose at Termination.[3]

Another and quite different area in which Applebaum's book has contributed to the total PRP structure, and more widely to the possibilities for psychotherapy research as a cumulative enterprise, is in its careful spelling out of the inherent problems in correlating the findings from one book on project results (his own on the psychological test data) with the findings from another (in the instance under discussion, that of Kernberg *et al.* [1972] on the quantitative data), despite the assumed commonality of theoretical perspective and the actual commonality of the patient population. In the particular comparison attempted — between psychological test ratings of Patient Variables, and the ratings derived from a modified Fechnerian paired comparisons method based on nontest clinical information — the correlations that emerged were quite low. Appelbaum adduces various possible reasons for this:

1. There may have been significant divergence in findings from the tests versus the other (interview) data sources.

2. The bases of judgment were different in the two instances: The test raters were explicitly rating change between their Initial and Termination test assessments, while the quantifying raters were using clinical write-ups of Initial and Termination assessments and applying statistical methods to establish the difference or change.

3. In one of the groups where different judges were used at Initial and Termination points (in order to avoid contamination of judgments), extraneous issues having to do with the presumed imperfect reliability between the two sets of judges could have been introduced.

---

3. The original Wallerstein–Robbins formulations of the variables formed the basis for most of the conceptualization of the Initial (predictive) full psychological test study of one of the project patients (No. 28, "Obese Woman"), which constitutes the overwhelming bulk — 53 pages — of Chapter 2 of the Appelbaum book. The process of reconceptualization of variables did not, however, start with the final Appelbaum book on the test data. It was preceded by a number of publications, most though not all produced by the group of clinical psychologists working with the psychological test protocol data. These included articles on Anxiety Tolerance (Siegal & Rosen, 1962), Motivation for Change (A. Appelbaum, 1972), Psychological-Mindedness (S. A. Appelbaum, 1973), and insight (S. A. Appelbaum, 1975, 1976), as well as the (abbreviated) glossary of idiosyncratically defined terms and concepts from PRP, published as Appendix 3 to the book by Horwitz (1974, pp. 349–361).

4. With many of the variables (especially those most based on theory, and thus most dependent on inference from observable data), the research testers and the paired comparisons judges could—despite all the care to prevent this happening—have been working from different understandings of the variables.

5. In a relatively small total sample size, just a few patients contributing a large deviation could have resulted in a nonsignificant finding for the group.

6. One or another set of judgments could simply have been faulty, in the sense of being poorly thought out, poorly linked to the data, and so forth.

What is the lesson of all this for the possibilities in psychotherapy research? It is, at its simplest, that at this stage of development of the field—both of psychotherapy and of psychotherapy research—each contribution should make its own statement of its own methods, its own data, and its own findings, and should not necessarily expect that these will always correlate well with findings from other contributors, even in regard to similar issues studied in relation to the same data base. This is a partially comforting and a partially very discomforting conclusion.

At the same time, the S. A. Appelbaum book is also one with which I want to draw out differences, especially in regard to what I feel to be an overemphasized point: the question of the *comparative* merits of psychological test data versus clinical interview data as predictors of treatment course and outcome. This is a scientific issue that can unhappily also shade over too easily into a linked political–economic issue of comparison between psychologist clinicians and psychiatrist clinicians. Chapter 8 of the book demonstrates quite convincingly the evidence that the clinical psychologists, who predicted treatment course and outcome on the basis of the projective psychological test battery alone, had a significantly better "batting average" for predictive accuracy than the psychiatrists, who made their predictive assessments on the basis of the totality of available clinical data (mostly interviews, of course, but also including access to the psychological test write-ups). That is, in a sequence of studies of the available data, in each study the research psychologist judging from test data was significantly more often in agreement with the criterion statements on issues of diagnosis, of treatment recommendation, and of predicted outcome than was the research psychiatrist judging from the total data, *including* the test write-up. It should be added that in just about every instance the discrepancy was that the psychologist working from the tests predicted a much lesser achieved change, based on a more solidly emphasized statement of difficulty and limitations; in contrast the psychiatrist working from the total data base predicted a more extensive range of achievable change, based on perceived potentialities within the presenting situation and the possibilities of the recommended therapeutic approach.

The findings of the Appelbaum book on this issue are quite unequivocal. What are the reasons that are offered? In his discussion, Appelbaum basically lists four:

1. The psychiatrists tended to ignore the clinical-psychological test report's findings of the severity of the patients' difficulties and chose rather to emphasize more hopeful indicators from nontest (interview) data as more compelling and/or more determinative of possibility for change.

2. The psychological testers were less involved with the patients personally than were the examining psychiatrists, and therefore were less subject to evoked ("rescuing") countertransferences or other interpersonally misleading effects.

3. Psychiatrists, who are less used to thinking in terms of "thought organization" as a central aspect of personality functioning, perceived fewer difficulties in this area and concomitantly made diagnostic errors, leading to overoptimistic assessments of the state of the patients' ego resources and of favorable indicators for the therapeutic task.

4. Psychiatrists, who are more intensely dedicated to a healing ethos as a centerpiece of their professional identity, were generally overoptimistic about the efficacy of their projected treatment efforts.

Because of these various factors, Appelbaum declares that overall a great deal of time, labor, and expense was wasted in the usual psychiatric case study: "The unvarnished fact of the matter is that major questions about these patients would have been better answered if the examinations had consisted solely of testing" (p. 260).

Without entering into discussion of the degree of cogency (or not) of each of these factors (and clearly they each do make a point), what additional perspective can nonetheless be brought to throw light on this issue? It is simply that there was yet another and perhaps even overriding factor in the (overoptimistic) judgments of the research psychiatrists, in their assessments of present status and prediction of future (posttherapy) status. This factor was a commitment, for each potential patient under consideration and for each prospective treatment plan, to think and to prognosticate in terms of its utmost reach — the best that it can do or could do — and then to try to see where and why it fell short of realizing this potentiality. This is, to me, not a matter of being poorer or better judges of illness severity or of treatment applicability, nor a matter of temperamentally or occupationally more optimistic or more pessimistic cast about the possibilities for personality change and illness amelioration; rather, it is a matter of strategic intent to pose what can be done under optimal circumstances and to see what we can learn from the extent that this is not achieved, and even perhaps to find new ways to try to narrow the gap between what is possible and what gets realized. I think that such a perspective could better take us away from the potentially divisive polemics to which Appelbaum's book can unfortunately be construed to lend itself.[4,5]

---

4. In stating this position, I have the crucial advantage and also disadvantage of being one of the two research psychiatrists (together with Robbins) who made the original clinical judgments and prognostications (from 1954 to 1958) that earned poorer "batting averages" than the later assessments and predictions done by others from the psychological test battery protocols. The advantage is that I feel I can speak confidently for what was self-consciously in our thinking at that time. The disadvantage, of course, is that my perspective can be seen as self-serving and exculpatory.

5. A very similar point has been made by a Philadelphia group of psychoanalytic psychotherapy researchers (Huxster, Lower & Escoll, 1975; Lower, Escoll, & Huxster, 1972), who were comparing the greater therapeutic optimism of the screening analyst in a low-cost psychoanalytic clinic center, who was directly evaluating potential patients for psychoanalysis, with the more guarded prognostications of the institute committee, which operated only from the secondhand written evaluation material. They noted that "the screening analyst is subject to the pressures inherent in his interaction with the applicant. He tends to respond positively, and in fact seems to look for appropriate reasons for accepting the applicant" (Lower *et al.*, 1972, p. 618), and that "examiners in a face-to-face situation are subjected to influences from which the committee members, who don't see the applicant, are shielded. We found one of the influences to be

THE PREDICTION STUDY: HORWITZ'S BOOK

I turn now to the Horwitz (1974) book on the Prediction Study, the tracing of the fate of the 1700 individual predictions (about 40 apiece for each of the 42 patients under study), together with the implications of the ascertained outcomes of these predictions for our psychoanalytic theory of therapy. Importantly for the reporting of findings and conclusions from large-scale and comprehensive psychotherapy research projects, the Horwitz volume has led the way (in which I trust to carry on) with an uncompromisingly clinical rather than statistical approach to the presentation of meaningful findings and persuasive conclusions. It has done this, incidentally, with elegantly composed vignettes that within a small space make the 42 patients come individually alive; these are all done interestingly enough so that repeated presentations of aspects of the same patients in relation to different issues do not become repetitive or boring. The degree of "intrinsic validity" achieved in the sense stated by Rapaport (1960, p. 14) becomes a matter of resonance with the clinical experiences of the informed reader.

A second and more substantive area of contribution of the Horwitz book to the field of psychotherapy research is in the support that it impressively marshals on behalf of its bold statement of overall conclusion: that within the realm of psychoanalytically based psychotherapeutic approaches, from the most specifically supportive to the most specifically expressive (like psychoanalysis itself), the supportive psychotherapeutic mode often accomplishes a good deal more than has been expected of it in terms of the heretofore conventional wisdom within the psychoanalytic perspective. This "more that is accomplished" can be in terms of amount, of kind, of duration, and of stability of change, and Horwitz makes an effort to understand the reasons and the mechanisms that account for that. To put it another way, supportive psychotherapies often seem to achieve changes (whether in amount, kind, etc.) approximating those that only expressive approaches with adequate "conflict resolution" and concomitant "structural change of the ego" have been anticipated to achieve.

This is put in the book's conclusion as follows: "Thus, in terms of the *extent* [and the word 'extent' could also be replaced by other indices] of change, supportive treatment has been underestimated by analytically oriented therapists as represented by our predictors" (p. 206). The counterpart is this: "Not only did the predictors underrate the potential influence of supportive treatment but they made the converse error of overestimating the necessity for conflict resolution in order to achieve certain results" (p. 208). The predictions that certain changes in various patients could only be achieved on the basis of a full working through

---

that of the interviewer's liking the applicant as a person and consequently wanting to see him accepted. We observed that this had on several occasions seemed to lead the examiner to make a recommendation in favor of acceptance for analysis, in spite of factual information in his own report which should have given rise to caution" (Huxster *et al.*, 1975, p. 91). Though the two situations (in PRP and in the Philadelphia setting) are not identical, the general point is enough the same, and for enough of the same reasons, that Bachrach and Leaff (1978), also writing from the Philadelphia group, could later state that "It [referring to the PRP data of the S. A. Appelbaum book] also confirms Huxster, et al (1975) in their claim that the subjective response of the interviewer is a major source of therapeutic overoptimism" (p. 898). My own way of assessing the basis of this kind of discrepancy has, of course, just been stated somewhat differently.

of the related underlying conflicts via the interpretive process earned the dubious distinction of garnering the highest percentage of *dis*confirmations (see p. 208). A whole linked set of questions on the stability of changes brought about via supportive psychotherapeutic means in the face of ever-changing life vicissitudes was again answered in the affirmative: At least within PRP's period of official follow-up inquiry, such changes proved (surprisingly?) sturdy.

What, then, do I point to as a possible limitation of perspective in the conclusions of the Horwitz book? It is precisely in the same area, that of explaining in the broadest sense the "bottom-line" basis for the surprisingly far-reaching and seemingly stable results obtained in many of the supportive (and therefore, less "ambitious") treatments, as against the counterpart failures of many of the more far-reaching reconstructive therapeutic efforts (the explicitly expressive psychotherapies and psychoanalysis) to achieve their predicted potential. Basically *the* major determinant of this significant degree of change in these supportive therapies is declared to be the capacity to develop, and the subsequent development of, a sound "therapeutic alliance." Horwitz puts it thus: "To the extent that a psychotherapy is supportive, the therapeutic alliance, with its various by-products, becomes both an end in itself and the *major vehicle* of the treatment. Thus, in a primarily supportive treatment the alliance is not only necessary, but often *sufficient*, for therapeutic change to occur" (p. 157, italics added). In regard to expressive therapies (and psychoanalysis), a far less sweeping and far less controversial statement is made: "The therapeutic alliance is a necessary, but by no means sufficient, condition for the success of the therapeutic process in psychoanalysis. It provides the framework within which the main work of the treatment, the development and analysis of a regressive transference neurosis, occurs" (p. 157).

Though Horwitz makes some effort throughout the text to develop some of the "various by-products" of the therapeutic alliance that he alludes to, in the direction of the delineation of a range of differentiated mechanisms that can be involved in determining change in supportive psychotherapeutic approaches, he seems unfortunately to place more emphasis on the therapeutic alliance per se. Moreover, he gives a particular and quite idiosyncratic meaning to that concept.[6] A strong or "positive" therapeutic alliance is linked to "a long-term supportive psychotherapy which excludes the negative transference" (p. 171), and this linkage is made explicit in the following question and answer:

> How is it possible to differentiate in advance between those supportive therapies which can be expected to ride smoothly and successfully on the positive transference from those cases where, despite the therapeutic efforts, the patients are unable either to repress or split off the negative transference elements? The differentiation would seem to be based upon a favorable balance of the internalized good and bad parental images, bolstered by some capacity to maintain the bad internalized object relationship in repression. (pp. 171–172)

That is, patients with some disposition (the favorable internal balance) to perceive benign object relationships in supportive treatments that afford a sufficient modi-

---

6. See Zetzel (1956b) for the original presentation of the "therapeutic alliance" in the psychoanalytic literature.

cum of need gratification will tend to develop a "therapeutic alliance" that is solid enough to be a sufficient vehicle to effect adequate and stable psychotherapeutic change—and without the need for interpretive work aimed to integrate negative transference dispositions, but rather with the "repression" or "splitting off" of such elements. Here again, I trust that the present book offers an alternative conceptualization of the *varieties* of change mechanisms operative in successful supportive psychotherapies. Put succinctly, my thesis is that a consolidated and successful "therapeutic alliance" is a necessary but by itself insufficient condition (or vehicle) for change in both expressive *and* supportive psychotherapies; in both types of therapies, there are *additional* specific operative mechanisms that account for the varieties of change and the varieties of bases for change, and these mechanisms differ in the supportive therapies and the expressive therapies. From my standpoint, the thesis developed in the book by Horwitz becomes a premature effort at oversimplified synthesis of an overall organizing framework for conceptualizing the mutative mechanism of all the diversity that is grouped under the rubric "supportive psychotherapy."

THE QUANTITATIVE DATA:
KERNBERG *ET AL.*'S MONOGRAPH

This brings me to the fourth of the outcome books from PRP published to this point, the monograph by Kernberg *et al.* (1972) on the (semi)quantitative data from the project. Here, as has been already stated, two basic approaches have been taken: (1) a statistical approach, leading to the extraction of factors by factor analysis from intercorrelational matrices of categories of variables (Patient, Treatment and Therapist, and Situational), rank-ordered via an adaptation of the Fechnerian method of paired comparisons at the three successive points in time (Initial, Termination, and Follow-Up); and (2) a mathematical but nonstatistical and nonmetric translation of 169 different variables (either scaled or dichotomized) via Guttman's facet theory analysis into a master mapping sentence of 17 facets, manipulated on a computer by the multidimensional scalogram analysis techniques devised by Lingoes. Mention has already been made of the place of these quantitative methods of analysis in the context of the total PRP contribution to this kind of clinical psychotherapy research, both in its potential reach and in its real limitation.

Here, I want to address the implications for the theory of technique, or rather for the altering of our conventional perspectives on issues of technique, that Kernberg and his coworkers have drawn from their quantitative work with the empirical data of PRP. Kernberg's theoretical writings on the psychopathology and the treatment of those sicker patients called "borderline" and "narcissistic," as gathered into his three published books (1975, 1976, 1980) in this field, are properly widely known in the psychoanalytic and psychiatric worlds. What is much less known is the extent to which his theoretical formulations have derived from his clinical experiences and his quantitative data work with PRP, as well as from his broader experience in the clinical context of The Menninger Foundation, an institution significantly dedicated to the psychoanalytically guided treatment of such "sicker" patients (with wider and deeper ego disorders) within the protective confines of a sanatorium setting, with a full panoply of care arrangements available.

The guiding reasoning in relation to these "sicker patients" that is developed in Kernberg *et al.*'s monograph is built on the quantitative data from the PRP patients treated in this setting. It is stated quite early as follows:

> These efforts [to focus on and work with the transference manifestations], maximal in psychoanalysis (a modality which strives to permit the development of a full-fledged transference neurosis), are minimal in supportive treatment (a modality which strives to reinforce defenses and prevent the development of regression). However, another important objective of supportive treatment is the encouragement of adaptive combinations of impulse and defense. We think adaptive combinations become more possible when the *negative transference is focused upon* and the therapist works with the pathological defenses related to the negative transference. This statement is particularly true in the treatment of patients with borderline personality organization whose severe negative transference predisposition mobilizes further pathological defenses in the therapeutic relationship. (pp. 44–45, italics added)

Further on, the authors suggest "a special form of modified analytic procedure or psychoanalytic psychotherapy . . . as the treatment of choice for patients with borderline conditions. . . . Unconscious factors would be considered and focused upon, especially in regard to the *negative transference* and to the consistent *interpretation in the 'here and now' of the pathological defenses* of these patients" (pp. 173–174, italics added). The total therapeutic prescription for these "sicker" (borderline) patients, then, is as follows: "[F]or the purpose of strengthening the ego it may be preferable to combine an expressive approach with relatively little structuralization in the treatment hours with concomitant hospitalization, rather than combining a purely supportive approach and highest structuralization in the treatment hours without hospital support. In more general terms, it may be that [for these patients] expressive psychotherapy is generally preferable to supportive psychotherapy" (pp. 168–169).

Supportive psychotherapy, as such, is in fact specifically declared unsuitable for such patients: "Supportive psychotherapy frequently fails because the characteristic defenses predominating in patients with borderline personality organization interfere with the development of the working patient–therapist relationship. When strong negative transference dispositions are not interpreted, these patients are prevented from accepting the supportive aspects of psychotherapy" (p. 184). In the face of this, what place do Kernberg *et al.* then leave for a predominantly supportive psychotherapy? They see two possibilities: One is "for basically healthy individuals overwhelmed by severe problems or anxiety temporarily paralyzing their optimal effective functioning" (p. 186), and the other is for "cases of chronic schizophrenia" (p. 186). They then state of both these categories, however, that "We had no such cases in our series" (p. 186).

One can readily see here the seeming stark contrast between these major clinical conclusions derived by Kernberg *et al.* from their study of the quantitative data of PRP, and Horwitz's major conclusion that the supportive psychotherapeutic approaches (which he essays to subsume under the umbrella concept of a successfully consolidated "therapeutic alliance") owe their success *precisely* to a "riding on the positive transferences," with the concomitant "repressing" or "splitting off" of (and specific avoidance of interpretive activity directed to) the negative transference components. In part, one can look at this as yet another striking example of the general problem described in S. A. Appelbaum's book—that is, failures of correlation between the findings and conclusions from one book in one area of project results and the findings and conclusions from another book in another area. From that point of view, one could regard even this dramatic lack of congruence of findings as not different in principle (i.e., in the kinds of factors that provide a framework of possibilities within which to endeavor to explain the perceived divergences) from the noncongruence already demonstrated between Voth and Orth's insistence on the overriding significance of engagement with or disengagement from "conflict triggers" as a determinant of treatment course and outcome, and Kernberg *et al.*'s inability to demonstrate any empirical relationship between any of the array of Situational Variables and any of the indices of treatment outcome.

I think that in this instance, however, a quite different and more consequential kind of conceptual consideration is involved. That is, in contrast to the relative conceptual clarity of psychoanalysis as a quite clearly demarcated psychotherapeutic method set within a well-articulated theoretical framework, supportive psychotherapy, even when limited to types that are psychoanalytically oriented or based, has never attained anywhere near comparable conceptual clarity. It encompasses many approaches; it also clearly means different things to different people, as witness Horwitz's *and* Kernberg *et al.*'s concepts of "supportive psychotherapy." I feel both of these delineations to be quite idiosyncratic and quite narrow, each in a different way. In the main bulk of the present book, I develop my own perspective—far broader, I trust, if less tidy—on the variety of ways of implementing a centrally supportive psychotherapeutic approach; I feel that this perspective can properly encompass as subsets the more particular (and, to me, far narrower) stances of both Horwitz and Kernberg *et al.*

Here I want only to quote from a discussion that I gave (Wallerstein, 1977a) of a presentation of Kernberg's entitled "Developments in the Theory of Psychoanalytic Psychotherapy," in which he developed this identical perspective on his "modified psychoanalytic" as opposed to "supportive" therapeutic approach to the borderline patient, from a clinical–theoretical rather than an empirical research perspective. I said in my discussion:

> [Kernberg] says that supportive psychotherapy (as he and I both have traditionally conceptualized it) fails whereas his new approach, embedded in object-relations theory built on incisive integrative interpretations [encompassing the negative transference dispositions] of primitive conflictual units of self and object representations together with a holding structuring of the patient's life, will succeed. I submit that what Dr. Kernberg is talking about is *bad* supportive therapy, in the sense of planless and conceptually unfocused, general almost do-gooding "supportive therapy" which it is true can only be variably and occasionally unspecifically helpful and thus often fails, in contrast to *good* supportive therapy in the best sense of the word which can combine this very kind of specifically needed integrating interpretive work together with the structuring of a supporting and controlling environment within which the expressive interpretive work can be received and sustained. To me, what he proposes is not a difference from what supportive psychotherapy is all about but rather a specification

of what it should be all about if it is to be a meaningful therapeutic modality at all and not just a variety of non-specific reassurance and transference gratification. (p. 13)

I only want to add in this present context what I try to develop throughout this volume — that what Kernberg has evolved is a specification of *one kind* of supportive psychotherapy, which he feels to be specifically geared to the therapeutic needs of a particular segment of the patient population. Unhappily, the kind of seeming conceptual and semantic unclarity that this whole discussion unfortunately reflects is at the moment too much the theoretical "state of the art" in psychotherapy (and in psychotherapy research). In the concluding section of this book, I specifically address the issue of "The Expressive–Supportive Dichotomy Reconsidered," in the light of the empirical studies of treatment courses and treatment outcomes to be herein presented.

POSTSCRIPT: THE CONCORDANCE OF THE CASES

This comparative overview of the findings and conclusions from the four major works from PRP that have preceded this one has referred a number of times to the common base from which they each have built: the intensive study of the same population of 42 patients in psychoanalysis and in psychoanalytic psychotherapy. To facilitate the going back and forth from the data and thinking of any one of these books to the others, as well as from all of them to this one, some shared convention on the common designation of the patients across the various publications should have been arrived at.

Unfortunately, such was not the case in the first four books. Voth and Orth designate the patients throughout their text by numbers from 1 to 42; then, in an appendix called "Case Histories," which occupies 257 pages (almost 75% of the total in the volume), they give a case-by-case "Synthesis of Situational Variables" in the sequential order of the number designations. Horwitz took a more imaginative leap in his book, with the creation of descriptive sobriquets for the patients. This practice has had an honored history in our field. Freud did it in two of his famous case studies, those of the "Rat Man" and the "Wolf Man," which have become famous through study by generations of students; in each of the two, the descriptive phrase refers to a central feature of the patient's fantasy system. In fact, a whole book has been written *about* the Wolf Man, including contributions *by* the Wolf Man himself (Gardiner, 1971). This same practice of Freud's was taken on more systematically in one of the first books on empirical psychotherapy research within a psychoanalytic framework, David Malan's *A Study of Brief Psychotherapy* (1963). (This book, incidentally, owes much of the structure of its design to a creative, simplified adaptation from our own psychotherapy project, which Malan came to visit and consult with when he was fashioning his project in 1959.) Malan's book contains very clear and compelling descriptive vignettes characterizing each patient; each is given a descriptive title, some of them charmingly English — "Articled Accountant," "Draper's Assistant," "Lighterman," "Storm Lady," "Student Thief," "Dog Lady," and the like.

Horwitz, following in this descriptive genre when he wrote his book, created phrases to capture something of the essence of each PRP patient — "Snake Phobia

Woman," "Claustrophobic Man," "Peter Pan," "Heiress," and so on. These designations then set the tone to Horwitz's own very aptly descriptive clinical vignettes as he presented the findings around the predictive outcomes with each case. I have for my purposes here, in the interests of both uniformity and dramatic representability, taken over Horwitz's designations, but have altered some of them. In some cases, I wished to make them even more precisely descriptive, as in changing "Bohemian" to "Bohemian Musician" and "Fencer" to "Intellectual Fencer"; in other cases, I thought a different phrase could better capture something central to the patient, as in changing "Playboy" to "Manic–Depressive Physician," or "Covert Addict" to "Sexual Masochist." I have, however, tried to keep these alterations to the minimal number that would enhance clarity and usefulness for the reader. To serve the purposes of easy transition from the designations in one book to those in another, Appendix 1 to this volume, "The Patient Code," lists the patients by number in accord with the Voth and Orth designations; opposite each number is the descriptive title from this book, and then (where it differs) the descriptive title from the Horwitz book.

Additionally, some of the other books, monographs, and articles from PRP have extensive write-ups of several of the patients. These are cross-referenced here as follows: The book by S. A. Appelbaum (1977) devotes 53 pages (almost 20% of the book) to a description of the complete psychological test data and inferences for one patient; this patient (with some demographic data altered in the interests of disguise) is No. 28 in the Voth and Orth book, and the "Obese Woman" in this book and that by Horwitz. The monograph by Sargent *et al.* (1968) stating the method for the Prediction Study devotes 70 pages (exactly half its length) to a description of the full prediction process for one patient, called there "Mrs. X.," with, again, some alteration of demographic data for purposes of disguise. This patient is No. 9 in the Voth and Orth book, the "Bohemian Musician" in this book, and the "Bohemian" in the Horwitz book. (The case material in this 70-page accounting uses verbatim almost precisely half of the Case Study that I wrote for that patient; as noted earlier, these Case Studies are the chief source for the presentation of data and the drawing of conclusions in the present book.) Finally, one article by myself (Wallerstein, 1968), an overview presentation to the third American Psychological Association Conference on Research in Psychotherapy held in Chicago in 1966, uses illustrative clinical material in considerable detail from one case to describe the state of the PRP at a point of "Semifinal View." The patient described in this overview is No. 5 in the Voth and Orth book and the "Adoptive Mother" in this book and that by Horwitz.

Conducting and Describing a Long-Term Psychotherapy Study: Questions and Issues

WHY THIS BOOK NOW?
AND THE STATE OF THE FIELD

There are always questions, at least implicit, concerning the scientific justification for publication, especially of books; such questions are heightened when the presentation of findings and conclusions is from data gathered in the course of a research study that was initiated some 30 years ago. In one sense, one can state, of course, that psychotherapy and psychoanalysis are in themselves long-term undertakings (in this project, some treatments studied ran over 10 years), and one can add that appropriate follow-up adds further years to the official span of study. One can then add the truism that a research study—the gathering of data, especially of such great volume, of such complexity, and over so long a span of time; analyzing the data in a variety of ways (clinical analysis, formal Prediction Study, quantitative study derived from the data of the paired comparisons); and writing all this up—also characteristically takes longer than originally projected. And all this then gives a certain comforting warrant to the long time span between the conception and inception of a psychotherapy project and the point at which final outcomes and results can be presented.

In these senses, psychotherapy research, if it concerns these kinds of long-term psychoanalytically based treatments, partakes fully of the usual problems of long-term growth and developmental studies—carrying out all that work, over all that time, while holding the research group generally intact enough to complete it.[1] It raises, too, an additional problem for the final write-up at the end: the fact that the field itself (whether it is psychotherapy or development) has itself moved significantly over that time span, both in terms of empirical work done and in terms of conceptual–theoretical advance. True, as compared with the natural sciences, the pace of movement and of change in psychotherapy is far slower, and the difficulty created by writing up today work that was undertaken nearly 30 years ago is less fatal—but it is nonetheless real. The field has moved, and so has the body of psychotherapy research.

Let me present just one reflection of this. The American Psychological Association sponsored a succession of three major Conferences on Research in Psychotherapy: in Washington, D.C., in 1958; in Chapel Hill, North Carolina, in 1961; and in Chicago in 1966. The proceedings of these were each subsequently published in book form (Rubinstein & Parloff, 1959; Shlien, 1968; Strupp & Luborsky, 1962). The first Conference brought representatives of eight major psychotherapy research programs together for scientific interchange; PRP, which had recently published its first sequence of five papers (Wallerstein, Robbins, Sargent, & Luborsky, 1956), was one of those invited to participate and make a scientific presentation. We were subsequently invited to make presentations at each of the succeeding Conferences. By the third Conference, there were 32 invited presentations, and two major sections that had not existed at the first Conference had been added—one on Behavior Therapy and one on Psychopharmacology in Relation to Psychotherapy.

On the other hand, at the time of this writing (the academic year 1981–1982), we are in a period of renewed and intensified interest in the scientific (and sociopolitical) study of psychotherapy of all modes, but perhaps in some sense especially of the avowedly more long-term, more ambitiously long-range and comprehensive, and more costly therapies. This is occurring in the context of the current wide-ranging debate in the social and political arena over the extent of appropriate coverage of psychiatric treatments (especially outpatient treatments) under both

---

1. This gets into all the problems of the sociology of psychotherapy research. I have written about this elsewhere (Wallerstein, 1966, pp. 509–511), and I also address these issues in this book at the end of Section II.

private and governmental health insurance plans; the related clamor, then, is for proper comparative outcome evaluation studies, for demonstrations of the safety and efficacy of psychotherapy, and (especially with the more costly treatment approaches) for demonstrations of cost-effectiveness.

Some of these pressures have been expressed in the demand that there be proper comparative Clinical Trials for each of the major proposed psychiatric treatment approaches (psychotherapeutic of various kinds, psychopharmacological, and others, either singly or in combination) to the array of mental illness categories. The National Institute of Mental Health (NIMH) has in effect responded to these pressures by setting up at great expense, over a considerable projected time span, and across a multiinstitutional clinical base, a study addressed to but one circumscribed disorder — depression — as comparatively treated by three reasonably circumscribed psychotherapeutic approaches.

I do not digress here into the scientific and also the ethical complexity of the Clinical Trials approach to the study of treatment outcome and effectiveness, let alone the almost insurmountable logistical and financial problems that would be involved in attempting to cover a whole field (mental illness) comprehensively and to assess the effectiveness in relation to each of the components of that field (the variety of mental disorder categories) of each of the treatment approaches that has an established theory, literature, and body of practitioners. These same issues have already been amply discussed in relation to the problems of clinical medicine and somatic illness. The proceedings of a distinguished review panel covering these scientific and ethical issues as confronted in clinical medicine have been recently published ("The Changing Scene in Clinical Trials," 1980).

My approach in this book is different: to contribute to the heightened current interest in, and dialogue centering around, the issues of the effectiveness of all the psychoanalytic psychotherapies by describing what transpires — and how effectively — when these kinds of psychotherapies are deployed with requisite diligence and skill in relation to that range of mental disorders for which they are felt to be appropriate. In that sense, the entire book is a statement about what we think can be learned about one kind of psychotherapy studied in accord with one research model (to be fully detailed in Section II). It is not meant to be a comprehensive statement about or review of the field of psychotherapy research as a whole or of its voluminous literature. That literature is indeed vast and has been amply surveyed any number of times. In 1964 Hans Strupp published *A Bibliography of Research in Psychotherapy*, and that endeavor, which he called "a reasonably comprehensive list of articles related [only] to *individual psychotherapy with adults*" (p. i, italics in original), comprised 999 titles. An update covering the period up to December 1967, prepared by Strupp and Bergin (1968) and incorporating the earlier list, comprised 2741 titles — almost a tripling over that short span of 4 years. Again, the focus was just on individual psychotherapy with adult patients. The rationale for that selective focus was explained in a critical review of the literature (its issues, its trends, and its evidence), published by Strupp and Bergin (1969b) under the title "Some Empirical and Conceptual Bases for Coordinated Research in Psychotherapy." The next issue of the same journal (Strupp & Bergin, 1969a) contained nine evaluations of the Strupp and Bergin article by psychotherapy researchers (two of them, Luborsky and Robbins, from our project), followed by a response from Strupp and Bergin.

Since then, there has been (as one might expect) a further almost exponential proliferation—not just of articles, but of critical, summarizing books, each presenting some aspect of the state of this rapidly burgeoning field. Among all of these, I only call attention to a few in order to follow a particular thread. In 1972, Bergin and Strupp published a book, *Changing Frontiers in the Science of Psychotherapy*, which reprinted all the material just mentioned from the two 1969 journal issues. It then reported the views of a widely divergent array of psychotherapy researchers (including Luborsky and myself from our project), who were visited by the authors and asked for their opinions—not just on the current state of psychotherapy research, but more pointedly on the future directions and prospects for the field. The central question that Bergin and Strupp carried to each of their interviewees was a request for an assessment of the readiness of the field for collaborative psychotherapy research studies across multiple institutions, multiple patient bases, and multiple theoretical perspectives through the use of consensually agreed-upon instruments and methods. The responses that they received (and recorded in the book) varied widely.

In 1975, NIMH, under the title *Psychotherapy Change Measures* (Waskow & Parloff, 1975), reported the results of a like-minded and parallel effort via a series of conferences to create a "core battery" of psychotherapy outcome measures that would be comprehensive enough and general enough ("general" in the sense of not being idiosyncratically linked to any particular theoretical position) that it might come into general usage in psychotherapy research projects across the country and allow for greater comparability in the assessment of outcome across the various studies. Again, several members of our project (Luborsky, Mayman, and myself) took part in the endeavor, either as a reviewer or as a participant in the Battery Conference. Again, the hope expressed by Hussain Tuma of NIMH in the preface has to this point been only very slightly realized: "We expect that the thoughtful application of the recommendations contained in this document will contribute to the development of a corpus of comparable data from a variety of psychotherapy investigators. Such information will expedite the progressive growth of cumulative knowledge in the broad field of psychotherapy" (p. vi).

A year later, in 1976, the outcome of another meeting—that of the American Psychopathological Association—was published under the title *Evaluation of Psychological Therapies* (Spitzer & Klein, 1976); at this meeting, "the participants . . . were required to present data, not mere speculation" (p. xiii). Here there was again the by now familiar set of groupings: Psychoanalysis and Psychotherapy (in which two of the presentations, by Kernberg and Robbins, were from our project); Aspects of Behavior Therapy; and Combined Drug and Psychological Therapies.

A very recent book by Smith, Glass, and Miller, entitled *The Benefits of Psychotherapy* (1980), undertook the highly ambitious task of finding and assessing "*all* the controlled studies of psychotherapy outcome [in the literature]; that is, *all* the research in which one group of persons was treated for psychological conditions and compared with another, roughly equivalent untreated group" (p. 4, italics added). Smith *et al.* subjected the data of these studies to a statistical summarizing method that they called "meta-analysis." The object of the meta-analysis was to give an integrated representation of the overall benefits of psychotherapy, doing so according to "a set of rules that can be specified and repeated so that prejudice and idiosyncrasy can fade into the background and the evidence can take its rightful place as the center of concerned attention" (p. 4). Happily for my intent in this present volume, their first major general conclusion was stated in their concluding chapter as follows: "Psychotherapy is beneficial, consistently so and in many different ways. Its benefits are on a par with other expensive and ambitious interventions, such as schooling and medicine. The benefits of psychotherapy are not permanent, but then little is" (p. 183). As might be expected, this book too has met a mixed reaction.

Finally, to demonstrate (if that be necessary) that this particular discourse is unending, I will only mention a specifically featured article in a recent issue of the *American Journal of Psychiatry*, entitled "Research on the Results of Psychotherapy: A Summary of Evidence" (Epstein & Vlok, 1981). No more of a reference to the vast literature already accumulated in the field of psychotherapy research is attempted here; each of the books or articles already referred to has its own listing of citations to the relevant literature, as does the present volume.

At this point, I rather turn very briefly to one other consideration that belongs here in answer to the question of "Why this book now?"; this has to do with its fit into the timing of my own life cycle. Most of the 42 Case Study documents— which, as noted, have served as my central data base for the presentations in this volume—were written by me during a first Fellowship year in 1964–1965 at the Center for Advanced Study in the Behavioral Sciences. In the years immediately following, I completed the write-ups on those dozen or so cases that had not yet come to official follow-up closure (though all had come to either actual or "cutoff" Termination Study by 1964). The opportunity to devote myself almost uninterruptedly to the writing of the present overview and clinical accounting—in the light of our fully completed studies on all the patients (including follow-up in one instance for as long as 23½ years), as well as in the light of all the sector summary books written in the major component areas of the project's work—was afforded me by the rare privilege of a second Fellowship year at the Center for Advanced Study, this one in 1981–1982.[2] I now need to turn to some of the complex problems that have arisen over this span of years regarding particular historical developments in this field of research and the social climate of research in general.

SOME SCIENTIFIC AND ETHICAL ISSUES

"Dated" Concepts and Language: A Problem?

I have already mentioned the fact that the field of psychotherapy and of research about psychotherapy has moved over the nearly 30 years that have elapsed between the first Initial Studies on the first patients taken into the project for study and the final clinical write-up now. Even a field as slow-moving and as seemingly "timeless" as psychoanalysis, with its telling literary habit of always returning to the wisdoms of Freud as the theoretical bedrock for whatever new proposition

---

2. The various vicissitudes of my own professional and academic life between these two Fellowship years are not germane to my purposes here, except as they again illustrate aspects of the sociology of psychotherapy research (or any other long-term psychosocial research), which, as I have already stated, is addressed in this book at the end of Section II.

is being advanced today, has seen major conceptual advances in the decades since the 1950s. We have only to think (just in terms of the American literature) of the integrations of the ego psychology development with object relations perspectives (Jacobson, 1964), of the developmental perspectives of separation–individuation theory (Mahler, Pine, & Bergman, 1975), of the evolving understanding of narcissistic disorders and the psychology of the self (Kohut, 1971, 1977), and of the delineation of the borderline personality organization and its treatment (Kernberg, 1975, 1976, 1980) to realize how much has changed since the mid-1950s in both the conceptualization and the language of our theoretical and clinical undertakings.

Precisely the problem that such major changes pose for longitudinal psychotherapy research was presented by Bachrach (1980) in a discussion specifically of our project (within an article devoted to the problems of psychoanalytic psychotherapy research in general) as follows: "The Menninger Project, for example, lavished great care on its assessment procedures and was built on the inspired ambitions and collective wisdom of the best in psychoanalytic and research thinking available *at the time*: But it required *two decades* to bring to completion and in the interim patients, therapists, and investigators had moved to different places and *the very nature of the clinical theory* it was designed to study had *undergone an evolution*" (pp. 111–112, italics added).

In terms of these new conceptions and their attendant new language, the Case Study documents written in the mid-1960s may in some sense sound "dated" when presented today in summary or abstracted form as illustrations of the various aspects of psychotherapeutically induced change considered in this book. To put it differently, those same Case Studies might be altered to some indeterminate degree, in language, in emphasis, in perspective, or in framework, if undertaken today in the light of the cumulated expansion of conceptualization over this span. The question of how much the cases themselves might be altered, either in our thinking about the patients or in our therapeutic interventions with them can certainly be a significant consideration in the reader's mind throughout the bulk of the clinical presentations that constitute the main body of this book. This is an especially pertinent issue in the discussion of the psychoanalysis of the Prince, an intensely narcissistic character.

However, though the Case Studies and the thinking reflected in them are cast in the idiom of "then," it is not as if there are wrenching discontinuities between the classical (ego-psychology-dominated) thinking of the 1950s and now. The fashionable emphases and formulations of today had their representations at that time as well. The concept of "borderline" patients as representing a broad and not clearly defined diagnostic grouping that partakes somewhat of the qualities and conditions of the neurotic and somewhat of the qualities and conditions of the psychotic—or, to put it differently, that often seems quite neurotic in functioning while unusually susceptible to psychotic or psychotic-like regressive sweeps and decompensations under conditions of psychological challenge—had already been well delineated in the pioneering paper of Knight (1953), himself one of the creators of the clinical thinking at The Menninger Foundation that served as a major part of the conceptual base for the PRP. And Kernberg (1975, 1976, 1980), identified today as the central contributor to our currently evolving formulations about borderline pathology and its psychoanalytic treatment, developed these ideas in part out of the object relations emphasis in his own psychoanalytic training background, and also in part (very importantly) out of his experiences with the patients in PRP and in the clinical ambience created by Knight and others. This thinking was, certainly in its beginnings, already reflected in our case protocols and in the formulations of conclusions and implications in the parts of the final project write-ups for which Kernberg took responsibility (as I have already discussed when presenting my own differing perspective on what we mean by "supportive psychotherapy" and how it relates to the treatment of precisely this group of borderline patients).

Similarly, the concern with the phenomena of narcissism and with their lack of conceptual clarity or of readily agreed-upon fit within the overall theoretical corpus of psychoanalysis has been with us ever since Freud's signal paper on that subject in 1914. This, too, has been a continuing focal point of theoretical and clinical interest. Within The Menninger Foundation milieu in which PRP grew, the contribution of van der Waals (1965) on that topic had a most influential impact. And Mahler's contributions in regard to early developmental stages and their relationship to some of the severer mental disorders go back to a whole series of papers from the early postwar years (see Mahler, 1952) through an earlier book (Mahler, in collaboration with Furer, 1968), and were well known to the psychoanalytic world through the whole period spanned by PRP. Perhaps somewhat less well known (in America) were the earlier contributions of the English object relations school (see Fairbairn, 1954, and Guntrip, 1961) before they were given new emphases here by Zetzel (1956a), Jacobson (1964), and Kernberg (1976). None of this is designed to deny the major conceptual clarifications and advances associated with the names of Jacobson, Mahler, Kohut, and Kernberg over recent years; rather, it is meant to indicate that the thinking that has come to fruition in their current work was not really entirely unknown earlier, or entirely foreign to the thinking that characterized the PRP group in Topeka and that was expressed in its formulations and case records.

Of course, it is not psychoanalysis alone but psychiatry too that has seen significant changes in its conceptualizations over this same period; for this context, I refer here particularly to its diagnostic and case-formulating understandings. We have moved from the era of the second edition of the *Diagnostic and Statistical Manual of Mental Disorders* (DSM-II) (American Psychiatric Association, 1952, 1968), an immediate post-World War II creation dominated by the broad psychoanalytic thinking that at the time was being incorporated wholesale into the psychiatric corpus under the banner of psychodynamics, to the current era of the third edition (DSM-III) (American Psychiatric Association, 1980), which seeks to strip the psychiatric diagnostic formulation of any presumed linkage to a particular theoretical perspective and at the same time to increase its precision and reliability through closer specification and narrowing of criteria (an atheoretical trend significantly influenced by the perspectives of the Washington University [St. Louis] school of psychiatry). In my view, the enhanced precision and reliability that DSM-III strives for may be purchased at the cost of an indeterminate loss of breadth, clinical complexity, and possibly validity. I should state here that the kind of diagnostic (and prognostic and therapeutic) thinking that characterized PRP in its clinical descriptions and in the diagnostic phrases attached like identifying tags to each of the patients stemmed from the more congenial (to the clinician) era of

DSM-II and has not been altered in any way to conform to the more precise (and narrower) criteria of DSM-III. In that sense, we did not establish diagnoses for our patients; rather, we arrived at diagnostic case formulations. Given the changes that psychoanalytic (or psychodynamic) thinking has undergone over these years, the thinking of PRP has remained unswervingly psychoanalytic. Despite the impositions of DSM-III as a system of diagnostic categorization for particular clinical or research or educational purposes, psychodynamic thinking remains as congenial to the general psychiatric and psychological readership today as it was all through the post-World War II period that was PRP's framework.

Ethical Considerations

Whatever the extent of these scientific issues of conceptual change and of adaptation to it wrought by the progression of the scientific knowledge base over this period, they are of far less importance to my immediate focus here than the profound changes in the climate of scientific research involving human subjects and in the conditions and rules governing it, which have become totally transformed over just the period covered by PRP.

As already has been stated, from its start in the early 1950s the project was committed to a "naturalistic study" of psychotherapy; I spell out in Section II all that such a commitment, *as we conceptualized it*, entailed in designing the research. This was done in large part for scientific reasons, which are indicated in the discussion of the various component features of our "naturalistic" study, but also to some extent for political reasons. In the climate of that time, and within a committed clinical community whose highest ethic was the commitment to the absolute primacy of the clinical treatment enterprise and the avoidance of any potential interference with it, intrusions into the clinical enterprise for research purposes, whether gross (in the form of audiotape recording) or more subtle (such as interpolating research-oriented interviews or questionnaires into the therapeutic stream), would have engendered intense and powerful resistance to the research study activity. The reasonably widespread acceptance of the possibility of introducing various research study instruments into an ongoing therapy, or even of recording it on audiotape (or, now, videotape), without necessarily vitiating the therapeutic process (though in some sense always affecting it or altering it) has been a phenomenon only of the most recent years, at least in analytic circles.[3]

In the PRP, the naturalistic commitment that was undertaken on both the scientific and political grounds indicated here, and that is more fully developed in the spelling out of the various features of that commitment in Section II, was carried to the extent of creating a design in which the research study of ongoing

---

3. There is now a body of psychoanalytic therapy research literature that deals with the scientific issues of the possibilities of conducting psychotherapy, even psychoanalysis, under conditions of, say, audiotape recording, without vitiating the unfolding of the therapeutic process (including the transference neurosis), while at the same time being mindful of the ways in which the therapy is thereby systematically affected, the manner in which this can resonate in different ways with the particular characterological issues in that patient (paranoid, masochistic, exhibitionistic, voyeuristic, etc.), and even the ways in which all this has been or can be successfully encompassed within the interpretive dialogue of the therapy. For my own discussion of these issues, see Wallerstein and Sampson (1971, pp. 21–26).

treatments (psychoanalysis and psychoanalytic psychotherapies) would be carried out not only with no research impingement *of any kind* on the clinical treatment activity, but in such a way that a treatment would go on throughout its entire course without the therapists' and the patients' even *knowing* that they were the subjects of a research study. The details of how we could do this, and did do it (successfully in all cases), are spelled out in Section II in the elaboration of the total PRP design.

Suffice it to state here that the Initial Study group for the research (Robbins and myself) could obtain the comprehensive clinical workups, case formulations, and treatment recommendation records from our medical record room on designated patients awaiting assignment to psychoanalysis or some other psychotherapy from The Menninger Foundation waiting list, and could then prepare comprehensive clinical assessments, research assessments, and research prognostications, without anyone other than a single medical records clerk's knowing which cases had been drawn for such study. Through a similar arrangement with another clerk, who kept records on terminating patients for the purposes of knowing who among the staff therapists would have time coming free for assignment to new patients from the waiting list, we were able to introduce *for the first time* the idea of doing a Termination Study of the now just-terminated therapy to therapist and patient alike *after* the therapy had completed its natural course. In other words, both therapist and patient had been unknowingly "drafted" into their participating roles in the study of the therapy that had transpired.

Of course, there could be clinical contraindications to the patients' participating in the retrospective research study of the treatment they had been through. When these could be satisfactorily substantiated according to agreed-upon criteria (to be detailed in Section II), they were unhesitatingly honored; in the few such instances that were raised by therapists and concurred in by the Termination Study research team, the patients were not even notified that a research study of their treatment was under way. In these few instances, a "truncated study" of the treatment, which did not involve direct access to the patients but which drew data from a variety of other sources, could be undertaken. There was only one project patient—the Fearful Loner, who was in ongoing psychotherapy at the time of "cutoff" Termination Study and was still in therapy at the officially designated Follow-Up Study point 2 years later (and gave indications of going on permanently, or at least indefinitely, in therapy)—whom it was felt to be clinically contraindicated to involve in the research project at both points, and who therefore probably never learned that his treatment was under intensive research study. (Even in his case, though, a very adequate "truncated study" could be accomplished, giving a picture of the transactions and achievements in his treatment that was quite comparable to those obtained in the overwhelming majority of the instances where the patients were fully involved and cooperated willingly with both the Termination and the Follow-Up Studies.)

In a few cases, although there was no perceived clinical contraindication to the patients' participation, the patients, once notified, refused to participate. We had two such refusals at Termination Study, the Suspended Medical Student and the Exhibitionistic Dancer, as well as a third, the Intellectual Fencer, who participated in interviews but refused to repeat the initial psychological test battery. Only one patient, the Suspended Medical Student, also refused participation at the Follow-Up point, but in his case too we had enough collateral information sources about not just his treatment but his posttreatment life to put together a very adequate treatment history.

The therapists who treated the designated project patients did not enjoy the same option to refuse participation in the project work. PRP was an official Menninger Foundation research activity, which received financial support from The Foundation in addition to the sizable extramural grant support it had garnered. Its plan had been presented for discussion at staff conferences, and those who worked for The Foundation in staff positions knew about the existence and working of the project and about their obligation to cooperate with it in all ways that would not be hurtful to their clinical commitment to their patients. In this sense, then, the therapists knew about the project while their patients did not. However, the project was only going to enroll 42 patients over a 4-year span; with there being some 250 to 300 patients in long-term therapies (psychoanalysis and psychoanalytic psychotherapy) at any one time, the likelihood was that in any given therapist's caseload, which could include 10 or more different patients, not more than 1 patient (or in some instances perhaps 2) might emerge at termination time as research project subjects. That this general awareness existed did not not seem to alter the general treatment climate within The Foundation in any way. It certainly *never* seemed to diminish the sense of surprise (and anxiety) that arose in each instance when a particular therapist was informed at termination time of our intent to do a Termination Study with him or her and a particular patient.

One other aspect of this way of organizing our "naturalistic study" is germane to the context of this discussion. As noted earlier, the Initial Studies, with all of their complex assessments, recommendations, and predictions, were done by two people—Robbins and myself. Again as part of our design, since a major part of the task of those who were to carry out the Termination and Follow-Up Studies would be to look for evidence to confirm or refute the initially made predictions, it was vital that they not be contaminated by knowledge of the precise predictions that had been made in relation to each of the different aspects of course and outcome that had been predicted, lest they shade the search for confirming evidence in wish-fulfilling ways. Therefore, the Termination Study and Follow-Up Study teams who would be (among other things) interviewing the patients and becoming well-known to them would not include either of us who had done the Initial Studies. For that reason—and also because, in the interest of keeping the research investigative group as separate as we could from the group of therapists of the project patients, we did not take any of our own therapy patients into the project pool—Robbins and I were at the time (and to this date remain) unknown to the project patients, except as they might be aware of us as members of the overall staff of the institution within which they were receiving their treatment. We were certainly unknown in our central role in the project and in their lives in treatment.

It must be very clear by now that nowadays (in the 1980s) such a project design could hardly be possible. Primarily, of course, it would now be considered improper to involve patients in a clinical research program without their thoroughly informed consent arranged ahead of time, and this stipulation is rigorously enforced by Institutional Review Boards or Human Subjects Review Committees (as they are variously designated) and insisted upon by governmental funding agencies. This means that this particular kind of naturalistic project design, if it indeed has the kind of scientific virtues that we hold it has—and these are spelled out in fuller discussion in Section II—can perhaps never be repeated.

How matters actually worked out when the secret was finally divulged at the Termination Study time has already been stated in part; a fuller account is given here. At the Termination Study point, 33 of the 42 patients were seen and participated fully in the interviewing and repeat psychological testing. As already indicated, 2 (the Suspended Medical Student and the Exhibitionistic Dancer) refused, and 1 (the Intellectual Fencer)[4] partly refused, permitting interiewing but not testing. Of the others, 1 (the Sociopath) had disappeared; 1 (the Alcoholic Doctor) had died while in treatment; and 4 (the Economist, the Housebound Phobic Woman, the Fearful Loner, and the Phobic Girl) were, for various clinically appropriate reasons, not seen. At the official Follow-Up Study point, 35 of the patients were seen and participated fully. A total of 4 were now dead: the Alcoholic Doctor, the Alcoholic Heir, the Car Salesman, and the Addicted Doctor. Of the remaining 3, 1 again refused (the Suspended Medical Student); 1 we felt it indicated not to interview or test directly (the Invalided Hypochondriac); and 1 (the Fearful Loner) was again not asked (being, as already indicated, the only patient in the sample who remained ignorant of his career as a research subject). As already stated, adequate "truncated" studies could be done in all these instances.

In all of this work at that time (the 1950s into the 1960s), we were as much guided by our sense of proper ethical and scientific considerations as any of us are today, albeit today within an altered context of what the boundaries of the "proper" are. At no time were research interests knowingly put ahead of the clinical interests of the patients and their therapists. Rather, the reverse was by policy *always* the case; in fact, a significant part of the scientific justification (to be elaborated in Section II) of our kind of "secret" naturalistic study was that in this way, the treatment that the patients came for and were receiving could in no way be affected because of research intrusion or even the knowledge that they were research subjects. And as part of safeguarding the patients' interests and privacy, we were committed to the absolute principle that whatever would be published from the project would be suitably disguised with all identifying data removed, so that we could be sure that no one else would be able to recognize the patients, whatever the details presented in terms of the treatment course and life course of the patients.

Over the years since the project's inception, a total bibliography of 68 items has accumulated (see Appendix 4), starting with the initial collection of five articles in 1956. In a very few of them, there have been rather extended individual case presentations, and these have already been mentioned (see pp. 19 and 28). Other publications have used group-averaged data handled statistically, like the monograph by Kernberg *et al.* (1972); or quite small piecemeal vignettes, like the book by Horwitz (1974) on the Prediction Study outcomes; or rather limited-sector accounts, like the book by Voth and Orth (1973) on the Situational Variables. Clearly, none of these has posed the same problems for publication that I face here today, with my intention of presenting a major *clinical* accounting of the treatment courses and subsequent fates of the entire sample of 42 cases, drawing on the de-

---

4. This makes it 34 who were actually seen in Termination Study, though in this particular instance not fully so.

tailed clinical material available in each case with as much specificity as necessary to establish my findings and conclusions in as persuasive a way as possible.

The issue I face today is how to proceed in this undertaking—whether or not to undertake to obtain the properly informed consent of the now ex-patients (whose actual treatments at The Menninger Foundation terminated between 15 and 25 years ago, with a very few exceptions of still ongoing treatment at the point that we closed off official Follow-Up contact), now that the properly informed consent of research subjects has become in the meantime a *sine qua non* of research conduct and publication. First, there are problems of situation. It is now nearly 30 years since the beginning of the PRP. When the cohort was taken into the project (1954–1958), the age range was 17–50, with an average age of 32. The range would today be nearly 47 to 80 and the average nearly 62. By the time we closed off contact, six patients were known dead (the four already mentioned by the time of official Follow-Up Study and two more, Peter Pan and the Suspended Medical Student, in the period subsequent to that about which we succeeded in gathering quite detailed information). The last official Follow-Up Studies took place in 1966, and the last recorded information we have officially within PRP files on any of the patients was in a long letter written by the Snake Phobia Woman to her ex-analyst in 1974, which he passed on to us. Clearly, if we located all the patients today, more of them (and/or their spouses) would now be dead; indeed, through my inquiries to the former therapists, I have learned of the subsequent deaths (of non-mental-illness-related causes) of two of the patients.[5] At the same time, incidentally, several of the therapists of these patients—many of them quite senior staff members of The Menninger Foundation when they treated them nearly 30 years ago—are now also no longer alive. Those concerned who are now living are at a much different point in their careers and in their life cycles, with all the varying vicissitudes of people's life course over nearly three decades.

If I were to take the course of obtaining informed consent, I would have to try to locate each of the ex-project patients and ascertain how many I could locate and what their present circumstances are, including how many they now are. Though Menninger Foundation patients, by virtue of who they are and how they characteristically get there, are more visibly located in their home communities (through family name or through business or professional status) than the usual highly mobile clinic population of lesser socioeconomic status, and though one of the conditions for inclusion in the project sample was that the patients be easily identifiable and likely to be readily available for later Follow-Up Study, tracking them each down after 30 years would nonetheless entail a considerable expenditure of money and effort, and clearly would not be completely successful.

Once the ex-patients were located, there would be the great expense and effort of my arranging to visit however many are today alive, wherever across the country (or possibly the world) they might be, in order to discuss with them what I am doing. I would have to explain how I—someone they have never met before—happen to know so much about them, or at least about their past; to show them what is to be published about them (which we can be reasonably sure they would want to see); and then obtain their informed consent to the publication, whatever

---

5. See footnote 1 to Chapter 1, pp. 6–7, for the detailed count on this latest effort at follow-up survey.

their possible personal discomforts or qualms, on the basis of their cases' imputed value to the scientific world and to the more informed psychiatric treatment of others like themselves in the future. Just because I am at this point a stranger to them, clearly I could not on the telephone or by mail give an adequate explanation of the enterprise; give appropriate and satisfactory assurances concerning the measures taken to guard against identifying disclosure, as well as concerning the tact and circumspection with which I would try to present material from their lives; or obtain the requested informed consent.

Clearly, also, should this tack of trying to elicit the informed consent of every locatable and available patient be pursued, the outcome would of course be variable. The great majority, who have after all participated before in the Termination and Follow-Up Studies of their cases (for all the varying reasons that motivate people at such times), and who of course were given to understand that the findings from the research were to be published at some point in the professional literature (with of course due safeguard for their privacy and the protection of their identity), would probably agree. An indeterminate number, perhaps only a small number (and this may or may not be a group critical to the illustration of one or another of the major directions of project findings), might at this point refuse for various reasons. Such an eventuality might or might not significantly impair the scientific worth that could be drawn from the whole sample if it were published in a completely untrammeled way. Untrammeled publication, however, could be seen as serving the interests of science, not necessarily those of the patients.

An additional consideration is that from the point of view of these ex-patients from so long ago, contacting them for the purposes of covering ourselves today with the now customary informed consent might itself not be in all cases a completely benign procedure. At the time of original Follow-Up Study, which in all cases the patients had been thoroughly prepared for at the same time of Termination Study as a request that we would be making, there was at least one patient (the Bohemian Musician) who, though eager to return for the study, stipulated that it be over a particular group of days when her new husband (she had met and married him during the 2-year interval since the Termination Study) would be away on a business trip. She indicated that he knew nothing of her previous (very severe) illness and her treatment, and it was important to her to keep her old sick life and her new healthier life totally apart from one another. It is this kind of situation that, perhaps rightly, should make us all take pause before we automatically or unthinkingly just go ahead and ask, in order to play it safe by today's new rules. Paternalistic or self-serving as such a line of reasoning can be construed to be, it is nonetheless worthy of consideration. Seeking out informed consent from all the locatable ex-project patients at this distant point in time would indeed be unpleasant and to some extent potentially psychologically disruptive to at least some of them, and this must be weighed in the balance in assessing ethically the good and the harm in this approach as against possible alternatives.[6]

---

6. For additional discussion of some of the possibly adverse consequences of the pursuit of informed consent, see the editorial by Loftus and Fries (1979) in *Science*, entitled "Informed Consent May Be Hazardous to Health." And for extended consideration of the ethical and cultural complexities of the informed consent doctrine, see the discussion by Cross and Churchill (1982) of such issues as "coerced consent," under the persuasive or manipulative pressures of the physician; "consent without hope," when patients are overwhelmed by potential complications and problems; "misunderstood consent," reflecting idiosyn-

What are such alternatives? Basically, the other main possibility is that of continuing along the way in which the project was originally conducted. It is to go ahead on the basis of its original assumptions: that we could carry out a research program as we designed it; that there were substantial scientific reasons for and scientific rewards in such a choice; that it could be done in an ethically responsible way that safeguarded the patients' interests and their privacy as best we saw them (while it enabled the maximal accrual of scientific knowledge); that the patients, as evidenced by their overwhelmingly willing cooperation in the Termination and Follow-Up Studies of their cases, concurred in our decision and trusted our integrity; and that we would do nothing that we felt could be to their individual detriment. Such a tack would mean, then, also going on now and publishing in the spirit of the original understandings, without reopening any of the old treatment and/or research issues with the ex-patients just for the purposes of conforming to today's standards for the conduct of scientific research involving human subjects.

What safeguards of the patients' welfare can be built into such a proposed course? First, of course, should be the tact and sensitivity that should always be employed in portraying the lives of the troubled and defenseless, for whatever purpose. And certainly this means a use of language that, to whatever extent it need be technical, should as far as humanly possible be kept from being pejorative. All this requires a vigilance that should never be relaxed. Linked, of course, to the style or language of case write-up is that of suitable disguise, with the elimination of all names and places and any other identifying data so that at least no one other than the individual portrayed could possibly recognize them. (Of course, it might not always be possible to insure that the spouse or significant other would not recognize them. That would all depend on many factors, such as the amount and kind of personally revealing data used, and the intensity and kind of relationship that existed between the patient and the spouse.) Certainly, in all of this, the intent should be that in the unlikely event that the ex-patient should ever read about himself or herself in the professional literature (or in the still rarer event of the spouse who could perhaps correctly guess at the identity of the patient described), the case should be written up in such a way that the individual concerned does not feel misunderstood, misrepresented, unfairly treated, or otherwise hurt. We should have a realistic perspective on this possibility, neither underestimating nor overestimating the potential for such hurt. One can readily enough go overboard in either direction (again, one must guard against falling into the trap of shading an argument that can after all become self-serving); one can exaggerate, as well as minimize, the risks of hurt and other damage to the surprised ex-patient being brought face to face with an intimate portrayal of himself or herself. In our field, we talk properly of the enormous difficulty of influencing, especially of changing, people. This entire book can be read as a spelling out of the various reasons why this is so and the various ways in which it is so. Yet here

---

cratic emotional loadings by the patient; and "crisis consent," in instances of real or imagined urgency. Though the references here are to problems in somatic illness and treatment, the same kinds of considerations can prevail, in altered form, within the sphere of psychiatric illness and treatment. The play of transference feelings, both positive and negative, in relation to willingness or unwillingness to give consent is of course under more explicit scrutiny in the realm of psychological therapies.

we can allow ourselves to conjure up all kinds of violent and harmful repercussions from an action intended only to be usefully informative. (Again, this is not an attempt to excuse well-intentioned blundering or thoughtlessness.)

In addition to the way things are written, one must of course consider the likely audience for whom they are written. This book is a report of a psychotherapy research project, a natural history of the lives of people in psychoanalysis and psychotherapy; the intended audience is that of the scientific readership, those persons interested in the intensive psychotherapies from the technical standpoint of how they work and what can be done to make them work better. Although it was not by itself built into the original design as an explicit exclusion factor, other aspects of the PRP selection criteria worked to insure that none of our research subjects or their spouses were mental health professionals in any of the traditional mental health fields that were represented in our Topeka professional community, though such professional colleagues and their spouses did form a very significant portion of the total number of patients in intensive psychotherapy at The Menninger Foundation.

Given that none of the patients (or their spouses) were mental health professionals; given that none were or became readers of our professional literature[7]; and given that nearly 30 years have gone by to attenuate any special treatment-related preoccupation with the world of mental health professional activity, we can safely assume, I think, that it is most unlikely that any of our research subjects will come across or feel an impulse to read a book about psychiatric treatments by an author unfamiliar to them. Should any one or more of them do so, I trust that the process would do no harm, for all of the reasons assembled to this point.

In summary, I have decided, after as thorough a consideration as possible of the pros and cons of each of the considerations reviewed to this point, and given the originating circumstances and the subsequent history of our project, to go ahead and write (as carefully and as concernedly as possible) and publish this book on what are to me ethically satisfactory grounds that do not involve seeking informed consent at this late date. That there are many scientific advantages to doing this, I think to be unarguable. That it also best safeguards the well-being of the patients (in the sense not only of their rights but also their best interests), and is therefore from their point of view also the best way to go, is I think at least an arguable proposition. That the argument carries some aura of a paternalism from an earlier day into today, where it is less fashionable and less acceptable, is one of the uneasinesses that accompanies this choice.

---

7. One patient, the Medical Scientist, was treated in psychoanalysis most successfully and was able to resume a productive professional career with interests, including reading interests, collateral to psychiatry. This patient, however, is one of those who we happen to know died of non-mental-illness-related causes a considerable number of years after his completed Follow-Up Study.

II

Overview and Organization

The Problem

The Methods

The Design

From its very first collection of five articles (Wallerstein *et al.*, 1956), PRP has been involved in presenting its methods and design to the professional world on the basis, which we felt important, that the field of systematic clinical psychotherapy research was still in that early developmental state where issues of methods advancement properly preceded attention to substance advancement.[1] Subsequently, as the project moved through its data-collecting phase in accord with the methods and the design that had been constructed, presentation was made (in the third collection, of three articles, in 1960) of what we called the "operational problems of psychotherapy research": the problems encountered, and the choices available to cope with them, in implementing such a naturalistic study of change brought about by psychotherapy (Hall & Wallerstein, 1960; Wallerstein & Robbins, 1960). The entire overall structure of methods, of design, of operational problems, and (sketchily) of paths of data analysis and the directions in which preliminary findings pointed has been presented in highly schematized and condensed form at a number of points in progress—updated each time (see Robbins & Wallerstein, 1959; Wallerstein, 1961, 1966 [midway point], and 1968 [semifinal point]). In 1977, this was all brought together into a total overview (again, necessarily abbreviated) (Wallerstein, 1977b). In Section II of this book, I trace the evolution of the PRP methods, design, operational problems, pathways to data analysis and write-up, and handling of the issue of controls, in the kind of full detail not possible to this point within the constraints of journal presentation. This detailed presentation of plan is a most necessary part of the evidential base for the subsequent assessment by the reader of both the "intrinsic validity" (see p. 12) of our findings and conclusions, as well as of the degree to which we have been able to subject the subtle and complex phenomena of subjective mental states to appropriate canons of scientific inference (i.e., proper regard for issues of objectivity, reliability, and predictability) in order to add sufficient warrant of confidence to the adjudged findings and the derived conclusions and implications.

---

1. For an extended discussion of this issue in the context of psychotherapy research in general, see Wallerstein and Sampson (1971). For discussion of these issues as reflected specifically in PRP, see our discussion in the second collection of three articles from the project (Wallerstein & Robbins, 1958).

Questions and Basic Premises of the Project

THE QUESTIONS OF THE PROJECT: PROCESS VERSUS OUTCOME

As described in Section I, the committed clinical community of The Menninger Foundation decided in the early 1950s to try to learn more from and about its central professional activity, and from this decision PRP was born. We sought more precise answers to what started out as two simple, though even at that first stage clearly not simple-minded, questions. The first was that of *what* changes take place in psychotherapy: What good can we, with reasonable confidence, say that it does? The second, immediately following, question was that of *how* those ascertained changes come about—through the interaction of what constellation of factors in the patient and in the treatment and the therapist, with the addition a little further along in the planning of factors in the patient's ongoing life situation as well? Clearly, specified answers to such questions would be critical to the improvement of clinical practice; we could expect to achieve more with patients through more appropriate attention to the particular factors that turned out to be the most critical to particular kinds of clinical outcomes.

Here we are immediately in the realm of *outcome* questions (What changes?) and of *process* questions (How do those changes come about?), and of our intent from the start to create a combined process–outcome study—at least at an exploratory level. The immediate overall goal was stated in one of the earliest publications (Wallerstein & Robbins, 1958) to be "one of hypothesis finding and refining and the development and testing of instruments suitable to this way of research" (p. 118). The ultimate object was stated to be "more specific knowledge of the process by which changes are brought about in treatment" (p. 118).

We were aware from the start of the conceptual and methodological problems involved in trying thus to combine process and outcome studies within the same project design. I quote our first statement of this issue at some length:

> We believe that in theory, process and outcome are necessarily interlocked and that the hypotheses that will yield the answers sought can only come from an exploratory study paying equal attention to both components. Any study of outcome, even if it only counts a percentage of cases "improved," must establish some criteria for "improvement," and these in turn derive from some conceptualization of the nature of the course of illness and the process of change, whether or not this is explicitly for-

mulated. Similarly, any study of process, in delineating patterns of change among variables, makes at varying points in time cross-sectional assessments which, if compared with one another, provide measures of treatment outcome.

However, the effort to separate psychotherapy research projects into process or outcome, or more often, polemically, into process *vs.* outcome studies continues apace. On practical grounds, this is often necessary. Though process is conceptually not separable from outcome, methods that yield the best judgments in one area or the other are often operationally opposed. For example, judgments of outcome will be scientifically most convincing if bias is minimized and absolute freedom from contamination maintained by keeping those who make the "after" judgments unaware of the "before" judgments and predictions. "Blind" psychological retesting is an obvious way to meet this research goal. Yet truly "blind" clinical interviewing, in which all knowledge of the "before" state is rigorously excluded, is by the nature of clinical interaction hardly possible. Any clinical interview, no matter how closely geared it is to an assessment of current status, will inevitably yield data comparing present states with prior ones. From the point of view of *process* judgments about the *same therapy*, such care to minimize contamination would be unnecessary. Indeed, it would be counter to the whole spirit of inquiry into process in which maximum knowledge of all the known determinants, as these have varied through time, is essential in order to understand the changes that occur. In this sense, in terms of relative emphases at different stages of their operations, psychotherapy projects can be designed with greater clarity and efficiency to answer questions about outcome or about process. (Wallerstein & Robbins, 1958, pp. 118–119)

In the extended discussion following this quotation from that article (see pp. 118–123), we discussed two common but, we felt, erroneous assumptions that tend to get linked to this pragmatic distinction between process and outcome studies. The one is that a study of process must necessarily be committed to microsize units of interaction and observation and cannot be done with a larger, "macro" perspective from the three widely separated points in time (Initial, Termination, and Follow-Up) that we chose as our windows of access to research data. The other assumption is one that distinguishes between the two kinds of studies on the basis of the level along which the change is measured: The process category is assigned to those studies in which change is evaluated at the level of intrapsychic configurations, and the outcome category is assigned to those studies in which change is evaluated at the "objective" behavioral level — as if the nature of the study were determined by the level of the criterion variables chosen. The reader is referred to our 1958 article for presentation of the reasoning behind our contrary assumption that neither the size of the unit of observation (micro *or* macro) nor the level of observation (intrapsychic *or* external behavioral) determines whether process or outcome knowledge is being obtained. We contended that either kind of knowledge can come from either micro or macro observational units, and from the most "internal" (inferential) or "external" (observable) level of observations, depending on how the research questions are framed. I trust to demonstrate this in the many pages ahead.

Clearly, not all researchers in this field fully shared (or share) these views. One of our chief project consultants, John Benjamin, expressed himself along such lines in a consultation visit in December 1957. Though agreeing strongly with our contentions that process and outcome studies are necessarily conceptually interlocked, and that neither kind of study is *necessarily* linked either to observational units of a particular size or to a particular level of observation, Benjamin nonetheless felt that practically, in terms of operational emphasis, process and outcome studies were more separate than otherwise, and that trying to encompass both at the same time would create difficult dilemmas of wanting in the handling of the various instruments of research access to be simultaneously as free from contamination as possible (for outcome purposes) and as fully informed as possible (for process purposes). This represented for Benjamin one of the kinds of choices that the researchers would inevitably be driven to make in terms of the specific research aim being particularly emphasized. He felt that in PRP, although we spoke of both outcome and process interests, the actual project design would lead to more insight and knowledge in the area of outcome than it possibly could in regard to process. And though he agreed that the size of the unit of observation was not determinative of the kind of data being elicited, he felt that, nonetheless, process did imply *continuity* of observation, regardless of the unit's size. In his view, getting down to observations at only three major windows of access, at three possibly very widely spread points in time, would make us too dependent on long-range retrospective filling in and correspondingly less able to minimize the inevitable distortions and memory fallibilities that would be introduced into the process assessment. Benjamin concluded that we would end in a much weaker position as far as throwing significant light on process aspects of change in psychotherapy was concerned, but also felt personally in accord (in terms of the research priorities in the field) with what he felt were the implicit strategic decisions made all along to emphasize outcome knowledge, even if at the expense of process knowledge.

How PRP did try to address these cogent objections should become clear through the remainder of Section II. Certainly, there was agreement within PRP with Benjamin's rightful emphasis on how much our methods were geared to the securing of the best possible outcome judgments. The disagreement was over how much could be learned about the *process* of therapy at the same time. Here a number of different definitions of "process" seemed to becloud the argument. Certainly, it was agreed that when one makes outcome judgments on intrapsychic variables, one is making judgments about changes in intrapsychic processes. Such judgments, however, have to do with outcome measures and would in no way constitute a process study. Process studies, rather, have to do with how the discerned changes (albeit in intrapsychic processes) have come about. Can one, in terms of one's theory and the observations at hand, construct a plausible set of explanatory sequences that help us understand more about how one got from position A to position B—that is, how a particular outcome came about?

Benjamin's position was, as stated, that although process studies are not necessarily linked to the size of the unit of study, they do imply more continuity of study than we had built in. A somewhat different position, PRP's as developed by Sargent, has been that this depends on exactly what is meant by "process." For instance, if a "process" is something that changes constantly over time, then the fullest understanding of the process would come about through the greatest continuity of observation in time. However, if "process" here is something akin to the "process of manufacture" (i.e., how some kind of intervention brings about some kind of change), then it might be possible to learn something (albeit perhaps not as much) about that process even from a lesser number of vantage points more

separated in time. How much the data-gathering methods of PRP, to be detailed
through the rest of Section II, succeeded in throwing light on "process" in this last
sense described can be judged best by the end of this book.[2]

THE BASIC PREMISES OF THE PROJECT

The basic premise of PRP can be grouped under three headings: those that had
to do with the carrying out of a naturalistic design as we conceived it; those that
had to do with the extent of hypothesis-testing as against hypothesis-seeking (hypothesis-creating) project goals; and those that had to do with the relationships
of the project's aims and activities to the psychoanalytic theoretical framework
within which it was constructed. These are discussed in turn.

Naturalistic Design

For all the scientific and sociopolitical reasons already elaborated, the very first
decision made in the planning of PRP was that the design would be thoroughly
"naturalistic," as we understood and could implement that concept. By this we
meant a study of psychotherapy in its natural habitat—that is, unencumbered by
the intrusion into it of any component (whether intermittent, like questionnaires,
interviewing, or other such periodic data-gathering instrument, or continuous,
like audiotape recording, even though the latter just because of its continuous
presence and relative inconspicuousness can appear to be "accommodated to" over
time) that would make the therapy differ from the usual clinical practice in our
institution at that time. Even the knowledge that the particular treatment was or
would be the subject of research study would in itself be an added dimension of
meaning and probably of concern that would have some impact on the "natural-
ness" of the study. Therefore, we undertook to devise a project design that would
somehow enable us to study the phenomenon of change in psychotherapy adequately, and yet to do so without either a therapist's or a patient's knowing at
any time throughout the course of the therapy that such a study was in progress
until the treatment came to its natural end. Such a design restriction would clearly
erect barriers against access to many of the usual kinds of research data, and would
of course certainly bar any kind of (experimental) manipulation and/or control.
How we did then try to construct adequate avenues of access to necessary knowledge—of outcome *and* process—is spelled out in detail through the course of Section II.
   Clearly, none of this is a commitment to the proposition that any other kind
of "less naturalistic" research study of therapy processes, involving any degree of

---

2. Some three different meanings of the concept "process" have by this point been stated. It was Ehrenreich
who, in the early days of PRP, first insisted that we should clarify these distinctions by defining them separately as "process 1," "process 2," and "process 3," and that we should so label the word on each use of it
in order always to keep ourselves and the readers clear as to which conception of the word we intended.
Rather than adopt this awkward convention, I trust in this book that the context at all times makes clear
how the word is being used. Mostly, when I talk of "process study" or the "process" aspects of the study,
I have something like the metaphor of the "process of manufacture" in mind.

intrusiveness into the therapy (knowledge that the participants were part of a research study, the introduction of instruments of inquiry at predetermined intervals, or even full audiotape recording and/or [nowadays] videotape recording), would necessarily vitiate it as a therapeutic process. Clearly, there have been enough research investigations (within psychoanalytic as well as nonpsychoanalytic frameworks, and even with psychoanalysis itself)[3] to establish that both psychotherapy and psychoanalysis can take place under such circumstances, as long as one takes care to encompass within the scope of the therapeutic inquiry and concern the impact of the device or the intrusion upon the therapy and its meaning in relation to the particular character configuration and problems of the patient (and also the therapist?)—whether masochistic, paranoid, exhibitionistic, voyeuristic, or whatever. Our contention was a different one. It was that any such therapy conducted within such less naturalistic research requirements is systematically different because of this introduced parameter or parameters, and that though one can thereby learn more of certain kinds of things, they are being learned about an entity altered to some undetermined degree. Given our way of conducting the research, less of certain kinds of things would necessarily be learned, but all that would be learned would be learned about the totally natural, unaltered entity.

Our commitment to a naturalistic study had other aspects as well. It meant that every patient being studied was in that treatment modality that was deemed on the basis of case study to be the most appropriate to his or her needs. This instantly meant that our study, with half the patients in psychoanalysis and half in less intensive psychoanalytic psychotherapy, was not a comparative study of psychoanalysis vis-à-vis other psychotherapy in relation to the same kind of patients, or matched patients. Rather, it was a study of each of these kinds of therapies against itself, against its own appropriate indications, in order to see how well each therapy could realize its own imputed promise and where and how it would fall short of so doing. Given all this, it follows that there was no randomization, no matching of patients for the purpose of contrasting their course and outcome within different therapeutic approaches; there were also no traditional controls, control groups of any kind, or other nonclinical research impositions. Nor, in a clinical setting where prospective patients came expecting (and did receive) the treatment felt indicated for and appropriate to them as expeditiously as possible, could there be groups of those assigned to nontreatment or deferred treatment categories. None of this, of course, abrogated one whit our scientific responsibility to introduce appropriate principles of control; they just needed to be implemented in other than these standard ways. Specifically, how we undertook to introduce adequate control of observation in this project is spelled out in the discussion of our control principles (see Chapter 7).

Hypothesis-Finding versus Hypothesis-Testing Goals

The second major set of operating premises of PRP had to do with the issue of where the project would (or could) lie on the continuum from the most wide-open, freewheeling, exploratory, hypothesis-finding (hypothesis-creating) research en-

---

3. These investigations are discussed at length in Wallerstein and Sampson (1971), pp. 21–28.

deavor, through to the definitive hypothesis-testing endeavor in accord with the usual and well-established scientific canons, involving close control over relevant conditions, appropriate narrowing of the field of inquiry, and even (usually) experimental manipulations designed to put the hypothesis at specific issue to an unambiguous test.

It should be clear by now that PRP was from the start avowedly primarily a hypothesis-seeking project—because of the relatively undeveloped state of knowledge of the field of clinical psychotherapy research (particularly at the time when the project was designed); because of the nature of the clinical psychoanalytic treatment enterprise and of psychoanalysis as a systematic theory of personality functioning; and, lastly, because of the way in which the project was conceived and structured (with reference, of course, to the first two considerations). In fact, PRP was not just a hypothesis-seeking project; perhaps even prior to that or certainly at least alongside of it, it was also a method-seeking project in this arena where the usual methods of inquiry created for the experimental psychology laboratory have simply not yet become applicable (assuming that someday they *might* be).[4] It is precisely because of these considerations about both the field of psychotherapy and psychotherapy research that there has inevitably been so much appropriate emphasis in this and in kindred research projects on the issue of methods advancement before substance advancement (see Wallerstein & Sampson, 1971, pp. 16–18). And, of course, in creating a project that was explicitly method-seeking and explicitly hypothesis-seeking and that was uncompromisingly naturalistic in all the senses adumbrated, we were far from the laboratory and its experimental norms, as has been clearly stated. Some observers have related this kind of study to at least the study of "experiments of nature," and perhaps the concept is applicable to the extent that one could consider psychotherapy at all as a natural occurrence. I prefer to see psychotherapy as a highly contrived and highly unnatural situation brought into being because it has been felt to be a way to influence psychological functioning in the direction of amelioration of psychic distress—an unnatural state, then, to be studied within the natural habitat that custom and usage have gradually carved out for it.

However, all this emphasis on the primarily hypothesis-seeking nature of the major PRP premises should not detract from the fact that, where possible and to the extent possible, more definitive and to some extent hypothesis-testing aims should be achieved. The three major lines of data study and data analysis marked out from the start for the project—the clinical case study and analysis, of which the present book is the final accounting; the formal Prediction Study with its analysis according to predetermined evidence of the fate of some 1700 individual

---

4. I do not want to enter at all here into the issue raised by some in the psychoanalytic clinical and psychoanalytic research literature that the standard psychoanalytic situation is itself, or can be considered from a perspective that permits it to be viewed as being, close to a research (or even a quasi-experimental) method. That literature is cited in detail elsewhere (Wallerstein & Sampson, 1971, pp. 13–15). Briefly, my own position as stated in the 1971 article is that this line of reasoning is specious; that psychoanalysis (and psychotherapy) as a clinical enterprise is a search, not a research; and that to make it into a research (or, better, to do research about it) takes the kind of formalization and systematization of which PRP is an example. PRP, in our view, is a formal research built upon a non-research-influenced natural psychotherapy, carried out in accord with its usual (and non-research-influenced) procedures.

predictions, of which the Sargent *et al.* (1968) monograph is the major formalization and the book by Horwitz (1974) the final accounting; and the quantitative
studies (both statistical and also mathematical and nonmetrical), all built out of
the data derived from the application of the Fechnerian method of paired comparisons to the phenomena under study, of which the Sargent *et al.* (1967) monograph is the major formalization and the monograph by Kernberg *et al.* (1972)
is the final accounting—have sought to throw as much definitive (tested) light upon
our guiding propositions as possible. Certainly the clinical case study method of
this book is the one that proceeds least in this direction. The concluding section
of the book, rather, contains statements about the major hypotheses that have
been constructed out of the observations made about the course and outcome of
therapy throughout the book; it also indicates various ways in which these hypotheses can be put to more definitive test in future projects that could be more
tightly constructed around them.

Psychoanalytic Theoretical Framework

The third set of basic operating premises of PRP had to do with its specifically
psychoanalytic theoretical framework and its operating within the specifically
psychoanalytic setting of The Menninger Foundation. Within this orientation,
its effort was to test the guiding assumptions of the theory of psychoanalytic
therapy—that is, the sets of theoretical and the derived technical propositions that
guide our understandings of how psychoanalysis and psychoanalytically based
psychotherapies operate to bring about change. Such a test had never before been
systematically made, and it is a large task. For, as Rapaport (1960) has stated,
psychoanalysis as a general psychological theory is a widely comprehensive,
coherent, and articulated rendering of the phenomena of the mind, and psychoanalysis as a theory of psychopathology, though less encompassing, is still a reasonably comprehensive formulation of normal vis-à-vis abnormal mental functioning. As a theory of therapy, however, psychoanalysis is still, and certainly
was when Rapaport wrote (and when PRP itself was being formulated), in a much
more rudimentary and fragmentary state—one he characterized as consisting essentially of "rules of thumb" (p. 17).

Several efforts have been made within the psychoanalytic literature to better
articulate a theory for psychoanalysis as a therapy, as well as for the psychoanalytically based expressive and supportive psychotherapies. Some of the best-known
of these efforts were made in the period during which PRP was being planned.
For example, Bibring (1954) discussed the differential "curative" and "technical"
application of the same group of therapeutic principles, in psychoanalysis proper
as opposed to the dynamic psychotherapies that are based on the theory of psychoanalysis; Gill (1951) described the mechanisms and procedures of supportive
psychotherapy, again as psychoanalytically conceptualized. Both of these papers
achieved instant "classic" status. The PRP likewise has set down its (psychoanalytic) operating assumptions very explicitly: Our assumptions about the
origin and the nature of mental illness were described on the very first page
of our very first publication (Robbins & Wallerstein, 1956, p. 223), and our very
specific assumptions about the nature of the presumed mutative mechanisms in

all the psychoanalytically based psychotherapeutic modalities have been set forth all through the various books on the outcomes of the project (S. A. Appelbaum, 1977; Horwitz, 1974; Kernberg *et al.*, 1972; Voth & Orth, 1973).

In briefest capsule, these basic assumptions about the theory of psychoanalytic therapy are as follows:

1. Psychoanalysis itself operates essentially through the establishment of a full-fledged regressive transference neurosis, and its ultimate resolution comes about centrally through interpretation leading to insight and mastery. It is the most thorough-going and long-range reconstructive therapy in its goals; it is the most unified and coherent in its techniques; and it is capable of achieving the most extensive and stable results, the ones that hold up best against subsequent life vicissitudes.

2. Expressive psychoanalytic psychotherapy is similar in mechanisms but differs sharply in degree. It is limited in focus to agreed-upon sectors of psychic distress and personality malfunction, and operates through means that do not evoke a full transference regression, all leading to less extensive (more "intermediate") results but similar in direction and kind.

3. Supportive psychoanalytic psychotherapies operate through varieties of mechanisms that are differently emphasized in different books and publications from PRP, but that variously invoke such concepts as "transference cure" (i.e., cure based on a transference trade—"I do it for you, the therapist, so as to earn or maintain your support, your esteem, your love, etc."); "corrective emotional experience," whether in the sense originally adumbrated by Alexander and French (1946) or in the more classically psychoanalytic sense specified by Gill (1954); "identification" with the therapist and his or her ways of behaving adaptively, of being in accord with reality, and so forth; defiance or "acting against" the therapist ("I'll do it despite or in spite of your negative and pessimistic expectations of me"); "disengagement" from specifically conflict-triggering, life-situational pressures; and "need gratification" within the therapeutic situation. All of these mechanisms lead to changes that are presumably the least extensive, the least enduring, and the most vulnerable to future adverse life circumstances.

Yet despite all this effort at delineation and clarification of the theory of therapy, major theoretical controversies have existed all along, and continue to exist almost unabated today, over such issues as the relationship of verbalizable insight to change (is it an essential precondition of change, a consequence of change, or an accompaniment of change, with either crucial or only incidental value?),[5] or again over the nature of "working through," or over the meaning of structural change in the ego and its relation to the nature and durability of change. In regard to just one of these issues, the role of insight in relation to change in psychoanalysis, the *Journal of the American Psychoanalytic Association* published a supplemental issue in the summer of 1979 on problems of technique; this issue included

---

5. See our own early extended discussion of this issue in our first collection of papers from PRP, where (in summary) we stated that insight is best conceptualized as the concomitant *ideational representation* of the change in ego functioning (Wallerstein & Robbins, 1956, pp. 258–261).

a sequence of four articles on the role of insight, in which the same debates of 25 years before were restated in almost the same words. (See, in this regard, Blum, 1979, and Neubauer, 1979.) In my own recent extended discussion of this same issue (Wallerstein, 1983b), I quoted, in regard to these continuing controversies, from Gill's (1979) plea concerning yet another technical controversy in the field (that over the position of the analysis of the transference in the "here and now" as *the* absolutely primary technical mode—or not—of the curative psychoanalytic process). Gill's plea could be taken as a credo for the PRP as a whole, and of course for this whole book.

> I close with a statement of a conviction designed to set this paper into a broader perspective of psychoanalytic theory and research. The points I have made are not new. They are present in varying degrees of clarity and emphasis throughout our literature. But like so many other aspects of psychoanalytic theory and practice, they fade in and out of prominence and are rediscovered again and again, possibly occasionally with some modest conceptual advance, but often with a newness attributable only to ignorance of past contributions. There are doubtless many reasons for this phenomenon. But not the least, in my opinion, is the almost total absence of systematic and controlled research in the psychoanalytic situation. I mean such research in contrast to the customary clinical research. I believe that only with such systematic and controlled research will analytic findings become solid and secure knowledge instead of being subject to erosion again and again by waves of fashion and what Ernst Lewy (1941) long ago called the "return of the repression" to designate the retreat by psychoanalysts from insights they had once reached. (Gill, 1979, p. 286)

This, of course, has been our chosen road—systematic, and as far as possible, controlled research. Based on the various kinds of assumptions about the psychoanalytic therapies referred to above, various sets of hypotheses have been elaborated within PRP; it has been the purpose of the project to explore and, as far as possible, to test these. The aim has not been to "validate" psychoanalytic theory, but to test a series of hypotheses derived from within that theory, bearing on the problems of treatment process and treatment outcome. A chief mode for doing this has been within the Prediction Study aspect of PRP, the mechanics of which are to be specified further on in this section. Basically, they comprise a mode of progressing from the clinical data of the consulting room to a series of testable (in ways to be detailed) predictions capable of throwing light on the propositions of that aspect of the psychoanalytic theor*ies* of therapy (Rapaport's "rules of thumb") in accord with which the data have generated the particular predictions.

A caveat needs to be stated here, however. What we will have learned from all this effort will be a further more credible specification of the theory of psychoanalytic therapy, a more articulated hanging together of its assumptions, linked in its (altered) emphases to findings from our project that have caused us to recast some of our initial assumptions about the mechanisms and the meanings (as well as the limitations) of achieved changes in psychoanalysis and psychoanalytic psychotherapies, having firmed up the credibility of some and diminished the role of others. To point, however, to a critical distinction made repeatedly for us by our consultant, John Benjamin, an enhanced theory of psychoanalytic therapy is not yet (and is far from) the same thing as an enlarged psychoanalytic theory of therapy. The latter, to which our effort does not aspire, would comprise an enlarged psychoanalytic understanding of *all* psychotherapy—that done within a psychoanalytic framework and that specifically not (the behavioral, the humanistic, etc.). This enlarged understanding would rest on a psychoanalytic study of other kinds of therapies, carried out within our explanatory conceptual systems, and satisfactorily explaining their data and their results within a psychoanalytic framework. This is all in theory possible, and it is also necessary if psychoanalysis indeed is a more encompassing and a truly general psychology.[6] Perhaps it is needless to say that it is my strong conviction that the overall field of psychotherapy research is at present far from ready for such a grand synthesizing effort.

Selection and Characteristics of the Patient Group

SELECTING THE SAMPLE

The research subjects for PRP were intended to be a usual population of patients in intensive and long-term therapy (either psychoanalysis or psychotherapy) at The Menninger Foundation. Because of the design requirements of our method of paired comparisons (to be described), the sample size would need to be a multiple of 6. Because of the very considerable time put into constructing each patient's Initial Study (about 40 hours apiece of each of the two collaborators in this, Robbins and myself), prospective patients were processed into the sample at the rate of 1 per month, or (given vacations and other absences from work) 10 or 11 per year. By the time Robbins left Topeka (summer of 1958), 4 years had been spent entering patients through constructing their Initial Studies, and the total sample size was 42. It was felt that that represented all the data that could sensibly be encompassed within the overall design requirements of the project and the time available (from even a large group of investigators) within which to meet them. The total n was therefore 42.

The patients were chosen to be half men and half women. In regard to some of the patients with some illnesses, we had specific hypotheses concerning the different meaning and treatment potential of the illness on a sex-linked basis. One obvious example is alcoholism—a severe difficulty with many in our sample, a much more frequent factor among the men than the women (a major symptom state in 12 of the men and troublesome with 2 others; a major symptom state with only 3 of the women and troublesome with 2 others), and a disorder that seems significantly different between men and women in terms of inner dynamic

---

6. Bibring (1954) tried this in a small degree when he (pp. 766–767) essayed to characterize the operations of Rogers's "nondirective counseling" (conceptualized by Rogers, 1951, and Rogers & Dymond, 1954, within his other, client-centered theoretical framework) in terms of the basic deployment of two of the five main therapeutic principles of the psychoanalytic psychotherapies—clarification and experiential manipulation, the latter "in the sense of offering the 'new' experience of being accepted, of successfully assuming self-responsibility, etc., thus gaining in self-reliance and independence." This statement of Bibring's was of course a conceptual speculation; it did not derive from empirical study of the course and outcome of Rogerian therapy, done by psychoanalytic observers trying to apply a psychoanalytic explanatory framework.

structure as well as outer social sanction and consequence. Half the patients were intended to be in psychoanalysis and half in other psychoanalytic psychotherapy. Actually, psychoanalysis was the selected treatment modality for 22 of the patients (12 women and 10 men), and psychotherapy for 20 (9 women and 11 men).

The patients were originally planned to be all adults and in the younger adult age range (between 20 and 45). This was intended to ease the task of delineating the changes that would take place consequent to treatment. Specifically, we hoped to eliminate the confounding effects with children of growth and development, with all of the inevitable changes wrought by the developmental (and the concomitant educational) process and all of the intertwining between treatment-induced change and developmental change (mental illness is often a significant inhibitor of aspects of development, and its successful treatment is often a significant release of developmental thrust). We also hoped to eliminate the confounding effect at the upper range of the age span of the physiological aging process and any concomitant physical or mental impairment. Actually, it worked out that the age range of the sample was from 17 to 50.

Since the intent was to study individual psychotherapy as the chief treatment vehicle, any patients in concomitant group or family treatment arrangements (very few in those days in that setting) were excluded, as were patients for whom hospitalization and hospital management under the direction of the hospital doctor were major therapeutic instruments. This latter stipulation would therefore exclude patients with overt psychoses, schizophrenia, the openly paranoid psychoses, or the manic and psychotic depressive states. This would not, however, exclude hospitalized patients per se from the sample. (Actually, 22 of the 42 were hospitalized one or more times during the course of their treatment; 15 of these were hospitalized only in the initial period—which could be rather prolonged—of the psychotherapy's getting under way and becoming established.) The stipulation was, rather, that in the cases included, the hospital treatment be intended to be only adjunctive and supportive, with the formal psychotherapy to be the major planned vehicle for change. Consequently, patients suffering from organic brain syndromes, dementia, and mental retardation were likewise excluded from the sample.

There were other specified exclusion criteria as well. These were as follows:

1. Patients for whom the intent was brief therapy. We were centrally interested in the presumably far more substantial changes in psychic functioning that could be achieved through long-term and intensive therapeutic endeavors, and thus we excluded all varieties of brief interventions, crisis treatment, prolonged time-stretched evaluations preparatory for other more definitive psychotherapy, time-limited "holding operations," and so on. Not only were all these a different species of therapy from that we intended to study, but the mechanics of our project, with the very time-consuming and at times quite prolonged Initial and Termination Studies, could logistically swamp the time compass of a brief therapy; there could be a more intensive evaluation period before and after (with the "after" almost immediately consequent to the "before") than the therapy itself would cover.

2. Old cases. Though we did not exclude patients who had had previous psychiatric evaluation and/or treatment prior to coming to Topeka (we would hardly have been able to accumulate a sample if we had), we did exclude "old cases" in our own setting—patients who had been in previous treatment at The

Menninger Foundation, where the present "beginning" of treatment represented a transfer or a continuation rather than an actual start. Patients transferred from therapists who were leaving the Foundation fell into this category, as well as some cases starting again with the same (or another) therapist after a lapse of time, either caused by the patient or planned as part of the treatment. Some "mixed-up cases" also fell into this category, where the patients, although never in formal psychotherapy before, had been in the hospital and in a therapeutic relationship with the hospital doctor over a considerable period of time, and where the present "beginning" was actually only a formalization of that ongoing relationship.

3. Patients who would not be readily available for Follow-Up Study. As already stated (p. 39), by virtue of who they are, Menninger Foundation patients are generally highly visible in their communities (often with important business or professional connections); we counted on this, of course, in planning the Follow-Up Study. In this we also succeeded: Unlike the usual such study— which draws subjects from the highly mobile clinic populations in publicly supported treatment facilities, and in which there is always significant subject attrition over the course of the study and particularly into the follow-up period—we did manage (in ways I later specify in detail) to obtain a 100% Follow-Up Study reassessment. To help in accomplishing this, we did, however, exclude patients where there would be lesser probability of securing their later involvement. This exclusion applied primarily to patients from abroad (other than from Canada, where we counted on them being as accessible as in the United States) and to personnel in military service who knew that an overseas assignment might soon follow.

4. Professionally/socially restricted cases. We excluded those patients, mostly but not all from our own professional community or their spouses, in whose cases it was felt that the lives of the research investigators did (or might well come to) impinge either professionally or socially on the lives of the patients or people closely involved with the patients. We also excluded other patients in the same general categories, where it was felt that it could be personally awkward or embarrassing for so many others (the large research group) to be privy to so many details of the patients' life, behaviors, and mental states.

This last type of exclusion had several skewing consequences for our sample and the work with it. First, since such patients, especially those from our own professional community, tended to be treated by the most senior and experienced staff members (the more so if they were psychoanalytic candidates being treated by the training analysts), it meant a skewing of our population in the direction of the often "sicker" and more "ordinary" patients, who were usually treated by the less skilled and experienced, albeit mostly with close supervision. This could lead to an unwitting skewing of the "goodness" of our overall PRP results into a factitiously more limited direction, since so many of the "best" (most amenable) patients treated by the most experienced therapists were systematically excluded from our sample. This might create an unhappily more "negative" overall results effect.

This issue was discussed most comprehensively by John Benjamin in a consultation visit in 1956. I can indicate the logic of his fuller discussion through a quotation (somewhat abbreviated) from the minutes I made of that consultation visit:

A general problem derives from the whole way in which clinical practice operates here. The most senior therapeutic group (the training analysts) have most of their therapeutic time given to candidates, who of course are not used as Project subjects. The next most experienced therapeutic group (graduates, Society members) for the most part treat confidential cases and of course most of these cannot be used (although it does not follow that all confidential cases need necessarily be excluded; judgment can be made in each instance as to whether the particular patient involved is one whose therapy can be studied without getting involved in the problems of a colleague). Patients who are not candidates and are not confidential cases have a difficult time receiving psychoanalysis unless they can qualify as [Topeka] Institute [for Psychoanalysis] control cases. Thus, the cases of analysis being studied in the Project are for the most part control cases, with only a handful being treated by more experienced analysts. Most of the analytic cases under Project study (certainly the better ones) are being treated by inexperienced analysts. Where we have the advantage of studying analysis done by more experienced analysts, for the most part these cases (fewer in number than the other group) are more difficult analytic cases, often of a dubious feasibility for analysis.[1] Overall, therefore, we will have a biased rather than a fair assessment of psychoanalysis as therapy, and the bias will be in the direction of analysis as a specific treatment modality not showing up as favorably as it ought to.

By contrast, the psychotherapy cases will by and large be treated by people with greater backgrounds of experience in psychotherapy than is true for those who treat the project's analytic cases. We have enough staff members doing psychotherapy (and there is a far larger pool of psychotherapy cases than of psychoanalysis cases to draw upon) that we can readily eliminate psychotherapy being done by relatively inexperienced or junior staff and can set our level of minimal technical skill required at an acceptably high enough level. The distortions thus introduced may bias our study of differential indications for different treatment modalities and will tend consistently to put analysis in a more difficult light.[2]

The skewing of our research sample by this necessary avoidance of "confidential" or otherwise restricted cases, however, also eventuated in some unplanned

---

1. Glover (1954), in an article on the suitability of various illness states for psychoanalysis as the treatment, divided the indications for analysis into three categories (each specified in considerable detail): those "accessible" to psychoanalysis, those "moderately accessible" and those "refractory." He felt that being only in the moderately accessible or even refractory group did not necessarily rule out a treatment effort by psychoanalysis. Though the prospect might be poor, it still might be for the individual patient the only treatment that offered any real chance (i.e., the best treatment available). It turned out that we had a fair number in our PRP sample of patients with such "heroic indications" for analysis. Study of the course and outcome of just this group of cases leads to a discussion in the final section of this book (see Chapter 36, "'Heroic Indications' for Psychoanalysis Reconsidered").

2. This, of course, gets to the whole question of the general level of skill of the therapists in such a study and its relation to the value of the findings. Ways need to be devised to correct for, or to encompass, the problem posed by the number of therapists (whose therapies are under research study) who are not yet optimally skilled and experienced. Otherwise, we can find ourselves too often in the position of saying that the predictions made in the Initial Study of the patient did not hold because the therapist carried out the treatment plan with less than adequate skill. If that happens, we cannot extrapolate and claim that the predictions would have held if the therapy had been optimally skillfully applied. We would like to think so, but we clearly have no substantiating evidence. In fact, of course, many of our predictions that relate to the course and outcome of treatment depend on the proper application of requisite therapeutic skill, for the valid assessment both of our ability to predict and also of the adequacy of the assumptions upon which we predict. In the absence of such requisite technical skill on the part of a therapist, the failure of a given prediction in no wise provides support for or against the adequacy of the prediction or of the inferential process on which it is based.

favorable research consequences, at least for the issue of publication. Because of the way our sample was drawn—that is, with the avoidance of these particular categories of patients—we readily ended with a sample that included no mental health professionals and only one patient, the Medical Scientist, whose posttreatment career interests brought him even tangentially into contact with the psychiatric professional world (and he is no longer alive). This fact, as already stated in the discussion of the scientific and ethical issues posed by this book's preparation (see Chapter 3), has made my resolution of the issue of how to proceed with publication much easier. As previously noted, it is highly unlikely that any of these particular individuals would ever chance to read this book.

Linked to this issue of the necessary exclusion from the research study of almost all of the professionally and socially restricted cases was the corollary avoidance, as the two of us (Robbins and myself) selected the sample, of either our own planned cases in treatment or those awaiting psychotherapy with another member of the research group. With our own cases, the proscription was absolute. It would contravene every element of our naturalistic design, constructed in the first instance on the clinical treatment's being carried out without knowledge of the coming research scrutiny; additionally, it would be scientifically untenable to do an Initial Study—and, as part of that, to formulate predictions about the treatment course and outcome—and then to be the one carrying out that treatment with full knowledge of how it had been predicted to develop. With other members of the research group, the proscription could be less absolute. If it turned out that a sample member on whom we were constructing an Initial Study subsequently went into treatment with a PRP member, we could simply ensure that that therapist would not participate in his or her usual role in the subsequent Termination or Follow-Up Study phase with that patient (and we always had a large enough research group to be able to make such substitutions).

Given all these exclusion criteria, how *did* we then actually select the sample? In an effort to have as high a level of chance operating as possible—and knowing that this would be in no wise a strictly "random" sample, even within the constraints and exclusions already specified—we undertook to do Initial Studies sequentially on the prospective patients who had undergone full Menninger Foundation psychiatric evaluations (to be specified further on), and who, on the basis of those evaluations, were being placed on the psychoanalysis or psychotherapy waiting lists (the usual wait for placement in therapy seemed to average 6 weeks to 2 months). Since each Initial Study took about 1 month to complete, each time that we would turn to the lists for the next subject, we would try to choose the most recent addition.

The sample that emerged from this process over the 4-year span was, in our best judgment, what it was intended to be: a "usual" and typical population of Menninger Foundation patients (modified to whatever extent by the various exclusion criteria just described)—that is, a fairly homogeneous group in terms of the nature and the degree of their illness and in terms of demographic characteristics (to be described below), but by no means representative of the whole universe of patients in intensive psychoanalytic psychotherapies in the varieties of private and public practice settings across the country. Their relative homogeneity in terms of nature and degree of illness should be specified. With our exclusion of the openly psychotic, the organically brain-damaged, the mentally retarded, and those for whom (for these or other reasons) hospitalization and hospital management were to be central treatment vehicles, our sample did not have the sickest patients—those most refractory to, or even inaccessible to, psychotherapeutic approaches. However, they were also patients who for the most part (with the exception of some who lived in or near Topeka and came for treatment in their local setting) came or were sent for evaluation and possible treatment from all over the United States (and the world), either because treatment was not available in their home setting or, more often, because their pathology was of such a nature (i.e., more severe) that they could not be treated readily in the usually available private practice outpatient setting, but were felt to require intensive psychoanalytic therapy within the context of a readily available and coordinated psychoanalytic sanatorium (inpatient) setting. In fact, many came or were sent to The Menninger Foundation for treatment only after they had proven refractory to (often highly competent) outpatient treatment efforts usually available in the urban centers of our country. This made them as a group, then, not a usual neurotic patient population.

The individual case formulations and diagnostic formulations on our research sample emerge in the context of appropriate discussions of our patients and their treatments throughout this book. Here I should simply characterize them as suffering from a group of very severe symptom neuroses (crippling phobic states, very constricting obsessive–compulsive states) and at least equally severe character and impulse neuroses (including many severe alcoholic, addicted, acting-out, and sexually disturbed states). A fair number of the total, as will become very evident in the individual case discussions, suffered from what, in keeping with today's emphases, would be readily labeled narcissistic character disorders, and even more would be said to suffer from severe borderline states. One was a (usually compensated) sufferer of manic–depressive illness.

Of all those who have written books on the overall PRP results, only S. A. Appelbaum (1977) has emphasized the relative smallness, the nonrepresentativeness, and the severe degree of illness of this population in relation to whom the effectiveness of psychoanalytic and psychotherapeutic results was being appraised. In Chapter 4 of his book, "Overall Assessment of Change for Better or Worse," he put it (appropriately) as follows:

> The degree to which patients get better or worse was studied by way of psychological testing at termination. Ideally such a study should have provided an answer to the question of how well psychotherapy works. But, as discussed, we found that our data provided a very limited answer to such a question. The results merely told us the fate of a small population of patients, who were among the most difficult for whom psychotherapy was recommended. (p. 215)

DEMOGRAPHIC CHARACTERISTICS

Age and Sex

What were the demographic characteristics of the research sample selected in the manner just described? As stated, there were 21 males and 21 females. The age range, though originally intended to be 20–45, was in fact 17–50 (17–47 among the men, 19–50 among the women). Actually, only 6 were outside the originally stipulated age range—3 males (The Bohemian Prep School Boy at 17, the Adolescent Grandson at 17, and the Claustrophobic Man at 47) and 3 females (Peter Pan at 19, the Actress at 19, and the Involutional Woman at 50). The average age of the sample was 31 (33 for the men and 30 for the women).

Marriage and Children

When the patients came for treatment, 19 were married, 7 were divorced, and 1 (the Tantrum Woman, age 24) recently traumatically widowed. The other 15 had never married. Division by sex was approximately equal except in the divorced category: Of the 19 married, 8 were men and 11 women; of the 15 single, 8 were men and 7 women; of the 7 divorced, 5 were men and only 2 women; the widow was of course a woman.

The 27 who had been married had a total of 50 children. Of these 27, 5 had no children, 5 had one child, 11 had two children, 2 had three children, 3 had four children, and 1 had five children. Issues concerning particular children played substantial roles in a few patients' evolving illness pictures. One of these patients, the Adoptive Mother, felt constrained by mounting inner discomfort to return her child to the adoption agency; this decision actually heralded the psychological collapse, under a burdening sense of guilt and shame, that led directly to her appearance for treatment. The Script Writer's long-time shameful mistreatment of her severely polio-crippled child was a central aspect of her progressively destructive (as well as self-destructive) life functioning. With the Snake Phobia Woman, the birth, and 6 weeks later the death, of her third child (born with a major congenital heart deformation) was a part of the immediate sequence precipitating the request for treatment: This painful period engendered a great deal of phobic anxiety, as well as a residual guilt feeling over not having done enough. And with the Bohemian Musician, a central dynamic of her illness revolved around an ill-considered adoption and the subsequent struggle in her family centering around her inability to cope with the requirements of motherhood.

With a fair number of the patients, their psychiatric evaluation prior to acceptance for psychotherapy revealed substantial psychopathology in their children; later in this book, I provide the data on how many of the spouses and children likewise found their way to psychiatric treatment, either concurrent with or subsequent to the treatment of the presenting patients. One particularly striking instance of such wide family disturbance was in the family of the Alcoholic Doctor, whose four children were a 14-year-old boy with severe antisocial proclivities; a 12-year-old girl who was obsessionally overmeticulous, complaining, and never satisfied; a 6-year-old very phobic girl; and a 3-year-old stubbornly negativistic little girl. Furthermore, in this particular instance, the patient's wife was an almost equally heavy drinker, and when the two brawled they often drank themselves into stupors.

Sibling Status

The patient's place in the family sibship is something that is usually not particularly attended to in conceptualization of personality structure or the dynamics of mental illness, unless it has in a particular instance some dramatic meaning (e.g., a firstborn girl abruptly displaced from her favored position by the birth of a first son); our formulations of our cases and their treatments by and large conformed to this norm. Of our sample, 6 were only children; 19 had one sibling, and of these 10 were the firstborn and 9 the second; 11 had two siblings, and of these 2 were the eldest, 4 were the middle child, and 5 were the youngest; 4 had three siblings, and of these 2 were the eldest, 1 was second, and 1 was third; 1 had four siblings and was the third in the line of five; and 1 had five siblings and was the third in the line of six.

With a half dozen of the patients, issues concerning their siblings were either sufficiently central or sufficiently traumatic to color the personality development and illness picture in ways that deserve special mention here. One, the Snake Phobia Woman, had a "younger" twin brother who, in contrast to the patient's healthy state, was sickly from infancy on. This twin brother was the spoiled family favorite; he grew into an irresponsible, selfish child and a depressed adult. The patient, growing up in the shadow of this twin brother, always sat hopefully in the wings seeking in vain for her share of attention. Mostly she was considerate; occasionally she was wracked by severe childhood temper tantrums. Another patient, the Heiress, was the third of six siblings (four were boys) born into an extremely wealthy family owning a large department store empire. Not only were the male children clearly preferred, but this preference had been institutionalized in the terms of the grandfather's will in regard to the inheritance of the retail store empire and the control of the very large estate. The patient grew up fiercely competitive with the boys, tomboyish and athletic. She had many temper tantrums and crying spells because she was not a little boy and could not share some family privileges with the boys. With a third patient, the Intellectual Fencer, the situation was almost the same. The father was a very successful physician, as was the mother's brother; in the families of both parents, only male children and their educations, professions, and accomplishments were considered important. The patient had a brother 4 years her senior, who had grown up the spoiled darling of the family, had been a world-class fencer, and was now a successful physician. The patient, by contrast, was made to feel unable to compete or to garner her share of family praise and affection. Though an excellent scholar, she was not allowed to aspire to a career in medicine (like her father, brother, and uncle), and took solace in training and employment as a medical lab technician in a university teaching hospital, where she worked in a cancer research lab and had visions of becoming a famous researcher and finding the cure for cancer. She had few dates but could attract some men by her "intellectual brilliance."

The Rebellious Coed was a third and last child, born when her older brother was 18 and her older sister 16. Her siblings each left home to make their way in the world at about 18 years of age but would come back for regular weekend visits. The patient grew up feeling like an only child with two sets of parents who often did not agree. With two of the patients, the Alcoholic Heir and the Masochistic Editor, the major psychiatric illnesses of siblings played direct central roles in their own coming to treatment. The Alcoholic Heir's father was retired from his position as a major executive in one of the nation's giant scientific–industrial enterprises and was an abstainer from alcohol, though the father's own father and brother had been very heavy drinkers. The patient had had an older brother (the original family heir) who had been a confirmed alcoholic and had died at 28 in a household fire that he had accidentally started when going to bed drunk. There was also a slightly younger sister who was labeled an "excessive social drinker." The patient's own progressive alcoholism—linked to his brother's illness and death in ways to be later described (see p. 126)—ultimately destroyed his career in the company his family had created and led finally to increasing family pressure to come to the Menninger Foundation for treatment, with the threat to commit him should he balk. With the Masochistic Editor, by contrast, the pressure for treatment came from the reverse direction—from the patient. The patient had had a brother 2 years younger than he, with whom he had become quite close; the brother had grown up severely depressed (and had been hospitalized for it), but the parents had ignored the patient's pressure to bring the brother to The Menninger Foundation for treatment. Shortly after his hospital discharge, the brother had committed suicide very painfully by strychnine poisoning, with the pharmacopeia open to the proper page so that the family (especially the pharmacist father) could realize all the horrible effects. The patient, after a 4-year effort then on his own behalf, could finally persuade his parents to bring him for psychiatric treatment at The Menninger Foundation because of his disordered and severely alcoholic life. The success of this effort was made possible after the brother's death, which shook the parents into an awareness that their two sons had indeed both been sick and both in dire need of expert psychiatric help.

Religion

The professed religious affiliation of 33 of the 42 patients was Protestant; of course, there were some declared agnostics among this overwhelming majority. Only 6 were Jewish, 2 Catholic, and 1 Eastern Orthodox. This religious distribution reflects more the specialized patient clientele of The Menninger Foundation than the spread of psychiatric patients in the general population, where Jews are much more heavily represented (often equal to the number of Protestants), and Catholics, though far less in usual number, would still be more than in this sample. Special note should be taken of religious persuasion for nine of the patients.

The Sociopath, who was Eastern Orthodox by birth, was the patient most profoundly in revolt against his heritage. The father had grown up struggling against the prejudices encountered because of his Mediterranean birth and his Eastern Orthodox religion. The family always was beset by considerable shame mixed with defiant pride over its foreign origin, and tried, in inconsistent ways (including change of name), to deny this heritage. The patient, in turn, was shielded against the ethnic prejudices of the neighborhood children by restrictions on his playtime freedoms; nonetheless, he grew up feeling inferior and bitterly resentful, hating the "established American families" and the "400 percenters." He became a trial lawyer (in practice with his very successful father) and used the adversary proceedings of the courtroom as a vehicle for personal combat with the opposing attorneys, particularly if the latter were "400 percenters."

Religion played a comparable part in the difficulties of other patients. The Alcoholic Raconteur, one of the two Catholics, expressed in his disorganizing and disruptive symptoms, severe alcoholism, and many other difficulties his profound rebellion against his devoutly religious "lace-curtain Irish" family, who were always preoccupied with presenting a faultless appearance to society, whatever their personal peccadillos in private. Another, the Housebound Phobic Woman, spent much of her life self-consciously trying to shake off what she felt to be the hurtful impact of her mother's fanatic Christian Science faith. The mother had actually died of severe hypertension and a stroke when the patient was 20, consequent to her lifelong refusal of all medical help. And yet another, the Bohemian Prep School Boy, who came from a wildly eccentric and highly intellectual home (the father was a well-known artist and the mother was the heiress to a great industrial fortune), expressed part of his severe identity confusion in the fashionable Episcopal prep school he attended through his statement of feeling always out of place and different, "neither a Christian nor a Jew." Two other patients, Peter Pan and the Intellectual Fencer—both Jewish and both single when they came for treatment— expressed their growing separation from their parents through the course of treatment, in part through intermarriages: The Intellectual Fencer took on the strongly religious Episcopal faith and practice of her husband, while Peter Pan joined her husband in an espousal of a "liberal religious viewpoint," with thoughts of joining the Quaker or Unitarian churches.

With three of the patients, issues of religion played a major role throughout their treatments and were related to the nature of the results achieved and their stabilization into the posttreatment period. One of these, the Snake Phobia Woman, gave up her church as a consequence of her (ultimately) successful analysis because she could no longer abide its fundamentalist and literal emphasis in church and prayer meetings. Her own ideas on God had become "more abstract," and the divinity of Christ was no longer a congenial doctrine to her. This was itself all part of a growing psychological separation from what she felt to be the petty small-town life to which she was tied by her husband's business (inherited from his father).

Events with the Adoptive Mother, the other Catholic in the sample, took the opposite turn. She had converted to the Catholic faith of her husband, having been aware as a child of the great crowds that seemed to go to the Catholic church and feeling that a faith that could draw so many people to church must be the "true faith." During her illness—precipitated, as noted, by the guilt-laden return of her adopted infant, which even a trip to Lourdes in search of a miracle that would enable her "to develop some feeling" for the baby had not been able to forestall— she had received no comfort from her religion, and this had consequently "shaken my faith." Going to church had become an empty experience. In church she now felt "lost"; she had certainly failed to be a "good Catholic mother." She emerged from her reasonably successful psychoanalysis with her religious convictions restored. When in the follow-up period she undertook again to adopt a child, she coped with the attendant anxieties in part through calling on her religion, lighting candles and going to Mass twice daily, praying and weeping, "storming heaven." This effort was undergirded by a stern priest who admonished her to "shape up," to do her duties as a Catholic wife, and to stop ruining her husband's life. With all this, and other helps, she did adopt again—this time successfully.

The most dramatic case in this sequence was that of the Exhibitionistic Dancer, who through her pretreatment life made sure to keep clear of her mother's Christian Science involvement (one among a variety of the mother's ill-sustained interests), but who ultimately ended her very stormy and most unsuccessful psychotherapy through propelling herself into an intense attachment to Christian Science and a Christian Science practitioner; this attachment seemed to become the one stabilizing and sustaining element in an otherwise continuing chaotic life. This story is recounted in detail, as one kind of "result," in the case descriptions in the main body of this book.

Family Socioeconomic Status

In terms of socioeconomic status (SES) and occupational groupings of the patients' families of origin, there was the expected clustering of the private practice psychiatric patient clientele of that time period (the 1950s) in a small Midwestern town. There were no blacks or other minority-group members in this all-white sample. What was less predictable was the actual class distribution. In contrast to the usual stereotype of who could get to treatment at the expensive Menninger Foundation, only five of the patients came from families of great wealth. These were as follows: the Heiress, from the great department store empire established by the grandfather whose will barred any female heirs from ownership participation; the Alcoholic Heir, who had succeeded in destroying his career in the giant scientific–industrial enterprise in which his father was a major executive; the Adolescent Grandson, whose life was totally manipulated and controlled by his grandfather, the head of a great industrial fortune; the Bohemian Prep School Boy, whose father was the famous artist and his mother the heiress to another great industrial fortune; and the Sexual Masochist, whose very wealthy lawyer father spent a good part of his working life managing the even wealthier mother's inherited fortune.

    Eighteen of the patients came from substantially well-off but not truly wealthy families. The fathers of five of these patients were physicians, two of whom were in academic medicine, and one of whom was married to a lawyer and judge who became "the first woman judge in the West." Six of the fathers were other professionals—three lawyers, an engineer, an architect, and a dentist. Another seven fathers were businessmen and bankers, mostly in small towns; one of these was a commodity broker and one an automobile dealer. The other 19 patients, almost half the sample, came from small-town petit bourgeois or rural backgrounds. Their fathers were farmers, laborers, mechanics, railroad workers, salesmen, small shopkeepers.

Family Alcoholism

In view of the high rate of alcoholism and other varieties of addiction in the patients (to be described), it perhaps should be no surprise that severe alcoholism played an important role in the family background of 15 of the 42 patients. With 10 of these, it was the father alone who was alcoholic, and 8 of those 10 were from the 19 patients from the lower-middle-class or working-class backgrounds; 1, the Actress, was the daughter of the architect; and 1, the Heiress, from the wealthiest group, was from the family with the retail store empire. With 4 of the patients, it was not the father but others in the family who were alcoholic, and these 4 all came from either the professional–business (2 of them) or the very wealthy group (the other 2). With 3 of these 4, the mother was the alcoholic: in the cases of the Adolescent Grandson, whose very wealthy grandfather headed the major industrial complex; the Alcoholic Raconteur, from the "lace-curtain Irish" family, where the father was a successful commodity broker; and the Car Salesman, whose father managed a successful automobile dealership. The fourth in this group of other-than-father alcoholism was the Alcoholic Heir, whose father (the scientific–industrial empire executive) was actually an abstainer, but whose paternal grandfather, paternal uncle, older brother (who had died in the fire he set while drunk), younger sister, and wife were all varyingly alcoholic.

In the last (15th) case in this group—the Sexual Masochist, who also came from the very wealthiest group (the lawyer father and heiress mother)—*both* parents were severely alcoholic. In this most extreme situation, the patient's major childhood memory of the father was seeing him sprawled at home in a chair in an alcoholic stupor. The mother was remembered as sweet and kindly when sober, but very seductive when intoxicated; she would insist on the patient's assistance to get to the bathroom, where he would be made to watch her urinate. After the father's first heart attack, he had no longer worked at all, but had just stayed home drinking. Shortly after the father's death, the mother had fractured her hip when drunk (at age 65), and thereafter she was invalided and continuously drinking.

What seems to emerge overall from the amount of family alcoholism in this patient population (15 of the 42) was that where the father alone was the primary alcoholic, the families were almost always (8 out of those 10) from the lower-middle-class or working-class backgrounds, but where the mother alone (3) or both parents (1) or other family members (1) were alcoholics, the families were all from the wealthier strata. In fact, among the five families in this group with alcoholic family members other than the father alone, three of them were among the five families of great wealth—the families of the Alcoholic Heir, the Adolescent Grandson, and the Sexual Masochist. Of the other two extremely wealthy families, one was that of the Heiress, where the father was severely alcoholic; only one, that of the Bohemian Prep School Boy, was not beset by severe family alcoholism.

Personal and Spouse SES

I turn now to the occupations and SES of the patients themselves and their spouses. Among the 21 males, 11 were professionals (5 physicians, 1 of those still a medical student; 1 lawyer; 1 civil engineer; 1 psychologist; and 3 college professors). Another 2 were businessmen, though 1 by that time had destroyed his business career through his alcoholism; 4 were various kinds of white-collar workers or salesmen; 2 were still young students (the two 17-year-olds in the project—(the Bohemian Prep School Boy and the Adolescent Grandson); and 2 were unable to hold any job and lived essentially as remittance men on their families' largesse. This last pair, the Sexual Masochist and the Alcoholic Raconteur, came from the more moneyed families, the first of them from the small handful (five) of the very wealthiest families.

Among the 21 female patients, 4 were nurses, though not all of them were working; 3 were other professionals (a lawyer, a nonpsychiatric social worker, and a teacher); 5 were in some kind of creative art endeavor (a musician, a script writer for the media, an editorial worker, an adjunctive therapist, and an occupational therapist); 4 were still students (ages 19, 19, 21, and 21); and 5, one of them the extremely wealthy Heiress, had no occupation. Of the 12 female patients who were married when they came to treatment, in 5 instances the husbands were professionals (2 physicians, a dentist, a lawyer, and a psychologist); 3 were businessmen; 1 was a civil servant; 1 was a journalist; 1 was still a student; and 1 (the husband of the Tantrum Woman, who had been killed in the auto accident that precipitated his wife's decompensation and turn to treatment as a freshly grieving and very distraught young widow) had been a cab driver.

It is clear from this account of the SES of the patients that as a group they were downwardly mobile from the parental generation. Of the five who came from great wealth, only two, the Heiress and the Sexual Masochist, were in any way able to live in accord with it. Fewer patients than parents were in professional and business roles. The fact of downward mobility becomes even more apparent when it is recalled that a fair number of the occupations listed for the patients were collapsed occupations. For example, the four established physicians were not able to function, three of them because of severe alcohol and drug addiction and the fourth because of the cyclical decompensation of his manic–depressive illness; the fifth medical person, the medical student, was a *suspended* medical student. Additionally, some of the occupations listed, especially among the women, were things that they actually came to be able to do in some productive fashion during, and as a beneficial consequence of, their treatments.

One patient, the Exhibitionistic Dancer, actually propelled herself by marriage into a far wealthier economic bracket. While in the hospital, she eloped with an even sicker hospital patient who was the young heir to a famous and large industrial fortune. This ill-starred marriage ended in divorce very shortly after the patient terminated her treatment; the divorce left her with two small children and a very adequate lifetime financial settlement.

Intellectual Capacity

In intellectual capacity as reflected by the IQ (as at least one measure of the requisite resources for psychotherapeutic work, as well as a dimension of demographic identification), the patients clearly were a superior group. The range at the point of Initial Study, as determined by psychological testing—even with all the evidence in numerous instances of adverse effects from the ravages of decompensated mental illness (ranging from constrictions and anxieties to frankly disorganized states)—was still from 111 to 141, with a mean of 124. The individual with the lowest score (111) in the group, the Housebound Phobic Woman, was at that point a chronically organically brain-damaged woman from her many years of severe barbiturate addiction (though by then recovered from the severe acute organic intoxication that had characterized her state when she had been brought to The Menninger Foundation 2 months earlier, at which point her IQ had only measured 98). The IQ figures given above are the mean of the Performance and Verbal components, which in almost all the instances showed but a small spread. One outstanding exception was the very motorically inclined and action-oriented Sociopath, whose Initial Study mean of 125 represented a spread between a Verbal IQ measure of 109 and a Performance IQ measure of 135.

Two articles from PRP (S. A. Appelbaum, Coyne, & Siegal, 1969, 1970) deal specifically with the issue of change in measured IQ during and after long-term psychotherapy — in an overall upward direction and to an unexpected degree — and the understanding of the routes to that change. This issue is discussed in some detail further on in this book, in the description of the results of therapy. At this point, I want only to emphasize that this particular relatively homogeneous but nonrepresentative population was indeed drawn from the intellectually more gifted end of the general population distribution spectrum. How representative it would be in this regard of the population that comes to intensive psychotherapy is of course not known precisely, though we all do have reason to believe that psychotherapy patients in general have considerably higher IQs than the population at large.

Previous Psychiatric Treatment

A last dimension to be discussed in this demographic description of our patient sample is that of the amount of previous psychiatric evaluation, consultation, or treatment received by the patients. Although I have indicated in the description of the sample selection that one of the chosen exclusion factors was that of "old cases" — that is, "old" in the sense of having had previous treatment in The Menninger Foundation setting — I have also noted in that context that a chief way in which prospective patients came to The Menninger Foundation for evaluation and/or treatment was through psychiatric consultation or failed treatment elsewhere. The decision was generally made in those settings that the special resources of The Menninger Foundation might be required in order to give the patients their best treatment chance.

Given this situation, it is not surprising that only 10 of the 42 patients had had no previous evaluation or treatment effort at all before the immediate events that led to their appearance at The Menninger Foundation. Another 6 had had no treatment effort but only psychiatric evaluations prior to referral to Topeka; however, for 1 of these, the Bohemian Prep School Boy, these consultations had covered an 11-year span, starting when he was only 6. All 26 others had had various treatment efforts, either single or in combination — some brief, some fitful, and some indeed very long-standing: The Phobic Woman, for example, had been in practically continuous psychotherapy for the preceding 8 years, and the Manic–Depressive Physician had had various treatment efforts, including hospitalization and electroconvulsive therapy (ECT), over a prior 11-year span.

Actually, a total of 20 of the patients had been involved in various efforts at systematic and formal psychotherapy. One of these patients, the English Professor, had had two different hospital doctors and three psychotherapists — a total of five different helpers over only a 4-year span. Another of the 20, the Housebound Phobic Woman, had in one of her periods in psychotherapy had a trial of "narcoanalysis." Still another, The Phobic Woman, had had 8 years of treatment (as indicated above) with two psychoanalysts — the first of these was also a child analyst — but the treatments had not been intended to be psychoanalysis. And yet another of the 20, the Sexual Masochist, had during one of his periods of treatment sat with his back to the therapist twice weekly for about 150 hours, trying to free-associate. In addition to the 20 in previous formal psychotherapy, another patient, the Masochistic Editor, had had a year's effort in formal psychoanalysis; however, he had often missed hours or had come to them drunk. The father, who had never been fully informed of the extensiveness of the patient's psychological difficulties or why they required so expensive a remedy, had been paying for the treatment most unwillingly, and when the patient had secured a temporary job, the father, feeling that the treatment objectives had been met, had ceased his payments. The patient, rather than doing anything about this (either to secure continued support from his father or undertake to try to support the treatment in any way himself), had let the treatment lapse, stating, "I was a failure."

In addition to all these patients in psychotherapy of one kind or another and of such varying durations and intensity, 12 of the patients (some of them of course overlapping with those in psychotherapy) had had varying periods of hospitalization—in general hospitals, in private psychiatric institutions, in Veterans Administration (VA) hospitals, and one (the Addicted Doctor) for a period at the Federal Narcotics Treatment Center in Lexington, Kentucky. Some of these had been repeated in-and-out hospitalizations, essentially for drying-out purposes (as with the Alcoholic Heir, who would be contrite and compliant when entering and then with recovered sobriety would be noisily clamoring for release); others had been more extended efforts at more definitive hospital management and milieu treatment. Four of the patients had had some combination of ECT and/or subcoma insulin treatment: These had included the Manic–Depressive Physician and the Involutional Woman, and also two others for whom the indications were more dubious, the neurotically depressed Silent Woman and the very alcoholic Car Salesman. Another four patients had had major treatment efforts with one or another of the behavior-influencing drugs. The heavily drinking Sexual Masochist had been on Antabuse for a substantial period of time; the Housebound Phobic Woman, who had had the earlier treatment effort with "narco-analysis," had for a considerable period of time before coming to The Menninger Foundation been using a psychiatrist mostly as an unfailing source of prescriptions for sedative drugs, which played their major role in her decompensation into the acute barbiturate-intoxicated state superimposed upon a (barbiturate-induced?) chronic organic brain syndrome seen when she arrived in Topeka; the very anxious and potentially decompensating Bohemian Prep School Boy had been put intermittently on large doses of Miltown; and the Fearful Loner, who had never before had psychiatric contact, had been put on Thorazine (with some relief of his high anxiety) by his general physician. It must be remembered that all of this took place in the mid-1950s, when the first of the psychoactive drugs were coming onto the market. A comparable patient population coming to The Menninger Foundation today would no doubt have a far more extensive history of psychoactive drug administration, perhaps somewhat less hospitalization, and certainly less ECT or subcoma insulin treatment.

Additionally, a few of the patients had had other kinds of treatment efforts, both within and without the limits of formal therapy. Only one, the Heiress, had had a trial of group therapy (again, this would be probably a much larger number today), which in her case had accompanied her individual psychotherapy. Another, the Obedient Husband, came to his own psychotherapy after about a year of casework sessions with the psychiatric social worker as the responsible relative in relation to the illness of his wife, who was hospitalized and in psychotherapy at The Menninger Foundation. The Adoptive Mother, the Catholic convert, had sought a very different kind of help: As noted, she had tried a visit to Lourdes in the vain hope that a miracle would enable her "to develop some feeling" for her adopted baby. And still another patient, the Medical Scientist, had engaged in a species of self-help endeavor. Several times he had struggled against his addiction (mainly to Demerol and codeine) by retiring to a hotel room in a city near his home town and living through the agony of an abrupt "cold-turkey" withdrawal. Unhappily, he had each time returned to his addictions.

One patient had had a particularly neurotogenic experience during her previous psychotherapy. This was the Snake Phobia Woman, with an intensely crippling and pervasive "classical" snake phobia, who had had two periods of prior weekly psychotherapy with a psychoanalytically trained psychiatrist. She had finally discontinued this treatment because of her therapist's "aggressive approach to treatment"; by this, she meant that he would have her sit on his lap while he caressed her, made advances to her, and insisted that she was unable to give love because she was fearful of what form treatment might take next. By the point of her arrival in Topeka, the patient was very panicky, and clearly iatrogenic issues imposed their additional burdens on the transference expectations in the subsequent psychoanalysis at The Menninger Foundation.

All told, this was a very considerable amount and variety of previous treatment efforts in this quite sick patient population before their entry into PRP.

The Three Phases of the Project

THE INITIAL STUDY: FORMULATIONS, RECOMMENDATIONS, AND PREDICTIONS

Description of Form A

PRP was built not just around, but also out of, the usual clinical operations of The Menninger Foundation. We began with the usual psychiatric case study routinely carried out with individuals who came or were sent to The Menninger Foundation for evaluation and possible treatment recommendation. As has been indicated, we (Robbins and myself) were able, with the assistance and knowledge of only one clerk in the medical record room, to obtain the complete case record write-ups of those prospective patients who had been evaluated, had been recommended for intensive analytic psychotherapy at The Menninger Foundation, had accepted the recommendations, and had been placed on waiting lists for psychoanalysis or psychotherapy; we were then able to use the data of this psychiatric case study (called by us "Form A") as the very adequate basis for construction of the PRP's Initial Study of that individual.

The usual psychiatric case study was composed as follows: The prospective patient came to Topeka accompanied by a significant relative—where possible, the spouse; otherwise a parent, an adult child, or some other involved and responsible individual. Records and letters were brought along from the referring sources.

The time period of the evaluation was 2 weeks, during which the individual and the family member lived in a local hotel, unless the illness picture was such as to require hospitalization during this assessment period. (As should be clear from much of what has been described about this patient population to this point, there were many in the PRP sample, especially among the drug- and alcohol-addicted and intoxicated group, who were immediately hospitalized when they arrived in Topeka.)

The patient was seen in daily interview sessions (a total of up to 10) with an examining psychiatrist during this 2-week period. A complete psychological projective test battery was administered and assessed by a clinical psychologist over that same span. At the same time, the accompanying relative was seen daily by the team psychiatric social worker, and a comprehensive family and situational history was developed. During this same period, the staff internist did a physical examination, and referred the prospective patient to a staff neurologist for a neurological examination if this was indicated. At the end of the 2-week period, a regular team staff conference was held (with up to a dozen participants), in which the psychiatric examination, psychological testing, social history, and other relevant data were presented for discussion and decision. Out of the conference a comprehensive case formulation emerged (the life history; the structure of the personality and of the illness; the diagnostic understanding), as well as recommendations for treatment (no treatment; continuation of treatment back in the home community with the referring therapist; or staying in Topeka for treatment, with or without concomitant hospitalization or other less encompassing life management [partial hospitalization, day care, foster home living, etc.], and with or without the whole family being asked to move to Topeka for the treatment duration) and some preliminary treatment planning and prognostication. These whole proceedings of this case conference were summarized in detail and likewise became part of the permanent case record.

The overall findings and recommendations from this case conference were then communicated to the prospective patient and the accompanying family member by the examining psychiatrist and the psychiatric social worker. If the recommendations were accepted, and if they included remaining for psychoanalysis or other intensive psychotherapy at The Menninger Foundation, the prospective patient moved into the indicated living arrangement and was placed on the appropriate therapy waiting list—a wait before starting of not usually more than 6 to 8 weeks. It was all this detailed clinical record (psychiatric case history; psychological test report; social history; physical examination and, if indicated, neurological examination; letters and summaries from all referring sources; and summary of the case conference—averaging usually a total of about 25 typed single-spaced pages) that we collectively called "Form A" and that comprised the basic study data for our research assessments.

The Form A data were of course written in the usual narrative clinical format, full of the usual clinical qualifications. They presumably contained the full and adequate information out of which one could construct the case formulation and make the appropriately indicated treatment recommendations. Most of the inferential reasoning process by which the elicited data were put together into a coherent formulation and the appropriate treatment plan derived was, as is usually the case in clinical documentation, *implicit*. On occasion, if debate had arisen at the synthesizing case conference concerning the nature of a particular recommendation (why psychotherapy instead of psychoanalysis, why with concomitant hospitalization or day hospital, etc.), there would then usually be, in regard to that particular issue of formulation or recommendation, a more explicit statement of the reasoning process that had led to it.

Description of Form B

PRP undertook to begin its research at this point by making more explicit and setting down in permanent documentation, to which subsequent observers could have recourse, as much as possible of this clinical thinking that is always present but usually only implicit in clinical discourse. We began by creating an assessment form for relevant Patient Variables, which we called "Form B." Appropriate treatment recommendations could only derive from an appropriate and adequate understanding of the patient; thus, we first undertook to specify those factors or variables in the patient, in the structure of the patient's personality or illness, that we felt were regularly relevant to a proper understanding of the patient, the illness, and the proposed treatment course. These were conceptualized of course within the framework of our psychoanalytic theory of personality, but were specified within the local and perhaps at times idiosyncratic usage of The Menninger Foundation clinical community. Except for sex, they did not include any of the demographic identifying dimensions already discussed (age having been removed as a significant factor by trying to restrict our sample to the young to middle adult years).

These variables, after much discussion, became a list of 28, grouped within eight general categories. They comprised, rather than demographic markers, assessments of that array of psychological attributes and patterns that would yield the kind of personality- and treatment-oriented understandings we sought—assessments that were many (or even most) of them complex clinical judgments to be arrived at by clinical inferential processes from the available data of Form A. As finally evolved, they were as follows:

FORM B: ASSESSMENT OF RELEVANT PATIENT VARIABLES

   I. Sex (and where relevant, Age)
  II. Anxiety and Symptoms
     1. Anxiety
     2. Symptoms
     3. Somatization
     4. Depression and Guilt Feelings
       a. Depression
       b. Conscious Guilt
       c. Unconscious Guilt
     5. Alloplasticity
 III. Nature of Conflicts
     1. Core-Neurotic Problem
     2. Current Life Problem
 IV. Ego Factors (and Defenses)

1. Self-Concept
2. Patterning of Defenses
3. Anxiety Tolerance
4. Insight
5. Externalization
6. Ego Strength
V. Capacities Factors
   1. Intelligence
   2. Psychological-Mindedness
   3. Constitutionally Endowed Aspects of Ego Strength
   4. Capacity for Sublimations
VI. Motivational Factors
   1. Honesty
   2. Fee
   3. Extent of Desired Change
   4. Secondary Gain
VII. Relationship Factors
   1. Quality of Interpersonal Relationships
   2. Transference Paradigms
VIII. Reality Factors
   1. Presence of "Neurotic Life Circumstance"
   2. Adequacy of Finances to the Treatment Requirements
   3. Attitudes of Significant Relatives
   4. Physical Health

Our definitions of these variables, and what we meant to be included under each variable in our Form B write-ups on each of the PRP patients, were spelled out in detail in the paper "Concepts" (Wallerstein & Robbins, 1956) from the very first collection of five papers from PRP. In order to convey some of the clinical comprehensiveness that we tried to bring into these assessments, I quote from the "Concepts" paper the description of just one of the 28 Patient Variables, Anxiety (admittedly one of the more complex ones):

> Anxiety: conceived of as a subjective experience, an inferred experience, and an observable manifestation:
>
> a. Intensity: extreme (panic), severe, moderate, mild, none or unobservable.
> b. How evident: How is anxiety expressed, dealt with or avoided? This involves, of course, a statement about which ego defenses are utilized in order to ward off or dissipate anxiety. These defenses should only be named here, being further individually assessed under IV: Ego Factors.
>   (1) Manifest anxiety: How does the patient consciously experience anxiety and what does he do to relieve it? Is it used adaptively (stimulating the ego to efforts at increased mastery) or nonadaptively (leading to further impaired mastery)?
>   (a) Free floating: A subjective experience which can be described by the patient or which can be inferred from specialized procedures, as psychological tests. It is usually diffuse and pervasive and may or may not be observable in behavior.

(b) Attached: Also a subjective experience which is, however, focused on a specific situation or idea. The patient may recognize that the situation or idea to which the anxiety is attributed is inadequate to explain it.

(c) Expressed as tension: This consists of behavioral manifestations of tension (reflecting for the most part autonomic or musculoskeletal hyperactivity) such as sweating, tremors, tachycardia, restlessness, crying, tics, mannerisms, word blocking, respiratory symptoms (the listed signs are intended to be suggestive rather than exhaustive). Some subjective experiences such as palpitations, soreness in the chest, also belong here. What characterizes this group is that it is the distressing "nervous symptom" that is primarily manifest rather than "anxiety" as a specific mental state of apprehension.

(2) Averted anxiety: This concerns anxiety which is kept from consciousness by some manoeuvre defensive in nature, and maladaptive in outcome (in terms of optimal psychic functioning).

(a) Bound anxiety: From the nature of the defensive operations of the ego one can often infer that they are designed to deal with inner tension in such a way that anxiety will be avoided. That is, if a compulsion neurotic is prevented from carrying out his prescribed compulsive ritual, anxiety will then become manifest. The intensity of the anxiety which is thus "bound" in the compulsive defense can be inferred from the strength of the anticathexis. The extent to which anxiety is thus partially or fully avoided and the defensive measures utilized should be stated.

(b) Discharge of anxiety-provoking tension: Under this category belong those actions which are used to discharge tension in order to ward off anxiety. Resort to alcohol would be a classical example of this (and is often referred to loosely as "discharging the anxiety"). By drinking, an infantile instinctual gratification is obtained (in fantasy) and the anxiety that would ensue from the awareness of the unfulfilled instinctual longing is warded off.

c. Awareness of anxiety: This is a more quantitative assessment of the extent to which anxiety is experienced or kept out of awareness. To what extent does the individual experience anxiety as a distressing symptom that furnished part of the impetus to seek treatment? The extremes can range from being overwhelmed by anxiety to a complete denial.

Although the "anxiety tolerance" is closely linked to all of the above (i.e., the lower the tolerance for anxiety, the more essential that prompt and vigorous steps be taken to bind it or to ward it off), it is more properly a specific ego operation and will therefore be delineated under IV: Ego Factors. (pp. 241–242)

For comparable descriptions of what was to be included under the assessment of each of the other 27 Patient Variables, the reader is referred to the "Concepts" paper (Wallerstein & Robbins, 1956, pp. 241–250). Once these Patient Variables had been formulated, agreed upon, and defined as above in this essentially theoretical and "armchair" manner, they were put to use by the Initial Study team (Robbins and myself) who had worked out these Patient Variables conceptually; the available Form A material was used in each of the project cases to describe the operation of that Form B Patient Variable (that function or that attribute) in the particular patient under study. In each instance, if the Patient Variable were indeed relevant and necessary to the understanding of the patient and of the recommended treatment course, there should have been adequate data available in the Form A material to come to a reasonable assessment of it—and in each case there was. (Presumably, if the Form A material provided insufficient data to provide the basis for an informed judgment on that particular Form B Patient Variable, the overall assessment of the patient on which the clinical treatment planning and assignment had been made by the examining clinicians would have been too shakily based, or the particular variable would not have been significant to the projected course and outcome.) In a departure from usual clinical practice (where, as stated, the inferential process is so often left implicit), when we made the Form B Patient Variable judgments in each case, we specified in detail the information in the Form A clinical material (whether psychiatric examination, psychological test, social history, or case conference discussion) that led to that overall assessment of the variable. This assessment of the relevant Patient Variables was a mutual, not an independent, process by the two of us on the Initial Study Team; our consensus, once arrived at, was dictated at that point into a machine by one of us in the presence of the other, who could and did offer amplification or correction as he felt it indicated. When transcribed, these Form B statements of the status of each patient on the 28 relevant Patient Variables at the Initial Study point in time usually ran to about 20 single-spaced typed pages.

As has already been described, the conceptualization of the Patient Variables arrived at by Robbins and myself did not remain static in use over the lifespan of PRP. The group undertaking the separate and parallel use of the psychological test data protocols as sources of assessments of patient variables and predictions to projected psychotherapy course and outcome found it useful to add two other variables, "Affect Organization" and "Thought Organization," to the assessment of which projective psychological test data particularly lent themselves; at the same time, that group could not from the psychological test data really assess any of the Category VIII (Reality Factors) variables, and only some of the Category VI (Motivational Factors) variables, that Robbins and I were making judgments on.

This process of additional conceptualization or reconceptualization of the relevant Patient Variables did not stop there, however. The Patient Variables were originally conceptualized for assessment purposes at the Initial Study point in time, where the major issue was that of the proper understanding of the individual as a prospective psychotherapy patient and an assessment of that individual's prospects in that undertaking. When the issue arose of reassessing all the patients' status on these same Form B Patient Variables from the standpoint of Termination Study or Follow-Up Study, it was found that some of the original conceptions were too limited or perhaps even faulty, and some were therefore rethought and redefined. Footnote 3 in Chapter 2 (p. 19) lists specific articles from PRP devoted to several of these reconceptualizations.

Description of Form C

Once the prospective patient had been initially assessed on all the Form B Patient Variables, the same Initial Study team (Robbins and I) went on to create "Form C," the clinical Prediction Study proper. This form was created as a dynamic case synthesis and then a series of predictive statements about the expected course and outcome of the recommended therapy, based on specified crucial aspects of each treatment process: the expectable vicissitudes of the transference (including the patterning and sequencing of transference models, major anticipated resistance patterns, and foreseeable likely external events that might be expected to bear on the course of the treatment, favorably or unfavorably); changes anticipated in the originally presenting (or in evolving) symptoms and complaints; changes in manifest behavior patterns; changes in the patient's characteristic impulse–defense configurations; expectable overall structural changes[1] in the ego; and, finally, the acquisition of insight through the treatment, and its relationship to change in attitudes toward the self, others, things, and the illness. The reader is again referred to the "Concepts" paper (Wallerstein & Robbins, 1956, pp. 250–261) for a full explication, with examples, of what was to be included in the Form C (Prediction Study) write-up under each of these various headings.

All of this Form C material was also arrived at by the same process of consensus and was jointly dictated in the manner already described. In the first part of Form C, the case synthesis and treatment recommendations, there was meant to be as full a statement as possible of how that patient, as defined by the Form B assessments of the relevant Patient Variables, would be expected to fit into the treatment plan recommended by the initial clinical examination process to which both the patient and the clinic had committed themselves. At times, it might be the case that the ideal treatment plan for the patient might not be possible, due to limitations posed by available finances or geography or life circumstances (e.g., not being available for daily psychoanalytic sessions); statements would then be built into Form C about expectations of fit (and prediction of the course and outcome) with the "ideal" treatment and the degree to which, or not, the expectations could be approximated in each instance with the alternatively chosen more feasible or available therapeutic plan.

Another kind of discrepancy could also arise. It might happen (as it did in several instances — the Alcoholic Raconteur's case was a striking example) that the research study group doing the Initial Study disagreed with the treatment recommendations that had been worked out by the original clinical evaluation team and that had been agreed to by the patient in consenting to remain in Topeka for the recommended treatment. For example, the Alcoholic Raconteur had been recommended for psychoanalysis (which actually he loudly insisted upon), and that was the treatment that was planned. With all of the (quite conscious) bias operating within PRP for its predictors to prognosticate in terms of the utmost reach, the best that it could do, for each treatment modality being studied, and then to see where and why it fell short of realizing this potential,[2] this particular case was nonetheless one that the PRP Initial Study team felt would end disastrously if psy-

---

1. The concepts of "structure" and "structural change" are used throughout in the sense — most clearly articulated by Rapaport (1960) — of a characteristic and relatively fixed *pattern of functioning*. How much of such "true" structural change is achievable (and achieved) in psychoanalysis on the one hand, as opposed to the more strictly supportive psychoanalytic psychotherapies on the other, and even, incidentally, how useful this concept proved to be in the empirical crucible of PRP, are themes that weave repeatedly through the description of therapy courses and outcomes throughout this book. This is all then integrated into a final statement in the final section of the book (see Chapter 38, "Insight, Structural Change, and Their Relationship Reconsidered").

2. See the discussion of this issue and its place in relation to the broader conceptualizations of the "results" from PRP in Chapter 2, pp. 20–21.

choanalysis were undertaken and persisted in as the treatment of choice. In a case such as this one, alternative statements were made about treatment fit and expected treatment course and outcome, based on the two possibilities: (1) that the selected therapist would agree with the recommendations of the examining team and undertake (and persist in) the effort at psychoanalysis; or (2) that the therapist would either from the beginning or after an initial period of trial at psychoanalysis come to disagree with those recommendations and alter the treatment mode himself or herself in the direction that the research study group had outlined as the more appropriate (though, of course, without any knowledge that there were such statements made about the patient he or she had taken into treatment). Clearly, quite different treatment courses and outcomes could be placed side by side in each dimension under study, each related to a different treatment plan. Again, in writing up Form C, just as with Form B, we undertook to specify under each heading not just the judgment made, but also the inferential process by which it was linked to the data about the patient in interaction with the described attributes of the selected treatment modality.

What is clear from all this is that this entire clinical Prediction Study was based on a series of theoretical understandings. First was the psychoanalytic conceptualization of the nature of the patient's personality organization and illness structure, as embodied in the Form B statement about the designated Patient Variables (which, in turn, was based on the data gathered about the patient in the clinical study contained in Form A). To this was then added a set of predictions about how that individual would fare in the prescribed therapeutic modality (administered of course, by a therapist of at least "average expectable competence"[3]), given our theoretical understandings (our theory of psychoanalytic therapy) about how that

---

3. The reader is referred to the earlier discussion of this issue in Chapter 5, footnote 2, p. 59. Since the Initial Studies were so often made prior to any knowledge of the identity of the particular Menninger Foundation staff therapist who would take on that treatment, this issue of the prospective therapist's presumed level of competence clearly raises a serious scientific concern—and it was one never completely satisfactorily resolved throughout the entire operation of PRP. Our consultant, John Benjamin, pointed to it in his 1956 visit as another example of the kinds of specific bias that we were building against ourselves throughout the predictive process. Not knowing who the therapist was to be—and thus with no knowledge of the specific capacities and possibly the limitations of that therapist, as well as the judgments that might be made concerning areas of specific fit (or not) between *that* therapist and *that* patient—we were unable to tailor our predictions of the outcomes to be expected to an understanding of how particular attributes or limitations of the particular therapist might interact with (or play into) the neurotic patterns of the patient in ways that could give special possibility to, or cause special difficulty for, the therapeutic process. This whole issue is of course highly relevant to the discussion in Chapter 2, pp. 20–21, of the degree of predictive accuracy achieved by the Initial Study team.

Clearly, the one way we could cope with *one aspect* of this issue—that of ensuring at least a minimal adequate skill and experience level of the therapist-to-be (apart from issues of personal style and idiosyncracy, as well as of special problems or attributes referred to above)—would be not to take into the project patients who had some likelihood of going into treatment with the more junior members of the therapy staff. The floor that we did succeed in building in was that all the psychotherapy patients would be with therapists with at least 5 years' experience at therapeutic work beyond their training years. With the psychoanalysis cases, for reasons already indicated earlier in this section, most of the "better" cases for psychoanalysis in the project would be the supervised training cases of neophyte psychoanalysts (although most of them were already quite experienced psychotherapists). There, our safeguard would have to be in the closeness and the overall adequacy of the supervision process in the Topeka Institute for Psychoanalysis (operating within The Menninger Foundation).

planned modality (within the range of psychoanalytically based psychotherapeutic modes) would operate to bring about the hoped-for and planned-for changes in psychological functioning. The Prediction Study could then become the basis for systematic testing of the various aspects of our "rule-of-thumb" assumptions that, in their totality, comprise this theory or these theories of the various modes of psychoanalytic therapy. Just a little further on, I specify the degree of precision with which we could try to accomplish that large goal within the PRP.

Overall, the Form C Prediction Study that then emerged was a document that ran about 10 single-spaced typed pages. Added to the approximately 20 single-spaced typed pages of Form B, this made a considerable body of sifted information and derived judgments about each of the patients in the study. Robbins and I could each devote 10 hours per week to this shared task. It took us about a month per patient studied, which accounts for the particular ultimate limit on the total size of the sample.

Use of the HSRS

The last task of this phase of the Initial Study was the designation of the patient's initial status and the prediction to the end-of-therapy expected status on the HSRS. This scale, the only effort at quantitative measure and the only rating scale employed during the assessment and data-gathering phases of the PRP (others were devised later as aspects of the data analysis in different categories), was, as already stated (see p. 5), a 100-point scale, anchored by 34 paragraph-long sample case descriptions covering the entire range of the scale. The scale (as earlier stated) was first created during the precursor period to PRP, in 1951–1952. Several articles specifically about its use in PRP, as well as in other projects through the country, have appeared in the literature (Luborsky, 1962a, 1975; Luborsky & Bachrach, 1974). For each PRP patient, the original Initial Study team made a judgment of the patient's Initial Study place on the HSRS, plus a judgment about the predicted HSRS at Termination. At the time of Termination Study, other clinical judges (the Termination Study team) would make an assessment of the HSRS as they judged it at that point, for comparison then with the adjudged level at Initial Study and with the predicted level for Termination. They would also then make a prediction to the expected Follow-Up Study level, at which time similar comparisons between prediction and outcome could be made, and the overall sequence (from Initial to Termination to Follow-Up Study) could be looked at as one numerical reflection of the degree of treatment gain and the degree of its stability into at least a several-year follow-up.

Description of Form S

In parallel with the Initial Study team's work in creating Form B and Form C out of the Form A clinical evaluation process material, another group, working according to the conceptualizations of Sargent, began undertaking a comparable assessment of environmental factors. This was called "Form S: Assessment of Relevant Situational Variables," and was based on the same available Form A data. These conceptualizations arose in the first instance out of considerations for control in the judgments to be made about the determinants of psychotherapy course and outcome. Basically, the question to be answered via the repeated assessments of Situational Variables was this: How does one know that these changes that took place in this patient during or subsequent to the course of his or her psychotherapy were not due to the favorable or unfavorable impact of some external life event—an opportunity that appeared or a trauma that impinged? To complicate this question somewhat, and to put it into a truly interactional context, the question could further become this: If this patient or ex-patient is now in a much more suitable marriage, job, or other major life circumstance, how does one know whether or to what extent this was the outcome of fortuitous happenstance (an opportunity not before present that had now materalized), or, alternatively, was itself *brought about*, wholly or at least significantly, by the patient himself or herself as one consequence of the treatment-induced changes in behavioral capacities and dispositions?

To attempt to answer such questions satisfactorily, it was clear that attention comparable to that minutely accorded to the array of psychological attributes and functions that comprised the Patient Variables would have to be paid to the relevant Situational Variables (and in parallel, at the same three points in time—Initial, Termination, and Follow-Up). In devising our listing of the relevant Patient Variables, we could of course be guided by the large body of clinical experience and theoretical conceptualization that existed within the psychoanalytic literature on therapy. No agreed-upon counterpart existed in regard to Situational Variables, especially to our own uncommon way of conceiving them. For, by "Situational Variables," we did not mean the facts of life environment embodied in the social history part of the Form A data. We did not mean, that is, any specification of the facts of parental or conjugal family constellation, education, occupation and position, wealth, activities, hobbies, friends, and so on. We meant, rather, a specification of their psychological impact, in the sense of the role of the whole array of such environmental factors within the psychological "life space" (Lewin, 1935) of the patient. Within such a conceptual framework, the Situational Variables (seven in all) were therefore conceived of as follows in Form S:

I. Degree of Relevance in the Individual
II. Amount of Stress Imposed
III. Degree of Support Afforded
IV. Degree to Which the Situational Factor is Conflict-Triggering[4]
V. Extent of Opportunity for Self-Realization, Growth, Autonomy, Success, etc.
VI. Congruence of Situations with Needs, Interests, Capacities, etc.
VII. Degree of Situational Mutability

---

4. How "conflict-triggering" a particular environmental event or influence is, in the sense of triggering the specific neurotic conflicts of that individual (say, the *conscious decision* on the part of a couple to stop the use of contraception in order to try to have a child, as it might reverberate with quite *unconscious* conflicts within the woman over becoming a mother and fulfilling the role of mother, especially in relation to all the specific unresolved neurotic conflicts in her own intrapsychic relationship to the internalized mother of her childhood), is obviously a crucial aspect of the effect of evolving life circumstance upon the precipitation of overt neurotic illness. It should come as no surprise that the Situational Variables group, in its work over time, felt "Degree to Which the Situational Factor Is Conflict-Triggering" to be the most critical of all

In assessing these Situational Variables, the Situational Variables team would need at each point in time to assess the impact under each of these headings of a whole array of life-situational events or factors: matters of background (cultural, religious and ethical, educational); of interpersonal relations (with parental family, marital family, friends, coworkers, colleagues); of marital–sexual relations; of living situation (home arrangements, financial situation, responsibilities); of occupation (stability, demands, compensation); of community and leisure time (recreational and avocational activities, group participation, civic and cultural activities); and of physical factors (appearance and physique, handicap, somatic illness). It may be readily seen in this most cursory listing that some of these factors (e.g., physical factors) did not really differ from some of those considered under Patient Variables, except that here the vantage point was a different one. For a much fuller description of how the Situational Variables were conceived, were described and defined, and were to be used, the reader is referred to the original article in that area by Sargent *et al.* (1958, especially pp. 151–155), in the second collection of papers published from PRP.[5]

Just two additional points (developed in fuller detail in Sargent *et al.*, 1958)—one major, and the other corollary to it—should be iterated here for their relevance to the discussions to follow concerning Termination and Follow-Up Studies. The first is that from the standpoint of the PRP research design, Situational Variables were not to be considered as criterion measures of improvement but as covariant factors, the precise role of which, in interaction with Treatment and Patient Variables in the determination of treatment results, would itself be a major focus of

---

the Situational Variables as an important element in the codetermination of treatment outcome. Indeed, I have already indicated (see Chapter 2, pp. 16–18) what I feel to be the severe overemphasis in the Voth and Orth (1973) book on the role of conflict-triggering situational factors in interaction with specific neurotic conflicts of the patient as (the?) major factors in the instigation of overt illness, and on the "disengagement" of patients from the conflict-instigating pressures as (the?) major factor in the degree of favorable result achieved, in the absence of demonstrable neurotic conflict "resolution" via interpretation, insight, structural change in the ego, and so on.

Clearly, by the way, specifications of what is conflict-triggering in the environment rest on an adequate understanding of what the specific core conflicts of that individual are, and this is one among many examples of the interdependence between the data and judgments in one area (Form S) and the data and judgments in another area (Form B). A last note at this point: Benjamin, in his 1957 consultation, suggested the even more felicitous phrase "conflict resonator," which serves even better than "conflict trigger" to capture the kind of feedback and reverberation that constitutes the vicious circle within which neurotic patients are caught. For some reason this phase did not catch on in our own PRP writings.

5. Among the inconclusively resolved major conceptual issues from the decades of PRP's work is that of the more precise and consensually agreed-upon assessment of the actual importance—empirically determined —of the role of Situational Variables as codeterminants, together with Patient and Treatment Variables, of psychotherapeutic courses and outcomes. The very strong emphasis (to me, overemphasis) on this in the Voth and Orth (1973) book has already been underlined a number of times. The completely contrary position arrived at in the monograph by Kernberg *et al.* (1972) (i.e., that no such significant role could be demonstrated in the various quantitative studies that they reported), and some of the reasons that Kernberg *et al.* felt could account for this, have also been presented (see Chapter 2, pp. 17, 26). Perhaps, as Kernberg *et al.* propose, all this is just a reflection of the conceptual newness of these variables, conceived and utilized in psychotherapy research study in this way; perhaps further empirical testing in concert with efforts at continuing conceptual refinement will bring us to a better research and theoretical consensus. Certainly, the conception as first proposed by Sargent has a considerable intuitive appeal. That is why we took it seriously enough to build it so substantially into our research design.

the empirical research investigation. In this role, Situational Variables were recognized to be continuously operating and requiring appraisal at each of the three vantage points in time — Initial, Termination, and Follow-Up — just like the Patient Variables.

The corollary point implied in this approach is a variation from the usual research design, in which situational factors are utilized primarily as "independent" variables. For example, when intrapsychic factors are recognized as determining the psychological meaning of events or circumstances, the situation, or the reality perception, can assume the place of the "dependent" variable. A familiar instance would be a domineering boss who is experienced by one individual as a protective father figure and by another as a resented, bullying rival.

In summary of the points just made, as well as the prior related discussion in this section (see Chapter 4, pp. 48, 49), our overall conceptualization of the Situational Variables rested on a series of linked assumptions:

1. Attention to the Situational Variables implies no change in focus or level of analysis of the data. Change in psychotherapy can be manifested at various levels, behavioral, experiential, and intrapsychic, and the proper assessment of each of the Situational Variables at each point in time rests, just as does the proper assessment of each of the Patient Variables, on the data and inferences drawn from each of these levels.

2. The Situational Variables are not conceived of as criteria of change, but rather as interacting contributing variables (of undetermined valence) helping to codetermine the attained changes.

3. As interacting codeterminants of change, Situational Variables are an essential background against which to assess the interactions of Patient and Treatment Variables. To put it differently, they would be variables to be controlled if, for example, we wished to contrast treatment-induced changes in patients matched on relevant Patient Variables and undergoing specified forms of treatment, coming from "high-stress" as against "low-stress" environments. (In this sense, psychiatric treatment itself is a special kind of environmental impact or Situational Variable; as such, it does not take place in a vacuum but against the background of a wider situational context, whether that is a relatively somewhat controlled environment or a complex interpersonal milieu.)

4. In apparent reverse, but in actual corollary, Situational Variables in one sense are a kind of Patient Variable, since they represent an aspect of the patient's psychological "life space"; in another sense, they represent an extension of Treatment Variables, in their negative and positive impacts as influences brought to bear on the patient — that is, as extensions of treatment, when it is conceived of as an aspect of environment.

I would like to quote one trivial but telling example from Rapaport (1960), in illustration of the central organizing thread in this statement of assumptions underlying the PRP conceptualization of the Situational Variables — that is, that external behaviors or situations take on relevance for our purpose here only in terms of their psychological meanings to the affected individual (just as do our Patient Variables): "[I]dentical typewriting speeds of applicants for a job provide insufficient information, since they may be products of maximal exertion or routine approach, disuse or peak efficiency, recent training or established working level. We must conclude that without the exploration of its genetic antecedents [read, for this, 'psychological meanings'] a behavior can only be described in terms of achievement concepts" (p. 44).

Finally, concerning the Situational Variables write-ups, it perhaps need not be stated that using the data of Form A (especially, but far from exclusively, the social history) and Form B (for the understandings of the patient) to construct Form S on each PRP patient took an amount of time from the members of the Situational Variables group fully proportionate to what Forms B and C took from Robbins and me as members of the Initial Study team.

Descriptions of Forms P and E

At this point, the overall Initial Study of each patient was still not concluded. What yet remained to be done was the process of translation of the clinical Prediction Study made by the Initial Study team into a form that would lend itself as far as possible to scientifically controlled efforts at confirmation or refutation. In order to permit valid overall estimates of the degree of agreement between clinical predictors and the later (Termination and Follow-Up) clinical judges regarding the subsequent intrapsychic and reality situations predicted, the precise predictions had to be rendered into as explicit a form as possible. And in order to safeguard against post hoc reasoning, according to which almost any outcome can be plausibly rationalized in terms of a retrospective weighing of contending forces, the acceptable evidence (in demonstrable event or in clinical judgment) that would subsequently be necessary in order to sustain or refute the predicted outcome likewise had to be specified in advance.

To accomplish these tasks, the Prediction Study team, led originally by Sargent, devised two additional forms in order to *formalize* the clinical inferences and predictions written out in the clinical discourse of Form C. Each predictive statement in that form, embedded in the usual clinical context and qualifications, was separately teased out and recast into a discrete and testable predictive statement in "Form P: Formalization of Predictions," specifying the response and/or change anticipated. Each such discrete statement was in accord with a tripartite "if–then–because" logical model. That is, each separately fashioned prediction started with an "if" clause, the conditions necessary for the expected event to occur or the contingency to which it related: "If this expectable external event happens . . . " or "If this development (of specific transference, or specific resistance) takes place within the analysis as anticipated . . . ". This was then followed by a "then" clause, the prediction proper or the nature of the expected consequence, given those assumptions: " . . . then a major transference problem will be between his overly compliant and obedient way of relating himself on the one hand and his extreme fear of free association (with the implication of absence of controls on his thinking) on the other hand." And third, and theoretically most critical in the sequence for our purpose of testing our theory of therapy, came a "because" clause, the statement of the assumptions in the theory of psychoanalytic therapy that underlie the prediction, in accord with which the observational data are meaningfully organized. Thus each prediction had the form: "If these considerations are fulfilled or come to pass, then these consequences will eventuate, because of these assumptions grounded in our theory of psychoanalytic therapy."

In accord with this logical (as contrasted with psychological) model, each Form C created by the Initial Study team was taken by the Prediction Study team and converted into such a sequence of discrete "if–then–because" predictions. As noted earlier, these numbered about 40 individual predictions per case, or approximately 1700 all told in our population of 42 patients. Each of these separate predictive statements, when teased out of its clinical context in the discursive Form C document and put in the single-sentence, tripartite form, was then funneled back to Robbins and me for checking to insure that the intended meaning had not been altered in the translation process. On this basis, some of the predictive statements were rewritten before being cast into the final Form P for that patient.

The second form devised by the Prediction Study team was "Form E: Evidence," which consisted of a series of at least two (at times three or four) outcome statements for each prediction: One of these gave the predicted change or outcome, and the others gave plausible alternatives that had not been predicted. Each such Form E statement representing a possible outcome could then be marked "true," "partly true," "false," or "no evidence" at the subsequent judgment points at Termination and Follow-Up Study. At the point that the individual Form E's for each patient were initially devised, they too were funneled back to Robbins and me and keyed by us in terms of how we expected them to come out. When these keyed statements in Form E (perhaps 100 per patient) were then compared at Termination and at Follow-Up with the same Form E as filled out then by new judges (the Termination and Follow-Up Study teams) who did not know the original predictions made and the original keying of Form E, one could readily determine the concordances between keying and outcome, where the prediction was confirmed, and also the discrepancies, where (for whatever reason) the prediction did not come to pass.

Since Form E was constructed from the Form P statements, each discrepant Form E outcome led back to a specific Form P prediction, where both the "if" clause, the contingency statement (had that contingency not come about, so that the consequent prediction would be inoperative?), and the "because" clause (where had our operating assumptions concerning the particular aspect of therapeutic process or outcome misled us?) could be examined. Thus the way was clear for us to test the operating assumptions of our theory of psychoanalytic therapy through this process of setting down, *in advance of* the patient's entering the planned therapy, the entire predictive complex—conditions, predictions proper, and assumptions clauses, as well as the predetermined evidence (in fact or in judgment) that would subsequently be necessary in order to sustain or refute the predicted outcomes.[6] With this task accomplished, the entire Initial Study was now complete: Forms A (Clinical Evaluation), B (Assessment of Relevant Patient Variables), C (Prediction Study), S (Assessment of Relevant Situational Variables), P (Formalization of Predictions), and E (Evidence), and the HSRS, both initial and predicted. For further detail concerning the construction of the prediction aspects of PRP,

---

6. The more this predetermined evidence necessary to confirm or refute a predicted outcome was anchored to observable behavioral facts that lent themselves to ready objective consensus, and the less it was anchored to judgments of intrapsychic processes that would rest on interpretations of the configural meaning of behaviors, the less the danger of circularity, of sneaking in the confirmation via the interpretation—an ever-present danger in theory validation in psychoanalysis, as pointed out so distinctly by Rapaport (1960).

both practical and theoretical, the reader is referred to the initial paper of design (Sargent, 1956a) and a later paper of theoretical statement (Wallerstein, 1964).

THE TREATMENT COURSE AND
THE TERMINATION STUDY: ASSESSMENT

Through Treatment into Termination

Sometime during the time period in which the Initial Study was being constructed for each selected PRP research subject, the patient would have started in the recommended psychotherapeutic course—in some cases psychoanalysis and in others psychoanalytic psychotherapy, but in each instance expectedly reasonably long-term (from 2 years to quite indefinite). From the point of view of PRP, the study was now in its indeterminate "silent phase," during which the treatment was going on without our making any research contact with either therapist or patient, or even informing them that they were and would be objects of research scrutiny. The research inquiry came into focus again each time PRP was alerted to a pending termination of a project patient.

This was accomplished through inserting a PRP eye into the therapy assignment process in operation at The Menninger Foundation. In order to accommodate the flow of new patients entering psychotherapy via the comprehensive evaluation process that has been described, to the staff therapists who would have time available for them, every staff member was asked each month to provide one centralized office with an account of the total number of therapy hours filled and to indicate whether any vacancies for new assignments were anticipated over the next month or two. The secretary in that office who routinely received these monthly time reports for these clinical operating purposes was provided with a list of the PRP patients (and was the only individual outside this research group itself who knew the identity of the patients in the project sample). When she was notified of a pending termination of one of our PRP-flagged patients, she in turn notified the project, and the Termination Study phase was formally entered upon.

Though the treatments were, as stated, expectedly reasonably long-term, in fact the actual treatment span was highly variable. Treatments could be terminated prematurely for any of a variety of reasons; three of them did end after only 7 to 9 months (the Bohemian Prep School Boy, the Script Writer, and the Invalided Hypochondriac), and another four ended at about 1 year (the Silent Woman, the Alcoholic Heir, the Rebellious Coed, and the Addicted Doctor). (Three of these seven had started in a recommended psychoanalysis—the Script Writer, the Silent Woman, and the Alcoholic Heir.) Again, though the anticipated termination was called "indefinite," we did originally expect all the patients to terminate. Yet when we had to do "cutoff" Termination Studies in 1964, for reasons imposed by the constraints of available time and money, there were five patients who had not yet terminated (the Economist, the Housebound Phobic Woman, the Involutional Woman, the Fearful Loner, and the Phobic Girl), and they had each been in treatment between 7 and 11 years at that point. (Two of them, the Economist and the Housebound Phobic Woman, had been started in psychoanalysis; the other three were in what were anticipated to be long-term intensive psychotherapies.)

At whatever point at or between these extremes the treatment was ending, the Termination Study team approached the therapist to plan a Termination Study just at or just after the actual ending. This approach was timed in order to make sure that the patient would still be in Topeka available for study, since so many of The Menninger Foundation patients who had been living in Topeka (for whatever the duration of their therapies) planned to return to their home communities directly upon their termination. As already stated, this was the point at which to his or her surprise (and at times, dismay), the therapist found out for the first time that the patient he or she had been treating for whatever length of time was a research subject of PRP, and that we desired to do a full-scale Termination Study on that treatment.

The need to do the Termination Study while the patient was still in Topeka did at times crowd the study upon the terminating hours of the therapy; whether they actually overlapped or were indeed separated in time, the Termination Study was always carried out in the shadow of the termination feelings themselves, whatever their individual range and complexity. It can certainly be reasonably argued that this would hardly be the best time to assess the changes the therapy had wrought, since they were then necessarily being experienced and perceived by the patient through the affective coloring given by the terminating process itself and its various overdetermined meanings and inner reverberations in the patient's psyche. Nonetheless, it was the only logical time that we could do such a study, in terms of best securing the patient's cooperation for it (before they were outside our therapeutic orbit) and in terms of preparing them for the planned Follow-Up proceedings several years hence. And, of course, trying to do it any sooner neither would have been possible in terms of the mechanics of our operation, nor would make any sense as a "termination study," nor would be consonant with our naturalistic, noninterfering design intent.

Given these necessities of time, we had to live with the consequences that one of the major tasks of the Termination Study itself would be to try to disentangle the achieved changes of the treatment that was terminating from the biases introduced into the perception of it by the emotions of the termination process and of the various termination meanings—from distressing to euphoric, from compliant to defiant.

Form A Data for the Termination Study

WRITTEN DOCUMENTATION OF TREATMENT

What the Termination Study ideally comprised (should the patient be willing to cooperate and should there be no clinical contraindication to the involvement of the patient) began with an assembling of the Form A clinical data. First, access was requested to all of the records that had been regularly kept on the patient's treatment for routine clinical–administrative purposes. At the least this was a monthly progress note, usually two paragraphs or so, entered into the clinical record by the therapist in fulfillment of the clinical record-keeping requirements of the institution. At this minimum—in a treatment, say, of 2 years—this would be a sequence of about two dozen such two-paragraph statements, from which some sense of the flow and the events of the ongoing treatment could be secured.

At the most detailed, if the case were of psychoanalysis and were a Topeka Institute control case (as the majority of our cases in psychoanalysis were), there would be typed process notes dictated after each session by that psychoanalytic candidate for supervision purposes. These were usually one to two typed single-spaced pages each and could exist for from 500 to more than 1000 analytic hours—clearly an enormous amount of available clinical data to be read.

TERMINATION INTERVIEWS AND RETESTING

In addition to access to the written documentation of the treatment, the Termination Study team sought to interview the following (usually more than once for each person):

1. The patient himself or herself. The therapist always helped in making the initial contact with the patient, who, after all, was even more surprised than the therapist at being included within a research study of the treatment; the therapist at least had had some general knowledge of the existence of the project, which of course the patient had not had.
2. With the patient's permission, other individuals who had been active in the patient's life through the treatment: the spouse; other family members; occasionally the employer; in the case of a young college student, the Dean of Students; and so forth.
3. The therapist, of course, and the supervisor where there was one (in all of the psychoanalytic control cases, and with almost all the other PRP cases as well, since in The Menninger Foundation system all but the most senior therapists had ongoing supervision of their therapy caseloads).
4. Others who might have been significantly involved in the patient's treatment life: the hospital doctor where the patient had been hospitalized, an activities therapy worker where that relationship had been significant, and the like.

In addition to all these interviews, the psychological projective test battery that had been administered at Initial Study was again administered. The only difference was that at Initial Study it had been administered by a staff psychologist as part of a clinical evaluation process, and now it was being administered by a research psychologist member of the psychological testing team of PRP (who was, in fact, among the more senior members of the regular clinical psychology staff). The psychological test battery had two special features as data that it is pertinent to mention here. The first was that the tests were the one data source where the stimuli were constant and where the responses could therefore have the most precise comparability. The second was that, because it was administered by different people and because of its nature, the test battery could be administered and scored at termination "blindly," with no contamination by any knowledge of the "before" state. (Clinical interviewing, by contrast, could hardly be conducted as a cross-sectional endeavor without gaining at least some knowledge of what the patient was like before and what the intervening events were.) This made the tests a unique source for contamination-free outcome assessments.

Reactions of the Patients

As has already been indicated, two of the terminating PRP patients refused to participate in the Termination Study—the Suspended Medical Student and the Exhibitionistic Dancer. A partial third refusal came from the Intellectual Fencer, who consented to interviewing but would not let herself be tested; she sensed rightly that she would be more likely to betray aspects of herself that she wanted to guard in the testing situation, where she could not as readily exert the same self-conscious censorship on what was being communicated. Also, as has likewise already been indicated, the PRP, committed to the primacy of clinical exigencies over research exigencies, unhesitatingly honored clinical contraindications to the involvement of patients in the Termination Study. Such contraindications existed for four of the five patients still in ongoing therapy, on whom the so-called "cut-off" Termination Studies were eventually done. Three of these four were not seen at all (the Economist, the Phobic Girl, and the Fearful Loner), while the fourth (the Housebound Phobic Woman) was not seen by the research team but was retested at the time of "cutoff" because of clinical indications, with the test protocols then being made available to the research team. The fifth of those in a still ongoing therapy (the Involutional Woman) was, with the therapist's and her own agreement, nonetheless seen in a full Termination Study. Two other patients were, for other reasons, not seen at termination. One, the Alcoholic Doctor, in psychoanalytic treatment over almost a 7-year span (1238 hours), died while still in treatment. He had been ill, apparently with the flu, and had died in a cyanotic stupor. At autopsy it was determined that the patient had died from a massive forceful aspiration of his vomitus into the far reaches of his bronchial tree. The other, the Sociopath, had ended his disastrous treatment by simply disappearing, with creditors, his landlord, his lawyer, the police, and his parents all looking for him in vain.

Of the two patients who refused to participate, one, the Exhibitionistic Dancer, with a basically unsuccessful treatment, was angry; she claimed she was too busy (though she was doing nothing in particular), wondered about the purposes of the research and what was in it for her, and stated that perhaps if we paid her $25 per hour for her time (which was the fee she had been paying), she might participate because she could use the money, but even then she might refuse. Finally she said, "I would be thinking and talking about the treatment and that's the trouble. It's not good for me to think along those lines. I should stay away from it. . . . I don't believe in treatment. I suppose it helps a lot of people but it didn't help me. As far as cooperating with the research study, I don't want to do it. There's not enough in it for me."

The other one who refused, the Suspended Medical Student, with an apparently successful psychoanalysis—during the course of which he had become able to return to and graduate from medical school—professed a great willingness to participate, because it would be "fun" and "Such research is important and it could benefit others. . . . But then there's the practical problem, I don't know when I could do it. Certainly, in the next 2 weeks, I'll be so busy. . . ." This heralded the beginning of a long and unsuccessful effort, pursued by numerous letters and phone calls over an 18-month period, to obtain the patient's participation in the research study. At each contact he was willing to come, eager to cooperate in research, but had some very plausible reason that rendered it impossible just at that point. But he always added that he might participate later, "if you're still interested in an evaluation of me, and I certainly am." On two occasions there were last-minute cancellations by the patient of carefully planned interview sessions and motel reservations. Regarding any *reluctance* to participate, however, he would only say, "Maybe there is but I don't know about it." He did adamantly refuse to have the research team members come to his home town to do the interviewing and testing at his convenience there. In the light of his subsequent tragic fate, which is described later in detail, his failures to appear—which always surprised and puzzled his analyst and the analytic supervisor—became more understandable.

Of course, not all of the patients who *were* seen participated equally willingly. The great majority were quite willing; a few, for their own reasons, were eager—either to complain about not having done well enough, or to proclaim how well they felt they had done. An example of the latter was the Bohemian Musician, with an outstandingly successful result in a supportive psychotherapy, whose gratitude toward her therapist spilled over into an overly cooperative attitude toward the research project. She offered to "place myself completely at your disposal." By contrast with this overeager individual, two patients were at the other extreme of being secured most reluctantly, basically through the vicissitudes of clinical happenstance. The Alcoholic Heir had at first paranoidly refused to participate, stating that there was some secret intent in this—probably our being out to get more of his money, or some secret conspiracy linking the research inquiry and his therapist. When, in a reversion to an uncontrolled drinking bout some 3 months after his treatment termination, he returned for a rehospitalization for 2 weeks, he made a complete about-face and presented himself cooperatively for research termination study. Even more dramatic was the case of the Alcoholic Raconteur. Like the Sociopath, he had essentially disappeared after his comparably disastrous treatment, but he returned eagerly some 9 months later after his hotel landlady wrote to The Menninger Foundation asking our help for the patient, who was drunk, sick (vomiting blood), losing weight alarmingly, and penniless. He was appealing, and she did not want to turn so sick a man out in the street. When we called offering him a research evaluation at our expense, he rushed to respond, asking only for transportation and expense money in advance. Before he arrived, he had to ask for more money (since the first advance was depleted), and then he arrived disheveled, drunk, and disorganized for his first research interview. He was hospitalized at PRP's behest (and expense) in order to be sobered up and physically rehabilitated, so that the research assessment would be rendered possible.

Having described the range of circumstances under which they came (or did not come), I turn now to figures. A total of 33 of the 42 research subjects had full Termination Studies, plus an additional 1 (the Intellectual Fencer) who had all but the repeat psychological testing, as noted. With 6 of the others—the 2 who refused to participate and the 4 who were not asked—we could accomplish a "truncated" Termination Study, based on the routine clinical records of the entire therapy (as completed, or if a "cutoff," to the point of cutoff) plus interviewing of the therapist, supervisor, and those involved with the patient's treatment life. What was not available in these instances were, of course, interviews with the patient, interviews with those in the patient's life (to whom access was only possible through the patient), and the repeat psychological testing. In the other 2 instances—the Alcoholic Doctor, who died, and the Sociopath, who disappeared—the families did cooperate fully with our information-gathering activities. In all these cases as well, therefore, where we had access to less than the full data called for by the designs, we could nonetheless do a quite satisfactory Termination Study; in this sense, then, there was 100% coverage of our research population at the Termination Study point.

Organization of the Data

With all of the Termination Form A data in hand, the Termination Study team could then turn to its data-organizing tasks. In carrying these out, they of course did *not* have access to the original predictive statements, or any of the research forms into which they had been cast—the keying of Form E, the HSRS judgments and predictions, and so on. These Termination Study tasks included carrying out the following:

1. Form B: *Reassessment of the Relevant Patient Variables*—the patient's present (and altered) posttreatment status in regard to each of the Patient Variables originally conceptualized at the time of pretreatment Initial Study.
2. Form S: *Reassessment of the Relevant Situational Variables*—again, a statement of present (and altered) status for the same comparative purposes.
3. Form E: Evidence—the response to the array of possible predicted consequences, as "true," "partly true," "false," or "no evidence."
4. HSRS termination judgment.
5. In the light of the patient's status at termination and how it had been adjudged to have come about, some predictive statements (in the same clinical discursive form as the original Form C: Prediction Study) geared to the expected status at Follow-Up—gains extended, consolidated, just held, or lost in part or wholly. These were then translated by the same process and the same Prediction Study team into a Follow-Up Form P (averaging about 8–10 discrete predictions) and a derived Follow-Up Form E (keyed in turn by the Termination Study team).
6. A predicted HSRS rating for the Follow-Up point.

Various aspects of these Termination Study tasks were parceled out among the Termination Study team: the Treatment Variables group, which conducted the bulk of the interviews and was responsible for the major statements about the patient (Form B) and about the course and outcome of the therapy itself (in Form T, which is described next); the Situational Variables group, which conducted additional interviews related specifically to issues of ongoing and altered life situation and was responsible for the statements in Form S; the Psychological Testing group, which administered the research test battery for its own comparative (test–retest) purposes, as well as for feeding into the overall assessments by the Termination Study team; and the Prediction Study group, which was responsible for the new Forms P and E.

Description of Form T

At each patient's termination, of course, a wholly new kind of data became available—that concerning the treatment itself, its course and outcome. This new information was conceptualized in another form to be completed at the Termination Study point, "Form T: Assessment of Relevant Treatment Variables." At the Initial Study point, the course and outcome of the recommended treatment could be predicted (and in some cases, where relevant, possible alternative treatment plans could be predicted). At the Termination Study point, with data in hand from many different sources—the clinical records routinely kept during the treatment, all the triangulating interviews (each from its own vantage point and its own perspective upon the patient and the changes wrought in the patient during the treatment), and the psychological retest report (with its more blind termination cross-sectional assessment)—the actual treatment course and outcome could now be judged.

Like Form S for Situational Variables, Form T for Treatment (and Therapist) Variables was likewise wholly a PRP creation, with minimal established consensus in practice or in the literature concerning the relevant factors or variables to be delineated and conceptualized. The psychotherapeutic or psychoanalytic process is clearly so complex that literally hundreds of possible variables could be extracted from it. It varies, of course, even for therapists of very similar training and theoretical persuasion. Some of the variables we chose as most relevant to our conceptions about treatment were central to psychoanalytic notions, covering our "rules of thumb" of the theory of psychoanalytic therapy (e.g., the variables dealing with transference, defense, conflict, etc.); others had no special theoretical anchoring (e.g., variables having to do with the climate of the therapy, etc.). In assessing the relevance of each of the selected variables to the treatment course, we were guided by criteria not only of frequency (how often things occurred, or occurred together), but also of pervasiveness (for which, unlike frequency counts, only a small sample might be a sufficient data base—even a single statement, if supported by adequate evidence), and of pivotalness (an important enough "once-only" instance).

The details of the conceptualization of the Form T variables are set down in the article on them in the second collection of papers from PRP (Luborsky, Fabian, Hall, Ticho, & Ticho, 1958; see especially pp. 129–147). Here, as in the descriptions of the other forms, the relevant variables are only listed:

FORM T: ASSESSMENT OF RELEVANT TREATMENT VARIABLES

  I. Formal Elements of the Treatment
    A. Treatment Modality (psychotherapeutic counseling, supportive psychotherapy, expressive psychotherapy, psychoanalysis)
       1. Variations Determined by the Nature of the Patient's Illness
       2. Variations Determined by Reality Events
       3. Variations Determined by the Therapist
       4. Variations Determined by the Supervisor
    B. Treatment Instructions, General and Special
    C. Special External Circumstances That Affected the Treatment Course
    D. The Basic Techniques of the Treatment
       1. Suggestion
       2. Abreaction
       3. Manipulation
       4. Clarification
       5. Interpretation

    E. Types of Subject Matter
       1. The Patient's Past Life and Memories
       2. Reconstructions and Memories of the Conflicts of Infancy and Childhood
       3. The Patient's Current Life Situation
       4. The Events of the Treatment Hour
       5. Dream and Fantasy Material
       6. Style and Form of the Patient's Expression
       7. Accompanying Affect of the Patient's Expression
    F. The Goals of the Treatment
       1. The Goals of the Therapist
       2. The Goals of the Patient
       3. Changes in Goals
II. The Process of Treatment
    A. Life of the Patient during Treatment
    B. Significant New History
    C. Course of Treatment
       1. Major Themes
       2. Major Transference Paradigms
       3. Changes in Symptoms
       4. Changes in Manifest Behavior Patterns
       5. Changes in Impulse–Defense Configurations
       6. Structural Changes in the Ego
       7. The Acquisition of Insight, and its Relation to Changes in Attitudes toward the Self, Others, Things, and the Illness
       8. Style and Form of Communication
    D. Termination of Treatment
III. Variables in the Therapist and the Climate of the Patient–Therapist Interaction
    A. Qualities of the Therapist
       1. Skill and Experience
       2. Need for Supervision and How It Was Used
       3. Personal Style and Attitudes
       4. Countertransferences
       5. Age and Sex
    B. Climate of the Therapy
IV. Synthesis of Factors Responsible for the Outcome
 V. Prognostic Estimate

This Form T, together with Form B and Form S, gave a comprehensive rendering of the total array of factors—in the patient, in the treatment and therapist, and in the interacting life situation—that through their interaction codetermined the treatment course and outcome. This accounting was synthesized in the Termination Study; it was, at that point and subsequently, compared with the course that had been predicted initially from the original status of the Patient and Situational Variables and had been projected to interact (in terms, of course, of our theory of psychoanalytic therapy) with the recommended treatment mode and its special attributes and consequences.

As a last part of the Termination Study, plans were worked out in each case to contact the now ex-patient 2 to 3 years hence, in order to ask him or her to return to Topeka for a week-long Follow-Up Study (accompanied again by the spouse or other significant relative), all at our expense.

THE FOLLOW-UP STUDY: REASSESSMENT

Follow-Up in Psychotherapy Research

Voth and Orth (1973), in the acknowledgments section of the preface to their book, stated their (and PRP's) credo as follows: "Dr. John Benjamin's observation that the most solid evidence regarding the efficacy of treatment is to be found in the way a patient lives his life after treatment served us well throughout the entire period of this project." And certainly adequate follow-up study is recognized everywhere in clinical medicine as a most vital aspect of the understanding of the course of an illness and the success of its treatment. In cancer research, the 5-year follow-up has been widely institutionalized; before this point one rarely speaks, even cautiously, in terms of probable cure.

For many reasons, follow-up has not had this established a position within psychoanalytic clinical work. In considerable part, this has had to do with theoretical considerations relating to the effort to bring the regressive transference neurosis to as full a state of resolution as can be achieved; thus psychoanalysts tend to avoid any devices, such as planned follow-up, that could play into the perpetuation of transference fantasies. And when I discuss further on in this book the various meanings the planned-for follow-up inquiries came to have in the lives of our research patients (including, for a fair number, the fantasy that the treatment itself would not really come to proper "termination" closure until after the official Follow-Up Study, which would put the old treatment issues to rest and in proper perspective), the reader will see just how realistically based these concerns about the possible intrusiveness of follow-up as a hindrance to the "natural" resolution of the treatment can be. In part, also, the lack of tradition for follow-up in psychoanalysis stems from the fact that psychoanalysis has had its main scholarly centers in the private consulting rooms of its practitioners, where whatever follow-up inquiry emerged has had to be the unorganized happenstance of the lives and interests of individual psychoanalysts. This is unlike the situation in clinical medicine, where the main centers of investigative activity have been the academic medical centers, their affiliated hospitals, and their organized clinics, where follow-up on treatments has been logically built into the proceedings.

Nonetheless, there are many reasons—the advancement of scientific knowledge in the discipline being a central one—why follow-up must find its rightful and honorable place in the psychotherapy arena as well, despite the psychological problems it may raise, which should be manageable. Though not planned that way, Freud's case of the Wolf Man (Gardiner, 1971) has become the single most famous psychoanalytic case—not only of long-term serial psychoanalytic work, but of detailed follow-up knowledge spanning more than half a century. Helene Deutsch (1959) added to the interest in and respectability of this area by reporting the longtime follow-ups that she happened to have with two former women patients in psychoanalysis, one 25 years and the other 27 years after the termination of the treatment. And, of course, the growth in the most recent decade of organized psychotherapy research (most of it in university centers) has given the most substantial impetus to this area of study as a necessary part of our enlarging knowledge concerning the mechanisms and bases of change in psychotherapy.

Establishing the Follow-Up Procedure for PRP

When PRP was being organized, follow-up was built into it from the start. The original intent was for a 5-year follow-up, in analogy to the well-established custom in cancer research, where the cure is equally uncertain. As already mentioned, funding and time constraints were such, and the projected lifespan of PRP already so long (with treatment durations up to 10 or even more years), that we compromised and set a time frame of 2–3 years for the formal, planned Follow-Up Study. In individual instances, the follow-up period turned out to be somewhat longer (never less). In 28 of the 42 cases (two-thirds of the sample), we have had additional follow-up information through contacts by the ex-patients with members of the Menninger Foundation therapeutic staff and/or therapeutic community, as recorded in the official PRP files, and supplemented by information garnered through my own most recent (spring 1982) contact with all the available ex-therapists of PRP patients. (For details of this, see Chapter 1, footnote 1, pp. 6–7.)

The first research decision about the official PRP Follow-Up Study was where and how to do it. In the interests of completeness of positive response and fullness of information to be garnered from each patient, we determined not to attempt this by mail or even by telephone. Rather from the start, we built sufficient funding into the extramural support that we obtained so that, as already stated, we could invite the ex-patients back to Topeka for a week-long follow-up visit, together with the spouse or other significant relative, at our expense. In this we counted (successfully) on the ex-patient's willingness to participate—not just for various treatment-related reasons, or altruistically for the furtherance of science, but out of their desires for a "vacation" return visit to a setting in which they had lived a most significant segment of their lives, and in which, in most instances, they now had a circle of old friends.

Nonetheless, the decision to do the Follow-Up Studies in Topeka, rather than to send the researchers to do the studies in the ex-patients' own home communities, was not arrived at except after considerable scientific debate. Basically, the issue was this: Where and how could we best gather the kind of data in which we were interested? Clearly, follow-up inquiries carried out in the patients' home communities could enable better assessments of raw, objective factual material, since we could have readier access to sources beyond the patients for independent and more objective verification of how the patients' lives were now being lived. Aside, however, from the logistical problems involved in such a strategy (clearing and coordinating the crowded schedules of part-time researchers, so that they could go as a team—psychiatrist, social worker, and clinical psychologist—for each visit to an ex-patient), as well as the issues of awkwardness if not embarrassment that would be raised for our subjects by this kind of intrusion into their "life space" in their home communities, there were also compelling scientific reasons for our selected strategy.

Since our central focus was that of obtaining assessments of intrapsychic shifts in the personality functioning of patients as reflected now in their lives and their behaviors, and since we were using Situational Variables as just one avenue of access to the patients through which we could then infer the phenomena of intrapsychic functioning, we were in effect after the kind of "clinical" data that can be secured most advantageously in a clinical setting. On our home ground we could, over a week, have daily psychiatric interviewing (albeit the interviews would be done by a group rather than an individual), social work contact with the accompanying relative (usually also by a team), and repeat administration (the third time now) of the psychological projective test battery. We could thereby have the most comprehensive assessment possible to us of psychodynamic (intrapsychic) phenomena, and would arrive at it in a manner as comparable as possible to the conditions of the Initial Study, when the patient came originally seeking therapy.

Clearly, we would not in this way be in as good a position to study the phenomena of a patient's social milieu, in and of themselves. These data could better be gathered if someone could see the patient in his or her home in interaction with the figures in it — in his or her native habitat, so to speak — but this would make it less possible to get some of the inner psychological data in which we were interested. To put it more specifically, the richness and diversity of a patient's life and contacts within his or her community, and the way in which he or she played a constructive or destructive role within it, would be better seen by visiting in the home community and observing the patient's interactions with the figures in it. However, whether or not a manifest complaint such as homosexuality was in effect cured,[7] and, even more significantly, whether the patient was still liable to homosexual panic states that were not overtly recognizable, would be the kind of information that would obviously be more easily elicited when the patient was back in Topeka, in a clinical rather than a home setting. The point need not be belabored.

This meant, of course, that our primary focus was on bringing patients back to Topeka wherever possible; only where this was not possible were patients seen in their home communities. As it actually worked out, of the 35 of the total 42 patients actually seen at Follow-Up Study, 30 were seen in Topeka and only 5 were seen in their own communities. These 5 exceptions were made for a variety of reasons. In one case — that of the Movie Lady, who was the one patient in our sample who had not been treated in Topeka[8] — it would have made no sense to

7. In speaking of homosexuality as a "complaint" and as being "cured," I am speaking of a homosexual individual who would have come to psychoanalysis or psychotherapy experiencing homosexuality as an illness and desiring and intending to become heterosexual in disposition and functioning.

8. The circumstances here were as follows: At the time that PRP was being constructed, Dr. X., a former colleague from The Menninger Foundation who had in fact been one of the prime movers in the original psychotherapy research planning group as far back as 1948, was now at the National Institute of Mental Health in Bethesda, Maryland, where he was the central figure in a new psychotherapy research project being built around the material from a videotaped analysis he was conducting with a patient who had been willing to volunteer for that research patient status. In the interest of comparing methods and data from two programs of study (The Menninger Foundation's PRP and the NIMH group) built around the material from the same case instance, an agreement was worked out that the initial evaluation material on the patient in videotaped analysis in Bethesda (dubbed here the "Movie Lady") would be sent to us in Topeka for assessment as one of our research sample of 42. Termination and Follow-Up Studies would then be planned for, but clearly not in Topeka (in Bethesda at Termination and then wherever she would be at Follow-Up time), on the same basis as if she had been a Menninger Foundation patient in Topeka.

ask her to "return"; thus the Follow-Up Study (and of course the Termination Study as well) was done where she was in treatment and where she was then subsequently living at the follow-up time. With another patient, the Heiress, who had followed her therapist when he had left Topeka to continue her treatment with him to its natural conclusion in another city, it just made more sense for the research group to travel to her rather than to ask her to do the reverse. Still another patient, the Masochistic Editor, refused to return to Topeka for a Follow-Up Study but was willing to be seen for interviewing and testing in his own city, and only over a weekend. In all of these instances where people were seen in their home communities, at least a pair of researchers always went, since we had used at least two observers at every other vantage point throughout the research project. In addition to the research team members who made the visit (preferably, at least one psychiatrist and one social worker), we enlisted the services of a nearby (if possible, Menninger-trained) qualified clinical psychologist to administer the repeat psychological test battery.[9]

In pursuing our Follow-Up Studies in this way, the intent, of course, was the one stated: to make the Follow-Up Study *as comparable as possible* to the Initial Study, when the patient came originally seeking therapy. We also recognized, however, that the two assessments could not be *exactly* comparable. Even if an ex-patient were to come back for an "evaluation" exactly comparable in its outer form to the one he or she had had initially, it would not be the same in psychological circumstances. Originally the individual came as a prospective patient — driven by psychic distress, seeking help, and ready (usually) to participate as fully as possible in the evaluation process, including trying to "tell all" in the interest of making the promised help more possible and more precise. Now the individual would be coming back as an ex-patient — altruistically helping contribute to "science" or to "research," and perhaps with an axe to grind in terms of an intended communication (positive or negative) to the ex-therapist and/or to the treating institution, but with neither obligation nor motivation to try to "tell all." Quite apart even from the group or team interviewing context, the relationship with the interviewer would be different, and what the interviewer might feel that he or she had a right and even an obligation to probe would no longer hold in the same way. Again, the differences are obvious. Recognizing that we would never have exactly comparable data, we could at least aspire to *comparably good* data.

In connection with this entire procedural discussion concerning the optimal format and circumstance for Follow-Up Study, the question was considered of having the former therapist contribute at this point — not as a subject of research study (the therapist's role in the Termination Study), but as a participating member of the Follow-Up Study team. There might, for instance, be cases where *only* the former therapist could on interview elicit the desired data; to pursue the example previously used, perhaps only the former therapist could really candidly ascer-

---

9. The considerable debate within PRP on the relative merits of doing the Follow-Up Study in Topeka versus in the ex-patient's home town was never fully resolved. The majority position, to do it (preferably) as described, was strongly advocated by Sargent and our consultatnt, Benjamin (and occupied a considerable portion of the time during the latter's September 1956 consultation visit). The contrary position was strongly argued by Gardner Murphy and some members of the Situational Variables group. Parts of this debate have been preserved in my write-up of Benjamin's consultation visit and in an internal memo from Sargent to Murphy.

tain whether the former overt homosexual still suffered from homosexual panic, or still had dubious orgastic potency, or was no longer actively homosexual but had simply learned to live better with homosexual longings and homosexual temptations. Theoretically, the former therapist would have a distinct advantage in eliciting this intimate and possibly embarrassing data, and this could lessen the inherent lack of full comparability of the Follow-Up data with that gathered during the other temporal phases of our work. But even then, under such theoretically more "ideal" circumstances, the original situation would not be exactly duplicated: The ex-patient would be in a different life situation, the therapeutic relationship would long since have been attenuated, and so on.

And, of course, having the ex-therapist as part of the Follow-Up team would have disadvantages (which caused us not to pursue the plan). We would have a biased judge who might have a need to see the patient's material in a particular light. The patient, for his or her part, might have a need to show himself or herself to the former therapist in a particular way, to hide certain things, to accentuate others, and so forth. Furthermore, beyond the research indications and contraindications, there would be all the (indeterminate) problems of the clinical indications and contraindications. How upsetting might it be to the former patient's equilibrium to have the former therapist see him or her and open up such potentially sore areas? Could this be known *a priori* in individual cases? Would such a risk be justified if taken just on research, and not on clinical, grounds? And then, of course, there was the practical problems that (in certain instances at least) the former therapist would have left Topeka and would no longer be available to undertake this task with us anyway.

Reactions of the Patients

Pursuing the Follow-Up Studies in the way in which we decided, then, we did secure full Follow-Up contact with 35 of the 42 patients in the sample, as noted—30 in Topeka and 5 (for the kinds of reasons indicated) in their home communities. Those who came to Topeka did so with a variety of central and auxiliary motivations. The Adoptive Mother, for example, was very eager to return when contacted at a point almost 4 years after her termination. She came with her husband, and also with her 3-year-old adoptive daughter. Strongly contributing to her eagerness to come was the voiced desire to see her ex-analyst and to show him the successful "fruit of his labor"—the daughter. At the other extreme, the Adolescent Grandson, now permanently living in Topeka, expressed a willingness to cooperate but at the last moment canceled each appointment set up for him, on one or another pretext. When the effort was renewed a year later, the patient came for interviews and testing willingly and agreeably. He offered no explanation of his avoidance a year earlier except to say, "I was up to my neck in the real estate leasing business at that time and wasn't interested in coming in for tests."

Some of the ex-patients came expressing very grateful feelings. The Bohemian Prep School Boy came readily and expressed surprise that we were willing to pay his expenses; he said he would have come anyway. (He was from one of the very wealthy families.) The Housebound Phobic Woman, who was still in Topeka and still in treatment at her Follow-Up time (as noted earlier, she had had a "cutoff" Termination Study during which she had not been seen, but had been retested for concomitant clinical purposes), actually refused all expense money, saying she had been amply repaid by all the help The Menninger Foundation had been to her all those years. And the Alcoholic Raconteur, who had only been seen for Termination Study when PRP rescued him from a skid row existence, hospitalized him, and sobered him up, was now working steadily (and was sober) at the Follow-Up time and came readily for the Follow-Up Study. More than that, he spontaneously kept in touch with PRP for another 18 months, during which he married and immediately wrote to the research group offering to come for study again (the only patient in the entire series who did this): "If you wish me to participate in your research program this year, please contact me." The opposite extreme to this was the Script Writer, who comported herself at Follow-Up in the way characteristic for her. She stated that she was no longer drinking except "socially in a conventional sense," and yet she came to an early-morning Follow-Up interview reeking of alcohol. She emphatically disclaimed the slightest interest in her lover from her treatment days in Topeka, and yet she sought him out and spent as much time as she could with him. Alone, of all the patients back for Follow-Up Study, she grossly overcharged for her expenses in a flagrant and obvious manner. Her continued ethical elasticity was but one reflection of her unsuccessful efforts at change in psychoanalysis.

Of the seven patients who were not seen at the Follow-Up Study, four were now dead, as previously mentioned. In addition to the Alcoholic Doctor, who had died of aspiration pneumonia while still in treatment, the other three now also dead of mental-illness-related causes were the Alcoholic Heir (of bilateral lobar pneumonia and pneumococcal meningitis acquired in an alcoholic stupor on a wintry night), the Car Salesman (of an alcohol–drug overdose), and the Addicted Doctor (of direct suicide with Nembutal while an inpatient in the local state hospital). Later on in this book, I give a fuller accounting of the relationship between the unsuccessful treatment course in these patients and the precipitation of their deaths, and I do the same for two others who died after their Follow-Up Study times (the Suspended Medical Student, who committed suicide by asphyxiating himself in his car 4 years after the Follow-Up Study, and Peter Pan, who committed suicide by jumping off a bridge 5 years after her Follow-Up Study).

The three others not seen at the Follow-Up Study, in addition to those four who were then dead, were these:

1. The Suspended Medical Student, whose long saga of evasion at the time of attempted Termination Study has already been recounted. At follow-up time, the urging to get him back was much less, for good clinical reasons that became clear to us from the successful effort to locate him and find out his circumstances. He had our letters and he clearly wanted to avoid us, with even more reason than he had had at Termination Study time, when presumably all had been going much better.

2. The Invalided Hypochondriac, whose precarious and grossly paranoid equilibrium at the Follow-Up Study time we decided not to jeopardize. We informed her that we were taking all of her misgivings and reservations very seriously (such as her demand, just one among many, to have an attorney present with her at the Follow-Up interviews) and thought it wiser that she not participate with us at this time.

3. The Fearful Loner, who was still in a continuing therapy where the therapist, for good reason, felt it still contraindicated that we contact him. As noted earlier, this made him the only PRP subject who was never informed officially of his research status.

Actually, of the five who had seemed at the time of Termination Study to be "therapeutic lifers," one had been seen in regular Termination Study anyway (the Involutional Woman); one had not been seen by us but had been retested, as noted (the Housebound Phobic Woman); and three had not been seen at all (the Economist, the Phobic Girl, and the Fearful Loner). By Follow-Up time, the Involutional Woman had actually terminated and the Phobic Girl was just terminating, and both of these were now seen in full study. The other three were still continuing in therapy, but now the Economist and the Housebound Phobic Woman were seen anyway, and only the Fearful Loner was excluded by agreement with the therapist on the strength of the clinical contraindication.

Just as at Termination Study time, we were able, in the course of our efforts to locate the seven patients we did not see at Follow-Up and to find out their circumstances, to gather enough collateral information about their lives during the follow-up period from family members, family physicians, and other sources to do satisfactory "truncated" Follow-Up Studies; in this sense, we again had 100% coverage of our research population at the Follow-Up Study point.

Organization of the Data

Again, with all of its Follow-Up Form A data in hand (the psychiatric interviewing, the third administration of the psychological test battery, and the social history data obtained from the accompanying relative, as well as all of the collateral information just mentioned that was obtained in the process of locating our ex-patients and ascertaining their present circumstances), the Follow-Up Study team could turn to its data-organizing tasks. These tasks included carrying out the following:

1. Form B: Reassessment (again) of the Relevant Patient Variables—the ex-patient's status at Follow-Up in regard to the selfsame group of Patient Variables originally conceptualized at the time of pretreatment Initial Study.

2. Form S: Reassessment (again) of the Relevant Situational Variables.

3. Form T: Reassessment of the Relevant Treatment (and Therapist) Variables—an evaluation with the retrospective cast now given to the events of the treatment period by the subsequent life events and the ex-patient's evolving status, in whatever direction, during the follow-up period. (This reassessment in theory gave promise of more illumination than in actual practice we found it to provide.)

4. Form E: Evidence—both the Termination Form E (now responded to again, with perhaps some retrospective revision in the light of the subsequent happenings during the follow-up period) and the Follow-Up Form E, representing the predictions made and keyed at Termination Study time for the follow-up period.

5. Follow-Up HSRS rating, plus again any retrospective alteration (from that perspective) of the Initial or Termination HSRS assessments.

These tasks were, of course, accomplished by the same kind of parceling-out process among the project subgroups as at the time of Termination Study. The earlier Treatment Variables group, whose members had originally interviewed the patients at Termination Study for purposes of assessment of both Patient and Treatment Variables, did so again at Follow-Up Study. The same Situational Variables group that had originally interviewed the patients at Termination Study for purposes of assessing Situational Variables also again did so at Follow-Up Study. And the same Psychological Testing group (though, in the interest of blindness and freedom from contamination, a different member of it) repeated the psychological projective test battery administration.

When this was all completed, not only did we have the complete Follow-Up Study; we now had the three studies (Initial, Termination, and Follow-Up) on each patient, each in a separate bound folio of many, many pages. (The Termination Study, which often contained in its Form A data a copy of the daily process notes—one to two single-spaced pages each—of a lengthy psychoanalysis, comprising in some instances upward of 1000 hours, was especially voluminous.) The studies on each patient were now available for varieties of comparisons with one another and with the comparable data on the other patients along our several designated avenues of data analysis.

Pfeffer's Follow-Up Studies

One last set of considerations should still be raised here concerning our Follow-Up Studies: that of the comparison of the methods and the kinds of findings that they generated with the methods and the kinds of findings in a different kind of follow-up study pioneered by Arnold Pfeffer (1959, 1961, 1963), and since then extended further by others.[10] Pfeffer was fashioning his type of follow-up study at about the same time that PRP was being constructed, and it elicited very widespread interest in psychoanalytic circles on both empirical and theoretical grounds when it was published. During this period (in 1959), Pfeffer made a consultation visit to PRP for initial exploration of the pros and cons of his and PRP's approaches.

In their theoretical framework—the psychoanalytic theory of personality and of treatment—both projects were identical. In this, they stood apart from all other organized research studies that we knew of at that time that were of similar design (i.e., that were trying through selected points in time, with a special focus on follow-up, to learn more about the changes that come about in psychotherapy). The other such projects that we then knew about (e.g., those that were represented in the various American Psychological Association Conferences on Research in Psychotherapy; see Rubinstein & Parloff, 1959; Shlien, 1968; Strupp and Luborsky, 1962) were all explicitly Rogerian, behavioristic, or avowedly eclectic in framework.

---

10. Two psychoanalytic research groups—one in Chicago (Schlessinger & F. Robbins, 1974, 1975) and one in San Francisco (Norman, Blacker, Oremland, & Barrett, 1976; Oremland, Blacker, & Norman, 1975)— sought to replicate Pfeffer's findings. They each used essentially his methods with some slight modifications, and came up with essentially the same observations and conclusions.

However, the data-gathering methods of our two projects, though similar in some ways, also differed substantially. Pfeffer's method of data gathering consisted of a series of analytic-like interviews (done by a designated "follow-up analyst") held at a follow-up time approximately 4 years after treatment termination. The guiding assumption was that the best way to obtain analytic-like data concerning intrapsychic processes was to approximate the previous analytic situation as closely as possible. The interviews therefore consisted of an open-ended invitation to the former patient to report his or her material in any way that he or she wished, to bring in dream and fantasy material if he or she desired, and to consider that the interviews would continue, on a once-weekly basis, until they came to a consensually agreed natural close. They actually averaged five to seven in number. In this "analytic-like" setting of interviews with a single "follow-up analyst," residual or long-dormant treatment transferences were regularly readily elicited; the course of their revival and mastery within the "minianalysis" that occurred (including reports of happenings, interactions, associations, and dreams and fantasies from the intervening week preceding each interview) gave important clues to the neurotic problems that had occupied the previous analysis, as well as the ways in which, and extent to which, new and more adaptive solutions had been arrived at for them—that is, the extent to which they had been "resolved." (See Pfeffer, 1959, 1961, 1963, for detailed explication and for illustrative examples.)

Our data-gathering methods were different in important ways. Although we tried for our interviews to be as open as possible, in order to enable the ex-patient to recount his or her experiences and impressions freely and in the way he or she found most meaningful, we nonetheless did a number of things that (structurally) worked against this clear and uniform elicitation of transference revivals; we only tended to experience such revivals with the still disturbed patients who had basically had quite unsuccessful treatments. For instance, our interviews were not open-ended but were predetermined in number, and this was made known to the patient, who thus paced himself or herself accordingly and could also more successfully hold out what he or she chose not to convey. We also had multiple interviewers (at least two) at each session, thus "diluting" the possible transference focusing; we had different groups of interviewers for different purposes (one group with a focus on Patient and Treatment Variables, another on Situational Variables); and we had additional modalities of approach to the patient (the concomitant psychological testing). And, finally, we were also eliciting data from collateral sources, including (very visibly to the patient) from the spouse or other accompanying relative. Our guiding assumptions were therefore different from Pfeffer's: We felt that data of analytic concern, to be understood within an analytic framework, need not be gathered only by analytic methods. For instance, we placed considerable reliance on what psychological testing (as opposed to clinical interviewing) could yield about the intrapsychic configuration of the patient.

Pfeffer had been most concerned when he started his research about possible difficult aftereffects of his kind of interviewing and his kind of data gathering on the psychic equilibrium of the former patients, but these had not come about. In one of his cases there was a real crystallization of a felt need for more treatment, and this was judged to be indicated and was therefore encouraged. Most of his interviewees had, however, at least toyed with this idea during the course of their follow-up inquiry and then decided for sound reasons not to do so: The old conflicts of which they continued to see evidence were now quite manageable, in marked contrast to their preanalytic status. As a rough rule of thumb, Pfeffer felt that the kind of symptomatic transference manifestations that he elicited were never more severe than the patients' initial presenting symptomatology. With the individuals in his sample ("good" analytic cases from the Treatment Center of the New York Psychoanalytic Institute), he was dealing with outpatients with essentially autoplastic symptom pictures (phobic, depressive, obsessional, etc.). A reactivated symptom flare-up might cause acute discomfort for a period of time, but would likely not turn out to have more serious consequences than that.

Our population, by contrast to Pfeffer's, consisted of far "sicker" patients on the average; many required some concomitant hospitalization, and many had alloplastic and destructive symptoms (addictions, alcoholism, perversions, etc.). The possibility of a reactivated symptom flare-up of that kind, no matter how transitory, in such patients would be of much more serious import. One drink for the "ex-alcoholic" during such a period could perhaps trigger off a renewed and prolonged alcoholic bout. Aside from all the other (positive) scientific reasons that had converged toward the creation of our PRP design, this caution by itself would have rendered Pfeffer's method of follow-up approach an unwarranted risk with our particular patient population. The findings and conclusions from the two projects would thus have significant areas of noncomparability.

Procedural Aspects of the Project

THE PATHS OF DATA ANALYSIS

It has been indicated, that PRP set out to pursue three main avenues of data study and analysis. The three—the clinical case study, the formal Prediction Study, and the (semi)quantitative studies—are now described briefly in turn.

The Clinical Case Study

The clinical case study is the time-honored method pioneered by Freud. It has flourished in the hands of its founding genius and of those who have come after him, and has provided a truly extraordinary range of insights into the structure of the mind, the organization of mental illness, the forces at work in the treatment situation, and the processes of change. It is the method of this book.

A full clinical case study was constructed for each of our 42 PRP patients. This was done as follows: All the material on each of the cases—the by now many hundreds of single-spaced pages that comprised the write-ups in the folios of the Initial Study, the Termination Study, and the Follow-Up Study of each case—was read and abstracted[1] into one four-part document, the "Case Study." This

---

1. In the interests of uniformity of organization, style, and conceptualization, and with the writing of this present book ultimately in mind, I undertook and mostly completed this task during a year of Fellowship

Case Study followed the by now familiar basic format. The first part, called "Initial Study," was a clinical summary in four sections:

1. "The Patient"—the presenting history of the patient's life, character development, and illness picture, leading up to his or her coming for evaluation at The Menninger Foundation. This was basically a synthesis of the Form A case history and cross-sectional examinational material.

2. "Form B: Assessment of the Relevant Patient Variables"—an account of these variables as they appeared at initial evaluation, in an abstracted and highlighted narrative form in which not each is necessarily mentioned, and in which the space accorded each one reflects its deemed importance to the understanding of that case.

3. "Form S: Assessment of the Relevant Situational Variables"—again, an account of them as they initially appeared, abstracted and highlighted.

4. "Treatment Planning and Prognostication"—basically a narrative summary of the Form C Prediction Study material, covering the major statements and predictions in regard to treatment recommendations, treatment planning, treatment course, and treatment outcomes. A final paragraph-length statement contained the overall diagnostic summary statement on that patient, a single-sentence overall global predictive statement, the Initial Study HSRS rating, and the predicted HSRS rating at Termination Study.

This entire first part of the Case Study was condensed into between 15 and 20 double-spaced typed manuscript pages.

The second part of the Case Study, called "Termination Study," was a clinical summary, again in four sections:

1. "The Treatment Period"—a narrative account of the course and outcome of the treatment (in interaction with the ongoing events in the patient's life), basically abstracted and summarized from the Form T material, and again emphasizing those parts deemed significant to the particular treatment course and outcome.

2. "Form B: Reassessment of the Relevant Patient Variables"—an account of the variables as now seen at Termination and as compared with their status at the time of Initial Study.

3. "Form S: Reassessment of the Relevant Situational Variables"—a similar comparative account.

4. "Follow-Up Prognostication"—a summary containing an overall single-sentence global statement of the results achieved in that therapy, the adjudged Termination Study HSRS, a brief statement of the new predictions for the follow-up period, and the new predicted HSRS rating at Follow-Up Study.

---

at the Center for Advanced Study in the Behavioral Sciences in 1964–1965. At that time a certain number of the Follow-Up Studies had not yet taken place, and in those instances I carried out the task of completing the Case Studies in the few immediately following years. I describe a little further on some of the scientific and language issues posed for the present-day publication of this book based on these Case Studies—issues that derive from their having been written in the framework of the state of the field and the sociohistorical context of the mid-1960s.

This second part of the Case Study was condensed into between 15 and 25 double-spaced typed manuscript pages.

The third part of the Case Study, called "Follow-Up Study," was another four-section clinical summary:

1. "The Follow-Up Period"—basically an account of the new Form A material gathered during the Follow-Up Study, plus any new Form T material that would add any retrospective revised insights to the understanding of the prior treatment as seen now in the light of the follow-up experience.

2. "Form B: Reassessment of the Relevant Patient Variables"—with comparative statements now covering three points in time.

3. "Form S: Reassessment of the Relevant Situational Variables"—similar comparative statements.

4. "Follow-Up Summary"—an account including a final global statement on the sustained results achieved in the therapy, the Follow-Up Study HSRS rating, and a summary of any post-follow-up information that happened to be obtained concerning the patient, over whatever time span.

This third part of the Case Study was condensed into between 10 and 15 double-spaced typed manuscript pages.

The fourth and final part of the Case Study, called "Synthesis of the Treatment Course and Outcome," was an effort to give an overall narrative summary of what we thought we learned about psychotherapy and how it works from the intensive study of this particular case. This was therefore an explanatory effort to create a plausible and persuasive accounting of why and how this particular patient, treated in this way, within the context of this life situation and setting, achieved these particular changes that had been documented to this point, and neither more nor less. This fourth part of the Case Study usually occupied about 10 double-spaced typed manuscript pages.

The total manuscript length for each of these 42 Case Studies therefore came to between 50 and 70 double-spaced pages; each one can be easily read in 1½–2 hours. They add up to about 2500 pages of text. Though available as rich data sources for study by qualified scholars,[2] they would hardly be read as a serial published collection. A few of them have been excerpted at some length in some of the other books from PRP (see Chapter 2, p. 28). Their primary use to date has been as the central data base for this book: All the clinical vignettes, case descriptions, clusterings, and comparative studies of patients and their treatments throughout this book come from and are built upon those individual Case Studies.

Something, however, still needs to be said about these Case Studies in regard to the issues of language and conceptualization that derive from their use for publication now, more than 15 years after they were originally written. My original intent was to avoid value-laden and judgmental terms as much as possible (though unfortunately even some of our most technical vocabulary has, through use and misuse, taken on unintended pejorative connotations), and simply to describe as best I could what transpired with the patients, their treatments, and their lives,

---

2. See footnote 3, Chapter 1, p. 8, for the statement of the conditions of availability of these documents.

with the reader left free to make whatever inferences or value judgments (good or bad for the patient, or for society) that he or she would wish. My intent was also as much as possible to use the language of observable phenomena, with as clear a distinction as I could draw between clinical observations and our inferences about what they all meant or how they made sense to us within our theoretical framework, and, as part of that, to try to minimize the use of higher-level meta-psychological language and its theoretical assumptions.

Nonetheless, there is always something "dated" when one writes within the language usages and the scientific thinking of a particular period of scientific development and its sociohistorical context, and this fact becomes painfully apparent when reading or rewriting from the vantage point of a later point in time. Here I want to sort out two overlapping but also distinguishable issues: that of the vocabulary and concepts of the scientific endeavor, and that of the context provided by the times. I have already in Section I (see Chapter 3, pp. 32–34) discussed the conceptual advances within psychoanalytic clinical and theoretical exposition between the period in the 1950s when PRP was being conceived and the time of present final write-up nearly 30 years later, and have noted that the intervening period has brought new conceptualization and new language that would no doubt be more reflected in these 42 Case Studies if they were being written today. And yet the actual difference and apparent discontinuity may, for the reasons spelled out in Chapter 3, be far less than one might at first blush anticipate. Science is, after all, a continuous and mostly a cumulative enterprise, and today's major developments had their clear earlier forerunners, as I have tried to make clear.

In the realm of public (political–social) discourse, the issue of language and conceptualization may be even more sensitive. We have only to think of the heightened public credibility accorded in today's world to protests from the homosexual organizations that traditional psychoanalytic theorizing has done them a great disservice by psychologizing and "pathologizing" what they feel to be an equally viable choice of alternative life style, or to similar protests from women's organizations that our views of so-called "normal" feminine psychology (and psychopathology) have, wittingly or unwittingly, contributed to the perpetuation of social and psychological disadvantage to women. Clearly, many rethinkings have been undertaken in response to these protests, and again such rethinkings would probably be reflected in these Case Studies if they were being written today.

But language, too, was an issue in the days when the PRP was being conceptualized, and we were burdened then as we are now by the kind of jargonish shorthand of words like "femininity," "passivity," "activity," or "normal masochism"—words that condense and can conceal so many discrepant and at times opposed meanings, quite apart even from their polemical uses (e.g., individuals who may have profoundly differing visions, about the "proper" or normal role of women in society). I use the word "femininity" first in this illustrative list of nodal words that capture and reflect some of our most passionate intellectual–scientific controversies, because it was the particular word used by Jane Loevinger in a letter to us written in 1968 to describe her view of some of the issues encountered in writing and reading our PRP Case Study material.

Loevinger was referring to a write-up in which mention was made, without (in her view) sufficient specification of what was meant, concerning a particular patient's problems with her "femininity." Of this she said, "One of the things that struck me in the case history you gave me was the dependence on the notion of femininity. As a class exercise, I have had students come up with varied connotations of the term." And she then went on to list a good many: (1) acceptance of woman's biological role in regard to child bearing and child rearing; (2) acceptance of woman's traditional social role; (3) submissiveness to men (once called "normal feminine masochism"); (4) subtle manipulation of men ("feminine wiles"); (5) appreciation of art and culture; (6) sensitivity and richness of inner (feeling) life; (7) an intuitive and empathic rather than an analytical turn of mind (with phobic avoidance of mathematical thinking); (8) preference for frilly clothes and high heels (the advertiser's "femininity"). Biologically, the concept could embrace both being a sexpot and enjoying breast feeding; so asked Loevinger, what about the women who won't nurse because it might spoil their figures? And is being motherly being feminine? Or being jealous of men? One could go on, but the point is clear. Loevinger stated that she was working on an objective personality test for women and was finding separate clusters of items uncorrelated and even slightly negatively correlated with each other. And of course none of this has any reference to the application of the term to men, with all the additional connotations, mostly pejorative.

The overall point about language usage and its possibilities for unintended misunderstandings and hidden prejudices is raised for two reasons. First, I mean to indicate that I have tried to be mindful of it in the writing of this text, and have tried to employ (and in the use of examples from the original Case Studies, to alter, if I deem it indicated) a vocabulary that is as unambiguous in connotations as I can make it and as free of possible covert biases as I have been able to control. Second, the discussion is also intended as a declaration of intention, and also a caution, to the reader reacting in the context of today's perceptions, both scientific and social.

The Formal Prediction Study

The second major path of data analysis was the formal Prediction Study. Its various formal components have already been described: Form C (the clinical Prediction Study), Form P (the formalization of the narrative, psychologically conceptualized predictions into the discrete sentences of the logical, if–then–because tripartite model), and Form E (the embodying of predictive statements into evidence judgments, along with plausible alternatives for keying in advance).[3] What this pro-

3. The original description of this overall conception and its detailed formal specification appeared in the "Design" article by Sargent (1956a) in the very first collection of five articles from PRP. The subsequent monograph elaborating the Prediction Study (Sargent et al., 1968) amplified tremendously the statement of rationale for prediction in science and psychology, set the PRP conceptions within a matrix of models for scientific prediction, and then gave a very detailed manual for use of our model. This manual used as an illustration one total case description: the data on the patient (the Bohemian Musician); the development of the 31 individual Form P tripartite predictions; the keying and outcomes of the 72 individualized Form E statements devised and keyed at Initial Study time for Termination; 18 additional individualized Form E statements devised and keyed at Termination Study time for Follow-Up; the 78 core Form E statements, devised for use as a common core series of possible changes and outcomes (the same for each patient, and keyed for that patient at the time of original Prediction Study); and then the use of the Form E (Evidence) results in that case to confirm or refute each discrete prediction, with discussion of the most probable meaning and basis for the outcome that eventuated.

cess of progressive data handling did was to start with the kind of clinical predictions (in Form A) that are typical of clinical discourse—that is, *implicit* statements of diagnosis and prognosis, of treatment planning and therapeutic expectation, all embedded in clinical context, qualification, and often ambiguity. It transferred these into the *explicit* statements of Form C (equally clinical, however, in narrative form and context), and then into the logical if–then–because *discrete* predictive statements of Form P. These were each in turn tested, through the outcome alternatives arrayed in Form E, by specified predetermined evidence or outcome criteria, which were keyed in advance to the predicted outcomes and presented for subsequent judgment according to the actual outcomes within the array of plausible alterna tive predictions. To underline what has already been stated, post hoc reconstruction and rationalization was avoided through setting down in advance both the specific predictions and the evidence necessary to confirm or refute them at the end, and then through having outcome judges with no knowledge of what predictions had been made among the plausible alternatives presented make the judgments as to which outcomes had actually taken place.

This process, of course, did not solve all the problems of making and testing predictions in clinical work—an issue discussed at considerable length in a theoretical paper elsewhere (Wallerstein, 1964). I quote from that extended discussion:

> Psychoanalytic theory is loosely coupled; any single prediction can be wrong—or right—for a multiplicity of reasons; the conditional clause may be wrongly specified or wrongly assessed; the assessment of the relative weighting of the predictive variables may be off sufficiently to alter their over-all balance; the specific outcomes predicted—the criterion variables-may be insufficiently tightly linked to the causal chain or their assessment in practice may be wrong; or the psychoanalytic theoretical assumption underlying the prediction itself may be faulty. Thus the outcome of no single prediction, or even of any given series of predictions underpinned by the same theoretical proposition, will provide a crucial and definitive test of the adequacy of that proposition; but certainly predictive success, and repeatable success, will strengthen the credibility of that proposition, and predictive failure will weaken it. In this sense, and granting the many difficulties adduced, we do believe we have followed a theoretically logical chain in trying to link explicitly the data of psychoanalysis to the theory of psychoanalysis via the method of explicated predictions and thus to use the predictions as a wedge by which to test theory.
>
> In doing this, predictions that go awry are intrinsically as valuable as those which come out correctly, and practically perhaps even more so. Our interest is not in predictive accuracy per se, in a scoreboard of predictive success, but rather in widening our understanding of the conditions that govern predictions and the theoretical assumptions from which they derive. While predictive success in any instance does not assure that this is due to the reasons adduced, predictive failure is a clear signal of inadequate observation or theory somewhere along the line, and is thus a prompt stimulus to searching inquiry and, if successful, a correction of faulty assumptions and hence a modification, however minute or gross, of a theoretical proposition. (pp. 686–687)

This statement puts the testing of theoretical assumptions about the theory of psychoanalytic therapy (Rapaport's "rules of thumb") at the heart of the research enterprise. Though our population of 42 cases, at about 40 predictions per case, produced about 1700 predictions all told, only about 300 distinguishable and separable assumptive statements were made (at varying levels of generality and specificity), since any number of them (relating to such ubiguitous psychoanalytic treatment concepts as transference, insight, resistance, etc.) ran across many cases and also across many predictions within a single case, and thus were subject to multiple tests. In this way, though no predictive success or failure could *definitively* confirm or refute any of the underlying theoretical assumptions (for the reasons developed in the quotation above), repeated predictive success in relation to predictions that shared a common assumption would indeed strengthen the credibility of that assumption about how therapy works, while repeated failure in relation to another assumption would weaken and could destroy its credibility.

Furthermore, an article by Horwitz and A. Appelbaum (1966) has spelled out and has also given a graphic representation of how the 300 or so assumptions have been interrelated through linkages within a hierarchical organization of the whole array of assumptions, based on their degree of generality and explanatory power. It is in the linkages of these assumptive statements—as refined, altered, rendered more precise, and rearranged by the results of our research studies into a (now modified) hierarchical system of assumptions in ascending levels of generality and explanatory power—that PRP will have made a contribution, via its Prediction Study component, to the more precise specification and systematization of the theory of psychoanalytic therapy. We hope that we have moved this theory well beyond just "rules of thumb." The outcomes and the conclusions in this area of PRP's activities have been presented in the book by Horwitz (1974).

The (Semi)Quantitative Studies

The third major path of data analysis consisted of the (semi)quantitative studies built on our application of the Fechnerian method of paired comparisons. With our intention to study the interactions of many variables in several domains as codeterminants of treatment effects, we were faced with the fact that for almost all of these variables, standardized measures, complete with established degrees of reliability and validity, simply did not exist. To devise even a single scale to such specifications is a most complicated and time-consuming undertaking, which PRP did undertake to do with one "outcome" measure, the HSRS. What we sought across the board was a rapid and easily used check upon Patient, Treatment, and Situational Variables that clinicians would employ because it would be clinically congenial, and that could lead in time to the identification of measures (of whatever attribute or function) that would warrant more laborious and precise measurement.

The use of rank-order statistics—assigning patients a higher or lower status on a given dimension—is such a clinically congenial task. Clinicians are not accustomed to "measuring" a patient, but they are used to thinking and judging one patient as being more anxious than another or possessing more insight than another, and one treatment as focused more on transference interactions or on dreams and fantasies than another, and one life situation as being more stressful or more conflict-triggering than another. Clearly, however, it would be difficult if not impossible to try to keep the relevant information on all 42 patients in mind concerning any variable, or to rank-order the whole array of 42 with any sense of confidence, let alone to guard against the intervention of the halo effect and other such confounding problems.

However, one could keep the relevant data on a particular Patient, Treatment, or Situational Variable in mind with perhaps a dozen patients at a time. Futhermore, very many (perhaps most, but certainly not all) of our chosen variables in these three domains could lend themselves—aside from all of their qualitative many-faceted complexity (as witness the example given on pp. 74–75 of the specification of one Patient Variable, Anxiety)—to a quantitative dimension that could be extrapolated out of them, on which patients could be adjudged as "more or less." For instance, one could ask which of the two patients in a pair was *more* (quantitatively more) anxious. Reading and fixing in mind the Form B assessment on that variable, Anxiety, at one point in time (say, Initial) for 12 patients, one could then present to clinical judges the task of making a more-or-less judgment in regard to that variable as each patient appeared in a pairing with each other patient in the batch of 12. The number of such possible pairings in a batch would be $n(n-1)/2$ or 66, and once the Form B data were read and memories refreshed, it would take about 1 hour to make the 66 judgments. If two clinicians were to do this separately (e.g., as Robbins and I actually did for the initial Patient Variables assessment), their reliability with each other could be checked, and the data could be used additively (where appropriate) in arriving at the number of times any patient was chosen. If one patient was clearly at the head of the list (more than any other patient he or she was paired with on that attribute), he or she would be chosen 11 times by each judge, or a high number of 22 times altogether; the low point, of course, would be 0. A rank ordering could be created, then, derived from this application of the Fechnerian method of paired comparisons.

In order to rank-order all 42 (not just 12) patients, 6 of the first 12 were put into another batch together with 6 new ones, and when that rank ordering emerged from that group of paired comparisons, the two lists could be merged (with some technical statistical corrections to cope with "batch drift," due to the same 6 bunching higher or lower within a batch, depending on who the other 6 happened to be)[4] because of the overlap of 6 patients in the two batches. Again, the new group of 6 could be placed into a third batch together with an additional new 6. This could continute until the last 6 were put into a batch with the original 6 who had been withheld from the second batch; and the total would now have been completely circled back so that every subject had been judged in two different batches of 12. It was because of this paired comparisons requirement for half batches of 6 that the total project n (42) had to be a multiple of 6.

What did ultimately emerge from all this, of course (after going around 7 batches of 12, each time consisting of 66 judgments), was a rank-order listing from most to least times chosen of all 42 subjects on *one* variable at *one* of the three points in time. Of course, not every variable (e.g., Self-Concept, in which every patient differed, but not in a way in which "more or less" made any sense) lent itself to extrapolation along a more-or-less dimension; however, 12 of the Patient Variables did, as well as 17 Treatment Variables and all 7 Situational Variables. Given, too, not only that this whole cycling of 7 batches per variable had to be done for each variable so used, but that the same entire process had then to be repeated for that variable at the subsequent points in time, the overall magnitude of the clinical judging task becomes readily apparent. Actually, all of the 12 Patient Variables and the 7 Situational Variables were used in paired compari-

---

4. For a full explanation of this, see Kernberg *et al.* (1972), pp. 7–11.

sons rankings at all three points in time. The 17 Treatment Variables, since they were first adjudged only at Termination, could only be first done then, and since the judgments on them rarely shifted in any significant way in the light of the retrospective look from the Follow-Up vantage point, they were only rank-ordered by paired comparisons once. The arithmetic of this endeavor is staggering: Making 66 judgments per batch, at 7 batches per variable, for 12 Patient Variables and 7 Situational Variables 3 times each and 17 Treatment Variables 1 time, resulted in almost 35,000 individual paired judgments.

Though this task was parceled out over a considerable time span and among several groups—in each instance, those research clinicians who had gathered that clinical data for that variable at that point in time and who therefore knew those patients intimately from that perspective—it was nonetheless an enormously time-consuming and tedious task. This was its central drawback as a research method in so large-scale a research enterprise with so many acts of judgment involved. On the other hand, it was inherently a clinically congenial task, and one that clinicians with research investments could be persuaded to undertake.

The rank orderings, as distributions of times chosen, could then serve as the basis for various quantifying and grouping activities. Profiles were created for individual patients, reflecting their patterning on a group of variables (Patient, Treatment, or Situational) at a particular point in time; these profiles could serve as a ready device to identify patients who had particular clusterings or patternings of the variables (with the caution that this was only of the quantitative more-or-less dimensions on those variables in that domain that lent themselves to such use). Such profiles lent themselves not only to ready graphic individual comparisons between patients, and to equally graphic before-and-after comparisons of the same patient as the variables might change over time (e.g., has this patient's Ego Strength been raised in its rank-order position as a consequence of a successful treatment process?), but also to various kinds of group comparisons. For example, patients who occupied similar relative positions on certain variables (i.e., these variables being held relatively constant) could then be selected in terms of gross differences on other variables) (e.g., the third highest vs. the third lowest on, say, Ego Strength, Anxiety, etc.), so that the relationship of the variability of those particular variables to different aspects of outcome could be assessed. For more detailed description of the profiles and of their uses, the reader is referred to the article by Luborsky and Sargent (1956) from the very first collection of five articles published from PRP; to the initial comprehensive presentation of PRP's approach to quantitative problems of psychoanalytic research (Sargent et al., 1967, especially pp. 271–279); and to an overall research accounting of a single case (that of the Adoptive Mother), in which the data of the clinical Case Study, the formal Prediction Study, and the profiles over several points in time are compared (Wallerstein, 1968).

Another use of our distribution of times chosen was the creation of intercorrelational matrices and derived factor-analytic studies. PRP owes to its chief consultant on quantitative issues, Wayne Holtzman, the statistical reasoning that gave it warrant to treat these ordinally rank-order-derived distributions of number of times chosen as if they had at least semicardinal properties, and to use them as if we had some sense of the metric related to the phenomena being judged. For one statement of the details of this argument—that is, that this kind of rank ordering of 42 patients strung out this way from most to least on any dimension would be spaced more clearly and more widely at both ends, and would be more bunched together and more difficult to distinguish in the middle—the reader is referred to Sargent *et al.* (1967, pp. 270–271). For the various publications showing the intercorrelational matrices and the various factor-analytic studies, see Luborsky and Sargent (1956), Luborsky (1962b), Sargent *et al.* (1967), and the Kernberg, *et al.* (1972) monograph of results of the quantitative studies (the first half of Kernberg *et al.* is devoted to these results in full detail).

A last aspect of our quantitative studies, a mathematical and nonmetrical approach, derived from a collaboration between PRP and the Israel Institute of Applied Social Research in Jerusalem; this collaboration was initiated when I presented the work and the problems of PRP in the course of a scientific visit to the Israel Institute in 1964. Louis Guttman, the Scientific Director of the Institute, felt that the facet theory method, using multidimensional scalogram analysis computer programs that he had worked out with James Lingoes at the University of Michigan, represented an ideal way to try to handle our kind of data with its great array of relevant variables, only some of them scaled (the rank orderings). Subsequently, a number of PRP staff members spent several months of collaborative work in Jerusalem, out of which came the ultimate creation of a 17-facet mapping sentence that handled the analysis of a total of 169 quantitative and category variables. The full results of this endeavor occupy the second half of the Kernberg *et al.* (1972) monograph, together with a final discussion of the concordances, as well as the discrepancies, between the findings and conclusions of the two quantitative approaches—the statistical factor-analytic approach and the nonmetrical facet theory approach.

THE PROBLEM OF CONTROLS

Central to the commitment to a thoroughly naturalistic study of psychotherapy course and outcome was the inability to use any of the usual accoutrements of a clinical-trials-type research design, such as a similarly constituted untreated control group, or even the type of design pioneered in psychotherapy research by Rogers and his coworkers (Rogers, 1951; Rogers & Dymond, 1954) of trying to use the patient as his or her own control through deferring the planned treatment, so that a pretreatment interval could be compared in its effect with a subsequent treatment interval. Such arrangements were incompatible with our intent to study psychotherapy as it regularly took place in its natural habitat. In addition, of course, the clinical exigencies of The Menninger Foundation made it impossible: Prospective patients came a long way and expected to spend a good deal of money to receive needed treatment, and could not be handled in any such research-dictated way that would have either delayed or denied them their treatment.

However, as has already been strongly emphasized, none of these design strictures abrogated in any way our responsibility to tackle the ever-thorny problem of controls in psychotherapy research. We were simply forced to consider afresh what to control, and how to control it, and by what specific control methods.[5]

---

5. The discussion to follow here is condensed from our fuller statement in an article from the earliest days of PRP, specifically devoted to this issue of controls (Robbins & Wallerstein, 1959)—see especially pp. 39–42.

Our overall premise was to base our major efforts at control more on appropriate *selection* of clinical material than on its *manipulation*. Our strategy, that is, was to set up criteria for the *selection* of instances that represented the hypotheses we wished to test. Nontreated control groups are usually set up on some matched basis, in which custom dictates the control of such demographic variables as age, sex, SES, marital status, duration of illness, formal diagnosis, or the like. Since we felt that these simple differential criteria simply did not distinguish individuals from one another along dimensions crucial to their psychotherapeutic course and outcome, we bypassed them and concentrated our attention on our assessments in depth of the three groups of variables, Patient, Treatment, and Situational, which we did deem centrally relevant to the course and outcome of treatment. How we used these assessments to match patients for similarity or contrast in regard to any grouping of them is discussed below under the heading "Interpatient Controls." We did not use these differential criteria to set up nontreated control groups, since that would mean withholding clinically indicated treatment (at least temporarily); as just stated, this would have violated our scientific commitment to a naturalistic research study and would not have been clinically possible in our setting. Nor did we try to set up a so-called "normal" control group. Often this means simply "not in a hospital" or "not in treatment," which is not a dimension crucially relevant to an understanding of either mental illness or its treatment.

Still another premise governing the use of controls in PRP had to do with the *level* at which the concept of control was to be introduced. In experimental work, controls are most often introduced at the level of data collection in the form of specifications and restrictions as to what the observer should look for. We chose rather to have the clinician work just as he or she was accustomed to do (the naturalistic design), to use whatever conceptual categories he or she found natural and congenial, and to gather and utilize in his or her formulations and judgments all the clinical data available at each point of study. Postaudit controls were then introduced at the level of data classification and analysis, as formalized in our various instruments, in which the data were recorded in defined categories.

Intrapatient Control

Within this conceptual framework, we then addressed ourselves to the "how to control it" question and selected four specific methods of control. The first, called "intrapatient control"—that is, using the patient as his or her own control—was accomplished via the individual Prediction Study. We used the concept of the patient as his or her own control not in the sense popularized by Rogers and his coworkers, which, as already stated, could not be a viable method for us,[6] but in the sense propounded by Gordon Allport (1937) in his exposition of idiographic versus nomothetic research inquiry. Within our longitudinal individual predictive study for each member of our research sample, having (as has been described) specified in advance for each prediction the contingencies to which it related, the

---

6. Many other arguments besides ours exist against considering a pretreatment "waiting list" period as a valid reflection of the course of illness without treatment, to be compared then with its course during treatment; see, for example, Frank, 1959.

assumptions on which it was based, and the predetermined evidence in subsequent event or subsequent judgment that would be necessary to confirm or refute it, we could learn to what extent and in what areas the underlying assumptions and the specific variables chosen did or did not permit adequate prediction. That such testing could not be definitive in the direction of either clear confirmation or refutation of aspects of theory has already been indicated, but it could and did strengthen or weaken the plausibility of given assumptions or clusters of assumptions, and thus could and did lead to an altered and now more empirically linked hierarchical organization of our assumptive network that in its totality constitutes our theory of psychoanalytic therapy. Our testing could, of course, also narrow the areas for future, more specific, and more definitive testing. The *control* over post hoc reconstruction and rationalization rested in setting down the predictions, the assumptive base, and the necessary evidence in advance.

Interpatient Control

The second control method, called "interpatient control," stemmed from the profiles of the different domains of variables at the different points in time derived for each patient from the paired comparisons judgments in the way already described. These profiles facilitated interpatient comparison and contrast, through permitting the selection of groups of patients who were alike in respect to certain of the variables and dissimilar in respect to other variables. Thus some variables could be controlled while the variability of others was investigated. Such profiles, useful though they could be for these purposes, were of course limited by the fact that clearly not all the variables we postulated to be relevant to psychotherapeutic course and outcome could be included in them.

Parallel Study of the Test Battery

The third control method was the parallel and independent study of the psychological projective test battery that was administered at the PRP's three vantage points in time. From the assessment of the Patient Variables from the test data alone, full individual prediction studies were made in many of the cases[7] that were exactly comparable to the Prediction Studies made from the full clinical evaluation material. At subsequent points in time, the nature and extent of the achieved changes in the variables under study could again by judged from the tests alone, parallel to, but independent of, the concomitant clinical restudy. In fact, Chapter 8 of the S. A. Appelbaum (1977) book on the test results, "Comparing the Usefulness of Tests with Other Psychiatric Information," represents the examination of this particular control method. My own reasons for differing with some of the conclusions drawn there (not with the data) have already been presented (see Chapter 2, pp. 20–21).

---

7. Not in all cases, in part because of the lack of availability of some of the research subjects at either Termination or Follow-Up Study time (the so-called "truncated" studies), and in part through lack of sufficient research time to deal with all the instances we did have.

Such psychological test studies of course had the advantage, already indicated, of being truly "blind" in the sense of not requiring any knowledge of preceding clinical or of preceding test data. The comparative judgments of the change in status of the variables studied could be made after they are independently assessed at each point in time. In this way, cross-sectional judgments could be made independently of knowledge of earlier stages. Therefore, we could have assessments that were not only independent of clinical data, but were also completely independent of previous assessments using the same test method. Successive clinical studies of course cannot be as uninformed with respect to the data from the preceding study period. Those doing the Termination and Follow-Up Studies did not know what predictions had been made, but it was not possible in the course of gathering interview data at Termination and Follow-Up to avoid acquiring knowledge of how the patient viewed himself or herself and how others viewed him or her over the course of time.

Thus, through the Prediction Study aspects of our design, the use of the patient as his or her own control was a major control method in both the clinical and the psychological test studies. The two types of studies, conducted concurrently but independently, acted as checks both upon themselves and upon one another.

Inadvertent Control

The fourth and last control method specifically built into the PRP operations was called "inadvertent control." This operated when, for whatever reason of finance, geography, or differing clinical judgments between the clinical evaluation group and the research evaluation group, the patient could not or would not receive the treatment approach deemed optimally appropriate by the research evaluation group. In those instances, as already indicated, differing sets of predictions were made out for the treatment actually to be undertaken and for the other form of treatment that the research group deemed ideally more appropriate. This lent itself to a specifically useful kind of control. For example, it might have been felt that the major conflicts that constituted the particular neurotic illness of a patient could only be resolved through psychoanalysis, and that various desired and specified changes would otherwise not occur. If the patient, for reality reasons, were in only a once-a-week psychotherapy, and some of the changes that had been postulated to be dependent on psychoanalysis with the working through of the full-fledged regressive transference neurosis nevertheless did take place in this far less intensive (and regressive) therapeutic effort, then the assumptive bases on which particular predictions had rested would be seriously shaken. We had a fair number of such instances, and the ways in which they helped shape our overall conclusions are demonstrated throughout this book.

THE SOCIOLOGY OF PSYCHOTHERAPY RESEARCH

The issues to be discussed here are the subject of constant discussion among gatherings of researchers (undoubtedly in every field), but are only occasionally addressed formally in the literature. They are the issues of the sociology of research,[8] already alluded to—of maintaining a more or less cohesive and harmonious working relationship among research colleagues of varying degrees of clinical and research motivation, sophistication, and determination, dealing with a population of research subjects who are at the same time clinical patients, subject to the vicissitudes of varying experiences in both their treatments and their lives that might or might not allow them to remain amenable and accessible to the research requirements over the projected lifespan of the research design. Add that, by its nature, research into the process and outcome of psychotherapy is long-term, that the subjects have a lifespan equal to that of the researchers, and that the researchers vary over the course of time in their research commitments and their personal commitments, and the difficulties that beset workers in this field become obvious.

These difficulties of conducting a research study into the nature of the mechanisms of change in psychoanalysis and in psychotherapy are all the greater in a dedicated clinical center like The Menninger Foundation, with its clinical service ideology and its strongly positive convictions about the high value, the seriousness, and the effectiveness of the therapeutic work that is its central activity. By and large, clinicians believe strongly in the great usefulness of their practical clinical endeavors and of their theoretical guiding principles. Research that explores as open questions the nature of psychotherapeutic change and the effectiveness of psychotherapists as the instruments of that change thus readily evoke anxieties and resistances in such a clinical community. This is the more so, since research data such as ours—clinical *judgments* about therapeutic changes and outcomes, and about the therapeutic process by which these changes have come about—can only with difficulty be separated from the *judge* who makes them, despite the utmost honesty in striving for such objectivity. And just as the judge is always part of the judgment, so, to the therapist whose work is being studied, must the assessment of the therapy always involve an assessment of the therapist. Indeed, an assessment of the therapist, with its inevitably heavy weighting of the unconscious predispositions and biases, the countertransference elements, was specifically built into our research design as part of the system of Treatment and Therapist Variables.

Such factors obviously give rise to interpersonal tensions that will beset and often seriously threaten research into the basic operations of a clinical community. That most research is free of such complications reflects the fact that most research is about phenomena that are not the object of such fierce subjective convictions. It is the difference between doing research on the things that really count within us emotionally, as against the things that are emotionally neutral or irrelevant. In the face of this array of considerations, we did succeed over the two decades of the operation of PRP in maintaining our complex research group intact in its vital functions, while inevitably losing and gaining individual members along the way, including a major change in working leadership in 1966 (when Kernberg succeeded me in the ongoing management role). During all this time

---

8. The discussion to follow here is condensed from my own fuller statement of just these problems (Wallerstein, 1966, pp. 509–511) as an important array of issues that must be successfully dealt with in order to be able to carry out the actual operations of this kind of long-range clinical research. Reference is made in this article to some of the other articles in the clinical research literature that also deal with these specific issues.

we were likewise successful in maintaining a good working relationship with the body of treating clinicians, despite the kind of problems discussed here, and also in maintaining contact with or adequate knowledge about a population of patient subjects with no loss, despite the passage of time and the wide vicissitudes of life. Obviously, all this could only be accomplished in a clinical institution that was at once large enough, tolerant enough, and convinced enough about the importance of the research enterprise.

Before I close this discussion, I should speak of the peculiar uniqueness of The Menninger Foundation as a possible locus for this kind of grand-scale longitudinal clinical research program—devoted to study of its own vital core, the clinical psychotherapeutic endeavor—from another angle: not that of difficulties to be patiently overcome, but of singular opportunities there available. Only in such a large clinical community, harnessed to such a common endeavor and common ideology (and doing its work within a common administrative framework), could such a large-scale and long-range study be constructed and carried out, with all of its requirements for total participation by the community. In the more individually controlled settings in which the overwhelming amount of psychoanalysis and long-term intensive psychoanalytic psychotherapy is conducted, obtaining such total cooperation would be neither logistically nor psychologically possible. Probably only at that place, and—as has been stated at length in Section I in the discussion of the scientific and ethical issues of this book (see Chapter 3, pp. 35–38)—at that time, could PRP have been carried out at all.

III

The Patients and Their Characteristics

In Section II (see Chapter 5), I have described the patient sample in terms of the criteria that governed their selection as research subjects (basically a series of exclusion criteria) and then have specified the characteristics of the patient group along the usual demographic identifying lines. As noted there, the population was reasonably homogeneous but very far from representative of the population at large, and probably also systematically somewhat different from that subset of the population at large who come (or are brought) to psychiatric treatment.

The sample, to recapitulate, consisted of 21 men and 21 women. The age range was restricted to the young adult to middle adult years. Not quite half were married, and those who were (or had been) married averaged not quite 2 children per family. They came from sibships that averaged about 2½ children per family. Their religious affiliation was overwhelmingly Protestant. They were all white. About half came from affluent families (with a small handful of very wealthy ones) and half from much more modest backgrounds. There was a surprising amount of severe alcoholism in the family backgrounds — in about one-third of them. The patients' own occupational and social status was at a somewhat lower level than that of their families of origin. Intellectually, they were in a clearly superior range, with a mean IQ of 124. Most of them came to The Menninger Foundation in the context of failed psychiatric treatment efforts in their home communities of varying kinds and varying intensities.

Both the nature of the institution in which the patients were treated (The Menninger Foundation) and the exclusion criteria that we used in the selection process served also to restrict the range of the sample. Coming to Topeka mostly on the basis of failed outpatient treatment efforts in other communities excluded the usual moderately neurotically ill psychiatric outpatient population; the patients had to be "sick" enough to come to The Menninger Foundation. Excluding those for whom hospitalization, other adjuvant care facilities, and somatic treatments were major planned therapeutic modalities eliminated the openly psychotically ill, as well as the organically damaged, the retarded, and the grossly physically ill; the patients had to be "well" enough so that the planned formal psychotherapy or psychoanalysis in Topeka would be the major therapeutic vehicle.

As stated earlier, this made for a group of patients with severe symptom neuroses, severe character neuroses, and impulse neuroses with various behavioral disturbances (alcoholic, addictive, and sexual), as well as a good many who would be conceptualized today as having narcissistic characters and borderline personality organizations. These various categories just stated, of course, overlapped in varieties of interacting ways, and together constituted a spectrum of patients between the moderately neurotic and the flagrantly psychotic. Section III of this book consists of a much more detailed clinical accounting of this particular patient population. I describe their character structures and their symptom and illness structures as they came to and entered their treatments at The Menninger Foundation, where they constituted a typical cross-section of the patients treated (modified somewhat, to be sure, by the skewing introduced by the kinds of exclusion criteria that we had to or did choose to employ).

In reading the descriptions of patient characteristics to follow, two considerations should be kept in mind. First, under each heading, I describe those patients for whom that particular characteristic represented a significant aspect of the patients' total psychological organization. A particular patient thus can be described under a number of headings reflecting various components of that individual's character functioning. For each patient, these various perspectives are all brought into a summary diagnostic statement in the final pages of Section III under the heading "Tabulation of the Patients."

The other consideration that I want to emphasize is that the nature of the diagnostic thinking and conceptualization described here is what was developed and was congenial within a psychoanalytic theoretical framework as applied to the range of psychiatric pathology. It is not bound by the particular categories of DSM-II, though it is certainly mostly compatible with those categories, because basically it derived from the same conceptual framework. Nor of course, is it bound by the newer categories of DSM-III, with which it is far less congenial. The patients are fully enough described so that the reader can readily make the translation into DSM categories. (For further discussion of this point, see Section I, Chapter 3, pp. 32–35.)

Symptoms and Illness Configurations

CENTRAL PRESENTING COMPLAINTS

Anxiety and Depression

Whatever their character problems and illness structures, the overwhelming majority of the patients (37 of 42) came with central complaints of severe anxiety or depression, or both in combination. Of the five who did not manifest open anxiety and/or depression, three were intensely and malignantly alloplastic in symptom expression: the Alcoholic Raconteur, with severe alcoholism; the Addicted Doctor, with severe barbiturate (and other) addictions, who was driven to treatment by revocation of his license; and the Sociopath, with a career of pathological lying, depredation, and embezzling, who had barely escaped criminal prosecution. In these three, the intensity and rapidity of tension discharge into destructively alloplastic directions served at least to preclude open anxiety and/or depression. Of the other two, the Obese Woman came for treatment because of compulsive overeating and severe obesity (also a way of warding off anxiety and/or depression); only the Prince came without the press of anxiety and depression (his complaints were of distressing personal characteristics that he called paradoxical and contradictory, like haughtiness and yet profound insecurity).

Of the other 37, 23 (11 men and 12 women), or more than half the total sample, came with significant complaints of *both* anxiety and depression. The primacy, the centrality, and the mode of manifestation varied enormously. Some patients had severe recurring symptoms of long standing. The Manic–Depressive Physician, for example, had suffered severe anxieties all his life, from intense separation anxieties when he started school to intense social anxieties through his adulthood; since age 13 he had suffered serious depressive–anxious episodes, occasionally interspersed with manicky and semidelusional paranoid episodes. In one suicidal depressive episode he had received ECT. The Involutional Woman had been phobically anxious since childhood, and recurrently depressed with a series of real and symbolic adulthood losses. She came with an involutional depression, with multiple sources, that had been unresponsive to psychoactive medications, supportive therapy, subcoma insulin, and ECT.

With other patients, the anxiety and depression were more constant and pervasive. The Obedient Husband, for example, was ever fearful that his wife would no longer need him and therefore would no longer love him. The Actress reflected

121

her pervasive distress in repetitive (nightmarish) dream and mood states; she acted out the latter through dyeing her hair black and making her college dormitory room black, with black curtains, rug, and bedspread, and black and white furniture (it was described as a "funeral vault").

With still other patients, a specific harrowing experience triggered the symptoms. The Claustrophobic Man was in a hospital operating room for cancer surgery when a surgical emergency came in; the patient felt everyone leaving him to attend the newcomer, at which point he felt helpless and abandoned—and panicked. And the Tantrum Woman, who was given to constant intrusive anxieties over her impulses to kill her children, came to treatment specifically because of an acute reactive depression following her husband's death in a car accident, which she (unrealistically) felt could have been avoided if she had behaved differently with him that morning.

Another group of patients resisted, or repressed these symptoms. The Movie Lady, for instance, habitually pushed away her phobic anxiety and depression by counterphobic maneuvers and a Pollyannaish facade. The Fearful Loner usually successfully kept himself under rigid repressive controls until he felt pushed or trapped, as in an evaluation interview just prior to his arrival in Topeka. He felt the evaluating psychiatrist to be too impatient and too intrusive in demanding that he talk about himself; this feeling suddenly led him to physically assault the psychiatrist, pinning him to the chair. (He never returned to him.)

A final patient in this group with depression and anxiety, the Car Salesman, had made a serious suicidal effort with 26 barbiturate pills, which rendered him unconscious for 24 hours; this effort led directly to his appearance for treatment.

In addition to the 23 with both anxiety and depression as strongly presenting symptoms, there were 9 others (4 men and 5 women) with significant, even very major anxiety but without evident depression, and 5 others (2 men and 3 women) with severe depression—leading in some instances to serious suicidal efforts (the Script Writer) or deflected in others into uncontrolled alcoholism or addiction (the Alcoholic Doctor, the Intellectual Fencer, and the Medical Scientist)—where anxiety was not remarked. The overall range of circumstances in these was similar to the others just described.

Phobias

With a total of 18 of the 42 patients (8 men and 10 women), the anxieties had crystallized into clear phobic attitudes and/or symptoms; however, with but a single exception (the Claustrophobic Man), the strength of these symptoms was much more massive among the women than the men. With five of these patients, the phobias were so dominant in the symptom picture as to be reflected in the titles given to the patients. The Snake Phobia Woman's dominant symptom was triggered at age 13 when her mother, who was fearful of snakes, casually remarked that someone had once found a snake in bed. The resulting snake phobia had grown in scope and intensity ever since. Everywhere the patient went she apprehensively looked for snakes, because "a snake could be there" even in a 10th-floor hotel room; every cord, rod, or pipe "could be a snake" and was examined critically. Whenever she noted a crack under the door, she would think that a snake "could crawl under," and trips to the basement of her home were postponed as much as possible. When going to bed at night, she would carefully examine the surface of the bed for any unusual contours, and then when getting in would ease her feet down, taut and apprehensive, relaxing only when she touched the footboard. She dreaded getting out of bed at night lest she step on a snake. And black snakes repetitively invaded her dreams as well, terrifying her till a voice told her that the snakes could be pacified with alcohol, or if that failed, chocolate milk. (The father, who was unrealistically seen as a slovenly, dirty man, was an alcoholic.)

The Housebound Phobic Woman became progressively incapacitated, to the point where she would remain indoors—sleeping, reading, watching television, drinking, and drugging herself with barbiturates—all day. She rarely if ever went out, but she did receive a married visitor, with whom she was involved in an affair; he became her one continuing contact with the outside world, bringing the mail (from her post office box), the groceries, and the laundry. The Phobic Woman would have been similarly housebound, except that she could keep her husband constantly at her side, since both of them were fully supported by her affluent parents. Because she was unable to tolerate the most minimal separation from him, he had to accompany her everywhere, including waiting outside during her psychotherapy hours (she had been in about 8 years of almost continuous psychotherapy before coming to The Menninger Foundation). And the Phobic Girl had, since age 10, suffered from panicky phobic episodes that would feel "as if my soul leaves my body." These phobias were multiple: of leaving home; of sunlight (from the moment she was informed on a bright day of her father's heart attack); of the dark (this would bring her mother to her bed nightly); of small enclosed places; of elevators; of being caught someplace without a toilet (this had led her at age 11 to refuse to go on a museum trip with her school class); and so on. Her parents did not see all this constriction of her life as illness; rather, they saw her as lazy and recalcitrant, and regarded her obesity as her only real problem. (And the mother suffered a separation anxiety equal to that of the patient when the latter entered the hospital.)

The only man in this severely phobic group, the Claustrophobic Man, traced the onset of his symptoms to the panicky episode in the hospital operating room where he suddenly felt unattended. Though he had had a series of operations for recurrent cancer of the thyroid and his prognosis was still not clear, he professed no concern about this, because his highly esteemed physicians were taking proper care of him and had that situation well in hand. Rather, he suffered from an intense claustrophobia—in business meetings, hotel lobbies, theatres, and social gatherings—which progressively narrowed down his business activities, his social life, and his travel; he also had an intense phobia of (nonexistent) heart disease, in which he persisted despite a series of negative workups by those selfsame esteemed physicians.

The phobic patients showed a considerable range in their handling of the phobic illness and in the constricting impact of the phobias on their environment. The Phobic Woman, as indicated, so constricted her husband's life that she had to attend his college classes with him; she could not even allow him to leave the house for a haircut, so that the barber had to be brought to the home instead. By contrast, the Movie Lady, whose main symptoms also consisted of a widening network of phobic restrictions (of 15 years' duration), would hold herself to her allotted tasks: For example, she would drive on back roads, where she knew she could always stop the car and run out at the side of the road and across the field if she felt desperate. It was important to her to try to keep from encroaching upon her husband's work life or their shared social life as much as she could. The Adoptive Mother handled her fears of being a parent counterphobically—by inducing her husband to go abroad, where they could adopt a baby and return it to the agency without any of their friends' finding out, should the adoption not work out. Actually she did, after experiencing a rising panic over intensifying hostile impulses toward the baby, return the infant to the agency; as noted earlier, this precipitated her guilt-ridden collapse into an acute depression, which finally led her to treatment. The English Professor was more successful in his counterphobic maneuvers, but at a severe price. He had "fear reactions" in almost every social and professional situation. These would occur when he was lecturing in class; his first impulse would be to flee, but he would feel trapped and somehow brave it through. Ultimately this effort collapsed and he began to dismiss his classes early. Finally, he abruptly resigned his position and sought therapy.

Aggressive Behaviors

Alongside the depressive, anxiety, and phobic symptoms, a surprising 26 of the patients (not quite two-thirds)—14 men and 12 women—suffered with varieties of uncontrolled aggressive behaviors, rage attacks, and tantrums, leading with some into verbally and physically assaultive situations. As might be expected, these were more dangerous with the men, especially as they were combined with drunkenness in 8 of the 14 men. In fact, this aggressive behavior was so compelling that, any number of times in the case studies, a note was made that the patient kept from being more depressed (or anxious) through being so constantly angry and raging. The cases of the Tantrum Woman and the Divorced Nurse were both good examples of that warding-off function of their angry outbursts.

Among the women, the Tantrum Woman had characteristic (and lifelong) temper tantrums, which then punctuated her analysis as increasingly unmanageable "affect storms"—repetitive episodes of torrential affective (and abusive) outpourings during the analytic hours. These inundated all reasonable and reasoning processes, so that she could hear neither her analyst nor herself. She was also regularly riddled with intrusive murderous thoughts toward her children. The Heiress suffered from incapacitating "turbulent periods," usually precipitated by an altercation with the husband or an upset with the children; she would sit with clenched fists, trembling in terror, going into a withdrawn, depersonalized, "unperson" state. Of these occasions, the husband said that there "seemed to be a tiger inside her which immobilized her." And the Bohemian Musician, when she was not lying in bed with the blinds drawn, her hands over her face, and wearing dark glasses, would be up screaming and moaning with wild temper outbursts, expressing thoughts that she would kill herself or that her husband would choke her.

By comparison, the situations with the men were far more dangerous. For example, the Suspended Medical Student periodically got involved in high-speed drunken driving, when he was clearly pushed by suicidal and homicidal ideation.

Once he rounded a blind corner at high speed and was hit by another car; his car was totally demolished, but the patient escaped miraculously unscathed. The Alcoholic Heir was one of those who typically got into drunken brawls with his equally hard-drinking wife: He would threaten to throw her out the window, and she would barricade the doors and call the police, who would cart him off to jail for an overnight stay. And the Alcoholic Raconteur's "crazy drunk" assaults upon his father ended many times in his dramatically ordering the father out of his own (the father's) house, with threats to kill him if he stayed. Twice the patient physically assaulted the father; after the second beating, the wealthy father, in the interests of family peace, moved out of the house into his club downtown.

Such verbal and physical assault was not always alcohol-related. The Sociopath, whose personal depredations, lying, swindling, and courtroom savaging of opposing attorneys who were hated "400 percenters" have already been mentioned, struggled with such throttled hatreds that when action discharge was precluded—as when he was confronted with Rorschach cards that elicited a welling up of savagely aggressive imagery—he jiggled his legs so severely that the whole room seemed to shake, while keeping his body stiffly immobile from the waist up. He was the individual of whom the testing psychologist said, "If ever we can say about a patient from his psychological test performance that he is a potential rapist or murderer, I think this can be said about this patient." With the Manic–Depressive Physician, we saw how far violent propensities could carry a patient. When he found his wife in bed in his house with a lover, he flew into a rage and proceeded to beat the other man over the head with a bed slat until he realized he might kill him. He then beat him with his fists and called the police. The other man was hurt badly and had to be hospitalized. The patient, in recounting the episode, was proud that he had overcome his own fear and had beaten the other man up. The patient's father commented, "The only difference is I would have killed the fellow." The Masochistic Editor, on the other hand, got into a jealous fight with a homosexual lover (who had brought a rival to their apartment) and in the encounter, suffered a severe blow to the head with a bottle; this caused a subdural hematoma that required surgical relief. In this context, it seems so much milder that the Economist, constantly paranoidly fearful of being assaulted, always carried a pistol and a club in his car in order to be properly vigilant against attack.

BEHAVIORAL DISTURBANCES

Alcoholism

Many different behaviors fell under the rubric of "behavioral disturbances." The amount of alcoholism in the families (mostly the fathers) of our patients has already been stated. It should be no surprise that alcoholism was in turn a major symptom disturbance in 15 of our patients and very troublesome in 4 more—a total of 19, or almost half the sample. Men outnumbered women 12 to 3 among the severe alcoholics; the sexes were evenly divided (2 to 2) among the moderate ones. Two of the severe alcoholics, the Alcoholic Heir and the Car Salesman, had received identical offers from their fathers (in the context of severe family alcoholic histories that did not involve the fathers) of $1000 if they would not drink before they became 21. (In one instance beer was excepted, and in the other the restriction also applied to smoking.) Each patient had successfully collected his money and then promptly embarked on an alcoholic career. With at least 7 of the severely alcoholic patients—6 men (the Alcoholic Heir, the Alcoholic Raconteur, the Alcoholic Doctor, the Car Salesman, the Sexual Masochist, and the Medical Scientist) and 1 woman, (the Script Writer)—the alcoholism was *the* central driving symptom of their illness (though in the Sexual Masochist's case this distinction was shared with his bizarre sexual perversion). Three of the six mental-illness-related deaths in our patient sample occurred in this group of 7, and two more of them occurred among the larger alcoholic group.

The story of the Alcoholic Heir is paradigmatic. As noted earlier, he was the very wealthy heir to one of the nation's giant scientific–industrial enterprises, in which his nondrinking father was a major executive. As he entered upon his foreordained career in the family firm, where he at first performed adequately enough to warrant his rapid promotions, he began to drink more and more heavily—to the point where he would retire to his room for solitary binges and where his work was progressively interfered with because of spillover from weekend drunks. Quite close to the 10th anniversary of his brother's death in a household fire the brother had set while drunk (about which the patient had always felt guilty, because he had failed that night to wait up for his drunken brother so he could put him to bed), the patient's own house burned down after a cigarette fire started when he was drunk; he escaped with burns only on his hands. His alcoholism intensified to the point where he often felt unable to go to work at all: He would become apprehensive and proceed no further than the door of the office building. Soon he received only a "horizontal promotion," which took him out of meetings of the board, and then an actual demotion. When things progressed to the point at which he could only enter the office building on Saturday afternoons and Sundays when no one was there, he was finally brought to the first of a series of hospitalizations at a psychiatric sanatorium. By then, his career was destroyed and his marriage nearly so. He and his wife, incidentally, would often get into alcoholic stupors à *deux*. On one such occasion, he jovially said to her, "We're just a pair of old drunks."

The case of two of the alcoholic patients had special twists. One of them, the Suspended Medical Student, was asked to withdraw from school because of episodes of unethical behavior in which he had performed capricious pelvic examinations on surgical patients who were strangers to him, without gloves, in the middle of the night. It turned out that these had occurred during fugue states triggered by alcohol; he was a heavy drinker. The other, the Medical Scientist, was someone whose struggle against his drinking (and drug taking) was as intense as his addictions themselves. He was extremely ashamed of his affliction. As noted earlier, he would embark periodically on self-withdrawal from alcohol and narcotics by taking himself to a hotel room in a nearby city, during which he would (painfully) withdraw completely. He did this several times, but his drinking and drug taking always gradually recurred. When drunk, he could be savagely destructive of furniture in his home and violently abusive to his wife. He said, "A man could kill a woman when drunk."

Drug Addiction

Related to alcoholism was addiction to a variety of drugs among 14 of our 42 patients (or one-third of the sample). The addictions were mostly to barbiturates[1] (in all but 2 cases); other drugs involved included amphetamine in 6 cases, psychoactive "tranquilizers" in 4 cases, peyote in 1 case (the Bohemian Prep School Boy), bromides in 1 case (the Addicted Doctor), and opiates (Demerol and codeine) in the cases of 2 physicians to whom these were readily available (the Addicted Doctor and the Medical Scientist). Of these 14, 8 were men and 6 were women. In 8 of the 14 the addiction was severe (6 men and 2 women), and in 6 it was moderately troublesome (2 men and 4 women). Like alcoholism, drug addiction, especially the more intense type of addiction, was preponderantly a symptom of the men. And of these 14, 10 were also addicted to alcohol. Only 4 (the Intellectual Fencer, the Bohemian Prep School Boy, the Bitter Spinster, and the Phobic Woman) were drug-addicted but *not* alcohol-addicted, and only 1 of these 4 (the Intellectual Fencer) suffered a severe drug addiction as the central presenting symptom.

With some of these addicted patients, the drug abuse had been carried to the point of major incapacitation and physiological damage. The Housebound Phobic Woman was brought to psychiatric care by her father after 14 years of a lonely, withdrawn, and severely barbiturate-addicted life. When she was brought she was in an acute barbiturate-intoxicated state, with signs of a chronic organic brain syndrome—neurological disturbances such as tremors and ataxia, failing memory, and confused thinking. On initial interview, she was disoriented and her affect was labile. She failed at one point to see her purse beside the examiner's chair; she got down on her hands and knees and looked under all the chairs for it, and then laughed inappropriately to cover up her aberrant behavior. Repeat psychological testing more than 9 years later at the time of Termination Study, and in the context of a life successfully stabilized without alcohol or drugs, nevertheless still showed subtle but definite perceptual and thought deficits. This had been reflected all during treatment in the patient's real inability, not just unwillingness, to engage in inner psychological exploration.

Only a little less dramatic was the case of the Intellectual Fencer, referred for treatment because of a 3-year intensifying barbiturate addition, which had culminated in an episode when she was found wandering about the hall of her apartment building, clad only in her undergarments, confused, ataxic, with slurred speech. With her there were no long-range sequelae. The Intellectual Fencer, like several other of the addicted women, was involved with only one drug, barbiturate. This was true of none of the men, who were all on some combination of barbiturate, amphetamine, and alcohol (and occasionally something else)—generally all of these substances, and severely so.

Among the men there were not only more instances of such severe addiction, but also a greater range of expression. The Addicted Doctor, who came to treat-

---

1. These were the illness pictures of the 1950s, it must be remembered, before the use of LSD and other hallucinogens, marijuana, heroin, and cocaine became widespread in upper- and middle-class circles.

ment after his medical license was revoked, had been involved with barbiturates and also with codeine and Demerol (when these were prescribed for sedation and pain control after surgery for a dislocated shoulder suffered during a grand mal seizure); had had an episode of bromide psychosis; had also taken Benzedrine and alcohol to excess; and had been in a period of treatment at the Federal Narcotics Treatment Center at Lexington, Kentucky. He was the most wide-spectrum drug user in the sample. The more usual pattern among the severely addicted and severely alcoholic men (the Alcoholic Doctor, the Car Salesman, and the Sexual Masochist), as noted, was the combination of barbiturate, amphetamine, and alcohol. The Sexual Masochist, when dried out from alcohol (in a hospital), liberally substituted paraldehyde, barbiturate, coffee (up to 20 cups daily), and cigarettes (three packs daily). During his psychotherapy at The Menninger Foundation, he constantly struggled over drugs; as he gave up alcohol, he went onto a tranquilizer (mostly meprobamate), which he mostly got through covert visits to other physicians and druggists (usually concealed from his therapist), until he got up to toxic and debilitating levels of 14,000 mg daily. He resisted going off the meprobamate because "all high-strung business executives" were on tranquilizers. The Alcoholic Doctor, with 10 years of uncontrolled drinking, began to counteract the alcohol with increasing amounts of Benzedrine, up to 700 mg daily. (Like the Alcoholic Heir, he shared his drinking with an equally alcoholic wife; they often brawled and drank themselves into shared stupors so that the patient's parents had to intervene, rescuing the couple from local taverns.)

Sexual Disturbances

Sexual disturbances of various kinds were even more prevalent than alcohol and drug-taking problems. Of the 21 men, 15 complained of some degree of potency disturbance (in some, of course, this was concomitant with their severe alcohol- and drug-addicted states); likewise, 15 of the 21 women complained of some degree of orgastic difficulty. This came to a total of 30 of the 42, or just over two-thirds of the sample.

Again, there were various patternings. For example, among the men, the Car Salesman, whose embittered relationship with his wife was marked periodically by impotence, would go off on drinking sprees with chartered planes and expensive prostitutes, with whom he could be potent. The Alcoholic Doctor also began to become impotent with his wife, who was, like him, a physician; when the testosterone injections that she prescribed for him failed to help, they discussed whether his potency troubles might be due to latent homosexuality, and together "decided he should see." His wife brought him books to read on the subject, and he embarked on a series of homosexual adventures, bringing his partners to live with them in their home (at her suggestion) so that they could be together more. His wife told him that he should give up medicine for interior decorating. The Masochistic Editor had had no heterosexual relations for 8 years; he was fearful of trying, feeling he would be impotent. Instead, he engaged in a predatory homosexuality, preferring to debauch normal, married, heterosexual males. After his mother died, however, his homosexual potency likewise became impaired. And with the Economist, it did not come out until the fifth year of his analysis that his avoidant sexual behaviors had been concealing a severe symptom of sexual impotence. This had been the chief problem in his recurrent past failures with women; he had ragefully projected his failures onto them, bullying them finally into fleeing him.

With two of the men, the potency disturbance was more nearly total and was quite central to their illness picture. The English Professor, at the time he entered analysis (at age 36), entered onto a courtship with a young woman. After 3 years of being with her (often five evenings a week), sexual relations were attempted for the first time and failed miserably. The pattern that finally evolved was of considerable foreplay with both of them nude, culminating in successive masturbation with his orgasm first, at which point he would often cry. (They subsequently were able to marry and have a child—in the follow-up period.) And the Homesick Psychology Student was finally able through treatment to get married, but the marriage was not consummated over a 2-year span because of the patient's defective erections with premature ejaculations. Though they both were bitterly disappointed by this failure in marriage, the wife was "taking it well." She did not overtly complain; each time they would "give it a try" and not succeed, she would dismiss it with some remark like "Worse things happen to some couples."

There were comparable orgastic disturbances in the 15 women, but for the most part they were less dramatic. A commonplace perception among the women was captured in the statement of the Adoptive Mother, who through her analysis became increasingly aware of her failures of sexual satisfaction. She spoke of her marriage as "the name without the game." At the Follow-Up point, within the context of her overall satisfaction with her treatment results, she still described her sexual life as limited and relatively infrequent. She wondered if this reflected her advancing age. (She was then 35.) The Involutional Woman, who was also quite satisfied with her treatment result, talked of the small change in her sexual life. She was still resentful, but had gradually better accommodated to her husband's impositions on her stemming from his sexual needs, though doing so was quite uncomfortable because of her arthritis. The situation with the Invalided Hypochondriac was more extreme. On her wedding night the husband had had to sleep on the living room couch, and in the first week of the marriage the patient had created an embarrassing scene in front of the landlord, demanding an immediate switch from a double bed to twin beds in their furnished apartment. Only when intoxicated would she permit a sexual relationship; the husband said that he could date exactly when each of her two pregnancies had started. And Peter Pan said at Follow-Up that through the years of her marriage she had rarely gotten "really excited" and had never had an orgasm—though in analysis, in regressive and excited states, she had twice wet the analytic couch.

Eighteen of the patients had significant, and in some instances pervasive and overwhelming, sexual dysfunctions, going beyond just potency and orgastic disturbances. With 10, 7 men and 3 women altogether (this may be a conservative count), there was a major problem of casual and promiscuous sexual relationships. In some cases, this had a particularly vicious cast. The Car Salesman, for example, in the context of his career of casual contacts, had seduced a close friend's fiancée, ostensibly at the friend's request "to test her out." When the friend had broken up with the girl, she had committed suicide. The patient expressed not the slightest pang of concern or remorse about this. He was equally callous about another young woman whom he had gotten pregnant soon after that: "She almost died—at least she was quite ill from having an abortion." (This was the same individual who was later impotent with his wife but went on extravagant alcoholic sprees in which he chartered airplanes and took expensive prostitutes along with whom he was potent.) The Sociopath was another sexual predator. At first he was fearful of approaching women because of his sense of inferiority, but with his successes as a lawyer, he became emboldened and set out after the most beautiful models and women in café society, particularly if they were "400 percenters." With them, he launched campaigns of sexual seduction and pursued these tenaciously until he succeeded. At that point, he would callously discard the women.

With seven of the patients (five men and two women), mention was made of a deeply troubling struggle with compulsive masturbation, and this is probably a sharp undercount. With the Homesick Psychology Student, the individual who was not able to consummate his subsequent marriage, his problem with masturbation emerged as almost his central symptom disturbance. He felt intense masturbatory pressures, most urgently before and after dates. In therapy, this pressure often similarly bracketed the psychotherapy hour. He often had to urinate before and after, and at times, driving to the hour, he would stop his car to urinate at the side of the road, or on occasion to masturbate. In therapy he began to feel this behavior as an expression of his hidden aggression against girls, "pissing on them." When he masturbated, he alternated between two fantasies: one of being an aggressive male raping a young, naive virgin but ejaculating as he undressed her and exposed the upper part of her body; the other of being made love to by a fascinating, tenderly loving motherly woman and ejaculating as she undressed him.

Eight of the patients (four men and four women) were homosexual. However, this was concealed by three of the four women at the initial evaluation and only became clear during the course of the treatment; with two of them, the Rebellious Coed and the Actress, it in fact became a central issue of the treatment. With the men, the homosexuality was much more blatant and more destructively expressed through their lives. The Alcoholic Doctor was the individual precipitated into his manifest homosexuality by his wife's suggestion; through his years of analytic treatment while living and fighting with his wife, he had recurrent homosexual escapades—anonymous encounters across adjacent booths in men's rooms in public buildings (always running the risk of public disclosure and disgrace). The Masochistic Editor, as has been said, was the most predatory. He would aggressively seek out "normal married men" who had never before been homosexually involved in order to despoil them. He felt guilty enough over these behaviors so that when he acquired a gonococcal infection from a homosexual prostitute he put off treatment and suffered through the acute pain, with the concomitant feeling of now "being destroyed."

Some of the patients had even wider perverse sexual disorders. Two of them displayed a defiant polymorphous perverse sexuality (the Addicted Doctor and the Exhibitionistic Dancer). With the Exhibitionistic Dancer, this began with constant teenage sexual play, starting when she was 11 ("everything short of intercourse") with her older brother, and going on to homosexual liaisons with older women flaunted before her parents, nude modeling for a photographer, and mutual masturbation and simulated intercourse with older (and married) men. The interaction with her parents concerning her sexuality was captured in an interchange during her initial evaluation (when she was 21). The patient was sitting with her mother in the motel lobby and at one point tugged her dress up over her hip; when the mother remonstrated with her, she replied "But, Mother, you know that I am a whore." Not too surprisingly, when this patient suddenly married (during her psychotherapy), she was a frightened virgin. Another patient, the Housebound Phobic Woman, pursued a perverse voyeurism through her teenage years. She would attend movies, often daily, with a girlfriend—not to see the pictures, but to sit next to men who might be masturbating. The girls seemed fairly successful in these quests, often getting involved with men who "forced" them to assist in the act. The opposite, exhibitionism, was a symptom of the Adolescent Grandson (age 17). He was brought to treatment when he was caught in one of a series of episodes in which he either scampered naked or rode a horse naked over his grandfather's estate. He said he had been doing this "to give me a sense of freedom." He denied the police charges of public masturbation and deliberate exhibitionism.

The most bizarre and probably most indurate sexual pathology revolved around the sexual masochistic perversion of several of the patients. This could of course be limited to fantasy, as with the Prince, whose masturbation fantasies were of being held and restrained and "women taking advantage of me," either fondling or raping him. Such fantasies, though not often elicited during initial evaluations, might of course not be that uncommon. With the Phobic Girl, the masochistic propensities were expressed in behavior. In intercourse she "did not want to go all the way," so she would ask her partner to withdraw and would then watch him while he masturbated. When she could persuade him to beat her, she would in return receive her pleasure. The Obese Woman carried this tendency further, to a sexual game with her husband in which the loser would be tied to the bed with rope during intercourse; they both enjoyed being the one tied up. And with the Sexual Masochist, the sexual behaviors were (along with the heavy alcoholism) the main, and very humiliating, expression of the illness. As an adolescent, he had enjoyed having his mother intoxicated so that he could take her to the bathroom and watch her urinate on pieces of toilet paper that he had placed in the bowl. In his young adulthood, he masturbated compulsively, accompanied by fantasies of a woman urinating upon a goldfish, a cat, a turtle, a slave, or himself tied in the toilet. In his marriage, he asked his wife to urinate or defecate on his face, which on three or four occasions she consented to do. He once designed a barrel with a hole along the side into which he could stick his head and look up at his wife sitting on a toilet seat on the top of the barrel. He did not enjoy intercourse and participated in it only under pressure from his wife. And these fantasies and practices were not confined to his home; he shared them with prostitutes and strange women he approached in bars.

Alloplastic versus Autoplastic Patients

Given this whole array of behavioral disturbances presented to this point—the widespread alcoholism, drug addiction, brawling and assaultiveness, suicidal and/or homicidal impulse, and sexual disturbance of all variety and intensity—

it should be no surprise that by a very conservative estimate, 18 of the patients (11 men and 7 women), or somewhat less than half the sample, were designated as alloplastic or predominantly "acting out" in their symptom and behavior dispositions. Some of these had a number of these behaviors in sufficient combination and intensity to be living almost totally chaotic lives. The Sociopath was a prototype for this group; his temper outbursts, lying, cheating, sexual predations against "400 percenter" women, and vicious courtroom tactics against opposing "400 percenter" lawyers have already been recounted. To satisfy his insatiable need to be a "big shot," to make and spend money profligately, he got into a variety of irregular undercover deals with shady characters. As these deals got larger and riskier, he tried ever more frantically to keep ahead of himself, with now more detectable falsifying of records, forging of documents, and embezzling of monies he held in trust — to the extent that considerations not only of morality and legality, but also of personal safety were left far behind. When the house of cards finally came apart, the patient had either embezzled or owed upward of $100,000, mostly to importunate gangster elements. It was his appalled lawyer father who undertook to make restitution on all thefts and debts (giving his whole accumulated fortune to this), to bring his son for psychiatric treatment in Topeka, and to plead for some statement from The Menninger Foundation that the patient was psychotic and therefore not responsible and ought not to be brought to criminal trial. At the time, there was pressure for the patient's extradition in order to stand trial on legal charges in his home state.

There was not, however, just an automatic summation of such alcoholic, addicted, perverse, and/or antisocial behaviors in arriving at the overall judgment of a predominantly alloplastically directed life and illness style in the 18 patients put in this category. In most of the cases, of course, the summation was more or less automatic. But the Medical Scientist (the alcoholic and drug-addicted individual who struggled to break himself "cold turkey" alone in hotel rooms and who tried to hide his illness and not to inflict its consequences upon others) was put in the autoplastic category (in terms of the targeted direction, outer or inner, of the distressed behaviors and symptoms), rather than among these 18. On the other hand, the Phobic Woman, who so crippled her husband's life (and before that the lives of her parents) by holding him to her to the point that he could not attend his college classes alone or go out to the barber, was numbered in this alloplastic group. Her parents understood very clearly that they had bought and were supporting the husband in order to get out themselves from under the burden of the patient's illness.

SOMATIZING DISTURBANCES

Like behavioral disturbances, somatizing disturbances were almost ubiquitous. A total of 31 of the patients (13 men and 18 women) had one or more symptoms of significant somatic distress — whether so-called "functional," or classically "psychosomatic," or (in some very few instances) somatic pathology usually seen as relatively remote from psychological influence. And 15 of the patients (9 men and 6 women) were significantly hypochondriacal, in some instances in quite major ways. Because of overlap, this totaled "only" 37 of the whole sample (or close to 90%). To put it the opposite way, only 5 of the patients (the Divorced Nurse, the Heiress, the English Professor, the Adolescent Grandson, and the Fearful Loner) were devoid of significant bodily complaint.

A truly partial catalogue of somatic symptoms, many of them complaints of many more than one patient, is the following (in no special order, other than as they appear in a listing of the patients): low back syndrome, rheumatoid arthritis, prolonged enuresis, open tuberculosis, menstrual irregularities, sterility, asthma, severe acne, headache, diarrhea, hyperventilation syndrome, vasomotor instability, hypertension, neurodermatitis, pityriasis rosea, infectious mononucleosis, rheumatic fever with pericarditis, colitis, hiatus hernia, hypothyroidism, migraine, epilepsy, cardiac arrhythmia, ulcer, bladder frequency and urgency, organic brain damage, stuttering, ptosis, recurrent accidents, hay fever, hepatitis, influenza and bronchopneumonia, sinus infection, gall bladder disease, toxemia of pregnancy, and a true anorexia nervosa with amenorrhea. The point is clear: Most of these patients presented themselves as having histories of significant recurrent, chronic, or sequential somatic afflictions, of varying degrees of seriousness and varyingly disabling. This is in keeping with a fair number of studies by now, from various populations sampled, showing significant correlations between histories of somatic and of psychiatric illness.

Primary Somatic/Hypochondriac Complaints

With some of the patients, these somatic (or hypochondriacal) complaints were to the fore of the problems presented at psychiatric evaluation. The Invalided Hypochondriac, with a very hypochondriacal mother who spent most of her life going to doctors or being in bed for some complaint, had had a childhood filled with one disease or complaint after another, often with some unusual debilitating complication. There were many months of intestinal disorder, ascribed to eating watermelon, and pain on exertion, attributed to a thickening of heart valves consequent to measles (this had kept her out of play for a year). As an adult she suffered gastrointestinal disturbances; bladder disturbances; menstrual difficulties; assorted allergies; sinus and other ear, nose, and throat difficulties; headaches; low blood pressure; and "chronic brucellosis." She went from one doctor or clinic to another and was in bed most of the time, abandoning the care of her house and children to her husband and hired help. Letters from general and specialist physicians were unreserved in their comments on the difficulties in filling her needs as well as managing her illnesses. Her obstetrician wrote that he had "never seen a patient demand or get the attention and all the extra care and consideration that this patient seemed to need and obtain." The Bohemian Prep School Boy, at 17, already had a similar though less severe picture, with headaches, stomachaches, asthma, urticaria, bulimia and anorexia, fainting episodes, sleepwalking, and nightmares, all going back to his earliest years; he also had a history of such severe nailbiting that he often had infected fingers. The Movie Lady had a history of obesity, severe acne, headaches, rashes and pruritis, diarrhea, vasomotor instability (in her square dance group she was known as "the lady with the cold hands"), and hyperventilation. Her frustrated therapist wondered for a while whether she had multiple sclerosis. There were clearly many others like these three, but less intensely so.

Specific Roles for Somatic Symptoms

With a number of the patients, their somatic and hypochondriacal symptoms played specific roles, sometimes primary ones, in their total life and illness expression. For example, the Claustrophobic Man, as noted earlier, came to psychiatric treatment in the wake of a series of operations for cancer of the thyroid (with a still very uncertain ultimate prognosis). He professed no concern at all about that, since he was in such excellent medical hands; however, his life was progressively crippled by intense fears of (nonexistent) heart disease. His many phobias (of hotel lobbies, business meetings, parties, theatres, heights, etc.) related to the fear that he might have a heart attack while momentarily alone and unattended; he would die suddenly and the fact might be unknown to everyone. The Adoptive Mother was torn by a conflicted desire to prove herself "a good Catholic mother," guilty over the adoption failure, and concerned that her apparent sterility was psychologically determined. She hoped that her analysis would succeed to the point where she would successfully become pregnant. The Alcoholic Raconteur, as part of his felt inferiorities during adolescence, was concerned that he might have tuberculosis (there were several cases of it in his family); he had tuberculin tests performed, repetitively and secretly. He was concomitantly involved in weight lifting to develop his muscles and build up his health, and he was very concerned with the lateness of his pubescent changes and his fear that his genitals would remain much below average in size. Another patient, the Bohemian Musician, signaled the start of her very unhappy married life by developing vaginal bleeding, abdominal pain, and an intense fear of having contracted a venereal disease (from a toilet seat) while on her honeymoon. This led promptly to workups and gynecological surgery, at which her Fallopian tubes and one ovary were removed. And with the Tantrum Woman, a significant part of her intensely conflicted and hostilely dependent relationship with her mother focused on her severe constipation, both in childhood and in its reactivation in her adulthood (as part of the regressive, depressive illness responses to her husband's death in the car accident). Her mother—with whom she could barely sustain a civil conversation—would give her the enema every 2 or 3 days that kept her from being "poisoned" by her wastes.

Weight-Related Problems

One particular somatic disturbance, obesity, is singled out here because of its focal relevance in relation to a significant number of the patients' illnesses. Actually, this was an issue of some moment with 11 patients; as might be expected, they were predominantly female (8 women to only 3 men). With some of these, obesity was mostly a symptom of adolescent years by now overcome, as with the Movie Lady, whose adolescent weight of 165 pounds was down to 118 pounds at the point that she sought treatment as an adult for her intensifying phobic illness. Obesity was very central to the presenting illness picture with three of the women: the Housebound Phobic Woman, who came weighing 180 pounds (this was overshadowed to some extent by her general physical dilapidation and her acute and chronic barbiturate-intoxicated state); the Phobic Girl, who came weighing 203 pounds (she had been very self-conscious all her life about this obesity and tried to carry it off by playing the buffoon, which led to a picture of dependence and immaturity); and the Obese Woman, who came weighing 238 pounds (in her case, the obesity itself was what brought her to treatment). The Obese Woman's weight problem had started in her earliest years, when she had sought to make friends by gathering a crowd around her and passing out cake and cookies from her father's bakery. She had been gaining and losing and dieting all her life. Her appetite would vary, from times of relative indifference to periods of nagging hunger. At times she would differentiate "a different kind of hunger—a need to put something into my mouth."[2]

Three of our patients—two men and a woman—had the opposite problem: physiologically and psychologically painful thinness. With the two men, this was a particularly significant psychological problem. The Homesick Psychology Student came to psychotherapy suffering intense feelings of inadequacy and inferiority in the educational–vocational sphere, and even more in the social–sexual sphere. He was 23 years old but still caught up in an intensely dependent adolescent relationship with his parents. What came first to his mind at his Termination Study interview as a marker of his therapeutic gains was that his long-standing very poor appetite had been overcome and he had gained some 20 pounds. This was very important to him, because he could now buy his trousers in the men's department and no longer had to go to boys' wear. With the Devoted Son, similar concerns were accentuated many times. From early childhood, his life and behavior had been seriously influenced by his self-concept of physical inadequacy. "I thought something was wrong with me, and I've always felt that I was defective physically. I have always been very thin, and my interests were never those of other boys." At school, he was jeered at as a sissy able to play only with girls. He was always afraid to appear in a bathing suit and avoided any sexual overtures to a woman— not out of fear of impotence, he said, but out of fear of undressing in front of her and exposing his "inadequate physique." In actual appearance he was thin and rather tall, looking somewhat cadaverous and vaguely aesthetic. He dressed in conservative, drape-styled, loose-fitting flannel suits selected to hide his asthenic habitus, which he at the same time accentuated by wearing shirts several neck sizes too large for him. The examining psychologist said of him that he could somehow leave a session without having made a dent in the chair.

The one woman in this thin group, Peter Pan, demonstrated the combined physiological and psychological disturbance characteristic of true anorexia nervosa with alternating anorexia and bulimia (and with attendant amenorrhea). Her problem with eating started at about puberty. She recalled a doctor telling her then that she would have to eat more if she wished to have a nice rounded female figure. Eating soon became a major focal arena of conflict with her parents (there were also others). She would sit at the table and refuse to eat, despite their entreaties. Afterwards she would secretly raid the refrigerator. By the time she went to college, her eating difficulties had invaded her whole life. She refused dates

2. This is the patient whose detailed study through the repetitively administered psychological projective test battery, including the test-engendered predictions and the inferential process by which they were arrived at, occupies 53 pages (almost 20%) of the book by S. A. Appelbaum (1977) on the psychological test study results.

involving dinner, making all kinds of excuses to get out of eating in public. Her correspondence home was filled with her eating problems. She often skipped regular meals in the dining room and then went on binges, eating great quantities of sweets in her room. Then she would starve herself for days to lose the weight she was sure she had gained. It was important to hold her weight down to 100 pounds and her dress size to 7 (the size she had reached at age 13). When her weight went up to 103, which she estimated from the way her clothes fit her or the size of her wrist, she went on a vigorous diet. She did not feel complimented if told she had a nice figure, preferring to be regarded as slim and petite. What led to her dismissal from college and coming to psychiatric treatment was being caught stealing candy from the college cafeteria. At The Menninger Foundation, she confessed that this was not an isolated episode—it was just the one time she had been caught—and that the preceding 4 years had been preoccupied with her compulsive stealing (mostly of sweets) and her struggle against it. This had the structure of a severe compulsion neurosis, daily repeated. She would be in her room studying and would begin to have intrusive thoughts about going out and stealing. She would try to concentrate harder on preparing her lessons. If this failed to distract her, she would undress, and would even go so far as to lock up her clothes and try to forget where she placed the key. Finally these various barriers would nonetheless give way before the pressure of the impulse, and she would hurriedly rush to dress, go out, and steal. Whatever she stole, she consumed. The next day the process might start all over again.

CHARACTER DISTURBANCES

Except for the group of strongly phobic patients, like the five whose phobias were incorporated into their patient designations, our subjects did not have classical symptom neuroses; even among the five "titular phobics," the phobic states were in some cases only part of a wider personality dysfunction. The Housebound Phobic Woman, for instance, also suffered from long-standing barbiturate addiction, which deteriorated finally into the acute and chronic intoxication that precipitated her hospitalization. As an overall group, our patients could rather be looked at in terms of severe character disturbance (and impulse neurosis), and it is the varieties of character pathology that are described here.

Hysterical Character

Among the very large group of patients beset with depression and/or anxiety, and especially among that group where these two central symptoms occurred together and were joined by phobic formations of varying intensity, were a fair number who represented basically hysterical character organizations. These are not described here, since to do so would be repetitive and would overlap with the descriptions for the most part already given under the "Central Presenting Complaints" heading. But certainly in this category of strongly hysterical character configurations were the Adoptive Mother, the Tantrum Woman, the Snake Phobia Woman, the Divorced Nurse, the Phobic Woman, and the Obese Woman. All of these were women. There was, of course, a wider group with prominent hysterical features but with them these features were less dominant in the character picture; this group included men as well as women. The Claustrophobic Man and the Phobic Girl are good examples from the wider group.

Obsessive–Compulsive Character

It is clear by now that relatively few among the whole sample could be thought of in terms of typically obsessive–compulsive character structuring, and this was no doubt a significant dimension of difference of our patients as a group from the "usual" patient population in outpatient psychoanalytic therapy. However, 12 patients (6 men and 6 women) had at least some obsessive–compulsive features. Of the men, 4 were actually predominantly typically compulsive characters. The Devoted Son (the individual troubled all his life by his painfully "inadequate" physique)—a civil engineer with high modern and progressive professional ideals, whose personal life consisted of devoted attention to his parents (with whom he spent every weekend)—had a rigidly routinized life and compulsive character organization, with massive inhibition and constriction of affect and impulse expression, both sexual and aggressive. Almost comparable was the Fearful Loner, who lived a life of apprehensive and watchful isolation from people; he was an accountant in a governmental civil service position, preoccupied all day with numbers and not people. He did the job well and secured quiet gratifications in its compulsive and isolated aspects. The English Professor, struggling counterphobically against his many phobic apprehensions, had a "looser," more obsessional character style; however, he also exhibited compulsively compliant traits, constant intellectualizing, and a compulsion since childhood of habitually counting objects in threes. And the fourth in this group was the Medical Scientist, whose desperate fights to break his alcohol and drug addictions in the "do-it-yourself" cold turkey regimen were aided by a compulsive character style (including tremendous isolation of affect) and compulsive life style—as a hard-working, conscientious, and competent physician, and an equally hard-working outdoorsman and athlete.

The other two men put in this group were much more "pseudocompulsive." With the Economist, the seemingly compensated and successfully functioning compulsive character style with which he presented himself at the time of initial evaluation gave way through the course of his analytic treatment to an obsessional indecision that at times was paralyzing; a severely borderline and paranoid character organization marked by paranoid fears (he was the one who always carried a gun and a club in his car for protection); and compelling bizarre ideation, like his classification of people and his assessment of their "sincerity" by the shape of their fingers and of their gums. And the Sexual Masochist, with bizarre masochistic perversion and heavy alcoholism all embedded in a schizophrenic character structure, also suffered from both childhood and adulthood compulsions: touching things in a certain order, opening and closing doors several times, knocking on doors or rapping his knuckles on the table in a particular ritual way, and so forth.

The six women as a group were even less compulsively organized. Only one, the 50-year-old Involutional Woman, was a true compulsion neurotic. She was a rigidly compulsive, conscientious, duty-ridden woman with lifelong perfection-istic strivings, anhedonic life style, and myriad somatic complaints and illnesses. She came to treatment when, under severe psychological pressure, she decompensated into an acute depression. The 19-year-old Actress made many unsuccessful efforts at a compulsive handling of her life and coping with her conflicts: taking three baths daily, keeping her room spotlessly clean, emptying ashtrays after each cigarette butt was placed in one, and so on. She came to treatment in a decompensated state marked by alcohol excess, homosexual activity, and grossly disturbed interpersonal relationships. Even less successful was Peter Pan, the young woman with anorexia nervosa whose obsessional preoccupations (verging on the bizarre) with food, weight, and study have already been described. The same was evident in her handling of social–sexual relationships, and particularly in her handling of money. For example, she rigidly compartmentalized her available money with certain portions only to be spent for certain things, so that while she might have plenty with which to buy, she might, by her manner of accounting, be broke—and therefore "driven" to steal. Her unsuccessful efforts to cope with her wild eating gyrations and her push to steal have already been amply detailed. And the even sicker Invalided Hypochondriac, an "infantile" character—functioning in an almost totally collapsed and chaotic way, and in no sense a compulsive or an obsessive character—was constantly beset by hostile, intrusive, obsessional thoughts of harm and even death to her husband and children. She had constant fears for her husband's life: that he would drive too fast and be killed in a car accident, or drown on a fishing trip, or be shot to death on a hunting trip. Two other women had somewhat obsessive–compulsive trends as part of a more complex character organization—the Silent Woman, along with hysterical features, and the Heiress, along with prominent masochistic features.

Sadomasochistic Character

A total of 23 of the patients—12 men and 11 women (a little more than half the sample)—had sadomasochistic components to their character organization, again of varying intensity. The 3 (the Sexual Masochist, the Obese Woman, and the Phobic Girl) who also had manifest masochistic *sexual* perversions were of course in this group. The sadistic component was to the fore in 5 of the 23, 4 of those being men. This subgroup of course included the Sociopath, whose "hate complex" and vicious depredations against "400 percenter" attractive women and court-room opponents have already been described. He was the one labeled on the basis of his psychological test imagery as a potential rapist or murderer. The sadistic subgroup also included the Manic–Depressive Physician, whose explosive murderous assault on his wife's lover with the bed slat was just part of a wider pattern of equally violent behaviors in his marriage. Whenever his wife failed to respond to him in the ways he desired, he could have rage outbursts, even assaulting her physically with his closed fist. Once she had a sore throat, and when she said she couldn't gargle as he had instructed, he proceeded to pour the lavage fluid forcibly down her throat, pushing her until she fell over backward into the bathtub. Another time, when she overcharged her account at a department store, he slapped her so severely that he left her with a severe cut under one eye and a bruised face.

He said he was frightened lest he kill her in one of his uncontrolled rages. The wife stated that he was always jealous of her and her musical career, and on occasion teased her in a menacing way with smashing her nose or cutting her vocal cords.

With the other 18 of this 23 (8 men and 10 women), the masochistic components were to the fore. With the Masochistic Editor, they dominated his character functioning. His family had found it difficult to punish him as a small boy. He seemed not to mind being beaten or sent to bed, where he could always take refuge in his books; what seemed most effective was to take his book away from him and shame him in front of other children. He was never an assertive child, either within the family or with his peer group. In keeping with this were two adulthood incidents: He left the painful gonococcal infection he caught while in the Army untreated ("I was passing blood and being destroyed") as proper punishment for his involvement with a homosexual prostitute; and he allowed his father to pull the financial support from his previous period of psychoanalytic treatment (opining "*I* was a failure"). In The Menninger Hospital, he was put on a full hospital activities schedule with much physical labor (the project group); he enjoyed this, carrying his work through compliantly and even masochistically (not seeking attention to painful blisters that arose, etc.). His sadistic side came out in his despoiling homosexual predations on normal, heterosexual, preferably married, males, whom he could then scornfully depreciate.

A more sublimated but equally extensive masochism marked the Homesick Psychology Student. He was shy, inhibited, and unassertive. He always saw himself in a "second-class position," which he accepted as his lot in life. This was reflected in his academic unhappiness in his graduate psychology department: He felt it not "progressive" enough, and would have preferred to transfer into clinical training in psychology, but he doubted that he would be accepted at a better place or in a clinical psychology training program (despite his excellent academic record). He was the individual who ultimately married but did not consummate his marriage; his wife accepted him as an infantile, presexual man to whom she could give maternal care and interest. The patient saw himself as a person of great potential mistreated by fate, always pushed into finding conflict "solutions" at his own expense. This attitude was similar to that of the Obedient Husband, whose wife was ill physically (with a chronically debilitating condition) and emotionally (depressed, apathetic, interested only in her numerous somatic complaints). The wife's therapist advised the patient to "go along with her wishes" when she gave up all responsibility for either his care or the care of the home. Quite uncomplainingly he soon became nurse, mother, and housemaid, as well as husband—roles he fulfilled over years. He would nurse his wife, clean the house, cook the meals, and do whatever she desired, as well as try to run his business. What seemed to bring him to psychiatric treatment was his fear that as his wife seemed to improve in her therapy, she might become less dependent on him, need him less, and leave him.

Of course, with most of the patients in this group, the masochistic trends were far less striking. In fact, for the most part they were typically quite muted, as with the Divorced Nurse, where, within the turbulence of her life and the struggles over her divorce and the custody fight for her children, there was the underlying masochistic theme of being "forced against her convictions": She experienced many of her behaviors as forced on her by circumstance, and against her wishes, convictions, and principles.

Narcissistic Character

Not surprisingly with this patient group, narcissistic character features were felt to mark 19 (almost half the sample)—8 men and 11 women. What was somewhat surprising was how much the narcissistic character trend seemed consistently underestimated at the time of initial evaluation, only emerging clearly in most of these patients during the course of the therapeutic effort. Of course, in some cases this was not at all true; The narcissistic issues were to the forefront from the start. The Prince was of course the paradigm instance. He came to psychoanalysis because of personal characteristics that he wanted to change. He described these as paradoxical and contradictory attitudes about himself: He felt insecure but could for the most part hide it successfully; it was important to him to be fully and immediately accepted; he felt alternately benevolent and haughty toward his colleagues; he was jealous of his superiors and would like to replace them; he was generally successful, at times feeling that he was "like a prince" and that the attention he got was due and proper ("this is neurotic, but I like it just the same"). He always liked the experience of dating two women at a time—"I get a secret pleasure out of being in demand." He liked being "treated like a prince. . . . And when I don't get it, I get depressed, not deeply, but with a feeling that things are out of joint." He expressed himself as reluctant to accept anyone as a wife, no matter how attractive, because someone better might come along the next day and he would be "tied down for life." Naturally, these narcissistic issues were the central concerns of his entire psychoanalytic treatment process.

With other patients, narcissistic issues were presented differently. The Exhibitionistic Dancer, had been specially indulged all her life and had been shown off for the narcissistic aggrandizement of her parents. The father was an achiever (a business executive) for whom ambition, accomplishment, academic standing, and intellectual performance were central values. He set these high expectations for all the children, declared he wanted to be proud of them, and acknowledged that he was not patient enough with them—in fact, that he was usually critical and nagging. The mother, having grown up feeling herself awkward and an ugly duckling, strongly pushed the patient's wishes to express her individuality through art forms (acting, dancing); the mother then gloried in the recognitions the patient received for her beauty and her talented performances. The mother also participated voyeuristically as a seductress in the patient's adolescent sex life. When the patient remonstrated at her mother's insistent probing into the details of her behavior with boys, the mother said, "You shouldn't object so to my questioning. Any mother has a right to live a little bit vicariously through her daughter." (This was the patient who, at the point of psychiatric evaluation, turned the tables by replying to her mother's remonstrances about how her dress was pulled up too high with "But, Mother, you know that I am a whore.")

The Actress was similar. She led a dramatic "as-if" life (she was the one whose college room was made into a "funeral vault"); she was never sure of what role she wanted to play out—a mature adult or a confused child. She was self-preoccupied and showed little concern for others. She had many superficial attachments but no real friends. Her most intense relationships had been with older women. She was very contemptuous of men. In the hospital, she was superficially cooperative but always manipulating. She was full of instant dislike for her first therapist at The Menninger Foundation, whom she called a "typical Babbitt"; she became convinced that he couldn't help her and felt unable (more, unwilling) to talk with him. After 20 fruitless hours, he gave up. The Bohemian Prep School Boy, with the heiress mother and the famous artist father, was incredibly indulged (and inconsistently handled) from the start. As a 2-year-old, he was taken to cocktail parties to be fussed over by people. He grew into adolescence intellectually gifted but depressed and bored; he said that "everything is like a stage setting." Intellectualizing was his chief interpersonal stock in trade—his way of winning acceptance and respect, and also his way of intimidating and alienating others. His relationships were consequently shallow, artificial, and highly intellectualized. He was deeply aware that heretofore his only sense of security in life had come through attracting attention to himself by being unique and special.

The Bohemian Musician constructed her life style (with her husband's acquiescence) around maintaining her narcissistic entitlements. He was a "philistine" businessman who moved with her at her desire to a major metropolis where she could pursue her desired cultural and intellectual activities. There they led almost separate lives. The patient taught music and went out often to the theatre, concerts, and restaurants. She abandoned any pretense at running the house. The husband attended to his business and also the housework (including often the cooking, and even the mending, washing, and ironing). He felt sadly that he had lost his wife to the attractions of the big city. Soon the patient became involved with another man—a relationship originally promoted by the husband, who brought this friend to the home as an intellectual companion who could share his wife's interests. This rapidly became a love affair in which the heretofore neurasthenic patient became again interested, vivacious, enthusiastic. The husband kept himself uninformed about this development. When after 5 years of this life the husband decided to return to his home town and family business (which the patient contemptuously referred to as her "home in a cornfield"), he acquiesced in the patient's decision to stay in the big city.

Infantile Character

The concept of the "infantile" character is an extension, beyond that of the DSM-II nomenclature, of the orally regressed and passively dependent character—an accentuation of a childishly indulged or helplessly dependent "infantile" stance toward life. And of course such fixations can overlap in major ways with alcohol and drug addictions and with regressive and borderline states. In the sense of strongly passive and dependent attitudes toward life, 18 of our patients (8 men and 10 women) could qualify as "infantile." In the more extreme way here intended, 4 in this group stand out. The Addicted Doctor's hospitalization came in the wake of a profound heretofore totally unsuccessfully treated drug addiction, an almost collapsed marriage, and a revoked medical license. Nonetheless, in the hospital he seemed cheerful and contented. He saw himself as a weak little boy who had somehow been forced to face adult responsibilities long before he was able to, and was now grateful for the haven from those responsibilities that the hospital afforded him. Here he could be his "real self"—a playful, self-centered youngster. On a ward picnic he amused himself by dropping lumps of ice into the blouses of the female aides, which provoked them to chase him about the park. He loved to acquire possessions, which he assumed should come to him without effort; thus he had been in debt for years, buying on credit many expensive things he could not afford. In turn, he used these things to purchase the attention and interest of others. He surrounded himself with the symbols of oral indulgences: Deprived of drugs, he filled his room with a large collection of pipes and tobaccos. His interest in his profession seemed slight, though he dutifully stated that he "loved" medicine. During this hospitalization, faced with his accumulated indebtedness, his wife went to work as a special duty nurse to support their two children.

Even more extreme was the case of the Invalided Hypochondriac. (She was the woman of whom her physicians had stated that they had never seen anyone receive or need so much indulgence and attention.) When her first child was born, the responsibility frightened her. The baby was colicky and allergic, and the patient "was sure he was going to die." When the child was upset at night, the patient could only lie in bed and cry, and her husband had to care for the infant. The patient would awaken each day exhausted and with a severe headache. She would insist that the husband tend to the child and keep it quiet. She couldn't eat breakfast at the table with her husband; he made too much noise, and this intensified her headache. A pattern developed in which the husband would get up in the morning, feed and clothe the child, and prepare breakfast for himself and his wife, which he took to her in bed. He could then go off to work when he turned the child over to the maid. The patient professed not to understand how her husband and others could "do things for him when I can't." With her second pregnancy, the patient was even sicker, remaining in bed throughout. She had constant symptoms; she often had to be fed intravenously; she couldn't urinate for herself. She was fearful at every point of losing the baby. As the patient's incapacities escalated over the years, the husband would often be called home from his business as many as five and six times in a working day. The patient was in bed practically all day, yet throughout this period she still had an "amazing ability" (to her husband) to pull herself together to go out to an evening cocktail party or bridge tournament.

Along these same lines were two other cases already described in some detail. The Phobic Woman was the individual who totally circumscribed her husband's life by her need for his attendance and care. This same total caretaking and attendance (because of her phobic constrictions) had been previously played out by her parents, who had been content to turn these nurturing chores over to the husband in return for supporting the couple. However, the parents also maintained a strong undercurrent of blaming the husband for their daughter's illness, because of his "not loving her enough." He should have made up to her for all the deprivations she had suffered in infancy from her parents, when they had raised her according to the book (she had been a "compliant baby" reared by the then "modern books," which advocated adherence to rigid schedules) rather than their hearts. And the Housebound Phobic Woman was the organically damaged barbiturate addict whose life had become constricted to a drugged, television-watching, housebound existence, with a 20-year-older lover who fled a psychotic wife at home to take refuge in the patient's apartment three to five nights per week. As noted, he became the patient's one continuing contact with the outside world, bringing the mail, the groceries, and the laundry. They would "save their pennies" together and when they had enough would make themselves a steak dinner.

Paranoid and Externalizing Character

From all that has been written to this point, it should be no surprise that 14 of the patients—10 men and 4 women, a full third of the sample—could be described as having a strongly paranoid character trend, and that another 5, though not strictly paranoid, were strong externalizers in their attributions of psychological responsibility. Typical of these 5 was the Car Salesman, who lived his life with the psychology of the "innocent victim" to whom things just happened. With the 14 really paranoid cases, the paranoia was a character trend that was usually quite successfully concealed at the time of initial evaluation, when it was either not evident at all or only evident in a muted way. Characteristically, it would come to the fore during the course of a psychoanalytic treatment effort; a paranoid transference psychotic state would either emerge in the treatment or threaten to emerge. The patient might then take various frantic steps to ward it off, such as fleeing the treatment (the Alcoholic Raconteur was an example), or the therapist might take various steps, such as converting the effort at psychoanalysis to an explicitly more supportive–expressive psychotherapy (the Economist's case was a good example) or delicately titrating the intensity of the therapeutic contact to the patient's tolerance (the Fearful Loner's case was a good example). Actually, 10 of the 14 paranoid patients came to this pass in treatment—of either an erupted or a threatened paranoid transference psychosis reaction—and these cases are described in detail in the discussion of the treatment courses.

Two examples of this covert but strong paranoid potential were the following: The English Professor presented himself with widespread phobic symptoms set within a compliant, compulsive character structure. Yet his responses to psychological testing were full of a consciousness of being watched, being sought after to be punished for misdeeds unknown to him. With irrational persistence he saw eyes and masked, disguised men staring out at him from the Rorschach cards. And the Fearful Loner presented himself as a lonely, fearful individual leading an isolated, schizoid life. But he was always hyperalert and suspicious; even when relaxed, he was very sensitive and touchy. He was especially sensitive to and suspicious of anything that he construed as a "demand," and he would closely query the person making the "demand" to make certain that the latter was really benevolently enough interested to be entitled, as it were, to do so. (He was the individual who sprang at the psychiatric consultant when he felt that the psychiatrist was too impatient and intrusive with his "demand" that he talk about himself.) The Sociopath, by contrast with these two, was more overt in his paranoia. He saw the whole world of white Americans (the "400 percenters") as out to get him for his Mediterranean background and his Eastern Orthodox religion, and he devoted himself to a lifelong process of revenge—of outsmarting them and turning the tables destructively upon them.

With two of the patients in this group, the paranoid potential never really emerged during their treatments (one seemingly successful, the other clearly not), but came out in each instance in their posttreatment downhill courses. The Suspended Medical Student was the seemingly successfully treated individual who (inexplicably at the time) could not be persuaded to participate in the Termination Study (which he professed he did want to cooperate with) or the subsequent Follow-up Study. During the Follow-Up inquiry, it was the family physician who described the patient's frenetic, disorganized, and drug-addicted life while trying to maintain a medical practice. The physician indicated his view that the patient's difficulties stemmed from an overly strict conscience and overly high professional demands that the patient just couldn't live up to; these factors then brought out the patient's paranoid streak ("With everybody, with his practice, with his wife, it's always everyone else who is wrong and causes the trouble—it's his persecution complex") and his megalomanic streak (he was accounting for his difficulties by more and more fanciful tales of the 250 cases of Asian flu he was treating at one time, the four sets of tire chains he wore out in one season, etc.). And the Invalided Hypochondriac blamed The Menninger Foundation for her husband's "personality changes" that led to his divorcing her ("He loved me when he brought me up there because no one would spend that kind of money for someone unless they loved her"), as well as for her loss of her children in the custody fight (though it was her lawyer who, at her insistence, used the subpoena threat to get summaries of her clinical record to introduce as court evidence). She then stated that, if she were to agree to Follow-Up interviewing, her lawyer would need to be present, since she was not convinced of our honesty; we would have to, without her telling us how, express something from our "heart and soul" that would be proof of our honesty.

All of the foregoing, incidentally, is small enough evidence of a major paranoid potential in so many of our patients (a third), which played a strong determining role in so many of the treatments that did not come out well. Paradoxically, there was one patient thought to be "paranoidly" fearful, the Divorced Nurse, whose every fear was actualized. She was afraid that her physician husband, who remained behind with his practice and the children in their home community while she came to Topeka for psychoanalysis, would be unfaithful to her (with his office nurse) and would divorce her—which is what happened. She was then convinced that, despite her apparently better case in the custody fight, he would win the children away from her—which is also what happened, despite a deposition entered on her behalf by her analyst.

Borderline Character Organization

In keeping with the paranoidly regressive potential of so many of our patients, there were many (even more, as a matter of fact) with "weak," borderline, or otherwise brittle and precarious ego organizations—20, all told, who were vulnerable in this way (12 men and 8 women). Of the 14 from the paranoid cohort, 12 were also (and for very similar reasons) among these 20. And, as with the paranoid potential, the borderline quality and the vulnerability to decompensating pressures were mostly not evident at the initial evaluation time, but emerged clearly in the course of the treatment effort, where they often became the central treatment difficulties.

Some of those with borderline (or at times psychotic) functioning who were *not* on the overlap list with the actually or potentially paranoid should be separately mentioned. One was, of course, the Manic–Depressive Physician, who had a history of recurrent depressions starting at age 13. He had been a shy, uncomfortable, isolated child who would spend days wandering by himself in the woods while his mother was in town at "study groups" to learn the correct techniques of child rearing. At 13 he had been depressed, but had confessed his concerns to his father; he felt he had been helped to some extent by the father's advice (though he found he could not follow it)—to stop masturbating. Between the ages of 14 and 17 he had had a depressed period annually, associated with fears of people, self-reproaches, and feelings that people were talking about him and calling him names. When he was elected vice-president of his class he was surprised, thinking his schoolmates mistook his depression for serious meditation. And when he received an honor award in high school, he tore it up in front of his parents, declaring bitterly that he would rather be a regular fellow among his peers. In college he had a suicidal period, and at age 25 (he had married at 22) he had his first psychiatric hospitalization, for a month. This had come in consequence of an episode where he was listening to records in the library and felt strangely affected by the play that he was listening to, *The Cocktail Party*. He wondered if he had powers over the people in the library and stared at them to see whether he could make them leave. On the way home, his wife felt that he stared at her and muttered gibberish. He was hospitalized, and during this hospitalization he was openly disorganized and facetious, making vulgar rhymes and puns. He responded to ECT and was discharged with the diagnosis of "manic–depressive psychosis, manic phase." His Menninger Foundation hospitalization came 2 years later (there was an intervening hospital episode when he was depressed and suicidal and again responded dramatically to ECT), after the brutal, near-lethal assault on his wife's lover.

In contrast to this, the regressive potential of the Bohemian Musician was much more sporadic and seemingly "hysterical." As has already been stated, she would remain in bed with the blinds drawn, her hands over her face, wearing dark glasses; these periods would be punctuated by screaming and moaning, temper tantrums, and wildly expressed murderous fantasies. And then she might get up and tear off on a wild, panicky car flight through a crowded suburban area at 90 miles an hour. When she was stopped by the police on one such occasion, she collapsed, lost track of time and place, and was in a completely dissociated state. It was this that brought her to psychiatric hospitalization at The Menninger Foundation. She was demoralized and almost incoherent when she came, moaning that she did not want to die. The Bohemian Prep School Boy shared some of this same dramatic quality, but in a more ominous way. He was beset by constant fears—of smothering, of knives, of needles, of going crazy, of fantasies of having his eyes poked out; he suffered frequent nightmares. He began to feel that the left side of his body was asleep, that he was insignificant in a big world, and that people were always staring at him. His fears multiplied: of disintegrating, of the dark, of looking in the mirror lest he not see anything there. He gathered like-minded schoolmates together into a salon that met in a closet to debate existentialist philosophy, and he wrote a final examination in the form of an allegory about the behavior of bedbugs in a bathtub. Together with his obsessional preoccupation, phobic concerns, and somatic complaints, these bizarre fears and the various estrangement and depersonalization phenomena led us to think of him as an overideational preschizophrenic. The endeavor to bind his anxieties into philosophical systems, Oriental and existentialist, was obviously a vain effort against the decompensating pressures. A final patient in this subgroup was Peter Pan; her near-delusional fixations about food, eating, and weight gain, together with the desperate behaviors to which she was driven to control her food intake and her kleptomania, have already been indicated. Not surprisingly, the lifelong very well-compensated, compulsive Involutional Woman, though she came with a severe, acute involutional depression, was *not* among those characterized by a borderline or overall weakened ego structure.

Two individuals with even weaker ego organizations, who *were* on the overlap list with the paranoidly organized patients, may have been the "sickest" in this regard among the entire patient population. The Sexual Masochist, though never openly psychotic to the point of requiring hospitalization, was nonetheless the only patient clearly felt to be a schizophrenic character. His bizarre masochistic perversion has already been spelled out in detail. He came to the point where he could only become sexually aroused if his wife would enter his perverse fantasies with him. For example, if she responded to his question "Would you rather have intercourse with a bum or urinate on him?" that she would rather do the latter, he could get sexually excited. Along with the perversion were the patient's heavy alcoholism; severe panic states; episodes of cheating to secure his entitlements; near-total abandonment to archaic and bizarre impulse without restraint (or seeming shame); and character style that was totally passive, masochistic, parasitic, and, if thwarted in any way, paranoid. And yet, aside from the episodic hospitalizations for uncontrolled drinking, the patient seemed able to function somehow outside a hospital (buttressed, of course, by the family wealth) as quite a "man about town," one "well worth saving."

The other very paranoid and borderline (or more) individual was the Alcoholic Raconteur. His chief symptom was his alcoholism: At one time he was essentially holed up in his room drinking for 8 months, during which his day–night schedule became reversed so that he was in bed all day and out drinking at night. He often passed out when drunk and was brought home by cab drivers and deposited at dawn on the front porch. His character trends were paranoid, megalomanic, and parasitic. He kept afloat because of his enormously compliant environment: It was his father who, after being physically assaulted by the patient, was willing to purchase peace in the family by moving out of his own home into his club. The formulation with the Alcoholic Raconteur was of an overideational preschizophrenic state; there was not quite the same degree of chronically decompensated ego functioning as with the Sexual Masochist.

Aside from these who have been individually described, all the others in the borderline group functioned at a seemingly more integrated level; the serious ego weaknesses only became openly manifest in the context of treatment-induced (regressive) pressures.

DISTURBANCES IN THE MARRIAGE

Given the severity and chronicity of the personality disorders and the illness structures in this patient population, it should be no surprise that of the 27 patients in the sample (13 men and 14 women) who had been able to marry,[3] almost every single one either was in a very disturbed marriage with an almost equally sick mate, or was using the marriage as a major vehicle for the recapitulation of lifelong central neurotic conflicts. Of course, many of these marriages could be appropriately viewed from both of these perspectives.

Shared Disturbances

Of the 27 patients who had married, 16 (10 men and 6 women) were caught up in a complementary or concordant neurotic interaction with an almost equally psychologically disabled mate. A few examples should indicate the issues. In the cases of both the Alcoholic Doctor and the Alcoholic Heir, the wife almost matched the husband in the intensity of her own alcohol problem. The Alcoholic Doctor's wife would drink herself into a stupor along with her husband, sometimes to the point at which both had to be rescued from local taverns by his parents; she was likewise the one who encouraged his trials at homosexuality, including bringing the lover into the household so they could all be together more. Also, like the patient, the wife had to all intents and purposes totally given up on responsibility and care for the children (four in number, and each psychologically disturbed). The patient's father, a 70-year-old physician wanting to retire, had had to take over the children's upbringing and continue in practice in order to finance his son's hospitalization, raise his grandchildren, and provide for their futures. The physician wife thereupon blithely went off to a major medical center in order to resume her uncompleted specialty training. The wife of the Alcoholic Heir was likewise a heavy drinker. During his analytic treatment they made a strange written compact that there would be no liquor around the home "except by mutual consent" and no drinking "except in front of each other." But then the patient would be enraged to find half-empty liquor bottles hidden about the house, and to receive reports that his wife was "drinking like a fish." They fought over the concealed bottles, which she would explain as having been packed for shipment to their new Topeka home by the servants, or as needed to cope with her medicinal needs (menstrual cramps), or as being hidden from him so that *he* would not drink. Each would accuse the other of trying to drive the partner to drink. This was the patient who once said jovially in a drinking bout, "We're just a pair of old drunks."

Alcohol was not the only shared pathology in a concordant neurosis. The Involutional Woman, a lawyer, and her lawyer husband were two equally rigid, compulsive, obstinate, and competitive people, locked throughout their marriage in a struggle for domination. They competed in law school (academically), in civic and church activities, in tennis, at playing bridge—even, it seemed, at symptoms and complaints (he likewise was hypertensive and depressed). Who was the "boss" was always an issue: The patient said that her husband was rightly the "boss," but in the same breath indicated that she did not like his monotone way of singing and would no longer let him participate in the church choir, which he enjoyed. The mutual involvement of the Obese Woman and her husband in sadomasochistic

---

3. As has been previously stated, only 19 of the patients (8 men and 11 women) in the sample were still married at the point that they came to treatment at The Menninger Foundation; 7 were divorced (5 men and 2 women), and 1, the Tantrum Woman, was a recent widow.

sexual games (taking turns being tied up during intercourse) has already been described, as has the degree of the wife's participation in the more extreme and bizarre sexual perversions of the Sexual Masochist. In this same category, but complementary rather than concordant, was the interaction already described between the Phobic Woman and her husband, in which her parents supported them both fully so that the husband could devote himself totally to being at his wife's side in order to ward off phobic panic states. Also in this mold of neurotically compliant environments were the similar positions of the husband of the Invalided Hypochondriac, whose total caretaking of the wife and children has already been described, or the husband of the Bohemian Musician, who was willing to let his wife live with her lover and engage in the cultural pursuits of the big city, while he took care of his business in his small-town "home in a cornfield."

Recapitulation of Lifelong Neurosis

The other pattern in these marriages, dominant with 9 of the 27 (2 men and 7 women), was the patient's imposition on the marital partner (and children, if any) of the lifelong neurotic conflicts stemming from the interaction patterns of childhood. The Tantrum Woman was quite typical of this group. She had been locked in a lifelong difficult relationship with a hard-working and extremely self-willed and controlling mother. She found it hard to be with the mother; their relationship had deteriorated so badly that a maternal aunt rather than the mother had been co-opted to accompany the patient as the responsible relative to her psychiatric evaluation. And yet the patient could also not detach herself from this mother, who, despite their hardly talking to each other, was the one who administered the enemas every 2 or 3 days in order to cope with the patient's returned constipation (part of her acute depression in the wake of the husband's death). This mother had always dominated and pushed aside the depreciated father. The patient in turn played out this relationship with her own acquiescent husband, and it was only the upsetting of this equilibrium by the husband's traumatic death in the auto accident that precipitated the patient's acute depression and turn to treatment.

The Script Writer's case was another in this pattern. Her mother was a domineering and sanctimonious person, who used her arthritic complaints to lessen her homemaking burdens; she could easily bully her easygoing, passive husband, who would respond to the pressures in the marriage by acceding to his wife's dictates (e.g., taking on much of the housework and cooking) and by fleeing for solace to card games at local clubs. In her own marriage, with a busy physician husband, the patient took to heavy drinking (she insisted that nothing else gave her relief from *her* painful rheumatoid arthritis); essentially gave over the care of her children to her husband; and insisted that they move from their very convenient home in town to a "country estate" in a remote suburban area. Though it would make the husband's medical practice much more difficult and time-consuming, he purchased the outlying home to buy his peace with her. Ultimately, the patient's uncontrolled drinking brought her to treatment.

There was one marriage, that of the Adoptive Mother, in which the neurotic pattern was somewhat differently re-enacted—not predominantly with the husband, but in regard to motherhood and children. With this patient, as noted earlier, it was the decision to adopt a child, and the taking on of the conflicted role of mother (and "good Catholic wife"), that triggered her acute illness. Specifically, this decision brought about an intensive revival of her lifelong difficulties with her own mother, and a hostile identification with the mother she had seen as affording *her* insufficient and/or improper care and nurture.

In only one marriage—that of the Claustrophobic Man, unable to face the reality of the threat posed by his cancer surgery and its still unsettled prognosis—can one speak of a reasonably healthy accommodation by a spouse to the patient's neurotic illness and neurotic impositions. This patient's wife had long accommodated to his ongoing needs for (covert) dependency gratifications, as well as to their massive pathological accentuation in his acute phobic illness, with its progressive almost total constriction of their lives. At the same time, she exerted a constant gentle pressure toward psychiatric treatment for the emotional repercussions of his recurrent malignant illness. It was only during the course of the patient's treatment that the wife (in a joint therapeutic interview) openly cried and protested against her husband's demanding behaviors. On that occasion, she stated that she felt chained by his symptoms and exhausted by what he asked of her. He was embarrassed and had an "anxiety attack" on the spot.

Unmarried Patients

Fifteen of the patients had never married at the time they came to treatment. In some, this reflected either manifest or still covert homosexuality. The Masochistic Editor was an example of the former, and the Rebellious Coed and the Actress were examples of the latter. In some it was a reflection of their youthfulness, as with the two 17-year-olds, the Adolescent Grandson and the Bohemian Prep School Boy. With most, however, their single state was the expression of their crystallized difficulties in working out (and fear of, on a variety of bases) a meaningful and enduring heterosexual social–sexual relationship. The various ways in which these difficulties manifested themselves and reflected the patients' underlying neurotic problems have already been presented in the descriptions of these patients under the various character headings.

Actually, of the 15 never-married patients, 9 married either during the course of their treatment or in the subsequent period of follow-up observation. Some of these marriages were grossly neurotic and inappropriate, in the sense of being flagrant enactments of dominant conflicts, often as part of an effort to preclude the intrapsychic exploration and resolution of those conflicts; in other cases the marriages seemed more like progressive adaptive achievements. Some of these marriages failed grossly (with some surprises), and some succeeded (again with some surprises). The stories of these marriages are part of the recounting of the treatment courses.

UNUSUAL SYMPTOMS AND UNUSUAL CONFIGURATIONS

The intent of a project such as PRP was to explore the "natural histories" of psychoanalysis and analytic psychotherapy as they unfolded with a "typical" or "usual" population of such patients, at least as the patients appeared in a particular institutional setting (The Menninger Foundation) and over a particular span of time (the 1950s and 1960s), and given, of course, the various exclusion criteria we used or had to use that helped shape the parameters of our research population. However, within such a group, we would inevitably nonetheless encounter quite singular or highly unusual cases that chance had just happened to place within the sample. Here I want merely to review the array of unusual symptom and illness pictures that we encountered in this population, and/or of unusual internal or external circumstances that helped determine their treatment availability and prospects. These are for the most part only reviewed here in brief statements, because by and large they have already been spelled out in one place or another in the recounting of the various patients' behavior and character dispositions.

Major Dissociative States

With as many as four of the patients, major dissociative or fugue states played a prominent role in the presenting picture. With all four, it was these episodes that led directly to their evaluation for treatment. The Suspended Medical Student suffered a succession of three such episodes, which began during the time of his psychiatry clerkship. One day he was restless and upset, couldn't study, and went to a movie. The next thing he remembered, it was after midnight and he was walking down the street toward the medical school hospital. He was frightened; he got a cab and went home, but couldn't sleep. He checked his billfold and found he had all his money. A week later he had a second episode, preceded by drinking, during which he came to on the surgical floor of the hospital. Again he was very frightened that he had been drinking, and that he might be discovered. He left the building as fast as he could. The third episode, preceded by heavier drinking, occurred several weeks later; again he came to in the hospital, and found this time that he had spent some money. The next morning he was called to the Dean's Office. A distraught patient had reported that he had awakened her at 2:00 A.M. in order to perform a pelvic examination, without wearing rubber gloves. Several weeks before (at the time of his earlier episode), there had been another such occurrence, for which one of the residents had been formally reprimanded. The patient claimed an absolute amnesia for these events.

The Adolescent Grandson was similarly precipitated toward his treatment. He was the individual who scampered naked across his grandfather's estate (and had previously ridden horseback the same way) "to give me a sense of freedom." He was accused of public masturbation and deliberate exhibitionism, but he denied both charges; it was unclear how much memory blanking he was claiming. The Bohemian Musician was the individual stopped by the police after a wild, panicky car ride through a crowded suburban area at 90 miles an hour. She appeared completely out of contact, mixed up fact and fancy, and had lost track of time and place. She was consequently referred for psychiatric hospitalization. The Snake Phobia Woman was driving home one day and found a large truck blocking her accustomed path. The driver showed no inclination to move to let her pass. She angrily called her husband and then the police; neither seemed helpful. She took another route home, feeling that she would explode or burst into uncontrolled sobbing. She then fled her home so that the children would not pester her and went wandering over the fairgrounds, feeling that all this was unreal, happening to someone else—that she was a mere onlooker. She saw two young boys approaching her, was frightened that they could kill her, and fled home. On her return, she insisted to her husband that they arrange psychiatric consultation, because she feared she was losing her mind.

Stealing

Four of the patients were involved with stealing as an active symptom. With one, the Sociopath, it was of course part of a total spectrum of psychopathic and predatory activities that have already been detailed. All of these activities were rationalized as his proper revenge against the "400 percenters" by whom he had always felt victimized, and all of it finally fell apart: Police, creditors, aggrieved mobsters, and his own family were all pursuing him, and not especially with his welfare in mind.

With the other three patients, the stealing was much more "neurotically" driven, a true kleptomania. I have already described the intensity of Peter Pan's urge to steal (usually candy and other sweets) and the lengths to which she would go (unsuccessfully) to control the urge. During her lengthy treatment, it came out that as a very young child she had tried to "steal" her brother's bottles when he was an infant and that she had had to be locked up to prevent her harming him. At that point, she had first begun to vomit and reject food (many years before her developing anorexia). When she was 13, some 2 years before her serious stealing and eating problems began, her mother had once shouted at her in a fit of pique, "I'd rather have a thief than have you."

With the other two, the kleptomania had been concealed at the time of initial evaluation. The Obese Woman had presented herself for treatment because of the emotional problems associated with her obesity. She was the individual who, as a young child, had curried favor with her friends by giving away cake and cookies at her father's bakery. During her psychoanalysis, among the new historical material that emerged was a long history of petty shoplifting and stealing money from her mother. Similarly, with the Economist, who had presented himself for treatment because of difficulties in establishing enduring heterosexual relationships, many symptoms concealed at the time of initial evaluation came to light during the course of the analysis. These included childhood symptoms during latency years, enuresis, stuttering, and stealing from his father. He stole money as a conscious symbol for what he felt he was not given—money that he rarely used and mostly gave away to friends.

Success Neurosis

Two of the patients could be clearly described in terms of a "success neurosis," in which every advancement in life signaled a further eruption of distress and disability. The Alcoholic Heir was a striking instance. As described earlier, he was destined to succeed his very wealthy father as a major executive in one of the country's giant scientific–industrial enterprises. Yet each step along the way intensified the struggle with the domineering father, who both promoted and simultaneously controlled every step of his son's career. A characteristic memory was from a hunting trip that the patient had taken with his father at age 16: He had felt keen, but unvoiced, resentment when the father publicly claimed a bird that the patient affirmed was his shot. When he attended college he gave up his own differing inclinations in order to take the scientific courses that the father dictated as the essential preparation for his destined career. However, when he collected the $1,000 reward from the abstaining father for not drinking (other than beer) prior to age 21, he promptly embarked on a career of defiant drinking. As noted earlier, he received successive promotions within the firm—guided and bullied at each point by the father, who always undertook to tell the patient how to do his job—with each new promotion then intensifying the recourse to alcohol. The story of his ultimate "lateral promotion" and then actual demotion has already been told.

The Bitter Spinster had a similar life story, but on a lesser and less destructive scale. She came to treatment at age 30 because of depressive episodes and chronic difficulties in relationships with people. In each of the major areas of her life—her work functioning as a nurse and nursing supervisor, and her social–sexual relationships with men—she could carry an involvement to the point where success threatened, and would then do something to make it fail and to waste her investment and her capacity. Of her latest firing, as a nursing supervisor, she first said, "I did it again"; however, she then rationalized that the head nurse had let her go because she was such a threat. Now, at age 30, she was no closer to either of her goals of marriage or professional success.

Accident Proneness

One patient, the Medical Scientist, whose "do-it-yourself" efforts at breaking his alcohol and drug addictions have already been described, also had a history of daredevil activity and accident affliction (accident proneness?). He had always been a fine athlete and an intense outdoorsman. Of a camping trip spent with his father during his adolescence, the father said, "He had me frightened all the time with the things he did—like riding his horse into a whole herd of moose one day." As a young adult, he had had a car accident in which he was thrown to the pavement; the wheel of the car had caught his right hand underneath and skidded along the pavement with the whole weight of the car on it. The patient's hand had been badly mangled and required reparative surgery over the next several years. Incidental to this, the patient had experienced a great deal of pain; this had initiated the drug dependence that had plagued him ever since. Years later—just prior to his coming to The Menninger Hospital—he had another automobile accident, in which he suffered a concussion with a head laceration, momentary unconsciousness, and some persisting posttraumatic headaches. A month after that, he came down with general malaise and lymphadenopathy, which led to a diagnosis of infectious mononucleosis. The patient found the further enforced work stoppage, bed rest, and mandated inactivity intolerable, and his barbiturate and alcohol consumption heightened to the point where he was finally brought to hospitalization in Topeka.

Solitary Life Style

One other patient, the Fearful Loner, should be mentioned in this context of unusual symptoms; it was his entirely solitary life style that marked his specialness. He was a withdrawn, schizoid individual, with no acute illness, but a lifetime of encrusted unhappiness and fearfulness of intrusions—he was a "turtle without a shell." He grew up keeping apart from groups and enjoying the solitary hunting, fishing, and trapping that his father had taught him. When he grew up he had been briefly married for 6 months, but of his marriage all he would state was "I prefer not to talk about that," and of the divorce "I could not live with her." He was an accountant in the civil service, finding his work with figures the best part of his whole life adjustment. He lived alone in a rented room and spent a great deal of time reading. He was interested in bridge, but was so perfectionistic and intolerant that no one would play with him. His only social contacts were with his brother and the brother's family: He would visit them irregularly, stay an hour or two, and then abruptly leave, rarely accepting their regularly extended dinner invitation. He showed no interest in the brother's two children, but occasionally sat around in their house listening to records. He was estranged from his parents. It gradually came out that the father had written to him expressing his concern that the patient was not having as full a social life as it seemed he should. The patient had felt that his father was "meddling too much"; he had angrily broken off relations with the father and had refused to see him ever since.

Unusual Internal or External
Circumstances

Another whole group of patients had their treatment surrounded by (or beset by) some unusual internal or external circumstance or pressure. Most of these have already been stated. The Movie Lady was the individual involved in the research filming of her treatment, in return for which she was treated by a very senior therapist at a most nominal fee ($1 per hour). For this competitive, somewhat exhibitionistic, and somewhat masochistic woman, this could of course pose special problems for her treatment. Since her whole treatment would be in a very real way an "exhibition," her competitive efforts to defeat the analyst, to show him up as ineffectual, would indeed be given added valence in this treatment setting. At the same time, there could also be a heightening of her masochistic willingness to persist in and display her suffering, particularly if it could be viewed altruistically as simultaneously serving a larger, social goal. All of these dispositions indeed appeared during the course of her treatment.

With the Claustrophobic Man, the whole psychotherapy was carried out in the shadow of serious somatic illness (cancer) with a still unclear prognosis. He had had three operations for recurrence of his thyroid cancer. The Bohemian Musician suffered a deepening depression with her hospitalization, and was the one patient in the group who had a major somatic therapy intervention as part of her Menninger Foundation treatment. A course of 20 electroconvulsive shocks and 10 nonconvulsive shocks promptly ameliorated her depression, at which point the formal psychotherapy could be initiated. (As already stated, several of the patients had had prior ECT and/or subcoma insulin treatment before coming to The Menninger Foundation.)

One patient, the Sociopath, was unfortunately allowed to strike a treatment bargain, which operated later to the detriment of his treatment. With his world collapsed around him, and both gangsters and the law after him, he finally came to treatment evaluation; at the same time he rejected, as unwanted and financially out of the question, the recommended treatment plan of long-term hospitalization concomitant with intensive psychotherapy. He demanded outpatient treatment and asserted that he could control his behaviors on the outside. He was told to do so, to maintain himself in some trouble-free equilibrium on the outside for a year, and, with that proof of his capacity, to return for psychotherapy. A year later to the day, the patient called, asking for his re-evaluation. His story of the intervening year was one of reasonable and quiet management of job and home, with now only some minor inconveniencing discrepancies, "white lies," and so forth. His wife's description of the same interval was a more flamboyant one. His lying, cheating, depredations, and playing the "big shot" had all continued, though indeed on a somewhat muted scale. But the bargain had been struck, and it now permitted the patient, by fulfilling his commitment (however marginally), to enforce a countercommitment to a less than optimal treatment plan (outpatient psychotherapy)—which led to treatment disaster.

And for some of the five patients who came from extremely wealthy families, their wealth posed special problems for their lives and their treatments. I have already detailed how the coercive molding of the Alcoholic Heir into a destined career as a captain of industry was the context for a living out of a total alcoholic collapse, with all the manifest dynamics of a so-called "success neurosis." With the Sexual Masochist, the great wealth of both his own and his wife's family allowed the indulgence of a wasteful and profligate life, of uncontrolled alcoholism, and of all his perverse masochistic enactments. He had never felt any pressure to seek any gainful employment, and always felt himself too tired and lazy to attend to any job. The Adolescent Grandson, whose alcoholic and promiscuous mother had deserted the family when he was 2, and whose cardiac-invalided father had died when he was 9, was the victim of the tyrannical upbringing of his enormously wealthy grandfather. This grandfather controlled the patient's life from an aloof distance through his stepmother, and treated the stepmother as a governess and servant hired to care for his grandchildren. Occasionally the grandfather would permit the daughter-in-law and grandson to visit with him at one of his various estates. When the patient did spend some summer vacation periods with the grandfather, he found him very hard to talk to. He ultimately did make a dramatic statement that called full attention to himself—his naked scamper across the estate, with his subsequent arrest and referral to psychiatric treatment.

OVERALL DEVELOPMENTAL AND CHARACTEROLOGICAL ORGANIZATION

From the overall picture drawn to this point of the ramifying and interlocking features of the character and illness structures of this patient population, it is clear that these individuals by and large did not fall into neatly circumscribed, "typical" neurotic illness structures, linked to particular psychosexual developmental fixation levels and to characteristic defensive and character constellations. The pictures were rather more mixed, more diffuse, and more complex. However, certain major groupings nonetheless did emerge, and they are indicated here as one way of synthesizing the many descriptive rubrics used to characterize the population elements to this point.

Oral-Infantile Character Organization

A total of 12 patients (9 males and 3 females) could be characterized in terms of an overall orally fixated conflict and character organization, with often some "pseudophallic" facade in the sense of apparent competitive, triangular, "Oedipal-like" strivings and conflicts. The preponderance of males in the group relates to the prevalence of this kind of character organization among the preponderantly male alcoholic and addictive population. A prototypical case was that of the Addicted Doctor, whose core conflicts were centered in his extremely infantile, narcissistic character; he looked upon the world primarily in a passively receptive and oral-dependent way. He seemed not to question the inappropriateness of his oral-demanding attitudes, and experienced only frustrations and rages against those who presented obstacles to his immediate gratifications. He blandly assumed his right to wreck his own life as an act of revenge against his parents, and narcissistically assumed that no greater blow could befall them. His current life problems represented only the current version of these conflict positions. His medical license was lost, he and his children were being supported by his wife, and he demonstrated a total unconcern about his future or planning; he was occupied in the hospital with the daily status of his privileges, and with playing childish games with the nurses and other personnel (e.g., putting ice cubes down their blouses at the hospital picnic).

The pseudophallic components among some in this group were epitomized in the Alcoholic Heir, the individual manifesting the "success neurosis." He did (conflictedly) attempt to live out his father's dictates, but at each step along the way he fell further into a deepening alcoholism, a phobic withdrawal from life, and a mutual indulgence with his equally wealthy wife in their shared drinking ("We're just a pair of old drunks"). During his illness (and treatment), he essentially abdicated any work responsibility; he had little contact with his children; and his sexual life fell away almost completely. His wife stated that they lived together "like a pair of grandparents" (or children).

Oral–Anal Character Organization with Prominent Masochistic Features

A group of four patients (three men, all alcoholic, and one woman) had a mixed orally and anally organized conflict structure with prominent masochistic features. The Sexual Masochist and the Masochistic Editor (a characterological masochist) were in this group. The one woman was the Obese Woman, who came to treatment because of her obesity, and whose sadomasochistic sex games with her husband were initially concealed. The more "anally organized" and sadomasochistic character components were expressed in the patient's hostile competition, hostile identification, and lifelong fighting interactions with her bullying, domineering mother. Characteristically, the patient took the masochistic position in this interaction: For example, she had learned not to cry during altercations with her mother, when the latter, given to tantrums, would hit and beat the patient and pull her hair, even up to the time of the latter's marriage at 22. The patient's not crying would reduce the mother to helpless fury. At times, in her identification with the mother, the patient took on the sadistic role: For example, when a little boy playmate (with whom she got into mutual sexual explorations) had bit her, the mother had told her to bite him back; she had done this, and the little boy thereupon had run home crying. The patient saw in these encounters one of the sources of the connection in her mind between "sexuality" and "orality." In the patient's marriage, these same kinds of fighting interactions were reduplicated, and the guilt generated by them could be overcome by masochistically perverted sexual relations, in which the patient would suffer physical pain that both aroused her sexually and atoned for the guilt feelings.

Oral–Anal–Phallic Character Organization

Another group of 12 patients (6 men and 6 women) were more complexly arrayed, with developmental conflicts across the whole span of oral–anal–phallic fixation points, and some of these with marked masochistic features. The Movie Lady, who came to treatment because of her widening network of phobic symptoms and restrictions, was a good case in point. Her core problems revolved around each of the several axes. She had intense wishes for nurture and dependency gratifications, which had to be strongly defended against and denied; she resented bitterly being cast so often, and starting so young, in the caretaking "little mother" role, from her childhood care of her sickly sister through her adult commitments as a nurse caring for the world of sick people. Her own dependency longings could only be expressed in her phobic incapacity, and even then she called on other people (her husband) much less than phobic individuals usually allow themselves to do. At the same time, she struggled, under relentless superego pressures, to repress her reactive oral-aggressive (and anal-aggressive) rages and jealous hostilities in order to be the good little girl, the rigidly conforming person. Any outward expression of her angers would jeopardize the dependencies she craved, and so they were turned inward and made self-punitive. Alongside this play of oral-level conflicts were the masochistic gratifications that went with the superego appeasement and the constant need to make a good impression; and the phallic-level conflicts of the unattractive, socially inadequate young girl with acne and obesity, growing up competitive with and hostile to men, of whom she was suspicious and distrustful, and to whom she wanted to feel superior (just as her mother had been a better provider than her father).

Oral–Phallic Character Organization

Another 10 of the patients (here the sex ratio shifted dramatically, to 1 man and 9 women) had their main fixations at the oral and phallic developmental levels without much evidence of anal-masochistic conflict issues. Many of these, of course (e.g., the Adoptive Mother, the Tantrum Woman, and the Divorced Nurse), were the kinds of individuals often characterized as so-called "good hysterics" (see Zetzel, 1968) or hysterical characters with strong oral fixations. The conflicts of the Script Writer were characteristic of this group. On the oral relationship level were intense feelings of oral deprivation, with no sense of ever having received nurture or loving care from a mother figure; the reactive oral demandingness on the model, "You have to extort the manifestations of love in order to get any"; and the frustrated wishes for affection and attention converted into self-punishing and self-destructive behaviors (her alcoholism and her suicidal depressions). On the phallic relationship level were the struggle against acceptance of any passive, receptive impulses; the destructive, competitive relationships with men, who were at once envied for their superior attributes, and at the same time chopped down and depreciated (as her mother had done to her father, and as she did by forcing her husband's move away from town to the remote suburban area, which complicated so much his capacity to carry on his medical practice); and her shameful and neglectful treatment of her rejected, polio-crippled son, who "should have been a girl." And oral- and phallic-level conflicts were fused in the lifelong openly hostile relationship with the mother (by whom she was now practically disowned), with whom she nonetheless had an intense hostile identification (manifested in ways ranging from the conduct of her marriage and the treatment of her husband, to her somatic affliction—the same arthritic complaints).

Phallic-Oedipal Character Organization

A final group of four patients (two male and two female) had no special oral-level components to their character functioning at all, but primarily demonstrated Oedipal, phallic-level conflicts, with regressive retreats to anal-compulsive organizations. The Snake Phobia Woman was typical of this group. Her major phallic-Oedipal conflicts centered around her sexual identity as a woman; her depreciation of "feminine" activities in identification with the mother, whom she at the same time resented for never having encouraged her in homemaking interests (the mother never seemed to have the time or the interest to teach her how to cook or sew); her intense penis envy (she felt herself "not perfect" and avoided awareness of sex differences—e.g., she had shared the same bed with her twin brother till age 5 and the same bedroom till age 12, but claimed never to have noticed the male genitalia), which was inordinately heightened by the patient's sense of rejection over the parents' seeming open preference for her male twin; and her hostile competitiveness with and retaliatory anger toward the weak, unreliable, and disappointing men in her life (father, twin brother). And all of this conflict structure was contained within a framework of compliant and compulsive character defenses.

Overall Summary

In overall summary statement of this assessment of the core conflicts of our patient population, I can state that the men were much more heavily represented in the more "primitive" or "regressed" fixation levels, outnumbering the women 12 to 4 in the first two categories listed—the primarily oral-infantile (or oral-narcissistic), and mixed oral–anal (with sadomasochistic accentuations). Contrariwise, the women were much more heavily represented (an almost exact reversal, with the women outnumbering the men 11 to 3) in the more "complex" or "advanced" psychosexual fixation levels — the oral–phallic (the so-called hysterics with oral features) and the phallic-Oedipal. To repeat, this bespoke the loading of our sample with so many strongly alcoholic and addictive men.

The counterpart (but not an exact one) of these developmental and conflict fixation levels can be seen in the preponderant defensive and character configurations of the patients. A total of 24 of the sample would be seen as varieties of clearly "psychotic" characters (7 — 6 men and 1 woman), or manifestly predominantly paranoid characters (4 — 3 men and 1 woman), or combinations of infantile and narcissistic characters (13 — 2 men and 11 women), with the great majority of all these suffering severe alcoholic, addictive, somatizing, sexually perverse, or "as-if" symptoms.[4] Another 4 (all men) could be seen as inhibited, passive, dependent characters, with degrees of depressive and "immature" characteristics but with less intense aggressive and reactive components. One patient, the Sociopath, could be placed in the antisocial character category. Finally, 13 (5 men and 8 women) were called obsessive–compulsive characters (5), or mixed character neuroses (4), or hysterical characters (4).[5] Individual case vignettes are not given here to illustrate each of these defensive and character configurations, since to do so would be clearly repetitive.

Issues of Diagnosis and Implications for Treatment

CLINICAL EVALUATION AND
THE CONCEALMENT OF INFORMATION

Concealment as a Major Phenomenon

The clinical enterprise is based upon the ability (through psychiatric interview, abetted by such auxiliary devices as psychological testing, social history, and information from referring sources) to conduct a clinical evaluation process that will lead to informed judgments about the nature of the patient's personality and illness history, as a basis for appropriate, differentiated treatment recommendations, treatment planning, and treatment prognostication. That this process operates reasonably well in practice is a working conviction of the mental health practitioner who sees prospective patients in evaluation, takes them into therapy, and

---

4. This listing is not identical with that given earlier in this chapter (see p. 144) in the description of those with borderline (or more than borderline) ego weakness or vulnerability (though 15 are on both lists), because the listing here of the 24 has 9 who are seen as infantile and oral-narcissistic in character organization, but without real vulnerability to psychotic regression, and the other listing of 20 contained 5 whose vulnerability to paranoid and psychotic decompensation was not evident at the point at which the diagnostic assessments were made initially.

5. Again, for reasons similar to those just indicated in footnote 4, the overall character designations here are not exact overlaps with the patients previously designated as portraying various character trends (obsessive–compulsive, hysterical, or whatever) as part of their overall character organization.

frequently enough experiences over time the reasonable concordance of initial expectation and achieved outcome. At The Menninger Foundation over its decades of operation, the conviction that such concordance would be brought even closer through an enhanced comprehensiveness of the initial clinical evaluation process led to the formalization of this clinical evaluation over a basic 2-week span that has been described in detail in Section II (Chapter 6, pp. 71–73) and that became known as the "Menninger case workup." Our own whole research enterprise was constructed upon this clinical operating structure, using its large information base to describe patients comprehensively and to predict their treatment courses and outcomes in research-testable terms (i.e., through making relevant variables explicit, through setting down predictions and the means for their subsequent confirmation or refutation in advance, through arranging for independent and blind judgments of outcomes, through using various control methods, etc.).

It came, therefore, as all the more a surprise to us that with 24 of our 42 patients (more than 55%), major symptoms, behavior dispositions, and personality trends were successfully concealed at the time of initial evaluation, and emerged as newly available historical data only within the growing confidences of the therapeutic relationships into which the patients entered. Here I do not mean issues of repressed infantile memories and fantasies emerging in the reconstructions of the infantile conflicts within an unfolding regressive psychoanalytic process; I mean major issues of clearly remembered experiences and clearly conscious behaviors and feelings that patients felt unable or unwilling to make available to the various members of the initial examining team. The extent to which this can be ascribed to the shortcomings of *these* examining teams—their not uncovering what they could or would have uncovered had they worked with more skill, or had they had more time—is of course an arguable proposition. Certainly, the dedication to this specific diagnostic and case formulation task has always been higher at The Menninger Foundation than almost anywhere else in the organized clinical world,[1] and stretching the process over a longer span than 2 weeks would not only raise many practical and logistical (and financial) problems, but would also turn the extended evaluation into a species of "treatment before the treatment."

Withholding of Specific Events or Behaviors

Given, then, a setting where the diagnostic evaluation process was (and is) as comprehensive as it could practically and should conceptually be, the extent of the major concealments here being talked about has been indeed one of our more unexpected findings. There were many different such concealments, all of them clearly related to the dynamic structure and needs systems of the patients, and many of them occurring with individuals whose "honesty" as people was never in ques-

1. And it is certainly carried out at The Menninger Foundation in a much more comprehensive way than anywhere in private practice at all. This is not just because of the availability of such comprehensive resources focused this way in an organized institutional clinical setting like The Menninger Foundation (although it would be correspondingly extremely difficult to assemble such coordinated diagnostic resources regularly within the usual private practice setting); it is also because of the usual outpatient private practice bias (under the most sophisticated of circumstances) that it is counterproductive, in the sense of possibly distorting the subsequent therapeutic work, to *try* to undertake such definitive diagnostic case study and case formulation.

tion, except as deformed by the pressures of the neurosis. The Adoptive Mother was an excellent case in point. As detailed earlier, she came to treatment distressed over her inability to conceive and to be a "proper Catholic mother," and guilt-ridden that her overpoweringly intrusive, hostile impulses had led her to return the adopted baby to the adoption agency. She spoke unhappily of her many inconclusive workups to see if there was some remediable physiological or anatomical barrier to conception. Yet the husband revealed, when he himself came to psychiatric evaluation 2 years after his wife, that in the very first months of the marriage the patient had become pregnant and then suffered a miscarriage. It was only in one of the dreams from the *termination* period of her analysis, in which the patient spilled her jewels and had these returned to her by the analyst, that her associations led to toying with this dream imagery as a symbol of the restoration of her femininity and—within that context now—to the revelation of the pregnancy and miscarriage. And yet no issue could be said to be more central to the whole analysis!

With other patients, the withholdings included a whole variety of other specific events and/or behaviors. The Script Writer, who displayed so much alcoholic pathology and depression (including two previous suicide attempts), nonetheless carefully hid rather severe lifelong phobias of thunderstorms and heights. These were only revealed during the course of her analytic treatment, in relation to recurrent childhood fantasies—that she and her mother would be in a boat in a storm together, that the boat would overturn, and that the mother, being the nonswimmer, would drown; or that the mother would fall from a high cliff and be crushed to death. The linkage of these childhood fantasies to the patient's lifelong, unresolved hostile–dependent relationship with her domineering and often neglectful mother, as well as to the patient's own phobic symptoms, was transparently clear. The Alcoholic Heir initially concealed the extent of the intense, drunken, brawling turmoil with his equally wealthy and just about equally alcoholic wife (with many accusations of extravagance, lying, deceit, intent to destroy him because of her own sick personality, etc.).

With all of the alcoholism that was blatantly rampant through our population, it was nonetheless at evaluation a specifically downplayed symptom with the Heiress, who during treatment made many drunken out-of-hour telephone calls to her analyst (during which she could pour out the tender feelings that were rigidly warded off during her hours), and otherwise gave evidence of how much her excessive drinking *was* an important ongoing behavior in her life. It was also concealed by the Obedient Husband, whose constant escapes into alcoholic excess, so evident during his treatment, had been carefully represented during the initial evaluation (to himself as well as to others) as nothing more than "social drinking." This patient, as it turned out, had concealed not only his drinking, but his even greater shame over his inadequacies as a businessman. It gradually came out over the first months of therapy that, contrary to the way in which he had initially presented it, his business had never been a successful proposition: It had been taken on (after his father's death) with the help of money put into it by his father-in-law; it had been progressively failing (he had concealed this from his wife "lest this burden distress her unduly"); and it was now nearly bankrupt. With the help of the therapist, the patient could now more openly begin to acknowledge his failure as a businessman and breadwinner—something he had denied to that point, not only to others but also to himself.

As already mentioned, the sadomasochistic perversion in the sexual behavior between the Obese Woman and her husband, as well as her long history of kleptomania (petty shoplifting and stealing from the mother), had for reasons of intense shame and embarrassment been initially withheld. Peter Pan's kleptomania, with a much more extensive history of compulsive stealing and of unsuccessful struggle against it, had similarly been withheld. For like reasons, several patients initially withheld the existence or the degree of prior homosexual involvements. The Intellectual Fencer, after 4 months of intensive therapy, confessed the until then closely guarded secret of a homosexual involvement with a motherly older woman over a several-month period several years before. It was in fact the rejection by this woman that had led the patient into the deepening barbiturate-drugged state of the following years, which finally brought her to psychiatric hospitalization. And, at a greater extreme, the Alcoholic Doctor—whose initial history included being provoked into homosexual trials by his wife's taunting suggestions— revealed in treatment an active homosexuality, starting with a seduction by the handyman when he was 12 and continuing all through his school years. (This had come after years of the mother's dressing him in girl's clothes, encouraging him to play with dolls, and seductively undressing and changing her sanitary napkins in front of him.) The homosexuality only became less of an issue when his severe alcoholism took over.

And half a dozen of the patients very knowingly concealed major problems of potency or orgastic disturbance. The Medical Scientist, for example, concealed a concern over sterility, lifelong troubling premature ejaculations, and flights into unfaithfulness (verging on promiscuity) that had marked the last 20 years of his 23-year marriage. These matters were never mentioned at all in the initial evaluation, though so much other symptomatic disturbance was (alcoholism, drug addiction, and assaultiveness). The others in this group were similar.

Large-Scale Withholding

With another group of seven patients, there was a much wider net of withholding. The Economist was typical of this group. He fiercely withheld a major potency disturbance until the fifth year of his analytic treatment—an impotence that he projected and attributed to his partners' being unable to behave properly sexually toward him. He would be enraged at them for his impotence, bully them savagely, and work to rid himself of them. This was a directly significant part of his presenting inability to establish enduring relations with women (which at evaluation he professed himself unable to explain). But this specific concealment was in the context of a much broader initial symptom and character concealment. What emerged as new history over the course of the therapy included childhood symptoms of latency years, enuresis, stuttering, and stealing of money from his father; adult compulsive symptoms, such as having to drive precisely down prescribed routes or step on cracks; adult antisocial behaviors, such as lying, manipulating his parents for money, and blatant cheating (he had been expelled from one university); long-time paranoid fears of being attacked, so that he always had to carry pistols and clubs on his person and in his car, in order to be "properly vigilant"; and, lastly, the severe impotence.

Clearly, the withholding of so much severe pathology could be reflected in a major underestimation of the scope of a patient's illness, and thus in distortions of the appropriate treatment recommendations. This issue of concealment's leading to possible misdiagnosis, and its implications both for research and for clinical practice, are discussed later in this chapter. Here I want to add what is no doubt the extreme example of pathological withholding, certainly in this sample—that of the Fearful Loner. This was the individual who cut off all contact with his parents because of the father's expressing his concern that the patient was not having as full a social life as it seemed he should, and who assaulted an examining psychiatrist because of his demand that the patient talk about himself. These incidents reflected a pattern of fearful guardedness and secretiveness, which persisted unaltered through 8½ years of observation to a "cutoff" Follow-Up Study. In fact, he did not inform his therapist that he had married (itself a minor therapeutic miracle), at a point about 7 years after the treatment onset, until 3 months after the fact, when he revealed it by way of a request for referral for marital counseling. The problem was that the patient felt unable to communicate with his wife (of whose existence the therapist had had no prior inkling), and the patient feared that his marriage might be endangered by this.

"Important" Issues at Evaluation Not Worked on in Therapy

Before leaving this issue of concealments during the initial evaluation process (no matter how seemingly comprehensive the evaluation), I should mention a curiously opposite, and of course rarer, phenomenon: that of issues that seem to bulk large during the initial evaluation process, and yet do not come into significant focus during the course of the subsequent ongoing therapy. This phenomenon could be clearly seen in three of our cases, and seemed to occur on a different basis in each. It was most sharply delineated in the Tantrum Woman, whose whole enormously hostile and dependent tie to her mother had been epitomized in the childhood interaction (revived in the course of the acute depressive illness that brought her to psychoanalysis) centering on the forced enemas, in which the mother intrusively extracted the "poisons" from her. As noted earlier, the relationship with the mother as a whole was so strained that it was a maternal aunt, rather than the mother, who accompanied this young widow to her psychiatric evaluation as the responsible relative. The treatment outcome was quite successful, but with some limitations (which are described in detail further on in this book); the central unfinished treatment task was the real resolution of the hostile dependency upon the mother imago, perceived as basically ungiving and malevolent (the mother–patient tie was muted at termination, with the two living far enough apart so that they could be more tolerant of each other when they did come together). In this context, it is not a total surprise that the "enema relationship"—so central at the evaluation point—did not come up as a major issue in the analytic work. Nonetheless, the discrepancy is also somewhat startling, and not altogether explicable in a treatment that, after all, was a long and serious effort at a classical psychoanalysis.

With the Homesick Psychology Student, something similar took place, but in a far less striking manner. When he came to psychotherapy with his feelings of inadequacy and poor school and social adjustment, a central dynamic of this immature young man (and only child) was his symbiotic dependent tie to pathologically overprotective parents. In his earliest childhood, he had slept in the same bed with his parents, and between them, until he was 4. While away at college, he never missed a chance to go home; at times, when he would get terribly lonely on a midweek evening, he would impulsively hitchhike home to spend the night. On weekends he was always the first in his boarding house to rush off home. And after longer stays at home (holidays, vacations), there would be especially emotionally painful good-byes. The father particularly would carry on, getting maudlin drunk or falling ill, and crying that he just didn't know how they could get along without the patient home with them. Yet these issues had a surprisingly small place in the total treatment picture that subsequently unfolded. Mostly, though, this was due to the patient's resistance: He was surprised and indignant that the therapist kept trying to bring this relationship with his parents up for discussion, and seemed to feel it relevant and important to the patient's current life functioning and difficulties. This was the young man who ultimately married (shortly after his treatment termination), but had not consummated the marriage by the Follow-Up point 2 years later.

The third such instance was equally understandable, but in a somewhat different way. The Rebellious Coed had come to treatment with depression and uncontrolled crying since her mother's death 6 months previously. She also had had progressive difficulty in getting along with family members, fellow students, and teachers, plus a deepening (albeit very conflicted) series of homosexual involvements in which she was feeling at last loved and appreciated, at least temporarily. But in the whole course of the subsequent supportive psychotherapy, there seemed to be an ongoing tacit collusion between patient and therapist to refrain from any therapeutic working with the homosexual conflicts; the therapy focused instead on everyday reality problems of schoolwork and of proper social behaviors, and avoided their anchorings in the patient's underlying intrapsychic life. By treatment termination, the patient had been able to return to college (after having been put on academic and disciplinary probation by the dean for the serious misbehaviors that had preceded her coming for therapy) and to graduate successfully. She ended the treatment with a grateful letter to the therapist, thanking him for all his help and indicating that all was going very well in her new employment; there was perhaps the expectation on both sides that she would lead a stable life, finding satisfaction as a (spinster) schoolteacher, with a discreet homosexual personal life. It was only in the Follow-Up Study that the patient could express her profound dissatisfaction with the outcome. She had to come to treatment with the feeling that if only things got bad enough, *somebody* would notice her condition and would do something about it. Yet once in treatment, she had not been able to discuss with her therapist the things that constantly bothered her. "If he had *made* me talk about them, I could have done it; if I had had to and really wanted to—but I couldn't bring myself to bring them up."

Clearly, the issues involved in the failure of crucial evaluation issues to bulk substantially in the subsequent treatment are quite different from (and in ways, opposite to) those of initial concealment of major relevant evaluation data. The former are treatment issues and are discussed in much fuller detail in the accounts of the treatment courses; the latter are central issues of proper diagnosis and of possible misdiagnosis and are discussed further at this point.

ISSUES OF MISDIAGNOSIS

The issue of misdiagnosis is much larger and more encompassing than the sole matter of the often successful efforts of potential patients to conceal (for whatever reasons) significant aspects of their symptomatology and conflict structure during their evaluations for treatment. Certainly, concealments do operate to limit the evaluation perspective on the nature and severity of the presenting illness. But even when there is no significant withholding of relevant data, there are other issues to be considered: failure to discern accurately the full extent and depth of the disorder, which perhaps becomes evident as the fuller treatment picture unfolds; and, in the context of PRP, the commitment of the research team predictors, for each potential patient under consideration and for each prospective treatment course, to think and to prognosticate in terms of the best that treatment could do, and to try to see then where and how it might fall short of realizing its potential. Both these considerations could readily translate operationally into "misdiagnosis" (albeit, with the research predictors, a *knowing* misdiagnosis or underdiagnosis)—again, of course, in the direction of underestimating the nature and degree of the presenting psychopathology.

Given such manifold considerations, it should come as no surprise that 18 of the 42 patients (11 men and 7 women) were substantially misdiagnosed in the broader sense of the term; in every instance, the misdiagnosis was in the direction of underestimation of pathology. The majority of this group of 18 (over 60%) were males, and this is in keeping with the observation that these underdiagnosed instances were heavily clustered among the alcohol- and drug-addicted cases and the paranoid–borderline cases (themselves categories that significantly overlapped). As already indicated (see Chapter 8, pp. 143–144), the extent of the "underdiagnosis" usually became apparent within the emergence during the course of the treatment effort of a decompensating transference psychotic state. A typical "milder" example was the Obese Woman. The original diagnostic summary of this young woman who came to psychiatric treatment because of her impulsive eating and extreme obesity (238 pounds) was of "mixed psychoneurosis, with predominant sadomasochistic, compulsive, and to a lesser extent, hysterical trends (with symptomatic severe obesity)." As already indicated, a long history of kleptomania and a true sadomasochistic sexual perversion enacted between the patient and her colluding husband emerged in the course of the psychoanalysis. There was also, incidentally, the complication of the severe neurosis of the husband, who was inconstant in the marriage; who made a brief foray into psychotherapy for himself (where he was diagnosed as an immature, dependent person); and who ultimately divorced the patient, only to stick around in order to continue to fight with her (he left her again a number of times after the divorce). The fuller diagnostic picture at the end of treatment was of a deep-seated oral-narcissistic character neurosis with manifest sexual masochistic perversion, set within the context of an unstable marriage with a severely neurotic husband.

A more malignant underdiagnosed pathology was that of the Alcoholic Doctor. This individual was recommended for an effort at psychoanalysis, with the diagnostic summary statement of "passive–dependent personality with manifest alcoholism, drug addiction, and homosexual activity." What emerged during the course of the long treatment effort was a picture of a far deeper and wider ego

deformation, and of much more deeply entrenched and chronic symptom and behavior disturbances, than had been initially presented. This picture included depressed feelings and open desires for death, back to the patient's earliest remembered years; intense homosexual activity through all the adolescent years (not just
when "suggested" into it by his wife); intricate bowel and genital rituals relating
to his fears of constipation and contamination, which he went through after each
defecation and each sexual experience; and even actual psychotic episodes, in which
he was seemingly delusional and hallucinated (running out of the house nude, or
barricading himself in the basement of his home against the people who were out
to get him). In all, his behaviors had been much more antisocial, paranoid, and
psychotic than had been evident at the time of initial assessment. During treatment, the patient suffered episodic regressions into a transference psychosis state,
during which the analyst (among other things) would sit the patient up and actively direct the associations away from material he felt the patient could not
handle.

Some of the misdiagnoses had some very special bases. In the case of the Housebound Phobic Woman, the acute, confusional barbiturate-intoxicated state in
which she came for treatment helped obscure for a long while the degree of *chronic*
organic brain damage that had been wrought by her 14 years of severe barbiturate
addiction; this then made ongoing trouble for her capacity for introspection, free
association, and so forth. With the Alcoholic Heir, the picture of the so-called
"success neurosis" served to obscure the intensely paranoid, megalomanic, and
near-psychotic character core that emerged in treatment. For example, he once
rummaged through some attic trunks and found "a jeweled ice pick," which he
brought to his analyst for safekeeping, fearful that his wife intended to use it on
him; another time, he asked the analyst's permission to hire a detective agency
to investigate whether his wife had purchased a gun to use against him. In the
case of the Adolescent Grandson, the initial presentation of a chronically unhappy, isolated, and inhibited youngster who had twice engaged in bizarrely out-of-
character activities served to cover over what he then "confessed" during the course
of the treatment—that his perverse exhibitionistic practices had been far more frequent (and far more ego-syntonic) than the two episodes initially indicated. At
the end of treatment, he again "confessed" to the hospital director that these same
practices had continued throughout the treatment and that he had never been able
to bring himself to discuss this in the therapy. He said he had been masturbating
in a lighted bedroom in full view of a young female neighbor across the street,
and had, on occasions when his foster parents were absent from the home, run
nude in the backyard or worn only a bathrobe that was flapping open. (Parenthetically, both the therapist and the hospital director were reluctant to believe these
termination confessions; they saw them as the patient's ambivalent expressions
of continuing illness and as a covert plea not to be allowed to terminate the treatment, which consciously he was vigorously trying to do.) And with the Suspended Medical Student, who was originally diagnosed in terms of a "dissociative reaction in a hysterical character neurosis," a kind of "professional countertransference"
(to be elaborated further on in connection with the story of this treatment) helped
keep from initial view—as well as from real exposure during the course of his psychoanalytic treatment—the full seriousness of his paranoid character, his alloplastic, impulse-ridden trends, and his major ego deformations.

These various issues of misdiagnosis, of course, led at times to overambitious treatment recommendations—for example, proposals for efforts at psychoanalysis with patients who then turned out to be clearly unsuitable for that treatment, unable to tolerate its rigors. The subsequent courses for such patients were of course variable. The alcoholic, depressed, and paranoid Script Writer went into psychoanalysis; when this proved totally untenable after 8 months (129 hours), she abruptly terminated her analytic treatment, with its regressive tugs which were so frightening to her, and stated the intention (never acted on) of going on in analytic treatment in her home town. She was aided in her pressure to rupture her treatment, in the face of her analyst's strong opposition, by her husband: She kept him in a state of constant emotional turmoil by flaunting a hospital romance (which made him fearful that he would lose her), by the ups and downs of her drinking, by her financial extravagances, and by a generally disordered life that taunted The Menninger Foundation's claims of the therapeutic usefulness of an imposed structure. The Alcoholic Raconteur, likewise severely alcoholic, as well as paranoidly and potentially psychotically organized, also went into psychoanalysis (though the research predictors felt it to be a totally improper treatment plan), spurning Alcoholics Anonymous (AA) and such efforts. When the recommended analysis indeed proved untenable after 2 years and 9 months (546 hours), he angrily broke off his treatment when the analyst, now fully cognizant of the initial overly optimistic assessment and of the inappropriateness of psychoanalysis, insisted on a conversion to a more supportive–expressive psychotherapeutic mode. In quitting, the patient declared that his treatment had to be psychoanalysis or nothing.

The Economist, on the other hand, continued his treatment under comparable circumstances. The crux of his case was, in fact, a major initial failure of assessment. He came to psychoanalysis because of "interpersonal difficulties," basically an apparent repetitive problem in working out enduring social–sexual relationships with women. He was initially diagnosed as an "obsessive–compulsive personality" who had on occasions lapsed into episodes of crippling obsessional indecision. In the process of a prolonged course in psychoanalysis, a much more flagrant psychopathology and ego weakness emerged. I have already indicated the array of withheld symptoms and behaviors that gradually surfaced within the treatment course (see p. 161). Ultimately, actual psychotic regressions took place. During such a phase, the patient once brought his mother, who was visiting him, to an analytic hour in order for her to meet the analyst; they had heard so very much about each other, and the patient felt that it would be very "important." The analyst tried without success to fathom the range of possible meanings in this intent. At the end of the hour, he finally agreed (reluctantly) to be introduced and went out to the waiting room with the patient. He and the mother shook hands and exchanged a few pleasantries about the weather. The next day, the patient came for his hour in a rage. That encounter had been the analyst's effort to seduce his mother, and that handshake had been the symbolic representation of the sexual contact that was promised. It was in the wake of this episode—coming after 6 years of analytic work—in which the patient "believed" with almost delusional intensity that the analyst was actually carrying on an affair with his mother, that the analyst undertook to shift the treatment modality from psychoanalysis to a supportive–expressive psychotherapy. The switch was uneventful, and the patient reconstituted over the succeeding years of psychotherapy to a compensated neurotic (predominantly obsessive–compulsive) ego organization, with a few sharply circumscribed inhibitions—partly in the area of work and more in the social–sexual sphere.

Two patients were examples of special kinds of diagnostic problems. The Bohemian Prep School Boy, who came to treatment at age 17, all along represented a diagnostic puzzle. One group viewed his disorder as a more than usually intense "adjustment reaction of adolescence," aggravated by his unstable and deviant family background (the eccentric artist father and the wealthy society mother, who between them each indulged the patient inordinately, while at the same time making him the focus of much of the parental conflict). Another group saw the patient as an overideational preschizophrenic on a decompensating course (e.g., he had a paranoid fear of looking into the mirror lest he not see himself). The clinical evaluation group held to the graver view (and the research evaluation group concurred), while the hospital staff, enthusiastically supported by the parents, held to the milder view. The psychotherapist took a somewhat vacillating stance between these two positions, and both the hospital treatment and the psychotherapy were played out within this ongoing controversy over the diagnostic understanding.

With Peter Pan, the diagnostic problem was different. Because of her clear-cut presenting history of a severe obsessive–compulsive character structure and illness, and the symptomatology of adolescent-onset eating disturbances reflected in alternating periodic anorexia and bulimia, she was readily assessed initially as a sufferer of "incipient anorexia nervosa in a decompensating obsessive–compulsive neurosis." It was also quite clear over the succeeding years of analytic treatment that an ever-graver picture was emerging—that of a profoundly infantile–narcissistic personality structure with massive fixations and conflicts at all psychosexual developmental levels. This ultimately progressed (in a retreatment situation that she got into during the period after her official Follow-Up Study) to a disorganizing psychotic process and a successful suicide by jumping off a bridge. The entire span of observation was 11 years: 3½ years of formal treatment, an official Follow-Up Study at the 6-year mark, and then the retreatment effort, starting at the 10-year mark and progressing to its doomed end not quite a year later. In overview, the diagnostic issue was not that of any initial misdiagnosis or underdiagnosis so much as a sequential unfolding of a progressively worsening clinical state, which was ultimately not influenceable (or at least not influenced) by all the therapeutic intervention.

MOTIVATION AND THE CONDITIONS
FOR TREATMENT

Motivation for treatment is universally regarded as one of the central determinants of treatment prospect, almost regardless of the theoretical persuasion of the therapist or of the manner of conceptualizing the factors determinative of therapeutic change. Within PRP from the beginning, issues of motivation were conceptualized as a major category of Patient Variables, and in our original formulation of Form B, the category of Motivational Factors was subdivided into four discrete variables: (1) Honesty, (2) Fee (meaning the psychological role that the fee and the responsibility for it would be expected to play in the treatment course), (3) Extent of

Desired Change, and (4) Secondary Gain (as a countermotivation).[2] Like so many of our other variables, these were reconceptualized in the crucible of our ongoing experience with their research utility, and these reconceptualizations were critically reviewed in a separate article by Ann Appelbaum (1972). Basically, her article dissected the issue of "motivation for what?". She proposed a threefold conceptualization—the wish to get help, the wish to continue the treatment, and the wish to change—and demonstrated the intricacy of both their intertwining and their variance one from another. She proposed that we may conventionally have cause and effect reversed, and that the real question is not one of *motivation* for change but rather that of the "capacity to change" (p. 57), which she felt to be "dependent upon something we could call ego strength, or 'general level of integrative psychological functioning', one aspect of which is the capacity to adapt to changed internal and external conditions by changing oneself" (p. 57).[3]

Degree of Inner–Outer Pressure for Change

In this present context, issues of motivation, as reflecting aspects of patient dispositions, are presented somewhat differently. At the first level, I consider the degree of pressure or duress (inner and outer) out of which the prospective patients came to The Menninger Foundation, granted the qualification adduced by A. Appelbaum that they could be coming with any combination of a variety of different and even discrepant purposes in mind. The 42 patients were divided into three approximately equal groups.

DEEP DESIRE FOR CHANGE

A group of 16, or close to 40% of the total (8 men and 8 women), came highly motivated—that is, deeply desirous of change. Some of these came despite substantial obstacles. For instance, The Economist entered psychoanalysis 5 days a week, willingly traveling 55 miles each way daily, commuting from his academic post in a university in another city. He undertook unquestionably to work out all problems of time and the commute, as well as the fee, which was not inconsiderable for him. Comparably, the Movie Lady undertook to do whatever her analytic treatment required, including car travel in defiance of her long-standing phobias. She indicated that she never quit anything she undertook (like the experience with her nurse's training); in addition, her guilts and masochistic proclivities drove her in

---

2. For the tabulation of the Patient Variables in this book, see Chapter 6, pp. 73–74. For the original extended discussion of the Patient Variables, see the "Concepts" article (Wallerstein & Robbins, 1956) in the first collection of articles published from PRP. Our way of conceptualizing the Motivational Factors at that time is detailed there on pp. 247–249.

3. A fuller quotation explicating A. Appelbaum's position on the issue of motivation for change is as follows:

"How much one 'wants' to change depends upon myriad learned attitudes concerning the desirability, the feasibility, the value of change as a goal to be striven for, or as a disaster to be escaped from. The more rigid, ineffectual and labored the equilibratory processes of the individual, the more will this be reflected in conscious attitudes against change, in fear of changed circumstances and in pessimism about or open resistance against change in one's self, as well as in unconscious mechanisms protecting against change and its attendant disorganizing experiences. (p. 58)

her treatment commitments. The Prince sought out academic employment in Topeka specifically for the purpose of obtaining analysis; he pledged his savings and his current income, and expressed a willingness to borrow, if necessary, toward that end. The English Professor had spent periods with five different therapists and hospital doctors over a 4-year span before finding his definitive psychoanalytic treatment at The Menninger Foundation. The push from within was at its extreme in Peter Pan, who propelled herself to a consultation with a physician of *her* choice while she was still in high school, and to psychiatric hospitalization and therapy at the point in college where her eating and stealing problems finally overwhelmed her. Yet the issue of the *kind* of motivation was very pertinent here: She desperately wanted to bring her uncontrollable impulses under control and to avoid the socially unacceptable behaviors that were consequent to her inability to control her cravings. It was not clear, however, that she wanted to alter in any way her desired state as a permanent Peter Pan, who would never grow to adult responsibilities.

Some of the patients had to overcome considerable opposition from others in order to reach their sought-for treatment. The Snake Phobia Woman had to overcome the objections of her family physician, who tried to dissuade her on the grounds that it was foolish and unnecessary. The Tantrum Woman wrote a desperate and pleading letter asking for psychiatric help, and then had to persuade her aunt to make all the practical arrangements and to accompany her as the responsible relative. The Masochistic Editor had to wage a real campaign to secure his treatment. It took him 4 years to talk his parents into bringing him to The Menninger Foundation, where they "should have brought" the brother who had so painfully committed suicide with strychnine. It was his playing on the parents' guilt in the wake of that death that finally secured their willingness to commit their modest resources (the father was a successful drugstore proprietor) to the needed treatment. But here, as in other cases, the patient's motivational picture was indeed mixed. First, he was quite happy that the parents *should* use their modest savings to underwrite the treatment of the psychic damages that were, after all, their doing. Beyond that, within the treatment, the patient's conscious motivational push was quite circumscribed. He wanted very much to overcome his general ineffectualness in life and his uncontrolled drinking. About his homosexuality, things were not that clear: He seemed to regard it as a physiological given, something he wanted help to live with more comfortably. And at an unconscious level, there was the strong push to use the analysis to perpetuate an infantile and masochistic dependency upon the analyst.

Lastly, some of the patients were aided in their strong motivational push. The Obese Woman was urged on by her psychoanalytically minded husband, who indeed fancied himself heading for a psychoanalytic career. The Obedient Husband, who was seeing a case worker in connection with his wife's treatment, was helped in that context to move toward a treatment decision for himself. And one patient should be specially mentioned for the particular quasi-religious quality of his motivation: The Alcoholic Raconteur, an individual of great intellectualizing pretensions, came to treatment disdaining AA and seeking psychoanalysis, which to him would place him in a state of grace comparable to giving himself up to almighty God—a view of analysis as an expression of magical intake and faith healing.

PASSIVE WILLINGNESS FOR TREATMENT

Another 14 (one-third) of the patients (6 men and 8 women) fell into a less motivated category: They were willing, but passively so. For example, the Adoptive Mother came willingly and was distressed enough, but she hoped that The Menninger Foundation would concur with a recommendation made elsewhere for carbon dioxide inhalation therapy, instead of talking therapy. The Phobic Girl came in response to a referral initiated by a college psychology instructor after the instructor read an autobiography in which the patient revealed the existence of her multiple phobias; similarly, the Actress came in response to a referral by the dean of her college, who was concerned about her school and behavior difficulties. Several patients, like the Alcoholic Doctor, came in compliance with family persuasion: The Medical Scientist came only when convinced by his father that his self-help methods of overcoming his alcoholism and addiction had each time failed, and the Claustrophobic Man had to be gently but insistently persuaded by his wife, in concert with the family physician, that psychiatric treatment was what he needed. The Adolescent Grandson was passively compliant with police-initiated pressures that the grandfather do something about him to forestall legal action in connection with his arrest for exhibitionism and public masturbation. Characteristically, the grandfather himself refused to be involved personally (he was preparing for his forthcoming fourth marriage — at age 70), so all arrangements were handled by the grandfather's private secretary. The stepmother was allowed to come along at the time of admission, but she had been shut out of all the planning. She was helplessly resentful about this, guilty that she hadn't even been able to talk over the pending psychiatric hospitalization with her stepson, and fearful that he might feel she was deserting him.

A few others came in even more passively collapsed straits. For example, the Car Salesman had just made a serious suicide attempt, emptying the medicine cabinet of all the barbiturates he found there (26 pills), which had rendered him unconscious for 24 hours. The Housebound Phobic Woman was brought by her father in a state of acute and chronic barbiturate intoxication, with tremors, ataxia, failed memory, and confused thinking. And the Invalided Hypochondriac came in what can only be described as a state of complete neurasthenic, multiply somatized, collapse. At initial consultation she cried uncontrollably for the entire hour.

COERCION NECESSARY FOR TREATMENT

A third group of 12, not quite 30% of the total (7 men and 5 women), had to be coerced into evaluation and treatment. Some of these patients were under extreme pressure (from outside agencies). For example, the Addicted Doctor had finally had his medical license revoked, and psychiatric treatment was held out as the only possible road to its restoration; the Suspended Medical Student was dropped from medical school as a result of his unethical behaviors in the fugue state, and he likewise knew that only psychiatric treatment offered a chance for him to resume his medical career. In the same vein, the Rebellious Coed had been put on both academic and disciplinary probation by her college dean for her misbehaviors, with psychiatric treatment again being offered as the only road to a possible return to college. And also along this line, the Bohemian Prep School Boy was withdrawn from his exclusive prep school at the request of the headmaster and pressed into the psychiatric evaluation that neither the patient nor his parents felt to be really necessary.

With other patients, the coercive pressures toward treatment came from within the family. The Phobic Woman came because the cozy arrangement she and the parents had worked out to comply with the phobias — "buying" (and fully supporting) the husband — was finally collapsing: The husband was threatening divorce if something were not done quickly to drastically alter the patient's symptoms and their demands upon him. Others of the patients, who on the surface came to treatment much more willingly (some even in the so-called high-motivation group), likewise were trying to fight off a lurking threat of divorce. (With the highly motivated Divorced Nurse, the divorce came anyway — as soon as the husband was satisfied that he had done enough for the patient in having her hospitalized and in psychoanalytic treatment far from home.) The Exhibitionistic Dancer was brought by her parents after she had been expelled from college; they declared that they could no longer cope with her immaturity and rebelliousness, or her constant involvements with undesirable companions in antisocial behaviors and in Bohemian atmospheres. The patient made it clear that it was her parents' idea that she come, that she saw her troubles as centering around her "inconsistent parents," and that what she needed was emancipation from their domineering and unsympathetic presence. The Alcoholic Heir came only in response to multiple family pressures — from his parents and his wife. According to him, they were "unnecessarily" concerned about his drinking. He ran home from the recommended treatment, promptly got drunk, and was contritely brought back. The changes this patient saw as indicated were in others — the family company which had treated him unfairly; the family members, who didn't understand; and so on.

With the Sexual Masochist, the external pressures were further escalated. He had first undertaken psychotherapy some 2 years before his initial presentation at The Menninger Foundation, under his wife's insistence that he finally do something about his "sexual problem" (accompanied by threats of divorce if he didn't). He finally let himself be brought to hospitalization in Topeka after an embarrassing episode while visiting his mother over the Christmas holidays, when he got drunk and called a "loose" cousin, asking if he might come over to see her. She refused to allow him to come, but he drank some more and drove over anyway. He climbed up the house wall and into her bedroom, and then asked her, "Would you urinate on a cat?"; following this, he fainted. When he came to, he found his cousin, his wife, and his mother standing over him, after which "the whole town knew about it." This brought him finally to The Menninger Foundation.

The most extreme case of coercion, of course, was that of the Sociopath. His father had just had to assume his cataclysmic indebtedness of more than $100,000 (most of it owed to loan sharks, or as restitution for embezzlements), and he was fleeing both criminal prosecution and legal disbarment proceedings. His family, his creditors, the police, and the underworld were all after him; the psychiatric hospital was his only possible haven.

Extent of Secondary Gains

Another and wholly different aspect or level of the motivation for treatment had to do with the kind and extent of secondary gains that these patients had evolved during the course of their generally chronic and deep-seated illness structures. Again, they broke into three relatively equal groups.

NO SECONDARY GAINS

A group of 16, or about 40% of the total (7 men and 9 women), had essentially no secondary gains from their illnesses, which brought them only trouble. Surprisingly, this group included one of the severely alcoholic and addicted patients, the Medical Scientist, who had managed to contain his illness within himself (including his do-it-yourself cure efforts) and to maintain an excellent record and reputation in his medical practice. The patient had throughout his illness only hurt himself and cost himself. And with another of this group, the Obedient Husband, there seemed even a reversal of the usual illness effects. His "psychiatric illness" and his accepting the psychiatric social worker's referral for psychotherapy stemmed from the threatened loss of the (primary and/or secondary?) gains of his previously passively obedient adjustment to his neurotic wife's demandingness, in which his hold on her had been through her need to have him cater to her. With the loosening of their neurotic equilibrium over the course of the wife's treatment, the patient feared he would no longer be needed in the same old neurotic ways—and would thus lose the rewards of their neurotic interaction; the gratifications of his masochism; the maintained image of an amiable, even-tempered, and good-natured man beset by extremely difficult life circumstances but bearing up admirably under them; the release from all expectations that he do otherwise with his life, considering its burdens; and so on. He had become anxious and resentful that he might lose his hold on her.

MILD TO MODERATE SECONDARY GAINS

Another group of 11 patients, or a little over 25% of the sample (7 men and 4 women), had the "usual" kinds of mild to moderate secondary gains that accompany reasonably severe symptom neuroses and character neuroses. Two of these cases are illustrative of the group. For instance, the Snake Phobia Woman's home and family, in an organized effort to ward off her crying spells, had begun to revolve more around her and her neurosis, thus reducing the demands upon her for normal coping behaviors. Or, more elaborately, it was quite clear with the Adolescent Grandson that only through the bizarre episodes of the seemingly out-of-character nude scampering across the grandfather's estate could he really elicit the concerted and shared concern of his otherwise distant and warring grandfather and stepmother.

HIGH SECONDARY GAINS

There was a group of 15, or 35% of the sample (7 men and 8 women), for whom the secondary gains of the illness (at times intermingled with the primary gains in ways difficult to distinguish) were extremely high and posed serious potential barriers to treatment progress. This group included many of the intensely alcoholic and addicted (most of this subgroup were men), but also included many of the generally acting-out and behaviorally disturbed, as well as one intensely phobic patient (most of this subgroup were women). An extreme case of high secondary gains was that of the Phobic Woman. Her whole intensely phobic illness and life, in which she had successively ruled her parents and then her husband, was almost completely ego-syntonic. She very willfully used her illness to tie people to her and to dominate them, and she openly recognized this and referred to her illness as the "only asset" that she could count on to get her anyplace. Up until the point at which the husband endangered this neurotic equilibrium by his threat of divorce if the patient did not drastically reduce the pressures on him, she had felt no urge to seek treatment at all. She had been able, to that point, to have an environment accommodating enough to try to provide her with total infantile nurture; now that she was driven to treatment by the threat of loss of that secondary gain, she would no doubt look to the prospective analysis itself for a continuance of the same care and succor.

Almost equal in its extreme quality was the situation of the Bohemian Musician. She had been able for years to maintain a life in which she amused herself with her equally arty lover amidst the cultural and musical life of the big city, while her husband compliantly supported her and their adopted son from his "home in the cornfield" in a distant city. It was only when the husband, after 5 years of separate living, put ultimatum-like pressure on the patient to return home or be divorced, and she could not decide upon marrying her lover, that she felt she had to return home. This collapse of the whole structure of her secondary gains precipitated the patient's drastic symptomatic decline into the acutely disorganized state that led to her psychiatric hospitalization.

And to round out a trio of bizarrely extreme situations, the Rebellious Coed, beset by her severe difficulties in getting along with people and her acutely depressive response to her mother's death, came to a treatment recommendation for an intensive psychotherapy that would happily (from her perspective) bend her entire family to her requirements. The father was a skilled laborer with a very modest income. Before coming to treatment, the patient had been (quite extravagantly) using up more than half of his earnings in living expenses and going to college. The whole family—the father and the two siblings—wanted to do this: to give the patient (at whatever sacrifice) the college education that no one else in the family had had. Now the expenses of treatment and a car to commute to it would be superimposed. How this could be managed at all was not clear, but the patient saw her father's uncertainty as stinginess. The elder brother and sister were both horrified at this interaction. They saw the patient as having advantages and opportunities that neither of them had had, as having everything that the father could provide made available to her, and as spitefully failing to appreciate any of this or to make any constructive use of it.

Among the seven men in this group with very high secondary gains were six who were extremely alcoholic and/or drug-addicted (the Alcoholic Raconteur, the Alcoholic Doctor, the Addicted Doctor, the Car Salesman, the Sexual Masochist, and the Masochistic Editor); several of these had open perversions, and four of them were from among the more affluent families. Their particular combination of blatant and destructive symptomatology, together with sustaining family resources for many, enabled them to live out a comparable pattern of secondary gain. Each in a way could be said to be typical of these kinds of secondary gains "commonly" secured by such pathologically acting-out characters. For example, the Alcoholic Doctor had succeeded in abdicating totally all responsibilities for work, home, and family. His 70-year-old father, on the verge of retirement and clearly aging (his forgetfulness and carelessness had gotten him into two automobile accidents within the last year, both of which had been his fault), had now to continue in medical practice, raise the four grandchildren, and provide for the patient's very expensive treatment. The patient readily took to his hospital treatment, while his equally irresponsible and almost equally alcoholic physician wife promptly moved to a distant city to pursue her medical specialty training, ostensibly on her doctor's "advice." The Alcoholic Raconteur succeeded equally in bending reality to fit the pressures of his illness, even to getting his father to move out of the family home into his club downtown in order to preserve the family peace and avoid confrontations with his son, who would get so "crazy drunk" and threaten to kill him.

Two other patients, not specifically among the group of alcoholic–addictive men, nonetheless had secured quite comparable situations of secondary gain. The Sociopath had pursued his destructive, sadistic, wildly extravagant, and profligate ways, always secure in the knowledge that his father would save him; the father did so dramatically, in the end, by spending his whole fortune to cover the patient's bad debts, embezzlements, and underworld and loan shark payments. Conceptually, it might be difficult here to separate the secondary gains from the primary gains in this extremely severe characterological disorder, organized around such untrammeled impulse expression and gratification. The Invalided Hypochondriac was quite comparable to the Sociopath in the intertwining of the primary and the secondary gains of her illness, though the symptomatic expression was different (i.e., her invalided hypochondriacal collapse). The husband had long been used to the total care of the house, the two very young children, himself, and his wife, who could no nothing but lie in bed and cry all day but did have the "amazing ability" (to her husband) to pull herself together to go out to an evening social engagement.

Complexity of "Motivation"

The following points about motivation should be abundantly clear by now:

1. "Motivation" in relation to therapy, and to the possibilities for change through therapy, is a complex cluster of dispositions with varying components, among them those delineated in our Form B Patient Variables.

2. It ranges widely in the nature and the valence of those component aspects, as the foregoing case vignettes illustrate.

3. It is of various kinds (cf. A. Appelbaum's tripartite division into the wish to get help, the wish to continue the treatment, and the wish to change).

4. It can operate at both fully conscious and dynamically unconscious levels, with the two at times in flagrant opposition (e.g., the conscious motivation to be unburdened of painful neurotic symptoms and behaviors, and the unconscious motivation to perpetuate the living out of the same neurotic interactions with the more benevolently caring and nurturing or idealized and messianic figure of the analyst).

5. It can differ between the patient and the concerned responsible family members (e.g., a rebellious adolescent may want help in emancipating himself or herself

from unsympathetic and oppressive parents, while the parents, who are paying for the treatment, want their wayward child restored to the obedient youngster he or she once was before falling on bad ways or in with bad company).

6. Lastly, it can itself change during the course of the treatment, either constricting and diminishing or enlarging and intensifying. (This was a major point in the A. Appelbaum article.)

The assessment of all of this is indeed complex, both at the time of initial clinical evaluation, and in its changing facets and its changing extent over the course of the subsequent therapy. It seems therefore oversimplified to look at motivation as a single, unidimensional, and fixed element, which conduces to positive outcomes when it is adjudged overall as high, and raises serious questions when it is contrariwise adjudged as low. Certainly, in our own sample of 42, more of those who ultimately did poorly in their treatments clustered among the so-called "least motivated" (those more or less coerced into treatment). This phenomenon, however, clearly might reflect many factors or Patient Variables involved in the nature and severity of the patients' illnesses, and it is also true that at least one of the best treatment successes of the PRP sample (the Phobic Woman) was also in that least motivated group.

Particular Problems for Assessment and Treatment

Additional points to be considered under the heading of "Motivation and the Conditions for Treatment" are a variety of traits of this (or any) patient population that do (or can) create particular problems for the treatment.

VERBAL CAPACITY AND WILLINGNESS

Since psychotherapy is quintessentially an activity of verbal interchange and verbal understanding, issues of verbal capacity and willingness became central to the conduct of the enterprise. By this I do not mean only intelligence as measured by an IQ test, although at least average intellectual capacity is of course a necessary underpinning to the effort.[4] In PRP IQ was not an issue, since our whole sample was in the intellectually superior range (a mean IQ of 124 and a range of 111–141 at the point of initial clinical evaluation). There were, however, some significant variations among the patients in regard to general articulateness—or, rather, a state of characteristic relative inarticulateness versus its opposite, an easy glibness of intellectual or intellectualizing thought processes.

Inarticulateness. Actually, with 4 of the 42 patients, specific note was made during the initial evaluation of their surprising inarticulateness; this group included one physician with a strongly academic background (the Medical Scientist) and one physician-in-training (the Suspended Medical Student). The Medical Scien-

---

4. I do not want to digress here into the issue of the kind of psychotherapeutic work that can be done with the less well intellectually endowed (the various degrees of the retarded) and their emotional difficulties. Suffice it to say here that for the purposes of this research project, such patients (and the special psychotherapeutic issues that they pose) were deliberately excluded from consideration.

tist was paradigmatic of the group. Though clearly extremely well endowed intellectually (IQ of 138), the possessor of both an M.D. and a Ph.D., and the recipient of honors and scholarships, he was at the same time quite inarticulate and unreflective about things psychological and about his relationship to himself. His insights at initial evaluation were extremely limited. He simply saw himself as unaccountably ill (with his alcoholism, his drug addiction, and his proneness to violent behaviors), and made no connection between his disordered behaviors and any other aspects of his life experience, except on the most superficial level of talking about the excessive demands of a busy medical practice which could result in irritable tensions and lead to drink. He did not try to rationalize away his difficulties; he simply did not undertake to try to explain them. In other words, he showed no evidence at this point of psychological-mindedness. (Psychological-Mindedness was another of the relevant Patient Variables; see p. 74.) In keeping with this were the patient's own prior efforts to handle his illness by the exertion of willpower (holing up in hotel rooms for his painful withdrawal efforts) rather than by any attempt to think things through and come to understand them. And when he came finally to psychiatric treatment at The Menninger Foundation, he was in the middle group I have designated as "passively willing" (when his self-help efforts all failed and his father talked him into this turn to psychiatric help).

In terms of the initial predictions for the Medical Scientist's subsequent analysis, it was thought that this psychological inarticulateness, plus his general characteristic reticence, would pose specific treatment difficulties and would certainly limit the kind and range of insights explicitly achieved. Actually, it did not work out that way: This analysis turned out to be one of the outstandingly successful ones in our series. The patient achieved, along with massive behavior changes, a significant range of analytic insights—into the true nature of his relationship with his parents, particularly the competitive feelings toward the medical scientist father, the distorted ways in which he had previously dealt with these, and why he had done so; into his homosexual strivings and the feelings connected with passive "feminine" wishes and passivity in general; into his sexual functioning and the forces responsible for his promiscuity and his sexual disability; and into the nature of his object choices, so that these could be appropriately altered. The patient spoke in his Termination interviews about having achieved two basic requirements for growing up: (1) to learn to share; and (2) to develop the capacity to wait—to tolerate the attendant pain, frustration, or anxiety, and to be able to sit still and not jump into action.

Obviously not all these cases worked out so well. The comparable initial inarticulateness and seeming lack of psychological-mindedness of the Suspended Medical Student, with the whole trend of his defensive organization toward the inhibition of psychological thinking and of making psychological connections, did not really alter through the course of his subsequent psychoanalysis, and no doubt played its role in his ultimate total treatment failure. As an example from his case, on a day almost exactly 4 years after the fugue state that had led to his initial suspension from medical school, he had an accident with his brand-new car, in which he rounded a blind corner with insufficient care and was hit by another car. His car was completely demolished, but the patient himself miraculously escaped unscathed. He was momentarily terribly shaken by this continuing evidence of his "self-destructiveness." When the subsequent trial officially exonerated him of responsibility, he marked the event as "just an accident" and dismissed any further thoughts about psychological determinants and meanings. Similarly, the Obedient Husband, with a more middling therapeutic outcome, was both inarticulate and underideational. When advised to alter his stance vis-à-vis his wife, he undertook to do so without reasoning or integrating, just on the basis of his respect for knowledgeable authority.

The fourth in this group, the Housebound Phobic Woman, was in a somewhat different situation. Her limited ability to free-associate, to make psychological connections, turned out to be a reflection of the degree of chronic brain damage sustained in her 14-year chronic barbiturate addiction. This limitation (which was not as clear initially, when so much was ascribed to the aftermath of the acutely drug-intoxicated state in which she came to hospitalization) necessitated a real shift in the therapeutic approach, from an effort at psychoanalysis to a much more sustaining supportive psychotherapeutic mode.

Glibness. The opposite problem to this inarticulateness is a verbal glibness linked to easy intellectualizing or formula creating. A total of six of the patients had this difficulty. With two of them, the Car Salesman and the Addicted Doctor (both of whom were alcoholic and drug-addicted), this was manifested in the easy substitution of verbal clichés for thoughtfulness. For example, the Addicted Doctor would offer easy clichés as insights designed to explain to himself what he was doing—or, even more, to find people (e.g., his parents) to blame for his plight, thus giving him some false degree of comfort. These offerings had the value of being partially and superficially quite true, enough so that they served their defensive purpose of covering up the more painful, fuller truth.

The other four patients in this group were more fully intellectual people. For example, with the very psychologically willing and verbal English Professor, a specific problem for his psychoanalysis was predicted to be that insights would outstrip effective translation into action and would serve instead, to a significant extent, as a vehicle for continued passive compliance. In this sense, there might always be a wider range of insights revealed within the analytic situation than would ever become manifest in behavioral consequences. And it worked out that way: Within the context of an overall satisfactorily improved state at the end of his treatment, the patient nonetheless emerged with a storehouse of undigested (in the sense of unapplied) intellectual insights. With the Intellectual Fencer (her physician brother, with whom she had always competed, had been a world-class fencer), who was in the very superior intellectual range (IQ of 138), much of her treatment (as well as the resistances in it) was in the nature of a competitive intellectual dueling—she was called aptly "a fencer of the intellect."

With both the Masochistic Editor and the Bohemian Prep School Boy, the issue of glibness was even more extreme. The Bohemian Prep School Boy had been both incredibly indulged and precociously exhibited; (he had been fussed over at elegant society cocktail parties starting as a 2-year-old). His whole life of turbulent interpersonal relationships had always been set within the context of his precocity and brilliance. He was always angling to garner attention and admiration by dazzling and overwhelming others with his erudition (e.g., the examination allegory about the behavior of bedbugs in the bathtub). This, combined with his tendency to think about people in terms of philosophical rather than motivational categories, created a readily apparent problem for an insight-aiming psychotherapy. The Masochistic Editor was similar. His chief stock in trade was his intellectuality and pretentiousness, turned to the service of his narcissistic enhancement in victories over others.

SILENCES AND EMOTIONAL OUTBURSTS

Quite a bit beyond these problems of verbal reticence or glibness for treatment and the character traits linked with them was another set of more "pathological" or extreme dispositions (and problems for psychological treatment)—silences and their opposite, inundation by emotional or affective storms. With 2 of our 42 patients, silences during treatment (analysis in each case) were a major problem. One of these was the Devoted Son, in psychoanalysis for 5½ years (1030 hours). His prolonged silences were a major technical problem for this modestly successful treatment. Many meanings were adduced for them through the course of the treatment effort. They were seen as reflecting the following:

1. A deliberate delaying of speech in order to force the analyst to intervene decisively (and helpfully).
2. The patient's unworthiness to speak—he was "grubby, cheap, unimportant."
3. An identification with the mother, who would sit silently, dreamy-eyed, staring off into space when they visited together on weekends.
4. An identification with the unlettered, stupid father, who could only have mundane thoughts not worth uttering, or hostile, rejecting thoughts that were better not uttered.
5. Revengeful rage against the inquiring mother (analyst), whose milk was watery and did nothing for him, as well as the ineffectual father, who neither protected him against the mother nor compensated for her.
6. Occasionally, recognizable direct transference thoughts, reflecting a varying mixture of sexual and aggressive interest in the analyst, dependency, disparagement, and so on. There was often a pouting, carping, sour-grapes, hypercritical attitude in the silence, verbalized finally as "I hate the whole damn world."

Despite all of this, the silences were never really analytically worked through and overcome. The patient never felt a free flow of communication. "I wish I had been more open, able to talk more freely—it wasn't his fault." On other occasions, instead of silence, there was bitter weeping—usually without mental content, other than a diffuse bitterness at the whole world.

The other silent patient, the Silent Woman, lasted in analysis only 1 year (228 hours), at which point she unexpectedly and abruptly disrupted her treatment. The silences in this case were even more of a problem. On one occasion early in treatment, after a weekend visit to her family in another state, the patient drove some 500 miles through a storm at unsafe speeds in order to get to her hour on time; she came in saying, "Whew, I made it," only to lapse promptly into a prolonged silence. In his interventions, the analyst focused on the silences mainly as resistances, in their negative aspects. According to the supervisor, he often made "unfounded suppositions about the silences, such as giving guesses and using gimmicks to get her to talk." The analyst himself, in retrospect, felt that he concentrated too one-sidedly on the negative aspects of this transference resistance, and that this was perceived by the patient as cold criticism and only intensified her negativistic counterstruggle in the form of taut, provocative remarks.

At least four of the patients, all within the group of roughly hysterical–phobic, depressed, and anxious women — the Tantrum Woman, the Divorced Nurse, the Snake Phobia Woman, and the Movie Lady — demonstrated the very opposite problem of being subject to sweeps of unmanageable affect, or "affect storms." The Tantrum Woman can be taken as paradigmatic of the group. She had repeated episodes of torrential affective outpourings during the analytic hours, which inundated all reasonable and reasoning processes in the patient, and which served less as abreactive discharge processes than as defensive barriers against hearing either herself or her analyst. When waiting them out seemed fruitless, and when interpretation of meaning alone was lost in the absence at the moment of cooperating ego, the analyst began to intervene firmly — not simply via a command to stop emoting, but with a firm and insistent reminder that he was present to listen to her: "Just a minute! There's no need to shout. I'm listening." To the patient, this marked the turning point of her ultimately successful treatment: "For the first year and a half I didn't feel I was getting anywhere. At the time he started yelling back, that was the first big turning point. He said, 'Shut up.' I needed someone to shut me up. I needed it then. . . . Before that I was running wild and he was letting me. Now I felt there was someone who would help me and not let me run wild. . . . someone was there who was interested." Clearly, both profound silences and massive verbal outpourings can pose major treatment problems — and can also be dealt with, with more or less success.

TABULATION OF THE PATIENTS

The relevant patient variables listed in Section II (see Chapter 6, pp. 73–74) comprised 28 factors, each deemed relevant to the proper understanding of the patient and the proper planning of the treatment. They have not all been individually covered in Section III. For example, among those not here specifically separately considered and illustrated through clinical vignettes are such variables as Anxiety Tolerance, Insight, Externalization, and Ego Strength. Some of these emerged as critical factors in the assessments of course and outcome in the write-ups of the results of the Prediction Study (Horwitz, 1974) and the quantitative studies (Kernberg *et al.*, 1972). Here, I have rather sought to describe the patients in terms of their crucial characteristics from the standpoint of clinical write-up and clinical accounting, and my selections of characteristics and my categorizations have been made accordingly.

In closing this chapter and this section, I want, in final summary, to list the patients by the title designations I am using throughout this book (in the numbered order that corresponds to their designations by number in the Voth and Orth [1973] book), and by the overall summary diagnostic statement arrived at for each one during the Initial Study. (I must, of course, add the caveat that these summary diagnoses were all subject to the issues of misdiagnosis and underdiagnosis that have already been discussed and that come more sharply into focus during the descriptions of the treatment courses.)

  1. Silent Woman—mixed character neurosis with hysterical and obsessive-compulsive features (and symptomatic chronic depression and anxiety).
  2. Car Salesman—narcissistic character disorder with severe alcoholism.
  3. Addicted Doctor—infantile personality manifested by intense infantile demandingness, inability to tolerate frustration or to delay instinct gratification, self-destructive behavior, multiple addictions, somatizations, and polymorphous perverse sexual behavior and fantasy.
  4. Claustrophobic Man—anxiety–hysteria in a passive–dependent personality, with premorbidly a compensated equilibrium with an effective life functioning.
  5. Adoptive Mother—hysterical character neurosis, with an admixture of obsessive–compulsive elements.
  6. Snake Phobia Woman—anxiety–hysteria in a mixed hysterical and compulsive character neurosis (phobic–obsessional illness).
  7. Script Writer—passive–aggressive personality disturbance with manifest alcoholism.
  8. Invalided Hypochondriac—infantile personality disorder, with severe hypochondriasis, and some addictive tendency.
  9. Bohemian Musician—narcissistic character neurosis with oral-infantile, sadomasochistic, and hysterical components.
  10. Intellectual Fencer—narcissistic personality with barbiturate addiction.
  11. Divorced Nurse—hysterical character neurosis with strong infantile, oral-narcissistic components.
  12. Tantrum Woman—hysterical character neurosis with a recent superimposed reactive depression of traumatic onset.
  13. Bohemian Prep School Boy—overideational preschizophrenia.
  14. Rebellious Coed—mixed character neurosis, with predominant sadomasochistic, obsessive–compulsive, and narcissistic features.
  15. English Professor—anxiety–hysteria in a compulsive, compliant personality.
  16. Alcoholic Heir—success neurosis with symptomatic severe alcoholism in a passive–compliant personality.
  17. Obedient Husband—depressive reaction in a passive–dependent personality.
  18. Prince—narcissistic character neurosis.
  19. Exhibitionistic Dancer—narcissistic character disorder.
  20. Suspended Medical Student—dissociative reaction in a hysterical character neurosis.
  21. Homesick Psychology Student—immature personality.
  22. Sociopath—antisocial personality.
  23. Peter Pan—incipient anorexia nervosa in a decompensating obsessive–compulsive neurosis.
  24. Devoted Son—obsessive–compulsive character neurosis.
  25. Adolescent Grandson—inhibited character.
  26. Medical Scientist—compulsive character neurosis with alcoholism and drug addiction.

27. Alcoholic Raconteur—overideational preschizophrenia with symptomatic severe alcoholism.

28. Obese Woman—mixed psychoneurosis, with predominant sadomasochistic, compulsive, and, to a lesser extent, hysterical trends (with symptomatic severe obesity).

29. Actress—narcissistic character disorder, of the "as-if" character type, with symptomatic alcoholism, confabulation, and sexual difficulties, heterosexual and homosexual.

30. Manic–Depressive Physician—schizo-affective disorder.

31. Heiress—obsessive–compulsive character neurosis with prominent masochistic components.

32. Phobic Woman—phobic reaction in an oral-infantile character neurosis.

33. Alcoholic Doctor—passive–dependent personality with manifest alcoholism, drug addiction, and homosexual activity.

34. Bitter Spinster—hysterical character neurosis.

35. Movie Lady—phobic reaction in a mixed neurosis with compulsive, hysterical, and masochistic elements.

36. Sexual Masochist—schizophrenic character with masochistic sexual perversion and severe alcoholism.

37. Fearful Loner—schizoid personality.

38. Phobic Girl—infantile personality with strong narcissistic trends, obesity, multiple phobias, perverse sexuality.

39. Masochistic Editor—infantile character, with manifest oral dependency, sadomasochism, alcoholism, and homosexuality.

40. Economist—obsessive–compulsive personality.

41. Housebound Phobic Woman—infantile personality with oral-addictive and phallic-hysterical components.

42. Involutional Woman—involutional depression in a compulsive personality.

IV

The Treatments and Their Characteristics

Treatment Modality: Plans and Changes

The original intent of PRP was to follow the treatment careers of a typical sample of Menninger Foundation patients in psychoanalysis and in long-term expressive and supportive psychoanalytically based psychotherapy, in order to learn more about the changes that can (empirically) be expected to take place and the basis for those changes. Though we planned on an equal number in psychoanalysis proper and in psychoanalytic psychotherapy, the intent was never to compare psychoanalysis with psychotherapy. Patients presumed comparable were *not* randomly assigned to these two major treatment modes in order to try to see which mode did better, and in what ways, with which kinds of patients.

Rather, in keeping with the naturalistic spirit and naturalistic design of PRP, each modality had assigned to it those patients for whom it was deemed the specifically appropriate treatment method (in terms of the clinical knowledge and the clinical practice of the 1950s); therefore, different kinds of patients (in terms of illness structure) were recommended for psychoanalysis and psychotherapy. Comparisons were then made internally: Each planned treatment and predicted outcome was compared with itself, in terms of reaching, falling short of, or exceeding the expectations for it.

For reasons already stated in detail, the total sample size accumulated over a 4-year period of doing Initial Studies was 42. Inadvertently it worked out that 22 patients (10 men and 12 women) were designated for psychoanalysis and 20 (11 men and 9 women) were designated for psychotherapy.

PSYCHOANALYSIS

Classical Analysis with Minimal Modifications

Of the 22 who started in psychoanalysis, with 10 (4 men and 6 women) the analyst adhered throughout, as much as possible, to an effort at classical analysis. There were, even with these, some departures from the classical procedure—"minimal" within the context of that group of quite sick patients within that setting, though obviously they would be seen as more consequential with the more usual (less sick) psychoanalytic population in the usual private practice outpatient setting. For example, 2 of these 10 were concomitantly hospitalized—the Script Writer for the first 2½ months of her treatment, and the Alcoholic Heir intermittently through the whole year of his analytic work. In both instances, however, the analyst endeavored to maintain the classical analytic situation unaltered within the analytic hours. The Tantrum Woman, already described, was given to "affect storms"; the analyst "handled" these by an implied interdiction, a directive that the patient "stop, look, and listen." The patient experienced this as his "yelling back," and she marked it as the positive turning point of the treatment, since the analyst had finally demonstrated his concern and his interest in her.

With the Snake Phobia Woman, who had the problem of a "weekend marriage"—living in Topeka during the week and at home in another city on weekends—the analytic frequency was reduced to four and then to three times weekly during the last year in order to give her longer weekends at home with her family. The Devoted Son's analyst pushed this kind of terminating process more steeply and more deliberately. Because of a "cloying dependency" that the analyst felt could not be satisfactorily resolved analytically, he undertook to terminate the patient gradually via a weaning process of having him sit up, and then systematically reducing the frequency and finally the duration of the sessions. The patient was unhappy and resentful over this. He felt that he was being shoved out of treatment (it lasted 5½ years, 1030 hours), and that the analyst was only cutting down on him because he complained too much; he insisted that he had no one else to talk to, and that was why he needed the time as much as he did. The analyst, for his part, felt that the termination was overdue and that this imposed weaning process was the only way he could draw the curtain on an unresolved (or unresolvable) dependency transference. In the case of the Divorced Nurse, the reality pressures of her husband's suing her for divorce and for the custody of the children in their distant home state led to many irregular and quite sudden treatment absences to visit with the husband and/or the children. For the most part, these were unauthorized, and at times were undiscussed. Except when she went home for the official court appearance during the divorce proceedings, the patient was always charged for these missed hours and paid without question. Meanwhile the analyst was trying to conduct an analysis.

The last patient to be mentioned here from this group is the Suspended Medical Student, whose situation was quite different from those of all the others. From the start of his treatment, there was evidence of a more disruptive anxiety and a more serious characterological illness with greater ego deformation—marked by poor impulse control and by self-destructive, alcoholic, promiscuous, and assaultive behaviors—than had been initially forecast. The patient was also desperately looking for life-giving advice that would promptly dispel his anxieties and resolve his problems, and throughout the long initial phase of the analysis, the analyst was often directly supportive of the patient's reality-oriented controls and cautiously withholding of interpretive effort. Yet, despite these sharp cautions, the analyst (who was a candidate in the Topeka Institute for Psychoanalysis and wanted this case to "count" toward fulfillment of Institute requirements) wanted to make the case as fully analytic as possible; he also felt under pressure from the supervisor to be more, rather than less, analytic and interpretive in his efforts to cope with the patient's impulse-ridden character. Out of this balancing of pressures, a treatment situation evolved that at the beginning was more cautiously analytic, and later on, more fully analytic.

"Modified" Analysis

With another six of the patients in analysis (three men and three women), the analysis was more significantly "modified" through a variety of alterations or parameters, but was still adjudged to be essentially analysis, albeit with modifications. In the case of the Adoptive Mother, the modifications were explicitly a matter of the analytic supervisor's theoretical position. He was an adherent of Wilhelm Reich, and under his aegis the analysis was specifically modified in the direction of a "defense analysis," in which major attention was paid to the formal aspects of the communication process in its defensive and resistance meanings, rather than to the interpretation of content meanings. Corollary to this was the giving of the basic rule of analysis in terms of *permission* to say whatever came to mind, rather than in terms of a *contract* to attempt to do so. The analyst clearly was restive under this regimen, and, as much as he felt able, he cautiously broadened the scope of his interpretive work in a more "classical" direction. He was able to do so quite fully after a switch in supervisors, which occurred during the termination phase of the work with the patient. At that time the problem confronting the analysis was the husband's and the patient's own pressures toward termination, and the analytic interpretations were consistently directed at the meaning of the patient's controlling behavior in its variety of current manifestations. The new supervisor saw it as his main task to help bring this treatment that seemed headed for an inevitable termination to a graceful close.

There was a little of the same tendency toward a defense-analytic stance in the work with the Medical Scientist, whose voice was described as "even and dull, his speech like a slow running river." His effort was to put the analyst to sleep, so he could slip out from under the analytic attention, as when he would wait for his father to nap after dinner so that he could slip away to forbidden games with his peers. In addition, this patient also had a tapered termination (like the Devoted Son). Though desiring to terminate, the Medical Scientist also feared it (as the destruction of the father imago) and was saddened by the prospect; he was reluctant to give up the analyst's abiding support, to come to the feeling that alone he "could put up with the way I am and the way I am not." The analyst handled this via a progressive gradual reduction in the frequency of the analytic hours. During the sixth year the frequency was reduced at several-month intervals to four, then three, and then two hours weekly; in the seventh year it was once a week for the first half of the year, and twice a month for the terminal half.

With the English Professor, there was a comparable special emphasis on a character-analytic approach to his quite frozen obsessive–compulsive character style, as well as a special modification in the termination process of his 6-year (1145-hour) analysis. The analyst felt he had to use a "parameter" or "manipulation." He felt that the patient had become completely comfortable within the ongoing treatment, had had sufficient symptom relief that he was mostly contented with himself, and had little impetus for changing his continuing difficulties (in the social–sexual area), which he seemed quite willing to maintain unaltered. The analyst, in effect, felt that the treatment was now on an unchanging plateau, with the patient shielding it from deeper explorations; he suggested that they spend 3 months discussing whether there was indeed any purpose to further treatment or motivation to further change, especially in the area of the patient's patently unsatisfactory heterosexual adjustment. The patient's surface reaction was one of equanimity and acquiescence. The underlying disappointment and anger, always hard for him to express, came through in a transient revival of the patient's old projective trend—a paranoid outburst that he had not been helped at all by treatment, that there had been no real change in his basic yearning to be mothered, and that this *proved* that the analyst had had no intention of trying to help him change with the treatment. The episode subsided (with interpretation), and at the end of the 3 months there was mutual agreement on a termination date 3 months later. On research interview, the analyst expressed some disappointment that this "parameter," the termination threat, had not jarred the patient into renewed effort at serious analytic work. The patient, in his research interviews, expressed his bitterness about the treatment's having been cut off without him having been given anything to take its place.

With two patients, the enforced modification of the analysis had to do with the need to deal with recurring emergencies that threatened the stability of the treatment situation. With the Alcoholic Doctor, whose analytic effort was persisted in for almost 7 years (1238 hours) up until the time of his death, the nature and severity of his character and illness picture enforced many deviations from classical analytic technique. The patient continued in his addictions (to alcohol and a variety of drugs) with varying severity; he had to be rehospitalized four times (albeit relatively briefly each time) for intoxications, and on one of these occasions for a toxic encephalopathy with grossly disorganized behavior. The analyst also permitted outside-the-hour telephone contact fairly frequently. During the hours, there were stretches of sitting up (usually initiated by the patient), episodes of major advice giving, and direct work with the patient in helping him secure suitable employment at one juncture. And at times, when the patient seemed unable to cope with the analytic regressive process and seemed threatened with a serious ego decompensation, the analyst actively led the patient away from unduly upsetting material—memories, fantasies, transference images, and the like.

Comparable emergencies came up with Peter Pan. Suicidal threats and gestures occurred periodically; the patient wanted to drown herself dramatically in a river, and once in the wintertime she lay with her feet in a lake in order to catch pneumonia. Twice the analyst took the initiative of (very briefly) hospitalizing the patient until her upset and her suicide impulse should quiet down. Once the patient came to her hour by bicycle and was drenched by a pouring rain, and the analyst had to wrap her in blankets to guard her against cold. Once when she failed to appear (and seemed to be in a suicidal mood), the analyst went to check on her apartment, only to be informed by the landlord that she had gone to play tennis with friends in a cheerful mood. Once when she stole again, the analyst called the business firm involved in order to get her out of the trouble, and once when she thought she might be pregnant, he helped arrange a pregnancy test. He also made himself available in emergencies between hours, and there were quite a few telephone calls and an occasional extra analytic hour.

With the last of these six "modified" analyses, that of the Phobic Woman, the modifications were in the greater than usual employment of suggestive and manipulative techniques directed toward dealing with the phobic anxieties and constrictions. The analyst directly guided and encouraged the patient to confront her phobic situations, have a child, proceed with her education, expand her social life, enter into a more active sexual life, and so forth. Sometimes this guidance was in the form of suggested behaviors, as in confronting the phobias: "Well now, I think it's something you ought to do." Sometimes it was in the form of reassuring the patient against the consequences of feared impulses: "You know you don't have to worry, you really just can't seduce people you pass in the street . . . or your father . . . or your analyst." In regard to her very inhibited sexual life, it was most direct and directive. In the patient's words, "He told me very directly that this is my husband, not my father. . . . He said *in no uncertain terms* that it's appropriate to have this sexual freedom with your husband whereas it isn't with other people, almost the way you would say this to a child really. Because at these times he thought it was very necessary that I quit acting like a child and talking like a child."

Explicit Conversion from Analysis to Psychotherapy

With all of the six patients just described, there were very substantial modifications of analysis, and yet clearly at the same time the analyst's effort in each case was to be as continuingly "analytic" as the patient and circumstances allowed. However, with another 6 of the 22 who started in analysis (again, 3 men and 3 women), the analysis was deliberately not just "modified" but altered into an explicit psychotherapy varyingly expressive and/or supportive in tone and intent. I discuss in the final section of this book (see Chapter 35, "Second-Guessing: Misdiagnosis and Wrong Treatments?") the wider technical issue of how many patients in the overall sample population *should* have been converted into psychotherapy, on the basis of the recommendation for analysis resting on a seriously overgenerous estimate of the patient's capacity for analytic work; I indicate there whether all these six should have been in that number. Here I want only to indicate what the patients therapists' decisions were and why.

The most dramatic of the six instances was that of the Movie Lady. Within the first 6 months, the analyst decided that he was dealing with a much sicker individual (a paranoid, borderline psychotic) than had been originally anticipated. He saw her as someone who clung anxiously to a "culturally approved average pattern" and would think paranoidly whenever she dared to deviate from it. After he altered both his diagnostic formulation and his handling of the case, he felt able to say, "I became more and more convinced that she did well for a psychotic person but poorly for a neurotic person." By the 6-month mark, the patient was sitting up. The frequency was then progressively reduced to four, then three, then two times weekly—ostensibly in response to the patient's claimed difficulties with transportation (her driving phobia), with babysitting arrangements, with available time, and even with money (besides the $1-per-session analytic fee, there were babysitters' and sometimes cab fares). Additionally, techniques within the hours were explicitly altered. In response to the patient's persistent demand that the therapist do something to help her overcome her "hyperventilation attacks" (as she called them), he introduced relaxation exercises (*à la* Jacobson) and advised that they be performed at home. The patient followed these instructions in a compliant but overliteral, self-defeating way, and after a while both agreed that they were not helpful. Besides this "homework," there were other treatment manipulations. At least twice, for example, at the therapist's request, the husband came along to the treatment hour, so that the therapist could talk both patient and husband out of the intent to move to new employment in their old home town (close to the patient's mother). Mostly the treatment could be characterized as one in which the therapist avoided clarification and interpretation in the usual sense; he felt that the patient reacted to all such activity as criticism, as a nagging that she was "wrong." Even the effort to stay at the level of reflecting the patient's feelings was taken as criticism that she had the "wrong feelings." So the explicit plan of the therapist became to be with the patient; to talk with her more than his usual wont; to be a person whom she felt was on her side; and, by being as natural and human as possible, to give her a "corrective emotional experience" that a man could be trusted and could help through caring.

Others in this group of specific conversions from psychoanalysis to psychotherapy were similar. The Heiress got into an analytic impasse with her first analyst, who devoted himself to an effort at classical analytic work; she experienced this as the unfeeling, ungenuine, and unhelpful activity of a "cardboard analyst" (no different from all other men), and she responded to it with hostile withholding and angry depreciation. When the impasse could only be resolved by a transfer to another analyst, the second analyst, in his effort to differentiate himself and get the treatment moving, systematically began to alter his technique. In effect, he undertook to present himself as (and to be) a real person, a father figure, steadily present, benevolently interested, and willingly giving—of transference gratifications, of allowing the patient the fantasy of the specially preferred one, of permitting her to pry him out of his analytic neutrality and off his "analytic pedestal." With the Economist, it was after 6 years of a classical analytic effort against stubborn resistances, when the patient was finally precipitated into a transference psychotic regression (in which the handshake between the analyst and the patient's mother in the patient's presence was delusionally interpreted as the confirmation of an illicit affair between the analyst and the mother), that there was an explicit turn to a supportive–expressive psychotherapy in order to foster reconstitution to the patient's better integrated (and much preferred) prior transference position. The patient wanted (and secured) a return to the passive gratification of a dependent transference attachment, and was willing to pay a high price for such a protected life in the shadow of, and under the guidance of, the analyst. He would forego real autonomy and independence, marriage, even his Ph.D., if he could once again continue to be permanently cared for by the nurturant parent and to be the permanently gratified dependent child.

In the case of the Masochistic Editor, the classical analytic effort was adhered to for over 4 years (despite increasingly evident severe ego deformation), until the supporting father's patience and money were depleted. When the father at last stated that henceforth he could only contribute $100 per month to the treatment (up to then he had defrayed the total cost of a five-times-weekly psychoanalysis), the therapy was reduced in frequency to twice weekly, with the patient agreeing to add the "token" $20 per month (to make up the total bill of eight sessions at $15 per session). This was the first time that the patient agreed to contribute at all to his tratment expense; however, he never kept his end of the bargain, always finding some suitable excuse for his failure to do so. Therapy from this point on was explicitly supportive–expressive, with many suggestions and pressures in regard to ways of effecting control over the patient's sadomasochistic and self-destructive interactions, curbing his very damaging homosexual involvement with a young boy, and taking a more active responsibility for his own life.

With the Alcoholic Raconteur, the proposed conversion to psychotherapy was never completed. Severely alcoholic and pretentiously disdainful of AA (as noted earlier), he was willing to come for psychiatric treatment, but only if it was psychoanalysis. He pleaded for the psychoanalysis and at the same time averred the importance of his Catholic faith, since no therapy could be effective unless the patient gave himself up to almighty God and was in a state of grace to receive it. He said that psychiatrists used the word "limitation" a good deal, and then stated, "In my life, the Catholic church is the most stringent, yet wonderful, limitation I have." When after almost 3 years of analytic effort (546 hours), interspersed with periods of face-to-face supportive expressive psychotherapy aimed at more direct behavior control, the analyst determined that only irrevocable conversion to psychotherapy could offer a proper prospect of coping with the surges of decompensation and of uncontrolled acting out, the patient refused to accept this decision. For him it was psychoanalysis or nothing, and he shortly thereafter precipitously broke off his treatment, ostensibly to try to make a fresh start in psychoanalysis elsewhere.

The last case in this group of treatment conversions, the Housebound Phobic Woman, was different from all the others. Though she was ostensibly in analysis, the patient's relative lack of psychological-mindedness and thinking and her constant great difficulty in associating, though understood as partly a resistance to analytic work, also began to be seen increasingly clearly as a reflection of the limitations imposed by her degree of chronic organic brain damage. The analyst, though never making this explicit with the patient, shifted very early toward a directly sustaining and supportive therapeutic work. He gave a good deal of direct advice in regard to the problems of job seeking and the timing of a steadily enlarging testing of the phobic restrictions that bound the patient. And he helped her set up a more organized and realistic life pattern, obtain and manage a job, and an apartment, and some semblance of a minimal social life for herself. It was never quite clear as to how much the patient still thought of this as a psychoanalysis. She did confess after almost 1000 hours that one of her "greatest fears" at the start of the "analysis" was that she would fall in love with or come to hate the analyst. This very affect-bound and inhibited woman expressed that she felt lucky that neither possibility had ever eventuated.

PSYCHOTHERAPY

The remaining 20 patients (11 men and 9 women) had been started in psychotherapy explicitly geared somewhere along the expressive–supportive dimension. For reasons that are discussed in detail in the concluding section of this book (see Chapter 37, "The Expressive–Supportive Dichotomy Reconsidered"), the effort to break the array down more specifically into the more purely expressive, the mixed, and the more purely supportive, either in planning and prognostication or in assessment of course and outcome, is not a particularly productive or useful endeavor. Furthermore, since in its nature (or at least in its historical development) psychotherapy—varyingly expressive and/or supportive—is inherently a more diversified activity or array of activities than is psychoanalysis, with its far sharper delineation of what the endeavor is and what constitutes a departure from it, it would not be appropriate at this point to try to indicate for each of the 20 what was felt to constitute the essence of the psychotherapeutic mode for that patient. This is done, rather, in the discussions of the treatment courses and outcomes for those patients, and of the varying bases on which each accomplished or fell short of accomplishing its intended results.

Here, just a few kinds of qualifying issues should be addressed. Though more than half of those who were started in psychoanalysis (12 of 22) had the analysis modified significantly in the direction of more psychotherapeutic interventions, and 6, or half of those, had such substantial modifications that they were considered cases of specific conversions from psychoanalysis to psychotherapy, there were no instances of a conversion or an attempt at conversion the other way around. In one instance, the case of the Bitter Spinster, it was felt at Initial Study that the ideal treatment would be psychoanalysis, in terms of the deep-seated nature of the patient's character problems (manifest in her recurrent life difficulties and her dissatisfactions in both the vocational and the social–sexual spheres). For practical reasons she could not afford analysis, and she was proposed for the twice-weekly expressive psychotherapy that, at the minimum fee, she could afford. The possibility was to be kept open that this might pave the way for later analysis; the treatment might help the patient achieve the kind of life adaptation (and security) in which it might become feasible to make a psychoanalytic arrangement. Actually, as it turned out, the patient was far more deeply ill (in a paranoid and acting-out way) than originally evident, and psychoanalysis would not have been the treatment of choice for her after all.

Three of the patients—the Adolescent Grandson, the Actress, and the Homesick Psychology Student—were, for appropriate reasons, recommended for psychotherapy at the time that they initially presented. It was indicated, however, that they might come to a more definitive effort at psychoanalysis after the completion of this course of psychotherapy (the Adolescent Grandson and the Actress), or might have the current psychotherapy, given appropriate clarifications and developments within the psychotherapy, evolve into psychoanalysis (the Homesick Psychology Student). As might be expected, these three were among the youngest patients in the project (17, 19, and 23, respectively). A fourth patient for whom a conversion to analysis might become indicated should all go well in her psychotherapy but for whom it was clearly not initially appropriate was the severely barbiturate-addicted, 30-year-old Intellectual Fencer, who was brought to her treatment in a thoroughly drug-intoxicated state. Her intellectual resources and propensities would be more than equal to the challenge, and it was questionable whether any treatment short of analysis would be ultimately sufficiently definitive. Yet her psychotherapy clearly fell short of developing in that direction. For example, the therapist did try to deal with some of the inner sources of the competitive strivings that suffused the transference from the start. But at points where the competitiveness was quite conscious in the patient's associations and where the therapist would try to point this out interpretively, the patient would stiffen either in resistant denial ("What you say isn't true") or in defensive competitiveness ("I know all that already; you're not telling me anything that changes anything").

At such points, the therapist would then characteristically desist instead of being able to go on effectively with the crucial (and required) transference interpretation—that here in this interaction she was re-enacting this very competitive striving that was the subject of inquiry. It was now manifest in needing to be a better therapist than the therapist, and incidentally to ward off the therapist's insights at the same time.

With still another of the psychotherapy patients, the Addicted Doctor—an extremely ill individual, with an infantile personality structure, multiple addictions, somatizations, and polymorphous perverse sexual behaviors—the second therapist, while treating him within the local state hospital inpatient setting (he could not any longer afford Menninger Foundation hospitalization), tried to treat the patient by way of a modified Aichhorn technique, allying himself with the patient's dispositions in the face of a hostile world. The therapist lacked the experience for this technique, and this therapeutic attempt was as unsuccessful as the first.

TREATMENT DURATIONS AND TERMINATIONS

Of the 22 patients (10 men and 12 women) started in psychoanalysis, 15 (6 men and 9 women) finished or terminated their treatments (with, of course, vastly varying degrees of adjudged success); 2 more (1 man, the Economist, and 1 woman, the Housebound Phobic Woman) had apparently become permanent patients, or "therapeutic lifers," by the time of "cutoff" Follow-Up Study. Counting these 17 together, their amount of treatment until the Follow-Up Study point ranged from 2½ to 9½ years in length (averaging 5⅔ years), or from 543 to 1601 hours (averaging 1017 hours). This number included, of course, those 6 who, after varying periods of time, from close to the very start of the treatment (the Housebound Phobic Woman) to as late as the 6-year mark (the Economist), were explicitly converted to psychotherapy. The figures for the 2 who had become "lifers" are notable: The Housebound Phobic Woman had had 9 years and 1356 hours when last officially counted at Follow-Up Study, and the Economist had had 9½ years (6 years of psychoanalysis, 3½ years of subsequent psychotherapy) and 1601 hours—his were the largest total figures of all 42 patients.[1]

Of the other 5 patients started in analysis, 1, the Alcoholic Doctor, continued for 7 years and 1238 hours until his death; his treatment was never terminated. The other 4 (2 men and 2 women) who actively disrupted their treatments were in analysis from 8½ months to 2¾ years (averaging 1⅓ years), and from 129 to 546 hours (averaging 281 hours). The only patient of this group of 4 who went for longer than a year—the Alcoholic Raconteur, who was in analytic treatment for 2¾ years and 546 hours—was the individual who would not accept the

---

1. Later on—in connection with the individual case write-ups of those who became "therapeutic lifers" (either on a continuous basis, or by posttreatment return to a continuing therapy), as well as in the discussion of the "therapeutic lifers" as a group—I indicate the extremely long treatment durations involved. With three patients, the treatments have lasted over 25 years each, and are still going on as of the present writing (spring 1982): the Economist at 28 years, the Sexual Masochist at 28 years, and the Housebound Phobic Woman at 25½ years. The frequencies are of course now much reduced (averaging now once a month), and there is no precise count any longer of actual treatment hours to date.

therapist's requirement that there be a firm conversion to psychotherapy, and left ostensibly to go on with analysis elsewhere. As noted, he did not do so.

Of the 20 patients started in psychotherapy (11 men and 9 women), 14 (8 men and 6 women) "terminated" their psychotherapy in some sense; however, as will be seen in the treatment descriptions, several of these terminations could hardly be considered appropriate or natural. The Sociopath is a dramatic example of such a pathological "termination." His disastrous treatment ended (after 2¾ years and 121 hours) at the point when he was fired from the last of a succession of jobs and everyone had given up on him except the therapist. Nonetheless, he canceled his last scheduled hour and simply disappeared. He could not be located for Termination Study—neither in Topeka, through his ex-employer, his lodging, the police, or his lawyer; nor in the other city in which he had business (to which it was rumored he had gone), through the hospital, the police, the jail, or the bondsman; nor through his parents. The various reasons why all these parties were looking for him are elaborated in the description of the treatment course. Adding to these 14 thus "terminated"—ranging from the most mutually satisfactory to the likes of the Sociopath—the 2 (both men, the Sexual Masochist and the Fearful Loner) who did not terminate, but also became "therapeutic lifers," we have a total of 16 (10 men and 6 women) whose treatment duration to its end or to the "cutoff" Follow-Up Study ranged from 6 months to 8½ years (averaging 4⅓ years), and from 46 to 900 hours (averaging 316 hours). The frequency varied from one to three times weekly, and with some of the patients this was of course altered upward or downward during the course of the therapy. Of the 2 "lifers," at the last official Follow-Up Study count (and still going), the Sexual Masochist had 8 years and 540 hours and the Fearful Loner 8½ years and 371 *sessions*. (They could not be called "hours," because after the first 66 hourly sessions, the time was cut to 30 minutes in order to keep the patient, who was often silent and unproductive and always guardedly fearful, from being too uncomfortable with time blocks and time pressures that seemed more than he could handle. He was the only patient among the 42 for whom the length of the regular session was altered from the standard 50-minute hour, except for the Devoted Son in the final weaning phase of his analysis.)

It should of course be noted in connection with the foregoing that these psychotherapies could have the same overall duration (with not quite the same *average* duration), including going over into permanent "lifer" status, as the psychoanalyses. (In fact, there would be a much greater propensity toward "lifer" status, because in theory some psychotherapies can be seen as permanently sustaining endeavors, and in theory psychoanalysis should always come to some natural resolution; indeed, the two "lifers" from the psychoanalysis group were among the six who had been explicitly converted to psychotherapy.) Though the durations of psychotherapy and psychoanalysis could thus be equivalent, the different frequency makes the total of hours far different (average 1017 among the 17 terminated or cut off in the psychoanalysis group, and average 316 among the 16 terminated or cut off in the psychotherapy group).

In addition, there were three psychotherapy patients (all women) who did not "terminate" in any way (in the sense of finishing a treatment, however successfully or unsuccessfully), but specifically disrupted ongoing treatments. And besides these three, there was a fourth (a man) whose ongoing treatment, rather than "terminating," ended with his death by suicide. This was the Addicted Doctor, whose first treatment at The Menninger Foundation had failed and who, at the time of his death 2½ years later, was in psychotherapy with a Menninger Foundation-trained therapist while an inpatient at the local (Menninger Foundation-affiliated) state hospital. The durations of these disrupted therapies were from 9 months to 3½ years (averaging somewhat over 2 years), and from 52 to 441 hours (averaging 202). This was quite comparable to the similar-sized group of patients in psychoanalysis who disrupted their treatments.

THE TREATMENT FEE

Fee Structure

The treatment fee structure needs to be understood in terms of both the time (the 1950s) and the clinical practices of The Menninger Foundation. At that time, the usual fee for outpatient psychotherapy or psychoanalysis throughout the country was $15 or $17.50 per hour, and 21 of the fees for this sample, or exactly half, were at that level (12 at $15 and 9 at $17.50).[2] The fees, in accord with Menninger Foundation practice, were set in relation to the assessment of the patient's financial status and ability to pay, without regard to who the therapist might be (e.g., how senior and experienced), and usually before it was known who the particular therapist would be. The therapist, however, had the option, in concert with the patient, to work out an upward or downward revision of the fee at the time of actual initiation of the treatment if fuller exploration of the patient's financial circumstancees indicated the appropriateness of such action, and of course, at any time during the subsequent course of the treatment if the patient's circumstances were to change.

In 5 instances lower fees were set (1 at $7.50, 3 at $10, and 1 at $12.50), all of these cases in psychoanalysis at five times per week; this was done, of course, to make it possible for these patients to secure the psychoanalytic treatment indicated for them. In view of the quite affluent status of so many of The Menninger Foundation's patients and the extreme wealth of some, it would be expected that a significant number would have higher than usual fees. Actually, 15 (just over one-third) were in a higher range (3 at $20, 2 at $22.50, 6 at $25, 1 at $30, 2 at $35 — and 1 at the extremely high fee, for then, of $75 per hour). The one fee set so extremely high was that of the Adolescent Grandson whose enormously wealthy grandfather arranged everything from a distance through his private secretary. Though the fee represented no significant problem to the family, setting it thus so out of scale from all others did actually pose specific psychological problems for the treatment: It allowed the patient to feel exploited, and it gave the grandfather a basis for prematurely terminating his support of the treatment.

---

2. Of course, a very significant number of the patients — 22 altogether, or just over half — were also hospitalized at one time or another during their treatment (averaging for the 22 about a 12-month hospital stay each). This very significant expense (again, at the private psychiatric hospital rates then usual) was an additional part of the overall financial burden of the treatment process on the patients and their families. The issues of hospitalization as a concomitant of psychotherapy are discussed in Chapter 11.

Actually, the grandfather had never been sold on the value of therapy, since he saw his grandson less as sick and more as just lacking in discipline. For his own part, he was old and wanted only to be left in peace. When his grandson was being treated while hospitalized, he found cause to complain of the expense to him; when the patient was out of the hospital, he found cause to complain of the youngster's unacceptable behaviors. At the crisis juncture—after almost 2 years of psychotherapy, partly at two and partly at three times weekly—the grandfather only wanted The Menninger Foundation to take his grandson off his hands. He stated that he would continue to pay for the more expensive hospital care, but would no longer support the psychotherapy fee, which he declared to be unnecessary and an upsetting influence on the patient. Under these circumstances, the whole treatment was reluctantly terminated.

The foregoing tabulation adds up to 41 patients. The other is the one patient not treated at The Menninger Foundation, the Movie Lady. Her husband was a governmental civil servant with an adequate income, but her analytic fee was set at just $1 per hour; the real fee was the patient's willingness to have her sessions recorded and filmed for research purposes. (Nonetheless, she often complained of babysitting and cab fare costs.)

Fee-Related Issues in Treatment

With a number of patients, there were special psychological features of the fee, and the handling of it, that deserve specific mention. Adjustments of fees either upward or downward in the light of changed circumstances were relatively commonplace, and such adjustments were almost always downward. The Tantrum Woman, for example, started her analysis at the usual fee of $15 per hour. When her insurance money (from the husband's accidental death) ran out and she had to maintain everything on her own earnings, the fee was lowered to $12.50; when her child went into treatment, it was further lowered to $7.50.

For a patient like the Devoted Son, the fee that was set fitted in with his need to see himself as handicapped and suffering. To make his analysis possible, a reduced fee of $10 was set; being frugal, he could manage this (with some hardship) and did, and always paid very conscientiously. In this way, it fitted very well with his need for masochistic suffering and acceptance. Since he was also self-conscious about his lower-than-standard fee status, he always felt limited in what he had a right to expect and also in how much he dared to complain. On the other hand, he was also confirmed in his feeling that with his second-rate fee, he was getting no more than he paid for (and than he deserved)—second-rate treatment.

Others, of course, had an opposite problem. The Car Salesman (whose fee was $20) could blithely keep himself totally uninformed about such mundane matters. All treatment expenses had been taken care of by his mother, and his detachment from them was complete; he didn't even see the bills. The Alcoholic Heir, who came from an enormously wealthy family and himself had trusts and inheritances, paid $35 per hour and always paid promptly, but also constantly complained loudly that The Menninger Foundation was cheating him because he was rich. At the time of Follow-Up Study he "misunderstood" the letter indicating

that the research project would defray all expenses for participation: His interpretation was that he could "charge" (at $25 per hour) for his 8 hours of co-
operating time, this "charge" to be then considered a donation to The Menninger
Foundation, which he could write off for income tax purposes. He was irate when
this scheme was not acceded to. A similar situation existed with the Sexual Masochist, who came from an equally wealthy family, and at $30 per hour always felt
that he was paying too much and was being exploited because he was rich. On
the other hand, he felt that if he were paying still more he would be getting the
properly preferential treatment that he really needed. There was a variant on this
issue with the 17-year-old Bohemian Prep School Boy (his fee was $17.50), who
was totally irresponsible in the handling of the monies entrusted to him to manage
his living expenses and treatment expenses. This was a constant complaint of the
father, who wrote that he felt his son to be in a "*Magic Mountain* atmosphere"
where "Everyone around him suffers, all are quite rich, privileged, forgiven, and
protected. . . . he plays the role of the misunderstood aesthete, wounded and
unable to do an honest day's work, be it at school or a job." This feeling that The
Menninger Foundation, in turn, had no regard for the parents' "limited" finances
(actually they were profligate but wealthy) was then used by the father as a basis
to terminate the treatment prematurely (after only 7 months) through withdrawal
of parental support.

As might be expected, there were also problems with payment with some patients. The Suspended Medical Student, who was paying $10 per hour for his
analysis, piled up a sizable analytic debt after he was able to return to school and
stopped working. Though he made an arrangement at termination to pay this off
in regular installments, over the succeeding year and a half he only partially lived
up to this agreement. His analyst saw the maintained indebtedness as a continued
combined expression of dependent attachment and rebellion, reflecting unresolved
transferences. With the Bitter Spinster, seen in twice-weekly psychotherapy at $15,
the fee was always a source of contention. A number of times she simply stopped
paying; once she obtained a fee reduction for a while, and in the last year (of an
8-year therapy) she did not pay at all, taking it for granted that this period
represented a gift to her. Yet during this same period she indulged in major spending sprees, once spending over $1000 on a hi-fi set, a record collection, and
clothing. The Addicted Doctor carried this tendency even further. In his 11 months
of Menninger Foundation treatment, he only paid the bills for the first 3 months.
For the rest of the time, his wild extravagances and his debts put him in a position that precluded his being able to make payment; despite a good deal of therapy
focus on this, it proved to be an unbudgeable pattern. His second period of treatment in the local state hospital cost him nothing.

As might also be expected, this kind of problem stretched to its uttermost with
the Sociopath. He was seen once weekly (all he stated he could afford) at $17.50.
With his wild extravagances, his neglect of bills, his promissory notes, and his
writing of bad checks, he was always in financial and legal troubles. At one point
during treatment, during which he bounced checks, was threatened with prosecution by angry creditors, and lost an insurance job because of financial irregularities,
he was suddenly revealed to have over $11,000 in outstanding debts, bad checks,
and illegal deals (e.g., selling property that he did not yet fully own). At this point,
his wife finally left with the children and sued for divorce. Surprisingly, she said

that she was not leaving vindictively—she just had to get out from under all these pressures and uncertainties—but that she still loved the patient and would be glad to return if she could be assured after an appropriate time (by the therapist) that her husband had at last straightened out. The patient was temporarily stunned by this blow to his narcissism, but was soon making what he considered restorative efforts. His financial and legal disaster he handled by declaring bankruptcy. His house, car, and furniture were repossessed, and his creditors received about 15 cents on the dollar; the patient declared that this served them right, because they were fools for having gotten mixed up with him in the first place. His therapy fee was treated the same way: He paid approximately 20% of his treatment bill, all told. The Menninger Foundation finally abandoned as fruitless its collection proceedings for the 80% still outstanding. In retrospect, the therapist, in what can only be called an understatement, expressed himself as having been insufficiently firm with all these delinquencies, accepting too often the patient's delays and ever-plausible excuses.

With two other patients, fee played a special or unusual role in the treatment. In the case of the Medical Scientist, the fee was used especially effectively as part of the treatment leverage (it was perhaps used as such in other cases as well but in less striking and manifest ways). His analytic fee was $15, and he was concomitantly hospitalized for a full year as part of the handling of his severe alcohol and drug addictions. But the patient's resources were limited, and, even with borrowing from his modestly well-off parents, the year in the hospital was about all that could be afforded. Through most of that hospitalized year, the analyst felt that little dent had been made in the patient's avoidant, isolating, and intellectualizing mechanisms (he would discuss himself like a scientific case report), and that the treatment was at an "almost complete standstill." In this context, renewed interpretive effort was directed to the patient's utter disregard of his apparently hopeless financial outlook, his deliberate undermining of his parents' financial security, and his lack of interest in securing employment for himself. All of this finally did take effect, and the patient was enabled to leave the hospital for the day hospital and outside living just before the money ran out. From that point, he was able shortly to obtain a state medical license, secure an affiliation with a local medical clinic, and begin his long and slow but ultimately successful rehabilitative effort as a physician and medical scientist.

And with the Fearful Loner, there was an unusual handling of the fee, in full keeping with his total character propensities. His once-weekly psychotherapy fee was $17.50, and, though he was on a very modest income, he could handle this readily within his frugal ways. He insisted on a very special handling of the fee, however. He questioned the usual Menninger Foundation procedure that the therapists hand the monthly statements to the patients; he demanded that this arrangement be bypassed in his case and that the business office send his bills directly to his home. He refused to discuss any reasons for or possible meanings of this demand. When the therapist tried to deal interpretively with it, the patient's sullen and angry resistance only stiffened. The therapist finally "gave in" to the demand; thereafter, with a succession of three therapists (the reasons for this are discussed in the description of the treatment course), the patient was billed in accord with his wishes. He always paid the bill promptly.

THE ACTUAL TREATMENT AND
THE IDEAL TREATMENT

In contrasting "actual" and "ideal" treatments, I do not discuss those instances (as is clear by now, they were considerable) where both the clinical examination team and the research Initial Study team concurred in a diagnostic misassessment—a major seeming underdiagnosis of the depth of the pathology and a concomitant overgenerous assessment of the treatment possibilities. There were several such shared "errors," and they are discussed in proper detail under the description of the treatment courses. In briefest summary statement, they represent the recommendations of marginally or dubiously suitable patients for psychoanalysis in terms of Glover's (1954) third category, of so-called "heroic indications"—that is, where the prospects with analysis may not be good, but analysis is deemed the only treatment that can give the patient a thorough chance at the desired result. The "errors" also represent willingness or desire within our group (already discussed in Section I, Chapter 2; see pp. 20–21) to reach for the potential of each modality (especially psychoanalysis) to achieve its uttermost, and then to see where and why it fell short of realizing such potential. In the light of the presentations of the treatment courses and outcomes to follow in this book, I develop a fuller "reconsideration" of such issues as "heroic indications," the possibilities for achieving enduring "structural changes" with psychoanalysis and psychotherapy, and so forth, in the concluding section of the book.

Here, then, I present two other kinds of discrepancy between treatments as recommended and treatments as carried out. The first has to do with those instances where the Initial Study research team (Robbins and myself) differed significantly in our understanding of the cases, and our judgments about the appropriate therapy from the clinical evaluation team who had made the actual judgments and recommendations, which were presumably to determine the treatment plan that would be carried out. All told, there were 5 such instances of some significance among the 42 patients. The second kind of discrepancy has to do with the instances where the research team (in accord with the clinical evaluation team) felt that the treatment of choice would not be available, usually because of limitations of finances or geography; therefore, the best possible treatment under the circumstances, but less than the ideal treatment, would knowingly be carried out. We felt that there were 6 such instances of some significance among the 42 patients.

Both of these kinds of discrepancies of course made possible the fourth kind of control method, called "inadvertent control," that was built into our project design (see Section II, Chapter 7, p. 114). In the situations where we disagreed with the clinical evaluation team, we made alternative predictions for how the treatment would turn out if carried out in accord with the clinical recommendations, as against how it would turn out if the treating clinician himself or herself came to see the situation as did the research group, and altered the treatment mode to be more in accord with what the research team felt to be indicated. Similar alternative predictions (and control possibilities) were set up for the other kind of discrepancy as well.

Differences between Clinical and Research Assessments

PSYCHOANALYSIS VERSUS PSYCHOTHERAPY

I turn now to the five instances of significantly different judgment between the clinical and the research assessments. In two instances (the Alcoholic Raconteur and the Alcoholic Doctor), the differences had to do with a clinical recommendation for treatment by psychoanalysis. The Alcoholic Raconteur, as noted earlier, came intent to be treated only by psychoanalysis—a treatment that to him combined a conviction of magical faith healing (consciously held) with an unlimited indulgence in regressive oral nurturant fantasies (less in conscious awareness). He utilized a preliminary 7-month period of hospitalization to seem to effect sufficient control over direct instinct discharge, and sufficient capacity for delay and modulation, that—together with his high intellectual endowment, his apparent introspective capacity, his intense discomfort, and his strong desire for change—he made out a persuasive case to be taken into analysis. There were, of course, no optimistic illusions about analysis; rather, there was a feeling that analysis alone (given adequate support from concomitant inpatient hospitalization) could offer some chance, even if not a very bright one, for real conflict resolutions and consequent enduring character and behavior changes. The research investigators held a contrary view: We felt analysis to be completely contraindicated in this individual, who had had no reality achievement his whole life long, was totally symptom-ridden, had decompensated defenses, and was flooded by constant impulse pressure toward immediate gratification. We pointed to the patient's very poor ego controls, very low anxiety tolerance, inadequacy of development of functioning neurotic defenses, withdrawal tendencies, and essentially narcissistic orientation. On these grounds, we recommended a supportive psychotherapy geared not toward conflict resolution and character change, but toward the institution of behavior controls based on processes of identification, of "borrowing ego strength," in order to effect improved reality testing and discharge delays, and to search out more socially syntonic substitute gratifications that would make for a more reality-appropriate life. We felt additionally that the supporting relationship within which this took place might have to be maintained indefinitely. And we further stated that, should the effort at psychoanalysis be undertaken and persisted in, the indulgence in free association would probably lead to a greater access of uncontrolled primary-process material, a flooding with concomitant unmanageable anxiety and dysphoria, and a further weakening of the defensive barriers against an open psychotic decompensation.

The situation with the Alcoholic Doctor was very similar. It was clear that, during the initial evaluation, both the severity and the long duration of the patient's behavioral disturbances—going back to clearly identifiable precursors in earliest childhood—were systematically understated, and correspondingly that the depth and breadth of the ego deformation was not adequately appreciated. The clinical recommendation was that the patient be taken into psychoanalysis, with, of course, concomitant supportive hospitalization during its initial phases. The research appraisal did not concur. A large number of factors were felt to militate against the prospect for psychoanalysis; including the severe and chronic disruptive and self-destructive alloplastic behaviors; the progressive decompensation of defenses; the low anxiety tolerance; the absence of psychological-mindedness or of insight (the patient's coming to treatment itself was at best an act of compliance with parental anxieties and pressures); the absence of sublimation potential; the high secondary gain; the passive, compliant, and masochistic character formation; and the highly unfavorable external reality situation (a very disturbed marriage to a sick wife with many of the same symptomatic behaviors as the patient—drinking, brawling, etc.). The most cogent caution of all against analysis, it was felt, rested on the patient's profound passivity and masochism, which would engender too strong a risk of his developing an insoluble and perpetual transference neurosis, or, alternatively, a defense against this development by an abrupt treatment disruption with prompt reversion to the pretreatment illness picture. On these grounds, our treatment recommendation was rather for psychotherapy, with (as with the Alcoholic Raconteur) a specification of the recommended characteristics of the psychotherapy (also, of course, combined with concomitant hospitalization).

OUTPATIENT VERSUS INPATIENT TREATMENT

With two other of the severely alcoholic and drug-addicted patients, the Car Salesman and the Addicted Doctor, the clinical recommendations were not for psychoanalysis but for a supportive–expressive psychotherapy. But, in both of these cases, the psychotherapy was projected by the clinical evaluation group on an outpatient basis, in order to avoid playing unduly into the patients' inordinate dependency strivings. In both these cases, the Initial Study research team felt that, despite the risk of intensifying the dependency dispositions of the patients, the psychotherapy still should start within the framework of preparatory prolonged periods of hospitalization. Otherwise, the opposite danger would dominate—of insufficient controls over self-destructive behaviors. There would thus be insufficient likelihood of the psychotherapy's being able to stop a regressive, destructive process, to help the patients effect better impulse control and tolerably stabilized lives, or to help them develop more socially acceptable discharge channels for drive pressures.

MULTIPLE DISAGREEMENTS

The fifth instance of discrepancy between the clinical and research treatment recommendations was of a somewhat different sort. This was with the Sociopath, whose flamboyantly (and luridly) destructive and self-destructive history has already been described, and who came with a totally unrealistic self-recommendation (supported by a referring psychiatrist) for psychoanalysis on an outpatient basis. The treatment plan recommended by the clinical team involved long-term hospitalization concomitant with psychotherapy. The patient demurred and indicated that only outpatient therapy would be acceptable and also financially feasible. The clinical evaluation team, to avoid the threatened flight from treatment, thereupon "compromised": It advised the patient to wait a year and to prove by the conduct of his life in the interim that he could handle the stresses of living satisfactorily enough to be able to tolerate outpatient psychotherapy. This challenge the patient accepted; after the year, he returned for re-evaluation, having lived up to his commitment "after his fashion" (see p. 154). Nonetheless, the clinical evaluation team now felt constrained to keep its side of the bargain, and it was agreed to take the patient into a once-weekly supportive psychotherapy on an outpatient basis.

The frequency of the Sociopath's treatment was set only partly in terms of the patient's limited financial resources. A larger consideration was the feeling that a more frequent contact would carry the danger of a too intense involvement with the risks of transference regression, and an increased potential for a linked destructive acting out. It was felt that the once-weekly contact would avoid the danger of uncontrollable anxiety and would encourage the therapist's most flexible activity in respect to the patient's current life, the putting of brakes on his impulses, and the improvement of his reality testing. Concomitantly, regular casework contact was recommended for his wife to aid her with the ever-difficult reality of life with this husband, and also to obtain from her a more objective appraisal of the patient's life functioning as a check on the reliability of his accounting.

The research study group was in accord with the recommendation for supportive psychotherapy. However, we still thought that long-term supporting hospitalization was also indicated in order to give this difficult treatment its best chance. In the absence of this hospitalization, we felt that the patient would then need the supportive psychotherapy at least three times a week, and that once weekly would be grossly inadequate. This was because the psychotherapy would inevitably engender anxieties, and only a more frequent therapeutic schedule, properly conducted, could have the necessary continuous steadying effect, could provide sufficient contact to permit effective control efforts, and could prevent the anxieties that would be generated from spilling over during the week's interim into constant crises, emergency situations, and destructive acting out. And even with all of this, recourse to at least temporary periods of hospitalization—it could be in the affiliated VA hospital—would still need to be available to cope with treatment emergencies from time to time.

Differences between Ideal Treatments and Reality Considerations

As stated, there were six patients for whom the clinical group and the research group agreed on the appropriate treatment recommendations, but for whom (for various reasons) the ideal treatment would not be feasible or available, and some other treatment plan needed to be worked out.

FINANCIAL AND RELATED BARRIERS

In two instances, with the Bitter Spinster and the Rebellious Coed, the treatment modality felt to be optimal was psychoanalysis. With the Bitter Spinster, the barrier was financial, and she was proposed for the twice-weekly psychotherapy that she could afford. The possibility was to be kept open that this could lead into analysis or that the psychotherapy could pave the way for an analysis later, through helping the patient achieve the kind of life adaptation (and security) within which it would become possible to make a more feasible analytic arrangement. With the Rebellious Coed, there were issues not just of money (she was the patient who was absorbing more than half her father's modest income in just her college expenses), but of commuting distance, of ongoing college pressures, and also of insufficiently clarified motivations. It was felt that one of the possible outcomes of the once-a-week psychotherapy upon which the patient was entering was that the patient would come to see the need for and would do all that was required to enter psychoanalysis (including shifting her college to Topeka, securing part-time employment, etc.). In both these instances, it actually turned out that psychoanalysis would not have been the appropriate treatment. This was unqualifiedly the case with the Bitter Spinster, who was actually harboring a far graver illness than was initially realized; rather than suffering with a hysterical character neurosis (she was one of the two initially conceptualized in terms of a success neurosis), she was at Termination Study adjudged to present a more serious (and more fixed) paranoid personality state. Her treatment effort in a prolonged (8-year) psychotherapy was totally unsuccessful. The Rebellious Coed had a better result, but one limited to some significant behavioral shifts, and without any mobilized real motivation to a fuller psychoanalytic reconstructive effort.

The Actress was someone for whom supportive–expressive psychotherapy was recommended—with concomitant hospitalization, however, which would give her the needed supportive and controlling structure in which to live, and which would not respond so easily to the vicissitudes of her moods (including her "as-if" characteristics) or to the roles she played (her histrionics offstage as well as onstage). The hospital, in short, would be an environment that she could not readily provoke or alienate (as she had usually done so "successfully" in her life to this point). The resources available to underwrite hospitalization were very sharply limited, however, and the great bulk of this treatment had perforce to be on an outpatient basis. The patient thus could not be prevented from living an unstructured, unsupervised life that provided easy and immediate sources of impulse gratification, and this made it extremely difficult for the treatment to compete with her very neurotically gratifying life situation.

VIEWS OF THE SUPERVISORS

With the Adoptive Mother, there was a special twist that altered the treatment plan. Both the clinical and the research evaluation groups recommended psychoanalysis, and this was the intended and available treatment. But, as noted earlier, this was the one instance in PRP where the supervisor happened to be a strict adherent of Wilhelm Reich's views on "character analysis" and undertook to hold the psychoanalytic interpretive effort within the more limited scope of just a defense- and character-analytic focus. Though the analyst himself was restive within this approach and sought to broaden its strictures, and though there was a change in supervisors during the last year of the analysis, which made it possible for the treatment to be more forthrightly broadened, this unintended variance from the recommended analytic approach held nonetheless through most of the course of the analysis.

PATIENTS' MANIPULATION OF CIRCUMSTANCES

Finally, two of the patients (much like the Sociopath), through the manipulation of circumstances, forced their treatments out of the recommended mode and into the far less suitable mode that the patients desired (though in these instances, it was against the strong expressed disagreements of the therapists, rather than with the collusive assent that the Sociopath had been able to secure from his therapist). The Exhibitionistic Dancer lasted for a year in the supportive–expressive psychotherapy with concomitant prolonged hospitalization that was initially recommended. She succeeded in disrupting the hospitalization after not quite a year: Abruptly (after 5 minutes of deliberation) and with no planning, she eloped from a hospital party with a wealthy, delinquent youngster (another patient of the same therapist; she was 22, he 18), with whom she had been carrying on a romance as best she could within the hospital, and drove off to a neighboring state to get married. The newlyweds were back in Topeka within a week; they said that they had come back to continue their treatments, which they would now need more than ever (to help consolidate their marriage), but would of course now have to have on an outpatient basis. The patient's family claimed that they were gratified by the progress they had seen in their daughter over the first year of treatment, were pleased and proud of the marriage (which linked them to one of the famous names and great fortunes in the country), and felt strongly that The Menninger Foundation would be shirking its responsibility if the treatment was discontinued in the light of the marriage. Professional opinion was partially in favor of discontinuing their treatments and referring them both elsewhere, and partially in favor of continuing them on their own (i.e., outpatient) terms (with one or the other being referred, however, to another therapist within the institution). On the side of discontinuation and referral elsewhere was the feeling that the patients had effectively destroyed the treatment program planned for each, and that accepting them now on the new basis would handicap their further treatment prospects: They would have strong needs to "prove" their marriage and the correctness of their defiance, and thus might feel they would have to remain together even if they later came to feel a lack of wisdom in the marriage decision. On the side of continuing treatment, and referring just one to another therapist, was the argument that our professional guilt feelings over not having prevented the romance and marriage should not be translated into a response that could be construed as reflecting exasperation and a wish to punish. After some period of indecision, treatment was resumed for the pair as outpatients; after a joint conference with the therapist, the patient remained with her, and the husband was put on a list for transfer to another therapist. The subsequent course of outpatient therapy was not a happy one for either of the two.

The other patient who enforced a drastic alteration in her treatment plan (also for the worse) was the Invalided Hypochondriac, who started as a hospital inpatient in psychotherapy three times a week. Throughout its brief course (only 42 hours), the therapy was stormy, tense, out of control. It was flooded from the start by explosive affects, intense and wildly fluctuating transferences, dramatically voiced fears and melodramatic blocking, and a disorganized, chaotic, "wild" (and often quite delusional) quality to the patient's ideational content and verbal expression. Yet, with all this, the patient was able to effect her discharge from the hospital—and subsequently from the psychotherapy as well. Within the hospital, she was busily convincing everyone of her readiness for discharge and manipulating the involvement of an increasing number of the senior administrative and supervisory staff members in her case. Within the psychotherapy, she was also pressing for discharge by, on the one hand, refusing to cooperate (toward the end coming late or not coming) and stating her feeling that she couldn't profit from the treatment, and, on the other hand, avowing her conversion to a new life—she could now see that she could and would be a better wife and mother (she had "talked to God" and he had "forgiven" her). To this pressure from the patient was added pressure from the husband. He was by no means as able to understand or to support the need for a long period of hospitalization and treatment as had initially been somewhat optimistically thought. He complained about the expense, and within a few months was quite angry at the doctors for having thus far failed to cure his wife more completely. (He was one of those not at all taken in by her "flight into health.") A number of times he threatened to take his wife out of the hospital, saying that if she needed this much hospitalization she could just as well go to a state hospital; he was readily enlisted alongside his wife in her insistence on hospital discharge and going on, if need be, as an outpatient. Faced with this solid front of the patient and her husband (who, however, presented opposite reasons for the demand), the hospital and the therapist capitulated and agreed to an ongoing outpatient arrangement on a weekly basis. This lasted only 10 sessions over a span of 3 months before it also collapsed.

ALTERATIONS OF TREATMENT PLAN AND COURSE

There is a widespread lack of clarity and consensus on what defines the essence of psychoanalysis as a therapeutic undertaking; there is even greater conceptual uncertainty on what constitutes the dimensions of psychodynamic (or psychoanalytically based) psychotherapy in its range over the entire expressive–supportive spectrum, as well as continuing controversy over the distinctnesses of or the differences between psychoanalysis *and* dynamic psychotherapy (do these constitute the endpoints of a spectrum, or a dichotomy?).[3] It is little wonder, then, that it becomes exceedingly difficult to bring any precision to statements about the extent to which treatment courses in PRP followed the recommended treatment plans and treatment modes, or deviated "significantly" from them. I have already, in the opening discussion in this chapter, presented the 22 patients recommended for and started in psychoanalysis in three groupings: the 10 patients for whom a "classical" psychoanalytic approach (with minimal modifications) was essentially adhered to; the 6 whose analyses were "modified" to a greater extent through a variety of parameters but were still adjudged to be essentially analysis; and another 6 for whom the alterations were so substantial that the treatments were adjudged to have become psychotherapy, varyingly expressive and/or supportive in mode and intent. I think I also make clear in that discussion of the various individual deviations from an unswerving psychoanalytic position that there is in the end

---

3. There is a substantial body of psychoanalytic literature on the nature of the theoretical and practical relationship between psychoanalysis as a specific treatment modality and the whole range of supportive–expressive psychotherapies that are based on psychoanalysis as a theoretical system (psychoanalytically oriented or psychodynamic psychotherapies). Two of the major statements from the debate that raged over this issue in the early 1950s (when PRP was being conceptualized) have already been referred to in Section II (Bibring, 1954, and Gill, 1954; see Chapter 4, pp. 53–54). For an update on this same issue a decade and a half later, and from a worldwide rather than a strictly American perspective, see my article "The Relationship of Psychoanalysis to Psychotherapy—Current Issues" (1969), which I presented as chair of a panel on this subject at the International Psychoanalytical Association Congress in Rome, 1969.

a highly subjective and idiosyncratic, if not quite arbitrary, assignment process involved, and that other people might assign some of these patients differently among these three categories, and with equal justification (though this would none of it really alter significantly the overall picture being drawn). I need hardly add that, since the defining dimensions and characteristics of psychotherapy are even less clarified and less consensually agreed upon than those of psychoanalysis, and since the distinctions between the expressive and the supportive components of the psychotherapeutic process (though clear conceptually) are very difficult to mark out convincingly in the empirical study of therapy records, the decision as to when a treatment that was supposed to be essentially expressive has become essentially supportive is perhaps even more subjective and idiosyncratic (and arbitrary).

Nonetheless, there is some rough value to this kind of effort. With the foregoing caveat in mind, I turn here to the viewing of these 42 treatment courses from the perspective of how well they seem to have fulfilled the initially recommended plan as against departures from it. If significant departures are deemed to have occurred, I examine the extent to which they were unwitting or inadvertent, as distinguished from having been deliberately planned (as a thought-out response to altered perspectives on the nature of the patient or the proper treatment), and the varying degree to which they were made explicit between therapist and patient. With 23 or 55% of the 42 patients (11 men and 12 women, 11 in psychoanalysis and 12 in psychotherapy), there seemed to be well enough demarcated shifts in the originally offered treatment modality to warrant closer consideration here.

Official Shift from Psychoanalysis to Psychotherapy

Of the 11 in psychoanalysis (4 men and 7 women), the 6 who were officially converted, or to be converted, to formal psychotherapy (3 men and 3 women)—the Movie Lady, the Heiress, the Economist, the Masochistic Editor, the Alcoholic Raconteur, and the Housebound Phobic Woman—have already been presented in clinical vignette (see pp. 189–191). The statements made there of rationale and justification for the change in modality from psychoanalysis to psychotherapy, based in each instance on the particular alterations in the understanding of the nature of the patient's problems and illness as these came into fuller view within the unfolding treatment, are not repeated here. Some additional facets of these cases should, however, be mentioned.

With five of the six, it was the therapist who made the determination to alter the treatment course and executed it. With the remaining patient, the Masochistic Editor, the pressure to change course came from outside, from the family. At first this patient gave indication of seeming to respond favorably to the classical analytic technique—certainly while he was concomitantly hospitalized (over the first 16 months of the analysis), and for a while during the subsequent outpatient phase. But gradually he gave progressive evidence—in his very borderline ego functioning with projective and megalomanic excesses, in his poor impulse control and delay capacity, and in the return of unbridled symptom excess, alcoholism, and predatory homosexuality—of his inability to utilize the analytic method properly. Nonetheless, the psychoanalytic treatment mode was adhered to for over 4 years, until the father (as noted earlier; see p. 190) indicated that henceforth he would only support it to the extent of $100 per month. In response to this withdrawal of support, the therapy was reduced to twice weekly. The patient, as already indicated, agreed to add $20 monthly to make up the total bill (an agreement that he then never lived up to), and continued for several more years in an avowedly supportive–expressive psychotherapy.

Again, with five of the six, the treatments continued on after these "conversions" to psychotherapy—in some cases with dramatic changes for the better (as with the Economist), and in some with no significant improvement in treatment progress or life functioning (as with the Masochistic Editor). One of the six, however, the Alcoholic Raconteur, refused to accept this "humiliating" change and disrupted his treatment, as already described (see p. 191). He had, during his total of 2 years and 9 months in analysis (546 hours), had a 5-month conversion in the middle of that span into a face-to-face supportive psychotherapy aimed at more direct behavior control, but he was able to convince his analyst to reinstitute the psychoanalytic effort, just as he had successfully pleaded for the analysis in the first place (on the grounds of his intense quasi-religious motivation). When the analyst finally concluded after the second trial at analysis that the analytic effort would be hopeless and insisted on a permanent conversion to psychotherapy, the patient declared the shift unacceptable, sought out a senior consultant, and there declared his intent to seek further analysis elsewhere in a big city; he abruptly stopped coming to his own analyst, disappeared from his lodging, and left the analyst to close out the treatment alone.

Another facet of interest is that with four of the six the conversion to psychotherapy was formal and explicit (involving reduced frequency, face-to-face interactions, etc.); with the other two, the Heiress and the Housebound Phobic Woman, the shift in approach was never formalized, and certainly never made explicit. The patients continued to come with unaltered frequency and to use the couch—that is, they saw themselves as conforming to the "requirements" of analysis, and they seemed to continue to view their ongoing treatments as analysis. The difference between the two patients was that with the Heiress the change of approach coincided with her transfer from her first, "cardboard analyst" to the second, more senior analyst. The second analyst began to alter his techniques systematically, presenting himself in various ways already specified (see p. 190) as a benevolent father figure, with whom the patient in turn was able to work much more effectively. The Housebound Phobic Woman's unsuitability for analytic work (linked at least in part to the chronic brain damage from the prolonged barbiturate addiction) was clear almost from the start. From almost the very beginning of treatment and over the 9 years (with two "analysts"; see p. 249) to the "cutoff" Follow-Up Study, the patient (though always using the couch) was in effect in a supportive–expressive psychotherapy, riding on a benevolent, positive, unanalyzed transference attachment. All during this time, this patient described herself as "in analysis."

Other Shifts in Modality during or after Analysis

Of the other five patients in analysis where there was at some point, some shift in modality, all but one were women. With two of them, the Snake Phobia Woman and the Divorced Nurse, the issue was one of a preliminary period of psychotherapy as preparation for analysis and as necessary clarification of the internal and external conditions for analysis. The Snake Phobia Woman, when she was seen in evaluation initially, was referred for once-weekly psychotherapy (with an analyst in a city close to her home) because of fears that she was in a near-borderline state, based on such evidence as the illusionary quality of the pervasive snake phobia. This therapy foundered after a year because of the therapist's "aggressive approach to treatment." The patient stated that she would sit on the therapist's lap while he caressed her, made advances to her, and insisted that she was unable to give love because she became fearful of what form treatment might take next. The patient fled from this treatment back to The Menninger Foundation in a panicky state, fearful of both suicide and of mental breakdown. Even with this worsened symptomatic state, it was nonetheless now clear at the (re-)evaluation in Topeka (based in part of course on how she had handled her life and her treatment course in the intervening year) that there was no borderline illness or real danger of ego disorganization; the patient was now recommended for, and taken into, psychoanalysis.

With the Divorced Nurse, it was clear from the start that psychoanalysis would be the definitive treatment of choice for her, but her life was at that moment in acute turmoil: The patient was pregnant, and at the same time her marriage was in deep trouble, with the husband uncertain as to whether he wanted to stay with it or seek a divorce. A recommendation was thus made first for a supportive–expressive psychotherapy three times a week, which would help her sort out the acute crisis, sustain her through the pregnancy, and make plans for more definitive treatment after the baby was born. Actually, this preliminary therapy took place intermittently over almost a year, during which the child was born, the patient began to work professionally half-time at a local hospital, and the husband filed for divorce but then agreed to withdraw the divorce suit pending the outcome of the patient's treatment. Having worked things out to that point, the patient opted to go into her definitive treatment — psychoanalysis — at The Menninger Foundation, where she felt protected and helped.

In each of the other three psychoanalytic cases where there was a change in modality, the change occurred during retreatment efforts that the patient undertook during or after the follow-up period — that is, well after the seemingly more or less satisfactory conclusion of the formal psychoanalysis under study in PRP. The Adoptive Mother (the individual whose analysis had been modified in the "defense-analytic" direction) terminated her treatment content with the result, and was determined to try again to adopt a child when she settled down in her new permanent community. She did successfully adopt a little girl during the follow-up period, but because of the reawakened anxieties over this process, she fashioned for herself the ingredients of a supportive–expressive psychotherapy that helped carry her through the stresses of the adoption period. These ingredients consisted of the help of (1) the friendly family physician, who stood by her and prescribed sedative, tranquilizing, and analgesic agents as needed to help her cope with her anxieties and her recurring somatic aches; (2) the social worker at the adoption agency, "an angel in disguise," to whom the patient could pour out her heart; and (3) the priest who admonished her to "shape up" and do her duty and stop ruining her husband's life. (This turn to religion was also manifested in lighting candles, going to Mass twice daily, praying and weeping, "storming heaven.") The patient specifically did not go into formal psychotherapy during this time, claiming that she could not afford the higher therapy fees that prevailed in her home community, compared with what she had been paying in Topeka. Yet when her sister suffered an episode of puerperal psychosis during this period and received electroconvulsive therapy, the patient was incensed; she felt her sister could have profited much more from psychotherapy, a chance to talk things over.

With the other two in this group, the retreatment effort was a formal psycho-therapy. The Prince, who ended 4 years and 3 months (950 hours) of analysis moderately successfully, nonetheless returned to his ex-analyst for treatment about a year after the Follow-Up Study. He returned because of "the same old prob-lems"—his discomforts in his work and marital relationships, and his continu-ing vulnerability to narcissistic hurts. It was not clear whether he sought more analysis, but the analyst, who now considered the patient "probably unanalyzable," did not wish to make this available. He saw the patient once weekly for about a year (43 hours); the patient then rather abruptly terminated, feeling improved and restabilized. He wanted to be assured that the therapist would see him again if need be.

The third in this category, Peter Pan, did not turn for her retreatment to The Menninger Foundation. The patient's analysis took place over 3 years in Topeka (510 hours), and then continued for another 6 months (almost 100 additional hours) with another analyst, to whom she transferred in a distant city where she went to live. During the second period of analysis the patient experienced a "rude awakening" in contrast to her treatment with the first analyst in Topeka, who she felt allowed her favors (out-of-hour contacts, etc.) and whom she experienced as "fatherly and gratifying." When confronted by her second analyst with a necessary choice, the patient opted to terminate the treatment: "The analyst just felt that I either had to settle down to a long-range treatment program and analyze my relationship to my boyfriend, as well as everything else, and just not think in terms of terminating quickly in 3 or 6 months. And my boyfriend was oppos-ing the treatment. He wanted me out. I had to choose." The patient returned to treatment 6½ years after her analysis termination and 10 years after she was ini-tially seen. Her illness and symptoms (the eating disturbances, compulsive steal-ing, depression, and suicidal actions) had all massively recurred; after a serious suicide attempt with barbiturates, which led to 3 days of coma, she was briefly rehospitalized at The Menninger Foundation. A renewed treatment effort—not outpatient psychoanalysis, but an active supportive–expressive psychotherapy with concomitant hospitalization—was now recommended. The patient refused this recommendation and returned to her home community for an outpatient, very succorant psychotherapy, not psychoanalysis. This, however, did not contain her. After a 10-month effort, punctuated by six brief periods of hospitalization (the longest 2 weeks), the advancing encroachment of a disorganizing psychotic pro-cess (clearly revealed in repeat psychological testing during this period) eventuated in her successful suicide by jumping off a bridge.

Shifts in Treatment Plan during Psychotherapy

For the 12 patients in psychotherapy who underwent substantial modifications of the planned treatment approach (7 men and 5 women), the alterations were of two basic kinds. With 5 of them (2 men and 3 women), it had to do with the requirements for concomitant hospitalization in supporting the treatment and making it possible; with the other 7 (5 men and 2 women), it had to do with the issue of how expressive versus how supportive the treatment was intended to be.

SHIFTS IN HOSPITALIZATION REQUIREMENTS

The five cases where the issue had to do with the role of the hospital were all instances where the planned treatment assigned a stronger and longer place for supporting hospitalization than the patients allowed; these treatments were each handicapped thereby, some to a disastrous degree. (These 5 were all among the 14 patients who were adjudged to have overall insufficient hospital courses; this issue is discussed in the next chapter.) With two of these, the 21-year-old Phobic Girl and the 19-year-old Actress, the issue was one of insufficient family resources for the optimal hospital stay. With the Phobic Girl, because of limited finances, the total initial length of hospitalization was curtailed to only 8 months, and the patient moved into the day hospital and a foster home before actually starting in formal psychotherapy (which started 2 months later). Because of these financial constraints, a more directly supportive, reality-focused, and behavior-controlling psychotherapeutic strategy was enforced, as against the original recommendation for a more purely expressive approach, even leading perhaps to psychoanalysis. The Actress was hospitalized for a total of 14 months; during that period (after 10 months), the patient entered a first abortive psychotherapy, which lasted only 20 hours over 2 months. She was full of instant dislike for her "typical Babbitt" therapist, as noted earlier (see p. 141); after the 20 fruitless hours, he gave up. By the time an appropriate therapy reassignment could be worked out, some 5 months later, the patient had had to leave the hospital some 3 months before and was now living alone in an apartment in town. Though the patient was adjudged now to be sufficiently stabilized to manage on the outside, her psychotherapy was from the start necessarily more supportive and controlling than was intended in the original treatment plan. Her severe character problems required firm stands by her therapist in regard to her destructive behaviors, in a therapy that perforce dealt almost exclusively with the realities of her day-to-day living—the patient (at this early point) was not working, but carousing and drinking, with indiscriminate homosexual and heterosexual promiscuity when drunk.

With the other three in this group, the problems related to insufficient hospitalization were even graver, and these have all already been presented. The Exhibitionistic Dancer was the patient who eloped from the hospital into her marriage with an even sicker patient and was able to use the fact of the new marriage as the basis for an agreement to allow a fully outpatient treatment effort. The Car Salesman and the Addicted Doctor were two severely alcoholic and drug-addicted individuals for whom the fear of unduly entrenching passive dependency gratifications resulted in the agreements to wholly unsuitable efforts at outpatient psychotherapy. It was only when these efforts failed abysmally that the patients were persuaded to accept hospitalization as the needed environment within which to pursue further therapeutic work, and then each of these treatments was burdened by the background of the prior failed effort.

EXPRESSIVE VERSUS SUPPORTIVE TREATMENT

With the seven patients (five men and two women) for whom the degree of "expressiveness" (i.e., an interpretive, insight-aiming, conflict-resolving approach) was at issue, the treatment in each instance became much more purely supportive than originally deemed appropriate and recommended. The Claustrophobic Man was typical of this group. The patient came after several operations, hoped to be successful, for cancer of the thyroid and local recurrences. His natural anxieties were displaced into the intensely constricting phobic concerns about nonexistent heart disease. A circumscribed, but definite, expressive psychotherapeutic course was planned; the main effort would be to help the patient face the cancer and its implications, to experience his fright and his dependency, even with the likely risk of precipitating a depressive episode. At its best, this could result in the patient's working out his regression and dependency in relation to the reality of the cancer threat, not in relation to lifelong dependent strivings that had heretofore been successfully warded off. This much might be ultimately acceptable — to see himself as psychologically healthy until the cancer onset, with his phobic and regressive illness a response to the need to deny the reality of the cancer threat. Thus there could be limited insight into the current triggers of his dependency, some gratification of it within the therapeutic relationship, and a simultaneous effective hiding of the lifelong characterologically rooted dependent strivings. Despite this intent, the treatment (only 46 hours stretching over 18 months) turned out to be essentially supportive therapy throughout, experienced by the patient in directly reassuring terms. A typical incident was an "anxiety attack" in the therapist's office upon which the patient turned to the therapist pleading, "Aren't you going to *do* anything to help me out?" He reported that the therapist answered, "Why no, there isn't anything I can do. It's up to you." The patient took this as follows: "And I think from that time on I had more confidence in him because I knew that—I told myself—he knew I wasn't going to die and he wasn't worried about it. I was the only one that was worried about the situation." The way in which the therapist's countertransferences played into this nonexpressive, supportive approach is described later in relation to the whole treatment course.

Most of the others in this group of seven were similarly shifted, albeit for varying reasons, into more purely supportive psychotherapeutic approaches. The one other case in the group where there was some special feature was that of the Sexual Masochist. The recommended treatment approach for this patient—in many ways, as noted, perhaps the most profoundly ill individual in the entire sample— was a prolonged supportive–expressive psychotherapy (three times a week), with concomitantly an almost equally prolonged hospitalization. His treatment span actually stretched over 8 years (540 hours) and his hospitalization was almost the longest (29 months), being exceeded only by the Addicted Doctor's 30 months of hospital treatment in the affiliated state hospital. With all of this, there was some stabilization and improvement of the patient's enormously chaotic and destructive life (his perversion, his alcoholism, his drug addiction, his panics), and at the end of treatment he was living outside, was off alcohol, was married, and was conducting his own affairs. This very wealthy individual had gradually come to replace his therapy sessions with a daily hour-long session with his lawyer, ostensibly to talk about his endless stock transactions and real estate dealings. The lawyer was clearly a combination of counselor, friend, legal advisor, business partner, and, not least, amateur therapist. After his treatment termination, the patient continued to live in Topeka; during the follow-up period, under the impact of renewed pressures, a return to drinking, and intervening serious heart disease (in this now 42-year-old man), the patient, under the implied threat of divorce, came with his wife to consult his former therapist again. This visit served as the starting point for a new, once-weekly, joint therapy for husband and wife as family counseling and family therapy, with attention directed ostensibly to the problems of each with the other within the marriage. On this basis, it was acceptable to the patient. This family therapy was still ongoing at the time of official Follow-Up Study.

Alterations in Procedural Arrangements

PSYCHOANALYTIC PROCEDURAL ALTERATIONS

One other aspect of treatment alteration has to do with modifications in the specific procedural arrangements of psychoanalysis or psychotherapy in the direction of one's approximating the other. With psychoanalysis, such alterations often involve the frequency of sessions and the recumbent position out of the line of direct visual contact with the analyst.

Session Frequency. At the Menninger Foundation, the usual procedure with psychoanalytic cases—five sessions weekly throughout the course—was substantially adhered to with the entire sample. A significant exception had to do with the termination "weaning process," which has been already described with two patients. One was the Devoted Son, whose 5½-year analysis totaled 1030 hours. Because of a continuing "cloying dependency" that the analyst felt could not be analytically resolved, he undertook a "weaning process" during the terminal 8 months: First, he had the patient sit up, and then he systematically reduced the frequency and duration of sessions—down finally to once weekly, and (during the last 3 months) only 30 minutes each. The patient's very unhappy and resentful response to this—that he was being shoved out of treatment—has already been elaborated (see p. 186). A very comparable termination "weaning process" has also been described with the Medical Scientist (see p. 187).

Face-to-Face Sessions. Of the 22 psychoanalytic patients, 14 (7 men and 7 women), or almost two-thirds, sat up for face-to-face sessions at one time or another. One of these, the Devoted Son, has just been mentioned; his sitting up was part of the termination "weaning" from what had until then been a process conducted along classical psychoanalytic lines. In four other cases already described (the Movie Lady, the Economist, the Masochistic Editor, and the Alcoholic Raconteur), the face-to-face sessions were part of the formal and explicit conversions of psychoanalysis to psychotherapy. The other two "conversions" to psychotherapy, with the Heiress and the Housebound Phobic Woman, were tacit rather than explicit and were manifested in the altered ways of dealing with the material that was coming from the couch; the patients were not sat up. The Heiress occasionally sat up spontaneously at times when she felt very distressed and unable to feel a real contact with her therapist. The Housebound Phobic Woman never sat up throughout her therapies with her two analysts.

In addition to the Heiress, two of the other patients, the very ill Alcoholic Doctor and Alcoholic Heir, sat up from time to time when very distressed. The stretches of sitting up during the course of the Alcoholic Doctor's 7-year (1238-hour) analysis were usually initiated by the patient; during these times he would be seeking practical advice on the handling of his life problems (e.g., on one occasion, he enlisted the analyst's help in securing suitable employment). With the Alcoholic Heir, who only lasted 1 year (221 hours) in analysis, the stretches of sitting up were more extensive. He was clearly frightened of the "unstructured" situation of analysis, and from the beginning he resisted the couch and the instruction to free-associate, which latter reminded him of stories of hypnotism and magic. He was often allowed to sit up and smoke. Additionally, he would often call the analyst when upset and would try to see him at unusual times. On several occasions, he showed up at the analyst's home when in trouble. On other occasions, he very directly tried to make social visits (e.g., inviting the analyst to go sailing on his boat or to come watch television on a rainy afternoon).

With the other six patients who sat up, the sitting up took place only during the initiation of the analytic work. The Snake Phobia Woman sat up on a single occasion: At the supervisor's instigation, the analyst asked that the patient do this in order to give an accounting "outside the analysis" of the precise nature of her experience in the previous therapy (where the therapist had had her sit on his lap, caressed her, etc.). The Script Writer, who expressed great apprehension when assigned to a woman analyst because she had always "had so much more trouble getting along with women than with men," also sat up on a single occasion—in her very first psychoanalytic hour, when she had an "inexplicable" panic reaction immediately upon lying down. Her associations led to her bad relationship with her "bitchy mother."

The initial periods of face-to-face work were more extended with the other four patients in this group. As already described, the Divorced Nurse had a whole year of psychotherapy in order to resolve her acute life-situational problems before she felt prepared for the definitive psychoanalytic treatment. The Adoptive Mother was recommended for psychoanalysis rather than the carbon dioxide inhalation therapy that had been recommended by the referring psychiatrist—a recommendation that she and her husband hoped The Menninger Foundation would concur with. For the first 40 hours of her 3-year analysis (677 hours), she sat up; she was "scared" and could not get on the couch. During this period she would cry bitterly, pouring out her many life dissatisfactions and berating the analyst. For the balance of the treatment, the patient was able to stick to the analytic structure, except for another almost equal period in the middle of the third year of treatment, when she was trying to resolve conflicting pressures around the question of possible termination, and again sat up. She ascribed this period to her anxiety, like the first period, but it was interpreted in relation to her needs to dominate and set the conditions for the structure.

The Suspended Medical Student was recommended for psychoanalysis with an inadequate appreciation of how disruptive his anxiety was and how serious his characterological illness and ego deformation were (with a grave paranoid and borderline potential). He was so fearful of the potential consequences of the un-covering analytic process and of the submissive meanings of the analytic couch that he insisted on sitting up from hours 10 to 46. He was even afraid at this time to give The Menninger Foundation his new local address. With the last of these six, Peter Pan, the situation was exactly the opposite. She very much wanted the recommended psychoanalysis, but was started for the first 3 months in a face-to-face expressive psychotherapy and was told that the analysis itself could only start when she could completely control her stealing, which would otherwise con-stantly endanger the treatment. A few times she was indeed apprehended by local merchants, who, after contacting The Menninger Foundation, agreed not to press charges; the patient was informed that there was no guarantee that this kind of protection could continue. The analyst showed the patient newspaper articles about the many theft detection devices installed in stores. She said that this shocked her out of her stealing. After 3 months, she demonstrated that she could abruptly halt the stealing, which till then had occurred almost daily; she was then formally started in analysis. Episodes of stealing indeed recurred only extremely rarely after that.

PSYCHOTHERAPY PROCEDURAL ALTERATIONS

Among the 20 patients in psychotherapy (11 men and 9 women), there were a fair number—in fact, 7 (5 men and 2 women), as just described—where the therapy shifted, deliberately or inadvertently, from a planned more expressive direction into an actual more supportive direction. With only 1 of these 20, the Bitter Spinster, was an effort made to shift the psychotherapy in the other direction—toward a more "analytic mode." This of course was a patient who, on original evaluation, had been deemed (mistakenly) to be very suitable for psychoanalysis, but because of financial limitations would be going into a twice-weekly, intensive, expressive psychotherapy. The therapist then tried to make this psychotherapy "as close to analysis as can be gotten on a twice-a-week basis." This included even an apparently standing invitation to the patient to use the couch if it would facilitate her communicative process. She declined this invitation during the early part of the therapy, but she periodically accepted it; in fact, for one period of a few months (over the course of her 8 years [560 hours] of treatment), she was on the couch all the time. This was never accompanied, however, by the requirement that she try to free-associate—and the treatment, because of inherent limitations within the patient's character and illness picture, never became really "analytic."

Summary of Alterations

Though the departures from the originally recommended treatment plans that have been described here were of various kinds—change of modality, modifications of psychoanalysis, change in degree of expressiveness versus supportiveness, change in the place and role of concomitant hospitalization, and change in some of the procedural arrangements for these various treatments—the overwhelming majority (though not all) of them were in the service of gradual acknowledgements that the patients were indeed "sicker" than originally understood and that their treat-ments had to be altered into less ambitiously reconstructive and more directly ego-sustaining and supportive channels. The one major exception to this trend had to do with some patients' serious financial limitations, which resulted in curtailments of needed hospitalizations, rendering those patients more vulnerable to disruptive pressures on their lives and their treatments.

Treatment Setting and Context

THE ROLE OF ADJUNCTIVE HOSPITALIZATION

The Place of Hospitalization in PRP

The Menninger Foundation was founded in the 1920s as The Menninger Clinic, a psychoanalytic sanatorium in which sick people could receive the intensive psychoanalytic treatment which they needed within a supportive and protective sanatorium environment, on the model originally established by Ernst Simmel at Der Tegel outside Berlin (see Simmel, 1929). Within such a setting, intensive analytic treatment could be provided to individuals who, by reason of their character structure and/or illness picture, could not be maintained successfully in intensive treatment in the usual private practice outpatient setting. And it was also possible then to develop within that setting a conjunction of therapeutic planning between the specific psychotherapeutic treatment mode and the concomitant psychodynamically planned impact of the hospital environment and milieu. This conjunction was guided by William Menninger into the Menninger-created concepts of psychoanalytically based "milieu treatment."

In its operation, the early clinical reputation of The Menninger Clinic grew out of just this rationale and this context, which were widely written up in both theoretical and clinical terms in many articles in the scientific literature by Karl and Will Menninger, by Robert Knight, and by their coworkers. (Many of these articles appeared in the *Bulletin of The Menninger Clinic*, established in 1937.) A significant milestone in this development was the series of articles by Knight (1937a, 1937b, 1938) on the psychodynamics of alcohol addiction and its psychoanalytic treatment within a sanatorium setting. It was this central feature of the history and the institutional setting of The Menninger Foundation that led so logically, in the setting up of PRP in the 1950s, to two decisions: (1) the theoretical (or the research) intent to explore the limits of the potential for far-reaching and reconstructive character change and illness resolution in intensive psychoanalytic treatments within such a sanatorium setting of patients considerably sicker (with deeper and wider ego deformations) than those usually considered "suitable" for such treatment; and (2) the practical decision that if we were to get a significant sample of psychoanalytic patients who would be available for research study in that setting (i.e., patients aside from the "restricted cases" among students and colleagues in the professional community, where issues of improper invasions of privacy would preclude their inclusion), we would have to study a population many of whom were not only "sicker" than usual, but in concomitant hospitalization as well. In this sense, we were in an excellent position to explore more empirically Glover's (1954) so-called "heroic indications" for analysis—its use in cases where it was felt that however poor the likelihood of its succeeding, only psychoanalysis would give promise of bringing any possibility for real resolution of the patient's conflicts and symptoms.

However, since PRP was to be a project focused on the study of psychoanalysis and psychoanalytic psychotherapy as central treatment modes, the stipulation was made early that we would only select patients where the psychotherapeutic activity was to be the *principal* treatment modality, and where the concomitant use of the supporting and protective environment[1] would only be adjunctive to and supportive of this main treatment approach. We thus did exclude patients (e.g., the openly psychotic) for whom hospitalization and the care of the hospital doctor was seen as the central treatment modality, and for whom whatever concomitant psychotherapy was engaged in was seen as ancillary. Drawing such a line can, of course, be an arbitrary enterprise, and many readers may perhaps wonder whether we did not include some sicker patients for whom the concomitant hospitalization in fact bulked larger than our presumed intent. This is again a matter of relative context. Within our setting, these 42 patients all did represent patients seen as being primarily in psychoanalytic psychotherapy, however prolonged or intensive their hospital care.

Types of Hospitalization within PRP Sample

INITIAL HOSPITALIZATION ONLY

Of our sample of 42, 19 (a little under half) were never hospitalized. These were 10 men and 9 women; 12 of these were in psychoanalysis and 7 in psychotherapy. Of the 23 (a little over half) who were then hospitalized at some time (11 men and 12 women, 10 in psychoanalysis and 13 in psychotherapy), 15 were hospitalized only once at the beginning of their treatment, usually prior to the onset of the formal psychoanalysis or psychotherapy and then overlapping for some variable period with the initial phase of the formal treatment. These 15 were more lopsidedly distributed—only 4 men and 11 women, 6 in psychoanalysis and 9 in psychotherapy. They were hospitalized for periods of from 3 to 18 months, the average being 9½ months. The overlap with the intensive analytic treatment could range from total, as with the Medical Scientist (who was in psychoanalysis for the whole 12 months of his hospitalization), to minimal, as with the Script Writer (who spent 9 months in the hospital altogether, but did not start her analytic treatment until after 7 months of that; she then went on to day hospital status after only 2 months of overlap between her hospital care and her analysis). In most instances, the period of prior hospitalization before the start of the intensive psychotherapeutic work was planned as a period of stabilization; with some (the drug-addicted and/or alcoholic patients prominently among them), it was a period of securing full symp-

---

1. The more comprehensive word "environment" is used here, rather than the narrower word "hospitalization," to indicate that under this rubric in this discussion, I mean to consider the planned deployment of the entire range of environmental control possibilities, from the most restrictive to the most open. This range includes inpatient hospitalization, full and partial day hospitalization, foster home living, living in a relatively unsupervised apartment complex that provides living quarters for Menninger Foundation outpatients, and participation in an organized Out-Patient Club for patients in ongoing therapy—all of this with or without concomitant social casework help and supervision for the patient and/or the family members.

tom cessation and control before embarking on the stresses of the planned psycho-therapy. In some instances there were unplanned delays in getting the patients properly placed from the psychoanalysis and psychotherapy waiting lists.

With 2 of the 15 patients who had just initial hospitalization periods, there were special features that should be noted. One was the Exhibitionistic Dancer, who was in the hospital for 12 months and in concomitant psychotherapy three times a week. It was never intended that her hospitalization would end at that point, but, as already described (see p. 204), she abruptly eloped with another young patient and ran off to get married in another state. When the couple returned, it was with an ultimatum (eventually accepted, as has been described) that they be allowed to go on in their psychotherapy as outpatients, a married couple living on the outside. A good number of the other hospitalized patients (actually the majority, as will be described) actually ceased to be inpatients before they were considered optimally ready, in consequence of a variety of pressures (often posed as family pressures, or the press of limited finances); however, in all these instances the agreement of the therapist and the hospital doctor was always somehow first secured, albeit often quite reluctantly.

The other case with a special feature was that of the Bohemian Musician, who came to treatment in a severely disorganized and depressed state and was hospital-ized with a strict regimen of hospital activities; in response to her deepening depres-sion in the hospital, she received a course of 20 electroconvulsive treatments and 10 nonconvulsive treatments. As noted earlier, she was the only patient in our sample who had such a major somatic treatment intervention as part of her total Menninger Foundation care. Of course, a number of patients—the Silent Woman, the Car Salesman, the Involutional Woman, and the Manic–Depressive Physician —had had somatic treatment (ECT and/or subcoma insulin) before coming to The Menninger Foundation, and a number (though probably fewer than in a com-parable population today) had various psychoactive medications as part of their care with us, or before they came. At the point of onset of formal psychotherapy, the Bohemian Musician was again in ready contact. The electroshock was behind her (it had been stopped several weeks before); and her initially presenting acute psychotic disorganization had considerably abated to her chronically agitated, im-pulse-ridden, but nonetheless (tenuously) controlled state. Her total hospital stay was 12 months, and her three-times-a-week psychotherapy started at the 6-month mark, so that there was a 6-month overlap.

INITIAL HOSPITALIZATION PLUS REHOSPITALIZATION(S)

With 6 of the 23 hospitalized patients (5 men and only 1 woman, 4 in psycho-analysis and 2 in psychotherapy), there was an initial period of hospitalization plus one or more rehospitalizations. These latter were usually of somewhat brief duration and were always needed to bring destructive symptoms back under con-trol. As would be expected, these patients were clustered in the severely alcoholic and drug-addicted group with whom psychoanalysis was being "heroically" at-tempted; they included the Alcoholic Heir, the Alcoholic Doctor, and the Maso-chistic Editor. The Alcoholic Heir was typical. His total psychoanalytic treatment lasted 1 year (221 hours); he was hospitalized for the first 2 months of it and then, because of pressures to join his wife and children (who had moved to Topeka), he had a 2-month period as an outpatient. In response to the stormy and extremely pathological family interaction (the wife, as noted earlier, was an almost equally excessive drinker, and the two of them had produced a strange written compact that there would be no liquor around the home "except by mutual consent" and no drinking "except in front of each other"), the patient was back in the hospital for another 2-month stay after the 2 months out. Actually, the entire treatment effort during that year was marked by constant turmoil, with episodes of hospital control (four hospitalizations totaling 8 months) alternating with periods of attempted outpatient life (three such periods totaling 4 months), each of which were marked by progressive and uncontrolled alcohol excess and by marital strife and violence. The outpatient episodes were usually climaxed by the wife's recourse to the police, an overnight stay in jail for the drunken, abusive patient, and a contrite acceptance of rehospitalization the next day. After a year of this cycle, the hospital, with the analyst's concurrence, insisted that a long period of inpatient care would be an essential condition to the continuation of the treatment; the patient refused and terminated his treatment.

The fourth psychoanalytic patient in this group of six was Peter Pan, the one woman among the six, whose hospitalizations were not related to control over drinking, but to control over the wild gyrations in her food intake—and even more, control over her compulsion to steal.

HOSPITALIZATION AFTER FAILURE OF OTHER EFFORTS

The 2 remaining patients among the 23 hospitalized at one time or another were the Addicted Doctor and the Car Salesman. They were the only ones of the 23 not hospitalized initially, but only thereafter when the primary effort at outpatient treatment had failed. With the Addicted Doctor, for example, there was a full 11-month treatment effort in outpatient supportive psychotherapy, first twice weekly and then three times a week (102 hours altogether). This was done first on an outpatient basis for a variety of reasons—the desire not to entrench the patient's dependent gratifications further, and also to make it possible for the patient to secure gainful employment in the protected setting of the state hospital, while having psychotherapy at The Menninger Foundation. This outpatient treatment period was constantly troubled by the patient's many symptomatic excesses —his alcohol and drug intake, an extramarital affair, and his wild personal extravagances and deepening debt-ridden status. The problems finally culminated in the patient's having a fight with his wife, taking 40 Seconal pills, and driving off to his therapy hour, expecting to fall unconscious and perhaps hit someone. He was found unconscious in his car and was hospitalized in a coma for 30 hours. An emergency tracheotomy and the use of an iron lung were necessary to save his life, but he recovered without any discernible harmful physiological sequelae. As soon as it was safe to do so, the patient was transferred as an inpatient to the affiliated state mental hospital, terminating his Menninger Foundation psychotherapy. He was then in psychotherapy as an inpatient at the state hospital for the next 2½ years until the even more disastrous end of that treatment—his successful suicide with a Nembutal overdose (in the hospital).

The situation with the Car Salesman was comparable and equally disastrous. He went through two periods (totaling 20 months) of psychotherapy on an outpatient basis (again because of the fear of playing unduly into his strong dependency strivings); these both collapsed. He was finally hospitalized for a 10-month-long third treatment effort with a hospital doctor but no formal psychotherapist. This ended equally unsatisfactorily, and the patient went on from there to his death during the follow-up period from an alcohol and drug overdose.

Altogether, for the eight patients who had hospitalization periods beyond the initial period concomitant with the start of their psychotherapy (seven men and 1 woman, four in psychoanalysis and four in psychotherapy), the total hospital periods ranged from 3 to 30 months, and the average was 16 months. As might be expected, this average was longer (16 months as compared with 9½ months) than the average for those hospitalized only once during the initiation of their ongoing therapy. For the 23 hospitalized patients as a group, the total hospitalization periods ranged from 3 to 30 months, with a 12-month overall average length.

Review of Hospitalization Decisions

NUMBER OF PATIENTS HOSPITALIZED

Given all of this, what can be said of the amount of hospitalization in the overall sample, and its relationship to treatment course and outcome? Though 23 (or over half) of the patients were hospitalized for some period of time, it is clear that this figure was not large enough. At least 2 of the 19 treated as outpatients should have been hospitalized; they were both, in different ways, major treatment failures. One of these was the Sociopath, who forced the detrimental "bargain" of outpatient treatment in return for his demonstration that he could survive for a year on his own first (which he barely did, in his symptom-ridden ways). His disastrous outpatient treatment career and termination have already been spelled out in sufficient detail.

The other patient who, in retrospect, should have been hospitalized was the Suspended Medical Student. The issue with him was that he seemed on Initial Study to be a most suitable candidate for outpatient psychoanalysis; he appeared to be suffering with neurotic (hysterical) character problems, marked by the several alcohol-linked dissociative episodes during which he got involved in unethical behaviors with female hospital patients. As this 4½-year psychoanalysis (672 hours) progressed, the analyst was caught between his desire to keep this a properly psychoanalytic case (for Topeka Institute for Psychoanalysis educational purposes), supported by the patient's evidence that he *could* manage his behaviors (effortfully) on the outside, on the one hand; and the telltale indicators that soon surfaced within the analysis of a more disruptive anxiety, a more severe characterological (paranoid) illness, and greater ego deformation than was initially understood, on the other hand. The analyst's gamble on outpatient treatment seemed to pay off during the treatment course, with a seemingly satisfactory termination: The patient returned to medical school, graduated, and was on his way into a general practice. It was only during the follow-up period, as the patient gradually decompensated into a totally collapsed state, that the various issues not worked out in the previous treatment came into clearer focus. Again, as with the Sociopath, intensive therapy with concomitant hospitalization might have given him a far better treatment chance.

LENGTH OF HOSPITALIZATIONS

In addition to how many patients should have been hospitalized, there is the related issue of how long these hospitalizations should have been. Similarly, the judgment is that they should have lasted longer. Of the total of 23 hospitalized altogether, in no case was there a judgment that the hospital period was unduly prolonged, or that it in any way contributed to the entrenching of neurotic dispositions (e.g., dependency gratifications) that was often a feared untoward consequence.

With 9 patients (2 men and 7 women, 5 in psychoanalysis and 4 in psychotherapy), the hospital stay was judged to be appropriate in length (ranging from 3 to 18 months and averaging 9 months). As might be expected, the more successful cases, both with psychoanalysis and psychotherapy, were clustered in this group (e.g., the Medical Scientist and the Phobic Woman in psychoanalysis, and the Bohemian Musician and the Involutional Woman in psychotherapy). But this is not just a circular argument: A case that ended in a dramatically unsuccessful way, that of Peter Pan, is also in this group whose hospital course seemed sufficient.

With the other 14 hospitalized patients (who represented one-third of our total sample and 60% of those hospitalized), it was clearly evident that their overall treatments were grossly handicapped because of insufficient hospital treatment. These 14 included 9 men and 5 women, 5 in psychoanalysis and 9 in psychotherapy. Again as might be expected, this group of 14 was heavily loaded with the failed cases—4 of the 6 who died of mental-illness-related causes, and 8 of the 15 who came with severe alcoholism (and often drug addiction as well); among those 8, not a single one did well in treatment. (By contrast, though, there were 4 severely alcoholic and/or drug-addicted patients among the 9 who were adjudged to have sufficiently long hospitalization periods; 3 of these 4 had successful outcomes, and 1 showed a moderate improvement.)

Purposes of Hospitalization

The purposes of hospitalization, though in general related to issues of need for protection and care, differed significantly in particulars among the patients. Horwitz, in his book on the results of the Prediction Study (1974), spelled out what he called "[t]hree major assumptions . . . regarding the need for hospitalization or other adjunctive supports" (p. 139). He described these as follows:

> Most important was the belief that patients whose symptoms were destructive or self-destructive needed hospitalization to supply the necessary controls to such behavior in order to protect the patient as well as the treatment situation. Prominent in this group were the addictive patients, but other kinds of acting out (promiscuity, antisocial behavior, suicidal danger) were also included. A second assumption concerned patients whose symptoms were not destructive or self-destructive, but who were seen as unable to form a stable therapeutic alliance without the support and gratification of a hospital, at least in the early phases of the psychotherapy. And last, individuals for whom expressive psychotherapy was deemed desirable or necessary but whose ego strength was not sufficient to tolerate the stress of such treatment required hospitalization in order to make expressive treatment possible. (pp. 139–140)

CONTROL OF DESTRUCTIVE SYMPTOMS

Here I would like to extend and further particularize this presentation of the different bases for hospitalization and the differing impacts of hospitalization. With at least 9 patients, control of destructive and self-destructive symptoms was put forth as *the* central and overriding purpose of the hospitalization; this factor also bulked to varying degrees with almost every one of the 23 who were hospitalized. Of course, control of addictive and alcoholic propensities was the behavior control goal most frequently adduced. For patients with histories of unremitting drinking and/or drug taking that had destroyed previous efforts at intensive outpatient treatment (e.g., the Masochistic Editor, whose year of previous outpatient psychoanalysis had been riddled with missed hours and with hours to which he had come drunk), the renewed effort at psychoanalysis within The Menninger Foundation was predicated on the hospital control that would insure their coming to the analytic sessions regularly and sober, and with their anxieties blocked from drainage via alloplastic behaviors. But other symptom expressions were also targeted for comparable hospital control. With the Script Writer, it was not just her drinking but also her hostile acting out and destructive interactions with her family that were so damaging, and with the Medical Scientist, it was not just his alcohol–drug intake, but also his proneness to rages and violent assaultiveness when drunk. With Peter Pan, it was her compulsion to steal and risk trouble with the law that was the target (as well as the possibility in the hospital of supervising her diet and seeing that her alternating anorexia and bulimia were regularized into a stable food intake). And in several cases, the target was severe suicidal impulses; in fact, some patients, like the Addicted Doctor, were precipitated into hospitalization by a serious suicide attempt.

REGULATION OF AND CAPITALIZATION ON CHARACTER PROPENSITIES

But there was also a whole array of other specific purposes for hospitalization. The ability to supervise diet and regularize food intake has just been mentioned in connection with Peter Pan. With the Alcoholic Doctor, the issue was not just one of control of his massive alcoholism, addiction, and homosexual activities; the particular use of the hospital environment was also planned to capitalize on his passive, compliant, and compulsive propensities in the service of having him follow his scheduled activities carefully and accomplish his tasks conscientiously, and in general of reinforcing his dependency and compulsivity through the congenial role of the "model hospital patient." Once this pattern was well re-established, it could then possibly continue as the patient transferred to outpatient status, with the therapist now assuming (even more than the hospital doctor) the role of the benevolent superego figure, encouraging this kind of compulsivity and compliance. Over the long term, this could lead the patient back to an academic or an institutional medical career (for which his training background had adequately prepared him), rather than independent private practice. In such a career choice, some of the patient's passive needs could be successfully met, but channeled into appropriate and highly socially approved directions. (There was already a model for just such a course in the patient's prior life, both in his success in Army medicine, and in his year of work in academic medicine subsequent to his military service.) How this would all then interdigitate with the expressive, insight-aiming aspects of his analytic therapy would, of course, be a crucial issue for the therapist within the treatment.

Likewise, with the Intellectual Fencer, the goal was not just the control of her addictive symptoms. In her case, there was the problem of mounting an expressive psychotherapy in the face of her proneness to deceptions and concealments in her interpersonal dealings; hospitalization and hospital observation would provide the additional channels of information that could support the therapist's confrontational activities in coming to grips with the patient's character propensities. Of course, these phenomena of interpersonal evasiveness and outright deceptions might also tend to drop away, just because she *was* under hospital control and supervision, and therefore both off drugs and separated from her parents. For the Phobic Woman, a different specific kind of therapeutic help could be offered by the structured hospital environment, as well as by the constant availability of the day hospital and the whole community of patients and ex-patients: These would, all together, provide a network of supports within which she could live a relatively freer life in the Topeka setting (i.e., perhaps phobia-free), albeit perhaps restricted as far as being able to move beyond it would be concerned. Such a development could then provide a "space" within which the patient could move and function tolerably well, while undergoing the more definitive and reconstructive intensive psychoanalytic work that was hoped for.

With the Actress, the role of the hospital would be the much more encompassing one of providing a consistent and acceptable form of nurture, of dependent gratification, while not being put off or repelled by her hostile testing devices, by her greediness, or by her tendency to play off people one against another. Within the context of such a setting, it was felt that the patient could enter an effort at an expressive psychotherapy in which she could gradually give up her constant role playing, her "as-if" characterizations, and her confabulations, and be enabled to confront herself as a disturbed person in need of psychotherapeutic help.

DOVETAILING OF HOSPITALIZATION AND PSYCHOTHERAPY

With two of the patients, the total hospitalization and psychotherapy efforts could dovetail in reinforcing ways: The psychotherapy itself could provide in a specifically focused and verbalized way the very same things that the whole setting—hospital, day hospital, family care home, and (in one case) school tutorial arrangements— was designed to provide. With the 17-year-old Adolescent Grandson, the object of both hospitalization and psychotherapy was the creation of strong and stable objects for attachment and identification. In the hospital, this would be encouraged through the concerted, non-warring, mobilized concern of a stable therapeutic community interested in his welfare and in his growth. In the very carefully selected foster home into which he would be graduated, he would experience an intact family—with a father with whom a positive bond could readily exist, as well as an affectionate mother, and without the estrangement that characterized the relationship between his own grandfather (the strong father in his life) and his stepmother (the tender mother in his life). Similarly, in the specific psychotherapy, the youngster's search for a strong masculine object to attach himself to, and to identify with, would be carefully fostered. And the patient quite explicitly aided this treatment plan when he asked to change his first foster home placement because he found his first foster father too remote and preoccupied with his business affairs (too much a new version of the grandfather).

A similar kind of coming together of the two influences (psychotherapy and hospitalization) was planned with the Invalided Hypochondriac, who came to treatment with an enormous sense of oral deprivation. This 30-year-old married woman with children burst into tears on initial interview and blurted out, "How can anyone live unless her mother loves her?"; she saw nothing especially incongruous in her still voicing this complaint with such present-day anguish. Her psychotherapy would be geared not only to working out the extent of these feelings of deprivation, but also to working with her distorted behavioral expressions of these needs for love, and to working out with her as much as possible the barriers that prevented her pursuing these needs in ways more likely to gratify them. She consistently frustrated the very satisfactions that she felt she wanted so much; it was hoped that she could be helped to work out more rewarding ways to secure them. The whole hospital treatment would be designed to pursue these very same goals, through the focus on the patient's actual behaviors within the hospital environment and the interactions she provoked with the figures in it.

Possible Adverse Effects of Hospitalization

UNDUE GRATIFICATION OF DEPENDENCY NEEDS

At the same time there were many cautions raised about the possible adverse effects of hospitalization (or at least of unduly prolonged hospitalization). The most often mentioned for many of the patients was the fear of unduly gratifying and further entrenching deep-seated passive dependency strivings, which often included an additional facet of masochistic willingness to endure restriction and frustration. This fear on our part served to keep some patients initially out of the hospital altogether, and to launch them rather into wholly unsuitable efforts at outpatient psychotherapy (as with the Addicted Doctor and the Car Salesman). These efforts generally collapsed out of their inherent nonviability, and the patients then had to be persuaded to accept hospitalization as the necessary framework for continued efforts at therapy. The Addicted Doctor's hospitalization, as noted, came only after his near-lethal suicide attempt.

With other patients, this fear of fostering dependency was a major factor in our agreement to what turned out to be very premature discharges from hospital treatment. This operated among many of the 14 adjudged to have an insufficient period of hospital treatment. The Alcoholic Heir was a good case in point. As noted earlier, he was one of that group of profoundly alcoholic and/or drug-addicted individuals recommended for psychoanalysis on the basis of the usual statement of heroic indications. Concomitant hospitalization was, of course, felt to be necessary to curb his unremitting drinking, but it was also clearly declared to pose a major problem for the treatment. On the one hand, it was indeed necessary: Whenever the patient left the hospital's security he reverted to uncontrolled drunkenness, which would be totally disruptive of his treatment chances. On the other hand, when in the hospital, the patient's profound passive needs seemed fully gratified: He quickly became anxiety-free, the pressure to drink ceased, and he became a "model" and totally problem-free patient. Perhaps the most therapeutically conducive course could be managed "in between" — time spent in the controlled environment, at least, of the day hospital, but a life outside with his own family. This would be a more nearly normal life situation, posing its demands to function as husband and father at least, even though not as responsible business-man and breadwinner. The actual treatment course did not work out that way at all, as detailed earlier (see pp. 217–218). This experience was a uniform one. Many hospitalizations were unduly curtailed because of this fear of digging in neurotic dependency patterns, and the therapies were then adversely affected in very ma-jor, and often disastrous, ways; on the other hand, in no instance was an unwork-able dependency problem created for an ongoing intensive therapy in any significant way by virtue of a long hospital stay, and some of these hospital stays went up to 30 months in length.

Other cautions concerning the possible adverse consequences of hospitaliza-tion were also raised. Very closely related to the issue of undue dependency was the issue of the secondary gains of hospitalization — the pleasure gratifications of total nurture, and the insulation from, and avoidance of, reality problems. This line of reasoning was used as part of the argument to allow the Sociopath to have the psychotherapy he demanded on his outpatient terms — to his total detriment.

SPLIT TRANSFERENCE

Another kind of potential danger that was raised was that of the possibilities for a split transference that could work out to the patient's detriment. This risk was especially highlighted with two of the patients. The Exhibitionistic Dancer could constantly experience the hospital's control efforts as the father's punitiveness, and its understanding efforts as the mother's seductiveness. Hospital personnel could thus readily be made to appear inconsistent. Similarly, in contrasting the hospital staff and the therapist, the patient could readily see the former in the father's role (the one who always demanded conformity and obedience), and the latter in the mother's role (the one who allowed impulse expression for her own neurotic reasons, her vicarious enjoyments, and never really tried to stop the pa-tient when she should have). Any evidences, then, of lack of perfect concordance between hospital and therapy could be distorted into replicas of the neurotic family interactions at home.

Similarly, the Bohemian Musician's evolving transferences could readily be split in the direction of a repetition of the neurotic life constellations on the out-side — that is, the therapist and the hospital doctor could be seen respectively as revivals of the lover in the big city and of the husband with the "home in a corn-field" (Topeka, Kansas). The therapist–lover would be intellectual, cultured, and sophisticated, appreciating the patient adequately, giving her narcissistic supplies on her own terms, and drawn to side with her against the cruel and arbitrary dic-tates of the hospital doctor–husband to whom she was bound by reality ties. Should this initial transference stance fail, the patient's frustration and anger could take a variety of turns — among them a renewed deepening depression (requiring fur-ther electroshock), or an abrupt treatment disruption, or a transference reversal (with an uninterested and uninteresting therapist versus a kindly, protecting hos-pital doctor).

Obviously, this problem of the possible fostering of tendencies to split the transferences could also be turned to psychotherapeutic advantage if properly recognized and dealt with, both in the psychotherapy and in the hospital management.

EVOCATION OF ENHANCED OR NEW SYMPTOMS

Other apparent problems could likewise be turned to potential therapeutic advantage. For instance, the possibility was specifically raised with the Bohemian Prep School Boy that enhanced or new symptoms might be evoked by hospitalization. When he came for treatment, he was flooded by a mounting anxiety and a growing awareness of the disorder and inner chaos of his life; when hospitalized, he responded rapidly to the ordered and structured environment, becoming considerably less anxious and stating, "I like it here in the hospital because everything is so orderly and efficient and I get the idea that people know what they are doing." At the same time, he became overtly more depressed. This evocation of symptoms, especially an emergent or intensified depression, was seen as well with many other patients as a major kind of response to the enforced self-confrontation that coming to this kind of treatment and this kind of hospitalization almost inevitably represented. It could as well facilitate as hinder the treatment effort.

Something of a different cast, but with a similar effect, was postulated for the Sexual Masochist. It was thought that his perverse behaviors might be brought under control not only because of the enforced hospital controls, but also because (psychologically) he could construe the hospitalization in a masochistically perverse way. His behavioral expression of his sexual masochism in his life outside would then disappear into his characterological masochism being lived out in his transferences in the hospital, especially with his intense feelings about his "inferior" position as a hospitalized patient. Again, a transference problem created for the therapy could be turned to therapeutic exploitation within the therapy.

MULTIPLE PROBLEMS

I have given an accounting of the pros and cons of the various ways in which hospitalization could operate psychologically as part of the whole treatment picture. Clearly, with all the good hospitalization could potentially do if used without fear when needed, and for a long enough period of time, it was by no means always capable of living up to its assigned tasks. The Addicted Doctor represented the most spectacular failure of hospitalization. His first outpatient treatment ended disastrously after 11 months (102 hours) with his near-lethal suicide attempt. There then followed his second treatment, now as an inpatient, for 30 months in the affiliated state hospital with the therapist who was intent on employing the "Aichhorn technique." Though he was officially a hospital patient throughout this time, his life and behaviors were never brought under proper hospital control. As a physician and former medical staff member in the hospital, he created a privileged position for himself. He was called "Doc" and was usually the buffer between the other patients and the personnel; he was, in fact, often the one the other patients approached first before seeking out the ward doctor. The patient used this favored role to instigate much turmoil; for example, he advised patients on how to engineer elopements and provided keys for them. In turn, the other patients covered up for him (as when he went on unauthorized leaves, fashioned a key to get in and out of closed wards, etc.), helped provide a chain for smuggling his contraband in and out of the hospital, and shared with him, especially money. Though he had no obvious source of funds (and could get no money at all from his wife), he always had money and was always able to buy things—candy, cigarettes, and most dangerously, drugs; the hospital could never discover the source of the money or cut it off.

The most dangerous traffic was in barbiturates, which, despite his hospitalization, the patient could get hold of, sometimes in large quantities. He carried on a *sub rosa* correspondence with wholesale suppliers; when he was out on passes, he bought supplies and stashed them away in his home. His wife knew of caches of up to 1000 pills hidden in the rafters, yet seemed to take no action to curb this. On one occasion when the patient's therapist was on vacation, he brought 500 Nembutal tablets onto the ward and hid them in two different places; he seemed to have these both for personal use and for sale to other patients. No wonder that when he felt he had played his desperate situation out to its bitter end, and he decided upon it, he was able to commit suicide with a large overdose of Nembutal.

Alternatives to Full Hospitalization

In addition to full hospitalization itself, other (lesser) adjuvant environmental control mechanisms, such as day hospital, the Out-Patient Club, or ancillary casework with the family could be used in very specific ways as part of the overall treatment plan. One example is given of the use of each of these mechanisms.

DAY HOSPITAL

The Involutional Woman was hospitalized for 3 months and then went for a prolonged period into the day hospital; this was combined with a return to school for refresher law courses, as well as for secretarial instruction. The therapeutic plan was for a circumscribed expressive psychotherapy, built around the working out of her massive inhibition of all expression of aggression, and of her deep denials and repressions in regard to her long-time competitive struggles with her husband. In view of her age (50) and her character rigidity, it was thought best to steer clear of the even deeper conflicts centered on dependency strivings and on her femininity. The concomitant day hospital care and the return to school—and, ultimately, the return to some professional (legal or paralegal) activity—would help to reinstitute working compulsive defenses, to channel hostile and competitive impulses more constructively, and to obtain enhanced narcissistic gratifications. Clearly, the patient's wish to return to some level of active career would not work unless the psychotherapy helped relieve the pressures of her hostilities and of her harshly punitive superego. Equally clearly, the psychotherapy probably would not work unless this concomitant rechanneling of aggressions and enhancement of self-esteem could occur in her life.

THE OUT-PATIENT CLUB

The psychotherapeutic use of the Out-Patient Club was best exemplified with the Fearful Loner. The goal of psychotherapy with this inhibited, isolated, compulsive, and paranoidly hyperalert individual was to give him an opportunity to find that he could have a relationship with another person that was not basically hostile and threatening, and, along with this, to come to recognize the extent to which his feeling that he was ever surrounded by menacing dangers was but a projection of his own inner turmoil and aggression. Along parallel lines, the recommended treatment plan also included participation in the Out-Patient Club, in which his involvement with a bridge-playing group was encouraged. Here, in a similarly appropriate manner, the patient could engage in interactions on his own terms, could engage in interpersonal exchange when he wanted, and could focus just on the cards when he wanted—always to the extent that he felt comfortable, and in a tolerant milieu. Here too, as he felt able and at his own pace, he might reach past the loneliness of his essential isolation towards tolerable interpersonal relationships.

CONCOMITANT SOCIAL CASEWORK

Lastly, of course, concomitant social casework—usually with the spouse—was an ongoing recommended process in many instances. With the Sociopath, for example, there were at least two specified purposes for his wife's recommended casework contacts. As already stated (see p. 202), the first was to provide her with specific aid for the ever-difficult reality of life with her husband. The second was to obtain from her a more objective appraisal of the patient's ongoing life functioning, as a needed check on the reliability of his accounting. On occasion, such a casework process would leave the involved spouse to seek separate psychotherapy on his or her own behalf. In fact, one of the PRP patients, the Obedient Husband, came to treatment in this way; it was the outcome of the intensive casework contact he had been having for a year in connection with his wife's treatment as an inpatient at The Menninger Foundation.

LIVING SITUATION AND LIFE CONTEXT

At the beginning of this chapter, I have indicated the original rationale and conceptualization of the then Menninger Clinic in the 1920s: a supportive and protective sanatorium environment within which very sick people could receive the intensive psychoanalytic treatments they needed—an environment that could not be successfully offered in the usual outpatient private practice setting of psychoanalytic work. A logical corollary of such a treatment mode and setting was the creation of an at least temporary disruption of the usual living situation and life context for the patients referred for such sanatorium care. At its best—for those affluent enough, as well as flexible enough in their life arrangements—it would mean that the entire family would move to Topeka, so that as the patient moved through the range from the maximum of inpatient care to the most open of outpatient care, the family could be living in the community and available for mutual visiting, and after the patient was out of the hospital (under partial care, day hospital auspices, or whatever), he or she could be again living in his or her own home together with the family. If the patient was a man or a working woman, there would be the issue of having sufficient financial resources so that gainful employment could be suspended during the hospitalization period, and/or the related issue of being able to resume work or find appropriate employment in Topeka during the balance of the treatment course. If the patient was a woman and the husband was the main income source, there would be only a slightly less complicated and stressful working and living situation to be negotiated.

All this of course was based on the expectations of the "usual" psychotherapeutic situation, in which it is better for the treatment course and also for the life course that the treatment be carried on in the closest possible juxtaposition to the patient's life situation, and that there be opportunity for maximum commerce between the ongoing treatment events and the ongoing life events as mediated through the patient's behaviors and reactions. There would, of course, always be instances where the pathogenic and mutually hurtful nature of the interaction between the patient and the family members would be so destructive that the separation of the patient from the family — at least for some period of time — would in itself be one of the positive aspects of the hospitalization and removal experience. In such cases, the family's continued location in the city of permanent residence during the hospitalization would not by itself pose a significant problem to the patient and the treatment, so long, of course, as there were the resources and the flexibility to enable the family to visit in Topeka whenever it was felt that that would be appropriate and helpful.

The opposite situation, however, would also exist — that in which the separation (for whatever period) of patient and family would be positively hurtful to the possibilities for proper therapeutic work and restored optimal living. Such a separation, where enforced by the exigencies of sanatorium hospitalization, would necessarily bring negative consequences to be considered, along with the therapeutic needs and the positive effects for which the hospitalization and separation were being recommended. Because of the whole institutional climate as well as the treatment rationale of The Menninger Foundation, such possible adverse effects of the hospitalization and separation experience tended to be insufficiently considered during the initial evaluation and treatment-planning process. This underrated possible adverse consequence of The Menninger Foundation treatment experience (at least with certain patients) could be highlighted even more in those instances where leaving the family and coming to Topeka for treatment were based not on the need for the concomitant hospitalization and its positive values, but simply on the fact that intensive long-term psychoanalytic treatment on an *outpatient* basis was not available in the patient's home setting or within nearby commuting distance (this was frequently the case with people from rural or small-town midwestern America). There were such instances within the PRP sample, and these were the patients who provided the strongest case for the thesis that is so dominant in the Voth and Orth (1973) book — the major contribution that proper engagement by the patient in the requirements of his or her ongoing life situation makes toward the possibilities for effective psychotherapeutic work. Here, I describe the treatment setting and the life context in relation to both the opportunities and the risks for the treatments in both directions: that of optimal separation from the family (usually by means of hospitalization), and that of maximal involvement with it (by means of living with the family in a home situation, usually transplanted to Topeka).

Patients Who Lived in Topeka or within Commuting Distance

Of the PRP sample of 42, 14 (exactly one-third), 7 men and 7 women, were treated as outpatients either living at home in Topeka or living at home within commuting range.[2] A fair number of these 14 had specifically moved to Topeka, either alone or with their families, in order to seek out their treatment at The Menninger Foundation. For example, the husband of the Adoptive Mother had obtained a relocation of his work assignment near Topeka so that his wife could apply for intensive psychotherapy. Similarly, the English Professor and the Prince had both sought out and obtained positions at the local university in order to be able to pursue psychoanalysis in Topeka. And the Bitter Spinster (a nurse), a patient in psychotherapy in Topeka, followed her therapist when he left to enter private practice in a nearby metropolis in order to continue her outpatient therapy and her livelihood in hospital nursing under, as much as possible, unchanged circumstances.

Of these 14 patients, 9 had to commute either all of the time or for a very large proportion of it; for at least 4 of them, this posed specific interpersonal or intrapsychic problems. The Claustrophobic Man, for example — bland about the threat from his recurrent cancer, but ever panicky about his nonexistent "heart disease" and its presumed threat of unattended sudden death — demanded that his wife accompany him on his weekly drive for treatment. This was given up after a while, but only after an episode of bitter protest by the wife during a joint interview, in which she stated that she felt chained by his symptoms and exhausted by what he asked of her. The specific masochistic propensities of both the Homesick Psychology Student and the Economist were fed by the inconveniences imposed by the commuting distance and schedule. For instance, the Homesick Psychology Student had no car at the start of his treatment. For his weekly commute (50 miles each way) from the city where he was pursuing his graduate studies in psychology, he had to arise at 4:00 A.M. to make the available train connection and then wait 2 hours upon arrival for his scheduled appointment. When he received his degree and undertook full-time employment, there was desultory talk of his doing so in Topeka and arranging for a more frequent (and much more convenient) treatment schedule, but nothing came of this. Somewhat later he did obtain a car, but he then did not feel free to use the very convenient and fast turnpike (presumably because of the expense) and usually came by the much slower

---

2. One of these 14 was living at home while in outpatient treatment, but, of course, not in or near Topeka; this was the Movie Lady, being seen in filmed analytic treatment on a research basis at the major mental health research institutiton in her home community, a large metropolitan area. Another of the 14, the Involutional Woman, had a brief 3-month period of hospitalization at The Menninger Foundation because of her depression, and then 9 months of living outside the hospital but away from her family as a day hospital patient in Topeka, taking courses at the local university. At the 1-year mark, she returned to her home and family situation while continuing to commute to Topeka, about 65 miles each way, for her then once-weekly treatment for several years thereafter.

and more tedious alternate route. The Economist had a similar pattern; he was always willing and even "eager" to maintain a similar long commuting schedule (in his case on a *daily* analytic basis for 6 years, or 1364 hours, plus another 3½ years, or 237 additional hours, of less frequent psychotherapy). He "enjoyed" having 3 hours a day for his analysis, which he ruminated on obsessively during the drive in both directions. With the Snake Phobia Woman, the specific conditions of her commuting to analysis posed a major treatment problem, to be spelled out further on in describing the instances of truly adverse treatment effects from enforced separations.

Patients Who Relocated Their Homes to Topeka for Treatment

Another 11 patients, 7 men and 4 women (just over a quarter of the sample), were in a slightly different category. They did not live to begin with in Topeka or within commuting range, nor had they come to live in Topeka with the intent to seek treatment. Instead, they were in a position, once their psychiatric evaluation resulted in a recommendation for treatment in Topeka, to move with their families and to have workable living situations set up for the families in Topeka. In some cases, patients and/or spouses found appropriate gainful employment as needed; in others, the families lived on family money (where the resources were available and the patients were too ill to be able to be self-supporting at the time of treatment initiation). In perhaps an extreme instance, the Obedient Husband literally sold out what was anyway a failing business in his home town, and after a period of dependence on the largesse of his rich in-laws, he secured a full-time position in a new kind of occupation (as an office manager in a moderate-sized business in a nearby small city).

Of these 11 who were able to bring their families to Topeka readily, 5 had periods of hospitalization, during which their families (spouses and children) lived in the community. All of the 5 (the Heiress, the Alcoholic Heir, the Alcoholic Doctor, the Addicted Doctor, and the Phobic Woman) were ill enough—4 of them alcoholic and addicted, and 1 of them phobically crippled—that they could not work; however, all but the Addicted Doctor were from the more affluent families in the sample and could well afford both the hospitalization and the concomitant extramural living of the spouses and children. The treatment career of the Alcoholic Doctor was typical of the severe problems that could be generated in connection with such an arrangement. His family had somewhat less money than the others (his 70-year-old father, as noted earlier, was continuing reluctantly in practice in order to support this expensive treatment plan), and his hospitalization only lasted a year. After a year and a half, when he was a full outpatient and was returning to work as a physician, his wife, who had been away pursuing her own advanced training in a medical specialty, joined him. Then the four children, who had been living with their grandparents (his parents), joined them—first the younger two, and then the older two. From this point on, with the ongoing workaday demands of the reconstituted family, things went less well. The patient and his wife both had a difficult time establishing themselves in practice. Homemaking and parenthood were difficult for both, and they slid back into a most unstable life together, with a full-scale reversion to fighting, mutual drinking, drug taking, and renewed homosexual escapades by the patient.

Patients Who Left Their Families for Treatment

The other 17 patients, 7 men and 10 women (40% of the total sample), came to The Menninger Foundation for treatment—in all but 2 of these instances, with concomitant much-needed hospitalization—that effectively removed them from their families for extended periods. In most cases, this treatment-created separation from the family was indeed necessary and highly beneficial, at least for an often prolonged initial period. For at least 2 patients, however, it had the opposite consequences—very detrimental ones. One was the Invalided Hypochondriac, who had to be hospitalized, to be sure, but whose enforced separation from her husband during this time played its major role in the subsequent downhill course of her treatment, her marriage, and her whole life. The other was the Divorced Nurse, who was one of the 2 among these 17 whose treatment in Topeka and separation from her family were not due to the need for concomitant hospitalization, but rather to the total unavailability of the recommended psychoanalysis in or near her home community, as well as to the husband's inability (or unwillingness) to relocate in a way that would keep the family together during the long treatment effort planned.

Beneficial Effects of Separation

But before discussing the three cases (these two, the Invalided Hypochondriac and the Divorced Nurse, as well as the commuting case previously mentioned, the Snake Phobia Woman) where the separation from the family had an adverse impact on the treatment course and life course, I want to describe something of those cases where such separation of patient from family was highly beneficial (and, incidentally, was not always of sufficient duration). The beneficial quality was strikingly manifest in seven instances, and moderately evident in a good many more. Of the seven, one, the Tantrum Woman, never needed hospitalization, but did need the separation. She was the young widow with the severe depressive and regressive reaction to her husband's death, whose relationship with her mother had so badly deteriorated that an aunt had had to accompany her as the responsible relative to her psychiatric evaluation, and who yet had maintained the intensely dependent tie to this same hated mother through the enemas that her reactivated constipation required in order to keep her from being "poisoned" by her wastes—a revival of the childhood hostile–dependent enema interactions with the mother (see pp. 148, 162).

Three of the six in this group who were hospitalized—the Medical Scientist, the Alcoholic Heir, and the Alcoholic Doctor (all three alcoholic and/or drug-addicted)—required separation from their wives and their very pathological marriages in order to give their treatment its best chance. With the Medical Scientist, the separation induced by hospitalization and the introspective turning induced by psychoanalysis in this relatively inarticulate individual led to a reassessment of a very difficult marriage, which had been basically an extension of a bad relationship with his mother. He gradually became convinced that his marriage to this highly competitive, sexually unresponsive, "sadistic bitch" was a total mismatch, and he decided on a divorce. One didn't have to be inextricably tied to a quarrelsome extension of one's mother: "You don't have to live with someone you feel this way about." Before his analysis, the patient had never dared to be critical of his wife or parents except when drunk.

With the other two, the Alcoholic Heir and the Alcoholic Doctor, the outcome was the opposite—totally unsuccessful. Both had wives almost as alcoholic as themselves. The Alcoholic Heir, as noted earlier, had made a strange pact with his wife in regard to liquor around the home, and had also said on the occasion of a shared alcoholic stupor, "We're just a pair of old drunks" (see p. 147). Yet he would not tolerate hospitalization (and separation from the wife) more than briefly, and four times during his year of analysis (221 hours), he was able to pry his way out of the hospital into outpatient status. During this whole period, as noted (see pp. 217–218) the patient's life progressively deteriorated, with increasing marital turmoil, drunken brawling, and fear-ridden paranoid decompensation. (He once found a "jeweled ice pick" in an attic trunk and brought it to his analyst for safekeeping, fearful that his wife intended to use it on him.) When the analyst finally firmly insisted that in order for the treatment to go on, the patient would have to agree to a prolonged period of hospitalization and separation, the patient abruptly fled. The comparable situation with the Alcoholic Doctor has likewise already been stated. When he began living on the outside with his disturbed and heavily drinking wife and his reconstituted family, both the marriage and the patient's working capacity went steadily downhill; the addiction problem grew ever more severe, until finally the patient died. In his case, unlike the Alcoholic Heir's, more hospitalization (and separation) was not financially feasible, and he and his wife were drawn to stay together out of their mutually reinforcing pathological dependencies.

With the other three of the six in this group who were hospitalized—Peter Pan, the Phobic Girl, and the Bohemian Prep School Boy, all younger patients (ages 19, 21, and 17, respectively)—it was the parents from whom separation was important to the chances for treatment progress. Peter Pan was first hospitalized in her home city at the point of intensifying anxiety and disturbance, with her eating and hunger behaviors completely broken down and out of control. The parents were not pleased with this hospitalization (which was in a first-class institution). They felt that the patient was being allowed too much free choice, receiving a diet tailored to her demands, doing pretty much what she pleased, and getting a great deal of time from the doctor. According to the doctor, the treatment was beset by the constant manipulations of the parents and their inability to refrain from attempts to interfere and dictate. For this reason, transfer to the (distant) Menninger Foundation was recommended and carried out.

The situation with the Phobic Girl was similar, but more intense and of longer duration. She had been in 2 years of prior outpatient psychotherapy on a twice-weekly basis in her home town. The patient's symptoms (her obesity, her self-destructive clowning, her social and academic failures) continued unabated, though the parents saw her only as lazy and recalcitrant and regarded her obesity as her only real problem. The mother had to take the patient, who was fearful of driving, to all the therapy hours. When the therapist became convinced that the patient required psychiatric hospitalization and separation from the intense symbiotic interdependency with the mother, he referred her to The Menninger Foundation. The patient received the recommendation with mixed feelings; she was afraid to go that far away from home. The mother had an even harder time accepting the idea of separation. She was not convinced that her daughter was so ill that she required it (obesity should be curable by proper diet and control); if the patient had to be hospitalized, the mother wanted to move to Topeka into an apartment in order to be near her. When she was actually hospitalized, the patient was very frightened, not wanting to leave her mother, and for her part, the mother had to be dissuaded from leaving her husband and moving to Topeka. While in the hospital, the patient intermittently pleaded to be sent home, but she admitted that she felt extremely secure in this request because she knew it would not be allowed.

The Bohemian Prep School Boy represented an instance where the desirable and recommended separation from the parents failed. As noted earlier, he was the brilliantly precocious youngster brought up in an incredibly indulged state within a totally chaotic family structure, marked by intense parental conflict between the creative artist father and the wealthy aristocratic mother. The 17-year-old patient had been in psychiatric contact on and off since the age of 6, and was referred to The Menninger Foundation when the psychiatrist thought he was decompensating into a paranoid schizophrenic break. The parents, though intensely conflicted about the patient (as about all else), were united in their anger at the referring psychiatrist, blaming him for all the poor advice over so many years that they felt had led them to their present plight with the patient (in part, at least). They also agreed, however, that he could no longer manage living at home. Nonetheless, when hospitalization at The Menninger Foundation was recommended, they pleaded that they all had to return home to work out plans for this; once home, they cooled off rapidly on the need for the hospital treatment. They wondered whether the clinical evaluation group had been misled into a misdiagnosis by their son's "exaggerated" stories. The evaluators stood firm and strongly urged that the family abide by the recommendations, which were then effected shortly thereafter. However, the parents never truly reconciled themselves to the patient's need for treatment in a hospital (and so far from home). They did not follow through on the recommended casework for themselves. The mother especially felt it hard to tolerate the patient's absence from home and became openly upset and disorganized, behaving strangely. The patient experienced all this as pressure on him to leave treatment and return to his family. The treatment always seemed tentative; the patient could never completely commit himself, always keeping an eye out for the expected adverse parental pressures. For his part, the therapist never took these external threats quite seriously until the very end, because the parents had always been so inconsistent. When the psychotherapy did end prematurely after only 7 months (71 hours), it was ostensibly because of irresistible adverse parental pressure. The father all along had been dubious about the nature of his son's illness and of his need for treatment. He saw much of the symptom picture as an unwillingness to assume appropriate responsibilities. He felt that his money was being used up unwisely and unwarrantedly both by the treatment and by his son's extravagant living (now day hospital and outpatient), which he felt was not sufficiently curbed. At the 7-month treatment mark, the father announced that they would shortly be selling their home and planning a permanent move to Europe, and that he had purchased a boat ticket for the patient as well. The parents promised that the patient could continue psychotherapy in Europe if he really wanted it. The patient felt that he had to run to be with his parents, not to be left behind when they went to Europe. Clearly, here, the recommended treatment separation from the highly neurotogenic parents failed to be really secured.

Adverse Effects of Separation

Yet it has been indicated that in other situations, and under other circumstances, separation of a patient from a conflicted and conflict-instigating home and family situation can impinge very adversely on the patient's prospects. The consequences can be even more unhappy when a separation is recommended or found necessary on other grounds. Three cases demonstrating the adverse effects of separation are described here.

The Snake Phobia Woman's case was an instance in which the impact was less severe and could have been overcome. The patient's life during her psychoanalysis (2½ years, 543 hours) consisted of living in Topeka during the week and commuting home most weekends for her "weekend marriage." Occasionally the husband and children came to spend the weekend with her in Topeka. This circumstance was felt by both the patient and her analyst to be the most outstanding and pervasively determining of the difficulties in the way of achieving a more complete treatment success: "She was always choosing throughout the whole analysis between a husband at home and an analyst in Topeka. This was important from the first of the analysis to the very last. We could never test the marriage in a realistic setting. It was always a weekend marriage." The patient constantly used and maneuvered the situation. Once, when the upset husband insisted upon and obtained a joint interview with his wife and the analyst, he revealed how she would browbeat him on weekends with talk about the "nice doctor" in Topeka who really understood her. All of this contributed to a treatment termination at a somewhat premature and incomplete point, without the fulfillment (or the resolution) of the patient's fantasy wishes: "I came. I saw. I conquered. But I don't have the trophy." But the continuing strain of the "weekend marriage" was becoming too much. The patient, throughout the treatment, did try to be a responsible wife and mother on weekends while living out incestuous fantasies with a father figure during the week—and rarely the twain did meet. Mainly, the patient could run from one situation to the other as things got difficult in either (threats of flight or actual temporary flights from treatment, etc.). And linked to this were the husband's constant antitreatment pressures, his impatience with the treatment, the many interruptions he suggested, and the financial crises that he always seemed able to precipitate by his ways of making and spending money. (He had been characterized as "a kind of psychopathic Babbitt.")

With the Invalided Hypochondriac, the situation was more serious and the outcome much worse. The patient had been extremely ill and had all but wrecked her husband's life by her literal invalidism, as described earlier. After each of their quarrels the patient would retire to bed completely for 2 or 3 days, abdicating any semblance of responsibility or concern for the house. The patient did have (to the husband) the "amazing ability" to pull herself together to go out to an evening cocktail party or bridge tournament. Perhaps this marriage was doomed in any case, and perhaps for the better. In any case, hospitalization and treatment in Topeka did not work out (it lasted only 4 months); it was terminated (the patient was supposedly to go on in outpatient treatment) with the husband's attitude expressed as "You guys have had your chance with her in the hospital. Now I'll straighten her out." What this finally came to was a transfer to a state hospital, where the admission was surrounded by considerable ceremony. The husband

and other accompanying relatives were taken on a tour of the institution by the superintendent, after which the family "in a somewhat condescending manner allowed [the staff] the pleasure of meeting the patient." During the patient's hospitalization there she had no formal psychotherapy, but did work in the hospital recreation department as a typist and "general office flunky." The husband meanwhile successfully sued for divorce and the custody of the children, which, according to a letter from the clinical director of the hospital, "did not have too much effect on her hospital adjustment." But, ever after, the patient persisted in being very angry at The Menninger Foundation for what she considered the total mismanagement of her case; it had led to adverse changes in both herself and her ex-husband, and to her mind had brought about the divorce. "He loved me when he brought me up there because no one would spend that kind of money for someone unless they loved them." And then he had changed and divorced her, and The Menninger Foundation had been derelict in its duty in just standing by and letting this happen.

The outcome with the third patient in this group, the Divorced Nurse, seems the most tragic because it seems to have been directly consequent on the unhappy necessity of her being totally separated from her husband and children in order to obtain the recommended and needed outpatient psychoanalysis. She came to analysis because of the severe deterioration of her marriage, marked by 6 years of bitter quarreling in which the patient felt constantly driven to question the love and fidelity of her husband. The husband, who accompanied his wife to the evaluation, was himself very tense and aware of his own very hostile feelings. He described the home atmosphere as so unpleasant over so long a time that he could only seek surcease away from home, sleeping frequently in his office. His efforts to reassure his wife regarding her suspicions of his office nurse were to no avail. Feeling unable to cope with the marriage, deeply hurt by his wife's constant recriminations over his confession that he had had a love affair with another woman prior to his marriage (an affair that had rapidly terminated after he met and began courting his wife), depressed about the likely outcome of the relationship, and even by now uncertain as to whether he wanted his wife back at all, he sought and obtained an outpatient evaluation of his own. He emerged from this determined to return home to his practice and his children, and not to enter psychiatric treatment himself.

The patient entered psychotherapy in Topeka, working out (as already recounted; see p. 208) many issues in her life (e.g., her pregnancy with the third child and potential working arrangements as a nurse). Within a month after the birth of the child, the now openly antagonistic husband filed for divorce. The patient made an angry, desperate trip home (across the country) to try to stave this off. They managed to reach an understanding that the husband would withdraw the divorce suit pending the outcome of the patient's treatment. In the meantime, however, he would move to the major metropolitan area where his parents lived, so that they could look after the two older children (whom he had with him) while he set up a new practice. Having worked things out to this point, the patient opted to go into her definitive treatment—psychoanalysis—in Topeka, where she had felt protected and helped to this point.

But the treatment did not help, at least not with the expressed intent to save her failing marriage. The analysis went on for 4 years (891 hours), coming to an agreed-upon but incomplete conclusion. It was beset by irregular and quite sudden treatment absences, in part for visits to her husband and children in desperate but unsuccessful efforts to save things, and in part for visits to her lawyers and for the divorce trial that did eventuate, during which the children's custody was litigated. Despite her analyst's giving a written deposition on her behalf and appearing in court to testify to the patient's fitness to be the custodial parent, the husband won the lengthy divorce proceedings and secured the custody of the two elder children. This was a great blow to the patient. Four months later the husband remarried; his new wife was his current office nurse, of whom the patient had been "paranoidly" suspicious. Not only was the marriage lost—and this loss was contributed to by the treatment arrangements that ensured the separation of the patient and her husband—but the analysis as well was adversely affected. The analyst said of her many absences, "In these flights, she was both flying to the transference father and trying to escape him, and we tried to make the analysis operate in between trips." The patient, too, saw her reality plight as constantly interfering with the analysis: "It would sidetrack me. . . . It was difficult for me to separate the two and to be able to forget my husband and choose the analysis." Here, more firmly than with any other case in the sample, one could say that the possibility for a different outcome in both the patient's life and/or her treatment could have been much strengthened if it had been possible (and agreeable to both) to arrange for the patient to have the analysis while living at home united with her family. After all, the husband did find it possible even to move and to relocate his practice—but to his parents' home city, not for his wife's treatment.

Therapist and Patient Factors Affecting Treatment

COUNTERTRANSFERENCES

Assessing Countertransference

Given the nature of countertransference, as well as the data-gathering methods of PRP (which depended so much on interviews with all the involved parties— especially the therapist, the supervisor, and the patient—as well as on the clinical records maintained routinely on that patient), access to understanding the role of the therapists' countertransferences (and transferences) in relation to the patients' treatment course and outcome is necessarily more limited, more inferential, and even at times more speculative than we would wish, despite the acknowledged importance of countertransference to the treatment process. Issues of ensuring some appropriate modicum of skill, experience, and requisite training for the therapists were, to a limited extent, handled through the case selection for the research sample.[1] Quite apart from the issue of requisite skill in the therapists, there is the further issue of therapist–patient match (or mismatch). Generally, this factor could not be predicted (regardless of the knowledge acquired of the patients' characteristics

---

1. See Section II, Chapter 5 (pp. 58–59) and Chapter 6 (footnote 3, p. 78), for discussion of this issue and the limited way in which PRP could deal with it.

and the therapists' characteristics), because in most of the cases—though not all—the initial Prediction Studies were done before it was known which therapist of those potentially available would be assigned to and would agree to take on the case.

On the other hand, for the assessment of operative countertransferences, we did have the advantage that the therapists were all members of The Menninger Foundation staff, within a shared professional community; we (the research assessors) knew them all as colleagues and as friends, and thus knew a fair amount about their characters and their life situations. This, of course, added occasionally to the interpersonal awkwardnesses in carrying out the research study, but it gave an additional (and often very illuminating) perspective on the countertransference issues in particular treatments—a perspective built, then, on far more than the data gleaned specifically out of the study of the particular treatment. Some examples of this added data base are evident in the descriptions that follow.

But, first, I wish to make a last general statement about countertransference and its assessment. There are few terms that are more conceptually clouded and beset by more widely deviating definitions than "countertransference," and a considerable literature on the attendant debates around this issue has accumulated within psychoanalysis. A recent and very thoughtful article by McLaughlin (1981) not only reviews this history and reframes the debate, but makes out a plausible case for the abandonment of the term altogether as having outlived its clinical and theoretical usefulness, in favor of just talking about the interacting therapeutic process to which both patient and therapist bring their personal transference dispositions. Nonetheless, I use the term "countertransference" here as if it still has unimpaired heuristic value, and without giving a specific definition, on the assumption that my way of characterizing each instance gives enough clues to my own conceptualization of the phenomenon under discussion.

In PRP, there were almost as many different styles or dispositions of countertransferences and their possible consequences as there were therapists. There were 42 patients in the sample, and since 5 of them had two official Menninger Foundation therapists (the Housebound Phobic Woman, whose first therapist died; the Involutional Woman, whose first therapist left Topeka; the Heiress, who at the point of treatment impasse left her "cardboard analyst" for another who was more feeling and accommodating; the Actress, whose first, "typical Babbitt" therapist gave up after 20 fruitless hours; and the Invalided Hypochondriac, ricocheting between the close therapeutic work of the hospital doctor who alternated in centrality with the formally assigned psychotherapist), and 1 had three (the Fearful Loner, who "fired" two therapists in succession before settling down uneasily with the third), there were a total of 49 psychotherapy assignments. However, since 13 therapists happened to have 2 of their patients turn up in the PRP sample, and 3 therapists each had 3, the 49 treatment courses were carried by only 30 different staff members.

These courses are not all mentioned here in their idiosyncratic postures, since our data were not as uniformly revealing in each case; additionally, in some instances, there were similarities enough to lend the cases to some grouping together. But very briefly for each, since there *were* so many variations, we found the following array of evident or clearly inferred countertransference dispositions and/or problems.

Defensive Reactions to Transference Pressures

The Exhibitionistic Dancer's therapist, who had no special experience with the psychotherapy of acting-out delinquent characters (and did not find this one especially appealing), tended to be correctly analytic, formal, and austere; the treatment climate was more analytic than personalized. In the treatment of the narcissistic Prince, both the patient and the analyst tended to be overformal, intellectual, overpolite, and avoidant of anxiety at the cost of circumstantiality. This, of course, made it more difficult for the analyst to work with just this character armor as itself a most important resistance barrier. With the Divorced Nurse, who, as noted, made endless trips home because of her failing marriage and her bitterly contested divorce, the analyst had special difficulties in distinguishing degrees of transference acting out from reality needs; at such times the supervisor felt that the analyst tended to be reproachful and didactic in his analytic approach. The Adoptive Mother's analyst, with a somewhat related problem, handled it differently. His characteristic mode was to wait expectantly (and defensively) for things to turn up with his patient and to accede permissively to her requests. She was a woman from whom the analyst was indeed willing to take a lot, whom he liked, and whom he would go to any length to help; she perhaps made him too anxious to cope effectively with her bossy, controlling tendencies. (He seemed to have a comparable problem of usually placating his very competent but also quite bossy wife.) Also in a negative direction was the countertransference to the alcoholic Script Writer, who withheld and concealed a great deal; the analytic climate became quite investigatorial with confrontations of the patient's recurring deceptions and their meanings. Similarly, in dealing with the Sexual Masochist's destructive acting out with secret drug taking, the therapist fell readily into the (appropriate?) role of a therapeutic detective and prosecutor—always suspecting the relationship in order to counter the evasiveness, lying, and withholding that marked the patient's behaviors.

Fostering of Positive Transferences

In the opposite direction of countertransference expressions were a group of therapists and analysts who undertook (deliberately or not) to foster the positive dependent transferences of their patients in the self-assigned role of the benevolent father. With the Intellectual Fencer, the therapist's style was warm-hearted and readily expressive; he did not control his expression of feelings and enjoyed the assigned transference role of being the approving, or sometimes disapproving, daddy. With the Heiress, the successor to the "cardboard analyst" allowed occasional physical contact (touching the patient's forehead), talked more, and permitted more knowledge of himself—all of which, as noted earlier, made him more real, more involved, a warm, interested, and spontaneous person who went out of his way to counter the distance and the frustration that the patient found so intolerable in the strictly analytic situation. Peter Pan's analyst was both permissive and self-assured, informing the patient that he was expert in gynecological diseases and could advise her forthrightly in these areas, while letting her play out the role of the helpless young girl with her father. The Housebound Phobic Woman's first Menninger

Foundation analyst deliberately minimized the rigors of the "analytic" situation by entering into the patient's life with advice and direction, in a warm and friendly manner; the patient in turn made strenuous efforts to improve in her work and living situation in order to demonstrate to her analyst how well she was doing. An almost identical situation prevailed with the Claustrophobic Man.

Therapist Overinvolvement

Even further in this same direction was the case of the Alcoholic Heir, in which the analyst "accepted" the transference assignment; he responded as though he had to "side" with the patient and to liberate him from the clutches of a bad wife (herself sick and alcoholic), and consequently could not focus sufficiently on the degree to which the patient used his wife in order to externalize his own problems. With the Alcoholic Doctor, the positive countertransference valence was reinforced by an unswerving therapeutic optimism: The analyst kept working doggedly (and sympathetically) in an analytic direction, despite his supervisor's advice to the contrary and despite the patient's progressively worsening clinical state. With the Fearful Loner, such aggressive therapeutic overoptimism ended less tragically. Both of his first two therapists, in their different ways, tried ambitiously to move in on the patient's fearfully guarded inner world—asking questions, confronting the patient with his behaviors, evoking feelings, all with the intent to scrutinize and change things. The patient simply "fired" each in turn.

Two other cases in different ways, represented even more extreme situations of the therapist's planned (or not) benevolent overinvolvement. The Bitter Spinster was in an unhappy psychotherapy for 8 years (560 hours), during which she moved along with her therapist, who left Topeka for private practice in another city. In the new city, she secured a position as head nurse in the psychiatric unit of the leading hospital in the area. Since the therapist often had patients hospitalized on that unit, this condition made for a good deal of extratherapeutic contact between the patient and the therapist, at times almost daily. The fact of these unavoidable extratherapeutic contacts—added to the feelings of responsibility that the therapist may have had for the patient who had moved her life for him (and added perhaps to his sense of guilt for the patient's continuing poor treatment course and unhappy life course)—undoubtedly increased the difficulty in dealing appropriately with the complex transference manifestations in this case. The patient would have jealous rages at the therapist's other patients and then would partially compensate for her frustrated feelings through the fantasy of indeed having a special relationship with him.

The situation with the Movie Lady was more deliberate. As noted earlier, her analyst felt she was "too sick" to be analyzed, and shortly shifted to a warmly supportive (and expressive) psychotherapy. There were many suggestions and manipulations (e.g., the relaxation exercises as "homework" to help the patient cope with "hyperventilation attacks"). Mainly, the therapist's explicit plan was to be "as natural and human as possible"—to give the patient a "corrective emotional experience" that a man could be trusted and could help through caring. He talked to the patient more than his usual wont, in response to her signal that she desired that. The therapist also, in honest response to direct questions by the patient (who prided herself on finding out a great deal about him), acknowledged that a treatment interruption had been due to his own illness with heart disease. This communication reverberated with the patient's own intense hostilities and her guilt that people might have died because of her hostile impulses (e.g., her father, her elder sister). It could well both have frightened and blocked the patient from fuller expression of her transference angers. She related on research interview that she had not displayed open anger at the therapist and that she had difficulty in feeling it—"whether it's because I know he's been ill, or because he's an older man, or because I just haven't gotten angry with him." The patient did express, through the therapy, concern for the therapist's health, commenting sympathetically when he appeared tired or preoccupied. In a first letter to her therapist after the termination of the therapy, the patient ended with the statement, "I hope you are enjoying your vacation and will be rested to face another year of comforting." In one of his letters in the posttherapy exchanges, the therapist wrote that the patient was right—his daughter could wrap him around her little finger. The patient felt that the therapist always wanted her to have warmer feelings toward him in the therapy, to feel toward him as one would toward a father. She indicated that he did seem like a father to her, and she worried about him as she would have about a father.

Apparent Therapist–Patient Collusion

A different kind of transference–countertransference problem was evident in a series of seeming tacit agreements to collude in seeing the world the same way, or to focus the therapeutic interactions selectively (with selective agreed-upon exclusions). For example, throughout the Devoted Son's treatment, much of the resistance focused around his attribution of so much of his maldevelopment and distress to his painfully thin physique. To him, this was a statement of his major reality, not in any significant way a reflection of a changeable state of mind. In his analysis, he saw all women as "cows" but his mother's milk as "watery"; he was brought up by middle-aged, poverty-stricken parents who provided insufficient food and love. It was a bleak childhood, in which they lived in a half-lighted world (always turning off the lights to save money), were never warm enough, and always seemed to be eating reheated leftovers in short supply. No wonder the patient never grew big enough. This picture, which emerged early in the analysis, never unfolded further; perhaps the analyst's own small stature contributed to the difficulty in developing these issues into a transference progression.

With three of the patients, there seemed an even clearer tacit conspiracy to set certain issues aside from therapeutic consideration. In the cases of both the Rebellious Coed and the Actress, the issue avoided was that of their homosexual propensities, which were more covert with the former, more blatant in the life of the latter. With the Rebellious Coed, the main treatment focus was on the everyday reality problems of school work and proper social behaviors. The patient occasionally went out with boys and tried to convey the impression that this was a more frequent event than it was. Meanwhile, she continued a clandestine homosexual relationship, which at one time she confessed was "driving her crazy"—especially since her partner (and roommate) also had a boyfriend and brought him around to their room, openly drinking and petting with him. The therapist was led to believe that he had helped pry the patient loose from this attachment, that she had moved out, and that he had succeeded in bringing her homosexual proclivities under control. He steadfastly focused in the meantime on the patient's improving school and social adjustment. At Termination Study interview he knew little of the patient's homosexual activities, or even how overt her homosexual relationships had been (or when), though she recounted these in great deal to the research interviewers.

Even though this was harder to do with the more openly homosexual Actress, her therapist too succeeded in deflecting the focus from her homosexuality. The therapy rode on the positive dependent (and *defensive*) transference attachment that he explicitly fostered, coupled with the displacement of aggression and overt sexuality into the acted-out patterns outside the treatment, so long as the latter altered in progressively less disruptive directions. How the therapist did this is described a little further on under the consideration of special issues surrounding the gender of the therapist. Here it should be added that the patient's urge to participate in this collusion was strengthened by her sporadic visits home, during which her father (who was now drinking more heavily) insisted on taking her to bars, introducing her to his young mistress, and pressing coarse and unwanted sexual talk upon her. He told her that, frankly, he didn't care whether she took a man or a woman to bed with her, but her trouble was that she hadn't had a good man and that was what she needed. He assured her that if she got pregnant he could help her take care of it. The patient was horrified and disgusted by this vulgar, thinly covered, incestuous seductive behavior. It strengthened her both in turning further away from men into homosexuality and in her unwillingness to talk about sexual issues in her therapy.

With the very disturbed and explosive Manic–Depressive Physician, the collusive exclusions went even further. The main focus of the therapy was on the patient's reality life, his precarious self-esteem, his strivings to improve his functioning. The issues specifically bypassed included the patient's continuing sexual difficulties (sporadic impotence, lack of sexual interest, guilt-ridden masturbation), his more-than-acknowledged continued drug taking, his apprehensions about the coming military life (he was about to become a doctor in the Army), and so forth. Wherever the values of the therapist and the patient clashed too much (sexual behaviors, drug taking), the therapist avoided these issues.

With the Sociopath, the issue was not one of collusion as much as of the patient's "conning" the therapist by his convincing manner, his glib rationalizations, and his defensive insights. Of this the therapist said in retrospect, "He was a pathological liar and I got sucked in by him. I didn't realize the extensiveness of his lying." Somewhat similar in outcome was the overidentification of the Addicted Doctor's second therapist, the one who pursued the "modified Aichhorn technique." He did not discuss the patient's massive behavior difficulties as things that it was urgent to try to control. That was the problem of the hospital doctor and the staff, and the therapist kept himself uninformed about the patient's privilege status, questions of drug supply, and the like. He steered clear of such "realities" and tried to "contact the patient as a person," placing himself on the patient's side in the face of a hostile world. Another kind of perceived dangerous mutual identification beset the therapy of the young Adolescent Grandson. An intensifying positive transference attachment could not be safeguarded from the disruptive effect of the uninterpreted, threatening, eroticized homosexual component in this transference submission. The patient could acknowledge considerable fantasying about the therapist from time to time, but this was always used more abreactively than interpretively. In his research interviews, the patient revealed a question that had always plagued him about the therapist all during the treatment: Why wasn't the therapist married? "I never could ask him . . . a good-looking guy like that with as much on the ball as he's got. I just figured he was more interested in his work."

Apparent Rejection by Therapist

With some patients, the countertransference problem was one of an experienced rejection by the therapist. With the very ill, alcoholic Car Salesman, the therapist initially applied himself in a dedicated, conscientious, and (over)enthusiastic way. When his treatment expectations were disappointed, the therapist reacted with marked frustration. His efforts to be supportive and directive had been either over-complied with, or, more often, flouted; in turn, he became bored with the patient's obsessiveness, his circumstantiality, his cloying compliance, and his over-weening need for approval. The therapist began to react in ways that the patient experienced as cold and sarcastic, as when he often confronted the patient with the latter's own son's comment on parental long-windedness: "Daddy, will this take very long?" In this way, the therapist played into the patient's image of his own father, with whom he had never been able to come to terms. Similarly, the therapist of the at least equally ill Invalided Hypochondriac felt all too readily provoked by her hostile barrages and in turn would become angry and fed up; he was quite relieved to have the therapy terminate prematurely. And in the case of the alcoholic and homosexual Masochistic Editor (every bit as ill as the preceding two), the whole 7-year-long (1107-hour) treatment effort, most of it psychoanalysis, could be characterized as the patient's living out in the transference of his need for punishment and his need to fail in the "negative therapeutic reaction"; he exhibited a masochistically self-defeating pattern of repeatedly snatching defeat whenever the jaws of victory gave promise of opening. The narcissistic injury suffered by the analyst in these repetitive interactions seemed to play its part in his redoubling the analytic treatment effort and not considering a change to a more appropriate treatment approach, until the father signaled the end of his financial support to the (by then) totally deadlocked treatment.

Therapist Intolerance for Hostility

With some patients, the therapists showed specific intolerances for hostile transference feelings. The analyst of the Obese Woman found it hard to work with her negative transferences, especially the exploitative, primitive mother-transference. His predilection was, rather, to see the (pseudo)positive transference phenomena in the same behaviors. He reacted to the patient's masochistic sexual fantasies about him in terms of the frustration of her positive Oedipal longings, and he did not see the aspect of the patient's need to ward off the savage oral aggression against him—developed as her response to her mother's hateful rejection, but leading to the danger of awesome retaliation. Similarly, with the Involutional Woman—a lifelong tightly bound and affect-inhibited compulsive—the therapist deflected the ongoing hostile competition with the representative superior male in the transference back into the relationship with the husband. Within the transference it could be denied, especially since from the patient's perspective, the therapist was "such a nice guy," someone you could not express hostile feelings to.

Therapist Difficulty with Dependency

With some other patients, the therapists' specific difficulty was in handling dependency issues. The therapist of the Homesick Psychology Student had a problem with weaning himself from a prolonged dependence upon supervisors and the supporting institutional matrix. At the time that he was quite abruptly declaring his own independence of the supervision process (a step his supervisor had for a considerable time been working to achieve), he equally abruptly terminated this patient with such major still-unresolved dependency problems. Similarly, with the Phobic Woman, who had a very good psychoanalytic result, the analyst nonetheless had a comparable problem with supervision: He used it less to enhance his understanding of the analytic process than to react to it as truly a "control," to which he could maintain a duly dependent position. In this respect, he paralleled within the supervisory process an important (and unanalyzed) component of the therapeutic process between his patient and himself. Nonetheless, the patient gradually became less overtly submissive, less openly fearful of how he might react, as (with his approval) she took her own steps toward greater maturity and independence in her life.

Insistence on Analysis for Institute Purposes

With one of the patients (the Suspended Medical Student) mention has been made earlier of a specific "extraneous problem"—the analyst's desire to keep this as a properly analytic case so that it should "count" toward Topeka Institute for Psychoanalysis credit. It has been noted that this might have played a role in this analyst's tenacious commitment to an analytic treatment process, despite the flagrant evidence of the major difficulties encountered with this treatment approach.[2]

Combination of Problems

With the last patient to be mentioned here, the Silent Woman, the combination of specific transference–countertransference interaction led to a "transference jam" that eventuated in an early disruption of this psychoanalytic treatment effort after

---

2. This same issue of the need to have the case "count" for Institute training purposes—with the manifold distortions that this could impose upon the analytic process, especially around the oft-recurring issue (with some of the sicker patients in analysis) of deciding whether conversion to a less demanding treatment approach (an expressive–supportive psychotherapy) was indicated or not—no doubt operated as well in more subtle ways in others of the psychoanalytic control cases in the PRP sample.

only 1 year (228 hours). The patient was the provocatively and stubbornly (and sadly) silent woman whose characteristic stance in the analysis has already been described (see pp. 178–179). The ways in which the analyst tried to deal with these silences technically are discussed in the description of the treatment course. Here I want to focus on the affective coloring of his responses and of his interchanges with the patient. The analyst seemed aware of the wistful waiting to be appreciated and loved that underlay the patient's frightened and angry exterior. He saw the evidence of the strong transference attachment, as in the patient's already described 500-mile drive at unsafe speeds through a storm in order to return from a weekend away and get to her hour on time. Yet he mainly focused on the silences as negative transference resistances; at least retrospectively, he saw these as being perceived to be coldly critical. The patient resented his interpretations. She said at the research interviews, "I was looking for a benevolent Santa Claus. I was disillusioned. There was nothing benevolent about him." She experienced him instead as undemonstrative, unresponsive, like her injuring, coldly analyzing, critical ex-husband (behind whom stood the father). Who would really listen to her? She was boring, not interesting enough, not important enough, just a country lass trying to relate to a city sophisticate. At his research interview, the analyst expressed himself as having indeed been too coldly neutral and too affectively inhibited in his contact with the patient, despite his feeling that his analytic work had been technically quite correct. For him, the analysis was always a hard job, in which he could never feel secure or relaxed.

THERAPIST REALITY FACTORS

Sex of Therapist

The reality factor in the therapist most often adduced as a variable significant to the patient's treatment course is the therapist's sex. This is especially true with younger, still adolescent patients, but at times it is also true with fully adult patients. Given the normal sex distribution of the component mental health professional groups in the 1950s before the recent accession of increased numbers of women into traditionally male-dominated disciplines, our sample of 30 therapists for the 42 PRP patients (23 psychiatrists, 6 psychologists, and 1 social worker) was overwhelmingly male (27 men, 3 women). Therefore, in most instances, there was the "usual" pairing of male therapists with both the male patients and the female patients. The three female therapists, two of the psychiatrists and the one social worker, treated a total of four of the project patients.

ISSUES CONCERNING FEMALE THERAPISTS

Special issues related to the sex of the therapist arose with some, but not all, of these four patients who had a female therapist. One female psychiatrist (and psychoanalyst) treated two of the project patients, both female—the adult Script Writer in an effort at psychoanalysis, and the still adolescent Exhibitionistic Dancer (age 21) in psychotherapy. With each of these patients, the initial prognostications concerning the projected treatment course posited a differential mobilization of transference dispositions, depending on the sex of the therapist.

In the case of the severely alcoholic and suicidal Script Writer, it was felt that the transference reaction to a male therapist would be predominantly envy and hostile depreciation. His analytic neutrality would be seen as the ineffectual passivity of the father (re-enacted in the marriage with the husband). The patient would assert her superiority through intellectualizing and aggressive competitiveness, while scornfully denying any envy over his imputed superior status. With a female therapist there would be equal hostility, but more fear of the vengeful, castrating, phallic mother image. Alongside the hostility would be, too, a deep wish to identify with "a successful professional woman" and an underlying erotic attachment (anaclitic and submissively homosexual) to the phallic mother. With the male, these erotic longings would be hidden under the surface of a seemingly more "heterosexual" attachment. Actually, within the analytic work with the female analyst, two themes that did emerge were in accord with these transference expectations. These were (1) fear and hostility in relation to the mother, who had always made life miserable for the patient (the patient, in turn, had characteristically responded all her life with withdrawal and avoidance); and (2) the direct linkage into the transference, starting with the anxiety attack in the very first analytic hour, followed by subsequent supporting dream material in which the analysis was likened to cold-blooded brain surgery. A related theme was the need to censor information given to this analyst, who was experienced as the bad, dangerous, and punishing mother. Yet the patient had to fight against seeing this transference projection, saying once, "If you ever would become a mother figure for me, I'd have to leave treatment immediately." Themes that were evident that the analyst felt unable to work with analytically included (1) the erotic transference tie, on a phallic-homosexual level and more regressively, on a submissive, oral-receptive level; and (2) the reactive competitiveness with the successful professional, the woman psychoanalyst. It was the struggle against awareness of such a growing positive attachment — at once a great temptation and a great fear — that generated the greatest intratreatment pressure toward treatment disruption.

It was predicted that the Exhibitionistic Dancer would develop a pervasive transference expectation of the analyst as someone with narcissistic goals of his or her own in relation to the patient, rather than as someone truly interested in helping the patient find her own life goals and shape her own gratifications. The patient would constantly doubt the sincerity of the relationship and constantly test it; she would seek to find out the therapist's hidden intentions and destroy them while seeming to meet them. This reaction could take different shapes, however, depending on the sex of the therapist. A male therapist would be conceived as a more coercive force, demanding conforming behavior quickly. There would be more initial resistance, readier mobilization of overt mistrust and fear, and more open struggle. A female therapist would be conceived as permitting and facilitating free expression (i.e., sexual and aggressive behaviors) in order to vicariously live out her own thwarted instinctual wishes. The neutrality of the therapist, and the invitation to discuss her inner life freely, would be to the patient a repetition of the mother's seduction. Initially, this might be more tolerable to the patient, but ultimately it might be even more frightening. The later reproach would be "You should have stopped me." That is, the male could be experienced as too controlling; the female might be seen as insufficiently controlling, with the complaints deferred till later. Though this whole range of issues was expected to unfold in the end with a therapist of either sex, it was felt that certain clear therapeutic advantages would accrue with a woman. The still adolescent patient needed a stable identification object alongside therapeutic work and insight. She needed to find herself as a young woman and to understand men in relation to herself as a woman, and it was felt that this could be more readily accomplished if the therapist was a woman.

Because of the situation created by this patient's elopement with the even sicker (but very wealthy) young patient from the hospital, their hasty marriage, and the forced agreement that they be allowed to go on as outpatients, her psychotherapy was more chaotic and more beset by life pressures and constant emergencies (in the ever difficult and stormy married life she had entered) than originally anticipated. Nonetheless, an intense transference involvement grew, within which the patient felt dependent; when under stress, she called at night, or on occasion obtained emergency appointments. In this transference the therapist was mainly the mother, and the relationship with the husband was primarily a repetition of her earlier sexual behaviors with her brother (the husband had started in treatment with the same therapist and at almost the same time). There was often a triangle involving the therapist as the corruptible mother and the hospital doctor as the rigid father. It was in a period of revived memories of the mother's jealousy of the patient's relationship with her father that the patient eloped with the fellow patient of her therapist (taking a man who belonged to the therapist–mother). The patient was always complaining about not getting enough gratification in the therapy. She was always being held accountable, and she felt this to be unjust and harsh: "You never say that I don't mean it, or that it's my father or my brother or someone else who is responsible. You always say it's I." Within this turbulent treatment very little of this transference material was, or could be, interpreted.

The other two female therapists each had one PRP patient, and each of these patients was a male. The Obedient Husband was treated by a female psychiatrist. No sexually differentiated prognostications were made at Initial Study. It was predicted that he would regard a therapist (of either sex) as the strong, admired father for whom he worked, and whose assent he sought to each major life decision — and also as the mother to whom he went when troubled, but in whose presence he remained silent, going merely to be with her and to feel close to her. In terms of these models, the patient would probably come diligently and faithfully to treatment but would have little to say. He would expect the therapist to set the topics, tell him what to do and how to feel, and comfort him. (He has already been described in these behaviors as a member of the group of relatively "inarticulate" patients; see p. 177.) Actually, at the start of the therapy, the patient felt openly resentful that he had a woman doctor: His self-esteem was low enough without having to come for help to a woman. To the therapist, there was an irony that this woman-ridden man, whose whole life had been a story of frustrated dependency relationships with women, should now once again confront this same dilemma. But as the therapy progressed, this issue proved not as important as was feared at first; it dropped away without specific working out.

The Fearful Loner had a female psychiatric social worker as the second of his three therapists. The first therapy (with a male psychiatrist) had foundered and the therapist had been "fired" by the patient, presumably over the therapist's too active pressures toward a changed and expanded life, with concomitant inadequate attention to the internal events within the treatment. The second therapist relaxed all pressures in regard to the outer behaviors and tried to focus on the patient's behaviors and attitudes within the treatment sessions, which simply then became the new battleground. The patient's bitter anger over this new variety of intrusiveness is described in the account of the treatment course. Suffice to say here that his final comment after many of his hours was "You did not accomplish anything today either." The therapist should "hire a private detective if you want to find out about me." He thought, more to the point, that they should reverse roles and examine the therapist's mistakes. He insisted at times that they talk about the therapist and what her neurotic problems were, all of which he promised to keep confidential. When the therapist finally (after almost 3 years), stiffened by supervisory backing, insisted that some limits would have to be set to the never-ending torrents of abuse, the patient in turn "fired" her and sought out the director of psychotherapy, demanding (and obtaining) his third therapist, a male psychologist. Here, even less than with the Obedient Husband, did the (female) sex of the therapist seem to play any special role. The first therapy (with the male) and the second therapy (with the female) had similar courses and similar unsatisfactory outcomes before the patient could finally settle down with the third therapist.

In addition to these four patients (two men and two women) who had female therapists within PRP while in treatment at The Menninger Foundation, one other patient, Peter Pan, sought out a female therapist in a distant city after two periods of psychoanalysis—3 years at The Menninger Foundation (510 hours), followed by another 6 months (almost 100 hours) with another (also male) analyst, to whom she transferred in a new city where she followed her boyfriend (see p. 253 for further details). For a while it seemed that these two periods of analytic work had been somewhat effective in mitigating the patient's symptoms and conflicts, but 4 years after the official Follow-Up Study and 10 years after having first been seen, the patient returned to Topeka to consult her original analyst. She had made a recent suicide attempt and was struggling with a total recurrence of all the original eating and starving behaviors. Psychiatric hospitalization and a renewed treatment effort (this time with a more active and supportive psychotherapy rather than psychoanalysis) was recommended, but the patient and her husband (the former boyfriend) chose to return to the university in her new home town, where she would enter outpatient therapy. She went into a 10-month psychotherapy (punctuated by six brief periods of hospitalization), this time with a woman analyst. The treatment course was essentially no different, and the patient's psychotic decompensation was steady, ending with her successful suicide by jumping off a bridge.

ISSUES CONCERNING MALE THERAPISTS

With the remaining 37 patients in the project treated by male therapists only, some special issue concerning the sex of the therapist arose with four patients, three female and one male. These were each quite different. As noted earlier, the Snake Phobia Woman had had a very disturbing, overtly erotic experience of psychotherapy with a very senior male analytic practitioner in another city (see p. 208). In view of the specific long-time snake phobia (with all of the obvious imagery and dynamics associated with it) that had brought the patient to treatment in the first place, it was expected that a very serious treatment problem would be created for the recommended psychoanalysis by the reality of the previous transference–countertransference acting out and the fearful confirmations of transference fantasies that had taken place. Actually, the patient's 2½-year psychoanalysis (543 hours) was quite successful, and it became clear within that treatment how she had played her part in maneuvering the acting-out situation with her former therapist, in which she had seduced the man, destroyed his therapeutic effectiveness with her, and later worked to destroy his reputation as well. (When she had sat on his lap, it had been ostensibly to learn directly that she had no need to be fearful of older men.)

In treatment predictions for the Obese Woman (who had a male therapist), differential transference expectations were raised that were similar to those already indicated for the Script Writer and the Exhibitionistic Dancer (who had the same female therapist). With the Obese Woman, the most salient transference problem was expected to center around her sadomasochistic relationship pattern. This would be mobilized earlier, and in a more explosively negative form, with a woman analyst. With a man, on the other hand, available positive relationship components could be mobilized earlier and an effective therapeutic alliance could be more readily established; this would later enable the more effective working through of the sadomasochistic transferences. What actually emerged in the transference with the male analyst over its greater course was (in keeping with this expected sequencing) open sexual fantasying about him, generally at points at which the analyst was trying to confront the patient with her aggressive, exploitative relationship pattern with men. This would lock into a power struggle with the analyst (could she force him to be other than a "cold fish"?); it became an effort to recreate the climate between the patient's mother and father—the mother who could simultaneously domineer and arouse, and thereby mistreat the father, who would be reduced to begging for intercourse. Only later did the analysis focus on the patient's intensive, primitive aggressive rages against the mother.

With the other two patients being described under this heading, the special gender-related problem resided in the open or latent homosexual impulses of the patient. The Actress was one of the two patients (the other being the Rebellious Coed) who entered into a tacit collusive bargain with her male therapist to keep her (homo)erotic thoughts and feelings outside the therapeutic interaction (see pp. 240–241). The patient used her basic dependent transference as a resistance against the exploration of the whole range of sexualized (and aggressivized) transference feelings, which were then lived out extratherapeutically in her life outside; this pattern persisted unchanged and unchallenged through the whole treatment course. The therapist, for his part, allowed this transference fixation, using it as leverage to influence the patient "educationally" via suggestions and manipulations directed toward altering her behaviors. He felt that the transference could not otherwise be worked with and that his few efforts to do so had been unsuccessful. Both the patient and the therapist seemed to agree that their acceptance of her gradually crystallizing homosexual life style (with more stable and less destructive relationships within it) was the best solution that the patient seemed capable of at the time. It enabled them both to guard against sexualized transference involvements.

The other patient for whom there was a specific transference issue focused around homosexual impulses was the Adolescent Grandson; he was the one male patient among the four in the project sample for whom the gender issue explicitly affected the work with male therapists. The specific transference issue had to do with the patient's strong latent homosexual impulses and their threatened burgeoning into the transference. His defensive wondering about why the therapist had never been married ("a good-looking guy like that with as much on the ball as he's got"), which he never dared bring up in the therapy, has already been indicated (see pp. 241–242). He *could* complain at termination research interviews about the therapist's "inconsistency." He said that at times the therapist was stiff and formal, and addressed him by his last name; at other times the therapist was warm and friendly, and used his first name. He complained that he knew nothing about the therapist's private life and contrasted him with the chatty hospital doctor, who would talk with the patient of his own adolescence. The patient said that he could work better with a doctor like that, who had once been a mixed-up kid like himself, living on "wine, women, and song" and yet now had achieved a solid position as a doctor, in contrast to the therapist, always a figure of great distinction with a presumably impeccable past. During the follow-up period, the patient, who continued to live in Topeka, returned at a stressful point to consult his former hospital doctor (with whom he maintained a periodic, friendly, "on-call" relationship) but not the therapist, and was willing to go for consultation to a senior psychoanalyst staff member. He declined further therapy, however (this time it was psychoanalysis that was recommended); he agreed to the recommendation in the abstract, but was reluctant to "start with a stranger" and unwilling to return to his former therapist.

Patients' Changing Therapists

Six of the project patients changed therapists while in treatment at The Menninger Foundation, and five others were recommended to or sought out other therapists for new treatment efforts after they left Topeka. In some instances, the shift in therapists made a significant difference in the treatment course for the better; in others, it seemed to make no difference at all.

UNPLANNED CHANGES AT MENNINGER

Of the six patients who changed therapists while at The Menninger Foundation, two had totally unplanned shifts. The analyst of the Housebound Phobic Woman, who had her in a psychotherapy that he allowed her to continue considering "analysis," died suddenly after 6 years (1056 hours) of treatment. At the time of "cutoff" Follow-Up Study the patient was still in treatment with the second analyst (she was a "therapeutic lifer"), though now it was clearly converted—with the established, clear-cut evidence of drug-induced chronic organic brain damage—to an explicit psychotherapy. The first analyst had from the start been aware of the patient's limited capacity (or unwillingness) for analysis and had been content to accept this (necessary?) limitation. He gave up the effort to bring transference thought and feeling into the treatment and spoke of it as a kind of "corrective emotional experience" in which he made himself available as a kind and understanding reality-oriented figure, "riding on the positive transference" and using it as a vehicle for helping the patient achieve a more satisfying pattern of functioning in her daily life. He had a special interest and talent for working with patients who required very long-term treatments and manifested clinical change very slowly and in small increments, if at all. The second analyst was therapeutically more ambitious and tried for a wider interpretive gain, but the patient proved equally refractory to this effort. When a repeat psychological testing gave conclusive evidence of organic impairment, with clear perceptual and thought deficits, the second analyst was willing to give up his efforts at "analysis" in favor of a more reality-oriented psychotherapy, and then later on switched from "regular psychotherapy" to "counseling and guidance." The patient never came to trust the second analyst as she had the first—it was like "comparing a pigmy to a giant"—and she was often angry at his "stupidity," such as thinking that her episodic behavioral upsets could be related in any way to vacation absences from treatment. But she continued to come and continued to maintain herself in a gradually widening way. In effect, the change of therapists, even with the differences that it brought in style and attempted technique, did not seem to alter her therapeutic progression in any way.

The other patient whose change of therapist was unplanned was the Involutional Woman, whose first therapist left Topeka after 3½ years of her treatment. For the first year, as noted earlier, the patient had been living in Topeka (she had been hospitalized for part of that time), but she had been subsequently living in her home in a nearby city and commuting to Topeka for her treatment. Her second therapist was a former senior staff member at The Menninger Foundation, now in private practice in the city where she was living. She went on with the second therapist for another 3½ years. The patient brought the same distrustful competitiveness to both therapeutic situations: She "checked up" on her first therapist with the hospital doctor, and diluted the relationship with the second therapist by employing two other supporting figures (her internist, with whom she discussed her numerous psychosomatic problems, and her minister, with whom she discussed troubling moral problems). The therapists, each in his own way, allowed this. With the first therapist, the transference was split; all the negative elements were shunted directly onto the relationship with the husband. With the second therapist, the hostile components were deliberately avoided; the transference was diluted over the patient's three "therapists," thus taking direct competitive pressures off the psychotherapy. The patient reacted similarly to both therapists. They were both "wonderful guys," equally beneficial to her. Thus, with the two patients who had unplanned transfers of therapists, the therapeutic course and progression seemed unaltered in each instance.

PLANNED CHANGES AT MENNINGER

Four of the patients had planned changes of therapists, due to difficulties perceived in the therapeutic relationship and in the treatment course. In one instance, with the Fearful Loner, the changes were essentially the patient's doing. The manner in which he successfully "fired" two therapists, the first a male psychiatrist and the second a female psychiatric social worker, has in part just been described (see pp. 246–247). At the time of "cutoff" Follow-Up Study he was still in his ongoing therapy (he was another "therapeutic lifer"), now at the 8½-year mark. With the first two therapists, the patient was hostile, abusive, and close to paranoid. With the first therapist, the patient's recurrent question, after long silences, was "When are you going to fix me up?" He constantly asked the therapist to admit that he had failed, and repeatedly called for his resignation from the case. When the therapist refused to "resign," the patient "fired" him (after a year of treatment) and returned, complaining, to the director of psychotherapy, seeking a new assignment. The second therapist pursued a somewhat different therapeutic strategy, as already indicated, but one that was to the patient equally intrusive. She lasted almost 3 years before she tried firmly to curb the patient's abusive outpourings; this led in turn to her being "fired" and the patient's demanding another change. The third therapist, a male psychologist, was mindful of the dilemmas that had arisen in the previous efforts at treatment. He acquiesced throughout to all of the patient's arrangements (being billed at home, 30 minutes weekly as the treatment desideratum, trials on tranquilizers when the patient desired, etc.) without comment or change. He accommodated the treatment to the patient's pace and to his silences (he did not question the silences or inquire into their meanings), and got into shared discussions with the patient as he wanted about books or wines or phonograph records. Mainly, the therapist engaged in "supportive management," supporting whatever efforts the patient would initiate, either inside or outside the therapy, to reach out for contact, "to come out of his shell." Whenever the therapist said anything that the patient construed as an unwelcome intrusion, the latter characteristically arched his eyebrows, and the therapist was immediately responsive to this gesture, halting the inquiry. In effect, then, the second of these "planned" changes resulted in a significant improvement in the patient's treatment willingness, and more important, in the life he lived on the outside. As already described, the patient even married during the course of this third therapy (see p. 162), but characteristically kept the fact of the marriage secret for 3 months, when he revealed it by way of a request for referral for marital counseling.

In the other three instances, the planned change of therapist was initiated by The Menninger Foundation itself. Two of these two also turned out to be changes for the better. The first was with the Heiress, who had gotten into a stalemated analysis with her first, "cardboard analyst" by the 2½-year mark (546 hours), at which point she was transferred to the second analyst, who was with her for the next 4½ years (809 hours) until her ultimate termination at the 7-year mark (a total of 1355 hours). The first analyst adhered to a classical analytic reliance on interpretation as the central treatment technique. The main transference relationship was that of hostile withholding from, and angry depreciation of, the analyst, who was perceived as unfeeling, ungenuine, and unhelpful, like all men. The hours were beset with silence, distance, secretiveness, and an intellectualizing and isolating of all interpretive effort. The patient projected her own throttling of affect and impulse expression onto the "cold" analytic situation and the "cardboard" figure of the analyst. When the analyst confronted the patient with the fact that their work together did not seem fruitful and suggested a change, the patient accepted the suggestion and made the change over one weekend. The second analyst got out of this impasse through a successful modification of the treatment in supportive directions, many of which have already been described (see pp. 190, 238). He talked with her more than analytically usual, including using her first name; he permitted and encouraged considerable information about himself as a real person involved in her life; and he even directly encouraged major life decisions (the move to accompany him for continued treatment when he left The Menninger

Foundation, and the subsequent remarriage she came to, toward the end of her treatment). Clearly, also, this was a change for the better.

The other beneficial change of therapists initiated by The Menninger Foundation was with the Actress, who was unwilling to talk with her "typical Babbitt" first therapist. He gave up after the 20 fruitless hours, and a second psychotherapy was then established (after a 5-month hiatus); this lasted for 4 years (318 hours) and ended with significant, albeit circumscribed, gains (see pp. 241, 248).

The last of this group of planned changes of therapists at The Menninger Foundation was with the Invalided Hypochondriac, and this one was not successful. The first psychotherapy effort—in the hospital—lasted only 4 months (42 hours) and got nowhere. In the hospital the patient played out the role of the "good little girl," compulsively productive in a variety of tasks in her organized activities program; her major symptoms (including the somatic ones) diminished in their overt expression. This was, however, the thinnest sort of "flight into health," accompanied by some specious offerings of insight: "I know what a mess of a human being I am and what I've done to my husband and children. I have a duty to return to them and to try to face my responsibilities that I've never faced up to before." With her own pressure in the psychotherapy for discharge (and her refusal toward the end to cooperate, through coming late or not coming at all), and her husband's joining the chorus with his complaints about the high expense, the hospital and the therapist finally capitulated and accepted her discharge from the hospital and the termination of her psychotherapy. It was not long before the patient's life outside was again as wildly disorganized and symptom-ridden as it had been initially; an effort at outpatient psychotherapy in her home city could not stay the regressive process, and the patient was becoming more openly suicidal. She and her husband finally accepted rehospitalization at The Menninger Foundation and this time the patient was under the care of the same hospital doctor, who now took on the role of therapist as well. He, however, was no more successful than his predecessor, and the patient was shortly transferred to a state hospital in her home state.

CHANGES AFTER LEAVING MENNINGER

Five other patients went to other therapists after leaving The Menninger Foundation. For the most part these were less-than-optimal, "compromise" arrangements forced by the patients, and were not helpful. For example, as noted earlier, the Addicted Doctor went from psychotherapy as an outpatient at The Menninger Foundation, which ended disastrously after 11 months (102 hours), to psychotherapy by a Menninger-trained therapist (using the "modified Aichhorn technique") as an inpatient at the affiliated local state hospital, which also ended disastrously in his suicide with a barbiturate overdose after 30 months. The Car Salesman (as intensely alcoholic and addicted as the Addicted Doctor) had three specific treatment periods at The Menninger Foundation covering a 3½-year time span (the first two with the same therapist, and the third, a 10-month treatment effort in the hospital, with the hospital doctor as his therapist); all three ended just as disastrously. Each time the patient had pried himself out of treatment, falsely buoyed up to feel that he "could make it." In the year subsequent to his third (and final) Menninger Foundation termination, he was in two further outpatient efforts with two more psychiatrists in two different cities. In his case, too, the treatment efforts finally ended with an alcohol–drug overdose death.

The third of this desperately ill group, Peter Pan, had three treatment efforts that were ultimately equally unsuccessful. The first was psychoanalysis for 3 years (510 hours) at The Menninger Foundation; the treatment seemed to have brought her distressing symptoms (stealing, eating and starving rituals, etc.) under enough control that she was allowed to leave in order to follow her boyfriend, who was leaving Topeka upon college graduation to pursue his graduate studies at a distant university specializing in his particular area of social science. The boyfriend was pressing the patient to come with him under the implicit threat of losing him, and the analyst acquiesced to these pressures and arranged that the analysis be continued with another analyst in the new city. The second treatment effort lasted only 6 months. The patient experienced this second treatment as a "rude awakening," in contrast with her first analyst, as noted earlier (see p. 209). The second analyst said of the first treatment, "She appreciated the fact that he apparently told her a good deal about himself. The patient perceived each hour with him as a feeding." The big issue in the second treatment was the patient's insistence that she be given a termination date from the start, so that she could know when she could marry. Both she and her boyfriend were pressing for this. The analyst never took the position that the patient could not marry; he did feel that she could not both marry and analyze properly. As noted earlier, she chose the boyfriend, left the analysis, and married instead. At the official Follow-Up Study time, the patient returned eagerly, together with her husband. She tried to present herself as continuing a slow but steady improvement in level of functioning. She and her husband were continuing their graduate studies; she hoped for a career in university teaching someday, after her own children (whom she hoped to have) would all be themselves in school. She was, in fact, a better scholar than her husband, and it was she who had won the fellowships that were their academic (and economic) support. But the gains were on the surface, and the patient's main eating symptom was by no means overcome. She was always struggling with it, in great apprehension and guilt. It was, however, not till 4 years after this Follow-Up Study that the patient sought out her original analyst, after a suicide attempt. At this time she felt she could not accept the recommended rehospitalization and renewed treatment (psychotherapy, not psychoanalysis this time); instead, she sought out the female psychiatrist in her home city, where she lasted in psychotherapy 10 months (punctuated by six brief hospitalizations, as well as many telephone calls and emergency contacts) before her progressive psychotic decompensation culminated in the successful suicide off a bridge. These three (the Addicted Doctor, the Car Salesman, and Peter Pan) who did so disastrously with the changes in treatment plan and therapists that they forced on The Menninger Foundation constituted three of the six deaths known to us of mental-illness-related causes among our sample of 42.

There were two other instances where a second therapist was involved. One was the case of the Rebellious Coed. Her first psychotherapy of 14 months (only 35 hours) ended inconclusively. The treatment, as noted earlier, focused on restoring the patient's progression in her college life, her social behaviors, and her peer adjustments, with the collusive arrangement to ignore her homosexual conflicts and behaviors. Termination of therapy came "logically" at the point of successful college graduation. Both the patient and the therapist accepted this as the proper goal, and graduation itself became the natural termination focus. The patient was going on into a life as a (spinster) schoolteacher, with perhaps a discreet homosexual personal life. It was at Follow-Up Study, as noted earlier (see p. 163), that the patient confessed her unhappiness over this earlier outcome, and the inability in the earlier treatment to talk about the things that constantly bothered her. She came to Follow-Up feeling that "this is my last chance." She was ostensibly always searching for an enduring heterosexual relationship, but could never meet a suitable man; she now acknowledged that overt homosexual relationships had continued unabated all through her period of psychotherapy and into the follow-up time. As a result of all this, the patient was referred for a renewed attempt at psychotherapy with a psychoanalyst in the city in which she worked. He saw the patient for about a year (74 hours). In contrast to the previous treatment, this therapist tried to work actively and interpretively with the patient's sexual problems. This treatment was however, a turbulent one, beset by emergencies (including suicide threats); it finally terminated after a major behavioral upset. The therapist felt that the patient had made some significant gains in some areas, but relatively little in others. The patient said (on research inquiry) that what had gone wrong in her treatment with the second therapist was that she found herself falling in love with him, and these feelings were, to her, unbearable. Here the two treatment periods with different therapists employing different therapeutic approaches (one more collusively covering, the other more actively uncovering) ended equally inconclusively.

The last patient in this group who changed therapists was the Bitter Spinster, who was able to make a very specific, helpful use of this referral. She was in an 8-year-long expressive psychotherapy (560 hours) with an unhappy course. The termination was a long-drawn-out affair; the therapist actively worked at it over a 3-year period, starting when he became convinced that the transference jam they were in would not be resolved and that no further treatment progress would be made. But the patient, despite the fact that she poured out a crescendo of complaints that she was no better, that she had not been helped, and that it was all the therapist's fault, still could not shake loose from the treatment dependency. And she felt that the therapist was only trying to get rid of an unwelcome burden (and reminder of his failure). To help get past this hurdle, and to facilitate the termination process, the therapist arranged for a series of consultation visits by the patient with another psychiatrist. The patient went six times and used the time to continue to complain about the therapist, but also to come to terms with herself about the need to terminate. She did not pay for these visits, just as she did not pay her own therapist's bills during the final year of her treatment.

TREATMENT OF THE "SPECIAL" PATIENT

In every setting there are categories of "special" patients—special in the sense of characteristic expectations and dispensations that they evoke, eventually usually in an exaggeratedly optimistic treatment perspective and prognostication given to them, combined with the unusual treatment arrangements that they are so often allowed. Obviously, many of the responses to these classes of patients can be considered under the heading of countertransference evocations. At The Menninger Foundation, three such classes of patients were represented significantly in the PRP sample. They were (1) adolescents/students, who exerted a pull to see their behavioral and symptom disturbances as aspects of adolescent turmoil and adjustment processes, rather than as reflections of more severe underlying psychopathology; (2) patients of great wealth (and often famous family names), who characteristically clustered at this very prestigious private institution, and whose privileged position in life could readily be translated into seeming advantage to their treatment prospects; and (3) physicians (and occasionally allied health professionals), who also clustered in a private sanatorium setting, who often had severe alcohol and drug problems, and with whom a "professional countertransference" would often operate, tempting the treating physicians and treating institution into according special privileges and expecting special progress. These three groups are considered in turn.

Adolescent and Student Patients

The original intent of PRP was to limit the sample to the prime adult age range of 20–45. The practicalities of accumulating the total sample for study in accord with the rhythm of the research led to the inclusion of four younger patients: the Adolescent Grandson and the Bohemian Prep School Boy (both 17), and the Actress and Peter Pan (both 19). In addition, the Rebellious Coed (age 20), the Exhibitionistic Dancer (age 21), the Phobic Girl (age 21), and the Homesick Psychology Student (age 23), could be considered, in terms of both educational position — college or other kind of student — and psychological position in life, to be part of our adolescent patient population. This "adolescent" group thus comprised eight patients, three male and five female. Of these, it seemed that with three (the Bohemian Prep School Boy, Peter Pan, and the Rebellious Coed), the temptation to see their illness picture somewhat overoptimistically did prevail; with one of these, Peter Pan, this overoptimism had the most serious of consequences. For both the Rebellious Coed and the Bohemian Prep School Boy, the generally overoptimisitic cast to the treatment prognostication stemmed from their precociousness and the kind of intellectual and emotional growth struggles they seemed caught up in. With the Rebellious Coed, the treatment recommendation for an interim psychotherapy was expected to operate as a preparation for the definitive psychoanalysis that would promise her the fullest (most far-rangingly reconstructive) treatment result. As has just been described, neither her first psychotherapy (the collusively covering one) nor her second psychotherapy (the actively uncovering one) reached any better than an inconclusive result (see pp. 253–254). At the end of it all, though she still turned urgently to psychiatric consultation when she was upset or depressed, she also felt that she didn't believe in psychiatry any more. She was at that point deeply entrenched in her homosexuality, without even a facade of interest in men.

With the Bohemian Prep School Boy, the misjudgment was perhaps more severe. Because of his precocious brilliance (e.g., his salon at school that met in a closet to debate existentialist philosophy) and the concomitant turmoil of his erratic and wildly eccentric family, he too was given a rather optimistic treatment prognosis with the projected supportive–expressive psychotherapy. This perhaps took insufficient account of the long duration of the patient's open emotional disturbance, going back to age 5, and the severity of his personality disorganization, which had led (properly) to the research group's diagnostic label of "overideational preschizophrenia." In his own eyes, the patient was Holden Caulfield in *Catcher in the Rye*—a part he played in an amateur theatrical, feeling that he was portraying himself.

With Peter Pan, as noted, the consequences were the most serious. Though clearly she was in the throes of a classical and severe anorexia nervosa, psychoanalysis was recommended and entered upon as the treatment of choice, and the presenting diagnosis was shaded to *"incipient* anorexia nervosa in a decompensating obsessive–compulsive neurosis"—partly because of her intellectual endowment, partly because of her age (19), and partly because of initial concealment of some of the symptom picture (the very extensive history of kleptomania and of the fiercely unsuccessful struggle against it). This assessment and the treatment plan based on it seemed for quite a while to be paying off, and actually her final decline toward psychotic decompensation and death by suicide did not take place until 11 years later. Whether her overall outcome could have been different is discussed further on, under the description of the treatment course.

Very Wealthy Patients

I turn now to the role that family wealth and position might possibly play in ultimately affecting the treatment course and outcome adversely, just because of initial expectations that were geared overoptimistically. Actually, there were fewer such patients in our sample (only 5 out of 42) than the popular stereotype of who can get to treatment at the expensive Menninger Foundation would imply. These five, already described in the discussion of demographic characteristics of the PRP sample (see p. 66), were the Heiress, the Alcoholic Heir, the Adolescent Grandson, the Bohemian Prep School Boy, and the Sexual Masochist. A sixth patient, the Exhibitionistic Dancer, eloped from the hospital with and married the (even sicker) scion of another famous and wealthy family. Perhaps just because such patients *are* more numerous (and thus taken more as a matter of course) at The Menninger Foundation, this potential issue turned out to bulk much less in the treatments of these patients than might have been anticipated or feared. Certainly the Alcoholic Heir wanted and demanded to be treated as special just because he was the scion of a great family; at the same time, in his very paranoid way, he complained loudly and continually about the high fees he was being charged ($35 an hour), which he could so easily afford. Nonetheless, he constantly felt that The Menninger Foundation was unfair and was cheating him because he had money. And with the Heiress, there was a hint of specialness in the solicitousness with which her second analyst treated her, though it was certainly not clear that this would have been different with a less wealthy patient with the same symptom and character pathology.

The one case where the existence of great family wealth clearly played a significant role in affecting the treatment adversely was that of the Adolescent Grandson. However, this occurred in a way perhaps different from what would usually be expected, because in this instance it was not the patient but the grandfather, as the responsible relative, who exerted total control over the family financial resources. The patient's hospitalization, as described earlier, was precipitated by his being caught scampering naked across his grandfather's estate; police charges of public masturbation and deliberate exhibitionism were hovering over him. The consulting psychiatrist made the referral for hospitalization, which was then arranged by the grandfather's private secretary, since the grandfather himself, occupied with his impending fourth marriage (at age 70), would not come. The patient's father was dead and the stepmother was shut out of the treatment planning, though allowed to come along at the time of hospital admission. The patient at the time of hospital admission saw himself as throwing in his lot more with the grandfather than the stepmother. He wrote a letter to his stepmother indicating that he felt he was growing up (he was 17) and that he probably would not be returning to live with her.

The patient was in therapy almost 2 years (224 hours), partly as a hospital patient and partly as an outpatient. The grandfather, though financially responsible, was never really supportive of the treatment effort. He never wrote to the patient, though occasionally his secretary did. Nor would he attend the patient's high school graduation (in Topeka while he was still a hospital inpatient), though the patient was pleased that his stepmother could be induced to think the occasion important enough to attend. The specific treatment termination came in the wake of an Easter visit home by the patient. He was delighted to find that he could present himself to his grandfather in such a way that he appeared quite well; in turn, this re-evoked the grandfather's own doubts about the need to spend all that money for continued treatment. The patient at this point readily acceded to the grandfather's pressure and was emboldened to talk about termination to the therapist. In an effort to rescue what appeared to be a disintegrating situation, the grandfather was called to Topeka for an emergency family consultation conference. At this conference the grandfather made his position very clear. He was old and tired and impatient. He saw his grandson not as that sick, but as just lacking in self-discipline. He would not longer support the psychotherapy, which he felt only upset the patient, but he might support hospitalization from time to time if the patient's behaviors became disruptive and intruded on his peace of mind. At this point, there seemed no leverage to hold the patient in psychotherapy, and he was reluctantly allowed to terminate. What is unclear is whether all this would have been acceded as to as readily if the grandfather were a "lesser" man—less domineering, but also less wealthy and less the kind of man who always had gotten what he wanted just because he was so powerful and wealthy.

Physicians and Other Health-Professions-Related Patients

I now address the issue of potential "professional countertransferences." There were 5 physician patients in the PRP population of 42—the Addicted Doctor, the Alcoholic Doctor, the Medical Scientist, the Manic–Depressive Physician, and the Suspended Medical Student. This was indeed a significant number (12%), and quite characteristic of the usual high representation of physicians among The Menninger Foundation patient population. And, as also was (and is) quite characteristic of the physician–patients in that setting, four of them (all but the Manic–Depressive Physician) were drug-addicted and alcoholic; with three of these four (all but the Suspended Medical Student), the addiction and alcoholism were their principal symptomatic expressions and main reasons for sanatorium treatment. In addition, the Script Writer was the alcoholic wife of a physician, who exploited the social and professional position this gave her to the fullest. And one further patient to be considered in this group is the Bitter Spinster, a psychiatric nurse, who through the course of her long-drawn-out (8-year) psychotherapy was able to use her professional capacity to place herself in a special working relationship with her therapist.[3]

With only two of these seven (the Medical Scientist and the Manic–Depressive Physician) was it clear that no "special" status or dispensation was sought or accorded by virtue of their profession. They seemed really to be treated just like everybody else (the Medical Scientist in psychoanalysis, the Manic–Depressive Physician in psychotherapy); both, incidentally, had very good treatment results. The treatments of the other five were shaded by their special claims and special consideration—in each of the five cases, to the patient's severe detriment.

The Alcoholic Doctor, for example, was recommended for psychoanalysis and treated then in a 7-year (1238-hour) effort at analysis, albeit with many deviations from classical technique enforced by the nature and severity of his character and illness picture (the severe alcoholism and addiction, his profound passivity and masochistic character, and the very unfavorable reality situation, with an extremely disturbed marriage to a very sick wife). This was one of those instances where the research team at Initial Study disagreed sharply with the clinical recommendations and felt the treatment prognosis to be a bad one. It was felt that the outcome would be either an unanalyzable and insoluble transference neurosis, or a treatment disruption with reversion to the pretreatment picture—unless the treatment plan was decisively modified into a more flexible psychotherapy. The basis for this research disagreement with the clinical recommendations has been spelled out earlier (see pp. 200–201). What is not emphasized there is the operative role played in the decision to recommend psychoanalysis by the fact of the patient's being a physician (and the son of a physician). His "achievements" had been in his professional education and activity, including a reasonably successful year in academic medicine following his wartime military service as a medical officer and before his embarkation on a private general practice career, at which point his troubles had begun in earnest. The subsequent fate of the treatment was in full accord (and more so) with the initial research apprehensions. The analytic effort went on doggedly over the full 7 years, with no real consideration of a formal alteration to explicit psychotherapy, despite the ample evidence of the patient's inability to tolerate the rigors of analytic treatment, manifested in the chaotic life he led. His steady downhill course finally terminated in death from a massive aspiration pneumonia in the context of his overall debilitated state.

A very similar situation existed with the Suspended Medical Student. In fact,

---

3. There were three other nurses in the group of health care professionals in the PRP population: the Divorced Nurse, the Adoptive Mother, and the Movie Lady. However, though nursing as a career had expressed and fulfilled various psychological needs for these women, in none of these three instances did this evoke any special concern or consideration that would affect their treatment courses in any way.

here it was even clearer that this patient's intellectual gifts, capacity for hard work, and commitment to his medical career all played a significant role in both the recommendation of psychoanalysis as the only treatment that could effect real resolution of the patient's deep-seated neurotic conflicts, and the undue optimism with which the projected psychoanalytic course and outcome was viewed. The patient seemed to do reasonably well in a 4½-year (672-hour) analysis, in the sense of bringing his disruptive behaviors under control and of being able to return to medical school and to graduate successfully. But it soon thereafter became evident— as he essayed the stresses of a medical practice—that his treatment gains had been tenuous, and that he could not tolerate the normal pressures of his chosen professional life. Nevertheless, the fact that he was now a struggling physician (and identified, incidentally, in an imitative way with an older physician friend and mentor) again played its role in persuading all concerned not to press too hard for renewed therapy, and to allow a dangerously deteriorating life (alcohol, drugs, reckless driving), as well as a clearly unsafe medical practice, to go on. His physician mentor, for example, saw him as a "brilliant boy"; he stated that "the boy always wanted to be a doctor and still wants to be." No one wanted to take any action that might jeopardize his medical licensure. Ultimately he was (through total incapacity) voluntarily withdrawn from medical practice, and went to live on his parents' farm; one night he committed suicide by asphyxiation in his car.

Another patient in this group, the Addicted Doctor, manipulated the treatment situation more explicitly (and more brazenly). The severity of his illness had been clear from the start, and the original treatment recommendation was (appropriately) for a supportive psychotherapy designed only to stop a regressive destructive process, and to try to hold things at some tolerable level of functioning, without further disintegration in terms of the patient's personality and life situation. For a variety of reasons, however—partly the desire not to entrench further the patient's dependency gratifications, but partly also to make it possible for the patient to go on working as a physician (in the protected setting of the local state hospital, to be sure)—this treatment effort was (inappropriately) allowed on an outpatient basis throughout. After 11 months (102 hours), it was clear that this had failed totally; the patient, who could not afford private inpatient care at The Menninger Foundation, was transferred after an almost successful suicide attempt with barbiturates to the local affiliated state hospital, in order to resume treatment on an inpatient basis. However, as already described (see pp. 225–226), he succeeded in manipulating a specially privileged position for himself, as a physician and a former staff member in the hospital. He was called "Doc" and was usually the buffer between the other patients and the ward personnel. As noted, his most flagrant misuse of this situation was to get access to large quantities of barbiturates, which he stored at home and in the hospital, and which he used for traffic with other patients as well as for himself. The patient was easily able at a point of real despair—after 30 months of hospitalization and fruitless inpatient psychotherapy, and with his wife finally filing for divorce—to commit suicide with a Nembutal overdose in his hospital bed.

These three physician patients—the Alcoholic Doctor, the Suspended Medical Student, and the Addicted Doctor—who were (or contrived to be) especially "favored" either prognostically or in their treatment circumstances, constituted three of the six PRP patients we know to have died of mental-illness-related causes.

The other two patients still to be considered in connection with the operation of so-called "professional countertransferences" had equally unhappy, but at least not lethal, treatment outcomes. The Script Writer was the severely alcoholic and suicidally depressed wife of a successful physician. She was aware of and exploited her social position and its perquisites to the fullest. Partly because of this, and partly perhaps because of her undeniable talents avocationally and vocationally (despite her illness, she had successfully operated a university radio program as script writer and interviewer), this patient was recommended for psychoanalysis; it was even stated that she had a much more favorable prognosis than the usual alcoholic. A variety of character attributes—her aggressivity, her phallic strivings, even her rebellious streak—were all adduced in support of this view. The effort at psychoanalysis lasted just 8½ months (129 hours), until the patient disrupted her treatment in order to return to her home and family, with the announced intention of going on in treatment with an analyst in her home town.

At the time of termination, there were only slight treatment-induced changes, and it was considered doubtful how well any of them might holdup in the face of the patient's return to the stresses at home. The drinking was somewhat controlled, her suicidal impulses had receded, and she was a little more attentive to her personal appearance; however, in a romance with a lover among her fellow patients (which she flaunted in front of her husband, thus making him anxious to get her out of the Topeka environment), she repeated exactly her long-standing pattern of exploitative and manipulative relationship with a passive–dependent and sexually impotent man. When the patient was seen at Follow-Up Study, she indicated that she had not gone on in analysis but in a "supportive psychotherapy combined with chemotherapy." But the psychiatrist was a social friend, who saw her only once weekly, let her cancel hours freely as she chose, and (as a physician's wife) did not charge her for the treatment—in contrast to The Menninger Foundation! The psychiatrist gave her a variety of sedatives and tranquilizers as needed, but could not secure her cooperation to a trial on Antabuse. He supposedly assured her that she was not an alcoholic and advised that she should resolve an "impossible marital situation" through divorce—which she promptly did. On her Follow-Up visit, the patient comported herself in a very characteristic way. She stated that she was no longer drinking except "socially in a conventional sense," and yet she came to her early-morning interviews on the third day reeking of alcohol. She emphatically disclaimed the slightest interest in her lover from her treatment days in Topeka, and yet she sought him out and spent a good deal of time with him. She was the one PRP patient who grossly overcharged for her Follow-Up Study expenses in a flagrant and obvious manner.

The Bitter Spinster, a psychiatric nurse, had the self-created situation of following her psychotherapist when he left The Menninger Foundation for private practice in another city. She secured there a position as head nurse on the leading psychiatric inpatient unit in the city—where her therapist often had patients hospitalized, and where inevitably she would have to have a good deal of extratherapeutic contact with him. There, sometimes on a daily basis, she and her therapist would be professional colleagues, discussing objectively the problems and behaviors of other, sick, hospitalized psychiatric patients. These "unavoidable" extratherapeutic contacts (by virtue of the professional association), added to the feelings of responsibility that the therapist may have had for the extremely lonely patient who had moved her life just for him, undoubtedly complicated the problem of dealing appropriately with the complex transference manifestations in this case. In any case, the psychotherapy went on over an 8-year span (560 hours) and was totally inconclusive in outcome. The patient could only be pried loose from it by the device of the six consultation visits with another psychiatrist (as already described; see p. 254). At Follow-Up Study time, she was still locked into the same life impasse as at her treatment termination.

It is clear indeed that, among the three varieties of "special" patients discussed here, it is with the last group (the physician and allied health professional patients) that the most adverse impact was manifested on potential therapeutic progress—an impact stemming from the specific complex transference–countertransference interplay into which these treatments could so readily fall. Such adverse effects were clearly manifest among five of the seven patients in this category; for three of these five, the treatments ended fatally.

V

The Treatment Course

*The Processes of Psychoanalysis
and Expressive Psychotherapy*

Analytic Cures

THE GOALS OF PSYCHOANALYSIS AND
THE CRITERIA FOR CURE

There is an abundant theoretical literature in psychoanalysis concerning the criteria for cure and for termination, as well as the goals of psychoanalysis against which its actual reach and limitations need to be assessed. I have in two previous publications from PRP discussed the conceptual dilemmas that make it very difficult to deal straightforwardly and definitively with these questions in a manner at all comparable to the (presumed) greater precision that operates in the realm of physical illness and its treatment. In a paper on "The Problem of the Assessment of Change in Psychotherapy" (Wallerstein, 1963), I indicated that posing the question of effectiveness of treatment (in reaching its goals, in "curing") implied at least tacit agreement that there exist *reasonably accepted* criteria of three kinds: "(1) criteria of illness—specifications of the degree and kind of deviations that merit the designation, pathological; (2) criteria of a state of ideal mental health (called 'positive mental health' in the current literature (Jahoda, 1958) and (3) measures of improvement as the degree to which the patient has diminished the gap between his state of mental illness prior to treatment and these desiderata of mental health" (p. 31). I then said that of the three, we only actually possess the first—criteria of illness—and that these constitute, of course, the whole body of knowledge of psychopathology and psychodynamics. I then tried to elaborate the conceptual complexity involved in trying to define criteria of optimal mental health and measures of improvement, including the central role of value judgments in hobbling the effort to give empirical psychological meaning to these criteria and these measures.

In a subsequent paper from PRP, written for a panel discussion on the limitations of psychoanalysis (Wallerstein, 1965), I tried further to outline the ideal and the practical goals of psychoanalytic treatment against which its inevitable shortcomings need to be measured. These goals, too, represent neither a set of simple and agreed-upon concepts nor an easily circumscribed range of delineated considerations. I focused in that article on the issue of goals from the standpoint of three major polarities, each of which at first glance seems to pose a paradox, or at least a complementarity, of viewpoints: (1) the paradox between "goallessness (or desirelessness) as a technical tool marking the proper therapeutic posture of analytic work and the fact that psychoanalysis differentiates itself from all other psychotherapies, analytically oriented or not, by positing the most ambitious and far-reaching goals in terms of the possibilities of fundamental personality re-organization" (p. 749); (2) the distinction between "the goals of psychoanalysis that are related to the outcomes striven for and the goals of psychoanalysis that are set in terms of the analytic process as an instrument to bring about those changes" (p. 752); and (3) the assessment of "average expectable accomplishments, along which Annie Reich (1950) has defined as nodal points the more pessimistic position of Freud and the more ebulliently optimistic position of Ferenczi" (p. 765).

Given this context of theoretical difficulty in reaching conceptual clarity and agreement on these (seemingly) straightforward issues of mental health and improvement, there is nonetheless a practical sense in which we do speak of "good analytic results," in a way comparable to Ernst Kris's (1956) description of the "good analytic hour" as a clearly recognizable, though hard-to-define, phenomenon. In this sense, I want to describe some typical instances of the kinds of analytic "cures" reached among the PRP patients, with the defining characteristics and the particular limitations of those cures. Among the 22 patients (10 men and 12 women) started in psychoanalysis (of whom 16 were maintained formally in analysis throughout their entire treatment, albeit with quite significant modifying parameters in 6 of these 16), a total of 8 (2 men and 6 women) fell into the category of very good outcomes, though 2 of these were among the 6 who were clearly converted to psychotherapy (the Movie Lady and the Housebound Phobic Woman—explicitly with the Movie Lady and tacitly with the Housebound Phobic Woman). Another 5 (2 men and 3 women) had reasonable but more limited outcomes, including 1 who was clearly converted to psychotherapy (the Economist); 3 (2 men and 1 woman) had very equivocal outcomes, including 2 who were clearly converted to psychotherapy (the Heiress and the Alcoholic Raconteur); and 6 (4 men and 2 women) were clear-cut failures, including 1 who was clearly converted to psychotherapy (the Masochistic Editor).[1]

Of the 8 patients with clear-cut very good treatment outcomes, I describe two here (the Medical Scientist and the Phobic Woman) to indicate the kind of results achieved, as well as the residual areas of incompletely resolved problems that seemed clearly evident in the treatment assessments.

ANALYSIS OF THE MEDICAL SCIENTIST

Background, Prognosis, and Early Course

Of the two, the Medical Scientist seemed to have the more thoroughgoing result. His good outcome was the more surprising, since he came from that sickest group of severely alcoholic and drug-addicted patients who were, by and large, dubious prospects for psychoanalysis. (He was the only one of the severely alcoholic and addicted group treated by psychoanalysis who did at all well.) His Menninger Foundation hospital admission was precipitated by recent erratic, bizarre, and violent behaviors superimposed upon his long-standing (since age 22 in this

---

1. See Appendix 2 for the tabulation of all the patients by treatment category and statement of the overall results achieved.

41-year-old man) barbiturate and alcohol excess. The behavioral eruption occurred in the wake of a bout of infectious mononucleosis, which imposed a period of inactivity on this very motorically oriented individual (given to hard physical labor, outdoor recreational activities, etc.; see p. 152). He found this enforced inactivity intolerable, and responded to it with a sharp increase of his "normal" very excessive barbiturate and alcohol intake; as a result, he became ever more irritable and impulsive, and began to behave bizarrely. When drunk he became violently abusive, threatening his wife, and on one occasion hitting her so that she became frightened of him (of this he said that "a man could kill a woman when drunk"). On other occasions, he was savagely destructive of furniture in their home. When the patient finally confided these difficulties to his physician father (along with the extent of the long-standing alcohol and drug intake), he was promptly brought to The Menninger Foundation for full psychiatric evaluation.

This patient has already been in part described under a variety of headings that each have some clear relationship to his psychoanalytic treatment prospects. He was the patient who, out of his shame over his illness, made the repeated, intense, secret (and always unsuccessful) "do-it-yourself" efforts at cure, holing up in a hotel room in a nearby city while withdrawing himself totally from drug and alcohol (see pp. 71, 126). It was the determination and the courage reflected in this behavior, channeled now away from the self-cure effort into the direction of being willing to seek help from others more expert than he, that was taken as portending a potentially strong motivational push and positive treatment influence. Also on the side of positive prognostic indicators was the issue discussed in connection with potential "professional countertransferences" (see p. 258): Along with only one other of the group of seven physician and allied health profession patients (the other being the Manic–Depressive Physician), the Medical Scientist neither sought nor was accorded any "special" status or dispensation by virtue of his privileged position or his professional position. This was certainly in marked contrast to the profound exploitation of the role by most of his medical colleagues in the patient population; in each case, this exploitation worked out to their severe detriment.

More problematic from the standpoint of its influence upon prognosis and course was the relative financial press of the patient's family, which limited the resources available for the support of the needed concomitant hospitalization and control to no longer than a year. The one major treatment crisis point came toward the end of the first year of analysis and hospitalization, when the analyst felt that little dent had been made in the patient's avoidant, isolating, and intellectualizing mechanisms, and that the treatment was at an "almost complete standstill" (see p. 198). At this point, renewed interpretive effort was directed to the patient's utter disregard of his financial outlook, his deliberate undermining of his parents' financial security, and his apparent lack of interest in securing gainful employment for himself. The patient was responsive to this effort (perhaps in analogy with his capacity to mobilize "willpower" in his previous "do-it-yourself" curative endeavors?); he was able to move successfully out of the hospital and (for a short time) into a day hospital setting, just before the available financial resources were exhausted. Hospitalization has effected a separation from what the patient had increasingly come to see as a very unhappy marital situation (see pp. 231–232); it also had effected a complete curbing of his drug and alcohol intake (with only two brief alcoholic bouts in the early months of treatment when he was away from the hospital on pass, one of those times during a holiday visit home). When after the year the patient could pull himself together sufficiently to be out of the hospital, he proved able to handle it. His addictive behaviors were now gone; he began to toy with the idea of divorce and began to see his (future) second wife. Within 4 months he had obtained his state medical license and secured an affiliation with a local medical clinic. Shortly thereafter, he went on to a position as a staff internist at a local VA hospital—a position he used as a base from which to restart his professional and academic career, with increasing consolidation and increasing success.

And last in this statement of aspects of this patient bearing on treatment prognosis and course that have already been described is the one factor that was thought initially to be handicapping but that did not turn out to be so. This was the relative degree of inarticulateness and lack of reflectiveness about things psychological that seemed to characterize this very intelligent but not psychologically minded individual. This verbal reticence has already been described in some detail (see p. 175), including the finding that it turned out not to limit either the symptom and behavior change achieved or the range of analytic insights acquired (see p. 176).

Overall Course of the Analysis

Overall (given the nature of the illness and the necessary start of the analysis within the hospital), the 7-year analysis (1147 hours) pursued a classically "typical" course. Initially, a good deal of previously withheld historic material emerged. This was mainly focused around the patient's checkered sexual history—his concerns over sterility, the ejaculatio praecox that had become a lifelong troubling symptom, and the unfaithfulness leading into promiscuity that marked his whole 20-year marital history. In the initial treatment period, the patient struggled at the same time to defend himself against feelings by avoidance and denial (he had no problems and could anyway solve them himself), and by intellectualization, isolation, and affective blandness (the giving of scientific case reports about himself). These same defensive functions had in the past been served by drinking and drug taking. In the transference, the patient behaved like a pupil with a stern (and remote) teacher who must be appeased at all costs. And the patient played the game of trying to put the analyst to sleep so that he could sneak out—just as when, as a young boy, he had waited for his father to nap after dinner so that he could run out and join his friends in forbidden games. Behind this facade of the good boy and diligent pupil lurked, of course, the flagrant disregard for reality strictures and for the parental financial sacrifices already mentioned.

As the therapeutic alliance gradually consolidated and the patient became convinced that the analyst was "really in his corner" (neither the remote father nor the bossy mother), deeper transference positions came to the fore. The turning point in this regard came when the patient could confess homosexual feelings for the analyst and was not driven out of the analysis in outrage, but was still accepted as a person whom it was worthwhile to try to help. For a while the patient felt that another analyst would be better for him, a tougher father, more like his grandfather; the analyst should fight back so that the patient could compete and outdo him. These feelings were also accepted in the same fashion.

Gradually the analytic material shifted to the mother-transference and the patient's lifelong effort to evade his cold and threatening mother, who had always tried to keep him from other women; she had told him in so many words that if he wanted to neck, it was better that he should neck with her. In this context, he came to understand his pattern of recurrent betrayal of his mother (i.e., his wife) with other women, and then in turn his feeling threatened by the new woman in the same way he had felt threatened by his mother–wife (hence, the restless promiscuity). From the second year of the analysis, the patient fluctuated in these alternating father- and mother-transferences. Toward the father he had always felt fiercely competitive; it was hard to be the son of a famous scientist. The patient had made it impossible to obtain the academic position he had so desired because he was afraid to work where his father had done so well. His father, a quiet man, was actually himself very competitive, and his mother was intellectually very ambitious. Neither had much respect for the patient's own intellectual capacity; in fact, his mother had tried to get him not to appear for his Ph.D. ceremony. He finally did go but he was drunk, and it was the mother who had started him drinking that day.

Gradually all these hostilities came to the fore. Prior to the analysis, the patient had never dared be critical of his wife or parents except when drunk. He had "drowned the hostility in alcohol." Gradually, too, the patient saw the relationship with his wife as but an extension of that with his mother. He had divided his life into two 20-year segments, the first of which was his mother's responsibility, and the second his wife's; in each instance he had been just the innocent victim. He had entered the marriage impulsively and regretted it directly thereafter. He was recurrently unfaithful in it, and when he was periodically drunk he could tell his wife off—"the only time I could." Then he would be guilty, depressed, and usually apologetic. During the course of the analysis, the patient became convinced that he and his wife were totally mismatched; as noted, he decided on a divorce. One didn't have to be inextricably tied to a quarrelsome extension of one's mother. The patient found it difficult to work out this decision to divorce with the analyst because he felt that the latter, like the parents, would doubtless oppose it. Nonetheless, he did, and he then moved into the second, much more gratifying marriage, marked by a mutuality and interdependency he had not known before. Within a year they had a child.

Status at Termination and Follow-Up

By the end of the analysis the patient was leading a contented married life with a multiply layered family: three children of his wife's, one of his own adoptive children from his first marriage, and their own joint child. His own competitive relationship with his new wife's three children (he had yearned to be her *only* dependent) had been transformed into an accepting and affectionate relationship. Though there were thus strong oral components to the entire illness picture, the main neurotic conflicts centered around the Oedipal developmental phase. This was clear in the variety of understandings worked out in regard to the central symptom of alcohol excess. The patient wanted to (1) appear virile to the mother, who respected hard-drinking men (he dreamed that she told him that drinking rye would put hair on his chest); (2) supplant the mother's alcoholic close woman friend and associate; (3) deny his passive homosexual longings for the father by assertively competing and drinking all the men under the table; (4) handle competitive situations with their castration dangers by hard drinking, which meant doing the rival in before being himself done in; (5) ward off depressive onslaughts; and (6) masochistically slip into a slow suicidal decline. Through this whole therapeutic course, the full-fledged transference neurosis thus unfolded and was subjected to interpretive inquiry.

At the same time, there was evidence at the end that the transference neurosis was incompletely resolved. Termination of the analysis, as noted earlier (see p. 187), took place at a slow and rather difficult tempo. The patient desired to terminate, but feared it since he could not shake the conviction that to terminate (to succeed) might really mean destroying the father imago. The patient was reluctant to give up this significant experience, to see himself as doing without the analyst's abiding support, to come to the feeling that alone he "could put up with the way I am and the way I am not." Thus, a long, tapered termination process was entered upon. For 5 years the analysis had been at a frequency of five times a week. During the sixth year, the frequency was successfully reduced at several-month intervals to four, then three, and then two times weekly; in the seventh year it was once a week for the first part of the year and twice a month for the terminal last part.

Perhaps related to the dynamics that underlay the need for this kind of tapered termination was the evidence, persisting undimmed into the Follow-Up Study time, of a strong residual transference identification and overidealization. Although the patient was not a psychiatrist, through his treatment he became strongly identified with the psychiatric community, interested in psychological medicine, and involved in (quasi-)psychotherapeutic relationships with students and medical patients. He went on after his treatment termination to develop a psychotherapeutically oriented psychosomatic training program for general practitioners at the local governmental hospital (and in affiliation with the overall psychiatric training programs of The Menninger Foundation). He saw this as a reflection of a consistent shift of his interests in increasingly psychiatric directions. He saw himself as a teacher of "barnyard psychiatry": "I focus a lot of attention on that part of medical education that's been neglected in the doctor heretofore. . . . And at the same time, I do think of myself as an internist—an internist who teaches a kind of psychotherapeutic approach. The patients I enjoy dealing with most are those who have medical problems, but also personality problems, or behavior problems, or emotional problems, which obviously need tending to also." In this way he claimed to maintain a medical identity—"by using a little psychiatry for a lot of people rather than a lot of psychiatry for a few people."

This work, though rewarding, the patient also felt to be challenging and difficult. He was out to help doctors make changes in themselves and in their way of working, "not in 3 years but in 1 year—and I'd like to know if it can or cannot be done." He felt that "these nonpsychiatrists whom I've chosen to deal with, they often look pretty blank when I try to get across that what I'm really interested in is not that they acquire a great set of facts here but that they develop certain different ways of feeling about themselves." He felt that time was too short to do all he wanted, and that needed being done. He felt more driven than he was comfortable with; he called this his tendency to "race my motor," and though he expressed concern about this, he also felt that he had it under fairly stable control. He felt all he was doing as "using the fruits of my analysis" in his work, but he seemed less consciously aware of the degree of identification with his own intensely admired analyst in his psychotherapeutic function that was involved. There was a further uneventful informal follow-up note 5½ years past the Follow-Up Study, 14½ years from the first contact with him (7 years of analysis, 2 years to official Follow-Up point, 5½ years beyond that). The patient had remained in the same position, with the same contented life, and had maintained the same high level of functioning. Some time after that, the patient returned to his home state to resume a more academic medical career in the institution to which he had originally aspired; where he functioned successfully there until his death of a heart attack about 12 years after his treatment termination, 19 years after his original turn to The Menninger Foundation.

ANALYSIS OF THE PHOBIC WOMAN

Background and Prognosis

The other patient to be described here of those with clear-cut good outcomes is the Phobic Woman, who likewise did not initially appear to be among the more promising psychoanalytic prospects. The first consideration in this regard was that of the pervasive scope and the panicky intensity of the crippling phobias of many years' duration, for which this 23-year-old woman had been in almost continuous psychotherapy since the age of 15. The related consideration was the enormity of the secondary gain garnered by this woman in the total bending of her environment (in earlier years the parents, and in more recent years the husband, who was supported by the parents) into compliance with her phobic requirements. (This enforced environmental compliance has already been described at several points; see pp. 123, 142, 171–173.) The patient's overt illness had started at age 4 when she cried and howled, terrified, when her mother was supposed to leave her on her first day of kindergarten. This separation crying typically occurred whenever the parents tried to leave her with a babysitter, so that the family ultimately took her everywhere with them if at all feasible (she was an only child). At 15, an embarrassing episode with her schoolmates (when she was censured for openly kissing several boys at a party) precipitated a phobic reaction to returning to school and a referral for the psychotherapy she had been in continuously since. Nonetheless, she suffered a widening fear of being left alone, and soon had to be accompanied almost everywhere by one of her parents or a close friend. When the patient was married very young, the husband became the talisman against experienced anxiety. The patient herself quit college, so that she could attend the husband's classes to be near him, until the school objected and asked him to pay double tuition under the circumstances. The mother (who lived in the same city) also could not leave the patient alone and insisted almost daily on coming to visit them and also on being invited each time they tried to have company. When things got to the point where the patient could no longer go to the movies or to a restaurant, ride elevators, or visit friends (even when accompanied), and the husband could not go out for a haircut but had to have the barber come to the home, the frantic husband came to the point of threatening divorce. The patient, who felt very badgered by this pressure from the husband, came up with the idea of transferring to The Menninger Foundation for continued treatment, where she could also enter the day hospital program (this would then free her husband to go about his affairs during the daytime).

The treatment recommended at the initial evaluation was psychoanalysis. In view of the long-standing nature of the patient's difficulties, so deeply ingrained in her total personality functioning, analysis was felt to be the only treatment that could promise her any real chance of resolution of conflict and any kind of autonomy and independence in her life. Yet cautions were of course also expressed. The patient's chief transference expectation would be for the increasing nurture and protection that she demanded and felt entitled to, in order to allay her anxiety—a more perfect living out of her neurotic dependency without the accompanying anxieties. A major treatment hazard would therefore be that of an insoluble transference neurosis, should the intensity of the patient's oral fixations (her oral cannibalistic impulses and the meanings of her phobic arrangements as protections against these impulses) prove too refractory to analytic resolution. The treatment might then bog down into a permanent anaclitic relationship.

Course of the Analysis

The patient was actually in analysis 4 years and 9 months (1012 hours). Though the treatment was avowedly classical analysis, the analyst also played a directly guiding and encouraging role in getting the patient to confront her phobic situations, and (as the treatment proceeded) to enter into a more active sexual life, have a child, go on with her education, expand her social life, and so forth. His specific ways of suggesting behaviors ("Well now, I think it's something you ought to do") or of reassuring the patient against the consequences of feared impulses ("You really just can't seduce people you pass in the street") have already been indicated (see pp. 188–189), as has his speaking to her "almost the way you would say this to a child really. Because I think at these times he thought it was very necessary that I quit acting like a child and talking like a child." In all of this the patient correctly understood the analyst's stance: that mature behavior is a good goal to strive for; that she should show more interest in her husband, her marriage, and in her social, cultural, and religious world (i.e., be less egocentric); and that he would be pleased if she could follow these indications. When he offered interpretations, he would, for example, combine the interpretation of sexual strivings toward the father with the comment that in reality, girls like herself just couldn't seduce their fathers. In this sense all the various techniques employed—suggestion, manipulation, and interpretation—were deployed not only in the service of analysis of transference and of defense, but also to strengthen defenses directly, through encouraging more adaptive combinations of impulse and defense.

To put it another way, though the analyst's goals were ostensibly to conduct a thorough analysis, more effort was often put into helping the patient overcome her symptoms and directly improve her adaptation to life than into helping her achieve the fullest understanding and resolution of her underlying conflicts. For example, the analyst was repeatedly struck by the fact that the patient could act so maturely and effectively in her life outside the treatment, and in so childish and self-centered a way in the hours. His approach to this was an effort to get her to behave in a more grown-up manner in the hours, rather than to exploit this difference for the more thorough analysis of the nature of the transference. In return, both inside and outside the treatment, the patient tried to please the analyst. In her life outside, there was a steady progressive improvement. She re-enrolled in college and could begin to go about town on her own (in the daytime) and out of town on trips (if accompanied). As the scope of her phobias continued to recede (she could, toward the end of treatment, stay home alone overnight when her husband had to be away) she became increasingly able to live a "normal"-appearing life again, though still restricted to Topeka and its environs. Her husband, freed from his bondage to her phobias, resumed his schooling, graduated from college, and went on to graduate studies at the university, while at the same time beginning to teach. After 2 years of analysis the patient became pregnant; she had a boy. In this period she was able to become an efficient homemaker, take affectionate care of her child, and participate in a widening social, religious, and club life. She completed college with honors and a teaching assistantship. At the time of termination she was doing part-time teaching, was 6 months along in another pregnancy, and was looking forward to living the next year in a near-by major university town where she and her husband would both be pursuing their graduate studies.

Throughout this course, two life events stood out as of signal importance intrapsychically. The first of these was having the first child. The patient was actively encouraged in this by the analyst; it was clear to her that he "looked on it with favor." She also was quite certain that without the almost explicit permission and encouragement she would not have had the child, falling back on the interdiction of major decisions during analysis to justify this. In her manifest fantasies it was difficult for the patient at the time the child was born not to feel that it was her father's child. The transference implication (i.e., that the analyst was responsible for the child), though patent, was less explicit with the patient. The second signal event was a $75,000 capital gift from her father, which had a dual (contradictory) meaning. It provided a perpetual gratification of the patient's dependency strivings toward the father, while at the same time creating the appearance of objective financial independence: She now "owned" the income-producing source, and would no longer be on a monthly allowance check directly from the father.

Within the analysis, a number of major interlocking themes unfolded:

1. The patient feared impulse, and feared the free-association process as opening the floodgates to impulse. She felt that she might yell out the word "penis" and this would be an irresistible seductive pressure on any males present. Hostile impulses were even more sternly forbidden, and she had many supporting childhood instances. With the analyst she could only tangentially talk about being angry, but she could be more aware of sexual feelings in the transference; at times she was convinced that the analyst had an erection while listening to her seductive talk, and she wanted to (and feared to) turn around to see.

2. There were Oedipal themes with sexual curiosities and fantasies in regard to her husband, her parents, other people she knew, but *not* the analyst (the patient avoided this). She had memories of her father scrubbing her in the bathtub until she grew frightened and put a stop to it when she was 13; her mother dismissed it all with "What of it? He's only your father." The patient grew up feeling that the father could be "seduced" into giving her anything she wanted, and she had sexual fantasies about most of the men she knew. She had constant prostitution fantasies about sexual seductions, and only the phobias could be relied upon to protect her against the realization of such forbidden impulses. At the same time, she was envious of her husband's successes, and she masked her competitive feelings toward him (and the analyst) by consciously imposed protective feelings.

3. Linked to the Oedipal dynamics were the problems of the patient's current sexual life with her husband. The analyst's specific encouraging "directions" in this regard have already been indicated. The patient ventilated her sexual fears, disgust, and excitement. She had been well schooled by her mother that women are supposed to be sexually passive, simply the vehicle of men's pleasure; whether women enjoyed sex or not, they must never let on. It became clear that her fear of a more active sexual life was based on the Oedipal meaning of the marital relationship, with the simultaneous fear of the father's angry retaliation if she truly tried to establish a mature sexual life with the husband. Gradually, under the analyst's persistent interpretive work combined with his encouraging pressure, the patient shifted her emotional tie and her loyalty from the parents to the husband. But even at the end of the analysis, the patient's new freer sexual life with her husband took conscious effort—she had to "fight to enjoy orgasm." She could not be wholly freed of the meaning that the more effective and assertive her husband became (i.e., the more he came to resemble her successful and powerful father), the more conflicted she would need to be about sexual intimacies with him.

4. The pregnancy and the baby became powerful themes. The initial anxiety and hostility were mixed with pride and the success of pending motherhood. The patient gained much support from the analyst's sympathetic approval of the baby while she simultaneously inhibited the transference meanings of the pregnancy.

5. The dependent transference was essentially stabilized (and never analytically reduced) through the whole treatment course. The patient at all times lived within the permission and encouragement of the analyst, and she worked to inhibit sexual and aggressive transference impulses lest they jeopardize the maintained dependency. Within this dependent equilibrium, the patient worked to do her part, in all the behavioral improvements already mentioned in her life functioning outside.

6. Gradually, as the improvement stabilized, the analyst moved to consider termination. This ran quite counter to the patient's now open fantasy of being in analysis indefinitely, dependent doubly on the treating analyst and on her father, who would continue to pay. The patient freely confessed her aversion to the idea of terminating; she didn't think it would happen, since up to then (with her father) she had always been convinced that she could have her way completely. But the analyst stood firm, despite symptomatic flare-ups, and the patient began to see the "justice" of termination. She was vastly improved, and gradually, through the analytic work (as she perceived it), her father and the analyst had both "grown smaller and smaller" while she and her husband had "grown bigger and bigger."

It was indeed time to terminate, but the patient couldn't rid herself of the feeling that the analyst was just "doing it because he was getting tired of me."

7. Absent from the explicit analytic interpretive work was the orally sadistic, hostile, revengeful, pre-Oedipal relationship with the mother. Hostile expressions toward the mother did come into the analytic material, including a recalled period of obsessional fantasies of strangling the mother (during which the patient had to be constantly at her mother's side, to reassure herself against these fantasies) and many dreams in the analysis of the mother dying. But these expressions always emerged at the level of Oedipal hostilities—desire to (and fear to) competitively surpass the mother in the quest for the father's attention and favor.

What can one make overall of this analytic outcome? Throughout the analysis, the main transference position and the central transference resistance was that of the good and ever-dependent little girl in relation to the powerful father who should protect and support her—whom she would try to please through her willing compliance in making the behavioral changes he desired toward being grown up and independent, if she could but then maintain the dependent, nurturant tie in perpetuated fantasy and as much as possible in reality (analysis forever, with the father paying forever). This transference position was counteractively fostered by the analyst in those mainly suggestive and manipulative maneuvers already detailed, which acted to guide and encourage the patient into desired responses and behaviors. Thus the dependent transference served as a defense against the fullest flowering of the complex transference neurosis. The analyst also fostered this trend by his particular interpretive style. At times, he prematurely interpretively deflected transference manifestations back out of the transference, to their prototypes in the patient's past; at other times, he stressed reality meanings, pointing out the irrationality of the transference feelings in terms of the reality. He also sometimes underemphasized sexual transference meanings. For example, the patient was upset at the prospect of being home alone one night when her husband would be away, and she fantasied calling the analyst, who would come over at 2:00 A.M. to give her an analytic hour in her living room. This was interpreted less in sexual terms and more in terms of the patient's infantile omnipotence—her assurance that the analyst would leave his home in the middle of the night at the slightest hint from her.

Thus, though the dependent transference came to full flowering, it was not interpretively resolved (especially in its defense meanings), but rather was counteractively fulfilled, and at the same time (unwittingly?) exploited to obtain the patient's cooperation in more mature, socially acceptable behaviors in her life outside. And that transference remained stable through the analysis as a defense transference, a defense against the fullest unfolding of the complex Oedipal sexual and aggressive strivings. And, *pari passu*, the Oedipal transference position that never developed fully could thereby be only partially resolved—more with the father than with the mother, but even there incompletely. Of this the patient said at Termination interview, "Other little girls quickly learn that they can't seduce their fathers. I didn't learn it. I snap my fingers and he *does* give me what I want. That $75,000 gift to me always meant that he took it away from Mother and gave it to me, although I know it really wasn't like that. I don't think I have ever *completely* believed that I couldn't seduce my father even to this day. I think that

I believe now that I can control wanting to." And, of course, much less worked out than these at least partially uncovered and worked-out aspects of the father-transference was the relationship to the mother, especially as the Oedipal aspects were so firmly linked to the almost completely unreached pre-Oedipal conflicts, the hostile identification with the orally frustrating mother. This last stood almost totally beyond analytic access in an analysis that rested on a compliant and positive dependent transference attachment, and that ended on the positive tie to an idealized "good parent" for whom the patient would even allow the analysis to be terminated.

Status at Termination and Follow-Up

By the end of analysis, the patient had made substantial major changes in remission of symptoms and in enhanced scope and style of life. But the changes were not total; there were residual problems. The patient had (almost defiantly) held on to two specific phobic areas—the fear of automatic elevators (especially in her parents' apartment house), and the fear of driving alone on the turnpike (equated with complete freedom of dangerous impulse). She hoped that after the termination of analysis, the natural pressures of life would enable her to conquer these. And she was well aware that her new freedom from phobic constriction was fullest in Topeka, a good deal less anywhere else, and least of all in her parents' home town. Once she had gone to visit there alone except for her infant son, whom she took along. She said, making a general point, "I have discovered a completely different sort of phenomenon and that's that I can do many more things without anxiety if I have my child along." A new protective talisman? Far less neurotically crippling for her, but what might be its ultimate impact on the growing child? And yet there was still a generalized phobic uneasiness: "The minute the sun goes down there's more anxiety; all the awful sexual things that I was always taught can happen to you when you walk around the streets in the dark."

But the general improvement held. At the Follow-Up Study point, the patient and her husband were living in the nearby university town and pursuing their graduate studies. They drove together for the interview because the patient was still fearful about driving alone on the highway. There had been a moderate symptom relapse coming to a head around the confluence of a number of influences, the chief one being getting pregnant with a third child. This was the first one decided upon and conceived on her own, without the analyst's benevolent encouragement. This was, to her, a significant "independent" step: "I could never have had any children if I hadn't been in analysis; it takes two to make a child and yet it always sort of took three to make my children." At that time the patient had been "ready to return to treatment," but the distress had subsided to the more chronic and usual (bearable) state.

The patient was still apprehensive when alone; she needed people around ("My children need me to be comfortable") and with her husband present she felt fine, relaxed. But it was not so focused as it once was. She could also use friends and neighbors as protectors against phobic apprehensiveness and could arrange it so that they were not aware of her neurotic binding to them. She still had the two residual phobias, riding in elevators alone and driving on highways alone. Though she was somewhat more symptomatic than at termination, her state was far, far better than it had been initially, and the patient felt it containable within the bounds of relatively innocuous protective maneuvers. Her husband said, "There are always people around if you need them." The patient felt that she had terminated her analysis when she was not yet fully ready; it had been done under pressure from her analyst. It might be paradoxically a mark of the patient's more secure achievement (and sufficient emancipation from the dependency upon The Menninger Foundation) that, should she feel her own continued efforts at mastery insufficient and wish to return for further therapy, she was thinking of seeking other kinds of (briefer) treatment, and of seeking them elsewhere (at her university counseling center).

We have additional follow-up information up to the time of this writing, 20 years after the treatment termination. The patient and her husband now live in another state. Both of them are mental health professionals; they practice together as "sex counselors" (at the Follow-Up Study, there was an evasiveness about discussing her own sexual life, and hints that it was still beset by inhibitions). There are now four children, all presumably doing well. The patient has had no further therapy; she seems to have no troubling phobic constraints.

Summary

In overall summary, at the Follow-Up Study point, the patient expressed herself as gratefully content with such a "successful" analytic result when she was only in part really analyzed; in part, she was riding on a "transference cure," changing for the beloved analyst. What had led to this particular oucome—part analysis, part "transference cure"—had been the very particular interlocking of the two major transference developments that each had served to block the possibility for the fullest unfolding and analysis of the other. One was the oral-dependent transference, which served (among other psychic purposes) as a defense transference, a regressive bulwark against the Oedipal transferences. The patient needed to maintain the compliant dependency of the good little girl to the powerful, benevolent, and protective parent and to inhibit the Oedipal flowering that could jeopardize this tie; the analyst played into these needs by virtue of his own countertransference tendencies toward a benevolent, guiding, suggesting, directing, and manipulating role. The other major transference development was the Oedipal transference, which nonetheless did emerge in truncated expression, and which in turn was either deflected away interpretively (prematurely) to outside reality or to the infantile past (reflecting yet another species of countertransference difficulty), or interpreted in relation to infantile needs for a controlling omnipotence, rather than in terms of evoked mutual sexual arousal and retaliatory sexual fear. In result, the overall transferences were in part not analyzed but used (the dependent transference, used as the basis upon which the patient would become more mature and independent in her life outside, as an act of compliant dependence within the transference inside); in part interpreted prematurely and/or deflected outside the transference arena (the Oedipal transferences); and in part bypassed (the Oedipal strivings, which were passed over in order to focus on the need for omnipotent control). And the pre-Oedipal relationship with the ultimately orally frustrating, pre-Oedipal mother was never reached.

Varieties of the Transference Neurosis

THE RISKS OF STALEMATE IN
THE "INSOLUBLE TRANSFERENCE NEUROSIS"

The Insoluble Transference Neurosis in PRP

The dangers of the development of a so-called "insoluble transference neurosis," leading to a stalemated treatment in certain classes of passively dependent or masochistic individuals, have been well-known to the psychoanalytic literature ever since they were focused upon and given that name by Alexander and his coworkers, who used this risk as a theoretical justification for many of their proposed modifications of the classical psychoanalytic technical precepts (see Alexander & French, 1946). Given the large number of alcoholic and/or drug-addicted, characterologically masochistic, and orally hysterical patients in the PRP sample, it is no surprise that the danger of this kind of development bulked large in the diagnostic and prognostic thinking with a very significant segment of our PRP population sample — actually, 16 out of 42, or almost 40% (9 men and 7 women, 8 in psychoanalysis and 8 in almost equally prolonged psychotherapies). And in fact it was the effort to avoid just this untoward treatment development that played a determining role in allowing some patients a treatment plan and course with either no concomitant hospitalization, or an inadequate hospital period, which on other grounds (the seriousness and self-destructiveness of their symptomatic behaviors, usually alcoholism and drug addiction, would have been strongly contraindicated. With two of the patients, the Addicted Doctor and the Car Salesman, this specific concern and the consequent willingness to allow trials of outpatient treatment figured importantly in the ultimate total failures of their treatments.

Actually, of the 16 patients "at risk" in this regard, the development of such entrenched dependency and masochistic gratifications was avoided with 6 — though, as just indicated, at too high a price with some. Of the remaining 10, these issues posed a serious treatment problem with 7 (4 men and 3 women, 5 started in psychoanalysis and 2 in psychotherapy). With 3 of these 7, 2 who had started in psychoanalysis but were subsequently converted to psychotherapy (the Housebound Phobic Woman and the Economist) and 1 who had started in psychotherapy (the Sexual Masochist), there was in fact no resolution of this problem. Those patients became part of the group of "therapeutic lifers," still in ongoing treatment when last contacted and with no plan for real termination. Their treatment careers are described further on under different headings. The remaining 4 were each "weaned" from the feared dependent and/or masochistic entrenchment in different ways. With the Bitter Spinster, I have already described (see p. 254) how her therapist felt that he could only detach her from her dug-in clinging to an 8-year psychotherapy, locked into a transference jam that he was convinced could not otherwise be resolved, by referring her for what turned out to be six consultation visits with another psychiatrist. This enabled the patient at least to come to terms with the need to terminate the treatment — an outcome that the therapist himself had not been able to effect in 3 years of work towards that end. In the case of the Phobic Woman, I have just described the weaning process engineered by the analyst, which the patient reluctantly but never fully accepted.

Two of the psychoanalytic patients for whom dependent and/or masochistic entrenchment was a very major treatment issue—one with a very good treatment outcome, and one with a very equivocal outcome—are described more fully here.

Analysis of the English Professor

BACKGROUND AND PROGNOSIS

The English Professor came to psychoanalysis because of anxiety attacks—"fear reactions" that gripped him in almost every social and professional situation. Things had deteriorated to the point where he had begun to dismiss his classes early, to avoid seeing his friends, and to spend his available time for the most part aimlessly driving around in his car. He finally had abruptly resigned his position and had started in a hospitalization that lasted 7 months, and a psychotherapy that lasted over a 4-year span (with a succession of therapists). During this period he was evaluated at The Menninger Foundation, and on psychological testing a pervasive paranoid condition was revealed that had not been detected on clinical interview. His projective test responses were full of a consciousness of being watched, being sought after to be punished for misdeeds unknown to him. With irrational persistence, he saw eyes and masked, disguised men staring out at him from the Rorschach cards. Because of the assessment then of his illness picture as representing an encapsulated paranoid state in a decompensated phobic–obsessional personality, the treatment recommendation at that time was for an expressive–supportive psychotherapy, to be initially very cautiously pursued. This therapy went on for the next 2½ years and led to enough reintegration and improved functioning (i.e., a return to college teaching) that he finally felt he could strike out on his own and left for free-lance writing in his home town, living with and taking care of his widowed mother. When this did not work out, however, for a variety of reasons, he came back to Topeka and to his previous faculty position, with the intention of seeking more definitive (psychoanalytic) therapy. This time the psychological test picture was that of a much better integrated individual; the paranoid coloration was no longer dominant, and was now also quite ego-alien. He seemed at this juncture to be a typically neurotic, well-compensated, compliant, obsessive–compulsive individual suffering from phobic and anxiety attacks.

The treatment now recommended was psychoanalysis. Among the major difficulties anticipated for the analytic work (alongside the tremendous inhibition of affect and impulse) were the patient's strong passivity, his deep dependent wishes, his willingness to suffer if he could in turn hope for gratification of these wishes, and his combined masochistic–passive tendency, which could all fit into a willingness to stay indefinitely in the analytic situation and to resist mightily efforts to change the dynamic constellations involved.

COURSE OF THE ANALYSIS

The patient was in analysis for 6 years (1145 hours); the treatment effort was classical psychoanalysis. The patient made no major life decisions during the course of the treatment. In fact, procrastination was for him a chief character symptom; it had the meaning both of avoiding commitment with all its dangers, and at the same time of affording the very eroticized gratification of sustained tension.

Through the course of the treatment, the patient made steadily progressive, undramatic, but consolidating changes in almost every sphere of his life functioning:

1. He was finally able to settle into a home of his own, and furnish it, with the implications of commitment and responsibility.

2. He was able to accept and settle into a tenured professorship, and felt improved enough in his public functioning to say, "Even though anxious, I can now stay with a big class—it's like leaving my penis in" (an allusion to his analogous difficulties in the sexual sphere).

3. He came to reasonable accommodations in his family relationships, including disentangling from an undue neurotic dependency upon his mother: "I have had to give up my immature dependence on my mother. I had had the idea that you can be in psychoanalysis and become a happy fellow and still be going home to Mother." He quoted Thomas Wolfe's *You Can't Go Home Again* many times in this connection.

4. He even worked out a stable relationship with a steady girlfriend for the first time, albeit in a mutually neurotically inhibited equilibrium. They had actually been with each other constantly (often five evenings a week) for 3 years before sexual relations were attempted. And then these consisted regularly of varieties of mutual masturbation, since he feared intensely the loss of control (and of identity) in sexual penetration with orgasm. In his analyst's words, sexual intercourse remained the "last refuge of the patient's phobias and defied further change via analysis." The patient was content to terminate his analysis this way, and was pleased that he had found a very special kind of woman willing to (masochistically) endure this situation indefinitely, hoping eventually that it would be overcome and that they would be able to marry.

The main themes of the analysis have been implied in this summary of the patient's life changes (and their sharp limits) during treatment.

1. The phobias were a central issue from the start. They were gradually (and with great difficulty in getting past the patient's vagueness and elusiveness) revealed as barriers against fears of fusion and annihilation. When pushed at this point, the patient was liable to quasi-depersonalization experiences; hence his borderline quality. By the end of treatment, the incapacitating phobic surges had remitted: The patient could comfortably enough do most of the things that scared him, (socialize, teach, etc.). His sexual inhibition, the "last refuge of the phobias," remained.

2. The patient's work problems and sexual problems were equally central to the treatment and linked to the phobic symptoms in the manner just indicated.

3. The patient's passive-phallic and oral-dependent (and orally frustrated) relationship toward powerful authorities—the analyst, the mother and so on— was a central focus. In connection with his fears of rejection and aloneness, to be expected at the hands of powerful adults, the patient recurrently brought three paradigmatic childhood memories: one of turning out not to be wanted by a woman who he thought had called him; one of being pushed out of his mother's bed when he put his hands on her breasts; and one of not being wanted by his father when he tried to help on a walnut-picking expedition. Linked to the fear

of rejection for attempted closeness was the concomitant fear of fusion and loss of himself should the move toward closeness be successful. Yet by the end he could overcome his fears in interpersonal relationships enough that he could step out of the ever-submissive role. He could say (and do) as follows: "I'm 42 now. I pay my taxes. I don't owe anyone anything, so I should be able to go to the toilet. If my bladder is full, I have a right to make a proper excuse to you and go." (This was a measure of the increase in his self-confidence and sense of being grown up, but it was still expressed in childhood, immature terms.)

Within the transference, all these themes were played out. The patient brought a deep dependent yearning (matched by a counterpart fear of rejection). As the distrust of the analyst was overcome, the patient settled into an anaclitic dependent relationship within which the work of the analysis progressed, but which also became ultimately itself a major source of gratification and a barrier to further analytic resolution. The whole analysis was felt as a probing, homoerotically tinged assault at the hands of a tremendously powerful figure—a very threatening, but at the same time a very gratifying, process to the patient. He began to become fearful of admitting further therapeutic progress, as measured by the mastery of his phobias (e.g., the stubborn phobic sexual symptoms); the therapeutic relationship might then have to be ultimately given up. Here was the evolved "insoluble transference neurosis."

TERMINATION

When the analyst, feeling that a plateau of improvement—and an impasse as far as further improvement was concerned—had been reached, moved to bring the analysis to termination, the patient turned on him with his feelings of being let down; he asserted that he still had his phobic potential, that "nothing had happened." This of course was his deeper perception. He had given his all, had tried to do everything that was required, had in turn not gotten everything he wanted, and now was being asked even to give this up. He felt like a stranded, helpless child. Thus a full-fledged transference neurosis had developed but could not be fully worked through and resolved. At the end, the patient felt a repetition of his fate with his frustrating mother, who didn't respond properly to his affection and his plea for closeness and could send him off.

The way in which the analyst terminated the treatment by use of "a parameter" or "a manipulation" has already been stated in detail in Chapter 10 (see pp. 187–188). Basically, it involved spending a fixed amount of time (3 months) in discussing whether indeed there was any purpose to further treatment or motivation toward further change. The patient's bitter and even paranoid outburst over this, and his ultimate acquiescence to the termination pressure, have already been described. The treatment ended with the analyst conveying to the patient that they both ought to consider this an interruption, and a trial at life without treatment, since they both knew that there were considerable conflicts not yet analyzed. The patient said of this in his Termination Study interview, "I'm dedicated to psychoanalysis and after it's over, it leaves me without anything to be dedicated to." And he added, "Analysis sounds good in theory, it looks good to a desperate person, *it feels good while you are in it*, but it's unproductive of a real change in feelings" (patient's emphasis). And because of this, he felt that some special arrangements should be made for those who have terminated analysis, for even a successfully analyzed person might be lost in the first year after treatment. "A guy could shoot himself" without anything to cling to.

STATUS AT FOLLOW-UP

At Follow-Up Study, the patient's life and adjustment were sustained, and even more consolidated than at termination. He now really accepted himself as a professor, "not one of the boys any more." He was still closely involved with the same girlfriend, was engaging now in a kind of half-intercourse with her, and was talking about setting a marriage date. He had given her an official engagement ring because people were beginning to say that she was a fool for going with the patient forever and she "needed something really tangible to show." At the time when he gave her the ring, he told her that he was not quite ready to get married, but that it did look "pretty promising."

The most striking change from treatment days was the patient's feeling that his life was now his own affair; there was no one to take over his responsibility for that. He now felt terminating his treatment when he did to have been the correct thing to do, because nothing but termination could have succeeded in driving that point home. Right after the termination he had been confused and in a vortex. Yet he had gotten up each morning and found that he was still alive, and gradually he came to feel that he could stand on his own feet. He found himself searching less and less for a mother. (His mother had died suddenly during the follow-up period and he could cry at the funeral, in contrast to his inability to do so at his father's earlier death.) He felt no desire to come back and throw himself upon the analyst's mercy. Evidently he had needed to terminate in order to show himself that he could live without treatment. In regard to the treatment, the patient mused about "what a more successful 6-year analysis would be—the maybe still childish and naive idea of it making a 'real' change, leaving one with no nerves, no anxiety." But the illusion of that kind of cure was now gone. He had been waiting for it for 2 years now after termination, and he was by now finally convinced that it would not come. Analysis, he said, tried to promise too much: "It's as though a fellow had his leg cut off and a group of individuals with a great deal of dignity and solemnity about themselves, and doctors' degrees after their names, would say, 'We are going, by this process, to regrow your leg.' He would be all full of false hope instead of just adjusting to the fact that he had no leg."

We have additional follow-up information to the time of the present writing, 24 years after the treatment termination. The patient did marry "on schedule" 3 months after the official Follow-Up Study. A year after that the patient sought out his ex-analyst for a consultation. His wife had an important job in the business world; though he was proud of it and of her capacity to handle it, he resented the inordinate pressures and time demands of the job, which all conflicted with his natural expectation that she should be home to attend to the marriage and to him. He was happy to receive the analyst's suggestion that he talk this whole issue out frankly with his wife, as if he needed the permission and this push to overcome his own procrastinating tendency before taking such a simple and logical step. Two years further along, the patient again sought out the ex-analyst to present him with an inscribed copy of a book of literary criticism he had just had published; he used this opportunity to complain about his life, and to state that his wife had not become pregnant after now 3 years of marriage. At the end of the visit he asked the analyst whether the latter thought he should come back for more treatment. When the analyst looked quizzically at him in response, the patient stated hastily that he personally saw no need for it, since he was doing so well. Somewhat over a year beyond that, with the patient now aged 48, his wife (who was only 32) became pregnant and a son was born; this happened about 5 years after the Follow-Up Study.

This account covers then, a 13-year span from the beginning of a 6-year analysis that the patient was manipulated out of (or weaned from) at a point of satisfactory achievement, and that otherwise might have bogged down into an "insoluble transference neurosis." It was also clear that the treatment outcome was sustained and even consolidated over a considerable follow-up span. Beyond that point, for the 17 years since, up to the present writing (24 years since the treatment termination), the patient has kept in touch with his analyst through an annual Christmas letter of varying length and confidingness. (The patient has lived on permanently in Topeka, while the analyst has moved to pursue his career in a distant city.) The patient's life has been monotonously stable, with the patient in the same job and home ever since. The marriage has been stable; the one child is now a college student. The patient is now close to retirement; he has over the years become a fairly well-noted expert in his area of specialization and has published substantially (publication had been another phobic inhibition). There has been no further therapy; the ex-analyst has usually responded briefly to the annual letter of report.

Analysis of the Devoted Son

BACKGROUND AND PROGNOSIS

The outcome was different, however, with the Devoted Son, the other patient to be described in detail here, whose treatment problems in regard to the termination issue were similar. He was a 32-year-old civil engineer who sought psychiatric evaluation with the following statement: "I am not acutely upset right now, although I was very upset earlier this year. It has been hard for me to admit to myself that I should go to a psychiatrist, although for the last 2 years I have thought a great deal about it and have even read some of the books by the Menningers. I know I am not getting what I want to out of life. I also know that I have not been able to realize what I really could do in my professional work. I am here to find out what can be done for me. If something can be done, I want to try and do it." He was the individual described earlier (see p. 135) who was so preoccupied with his painful thinness and his lifelong sense of physical inadequacy, and of whom the examining psychologist had said that he could leave a session somehow not having made a dent in the chair. He was also the individual who expressed his sense that he had never been loved or nutured properly, via his vision of all women as "cows" but his mother's milk as "watery," and via his memories of bleak, poverty-stricken childhood (see p. 240).

On the other hand, his only close relationship as an adult was with his parents.

He had had some intellectual friends, especially among homosexual classmates at the university. They avoided discussing homosexuality in his presence, and he tried not to be anxious about these relationships: "I didn't have any concern that this meant anything about myself, since I had no conscious homosexual wishes." In later years he brooded about this period, haunted by the thought, "It takes one to know one." He was very devoted to his parents, spending nearly every weekend with them in their home town. He worried constantly about what would happen to them when his father could no longer work. He anticipated the death of either of them as a period in which he might become very upset. His hyperconcern about his parents had led him to buy many things for their home—these gifts usually being for the mother, "things my father could never get her." He had thought of building a home in Topeka and having his parents move in with him, and the conflict over this impulse seemed central in precipitating an acute anxiety attack some 8 months before he sought psychiatric consultation.

The treatment recommended was psychoanalysis, the only treatment that offered hope of substantial modification of the patient's deep-seated characterological problems. There were no specific symptoms that might be relieved, if even temporarily, by other treatment modes. The chief handicap to the analytic effort would be the extreme rigidity of the patient's personality around its anal-compulsive core (amply evident in both the life history and the character functioning), and the difficulty of bringing the very strongly warded-off affects within the scope of the analytic work.

COURSE OF THE ANALYSIS

The patient was in psychoanalysis for 5½ years (1030 hours). A major technical problem of the analysis were the many and prolonged silences. The many meanings adduced for these silences have been previously detailed (see p. 178). With all of this understanding, however, the silences were never really analytically worked through and overcome, and the patient never felt a free flow of communication in the analysis. In the early period, an anamnestic picture somewhat amplified over the evaluation data emerged—basically that of the deprived and impoverished childhood just indicated. The patient saw himself as a gloomy person, thin, hungry, bitter, unwanted, a mother's boy with parents who were always middle-aged and poor. This picture never unfolded further from this early point. The analyst said that after a short period of work with the patient he knew everything about him that he actually ever learned in the whole course of the treatment.

Within the transference, the patient came initially fearful of the analyst as someone who would disapprove of him, would not care *about* him, and hence not be willing to care properly for him. Behind this emerged early, and massively, the expectation of the magical change of the patient into the heroic superman figure—a change to be wrought by the analyst. This expectation emerged in its total expression of helplessness, dependency, and compliance, as in the relationship of the infant child to the expected benevolent, nurturant, and protecting mother. The analyst tried throughout to interpret this expectation of the patient, as well as the (covert) negative accompaniments stemming from the inevitable disappointments and frustrations of this vision. The interpretive unraveling of this transference pattern was largely unsuccessful, and it was at this point that further analytic work foundered. With this impasse, the patient became ever more open in his transference dependency. He had periods of weeping bitterly and of feeling utterly helpless just with weekend interruptions.

TERMINATION

With the analysis of the transference proceeding no further despite all efforts, the analyst gradually shifted his tactics toward using this uninterpreted (uninterpretable?) positive dependency transference as a vehicle within which to help the patient to his best possible level of functioning, and from which the analyst would gradually detach himself through a process of stepwise, supportive weaning, rather than interpretive transference resolution.

Notwithstanding the very partial nature of the analytic work accomplished, and the substantial overall anhedonic sameness of the patient's life, there was evidence of some degree of treatment-related change. He got along better with his coworkers; he could at times join them for lunch or a few beers after work. He could be more comfortable with his parents, accept (and enjoy) his dependency, and no longer be troubled by intrusive, hostile fantasy. He still visited them regularly over weekends, at least every second or third one. He could be less obsessive about his work, complete it on time, and accept suggestions and criticism from superiors and colleagues with some grace. He had gained some weight and could frequent the swimming pool, without the former horror of people seeing his pathetic physique. He could (a trivial, but telling, example) accept the existence of television, without his tirades about the low-brow tastes of those who watched it. He could be a little bit more aware of and tolerant of anxiety, affect, and impulse. At the same time he was more resigned to limitation: He expressed willingness to accept himself as an unfulfilled man who shouldn't expect his life to be different. He said, "I don't feel that the analysis was a rousing success with me, but I think I got some benefit out of it."

How the analyst weaned the patient, via a systematic and progressive reduction in the frequency and then the duration of the analytic sessions, from what he called a "cloying dependency" that he felt could not be analytically resolved has already been detailed (see p. 186). During this process the patient cried many hours; the analysis was the greatest disappointment in his life, but bad as it was, it was far, far better than nothing, and now it was ending. With concealed bitterness and open disappointment, the patient said at the end, "I had a feeling that too much was being expected of me in the analysis. I was having to do the work and the thinking and the figuring out, treating myself almost. I suppose a person goes into analysis sort of expecting a miracle."

STATUS AT FOLLOW-UP

Certainly the treatment results were very modest, and the expectation at termination was for little change during the follow-up period. And at Follow-Up Study, the patient said that his life and he himself were much the same as at termination: "I have gone in the same grooves, wearing a little more deeply." He illustrated this with accounts of his work relationships, his living arrangements, his leisure-time pursuits, his friendships, his lack of social–sexual contacts (he avoided dates—"It doesn't take much avoidance, really"), and his continuing major relationship with his parents. He still visited them on weekends and took them along on his summer vacations, automobile trips around the country. They were both elderly; the father, however, was hale and hearty, while mother was quite crippled with arthritis and chronically depressive. The patient's future worries concerning this relationship centered in himself: "I've spent a great deal of time worrying what's going to happen to me when they've gone because they've played such an important part in my life." About his years of analysis, the patient expressed a variety of thoughts. First came the positive responses: "I feel that the analysis was undoubtedly a help to me. . . . What it has helped me do is when I get to feeling frustrated or in the dumps, to examine it a little more, maybe a little more objective about why I feel the way I do. But I don't think that it changed me very much or that I was able to really do much changing, I mean in basic ways of feeling or thinking. . . . I think I had unrealistic hopes—to become a more outgoing person, to get married."

The patient was reluctant to see his former analyst in connection with the Follow-Up Study, perhaps because of temptation. "I have a tendency to sort of want to become dependent on somebody like that and it was hard to break off, and I, you know, would hate to start it again." And then he spoke more negatively: "I often thought the analyst couldn't possibly really quite understand me because he didn't seem to like any of the things that I liked, like art and music. . . . I think I certainly got more freedom, but I don't know if I ever got complete freedom. . . . And the feeling that he was very critical of me, I never entirely got over that because I still have that feeling. . . . I did have the feeling that it really didn't make any difference what I did, I would never please him, it's that sort of a feeling I had toward my father." And during the long termination weaning process, "he was easing me out of treatment—I always resented cutting down on it."

In overall judgment the patient said, "The changes in my life have been conspicuous by their absence, I guess." Now at follow-up, 40 years old, still unhappily alone and constricted, the patient felt a little more resigned to feeling unable to live a fuller or more gratifying life. He had just dug in at a stabilized level of limited achievement that was paid for by acquiescence in (and resignation to) sharp curtailments in allowable present functioning and future hope. Here a patient seemed successfully weaned out of a dug-in, seemingly insoluble transference dependency, but at an overall much more modest gain in improved functioning and contentment with life than that of the English Professor—a very equivocal as compared with a quite substantial result.

Further follow-up until the present writing (22 years since treatment termination) has more than confirmed this assessment. Some 13 years after his treatment termination, the patient, living on in Topeka in the very same life situation, returned for sporadic contacts with his ex-analyst. He was still single, though his social sphere was somewhat enlarged; he had achieved a somewhat greater adeptness with the aid of Valium to help squelch incipient anxieties. He had continued with the same engineering firm. His renewed therapeutic contact was precipitated by his father's aging and physical decline. When his ex-analyst left Topeka 2 years later, the patient switched to another therapist who has seen him regularly—30 minutes each week for the 7 years since. He has now joined the group of "therapeutic lifers," with his "weaning" from his threatened lifelong treatment having lasted some 13 years. There is no expectation at this point of his current treatment's terminating. His parents are now both dead; the therapist is trying to help the patient "expand his life" bit by bit. The patient has achieved his aim of a permanent treatment dependency.

WAS THIS TRIP NECESSARY?

Certainly, such a result with so extensive a process as analysis does raise the very real question of "Was this trip necessary?" In order to achieve what he did, need the patient have been treated by psychoanalysis for so long, or at all? To put it even more sharply, couldn't the kind of treatment carried out in the actively supportive termination phase (the final 8 months) of the original treatment, and continued now in the still ongoing supportive treatment, been able to accomplish the whole of the therapeutic change achieved? Or, to put it contrarily, could a deeper or a better (more skillful) effort at classical analysis have yielded a higher likelihood that the bogged-down submissive–dependent transference neurosis could have been worked through adequately toward real analytic resolutions—with therefore more analysis, rather than less being the remedy? That is, was the limitation with this rigidly inhibited and overwhelmingly dependent patient in the applicability of psychoanalysis as a method, or in the efficacy of its application?

This issue is discussed at length in the light of the total PRP experience in the concluding section of this book (see pp. 661–662); it is a question that rose with more than the one patient. Further on in the description of treatment courses, I also discuss those cases where the therapist felt unable to detach the patient even temporarily from the perpetuating "insoluble transference neurosis," and where the only solution thus became a mutual commitment to an uninterrupted and apparently endless treatment. These cases constitute the largest group among the so-called "therapeutic lifers."

WORK WITH THE DEFENSE TRANSFERENCE (AND THE "TRANSFERENCE JAM")

Nature of the Defense Transference

The "insoluble transference neurosis" is of course not the only kind—and, in the case of a more "normally" distributed psychoanalytic patient population with proportionately far fewer of the tenaciously orally entrenched (alcoholic, addictive, profoundly dependent, masochistic, etc.) kinds of patients, not even the chief kind—of severe transference difficulty over which treatments can stalemate and/or founder, ending then in some kind of unresolvable "transference jam" (and the latter often abetted from the side of the analyst's countertransference propensities into a "transference–countertransference jam"). Transference difficulties are indeed ubiquitous, not just in psychoanalysis but in psychotherapies as well; in psychotherapies, they are often even more difficult to discern clearly and therefore can be even more difficult to handle appropriately.

And since transference difficulties are indeed ubiquitous, in one way or another almost every one of the PRP patients could be viewed from this vantage point, and the patients could be then catalogued under this heading in terms of what kind of transference difficulty seemed to prevail in their case, the particular way it was worked with, and the specific extent to which this was successful. What I want to do here specifically, however, is to highlight a special (though common enough) kind of difficulty, in which an early transference position gets crystallized and then is used defensively (as a defense transference) against the further mobilization of successive transference positions — that is, against the fuller unfolding of a regressive transference neurosis. Depending on the centrality of the transference position reached and worked with, and on the degree to which neurotic conflict gets adequately resolved at that level, such an analysis can terminate or be terminated at varying degrees of neurotic conflict resolution, and with varying degrees of psychotherapeutic relief of presenting symptoms and problems. This can be illustrated by highlighting two opposed such instances, one less successful and one more successful. The less successful outcome of such a crystallized "transference jam" was with the Silent Woman. Her analytic course is described further along, however, in order to illustrate what I have called the mechanism of the "anti-transference cure," by which she succeeded in freeing herself from the analytic impasse she was in. The fuller analytic working was with the Obese Woman, whose analytic course is described in detail here. In both these instances, it should be added, there were important evoked countertransference contributions interacting with the transference dispositions of the patients, in the fashioning of the precise configuration of transference dilemma that characterized each treatment (discussed on pp. 243–244 for the Silent Woman and pp. 242–243 for the Obese Woman).

Analysis of the Obese Woman

BACKGROUND AND PROGNOSIS

The Obese Woman sought psychiatric treatment because of severe obesity (she weighed 238 pounds when she came to treatment), compulsive eating, and a strong feeling that her obesity was related to emotional conflicts and that psychiatric treatment might help her. She also complained of tension, nervousness, and guilt feelings. She was the patient whose weight problem had begun in her earliest years when she had sought to make friends by gathering a crowd around her and passing out cake and cookies from her father's bakery. Though preoccupied all her life with eating and hunger, with gaining and losing weight, she would at times differentiate "a different kind of hunger — a need to put something into my mouth."

The treatment recommendation was psychoanalysis, for which the patient seemed an excellent candidate. She suffered with deep-seated (sadomasochistic) character problems that went back to earliest childhood, and with the chief presenting symptom of obesity, overt since age 6. She came to treatment at no point of acute crisis or life stress, but because of a growing dissatisfaction with her entire character patterning, her obesity, and all the secondary consequences of each. And she had many assets for analysis: a strong ego, youth (age 24), requisite intellectual capacity, high motivation, psychological-mindedness, a large ability to make use of insights, and a supportive family structure (especially the husband). The husband actually was very knowledgeable about psychoanalysis and was strongly supportive of the patient's securing treatment; he himself hoped to become an analyst (he was a premedical student).

COURSE OF THE ANALYSIS

The patient was in psychoanalysis for 5 years (1142 hours). The analysis was marked by one major life change, divorce, which came 2 years after the start of treatment. This was initiated by the husband, and the patient concurred in the action after she and the analyst both felt that they had analyzed its meanings sufficiently. The patient had always been fearful that her obesity would render her unattractive to her husband and that she might lose him to a more presentable competitor. This was indeed what happened. Nonetheless, after the divorce, the ex-husband, himself an immature, dependent person, seemed to be in and out of the house almost as much as when they were married. He would stick around a while, fight with the patient, leave her, and after a while return, at least all through the year following the divorce; after this, he gradually dropped more permanently out of sight. He never gave a penny of the child support money that was required by the divorce settlement, and the patient never pressed for this. During the latter part of the treatment, the patient lived alone and lonely, with her small son. She had some superficial friendships with men, but her social life was minimal, and after her divorce she had no sexual life at all. Her father had died (at about the time of the divorce), and she drew closer into an ambivalent, highly charged relationship with her mother.

Within the treatment, new historical material that had been withheld on initial evaluation emerged quite early. This included a long history of petty shoplifting and of stealing money from her mother, both of these exacerbated during periods of overt hostile struggle with the mother; it also included the sadomasochistic sexual perversion between the patient and her husband, during which they would take turns being tied to the bed with rope during intercourse. They each enjoyed being the one tied up in this sex game, and they rationalized this behavior as an expression of their uninhibited sexuality.

A number of major themes characterized this analysis in sequence.

1. The patient's presenting character defense was her expectation that her analysis would be a never-ending source of narcissistic gratification from which she had a right to expect and extort what she wanted for herself, without responsibility, shame, or guilt. She would fudge on the payment for the analysis, would steal from her mother and shoplift in the stores, and would criticize her father mercilessly while accepting (ungratefully) his total support for her life and treatment, all the while vowing awesome revenge on her parents for the rejection experienced at their hands in her childhood.

2. The patient's provocativeness in her relationship with her husband, quite apart from his own psychopathology, played its signal role in pushing him toward the divorce. Her attitude was always exploitative, seeing him "like a toy soldier with whom I can play"; when he was provoked to respond defensively, she suffered injured pride. When he decided on divorce, her reaction was one of great anger, with open fantasies of murdering him. After the divorce, she enjoyed masturbating, with the feeling that she could do without men.

3. Set in the midst of this was the father's death. This provoked no mobilization of mourning or guilt, only a berating of those who failed her, who did not do enough.

4. There was open sexual fantasying about the analyst, accentuated at points at which the analyst was trying to confront the patient with her aggressive, exploitative relations with men. This would lock into a power struggle with the analyst—could she force him to be other than a "cold fish"?—and become a re-enactment of the interplay between the patient's parents: The mother would simultaneously bully and excite the father, who would finally be reduced to begging for intercourse.

5. Toward the latter part of the treatment, the major focus was on the patient's intense primitive, aggressive rages against her mother. There were violent, sadistic fantasies of grabbing hold of "mother's ample bosom," and of digging her nails in, tearing, biting, devouring; or of a bloodthirsty vampire sinking its teeth into someone's throat. And at the same time, in defensive expression of the opposite dependent, nurturant yearning, the patient would fall asleep during the hours with weird hypnagogic experiences. Faced with the savagery of this primitive aggression against the mother, and with the increasingly ill-controlled, angry struggle in the current relationship with the mother, the analyst consistently interpreted the patient's responsibility in provoking the quarreling interactions she had with her mother. Under this confronting pressure, there was a progressive change in the patient's behaviors with her mother—an improved comportment, and simultaneously a disappearance of the violently hostile fantasies. The analyst was now experienced as a "protecting father" who was helping the patient improve her relationship with the fearsome mother.

6. And, of course, throughout the whole analysis ran the theme of obesity and overeating in all its richly overdetermined meanings. It was variously a protection against sexual attractiveness and adult sexual activity, and at the same time a substitute for genital sexual gratification; it was a cannibalistic incorporation of and destruction of the hated mother, the punishment of the mother, and at the same time the self-directed punishment for her hostility to the mother; it was the identification with the strong, powerful, dominant mother and the growing into strong, powerful adulthood, and at the same time the overcoming of an inner sense of emptiness and rejection; it was the maintenance of a comfortable self-image as an obese person who couldn't even conceive of herself as being slender, and at the same time the maintenance of a large pendulous abdomen to cover over the lack of a penis and partially to overcome this painful defect; it was an angering of the parents, and at the same time a way of pleasing them, since the brother had been a finicky eater and this had always distressed them; it was a revengeful weapon against the analysis, and at the same time a way of hanging onto the treatment, of being too sick to terminate. It was, in each of these polarities, both a gratification and a punishment. And all through the treatment, the obesity and eating binges were used as ways of expressing the patient's fluctuating transference feelings. More than once, the patient verbalized the conviction that she would never give up the obesity while she remained in treatment with the analyst. These varied meanings could not be worked through in the analysis to any point of consistent modification of the patient's cyclical eating behavior and weight fluctuations.

These themes of the treatment were all clearly expressed in, and interwoven with, the main transference positions that unfolded. The patient's presenting and central relationship was her oral-aggressive and oral-sadistic orientation to the analyst, from whom she expected increasing gratification of her narcissistic wishes —interest, love, and support—without feeling the need to give anything in return.

This continued unabated throughout the analysis. Despite analytic effort, it was never adequately worked through in all its intimate interconnections with the whole exploitative, sadomasochistic character orientation of the patient. When the analyst worked to bring this character attitude into interpretive focus, the patient would characteristically react with great anxiety, and would then bring up sexual fantasies directly or indirectly connected with the analyst, and all masochistically colored. These fantasies would be seen as transferences to the sexually aggressive father and would be interpreted as fear of Oedipal assault within the father-transference. On this level, the patient would respond with complaints about the analyst's lack of interest in her and lack of involvement in the treatment. Gradually then she would revert to her oral-aggressive demanding transference stance, and the transference cycle would repeat itself. That is, the major transference interpretive work turned out to be with the sexually and aggressively fused Oedipal father-transference, rather than with the orally devouring, hating, pre-Oedipal mother-transference; the "transference switch" to the defensive Oedipal transference position securely safeguarded the hating relationship to the pre-Oedipal mother from fullest exposure.

In the last 1½ years of the analysis, as the analyst focused the hateful complaints against the mother (which nonetheless ever persisted in intruding) into the patient's own role in nourishing the continuing present-day hostile interactions, the analyst helped the patient mold her actions toward more realistically appropriate behaviors toward the mother — rather than toward further uncovering of the basic conflicts with the mother. The patient was stimulated to act more appropriately toward her mother in reality, and in the transference more and more Oedipal material came up in which the patient now experienced the analyst as the protecting father, quelling the erstwhile tensions and dangers emanating from the relationship with the mother. In this context, the patient began both to separate herself from her hostile identification with her mother, and to get along better with her. The patient said of this, "Somewhere along in the course of analysis it came to me that all of the things that I dislike so much about my mother were faults or attitudes that I found in myself, and I didn't want to acknowledge them, of course, as being faults of mine; and here was a person on whom I could pin them all and so she kind of represented the unpleasant side of my personality. . . . She is not just heavy, and she is not just overbearing, she is not just all of my faults, she is a person in her own right." At the same time, the incompleteness of this whole "resolution" was attested by the reappearance during this whole terminating period of all the patient's more serious symptoms (her shoplifting, her overeating, etc.), and also her decision to go ahead with the termination of the analysis despite the fact that a main reason for entering into it, the obesity, was overall totally untouched (though her weight had fluctuated very significantly up and down during the course of the treatment).

What had transpired, then, in the analytic work with the transference? The main work of the analysis was with the transference, but with the Oedipal transferences used as a "defense transference": When the conflicts with the mother were more directly focused on, the analytic confrontation with the patient's own provocative role in the interaction stimulated her (defensively) to modify her behaviors favorably in reality, thereby succeeding in re-repressing the conflict rather than having to expose it for fuller analysis. From the analyst's side, it seemed more difficult for him to work consistently with the negative transferences, especially the exploitative, primitive mother-transference. His predilection was to see the (pseudo)positive transference phenomena: When the patient brought up her masochistic sexual fantasies about him, the analyst saw them in terms of the frustration of her positive Oedipal longings, not as defenses against his (maternal) retaliation for her savage oral aggressions. These interpretations then worked to alleviate the patient's deeper anxieties, to enable her to slip back to her basic orally exploiting position without having to fully uncover it analytically. In this sense, the transference neurosis developed to a point, but the main character defenses that became the main transference resistances were not resolved. And indeed, there were transference aspects that were (unwittingly?) used as vehicles of the treatment just because they were systematically underinterpreted. When the analyst sensed that he was not working through the aggressions directed at the mother to thorough conflict unfolding and resolution, he began to "insist" that the patient could at least behave better toward her mother, toward whom she had been behaving so provocatively and inappropriately. The analyst thus used the (pseudo)-positive Oedipal attachment to help repress the deepest layers of the hostile oral mother-transference tie in favor of a more harmonious manifest relationship. The unanalyzed transferences could thus be used to influence the treatment behavioral outcome directly.

TERMINATION

On this note, the patient chose to terminate her analysis. She had been informed at initial evaluation that there was "no guarantee" that analysis would bring about substantial permanent weight loss. At the termination point her obesity was in fact unchanged (up even to 258 pounds), but she anticipated somewhat wistfully (as did the analyst) that after the termination of treatment and the quieting of the termination upset, she would be able to make the consistent inroads into her weight problem that the analysis itself, with all its turmoils, had never effectively achieved for her. For the rest, the patient's social behavior was improved, most markedly in the enhanced relationship with the mother, which was now more appropriate (and tolerant) on both sides. "I used to hate my mother, I had to acknowledge that I also loved her, but now I like her." The shoplifting and stealing tendencies had again abated as part of the patient's overall improved interpersonal relationships; the sadomasochistic sexual perversion had, of course, disappeared with the cessation of all overt sexual life. All in all, the outcomes achieved were most uneven. Of the treatment, the analyst said, "This case was analyzed more deeply than any of my others." The patient said to him at the end, "I have no resentment of you even though you didn't give me a penis."

In overall assessment, the consistent interpretive focus on the Oedipal father-transference (the simultaneously desired, admired, depreciated, and envied Oedipal father), while an important and valid component of the total transference picture, also served importantly as a defense transference. It defended against the fuller working out and uncovering of the orally aggressive, orally devouring, hating transference to the pre-Oedipal mother, within which relationship was the genesis of the patient's sadomasochistic relationship patterns (and, no doubt, also her obesity). This successful "transference switch" to erotic fantasies and (pseudo)-positive Oedipal transference ties whenever the deeper layers of hostile identification and hostile encounter with the malevolent pre-Oedipal mother imago threatened was fed by a shared collusion from the two sides. The analyst had his countertransference difficulties in working with these primitive hating transferences, some of which have already been referred to. He was himself a somewhat shy and reserved person, who had suffered much in his life. He also seemed to have problems in dealing with his own very assertive wife, herself an obese person. In terms of the rubric under which this case has been presented, a potential "transference jam" was averted by the tacit collusive agreement on the level at which to keep the joint analytic work and the basis on which to terminate it.

STATUS AT FOLLOW-UP

The follow-up on this patient is rather limited. About a year into the follow-up period, the patient called on her ex-analyst in the rather distant city to which he had moved. She seemed to be getting along well in her job then and was down almost 80 pounds in weight (at 176) from her termination high (of 258). She said to her analyst, "I couldn't do it for you while I was in treatment." They both seemed rather pleased by her progress. At the official Follow-Up Study a year later, the picture was less positive. The patient's weight was again up to 200 pounds, and it was ill-managed with diet and adjuvant amphetamine. She had not worked out in her job as a counselor in the school system; she was dissatisfied with the field, which "only treated symptoms and didn't get at basic causes." She was living mostly on her inheritance income and was having a hard time managing. She expressed happy surprise that her other symptoms were gone—the shoplifting, the stealing ("I had completely forgotten that I used to do that"). Her relationship with her mother was rather strained, albeit improved. She was concerned that her son, now 8 years old, had a tendency to "compulsive eating" when he was bored or lonely and that he was gaining too much weight. She now had a new fiancé (of whom her mother disapproved), a severely inhibited and quite hypochondriacal individual. He was in psychotherapy and hoped to marry the patient when he could support her adequately. He was a music teacher in the school system, and the two of them dreamed of doing a Broadway musical together. There is no further follow-up information on this patient beyond the official Follow-Up Study point. In the other psychoanalytic treatment course with similar problems within the therapy (and an equally circumscribed treatment outcome)—that of the Silent Woman, to be discussed further on—the "transference jam" that eventuated totally deadlocked all analytic work, and the patient disrupted her treatment after only 1 year (228 hours).

The Analysis of the Hysterical Patient: Limitations?

HYSTERICAL PATIENTS IN PRP

Hysterical patients were the ones around whom both the theory and the therapy of classical psychoanalysis came into being, and for a long time they were considered the patients most amenable to, and with the best prognosis for this treatment. These considerations stemmed centrally from Freud's original conceptualization of the phallic-Oedipal nature of the salient psychosexual developmental fixation points and conflict loci in patients with hysterical symptoms; this conceptualization was later extended to the hysterical character formation as well. It was Marmor (1953) who, in a widely noted paper, so strongly underlined the often equally strong oral-level fixation points in the hysterical personality organization. Zetzel (1968) then elaborated these considerations of the range of developmental fixation levels and concomitant neurotic conflict that characterized the array of hysterical character organizations into prognostic and therapeutic prescriptive counsel. Zetzel distinguished patients with truly excellent prognoses, from the "so-called good hysterics," with much more problematic treatment prospects. This whole field of the diagnostic understanding of the phenomena of the hysterical personality, as well as of the technical prescriptions for therapy, has thus grown considerably in complexity (and, alas, also in ambiguity) since the original Freudian conceptualizations. For one overview of present-day psychoanalytic thinking on these various diagnostic, prognostic, and therapeutic issues—one that is at the same time linked firmly to the empirical experiences with the PRP sample—see a discussion of mine (Wallerstein, 1980–1981).

The PRP experiences had to do with a cluster of patients with certain marked similarities in personality structure and in the nature of their illnesses; incidentally, all of these were thought originally to be among those with the best prognosis for thoroughgoing neurotic conflict resolution in psychoanalysis. Those most clearly in this group were six in number, all women: the Adoptive Mother, the Tantrum Woman, the Snake Phobia Woman, the Divorced Nurse, the Phobic Woman, and the Obese Woman. They ranged in age from 23 to 32 (average age 27); were all married (the Tantrum Woman, however, had just been widowed in the car accident); and mostly had children, except for the youngest, the 23-year-old Phobic Woman, who was still in college, and the Adoptive Mother, who had tried unsuccessfully to conceive. They had different combinations of depression and anxiety among their presenting complaints, except for the Obese Woman, who came to treatment because of her distressing uncontrolled obesity. Four of them were phobic to varying degrees, with this being the central symptomatology in the diffusely pan-phopic, totally constricted Phobic Woman, and more focused (but not completely) in the Snake Phobia Woman. Three complained specifically of impaired sexual functioning, called by the Adoptive Mother "the name without the game." They were all diagnosed and understood as individuals with hysterical character organizations, with varying emphases along the axis from those with more salient phallic-level fixations to those with more salient oral-level fixations; of course, in some instances, there were admixtures of features from other character styles. They were each recommended for psychoanalysis as the best and most appropriate treatment for them, and their prospects were considered to be among the best. Beyond these six, there were perhaps another six (and among these latter six, some men) who to some extent shared features of illness picture and personality organization with the patients just described (and, incidentally, were also all recommended for psychoanalysis); however, these additional six had other more complexly ramifying personality features as well, with the hysterical components less salient.

To our surprise, as a group these patients achieved psychoanalytic outcomes that fell short of the ambitious goals originally posited for them. Characteristically, they mostly reached very (or at least reasonably) satisfactory *psychotherapeutic* goals in terms of symptom amelioration and favorable change in life functioning, and they expressed that satisfaction at termination and follow-up (though mixed with some disappointment and some awareness of limitation). At the same time, they fell short of psychoanalytic goals, and it became clear that they did so in very similar ways. The full treatment courses of two of the six (the Phobic Woman and the Obese Woman) have already been described, but not with special focus upon the issues I am here highlighting—though, indeed, in both cases these issues were clearly evident in the treatment course and outcome. One of the group, the Adoptive Mother, who in many ways can be considered paradigmatic in relation to the phenomena I wish to illustrate here—the particular kind of limitation upon the psychoanalytic outcome that was characteristically achieved—is described in detail from this particular perspective.

A PARADIGM: ANALYSIS OF THE ADOPTIVE MOTHER

Background and Prognosis

The Adoptive Mother was a 28-year-old married woman who sought psychiatric treatment because of her inability to be a proper mother, culminating in returning an adopted child to the adoption agency after 4 months of mounting distress. Of her family background and life history, I will only indicate that the father was an improvident, alcoholic, depreciated person, invalided in a nursing home when the patient came to treatment. The mother was the dominant parent—on the one hand devoted and concerned, on the other controlling and rigid. The patient was never able to feel close to her mother, though she grew up siding with the mother in shared hostility to the father. She was never allowed to touch the father's personal effects or utensils, and learned years later that this was because he was suffering from a venereal disease.

In equally brief capsule, the story of the patient's marriage and motherhood consisted of the following: From the start of her marriage she was intensely eager to have children, though inexplicably also fearful over the idea. She viewed her inability to conceive as itself reflecting her grave deficiency as a proper Catholic woman. When the patient's husband, an Army officer, had an option on an overseas assignment, she prevailed upon him to take it so that they could adopt a child more easily, away from the scrutiny of their family and friends—and return the child to the agency if the adoption didn't work out, without others knowing about it. She wanted to adopt "in order to be like other women." Within 6 months they were able to adopt a 1-month-old baby boy. The patient was excitedly happy for the first few hours, but that evening when tucking him in, she suddenly felt that she did not like him being "so cute and happy." She had an impulse to shake him "as if you are mad at somebody and you want to hold him and shake him." During that first night, when the baby cried and she got up to attend to it, she suffered an anxiety attack. In telling her husband about this, she said that she felt there was something wrong about having taken the baby.

These upsets increased as the days and weeks went by and the patient became increasingly concerned about her ability to care for the child. She went through the motions of giving him good care and was proud of his rapid weight gain. But she did not feel "as a mother should," and bitterly had to pretend maternal affection. She had an insistent urge to hurt the child whenever he looked happy and contented, and once or twice she actually took hold of him and shook him. She began to see an Army psychiatrist who treated her by "encouragement." She even went to Lourdes in the hope that a miracle would enable her to "develop some feeling" for the baby. None of this availed. When she could barely control an impulse one day to push the baby buggy into the face of oncoming vehicular traffic, the patient got herself hospitalized and, in panic, returned the baby to the adoption agency.

The patient was in a depression. She had failed in her eyes as a woman and a mother. The husband was given "a compassionate transfer" back to the United States. As soon as they could arrange it, the patient came to The Menninger Foundation for definitive psychiatric evaluation and treatment planning. Psychiatric evaluation (based of course on wider data than just what has been highlighted here) led to a diagnostic formulation of the core-neurotic conflicts as follows: (1) in the area of feminine sexuality, of her basic sexual identification, of activity–passivity, of her competitive rivalry with men and need to dominate them; and (2) in the area of oral-dependent deprivation and frustrations—in essence, the phallic–oral constellation so often characteristic of the hysterical personality. As might be expected, her proposed treatment (psychoanalysis) would revolve around the patient's problems in being a mother counterposed against her problems *with* her own mother, the unconscious hostile identification with a feared malevolent mother imago. Although the patient and her husband hoped for the recommendation of carbon dioxide inhalation therapy that a previous psychiatric consultant had proposed, she readily accepted The Menninger Foundation's recommendation for outpatient psychoanalysis.

Course of the Analysis

The patient was in psychoanalysis for 3 years (677 hours). As already mentioned (see p. 213), this patient sat up for the first 40 hours; she was "scared" and could not get on the couch for that time. This was also the case in which the analysis was specifically modified (under the aegis of the supervisor) in the direction of a Reichian "defense analysis," with more interpretive attention paid to the formal aspects of the analytic process in its defensive and resistance meanings than to the specific interpretation of content meaning.

In the course of the analysis, many themes emerged, but they did not seem to unfold or develop in any systematic way, partly perhaps because of the less than fully consistent interpretive work. They included the following: (1) her unhappiness derived from wanting a child but not feeling able to have one, and especially from adopting a child abroad only to feel impelled to give it up; (2) the feeling of not getting what she wanted out of treatment, for which she partly blamed the analyst and partly herself; (3) the feeling of being the innocent little child who does not understand what is going on; (4) the deep yearning for closeness, which had to be simultaneously pushed off; (5) the need to dominate and control the treatment and the therapist in the service of her assertive and aggressive strivings, all of which could be denied blandly and peremptorily when remarked by the analyst; (6) the closely related severe and basic problem of her sexual identity and her manifest penis envy; (7) the constant theme of having to choose between husband and analyst, playing one off against the other—by conveying to the husband, for example, that she did not know what the analyst was talking about, and getting the husband to come in to complain on her behalf (recapitulating her childhood triangle with her father and mother); (8) her desire to be a small child, to have no responsibilities, to be lovingly and appreciatively taken care of by a good parent; (9) her desire that the analyst be her lover; (10) the doubts about the strength of her religious convictions and her effort to resolve these in the direction of increased faith (which she did); and (11) the similar doubts about whether she could ever believe in or love her husband or ever be a good wife to him, with the concomitant feeling that she had married him only for material security.

A variety of transference models were successively activated through the course of this analysis. First was that of the nurse (the patient was a nurse), reporting objectively to the physician about the difficulties of a third party—herself, the patient. This reflected her distrust of people and her constant struggle between detachment and involvement: How distant or close a stance was it most worthwhile to take? Side by side, however, in the patient's affect surges, were the outpourings of the confessional to the (hopefully) forgiving priest. As the analysis got past these initial positions, the themes of the terrible father who mistreated and disappointed the mother, and of the good, kind, understanding mother who cared, who tried, and with whom one could be reunited, came to the fore and occupied the center of the analytic stage over its major course. Conspicuously absent throughout the entire course of the treatment was the negative image of the powerful, malevolent, vengeful mother. It is not that such material was not there. For instance, in a dream from the terminating period of the treatment, the interfering mother interrupted the patient and her husband during intercourse; in a rage the patient beat her mother to a pulp. Associations to this dream, however, were sparse and not pursued. At other times the analyst was berated for nagging like the patient's mother, but this aspect of the material was not vigorously pursued either. To the end the analyst was seen only as a warm, accepting, good parent (the good mother, the father she had never had), and of him the patient said afterward, "I think he's wonderful. I love him to death."

Status at Termination

The treatment terminated after 3 years, ostensibly under reality pressure from the patient's husband, who was insisting on moving to undertake his lifetime professional practice in their city of choice now that his military service obligation was fulfilled. From the patient's point of view, she had by then experienced major improvement in her work capacity; she stated with pride that she could again work comfortably, even on a pediatric ward. On the other hand, her central problem had not been definitely resolved. To her regret, the analysis had not made it possible for her to conceive. She wanted to be assured by the analyst that perhaps she could now adopt successfully—but the proof of that pudding would be very much in the eating. And she acknowledged that it was certainly hard to be comfortable with children, or with women who sit around and talk about their children. On that somewhat muted note the analyst and patient ended the treatment by mutual consent, at a point of significant symptomatic relief, but certainly sooner than the analyst thought optimal. The transference neurosis had indeed unfolded—to the point where the hostile relationship with the pre-Oedipal mother imago was pressing to the fore—but was not resolved. There was incomplete resolution of intrapsychic conflict, and incomplete cure of the presenting distress.

The process notes of the analysis from its terminal phase amply support this view. During the same period as the dream referred to above, there were fantasies of the mother indulging in the very same forbidden sexual behaviors that were interdicted to the patient; a memory of the mother having told her about degenerates (men) and what they do; the childhood fear of the mother catching her masturbating (and the association to the analyst peering at her); the fear of the homosexual fantasies that she might have if she had had a woman analyst. Hatred was gingerly expressed toward the mother and father as partners in crime, and the patient stated her strong discomfort on kissing her mother-in-law in greeting or on parting. In another dream of this period, the patient spilled her jewels, and these were restored to her by the analyst. In her associations she toyed with this as the symbol of the restoration of her femininity, and then brought up the pregnancy and miscarriage she had had early in the marriage (which had been withheld from the initial anamnesis). But then she veered to a bossy reaction to the analyst's presence, taking up a critical, defensive position. All these conflicts were active in the material of this termination phase of the analysis, without concomitant evidence of insightful mastery or of new ego positions.

Nonetheless, the patient felt pressured to draw the analysis to a premature close before this material was ever worked through. Her own awareness of this was caught in the complaint about "orders from headquarters" (her husband) pressing her to terminate so that she and he could move together to their new home. To this she asked, "How can I go when I can't make peace with my own dead mother?" Despite this, she did leave, alternately ascribing her departure to the increasing importunities of an ever more demanding husband, or at other times admitting "that I could have stayed longer if I really wanted to and that my husband would have been ready to wait for me." Certainly at the point of leaving it was clear that the analysis ended on the same note of positive attachment and sustained good feeling toward the analyst that had characterized the predominant transference mode throughout—gratitude toward the fatherly analyst, the good mother who cared.

Reasons for Limited Outcome

What accounted for this limited outcome, with termination prior to the analysis of the negative mother imago, which was so centrally tied to the patient's core conflicts and their symptomatic expression? A number of influences within the treatment contributed to this outcome limitation.

1. The supervisor tried to hold the analysis to a "defense analysis" that focused more on interpretation of defense and resistance, and less on specific content meaning of inner impulse or its transference manifestations. Interpretive effort was thus often partial and incomplete.[1]

2. These injunctions from the supervisor interlocked with a specific learning problem detectable in the analyst's work. This was the analyst's difficulty in showing the patient the transference meaning of phenomena — for example, acting out — without becoming punitive. For the analyst, acting out was characteristically to be directly suppressed, or ignored. He did not rely on the fact that the patient could come to understand its meaning in a way that would be sufficient to control it.

3. In addition to this specific learning problem, a particular countertransference problem seemed to limit the full effectiveness of the analyst's work, as noted earlier (see p. 238). The patient was a woman whom he would go to any length to help, from whom he was willing to take a lot, and who perhaps made him too anxious to deal effectively with her bossy, competitive ways. (As noted, the analyst seemed to have a comparable problem with his very competent but also quite bossy wife.)

4. A last problem specifically noted within the conduct of the treatment lay in the analyst's tendency to tread lightly in analyzing the meaning of the patient's religious beliefs and feelings. In part, this may have been in defensive deference to the husband's (and the patient's) anticipated fear that psychoanalysis would undermine (i.e., take away) the patient's religious faith; in part, it may have been a reflection of a more general attitude of reluctance to explore the meanings of religion in intrapsychic life. In any case, it is clear that the meaning of her religion and of her relationship to God was never brought into explicit analytic focus, despite its obvious connection with the unexplored aspects of her relationship to her mother. Rather, the disappointment with her religion with which she began the analysis shifted to the same note of heightened faith and good feeling that characterized every other aspect of the termination state of the analysis. The treatment never explored the question of how much her religious fervor represented the coin she paid to keep her husband's love, or the question of how much the sexual inhibition with which she ended the analysis represented the conviction that sexuality, to be moral, must be paid for by pregnancy, and that therefore if pregnancy were barred, sexuality at least should be muted.

Thus a variety of influences within the specifics of the analysis could be felt to contribute to the limited outcome. That they by themselves did not necessarily account for this outcome or for its specific form is attested by the other side of the coin — the limitations on the possible outcome of the analysis that were pre-

---

1. Stone (1981), in a recent article addressed to the issues raised by the current re-emphasis by Gill (1979) on the "here and now" in psychoanalytic technique and process, stated the following, which is equally applicable to the earlier emphasis by W. Reich on "defense analysis," and the limitations of these different technical approaches as seen from within Stone's more encompassing (classical) perspective:

> [D]espite special attention to the "here and now", the essential importance of the past remains unquestionable, not only in psychogenesis, but in the need for its technical reinstatement, to the degree reasonably and effectively possible. . . . is analytic work conceivable without resort to the influences and impacts of infancy and early childhood? It is thought that while such effort might provide productive experiment and be capable of certain useful therapeutic effects, it would be severely (and unnecessarily) limited by its omision of ultimately decisive factors in the understanding of current distortions. (p. 730)

dicted at the time of Initial Study from the psychological test protocols (i.e., from the side of the patient). It was observed that the nature and form of the acute decompensated state in which the patient presented herself for treatment gave evidence of the disorganizing anxiety that could potentially be generated by the regressive experience of psychoanalysis. The patient's own awareness of this was reflected in her panicky "fear of losing control." It was predicted that at a point of achievement of sufficient symptom relief, and of substantial if not complete gains toward more adaptive reaction patterns, that, rather than face the dangers of further regression, the patient would prefer to consolidate at that point and "quit while she is ahead"; it was felt that she could do this by invoking reality pressures from without, and by remobilizing her potential for counterphobic mastery from within. All this, of course, was exactly what happened. Furthermore, it was specified that the area of incompleted work would be in relation to the negative mother-transference, and her own hostile identification with this malevolent, feared, and hateful mother imago. Again, this was exactly what happened. In fact, the very life solution that she came to at the end of the analysis—to have a grateful feeling toward mother figures, to maintain her marriage with its problems glossed over, and to adopt children (again) even at the cost of considerable suffering—was in itself an expression of the unresolved identification with the mother: She chose to be a martyr like the mother, burdened with children and with an unsatisfactory husband.

Thus, in terms of this major limitation on the expectable outcome of the analysis, arising from the nature of the patient's personality structure and of her illness, the termination perhaps took place at the best possible point—whether it was deliberately planned technically (for which we have no evidence), or sensed intuitively and pushed for by the patient. The outcome was further influenced by the already stated problems within the handling of the treatment, which likewise worked to keep it less than fully interpretive and to allow significant sectors of intrapsychic functioning to remain in repression and unanalyzed.

Two corollary predictions had been made initially—one having to do with the first phase of the treatment, the other with the prospects of further, postanalytic, treatment. The first prediction was of the desirability in this case of an initial period of preparatory psychotherapy in order to help arrest the presenting acute decompensation. Again, though this does not seem to have been done deliberately, the actual treatment worked out that way. The patient spent the first 2 months (40 hours) sitting up rather than on the couch, as already noted. She expressed herself as too anxious to accept the analytic structure directly.

The other prediction, which was based on the expectation that the analytic result would be incomplete and that the patient would be left liable to recurrent anxiety and perhaps even transitory symptom formation in the face of continued environmental triggering of her core conflicts, had to do with the form of future treatment. It was stipulated that this should not then be an effort to analyze further what had remained unanalyzed from the first treatment (for the same reasons), but that this should rather be a supportive–expressive psychotherapy aimed at helping her utilize the previous analytic accomplishments to stabilize herself in the face of the new stresses. In effect, though not in formal terms, this is also exactly what happened.

Status at Follow-Up

When contacted for Follow-Up Study (nearly 4 years after the termination of the analysis) the patient returned eagerly with her husband and her 3-year-old adoptive daughter. Strongly contributing to her willingness to make the trip was the voiced desire to see her ex-analyst and to show him the successful "fruit of his labors"—the daughter. When she had come to live in her new community, the patient had continued to be beset by anxiety over her wishes to adopt. At times of special stress, she took sedatives and tranquilizers. She lit candles and went to Mass twice daily, praying and weeping, "storming heaven." When she put herself on an agency adoption list she had more anxiety, took more tranquilizers, and prayed harder that she would be able to love the baby she was going to adopt. During this waiting period, she forced herself to work with babies—as a pediatric nurse in a local hospital, and as a volunteer in the infant adoption agency to which she had made application.

In this period, the patient did not seek further psychotherapy in an explicit way. She rationalized this on the basis of the higher treatment fee in her new community than in Topeka; she stated that she could not afford the higher fee. What she did instead was to call on a variety of helping hands, none of which were specifically psychotherapy. There was the priest who admonished her to attend to her duties to her husband and to their proper future together, including the child he encouraged her to adopt. There was the friendly family physician who prescribed the medications to help her cope with the tensions and anxieties any such moves would generate. And there was the understanding social worker at the adoption agency ("an angel in disguise"), to whom the patient could pour out her burden of grief, of worry, and of discouragement. In combination, the patient had put together the ingredients of her own supportive–expressive psychotherapy, and had insured that any more ambitious psychotherapeutic effort would be precluded.

And this "package" worked. After a 6-month wait, the patient was able to adopt a 5-month-old baby girl. The patient had fallen in love with this particular child and had hoped that this would be the one she would get. When she did, she felt that her prayers had been answered. In the subsequent 2½ years the patient established that she could manage this relationship, even if never fully comfortably. At times she would be too irritable with the child; she would feel nervous when the child cried; and she would blame herself for her own childish attitudes toward the child. More important, however, she was no longer beset by fears of harming the child. In fact, at the time of the Follow-Up visit, the patient and her husband were on the list for a second adoption. She was fearful that this might be a boy, though, and she wondered whether she could tolerate a male child. Perhaps if she really felt fully cured, she could dare to adopt a boy. Less than a year after the Follow-Up Study came an announcement of the adoption of a 9-month-old baby boy. Accompanying the announcement, which was sent to the ex-analyst, was a letter stating, "Heaven has blessed us again." The patient had "made a weekend retreat and a nine-day Novena and stormed heaven before bringing him home, and so far (one week), so good, and we have so much to be grateful for." There were specific references to similarities to the little boy that had been returned to the adoption agency abroad, but so far, "I don't believe that my problems with myself over this will throw me like the other time. I'll be able to get through them."

Thus the patient was able to go ahead and twice adopt successfully (including even a boy), albeit with considerable psychological strain. With the consolidation of the success of the first adoption (the girl), she experienced enough accrual of circular gratifications and enough increment to her self-esteem and her self-confidence that she could adopt the boy 3 years later. Thus, with an analysis that was incomplete, with important transference components unanalyzed, the patient could nonetheless achieve her original treatment goals—to be able to be a wife and a mother. There is no further follow-up information on this patient beyond the official Follow-Up Study and the subsequent announcement by letter of the second adoption.

ANALYSIS AND REANALYSIS: ANALYSIS OF THE TANTRUM WOMAN

The account just given of the case of the Adoptive Mother leaves unanswered a critical question in regard to the achievable psychoanalytic result in such an instance. The question still at issue is this: To what extent was the failure of thorough conflict resolution (i.e., of a more complete psychoanalytic result) a consequence of the various limitations that were adduced in the analyst's technical handling of the therapeutic issues of the analysis, and to what extent was this limitation of result—to a very good psychotherapeutic outcome, albeit a limited psychoanalytic outcome—a consequence of the kinds of issues in the character structure of this "typical hysterical" individual that were noted ahead of time, and that were felt might preclude treatment gains beyond those that were in fact achieved? In other words, could we, based in part on the conclusions from this study, fashion technical approaches that could indeed carry such treatments to a fuller psychoanalytic conflict resolution, or are we up against limitations in the method itself—at least in terms of present-day knowledge of the application of the method (modified or not) to patients with these particular kinds of character problems?

At least a partial approach to answering this question would be to examine the happenstance of a patient "of this kind" having a second effort at psychoanalysis after the first one had left her at a point comparable to that described with the Adoptive Mother, rather than having a subsequent course of supportive psychotherapy (or, as with the Adoptive Mother, quasi-psychotherapy) to help overcome renewed life stress, on the grounds that that would be all that could or should be done. Fortunately from this point of view, we had one such patient in PRP, one of the "hysterical" group named at the beginning of this chapter. That was the Tantrum Woman, who indeed had two periods of psychoanalysis under just this kind of circumstance. And yet, of course, in deference to the fact that the comparability between psychoanalytic patients is never total, the phrase "of this kind" is put in quotation marks above.

Background and Prognosis

The Tantrum Woman, the 24-year-old recent widow, was indeed similar to the Adoptive Mother in many ways: She was phobic, anxious, and depressed. The phobic concerns centered around her body and physical illness. They included agitated cancer scares, as well as a lifelong concern with "asthma" and proneness to respiratory disability; the respiratory concerns were fed by an overprotective, hypochondriacally fixated mother, who moved the family to a mild sunny climate, forbade the patient most childhood activities, made her start school 2 years late, and made her wear long woolen stockings and unattractive dresses as constant guards against the weather. This was also the patient whose lifelong preoccupation with constipation (with its danger of "poisoning") was guarded against by the frequent enemas administered by the mother, both in childhood and again in her presenting adult acute illness. The anxiety was linked to the patient's distressing intrusive thoughts about her impulses to kill her children, and her explosive rages (and childhood temper tantrums) usually directed at her mother. The depression was consequent to her husband's traumatic death in the auto accident, superimposed on lifelong unhappy interpersonal stresses, particularly with the mother. There was also another symptom, sexual frigidity, fostered by the mother's moralistic and fear-arousing upbringing.

Basically, the patient came to treatment with an acute regressive and depressive reaction after her husband's death; this threw her back into the intensely hostile–dependent relationship with her mother (including the renewed enema administrations), from which she had rescued herself through her marriage. She was preoccupied with angry thoughts about her husband's desertion and her distress at feeling so intensely her yearning to be loved and understood. Psychoanalysis was recommended as the treatment of choice. The chief problems anticipated for the treatment centered around the hostile–dependent tie to the mother; this would now be transferred into the analysis, where the patient would be seeking not only realistic help in the resolution of intrapsychic problems and amelioration of psychic distress, but also fulfillment of the neurotic expectation of at last finding a long-term benevolent nurturing figure who would give unlimited love and gratification without frustration.

Course of the First Analysis

The first analysis of the patient lasted 4 years and 8 months (835 hours). There was one major deliberate variation from classical technique, described earlier (see p. 179)—a parameter introduced after more than a year of analysis to cope with the patient's increasingly unmanageable "affect storms" (repeated episodes of torrential affective outpourings during the analytic hours). When waiting them out further seemed fruitless, and when all effort at interpretation of meaning was lost in the absence at the moment of cooperating ego, the analyst began to intervene firmly with a direct and insistent statement that he was present and listening: "Just a minute! There's no need to shout. I'm listening." To the patient, these interventions marked the turning point of her treatment: "He [finally] said, 'shut up.' I needed someone to shut me up. . . . Before that I was running wild and he was letting me. Now I felt there was someone who would help me and not let me run wild."

Within the analytic work that was then carried out, a variety of themes were interwoven:

1. There was an initial period of delayed mourning for the husband.
2. There was long, intensive work on her Oedipal struggles; on her penis envy

and the linked preoccupation with her small breasts as against the big breasts of the dangerously powerful mother; on her relentless ambitiousness and competitiveness, especially with the envied but also derogated men; on her phobic concerns about "an intruder" coming into the house; and on her conflict over exhibitionistic tendencies.

3. Linked material was built around reconstructions and infantile "memories." For example, there was an insistent obsessional thought, a "memory" that the patient had had a younger brother when she was 5, whom she had killed. She made efforts to find out if indeed this had been true, and when she could secure no such evidence, could begin to accept that this was the screen for her perception of the ineffectual, drinking father, who had left the family when the patient was very young, had come back to claim his place with the mother, and then had left again.

4. In the transference, absences of the analyst were linked to absences of the father, just as the affect storms were seen (among their several meanings) as transference defenses against the erotic longings for the father.

5. The issue of "control" over impulses was most marked in relation to the affect storms, but also surfaced in relation to a periodic symptom of urinary frequency, which came on during situations that the patient felt she could not control (a displacement from the menstrual function, which indeed she could not control).

6. Sexual impulses were channeled mainly into masturbatory activity and fantasy — fantasies initially that she was a man, or homosexual fantasies of a fat naked woman with big breasts (like the mother), and, toward the end of her analysis, heterosexual love-making fantasies.

7. The concomitant actual loneliness of her life, which centered so completely around the analyst, the wishes for love from him, and the consequent frustrations and angers, were all interpreted in terms of longing for the Oedipal father.

8. The hostile–dependent relationship with the mother was prominent throughout the analytic work, but not equally central to the perception of the transference manifestations. Transference interpretation was most vigorous in relation to the positive Oedipal strivings toward the father, and their counterpart, the competitive Oedipal rivalry with the mother. But the yearning for (and fear of) dependence upon and homosexual submission to the controlling pre-Oedipal mother was much less worked out, though evident in dream, masturbation fantasy, and other aspects of the material mentioned. As part of this, the kind of manipulation by the analyst in the parameter introduced to control the patient's affect storms was not specifically analyzed in terms of the patient's childhood behaviors toward the mother, which were also designed, and in the same ways, to elicit the mother's suppressive control.

Though the analytic course was stormy, the patient's ongoing life was correspondingly quiet, uneventful, and progressively stabilized. She established a home for herself and her two children. She returned to college, and then, in identification with her analyst and the therapeutic role, went on (successfully) to a graduate clinical program in order to enter a clinical helping profession. She got into some difficulties with her children, and both youngsters entered into psychotherapy, in which they seemed to do well; out of their combined treatments, mother and children worked out a much improved relationship. The patient's social life was the least satisfying part of her life adjustment. She had rare dates and only one close woman friend, and was mostly emotionally involved in her treatment and her tie to the analyst.

Status at Termination of First Analysis

By the end of the treatment, the patient's initially presenting symptomatic picture had altered markedly. The affect outbursts were gone; the patient was now in control, and life could be pleasant for her and for others. The hostile dependence on the mother was now muted; they lived far enough apart that they could now be comfortable when they did come together or help each other. Termination came as a gradual response to a mutual agreement that this degree of resolution of problems represented the most feasible stopping place. The patient seemed less sure of this than the analyst, and twice made a delay in termination dates that she had set herself. She was disappointed. She said, "I'm really a lonely person. There is no one I have to talk to, so it's hard to give such a thing up." She was in a termination mourning process. Actually, it took the financial pressures of her children's continuing treatment needs to push the patient to allow termination.

In overall summary, just as with the Adoptive Mother, important aspects of the Tantrum Woman's hostile–dependent mother-transference — actually the central core of the neurosis — were incompletely analyzed. The patient's conscious goals in the analysis had been to be relieved of symptomatic distress, to regain control over impulse, and to secure her independence from the mother. These she had achieved. Her unconscious goals were, not to free herself from her dependent tie to the nurturant figure with its inevitable frustrations and reactive hostilities, but to restore it on better terms. She sought a more steadily giving anaclitic relationship, without the concomitant hostile turmoil engendered with her mother. She had indeed found just this in the marriage that had been so abruptly shattered. And she sought to regain it in her analysis — that is, not to analyze the nature and roots of the dependency and the hostility in relation to the mother, but to replace it by a better dependency without the same hostility, in the relation to the analyst.

It was just this result that was achieved in the analysis. Intrapsychic conflicts were partially worked through — substantially so at the Oedipal level, in regard to the relationship with the father and the rivalrous aspects of the relationship with the mother, but much less so in regard to the tie to the pre-Oedipal mother and the unconscious hostile identification with her. The changes that occurred in the relief of symptoms and in the major alteration of the patient's life adjustment rested only in part on the analytic resolution of conflict; they also rested on the identification with the therapist and the therapeutic task (in her choice of profession and of Topeka as the location in which to pursue it), and on a transference shift from a basically hostile tie to and identification with the negative mother imago to a loving tie to and identification with the benevolent analyst (the new, better imago). To make this transference shift and the behavior changes built upon it possible, the mother-transference had to be repeated (in altered form and with a new balance, of course) and not analyzed to resolution.

On this basis, the analysis officially "terminated." It became transparently clear at the Follow-Up Study inquiry that in the patient's mind it had never terminated. Monthly she found causes to return for follow-up interviews with her analyst and, in different ways (in relation to periods of transient symptom formations), to renew her plea for further treatment. The analyst was at first unconvinced, which angered the patient. He wanted the patient to give herself a chance, to try herself out in life, to give up her attachment to him as the idealized father, in order to effect an attachment to a suitable man as suitor and husband. He said, "Who knows, your future husband might live in the very next block." Quite promptly thereafter, the patient reported that she had met a lonely widower (of 3 years) living in the very next block, a man with three children ranging from 7 to 13. This quickly blossomed into a very intense involvement and a proposal of marriage. This man was affectionate and thoughtful, and his children seemed receptive, but the patient was undecided and anxious. She finally rallied and quit her job in order to take on her new family, with the combined total of five children.

From the start the marriage made the patient uneasy and guilty; it was finally "an Oedipal triumph"—taking the place of the other woman, the rightful owner who had been there first. Within the marriage there was friction and anxiety. There were sexual problems (the patient continued to be relatively frigid and unsatisfied) and religious differences (the husband and his family held to strict Lutheran tenets—"I feel guilty enough without them piling all that original sin on top of me each time"). There were also problems with the husband's expectations that the patient would be the same kind of meticulous and competent housekeeper that his mother and first wife had been before her. And basically, the patient brought into the relationship with the new husband the same unanalyzed problems of her dependency upon the negatively controlling mother that had dogged her life with her own mother and each mother-substitute figure. Finally, on top of this marriage, which thus exacerbated rather than abated her still unresolved conflicts, was the added spectre of the research Follow-Up Study, which would finally "officially" terminate her connection with The Menninger Foundation and thus would force the separation from the object of her dependent ties (the ex-analyst) that she was not yet psychologically capable of. Under these pressures the patient's symptoms returned in full measure—centrally anxiety, rising to panic proportions.

Course of the Reanalysis

Now that she had established that remarriage, by itself, was not enough, the analyst was willing to take the patient back for a second period of analysis (the intervening period was more than 2 years). The analyst saw it at this time as a return to work out problems previously insufficiently worked out—problems that could not be worked out "until she got into a situation like a marriage which would bring them actively to the fore again." The reanalysis spanned 4 years for a total of 481 additional hours (much of the reanalysis being at a reduced frequency).

In the reanalysis, many familiar themes were again evident: (1) the patient's difficulty in sharing her husband—with his parents, with his children, or with the demands of his work; (2) the less intense direct transference involvement (the patient was no longer a lonely individual whose whole real life centered around her treatment); (3) the disappointment and disillusionment with a marriage that did not automatically solve all her problems and, in fact, brought new ones (her anger at the husband's passivity, her being overwhelmed by the responsibilities in this marriage with this large family, her yearning for a dependency (which she resented), and her pain at the prospect of "separation" from her dependent position; (4) her sexual difficulties, with frigidity, masturbation, and overt masochistic sexual fantasizing; (5) her return to full-time clinical employment, and its problems as well as gains; (6) the marital discord, growing into a sense of "armed truce," with a waning of interest in the husband—all comcomitant with a growing transference attachment, with all the yearnings and fears about dependency and separation fully reawakened; (7) the redeveloping transference neurosis, with a reactivation of the dependent and orally aggressive relationship to the analyst, who this time was much more clearly in the transference position of the mother; (8) the effort at fuller analytic working through, then, of the patient's whole hostile identification with her "dirty, punitive, argumentative mother" and of her concomitant remaking of her husband into the image of her father, the passive male who could be safely depreciated; (9) the concomitant work again with the themes of disappointment in the husband and of unrealizable yearning after the analyst, in both Oedipal and pre-Oedipal meanings; and (10) the continuing, nonresolving tension between the patient and her adolescent stepson for first claim on the husband's attachment and concern.

Status at Termination of Reanalysis

When this whole period of reanalysis came to its close, the patient's problems were indeed more thoroughly worked out (if not fully), and her life and marriage more stably established (if not fully). Remaining tensions with the intruder stepson, remaining disappointments with the too passive and ineffectual husband, and remaining yearnings for the idealized analyst reflected some residues of incompletely resolved Oedipal and pre-Oedipal conflicts.

Questions about this analytic treatment obviously still remain. Could the two-part analysis have been carried through to at least this degree of further resolution the first time? Or did it require the intervening period, the pursuit of her life, and the patient's remarriage to bring the still unresolved issues to the point where they could come to these further increments of beneficial analytic scrutiny? And were these further results that were finally achieved the best reachable with this particular kind and severity of hysterical psychology? What seems clearly demonstrated is that a basically good analytic process, set into a good analytic situation, can, when aided by situational pressures, be resumed and carried significantly further—to the limits, perhaps, of the particular participants' capacities in working together. Further follow-up study after another several years would be needed, of course, to determine how much more adequate the additional degree of resolution reached in the second period of analysis would be in achieving a more enduring result, and one no longer dependent on the maintenance of a particular configuration of unresolved attachment and identification. With this patient, no further follow-up information is available.

ANALYSIS WITH A 22-YEAR FOLLOW-UP:
ANALYSIS OF THE SNAKE PHOBIA WOMAN

Another way of approaching the same issue of how much change can indeed be achieved in the psychoanalysis of the hysterical character and what the expectable (or inevitable) limitations upon that change might be—in terms, at least, of our present state of knowledge—would be truly long-term follow-up in a patient with no or minimal subsequent psychotherapeutic work, and, of course, no further analysis. Again, within the same cluster of similarly constituted "hysterical" patients in PRP, we happened to have one of our longest spans of follow-up contact with one, the Snake Phobia Woman. In her case, the follow-up covered 22 years after the original 6 years of pretreatment and treatment contact.[2]

Background and Prognosis

This patient was the 28-year-old woman who had suffered the intense and pervasive snake phobia for 15 years, triggered by a casual remark of her mother, herself fearful of snakes, that someone she knew once found a snake in bed. The various manifestations of this severe and long-standing snake phobia have already been described (see pp. 122–123). Actually, it was not the snake phobia (to which she had accommodated as a constant part of her ongoing life) that brought her to seek psychiatric treatment, but, rather, temper outbursts increasing in tempo and intensity, directed at her children. She feared that her episodic loss of control presaged her losing her mind. Her fear came to a head in the episode already recounted (see pp. 150–151), in which a large truck blocked her accustomed path in driving her car home one day; this event led to an acutely decompensated episode, with uncontrolled sobbing, a feeling of depersonalization, and the paranoid fear that two young boys approaching her might kill her. She insisted on a prompt psychiatric evaluation, despite the strenuous efforts of her physician to dissuade her from this step, which he felt to be unnecessary and foolish. This was also the patient who then went into treatment first with an analytic psychiatrist in another (closer) community, who treated her phobic concerns "aggressively" by having her sit on his lap, caressing her, and insisting that she was unable to give love because she felt so fearful of what form treatment might take next (see pp. 71, 208).

It was at this juncture that the patient returned to The Menninger Foundation, panicky, fearful of both suicide and mental breakdown. She saw herself get-

---

2. The Snake Phobia Woman, of course, is not the only patient with whom we have had such long-term follow-up contact of 20 years or more postanalysis. The treatment courses of three others have already been described: (1) the Phobic Woman (see pp. 271–277), who is also in this cluster of patients with "typical" hysterical character neuroses, but whose treatment course is not described with the special focus on the issues being highlighted here; (2) the English Professor (see pp. 279–283), of a very different—phobic-obsessional, and compliant—character structure; and (3) the Devoted Son (see pp. 283–287), very compulsive and inhibited, who returned to The Menninger Foundation 13 years after his treatment termination and has now become a "therapeutic lifer" in a still ongoing therapy, a half hour each week. In addition, the treatment course of the Divorced Nurse, another patient with a hysterical character neurosis, is described immediately following. And, in further addition, two others of the originally psychoanalytic patients, the Housebound Phobic Woman and the Economist, who were subsequently converted to psychotherapy, have been in continuous treatment ("therapeutic lifers") ever since, with spans of 25½ and 28 years respectively. Their treatment courses are described further on.

ting into a dream-like state, a "whirl of unreality"; she feared going into "a severe psychotic process, with deterioration" and ending in a state hospital. The treatment recommendation was for psychoanalysis, with the patient living (during the week) on an outpatient basis in Topeka. The three living children (there had been a third child born with congenital heart disease, who had died after 6 weeks—this event had preceded the episode that instigated the initial evaluation—and then a fourth child, born during the treatment with the psychiatrist from whom the patient fled) would remain at home with the father, and the patient would commute home each weekend.

Course of the Analysis

This analysis, starting some 3½ years after the patient's original Menninger Foundation evaluation, lasted only 2½ years (543 hours). The patient's life during treatment consisted of living in Topeka and commuting home most weekends for her "weekend marriage." Occasionally the husband and children came to spend the weekend with her in Topeka. I have already described in detail (see p. 234) how this circumstance was felt by both the patient and her analyst to be the most important and pervasively determining of the issues that stood in the way of achieving a more complete treatment success. As her analyst noted, "She was always choosing throughout the whole analysis between a husband at home and an analyst in Topeka. . . . We could never test the analysis in a realistic setting. It was always a weekend marriage."

And within this context, the husband made difficulties all through the patient's treatment. He was an irresponsible man, described as a kind of "psychopathic Babbitt." He was much involved in his hobby of buying and selling (and flying) airplanes; he was less interested in his wife, and the marriage was beset with constant strife. He was always on the threshold of great business successes, but at the same time was often courting bankruptcy. This, of course, created constant financial pressures upon the treatment. Indeed, he was often delinquent in meeting the bills and exerted a chronic pressure toward treatment termination.

Given this context of the difficulties of the "weekend marriage," with its vulnerability to the neurotic manipulations of the various protagonists (e.g., the patient's browbeating her husband on weekends with talk about "the nice doctor" who understood her so well all week), as well as the realistic and the psychological antitreatment pressures constantly exerted by the neurotically acting-out husband, the analysis proceeded with (as much as possible) classical intent. A number of themes ran through the analysis. First, and most completely worked out, was the snake phobia itself. There were many dreams about snakes: dreams of little snakes (her children, her favored twin brother and herself, father's sperm), which could be "placated" by chocolate milk; dreams of being concerned for her children's safety with a snake in the bathwater, and linked images of being in the bathtub with her twin brother; dreams of little snakes coming out of the faucet into the bathtub, and even more, of concern that the water would run out and she would lose things irrevocably down the drain. With the snake preoccupation, the patient was always "looking for something," and there were repetitive dreams of searching for something small—in cracks, between pillows, in books, and so forth. The meanings worked out were manifold. The patient said the snakes "stood for *so many* things."

These included fear of sexual assault ("I learned that such fears were really temptations and attractions"); identifications with the mother, who also had a snake phobia, and instigated that of the patient; a search for the "answer to my life, to be a man instead of a woman," linked then to the hostility toward and rivalry with the resented twin brother; and reflections of her own hostile destructiveness, since a snake could get loose "which I could step on." (It was the eruption into full consciousness of intense hostile feelings toward her children, with the death of her defective infant, that had precipitated her coming into treatment in the first place.) At the end of treatment the patient said, "Believe you me, there are times when I would like to have the phobia back. . . . It's much more comfortable sometimes just to be looking for snakes than to be trying to figure your way out of situations."

A major related theme was the childhood incestuous longing for the ever-disappointing father. There was a dream of a weak old man (her father, her former therapist, etc.) who wanted her to fondle him in the bathtub, and there were recovered memories of her sexual excitement when bathed by the father as a child. But the father did not respond to her infantile sexual wishes (projected as her disgust at *his* dirtiness); she was angry and guilty, and she was envious of the father's greater ease with her twin brother. She resented and envied the male who could be close to the father, while she was only an unlovable girl. As revenge, she had to seduce men and depreciate them—render them ineffective like her own father. Her problem was expressed in the obsessional dilemma, "How nice if only I were a man! . . . but that's no good because men are no good."

And related in turn, was the theme of hostile competition with the favored brother, heightened in intensity because of the twinship. Around this were focused the open wish to be a boy, the intense penis envy, the competitiveness, and the need to depreciate. The patient came to analysis able to "prove" the open preference for the brother on the part of the parents. These perceptions were progressively revised. She came to see the past differently: The parents hadn't differentiated between them and favored the brother as much as she had supposed. It was not only the patient who had been forced toward her brother in such matters as dress; he had been forced toward her as well, to his equal discomfiture (with Buster Brown haircuts, etc.). And what the patient in childhood had taken as the burdensome imposition of tasks, she could also come to see as evidence of trust and responsibility accorded her.

Reflecting the hypercritical, hostile, and depreciating relationship to weak and inept men (the father, the twin brother) was the patient's marital relationship and all its tensions. This was further complicated (and made harder to resolve) by the husband's own neurotic character, and also by the fact of the weekly separation—the to and fro, the struggle over whether to go back home to live or to stay in Topeka for fuller treatment, and all the pressures toward termination that the husband constantly generated in this interaction (the financial crises that he periodically precipitated gave great force to these pressures). Linked with this theme and never fully explored, were sexual difficulties in the marriage (the patient's inhibitedness and the husband's tendency to potency disturbances).

These, then, were the major treatment themes. As with the Adoptive Mother and the Tantrum Woman, there was much less analytic work with the mother material—the mother who stood behind the father and was chiefly responsible for her difficulties, for making her a woman in the first place. Within the transference, the major analytic themes were manifest in the patient's struggle to render the analyst as impotent as all other men. The effort to destroy the analyst was also revenge against the mother for not making her a boy, a denial of the feeling that men are better (more lovable) than women, and a killing of the twin brother (who had the power—the penis— that belonged by rights to her, which he could not properly use anyway because men are weak even if lovable, and women are stronger even if they are not lovable and have their birthrights stolen away). Side by side with this destructive intent was the effort also to identify with the favored man: The patient switched in her resumed college education to a psychology major, then took on a position as an adjunctive therapist in a mental institution, and later took flying lessons (to share with her flyer husband).

Status at Termination

Up to the end of the analysis, these major transference models hardly changed. The patient found it very difficult to face hostile transference fantasies explicitly, and just as difficult "to verbalize the attractions." The analyst felt unable to elicit and analyze the full scope of the positive transference longings, and the patient terminated in defense against (and unresolution of) her terrifyingly strong erotic transference feelings. Triangular situations were repeatedly set up by the patient: her shift from home economics to psychology and its symbolic meaning; her engineering of the confrontation between husband and analyst (so that *they* should quarrel about her); her running back and forth from one to the other. All this kept the patient's reality sufficiently in turmoil so that the patient could end the analysis (could "quit while she was ahead") with significant elements not thoroughly analyzed—its "positive" components, the disappointment in the ineffective analyst (who, in the end, did not fulfill her fantasy wish: "I came. I saw. I conquered. But I don't have the trophy," i.e., the penis), and the underlying relationship with the depriving mother who stood behind it all.

　　Yet the patient ended under the combination of the pressures of her own disruptive and avoidant impulses, the difficult realities of her "weekend marriage," the constant antitreatment pressures of the husband, and the patient's clearer perception of her using the *husband's* neurosis as a limiting factor to rationalize her feeling that things could not be fully resolved just in her treatment. And significant changes had occurred. The snake phobia was gone (she was at times quite rueful about this). The patient's relationship with her children was improved, and she looked at this as her greatest treatment accomplishment. Relations with the parents and the wider family were likewise improved. The "foggy states" (the decompensating hostile upsurges), the acute depressive bursts, and the asthmatic attacks had become only occasional shadows of their former selves. However, the patient was also well aware that what had before been expressed via the snake phobia and the other symptoms was now experienced directly in the still very troubled, quite unresolved relationship with her husband. This was the major area of acknowledged disappointment in the treatment outcome. The fact that the husband was himself disturbed and that they both brought unresolved problems with each other to the relationship was now "something you have to face." The patient had given up the expectation that treatment would somehow change all this.

Status at Official Follow-Up

The official Follow-Up Study took place 4 years later. Treatment termination had been difficult for the patient , but she had put a brave face on it. "Emotionally I had changed so much. I wasn't the same person—but I was going back to the same situation. . . . I talked myself into living a little bit in a fool's paradise at the end." And (expectedly?), in her struggles to get along with her husband during the posttreatment period, the patient was troubled by some of her old symptoms in somewhat different guises. A kind of neurasthenic–depressive picture came to the fore. Some days the patient would sit at the breakfast table with a sadness of unknown sources, tears brimming in her eyes. She ate poorly and was underweight.

It took the patient a good 6 months before she felt badly enough that she just had to consult her analyst again. She said critically that she had felt at termination that that should be it; there should be no further contact. "It would have been a big help to feel that I could come back and not feel that the only way I could return was to have failed." Once this reluctance was overcome, and the patient initiated the contact, she did feel welcomed. With considerable relief she embarked upon a series of follow-up contacts; at times she was accompanied by her husband, and occasionally contact was made by letter instead of visit. The contacts continued on this ad hoc basis over the entire period before the Follow-Up Study.

The patient felt, and the analyst agreed, that she needed more treatment, "especially in the area of day-to-day adjustment to the life situation with her husband." But the analyst strongly advised that for further treatment to be maximally fruitful, it should not be on the commuting basis in effect till then. The patient and her family should all move together to Topeka, or wherever else the treatment would be available. However, much as the husband accepted his wife's need for more treatment, he was unwilling to do this. His business was ever better established. It would be such a major uprooting, such a sacrifice, without even an assured gain in return.

But the periodic return visits continued, and they helped give the patient a sense of both continuity and mastery. In this context her work went on, and her open sexual fantasying about the ex-analyst gradually dwindled away. Another pregnancy came—this was the fourth living child, since a third child had been born during her treatment—and the patient could bring her treatment to a clearer "psychological termination." Meanwhile the husband, prompted by the joint interviews with the analyst, went into a once-weekly psychotherapy, which was available in his home town. To his and his wife's surprise, he stayed with this treatment for about 1½ years, and he felt much benefited. In fact, he said, "It saved the marriage." In the treatment he worked mainly on his own problems with a dominating father, but also substantially on the discordant marriage relationship.

In his discussion of all this at official Follow-Up the husband was quite critical of The Menninger Foundation. He felt that we should not just have sent his wife back to him at the end of her treatment, but should have "forced" him into psychotherapy for himself. He admitted that his attitude toward his wife had been coldly unsympathetic, on the model, "You've been away up there getting treatment all this time: I've had the burden of the household and the children and I've resented it. Now you buckle down and take over and make up for all that or I'll get a divorce." He agreed, though, that if pressured toward treatment for himself at that time, he might well not have accepted it.

As a result of all this, the patient's symptom distress steadily declined, and the marital relationship steadily improved. The patient and her husband found each other ever more interesting to be with—"We never run out of things to talk about." The patient's return visits to her analyst were in almost all instances prompted by renewed squabbles with her husband, and thus represented running to the understanding father for solace and support in these recurrent difficulties. On one occasion, when the analyst brusquely confronted the quarreling couple with the question, "Are you two considering a divorce?", they felt themselves shocked into considering more fully the implications of their behaviors. They subsequently described themselves as having been drawn closer "by this bombshell."

At the time of the official Follow-Up Study, the equilibrium was more stable. The husband's therapy was by now concluded. The patient said of hers, "I think it is still a working-through proposition and it continues. . . . I think 2½ years is rather short for analysis from some other cases I've heard of." The relationship with the children and the parental families was meanwhile greatly improved. But the patient also felt much less at home in what she experienced as the petty small-town life. And she had given up church attendance because she could no longer abide the fundamentalist and literal emphasis in church and prayer meetings. Her own ideas in God had become "more abstract," and the divinity of Christ was no longer a congenial doctrine.

Continued Follow-Up

Six years after this Follow-Up Study (now 10 years after treatment termination), the patient was still returning for occasional visits with the ex-analyst. These were now quite infrequent, and any idea of a return to intensive therapy had vanished. But as the tensions and misunderstandings within the marriage took an occasional more acute turn, the patient found it helpful to return for a few interviews. The ex-analyst ultimately reconciled himself to these continuing follow-up visits, now often spaced 6 to 12 months apart. He now more explicitly encouraged the patient to get in touch with him as she felt the need: "I have been trying to push her away each time in the past. I reversed that in this last discussion."

Ten years after that (now 20 years after treatment termination), the analyst sent us his most recent—and quite long—letter of report from the patient. She gave an account of her own busy life, including work in a mental-health-related area, as well as all the busy and happy family news. The four children seemed to be doing well, each in his or her own way. One had had a successful psychotherapy. Two were married, and the patient reported excitedly, "We're grandparents! . . . I'm adding some babysitting to the schedule." She stated that her husband and the 17-year-old youngest child, who was still at home, "deserve some sort of recognition for all they've done to keep the home fires burning as well as not letting me throw in the towel when priorities were hard to sort out." Her aging parents were living in a nursing home in their same city, and they visited them regularly. She was finding it hard to "find a stopping place" in this long letter of report, and went on at the end to say that she and her husband "are looking forward to the end of parenting and we want time together—how about that?" She decried the "crazy Pollyanna letters that some of our friends send out at Christmas," but put a handwritten addendum to her own typed letter in which she called attention to the stamp she had put on the envelope—the Robert Indiana painting with the word "Love" emblazoned across the stamp. She ended the letter with "not hard to make this choice for you." Thus, the patient had consolidated a now reasonably contented life with herself, her husband, and her family; the conclusion of her letter indicated a note of continuing attachment to the analyst as the architect of it. There was some further follow-up contact with this patient for another 2 years beyond this letter. The analyst had just moved to a distant part of the country. Ostensibly without knowing his whereabouts, the patient and her husband had just moved to the adjacent community, presumably for a better job opportunity for the husband. There were a few semisocial contacts initiated by the patient. All seemed to be continuing pretty much the same. The patient's life was going well, but she did let her analyst know that over all these years the marriage itself had never been truly fulfilling or happy; they had both just accommodated to it. A short time later the patient and her husband returned to Kansas, their home state, and have not continued any further contacts.

ANALYSIS IN AN UNFAVORABLE LIFE SITUATION: ANALYSIS OF THE DIVORCED NURSE

The last in this cluster of patients with basically hysterical character structures who did reasonably well in terms of the therapeutic outcomes of their analyses, but with clear (and comparable) limitations on the fullest psychoanalytic resolution of underlying conflict, was the Divorced Nurse. Actually, her therapeutic outcome was not as good as that of most of the group, and in many ways she had the most unfavorable life and treatment circumstances to contend with of any in the group. Unlike the Snake Phobia Woman's adverse treatment circumstances (the commuting back and forth between treatment and the "weekend marriage," together with an antagonistic husband who opposed the treatment), which could be dealt with, and over time (albeit a long time) could be overcome, the Divorced Nurse's circumstances were more severe and her ultimate outcome much more seriously affected.

Background and Prognosis

The Divorced Nurse's situation has already been described in considerable detail (see pp. 235–236). Basically, it had to do with the patient's coming for her needed psychoanalysis in Topeka while her physician husband, himself much conflicted about continuing their storm-wracked marriage, opted to move to a major metropolitan area close to his home city where his parents lived (so that they could look after the two older children, who stayed with the father) while he set up a new practice. The 4 years of the patient's analysis were marked by the husband's definite decision to divorce, the patient's futile struggle to ward this off, and then the long and bitter custody battle over the children, all of which made for frequent irregular and sudden treatment absences by the patient. How all this operated to the major detriment of the analysis and what could be achieved in it has been already, in part, stated. Here the story is filled out from the perspective of the intra-analytic treatment course itself.

Actually, the 30-year-old patient had come to analysis determined to try to save her badly deteriorating marriage, which had been marked by 6 years of bitter quarreling. This had started during a discussion (after more than a year of marriage) about love and morals, during which the husband acknowledged, in response to a question, that he had had a love affair with another woman prior to his marriage—an affair that he promptly terminated when he met and began courting his wife. Despite this evidence that she was clearly the preferred love object, the patient was deeply hurt, shaken, and let down. She felt that her beautiful but unreal dream was irrevocably shattered. She became openly antagonistic to her husband, repeatedly harped on the subject, and harried him for further details. She became distrustful and now constantly questioned the husband's love and fidelity. Though two children were subsequently born and she was 4 months pregnant with the third when she finally came for Menninger Foundation evaluation, the patient's agitation and symptoms, her doubts and accusations, continually intensified. During her evaluation process, she castigated herself unmercifully and desperately reached out for help. Depressive moods alternated with irritable outbursts, mild elated feelings, and even momentary calm. Mostly, she felt that her case was hopeless and that she had brought it all upon herself.

The patient was first entered into a supportive–expressive psychotherapy, which took place over almost a year and was designed both to help stabilize the patient's life and to help her work out more definitive treatment plans. During this time she began to work again professionally, half-time in a local hospital, and she set up a home for herself and her newborn third child. Her husband filed for divorce during this time but then agreed to withdraw the divorce suit, pending the outcome of the patient's treatment. It was then that he worked out his long-term plans for relocating his practice in his parents' city, and the patient entered psychoanalysis in Topeka, where she felt protected and helped but very far away from home—from her husband and the two older children.

Course of the Analysis

As noted, the patient's analysis lasted 4 years (891 hours). How this analysis was beset by the marital turmoil, the divorce litigation, and the resulting treatment absences (for the most part unauthorized, and even undiscussed) has already been recounted, as just indicated (see pp. 235–236). Despite these deforming pressures, the analyst tried as much as possible to abide by classical analytic procedure. There was a good deal of abreaction stemming from the patient's explosive handling of her affects. In this affect flood, which inundated the beginning period of the analysis, the patient expected in turn to be scolded, shamed, rebuked. She did not want to turn these "affect storms" introspectively into understandings. The patient's reality plight also constantly interfered. As already stated (see pp. 235–236), the analyst put it thus: "In these flights, she was both flying to the transference father and trying to escape him, and we tried to make the analysis operate in between trips." As the patient put it, "It would sidetrack me. . . . It was difficult for me to separate the two and to be able to forget my husband and choose the analysis." And complicating all this was that, quite contrary to the explicit analytic goal of being cured of her neurosis and recovering her husband and children, there was an unconscious thrust toward ensuring the husband's loss through the treatment plan that the patient so much desired and secured—to be analyzed in Topeka, far away from him.

The intra-analytic material was organized around a number of themes:

1. The separation from the husband and children, the desire to regain them, and the vicissitudes of the divorce were of course primary themes. They were predominantly interpreted in resistance terms, as a focusing elsewhere of feelings that belonged rather to the transference. Even more one-sided was the analyst's confidence that the patient would not lose her children and probably not even her husband. The husband, it turned out, was by now much more hostile and uninterested, and more determined on the divorce, than had been realized. Once the divorce action was under way, the analyst felt that the patient in any case would win the children. He tried to interpret her expectation that she would lose the custody battle (in her home state court) as a reflection of her neurotic guilts. (She later did lose the custody fight, despite her analyst's deposition and testimony on her behalf; see p. 236).

2. Another focus was the driven, gushing quality of the patient's manner of presentation in the analysis, alternating with her temper outbursts. There was considerable attention to the "ungenuineness" in this, and to its possible meanings, mainly as a defense against real transference feelings.

3. A sexual involvement, initiated coincident with the start of the analysis, served as a vehicle for "ready-made transference acting out." This was interpreted as a displacement of the loving father feelings from the transference, an unconscious love affair with the father.

4. The patient battled out her penis envy in sadistic, vengeful attitudes against the seductive father (analyst). In this sadomasochistic interplay, the patient would provoke the "rape" that was both seduction and punishment, and in turn would revengefully fantasy tearing off and devouring the penis, the maleness of the father figure.

5. This involvement in the seduction–punishment–revenge sequence in the love attachment in the father-transference was in turn linked to and underlay the material related to her turbulent marital situation, and her outside love affair.

6. A less vivid but ever present theme was the patient's masochism expressed in her "forced against her convictions" principle: So much of her behavior was experienced as forced upon her by circumstance, and against her wishes and convictions. This was built upon the patient's latent homosexual submission to the mother (as manifest in a dream of being strangled by a woman opponent, and another in which her mother was sealing over her vagina), and emerged in the transference as her perception of the analyst as someone who sealed her off from any man. This was her view of the analyst's constantly interpreting her efforts to restore her marriage in transference–resistance terms.

The transference modes activated through this course were mainly of the analyst as the forbidden sexual object, the father, followed by the emphasis on having to give up the man in submission to the nagging, critical mother, who demanded the suppression of sexuality. In these relationships the patient was at times a helpless, floundering, and devalued little girl, and at other times a greedily demanding one. The major analytic work accomplished was clearly in relation to the father-transference. By comparison, the infantile relationship with the mother was much less fully worked with (just as with all the other patients already described from this same hysterical grouping).

Through the course of the analysis, there was, at the same time, considerable amelioration of the patient's symptoms. Her anxiety and depressive episodes came under control, her masochistic stance was somewhat moderated, and the disturbed behaviors with the husband dwindled away, though this turn of events did not alter his determination to pursue the divorce. For her part, even at the end, the patient still clung to the fantasy that if she settled near her ex-husband after her treatment termination, things between them might yet somehow work out, and she would be able to win him back.

Status at Termination

The actual treatment termination was difficult and was hesitated over by the patient, who, since her divorce, had felt an intensified tie to the therapist (the little girl submitting to the controlling mother?). When she actually did terminate, it was done somewhat abruptly, under the pressure of the pending judicial review of the custody decision. Her lawyer argued that the patient's chances of regaining custody of her children would be greater if she were actually in residence in her home city, and no longer in treatment in Topeka.

After her treatment termination, the patient did return initially to her home town. She was uncomfortable there with the curiosities of all those who knew her about what had happened to her marriage, and she found that she got along better with her mother when she was not too closely involved with her. She ruminated over whether to reopen the full custody fight for the children; finally, she decided just to ask for improved visitation rights and more alimony (and travel money). She did not secure even that, and at the time of the Follow-Up Study had this adverse ruling on appeal in the courts. She pondered where to move and finally decided not to move close to her husband and her children: "Suppose I get there and I just can't work things out there and then have to leave. That would be worse for the children than if I hadn't gone in the first place." She then decided upon Topeka, partly on the conscious basis of having her young son (who had been born during her preparatory period of psychotherapy in Topeka, and whose custody the ex-husband had never made any claim upon) evaluated and, if need be, treated psychiatrically; the relationship between the two of them was not an easy one.

The son did go into psychotherapy at The Menninger Foundation, and the patient—fearful that she might lose him to his female therapist, who would be a better mother and succeed where she had failed—went into concomitant intensive casework. This did help the patient reach altered attitudes toward her son, with whom she then became able to effect some appropriate behavior controls, without having to suffer guilt over this. During this same time the patient was working steadily and effectively as a nurse; however, she was beset with social anxiety, felt a lonely longing for friends and companions, and felt cut off from her older sons (her ex-husband and his new wife were being more difficult about visits all the time). She felt she couldn't succeed in securing a new husband herself because she still felt so guilty about the failure in her marriage. She felt she had no roots and no meaning: "I feel so gloomy, I do not want to meet people and any good excuse is used to avoid meeting them."

Status at Follow-Up

During the succeeding 2½-year follow-up period, the patient continued her direct contacts with her analyst. In the 18 months that she lived in her old home town she wrote him some 25 long and detailed letters, 13 of them in 1 month when the turmoil over whether and to what extent to pursue the custody fight was at its height. The analyst responded to a number of these. He advised her to stop the fruitless legal fighting, and to consider carefully whether Topeka would indeed be the best place to move to, in order to get her young son into treatment. In the last letter, he noted that she was busily engaged in her old habits of heaping ashes on her head, gaining herself nothing, and getting nowhere. He pointed out that she was forgetting her hard-won knowledge and that her sense of guilt came from elsewhere, and told her that he believed she was capable of exercising better controls. After the move to Topeka, the son's treatment and the patient's casework took up the therapeutic burden.

The patient's attitude toward the Follow-Up Study was reluctant. She was afraid of showing that she hadn't done as well as she had hoped she would, and didn't want to suffer further blows to her self-esteem. She stated clearly her view of the limited treatment achievements: "I feel I'm keeping my head above water because I had that treatment, but I want more out of life than that." For this, she partly blamed the situation in which the analysis took place. "If only I had gone East for the analysis—before the divorce . . . if my husband had given me one bit of encouragement. I would have. . . . Topeka was familiar to me and friendly. . . . How could any two people possibly work anything out when they are so many miles apart?" In part she blamed herself more directly: "I'm not any better than I used to be; if you get out and use what you've learned, then you *are* better, and I feel that this is what I'm not doing." About her future, she was downhearted. She expressed the fear of being alone and growing old, and that this feeling would get worse as the years went on. When her son grew up she wouldn't have anything. In all, she was depressed, lonely, masochistically resigned, and feeling martyred.

Beyond the Follow-Up Study, there has been sporadic contact with the patient for another 18 years; she has lived continuously in Topeka ever since, as has her ex-analyst. These half-dozen contacts clustered actually across a span of 4 years, between 14 and 18 years after the Follow-Up Study (16 and 20 years after the treatment termination). They had to do with issues of growing older, problems of encroaching illness, and difficulties with the patient's aging mother. The patient herself began to suffer progressive orthopedic disease, which brought her finally to surgery (spine fusion). The increasingly senile mother was brought to live with the patient, was then put in a nursing home, and from there went back to live with the patient again. The patient's grown children were a problem: One of her sons was emotionally quite unstable, while another was suffering with some neurological disease. The patient often had a sense of diminished self-esteem and felt as though she were indecisively spinning her wheels in what often seemed like a bleak and effortful life struggle. The ex-analyst saw his role in these sporadic consultation contacts to exhort the patient to a renewed effort to her best functioning (as in the contact described during the immediate post-treatment period).

Reasons for Limited Outcome

Clearly, this overall result was more limited than that obtained with the other patients described from this group with hysterical character formations. This patient ended her treatment without really feeling free to start a new life and seek new attachments. This reflected not just the continued dissatisfactions with what she could reasonably expect and get in relationships, but the incompletely resolved intrapsychic problems as well—her continued inner submissiveness and masochistic stance toward repressive (mother) figures, which caused her to sustain situations in which she could not get what she would want and would even give up what she did have.

This overall sharply limited analytic outcome reflected the confluence of an array of forces. Some of them resided in the reality circumstances of the treatment in the face of the imposed separation of the patient from her husband, children, and home:

1. The effort to carry out a psychoanalysis in the context of this life situation of separation of the patient from her family was aggravated all the more by the conflict-wracked and deteriorated status of the marriage, with the husband set on divorce and seeking every opportunity to facilitate this outcome, and the patient so conflicted over her ostensible desire to salvage the marriage while her neurosis was pushing her to destroy it. In effect, life was set up to favor a particular major life decision, in contravention of the usual analytic requirements.

2. The linked difficulty for the analyst under these circumstances was in distinguishing clearly between reality and transference. What the patient impulsively wanted to do—and did—was so often close to the proper action that she would have to take in any serious effort to win her children that the meaning of any particular impulse to rush off from the analysis to be with them could become hopelessly entangled. Reality requirement and transference acting out coincided very closely.

3. The analyst's natural desire to support his patient in the face of a difficult and often unfair reality led him to encourage her that she could and would hold her husband, and, failing that, could hold her children (indeed, he testified on her behalf to help toward that end). Yet reality seemed constantly to confirm the patient's "neurotic fantasies"—that her husband would divorce her, and even more, win the children away. The analyst's more "realistic" appraisal turned out to be the fantasy.

4. Basically, the agreement to take the patient into psychoanalysis under these circumstances actually allowed the fulfillment of the patient's unconscious destructive impulses against her marriage, and increased her chances of losing her children, both psychologically and legally. At the same time, it represented falling in with the husband's maneuver; it enabled him to use the reality that the patient was now in long-term psychiatric treatment far away from home, both to strengthen his own emotional detachment from her, and to strengthen his legal case in winning the custody of the children.

And yet it has been abundantly clear in the description of the intra-analytic events in this case, and in the context of the individual discussions of the treatment events with the other patients who shared this hysterical character configuration, that there was also an internal push from within the patient toward particular outcome limitations. Again, the transference neurosis had evolved toward a level of uncovering at which it rested, incompletely resolved, and acted as a "defense transference neurosis." Behind its Oedipal manifestations stood the frustrations of the oral-submissive attachment to the nurturing (and depriving) mother, and an infantile paradise in which the childhood father, who came and went, was but a distracting intruder. This was the theme of homosexual submissiveness to the mother—the masochistic trends (always being forced to act "against her principles"), the oral possessiveness, and the regressive helplessness. The very first dream of the analysis depicted a sexual situation with the patient's lover, who abruptly turned into her girl cousin. At that point, the dream stopped and the associations were blocked. This was the guilt-laden and potentially disorganizing oral-dependent homosexuality that the analysis hinted at but never explicitly worked through. The very flamboyancy of the heterosexual analytic material bespoke its defensive nature and its contamination by the pre-Oedipal problems with the mother. But much of the analysis was living through, not working through: The patient's dozen absences during 4 years of analytic work were the father's many absences from home; the patient's initial insistence that only the (idealized) Menninger Foundation could treat her was the repetition of the only (idealized) husband who must, like her, never have loved another.

This case description has therefore been presented from two points of view, that of the patient's life circumstances and that of the intra-analytic limitations. Both sets of factors contributed (additively or interactively) toward limiting the analytic outcome even more sharply than with the other patients in the cluster with hysterical character organization, each of whose treatment courses has now been described. The one perspective (shared with the other patients in the group) has been that of the actual (and expectable?) limitations in fullest psychoanalytic conflict resolution in a particular personality sector—that of the hostile–dependent attachment to the variously frustrating pre-Oedipal mother imago. But the other, and special, perspective with this patient has been the issue created by the particular treatment setting and context—the question of analyzing under (too) adverse reality circumstances. This whole issue of the different kinds of life setting and context for the treatments (the patient's living and being treated in the home setting, or commuting to treatment from the home setting, or bringing the family and home setting to Topeka for the duration of the treatment, or being removed from the home setting while in treatment in Topeka) has already been discussed at length in Section IV (see Chapter 11, pp. 227–236). There I have reviewed the PRP experiences with each of these different settings and contexts, and have described both the circumstances under which enforced separations between patient and family would be vital to the treatment prospects (i.e., those where the interaction between the patient and family was destructive and in itself part of the pathogenic pressures), and those where the treatment would, contrariwise, proceed best under the "usual" psychotherapeutic arrangement of being carried on in the full context of the patient's usual life situation, with maximum interaction between treatment events and life events.

The Divorced Nurse was clearly the most extreme example of a patient who should have been treated in her usual life situation and was not. The question of whether she should have been treated at all under such major adverse environmental circumstances is, at least retrospectively, a real one. In retrospect, the patient too felt that it had probably been a mistake to stay in Topeka for her analysis. But she rationalized this decision in many ways. Her husband and her mother-in-law had not wanted her with (or even near) them during her treatment; they claimed that she disturbed the children and couldn't provide properly for them. She herself had felt unfit and undeserving. And she had been clinging, hanging on to the one place that had not been alienated by her and was sympathetically interested.

Analysis of a Narcissistic Patient

THE PRP CONTEXT AND SELF PSYCHOLOGY

In Section I (see Chapter 3, pp. 32–42), I have already discussed some of the implications for our understandings and formulations concerning the PRP research population that might stem from the conceptual advances in theoretical and clinical understandings between the state of the field in the 1950s, when these case studies were originally formulated, and the state of the field today in the 1980s. Of particular moment to this concern have been the formulations about the borderline personality organization and its treatment (Kernberg, 1975, 1976, 1980); the formulations about the narcissistic disorders and the derived theoretical perspectives of self psychology (Kohut, 1971, 1977); and the object relations and developmental personality perspectives (see Jacobson, 1964, in regard to object relations theory, and Mahler *et al.*, 1975, in regard to separation–individuation theory). I have stated in the earlier discussion (see pp. 33–34) why I feel that there is less substantial difference than might at first be thought between the emphases and formulations reflected in our case write-ups of that era, which have been drawn upon for the presentations in this volume, and the ways in which those same cases might be formulated and described if studied *de novo* today. Certainly the concept of "borderline," in much the way that Kernberg later came to delineate and articulate it, inheres in our PRP clinical thinking, partly because (as already indicated, pp. 33–34) it was out of the history and clinical milieu of The Menninger Foundation, and the treatment of the PRP patients within it, that Kernberg began to develop his formulations about borderline personalities and the object relations perspective as a means of understanding them. Later, as I describe more fully the treatment courses with the sicker PRP patients, this complete congeniality between the original ways of conceptualizing and describing the patient population and the ways they would be conceptualized and described in today's idiom should become quite clear.

In regard to the formulations of the narcissistic character and the perspectives of self psychology associated with Kohut and his followers, the seeming discontinuity or difference between concepts of the 1950s and the 1980s might be thought greater. Certainly the theoretical language is more different, more at odds with classical psychoanalytic (ego-psychological) formulations couched in terms of the psychology of conflict and its resolution. I have elsewhere (Wallerstein, 1981, 1983a) given my own perspectives, both in more clinical terms (1981) and in more theoretical terms (1983a), of the relationships between self psychology and classical psychoanalytic psychology. Most briefly put, I feel that the clinical perspectives deriving from consideration of the range of selfobject transferences (the mirror transferences and the idealizing transferences) and of the countertransferences they characteristically evoke have been a most valuable specification and delineation of the transference and countertransference phenomena that are manifested characteristically with patients with narcissistic problems and narcissistic character structure (of course, the phenomena are not limited just to these particular patients who do happen to highlight them). At the same time, however, I have questioned sharply the need for the new theoretical structure of self psychology, with its dichotomizations between a psychology of conflict and its resolution (the fate of Guilty Man) and a psychology of deficit and its restoration (the fate of Tragic Man). I have instead tried to demonstrate the operation of a both–and, rather than an either–or, principle, and to make clear my feeling that the psychic states underlying the selfobject transferences (and countertransferences) are themselves but variant expressions of intrapsychic conflict and can take their place within, and as part of, the mainstream of psychoanalytic (conflict) theory.

Given, however, that the clinical formulations of the selfobject transferences (earlier labeled "narcissistic transferences") did not exist in the form given them by the proponents of self psychology, prior to the formulations of Kohut (1971, 1977), it may well be both that some of our PRP cases (the more narcissistic ones) might have been clinically formulated somewhat differently — or at least with different language emphases — had they been evaluated and treated today. Furthermore, it may be that such consideration from the perspectives of the selfobject transferences might have led to some different treatment emphases and perhaps some different courses and outcomes if treated today rather than some decades ago. Among all the 42 PRP patients, this could be an especially pertinent issue in the consideration of the psychoanalysis of the Prince, an intensely narcissistic character, to which I now turn.

ANALYSIS OF THE PRINCE

Background and Prognosis

Like many such narcissistic characters, this 34-year-old single college professor and administrator applied for psychoanalysis not because of specific symptoms or anxieties, but rather because of a general and pervasive dissatisfaction with himself and his life. He described holding contradictory and paradoxical attitudes about himself: He felt insecure, but could for the most part hide it successfully; it was important to him to be immediately and fully accepted; he felt alternately haughty and benevolent towards his colleagues; he was jealous of his superiors and would like to replace them; he was generally successful, feeling at times "like a prince"; he felt that the attention he received was due and proper, but that "this is neurotic, but I like it just the same." He also complained, more focally, of great uneasiness in close relations with women.

The patient had "grown up successfully." Though the parents always lived in conflict, unavoidably antagonizing each other, the patient was preferred by both (over his brother), and became the mother's confidant to some extent. The father was a skilled mechanic, but the patient decided, to his father's discomfiture, on a higher education and an academic career. In school he was popular and successful. He was valedictorian of his class, was active in the student council, and played on the basketball and football teams. His mother taught him to dance, and he became an excellent dancer: "In a new situation I sell myself with this more than with anything else." His career in college, in his first jobs (as a radio announcer and an assistant in a college speech department), and as a Marine officer in World War II were equally successful. Directly after the war, he secured a position as assistant executive alumni secretary at his college, and felt so confident and competent in this role that he enthusiastically saw himself rising to become the college president. In his social–sexual development, the patient had always felt more immediately comfortable with women than with men, and attributed this to what he had learned in his close relationship with his mother. As a high school senior he was dating two girls alternatively, both of whom liked him. "I got a secret pleasure out of being in demand." He liked being "treated like a prince. . . . And when I don't get it, I get depressed, not deeply, but with a feeling that things are out of joint."

Nonetheless, his social relations with women were always uneasy, and he avoided intimate contacts; his first sexual experience was imposed upon him by an old college friend, "a sick mixed-up girl." While pursuing his graduate education, the patient met a young married woman who was obtaining a divorce. She was patient with him in developing the relationship; he was tense and lonely, and they decided to marry (her husband having presumably gone off to Reno for a divorce). From the first, the marriage went badly; the patient felt that he could never satisfy his wife sexually. It turned out that the wife had never been legally divorced, and so the two of them dissolved their relationship without legal action. When the patient came to psychoanalysis, he was again single. With regard to a new marriage, the patient was reluctant to accept anyone, no matter how attractive, because someone better might come along the next day and he would be "tied down for life."

The patient was recommended for psychoanalysis. In the presence of such deep-seated but clearly neurotic-level character problems, with no focal neurotic symptoms per se, there would be no special or even palliative indications for any other kind of treatment. The patient's severe narcissism was felt to be a defensive envelopment, representing the denials of the hysterical-level character formation rather than the intense oral fixations of the infantile character. (He would shut his eyes to disagreeable features of his inner or outer reality and live out the belief that everything would work out for *his* best.) His needs to protect his narcissistic integrity at the expense of genuine object relationships were clearly recognized, and it was felt that as this position came into analytic focus, possibilities for considerable discomfort, anxiety, even depression, and perhaps symptomatic acting out (on his job) might emerge. His overall prognosis for analysis was considered excellent, however. The patient himself wanted only analysis, since he had to have the very best treatment (analysis was "better" than psychotherapy) so that he would achieve his full productive and creative potential.

Course of the Analysis

The analysis lasted 4 years and 3 months (950 hours). The themes of the analysis unfolded within a particular kind of analytic content and climate created by the patient. These themes centered less around intrapsychic configurations and historical unfoldings than they did around an ongoing description of the patient's current life activities and struggles. And these accountings were cast in a particular way—as repetitious recitals of the day's events and the patient's role in them, for which the analyst was supposed to provide an admiring audience. The patient would be troubled when he was not sure that the analyst provided the necessary measure of admiration. The analyst said that it was difficult to get any word in, to which the patient would listen more than politely. The patient began his recitals with an expressed set of dissatisfactions with his life. He wanted a marriage, a home, and a family as others had; he was deeply ashamed of his divorce, his failure at marriage, which he hid from his old friends. He was pleased to quote a previous therapist's frequent statement that he always wanted to prove that he had the biggest penis in the world.

During the first long period of the analysis, the patient was much occupied with the vicissitudes of his life at work. At the university, he saw himself as a progressive force and a remarkable asset in an old-fashioned and rigid environment. He always wanted to "knock 'em dead" through demonstrating the superiority of his ideas over theirs. In conflict situations with the president he thought of himself as a better president whose will should prevail. The showdown came when, without the concurrence of his administrative superiors, the patient worked out with the students a liberalization of the rules governing the holding of campus social events (including serving liquor if this were done "discreetly"). This action led to the patient's dismissal. This event turned out to be the one occasion in the analysis when the patient could be made to see somewhat his endlessly provocative behaviors, the aggression underlying his usual pseudocompliance with authority.

At the same time, the patient was also intensely occupied with the nature of his interpersonal difficulties in general, and also his difficulties with women in particular. He could see his own bitter and critical attitudes toward those who denied him special appreciation; the world was supposed to be his "lover," and he required repeated adulation. But hiding behind the patient's flowery exhibitionistic talk of his strengths and his virtues were his inhibitedness, his fears of involvement and giving, and his sense of social inadequacy. One woman scornfully called him "my cautious friend." The kind of juggling involved in these encounters was not easy for the patient, who sought to avoid real commitments, and yet was also anxious to avoid this kind of disapproval and criticism, which made him equally anxious. In the analysis he was always concerned about his "performance" during intercourse, alternately bragging and anxious. It turned out that he had more of a problem with both promiscuity and potency than had been initially revealed. Sexually he was quite exhibitionistic, getting involved in counterphobic covering up of his latent homosexuality and his fear of attack and submission by a "hypermasculinity" in the form of sexual promiscuity and a facade of forcefulness. He liked best sexual relationships with older women; he felt he was doing them a distinct favor in relieving their sexual frustrations.

Gradually, though, the patient's conduct of his life shifted. He secured an executive position (at a higher salary, even) with a major nonprofit foundation as head of the public education department. This job he successfully held onto. He identified submissively with an admired boss, and in turn felt supported by the boss's respect for him. He met and began to court his wife (a university student 12 years younger than he)—a perceptive, intelligent, and strikingly pretty woman. He gave up seeing anyone else and willingly let himself be led toward marriage. The marriage itself was forced by the patient's fiancée's becoming pregnant; shortly after the child (a son) was born, the analysis was terminated, freeing the patient to devote himself to his obligations to a new home and the new baby. Despite the signs that seemed not to augur very well—the intrapsychic basis of the courtship and marriage (on both sides resting on incompletely resolved Oedipal fixations), and the conditions under which the marriage took place—things seemed surprisingly stable. The much younger wife was willing to be protective and nurturant, and the patient was willing and able to moderate his demandingness. They were experiencing tensions (e.g., the wife had orgastic difficulties and was frightened of intercourse), but they were working together to overcome them. And concomitant with the re-enactment of and working with the patient's difficulties with the significant figures in his environment (the college president, colleagues, women friends, his wife), the patient revived many facets of his lifelong complex relationships with both parents. His intensely ambivalent relationship with each came under therapeutic scrutiny: the critical father, whom he never felt able to please, and whom he depreciated and covertly rebelled against while remaining manifestly passively submitted to him; and the close, appreciative, but dangerously seductive mother, satisfying her sexual hungers through him while pressing him into a pattern of small-boy submission and dependence.

Yet none of all these interactions from past or present came sufficiently within the scope of the transference. The patient felt himself in constant conflict with every significant figure in his environment, but he studiously avoided it in the transference; he warded off every possibility of transference confrontation or criticism by the analyst. He came precisely on time to every hour, and always paid his bills promptly, despite his sometimes strained financial resources (often with a projective remark like "You probably thought I wouldn't be able to pay the whole amount this month, but I did"). He never requested change in any aspect of the analytic routine. He worked to isolate the analytic experience both from his outer life and his inner affects. "It was too rare that I could experience at the moment what was happening. It was like painting the experience on the wall and looking at it. . . . My defense was intellectualizing and to massage the event with words. . . . I used it in analysis." Not being emotionally involved, he could avoid the inferior status of patient and could better maintain his narcissistic position. He would always work to be more involved with issues than with relationships. And when he left the analytic hour, he typically forgot its contents.

All in all, the patient successfully used the analytic interactions to protect his narcissistic integrity. He exhibited himself in various symbolic ways; he tried always to charm the analyst and to provide an exciting though platonic homosexual liaison within which he could secure for himself enduring supplies of narcissistic gratifications. He used his facility with words, his talent for flowery and highly intellectualized talk, as a major vehicle in the service of these resistances (just as it was a major vocational tool of his, and a major weapon for interpersonal competitiveness). Transference hostility was therefore most stringently avoided. The patient admitted on Termination Study interview that with his wife he would poke fun at the analyst, ridiculing him with a derogatory nickname, but that he never dared to bring this material into the analysis. In this way he recreated his childhood situation, when he spent much time talking intimately with his mother about his father's shortcomings. Thus real transference interpretations were never successfully pursued, and the transference positions and the defenses against them that emerged in the analysis were not successfully resolved.

But the patient's life changes were substantial, and he was getting along much better on the job, with his wife, with his parents, and with his friends and co-workers. He still felt the same, but he also felt that he knew more. He felt better able to recognize potential dangers, to mitigate situations in which he would feel the press for the fulfillment of narcissistic wishes. He was more aware of his competitive pressures and could stop himself on the verge of an argument with his father, or apologize after a quarrel with his wife. He had become more aware of how he had so often thoughtlessly hurt people through lack of sensitivity or of interest; his narcissistic preoccupations had always depleted his capacity for this kind of empathy.

Termination

Termination occurred under the conjunction of several circumstances. The analyst had been trying to cut into the avoidant defenses that safeguarded the patient's narcissistic integrity, and to deepen the analysis. He began to touch on the latent homosexual themes, vaguely emergent in some of the dreams, hinted at in the patient's descriptions of his encounters with his father and his friends. The analyst felt that these efforts frightened the patient. Simultaneously, in reality, the patient's fiancée became pregnant and they married. (How much was this timing defensive against the emerging homosexual impulses?) The idea of termination thus seemed to fit naturally into both the new reality pressures upon the patient, and the patient's own fears of deepening the analysis and the transference involvement.

Termination was therefore readily worked out and took place over a span of a few months. The patient ended with a quite realistic appraisal of his analytic accomplishments. "Psychoanalysis gave me considerable awareness of what I'm doing and perhaps why. Sometimes I think my original expectations were immeasurably high. I wish I had more confidence that I can do differently. I think I have more control. . . . I know I don't have more than intellectual recognition of my danger tendencies. But I do have that. I'm very aware that my analysis is not completed." In the description of countertransferences in Section IV (see Chapter 12, p. 238), I have stated how the analyst's own style—somewhat stiffly formal and polite, as well as admiring of the patient for his talents and accomplishments—played its role in the analyst's difficulties in working toward more incisive resolution of the patient's character defenses and the conflicts that underlay them.

Status at Follow-Up

At the time of the Follow-Up Study, the patient's life had stably advanced in every sphere: in his work functioning, in his marriage, in his relationship with his (now two) small children, with his parents, with his friends and colleagues, and in the wider sphere of recreational, avocational, and community involvements. Yet the patient was also everywhere still uneasy. Though everyone saw him as a competent executive at work, he could never be sure of his own assessment of his worth, and he found himself still unduly dependent on external cues (direct praise, etc.). Similarly, in his marriage, "I married her for certain things and if she doesn't come through with them all the time I feel I have been deceived or I have been let down—I haven't got all I want—I mean that kind of adolescent feeling. And I can get pretty harsh under those circumstances." Overall, he said, "There is a certain shallowness to me. That is, I don't enjoy my work strictly on its intrinsic value. When I say I enjoy my work, I know immediately that I'm talking about a setting in which there is a lot of evidence that other people enjoy my work, and where there is status. . . . Much as I deplore that intellectually, emotionally it is true."

About his analysis, the patient could express his direct dissatisfactions. "I have difficulty knowing what analysis did for me. I raise the question frequently: What would be the difference in me now if I had not been in analysis? Or, what can I attribute directly to the analysis? I am not able to specify at all." (Here he was selling the analysis short.) He was not sure what or whom he blamed for the state of affairs. Was it a disappointment in the treatment, or in the analyst, or in himself? Was the treatment not long enough, or perhaps not the type best suited to him?

Of the analysis directly, he said, "I was aware of how infrequently, really, the stuff that I ought to be getting out ever came out. . . . It seemed to me that what should be happening was not happening. It was clear to me that what I was doing in analysis was what I was doing in the outside world, and that was simply using every situation to protect myself from a reservoir of feelings. . . . And there were just not enough moments when I came right up against feelings that I ought to be expressing in a situation that would handle them. The only legitimate place I ought to be expressing them, they were not being expressed, and I was aware of this. Now this is my problem, in analysis or in any place, it is my problem."

Though he was now dubious about his treatment, and certainly about more treatment, the patient nonetheless did return to his ex-analyst for more treatment about a year after the Follow-Up Study. It was not clear whether the patient sought more analysis, but the analyst chose not to make this available. He saw the patient once weekly over a year's span (43 more hours). The patient had returned because of a recrudescence of "the same old problems." The analyst strove to mitigate the returned distress by a more confronting and suppressive approach: "I tried to help him develop a 'so what' attitude toward his own impulses. . . . So what? If he could be more aware of these impulses and realize that he doesn't have to act on them, he might again be more comfortable." During this retreatment period for the patient, his wife was emboldened to decide that she wanted some help for herself. This development shocked the patient (in a salutory way): He was upset that his wife no longer saw him as her all-sufficient emotional counselor. When the patient terminated this retreatment period, he was feeling much improved and restabilized. The analyst said of this, "He was able to tell me that he had feelings of resentment that I had not done as much for him as he wished during his analysis. At the same time, he recognized that it was he, himself, who stood in his own way of getting 'well.' He was able to tell me that he not only recognized but really 'lamented' his inability to invest himself more in any other

person, including his wife, or in his job. There was far more sincerity in his statements about such matters than I had observed at any time during analysis. Then
it had been a far more intellectual process—thinking that he had to think well
of himself in order to cover up feelings of being nothing. But this time he could
really experience the feelings he used to talk about." At the end the patient wanted
to be assured that the analyst would see him again if need be. All that is known
of further follow-up is that, at some point shortly thereafter, the patient informed
his analyst that he was moving to a higher-level executive position in the national
headquarters city of the nonprofit organization for which he worked.

Final Questions

To circle back to the starting context of the discussion of the Prince's treatment,
the issues raised by this patient's treatment course and outcome can be considered
from two vantage points. One has been stated already in the presentation of the
5½-year (1030-hour) psychoanalysis of the Devoted Son (see pp. 283–287), who
also had a very rigidly defended character organization, though in his case it was
an extremely inhibited and dependent obsessive–compulsive character structure
that marked his functioning in life. The question posed in relation to his analysis,
which was also of rather limited accomplishment, was "Was this trip necessary?"
Need the maximum treatment effort have been mounted to achieve this much less
than (potentially) maximum gain? As indicated at that point, this question is discussed in the concluding section of this book (see pp. 660–661), in the light of
the total PRP experience.

The other vantage point, and one much more specific to the case of the Prince,
raises an exactly opposite question: Could more attention specifically to the grandiose and idealizing selfobject transferences, and more focused awareness of the
countertransferences that they in turn successfully played upon and/or evoked—
the interplay of respectful admiration, avoidance of interfering negative affect,
and politely formal, intellectual discourse—have enabled the patient and the analyst to come jointly to a more successfully accomplished analytic resolution? In
other words, would more rather than less analysis have been the proper prescriptive remedy, albeit analysis focused more sharply on the world of selfobject
transferences? Certainly, as indicated in the introduction to this case description,
this is an especially pertinent issue for the treatment of the Prince. There were,
of course, many other cases among our 42 where narcissistic trends were evident;
in the description of these (see Section III, Chapter 8, pp. 140–141), it was noted
that these narcissistic features seemed consistently underestimated at the time of
initial psychiatric evaluation, only emerging clearly in most of these patients during the course of the therapeutic effort. In all, narcissistic character features were
noted in 19 patients (almost half the sample), 8 men and 11 women. In the description of these cases just referred to, the special narcissistic configurations (and the
potential problems these could create for the projected treatment course) have been
indicated for 5 of them: the Prince, the Exhibitionistic Dancer, the Actress, the
Bohemian Prep School Boy, and the Bohemian Musician. Nonetheless, the issue
raised here of the special value that could accrue to the treatment prospects through
more focused attention on the specific selfobject transferences and countertrans-

ferences, though indeed a more general issue than just with the Prince, was not highlighted in so clear-cut a way in the actual treatment courses of any of these other patients (still to be described).

The "Transference Psychosis"

PARANOID PATIENTS IN PRP
AND TRANSFERENCE PSYCHOSES

Of the 22 patients recommended for and started in psychoanalysis in PRP, the 10 whose treatment courses have been described in detail to this point include 6 of the 8 (4 of those 6, women) who had really good treatment outcomes; 3 of the 5 (2 of those 3, women) who had moderate treatment outcomes; 1 of the 3 (a man, the Devoted Son) who had equivocal outcomes; and none of the 6 with failed outcomes. That is, they represent as a group the better psychoanalytic results (whatever the individual limitations of those results may have been), and they contain among them all those in the cluster of patients with hysterical character formations. Another large grouping that emerged in the PRP population was one of patients with a strongly paranoid character trend. These have been described in Section III (see Chapter 8, pp. 143–144). Fourteen patients (10 men and 4 women), a full third of the total research sample, are there identified as sharing this trend; another 5 are seen as strong externalizers in their attribution of psychological responsibility (though not strictly paranoid).

Of those 14 with paranoid attributes, 9 were recommended for psychoanalysis and 5 for psychotherapy. One of those among this group recommended for psychoanalysis, the English Professor, has already been described among the very good analytic outcomes (see pp. 279–283). As noted, at the time of initial evaluation, he was in an acutely decompensated phobic state marked by an (encapsulated) paranoid trend that emerged most clearly in the psychological projective tests—the disguised men peering at him from the Rorschach cards; the consciousness of being watched and sought out for punishment for unknown misdeeds; and so forth. It was because of this trend that he was initially recommended for an expressive–supportive psychotherapy, in which (over a 2½ year span) he came to a much improved life functioning and a psychological reintegration (confirmed by changes in the psychological test picture obtained on repetition of the original test battery). He was then taken into the more definitive psychoanalytic treatment effort; that analysis, as described, lasted 6 years (1145 hours) and came to a successful conclusion. The technical problems of the analysis derived not so much from the patient's paranoid potential as they did from his powerful masochistic and submissive character trends, with the threat of a developing insoluble transference neurosis. It was this danger that had to be overcome, which the analyst did through a manipulated weaning process, before the patient could achieve the good treatment resolution that he did and could go on to very impressive progressive consolidations over a 24-year period of follow-up observation to the present time.

The other of the nine patients with paranoid trends recommended for psychoanalysis who had a good treatment result was the Movie Lady, whose treatment course has not yet been described. Briefly, she was a patient originally recommended as an appropriate prospect for psychoanalysis. However, after 6 months of analytic effort, she was specifically shifted to an explicitly supportive–expressive psychotherapy, which, after a total 4½-year effort (652 hours), brought about a very good overall treatment result. The alteration in treatment modality was made because the analyst shortly came to see the patient as more seriously ill than originally anticipated, paranoid, potentially psychotic; he saw her as clinging anxiously to a "culturally approved average pattern," since she would begin to think very paranoidly whenever she let herself deviate from that limited, stereotyped pattern. The analyst felt that, with the alteration in treatment structure and techniques, he had successfully warded off the potential of a paranoid and regressive treatment eruption. Incidentally, the experience here described with the Movie Lady was a common one among these 14 paranoid patients: The paranoid potential was often (not always) quite successfully concealed at the time of initial evaluation, or was evident in only a very muted way, but in either case would then become fully evident during the subsquent treatment course.

The other seven (six men and one woman) among the nine paranoid patients recommended for analysis all fell into the group where a paranoid transference psychosis either emerged in full during the treatment, or threatened to emerge, with the patient taking frantic steps to ward it off (e.g., the Alcoholic Raconteur fled his treatment). These seven (the Alcoholic Doctor, the Alcoholic Heir, the Suspended Medical Student, the Alcoholic Raconteur, the Masochistic Editor, the Economist, and the Script Writer), incidentally, were in many ways among the sickest patients in the total PRP sample. Six were severely alcoholic (two of them also severely drug-addicted), and six had major disturbances of sexual function, including blatant promiscuity, predatory homosexuality, and so on; five of them were looked at initially as functioning in the borderline range of personality organization. Not surprisingly, as a group, they did very poorly in their treatments: Five were total treatment failures (including three of the six who died of mental-illness-related causes in the course of their treatment and posttreatment follow-up observation), one had a very equivocal treatment result, and only one (the Economist) could be said to have done moderately well.

Additionally, of the five among the paranoid patients recommended for psychotherapy (three men and two women), two (the Sexual Masochist and the Bitter Spinster) fell into the group where, despite the less intensive regressive pressures of psychotherapy (as compared with psychoanalysis), psychotic transference reactions nevertheless emerged. Of these two, one (the Bitter Spinster) ended as a treatment failure, and the other (the Sexual Masochist) achieved a moderately good result over a 28-year career as a "therapeutic lifer." With another of the five (the Fearful Loner), the development of a potential psychotic regressive process was forestalled by the therapist's skillful titrating of the intensity of the therapeutic contact to the patient's very fragile tolerance.

To look at the relationship between transference psychoses and paranoid character trends from the other side, transference psychoses with a paranoid cast emerged or threatened to emerge with a total of 13 patients; 7 of these were from the group of paranoid patients started in psychoanalysis, and 3 were from the group of paranoid patients started in psychotherapy. The other 3, 2 in psychoanalysis and 1 in psychotherapy, had not been among those seen initially as paranoid or potentially paranoid. They were, however, also among the sicker patients—not paranoid, but with clearly borderline personality organizations (see pp. 144–146). To illustrate, Peter Pan (in psychoanalysis) had near-delusional fixations about food, eating, and weight gain, as well as bizarre and reality-deviant behaviors desperately geared to try to control her food intake and her kleptomania; the Bohemian Prep School Boy (in psychotherapy), with his bizarre fears and various estrangement and depersonalization phenomena, was formulated diagnostically as having an overideational preschizophrenic character organization; and the Heiress (in psychoanalysis) suffered with disorganizing "turbulent periods," marked by schizoid withdrawals into inner fantasies, with major abdication of reality concerns.

NATURE AND PREVALENCE OF THE TRANSFERENCE PSYCHOSIS

It is the characteristic treatment course(s) of the 13 patients out of our 42 who developed or threatened to develop "transference psychoses" (9 of the 22 who started in psychoanalysis and 4 of the 20 who started in psychotherapy; 10 of the 13 were among those who had paranoid character trends, and 3 others, mentioned above, were not paranoid but clearly borderline in character organization) that I want to describe here. The phrase "transference psychosis" was first used as the title of a paper by Reider in 1957, and he said that it had been suggested to him by Gitelson some 6 years earlier. From the first, there were misgivings and differences of viewpoint about the construct—misgivings (voiced first by Reider) about the dynamic and etiological features implied in the descriptive analogy to the transference neurosis, and differences of opinion about the distinctness of this phenomenon from the considerations related to the problem of taking frankly borderline or overtly psychotic individuals into psychoanalysis, with the activation, then, of characteristic psychotic ideation and behavior during phases of the treatment. In 1967, I published a case report comprising two patients in psychoanalysis who developed transference psychoses (these patients were not from the PRP sample). In that report, I reviewed the psychoanalytic literature on the subject to that time, covering a total of six clearly described cases in four articles; presented my own two clinical instances; and indicated that I did not include the phenomenon of the "delusional transference" activated in the psychotic or markedly borderline patient in psychoanalytic treatment, but was rather confining my usage to patients considered "within the neurotic range in terms of character structure and adjudged appropriate for classical analysis, in whom nevertheless a disorganizing reaction of psychotic intensity occurred within the transference" (Wallerstein, 1967, p. 553). Among the issues I discussed that arose from this case material was the diagnostic question of the prevalence of such a severe regressive transference reaction. The fact that two such quite extreme deviations from the more usual transference course were being reported from what was then a still small analytic experience lent support to a suggestion first raised by Hammett (1961) of the wider prevalence of this phenomenon than the sparse literature to that point indicated.

The existence of 13 such reactions among 42 patients (and 9 among 22 specifically in psychoanalysis) does indeed lend weight to that concern, granted the
fact that, as has been stated in a variety of places, our "usual" Menninger Foundation psychoanalytic patient population is heavily weighted toward the sicker
patients, among whom such regressive transference reactions might be more common, and granted also that a fair number of these 13 would not be seen as having
at least started their psychoanalytic treatment within the clearly neurotic character
range. (But, as has been said, the paranoid propensities of many of these patients
were carefully concealed at the time of initial evaluation, and their borderline
features were thought mild enough not to preclude a recommendation for classical psychoanalysis.) Of the 13 patients, the treatment courses of two are detailed
here: one, the Alcoholic Doctor, from the group with disastrous outcomes, and
one, the Economist, from the (much smaller) group of those who did better. Others
of the group are discussed in other contexts in the next chapter.

ANALYSIS OF THE ALCOHOLIC DOCTOR

Background and Prognosis

Aspects of the Alcoholic Doctor's illness, character structure, and treatment features
have been described at various points. He came to psychiatric treatment as a 43-
year-old failed physician, with a chief symptom of 10 years of totally uncontrolled
heavy alcoholism. He also suffered with severe drug addiction (barbiturates, amphetamines, and tranquilizers), raging episodes of drunken brawling, severe potency disturbances, and the progressive homosexuality instigated at his wife's suggestion (see pp. 128, 130, 147, 161). However, though he turned out to be one
of the project's most paranoid patients, his paranoia was initially well concealed
(including even an acute seemingly delusional and hallucinated state at the height
of his pretreatment collapse—see pp. 164–165), and though 20 of the 42 PRP patients
were thought initially to have more or less borderline features, this patient was
not considered one of them. He was felt initially to be neither paranoid nor borderline, but rather someone with a passive–dependent and compliant–compulsive
character. This presumed neurotic-level character organization certainly played
its strong role in the treatment recommendation that psychoanalysis be tried. However, this was one of those five instances where the research evaluation team clearly
disagreed—calling instead for a supportive–expressive psychotherapy, based on
both the severity and the long duration of the patient's very crippling symptoms,
as well as the inertias built into his passive, compliant, and masochistic character
formation (see pp. 200–201 for this discussion, pro and con). There was also here
the highly complicating issue of the very disturbed marriage to an almost equally disturbed wife, who also drank heavily, brawled constantly with the patient, and
colluded with the patient's homosexual behaviors (even arranging the *ménage à
trois* that included the patient's male lover).

Course of the Analysis

The patient was taken into psychoanalysis, and this treatment went on for almost
7 years (1238 hours), up until the time of his death. The analyst tried throughout
to maintain as close to an analytic situation as he could, though the nature and

severity of the patient's illness enforced many deviations from classical analytic technique. The patient (who started his analysis in the context of a total 13-month period of hospitalization) was subsequently rehospitalized four times—albeit all too briefly each time—for intoxication, and one of these hospitalizations was for a toxic encephalopathy with grossly disorganized behaviors. There were also out-of-hour telephone contacts, stretches of sitting up (usually initiated by the patient), episodes of advice giving, and direct work in helping the patient secure suitable employment at one juncture. Through all the long treatment course, incidentally, the patient's drug taking was a continuing problem, and episodically it became more severe. He was never off drugs completely, and the analyst felt that he could never insist on total abstinence; to do so, he felt, would have been tantamount to forcing the discontinuance of the patient's treatment. The times of most dangerous drug intake were the occasions when the analyst could effect (very temporary) hospitalizations.

From the beginning, interpretive work in this treatment was limited in its range by two factors: (1) the patient's proneness to disorganizing regressions in the transference, which caused the analyst to back off from the more intensive interpretive efforts; and (2) the destructive acting out, which forced the analyst often to focus on the reality consequences of the behaviors, at the expense of the fuller interpretation of their meaning in terms of the transference and the infantile conflicts. The analyst was concerned constantly for the patient's working and occupying his time in a reasonable and productive manner, and the fact that the patient could respond effectively to this concern was a major element in encouraging the analyst to maintain hope and pursue his patient treatment effort.

Through this effort, the patient came to manage his life more adequately. He got out of the hospital, and then the day hospital, and did secure employment as industrial physician to a major industry in a nearby town. He performed competently and won the esteem of his confrères and his patients. His wife, who had been off pursuing her own medical specialty training, came back to rejoin him, and for a while they had together probably the most harmonious period of their married life; their mutual fighting and mutual alcohol and drug taking were at their lowest ebb. When the patient and his wife decided to start a joint private medical practice, and when at the same time they began to bring their children (who had been living with the paternal grandparents) back to them—first the two younger, and then the two older—things began to go less well. They had a difficult time establishing their practices; they were erratic parents, and felt homemaking and parenthood a difficult strain. There was a reversion to mutual drinking and brawling, and, on the patient's part, increased drug taking and a return to promiscuous homosexual episodes (anonymous encounters across adjacent booths in men's rooms in public buildings).

The wife, though herself severely mentally disturbed, declined all suggestions of treatment for herself. She stressed her external difficulties, especially having to cope with an alcoholic, homosexual husband; she felt that she had "a right to drink as this is my only pleasure." Their sexual life together fell away over the patient's potency problems, and he reverted wholly to homosexual foraging, where he would engage mainly in mutual masturbation. They talked about divorce, but the wife would have none of it and threatened to expose the patient's addiction and homosexuality to the community should he ever try to institute divorce proceedings. The analyst finally actively intervened to get the patient out of practice and into a staff job in internal medicine in a local federal hospital. There he worked for 2 years until his death; for long stretches, he lived in a room in the hospital and was there all the time except for his daily analytic hour and weekend trips home to his family. At first the patient worked hard and diligently in the hospital and became a valued staff member, but, over time, here too he bogged down. His chief felt that he was "too conscientious, stayed too late, got there too early, took too much time with his patients, became inefficient, was such a talker." He talked over all his personal problems with some of the nurses, whom he made mother–confidants. They, in turn, would cover up for him on nights when he was on call and couldn't be found, or when he could be found but was so drugged that he couldn't be wakened.

What was occurring in the analysis during this long, unhappy life course? Much new anamnestic material emerged that indicated a deeper, wider ego deformation and a more deeply entrenched picture of symptom and behavior disturbance than had been initially presented. There had been a long early childhood separation from the mother (over a year), and, after their reunion, a locking together in a guilt-ridden close symbiotic bond. The mother dressed him in girls's clothes and encouraged him to play with dolls. He often saw his mother nude, changing her sanitary napkin, and the like. He was trained to bring her breakfast in bed. When he was 5, the patient's father had had him circumcised by an uncle while he (the father) assisted, because of all that "irritation." The patient was ever after troubled that they "had cut off too much." The father was a man of violent rages and cruel behaviors, of whom the patient was always fearful. When the patient was 12, he had been seduced into homosexuality by the handyman, and had continued in rather frequent homosexual activity thereafter through his school years. What his wife subsequently instigated in the marriage was but a revival of the earlier homosexuality. Throughout his life, the patient had many involved bowel and genital rituals, which he felt to be necessary after each defecation and each sexual experience. When he wanted to marry, he felt his mother would not allow it; he fell ill immediately after the wedding and was taken home by his mother to be nursed, deferring the honeymoon and leaving his wife stranded. The patient's accelerated decline set in with his early successes in his beginning medical practice. Then he had actual psychotic episodes, in which he would run out of the house nude; and on one occasion, he barricaded himself in the basement of his home against the people who were out to get him.

Much of the initial analytic work centered around the transference fears relating to the image of the violent and cruel father. The patient once had to get up from the couch in order to look for a knife he was sure the analyst concealed in the stand next to his chair (the circumcision knife?). As the relationship with the father was analytically somewhat worked out, the patient could become more trusting of the analyst, was able to start again in medical practice, and was able also to work out a new understanding and closeness with the father. This process was not aided, however, by the father's taking the occasion to confess all his own failures as a parent, and to inquire whether the patient had ever actually desired intercourse with his mother.

But the main thrust of the analytic material shifted to the mother-transference and continued with it throughout. The patient revived his intense fears of separation from his mother, and linked these to his inability to give up his sedatives and alcohol. They were mother's milk, vital to his survival. He saw his sexual anxieties, his many vagina dentata dreams, and his homosexual activity going back to childhood as various ways of denying his direct sexual interest in his mother. As he lapsed into his sick, helpless, infantile state in the latter part of the analytic work, the patient began to take on all the mother's abdominal symptoms, and even began to take the same catalogue of medications. He was frightened when the extent of his symbiotic union fantasy became clear. He and his mother were one. If she were to die (and she was gravely ill at the time), he too would have to die. Gradually all sexual activity (even the homosexuality) disappeared, and the patient began to spend all his time fantasizing about dying and how he would accomplish it.

At the same time, the murderous hostility against the mother was concomitantly evoked by the analysis. He wanted to tear his mother out of his stomach, where she gave him his pains, his nausea and vomiting (his symptomatic hiatus hernia). He purchased a gun to shoot himself in the stomach and get rid of the mother and her pain once and for all. It was at such times that the boundaries between fantasy and reality blurred, and the patient could no longer take distance from the transference distortion, could no longer treat it "as if." In connection with the impulse to shoot his internalized mother, the patient when drunk would call the analyst, "telling me, 'I'm going to kill you tonight,' but in a meek way that nobody would believe." At the same time he once crawled over to the analyst to be petted, and another time voiced his heartfelt wish that the analyst could be a kangaroo with a pouch, who could then give up everything else and just carry the patient around close inside him—"this isn't homosexual either; it's earlier than that." During these times, the patient would initiate periods of sitting up: "He wouldn't know who I was and he would have to look at me to see that I was his therapist." The patient had a recurring frightening dream of a disembodied spirit consisting of four nuclei, which had to be properly arranged so he could live at peace with himself. One of the nuclei was his mother, one his father, one his health, and one his spirit. He could almost succeed in getting them in the right places, but couldn't put his mother where she belonged. At home he would have sleepwalking episodes, and when extremely miserable would go down into the basement and sit in his mother's old chair. His drug taking often seemed to be an effort to take the intensity off the psychotic transference regressions.

Termination: Death of the Patient

In the last 6 months of treatment (and of his life) the patient was severely depressed, going into an autistic retreat almost, in his withdrawal from his intense angers at his mother. His drug intake rose; he dreamed of death; he purchased the gun; he wrote suicide notes; he had a series of three auto accidents and a personal accident when he injured himself falling down a flight of stairs. He was coming to his analytic hours hopeless and helpless, with the repetitive statement, "I want to die." His mother was herself dying during this period. The analyst was pressing for rehospitalization, but the patient fought this off, claiming it would destroy the one thing he had left—his functioning as a physician. He threatened to commit suicide if a serious hospitalization were forced. At the very end the analyst felt the patient had almost come around to accepting the need for a prolonged hospitalization in order to go on in treatment, free of drugs and away from his family turmoil.

The circumstances of death and of treatment termination were as follows: The patient became ill at work with an apparent flu; he was aching all over and was nauseated and vomiting. He was sent home from work, arriving at midday. In the midafternoon he received a telephone message for his wife, which he relayed to her by phone. She detected nothing unusual. When she came home in the evening to prepare supper and tried to rouse the patient from his sleep, he was cyanotic and dying. Vigorous resuscitation efforts on her part, and that of some other neighbor physicians (who came within seconds after being called), failed. At autopsy, it was determined that the patient had died from a massive, forceful aspiration of his vomitus into the far reaches of his bronchial tree. It was not clear how depressed and how drugged the patient was that day, and how much this state, together with the weakening by the viral infection, had so blocked his protective reflexes as to allow the fatal aspiration. The analyst called it "an unconscious suicide."

Here ended—disastrously—a psychoanalysis, undertaken and persisted in over a 7-year span, that could not carry the patient out of the psychotic transference regression that developed during the treatment course. The analyst saw this clearly as a struggle within the transference with the mother of the patient's regressive infancy, who was supposed to nurture and gratify limitlessly and make up for past misdeeds. "Mother was the crux and the couch was the womb and he curled up in it." But this could not be worked out interpretively. The patient often responded with "I see this clearly, I understand what it is all about, but it doesn't make a goddamned bit of difference to me." In fact, interpretations were often used negatively to indicate how bad they proved him to be. He constantly reiterated, "I don't deserve to get well." The analyst said, "The material was all there. I had everything in the case except I didn't get him well."

TREATMENT OF THE ECONOMIST

Background and Prognosis

By contrast with this treatment outcome, I turn to the (even longer) treatment course of the Economist. He was a 31-year-old college instructor who came to psychiatric evaluation because of a seeming repetitive problem with women. His first marriage had failed, and he was now going out with another woman, was wanting to marry her, and was concerned at finding himself getting into the same kinds of difficulties that he had had with ex-wife. He had been married at 23 to someone he had been seeing often, though he had not been exactly serious about marriage. However, one day, in one of his infrequent long talks with his banker father, the father asked the patient whether he were serious about the young woman. He indicated that he was. His father told him that there was some money set aside for his college education (which had been delayed by his military service), and it was enough to enable him to go to college and support a wife too if he wished it that way. With this inducement, the patient married promptly; he said that it was like offering a new toy to a child. From the start, however, the marriage was a quarrelsome one that did not go well. The serious break came after about 2 years, when the patient's wife started going out with another man. The patient was suspicious and set out to do some "private shadowing." He came in on the two of them when they were out together. He said that both of them claimed they loved each other and there was nothing he could do about it. The marriage ended over a year later with mutual recriminations; each of the couple separately secured a divorce, and neither of them (or their lawyers) recognized the divorce settlement obtained by the other.

Two years before coming to The Menninger Foundation, the patient got involved with another young woman, and again began to think in terms of marriage. They were comfortable together and seemed to have much in common; however, as they drew closer, the same kinds of things began to happen as had happened in the relationship with his wife. They began to quarrel, and over similar issues—primarily that the girlfriend's parents disliked him (as had occurred with his wife's parents) and were propagandizing against him. He accused his girlfriend of not sticking up for what she supposedly wanted, namely him. After many heated quarrels, they finally broke off; she went off and shortly thereafter announced her engagement to another man, someone liked by her parents. Over the next several months, the patient oscillated between vigorous (quarreling) efforts to win back his girlfriend, and the pull toward psychiatric consultation in order to assess his own role in these recurrent events. If the same pattern that had transpired with his wife were repeating itself, then this marriage would not be happy either, and perhaps he should forego the marriage and work at these issues in treatment. On the other hand, he claimed to love the young woman very much and wished that they could get married. He bombarded her with quotations from Shakespeare: "To thine own self be true," and the like.

At his psychiatric evaluation, the patient specifically sought psychoanalysis and made it clear that no reality obstacles would bar his way to this treatment. Though he was on a relatively low income and was teaching at a university 55 miles away, he indicated that he would be able to work out all problems of fee, time, commuting distance, and so forth. And the treatment recommended was analysis, the only treatment felt able to offer the prospect of adequate resolution of the patient's deep-seated obsessive–compulsive character neurosis, with its series of derivative neurotic life problems: (1) his inadequate heterosexual adjustment, marked by the failures of the two serious attempts at relationships with women; (2) his search, ever to be disappointed, for the adequately nurturant mother; (3) his fear of the normally assertive and competitive male role; and (4) his struggle over strong latent homosexual strivings (all of the foregoing was amply documented in the total anamnestic material).

The major problems anticipated for the analysis would stem from the patient's ready capacity for positive attachments—the expectation that he would fall promptly into a dependent, passive transference relationship, with the unconscious intent to be in it (and to enjoy it) forever. This would make for ease in getting into the analytic situation, but would also become one of the major obstacles to its ultimate successful resolution. Within that transference relationship, the patient would search for the gratification of his oral-dependent yearning toward the mother, as well as a noncompetitive and hence nondangerous relationship with the benevolent and strong father. In creating this transference fantasy, the patient could come to feel indefinitely protected and nurtured in his little-boy status; he might never need to challenge it, or to grow toward real autonomy. And the considerable sacrifice in time and money involved in securing the treatment would fit in well with his passive and masochistic trends.

Course of the Treatment

PSYCHOANALYSIS

At the time when the treatment period was "cut off" for research Termination Study, 9½ years after its start, the treatment process was tapering off and terminating, but had not yet terminated. The patient had been in psychoanalysis for almost 6 years (1364 hours), followed—after a review conference, at which time a change in treatment strategy was decided upon—by a supportive–expressive psychotherapy for another 3½ years (237 additional hours). This phase of the treatment had still not ended, though, as noted, it now seemed to be tapering. During the whole of the treatment, the patient's life was less life than treatment. Most of his life activities slowed up. He stopped going out with women altogether; when this was pointed to, he quoted Freud to the effect that "psychoanalysis has to take place in a setting of abstinence." When, under what he felt was analytic pressure, the patient got involved sporadically with girlfriends, these relationships were mostly stormy and short-lived, ending in quarrels brought about by the patient's suspicious and demanding attitudes. Sexuality itself was eschewed for several years; once in analysis, the patient did not have intercourse for a 3-year period.

The patient developed a gradually improving relationship with his family as the various layers of his attitude toward them came up and were at least partially resolved during the treatment. Initially, his relationship toward them was much more exploitative than originally realized. Similarly, at work, there was evidence of much more difficulty than originally revealed. There was constant friction with his more senior colleagues, with an ill-concealed grandiose and sweeping denigration of them for their conservative economic views (like those of his father), in contrast to his own more liberal, Keynesian economic position. These attitudes, too, gradually abated. At the Termination Study point, however, the patient had not yet secured his Ph.D. The need to work single-mindedly on his thesis was the current rationalization for his almost total noninvolvement in any ongoing social and sexual life. Mostly throughout the whole 9½ years, the treatment stood at the center of his life. He spent 3 hours each day at it, counting commuting time. He asked a number of times to be allowed to come seven times weekly.

During the years of treatment, much new anamnestic data emerged that had been concealed at initial evaluation (see p. 161 for the full details). These included childhood symptoms (enuresis, stuttering, and stealing), current antisocial symptoms (manipulating and cheating, as well as specific compulsions) and—especially to be noted in this present context—paranoid fears of being attacked, which led to his always carrying pistols and clubs on his person and in his car, in order to be properly vigilant against attack. And, most centrally humiliating, the patient's long-time potency problem surfaced in the fifth year of treatment. This was what had wrecked his marriage, the fuller history of which now unfolded. The patient blamed his father for the marriage: He had interpreted the father's offer of support as forcing his hand, and he ever after resented that he had felt driven to do something that he was not fully ready to do. In his marriage he was often impotent, and it was his reproachful raging over this that had all but forced his wife into her infidelity. His sexual fantasy life was preoccupied with his feeling that his penis was too small and that vaginas were too large.

From the beginning of the analysis, there wre fateful indications of proneness to ego weakness. In the initial anxieties of starting, there was some bizarre ideation—the patient's (quite fixed) conviction that he could classify people and tell how sincere they were by the shapes of their fingers and of their gums. But the analysis settled into a first 4-year-long phase, characterized mainly by the oral-dependent transference yearnings toward the analyst as the (hoped-for) reliable, benevolent father and the giving, nurturant mother, for whom the patient had heretofore lifelong searched in vain. Toward this figure the patient assumed an ever-compliant position, since he did not dare jeopardize potential dependency gratifications. He was preoccupied with images of food and being fed; of the good uncle and good aunt who had treated him better in childhood than his own parents had (but who had "deserted" him by dying); and of the need to be cared for at the mother's breast and the feeling (almost literally) that the analyst should provide a proper breast for him. This gradually settled into an ego-syntonic passivity (in his life and in the analysis) as the appropriate way of being, which would lead to ultimate gratification: to be fed, cared for, masturbated. In effect, the patient gave up his adult social and sexual life and substituted for it the passive gratifications he received in his transference fantasies. Interpretive efforts directed to the inevitable frustrations of such guiding fantasies led to explosive rages—the revival of lifetime rages over oral deprivations, which the patient had always struggled to inhibit.

The next 2 years of the analysis were characterized by a gradual shift in the interpretive focus, from the pre-Oedipal dependency and passivity relationship (which had not been analytically dislodged) to the Oedipal fears and inhibitions—to the analyst as the dangerous father–rival more than as the withholding mother fused with the father. This was a much more stormy, negatively charged period. It was during this time that the patient first revealed his severe potency problem, withheld from the analysis till then. And the more the Oedipal rivalries and fears were probed, the more the patient's compliance gave way to fierce underlying anger, which at the same time he often felt terrified of expressing in the face of the dangerous father–analyst.

It was under the pressures of this effort at Oedipal interpretations that the patient's psychotic regression unfolded within the transference. A characteristic episode (already described; see pp. 166–167) took place when the patient brought his mother to an analytic hour. He wanted her to meet the analyst after the hour; it would be very "important." The analyst tried unsuccessfully to fathom the range of possible meanings in this request. At the end of the hour, he finally (reluctantly) agreed to be introduced; he and the mother shook hands and exchanged a few pleasantries. The next day, the patient came for his hour in a rage. That encounter had been the analyst's effort to seduce his mother, and that handshake had been the symbolic representation of the sexual assault that was promised. It became clear that, in this projection of his own archaic wishes and fears onto the analyst, the patient "believed" with half-delusional intensity that the analyst was actually carrying on an affair with his mother. Similarly, the patient held the conviction for periods that all women in the world belonged to the analyst and were barred to him; he would not see this as a revival of infantile positions. He asserted against this that he had a right to have intercourse with his sister and with his mother if he wanted, and that no one should stop him. Every woman was, after all, an incestuous object, and every man, correspondingly, someone to fight and overwhelm—or to submit to. He said in the analysis, "I'll kill you and marry your wife." And at the same time he accused the analyst of spying on him, and trying to force him to submit to a homosexual assault.

PSYCHOTHERAPY

It was because of the widening, nonreversing paranoid psychosis that was thus unfolding, under the interpretive prressure directed at the Oedipal dynamics, that the decision was made to cease the psychoanalytic effort. It was hoped that a turn to an explicitly supportive–expressive psychotherapy would foster the reconstitution to the patient's better-integrated (and much preferred) prior transference position. The patient also wanted a return to the passive gratifications of a dependent transference attachment. He was, after all, functioning better in life, getting along better with his family and his university colleagues, filling his teaching niche productively. He was willing to pay a high price for such a protected life in the shadow of and under the guidance of the analyst—to forego real autonomy, marriage, even his Ph.D., if he could continue to be cared for by the nurturant parent. This he much preferred to the effort to work through inner conflict with its attendant psychic pain (which pushed him into the feared psychotic regression) and the ultimate "promise" only of autonomy and separation. The patient was enraged by this pressure to "analyze," which to him meant only giving up his neurotic gratifications and ultimately giving up the analysis—his chief gratification—itself.

Thus was ushered in the third time period of the analysis, that of the phase of explicitly supportive therapy. This was the period of recovery from the psychotic regression and of reconstitution of the dependent transference, within which "magical" relationship the therapist reinforced (rather than uncovered) the dependency gratifications. He lent himself as a reality model, helped the patient in the management of his ongoing life (problems with his Ph.D. studies, his relationships with colleagues, his attitudes toward women, etc.), and then gradually worked within this relationship to try to wean the patient from the continuing close and direct need for dependency reinforcement. The transference by then had evolved through the various vicissitudes concomitant with the changing phases of the treatment. The subservient and dependent transference model of the first phase of the analysis had stood in defense against the underlying negative fused image of the dangerously rivalrous Oedipal father and the ultimately withholding mother. This first transference paradigm had been stable and self-reinforcing; the patient had been not only comfortable, but willing to persist with it and masochistically pay for it, in both reality sacrifices and neurotic ego restrictions. The effort to work analytically with the hostile transferences that underlay the positive dependent transferences could not be tolerated by the patient without a psychotic regressive process, and the analytic effort proper was therefore drawn to a close. The succeeding psychotherapeutic phase of the treatment did succeed in re-establishing the dependent relationship to the protective parental imago; within this dependency and idealization, the therapist now strove to help the patient again consolidate his level of functioning, while gingerly cutting down the intensity and the frequency of the necessary supporting contacts.

Status at Termination Study and through Follow-Up

Whether this weaning process could proceed to actual complete termination was, at the time of the "cut off" Termination Study (at 9½ years), not yet decided. The patient was at this time coming in only once monthly, and sometimes for not more than 30 minutes. It was the therapist's hope that the need for treatment continuation could just wither away. He felt satisfied that the transference regression was undone, that the patient's manifest behaviors and symptoms had markedly improved, and that the patient was a more appropriate person in his relations with his family and his colleagues. The patient, for his part, at this point felt gratified for the help he had experienced—for the ongoing support from a benign father in whom he could confide at any time, and who yet remained a parental figure that the patient could control and keep from getting too close.

Much then happened in a consolidating way during the subsequent follow-up period. The details are not recounted in full here, but with the prodding of his academic superiors and the encouragement (and coaching) of the therapist, the patient completed his long-deferred doctorate with flying colors. At the point of Follow-Up Study, he was going to a professorship at a larger university, with a salary double what he had been earning but two years earlier. In his relationship with his family members, the patient was more at ease (and less neurotically involved) with his mother and sister; the father was now dead. With people in general, he enjoyed a more active social life than had been his wont, with a real circle of faculty friends. His primitive fears of literal assault were totally gone, and he no longer felt the urge to carry concealed weapons for protection. He had widened hobby interests: Shakespeare had become a passion, pursued through a detailed trip to the Shakespeare country and to the English museums and galleries focused on Shakespeare and Elizabethan England. He felt, however, that social contacts with women were a large "remaining unresolved problem." He somewhat wistfully said, "I would like to get married again." He had some casual liaisons with women, and in these his impotence seemed in considerable measure overcome. But the therapist probably correctly assessed that the patient "wouldn't be able to be potent with a woman whom he would be more interested in."

Through this whole follow-up period, therapy appointments continued on a fairly regular but widely spaced basis, monthly or even somewhat less often. Appointments would be made one ahead, or by mail. They would usually be preceded by a letter stating the issues (e.g., concerns over his handling of classroom problems) that he intended to talk about, and then a reinforcing written agenda would be brought along to the actual session. Sometimes dreams would be detailed in these letters. The patient felt the therapist's intense interest at all times: "He was interested. When the heat was off in the building one day, the others canceled their appointments. He put on his overcoat and kept our appointment." Or, "He's the only person I've ever met who, when he said something about me, I had the feeling he only had my best interest in mind." This led to the overall statement, "I idealize him—and he's cautioned me on that." The periods of deep distrust that the patient remembered from the therapeutic past no longer existed. Underlying negative elements in the transference now could only be read in the patient's dreams and fantasies. In the patient's dreams, the therapist could be dying, dead, disgraced, or fired from his job; or the patient could be poring through obituary columns with the fantasy that the therapist died. All these usually occurred at times when the patient could not get in touch with the therapist immediately upon need; in the next hour, however, trust and confidence would be again to the fore, and transference fears brushed aside. The patient liked to identify with the therapist in his mode of dress, his hobbies, his interest in sports cars, and the like.

Within this benevolent and warm therapeutic relationship, the patient could examine his ideas and feelings and allow them to be "corrected." He said, "One of the benefits of analysis is that over a long period of time, I've had a lot of talks with him, and on a lot of different subjects. So I will, often, when I'm in a period of uncertainty, I'll say, 'What would he say about this and what would he think about this?' Well, chances are I know. We have talked about it. And usually I'll swing over and follow what I think he would do or think. I've found that quite satisfactory, *better than my own way*" (patient's emphasis). He also stated, "I want to conduct my life so that he would be pleased. He's got a big investment in me. I have an obligation to myself and also to him, to try to do things that are in my best interest."

Officially, by now, the patient's treatment had been terminated, but it turned out that this was only an "administrative termination" (an alteration in the patient's official status to that of a discharged patient being seen now only in "follow-up interviews"), and that the patient had not been informed about this. Neither the patient nor the therapist expected any actual change in the frequency or nature of the contact between them. Indeed, the patient saw the future as an unchanged continuation of the present. He looked forward to the regular mail contact, the periodic weekend visits, all on the same open-ended basis. "He is available to help me when I need help. I don't know what I will run into." He certainly did not anticipate terminating. He emphasized to the research group, "I like that man. . . . I'd like for him to know that I am content that I have benefited from treatment."

Actually, the patient was able to fulfill his wishes and his expectations for permanent treatment nurture. He has remained in continuous therapeutic contact with his original analyst until the time of this writing, 28 years from the time of his original entry into analysis. For a number of years, he continued to see his therapist on periodic weekend visits back to Topeka from his university post in another state, where he had by then become director of a specialized postgraduate program of studies. Then, feeling under some intensifying pressures, he returned to Topeka and a lesser academic position in the local university. At this time he was unsettled in his life directions, still unhappily single, at odds with his family, and depressed about his future prospects. But with his therapist having moved to another part of the country, Topeka had lost its allure, and so the patient moved on to a university position in the therapist's community, where he could resume his therapy on a more regular basis. This kept up over another span of years, and, at a point of renewed stabilization and regained self-confidence, the patient moved for an academic opportunity across the country (in a quite noncompetitive setting). He is there now, functioning well in his position, doing very well financially on the side (in the stock market), and now more resigned to accepting a single life. He continues to this day to keep in touch with the therapist, by phone or by mail, about twice a month.

Comments

Certainly, this final moderate improvement in a psychoanalytic patient who passed through a long and alarming psychotic transference episode in the course of his treatment represents a far different outcome than does the contrasting case of the Alcoholic Doctor. Yet there was indeed a heavy final price paid for this improvement—a settling down into a nonterminating therapeutic tie. This is the issue of becoming a so-called "therapeutic lifer," which is later discussed in more detail in relation to a group of (quite variously constituted) patients who all ended up in this same status. Actually, the treatment course of the Economist touches on a whole range of major issues that have arisen out of the experiences of PRP, each of which is separately considered in this book: (1) the issue of possible misdiagnosis, stemming at times from the often successful efforts of potential patients to conceal significant aspects of their character and illness structure during their initial psychiatric evaluations (see Section III, Chapter 9, pp. 158–167); (2) the issue of the transference psychosis, elaborated here; (3) the issue of the dangers of the insoluble transference neurosis (see this section, Chapter 14, pp. 278–287); (4) the issue of the conversion of psychoanalysis to psychotherapy (see Section IV, Chapter 10, pp. 185–193, especially pp. 189–191); (5) the issue of the "transference cure," established and maintained on the basis of continuing transference gratification (to be discussed in Section VI); (6) the issue of the "therapeutic lifer" (to be discussed in Section VIII); and (7) the question "Was this trip necessary?", already raised in connection with the psychoanalysis of the Devoted Son (see this section, Chapter 14, p. 287) and the Prince (see this section, Chapter 16, pp. 328–329), and to be discussed further in Section IX.

OVERALL SUMMARY

In overall summation at this point, of the 13 patients of our 42 who had actual or threatened transference psychoses (9 within the context of psychoanalysis as at least the starting treatment, and 4 within psychotherapy from the start), 7 had totally failed treatment outcomes (the Alcoholic Doctor, the Alcoholic Heir, the Suspended Medical Student, Peter Pan, the Masochistic Editor, the Bitter Spinster, and the Script Writer); the first 4 listed of these 7 were among the half-dozen known deaths of mental-illness-related causes among our PRP population. Another 3 had very equivocal treatment outcomes (the Heiress, the Alcoholic Raconteur, and the Bohemian Prep School Boy); 2 (the Economist, whose treatment course has just been described, and the Sexual Masochist) ultimately did moderately well through becoming "therapeutic lifers," continuing in uninterrupted therapeutic contact up to the time of present writing. Only 1 (the Fearful Loner) is in the group with very good outcomes, but with an extraordinarily difficult treatment course and also at the price of becoming a "therapeutic lifer" up until the point of his retirement and his move finally away from Topeka. However, to complete this perspective, it should be recalled that not all of the 14 paranoid or potentially paranoid individuals developed or threatened to develop transference psychoses in the course of their treatment; 10 did, but 4 did not. Of the 9 who went into psychoanalysis, 2 were carried through their treatments without such an untoward development and emerged with successful outcomes from their treatments. These, as already stated, were the English Professor and the Movie Lady (see pp. 329–330). And 2 of the 5 who went into psychotherapy (where such untoward developments can be more readily guarded against) did not develop or threaten transference psychoses. These were the Invalided Hypochondriac and the Sociopath—though both of these had differing treatment developments that were equally ominous.

Other Psychotic Treatment and Posttreatment Reactions

THE "SUCCESS NEUROSIS": SUCCESS *PSYCHOSIS?*

Under the subtitle, "Those Wrecked by Success," Freud (1916) called attention to a particular character type met with in psychoanalytic work, those people who "occasionally fall ill precisely when a deeply-rooted and long-cherished wish has come to fulfillment" (p. 316). He accounted for this "surprising, and, indeed bewildering" (p. 316) turn of events—at least in terms of the dictates of ordinary common sense—as follows: " [O]n closer examination we shall reflect that it is not at all unusual for the ego to tolerate a wish as harmless so long as it exists in phantasy alone and seems remote from fulfillment, whereas the ego will defend itself hotly against such a wish as soon as it approaches fulfillment and threatens to become a reality" (pp. 317–318). Freud's case illustrations consisted of two very brief vignettes from individuals who had consulted with him, plus more extended examples from literature—Shakespeare's Lady Macbeth and Ibsen's Rebecca Gamvik from *Rosmersholm*. In the concluding sentence of his discussion, Freud linked this phenomenon to the Oedipal dynamic: "Psychoanalytic work teaches that the forces of conscience which induce illness in consequence of success, instead of, as normally, in consequence of frustration, are closely connected with the Oedipus complex, the relation to father and mother—as perhaps, indeed, is our sense of guilt in general" (p. 331).

It is perhaps because of this last statement—the close tying of this phenomenon of being wrecked by success to the vicissitudes of Oedipal, higher-level conflict—that such patients have often been given favorable prognoses for psychoanalytic treatment, despite the total shambles that their illness may have made of their lives. Within our project sample, we had two patients, the Alcoholic Heir and the Bitter Spinster, who seemed quite clearly of this type. Though the one was severely alcoholic, and both were seen as individuals with paranoid potential and with borderline proneness (and both, indeed, did develop psychotic transference reactions within their treatments), both were nonetheless given initial good treatment prognoses, specifically linked in part to this Oedipal cast given to their conflict structures by their history of seeming "success neurosis." The Alcoholic Heir was recommended for psychoanalysis with the specific predictive statement, "These many expected changes add up to an analytic prognosis more favorable than usually offered for patients with severe alcoholism. The patient's alcoholic self-destruction is in this instance tied so closely to the dangers of actual Oedipal succession in life; it has supervened therefore at a higher psychosexual developmental level and fixation point." Similarly, the Bitter Spinster was thought to be ideally suitable for psychoanalysis, a treatment that would, however, be barred for practical reasons of limited financial resources. It was hoped that her fully expressive psychotherapy could pave the way for later analysis through helping the patient to achieve the kind of life adaptation (and security) in which it might become possible to make a feasible psychoanalytic arrangement.

Here I illustrate the issues at question at greater length with the treatment course of the Alcoholic Heir, who, of the two, had the graver (fatal) treatment outcome, and then, somewhat more briefly, with the treatment course of the Bitter Spinster.

Analysis of the Alcoholic Heir

BACKGROUND AND PROGNOSIS

The Alcoholic Heir came to hospitalization at the urgent insistence of his family because of his uncontrolled chronic alcoholism and consequent total inability to work. The story of his "success neurosis," described earlier (see pp. 63–64, 126, 147, 151–152), is recapitulated here. The patient came from one of the country's wealthiest and most powerful families and was destined to follow into the giant scientific–industrial enterprise founded by his family, in which his father was a major executive. The father was a powerful, competent, and subtly tyrannical man of great drive and determination. He was, incidentally, for most of his life an abstainer from alcohol; his own father and brother had been heavy drinkers. The patient had had a 4-year-old brother, a childhood rival. This brother had been a confirmed alcoholic and had died at 28 in a household fire that he accidentally started when going to bed drunk one night. The one sister was an excessive social drinker. The patient had been an excellent scholar and school athlete. He resented that he was always coerced by the father; in college he had prepared, without protest, for his destined position in the family firm, taking the necessary science courses and foregoing his own, different, inclinations.

The patient was one of the two in our project whose father had promised him $1000 if he didn't drink until he was 21, and he had qualified for this reward.[1] He had then begun his drinking while in the graduate school of business to which he had been sent by his father. The brother had died one summer vacation right after the patient completed graduate school. The two brothers had had a fist fight when the patient accused the brother of reneging on a promise to curb his drinking. The night of the accident the patient, who usually helped to put his drunken

---

1. The other was the equally alcoholic Car Salesman. See pp. 125, 126 for more details.

brother to bed in his houseboat cabin, had failed to wait up for him; he had been guiltily regretful ever since.

The patient married a woman of comparable social position to his own, who herself turned out to be a "moderate social drinker." After his World War II military service (as a Marine officer), he entered upon his preordained career in his family's firm, in which, at first, he performed productively and earned justifiably rapid promotions. When his father retired from his own active position, the patient became a high financial officer in the firm. It was at about this time that the wife dated the onset of his increasingly heavy drinking. The patient became irritable and withdrawn and would retire to his room for solitary binges. These seemed to come in response to the now retired father's active interference in the patient's business activities. The father was always offering gratuitous advice, and the patient felt unable to assert himself against this. The father had always been that way.

Within a year, the patient's alcohol intake had increased to the point at which a warning was passed on from the president of the firm (through the father) that the patient was drinking too much and that this was interfering with his work, especially Mondays after weekend binges. That night (which was close to the 10th anniversary of the brother's death by burning), the patient's house burned down and he escaped with burns only on his hands. The father indicated that it was a cigarette fire started when the patient was drunk. Through this time, the patient was beginning to experience acute anxiety episodes. He would go to work and return home soon, visibly shaken, having become fearful and unable to proceed past the office building door. The family doctor prescribed rest and a lessening of business pressures. The patient was next disappointed that he received only a "horizontal promotion" to controller, without salary increase, and that he was no longer entitled to participate in meetings of the board. Since his start in the company, he had been sensitive that he was being promoted mainly because of his family connections. Now he began to see his juniors promoted past him, and he became resentful of that. Through all this time, he developed one "psychosomatic" affliction after another. He took a prolonged vacation and drank more heavily. When he returned to work, he was demoted because of his long absence. He promptly developed another affliction—this time, infectious mononucleosis— and again was away from work a long time.

When the patient finally returned to work, he found himself completely unable to enter the office building door except Saturdays and Sundays when no one was there. He would suffer extreme panics; his drinking intensified, and his family finally instituted the first of a series of hospitalizations in a sanatorium devoted to alcoholic patients. In between these hospitalizations, the patient was shocked to learn that the company was arranging to carry him in a sinecure just because of his family. In an act of bravado, he impulsively resigned completely and proceeded to drink yet more heavily. By now his marriage had also markedly deteriorated. The patient's sexual life had become sparse, and he was intermittently impotent; both he and his wife attributed this to his drinking. In this context, and after a number of false starts, the patient was finally brought to The Menninger Foundation in an intoxicated state, with gross tremors of his head, tongue, lips, and limbs.

As has already been indicated, psychoanalysis was recommended and embarked upon with the statement (already cited) of a "more favorable than usual" prognosis for a patient with severe alcoholism. This was said despite the clear evidence of very poor motivation and bland denial of treatment need. And concomitant hospitalization, which was so essential to control the patient's drinking, clearly drained off all anxiety each time it was instituted, through its total indulging of the patient's passive impulses; he would become a "model," problem-free patient, clamoring for his release and hotly denying any further distress.

COURSE OF THE ANALYSIS

The patient was in psychoanalysis only 1 year (221 hours), at which point he terminated the treatment because of the insistence of the hospital—concurred in finally by the analyst—that prolonged concomitant hospitalization would be an essential condition to the continuation of the treatment. The patient's entire treatment effort during that year was marked by constant violent turmoil: With episodes of hospital control alternated with periods of attempted outpatient life, each of which was marked by progressive and uncontrolled alcohol excess, as well as by marital strife and violence, usually climaxed by the wife's recourse to the police and rehospitalization of the patient. Some aspects of this treatment course and life, especially the drinking involvement with the almost equally alcoholic wife, have already been described (see pp. 147, 217–218).[2]

Here I focus especially on the evolving transference psychosis. The patient's paranoid propensities first emerged around his struggles with his wife. He accused her of driving him to drink; to the analyst, he stated his belief that his wife was a Communist trying to drive him to alcoholic ruin, and thus to revenge herself upon his wealthy family and what they represented. Also, though wealthy, the patient was extremely frugal in the management of money, and felt that his wife's carelessness and extravagant inability to abide by any household budget was further evidence of her intent to destroy him. During the latter part of his treatment year, the patient's relationship with his wife took a more fearful and even more paranoid turn. Once he rummaged in some attic trunks and found "a jeweled ice pick," which he brought to his analyst for safekeeping, fearful that his wife had intended to use it on him. On another occasion, he asked the analyst for permission to hire a detective agency to investigate whether his wife had purchased a gun to use against him. This same paranoia colored the patient's other life relationships as well. He had a sailboat and would invite friends (usually other patients) sailing, but they were gradually alienated by his bullying manners and were afraid to go sailing with a drunken skipper. The patient attributed this to the hospital's interfering with his social life; he claimed that the doctors were "blacklisting" him with their patients.

All of these paranoid trends had their counterpart within the analytic hours. The patient was clearly frightened of the "unstructured" situation of analysis, and the request to free-associate reminded him of stories of hypnotism and magic. He was afraid of his aggressions and of losing control over them. He berated his analyst because his resentments had all been opened up by the treatment and now he had

---

2. The Alcoholic Doctor, whose full treatment course has already been described (see pp. 332–336), was the other PRP patient whose wife was equally ill and equally alcoholic, and who came to an equally tragic (lethal) end.

been left with nothing but alcohol. At the very end, he said to the analyst (on the phone and when drunk) that he "couldn't come back for treatment because I would punch you in the nose if I did, or I would throw you out of the window." Efforts to get the patient to become introspective and to free-associate were variously met. He would pseudocomply in a passive–aggressive manner, or he would openly mock the procedure, or he would point at his difficult reality (living with his sick wife, who refused several times to enter the treatment recommended to her) as the source of his troubles. He would try to divert the analyst into making their session a social visit, and he would invite the analyst to go sailing on his boat or to come watch television with him on a rainy afternoon. Transference interpretations were treated by the patient as high jokes: In his view, his father had so much more stature than the analyst that it was impossible to compare the two, or to see any relationship between his reactions to the one and to the other. In all of this, if the patient were pushed too hard toward introspection, with too distressing consequences, he would counter with a paranoid flare-up or an alcoholic binge.

DISRUPTION OF THE TREATMENT

In all, both the life situation (turbulent, strife-ridden, alcoholic) and the treatment situation (defensively paranoid) could not be controlled within the context of the original treatment plan—psychoanalysis as much as possible on an outpatient basis—and when the requirement for prolonged concomitant hospitalization was set, the patient balked and disrupted the treatment. Parenthetically, this patient was one of that group of severely ill, mostly alcoholic and/or addicted individuals recommended for psychoanalysis on the basis of so-called "heroic indications"— where concomitant hospitalization was felt to be essential in order to bring the destructive symptoms under control, but where the feared opposite danger of fostering an undue dependency led to a treatment plan with fewer external controls (day hospital, or even wholly outpatient) and more responsibilities on the patient's part for the requirements of an ongoing life situation. As already stated in detail, both in regard to this particular patient and in general (see pp. 223–224), many hospitalizations were unduly curtailed among our patients because of this fear of entrenching potentially difficult neurotic dependency patterns, and the therapies were indeed adversely affected in very major and often disastrous ways. In no instance, on the other hand, was an unworkable dependency problem created for an ongoing intensive therapy by virtue of an overlong hospital stay. It can be assumed that the common poor treatment motivation of these patients, and their often loudly proclaimed unwillingness to accept hospitalization as a necessary part of the treatment effort, would often play a major role in the willingness to try a less restrictive treatment plan, such as that carried out with the Alcoholic Heir.

FOLLOW-UP PERIOD AND DEATH OF THE PATIENT

The follow-up period lasted only 6 months. The patient's life continued as before— chaotic, with solitary drinking and frequent stupors. When his wife began seriously asking for legal separation, preparatory to divorce, he permitted a brief rehospitalization at The Menninger Hospital; he expressed himself as afraid to be alone and "fearful that he might have too much to drink and set fire to his clothes." Within 2 weeks he was again discharged under his insistent pressure, and against medical advice. He had already contacted a lawyer to get him out of the hospital, and he was not legally committable. He was in sporadic communication with his wife, and drinking sprees would frequently follow upon telephone conversations with her. Of his children, he said during his brief rehospitalization, "I hardly know the children—I write them every week and call them up now and then." He called his parents frequently, often becoming complaining and abusive. Finally, his mother wrote to him that she and his father wanted to have nothing further to do with him, because they were too old and frail to permit themselves to be disturbed by his senseless denunciations. The one perhaps bright spot in this whole picture was an employer and mentor (in a financial planning office), who felt the patient had talent and could be "potentially very successful"; this individual ended up spending an average of three evenings a week with the patient for the purpose of helping him stay sober and regain his self-confidence.

Then suddenly, 4 days after he was last seen by his employer, the patient called a new physician, complaining of feeling ill for a week with headache and backache. He was confused and inconsistent and clearly had been drinking. He had evidence of bilateral lower-lobe pneumonia, and the doctor thought him also to be suffering with delirium tremens. He was immediately hospitalized and placed on antibiotics. Nonetheless, he sank rapidly into a stupor, with meningismus and focal neurological signs. A lumbar puncture revealed an acute, purulent pneumococcal meningitis. Though, over the next 4 days of massive antibiotic therapy, the patient's meningeal signs and pulmonary signs all improved, his temperature became normal, and his spinal fluid clear and bacteria-free, he never regained consciousness. His white blood cell count, even at the height of the infectious process, had never been higher than 6000—an indication to his doctors of the massiveness of the infection and/or the low ebb of the patient's resistance. He died after 4 hospital days.

Treatment of the Bitter Spinster

BACKGROUND AND PROGNOSIS

Clearly, the conceptualization of the Alcoholic Heir as one of "those wrecked by success," a sufferer with centrally Oedipal conflicts and Oedipal pathology, turned out to be a serious misperception. The case of the Bitter Spinster turned out to be a similar instance. She was a 30-year-old nurse who came to treatment because of difficulties in her relationships with people, especially men, accompanied by depressive episodes and feelings of being unloved and unwanted. She had just been dismissed from her latest job—a dismissal that she, characteristically, felt was not warranted. Her life story was comparable in its dynamics to that of the Alcoholic Heir. She could never consummate an actual success. Though she was able to attract men very readily, and never lacked for dates, she found herself unable to become serious about a man; if she found one becoming serious about her, she engineered some reason to discontinue the relationship. Her work history was similar. She was an extremely competent psychiatric nurse who rose to supervisory posts but was in recurrent troubles on her jobs, with students, and with colleagues and superiors. Of her latest dismissal she first said, "I did it again," but then rationalized it by implying that the chief nurse had let her go because the patient was such a threat to her. Her repeated pattern, which she did see clearly, was to carry each involvement to the point where success was imminent, and then to do something to make things fail and to waste her investment and her capacity.

Since the patient's symptoms were so autoplastically contained (the very opposite of the extremely alloplastic, alcoholic, and brawling Alcoholic Heir), her ego resources seemed so adequate, and her conscious motivation so strong, psychoanalysis was, as already stated, deemed the treatment of choice; for practical reasons of limited finances, however, the patient was taken into an expressive psychotherapy "as close to analysis as can be gotten on a twice-a-week basis."

COURSE OF THE THERAPY

The therapy, which went on over an 8-year span (560 hours), never realized these high hopes. The patient's life continued its frustrating and problem-ridden course. She was lonely, usually living alone; occasionally she would acquire a roommate, but each time the arrangement would break up with a bitter fight. Her social–sexual life consisted of casual liaisons, usually with physicians or hospital colleagues. She usually treated these boyfriends shabbily and had little conflict over successively throwing them over. Once a physician got her pregnant and then performed the abortion on her. Losing the baby meant nothing to her; she wanted a baby only by the therapist ("With you I could be a woman"). Her estrangement from her own family intensified. Her work as head nurse on the leading psychiatric inpatient unit in the city, where her therapist often had his hospitalized patients, was marked by the special manipulations and special fantasies already described (see pp. 260–261) under the concept of evoked "professional countertransferences" (pp. 257–261). This job, like her others, ended with a pressured resignation (in the terminating phase of her psychotherapy).

The counterpart to this nonprogressive life course was an equally nonprogressive therapeutic course. The first transference phase was marked by an intense eroticization and total suppression of any hostile components. This could take on a bittersweet and resigned quality (e.g., she offered the fantasy of attending a lecture by the therapist on the nature of happy married life, in which he was going to talk from his personal experience; the patient felt she couldn't tolerate this and visualized herself walking out on the lecture). The therapist's lack of direct, counter-acted-out response gradually induced the feeling in the patient that this proved he was rejecting her as a woman. This stance could not be shaken interpretively. The patient then blatantly acted out her transference frustrations in a sequence of sexual involvements, usually with professional colleagues of the therapist (these were usually also married men), most intensively when the therapist was on vacation. Over the whole middle phase of the treatment, the patient's rage over the transference frustrations steadily mounted. She felt the therapist did not like her, had lost interest in her, and desired only to be rid of her. There were jealous scenes about those of his other patients whom she knew about through her hospital work. The final years of the treatment were a period of angry, repeated, directly vindictive accusations against the therapist for all his malfeasances. The acting out became concomitantly more violent. The patient loudly berated the therapist for not having helped her at all, for having in effect ruined her. She deliberately withheld more from the therapy; to the silences and latenesses that had characterized the treatment all along, the patient began to add frequent missing of hours, punctuated then by frequent late-night phone calls. A constant accusation was that the therapist was exploiting her. In fact, she acted to exploit him by not paying her bills and deflecting her money into extravagant "buying binges" that she could not afford; she also obliged the therapist to consent to frequent changes of hours, and in other ways forced him to treat her as someone very "special." At the same time, the patient used her jealous rages at the therapist's other patients and her extratherapeutic contacts with him at the hospital as partial compensation for her frustrated transference feelings; at work she could nurture the fantasy of indeed having the "special relationship" that she always demanded.

The specific nature of this transference interaction became crystal clear to both participants. The therapist, in describing the treatment course, said, "Little by little she began to express the feeling that I wasn't taking care of her, that I was not sensitive to her feelings and her needs as I once had been, and that I was more interested in other patients than in her. She said that in this I was like her mother, and here she was giving me the best years of her life and she was getting nothing from it and that this was just the way it had been with her mother." The patient, from her side, linked this to her own hostile identification with her mother. "I'm too suspicious, I'm suspicious of everyone. I hate suspicious women. My mother was one. I hate being like her this way."

TERMINATION

Though not as flagrantly psychotic as in the other cases described to this point (the Alcoholic Doctor, the Economist, the Alcoholic Heir), the patient's transferences had become paranoidly suspicious and reality-deviant in fixed, unshakeable ways—enough to warrant placing her too with the group of evolved psychotic transference reactions. (Could the fact that in contrast to these others, this patient's treatment mode was not psychoanalysis, but a somewhat less regression-inducing psychotherapy, have accounted for the lesser intensity of the disorganizing trend within the transference?) When, despite all interpretive efforts, this entrenched transference position (transference impasse) could not be resolved, and an insoluble transference jam seemed to be developing, the therapist moved the treatment toward termination through the manipulative device already described (p. 254): referring the patient for six sessions to another psychiatrist, with whom, as an uninvolved and disinterested outsider, the patient could discuss her entire predicament—including the therapist's conviction that he could help her no further. The patient spent these 6 hours of consultation complaining bitterly about the therapist, but she did come to terms with herself about the appropriateness of termination. As has also been already described (see p. 197), the patient, who had always been delinquent in the handling of her fees and had obtained a fee reduction during a period of difficult economic circumstances, made another point of being a "special" patient getting special indulgences by not paying at all for her entire last year of therapy or for the six consultation visits with the colleague. She considered all this a "gift."

STATUS AT FOLLOW-UP

As might be expected, at the time of Follow-Up Study, the patient's situation was unaltered. She presented herself with the statement, "I haven't done a thing in 2 years, really not a thing." She had worked only sporadically over this period, usually at private duty nursing. Her unstable and unsatisfactory work record she attributed not to any difficulties in obtaining employment, but to her own increasing depressive trend: It was harder to get herself to make the effort. There were considerable stretches of not working at all, and in order to manage financially, the patient had to ask her family for money. This they gave when asked, even giving a little more unasked. The patient's social involvements had all dropped away. She was living totally alone; she had few dates, and she indicated that she had had no sexual desires for a long time. She wondered whether she was getting old (she was now 40), or just denying her sexuality. She was not interested in doing anything most of the time except sitting around and sometimes reading. Her relationship with her family (her mother and father) continued estranged, though when she needed money they unquestioningly gave what was asked.

On occasions of heightened stress, the patient called her ex-therapist, but office appointments were usually not offered — or directly asked for. The therapist was discouraging of her tentative and hidden overtures toward further therapeutic contact. Once he did see her and tried to reassure her in the face of her difficulties and complaints by telling her. "You're the best psychiatric nurse around in this part of the country. You know that, don't you?" Yet to the patient this was no reassurance. To her it sounded as though he was saying, "You're good at washing dishes." She frequently slept with a bottle of sleeping pills at her bedside, and occasionally seemed seriously to consider suicide. But she was emphatic that she did not desire more treatment, either with the previous therapist or anyone else. "Treatment would make me worse. I want to get better." Of her future she said that she thought she ought to get out of that town and start over somewhere else, but she had been apathetically unable to take any steps toward even planning such a move. She was in a total impasse. There has been no further known follow-up contact. The patient's therapist died a fair number of years ago.

COMMENTS

This treatment, too, like that of the other patient characterized as having a "success neurosis" (the Alcoholic Heir), also ended in failure, though not lethally — and this occurred despite the Bitter Spinster's being a less sick, even more "hysterical"-looking patient at the time of initial psychiatric evaluation. In fact, the overall diagnosis given her at that time was "hysterical character neurosis." But here, too, a paranoid decompensation developed within the transference and seemed impervious to 8 years of highly skillful therapeutic effort. Certainly, these experiences (though there were only two such in PRP) raise two questions: (1) What is the essential nature of the pathology in these "success neurosis" individuals, and how amenable is it to psychotherapeutic amelioration? (2) What is the best treatment approach — how expressive–analytic versus how frankly supportive and reality-oriented should it be?

The conclusion reached at the time of writing the original Case Study document for this patient was that the treatment plan that was tried was not sufficiently developed in the one direction *or* the other. I quote it in full:

> The technical error seen clearly in retrospect in this therapy was that of following neither of the opposed alternatives — the one, psychoanalysis, being precluded by lack of financial resources, the other, a fully supportive therapy, avoided as being thera-

peutically insufficiently ambitious—and riding, then, a middle course that precipitated the weakness of each and led into the dangers of both. The expressive, uncovering effort led to the analytic-like regression but without the analytic structure within which to cope with it (and unfortunately in a patient whose own ego weakness proved such that she could not herself put the appropriate internal brakes on the regressive process). And the treatment conditions (only twice weekly) required energetic controlling measures in the face of the paranoid transference regression and the concomitant dangerous acting out, that were inadequate to stem the regressive sweep, and at the same time tended to vitiate the counterposed interpretive efforts. The patient thus suffered the consequences of a handicapped treatment strategy composed of the most ambitious therapeutic intentions stymied by lack of resources for psychoanalysis (which might have worked could it have been tried?), and equally stymied by lack of initial clarity of the seriousness of the potential ego pathology, which if it had been initially manifest might have deterred the therapist from an expressive attempt under less than optimal auspices, and might have led him to institute a more fully supportive therapy (which might also have worked had it been tried?) in which the patient would not have been relied on to have such consolidated inner ego resources.

THE NEGATIVE THERAPEUTIC REACTION

Nature of the Concept

Related in its structure to the concept of "those wrecked by success" is the comparable concept of the "negative therapeutic reaction," which can be put in the variant form of "those wrecked by treatment" or, more precisely, "those wrecked *in* treatment." Though Freud made a passing reference to the concept of the negative therapeutic reaction in his account of the treatment of the Wolf Man (1918, p. 69), he fully developed this conception and the linked notion of the unconscious sense of guilt in his definition of the tripartite structural model of the mind in "The Ego and the Id" (1923), when he used this clinical explanation as a centerpiece in his conceptualization of the nature of the superego in its conscious, and more, in its unconscious functioning. There he said:

> There are certain people who behave in a quite peculiar fashion during the work of analysis. When one speaks hopefully to them or expresses satisfaction with the progress of the treatment, they show signs of discontent and their condition invariably becomes worse. One begins by regarding this as defiance and as an attempt to prove their superiority to the physician, but later one comes to take a deeper and juster view. One becomes convinced, not only that such people cannot endure any praise or appreciation, but that they react inversely to the progress of the treatment. Every partial solution that ought to result, and in other people does result, in an improvement or a temporary suspension of symptoms produces in them for the time being of exacerbation of their illness; they get worse during the treatment instead of getting better. They exhibit what is known as a "negative therapeutic reaction." (p. 49)

The explanation for this phenomenon Freud linked a little further on in the text to what he called "a 'moral' factor, a sense of guilt, which is finding its satisfaction in the illness and refuses to give up the punishment of suffering" (p. 49). But "as far as the patient is concerned this sense of guilt is dumb; it does not tell him he is guilty; he does not feel guilty, he feels ill" (pp. 49–50). And later on, in another paper (1924b), Freud clearly labeled this "an 'unconscious' sense of guilt" (p. 166), which is recognized by the "negative therapeutic reaction," and said of it: "The satisfaction of this unconscious sense of guilt is perhaps the most powerful bastion in the subject's (usually composite) gain from illness—in the sum of forces which struggle against his recovery and refuse to surrender his state of illness. The suffering entailed by neuroses is precisely the factor that makes them valuable to the masochistic trend" (p. 166).

I have previously called attention (see Section III, Chapter 8, pp. 138–140) to the fact that 18 of the 42 PRP patients (8 men and 10 women), or almost 45% of the sample, had significant masochistic character trends; these trends are there especially described for three of them (the Masochistic Editor, the Homesick Psychology Student, and the Obedient Husband). Among these 18, a fair number lived out these masochistic propensities not just in their lives, but to some significantly discernible way in their therapeutic course as well—as negative therapeutic reactions, and expressions of the unconscious need for punishment. For example, one could readily look very profitably at the treatment courses of the Alcoholic Doctor (pp. 332–336), the Alcoholic Heir (pp. 345–349), the Divorced Nurse (pp. 314–321), and the Movie Lady (not yet described in detail) from this particular vantage point—treatments that have instead been highlighted from the perspective of the transference psychosis (the Alcoholic Doctor), the "success neurosis" (the Alcoholic Heir), and psychoanalysis carried out against the background of an unfavorable reality context (the Divorced Nurse). Here, however, within the specific framework of the concept of the negative therapeutic reaction, I want to describe the treatment course of the Masochistic Editor—one of the group of severely alcoholic, paranoid, and borderline individuals who was taken into psychoanalysis (at his insistent entreaty), and who got to the edge of a fully erupted transference psychosis within his analytic treatment. He was also the predatory homosexual who delighted in debauching "heterosexual males" (see pp. 128, 130). For the purposes here at issue, he had one of the most pervasively organized masochistic character structures within the whole PRP population (see p. 139). With him, therefore, the role of the "unconscious sense of guilt" and the derived "negative therapeutic reaction" in affecting treatment course and outcome adversely can perhaps be seen with the greatest clarity.

Treatment of the Masochistic Editor

BACKGROUND AND PROGNOSIS

The patient, a 33-year-old single man, a clerk in his father's drugstore, sought both psychiatric hospitalization and psychoanalysis because of years of uncontrolled drinking, involvement in constant predatory and degrading homosexual relationships, and an inability to get away from his parental home or to use his high intellectual capacities to make something of his life. His masochistic posture was evident almost from the beginning of his life. It had been difficult to punish him as a child. He seemed not to mind being beaten, or sent to bed where he could take refuge in books; what seemed most effective was to take his book away and shame him in front of other children. He had had one sibling, a brother 2 years younger with whom he did not get along as a child, but to whom he drew closer in adulthood. The brother had had his own psychiatric difficulties (depression), for which he was once hospitalized; the patient had urged the parents in vain to bring the brother to The Menninger Foundation for more comprehensive treatment. Shortly after his hospital discharge, the brother had committed suicide very painfully by strychnine poisoning, with the pharmacopeia open to the proper page so that the family could realize all the horrible effects. The patient blamed the father's inaction in the face of such overt illness for this unnecessary death.

Though the patient had been an outstanding scholar and leader during school and college days, he never found life directions for himself as an adult. Periods of hard work and productivity in different settings seemed to alternate unaccountably with slack, depressive periods. His overt sexual activities had begun early. At age 11 he began to be involved in mutual masturbation with other boys, and by age 18 he had had a variety of both homosexual and heterosexual experiences. While in overseas combat during World War II, the patient acquired gonorrhea from a homosexual prostitute and again (masochistically) punished himself with it for 2 weeks before reporting for treatment: "I was running with venereal disease; I was ready to go out of my mind; I was passing blood and being destroyed." After the war, when he felt he could neither return to school nor work steadily, he began to drink heavily and when drunk would solicit homosexual encounters in which he was always the aggressor.

One of the patient's homosexual adventures lasted 3 months and ended with a jealous fight when he brought a rival to the apartment. In this fight, the patient was hit on the head with a bottle, and this resulted in a subdural hematoma requiring surgical intervention. At this point, the patient returned to his parental home, alternating between doing nothing and clerking in his father's store. During his time away from his home city, the patient had been in outpatient psychoanalysis for about a year. The father had paid for this, though he couldn't really understand why the patient's inability to settle down in life required so expensive a remedy. (He was only vaguely informed about the drinking problem and not at all about the sexual disorder.) The patient often missed treatment hours or came drunk. When he secured a temporary job, the father, feeling that the treatment goals had been reached, ceased paying for more posttreatment. The patient did nothing either to secure continued support from his father or to try to support the treatment in any way himself. He meekly let it lapse, opining, "I was a failure."

While living at home, the patient drank steadily in a daily ritual: He would consume a huge quota of beer, gin, and whiskey, each at carefully prescribed times, scheduled around his working hours in the drugstore. When drunk, he would initiate repeated homosexual encounters, preferably with married "heterosexual" males whom he delighted in debauching (his sadistic side came out here). He became frightened when he began to suffer with blackouts and would awaken amnesic. He began to eat greedily and gained 35 pounds. He had had no heterosexual relations for 8 years now and was fearful of trying, feeling that he would be impotent. He finally persuaded his parents to bring him for psychiatric treatment to The Menninger Foundation. This climaxed a 4-year effort to effect this step. His success came after the brother's suicide, which shook the parents very much into an awareness that their two sons had indeed both been very sick, and both in need of expert psychiatric help. The patient was hospitalized directly while being evaluated for psychotherapy. He settled very contentedly into the hospital routine. He went on a diet and began to lose weight steadily; he gave up his drinking and his homosexual behaviors. He was put on a full hospital activities schedule with much hard physical labor, which he seemed to enjoy, carrying it through compliantly and even masochistically (not calling attention to painful blisters that arose, etc.).

Mostly on the strength of the patient's strong motivational push (whatever its neurotic determinants were), as well as his high intellectual endowment, the patient was recommended for psychoanalysis (with concomitant hospitalization of course), despite all the adverse indicators: the strength of the pregenital fixations; the driven, perverse behaviors that they led to; the low anxiety tolerance; the vulnerability of the ego to discharge pressures in severely distorted pathological directions; and the patient's strong self-destructive bent. And overshadowing all that, the patient's strong passivity, masochism, and need to comply could obtain powerfully reinforcing secondary gratifications from the perpetuation of a perennially unresolved dependent transference relationship.

COURSE OF THE TREATMENT

Psychoanalysis. The patient was in analysis for 4 years and 4 months, and then in a specifically supportive–expressive psychotherapy for another 2 years and 8 months, a total of 7 years (1107 hours) altogether; then, because of the nature of the ending, the therapy was not declared officially terminated until another 2 years had gone by.

The patient's life throughout his 7 years of treatment was most turbulent. His calmest period was the first 1½ years, when he was hospitalized (16 months) or in the day hospital (another 2 months). There was at that time almost no drinking and only very sporadic homosexual activity. When he was out of the hospital he secured a position as general editor of an alcoholic beverage trade journal (ironically!). His relations with his parents were more tolerable, less tension-arousing. The patient felt himself at a high point when, after about 3 years of analysis, he entered into a heterosexual liaison (with a young nurse)—his first in 11 years. This progressed to a relatively close emotional involvement, but the girlfriend finally left him when it became increasingly clear that the patient would not commit himself to a course that would lead to marriage. The patient felt unexpected relief mingled with the regret when she left.

During this time, the publisher of the journal wanted to liquidate the business, and the patient faced the alternative of either losing the job or buying his boss out. He responded by getting "stinking drunk"—his first major binge since the start of his treatment. From this point on, his situation deteriorated. Periodic drinking bouts recurred with each new life pressure. The patient's homosexual adventuring returned in full force, always intensely sadomasochistically colored. He tried to keep up with his work, having bought out the journal on the installment plan, but the issues of the journal became very irregular in appearance. With his drinking, his homosexuality, and his work all out of control, the patient had the first of a number of (brief) hospitalizations for stabilization purposes. Shortly after the end of his first rehospitalization period, one of the patient's homosexual partners walked out on him after an argument, drove off in the patient's car, and was killed on the highway (the highway patrol reported at first that it was the patient who had been killed, since his identification papers were found with the car). This precipitated another brief hospitalization with a guilty depression.

Things kept getting worse. The magazine went bankrupt. The patient's homosexuality was beset now by occasional impotence and by renewed infections with gonorrhea. He became involved homosexually with a young boy. He also got badly beaten and robbed by a homosexual contact he picked up when drunk. His drinking was now on what he called "a rigid schedule of dissipation." When in the midst of this period he obtained a new job (in a federal agency), he worked hard but at the same time drew a warning from his boss that his many absences (because of hangovers) would not be tolerated much longer. He "straightened up" for a while, secured a major salary increase, and promptly embarked on a campaign of heightened drinking, including drunken sprees that landed him in jail. He called this "a vested interest in chaos," and it finally lost him this job.

Psychotherapy. It was in this context (after 4 years and 4 months) that the father, who saw no visible progress, declared his loss of faith in the treatment and his unwillingness from that point on to put in more than $100 monthly. The analyst felt the patient's status to be too precarious to consider terminating, and was disillusioned anyway by now with the possibilities of analysis; the treatment was switched to a twice-weekly supportive–expressive psychotherapy, with the patient agreeing to contribute the balance of the fee (only $20) each month. The patient resentfully accepted this reduction in sessions, and never kept his end of the bargain on payment; he always found suitable excuses for his failure to do so.

In this altered treatment mode, things went no better with the patient's life. His employment was sporadic, and his attendance at treatment was often interrupted. He was frequently picked up by the police for drunken driving, and he was in a pattern of periodically being attacked and robbed by his homosexual pickups. Once he came to the therapy hour with the story that his car had been stolen. He had finally made the last payment on it, and for the first time in his life owned a car outright. He told the therapist, "You can put the rest of the story together." That very night he got into a drunken brawl with a homosexual pickup and was robbed of his money and his car. At a point 6 months later (now 7 years from the start of his treatment), he lost his latest job; now moneyless and behind on his rent, he came for a last therapy session, since he was returning to his parents' home (in a distant city) for a visit of uncertain duration.

Over the next 2 years, there were sporadic telephone contacts between the patient and the therapist. The patient was working again, discontentedly but steadily, in his father's drugstore. They got along tolerably well, and the patient's drinking and homosexuality were now moderated and more discreet. At about the 9-year mark, the therapist officially "terminated" the treatment. Shortly thereafter, the patient was able to pull up stakes and take on a journalistic–administrative job in an overseas aid program. But almost immediately after he started in that position, the patient's mother died, and he hurried home for the funeral. At this point he again fell apart, going on a 5-month-long drunken spree; he was "unconscious all the time," was getting physically run down, and was obese again. The last of the two people (his brother and his mother) to whom he had ever felt close was now dead. The patient eventually rallied from this despondency, and left his father's home for a new editorial job with a university press. It was there that he was relatively contentedly working when contacted for official research Termination Study, 10 years after the start of his treatment.

Themes of the Treatment. Through this long and checkered outside life, a few themes wound through the patient's treatment:

1. His work career. His father had never thought that he could work at anything except in the family drugstore and implied that he was too much of a coward for anything else. The patient had experienced lifelong shame over feeling himself a sissy, avoiding boyhood fighting, running away even from girls, and having to rely on his brother to protect him. He felt that neither his father, nor the analyst, nor he himself could ever believe that he could succeed at anything. When he secured his first job (with the beverage journal), he elaborated paranoid fears (almost delusions) that his father would undermine it. This progressed to the verge of, but did not quite become, a psychotic transference reaction.

2. The intensity of the patient's aggressions and the linked guilt (the latter reinforced by the brother's death by suicide). The patient had intense wishes to beat and be beaten, to kill and to commit suicide. Behind the primitive violence of these urges was the fantasy of coming through all these adventures unscathed. The patient held to this fantasy of narcissistic omnipotence with such fixity that it was hard to confront him successfully with the great dangers involved in his actual behaviors.

3. His sadomasochistic interactions. Sadomasochistic homosexual contacts when drunk were means of overcoming the superior brother, and also the father. In the childhood confrontations, the athletic brother had always been the victor and was the one who had to protect the patient from the attacks of his peers.

4. The expression of sadomasochistic impulses in the transference, in the need to defeat the analyst and the fear of being destroyed by him. The patient either scorned the analyst as of no help, or was himself powerless even to reflect on his dilemmas with the analyst, leaving the analyst to carry the full burden of managing the treatment and the patient's life.

5. The effort to destroy the treatment by exploiting the financial difficulties that arose when the father refused to continue his previous high rate of support. To that point, the patient had never contributed to his treatment costs at all, even when working; he was content to keep that burden on his father. This hostile aggression continued under the new treatment arrangement, in the patient's irresponsibility even in regard to the token aspect of the continued financing of his treatment that he agreed to undertake.

6. And throughout the treatment, the repetition of, and the many meanings of, his drunkenness, his homosexual prowling when drunk, and the sadomasochism that was at its most exaggerated in the alcoholism and the homosexuality. Toward the end of the treatment, this sadomasochism was expressed in both self-destructiveness and treatment destructiveness; the latter was carried to missing sessions, taking long interludes, and finally just dropping coming altogether.

Within the transference, the chief manifestation was the patient's sadomasochistic disposition always to re-enact his submissions, his hostile dependency, and his rebellions against the father (and ultimately, also the mother). This was combined with his need for punishment for his rebellious aggressions by the masochistic destruction of all his life opportunities and treatment opportunities. He was characterized as repeatedly snatching defeat from the jaws of (possible) victory. The episode with the car was a prototypic instance: The very day that he had made a final payment and for the first time in his life owned a car outright, he got into a characteristic drunken brawl with a homosexual pickup and thus arranged to be robbed of both money and car. In this sense, the dynamics of the need to fail and the unconscious guilt and need for punishment are closely related to the dynamics of the "success neurosis" considered earlier in this chapter. It became clear with the Masochistic Editor that the total constellation of adverse factors—the severity of the disturbed behaviors and acting out; the precarious (close to paranoid) level of ego functioning; the intense impulse pressure; and, perhaps above all, the extreme masochistic entrenchment with a consequent profound negative therapeutic reaction (a determined push to destroy any potential for therapeutic advancement)—all made it extraordinarily difficult for the patient to respond constructively to the prolonged psychoanalytic interpretive effort.

When the treatment mode was altered, the burden of the transference interaction passed from interpretation to a more directive effort at confronting the patient with the inappropriateness of his behaviors and their reality consequences, hoping to provide external coercive pressures toward more controlled living. A fully regressive transference neurosis had unfolded with the uncovering of the patient's primitive sadomasochistic conflicts in his fused relationship with his archaic parental imagoes. But the transference neurosis could not be brought to successful resolution, and the treatment was ultimately "interrupted" with the major transferences unaltered.

STATUS AT FOLLOW-UP

The 2½-year follow-up period seemed somehow just to recapitulate in a far briefer time compass the whole history of the patient's many previous years of treatment in Topeka (including a new trial of therapy). His own beginning assessment at Follow-Up interview was, "In a general way, I am just making it on the positive side." He was still on the same job with the university press, in which he did feel secure. "But if it weren't for the fact that I am so expert at the job, I would have been fired a long time ago because my absenteeism (because of alcohol excess) is so hideous. But the job's in no danger." He had quit a doctorate program in which he had briefly enrolled, "because school interfered with the whole ridiculous pattern of drinking every night." His wasteful financial ways had now been curbed by an outside regulatory arrangement his father had pressured him to set up: He turned his entire paycheck over to an accountant, who paid all his bills for him and gave him a regular allowance of spending money.

Overall, the patient's life still revolved around his two major symptoms, his alcoholism and his homosexuality. His drinking was maintained on a continuous high level bordering on constant drunkenness; only his job performance was spared (even that not fully). He would drink all weekend, and would have six to seven martinis each evening, "so that I am virtually unconscious except for going to work." His homosexuality had temporarily altered in pattern. For the first time he had entered a sustained homosexual liaison—with a 20-year-old, almost illiterate farm boy (25 years his junior). This improbable relationship lasted for 3 months of living together. The patient took a parental interest in the youngster and was teaching him to read. The care went even more the other way: The patient was drinking very heavily and relied on the boy "to get me up in the morning, and drive me to work, and make lunch, and clean the house." Yet the patient could not maintain this "marriage"; to his surprise, he found himself undermining the relationship by occasional turns to outside partners. "I was mystified at myself, because without ever openly quarreling, I did everything that I could to get rid of him, which I finally succeeded in doing." When the youngster was "driven out," the patient reverted to his previous pattern of predatory encounters when drunk, with pickups in bars. He was, however, a little more careful than in the past to avoid situations where there was a high risk of being beaten and robbed. He was also now beset by potency disturbances in his homosexuality.

With his behaviors unchanged, the patient was now chronically overtly depressed. "I'm unconscious most of the time. I'm either working or I'm drunk. When I'm not doing either, I read continuously in order not to think. . . . It's just sort of death on the installment plan." But he denied a more active suicide push: "I'd like to die but I couldn't kill myself." The patient's contacts with people (other than as drinking companions in bars, or in homosexual pickups) had ebbed even further; he had no friends. He still visited occasionally with the few family members from whom he was not totally estranged. But he was quite alienated from his father. When his father had been away on vacation, the patient had entered the father's home and "simply lifted the porch furniture—for my living room." Since then, the father had practically ceased seeing him, which the patient took in stride. "Actually my father and I seem to get along much better now when we don't see each other."

During this 2½-year follow-up period, the patient's symptomatic ups and downs had brought him back into a temporary renewed treatment effort with a local psychiatrist (who had been on The Menninger Foundation staff and had for a while been the patient's hospital doctor there). The patient came to this treatment because he feared the loss of the one stable and (partially) productive aspect of his life, his job. He told the psychiatrist, "I've got a good thing going and I just don't want to screw up again." The therapy was once weekly, and its honeymoon phase lasted 4 to 5 months. The patient cut down his alcohol consumption and his homosexual prowling; he entered the "restricted" relationship with the farm boy; he employed the accountant to help rescue him from his profligacy. But in this therapy, too, the patient's masochistic push to fail could not be contained. He had very little impulse control; even with very little alcohol in him, he began to do bizarre things and talk in bizarre ways. The therapist felt the patient to be quite vulnerable to regressive sweeps into frankly minipsychotic episodes, after which he would drink more intensely to cover them over by an alcoholic rationale: "He would rather be thought of as a drunk than as crazy." The reprise of the patient's former treatment course became more exact when the patient's bill began to accumulate unpaid in this treatment too. Over this issue, the patient finally then also disrupted this treatment after 9 months.

Of all his experience in treatment, the patient said that he had had "too much psychology, too many years, too many doctors. I'm immune to treatment now.

When you've talked about yourself for so many years it becomes humiliating, if nothing else." He doubted that he would re-enter treatment. He had spoken bitterly of his analyst in Topeka to his more recent therapist: "He had been talking to his analyst about some heterosexual feelings he had a hint of, and he looked over, and he saw a sort of self-satisfied look on his analyst's face and he just felt rage within himself as if he had been capitulating to what was wanted and expected of him." The patient himself ended his follow-up contact (which had begun with the remark about "making it on the positive side") with the statement "As you can see, I don't feel so hot this morning."

The next contact with the patient was 13 years later, 17 years after his treatment termination. The patient's situation was sadly the same. He was now 59. Both parents were dead. The patient was still single and alone. He had seemed to have somehow supported himself in the intervening years doing "editorial work," living still in his home state. He returned at this point to a special inpatient Alcoholism Recovery Program at The Menninger Foundation, stating that he had been "drinking excessively"; he also stated that he was continuingly openly homosexual but couldn't establish relationships without drinking. He wanted help in giving up alcohol, having finally abandoned the goal of being a "social drinker." He was described by one observer as a "fat, balding, homosexual alcoholic." The psychological test battery at this point still reflected the same sadomasochistic character organization. There was also evidence of an advancing psychotic process, with primary process thinking, overelaborated and confabulated associations, and a dysphoric or overtly euphoric affect, characterized by frantic pacing of thought and speech.

The patient's behavior in the hospital was quite disruptive and alienating. His verbosity, his jocularity at his own expense, and his proneness to grandiose and paranoid flare-ups tended to isolate him from other patients and staff. He spent most of his time alone, reading or writing in his room, or taking walks or bike rides on the grounds alone. His underlying mood was always depressed. With his hospital doctor, he was submissive and rather seductive. He said that he knew that some psychiatrists were homosexual.

The hospital's treatment plan was to involve the patient in participation in AA, and also in long-term psychotherapy to be continued via an aftercare arrangement, with the patient again settling in Topeka. The whole hospitalization and treatment period lasted less than 2 months, however. Because of the diagnostic issue raised at this time of a manic–depressive psychotic process, now in a manic phase, a trial of lithium was proposed. This the patient flatly rejected, declaring that "a chemical will not be used to alter the composition of my body fluids." Over this issue, the patient left the hospital against medical advice; typically, he left an unpaid bill for over $9000. He has not been heard from further in the 2 years between this hospitalization and the time of this writing. Nothing seems to have altered over the entire 26-year period of contact and observation.

COMMENTS

Clearly this was the most extreme and severe instance in our patient population of the "negative therapeutic reaction": The Masochistic Editor proved impervious to a prolonged and careful trial of psychoanalysis, and fared no better when switched to a more directive psychotherapy, with two different therapists. His was a totally failed treatment. Other patients for whom such severely masochistic tendencies played some significant treatment role had varied treatment outcomes, but mostly they did very poorly under this adverse impact. Of eight who could be so characterized (in terms of thrust toward negative therapeutic reactions), actually six ended among our treatment failures (the Masochistic Editor, the Bitter Spinster, the Alcoholic Doctor, the Alcoholic Heir, the Addicted Doctor, and the Car Salesman), and four of these six (the last four listed) were among the six mental-illness-related fatalities in our PRP population. The two with better outcomes were the Divorced Nurse, who did moderately well, all things considered (see this section, Chapter 15, pp. 314–321), and the Movie Lady, who had a good result (her treatment course is described in detail later).

Certainly, major questions were left unresolved by the treatment effort, course, and outcome with the Masochistic Editor (and with other masochistic characters with comparably intense unconscious needs to fail?). First, there is again the question, "Was this trip necessary?" Did accomplishing what was minimally achieved (precariously stabilizing the patient at a barely tolerable level of extramural adjustment) require all that analysis and all those treatment years? Or, to put it differently, was this the wrong trip? Was an inappropriate treatment modality recommended and persisted in, on the basis of an overly optimistic diagnostic assessment, and did this make more difficult the kind of treatment outcome that might have been achieved if a less reconstructively ambitious, but perhaps more suitable, treatment modality had been implemented from the start? Or would even a more accurate initial appraisal and a "more appropriate" treatment recommendation and therapeutic handling from the start have enabled any better outcome with this very ill individual, dedicated so unswervingly to a failing and self-destructive course?

THE PROFESSIONAL COUNTERTRANSFERENCE

The Professional Countertransference and the Negative Posttherapeutic Reaction

Under the rubric of "professional countertransferences" (see Section IV, Chapter 12, pp. 257–261), I have described the special treatment problems, in the sense of "special" countertransference expectations and dispensations, that can be characteristically evoked in the treatments of physicians, sometimes their families, and sometimes allied health professionals. Seven patients are discussed in Chapter 12 for whom such issues in fact arose or were at least potentially present—five physician patients, one wife of a physician, and one psychiatric nurse. I indicate there that in only two instances among the seven was it clear that no "special" status or dispensation was sought by the patients or accorded by virtue of their professional position, and both of these had very good treatment results indeed. With the other five this factor did operate, more or less importantly, in the interaction between patient and therapist, and to the severe detriment of each of the five. All five were failed cases, and three of them were among the six who died of mental-illness-related causes.

Here I describe the treatment course of one of these patients, the Suspended Medical Student. I do so, in part, because he is such a good example of the more subtle (but equally pervasive and detrimental) impact of such professional counter-transferences upon treatment course and outcome (as opposed, say, to the treatment career of the Addicted Doctor, who brazenly manipulated special privileges and ruthlessly and self-destructively exploited them—see p. 259); and, in part, because he represents a unique instance of someone in a full psychoanalytic treatment who seemed to have an adequate and a promising outcome, only to collapse disastrously when no longer artificially propped up by the treatment, in what can only be called a "negative posttherapeutic reaction" (akin to what extent with the kind of negative therapeutic reaction just described with the Masochistic Editor?).

Analysis of the Suspended Medical Student

BACKGROUND AND PROGNOSIS

The Suspended Medical Student was the individual suspended from medical school and referred for psychiatric examination by his school authorities because of episodes of unethical behavior in which he performed unnecessary pelvic examinations on hospitalized surgical patients, without gloves, and in the middle of the night. There was a succession of three such episodes, the details of which have already been presented (see p. 150). The patient claimed amnesia for each episode, and at least two of them were preceded by drinking.

The patient's life history is presented here in briefest capsule. He had always been shy and uncomfortable in his growing-up years. He had been an outstanding student, scholastically ambitious, though coming from a farming family. He had also worked a good deal all along on the family farm, attempting from the first to do "a man's job." He took pride in how hard he could work: He "could work around any other farm hand." His adolescent years had been preoccupied with great conflict over his compulsive masturbation, which he fought unsuccessfully to control, and with varieties of somatic, autonomic symptoms. After combat service in World War II, the patient, now 21, began to drink heavily and had his first heterosexual experiences. He worked very hard in college and made very high grades, and his drinking abated. The hard work alternated, however, with periods of increased tension, including a frankly depressive reaction to a grandfather's death; this resulted in a return to heavy drinking and dropping out of college for a semester to work on the family farm. Over these same years, he was successively involved in courting two girlfriends, but with each, as marriage planning was imminent, the patient's drinking intensified. When his fiancées finally each broke the engagement, the patient was privately relieved as well as publicly outraged.

When applying for medical school, the patient fell ill and missed the entrance examination. On the day of his interview with the dean, he felt very sick but forced himself to go, even though he was vomiting right up to the time that he entered the building. Once he was admitted to medical school, the pattern was the same—of hard work and diminished drinking, alternating with increased tension and renewed drinking. In the summers he would give his father much-needed help on the farm, and toward the end of summer, with most of the farm work done, he would again feel at loose ends, tense, and depressed, and would resort to heavier drinking. His failed courtships occurred over this span. And his illness preoccupations persisted: He was much concerned about organic heart disease as the underlying basis for his autonomic cardiorespiratory symptoms, and, after a brief febrile illness, was very worried about the possibility of having suffered irreparable organic brain damage. He had to be medically reassured about these matters more than once. All told, this is the story of a very troubled young man, struggling with intense inhibitions and life conflicts, and given to potentially dangerous behaviors (his alcohol excess), who had somehow all through this avoided or escaped notice as someone in need of psychiatric help.

It was in this context, and while on his third-year clinical clerkship in psychiatry, that the three amnesic episodes with the attendent improper behaviors occurred (over a 1-month span); the patient was referred for psychiatric evaluation and asked meanwhile to withdraw from medical school. It turned out during the evaluation that there had been an earlier amnesic episode 6 years before. At that time the patient had been the life of a New Year's Eve party, drinking, carousing, and dancing, but he had awakened in bed at home the next day with no memory of having attended the party. On examination, the patient was anxious, depressed, and (for a medical student) suprisingly naive. The parents participated in the evaluation. The father stoically accepted the accounts of the school incidents, but insisted that such things were common among medical students under stress. The mother clung to the hope that maybe there was some mistake in the identity of the offender.

The treatment recommended was psychoanalysis, the only treatment felt able to effect real resolution of the patient's deep-seated neurotic conflicts. The patient seemed endowed with the requisite psychological resources and strengths for this treatment. He was considered to suffer from "dissociative reactions in a hysterical character neurosis" and was given an excellent prognosis.

COURSE OF THE ANALYSIS

The analytic treatment lasted 4½ years (672 hours). From the start, there was evidence of a more disruptive anxiety and a more serious characterological illness with greater ego deformation (marked by poor impulse control and impulse-ridden behaviors—self-destructive, alcoholic, promiscuous, and assaultive) than had been initially forecast. The patient was so fearful of the uncovering analytic process and the submissive meanings of the analytic couch that he insisted on sitting up for the whole stretch from hours 10 to 46. He was even afraid to give The Menninger Foundation his new local address. At the same time, the analyst (a psychoanalytic candidate) was very concerned to keep this case as properly analytic as possible.

From the beginning, it was also clear that the patient was in treatment under duress, forced to it by his understanding that his return to medical school was contingent upon the satisfactory resolution of his problems in the treatment. He saw himself in the treatment as a "punishment." He brought an expectation that his analyst could be gotten to side with him in his struggle against the denying school authorities. At other times, he was very suspicious that the analyst was only the extended punishing arm of the school. For his part, the analyst (in the earlier phases) was "working hard at trying to keep the patient alive and in treatment" — for example, helping him curb his proneness to respond to intrapsychic pressures with sprees of heavy drinking, followed by reckless, high-speed drunken driving. It was the patient's compulsive nature and drive to finish what he started that did keep him coming to the analysis, even though he often saw it as of little use to him — indeed, something that at times actually complicated his life and increased his suffering.

The patient's life over the course of treatment nonetheless underwent progressive steps of achievement and consolidation. He secured a job as an aide at the VA hospital, and when he revealed his medical school experience to the doctors, he elicited much supportive interest from them. When he was given permission to attend grand rounds, he was elated and yet guilty over the undeserved "advancement." Through an act of blatant insubordination, he got into a fight with the chief nurse and was fired. He became panicky, tried to get the job back, and in his analysis revealed an angry, paranoid misinterpretation of what had happened. The patient then secured a comparable job at the state hospital. Here he managed to stay on the safe side of overt confrontation and punishment. On one occasion a patient reported to the nurse that she had been raped, and the patient was worried that he might be accused. A number of times he pre-empted the doctor's role, reinserting fallen-out catheters and replacing infiltrated intravenous infusions, and was proud and guilty that in these instances he was a "doctor," not just an aide. Rocky though it was, this job went progressively better over time. Over this span, the patient had gotten back together with his second girlfriend, who, it turned out, had been willing to wait through his many vicissitudes. The patient experienced setting the wedding date as a rebellious act for which he feared punishment. When he married, the patient fortified himself with some "magic" — a small amount of barbiturate. But following the marriage, the patient's excess drinking and reckless driving finally dwindled away, and the marriage seemed to settle into a stable arrangement.

The patient now began to think about a return to medical school. At first he saw the analyst as standing in his way; he had the paranoid suspicion that the analyst had intervened to instigate the rejection of the patient's application for an externship experience at a local hospital. When the analyst (after not quite 3 years of analysis) wrote a letter to the medical school indicating the patient's present status, the patient was readmitted as a third-year student for that fall. The patient saw this as surpassing his analyst and as indicating his readiness to dispense with him. When he returned to medical school (75 miles away), the treatment frequency dropped to once weekly, which was held to for the subsequent 1½ years until termination. The patient worked very hard, was at the head of his class, and yet worried excessively about failing every examination. On a day that was almost exactly the fourth anniversary of the fugue state that had led to his initial suspension, he had an accident with his brand-new car, in which he rounded a blind corner and was hit by another car. His car was demolished, the patient himself miraculously escaping unscathed. He was terribly shaken by this continuing evidence of his "self-destructiveness."

Within the analysis, the patient presented his core Oedipal difficulties along two thematic dimensions. The first was the theme of hostile competition with the beloved father, against which he needed to defend—at first mostly with passivity, later with self-destructive and self-punitive acting out. The other was the theme of temptation toward, and fear of, passive submission to the father, which in turn was defended against by a renewal of competitive feelings and hostile acting out. These defensive acting-out behaviors (fighting, drinking, promiscuity) served as combined masculine assertions and self-destructive punishments ("safety valves"). As the patient oscillated in his outside life, and in his presentation of it within the treatment, between his "constructive and destructive" behaviors, the patient was alternatively a helpless little boy and a turbulent angry one. At times he experienced his alternating impulses—to outdo the father competitively, and to depend on him and be protected by him—projectively as what others (his family, his analyst, etc.) expected of him, and he then had to fight against this.

The whole course of the analysis consisted in the repetitive reworking of these themes—the positive and the negative Oedipal position in regard to the father—in the context of both the patient's current and past life situations. Every progressive step in life reactivated this ambivalent competitive struggle. The dissociative states that had brought the patient to treatment were now understood in these terms. The patient had been commended for his outstanding medical school work by the much-admired dean, and had begun to feel that his good work had emerged from his competitive wish to destroy the dean by outdoing him. He had become very frightened and had thought of giving up all competition, but then "the other students would think I'm his pet (i.e., his woman)." He had panicked at this thought, gotten drunk, and done the pelvic examinations. His fantasy during these examinations had been that he was showing the dean that he (the patient) was king, and that all the women around there were his. The method chosen to demonstrate his prowess had led to his being dropped from school (from further competition).

Within the transference the same themes were, of course, enacted, but more indirectly. The patient wished to depend on the analyst and be told what to do, but at the same time he was terrified of his submissive wishes and so had to sit up over the beginning stretch; he fought off seeing the transference meanings in this. He tried mostly unsuccessfully, to deflect the hostile competitiveness with the father out of the analysis, as if it existed only with the (other) figures in his outer environment. Only toward the end could the patient sporadically acknowledge the destructive fantasies within the transference. "It's even hard to remember dreams sometimes—if I do remember them, somehow I feel that then *you* won't be able to." He saw himself trying to identify with the analyst (returning to medical school) while avoiding an interest in psychiatry ("If I become like you, I destroy you"). And at the end, the patient put the completion of his treatment (i.e., success) into a farm metaphor: "to be high on the tractor with the woman, and leaving Dad behind." And so, at the very end, the patient expressed—but only by projection—the thought that he was not ready to terminate. He imputed this thought to the analyst and fought against it. Thus the patient ended the analysis with incompletely resolved transferences to the Oedipal parents, namely the positive and negative father-transference elements. And behind these stood the transferences to the pre-Oedipal mother that were linked to the patient's passive–dependent, addictive, and depressive trends. These mother-transferences had not come to the analytic fore at all.

STATUS AT TERMINATION

At the time of actual (uneventful) termination in the last half year of the patient's medical school work, the patient was actively searching for some talisman. He wanted to take a record of the analyst's voice; then, if he subsequently got upset, he could play the recording and "avoid something happening." The analyst felt that he learned from this case "how much change can come in a very seriously disturbed person if one is only patient enough." If this accounting had stopped here at the moment of actual treatment termination, it would stand as a reasonably successful outcome of an analysis of an individual with very refractory character pathology (impulse-ridden, paranoid, and self-destructive). Subsequent events, however, proved dramatically otherwise. The first inkling of things not being as well as they seemed was the problem of arranging the patient's participation in the research Termination Study. The patient felt that it would be "fun" but that "It would tie in with feelings I have that I could go further in treatment." He also said, "Such research is important and it could benefit others. But then there's the practical problem. I don't know when I could do it. Certainly in the next 2 weeks, I'll be so busy. . . . "

As described earlier (see pp. 88–89), this heralded the beginning of a long and unsuccessful effort—pursued by numerous letters and phone calls over an 18-month span—to obtain the patient's involvement in the research Termination Study. At each contact, the patient was willing to come, but had some very plausible reason why he could not just then. On two occasions, as noted, the patient actually canceled interview sessions and motel reservations. Each time the patient would hold out the possibility of future cooperation, but as these contacts went on, he became more lackadaisical about them. He denied actual *reluctance* to participate; he was quite definite, however, that he did not want the research team members to visit him at his convenience in his home town. At each failure of contact, the analyst expressed his surprise to the research group, feeling that the patient yet might come. He thought it might have to do with the patient's fear that if more people knew of his past history, this could work detrimentally to his securing his medical license. The research team saw it as a hostile continuation of an unresolved transference component, a refusal to make a gift of gratitude toward the analyst. At the same time, the patient had left treatment with a sizable unpaid bill. He made a termination agreement to pay this off in regular installments, but over the next 1½ years and a half he only partially lived up to his agreement.

STATUS AT FOLLOW-UP

The follow-up inquiry, 18 months after the last unsuccessful Termination Study contact (now 3 years posttermination), proved equally fruitless. Letters to the patient's last known address and also through the state medical society went unanswered. An inquiry directed to the town in which it was known that the patient had first gone to practice led first to another town, and finally through druggists to the patient's family physician, from whom the patient's follow-up story was put together. The patient was first in a very busy small-group private practice, seeing 75 to 100 patients a day. "All you could do was say 'how do you do' to them, and that was certainly not a right way to practice." To keep up with his rival for the favor of the chief of the practice group, the patient was soon taking amphetamines by day and barbiturates by night. The patient finally escaped from this pressure into another situation—a solo practice in a small town where the townspeople had built and equipped an office in order to entice a practitioner to their community. Here, too, however, there were the responsibilities and stresses of a very busy practice, and soon the patient was again heavily on drugs, his speech at times almost incoherent and his dress disheveled.

The patient's marriage was by now going badly. His wife at times had difficulty locating him; he might be frantically seeing one patient after another, or might be out at night, driving dangerously on the highway. On one occasion when he was racing home to his parents after an argument with his father, his frightened wife called the highway patrol, who stopped the wildly driving patient and held him in jail overnight. By this time the town was fed up and was pressuring the patient to withdraw from the practice. The probate judge wanted to remand him to the state hospital, at which point the family physician intervened; he arranged for the patient's retirement from practice because of "nervous exhaustion" and for his return to his parents' farm.

At this point of follow-up contact with the family physician, the patient had been living and working on the farm for 8 months, and was no longer on drugs or alcohol. He and the parents were reconciled, and they seemed happy to be able to provide this "haven" for him. The patient and his wife were separated, however, and their relationship was touch and go. She was living with her parents in her home town, working. Once, after a family argument there, the patient had assaulted her father. Nonetheless, the patient and his wife were still talking of getting back together, not of divorce. The main stabilizing relationship was with the family doctor. This man had been the patient's avowed ideal all his life, had originally strongly encouraged him to go into medicine, and had recommended him for medical school. "The boy always wanted to be a doctor and still wants to be." He felt that the patient was a "brilliant boy" but that he was suffering with an "anxiety neurosis" and was always unjustifiably complaining about how people were against him. Because of the amount of family alcoholism, the doctor had always warned the patient about drinking and about his driving.

The doctor saw the patient's difficulties as stemming from overly high standards of duty and conscience that he couldn't live up to. This was what he felt brought out the patient's projective streak: "With everybody, with his practice, with his wife, it's always everyone else who is wrong and causes the trouble—it's his persecution complex." It was the growing drug taking that had ultimately forced the doctor's intervention. He told the patient that "pills are for patients. If you have to take them yourself, you have no business being in practice." During this current period, the doctor and the patient were spending a good deal of time together chatting informally; the doctor felt that they had such a good relationship that the patient would no doubt consult with him prior to making any major decision about his future. The doctor indicated that the patient had not felt at all helped by his "1600" hours of treatment at The Menninger Foundation (actually it was 672). The doctor tried to make referrals to psychiatrists elsewhere, but the patient rejected all such efforts. The doctor also broached the idea of the patient getting training in a less emotionally demanding facet of medicine, like X-ray or pathology, but the patient violently rejected this idea as well; he insisted that when he worked he wanted to work directly with people. His doctor clearly saw himself as the patient's protector. He wanted him in some way to be able to return to medicine, and was clearly reluctant to press any action (especially in regard to further psychiatric treatment) that might jeopardize the patient's license and handicap his future right to return to practice.

DECLINE AND DEATH OF THE PATIENT

Under these circumstances, direct follow-up contact with the patient was not pursued, but his unfortunate further history subsequently did become known to us. Some 6 months after the contact with his physician, the patient did try to negotiate a return to a small-town solo practice without discussing this with his physician–mentor. When inquiry was made of the physician, he indicated that the practice under the conditions offered might be too much of a strain for the patient; the offer was withdrawn. At this, the patient angrily turned on his long-time friend for presuming to play God and severed the relationship. Thereafter, the patient was on his own; he again made plans, this time to open a medical practice in his own home town.

Meanwhile, the patient's wife finally moved to divorce him. In a letter to The Menninger Foundation explaining why the patient was not paying off his long-overdue treatment bill, the mother wrote that "out of the blue, with no warning whatsoever, his wife, to whom he had been married 5 years, walked out on him. Unbeknownst to any of us, she had started divorce proceedings. This was a terrific blow." Nonetheless, he opened the medical practice in his home town. According to the mother, "business was going beautifully" until a series of somatic illnesses and hospitalizations supervened, and then the patient suffered a broken jaw (the mother did not mention how). Finally, after running himself into the ground, he ended up in a renowned medical center for "a complete overhaul." He came back from there imbued with "positive thinking," under injunction to rest and go slow; he was now back on the farm, but medicine was still "his love and life." According to the mother, he had "taken all this adversity in stride."

According to the family physician and old friend (who was subsequently recontacted), the patient's efforts at practice in his home town were beset by a recurrence of the same turmoils and irresponsible behaviors. He had constant troubles with the townspeople, his patients, his fellow physicians, and the police. He got into medical difficulties because of bad professional judgments, and had to be rescued from these by other physicians. He was not accepted at the county medical society or the staff of the local hospital—he would have to prove himself first. (For this, he turned more angrily on his former sponsor.) He threatened various lawsuits. He was back on drugs (though not alcohol), and was again driving wildly and dangerously. Only his mother would work as his office nurse. He finally collapsed completely with a variety of self-made ominous somatic diagnoses. The patient's physician–mentor now thought of him as clearly schizophrenic. He felt that all the patient's hostility and persecutory fear had come to focus on him. He averred that the patient was a danger to the medical profession and to patients, but that no one wanted to move to revoke his license. He came from a respected family, and no one wanted to hurt them. The doctors were content to make good his mistakes, and everyone was relieved when he gave up his efforts at practice.

The final event took place 7 years after treatment termination, 4 years after the Follow-Up Study. The patient went out for a drive one evening. It was not unusual for him to "prowl about at night," so no one was alarmed when he did not return. He had not been obviously depressed. When he was found the next day, his car was parked off the road; the windows were closed, the engine was still idling, and the patient was dead, slumped over the wheel. There was no evidence of foul play. The coroner accepted the family's statement that the patient had been ill with heart disease, and called it a death from coronary thrombosis. The patient was 40 years old.

COMMENTS

Clearly, the patient's total collapse and fatal course after his treatment and after his medical school graduation, as he undertook the responsibilities of medical practice, of marriage, and of citizenship, can be conceptualized in terms akin to the two other perspectives discussed in this chapter—as a species of "success neurosis" (or, better, "success psychosis"), or as a self-destructively driven "negative posttherapeutic reaction." The fact that this trend was not clearly evident during the psychoanalytic treatment course, and that the commanding psychological forces that powered this downward drive never came to full psychoanalytic confrontation, had many determinants. These included the nature and severity of the patient's psychopathology; his countertherapeutic orientation; the forced motivation and treatment under duress; and the lack, not only of insight, but of psychological articulateness and willingness as well. Here I want especially to highlight the role of what I have called the "professional countertransferences" that are often evoked by patients fearing, claiming, and striving for their status and prerogatives as physicians and health professionals, and the special niches and considerations that these countertransferences enable them to carve out.

Such evoked responses operated more subtly with the analyst, and more blatantly (but under more handicapping circumstances in reality) with the physician–mentor in the patient's posttreatment (and also in his pretreatment) life. Within the analysis, this could have been a potent influence in the artificial propping up of the patient to a socially expected level of performance and achievement, to the extent that both analyst and patient ended the treatment reasonably contented—the analyst quite satisfied, the patient more cautious, more aware of continuing vulnerability and danger. Within the posttreatment life, the physician–mentor quite deliberately threw the weight of his influence (while it lasted) on the side of maintaining the patient's self-esteem and capacity (and livelihood) as a physician, rather than toward convincing him that—for his own sake—his needs as a patient should be made paramount. It seems unnecessary to add that this case history makes a powerfully convincing argument for the absolutely crucial role of extended follow-up observation in assessing the course and the outcome, and the basis of the course and the outcome, in psychotherapy and psychoanalysis.

VI

The Treatment Course

*The Processes of
Expressive–Supportive Psychotherapy*

The Expressive Psychotherapeutic Mode

EXPRESSIVE VERSUS SUPPORTIVE: DICHOTOMY OR CONTINUUM?

Psychotherapy conceptualized within the framework of the psychoanalytic theory of mental functioning—usually called "psychoanalytically oriented" or "psycho-dynamic" psychotherapy—has been traditionally divided into the expressive psy-chotherapeutic mode (also called "uncovering" or "insight-aiming" psychotherapy) and the supportive psychotherapeutic mode (also called "suppressive" or "ego-strengthening" psychotherapy). The traditional distinction has been between the therapy (called "expressive") that is basically geared toward *analyzing* defenses and resistances in order to uncover conflict (i.e., to make unconscious conflict conscious, as a step toward an eventual reintegration)—albeit, in distinction from psychoanalysis proper, within limited and prescribed sectors of personality func-tioning—and the therapy (called "supportive") that is basically geared toward *strengthening* defenses and resistances in order to make the repression of conflict more effective (i.e., to reduce the inner conflict pressures that have led to the erup-tion of symptoms and behavior disturbances). Our own original PRP concep-tualizations of this distinction in psychotherapeutic approaches as providing the basis for our treatment planning and prognostication, as well as the framework within which the subsequent treatment course and outcome would then be assessed, were set forth in our initial PRP publication (Wallerstein & Robbins, 1956, pp. 252–257). A much more detailed spelling out of these counterposed approaches along all the relevant dimensions of the psychotherapeutic process has been of-fered in Section III (pp. 93–302) of Paul Dewald's *Psychotherapy: A Dynamic Ap-proach* (1964).

In the introduction to his book, Dewald says of his approach: "In Section III on psychotherapy, the material is deliberately presented in the form of a somewhat artificial dichotomy of supportive versus insight-directed psychotherapy. This is being done for pedagogic reasons, with full recognition that in the usual clinical situation such sharp dichotomies do not always exist or persist" (p. xvii). Schlesin-ger (1969) has made this last point—of the "artificial" nature of such a pedagogical-ly justifiable dichotomy between the expressive and supportive modes—even more sharply. His thesis is that these are ways of thinking (and of interacting) that are necessarily intermingled. After all, all therapy is and must be fully "supportive" in order to be at all viable, and perhaps no therapy is more fully supportive than

373

psychoanalysis—the quintessentially expressive and uncovering mode—in its commitment to take all the time that is needed (possibly 1000 hours or more) for two people to focus together on the psychological conflicts of the one, to try to understand these as comprehensively as two individuals can, and to work toward their optimal amelioration and resolution as the overriding shared task. The important issue in a therapy characterized as "supportive" is really the question of *what* in the patient needs support, and Schlesinger (1969, p. 272) elegantly lists the various psychological attributes or areas of mental functioning that might need to be supported at different times. Schlesinger's next question, "Support *how?*", enters into the various mechanisms of supportive psychotherapy, which are more fully delineated in this section of this book. Lastly, Schlesinger raises the question of "Support *when?*" or "When is support *un*necessary? After support, *then what?*" (p. 273).

On the other hand, all therapy worthy of the name is also "expressive," for "A psychotherapy in which the patient is not helped to express something of the depth of himself would be quite unthinkable" (Schlesinger, 1969, p. 274). And further, "when we consider that a psychotherapist may help a patient *suppress* something by encouraging the *expression* of something else, the clarity of the logical distinction is lost" (p. 274). This leads to Schlesinger's overall categorization of these notions of "supportive" and "expressive" as defining dimensions of psychotherapy, as "widely-spaced categories" (p. 269) that "have come to be misapplied and as used, no longer capture with any precision the distinctions they were coined to preserve" (p. 270).

The degree to which, out of the crucible of the PRP experience itself, we have come to agree with Schlesinger's conceptual stance is presented in detail in the final section of this book (see Chapter 37, "The Expressive–Supportive Dichotomy Reconsidered"). At this point, given the various caveats properly adduced by Schlesinger and Dewald, I nonetheless proceed on the heuristic and pedagogically useful basis stated by Dewald: that, conceptually at least, "expressive" and "supportive" are distinctions that help us conceptualize the different possibilities in the psychotherapeutic endeavor. As starting points, at least, they are adhered to in the descriptions of the various psychotherapeutic courses in this section of this book. Of course, we ourselves have recognized the artificiality of a hard and fast distinction from the start—enough to have planned in terms of "purely" expressive psychotherapy for very few of the patients, in terms of "purely" supportive psychotherapy for equally few, and in terms of some admixture of expressive and supportive approaches for the great majority recommended for psychotherapy.

I must add one last caveat here: In accord with the distinction first made in PRP by Benjamin (see pp. 55–56) between a theory of psychoanalytic therapy (which this book is about) and a psychoanalytic theory of therapy, of *all* therapy, whether conceptualized by its proponents within a psychoanalytic framework or not (a much wider task, which this book is not about), I am here considering only psychotherapy (whether expressive, supportive, or some admixture of the two) conceived and carried out within the framework of psychoanalytic theoretical understanding, and within a psychoanalytically guided clinical institution.

In this chapter, then, I discuss those therapies intended to be only or overwhelmingly expressive in intent and execution. There were a few such. The Bitter Spinster was a patient who, in fact, was thought to be well suited for psychoanalysis; however, because this treatment was precluded (at that time, anyway) by lack of the requisite financial resources, she was recommended for an expressive psychotherapy "as close to analysis as can be gotten on a twice-a-week basis." Her treatment course has already been presented (see Section V, Chapter 18, pp. 349–353). As noted there, her 8-year-long psychotherapy bogged down into a developing paranoid psychotic transference reaction; the unsuccessful treatment was only pried loose from a tenacious transference dependency and brought to an end through the manipulative device of referring the patient to a psychiatric colleague for a series of six stock-taking sessions.

Two other patients whose treatment plans and courses were intended to be within a primarily expressive framework were the Involutional Woman and the Bohemian Musician, the first of whom had an expectedly very good outcome, and the second an unexpectedly good outcome.

THERAPY OF THE INVOLUTIONAL WOMAN

Background and Prognosis

The Involutional Woman was the oldest patient in our sample (age 50); she came to psychiatric hospitalization because of a severe, acute involutional depression. The patient was the only child of a self-taught lawyer who was a very successful practitioner. As a child she had been an excellent scholar, making her intellectual parents very proud of her. At the same time, they had been very strict in their upbringing; the mother had taught the patient in early childhood to be afraid of the dark and of storms and lightning, and the patient carried these fears all her life. When she grew up, she decided on a university education in law and was proud that she was the only woman in her law school class.

The patient met her husband in law school; they were engaged a month after their first date and were married 3 years later. The patient had worked after graduation for a year in her father's law office, but, once married, she dropped her own career completely. The husband said that he doubted that she would ever have gone into law, except that her father expected her to do so. There was always a constant, barely suppressed competitive theme in the relationship with the husband. They were each, in successive years, valedictorian of their respective law school classes. The patient was a good tennis player and consistently beat her husband; they also actively played bridge together. The patient maintained that her husband was the "boss" in the family, and yet she indicated that she could not abide his monotone way of singing and would not let him participate in his church choir, which he enjoyed. When the patient became responsible for the church choir, the husband became a member of the lay board; when she was an active leader in the association of university women, he became national president of his college fraternity. They were both always busy on parallel tracks.

During her years away at college, the patient started the habit of writing to her parents each day, because "this is the least I could do." She continued this pattern after her marriage and until the parents' deaths. On weekends the patient sent her daily letters special delivery. If on any day a letter failed to arrive, the parents would call long distance to find out what was wrong. The patient had always been considered frail, and as an adult she had a whole series of fairly major illnesses requiring frequent medical attention. During the early years of her marriage, when the patient's husband was not making much money, her parents financed the medical bills. Because of her illnesses, the patient always had household help, and her husband helped in the direct care of the two children. Everyone in the family was conditioned to the patient's being sick so much, and when she was not sick, she was tired. She seemed not to enjoy the care of the home, and her daughter said that the patient would have been "happier as a man." The patient herself felt women to be "two-faced"; she much preferred men, who were "practical-minded." With her children, she took the most interest in their intellectual development.

After the patient's mother died, some 11 years before the patient's turn to treatment, the father "seemed lost." During the last 2 years of the father's life (when he was gravely ill), the patient commuted constantly between her home and her father's (300 miles away) to help care for him. She spent most of her weekends there, leaving her college-student daughter to run her home. During all this time the father was quarrelsome and depressed, and "moaned piteously" that his daughter did not love him enough and was not doing enough for him. When the father finally died, the patient, exhausted with caring for him, again contracted pneumonia and was in the hospital. She was upset that she could not attend the funeral and "get to finish the job."

Approximately 2 years before coming to hospitalization at The Menninger Foundation, the patient suffered the onset of her menopause, and with it a severe, acute rheumatoid arthritis, controlled by corticosteroids. During this same period the patient's husband was working very hard, was found to be suffering with hypertension, and became depressed enough to be hospitalized for a week. The patient herself was suffering with intense headaches (like her husband), and was hospitalized for a workup for a brain tumor, for which no evidence was found. As the time approached for the patient's son to leave home for college, she became openly anxious and depressed. There had been an earlier depressive reaction when the daughter had left home to be married. But the son had always been more important to her, ever since he was the one who had been kept in the parental bedroom as a child. With this depression, the patient was hospitalized and treated with subcoma insulin. When this did not help, and the patient talked increasingly of suicide, she was again hospitalized, with a course of ECT this time, and was then referred to The Menninger Hospital.

The patient's own view of her illness was that she had always been an extremely active woman and that part of her depression was that she had not had enough to do. She vigorously denied ever having angry feelings, and refused to see that there might be sources of conflict or tension in her marriage or in her relationship with her parents. She was dissatisfied with being "just a housewife" and felt that in many ways she had not put her mind to its best use. A central difficulty was that she no longer felt that she knew what she would like to get out of her life. She was perfectionistic, and her life was full of "oughts."

The patient was clearly suffering from an involutional depression, set (typically) into a lifelong inhibited and compulsive personality structure. The treatment recommended was an expressive psychotherapy combined with half-time day hospital participation and half-time school attendance, including auditing law school classes and learning typing and stenography. This was envisaged as a twofold treatment plan: (1) to reinstitute working compulsive defenses by way of reopening a legal or paralegal work career, and (2) to help the patient in the formal psychotherapy to deal with her aggressions—the competitiveness and the hostilities—that were always crowding consciousness. She needed to express and work out her resentments over the menopause, the son's going out of her life, and the denied conflicts with the husband. If this could be accomplished, then many of the patient's symptomatic compromise positions (including perhaps even her recurrent somatic illnesses) could be attenuated, if not altogether relieved. That is, the major psychological intervention would be directed to the resolution of the patient's hostilities and their reflection in her current interpersonal relationships. In view of her age and her lifelong character rigidity, her deeply set problems in regard to her intense dependency needs and her conflicted femininity would not be dealt with.

Course of the Therapy

At the time of "cutoff" Termination Study, the patient had been in psychotherapy for 6 years (362 hours); she was now with a second therapist, a former Menninger Foundation staff member in private practice in her home community, to whom she had transferred when her first therapist left Topeka 3½ years after her treatment start. Her life over the 6 years was a progressively unfolding one. She left the day hospital, completed her school work, and sought full-time employment. Her husband did not wish to have her in his office, saying, "It wouldn't work out"; other attorneys were unwilling to hire her, since she might be a "spy" in their office for her husband, himself a very prominent attorney. So she secured a full-time position as administrative assistant to the executive of a nationwide women's organization. She maintained this job until increasing competitive rivalry with her boss, an older woman jealous of the patient's competence, began to make her office life increasingly unpleasant. The patient then resigned (shortly before the Termination Study) and decided not to seek another job, stating that her advancing arthritic condition rendered this unrealistic.

Meanwhile, the patient's relationship with her daughter, always strained, became more tolerable as the therapist helped her to work out the frictions over such issues as the daughter's expectation that the patient babysit for her as needed. She also came to accept more gracefully her son's being away at college, and even the subsequent shock of his becoming engaged. With her husband, the patient was becoming concomitantly more openly aware of her long-time anger and jealousy directed at his professional and organizational successes and leadership. Her hypertension (like her husband's) was under good control, her arthritis less so; both were under the constant care of her devoted internist. Through all this time, there were recurrent periods of depression and of need for support. In such periods during her work with the second therapist, she distributed her troubles among three "therapists," to each of whom she addressed but a partial accounting: psychosomatic problems to her internist, moral problems to her minister, and emotional problems to the psychotherapist.

Within the psychotherapy, the main themes were the patient's daily life and current problems, with only occasional "flashbacks" to her past. The main focus was on the relationship with the husband and the patient's gradually growing awareness of her competitive rivalry and envy, all heretofore strongly suppressed "by sheer willpower." The hostility centered around the husband's being a man, a professional man, and a successful man. The patient felt only envy and no pride in his accomplishments. She complained in turn that he was "domineering, opinionated, overbearing, assertive, loud." At the same time, "He is all I wanted to be," and she envied his poise, his good memory, his prestige. She herself was in the degraded "satellite role" of a housewife; she felt constantly torn by her own struggle over being a housewife or a career woman, "doing a man's job." And yet, she said, "How can you get mad at a guy who is wonderful to you?", and she came also to the point of saying, "He is a remarkable man; I came close to being proud of him rather than competing with him." By the end of treatment, the patient had come only to partial resolutions of her struggles with her resentment and her envy.

These same themes reverberated in other life arenas. Within her marital relationship, the patient tolerated sexuality; she dreaded it (and she felt frigid), but the husband wanted it, and she resented this. By the end of treatment, the patient was no longer using an aggressive withholding of sexual relations as a weapon to express the fluctuations in her feelings toward her husband. Similar developments took place in the difficult competitive relationship with her administrative superior on the job; the effort to work out a tolerable *modus vivendi* with her daughter; and, even more, the marriage and thus the final loss of the son (the latter was seen as a repetition of the loss of the father to whom she was so ambivalently attached). In all these areas, she became more aware of her resentments (and achieved some mitigation of them), but at the same time she continued with the firm repression of the countervailing libidinal and dependent ties that were also powering those same relationships.

Within the transference, the relationship had three discernible strands: (1) the ongoing hostile competition with the therapist as the superior male (but how could she be angry at him since he was "such a gentle guy"); (2) the insistent (and successful) search for a dependent relationship to the powerful but benign father (in the permissiveness of each therapist, in their helping the patient to "unload" her pent-up angers and her resentments over her unfair fate in life, and in their encouragements to return to her studies, to turn to full-time employment, etc.); and (3) each therapist as the projected repository of the patient's own very severe conscience pressures (e.g., in the patient's fears of discussing her intimate sexual feelings; in her distrustful competitiveness with the first therapist in having to "check up" on his perspectives with her hospital doctor; or, comparably, with her second therapist, in having to dilute her relationship by employing the minister and the internist as supporting therapeutic figures as well). None of these father-transference strands were significantly worked through in any way. With the first therapist, the transference was split, and all the negative elements were shunted directly onto the relationship with the husband. With the second therapist, the resentful components were softened by dilution across her three helpers, thus enabling the patient to keep each relationship free of undue competitiveness. Each therapist thus differently avoided the negative components and sought to strengthen the positive dependency gratifications in relation to himself as the good father.

In both cases, their patience, their persistence, and their friendliness helped. Both were described as "wonderful guys," equally beneficial to her. Each left the transference uninterpreted.

Status at Follow-Up

At the time of Follow-Up Study some 2 years later, it turned out (to the researchers' surprise) that the patient had indeed terminated her therapy during the interim, and expressed herself as being better off in every way (except for her progressive arthritic disability). Her mood oscillated between feeling bored (because of her physical limitations) and feeling that the days just weren't long enough to do all the things she wanted to do—"Now this is a change." Actually, she kept involved in a great variety of ways in various volunteer and organizational activities, though in terms of social life, she described herself as "kind of a loner." Besides, her husband was usually too tired and too busy himself with his own active professional and organizational life.

The patient felt that her one difficulty was the continuing arthritis, which seemed to be steadily worsening. The internist whom the patient saw constantly was an enthusiastic medicine giver and trier of new approaches; the patient was in a ceaseless, changing round of new drugs offered with persistent enthusiasm, and often procured for her prior to their official marketing. The patient was wryly proud of her great capacity to absorb medications: "Doctor, you can see that I'm a customer who has to have heavy doses of medicine and it doesn't affect me." She was proud that she pushed herself and stubbornly fought the inroads of the arthritis.

The patient's major life relationship, that with her husband, she felt to be considerably improved—a consequence, she felt, both of her treatment and of the work the therapist had done concomitantly with the husband: "He talked tough with him. You see, my husband needed to change a bit, too." The problems between them seemed to be mainly in the areas of expressing differing opinions and strong feelings. "We're both very strong personalities, with strong opinions. . . . But now we get along reasonably well. *He* changed. He decided to accept some of my opinions, which he had not been doing. . . . I didn't used to be able to express my angry feelings and now I can. We had our first knock-down drag-out fight right here on the grounds. We had never had a fight in all our married life, which of course was wrong. . . . Now in a difference of opinion I can express my viewpoint more freely and he accords me the right. But he also feels free to disregard me and do it his way. But sometimes I can finagle around. That's a female, I guess." In this tactic, the patient was encouraged by her therapist, whom she quoted as saying, "If you can't get around that man, one way or another, I'm ashamed of you." Overall, the patient seemed involved in a deliberate and successful effort to foster a more compatible relationship with her husband—one in which she could distinguish more realistically when it was appropriate for her to recognize the primacy of his wishes, and when she could stand her own ground, even to the point of expressing disagreement or anger.

Concomitantly, there was a mildly improved and relaxed sexual adjustment, though the husband was still distastefully described as sexually impatient: "I'm getting to be an old man; I can't wait.' . . . This is his problem." Toward her children and their absence, the patient professed herself more reconciled. Relations, especially with the daughter and son-in-law, were at times complicated and strained, but overall the patient felt that she had succeeded in establishing more stable and appropriate relationships with both her children. And a major area of the patient's ongoing activity was the active management of her own financial affairs. She kept her own money (basically her inheritance) in a separate account from her husband's, and it actually generated more income than her husband's law practice did. This she managed through the stock market, other investments, real estate speculation, and the like—all pursued knowledgeably, and often proudly contrary to her broker's advice.

About her psychotherapy, the patient expressed herself in glowingly positive terms. For a considerable while, as noted, she had seen her minister concomitantly with the psychiatrist, but she claimed that this had caused no confusion: "They supplemented each other. There's no question about it." She had continued longer with the psychiatrist, and when she stopped he had said, "I keep my telephone bill paid, and if you need help, I'm on the other end of the telephone." She was gratified that she had been treated by one of the country's great psychiatrists. She said, "You are supposed to hate your psychiatrist, but I never did. I'd get angry with them but they were awfully wonderful. . . . I worked hard. We'd peel off layer after layer. The first psychiatrist dug into the childhood angles and the sexual angles. The second psychiatrist was a more down-to-earth kind of person. He led me to face reality and to adjust to it." When the patient terminated, her main reaction was in the form of hypochondriacal and exacerbated arthritic complaints, not depression, and the positive transference attachment was untouched. For the future, the patient expressed herself as guardedly optimistic. She had learned from her psychotherapy to try to live contentedly "one day at a time." Mostly, she didn't want to think about the future, because "there is probably a wheelchair just around the corner." She was very grateful to The Menninger Foundation.

Comments

How can we understand this overall therapeutic course and good outcome? The original therapeutic plan and intent were for a clearly circumscribed, fully expressive psychotherapy, focused around helping the patient work through her tremendous throttled aggressions, especially as these were expressed in her current interpersonal relationships (centrally, that with the husband). In view of her lifetime character rigidity and her involutional position, any effort to work with the deep-seated problems in the areas of the patient's femininity and dependency conflicts was explicitly eschewed. Concomitant active work in regard to school and career planning was intended to serve meanwhile to reinstate compulsive working defenses.

The expressive therapeutic intent, as it turned out, was only very partly realized. Neither therapist really got very much below the surface of the feelings of this woman, who was always inhibited and polite but fiercely angry and resentful underneath; certainly there was no meaningful working out of any linkage of current angers and resentments to earlier attachments and formative experiences, and no emergence of the aggressive impulses into the transference, which was always maintained benevolently positive and uninterpreted. In fact, it was just this—the maintaining of an avowedly supportive, benevolent, dependent, and encouraging relationship, in which each therapist (especially the second) was very self-consciously protective of the patient's narcissism, guarding her against transference discomforts and against any real awareness of her insecurities—that became one of the two main vehicles of the achieved degree of improvement. (The other was the degree of expressive work that *was* done with the patient's current angers and resentments, bringing her, then, to some psychological accommodation to these feelings.) Within this consolidated transference attachment, this inhibited patient could become more safely assertive in her outside life with her husband; she could also, in part, shift the transference and the transference continuity onto the benevolent and enthusiastic internist, whom she continued to see regularly and indefinitely.[1] And, concomitantly, the arthritis itself could serve to take the heat off the patient's psyche—she was now resigned to (and even drew some satisfaction from) what she saw as her valiant struggle against the inroads of progressive arthritic disability. On these several combined bases, the patient could give up her direct tie to the therapist and could avoid directly becoming a "therapeutic lifer" (which at the time of "cutoff" Termination Study had been anticipated).

In the original Case Study write-up of this patient, these converging mutative mechanisms were described as follows (I paraphrase here):

> (1) Circumscribed as it was, the 6 years of therapy, talking about her difficulties and the discerned or imputed causes of them, was a definite, albeit piecemeal expression of troubling (aggressive–hostile) impulse and affect in this heretofore very rigidly inhibited and guilt-ridden woman. At its most unexpressive, the therapy could not help but be expressive in its cumulative impact, of just the range of her competitive, envious, and aggressive feelings. (2) Within the safety of the therapeutic situation and the benevolent encouragement of the therapist(s), the patient could change from her compliant and suppressed state to the trying out of a more assertive state of being in her life—on the basis of a new, uninterpreted compliance with the therapeutic expectation (she could be more assertive in life, as a new submission within the transference—moving the massive inhibition from her life where it caused trouble, to the therapy where it became converted into a mechanism of cure). (3) On this basis, then, there was a transference cure, of doing things differently "out there," for the (covert) trade-off "in here." (4) There was a shift, then, from a despairing sense of *unfulfilled* (oral and narcissistic) needs, not to any resolution of the problems of demandingness and felt needs, but to a sense of now, at last, (therapeutically) *fulfilled* needs.

And how would this all last? Fortunately, it might turn out that the internist would now carry (covertly) the supportive psychotherapeutic function, and that the arthritis would continue to stand in for the psychic difficulties, enabling the patient to function manifestly better on the psychological level and without manifest reliance on formal psychotherapy. Actually, this was what happened. The patient lived another 13 years, 15 years following the treatment termination. She

---

1. Two specific mechanisms were at work here—the "displacement of the neurosis into the transference," so that the patient could behave more appropriately in her outside life with the husband, and the "transfer of the transference" onto the internist—that are discussed in detail in the next chapter.

had no further psychotherapy and experienced no need for any. She was, however, progressively incapacitated by her arthritic invalidism, and finally had to enter a nursing home, where she died at age 72.

THERAPY OF THE BOHEMIAN MUSICIAN

Background and Prognosis

The operative mechanisms in the Bohemian Musician's expressive psychotherapy were, in some ways, altogether different. She was the woman with the strange marital situation already described (see pp. 141, 173). The patient saw herself as an arty and unconventional woman, married to a well-to-do, passive, and devoted businessman, who had none of the intellectual and artistic interests that she had cultivated. In her marriage she suffered with endless somatic and hypochondriacal ailments, and was usually tired, weak, and lying abed for long periods. She consulted a wide array of physicians and was always on a variety of medications. She had two full-time servants and spent most of her time reading and listening to music; her own work at the piano was mostly quite desultory.

After some 8 years of marriage, the patient decided quite abruptly, and surprisingly to the husband, to repair the sagging marriage by adopting a child. The husband went along with this desire in order to please her. Yet, from the very start, the patient felt totally incapable of child care and unwilling to engage in it. The husband had to take the baby from the nurse's arms and carry him home. At the first soiled diaper, the patient seemed astonished that such things occurred; the husband had to change it. The husband felt that his wife was afraid of the child, and he soon reconciled himself to taking over a large part of the nursing and rearing functions. The patient never did more than guiltily run through the motions of child raising. "I have no real wish for children. They bore me." The husband dated the subsequent total deterioration of the marriage to this ill-starred adoption.

Shortly after the adoption, the patient was able to pressure her husband into a move to a major metropolitan center—ostensibly so that he could be in business away from his father, but mostly so that she could better pursue her desired cultural, intellectual activities. In the big city, as noted (see p. 141), they led almost separate lives. The patient taught music and frequented the theatre, concerts, and restaurants; she abandoned any pretense at running the house. The husband attended conscientiously to his business and also to the housework. Soon the patient became attached to another man, originally introduced by the husband as an intellectual companion for his wife. This relationship rapidly became a love affair; the husband kept himself uninformed about this development.

After 5 years in the big city, the husband decided to return to his home town, referred to derisively by the patient as the "home in a cornfield." The husband, always a relatively passive man, acquiesced in the patient's decision to stay on in the city, separated from him. There the patient supported herself rather well (through her music lessons), and lived with her adopted son and her lover. This equilibrium came apart, however, in another 5 years, when the husband—finally fed up with the separate living—put ultimatum-like pressure on the patient to return home or be divorced. When she could not decide upon marrying her lover, she returned home; with this collapse of the whole structure of her secondary gains, the patient's precipitous symptomatic decline set in. Her wildly disorganized state, with panics, agitated depressive outbursts, and disturbed histrionic behaviors, has already been described (see pp. 124, 145, 150). What finally brought her to psychiatric hospitalization was the episode of the panicky car flight through a crowded suburban area at 90 miles an hour. When she was stopped by the police, she collapsed and seemed completely out of contact.

This was also the patient who, despite her immediate hospitalization and the immediate institution of a firm and restrictive hospital management regimen, including an active work schedule, went into a deepening depression; she began to talk insistently about her *right* to leave the hospital and commit suicide. She became the one PRP patient who was given a course of electroshock therapy (20 ECT treatments), subsequent to which the depression lifted and effective contact seemed restored. Concomitantly, the patient became a more difficult, angry, and openly complaining individual. In this context, the patient was now recommended for an expressive–supportive psychotherapy, with its explictly supportive features to be carried mainly by the hospitalization and the hospital doctor. Within the expressive psychotherapy, it was felt that the patient could look at the impossibility of her current life dilemma; the marriage that was and wasn't, her two different lives and life styles, and what each meant to her. What stood in the way of living the life with which she felt most comfortable (the "Bohemian" cultural and intellectual life) were the ties to her marriage—both the hidden gratifications involved in it, and the hidden guilt experienced in it. These gratifications and this guilt were linked to older problems of which they were the current edition.

Two differing outcomes of this therapy were envisaged. One was a kind of asexual outcome—a life perhaps with a woman friend, of teaching, of cultural and intellectual activities, of gracious living. It would not be a change of character, but rather a fuller acceptance of the predominant strains within her character, a giving up of the wish to be or to try to appear to be otherwise; the symptoms associated with these conflicts could thereby dwindle away. The other outcome that could be reached would be the achievement of a better sexual adjustment (this had been difficult with both her husband and her lover, in different ways), perhaps in a marriage with someone who shared her interests and with whom gratifications came from the elegance of their living and the cultural orbit in which they moved. Whichever of these outcomes were reached, the patient would be enabled to use her music more successfully as an important conflict-freed activity. And in either case, as the patient worked her way out of the marriage that seemed doomed, it seemed probable that the youngster would probably go to the husband, to the satisfaction of all concerned.

Course of the Therapy

The psychotherapy went on over 3 years (324 hours), with the patient remaining a hospital patient for 7 additional months after the start of her psychotherapy. Throughout, the patient made consistent progress in the effectiveness of her life adjustment—albeit with periods of uneven advance, even temporary setbacks. She began to work first as a volunteer music therapist in an outpatient state institution for the rehabilitation of the handicapped. Her job performance was, from the start, extremely good. According to her supervisor, "She was reliable, never late, never away unless physically ill. She was interested, she didn't mind at all spending additional time on something if it was necessary." Within 2 months she was offered a full-time staff position, and she held this job at the same high level of job performance and job morale until the termination of her psychotherapy. Meanwhile she was living alone in Topeka, separated from both her estranged husband and her (now also estranged) lover. She was bothered by the absence in Topeka of the usual cultural activities of a large city.

Meanwhile the patient's husband, though willing to support her treatment indefinitely, was increasingly unequivocally talking divorce. When he did file for divorce, the patient, with the advice of attorneys, cross-petitioned and asked for substantial alimony. The divorce proceedings dragged on, with many postponements, over 2 years. When the issue was finally settled, the patient received only $200 per month in alimony—far less than she had expected to obtain from her wealthy husband—and she failed to regain custody of her child. The patient was bitter about this last decision. Though she had always had great difficulty in tolerating her son, she fought strangely hard for his custody. She made clumsy efforts to influence the son to make statements that he loved her more than he did his father. When he rebuffed her and indicated his unwillingness to live with her, the patient experienced it as a severe narcissistic blow. It also seemed to the therapist that this fight over custody reflected the patient's spiteful attitudes toward her husband more than affection for the child.

Meanwhile, the patient was involved in another affair, this one with a severely handicapped staff colleague at the workplace. She was thus caught up in a new triangle: The first one had been with her husband and her lover; the second one was with the therapist and the hospital doctor; this one was with the therapist in the treatment and the lover outside the treatment. When the patient terminated her therapy, she encouraged her lover to follow her to a job in her home city, because she wanted his companionship through the new transitional period. She had no intention of marrying him, however, because he was such a *dependent* man (necessarily so, with his handicap), and because in turn an aged mother and an emotionally ill son were totally dependent on *him*. In encouraging him, therefore, she was just as exploitative of men at the end of her treatment as she had been at its beginning.

A series of themes moved through the treatment:

1. The dilemmas of the patient's eternal triangles. Should she try to live a respectable life with her husband, or return to her stimulating paramour and the culture of the big city? Neither seemed possible: She could neither be domestic with her husband nor feel secure and respectable with her lover.

2. The hospital battles—her push to break out versus submitting to the controls, with all of the maintained split transferences, and the hospital doctor absorbing all the negative elements.

3. The divorce proceedings and the custody fights.

4. Her job.

5. Her difficulties in social relationships, especially with attractive, "mascu-

line" women, where the repressed phallic-homosexual and oral-anaclitic tie to her mother threatened to surface.

6. The mother. The patient became somewhat aware of her fierce hostility toward her mother; she recaptured childhood death fantasies, and took note of her anger at the strictures by which she was controlled as a child, and yet her need to impose equally strict schedules upon herself.

7. Her exploitative relationships with men, including, in the newest version, her handicapped lover—a relationship that she withheld from the therapy for a while and then would only talk about most guardedly, since it was "love" and not an aspect of her problems.

Within the transference, the patient brought many expectations. First, there was her desire for the benevolent father, unknown and distant like her own father (who had taken ill with cancer when she was 1 year old and died when she was 3), but a figure who (like her lover) would side with her against her husband or her hospital doctor. Unhappily and contradictorily, however, she also seemed to expect a father who was weak, who could be pushed around just as the stronger women always pushed the weaker men around (the mother did to the father, as the patient did to her lover). Finally, at a deeper level, there was a desire for the controlling mother in a new, more benign version—setting the expectations, enforcing the schedule. Though these were all evident transference models, none of them were systematically worked with or uncovered in their contradictions. Efforts at transference interpretation were strongly rebuffed and readily given up. The therapist stayed then in the position of riding on the uninterpreted positive transference, allowing the negative feelings to be deflected onto the hospital doctor and other outside figures.

Termination

The patient ended her treatment on a sustained note of undiluted positive regard for the therapist: "He treated me as an adult; it increased my self-respect. I liked him. I admired him." Her gratitude toward the therapist spilled over into an overcooperative attitude toward the research project. She offered to "place myself completely at your disposal." For herself at the end, she expressed as her chief wish "A reliable flow, for as long as I live, within reason, of inspiration and creation and expanding satisfaction in accomplishment." Manifestly, she meant her work and her music achievement, and an appreciation of her special talents. More deeply, this could be linked to the sought-for ever-abundant flow of oral supplies and the sexual quest for eternal youth (a concern to her now at age 44). The patient was returning to her home town to live, ostensibly to be near her son.

Status at Follow-Up

The patient remarried a year after treatment termination. She came eagerly for Follow-Up Study, but insisted that it take place over a particular group of days when her new husband would be away on a business trip, since he knew nothing of her previous illness or treatment. She was sensitive about having been a psychiatric patient and was trying to live a normal life. Besides, her husband had had a previous long and unhappy marriage with a seriously ill, manic–depressive wife who had led him a wildly disruptive life. The patient felt that he had had enough illness imposed upon him in his life (how differently she was treating this husband than the first one!). She dissembled to her husband, telling him that she was going to Topeka on a consultation visit to the center for the handicapped where she had previously worked.

The patient had lived a very orderly life during this follow-up period. She had a successful career as a music teacher. She had friends, coworkers, students. She maintained an orderly home and had a new interest in rather elaborate gourmet cooking, a "minor but creative activity." She had met her new husband at a dinner party given by a good friend with matchmaking intent. He was an executive in a major industry, the scion of a distinguished and aristocratic family; he shared her serious interest in music and was himself an amateur musician, as well as intensely involved in camping and outdoor life and in elaborate foreign travel. Before marrying him, however, the patient had come back for a consultation visit with her ex-therapist. She brought along a variety of papers covering her prospective husband's financial condition, income, family responsibilities, and work plans, and after spreading them out all over the therapist's desk, wanted to know whether she was overlooking something. At the same time, she spoke of her fiancé in a genuinely affectionate manner. She also discussed how to sever her ties to her handicapped boyfriend, whom she still saw periodically; following this session, she was able to withdraw from that relationship in a direct, yet kindly way.

Thus fortified, the patient went into the new marriage a few months later. At Follow-Up Study, she talked only enthusiastically about her happy marriage and their shared life. The husband was an ideally sensitive man, interested in cultural and aesthetic things, and also a practical and orderly man. The patient, of course, had "always had all kinds of feelings about the responsibilities associated with marriage, especially the domestic ones, but here it didn't seem to be a problem." She was an adequate housekeeper and a willing cook. The couple had an active social life and many friends; they were involved in many musical activities, went on weekend camping and canoeing trips, and were planning a good deal of foreign travel. The patient stated her sexual adjustment to be most satisfactory. The patient was also (for the first time) getting along well with her now 16-year-old son. At first, the patient had felt that her son worried about her; she noted that when her new husband was courting her, the son had said, "Mom, you ought to get married." And now that she was married, the son joined them on occasional weekend trips. Finally, the relationship with the ex-husband was reasonably amiable. There had never been any need to legally formalize visitation arrangements with the son, since conflicts did not seem to arise.

Clearly, the patient felt all her goals to be achieved. Within a marriage with a husband who seemed very devoted to her, she felt assured of a reliable flow of narcissistic supplies. The patient, in turn, could be more giving and more understanding than had ever before been possible to her; to those who saw her, she appeared more relaxed, rather vivacious, and, for the first time, femininely attractive. (When originally seen, she had been gaunt, graceless, and unfeminine, and had talked in a psychological test response of "technical breasts"). The patient attributed all of this change directly to the psychotherapy, which she felt had made her present very satisfactory marriage and all its gratifying derivatives possible.

She spoke warmly about the therapist as a very kindly, sympathetic man, and indicated her sense of security in knowing that she could come back to him if she ever felt the need. She described too, how she continued to work with the internalized image of the therapist. Whenever she found herself tending to get depressed, she would sit down and try to recall her therapist's voice. She would remember what he said—that depression is a product of anger that is not consciously experienced. She would then try to search out what she was really *angry* about. Usually this search would be successful, and the depressed feeling would recede. Over the 2 years of follow-up, this endeavor became less necessary and less frequent.

Comments

Here was a result even more gratifyingly successful than that with the Involutional Woman, just described. Though again intended as an essentially "expressive" psychotherapy, the actual treatment implemented with the Bohemian Musician turned out to be much more a blended, supportive–expressive effort. In this therapy, the therapist played a variety of roles. He deliberately fostered a sustained, benevolent transference attachment. He was the resurrected benevolent father, a kind counselor, concerned, respectful of her, even if not always effectual (since men were always the weak and unneeded appendages to the strong woman). He was also the new version of the mother, more benevolently guiding the patient to standards of performance and achievement. And in each of these guises he could tolerate the patient's "badnesses"—the fierceness of her hatreds, the hurtfulness of her interpersonal relationships, the insatiable demands for oral-narcissistic fulfillments. And within this context, the patient gradually came to feel that the therapy did not pose a pressure to change herself. She could remain herself, as she was, and give up trying to do what she felt impossible; without having to feel regrets or guilt, she could get out of a very conflict-triggering environment in order to seek one more attuned to her own character and behavior dispositions.

The successful result was partly accomplished through the therapist's assumption of a direct advice-giving role in relation to the myriad of life situations the patient faced—the problem of the divorce, her living arrangements and life style, the pursuit of her music and her other interests, the custody question with her son, the handling of money. At each point, the therapist could give advice skillfully enough that the patient always felt that *she* was working out the solutions. Of her return to music, for example, she said that the therapist was right, that "I would play again when my life was more straightened out, not to worry about it or force myself." And partly, the therapist took advantage of the patient's intellectualizing propensities (and pretensions) by giving her formulas—for example, the statement that depressed feelings represent anger that is out of awareness—that she could then use in the continued service of self-mastery, to unravel and dissipate each new wave of depressive feelings. It was this formula giving that was the major "expressive" component of the psychotherapy, rather than interpretive work, which was in fact consistently underplayed. The therapist, by and large, did not focus interpretively on intrapsychic conflict; he did not relate the present to the unconscious past to any great extent. And he avoided major transference battles by riding throughout the therapy on the basically uninterpreted positive affects; negative transference components were allowed to be drained off onto the hospital doctor. When transference responses were (gingerly) interpreted, the patient would rebuff such efforts.

Thus, with this patient of very weak ego structure, who had been coping unsuccessfully with very intense conflict pressures, the therapist had pursued a course more explicitly supportive than expressive. It was designed, within the framework of a positive transference attachment, deliberately to strengthen the defenses in their struggle with drives (i.e., to support her intellectualizations, her reaction formations, her avoidances, etc.) and to encourage and approve more adaptive behavioral patterns (a return to her interests, namely, music, and renunciation of her anti-interests, namely, her home, husband, and child). That this kind of cure not only maintained itself, but consolidated significantly to considerably higher functional levels by the time of Follow-Up Study, reflected an interacting facilitation between treatment and fortuitous life circumstances. The patient found the latter in the coming into her orbit of the new husband—a man who constituted for her the kind of culturally and intellectually appreciative and emotionally nurturant environment that exactly fulfilled her narcissistic needs, and for which she was now willing (for the first time) to return an emotional *quid pro quo*. In contrast to the first marriage, which had involved too little emotional gratification and too much emotional demand, the new marriage precisely altered this balance. The intervening treatment had made it possible for the patient to get out of the one and to secure the other when it became available. But to make the transition, she had sought and obtained the explicit approval of the therapist. With this, enough of the therapist was now, in her, "transferred" to the husband, so that—at follow-up—the patient could have the true psychological termination of her psychotherapy.

At this point, the originally presenting characterological picture of a narcissistic character neurosis was still evident; the difference was in the progression from a destructively decompensated state to a fully compensated state, balanced in a mutual give-and-take in a marriage with an individual constituted quite similarly to herself. There was at the end, of course, still the cautionary question of just how resilient this new-found level of functioning would be, how well it would hold up against future stressful vicissitudes. The most likely danger points stemmed from the hints of concern about aging, declining beauty, and declining sexual attractiveness—all narcissistic blows striking a very vulnerable area in this still very narcissistically organized woman. Actually, we have very little further follow-up information. The patient had one further contact with the therapist, a single consultation 2 years after the Follow-Up Study. This came at the point of a projected move by the patient and her husband from their home in a nearby state to a locale much more distant from Topeka. All still seemed to be going well with them.

Supportive Psychotherapy: Varieties of the Positive Dependent Transference

THE MECHANISMS OF SUPPORTIVE PSYCHOTHERAPY

Within psychoanalytic theory, the *modus operandi* of the expressive psychotherapeutic approach (modeled as it is after the theory of therapy of psychoanalysis itself, as the quintessentially expressive, uncovering treatment mode) has always been conceptually much better delineated than that of the supportive psychotherapeutic approach. As has been clearly stated, its basic mechanism is interpretation directed toward full or partial analysis of defense and resistance, leading to the uncovering (making conscious) of unconscious conflict; as has been made evident in the preceding chapter, however, it does not (cannot?) exist in pure culture. Gill (1951) put this as follows: "While the two poles of either strengthening the defenses, or of analyzing them as first steps toward reintegrating the damaged ego, stand as the gross opposites of two theoretical modes of approach, the psychotherapy of any specific case will show intricate admixtures of both" (p. 65). Bibring (1954) developed the same idea differently: He outlined five major mechanisms that could, together, comprehensively characterize the technical and the curative operations of psychoanalysis and psychoanalytic psychotherapies. He called these "abreaction," "suggestion," "manipulation," "clarification," and "interpretation," and he sought to distinguish the different psychotherapeutic modes in terms of the differential deployment and saliency of each of these mechanisms. Psychoanalysis itself, of course, was described as that therapy in which interpretation is given overall primacy, and all the other mechanisms are employed only in the service of furthering the fullest interpretive effort. Within the range of psychoanalytic psychotherapy, however, Bibring did not distinguish the expressive from the supportive mode as sharply and explicitly as Gill did.

In Gill's conceptualizing, the concept of "strengthening the defenses" provides the organizing framework for all the supportive approaches, though its operational implementation is not self-evident. As he said, "the expression 'strengthening the defenses' has come into quite general use in the literature of psychotherapy, but the techniques to be used for this purpose are not sufficiently specified, and the theory of these techniques, from the point of view of our knowledge of the structure of the ego, insufficiently systematized" (p. 65). He himself then specified three ways in which defenses can be strengthened, as follows:

1. "A first principle for techniques of strengthening defense is to encourage, praise, or in general, to give narcissistic support for those ego activities in which defense is combined with adaptive gratifications, and to discourage by subtle or direct techniques those activities which are maladaptive gratifications" (p. 66).

2. "A second principle in the technique of strengthening defense is that one must take care not to attack unwittingly an important defense. . . . An example is that of a patient in whom the denial of dependent wishes is a particular important defense. The treatment must be so handled that it is not felt as an intolerably dependent situation" (p. 66).

3. "Another way in which the theory of strengthening of defense may be formulated is the one proposed by Glover (1931). He suggests that artificial neuroses of various kinds may be set up which offer a partial discharge for derivatives of instinct. . . . For the theory of the results achieved by such a technique Fenichel (1941) suggests that 'by this partial discharge the instinct becomes relatively weaker and the work of defense against the remainder becomes easier' (p. 15). The defense may then be said to have been relatively strengthened" (pp. 66–67).

Within PRP, our intent from the first was to move toward the development of an expanded, and (we hoped) more comprehensively integrated, theory of technique for the supportive psychotherap*ies*. Earlier in this book (see p. 54), I have outlined an array of six different (or at least differently named and conceptualized) operating mechanisms that can be said (or have been said) to characterize different supportive approaches, each to different extents. That conceptual display in part informed the original theorizing within PRP, and in part was derived from it. In the next two chapters of this section, I try to develop a more comprehensively data-based and therefore fuller array of operative mechanisms in supportive psychotherapy, aiming, if possible, toward a more comprehensive rendering of their conceptual linkages and their semantic overlaps.[1] In the preceding chapter, I have already referred to a few of these supportive mechanisms, which are elaborated more fully in connection with specific cases further on. At present I want to turn to a detailed discussion of one of these mechanisms—the establishment of a positive dependent transference attachment, within which varieties of unmet conflicted needs and wishes achieve gratification.

This particular mechanism is delineated first because it seems to be a basic feature of most (if not clearly all) supportive psychotherapeutic approaches, and an essential precondition to the operation of various other mechanisms that are admixed with it in different cases. It is also a basic element in the operation of the so-called "transference cure"—a concept often used too pejoratively, simply implying transience and instability. The concept is used here to indicate the willingness and desire of the patient to reach certain goals and achieve certain changes as things being done "for the therapist," in gratitude for the gratification of needs within the positive dependent transference attachment.[2] To anticipate one of the major conclusions of this entire volume (and of our whole study in PRP), this

---

1. However, I do feel it an oversimplifying generalization to assert at this time (as Horwitz [1974] from our project, for example, did; see pp. 23–24, this book, for my prior discussion of this point) that one conceptual category—the capacity to develop, and the subsequent development of, the "therapeutic alliance"—both (1) encompasses *the* major determinant of significant change in supportive psychotherapies, and (2) sufficiently integrates the various distinct operating, mutative mechanisms delineated in the supportive approaches. It is too heavy a burden (and also, I feel, an inappropriate burden) to try to put on a concept that not only is itself insufficiently consolidated, but enjoys insufficient consensual agreement on its value in our clinical and theoretical literature.

2. Horwitz (1974), in his book, distinguishes two major classes of need gratification that marked many of the PRP patients. The first was a "parental function," which "included gratification of dependency needs, bolstering of impulse control, clarifying reality and direct advice-giving" (p. 160). The other was a "special hypothesis particularly applicable to young, psychologically immature patients . . . these patients required the provision of suitable identification figures in the treatment situation as a necessary part of the change process" (p. 162).

mechanism of the transference cure operates widely, if not totally pervasively, in the supportive psychotherapies, and to varying degrees in the expressive psychotherapies (even psychoanalysis) as well—in fact, wherever there are unanalyzed transference components in the context of therapeutic changes. And a further conclusion to be based on the empirical evidence, especially from the Follow-Up Studies, has to do with the surprising (to us) durability of such changes. The varieties of these changes, and the varieties of reasons for them, are specified in this chapter in individual detail.

"PURE" CASES OF THE TRANSFERENCE CURE

I begin with the least complicated situations, where this mechanism has seemed to operate in almost pure culture, with minimal admixture with other factors. Two such examples are used: one, the Housebound Phobic Woman, originally recommended for psychoanalysis, and the other, the Claustrophobic Man, originally recommended for psychotherapy. These two examples are taken from a total group of 21, or exactly half our PRP sample (10 of the 22 in psychoanalysis and 11 of the 20 in psychotherapy; 9 men and 12 women), in whom clear-cut evidence was adduced of the important operation of this mechanism of transference gratification and transference cure in the result achieved, admixed with whatever other supportive and/or expressive mechanisms also characterized (or predominated) in their treatment courses. These 21 included 5 of the 8 who had good results in psychoanalysis and 8 of the 9 who had good results in psychotherapy, or 13 of the total of 17 with good results; 2 of the 5 who had moderate results in psychoanalysis and 2 of the 3 who had moderate results in psychotherapy, or 4 of the total of 8 with moderate results; 2 of the 3 who had equivocal results in psychoanalysis and 1 of the 3 who had equivocal results in psychotherapy, or 3 of the total of 6 with equivocal results; and 1 of the 6 failures with psychoanalysis and none of the 5 failures with psychotherapy, or only 1 of the total of 11 failed cases.[3] (The relationship of this mutative mechanism to the result achieved—it was present in 13 of the 17 overall good results and in only 1 of 11 failed outcomes—seems clear-cut.)

Treatment of the Housebound Phobic Woman

BACKGROUND AND PROGNOSIS

I turn now to the two case exemplars. The Housebound Phobic Woman was the patient brought to psychiatric examination by her father because of a severe, acute toxic state (with evidence of a chronic organic brain syndrome as well)—the consequence of 14 years of a lonely, withdrawn, totally phobically constricted life, marked by severe and constantly increasing barbiturate addiction. The severity of her prolonged phobic state (she was practically totally housebound) has been

---

3. This tabulation comes from counting as cases of psychoanalysis all 22 patients for whom this treatment modality was recommended and entered upon. It includes, therefore, the 6 who were explicitly or tacitly switched to psychotherapy sometime after the start of their treatments.

indicated on pp. 123 and 142–143; the severity of her prolonged addiction (she was the one patient among the many alcoholic and/or drug-addicted patients in our population—22 such in all—who had developed demonstrable and persisting organic brain damage) has been indicated on p. 127.

The aspects of the patient's life history most relevant to the understanding of her therapeutic course were her relationship with her father and her subsequent relationships with other men. The father was a very able and powerful public official, and a very strong-willed and controlling individual. He dominated the family; he was never aware that the patient grew up intensely fearful of him, and that she always resented his treating her like a little child who could not be trusted to make her own decisions. To him, she was always his overindulged, favorite child. As a teenager the patient and a girlfriend attended movies daily—not to see the picture, but to seek out men who might be masturbating, so that they could be "forced" to assist in the act. She never engaged in homosexual activity but wondered about this, declaring during her evaluation, "If I am a homosexual, I just want to know about it." After her mother died, when the patient was 20, she returned from college to be her father's housekeeper. Their relationship was difficult. The patient always felt inferior, unable to live up to the father's high expectations. They were tense together and had little to say to each other, spending periods sitting on the porch together in "strong silence." But at nights, the patient would suffer abdominal pain and crawl into the father's bed, complaining of the pain and the fear of appendicitis. After a period of easy alliances with older men, on trains, in bars, and in bed (she talked of this period at psychiatric evaluation as seeking "love and affection from a father substitute"), she entered a marriage "to spite my father" when she was 30. This marriage, to an alcoholic—a "shiftless no-good whom I had to support," and who was physically abusive to the patient in the bargain—lasted only 2½ years before it ended in divorce.

It was all during this time (starting actually in her early 20s) that the patient's drinking, her severe drug addiction, and her progressive phobic incapacitation carried her on a progressively decompensating course. Along the way, she had two unsuccessful periods of outpatient psychotherapy. The first was a brief period of explicit "narco-analysis"; the second drifted into the use of her therapist mostly as an unfailing source of prescriptions for sedative drugs. At the point when her father brought the patient to The Menninger Foundation (she was now 37), she was involved in another affair with a man 20 years older, "another weak person who is wonderfully kind and affectionate and does many things for me." As noted earlier (see pp. 123, 142–143), he was the patient's one regular contact with the outside world; he came to her apartment several nights a week, and ran all necessary errands.

Perhaps because of the failures of the previous periods of psychotherapy, psychoanalysis was recommended as the only treatment that offered the patient any hope of resolution of such deep-seated and lifelong neurotic conflict (together, of course, with concomitant prolonged hospital management). Needless to say, it was recognized that she was hardly a good psychoanalytic prospect: Her long period of addiction, her totally disorganized life, the superimposed organicity, the diffusion of her problems, and her barely minimal capacity and motivation for analysis all bespoke the difficult psychoanalytic prognosis.

COURSE OF THE TREATMENT

At the time of "cutoff" Termination Study, the treatment had been in process for over 7 years—6 years with the first analyst (1056 hours) until his unexpected death of heart disease, and then 1¼ years with the successor analyst (154 more hours), or a total of 1210 hours. It was unclear whether the treatment could be expected to terminate; in view of the nature of the ongoing treatment climate, the patient was not interviewed, though she did have repeat psychological testing. Although the patient was ostensibly "in analysis" throughout (and was always on the couch), the treatment was actually systematically altered almost from the start into a supportive–expressive psychotherapeutic mode. The basis for this shift has already been described (see p. 191) as a consequence of the patient's very limited capacity for an introspective and self-reflective process (a reflection of the limitations imposed by her degree of chronic organic brain damage?) and of her concomitant powerful thrust to search for dependent support and direction.

The first analyst was willing to meet the patient on these terms. He sought to free her of her dependency upon alcohol and drugs and to help her achieve some stable level of functioning outside the hospital setting. Beyond that, he hoped to help free her progressively of her phobic restrictions and enable her to lead a fuller and richer life. There was a good deal of suggestion, in the sense of direct advice giving concerning the importance of a steady job and the problems of job seeking, the timing of a steadily enlarging testing of the phobic restrictions that bound the patient in, and so forth. There was also manipulation—in the sense of helping the patient set up a more organized and realistic life pattern, obtain and manage a job and an apartment, and maintain some semblance of a minimal social life for herself—as well as manipulation within the treatment (a retroactive fee reduction when the father's death after 3 years of treatment left the patient a far smaller than expected inheritance). There was a good deal of clarification directed toward helping the patient develop a clearer picture of her life situation and a more realistic understanding of her behaviors. Characteristically, the patient then sought to alter her behaviors as a way of pleasing the analyst and of defending herself against the need to experience or to understand the nature of her conflicts within the analysis. The analyst, in turn, tended to accept the evidence of changes at their face value.

The patient's life during this treatment evidenced the kind of unspectacular but steady progression that encouraged both her and the analyst. From the start of her hospitalization, the patient gave up drugs and alcohol and immersed herself in a compulsive routine of scheduled activities. Over time, she moved into a foster care home and full day hospital status, succeeded in turn by independent apartment living and her first full-time job, as a saleslady. Her job history was checkered but also showed a steady progression. Early difficulties with coworkers and supervisors led to discharge from her first jobs; at the time of Termination Study, however, the patient had held her current (secretarial) job for a 2-year period and was managing creditably. She never required rehospitalization, nor did she ever revert to drugs or alcohol. When her father died, not unexpectedly, she lost her only close family member, real friend, and source of financial support. About 3 years later, she additionally lost her analyst through death from heart disease, this time totally unexpectedly. The patient coped with both deaths with some truncated expression of mourning, and without real disturbance of either her work or her level of functioning.

The themes of the treatment were fully consonant. The patient worked throughout to please the analyst, to be a good patient, to improve. She was not able (or willing?) to free-associate; she was rather inclined to emphasize her good functioning outside the hours as a resistance to analyzing her thoughts and her feelings within the hours. Transference feelings rarely surfaced. It was after almost 1000 hours of treatment that the patient confessed to the analyst that one of her "greatest fears" at the start of her treatment was that she would fall in love with or come to hate the analyst; she declared that she felt lucky that such had never eventuated. The mother did not enter the treatment very much at all, and when she did, it was in an idealized way, with all negative feelings blanched out. With the father, there was an effort to fight off the aroused affects (which were closer to consciousness) by acts of suppression and reaction formation. She held to the strong conviction that, in the end, her father or his surrogate would always rescue her.

The work with the second analyst began with the (brief) mourning for the first. Then came disparaging comparisons of having to accept a pygmy after having had a giant. When the second analyst handled the patient's worsening financial plight with a reduction in hours rather than a further reduction in fee (as she felt sure the first one would have done), she reacted angrily to this "realistic deprivation," and for the first time mobilized and expressed real anger within the therapeutic situation. The second analyst was also less willing than the first to settle for the secure and permanent relationship with a nurturant, protecting, ever-available figure that was a chief (unconscious) goal of the patient's. He thought in terms of a fuller and more vigorous interpretive analytic undertaking, in an effort first to effect whatever degree of real conflict resolution was reachable, and then to work for a proper termination within the context of the analytic understanding achieved. In this phase, the treatment material revolved around the sister's epileptic seizures, the patient's own childhood blackout spells, the relationship of fear of seizures to the patient's phobic concerns, and the relationship of her fear of loss of control during seizures to her fears of loss of control in the sexual experience. As with the first analyst, the patient markedly resisted analyzing the transference implications of such material. She would alternately deny, repress, and isolate.

The single major transference paradigm that unfolded (with both analysts) was to the strong, protecting, nurturing figure who would be ever helpful, ever available, ever willing to make special concessions (given reality by the first analyst's willingness to make a retroactive fee reduction when the patient's inheritance turned out to be less than expected). The first analyst accepted all this as the (necessary?) limitation of the analytic work and gave up any effort to bring transference thought and feeling into the analysis. Rather, he spoke at times of the entire treatment's being a kind of "corrective emotional experience," in which he made himself available as a kind, understanding, reality-oriented figure, "riding on the positive transference" and using it as a vehicle for helping the patient achieve a more satisfactory pattern of functioning in her daily life. The second analyst tried for a wider interpretive gain, but the patient resisted this. In sum, a full-fledged transference neurosis was not interpretively unfolded.

STATUS AT TERMINATION STUDY

At the time of "cutoff" Termination Study, the patient was symptomatically vastly improved. Her addictions, her organic brain syndrome, her hypochondria, and her (moderate) obesity were all remitted, and her anxiety and phobias were significantly diminished. Her disorganized living pattern had totally vanished. She was living alone, caring for her house and maintaining her secretarial job adequately. She had gradually widened her available sphere of activity. She had first taken bus rides (after having avoided them for 20 years), and then automobile rides. At the time of her first analyst's death she had purchased her first car and was driving it all over town, on *almost* every street; she was sorry that he was no longer present to share with her the triumph of each new street conquered. She still did not dare to drive out of town. However, she had no close friends, had no ongoing relationship with a man (there had been none since the start of the treatment), and showed no apparent interest in one. The patient continued to be openly and inordinately dependent on her treatment and on the total relationship to the institution.

STATUS AT FOLLOW-UP STUDY

At "cutoff" Follow-Up Study, the treatment with the second analyst was still continuing; by now the patient had reached an overall total of 1356 hours. This time it was felt that the patient could be interviewed, and she participated very willingly. In fact, she did not even want any expense money; she felt she had been amply repaid by all the help The Menninger Foundation had been to her over all those years (now 9¼). The patient's life during this 2-year period had continued to widen, very slowly but again perceptibly. She was in the same job, and her sporadic difficulties with supervisors had now flattened out. She had few friends, because "it was hard to get to know people in this town." She still yearned to meet people; life had been dull and lonely, especially after the deaths of her father and the first analyst. The main limitation in the patient's life was her continuing (though slowly still lessening) phobic constriction. Her improvement was a matter of an almost inch-by-inch extension of the streets on which she felt able to drive her car with comfort and familiarity. When she would venture beyond her self-imposed confines, she would get panicky or "lost." Gradually her domain extended to include the whole of Topeka, including its main avenue (but not outside city limits). There was little insightful understanding of the nature of the lessening phobic limitation. The phobic danger was greater with men around, and the patient felt it must be linked in some way to her relationship with her father. All her other symptoms were more thoroughly eradicated. The patient was now menopausal (47); she experienced "hot flashes" and with muted recriminations spoke of her life having passed "from teenage straight into old age." In regard to this, she felt lonely and depressed.

One differing interlude had been interpolated into this otherwise drab and unrelieved picture. During this follow-up interim the patient had met a car salesman and had had a brief romance, four dates. She felt suddenly and intensely close, though it did not come to an actual sexual relationship. Once he took her for a drive for a bite to eat, and before she knew it the patient was on her way to a restaurant in another town 30 miles away—her first and only venture outside

Topeka in the whole 10-year period of treatment since her initial hospitalization. She did not panic during this outing. But then the patient demurred at a whole weekend to be spent in another city, and the boyfriend never called again. The patient suspected, and later confirmed, that he was a married man. This brief, disappointing affair was described in the most (overtly) glowing terms. It "opened all of life . . . brought out the softer side in me. . . . it seems I recall feeling that way many years ago." The patient was determinedly "not bitter—as I would previously have been." Rather, the episode made her feel "terribly restless with the life I was leading." It was "a brief sort of sad affair—I had a man about a year ago but he got away."

Meanwhile, the patient's treatment course was like her life course, a steady undramatic continuation. The second analyst's industrious interpretive effort had finally bogged down, foundering on the patient's lack of comprehension (at the least), and more often her anger (over his "stupidity" at, for example, offering connections between the patient's episodic behavioral upsets and his vacation absences). He switched finally to a more "reality-oriented psychotherapy," and then from "regular psychotherapy" to "counseling and guidance." The therapist hoped that within the context of an unbridgeable anaclitic transference—once more generously gratified, now less so—the patient could gradually be moved toward treatment termination, perhaps within another year. But he wasn't sure.

The patient presented the contrapuntal perspective of the therapeutic interaction. It had always been very hard for her to talk about personal feelings. And, in addition, "I'm so poor at expressing myself that you'll have to take that into consideration. My vocabulary isn't what it used to be." Of the first therapist, she said, "At my worst moments I felt that maybe I could live through whatever it was I was experiencing because I had such confidence in his being able to at least hold me together until the thing was worked out or I got through whatever it was." She could never tell her first therapist how much she cared for him, because "I was kind of panicky." She was upset when she glimpsed him "playing rotten tennis," but she was thrilled when he came dashing by the waiting room with the wind rumpling his hair; "it sent my little heart just pitter-pattering." He was almost literally on a pedestal: The patient always saw "that statue of Lincoln in Washington" with the first therapist "sitting in that chair sort of like a carved statue—stern and judgmental, but kind and thoughtful."

By contrast, the second therapist was a very different person, "seen in a neutral light." He was a nice person, but evasive: "I have no confidence in him." With him, the patient could no longer bring up "real deep conflict things," but he was "certainly better than nothing—lunch is better than no meal." However, he "said stupid things. Whenever I was upset about anything in the summer, he mechanically related it to his coming vacation, even when he hadn't yet informed me about his vacation." But the patient was reluctant to think of changing therapists. "After all, it may be me—and I may be no better off with a change." And at this follow-up point, both the therapist and the patient could agree on the assessment of the patient's accomplishments in her treatment to date and the (somewhat wistful) goals she still held for herself.

COMMENTS AND QUESTIONS

In overall summary, this was a severely ill and disorganized woman, crippled by phobias and an intense barbiturate addiction (which had decompensated into an acute and chronic organic brain syndrome), with powerfully childlike dependent attachments to nurturant imagoes. She was taken into a benevolently support-ive–expressive psychotherapy (masquerading as psychoanalysis), developed a seemingly insoluble transference tie (insoluble transference neurosis), and became, potentially anyway, a "therapeutic lifer." Within this benevolent dependent trans-ference attachment, the patient could do things for the therapist, improve *for him* (i.e., the transference cure); she could disengage from the conflict-triggering pressures in her environment and accept a still phobically limited existence in a routine job and with the sparsest interpersonal interactions. She was able to do all this with some degree of contentment, and some sense of overall great change and still continuing steady improvement.

At the same time, this status at Follow-Up Study left still three major ques-tions at issue:

1. Was the treatment result all that could be reasonably achieved, given all the circumstances? On balance, one would have to give a positive response to this question and ascribe the initial more optimistic prediction to an incomplete pic-ture of the patient's illness, with its combined psychologically and organically deter-mined limitations in functioning and in possibility for reversal.

2. In order to achieve this treatment result, was this trip necessary? Did it require over 1300 hours of intensive treatment with the end not yet in sight? Here the response would probably be negative. Clearly, an unmodified psychoanalysis could never have been carried out, and the effort to become "more analytic" as attempted by the second analyst confirmed, as might be expected, that more hin-drance than help would come of this effort. Clearly, also, the more proper treat-ment encouraged a life of guided disengagement from external conflict-triggering pressures, plus an acceptance of an unanalyzed transference dependency within which the patient would improve *for* the therapist. Though the treatment, there-fore, did not need to be so intense or so frequent, probably it did need to be quite prolonged. Just how prolonged is an aspect of the third major question posed by the overall course of the case.

3. Could the patient terminate the treatment in a way that would preserve the therapeutic gain, through maintained introjection of the dependent transference gratifications combined with a supporting life structure, as the second therapist expected (hoped?) was the case? Or was this transference-based cure so incapable of dilution or symbolic substitution, that the patient's achieved level of function-ing had become dependent on an indefinite maintenance of some kind of thera-peutic tie? Would she become a "therapeutic lifer," tied to Topeka, as the first therapist expected and was willing to settle for? This issue was still to be resolved at the Follow-Up Study point after almost 10 years of ongoing observation and treatment.

CONTINUED FOLLOW-UP

We have an account of the 16 years after the "cutoff" Follow-Up Study up until the present writing (25½ years of continuous observation). The patient has in-deed become a "therapeutic lifer," and has remained in Topeka. She continued with her second therapist for 5 additional years until he left Topeka; she was then with a third therapist for another 5 years until he too left Topeka; and she has now been 6 years with her fourth therapist, a social worker. She is currently still being seen regularly, but only once a month. Occasionally over the intervening years the patient has experimented with relaxation techniques, with efforts at hypnosis, and with Valium medication. She has lived and worked in Topeka all this time, but her life has gradually expanded to include air travel for visits with relatives across the country. She has not been on drugs or alcohol. She has not married, and has now a dwindling circle of friends. She looks forward to retiring shortly (she is now 63); her postretirement plans are not yet crystallized.

Overall, the Housebound Phobic Woman had the second largest number of officially counted treatment hours in our PRP sample (1356 at the time of "cutoff" Follow-Up Study), exceeded only by the Economist (1601 hours officially at the time of his "cutoff" Follow-Up Study). (The Economist was also someone caught up in an insoluble transference neurosis who had also become a "therapeutic lifer"; see pp. 336–343 for the description of his treatment course.) The other patient to be used here to exemplify the operation of the positive dependent transference attachment (the transference cure), is another phobic patient, the Claustrophobic Man. In contrast to the Housebound Phobic Woman, he was originally recommended for psychotherapy (not psychoanalysis), and he also had the very shortest treatment course of any of our PRP patients (only 46 hours).

Therapy of the Claustrophobic Man

BACKGROUND AND PROGNOSIS

The Claustrophobic Man was the 47-year-old somatically afflicted businessman who came to psychiatric treatment because of severe "nervousness" and intense phobic anxiety relating to nonexistent heart disease, which had started in the wake of a series of operations for cancer of the thyroid. Aspects of his illness and character picture have already been described (see especially pp. 122 and 123 for a description of his phobic states, and p. 134 for a description of his crippling hypochondriacal concerns about possible heart disease and corresponding lack of concern about the ultimate prognosis of his cancer surgery). The patient's first cancer surgery had been at age 39, the same year in which his father had finally stepped down and turned the family business over to the patient. There were two subsequent cancer recurrences, each treated surgically (plus X-ray the third time), leaving the patient with permanent hoarseness and marked postirradiation scarring of his neck. It was during the third surgery that the patient suffered the harrowing experience of feeling abandoned in the operating room, which triggered his first severe anxiety attack. The subsequent rapidly progressive phobic constriction quickly totally crippled his own and his wife's lives. He became completely dependent upon his wife and could go no place without her and few places with her. His central fear was that he might have a heart attack while unattended; he would die suddenly and the fact would be unknown to anyone. The patient denied heatedly that his many symptoms (there were others, such as intensified "social drinking") and attitudinal changes were related in any way to fears concerning the malignancy. Both the patient and his wife claimed that the marriage had long been compatible and satisfying in every way. Only one discordant note was struck about the marriage: The patient reluctantly admitted a marked jealousy of all the attention his wife had always given their only child, a son, now 23, married, and in the Army.

A supportive–expressive psychotherapy was recommended, directed to the twin aspects of the illness picture—the denial of the reality threat of the cancer, and the activation by way of the neurotic symptoms of open and intense dependency needs. The patient was seeking the omnipotent and magical therapist who could make his distress disappear, while sparing him from having to face either the somatic threat or the meaning of the reactivated dependency. The therapeutic effort would be to help the patient face the cancer and its implications, to experience his fright and his dependency—with the risk, of course, of precipitating a depressive episode. If successful, this would result in the patient's experiencing his regressive symptoms in relation to the cancer threat in reality, not in relation to heretofore warded-off lifelong dependent strivings. This much might be an acceptable therapeutic solution: for the patient to see himself as psychologically healthy until the cancer onset, and his phobic and regressive illness as a reaction to the need to deny the reality of the cancer threat. Thus there would be a limited insight into the current triggers of his dependency, some gratification of the dependency within the therapeutic relationship, and a simultaneous, effective hiding of the lifelong characterologically rooted dependency strivings.

This "cure" of the illness would thus result largely in a restoration of the premorbid life adjustment, with perhaps some readjustments in view of the reality of the patient's potentially altered life expectancy (e.g., he might gratify his wishes for travel, which had been long postponed). A lesser treatment outcome would be the patient's turning out to be unable to face his difficult reality, with a need then to hold on to his intense defensive denial. In that case, the treatment would become a more permanently supportive effort, sustaining the patient by enabling the symptoms to be transferred into the maintained dependent relationship with the therapist; this would take the pressure off the wife, and thereby would attenuate somewhat the patient's embarrassments and guilt feelings. Either way, presumably the patient's symptoms (his hypochondria, his phobic constrictions) would dwindle away, and his dependency on his wife would be well back within its normal limits (and thus well within her capacity and willingness to meet). Though the patient might continue to need his wife near on many occasions, he would no longer be as liable to panic if she stepped out of the room.

COURSE OF THE THERAPY

The actual therapy was only 46 hours, spanning 18 months. It proceeded throughout along the "lesser" line anticipated. The patient was disposed to experience the whole course in supportive, often directly reassuring terms. The model was an "anxiety attack," experienced early on in the therapist's office. When he turned to the therapist, pleading, "Aren't you going to *do* anything to help me out?" he reported that the therapist answered, "Why no, there isn't anything I can do. . . . It's up to you." The patient described the positive way in which he took this: "And I think from that time on I had more confidence in him because I knew that—I told myself that he knew that I wasn't going to die and he wasn't worried about it. I was the only one that was worried about the situation." The therapist also offered no somatic care and gave no medications, though he was well aware that, throughout the psychotherapy, the patient was under the continued care of two internists who kept him on reserpine for his mild hypertension and his "nervous state."

The therapy throughout was marked by much direct suggestion and reassurance. The therapist constantly supported the patient's own mobilized wish to master the anxiety attacks by insisting that he enter the phobic situations. The theme of the counterphobic push was always "It won't be so bad. You won't die." At first the patient was scared by this, felt he was getting nowhere, and later admitted that he would have quit a number of times at the beginning if his wife hadn't forced him to keep coming. But quickly he felt encouraged, and within a month he took a brief hunting trip away from his wife. It was not until much later that he confessed that he had arranged for a physician to be a member of the hunting party. In 2 months he was again handling stressful business deals. Abreaction also marked the therapy, in the form of repeated "anxiety attacks," as noted; there were also episodes of fear and rage, usually linked to frustrations with his wife or his son. And there were manipulations of many kinds. There was a direct interdiction of drinking before coming to his hours, and the patient abided by this rule. The therapist saw the wife and the son—at the patient's behest, to be sure, but in part to try to arrange a more accommodating life situation for the patient. The therapist also threw his influence very vigorously against the patient's retreating any further from business or personal responsibilities, despite the patient's often-voiced belief that if only he could get out of the business, all would be well.

Within this overall context, the patient overcame his initial fear and mistrust of the therapist. "He won my confidence and I stopped lying to him. He wasn't taking advantage of me, he was there to help me, he knew what my trouble was." By contrast, his internist never succeeded in reassuring the patient about the normality of his heart. He would feel that the doctor was lying and giving false reassurances. But the therapist's assurances took hold: "You die a thousand deaths and yet everything is always going well." To the patient, this "restored my confidence, my courage, my enthusiasm. . . . Before that I had thoroughly made up my mind that I was going to die, that I had a bad heart or something wrong with me."

Alongside the effort to master the phobias and the constant reassurances toward that end, the therapist kept the patient's troubled interpersonal relations in focus. Panic episodes in the office were utilized, and the rage alongside the fear was pointed out. The inordinate dependency on the wife, the unreasonableness and irritability with employees, and the running conflicts with the patient's father and with his son were all worked with. The patient could accept some degree of awareness—for instance, of the difficult relationship with his father, who had formally turned the family business over to him, but was always around criticizing. But he insisted that even these troubles had all started *after* his surgery. With even these limited awarenesses, though, the patient achieved increased controls. "The major benefit that I've gotten in my treatment is that it has calmed me down to a point that I can assume friendly relationships with people, which I couldn't do for several years. . . . I was very unreasonable with my employees if they didn't do exactly as I wanted them to."

Within the transference, the concomitant trend was the development of a strong positive attachment to the therapist and to the institution. The therapist became the good protecting father with whom the patient could transcend his ambivalence (the distrust, the lying), and could even express his angers a little. He identified strongly with the therapist and with the therapeutic role, which he took home and to his business to pursue with fervor. (His proselytizing efforts on behalf of psychiatry are noted below.) These transference manifestations were never touched interpretively. Nor was the main defensive position—the denial—altered in any essential. Everything was "nice"; the therapist was nice, and was nice to see him. The patient had no fear of cancer, and his only trouble was fear of death from a heart attack. Upon Termination Study interview he rationalized the relation of his emotional illness to the antecedent cancer as follows: "The surgery and the X-ray destroyed my thyroid and made me nervous." A little later he spoke of his illness as "my glandular upsets." The therapist felt he had made a little dent in the denial in relation to the repressed angers and the interpersonal difficulties, especially around such episodes as an occasion of a joint interview with the wife. There was realization by the patient, too, that his was not a physical illness. "The thing that impressed me most is the fact that your mind is so important in your whole physical being—that you can make yourself sick or make yourself well, or that—that the mystery of your imagination is so important."

TERMINATION

When the patient felt ready to terminate, the cancer had this time not recurred (and 5 years had by now elapsed since its last appearance); though this was not talked about, it was nonetheless in the background. The therapist was willing to accept these limited goals and let go, which the patient wanted. The positive transference was consolidated, and the door was left open for him to come back. Both the patient and his wife were very grateful for the results achieved (the symptom remissions), and told everyone what a fine doctor the therapist was. The research interviewers said of the patient at this point: "He feels that he has been through a remarkable experience which he never tires of telling people about and recommending to them. He is like a man who has been to a famous place of healing, received its benefits, and is ever after a special person because of it."

STATUS AT FOLLOW-UP

The patient had indeed left treatment with an intense positive glow. Through the follow-up period, he continued his strong effort at identification with his therapist by taking on the role of popularizing psychiatry in his home town. Psychiatry became his new civic duty. In his business, he got his foremen together for periodic discussions on emotional problems and on mental health within the firm. He referred a succession of friends and five of his employees to The Menninger Foundation for psychiatric evaluations. During this same time, the patient's business boomed, and profits went up some 500%. But at the Follow-Up Study interview he wistfully indicated a desire to sell out at least some of the business, get out from under its increasing management burdens, and go into semiretirement. He said, "I still dislike my business."

The patient's chief difficulties during this follow-up period were, as expected, in the relationship with the father, and it was this that brought him back for a series of five interviews with his ex-therapist about a year after the treatment termination. The father had retired from the business but still kept an office there, continued to come around regularly, and played an interfering, prying, critical role. The patient said, "He just comes in and stays there and glares at people.

He is a very stubborn man. . . . The fact that I can cope with it is shown by the fact that I'm doing okay. . . . Once I had to duck out the back door when I thought he was going to come in and corner me again and be critical." The patient's plaintive statement that father never complimented him on his running of the business, but only criticized him, belied his assertion that he could now "cope with it"; the father continued to upset him as much as ever. He finally did say during the five renewed therapy interviews—concerning a minor coronary attack that the father had had—that he "knew darn well that the thing that was causing him trouble was that every now and then he found himself thinking how much more pleasant life would be if his father died." After the 5 hours, the patient had said, "I no longer need you to act as a buffer between myself and my father."

At the same time, the patient also continued in a troubled relationship with his son. The son continued to balk at coming into the family business. Though the patient still smarted at the way his father had originally impressed him into the family business, he found it very hard to give up the effort to do the same to his son. The patient could see some of the parallels in this repetition across the generations. He felt keenly his father's jealousy of him; he saw his own jealousies of his son. And with these life troubles at the time of Follow-Up Study, the patient reported a concomitant partial relapse of his symptoms. He was again chronically more tense: "A lot of things irritate me that I could control before." Fear of cancer death was, as always, completely disclaimed (it was now 7½ years since the last surgery). But he was again somewhat phobic, especially of crowds in closed places—"it's something I could get over if I wanted to." He was also phobic with barbers (he would never go to a strange barber, but only to his own barber, who could give him a quick haircut), with the dentist (when in the dentist's office, he would have to get up and walk around every few minutes), and at business meetings (he was due at a meeting next day "and I dread it because I haven't been in that place before, so I'll go down there today and look the room over, so I'll be familiar with it").

From the wife's point of view, though the patient still had problems, he was nonetheless still much improved in all respects. She felt that indeed he still got despondent, mostly in connection with the chronic friction with his father. She reported that the father taunted the patient ("You will never be the man I was") and was old and crotchety. The patient would like to get out of the family business, but his wife felt that he dared not while his father was alive: The father might turn on him, and he had to please the old man. In all other respects—the patient's relationship with herself and with the son—she felt all was still "back to normal."

Some further follow-up information is available. The patient continued in sporadic contact with his ex-therapist at least 3 more years, a total of almost a dozen times over the 5 posttreatment years. During that time, he cut the Gordian knot by resigning from the family business and selling out to his brother. He then went on an extended vacation, followed by a new business venture, which he pursued part-time. In effect, he was semiretired, and he and his wife traveled extensively. He had an episode of transient visual difficulty (linked to carotid artery insufficiency resulting from the postirradiation scarring), and the patient was uneventfully reassured about this. He and his wife had new worries about their son, who was now divorced and running around irresponsibly with "a fast crowd." The wife was worried over the son's failure to mature and be responsible. The patient characteristically tried to minimize the significance of his concern over the son's behavior. There is no further follow-up information past this point.

COMMENTS

Thus, via a supportive psychotherapy, a strengthening of the premorbid defense structure, and an unresolved positive dependent transference, relief of the illness symptoms occurred—a transference cure. The implied promise of the therapist never to abandon the patient ("If I were to leave, I'd be obligated to inform him and make substitute arrangements") helped underwrite and maintain this. In terms of the Initial Study predictions, this was the lesser therapeutic outcome that was achieved: The symptoms were relieved, but the conflicts and the transference remained unresolved. The combination of the patient's own limited motivations and the therapist's supportive propensities in the face of such massive and pervasive denial mechanisms together conduced toward this outcome.

On the other hand, this psychotherapy did lead to sustained symptom relief and improved functioning. A variety of influences converged toward this end:

1. The reality factor of the passage of time: The patient passed the magical 5-year mark with no sign of cancer recurrence.
2. The patient's "healthy" premorbid personality—healthy in the sense of a well-compensated neurotic character structure, set within the context of a gratifying life situation that willingly met both his adaptive and his neurotic needs.
3. The reactive nature of the symptomatic illness and its abrupt onset.
4. The readiness of the patient for a positive dependent transference.
5. The therapeutic push toward counterphobic mastery and the restoration of the *status quo ante*.
6. The supportive environment—the wife who kept him coming to the treatment through the initial mistrust and discouragement.

Since the reality factor—the passage of time without cancer recurrence—played so large a role (albeit an unacknowledged one) in effecting the therapeutic outcome, might this acute neurosis have remitted anyway, even without specific psychotherapy? Probably not. The enormous secondary gain of the illness would have helped to fix and perpetuate it. It took the work of the psychotherapy to absorb the secondary gain into the treatment, specifically into the transference. And what of the future of such a "transference cure"? It had not been anticipated that taking this therapeutic tack would permit so clear-cut a treatment termination, with the necessity for only sporadic reinforcements of the therapist introject in the face of acute problems. This was probably because the initial evaluators did not stress sufficiently the silent working of the passage of time, with its increasing reassurance against cancer recurrence (particularly past the 5-year mark). When the reality danger had sufficiently dwindled, it became psychologically "safe" for the patient to terminate the therapy.

THE BENEVOLENT DEPENDENT TRANSFERENCE AND THE "THERAPEUTIC LIFER"

Varieties of "Therapeutic Lifers"

The risk of the treatment that rides on what I have called the "fostered benevolent dependent transference," with its built-in transference gratifications (usually of passive, dependent, and/or masochistic propensities) and its concomitant returns on the part of the patient (the transference cure), is of course that of getting locked into an ongoing therapeutic relationship that needs to be maintained indefinitely. This is the risk of the truly "insoluble" transference neurosis[4]: If it cannot somehow be resolved, or at least sufficiently attenuated or "transferred," it develops into the situation of the "therapeutic lifer"—the ongoing therapy with an explicit or implicit commitment to an indefinite relationship that does not necessarily include its own termination (ever) as a goal. This whole problem of the insoluble transference neurosis has been presented in Section V (see Chapter 14, pp. 278–287). There, it is indicated that this potential treatment development was thought to be a risk with as many as 16 (almost 40% of the 42) of our patient population, and did in fact become a serious treatment problem with 7 of them. Of these 7, 4—the Phobic Woman, the English Professor, the Devoted Son,[5] and the Bitter Spinster—were more or less successfully, and more or less abruptly, "weaned" out of this treatment dependency. Their treatment courses, along with the ways in which these weanings were accomplished, have already been described in Section V.

The other three individuals who developed insoluble transference neurosis reactions could not be successfully weaned, even temporarily, from the treatment dependence; they thus became "therapeutic lifers." Actually, at the time of "cutoff" Termination Study, there were five patients still in treatments that had to that point already been between 7 and 11 years in duration. Two of these, the Economist and the Housebound Phobic Woman, had started in analysis (though, as already described, these were among the six psychoanalytic patients who were converted to psychotherapy). The other three, the Involutional Woman, the Phobic Girl, and the Fearful Loner, had started in psychotherapy. Two years later, at the time of Follow-Up Study, the Involutional Woman had actually terminated her treatment, and the Phobic Girl was just terminating. The other three of these five (the Economist, the Housebound Phobic Woman, and the Fearful Loner) were

---

4. The concept of the "insoluble transference neurosis" was advanced originally by Alexander and his coworkers (see Alexander & French, 1946; also, this book, p. 278) as a theoretical justification for the modifications that they proposed in classical psychoanalytic technique, which were designed to ward off the dangers of potential treatment stalemate in certain classes of passively dependent or masochistic patients in analysis. It should be clear here that I have broadened the usage to encompass these and other patients, whether in psychoanalysis or in psychoanalytic psychotherapy, who spontaneously develop or are deliberately encouraged into a regressive dependent transference attachment—what I have called the "benevolent dependent transference."

5. The Devoted Son was, of course, the patient in this group of four whose weaning from his analytic treatment was less successful. In effect, he "outwitted" the attempt to separate him from his treatment dependency through his return to treatment at The Menninger Foundation 13 years after his analytic "termination." For the 9 years from that point to the time of the present writing, he has been in a renewed psychotherapy, 30 minutes each week, as the "therapeutic lifer" he had all along aspired to be. (See pp. 286–287.)

still in an ongoing treatment relationship with no plan or thought of termination, and in that sense were settled into the status of "therapeutic lifers."

The treatment course of the Fearful Loner has not yet been described, but it is made clear later that his becoming a permanent patient was on a very different basis than that of the developed or fostered benevolent dependent transference and the insoluble transference neurosis. For the other two, the treatment course and the operative mechanisms have already been discussed. The Economist (see pp. 336–343) has been described in connection with the transference psychosis. Because of the emergence of this paranoid psychotic decompensating process, the patient was explicitly converted from psychoanalysis to a supportive–expressive psychotherapy at the 6-year mark, and this psychotherapy in turn gradually developed into the maintained (and seemingly insoluble) transference dependency. The Housebound Phobic Woman has just been described in connection with the transference cure. Though ostensibly in psychoanalysis all along, she was from almost the start tacitly switched into a supportive–expressive psychotherapy because of her drug-induced brain damage and limited capacity for introspection. The benevolent dependent transference and the transference cure led, in her case, into the status of "therapeutic lifer."

In addition to these three, however, there was a fourth patient, the Sexual Masochist, who should be counted among the "therapeutic lifers." This patient did officially terminate his psychotherapy after 8 years (540 hours). However, the subsequent events during the period of follow-up observation brought him back into renewed treatment with the same therapist, under arrangements that qualify him for inclusion in this group of "therapeutic lifers," though at the time of his termination it was not at all clear that his case would necessarily work out that way. He was also 1 of the 12 patients who developed a transference psychosis reaction in his treatment (psychotherapy, in his case). More than that, he was among the two very "sickest" patients in the entire research population (for details of the degree of ego weakness that led to his characterization as a schizophrenic character, p. 146; for details of his bizarre masochistic sexual perversion, see p. 131). He was among the 4 patients of the total PRP sample of 42 who—in retrospect, and with all the knowledge of hindsight—came to be viewed as essentially untreatable within any available or known psychotherapeutic approach.[6] And yet the Sexual Masochist emerged as the one "untreatable" who was paradoxically able to establish some sort of equivocal equilibrium, and ultimately a moderate level of improvement, by virtue of a developed insoluble dependent transference attachment. This was a long time coming into being, and it progressed into a face-saving and tolerable permanent therapeutic relationship.

Therapy of the Sexual Masochist

BACKGROUND AND PROGNOSIS

The Sexual Masochist came to psychiatric evaluation because of his perverse sexual practices, heavy alcoholism, and intensifying severe panic states. His lifetime was a parade of psychopathology. The parents were extremely wealthy, with the lawyer

---

6. The other three "untreatables"—the Addicted Doctor, the Car Salesman, and the Invalided Hypochondriac—were totally failed cases; the first two of these three were among the six patients who died of mental-illness-related causes.

father doing little work except to manage his wealthy wife's estate. Both parents were severely alcoholic. A major childhood memory for the patient was of his father reclining at home in a chair in a drunken stupor. And the mother, when drunk (which was often), would need the patient's assistance to get to the bathroom, where he would watch her urinate. The patient was always fearful of bringing any friends into the home lest they find the parents intoxicated.

The patient's symptoms had started early, with his perverse sexual practices earliest. When he was 8, he and his sister would place bugs in the toilet bowl and watch each other urinate and defecate on them. As an adolescent, it was his intoxicated mother he watched urinate on pieces of toilet paper he placed in the bowl. This progressed to adolescent masturbation fantasies of a woman urinating upon a goldfish, a cat, a turtle, a slave, or himself tied in the toilet. And finally as an adult, with his wife or with drunken women he picked up in bars, he could talk about his perverse sexual fantasies and seek enactment of them (e.g., by getting his wife on several occasions to urinate or defecate on his face, or by sticking his head into a barrel he designed so that he could look up at his wife sitting on a toilet seat on top of the barrel).

The patient's heavy drinking began in college years and dogged his life thereafter. Along the way, a severe barbiturate addiction was superimposed. Inveterate cheating as a way of coping started in schoolboy years and led to his being ostracized by his fellows. At college he made up for his "laziness" and indifference to his studies by cheating his way through. He was set back a term because of this, but was in the end allowed to graduate. In latency years he developed a number of compulsions (touching things in a certain order, opening and closing doors several times in accord with a particular ritual, etc.); in adulthood, these returned (e.g., he would repeatedly check the car, or lock the door, or rap his knuckles on the table in a particular manner). In adulthood, the patient also began to have panic attacks while driving across a bridge or over an open space, so that he found it increasingly difficult even to leave the house. All these symptoms he dealt with through drinking, and the patient felt that he would therefore need to continue his excessive drinking until his "underlying problems" (especially his sexual problems) could all be cleared up.

Given all this symptomatology, the patient's interpersonal relationships were quite disturbed, as might be expected. He related to people in a parasitic and masochistic manner. He expressed much hatred toward his father and his father-in-law, who he felt supported him inadequately; he was also abusive of his mother, but this was tempered with expressions of affection. He was married and had two children (both sons), and was mostly unresponsive to his wife's pressure that he do something about his sexual problems and his drinking. Finally the wife left him to procure a divorce, and the patient was bitter about that "because she didn't give me any warning. She could at least have done that."

Before settling into treatment at The Menninger Foundation, the patient had had several prior treatment efforts, including psychotherapy, a psychoanalytic effort, concomitant Antabuse, and periodic hospitalizations. All had failed. The patient was finally brought for his treatment effort at The Menninger Foundation by his attorney, the one individual in the world concerned with him. His parents were now both dead, and he was divorced. He stated, "I have got to get cured of this alcoholism—and get my wife back."

COURSE OF THE THERAPY

The patient was in a counseling, supportive psychotherapy over a span of 8 years (540 hours). For the first 1½ years he was also hospitalized, and after that he had periods in the day hospital and two episodes of rehospitalization; mostly, however, because of his insistence on outpatient therapy or no therapy, he was primarily an outpatient.

The patient's life and treatment over this 8-year span were marked by many vicissitudes and crises. For the first 1½ years, in the hospital, the patient played out a peculiar role. He was the perennial butt of the good-natured practical joking of both fellow patients and hospital staff. Much of this centered around his large size, combined with his awkwardness at manual activities, handicrafts, and athletics. Once out of the hospital, he began his extramural life in a succession of menial jobs — at day labor, or selling tickets at night in a bus depot. He complained bitterly about the hard work, the hot weather, and the strict bosses, and he ended up losing each of these jobs through sheer ineptitude. He decided finally that he should be self-employed, or rather self-occupied as a businessman, handling his own considerable fortune (playing in the stock market, investing in oil wells and in rental properties, etc.). His business life consisted of daily visits to his stockbroker to discuss the market, followed by daily visits to his (new) local attorney to talk things over, at length and in endless repetitive detail — under the guise of obtaining necessary legal counsel. After such "fatiguing days," the patient came home exhausted, exhilarated, tense, and feeling the need of medication to calm his nerves. He had an actual trust income of about $25,000 per year, and made an additional $5000 to $10,000 in his various deals and manipulations. He regarded all of this as money he had shrewdly "earned," and thus saw himself as a successful businessman.

During all this time, the patient's alcohol intake had dwindled away, except for two intense drunken sprees — one after a tragedy to his ex-wife and children (see below), the other after an automobile accident in which he injured a pedestrian. However, he had meanwhile become heavily habituated to meprobamate, given originally by a local physician to "calm him" without a "no-refill" warning on the prescription. This the patient took as license to have repeated refills thereafter, to shop from physician to physician and druggist to druggist for additional supplies, and to cover up his intake by evasion and lying, as well as to forge prescriptions when indicated. At times, when his meprobamate intake was at the dangerously intoxicating and debilitating level of 14,000 mg daily, the patient would acquiesce in a brief stay in the hospital or the day hospital for withdrawal purposes. Mostly he struggled defiantly and evasively against the therapist's efforts to bring his drug intake under control. He complained that the therapist was cruel and did not want him to be comfortable; he also averred that *all* the successful businessmen and financiers he knew (among whom he counted himself) were highstrung, burdened by enormous financial responsibilities, and necessarily sustained themselves on both tranquilizers and alcohol.

Early in his treatment course, the patient continued to harbor the idea that he might yet win his ex-wife back. Once he talked her into making a visit, and was painfully distressed that she appeared pregnant and was always holding a fur scarf over her dress, even in the hot summer weather. He confronted her with this, but she indignantly denied the allegation (though she was indeed pregnant at the time and later had a stillbirth, fathered by a mutual friend she was planning to marry). The patient subsequently got his ex-wife to agree to a second visit (this time with the children). Though forewarned that she was coming to inform him of her intent to marry the friend, the patient clung to the forlorn hope that he could perhaps yet win her back. On this trip, the ex-wife and children perished in a tragic travel accident, and this precipitated one of the patient's two major alcoholic relapses.

The patient had a succession of girlfriends after the ex-wife's death, but was always concerned lest he be victimized by gold diggers. He was often impotent and would often just talk about his perverse masochistic fantasies; he insisted that he no longer acted on these. Until his remarriage, there were no lasting attachments. His second wife, the last in the succession of girlfriends, was the most tenacious. She wanted very much to marry him and could not be dissuaded by all his vacillation or even his outright refusals. At the patient's request, she saw his therapist with him; with the patient's assent, she was fully informed by the therapist concerning the patient's extensive psychopathology, including even the nature of his perverse tendencies. This did not deter her. The patient set many conditions to the proposed marriage: that the girlfriend sign an agreement that she would continue to support herself as a secretary, that he be responsible only for himself out of his income, that food expenses be split equally, and that she forfeit all future claim to any share in his inheritance. She assented to all of these. He asked that she agree to see no other man, while allowing him to visit old friends as he desired; again, she assented. When, under such pressures, the patient would finally agree to a tentative wedding date, he would turn to his therapist, pleading for rescue from "the trap."

The immediate precipitant of the marriage, when it finally occurred after a 4-year "courtship" (and struggle against courtship), was an intervention of the therapist's. The patient was, as always, on heavy doses of tranquilizers and was struggling to reduce the frequency of his psychotherapy hours. As he became less regular in his attendance at the therapy, he became religiously regular in his daily sessions with his lawyer (as friend, legal advisor, business partner, and, not least, amateur therapist). These sessions were filled with endlessly repetitive "business questions," and the lawyer was charging a regular fee. At one point, the therapist had not seen the patient for a while and was becoming alarmed by reports he received from town physicians concerning the deteriorating state of the chronically drugged patient, who was pestering them for prescription renewals; he succeeded in cajoling the patient back to his office. The patient came, cadaverous with weight loss and heavily drug-intoxicated, and the shocked therapist employed strong pressure toward immediate hospitalization. The patient demurred. He would have to think it over, "because I have my reputation to look out for." The patient then wanted to know whether he should get married. The therapist indicated that this was not a decision that could be made properly while the patient was in this intoxicated state. The next the therapist heard, the patient had promptly turned around and married. The patient did not return, and a while later (8 years now from the start of treatment), the therapist wrote a letter to him officially terminating the therapy, but leaving the way open for a return whenever the patient might desire.

What had gone on all along within this therapy? The therapeutic plan from the very beginning was geared toward behavior control and life management. It involved a combination of direct advice giving; encouragement; environmental manipulation; discussion of pressing life issues and how to deal with them most realistically; the offering of a stable, enduring, and incorruptible identification figure; and the provision of a long-term, nonthreatening, and nonjudgmental relationship. The patient was encouraged to discuss all contemplated life decisions, and the therapist felt it essential to enter with direct advice (which was, however, often rejected, as in the case of the second marriage). The therapist allowed out-of-hour and emergency contacts; these were not infrequent. The conditions he most firmly tried to impose on the treatment were abstinence from alcohol and sharp limitation of tranquilizer intake. These interdictions could only be sporadically enforced. Often it was a struggle just to keep the patient in treatment on any basis, since the patient, in his denials, played out the role of the independent and successful business entrepreneur ("high-strung" and therefore needing surcease via tranquilizers), and often used the therapy mainly to keep from being overentangled by his importunate girlfriend or to deal with other "emergency situations" as they came along. When not seeing the therapist regularly, the patient had his three major substitutive "therapeutic" vehicles: his burgeoning meprobamate addiction, his auxiliary therapy (in the daily visits with the lawyer under the guise of legal and financial counsel), and the devoted girlfriend (who was willing to be totally supporting and nurturant to the patient).

In all of this, the major transference expectation was that of the relationship of superior to subordinate, of detective to miscreant who was to be found out and punished. The patient always expected to be mistreated, degraded, injured—by hospital staff and patients, who made him the butt of practical jokes; by employers, who exploited him; by people like The Menninger Foundation, who would cheat him of his wealth by their high fees ($25 an hour!); by gold diggers, who catered to his perverse impulses. The patient's response was a perenially fearful and suspicious attitude. This grew toward the end into the paranoid, frankly delusional belief that the therapist was actually shielding a murderer from the police (the flowering of his psychotic transference reaction). These transference positions were enacted (uninterpreted) in the therapy, and in the extratherapy relations as well (the defiant, evasive drug taking, the cavalier attitude toward therapy appointments, the deviant life behaviors, etc.). Actually, also, the transference phenomena were often blurred by the constant focus on conflicts in living, which were dealt with on a day-to-day reality basis.

STATUS AT TERMINATION STUDY

Despite all the turmoil during treatment, the patient's alcohol intake had dwindled away altogether by the time of his termination. And there was a seeming dropping away of the perverse sexual *behaviors* (the fantasies persisted unabated), together with a real improvement in the manifest aspects of the patient's personal, social, and "work" adjustment. The facts that his anxiety was now more intense than ever and that he was on a steady high intake of tranquilizers, he refused to regard as significant symptoms. It was mostly, though, the fact of the marriage that precipitated the termination. When the couple was seen during the Termination Study interviews, both partners attested to the happy and successful marriage, then 6 months old. The wife allowed the patient total infantile dependency within the marriage and apparently tolerated the fact that he gave little in return. The wife acknowledged some *small* problems within the marriage, including the patient's sexual difficulties (his potency disturbances, his need to talk about his perverse fantasies). Both felt his drug problem to be under control, and that anyway it had been much exaggerated by the therapist. And both were contentedly settled in Topeka — chosen because it was so fast-growing and gave the patient such wonderful business opportunities. He was emphatic that The Menninger Foundation and the therapy had had nothing to do with the choice.

STATUS AT FOLLOW-UP STUDY

Given this totally unpromising treatment termination with this gravely ill individual, there was a surprising turnaround for the better by the time of Follow-Up Study, 2½ years later. For about a year, there had been a steady physical and mental deterioration. Then an acute physical illness (an acute myocarditis) had frightened the patient very seriously. At his physician's urgent instigation, he promptly and totally gave up tranquilizer drugs (30–40 pills daily, about which he said at Follow-Up interview, "This will shock you") and smoking (four packs daily). He said, "I think I had enough. I had a bad scare and it was about time I grew up." He thereafter remained under the constant care of his physician. When he began again to substitute alcohol for drugs, there was an episode of drunkenness and physical abuse of his wife; after this, he allowed his wife (under threat of separation otherwise) to bring them both back to the therapist as the starting point for a new (and, since then, continuing) period of therapy. This was now conjoint weekly family counseling, with attention directed ostensibly to the problems of each partner with the other within the marriage. On this basis, it was acceptable to the patient.

At the time of Follow-Up Study, there had been no drinking, drug taking, or smoking for over a year. Of his previous drugs, the patient said, "Those damn tranquilizers . . . they can really lay you low. . . . I'm getting along a lot better now." His previous anxieties mounting to panics had largely subsided, and his touching compulsions and phobias had further receded. (He still went throught a ritual locking up of the house each evening, door by door, basing this on his instilled fear of intruders and of assault.) His outward social and work adjustment was improved and stabilized. His daily visits to his lawyer and stockbroker had diminished in frequency and intensity; these were now replaced in emotional valence by visits with his internist and his therapist.

The main focus of the recognized problems was the marriage. The patient resented the wife's attention to her parents, who lived nearby. To the patient, this "problem" of his wife's was one of the reasons for their joint marital counseling. The patient's sexual problems had continued. Overtly, his previous sexual activity and fantasies had given way to a massive sexual inhibition, with almost total impotence. Sex was now seen as dirty and evil. He said, "We practice no perversions at all. This is why the sex has stopped. . . . I'm afraid if I got started in talking about the perversions . . . I mean I still have to be prompted by talk. Talking about it could arouse me." Concerning his sexual avoidance, the patient said of his wife,

"She understands this. . . . she understood this before we got married . . . although I know that it bothers her." His summary statement on all this was "I'm happy the way I am. . . . I don't particularly give a damn about sex. I don't know as I want to try to cure the sex problem. I halfway want to and I halfway don't." The wife, though troubled by all this, was nonetheless sticking by the marriage. She still hoped for improvements. She saw her role as that of (partially unwilling) mothering of a disturbed and at times potentially dangerous, but appealing, son.

What was happening in this renewed therapy to underpin this new stability? The therapist was finally securely in the role he had long struggled to establish. He was a nonintrusive, friendly family counselor, providing ongoing support against family stress and a forum for discussion of family problems. The therapy was now freed of the ongoing struggle centered around drug intake (the internist was holding this line, abetted by the patient's fears for his heart). The therapist made special efforts to steer clear of the patient's essential defensive constellations; he especially avoided challenging the always latent paranoid orientation. The exclusive content of the treatment was the current life situation. It was "family therapy," focused on the ongoing family interactions, the patient's complaints about his wife's ties to her parents, and the wife's complaints about the patient's demandingness and possessiveness. The sexual problem in the marriage was an ever-present but unexpressed item on the agenda. The patient's transference in this new therapy was less fearful, less manifestly paranoid, burdened with a lesser intensity of projected sadism. The transference psychosis was now in abeyance. The dependent transference was to the fore, though diluted also in the simultaneously ongoing relationships with the internist, the therapist, and the wife. The patient's goal was clear: to live out his controlling dependency via the therapy, while yet maintaining a needed psychological distance. He implied that he came to therapy only because of his wife's and the therapist's desire that he do so, but he came.

COMMENTS AND CONTINUED FOLLOW-UP

Thus over a 10½-year span, this sickest and unlikeliest patient in the whole PRP population could be stabilized within the gratifications of a dependent transference (properly diluted and properly disguised), in return for which his defensive organization could be resolidified, his behaviors changed, and his extremely damaging problems abated (the giving up of the addictions, the change from extreme sexual perversion to almost total sexual abstinence, etc.). Two "external" circumstances buttressed the psychotherapeutic endeavor. The first was the severe cardiac episode, which frightened the patient extremely, which thus successfully motivated him to give up all drug intake (and cigarettes) once and for all, and which opened the way to establishing his dependent tie to the internist in whose care he placed himself. The second factor was the insistence by the wife that he return to therapy (lest she leave him) and her (to him, face-saving) willingness to participate with him in the "family therapy" arrangement. It was the combination of the threat of losing the marriage and his dependency support if he demurred, and the promise of full dependency support (in a form tolerable to him) if he accepted, that enabled the patient to enter and use therapy on this new "family" basis of shared responsibility and new gratification. All of this was, of course, underwritten by the patient's ample financial resources. And if the patient were to continue indefinitely in this supportive therapy, there probably would be a fair chance for him at least to hold his gains and his present level of functioning.

The patient *did* continue in his supportive therapy indefinitely. He stayed with his original therapist for 9 years after his return for the joint "family therapy," until the therapist left Topeka. At that point, he accepted a referral to the local AA group; he was never a devotee of AA, and mostly was not drinking, but he developed a very dependent attachment to a devoted married couple who were dedicating themselves to a quasi-professional leadership role in the local AA organization. He has continued with this involvement with this couple until the time of the present writing, a total of 28 years since the start of his psychotherapy. Over this whole time he has continued in his business dealings; economically, he has done fairly well. His somatic symptoms and his perverse practices have dropped away completely. He and his wife have had two children; one of them is handicapped, and they have coped with this quite adequately. The patient has come to lead a reasonably normal-appearing life. This can certainly be considered a very substantial improvement indeed, in such an extraordinarily ill ("untreatable?") patient, sustained via a 28-year-long continuing treatment (with but one short hiatus when the patient was "terminated" at the 8-year mark).

THE TRANSFER OF THE TRANSFERENCE

Nature of the Concept

Throughout this chapter, in connection with the various presentations of benevolent dependent transference attachments and the concomitant transference cures built on them, I have mentioned a variety of resolutions of this course: "weaning" and self-maintenance thereafter (the English Professor and the Phobic Woman are signal examples); transition into "therapeutic lifer" status (the Economist and the Housebound Phobic Woman are examples); and a third, intermediate outcome, not yet fully described in its own right, that I have come to call the "transfer of the transference." What I mean here is more or less self-evident in the designation. The transference attachment in the therapy, and the gratifications obtained within it, are somehow transferred to and are then carried by the appropriate figures in the patient's real world—usually, of course, members of the family, but sometimes other kinds of external helping professionals. This transfer carries enough valence and durability that the manifest tie within and to the therapist in the therapy itself can be relinquished. This is, of course, the result of a favorable enough external reality situation, or what is often called today the adequacy of the available "support systems." Sometimes this transfer of the transference is maintained admixed with the continued therapy of the therapeutic lifer, as just described with the Sexual Masochist, whose continuing attachment was divided among the therapist, the wife, and the sustaining internist.

As would be expected, the transfer of the transference operates widely over the patient population; it is built upon all of the supportive elements of this kind of transference tie and transference cure, whether the patients are also formally in psychoanalysis, as some of them are (again, the English Professor and the Phobic

Woman are good examples), or formally in varieties of supportive–expressive psychotherapy, as most of them are. Indeed, it is basically because of this mechanism that, contrary to the initial theorizing about the inherent instability of so-called transference cures within less than fully definitive psychotherapies, such cures can turn out to be surprisingly enduring and surprisingly proof against future stressful life vicissitude. Within the PRP sample, the transfer of the transference was very clearly manifest and prominent with nine of the patients (over 20% of the sample), three men and six women. Of the nine, five were in the group with good outcomes, two had moderate outcomes, one had an equivocal outcome, and only one patient (Peter Pan) was among the treatment failures. Clearly, the existence of this capacity in the patient—combined, of course, with the availability of favorable life circumstances—is an important favorable prognostic indicator.

Among these nine patients, the treatment course of four have already been described. With the Involutional Woman (see pp. 375–382), it was the minister (temporarily) and the internist who treated her for her progressively disabling arthritis (for a much longer time) across whom the transferences were diluted, and toward whom—the internist especially—they were enduringly transferred. With the Bohemian Musician (see pp. 382–388), it was the new husband, so much more congenial to the patient's needs and interests than the first one, who now willingly carried the task of providing the desired need gratifications. With the Claustrophobic Man (see pp. 398–403), it was again a supportive spouse, his wife, who undertook to maintain and gratify the patient's continued deep-seated characterological dependency. (As noted earlier, her efforts were abetted by the reality circumstance of the actual receding of the danger of cancer relapse with the passage of time.) And with the Sexual Masochist, just described, the dependency finally established and now maintained on a permanent basis with the therapist (and, later, the leadership couple in AA) was supplemented both by the wife and by the internist who was overseeing his cardiac condition. The fifth of these nine patients, the Phobic Girl, whose transfer of the transference was to the husband, is described further on in connection with another change mechanism—disengagement from an unfavorable life situation—which was more salient in her case.

The other four patients who were importantly in this category are described here in order to illustrate the range of possible outcomes observed. In the case of the Movie Lady, who indeed made a successful and enduring transfer to her husband *and* her mother, the overall outcome was quite successful. The Homesick Psychology Student made the transfer to his wife, but at a significant psychological price that made the overall outcome only moderately positive. The Heiress's transfer to her second husband did not hold because of the inadequacies in the husband, and the overall outcome was thus equivocal. Lastly, Peter Pan's transfer to her husband was totally unsuccessful in staying the downhill course to her death.

Treatment of the Movie Lady

BACKGROUND AND PROGNOSIS

The Movie Lady, the first of these four, sought psychiatric treatment because of severe anxiety attacks and a gradually widening network of phobic symptoms and restrictions of 15 years' duration. The special circumstances of her treatment (in another city than Topeka), which was filmed for research purposes, have already been described (see pp. 95–96, 153), as has the special low fee arrangement of $1 per hour (see p. 196). The most salient points from her life history were these:

1. The patient's sense of childhood deprivation. She had an older, sickly sister who died when the patient was 13, and a sister 6 years younger who was born the year the father died and the mother had to go out of the house into the employment market. The patient was thus often the "little mother" to both her sisters, a role she acquitted dutifully but with clear resentment. The younger sister got the attention as a baby that the patient felt she had never had.

2. The patient's chosen profession as a nurse. She resented her subordination to the doctors, whom she often saw as unfeeling and inept. In addition, she felt pushed into a recapitulation of her childhood role of having to care for others, despite resenting this seeming one-way street. She only stayed with nursing because she did not wish to displease her mother; in any case, she had a determined streak and never quit anything that she undertook. She always struggled the same way against her phobic constrictions, not wanting to encroach upon her husband's work life or their shared social life (as described on pp. 123–124).

COURSE OF THE TREATMENT

The patient's treatment, started as psychoanalysis, was explicitly shifted to a supportive–expressive psychotherapy within 6 months, when the analyst decided that he was dealing with a much sicker individual (paranoid, borderline psychotic) than had been originally anticipated. This conversion and the specific characteristics of the new treatment approach (which included sitting up, a reduced treatment frequency, "homework" relaxation exercises, counseling with the husband, eschewing interpretation or any other activity that could be experienced as "nagging," etc.) have all been described in detail (see pp. 189–190). The therapist was convinced that this shift successfully warded off the danger of a pending psychotic transference regression.

The treatment went on for 4½ years (652 hours). The patient's external life over the treatment course was uneventful, with a gradual amelioration of her initially presenting symptoms (the anxiety and the phobic constrictions); the patient also became easier for the husband to live with. The relationship with the husband had always been more troubled than the patient had initially admitted. They had married when he was still a student, and, from the start, the patient had resented that once again she had to help out in the providing role while he went on to finish his graduate education. Through much of her therapy the patient would lie to her husband, invoking certain behaviors and pressures on him as things her therapist had purportedly recommended that she should do. At sporadic intervals, they quarreled openly, with angry talk on one side or the other of divorce, but neither of them ever seriously meant it.

Within the treatment, the patient constantly sought encouragement and praise, and the therapist tried always to give it. He encouraged the more and more overt expression of the patient's dependent strivings—of her feeling immature, inadequate, and in need of support. Her transference expressions were mostly negative: to the ineffectual but bullying father, who died; to the busy, uninterested mother, who dumped caretaking functions on her; to the well-intentioned but unavailable uncle, who was supposed to stand *in loco parentis*. She saw doctors as incompetent pseudoauthorities, who pretended that they were superior and knew how to help (like the father), but basically didn't care (like the mother). With the therapist she was competitive in the extreme, and yet she always insisted that all her attitudes were based on the current real relationship. How dare the therapist even hint that any of her feelings stemmed from earlier relationships to her idealized parents? I have already described (see pp. 239–240) the deliberate plan of the therapist to be in return "as natural and human as possible" and to give the patient a "corrective emotional experience" that a man could be trusted and could help through caring, together with the countertransference propensities that led the therapist to "honestly" discuss with the patient his own intercurrent serious heart illness (the same as her father had died of when she was little).

TERMINATION

Within this total context, the patient felt that she improved steadily. She eventually pushed for termination through prompting her husband to obtain a new government job in a transfer back to their original home city, back close to her mother, and away from the temptation to become openly dependently attached to the therapy and the therapist. At the Termination Study, the patient said, "I'm not sure how much I gained from treatment per se—or might have improved without treatment specifically, just through a close relationship with someone who cared for me, like a close relative, but not as involved with me as my husband is. . . . I think the therapist is a wonderful person but I'm not sure that I have gained a good deal. . . . My children are older."

STATUS AT FOLLOW-UP

During the follow-up period, there were regular exchanges of letters about three or four times a year between the patient and the therapist. They were chatty, newsy letters, as between old friends, with exchanges of personal information and family news both ways. On one occasion, when the therapist had not heard from the patient for a considerable interval, he called her; she apologized for being remiss in her correspondence. The therapist also took occasion to insert optimistic advice and assessments of the patient into the letters. And at the Follow-Up Study point, all did seem to be going even better. The patient's symptoms were sharply diminished ("faded away"). Her anxiety attacks and rage outbursts had disappeared completely, and only the phobia of driving was still something of a problem. She still avoided tunnels and freeways and still preferred the back roads. But her life with her husband was almost completely unhampered, and the two were active in a wide network of social and community involvements. Her mother lived close by; she and the mother were seeing each other regularly and got along much better, though they still argued periodically. The patient indicated how upset she would be should serious illness or death befall the mother, now very vigorous but in her 70s. The patient's children were doing very well indeed. The patient was aware of problems that the children had, and wistfully indicated that they were getting all kinds of help and understanding (from herself and others) that children of her own generation had never gotten.

The patient's marriage was not always smooth, but it was very tolerable. The patient felt that her husband was at times hard to live with, oversevere with the children, grouchy, going through a "change of life." There were irritable tensions between the two of them. The patient also acknowledged that she could be "crabby" (not with other people, but with her husband), and that she often had the better of their altercations, since her husband was afraid of her anger and wanted to keep the peace. But mutual agreement, their sexual life together was sharply curtailed. "One finds outlets through other activities and interests. . . . We don't have intercourse as often now because we are so darned busy all the time. We don't make up by sex any more." None of these expressed dissatisfactions really seemed to threaten the marriage. Occasionally when they quarreled there was still talk of divorce, but the patient was sure it would never come to that.

Retrospectively viewing her treatment, the patient was not sure how much change it had brought about. She still professed not to understand the process: "Maybe everybody needs a grandmother to listen." She didn't know what the job of the therapist was except to listen. She did emphasize a number of times that the one thing that was very important to her and had helped the most in her treatment was that she felt somebody really cared and was interested in her. It gratified her that the therapist liked her, understood her needs, and would go along with her requests (e.g., reducing the treatment frequency, answering her question about himself, or letting her sit up). Sitting up made her feel more like a friend, and she was pleased that the therapist had understood that and accommodated to it.

The patient had finally left the treatment when she felt she no longer needed it. During the first 3 years, she had felt that she needed a crutch, and he had given it to her. She didn't know whether it had helped specifically as *treatment*; maybe if she had had her mother around, she wouldn't have needed it. If indicated, she would certainly do it again. The patient felt that all through the therapy, the therapist always wanted her to have warmer feelings toward him in the therapy, to feel toward him as one would toward a father. She indicated that he did seem like a father to her, and she worried about him (his well-being and his health) as she would have about a father.

COMMENTS

Clearly, over this whole span of treatment and to the point of follow-up, the patient improved and felt improved. The mechanisms seemed clearly to consist in the establishment of a supporting, gratifying relationship with a new, temporarily all-important object who cared, who significantly gratified her needs, who helped structure the patient's external and internal environment in more supportive ways, and for whom the patient improved through her wish not to displease him or to hurt him unduly (the latter especially because of the therapist's suffering from heart disease, just as her father had). The continuation and consolidation of this improvement seemed clearly to rest on two bases. First, there was the continuation of the same kind of therapeutic support from the therapist, via the posttherapy correspondence in which he was ever the concerned and devoted friend, always reinforcing what he had done with the patient in the therapy. (His kind of therapy seemed to lead naturally into this kind of continuation, this particular sort of two-sided, mutually equally involved correspondence.) Second, there was the move to a more sustaining, supporting, and gratifying total environment in the old home city, with the mother and the husband both there to be close to—and dependent upon. The partial continuation of the dependent transference and its partial transfer to the real life figures was thus quite successful, and the good treatment result indeed seemed to be more than sustained. There has been no further known follow-up contact. The patient's therapist died a good number of years ago.

Therapy of the Homesick Psychology Student

BACKGROUND AND PROGNOSIS

With the Homesick Psychology Student, a considerable psychological price was paid in the process of transferring the transference. The patient, a 23-year-old but still quite adolescent, applied for psychotherapy because of feelings of inadequacy and inferiority and a painful school and social adjustment. He had had a prior 2- to 3-year unsuccessful psychotherapy while in college for the same symptoms—anxiety, feelings of inferiority, and painful shyness with girls. He was the only child of pathologically overprotective parents, an ineffectual and alcoholic father and a martyr-like mother. As a child, till the age of 4, he had slept in the parental bed and between the parents. At 4 he had been put in a bed of his own, and at 6 into a separate bedroom, but the doors to the bedrooms were always kept open at the patient's insistence. He remembered hearing the sounds of parental sexual intercourse. When his parents quarreled, he would feel it his mission to restore harmony between them. He had suffered constantly with enuresis until he was 13.

The patient was always an excellent scholar. He went to college at the state university only 35 miles from home. As noted earlier (see pp. 162–163), he never missed a chance to go home, sometimes impulsively hitchhiking home to spend the night in midweek and always rushing home on weekends. After longer stays at home (holidays, vacations), there would be especially emotionally painful goodbyes. When it was time to seek graduate training (in psychology), the patient was determined to go to a more distant university in order to loosen his overintense involvement with his parents. He went ahead with this plan, despite their protests and offers of many concessions if he would only stay at the same university where he had attended college.

For a while the patient was contented at the new university. He met a girl he liked very much, and they dated often. (There had been an earlier girlfriend in college, who he felt had seen him only because she felt sorry for him.) The patient felt that in this relationship he was finally overcoming his shyness and timidity, but then something went wrong; the girl seemed no longer interested, and the relationship broke up. The patient was disconsolate, and his schoolwork began to suffer. He also felt unhappy that he was not in a "more progressive psychology department." He would have liked to transfer into clinical psychology training, but he doubted that he would be accepted at a better place or in a clinical psychology program. He felt totally indecisive about his future, and at this juncture applied for treatment at The Menninger Foundation.

The treatment recommended was the once-a-week psychotherapy that the patient could afford. The patient's desired treatment goals were unclear at the outset: Did he just want a consolidation of the separation process from his parents (which could indeed be expected to be achieved within this therapy), or did he want a more thoroughgoing working through of the entrenched neurotic character configurations that had hampered his fullest adaptive unfolding? The latter would ultimately require transfer into psychoanalysis.

COURSE OF THE THERAPY

The patient actually remained in the once-weekly psychotherapy for 4½ years (222 hours). The therapist tried to make the treatment as expressive (as analytic) as he could, since, from the start, he was convinced that psychoanalysis was the properly indicated treatment for the patient. It was over this issue that the psychotherapy ultimately ended.

The patient's life through the treatment was marked by outward signs of steady progression—but always, also, less than there might have been. He was the individual who at first had such a difficult commuting schedule. He had no car and thus had to rise at 4:00 A.M. to make the available train connection for the 50-mile ride, and then, upon arrival, had to wait 2 hours for his appointment. Later, when he had a car, he did not feel free to use the convenient and fast turnpike because of the expense, and usually came by the slower and more tedious alternate route. When he earned his master's degree he dared not go on for the doctorate in clinical psychology (which he treated as a forbidden area); he took a social work job for which he was not properly trained, which paid less than he aspired to, and which he regarded as second-rate. The infantilized relationship with his parents gradually altered under the therapeutic pressure. He had still felt compelled to write home at least twice weekly lest he suffer his mother's reprimands, and had still been allowing them to shop for all his clothing needs. This he could finally change, and he could even return from visits home without tearful separations. By the end of treatment, the patient at least *felt* independent.

The main behavior problem and main treatment issue was the patient's difficulty with women. He came to treatment shy and fearful, and felt that every relationship was doomed to end with his being rejected. At first this pattern repeated itself, but then he got involved for the first time in a seemingly stable relationship with a new girlfriend he met in church club work. He thought they loved each other, but when the girlfriend began to press marriage, the patient demurred, claiming his sexual disability as a barrier. When the patient came initially to treatment he was suffering from spells of unaccountable weeping, urinary frequency and urgency, and episodic intense masturbatory pressure, usually before and after dates. In therapy, similarly, the patient often had to urinate before and after the hour; later, driving to the hour he might have to stop his car by the side of the road and urinate, or, on a few occasions, masturbate. In therapy he began to see this behavior as an expression of hostility against women, "pissing on them." He had perverse (exhibitionistic and voyeuristic) childish masturbatory fantasies. He could not engage in "necking and petting" on a date without getting an erection (sometimes only partial) and quickly ejaculating. In therapy he brought up the fantasy that his girlfriend "should do something" about this, by which he meant that he was soiled, and that she should wipe and clean him. The patient never actually attempted intercourse, fearing that his premature ejaculation would lead to dismal failure. He called this his "impotence," and therefore he demurred when pressed to marry. His girlfriend's response to this explanation was "How do we know until we try?" The patient reacted with both fright and disgust to this, asking in the therapy, "What kind of woman is she if she makes such a proposal?"

Within the therapy, the patient's life course and interpersonal behaviors were reflected along a number of interrelated thematic lines. Alongside the patient's infantile helplessness and efforts to grow out of a smothering dependency was a counterposed grandiose and megalomanic view of himself. In this, he was occupied with fantasies of omnipotent control over his fellow men. He looked at each new relationship (with professors and with his therapist) as a way of parasitizing the other person, sucking him dry of knowledge, and then discarding him as useless. His intense social anxiety, timidity, and fears of rejection were paralleled by covert hostility and fearful competitiveness with authority figures. He believed he knew more than all his teachers and would make fun of them from a safe distance, but when with them would instantly retreat to a submissive position. Throughout all this ran the theme of inferiority–superiority. The patient clearly felt inferior, with a second-rate training at a second-rate university, ending with a second-rate job. He had second-rate treatment (not psychoanalysis) with a second-rate therapist. At the same time he was a superior person, discriminated against by a world that did not recognize and appreciate his gifts and talents. He could see all this much more clearly in his life outside the treatment than in the transference relationship inside the treatment.

TERMINATION

The termination of this therapy (which took place rather precipitously) was initiated by the therapist. The therapist felt the treatment to have reached an unsatisfying plateau, with a more stable vocational and life adjustment but with a fixed sexual difficulty and an impasse over marriage. The therapist felt that only psychoanalysis gave promise of carrying the patient further, and that he had waited overlong in conveying this conclusion to the patient. The patient's reaction to this statement was one of carefully guarded upset and resentment: It meant that he had failed, and, furthermore, that the therapist had failed him—that he had all along had second-rate treatment to which he had been relegated by the powerful therapist competitor. The therapist indicated that he would help the patient find a relatively low-cost analytic placement, and the patient, in order to make some more money toward analytic fees, promptly secured an evening job driving a cab. With the "demands" of the double employment and the pending analysis, the patient felt that he had to set aside for the time being any plans for further education toward his doctorate or for marriage. In assessing his therapeutic gain at this termination point, what curiously came first to the patient's mind was that he had overcome his lifelong poor appetite, had gained 20 pounds, and could now buy trousers in the men's department rather than having to go to boys' wear.

STATUS AT FOLLOW-UP

When the patient returned for Follow-Up Study, it turned out that he was married, and his wife accompanied him. He had not gone into analysis. What had happened was that the analyst he consulted in his home city had advised against it; not only was the patient's financial situation too precarious, but it would be hard to work with his sexual difficulties in the absence of a reality situation in which there was an opportunity for a regular sexual relationship. This statement the patient took as a "command," and within 3 months he was married, with all thoughts of analysis indefinitely shelved. His life then began to prosper. At the Follow-Up Study point the patient had a good job as a psychologist, and by now was earning more than double what he had been making in the social work agency. He and his wife had a widely active social life with friends, which included dancing (that he had always avoided out of shyness) and judo with a friend. His relationship with his parents was attenuated, though his wife felt that he was still unduly dependent on them; to her discomfort, he was still accepting gifts that were inappropriately pushed at them.

However, the patient's sexual difficulty was still a continuing problem. The marriage (now 2 years old) had never been consummated because of the patient's totally defective erections with premature ejaculation. They were both bitterly disappointed. The wife was "taking it well," and with each failed effort would say something like "Worse things happen to some couples." She felt that, rather than more therapy, the patient needed more self-confidence; she believed that he could work it out on his own. She said, "He is going through a learning process, which I know, these things you don't just change overnight." She felt that it was the patient's exposure to domestic scenes in childhood that had sickened him on things pertaining to sex, and that she herself could provide the corrective experience that would gradually overcome this. The patient was less sanguine about his troubles and had less heart to keep trying. He said, "At first my wife said patience would take care of everything, which I never did feel that it would. That was, to me, wishful thinking." The patient was thinking of outside recourse—occasionally wistfully of psychoanalysis, which he *could* now arrange, but also of drugs, hormones, and the magic of hypnosis, "maybe not for a cure but for whatever it might do." In a desultory fashion, he was consulting a number of physicians. Between the patient and his wife there was little overt tension; she was masochistically accepting and "understanding" of the patient's disability. The overtolerant wife accepted the expression of the patient's psychopathology (at her expense) and thus minimized the pressure of conflict that might otherwise be pushing him to more vigorous remedial action.

COMMENTS

How should this entire treatment course and outcome be understood? At the beginning, and even more strongly at the end, it was clear that a much more intensive, expressive psychotherapy, preferably psychoanalysis, was indicated. Perhaps if the patient's illness structure had been initially conceptualized less as an adolescent immaturity reaction, and more in relation to his very deep-seated oral-dependent and masochistic dispositions, it might have been possible to work out an overall plan that would have deferred immediate psychiatric treatment (there was no urgency) in favor of resolving the patient's problems of completing schooling, settling him into professional employment, and then working out the conditions for the more intensive and more definitive psychoanalytic treatment. Actually, of course, this is exactly what the once-weekly psychotherapy was intended to help the patient achieve. What it did achieve, however, was to enable the patient to carry his humiliating dependency upon his parents (he was 23 years old at the start of treatment) into the treatment transference situation; it then enabled him to use the treatment transference attachment both to help toward an enhanced life functioning (progressively less "second-rate") and (with the helpful prod of the consultant analyst) to make the transition into a marriage within which all the dependency needs would continue to be gratified, though more adaptively. But all this was achieved at a very significant price—the continued very severe sexual disability, which left the patient (in this major sphere) in a perpetuated infantile and presexual position. The patient and his wife were both enduring this solution, each for masochistic reasons of his or her own. There has been no further follow-up contact with this patient.

Treatment of the Heiress

BACKGROUND AND PROGNOSIS

The Heiress was a patient in this group for whom the outcome was even more uniformly limited: The effort to transfer the transference failed because of the deficiencies of the new object, the second husband. She came to psychiatric evaluation because of disorganized, "turbulent periods" of several years' duration. She was the third of six children, born to a very wealthy family and largely raised by numerous servants; the parents (an alcoholic father—the patient was supposedly unaware of his alcoholism—and an unfeeling, rejecting mother) pursued an active business and social life, literally traveling around the world much of the time. The father was nevertheless a much idealized figure, and the patient tried fiercely to be his favorite and was very jealous of attentions he gave to the others. She fought all her life against the clear family preference for the male offspring—a preference institutionalized in the terms of the grandfather's will in regard to the inheritance of the family department store enterprise and the control of the family estate. The patient always fought to outshine the boys; she cried often because she was not a boy or could not share some privilege with the boys, often a matter of accompanying the father on some trip. The patient grew up tomboyish and excelling in competitive athletics. At school she was an erratic, mediocre student; at college she did well, and there she was scornful of the boys, who struck her as immature and dull.

She was involved after college in a number of jobs, and got into a number of social involvements with unsuitable, unstable men; she also "had a hell of a good time, drinking a lot." At 25, after a whirlwind courtship, she married a "dynamic and brilliant" but unpredictable and irascible man who "would set the world on fire." He had been married twice before and came from humble origins. Together they were going to take over the family empire and move it in more progressive directions "as Grandfather would have wanted it." The marriage was, however, continuously unhappy and marked by open fighting from the start. The patient berated her husband for being improvident and living on her wealth; in turn, he berated her for her severe demandingness and dependence on him, which he said rendered productive work impossible. When she came to psychiatric treatment, the husband declared that his only occupation for the preceding 7 years had been to be a male nurse for his wife. The marriage was also sexually incompatible from the start, and the husband was constantly philandering—in fact, he returned to a former mistress after the very first week of the marriage. Over time, there were four children; during each pregnancy, the husband would intensify his extramarital involvements, delighting in telling the patient about them. She retaliated with a number of affairs of her own. Despite the husband's being even physically abusive, the patient masochistically endured this state of affairs. She said that she felt "some solution" could be worked out, and that it was wrong to give up. The four children were proof that, after all, there were "enough good times together to conceive a family." Once, though, during the third pregnancy, the patient attempted suicide with a barbiturate overdosage. She pitied herself as the "poor little rich girl."

It was within this situation that the patient began to experience "turbulent periods," lasting from a few hours up to a week. They would be triggered by a hostile upsurge, and during them the patient would sit with clenched fists, trembling with terror. The husband said of these, "There seemed to be a tiger inside her which immobilized her." She said that her "mind was working like a trip hammer." She would have to withdraw, to try "to organize my thoughts . . . arrange them in order . . . organize things into file drawers." If she proved unable to "think out the problem properly," she would become apathetic and feel disgusted with herself. There was no actual loss of reality contact; people "seemed to have the same faces," but she felt unattached to them, neutral, a mechanical "unperson." The patient would drink heavily during such a period of painful confusion and depersonalization, which could then cease rather abruptly. Because of these frightening episodes, she was referred to The Menninger Foundation for evaluation and hospitalization.

COURSE OF THE TREATMENT

Classical Psychoanalysis. The patient was recommended for and was in "psychoanalysis" for 7 years (1355 hours)—2½ years (546 hours) with the first analyst, and then 4½ years (809 hours) with the second. The first analyst held to a classically psychoanalytic approach. During the time with him, there was a significant widening and improvement of the patient's life functioning. She progressed from hospital inpatient status (where she had pursued chiefly intellectual activities with an elite little coterie) to a life outside. The husband initiated a divorce, the terms of which were promptly agreed to by both. (The husband then promptly remarried, and as promptly again, separated from the new wife.) The patient obtained custody of the children and then spent time preparing for their coming to her, with her mother meanwhile taking care of them. The patient was actually strangely avoidant of and cavalier toward the children. After they did come to her, her care of them was sloppy and rather neglectful; she was also still drinking quite heavily, and became involved in some casual sexual liaisons. Gradually, however, the patient's behaviors steadied into more respectable and reasonable directions.

Within the analytic transference, however, a stalemate was concomitantly gradually developing. The main relationship that developed—and that could not be interpretively modified—was the hostile withholding from and angry depreciation of the "cardboard analyst," who was unfeeling, ungenuine, and unhelpful, like all men. I have already described (see pp. 251–252) the failure of the effort to resolve this impasse, and the promptness and sense of relief with which the patient made the transition to the second analyst.

The Second "Analysis." With the second analyst, things started in much the same vein. The patient was intensely fearful of the invitation to free-associate. She had been well schooled in the family debates presided over by the father when she was a child: "If you lose your temper, if you're overcome with emotion, you're lost." The analyst could be dangerously seductive, could get her to reveal her impulses, and could then punish her severely for them. "The minute I walked into his office he became something on a pedestal and something to be afraid of." She could talk about her dreams quite impersonally and intellectually because she was only "partly responsible for it as my own . . . it's something you did unconsciously." Feelings about the analyst were specifically most difficult for the patient. "It was very difficult to feel much of anything during an hour. It would be after an hour that generally it would start. I would feel things, and drink, and call him up on the telephone and express myself"—often in outpourings of tender and sexual longings. But the next day the patient could hardly remember what she had said, and then would deny it: "I was drunk; I wasn't really feeling that way." And then there would follow hours in which the patient was particularly distant and aloof.

It was in this context—of rigidly blocked affect; of excessive fear of free association; of isolated and intellectualized interpretive work; and mostly of fearful distance, aloneness, and sense of loss of contact with a real presence (and, with the history of the "turbulent periods," there was always a real potential for a truly disorganizing transference regression)—that, without ever making it explicit, the analyst systematically began to alter his techniques (i.e., made a tacit conversion) toward a sustaining psychotherapy. (See pp. 190, 238, 251–252 for descriptions of some of the specific technical parameters that he introduced.) The changes were all in the direction of presenting himself as a real figure—a steadily present, benevolently interested, willingly giving father figure. He gratified several needs systems of the patient:

1. He allowed the patient the fantasy of being the specially preferred one—the one he took along with him when he left Topeka for practice in another city, the one who was allowed special emergency contacts with him. In all this, the patient at last had the fantasied reunion with and nurture from the father who had disappeared from her life just as she was struggling toward a finally won position as his favorite child.

2. He encouraged a romance with a new suitor, a musician and composer who appeared warm and friendly as well as talented, though financially never successful. In this the analyst was accepting the patient as a woman, increasing her self-esteem in the feminine role, and tempering her heretofore destructive competitiveness with men. In return, the new husband, unlike the first, proved affectionate and dependable (at least early in the marriage). (And when the patient became pregnant and was 6 months along, she could bring herself to terminate her treatment.)

3. In permitting the patient to pry him out of his analytic neutrality, off his "analytic pedestal," the analyst allowed the patient a covert triumph over him, a gratification of her lifelong competitiveness with men.

Within this analytic effort, though work with the transference was done, it was directed for the most part toward strengthening the positive dependent transference attachment. The very eroticized transference was not worked out, being deflected into the drunken telephone calls under stress, which could be disavowed when sober in the analytic hour. The negative transference components never developed fully. By being the benevolently interested father figure, who reassured the patient of his unfailing presence and assuaged her suspiciousness and fears of dangers, the therapist helped suppress rather than uncover the negative feelings. And, in the end, even the positive feelings were directly manipulated: The analyst encouraged the patient into the second marriage, thereby deflecting the positive transferences onto the husband, reducing the intensity of transference involvement within the treatment, and paving the way for a treatment termination that would not require transference resolution. When the patient then became pregnant, with her symptoms much alleviated (except for some drinking that never came completely under control), her life more stable, and the care of the house and children now more appropriate and more rewarding to her, the termination (after now 7 years) seemed to come quite naturally. At the time of termination the patient was busily planning to resume some intellectual pursuits (free-lance writing, etc.).

STATUS AT FOLLOW-UP

But at Follow-Up Study it was clear that things had not gone at all well in the interim. The patient did not look well, and her symptoms had been reactivated. The main troubles were in the marriage. The husband was an engaging and affable man on the surface, but had turned out to be very rigid and narcissistically preoccupied underneath. The patient complained of his dogmatic manner, his uninformed (but loudly proclaimed) opinions, and his fixed and peculiar ideas, all of which he imposed on the patient and on friends in the form of long soliloquies. He was a food and health faddist and a devotee of Hindu breathing exercises. He opposed immunizations and polio shots for the children as "not natural." Most importantly, he was very much opposed to smoking and drinking ("drinking depletes the vital nutrients of the body").

The patient and her husband fought constantly, often bitterly. They fought about the patient's drinking, which was increased and which she would not give up. She felt she needed it to assuage her angers and to comfort her in her loneliness: "I'm cornered. If I gave it up, I couldn't stand it another minute." They fought over the increasing seclusiveness of their lives; they now seldom saw their friends, who found the husband so often offensive and/or boring. They also fought over the husband's work. The patient was disappointed that not much had come of his music: He neglected it and hung around the house (hovering critically around her care of the new baby); she often had to push him to his studio; and when he was there she suspected him of "just dreaming," for he had little progress to show. Furthermore, their sexual life was not satisfying (the patient had intrusive masochistic fantasies of being degraded and raped during intercourse). Finally, they fought more than anything else over the children. The husband didn't get along at all with the patient's own four children. He tried to be a strict disciplinarian and curb their "natural noisiness," but he couldn't control them and only earned their antagonism. With their new baby, he was impossibly anxious and critical; for example, he voiced loud worries about "what angle the baby should be held during bathing."

With all this, the patient was again drinking excessively, was socially secluded, and was chronically depressed. But the "turbulent" periods had not returned, and the patient's treatment gains also held in the vastly improved relationship with her children and her care of children and home. In addition, she got along much better now with her mother, now over 70 and failing in health. But she felt caught in a hopeless bind with her husband. Though it was unthinkable to him, "the idea of divorce is almost constantly in my mind." At the patient's insistence, they had gone jointly to a marriage counselor, and much of their time there had centered around their struggles over raising the baby. The husband had finally broken it up, accusing the counselor of always siding with his wife because she was the one who paid the bill.

Through this whole follow-up period, the patient maintained a friendly relationship with her analyst. She had only very sparing contact with him, however—an occasional phone call or letter, exchanges of Christmas greetings, one social visit. She felt in retrospect that she had been allowed to terminate her treatment prematurely on the basis of her euphoric state at the time she married. She should not have been allowed to marry so hastily, and she should have been held in treatment longer. She was disappointed that she had not gotten more help from her analyst; he should have curbed her drinking more decisively—by prohibition. But it was not till after she was out of treatment and after the baby was born that the honeymoon glow vanished, and the patient really realized how unsatisfactory the marriage was turning out to be. And nothing had replaced the void left by the termination of treatment: The patient felt she no longer had a central purpose in life.

Whether even this new position, perhaps midway between the patient's initial starting level and her achieved termination level, could be maintained was unclear. Two years after the Follow-Up Study (12 years from the patient's treatment start), there was further follow-up news. The patient, when drunk one day, had attempted to kill her husband, chasing him with a knife and hammer. She was a patient for a period in a state hospital. The couple then again began to see a marriage counselor. The patient was holding onto a sense of good relationship and warm affection with her two children of this marriage, a boy now aged 4, and also now a baby girl. This was the last follow-up information concerning this patient.

COMMENTS

How is one to characterize this overall treatment course and outcome? The first effort at a full psychoanalysis was stalemated over a transference impasse, over rigid defenses and blocked affects, and over fear of a potential psychotic transference regression. The altered effort in a supportive–expressive psychotherapy succeeded in establishing a benevolent dependent transference relationship, within which the patient's life functioning improved greatly. She found a new, idealized suitor and married him, in an acting out of the positive Oedipal transference (which was kept out of the treatment). This acting out was encouraged by the analyst as a way of reducing the transference involvement with him, "transferring" it to the husband, and thus enabling treatment termination (with the husband taking over in real life the role being given up by the analyst). That this manipulation did not succeed reflected the fact that the patient had not been sufficiently freed in treatment of the grip of her own self-damaging impulses (masochistic, competitive, etc.). The man she chose for her second husband, though a toned-down version of the first, was in certain salient respects not that different, and the romanticized glow with which the patient had initially invested him prevented her from seeing it at first. Sustaining the therapeutic result after therapy was dependent on the creation of an external reality as benevolent as the treatment situation, and the patient was still too neurotically limited to be able to do this adequately. And by virtue of her overidealized transference fantasy, the patient had been kept from realizing that she had been unable to do it.

Treatment of Peter Pan

The fourth in this sequence of presentations illustrating varying levels of success in transferring the transference is Peter Pan. Though the Heiress's husband was not a strong enough figure in her life to make her transfer successful, and the overall outcome was disappointingly equivocal, one could still say that the patient's life was somewhat improved, and perhaps even that the second marriage was somewhat better than the first. Peter Pan, the only totally failed treatment case among the nine listed at the beginning in this category, had an unmitigated disastrous course.

BACKGROUND AND PROGNOSIS

Several aspects of Peter Pan's illness and character pathology have been described in detail: her history since the onset of puberty of a progressively crippling anorexia nervosa, with alternating anorexia and bulimia (see pp. 135–136); her compulsive stealing, usually of food, especially sweets (see pp. 135–136, 151); her unsuccessful compulsions and obsessional character structure (see p. 138); and her borderline ego organization with near-delusional fixations (see pp. 146, 167). What brought this 19-year-old college student to psychiatric treatment was not her chief complaint of anorexia and bulimia, but her kleptomania, uncovered when she was caught stealing food from the college cafeteria. Because of her capacity to neurotically entangle her parents in her illness and her treatment, to the point where the entanglement was grossly disruptive, she was transferred to The Menninger Foundation from the psychiatric hospital in her home city where she had first gone. An additional conscious motive the patient had for preferring treatment in Topeka was her terror of her compulsive stealing and the disgrace should she be caught, though she had only been caught the one time. The Menninger Foundation would be in a better position to protect her, she felt, should she again get into trouble with the law.

The patient's youth, charm, many gifts, and life history of energetic and excellent scholarship helped make for a recommendation of definitive psychoanalysis—to be preceded, however, by a period of preliminary psychotherapy, designed to bring the symptom excesses (the stealing and the disordered eating) under reasonably rapid and consolidated control, and thus to protect her (and thereby the analytic situation) against the ongoing dangers to her health and from the law.

COURSE OF THE TREATMENT

Analysis in Topeka. The patient was in psychoanalysis in Topeka for 3 years (510 hours), and then for another 6 months (almost 100 hours more) with another analyst to whom she transferred in a distant city where she went to live. Her initial period of hospitalization was very short (only 6 weeks), and she had two very brief rehospitalizations at times when she was suicidally upset. The initial period of face-to-face psychotherapy was 3 months, during which she continued to steal and was apprehended a few times. She said that the analyst finally shocked her out of her stealing with his horror stories. She then demonstrated that she could abruptly halt the stealing, which till then had occurred almost daily, and she was formally started in analysis.

Though the Topeka analyst tried to maintain a fully analytic structure, there were many enforced departures from it, determined by the constant emergencies created by the patient. These have been previously detailed (see p. 188); their common structure was that they forced the analyst to intervene protectively (when the patient exposed herself to pneumonia in the winter, was thought to be suicidal, was caught stealing one more time, thought she was pregnant, etc.). These emergencies involved many phone calls and occasioned extra analytic hours, and, as a result of them, the patient's life during treatment was checkered and eventful. Nonetheless, she had also started back to college, and completed it successfully. She lived by herself in a minimally furnished apartment, but she did visit her parents rather frequently and sometimes rather precipitously. At such times she would flee treatment for a few days and then return after the brief respite at home. It was a major but successful undertaking by the analyst to keep the parents from trying to manage the treatment from afar in response to their daughter's frequent (and contradictory) importunings.

The patient was constantly preoccupied with the analyst. She would often hang around the grounds for long periods of time to catch a glimpse of her analyst's going to and fro; at times she appeared for her hours with many cuts and scratches from time spent in the brambles. She made it clear that her dramatic suicide threats, her exposure to pneumonia, and the like were all attempts to force rehospitalizations: "I'll commit suicide if you don't admit me." When the patient first used the couch, she had a direct sexual dream about the analyst and then had to flee to her parental home for a few days. When the analyst declined to take the patient into his home (as his daughter), she reacted angrily with an episode of gorging herself, followed by a guilty starving of herself.

When the analyst would not respond directly to the patient's erotic overtures, she got involved with boyfriends. There was a very brief involvement with a young man sexually even more timid than she; the analyst called this a "practice relationship." Shortly thereafter, the patient met her future husband. Within 2 months, this had progressed into an intense mutual involvement, with an active sexual life for the first time in the patient's life. Both the patient and the analyst considered this the best relationship she had yet been able to establish and sustain with anyone. It was not interpreted in its transference acting-out aspect. The patient and the boyfriend soon began to plan marriage; she wanted to do this when she "recovered" from her illness. The boyfriend instituted a campaign for more immediate closure. He conceded that she had been sick and had been helped by treatment; he now wanted to break into what he feared was the danger of a prolonged and inordinate dependency upon the treatment. It was his decision to pursue his graduate studies at a distant university (which specialized in his particular area of social science scholarship), and his pressure on her to follow him under the implicit threat of perhaps losing him, that led to the patient's decision to terminate the first analysis and transfer to another analyst in her fiancé's new city.

Within the analysis, the main themes centered first around the patient's eating symptoms. New childhood history emerged—of her trying to steal her baby brother's bottles when he was born, and of first beginning then to vomit and reject food. These lifelong eating symptoms were related to the patient's conflicts on all developmental levels, and to the vicissitudes (again on all levels) of the relationship with her parents. "Deep" interpretations linked these symptoms to fantasies of cannibalistic incorporation and destruction, devouring the father's penis and the mother's breast. The patient gave up her stealing and eating of cashew nuts (symbolically "father's testicles"), and thenceforth rigidly abstained from nuts. On the Oedipal level the patient came to understand her unreasoning hostility toward her mother and her frustration in her possessiveness of her father. In her visits home, she experienced the actual seductiveness of her father (e.g., he once stroked her thigh and stated that if it were not for the mother, he would marry her himself). The patient said on Termination Study interview, "I was not aware of being *too* close to my father when I came into treatment, but I came to realize that this was a fundamental problem."

The analyst felt that the patient's improvement stemmed from the period of working with this material. The patient said that many of the analyst's interpretations were not of real use to her and only upset her. On the other hand, direct transference interpretations were worked with less fully. The patient lived her transference fantasies to the point that she really wanted to move into the analyst's home, to become his wife or daughter. She could never quite understand why this wasn't possible in reality or what all the transference meanings of this wish were.

During the latter half of the work with this analyst, the focus was on the relationship with the boyfriend. He was perceived as someone who made demands (e.g., not tolerating sick behavior) that the patient struggled (ambivalently) to live up to. In the vicissitudes of this relationship, the patient experienced again the phallic-Oedipal dynamics of jealousy, competitiveness with other girls, and the like. She was mostly frigid in their sexual relationship; she was ashamed of this and tried to deceive her boyfriend about it. When the parents, who were at first opposed to this relationship, came around to supporting it, the patient in her ambivalence responded with disappointment "because they must not care for me very much if they are willing to give me up so easily." At her most regressive turn in the analysis (during the time she was rehospitalized), the patient twice wet the analytic couch and made no mention of it until the analyst remarked upon it.

Within the transference, the analyst was experienced as a magically powerful, seductive, and protective father. The blatantly erotic aspects of this transference were underinterpreted; they were funneled into the enactments with the boyfriend.

In addition, the therapist was the focus of the infantile feelings toward the mother, alternately experienced as gratifying and frustrating. The patient was able to terminate this treatment and transfer to another analyst, partially riding on the transference experience of a now gratifying mother who arranged for a substitute figure and allowed her to go on to the new city to continue her relationship with the boyfriend.

Analysis in Another City. The short experience (6 months, not quite 100 hours) with the second analyst was altogether different. He was "stricter," less permissive of skipped hours or other manipulations. His interpretations were more "down-to-earth" and "corny," but the patient said that they were more useful to her because she could understand them better. His initial analytic focus was very clear: to get the patient to commit herself fully to the treatment with him, and to resolve her current dilemma by suspending her living arrangements with her boyfriend and her marriage plans, so that she could first work out her problems (including the problems in the relationship with the boyfriend) fully in analysis. The analyst felt that the patient was inordinately dependent upon the boyfriend, who daily brought her to her hours and waited outside to escort her back afterwards. He was also exerting a counterpressure upon her to terminate the analysis promptly (since she was now well enough to stand on her own) and get married directly. He would not marry her and allow her to continue in treatment, since, among other things, this would make them financially dependent upon her parents, which he fiercely resisted. The patient responded to these opposed pressures by insisting that she be given a treatment termination date from the start, so that she could at least know when she could marry. The analyst never took the open position that the patient could not marry; he did make it clear that she could not both marry and be free to analyze properly.

During this period of analytic jockeying, some analytic work was also accomplished. There was some increased insight into the mutual hostile interdependency with the parents, and some further consolidation of the emancipation from them. There was some awareness of the new transferred dependency onto the boyfriend, with whom the patient seemed to have a regressive child–parent relationship (as noted, he brought the patient to her hours, waited for her, and supervised her closely). The nonfulfillment in their sexual life was in keeping with this nonmature love relationship. Only a little headway was made into this. "The analyst just felt that I either had to settle down to a long-range treatment program and analyze my relationship to my boyfriend as well as everything else, and just not think in terms of terminating quickly in 3 or 6 months. And my boyfriend was opposing the treatment. He wanted me out. I had to choose." At this point, the patient then chose to marry and give up the treatment, rather than the other way around. She believed that she could get along without the treatment, and she was willing to run that risk rather than the other, more feared risk of losing the suitor. The analyst was a little surprised: "I thought she would come back to see me. But she never really became committed to the idea of treatment with me at all." Of the period with the first analyst, the second analyst said, "The patient appreciated the fact that he apparently told her a good deal about himself. She perceived each hour with him as a feeding."

STATUS AT FOLLOW-UP

At the Follow-Up Study, to which the patient and her husband came eagerly, the patient's status seemed far less secure and far less stable than at termination. The patient tried to present herself as continuing her slow but steady improvement. Her graduate studies alongside her husband were progressing well, and they both hoped for careers in university teaching. She was actually the better scholar, and won the fellowships that were their academic (and economic) sustenance. But the patient's main eating symptom was far from overcome. "I don't feel that I have a normal outlook on food at all, which is the basic symptom that I had. . . . I don't eat normally at all. . . . It's just a symptom; I can't see why I shouldn't be able to discipline myself and eat normally now." But "when I eat, I overeat." It continued to be just as magically necessary to maintain her weight at 100 pounds, her clothing size at 7. The patient continued to try to control food intake at each meal in compulsively ritualistic ways, but in between she would gorge herself on sweets and snacks (chocolates, candies, Life Savers, doughnuts, licorice, ice cream, nuts, potato chips)—all in set routines, ritualistically prescribed. Then there would follow days of total fasting, with a rapid subsiding of her anxiety. And then the whole cycle could start once again. These eating disturbances made for constant social problems; the husband often had to explain awkwardly to friends that they just didn't eat meals out.

The patient felt the other symptoms to be under somewhat better control. The stealing had not recurred. She was trying to relax her compulsiveness, especially her frenetic, immaculate housekeeping. Her husband applied a friendly, relaxing pressure, saying that he would be delighted to drink the water off the floor she was so continually cleaning. The patient had the same compulsion about time: "I feel that the world should be a much more ordered place than it is and that when the world doesn't go in an extremely ordered manner, I'm unable to cope with the situation." About her marriage, the patient also struggled to put up a brave front. "I feel that if I had known how difficult I would be, I probably would not have gotten married. But I am becoming less difficult . . . and my husband feels even if he had known how difficult things would be, he would have gone ahead just the same. I've been a difficult partner, but he says I've given him a lot more pleasure than anyone else could."

The patient was actually more satisfied with her achievements than her husband was. He was impatient with the way her symptoms interfered with their social life. He was primarily distressed with her continuing eating problems, but he spoke too of her rigid routines, infinite orderliness, and compulsive cleaning. He felt that things *could* improve if the patient would put her mind and her willpower to solving her difficulties by herself: "By thinking about getting more treatment she is excusing herself from working harder to overcome these problems on her own." They had talked fitfully of divorce. The patient mused that if she were divorced she could return to psychiatric treatment, which, in view of her husband's attitudes, it would be "impossible to do with an open mind" so long as they lived together. Not unexpectedly, their sexual life together was unchanged and unsatisfying.

The relationship with the parents continued to be stressful. They were critical of the husband and the marriage in several respects. They argued that he was not a good enough provider, and they also held him accountable "for a lot of things that he has no fault in"—namely, the patient's illness. They felt that the husband brought out the patient's poorest points; as evidence, they stated that the patient's taste had deteriorated, that she used to be interested in clothes and wasn't any longer. (There was no mention of her eating problem.) The patient's attitude toward her analyst and her treatment experience was openly mixed. Maybe she should have had more treatment, but then she looked at all these "long-termers" in therapy and wondered. On the one hand, she felt that her husband had done as much for her as treatment had; on the other hand, she had been in a position before treatment where she never could have let her husband or anyone else do anything for her. If her husband had let her remain in treatment longer, she would have been left in a better position to cope with things, but therapy alone could never help her cope with everything. About retreatment, the patient called herself ambivalent. It could be beneficial, but she should be able to handle her continuing problems on her own. Her husband was strongly against it; he felt that their careers came first, and he didn't want to be financially dependent on her parents. Her "leftover symptoms" were only bad habits, discipline problems. She should be able to control them without more treatment. For her part, she wasn't convinced anyway that it would make that much difference.

RENEWED THERAPY, DECLINE, AND DEATH

This was the unsettled state at the time of Follow-Up Study. Four years later (10 years after being first seen), the patient returned for consultation to her original analyst. There had been an unremitting struggle with the selfsame eating and starving behaviors; with the stealing, which now periodically recurred; and with her compulsive and ritualistic scheduling of every aspect of her life. She had made several suicide attempts, once with barbiturates that had led to a 3-day coma. Psychiatric hospitalization and a renewed treatment effort—this time with a more active supportive–expressive psychotherapy—were recommended. The patient and her husband decided, however, to return to their home city, where the patient would enter outpatient therapy.

The new therapy lasted about 10 months and was punctuated by six brief hospitalizations (the longest for 2 weeks). In one of them, repeat psychological testing was done. This revealed the advancing encroachment of a disorganizing psychotic process. The patient's tenuous hold on reality and her pedantic, intellectualized front were weakening. During this therapy, the patient's eating symptoms worsened. She would fast for 6 days at a time and then would have a seventh day of animal-like ravenous eating. Her stealing (of clothing) increased in frequency. She was seen as often as five times weekly in psychotherapy, plus many telephone calls and emergency contacts. A general practitioner would make house calls to give her parenteral sedation. The patient and her husband began to talk seriously about divorce. The patient said that her life was intolerable; she would be happy to spend the rest of her life in a state hospital. She made another serious suicide attempt and was only saved when her husband (who was now separated from her) came home unexpectedly and found her comatose. Following this episode, there was more open talk of both commitment to an institution and suicide. She ended this unhappy period by doing the latter—jumping off a bridge.

The husband thought afterward that she must have been planning this for a week or two. She had sent him and other relatives what he now considered to be farewell snapshots. She had seemed particularly moved when he had assured her of his continuing love for her during their last phone conversation, "as if she could now die happy."

COMMENTS

In overall course, this tragic case reflected a total failure of the transfer of the transference to hold, or to compensate for what had not been accomplished in the treatment. Despite the deceptive facade and the many gifts and capacities of the patient, she was severely ill, with a classical anorexia nervosa as the symptomatic expression of an ominous and progressively decompensating psychotic process. The patient was taken into an effort at psychoanalysis, which was combined with the active fostering of a dependent transference attachment, within which expectations for change were placed upon the patient. However, the cessation of the treatment effort, and the shift or transfer of the burden of need (or transference) gratification from the therapist to the husband, were not planned by the analyst as much (though they *were* aided and abetted by both the analyst and the patient) as they were demanded by the husband, with the analyst and the patient acquiescing. In effect, the husband promised to replace the transference cure by a love cure, and this is what he could not do in the face of the malignantly advancing disease process.

Could things have turned out otherwise? The patient gave some clues when she addressed the same issue during her Follow-Up Study interviews. She opined that she "should not have been allowed to get away with" what she did—the many pressures and disruptions in relation to the orderly treatment process. Primarily, she had not been stopped from following her lover and using that as the basis for prying herself away from the first analyst. Nor had she been stopped from marrying her lover and using that as the basis for disrupting the treatment with the second analyst. In both these instances, she had acceded to the boyfriend's pressure and his promise of a cure by love. If those central issues had been (could have been?) more thoroughly analyzed—rather than being allowed to become the carrier of the acted-out transferences, and the bearer of the burdens of the patient's whole neurosis (really psychosis)—perhaps things would have gone differently, to the profit of the patient, the husband, and the deferred marriage.

THE DISPLACEMENT OF THE NEUROSIS
INTO THE TRANSFERENCE

Nature of the Phenomenon

The development of a benevolent dependent transference relationship between therapist and patient, and the subsequent mechanism of transferring this attachment to a reality figure (usually the spouse) who, one hopes, is willing and able to maintain the interplay of support and gratification on an indefinite basis, constitute only one of the ways in which this kind of established transference tie can be exploited in the service of enduring therapeutic change. Another is to take the new consolidated dependency within the treatment as the basis for requiring desired behavior changes in the outer world—not just as the *quid pro quo*, but indeed as the price for being permitted the continuation of the transference gratifications within the therapy. With dependent and submissive individuals, who are so prone to this kind of transference attachment, and who often come to treatment because of the unhappy constriction of their lives and the desire to become more assertive in their lives, the new behavioral assertiveness in the outside life can be exacted as the price of the continuation of the dependent gratifications within the treatment. That is, the patient can become manifestly more assertive "out there" on the basis of a hidden (i.e., unanalyzed) new submission "in here." If this therapeutic maneuver succeeds, the hitherto unduly inhibited and submissive individual becomes newly (and proudly) assertive in the world—has achieved the desired therapeutic success—on the basis of a continued but hidden submission, now to the therapist in the transference. In effect, the behaviors have changed, but the character structure has been essentially unaltered; the burden of the neurotic inhibitions has been moved from the life arena to the therapeutic arena. This is what I call the "displacement of the neurosis into the transference."

This phenomenon differs from what takes place in proper psychoanalysis, where of course it was one of Freud's fundamental early insights into the analytic process that the developing transference neurosis—the folding of the neurotic illness into the interactions within the transference situation—is used in the service of its own undoing, its thorough analytic resolution. Freud (1912) said of the fully developed transference (i.e., the enactment of the neurotic illness within the transference as it occurs within the properly proceeding analysis) that "It is on that field that the victory must be won—the victory whose expression is the permanent cure of the neurosis. . . . For when all is said and done, it is impossible to destroy anyone *in absentia* or *in effigie*" (p. 108). By the "displacement of the neurosis into the transference" as I am presenting it here, I mean the same transference enactment; however, it is used, not in the service of its own analytic undoing, but rather in the unanalyzed service of being used to enforce new behavior expectations. One can then become more assertive, not because one has analyzed the roots of one's own submissiveness and no longer needs it as a neurotic compromise, but because one is fearful of losing the vital submissive tie to the new powerful object (the therapist), and in order to maintain this tie is willing to chance the lesser risk of obedient assertiveness in the outer world. The factors that then serve to maintain these newly won behaviors in life are not analytic understanding and resolution of underlying neurotic conflict, but reinforcing positive feedback and enhanced self-esteem when the new behaviors bring, not neurotically feared disaster, but real reward and gratification. On this basis, such therapeutically induced changes can be reinforced and can endure.

Actually, within the PRP sample, there were 12 instances (almost 30% of the sample)—5 in psychoanalysis and 7 in psychotherapy, 10 men and 2 women—where this particular mechanism seemed to play some significant role in the treatment outcome, and quite importantly in 7 of them.[7] Two of them can be taken

---

7. This great disparity in sex distribution (10 males to only 2 females) seems a striking finding. One wonders whether it reflects, not any real difference in the illness patterns along this dimension between the male and female patients in our research sample, but rather the culturally greater premium in our (sexist?) value commitments on seeing characterological submissiveness in males as more inherently psychopathological, and hence a more appropriate target for therapeutic activity.

as paradigmatic of the group. One of these two, whose treatment course has been described in Chapter 19 (see pp. 375–382), was the Involutional Woman. In that description, it has been made clear how a significant part of the therapeutic result rested on the maintenance of an avowedly supportive, benevolent, dependent, and encouraging relationship, within which this always inhibited (and recently progressively depressed) patient could become more safely assertive in her outside life with her husband.

Therapy of the Obedient Husband

BACKGROUND AND PROGNOSIS

Here I describe the other of these two exemplar cases, the Obedient Husband, whose very designation carries in it the statement of this particular problem. He was a businessman, who, alone of all our 42 patients in the sample, came initially to The Menninger Foundation not in his own right, but as the spouse of a sick wife who was in analytic treatment. Our patient (the husband) was having regular casework interviews with the social worker, and, as a result of her urging and his wife's, brought himself to psychiatric evaluation. He was distressed (and becoming depressed) that, as his wife seemed to improve in her treatment, he felt himself increasingly inadequate and unaccountably resentful.

All his life the patient had been quiet and shy. As a schoolboy he had learned quickly and done well, but had always been timid and reserved, and limited in his peer relationships. At sports he had always been a spectator. For no clearly specifiable reason, he had felt inadequate and inferior throughout his growing-up years. When troubled he would turn to his mother, not to discuss his difficulties but to get comfort "just by being close to mother." He grew up to take a job in his father's business, and, with his parents' support, married rather early. The marriage went well for only about a year. His wife became ill physically (with a chronically debilitating condition) and emotionally (she was depressed, apathetic, interested only in her numerous somatic complaints). The wife was in psychotherapy and made herself completely dependent on the patient. He was advised by the wife's therapist to "go along with her"—to press no demands, but rather to accede to her wishes. She gave up all responsibility for either his care or the care of the home. The patient was soon nurse, mother, housemaid, and husband, roles he fulfilled over the succeeding years. He would nurse his wife, clean the house, cook the meals, and generally do whatever was her desire. Because of her increasing disturbance and suicidal gestures, he brought her to a variety of psychiatric sanatoria. His business suffered accordingly, but he did not complain about any of this.

After a variety of treatment vicissitudes, the patient finally brought his wife to The Menninger Foundation, where she was hospitalized and shortly thereafter entered analytic therapy. As his wife began to show real improvement after about a year of treatment, the patient paradoxically began to feel troubled, depressed, angry, and insecure. He felt less needed, now that his wife was becoming less dependent upon him. With the help of the social worker, he could see that his own self-esteem had been importantly buttressed by his wife's extreme dependency. Now he began to feel neglected and useless; if he should die it would not be very important, since he was not of much real use to anyone. He was frightened of intrusive suicide thoughts (e.g., fantasies of driving off a bridge) and fearful that he might try it. Nor had he been able to follow the social worker's counsel in his dealings with his wife. He came to realize that his constant acquiescence to her helpless, demanding state had not been helpful to her. He tried to be more realistically firm, but he was uneasy at this behavior, which he experienced as being party to "ganging up on her." He was fearful that this might simply lead to his loss of her love. He was afraid also that she might turn to other, more attractive men now that she no longer needed his devoted nurturant care so much.

Under these circumstances, the patient had his evaluation. All this time the patient had been carrying on his business in his home town and making regular visits to his wife in Topeka. Now he readily agreed to move to Topeka for treatment, to work there as well, and to maintain contact through his partners with his business at home. The treatment recommended was supportive–expressive psychotherapy. Psychoanalysis was specifically advised against because of the patient's very passive–dependent character traits, his lack of psychological-mindedness and reflective bent, and, above all, his massive constriction of personality and profound masochism. It was felt that with this constellation of operative factors, the psychoanalytic situation could well conduce to an interminable perpetuation of the wellsprings of his neurotic character.

COURSE OF THE THERAPY

The twice-weekly psychotherapy lasted 18 months (124 hours). Supportively, the therapist was a sympathetic listener, an encouraging influence, the provider of a better reality guide; expressively, she helped constantly to elucidate the patient's predominant character pattern—his abdication of responsibility for himself and his masochistic submissiveness to others. A "turning point" came in the treatment some 3 months before the end, when the patient quite abruptly gave up his constant, too-heavy drinking (concealed at the time of initial evaluation) in response to the therapist's insistence that he would never know the "escapist meanings" that went into his drinking behavior unless he stopped. This the patient took as an "order," and he proudly responded positively; the episode proved that he *could* take charge of himself and effect changes. At the same time he dropped his (up to then, constant) refrain that he was only coming to treatment because his wife pushed him.

During the 18 months of treatment, the patient's reality situation progressively altered. His wife was discharged from inpatient status at about the same time that he moved to Topeka, so they again set up housekeeping together. And in response to the wife's resumed intense demandingness, to which he again acquiesced, the patient found himself once more with a practically full-time job as nurse, companion, housekeeper, mother, and maid. The patient tried to keep up with his business in his home town on weekends, but it turned out that the business had been progressively failing and was now nearly bankrupt. With the help of the therapist, the patient could now, for the first time in his life, acknowledge to himself his failure as a businessman. He sold out, salvaged what he could, and settled down into open dependence on the largesse of his rich in-laws (who supported both their living situation and their combined psychotherapies); he thus accepted openly what had anyway long since been the actual state of affairs. A second child was born shortly—an event that depressed his wife, but that the patient ostensibly welcomed. His home and parental duties naturally increased to take on the added burden of care and nurture of the infant, which he accepted with his usual resigned passivity.

Through the patient's whole treatment, he made desultory efforts to widen his social life and to find gainful employment. Most of these were ineffectual, since he was so bogged down in the nursing and caretaking role with his wife (e.g., he would go to bed with her most nights at 6:30 or 7:00 P.M., according to her desire). This all changed dramatically in the wake of his stopping drinking, however. He now began diligently to go to business school; he intensified his job hunting, and he began to insist on a wider social life, with or without his wife. At the point of termination, he had secured an office manager position in a moderate-sized business. He was proud of the job (the first he had ever secured for himself), and for his assertiveness in being thus able to disentangle himself from being the maidservant to his wife's neurosis. He attributed this significant improvement to his therapy and felt himself ready to terminate.

The themes of the therapy unfolded alongside the progression of the patient's ongoing life. They included the following:

1. The patient's coming into therapy in resentful compliance with his wife's demand (reinforced by others) that he do so, without his conceiving any possible gain for himself.

2. The network of deceptions concerning his failing business. It came out that he had never felt that the business had belonged to him; there was almost relief in accepting openly his total dependence upon his in-laws. After all, he felt, he was only competent at housework and home nursing.

3. The unfolding of the heretofore hidden story of the "escapist" alcohol excess. This had been covered over as nothing more than "social drinking," three to five cocktails each night; as with most of the patient's behaviors and activities, he never saw that he could do anything about it. It was his capacity to respond positively to the "demand" to stop drinking, and his exertion in making this stick, that the patient felt paved the way for all the other changes he could then bring himself to make: disengaging himself from his attendance on his wife, securing and holding a self-respecting job, involving himself with friends, and so on.

4. The revision of the relationship with his wife. Up to the "turning point," the patient did not work, but stayed at home, treated by his wife as a combination of housekeeper and nursemaid. When he could escape this bondage, under the therapist's aegis, he found that he welcomed the more assertive and productive role. It had been less the danger of the wife's improvement than the constant erosion of his dignity by her massive demands that had led to the patient's helpless symptom expression. He could see, also, that she was not getting that much better—that she was still extremely ill in her regressive and infantile character position.

5. And, linked to all of these themes, the unfolding transference position. The transference expectation that the patient initially brought was that therapy was a situation where responsibility would be taken off his shoulders, and where he would receive advice on how to run his life more satisfactorily. The patient brought his ineffectiveness and his helplessness, and then his frustration and anger that the therapist would not fully play out her assigned transference role.

Suddenly, with the stopping of drinking (the "turning point"), the patient proved that he *could* assert controls and resist temptation; he promptly expressed his new effectiveness and manliness in each of his major life areas—with his wife, his position in the home, his newfound job. What was not made explicit was the transference position that was the vehicle for this shift in behavior. The patient submitted to what he experienced as the transference demand that he at last be assertive in his life, and the new assertiveness in outside behaviors covered over the transference submission on which it was based. It was this shift in the direction of the submission from his wife (and his total life situation) to the therapist that represented the major transference effect of the treatment—an uninterpreted transference effect. The therapist put it thus: "I just helped him into a pseudoactiveness. It was all unspoken. . . . I was a kind of countermagic for the patient with regard to his wife. He used my white magic against her black magic."

TERMINATION

The treatment thus ended at this unanalyzed transference level. At this point, the patient's treatment goals were realized and his symptoms had largely remitted: He had stopped drinking; his other symptoms (sense of inadequacy, anxiety, depression, somatizations, sexual difficulty) had fallen away to varying degrees; he had gotten out from under his wife's tyranny; and he had secured employment for the first time ever on his own. Suddenly this all built up to an abrupt pressure to terminate treatment, to which the therapist acquiesced.

STATUS AT FOLLOW-UP

The patient's life continued and consolidated in Topeka during the follow-up period in a progressive but unspectacular way. He did not seek further formal psychotherapy, though he did have three consultation sessions with his former therapist at about the 1-year mark, for reasons that never seemed to get very clear. The patient was with the same firm and was very contented with his job. The scope of his responsibilities had increased significantly, as had his pay. He emphasized his very close and open relationship with his top supervisors—his willingness to be directly dependent on them for guidance, in return for which he loyally and effectively implemented their policy directions. His confidence was high: "I'm capable of handling the demands of this business."

With his wife, the patient had settled into a new and improved equilibrium, limited still by her immersion in her severe psychological illness. But the patient was no longer intimidated by her. "So many things in the past I used to just go right along the line with her in whatever she wanted with the feeling that maybe it would make her feel better. Now if I disagree with her, I tell her." He saw, however, his wife's continued need for the psychotherapy that helped her tolerate this altered relationship. "She'll never be completely free of her feelings of depression and her insecurities." She would "always" need treatment: "I'd settle for her being strong enough to have only 1 hour a week." And their life together was described as much improved and widened in scope. To the social worker who was seeing the couple in casework guidance related to their son's psychiatric treatment, this was perhaps an exaggeratedly rosy portrayal. He felt their life together to be devoid of interests; much of their time was spent in watching TV and escaping each other's company by recourse to sleep. In this connection, it emerged that the patient had again picked up his predinner cocktail custom at a lessened level. He made sure to deny that it now represented a problem or an "escape."

When the son's psychotherapy terminated, it became clear that the patient (and to some extent the wife) wanted to continue the family-centered casework process that they were in. He was asking that it go on now as marriage and family counseling. There was a proposal that the son could soon be going to a private boarding school (he was now 10), and the patient thought that that might be easier on all of them during the boy's coming adolescent years, especially with the youngster feeling the same issues in regard to his mother (the patient's wife) of her working to thwart his expressions of autonomy and self-assertion. The patient's reluctance in regard to the boarding school plan was that it would deepen his financial dependency upon his father-in-law. Actually, the father-in-law was paying the total treatment costs of all the family members, plus a varying amount toward the regular household and living expenses. With each raise the patient secured on his job, he was quick to lower the requested monthly supplement, and he expressed pride in this. He did not realistically foresee that he would ever dispense totally with this maintenance allowance; he had come to accept that.

All in all, the patient professed himself very satisfied with his treatment outcome. This was the more notable, since the time of the Follow-Up Study was a period of double stress for the patient. His emotionally disturbed and mildly brain-damaged young son was just terminating *his* therapy, and the patient did not yet feel completely up to coping with the boy's behaviors. Even more stressful was the fact that the patient's wife was suffering a relapse in her emotional state, necessitating a period of rehospitalization for the first time in several years. The patient, nonetheless, was holding up well, though his continuing dependencies were still discreetly evident. They were diffused over a variety of settings: (1) onto the father-in-law, who underwrote the marriage, as noted; (2) onto the company bosses at headquarters, on whom the patient could be comfortably dependent; and (3) onto the social work counselor, who afforded some continuing guidance under the guise of help with the family's concerns in regard to the son in treatment. For the patient, it suited his psychological needs to pause midway in the spectrum of possible change—to shift to more adaptive and assertive behavior patterns in relation to his wife, his work, and his social world, while less manifestly continuing to live out his deeper dependency. During treatment, he did this in relation to the therapist; by the time of Follow-Up Study, the dependency was more spread over the various supporting influences.

This same pattern has continued essentially unaltered up until the time of present writing, 23 years after treatment termination. The patient and his wife have continued to live in Topeka, where she has continued permanently in therapy (a "therapeutic lifer"), and the patient has continued in the supporting and caretaking role, though never himself returning to therapy. The wife is continuing to be seen, on a once-monthly basis at present, for her continuing combined somatic and emotional complaints; she drinks too much, and is confined pretty much to a wheelchair. The patient is visible as he brings her to and fro for each hour. The patient also continues with something of an alcohol problem; as he said to his wife's current therapist on one of their rare joint interviews, neither he nor his wife really want to give up drinking, which is one of their few shared pleasures. Currently the patient is no longer working, having recently retired from his job.

It is not clear from all of this how well the patient has maintained his more assertive stance in his life and his relationships over these years; he has never expressed any feeling of need or desire for renewed treatment.

INVERSE OF THE POSITIVE DEPENDENT TRANSFERENCE: THE ANTITRANSFERENCE CURE

The concept of the transference cure, put most simply, consists of the willingness of the patient to do things (i.e., to make life and behavior changes) *for* the therapist—to risk the lesser anxieties of change, rather than the greater anxiety (in the transference) of loss of the therapist's approval and love. Clearly, such willingness and capacity rest on the prior establishment of a sufficiently compelling dependent transference attachment that the patient finds gratifying and feels it important to maintain, and within which he or she can be asked for an emotional *quid pro quo*. Other patients, however, are oppositely motivated, for whatever reasons. These patients do things not for, but (in their perceptions) *against* the therapist—whether in spite of the therapist's contrary expectations, or defiantly because of such (perceived) contrary expectations. Such situations, which I have designated as representing an "antitransference cure," are of course less frequent than those of the so-called "transference cure," but they can have the same diversity of psychological causation. Two patients in our PRP sample, the Intellectual Fencer and the Silent Woman, represented clear instances of the significant operation of this antitransference cure; each, however, was differently based, and each achieved a different outcome.

Therapy of the Intellectual Fencer

BACKGROUND AND PROGNOSIS

I first describe the treatment career of the Intellectual Fencer, whose overall course was the more successful one. She was hospitalized because of her increasing barbiturate addiction, culminating in an acutely confusional and intoxicated state. The patient was the younger of two children of an emotionally labile and ineffecual mother and a coldly bullying physician father who was "very well liked by people who did not have to live with him." The father seemed only interested in making money, which, in turn, he stingily withheld from the mother and the house. "He seemed to enjoy the feeling of power he got from making people ask him for things." The father worked hard, 7 days a week, and never took a vacation.

In the families of both parents, only male children and their educations, professions, and accomplishments were considered important. The mother's brother, also a physician all his life, had been "the little God in the family." Similarly, the patient's 4-year-older brother had grown up the spoiled darling of the family, had been a world-class fencer, and was now a successful physician, married and with four sons. The patient had disappointed the father greatly in not being born a boy; so sure had he been that this second child, like his first, would also be male, that he had called all his relatives to announce the birth of a son before checking with the hospital and finding out that he had a daughter. The patient's growing up was difficult. The brother was so obviously the preference and pride of the father that, no matter what her accomplishments, the patient felt unable to compete or to garner her share of family praise and affection. The brother (taking his cues from the father) was contemptuous of the patient; he would correct her behaviors, and would indicate that he had always done everything better than she could. The patient was an excellent scholar who consoled herself with cultivating a wide range of interests. She enjoyed besting teachers in classroom debates.

The patient had few friends and few activities; she grew up lonely. Contact with her father was so formal and distant that she had to make appointments like a patient to see him, and even then he would often abruptly cancel these. She wanted very much to follow her father and brother and uncle into medicine, but her father was set against girls' preparing for any career other than marriage, and repeated conversations with him could not change his mind in this matter. When the patient was in college, her always unhappily married parents separated; this upset her greatly, and she tried unsuccessfully to reconcile them. Midway through, the patient was asked to leave college because of "unacceptable social behaviors." When the mother protested, she was told that if she did not press the issue, the college would let the patient leave in a way that would not prejudice her chances elsewhere. The father felt that the dismissal was for homosexual activities; he "accused" the patient of this, but she stoutly denied it.

After leaving college, the patient spent the following years living with her mother, working and/or going to school again for stretches. She finally took medical technician's training, followed by employment as a lab technician in a university hospital. She worked in cancer research and had visions of becoming a famous researcher, finding the cure for cancer. She also returned to complete her college education at night, and this exhausting schedule of work and school was leavened with gradually increasing doses of sedatives. She had a few dates, attracting some men by her "intellectual brilliance" and her wide range of interests. She had two sporadic suitors. Her father hired a private investigator in order to expose one of them as an imposter who was already married. The other seemed mainly to be used as a source of drugs (her other source was stealing from her father's office).

Over the whole 3-year period prior to her psychiatric hospitalization, the patient's drug taking became gradually more overt and more self-damaging. Her mother was first made forcibly aware of it when the patient fell over in a stupor at the dinner table one evening. Though the mother worried over this very much, the disgusted father and brother did not take it seriously as a problem or an illness. The patient herself denied taking drugs; her drug supplies were concealed around the house, but even when a cache was discovered, the patient denied that this reflected a habituation. With this constant drug intoxication, however, the patient lost some 30 pounds, suffered two episodes of pneumonia, and finally lost her job because of absenteeism (as well as coming to work obviously drugged).

The patient was finally referred for outpatient psychotherapy, which lasted only 3 months. Just as she had always denied the "insinuations" of homosexuality, she indignantly denied having any drug problem, though she often came staggering to her hours. Finally she dropped out of college 1 month short of graduation, and everything collapsed; this collapse culminated in the episode in which she was found intoxicated and wandering about the hall of her apartment building clad only in her undergarments. Her therapist then insisted on referral for immediate psychiatric hospitalization. Though the patient arrived in an organic confusional state, ataxic, and with slurred speech, she was resentful of both her therapist and her family for pressuring her to come. Once in the hospital, gradual withdrawal from all drugs was completed uneventfully over a week's time. The patient settled with some enthusiasm into a very full and compulsive work activities schedule.

The treatment recommended was expressive psychotherapy. Because of the nature of the patient's symptoms, as well as her deceptions and concealments, it was to be supported through a considerable phase by concomitant hospitalization. If it went well, this therapy might "prepare her for subsequent psychoanalysis."

COURSE OF THE THERAPY

Actually, the patient was in an expressive psychotherapy for 2 years (263 hours), with concomitant hospitalization for the first 6 months. The expressive treatment focus was consistently on her competitive strivings, their inner sources, and their frustrations. This was a constant struggle, in which the patient might stiffen in resistant denial ("What you say isn't true") or, alternatively, in defensive competitiveness ("I know all that already; you're not telling me anything that changes anything"). She was aptly called "a fencer of the intellect." But the therapist was characteristically unable to bring this interpretive effort effectively into the transference interaction, where the patient was ever re-enacting the very competitive strivings that were the subject of inquiry—manifested in her need to be the better therapist, while defensively warding off *his* insights.

The patient's life through this treatment was a steadily progressive one. For the first 6 months as a hospital inpatient, she worked compulsively and successfully in a variety of diverse activities, including the patient newspaper. She read widely and listened to her vast record collection (2000 albums), which she had with her. Subsequently she went on to complete college with honors as a literature major. She began to work full-time, first as a volunteer and then as the paid chief of occupational therapy at a local rehabilitation center for the handicapped (in her words, "a junior-grade psychiatrist"). At each step of demonstrated increased competence along the way, the patient felt strengthened in her competitive position vis-à-vis the therapist. She could utilize her achievements to force respect and acceptance, in place of having to understand the full nature and source of these inordinate yearnings for voiced respect and acceptance.

Alongside these life and work activities, the patient became gradually involved over the last year of her treatment in a growing attachment to another patient, a sensitive, intelligent, quite passive individual with known severe alcoholism and homosexuality. After about 4 months in therapy, as a measure of her growing trust within the therapeutic relationship, the patient had confessed the secret (until then, closely guarded) of a homosexual involvement with a maternal and succorant older woman about 2 years before her hospitalization. It was the rejection finally by this woman that had led the patient into the deepening barbiturate addiction of the next 2 years. In the romance with her present suitor, the patient held a clear rescue fantasy: "If only someone had come along when I was involved in homosexuality like I'm doing for him now, and tried to help me get out from under it, I might have made it." And in this role she would now competitively prove her own therapist wrong for his misgivings, and would also be a better therapist than her lover's therapist, who had not yet cured him. Thus after their first sexual experience, she came back triumphantly: "I slept with him and he's not homosexual." She considered herself wiser and stronger than any of the therapists. When her therapist counseled delay and consideration in her marriage plans, she pushed them forward more determinedly in order to thwart him. When she finally married, 2 months before her treatment termination, she used the fact of the marriage to prove that she was now strong enough to discard her therapist (besides, of course, she now had a substitute for him); at the same time, she used the achievement of the marriage goal to win the acceptance of her therapist and also of her father. The patient's father, in fact, for the first time thoroughly approved of her: Her wedding was her fulfillment as a woman in his view, and it stilled his concerns about the stigma of having a homosexual daughter.

The themes of the 2 years of therapy unfolded in orderly sequence:

1. Initially there was a sense of futility, stemming from the patient's lifelong hopelessness in getting close to people or trusting them, and her bitter feelings toward her family members.

2. After 4 months, as noted, there was the confession of the previous homosexual liaison. This was a mark of growing trust within the therapy, and, at the same time, a defensive response against the growing awareness of a positive transference attachment. That is, homosexual impulses were used as a defense against heterosexual (transference) impulses, and transference hate (directed against her stupid and bungling hospital doctor) was used as a defense against transference love.

3. Each forward step in her life represented to the patient a continued living out of competitive conflicts with the father (becoming a "junior-grade psychiatrist"), as well as a testing at each point whether or not this would be acceptable.

4. The romance with her husband-to-be stilled the rising concern about her own homosexual inclinations. The patient used her age (now 31), her desire for children, and her avowed feeling that this might be her "only chance" to push ahead with this marriage, which would anyway be curative of the illnesses of both her husband and herself—so how could anyone object?

5. Once married, the patient promptly pressed for a reduction in treatment frequency, and then for termination. She was surprised and frightened when the therapist agreed more readily than she had expected. She had married someone she saw as a weak man (she would be "uncomfortable with aggressive domineering men like my father") and as still a sick man (needing to go on in his treatment), and she realized that her whole new marriage was not in a solid state. She was wondering, "Am I ready? Will it last?" But she decided to go ahead anyway.

In the transference, the patient split her feelings from the start and maintained the situation in this way to the end. She was openly hostile and competitive with men, and, the hospital doctor bore this burden throughout. The therapist, on the other hand, immediately reminded the patient of an old, good friend, one of the few men she had felt kindly toward in her life; however, she never told him of the resemblance and the feeling it stirred. She "rode" on the positive attachment, but always warded off explicit awareness of its erotic components (via her homosexual inclinations, or via her courtship and marriage). With the therapist, she kept the feeling one of constant liking and admiration. "When I got mad, I got mad at the therapeutic situation, but I never got mad at the therapist." The patient at the same time used the marriage to achieve a newfound rapprochement with her father; as the father became a more benign figure, the mother became a more baleful one. The mother was suffocatingly devoted, and "you have trouble keeping her off your back. She fosters dependency. If you're not dependent she will take over and make you dependent." She was fearful of succumbing to the temptation to be close to the mother, with its homosexual overtones.

The therapist never succeeded in bringing either the explicitly erotic or the explicitly hostile components into the transference. Here, he was also inhibited by his own need to be the liked one; this made it more difficult to deal with the patient's triumphant competitiveness *with him* as a re-enactment of her hostile struggle with her family members. And when the patient pressed him hard (in regard to marriage, to decreasing the treatment frequency, to termination), he capitulated readily.

TERMINATION

At the termination mark, transference phenomena had not been worked past their initial positions. The therapist, rather, played out his various assigned transference roles; these were mostly in the image of the benign and understanding father, an image that was fostered at the expense of a multifaceted experiencing the full range of transference manifestations. Of the termination, the therapist said that the patient's feelings of love and gratification put her into an intoxicated state in which she could no longer be held still to examine her feelings.

The patient said of her termination, "My goals were achieved. Here I was definitely and decidedly a woman, an adult woman, very much in love, walking on pink clouds in a world full of light and beautiful and meaningful things." When the therapist insisted to the end that he would consider this only an interruption, not a settled termination, the patient responded with relief: "To be honest, I'm worried. I'm glad to know the door is open." And perhaps because of these fears, the patient, though willing to be interviewed for research purposes at termination (in her identification as herself a researcher), would not allow a repetition of the psychological test battery, where she could not control as well what she might reveal.

The treatment thus ended in a (not quite consolidated) competitive triumph for the patient; the therapist's acquiescence to the marriage and to the termination was his acceptance of defeat. The mate she chose also reflected the patient's need to continue her dominant role with the willing man. Rather than the treatment's having ended through the resolution of this conflict, it ended in the acting out of it.

STATUS AT FOLLOW-UP

At the Follow-Up Study point, the patient made an upbeat presentation. She had continued with her job for 16 months, but then had stopped in order to "concentrate on getting pregnant." The patient became at this point "a complete suburban housewife and loving every minute of it." The marriage became "sheer heaven" because now the pair could really live together (they had had jobs on different time shifts) and "I love it very much." The patient did become pregnant quite promptly, but then suffered a spontaneous miscarriage. The patient took this better than her husband did; she felt reassured by the obstetrician that this was a frequent occurrence with first pregnancies and that there was no reason why she couldn't "go on and have 50 children."

The husband, meanwhile, was finishing his own long-delayed college career (after the patient had finished hers), finally graduating with honors in one of the humanities. He was shortly admitted to an outstanding graduate department elsewhere in the country, and they were on the verge of leaving for their new home. This was a stressful time for the husband, and the patient saw her job as "getting him through these couple of weeks." She would do this by "keeping him fed, companioned, and entertained. . . . Just be there with him, help him, understand him. . . . I pamper him, spoil him, fuss over him—I'm very fond of him." Nonetheless, right after his graduation, the husband went on his first drunken binge in over a year. The patient's whole view of her life and marriage, though, was one that denied all problems and difficulties. Her job with her husband was "his improvement. He's not nearly the problem husband he used to be. He now knows what he wants to do with his life, and he's doing beautifully at it." As for herself, "I know where I'm going—to be a wife and a mother, and I'm getting right there." The patient's relations with her parents, she stated, were now "incredibly good." Her father, who had left his practice for the first time in his life to attend her wedding, had now invited the patient and her husband as his guests on a Christmas Caribbean cruise over his birthday. Of her mother, she said, "She is difficult but not unmanageable any more." The mother's constant "griping and criticism now slides off my back." Financially, the couple were living on the patient's trust income and her savings. She looked at this as an investment in their future, and declared her husband's academic record an ample return. But he resented as well as appreciated this. He didn't always take it kindly when she was too blatantly "making a man out of him."

From his side, the husband was aware of more problems. He took pride in the patient's superiority, but he resented her domination. When upset, he could still blow up and get drunk (though his overt homosexuality had vanished). He was maintained on Antabuse, and the patient would taunt him about not being able to drink socially with her and her friends. Of her own psychotherapy, the patient said retrospectively that it helped get her back on the track: "The Lord knows I was off the track and now I am back on it." And after a considerable pause she added, "How, I don't know."

COMMENTS

How, indeed, could one account for this seeming stability (at least over this period of time) of a marriage between two people, each with severe and very incompletely resolved problems of sexual identity and of addiction potential—a stability achieved, incidentally, in the face of near-universal prediction to the contrary?

Clearly, the marriage, a manifestly heterosexual relationship on both sides, could simultaneously be the vehicle for the concomitant covert expression of underlying homosexual strivings of *each partner* in a stabilized interaction, in which each helped the other to maintain self-esteem, to demonstrate that they were not homosexuals, not failures. The husband was clearly in a submissive relationship to a phallic woman, the partner with a fantasied penis, and hence in underlying symbol and fantasy was clearly still in a homosexual relationship. At the same time, his "pseudoheterosexual" attachment also masked an underlying infantile dependency born out of the original anaclitic relationship with his mother. What he acquired was a nurturant mother who married him to cure him of his homosexuality and his drinking, and to enable his growth under her protective wing. (All this interpretation was derived not just from his research interviews, but from his own therapy record as well.) The patient, from her side, exhibited the counterparts of each of these libidinal dispositions. She was the aggressively successful partner in the marriage—the one who made it go, and who led the way to each achievement. At the same time, the patient was the nurturing and rescuing maternal figure in the marriage. She took care of and "cured" her husband.

This marriage, therefore, had built-in stabilities. It could endure precisely because it so clearly operated on both levels at the same time—that of unconscious homosexual union of phallic woman with submissive man and of nurturant mother with orally dependent child, and at the same time that of conscious heterosexual union, albeit of a pseudoheterosexual variety. The patient, in her treatment, had probably worked through sufficiently to the point where from her side this solution in this marriage could be stable and enduring. The husband's psychic equilibrium was less certain, and the marriage would likely continue or founder depending on the vicissitudes of his life and his continuing treatment.

There was a fragment of post-follow-up information 4 years past this point. The patient and her husband had successfully had a child. But then, some time later, they had separated and divorced. The patient was living in the same city with, but separate from, her family. She was not in further treatment. She was "making it" as a woman with a child, but without a husband.

Analysis of the Silent Woman

BACKGROUND AND PROGNOSIS

The other patient whose treatment course, overall somewhat less successful, is used to illustrate this same mechanism of the antitransference cure is the Silent Woman, who was recommended upon evaluation for psychoanalysis. She was a divorced woman with two sons, aged 11 and 6; she sought treatment because of depression, anxiety, and indecisiveness, which had begun after the birth of her second child and had been increasing in depth and tenacity ever since.

The patient was the second of four daughters in a closely knit farm family of pioneering stock. The father was domineering—a strict disciplinarian, but also lovable and admired, "as exciting a person as I have ever known." The mother, by contrast, was a gentle, devoted person, around whom the whole household could relax, but subordinate in all things to the father. As a child the patient had been a good scholar, and also the local tomboy. "When it came time for me to be a young lady I had trouble making the shift." Like the Intellectual Fencer, she had also aspired to be a physician; when ill at ease socially, she consoled herself that she would become a doctor and that people would then, at least, respect her.

In college, however, the patient became frightened of the difficulty of premedical courses (especially physics), and she gave up her medical aspirations. This was a surprising turn to her: "I had never done that—given up—before." Very shortly thereafter she was found to be suffering from pulmonary tuberculosis and was hospitalized in a sanatorium for what turned out to be a refractory 2½-year stay. When she recovered, she made another career effort, studying to be a lab technician (again like the Intellectual Fencer), but this was halted by a relapse of the tuberculosis and another 6 months in bed. Thereafter, she was even more inhibited socially: "I was prepared for people not to want to have anything to do with me because I had had tuberculosis."

The patient then prepared for a business career, and at the same time got into a marriage that was disappointing from the start. Though warned against pregnancy because of the recent tuberculosis, the patient nonetheless became pregnant almost immediately. She then found her husband withdrawing from her. Through the years of the marriage, the estrangement grew, and there were repeated separations. With the second pregnancy, the husband backed away even more completely; shortly thereafter he left, never to return. The patient secured a divorce and returned to her parental home.

The patient had a severe postpartum depressive period following the birth of the second child. Ever since, she continued to be chronically depressed, anxious, and indecisive. She was fitfully aware of a continued emotional attachment to her ex-husband. Her father turned the ownership of a 400-acre farm over to her and bought her a home in town near the farm, from which she could rent and supervise it. She had a sporadic and unsatisfying social life. She had a brief period of unsuccessful psychotherapy; another psychiatrist then tried ECT and insulin, also to no avail. At this point, the patient welcomed the referral to The Menninger Foundation, and was brought by her elder sister acting *in loco parentis*. The patient came prepared to stay for the long-range treatment that she expected would be recommended. Her children had been left with her parents with arrangements for their care there "as long as necessary."

The treatment recommended was psychoanalysis. Based on the patient's compulsively anchored negativistic streak, as well as the lifelong nature of her interpersonal relationships, the caution was raised that periods of stubborn and pouting silences could pose a real problem to the analytic work. This might be accentuated by fears based on the interactions with the ex-husband, who had always unsympathetically "analyzed" the patient (i.e., had maliciously dissected her character traits and "faults").

COURSE OF THE ANALYSIS

The analysis actually lasted only 1 year (228 hours), at which point it was unexpectedly and abruptly disrupted by the patient; this act dislodged a "transference jam" that had developed around the intense silences that had come to characterize the analytic interaction.

The patient's life during the 1 year of analysis was one of consistent forward movement. She moved to Topeka without her children. Between her farm income and work, she planned to support herself and her treatment expenses fully. She rapidly secured a clerical job, while going to business school to prepare for a better one; within 6 months she had a second job, a managerial position with a public relations firm. Her work there was very successful, and she had good working relationships with fellow employees, especially her female immediate supervisor. But beyond the job she had little social life, and almost no men friends; she limited herself mostly to her several visits home and to her children during the year. She rationalized that, between her work and her treatment, she had not much time left over. Toward the end of the year, in opposition to the voiced skepticism of her family, she was able to bring her two children to Topeka and successfully set up a household with them and away from her parents for the first time in her life. The children's difficulties with each other she found not unmanageable. The patient indeed very successfully juggled the responsibilities of home, children, job, and treatment.

All of these developments in her life were accomplished by the time the patient terminated her therapy, despite all the feelings that she was helpless, and despite the guilt aroused with each achievement. Though she was unclear about what else she might have accomplished in analysis, she felt she owed these life changes to it. Being in treatment made her "more secure"; it gave her "an anchor—a stabilizer." "If not for the treatment I don't think I would have gotten a job, or held on to it." However, within the analysis, there was no such sense of movement or accomplishment. Retrospectively, the treatment impasse was dated to an encounter at the very beginning, in the second analytic hour. In that hour the patient had to sit up to make a "confession" about a recent diagnosis of "psychomotor epilepsy" made on her younger son, and her forebodings for his future, as well as her guilt over her current separation from him. The analyst's response was in terms of possible barriers to treatment becoming evident at the very start. The patient perceived this as accusatory, and the analyst himself felt with hindsight that it was perhaps "too scientific" and insufficiently empathetic with her plight.

The chief technical problem throughout the treatment was that of the stubborn and lengthy silences right from the start. Many meanings for these were adduced: the patient's difficulty in accepting the enforced passive and "feminine" position vis-à-vis the analyst, represented by the couch and the pressure to free-associate; the phallic-competitive struggle for supremacy in the analytic encounter with a man; the fear of revealing feelings of inadequacy and her sense of failure in life; doubts about treatment and its efficacy (she even feared that it could make her worse, that "taking a chance" and "letting go" would only lead to disorganized "hysterical babbling"); avoidance of forbidden affect expression (she expressed fear of her "clobbering impulses"); her perception of analysis as a fighting (and perverted love-making) relationship, on the pattern that that was what was expected and respected by the father; and alongside all of these, constant, stubborn, angry rebelliousness—"I felt rebellious toward the whole thing from the first." The analyst felt retrospectively that he had concentrated too one-sidedly on the negative components of this transference resistance, thereby intensifying it (see pp. 178–179, 243–244).

At the same time, the analyst was aware of the wistful waiting to be appreciated and loved under the frightened and angry exterior. Strong evidence of transference attachment appeared. This was the patient who once drove 500 miles and through a storm in order to get to her hour on time, came in saying "Whew, I made it," only to lapse promptly into a prolonged silence. The patient was distressed by emerging erotic and dependent transference longings. The analyst saw the patient as a frightened little girl with a tough shell, one who wanted to cry but couldn't let herself because it would destroy her image of herself as her father's fighting little girl. Material did emerge in the analysis enlarging the picture of the father and the relationship to him. Though intensely admired, he was also seen as a very pressuring and disparaging figure. No one could meet his demands. Others had given up trying, but the patient lived always emotionally tied to him, continuing in vain to try to satisfy and please him, but feeling that she could never win through to this. In a parallel way, within the transference, the patient saw the analyst as undemonstrative and unresponsive, like the coldly analyzing husband, behind whom stood the equally critical father. "I was looking for a benevolent Santa Claus. I was disillusioned. There was nothing benevolent about him." In effect, who would listen? She was just a country lass with a city sophisticate.

Thus there was an intensifying treatment impasse within which all interpretations were wrong and the patient felt reproachfully misunderstood; however, this was accompanied by an outside life of ever more independent and successful management and living, and a falling away of the patient's symptoms (her depression, her anxiety, her diminished self-esteem). There was inordinate satisfaction in proving to her father that she could handle a job away from home and on her own, and not the one near him that he had selected for her and was pressuring her toward. The patient said of these changes consequent to her treatment, "I got a lot out of it. I don't suffer as much as I did a year and a half ago. I don't consider myself well, but then I am much improved."

DISRUPTION OF THE TREATMENT

The termination of the treatment came unexpectedly for the analyst, who felt that the analytic process was moving, albeit very slowly. A series of interlocking events took place. The patient's important elder sister was visiting, and at the patient's insistence was brought along for an interview with the analyst. The sister was not impressed with him; of this, the patient said, "He didn't make any sense to her, any more than he ever did to me." The analyst also had not noticed (or at least had not paid attention to) a change in the patient's hairdo and an effort to make herself more attractive, which disappointed her. In this context, the patient sought a week off because of some unusual work pressures, and wanted not to pay for that week. When the analyst insisted on treating these requests analytically, the patient angrily walked out, announcing that she would not return to treatment. She did not return, nor did she respond to a letter from the analyst asking that she come in to try to discuss the termination and to bring closure to the many issues involved in it.

On what basis was the patient thus able to terminate this analysis? Two major factors converged—one negative, the other positive. The first was the deepening transference–countertransference jam, the degree to which the analyst allowed himself to conform to the transference expectation of the demanding and cruelly disparaging father by his primary focus on the silences in their negative transference-resistance aspects. The patient then readily fell into the position of the disappointed, sullen, and stubbornly rebellious child, and the analyst in turn reacted by "trying to push a truck uphill"; he was not able to analyze the interplay that made him into the truck-pusher. The patient's frustration with this impasse was expressed as "never being able to see the relation between what I came for and what the treatment was about." To the resulting desire to break off treatment were added the willingness and confidence to do so that came from the other, positive factor operative in this decision—the courage of the patient's improved life functioning in every area, achieved in independence of (and in defiance of) her father. This freeing herself from (and triumphing over) the father, which the work of the analysis itself had made possible for the patient, she now turned into a further freeing: an independence of (and defiance of) her analyst.

STATUS AT FOLLOW-UP

At the Follow-Up Study, the patient indicated that she continued to live successfully in Topeka, and had had no psychiatric treatment or even contact in the interim. She had increased responsibilities at work, involving aspects of programming. She had a larger, more comfortable house, a good housekeeper, and a roomer who helped share the expenses and gave her some companionship as well. The children were individually doing well, though they continued to scrap constantly. When it was suggested that she might consider psychiatric consultation for them, she froze. She said, "Anyway, if I have difficulties with them, it's not really them. It's me." She thought she wasn't firm enough with them. Sometimes, trying to fulfill both parental roles seemed too much, but she was afraid that if she got into a new marriage, the new husband wouldn't be of much help to her either (her views about men had not significantly altered). She had occasional dates, though there really were no men in her life. She didn't have enough in common with the men she did go out with. She denied manifest sexual feelings: "I like it this way." Contact with the patient's family had settled into friendly holiday visits back and forth. And her symptoms, she felt, were all much better. She did have mild episodic depressive swings, which she linked to premenstrual tensions. She was somewhat more irritable as a person than formerly. Her long-range attitude was a resigned one. But she said sharply, "I have no time to get lonely."

In all of these resolutions, the patient felt that her treatment had bolstered her. She said she often wished that she had gotten more out of treatment, but that the conflicts that brought her to treatment didn't bother her as much now. And she revealed more of the antipathy she had felt toward the analyst all through the treatment, and in fact from the very start. She had kept doggedly at it as long as she had, even though it was never pleasant, just because she had started. She saw it as a problem of the analyst's never understanding her, nor she him, and as something useless to discuss between them.

A post-follow-up contact 6 years later provided a glimpse of the patient's future fate. She called asking to see one of the research interviewers in consultation. She had left her job in order to return full-time to college for a degree in business administration; she had worked hard and was soon to graduate with honors. A few weeks before graduation she was seized with sudden panics, began to go blank when faced with term papers, and became fearful that she would fail to graduate at the last moment. The interviewer told her that she was a worn-out student, exhausted from chronic sustained overwork; he advised her to take a 48-hour respite from her studies. He also made a cautious interpretation that now that she was about to achieve something that meant so much to her, she couldn't stand it. She responded with a confirming awareness that this was an old pattern with her; she thanked the interviewer and took his advice. She called back a few days later to say that all was going better again and that she was now sure she would make it successfully. She subsequently obtained a sought-for position as information officer in a local governmental agency.

COMMENTS

It was clear at Follow-Up Study (and at the 6-year post-follow-up) that, despite the limited analytic (i.e., intrapsychic) change, the patient had accomplished and sustained a significant degree of behavioral change. Her life patterns had been constructively altered: She could successfully establish herself away from the parental home, could secure and maintain a job of her own choice, and could undertake to provide a home for her children. She was now for the first time a successful homemaker, breadwinner, and parent. The patient herself felt that the support she had gotten within the treatment itself—its concern with her and her doings—had been instrumental in making these many worthwhile life changes possible. But beyond that, and this was not at all worked through analytically, the patient herself cast the die for the behavioral "resolution" of her conflicted tendencies by strengthening the aggressively doing, competently managing (hence, to her, the masculine–intrusive) mode. She did this in protest against and in defiance of the father and of the analyst as father, who each had foretold her failure: The father had predicted failure unless she submitted to his direction over her affairs; the analyst had analogously implied failure unless she submitted to analytic work as the road to effective living.

Thus the patient's time in analysis enabled her to defy the father and in fantasy to triumph over him, and this victory in life strengthened her to act out in similar defiance against the analyst as father. She engineered her triumph over him by managing her life more effectively not only because of him, but also despite him, and then without him. The patient paid some price for this result, so far from thorough psychoanalytic conflict resolution. The price was her resigned acceptance of an essentially manless life, a life without marital or heterosexual fulfillment, and a consequent chronically moderately anhedonic state. It was, for our present expository purposes, another example (this one from a patient in psychoanalysis) of a therapeutic result that rested primarily on what I have called the antitransference cure.

It was exactly in this state that things seemed to continue to be maintained. Six years later still, now 14 years after the treatment disruption, the patient again contacted the same research interviewer (again, not her ex-analyst). A variety of stressful circumstances obtained in her life at this point. Her father had just died. She herself was somewhat entangled in an importunate romance with a very disturbed man, who had been an old high school boyfriend of hers. Her job was going well, but she was facing a possible interruption because of surgery that was being strongly urged for her severe lumbar disc problem. The only smooth area was her relationship with her sons—one a practicing architect, the other in architecture school, and both doing well. With the help of the consultation, the patient detached herself from the unsuitable romantic involvement and reset her life course. She was now over 50, functioning and managing well, but certainly in the state just called "resigned acceptance" and "moderately anhedonic." There is no further follow-up information beyond this point.

Supportive Psychotherapy: Other Supportive Mechanisms

THE CORRECTIVE EMOTIONAL EXPERIENCE

Nature of the Concept

Ever since it was advanced by Alexander and French (1946), the concept of the "corrective emotional experience" has been *a* central, or almost *the* central, explanatory construct invoked in the psychodynamic literature to elucidate the mechanism of the supportive psychotherapeutic approaches (plural); as such, it has been used to explain almost all therapeutic change other than that resting, in the expressive approach, on the operation of interpretations leading to mutative insights. It should be clear by now that I am using the concept here in a far more sharply circumscribed manner: I consider it as *one* of the possible supportive technical mechanisms operating (usually) within the broader framework of the more encompassing positive dependent transference attachment, with its transference gratifications. It may be less clear that I am not using the concept in the sense adumbrated by Alexander and French (1946)—that of attempting to alter or resolve expectations and behaviors of the patient by a planned counteraction within the transference situation, in which the patient is directly confronted with attitudes or behaviors of the therapist that are deliberately contrary to the patient's transference expectation. I am, rather, using it in the more classically psychoanalytic sense advanced by Gill (1954)—that of providing a steadfastly concerned therapeutic stance, equidistant from (and therefore neutral in relation to) the conflicting intrapsychic forces within the patient, and corrective in precisely the sense of *not* being drawn to respond in counteraction to the patient's transference expectations and pulls.

Within this usage, though the concept of the corrective emotional experience could probably be invoked, to some extent or other, in relation to the change process in a fair number of the PRP patients treated with the more supportive therapeutic approaches, it stood out most particularly in relation to three of them. The treatment courses of two of these three have already been described. Though the Housebound Phobic Woman (see pp. 391–398) was recommended for psychoanalysis and ostensibly taken into analysis, her treatment was systematically (though never explicitly) altered from the start into a supportive–expressive psychotherapeutic mode, because of the residual organic cerebral damage consequent to her 14-year-long severely barbiturate-addicted state. The analyst spoke of the entire treatment's being a kind of "corrective emotional experience" in which he was a kindly, understanding, reality-oriented figure, using the maintained positive transference as a principal vehicle for helping the patient achieve a more satisfactory pattern of functioning in her daily life (see p. 394). The Movie Lady (see pp.

413–417) was also recommended for and taken into analysis, but the analyst decided within the first 6 months that he was dealing with a much sicker individual (paranoid, borderline psychotic) than he had initially anticipated, and therefore explicitly shifted to a supportive–expressive psychotherapy. He too talked of his plan to be "as natural and human as possible" and to give the patient a "corrective emotional experience" that a man could be trusted and could help through caring (see p. 415).

Treatment of the Fearful Loner

BACKGROUND AND PROGNOSIS

Here I describe the treatment course of the Fearful Loner in order to illustrate most clearly the operation of the "corrective emotional experience" in the more constricted sense in which I use the term. This patient came to psychiatric treatment with chief complaints of loneliness and unhappiness with his asocial life style. His extremely solitary and constricted life style has already been described (see p. 153): He was estranged from his parents, and his only social contact was with his brother and the brother's family, where he would visit irregularly, stay an hour or two, and then abruptly leave, rarely accepting their regularly extended dinner hospitality. His pathological oversecretiveness has also been described (see p. 162). Even with his third therapist (the only one with whom he got along), he withheld the fact that he had married until 3 months after the wedding, and then revealed it only by way of a request for referral for marital counseling. He was also the patient who physically assaulted an examining psychiatrist whom he felt to be too impatient and intrusive (see p. 122), and who was especially harsh and abusive with his second therapist, a woman (see pp. 246–247).

This patient had grown up lonely and isolated on his parents' farm; he led an active but isolated life at the skills his father had taught him as a hunter, fisher, and trapper. He was always on the periphery of social groups, and disdainful of others in not very tactful ways. He had been a good scholar all through his school and college years, but was indecisive about his career directions until he settled into a civil service position as an accountant, finding his work with figures the best part of his life adjustment. He was naturally distrustful of women, but had gotten into a brief marriage that had lasted 6 months before he divorced his wife because he "could not live with her." When asked about his marriage, he said, "I prefer not to talk about that." His only relationship, carefully dosed and distant, was with his brother, and this has already been described. The brother felt that their relationship might be closer if he were willing to spend a lot of time hunting and fishing with the patient; the patient did not seem to understand the brother's sense of domestic responsibilities to his wife and children, and the patient did not really seem to enjoy visiting with them. The estrangement from the parents has also already been mentioned. As noted earlier, it stemmed from the father's expressed concern that the patient was not having as full a social life as it seemed he should. It was this that the patient called "meddling too much" and led to his angry total break with the parents.

The patient was gradually driven to seek help because up until recently he had felt that his life was future-oriented and advancing toward career goals, and he could hope that somehow things would change for the better. Now he had come to feel life as static and routine; it seemed to be slipping by and giving him very little. His first psychiatrist, whom the patient saw only three times, was the one he physically attacked, pinning him to a chair when he felt his questioning to be too impatient and intrusive. The patient did not go back but came to The Menninger Foundation for evaluation. It was considered a minor triumph when the patient reluctantly agreed to have his brother participate as family informant in the evaluation process. He would, of course, not allow his parents to be seen. Through the whole evaluation process the patient was anxious and fearful, alternately lapsing into silences or responding with a near-paranoid suspiciousness and evasiveness.

The treatment recommended was a once-weekly supportive–expressive psychotherapy. The patient was felt to be so sensitive to unwelcome involvement that any more intense contact at this beginning state might just frighten him off altogether. Treatment would have to proceed solely at his pace and at his degree of willingness for a long time, if not indefinitely. The main therapeutic goal would be to give the patient an opportunity to share a relationship that was not experienced as hostile and threatening (the corrective emotional experience), and, along with this, to come to recognize the extent to which his feeling of being surrounded by menacing danger was but a projection of his own inner turmoil and aggression. Along parallel lines, he was recommended for participation in a bridge playing group in the Out-Patient Club; there he could engage in interactions on his own terms, in a protected setting. His loneliness could be combated via interpersonal contacts whose closeness he could at the same time safely monitor.

COURSE OF THE THERAPIES

At the time of "cutoff" Termination Study, the patient had been in psychotherapy for 6½ years (281 sessions) with three different therapists: a male psychiatrist for 1 year, a female social worker for 3 years, and then a male psychologist for over 2 years. There was a short interim period after the patient "fired" each of the first two therapists and was seeking a reassignment. With the second therapist, the sessions had been reduced to 30 minutes each—the patient was so often silent, and sessions of the usual length were experienced as too much pressure—and this arrangement continued throughout that and the subsequent therapy.

The therapy with all three therapists was purely supportive throughout. The content was always controlled entirely by the patient; he would decide what he would and would not talk about. The third therapist in particular refrained totally from asking any questions about the patient's personal life, or threatening any kind of emotional closeness, anything that might arouse anxiety or provoke potential hostility. Being together in a "social, friendship-oriented" contact, and the patient's increasing capacity to tolerate this comfortably, took precedence over anything that might be said in terms of content. One condition of this type of contact was the patient's total freedom to make any move, any decision in his life, without any constraint that he bring it up for discussion in treatment unless he wished to. When the therapists were on vacation, the patient sought (and utilized) interim appointments with substitutes. He was loath to let time go by without seeing someone; it seemed less important whom he saw. He did join the Out-Patient Club bridge group and gradually made some minimal friendships there.

The patient brought special restrictions and expectations to the treatment.

He felt that he had already told about himself during the evaluation process. The therapist should now, in turn, make him well, and under the conditions that he, the patient, set down: that the therapist was not to pry, not to ask questions, not to try to clarify the nature of internal processes and events, not to create a situation that the patient would experience as uncomfortable in any way. When these conditions were violated, as the patient felt to have happened with the first two therapists, therapeutic impasses escalated rapidly. In regard to subject matter, the past was never brought into the treatment, except as the patient on rare occasions commented tersely that he had been most unhappy as a child. Nor did his current life come much into treatment. He bought land, built a home, entertained in it, sporadically dated women, and bought a flashy, fire-engine-red sports roadster—all without ever mentioning these happenings to his therapists, who usually learned about them from colleagues who were treating friends of the patient. Likewise, the interactions of the treatment hour were largely avoided, especially by the third therapist, who profited from the unsuccessful experiences of his two predecessors. Fantasy rarely entered; with the third therapist, the patient brought in mention of one dream. When the patient's silences became unproductively long, the third therapist simply filled in and picked up the continuity of the material. He did not focus on the thoughts during the silent period—when he tried, he got nowhere.

The therapeutic goal with all three therapists was explicitly the same: to provide the patient with a truly "corrective emotional experience," within which he could slowly become more comfortable, more trustful, more willing to express himself and his concerns, and less poised always to withdraw or to attack; it was hoped that the patient could then be encouraged to a wider participation in outside life activities. The patient, from his side, consciously sought relief from his tension states and his loneliness. At a deeper level, he sought a relationship in which he could experience the gratifications of human contact without the dangers of being dominated, or of being overwhelmed by his own aggressions; he could achieve this within a therapy he could completely monitor and control. The risk was that, having achieved such equilibrium within the treatment, the patient might use it to avoid facing any changes in his everyday life outside the treatment.

The patient's ongoing life and the events he allowed into the treatment fared differently in the three treatment phases, as noted earlier. The first therapist undertook to be actively encouraging in regard to the patient's life outside the treatment and the many stagnant silences within the treatment. He made many suggestions concerning the patient's life and activities (e.g., encouraging him to use the YMCA gym for workouts). Of these suggestions, the patient might ask, "Is that a long shot or do you think it will really help me?"—but then he might well follow through with them. The therapist was preoccupied with "getting to the patient" and cracking the shell of his resistive silences. The patient's recurrent question, after long silences, was, "When are you going to fix me up?" This therapy finally foundered around a struggle over the handling of the bill. I have already described (see p. 198) the patient's insistence on a different than usual way of handling the billing and payment. When the therapist tried to elicit the reasons for this request, the patient stiffened in a sullen resistance. The therapist finally "gave in," but the therapeutic situation could no longer be restored. The patient asked the therapist to admit that he had failed and called for his resignation from the case. He became hostile and abusive, and expressed his resentment over the many suggestions he had been given over how to expand his life, which up to then he had been dutifully (and seemingly contentedly) following. When the therapist pointed to some of these new activities as evidence of beneficial change, the patient said scornfully of them, "So what? I don't enjoy them." When the therapist refused to "resign," the patient "fired" him and sought reassignment. This therapy had lasted 1 year.

The second therapist, the female social worker, pursued an altered strategy (see pp. 246–247). She relaxed all pressures in regard to the outer behaviors and tried to focus on the patient's attitudes and behaviors within the treatment sessions. These then constituted the new battleground. The patient resented her "intrusive" efforts. He berated the therapist for being nosy, useless, worthless; she had better "get on the ball and accomplish something." His comment at the end of many of her (prying) hours was "You did not accomplish anything today either." He advised her to "hire a private detective if you want to find out about me." He thought, more to the point, that they should reverse roles and examine the therapist's mistakes and "neurotic problems," all of which he promised to keep confidential. Yet all through this relentless hostile barrage, which went on over the whole span of this therapy, the patient showed a steady expansion in his life outside the treatment; he hid this from the therapy itself, but the therapist learned about it in fragments from outside and collateral sources. Within the treatment, he admitted nothing. Even when he made a request for renewal of a sedative prescription, and was asked how much he needed it, his response was "You don't need to know." Yet with all his secretiveness and abusiveness, the patient never missed an appointment, nor did he try to disrupt the therapy. He felt that as long as he paid his bill, he could talk and act any way that he pleased. This therapy ended after 3 years, following a series of sessions that the therapist missed because of illness. When after her return, the therapist insisted (for the first time) on scheduling the patient during the regular working day, he flared up anew with insults. This time, however, the therapist indicated that some limit would have to be put to the never-ending torrent of abuse if they were to continue working together. The patient promptly "fired" her and again sought reassignment.

The third therapy had been going on for over 2 years at the time of "cutoff" Termination Study, with no sign, at that point, of major alteration or of termination. This therapist, as noted, accommodated the therapy totally to the patient's requirements, his pace, and his silences. He reached out in what he called "supportive management" to help the patient "come out of his shell." They had many shared discussions about books, wine, phonograph records, and the like. Whenever the therapist said something that the patient construed as an unwelcome intrusion, the latter characteristically arched his eyebrows, and the therapist was immediately responsive to this gesture, halting the inquiry. The therapist's didactic and quite general empathetic comments about the patient's state of tension, his hurt and angry feelings, were never in the context of the here and now of the transference (as the second therapist had tried unsuccessfully to do), or admixed with any suasion to behave differently (as the first therapist had tried unsuccessfully to do). Within this third relationship, the patient tentatively revealed some of his hurts and complaints. He talked of his "emotional deadness" and his alternating "tension states." He also mentioned his bitter anger at his parents and his fundamentalist church for a very punitive upbringing, and for "cheating" him of fun of any sort with their many prohibitions. The therapist would, at most, gently indicate that all of the patient's constrictions and withdrawals were by now self-imposed; the restrictive parents and church were no longer with him, and the limits on his life were now something that he himself would ultimately be able to change. The patient did not like to hear this and told the therapist that "those are *your* theories." He did not become abusive, however, and he acknowledged, "You encourage me when I get into negative thinking." Throughout all this, the patient's life continued (silently) to widen, and when the therapist found out something from other sources (like the flashy new sports roadster), he could jokingly ask what the "big secret" was.

The transference manifestations throughout the therapies were evident on several levels. To the forefront was the shy, sensitive, vulnerable "turtle without a shell," and just behind it the injured victim. Beyond that was the reverse: the patient as hunter, openly and sadistically attacking the therapist as the carrier of the patient's projected unacceptable self. The third therapist maintained the structure by carefully keeping the transference phenomena at the topmost superficial level and nurturing them there. The first two therapists had each differently tried to deal with the transference phenomena; in effect, mini-"transference psychoses" had ensued, in which the patient never fully realized the severe reality distortions involved in his angry and abusive outpourings. These could not be dealt with, and those treatment efforts had thus been disrupted.

STATUS AT TERMINATION STUDY

Overall, over the course of the three therapies, the patient's life had expanded (his social life with friends, his home and entertaining, his office promotion, etc.), but it seemed still in sum a rather bleak and withdrawn existence. The therapist had absolutely no idea of what kind of overt sexual life the patient had, if any. The patient had stopped mentioning any contact of any kind with the brother, and the therapist had never inquired into this. At the time of "cutoff" Termination Study—when, incidentally, it was agreed that it would be too risky to the patient's fragile therapeutic equilibrium to try to interview him—there was no thought by either therapist or patient of termination, either soon or even remotely.

STATUS AT FOLLOW-UP STUDY

At the time of "cutoff" Follow-Up Study, the patient was still in the same treatment situation with the third therapist, a treatment that was clearly going on indefinitely. Again, it was felt contraindicated to try to involve the patient in the research study.

The signal event of the follow-up period was that the patient had married. Characteristically, as noted, he had kept this entirely secret from the therapist, only revealing it some 3 months after the fact by way of a request for referral for marital counseling. He felt unable to communicate with his wife and feared the marriage might be endangered. When seen in joint consultation, the couple had little to talk about. They admitted some difficulties earlier in the marriage, but things were going along well now. The wife was an equally shy and withdrawn person, fearful of family strife; she couldn't stand quarrels. These were clearly two lonely and schizoid people finding emotional surcease with each other. Psychotherapy was offered to the wife on an open basis, but she decided not to undertake it at this time. Actually, what seemed to have instigated the consultation was the patient's narcissistically absorbed and demanding behaviors. His desire that his wife "should talk with someone here" was to have someone in authority explain to her that he had serious emotional limitations so that she would be more accepting of his demandingness and cater to it more wholeheartedly. He seemed oblivious of *her* emotional needs.

The marriage was mainly characterized by the partners' doing things together, and somewhat more than each had previously done alone. The other fact of this clinging togetherness was the patient's strong possessiveness in regard to time his wife spent with neighbor women, indulging in behaviors he disapproved of, such as gossiping and smoking. This was not a jealousy of potential rivals so much as a resentment against anything that might interfere with his wife's total commitment to meeting his enormous dependent urges (e.g., she might not remember to get back in time for his lunch). At one point, the wife mentioned her desire that they have a child. The patient was deeply frightened by this prospect, and angered that his wife could so fail to understand him. He pouted, with a "How could she do this to me?" attitude. He stated his feelings very directly to the therapist: "I just don't think I could be interested in a child. . . . they make me feel uneasy. I don't know what I would do with a child. . . . the child would be a rival for her attention." The patient's sexual adjustment was declared satisfactory by him. The therapist was able to ameliorate the wife's lot in small ways. He got the patient to allow her a TV set—after all, she was home alone all day long. And the patient wanted very much to hold his wife. (Where could he find another like her?)

In other respects, the patient's life had continued in the identical channel that it had throughout the treatment and before the marriage. He was contented in his same job, and talked only a little of his work and its problems. He had hobbies: reading, a hi-fi set, fine wines, cooking. The patient's "symptoms" were all syntonic. He was vaguely paranoid; people on the job were talking about him and not treating him right. He was very self-righteous. His previous anxieties (called "tensions") were now lessened. Throughout this whole 2-year follow-up period, the therapy had continued in the same even and low-keyed way as previously. There was a pleasant and stable rapport; transference phenomena were consistently avoided. In regard to vacations, the patient did mobilize an expression of transference attachment: "You doctors go away and make it very hard on the cash customers around here." Of their relationship, the therapist said, "I see as one of my tasks helping both of them in the marriage by making him more aware of the realistic needs of the wife, and helping him to accept them, and teaching him a little bit about what women need and what they expect in a marriage." Mostly, this worked. From the therapist's perspective, he was "settling for a long-term, perhaps lifetime, patient—with the hope that through these kinds of supportive interventions his life can go somewhat better for him than it would if he didn't have them." From the patient's perspective, his tension and his loneliness were relieved.

COMMENTS AND FURTHER FOLLOW-UP

Unlike so many of the other PRP patients with central problems in regard to dependency strivings, who did well with supportive psychotherapeutic approaches, this patient did not come to therapy with a readiness for a sustaining positive object attachment. Rather, he came intensely fearful, poised for flight or fight, and had to be won to some wary acceptance of a tolerable two-way rapport; in this task, the third therapist—perhaps building on the experiences of the first two—finally succeeded. This became then an indefinite and unchanging endeavor, probably leading to the "career" of a "therapeutic lifer." And within this endeavor, gradual changes in the enlargement of the patient's living sphere did take place, including even the surprise of his marriage—to someone, incidentally, very much like himself. And the marriage seemed not to significantly alter the patient's expression of tension and/or symptomatic behavior, either for better or worse; it simply seemed absorbed into the sameness of his psychological functioning. The chief operative mechanism throughout seemed to be the provision of a truly corrective emotional experience in just the sense articulated by Gill (1954): "To meet the patient's transference behavior with neutrality *is* to give him a corrective emotional experience without the risks attendant on taking a role opposite to that which he expects, as Alexander suggests" (p. 782). What made this all the more striking as a favorable outcome, and also allowed the clearer delineation of the corrective emotional experience as *the* salient mutative mechanism, was that this process took place in a patient who never dared allow the unfolding of a comfortably dependent transference attachment and a really stable therapeutic alliance.

With this case, there is further post-follow-up information for an additional 10 years. At the time of the official Follow-Up Study, the patient had been with the third therapist for 4 years. They continued working together another 8 years, making a total therapy span of 16 years (always at the rate of 30 minutes a week). At that point, the patient retired from his governmental position, and he and his wife moved to an isolated farm in a nearby rural state. The patient had become a health food enthusiast and was much concerned with issues of environmental pollution. On their farm, they could do organic gardening and cultivate much of their own food supply. They could continue their contained, cloistered life together, two lonely and schizoid people drawing sustenance from each other. They had thought briefly about adopting a child, but had discarded this notion. The move to the farm in another state of course drew the formal treatment to a close after 16 years, and this the patient at last accomplished successfully. In the new setting, there was no possibility for psychotherapeutic help. There was a last telephone contact with the therapist 3 years or so after the move and retirement; all was going "well," meaning the same (now 19 years from the patient's initial evaluation).

REALITY TESTING AND RE-EDUCATION

The Role of Education in Psychotherapy

The relationship between psychotherapy and education has been a significant conceptual issue for psychoanalytic theory almost since the inception of psychoanalysis as a psychology, simultaneously, of normal and abnormal human mental functioning, and of planned change in mental functioning. This issue became even more sharply focused with the rise of the behavioral psychotherapies based explicitly on psychological learning theory—models from which psychoanalysis has at all times clearly differentiated itself. The overall question for the field is by no means securely resolved. Freud talked at several times of psychoanalytic treatment as re-education, or as aftereducation. He did this first as early as his 1905 lecture and paper, "On Psychotherapy" (Freud, 1905), where, in explaining the concept of unconscious resistance, he stated that "Psycho-analytic treatment may in general be conceived of as such a *re-education in overcoming internal resistances*" (p. 267, author's italics). His fullest statement on this issue was in 1916. He said then,

> Psycho-analytic work is continually confronted with the task of inducing the patient to renounce an immediate and directly attainable yield of pleasure. . . . Under the doctor's guidance he is asked to make the advance from the pleasure principle to the reality principle by which the mature human being is distinguished from the child. In this *educative process*, the doctor's clearer insight can hardly be said to play a decisive part; as a rule, he can only tell his patient what the latter's own reason can tell him. But it is not the same to know a thing in one's own mind and to hear it from someone outside. The doctor plays the role of this effective outsider; he makes use of the influence which one human being exercises over another. . . . Let us say that the doctor, in his *educative work*, makes use of one of the components of love. In this work of *after-education*, he is probably doing no more than repeat the process which made education of any kind possible in the first instance. Side by side with the exigencies of life, love is the great educator. (1916, pp. 311–312, italics added)

Here Freud, in his talk of educative effects, touched on issues—the nature of the relationship between analyst and analysand, and the way in which the analyst's interpretive work helps the patient toward insight and change—that are today usually discussed under the rubrics of the "therapeutic alliance" (Zetzel, 1956b) and the "working alliance" (Greenson, 1967).[1]

At this point in this book, I am talking not about "education," "educational influence," or "aftereducation" in any of the senses used by Freud or continued in current debate within an altered conceptual language. Rather, I am talking much more specifically (and traditionally) about directly educational (teaching) activities as part of the *content* focus of certain supportive psychotherapies. For the most

---

1. Freud made essentially the same point—each time using the same phrase, though with perhaps some varying nuances—several more times over the span of his writing. "Psychotherapy seeks to undo the less stable of the two outcomes [neurosis and perversion] and to institute a kind of after education" (Freud, 1913, p. 330); "This work of overcoming resistances is the essential function of analytic treatment; the patient has to accomplish it and the doctor makes this possible for him with the help of suggestion operating in an *educative* sense. For that reason psycho-analytic treatment has justly been described as a kind of *after-education*" (Freud, 1917, p. 451, author's italics); and "The new super-ego now has an opportunity for a sort of after-education of the neurotic; it can correct mistakes for which his parents were responsible in educating him" (Freud, 1940, p. 175, author's italics). But Freud also warned against misconstruing this repeated statement to mean that psychotherapy and education are equivalent processes: "One should not be misled by the statement—incidentally a perfectly true one—that the psycho-analysis of an adult neurotic is equivalent to an after-education. A child, even a wayward and delinquent child, is still not a neurotic; and after-education is something different from the education of the immature" (Freud, 1925, p. 274).

part, such activities are properly eschewed in both the expressive and the supportive therapeutic modes; as Freud has just been quoted as saying, "he [the therapist] can only tell [i.e., teach] his patient what the latter's own reason can tell him." But there are instances, especially in some supportive therapies, where this is not quite so (Freud allowed for such instances by prefacing his statement with the phrase, "as a rule"). In such cases, for whatever reasons, the therapist can play a directly educational role through giving advice, transmitting information, and guiding the patient toward normative behavioral standards and expectations, and this role can be a significant component of the therapeutic change process. Within PRP, the case of the Manic–Depressive Physician was a quite clearcut instance of the importance of such education, and his treatment course is described here.

Therapy of the Manic–Depressive Physician

BACKGROUND AND PROGNOSIS

The patient, a 27-year-old married physician, sought psychiatric treatment with a history of recurrent depressions since the age of 13 and a self-diagnosis of "manic–depressive psychosis." (This was in 1957, when such diagnoses were made far less frequently, and when lithium was not yet available in the United States as a specific therapeutic agent for this disorder.) He also complained of an unhappy marriage, and of work difficulties centered around his avoidance of unpleasant tasks and conflicts with his superiors. The history of his regular depressions, of his suicidal danger, and of the psychotic episode in which the diagnosis of manic–depressive psychosis (manic phase) was made has already been presented (see p. 145); his propensity for violence, with its most flagrant eruption in his near-lethal assault upon his wife's lover, has also been indicated (see pp. 125, 138–139).

The patient's father was a prominent physician, from a distinguished family, and active in community affairs, but a cold man: "He doesn't show his love." The mother was a schoolteacher, described as sensitive and loving, but as someone who "raised me by the book and kept me on the book's schedule." The patient had been a bright and tractable child, but always shy and uncomfortable with peers. He would spend days wandering by himself in the woods, while his mother was often in town at "study groups" learning the correct techniques of child rearing. He had had intense separation anxieties in his first school years. Though always large and strong as a youngster, he would never fight, allowing himself to be bluffed or bullied by even the smallest boys in the class. His first openly depressed episode occurred at age 13, as already stated, and these then seemed to recur with annual periodicity (see p. 145).

Though he had been an excellent scholar as a youngster, in college the patient's academic achievements faltered. The college authorities summoned his father to a series of conferences over a several-year span to discuss the patient's poor adjustment and poor scholarship, his talk of suicide, his excessive drinking, and his "crude and insulting" behaviors with classmates. He failed to graduate with his class, and was sure that he never would have been accepted at medical school except that his father was an important faculty member and a member of the admissions committee; he felt that he was voted in out of respect for his father's position. In medical school, the patient's borderline grades continued, and he was certain that but for his father's influence he would have been asked to leave. He berated himself, complaining that people thought him "chicken-hearted, a shit, and a fairy"; he wondered about homosexuality and pleaded for help. A psychiatrist he consulted advised him not to rush into dates but to "practice on your mother, a sort of courtship proposition. . . . Every boy has to start with his own mother and develop that protectiveness and manly interest in her as a woman. . . . You have to think now that your mother is a woman and you are a man, and that you are really going to play up to her. Remember every boy is in competition with his father."

While in medical school, the patient married. The marriage was stormy from literally the first day. The patient felt his wife to be unresponsive, cold, and distant. She complained that he was never affectionate, had a wild look in his eye, acted brutally like an animal, and was interested only in his own crude gratifications. She had married the patient with the frank hope of being admitted to a wealthy and socially prominent family. She was disappointed in this, never securing her in-laws' approval; they saw her as a social climber. At age 25, the patient suffered the openly psychotic episode (see p. 145) that led to his first psychiatric hospitalization, the diagnosis of manic–depressive illness, and ECT treatment. There was another psychotic episode about a year later, this time diagnosed as the depressive phase, which again responded to ECT. During this, he questioned "whether he was a good doctor or would be any kind of doctor at all."

The patient failed at several successive residency attempts—first in his father's surgical specialty under the auspices of his father's close colleagues; then in internal medicine, where he spent more time playing bridge with the patients than carrying out his professional duties; and then in neurology, where he often failed to show up altogether on good golfing days. He enjoyed talking to patients and was fascinated by their psychopathology. When he applied for transfer to a psychiatric residency, he was rejected on the basis of his poor performance and his own known psychiatric difficulties. This made him very angry. During all this time, increasing troubles were brewing in the marriage. The patient was enraged by his wife's unresponsiveness, and he felt driven to assault her physically in various ways (see pp. 138–139). The patient said that he had never been able to be overtly angry with anyone except his wife, but with her, he was frightened lest he kill her in one of his uncontrollable rages. His wife, as noted, stated that he was always jealous of her and her musical career, and occasionally teased her in a threatening way with smashing her nose or cutting her vocal chords.

The incident that was the immediate precipitant to the patient's appearing for psychiatric evaluation—the violent, near-lethal assault with a bed slat on his wife's lover—has already been recounted (see p. 125). Subsequent to this, the patient filed public charges of adultery against the other man, and was pleased to disgrace his wife before the citizenry. His parents supported his push for divorce, the mother saying, "What is there left for them to try to build a marriage on?" The patient was fully cooperative with the psychiatric evaluation, but needed some persuasion before he came around to accepting the recommendation for supportive–expressive psychotherapy (rather than psychoanalysis, which he had come seeking) with concomitant hospitalization. He was actually hospitalized for 6 months; when he moved out into a foster home and part-time day care, he also took on a full-time medical job in a local hospital. Meanwhile, he had secured his divorce, and now undertook a rather promiscuous "scouting around to find other women."

COURSE OF THE THERAPY

The patient was in a primarily supportive psychotherapy for 4 years (321 hours). The interlocking salient features of the therapy included the following:

1. The therapist offered himself from the start as an explicitly helping, benevolent authority figure who would not knowingly distress the patient by expecting him to talk about any issues upsetting to him. When the patient did seem upset within the therapeutic interaction, the therapist would invariably ask whether the patient felt that he was being pushed too hard; if the patient responded positively, the therapist would promptly drop the matter.

2. The transference, thereby encouraged, became a positive, friendly, dependent relationship to the therapist as a benevolent and authoritative father. The patient liked the therapist from the start and had the fullest confidence in him. He felt that through his own good behavior he would obtain support and guidance from this good father, and this was indeed what he felt happened. Toward the end, "the feeling got pretty strong. I was almost willing to say I loved him." Behind this, there always hovered the more threatening spectre of the relationship to the actual father—in the patient's fear of confiding fully in the therapist, especially in regard to his sexual behaviors. This discomfort never fully subsided (nor was it ever interpretively dealt with); mainly, however, the positive aspects of the dependent tie to the father figure were to the fore.

3. Within this relationship, the therapeutic content centered mainly around day-to-day problems. The therapist encouraged the patient to try to understand these in terms of their immediate reality circumstances, and then to search out reality-appropriate solutions for them. This was indeed the heart of the therapeutic effort. The patient was to be fully responsible to his realistic professional obligations and would be allowed to cancel appointments if his medical duties obliged him to do so, as long as he made every effort to give reasonable notice. In return, the patient was expected to recognize the importance of the therapist's responsibility to *his* work: The hours would only be replaced during the regular working day, and, if a substitute could not be found, the patient would be charged for the ones missed. Similarly, the therapist gave the patient full responsibility for monitoring his own use of sedative drugs, and expected that this would be reasonably and appropriately handled.

4. Concomitantly, there was very limited focusing on the patient's basic characterological problems (e.g., his strong narcissistic orientation), or the dynamics of his mood swings (basically, the therapist just stressed that what the patient experienced as his "high points" were really times of justified satisfaction with himself, which the patient in turn used to bolster his self-esteem, as well as to defensively shut off any deeper inquiry). And, of course, there were only occasional references to the past, such as the relationship with the former wife and its linkage to the lifelong relationship with the mother. There was more talk of the father, whom the patient did come to see in an altered light. At the end he said, "I don't feel like a boy any more. I'm another man alongside my father."

The patient's life through the course of this psychotherapy progressively improved and enlarged. He started in an institutional position in medicine in a local hospital while living in a foster home, and from there he moved (with much trepidation) into a general practice in medicine offered to him in a nearby small community. Within a short time the patient was established in this practice, had stopped all drinking, and was discharged from the day hospital, which he no longer utilized. After 2 years of therapy the patient met his second wife, a schoolteacher like his mother. They were immediately attracted to each other, courted, and were married within 3 months. Considering the patient's prior marital history, this marriage went surprisingly well. The wife was initially unprepared for the patient's episodically moody behaviors and his nagging criticisms of her. Their greatest difficulties were in the sexual sphere. The wife was troubled by the patient's cold, aloof manner and his mechanical sexual behaviors. She was often unsatisfied, since he was so rough, clumsy, and at times, physically hurtful. His attitude was to hurry up and get it over with, lest (he feared) he be unable to perform. Yet his wife was reluctant to discuss these problems openly, since the patient "needed his self-confidence." When she did raise questions about their sexual life, the patient said that nowadays women were raised to expect too much in sex. Yet both of them were determined to make a go of this marriage. To the patient, another divorce would be unthinkable (too much of a blow to his narcissism?). The wife felt loyal to him, and was troubled that he had another loyalty (to his treatment).

At one point, the wife came for 8 hours of social work counseling. She expressed her jealousy of the patient's treatment, and yet, paradoxically, her fear for how things would go between them after his treatment terminated. She hoped to take the therapist's place, and yet she feared this too. She had come to accept the therapist as "a part of the family." And then, in a turnabout, she blurted out that it was also unfair that her husband had someone to help him with his problems, while she did not. She felt these eight counseling sessions to be helpful, and when the patient's therapy terminated after 4 years, both partners felt that the now almost 2-year-old marriage was going considerably better. Both of them were willing to defer indefinitely any decision about children.

The main themes of the treatment centered always around the patient's reality situation, his problems in regard to his work, his marriage, his mood swings, and his self-esteem. Difficulties in reality were taken up only as the patient brought them up, quite dependent on how his actual life situation was developing. The patient enacted the role of the good boy receiving support, advice, and approval for behaving well. The therapist gave advice, guidance, and approval in the full measure asked. And the therapist and patient together maneuvered to prevent the development of any situation that would be too anxiety-provoking for the patient. The transference, as noted, was consolidated at the level of a positive dependent attachment, which was then used by the therapist as a vehicle to reinforce the patient's capacity to go along with the recommendations of the therapist and thereby to improve his patterns of day-to-day behavior. This transference state was maintained intact until the very end. The twin transference risks were successfully avoided—that of an uncontrollable transference psychosis, leading to clinical worsening and possible treatment disruption, and that of an insoluble transference neurosis, perpetuating a tolerable but unresolvable permanent treatment dependency.

TERMINATION

The treatment termination was brought about under the impact of the patient's commitment to a period of military medical service. He was encouraged by the therapist not to try to defer this, but to undertake it on schedule; it would be yet another way of overcoming his insecurities, increasing his feeling of manliness and social responsibility, and (incidentally) achieving some immediate social status.

By the time of his termination, many changes seemed consolidated. The patient's mood swings had flattened out. His behavior with his wife, though it continued to present childlike and self-centered narcissistic traits, had become less directly hostile and demanding. He could carry his medical practice responsibly, though his compassionate involvement with his patients was within the confines of what his ministrations would do to his patients, what their outcomes would be, and how that would reflect on him as a physician. He was much more aware of (and certainly much more able to curb) inappropriate ways of impulse expression. In return, he now achieved narcissistic gratifications via the successes of his professional life, his more satisfactory marriage, and the concomitant societal approval that he received. The therapist felt that the treatment, now ready to terminate, could not have been shorter.

STATUS AT FOLLOW-UP

The Follow-Up Study was conducted 3 years later, upon the patient's return from his service with the Army (at an overseas base in Europe), and just prior to his taking on his new (civilian) medical practice career. The patient and his wife had enjoyed the Army life. The patient's job was routine and not intellectually taxing, and he had received a work rating of "excellent." For the most part, his time in service, with its opportunities for travel in Europe, had provided the setting for "an ever-increasing happy marriage and satisfaction with each other." The marriage was "tremendous": "We love each other almost as much as any married couple could. . . . And when we quarrel we no longer need order the other out of the house or think of divorce." There *were* sources of tension. The patient was critical of his wife's housekeeping and grooming, but proud of her attainments as a schoolteacher. She said she now felt more content with their relationship after the patient's psychotherapy had terminated, because "now he could talk over his worries with me."

Their sexual life was only partly satisfactory. The patient had sporadic potency disturbances and masturbated fairly frequently to heterosexual intercourse fantasies involving other women he had had, with the excited thought, "Let's get a scene going." But he was also proud of his fidelity in the marriage, averring that "I got that wanderlust out of my system between my two marriages." And he was proud, too, that he had his propensity to morbid jealousy under strict control. When his daughter was born, he had had momentary thoughts about others who could be the father but he had brushed these thoughts aside: "These things come up and I just try to get rid of them," since "my wife is not the kind of girl who would do anything like that." The daughter (2 months old at the time of Follow-Up Study) had been born after 5 years of marriage, and after the patient and his wife had become quite discouraged; he had been checked and had been informed that he had a borderline sperm count. Though the patient said "We get so much thrill and pride out of the baby," each of the parents felt that the child made the other quite anxious. The wife indicated that when the baby cried and would not stop, the patient would become exasperated and would have to be restrained from shaking her too hard. In other respects, the husband and wife shared their life and activities. They would sing together, with the patient playing country and Western songs on the guitar, or his wife playing the piano. They also went to a weekly Bible reading group, attended church regularly, and "did a lot of praying together."

The patient was now returning to the United States to a group practice of general practitioners in the suburbs of a major metropolis. He was starting on a salary arrangement that would become a full partnership, assuming mutual satisfaction. One of his avowed reasons for going into a group rather than starting a solo practice was the help it would be in maintaining a structured life situation, especially in regard to the management of his finances. In other respects, too, the patient's life seemed more secured. Even his relationship with his father had eased, and was now "OK." The father was no longer held so pervasively responsible for the patient's difficulties. "I used to think I feared people and had so much anxiety because my father was an ogre," but he no longer held "one factor" responsible for his emotional distress and felt it "unreasonable" to blame his father for everything. He got along better with his mother as well.

In terms of specific symptoms, the patient had maintained all the termination point gains. His major cyclical mood swings were now a thing of the past. He complained of "tension headaches" about twice weekly; he denied any consistent drug taking. He did admit to still having a "pretty hot temper." He insisted that he would be firm in child discipline and "be liberal with the threat of spankings." Once, overseas, he had almost hit his wife; he had "grabbed her arm and gripped it real hard." He "realized" now that there was no justification for letting himself go this way. All in all, the patient declared himself to be now in "excellent mental and emotional health." This was not all attributed to the therapy: "I was maturing in the practice of medicine and finding out that the things I did didn't damage people as much as I thought they might at the time." But the therapy too was duly credited. Of the therapist, the patient said, "I liked him. In a way psychiatric treatment has been a wonderful experience for me. He seemed to be a mature person. I used it as a confession. I liked to come in and talk things over. He just let me talk on what was on the surface of my mind at the moment."

When the patient heard of his therapist's death, he did not seem especially distressed. "I did not feel it as a personal loss because I did not expect to see him again." As for the future, and possible needs for more treatment, the patient thought that it would be "a nice luxury" to have someone to talk to. There *were* things he felt uncertain about, matters of "self-discipline" — difficulties in studying, in curbing his appetite, and (he almost acknowledged) his sexual functioning. In regard to the PRP research, the patient expressed himself as glad to have been of help; he said that later, when he would be able, he would like to make a financial contribution to the project.

COMMENTS

Overall, within an established dependent attachment to an idealized benevolent therapist, the patient had been supported and re-educated: to curb his impulsivity, to talk and think before he acted, to solve day-to-day problems in accord with the constraints of reality, and to do this on the basis of the "borrowed ego strength" that came from his identifications with his therapist in the role of medical healer. Within this therapeutic structure, significant character and behavior realignments had taken place. First, there was a major shift from the (often psychotic) turmoil of the schizo-affective state (alternately depressive, manic, and paranoid) to a narcissistic characterological hardening and sealing over. And, second, there was a more ego-syntonic acceptance of this basically narcissistic orientation, which was at the same time better bent behaviorally to the requirements and possibilities of reality. That this could work adaptively depended on the appropriate feedback reinforcement from a fulfilling environment that was set up in the patient's therapy, and was carried over into his new marriage and his professional work. The success of the second marriage, as compared to the catastrophic troubles of the first, came out of the combination of the patient's therapeutically tempered behaviors and the new wife's more willing understanding and compliance; the success of the patient's return to the practice of medicine came from a similar fortunate conjunction of circumstances. By the time of Follow-Up Study, the edifice seemed enduring enough that the removal of what had heretofore been the key piece—which had catalyzed the emergence of the others—did not seem to shake its stability (at least within the requirements of posttreatment life thus far). The therapist, at this point, was dead, and there has been no further follow-up information about the patient.

DISENGAGEMENT FROM AN UNFAVORABLE LIFE SITUATION

Removal from versus Engagement with the Life Situation: A Recapitulation

A major pillar of the original conceptualization within PRP (see Sargent, 1956a, 1960; Sargent et al., 1958; Voth, Modlin, & Orth, 1962) was the central positioning of the Situational Variables—not as criterion measures of therapeutic change and improvement, but as coequal determinants, in interaction with the designated Patient Variables and Treatment Variables, of the discerned changes over the course of the ongoing therapies. The precise role of the variables within each of these sets, in interaction with the variables in the other sets, in bringing about those changes was to be itself a major focus of the empirical research investigation. Earlier in this book, I have summarized how the Situational Variables were operationalized within PRP (see Section II, Chapter 6, pp. 79–83). I have also discussed the (I feel, strangely overemphasized) thesis of the Voth and Orth book (1973, p. 86) that "The process of decreasing the level or intensity of environmental commitment [either by 'shedding' of life responsibilities through illness, or through coming to Topeka, or as a consequence of treatment in some other way] appears to us to be the primary basis for the symptomatic improvements of many of the patients" (see Section I, Chapter 2, pp. 15–18, especially p. 16).

   Certainly it is true that a number of the PRP patients became much sicker (i.e., more symptomatic) in direct proportion to the requirements for "engagement" in their usual life interactions, and the pretreatment courses of several make that point compellingly. For example, the Bohemian Musician's symptomatic collapse into an acutely decompensated state came in the wake of the patient's decision, in response to her husband's threat of divorce, to leave her arty lover in the big city and return to the responsibilities of home, marriage, and motherhood (see pp. 382–388). A number of other patients had such neurotogenic life situations that removal from them was a first prerequisite to a serious treatment effort. Typical of these was the Housebound Phobic Woman (see pp. 391–398), debilitated and organically damaged by a prolonged, intense barbiturate addiction, which kept her housebound and enthralled in a mutually supportive symbiotic union with a lover who was her one link to the outside world. Still others had such interfering life contexts that treatment could not proceed without complete physical removal. For instance, Peter Pan's first major treatment attempt (psychotherapy with concomitant hospitalization in her home city) was rendered ineffective by the constant manipulations and interferences of her parents, and these led to a recommendation for treatment far away at The Menninger Foundation (see pp. 426–432).

And certainly, also, there were patients within PRP whose treatment courses seemed to go well (or reasonably well) while they were "disengaged" from their usual life requirements and life stresses, only to decompensate again as they resumed those commitments with treatment support. The Alcoholic Doctor and the Suspended Medical Student were two especially tragic examples of this phenomenon. The Alcoholic Doctor (see pp. 332–336) seemed to be doing well enough in his psychoanalytic treatment that he could undertake a return to outpatient life, start a private medical practice, and be rejoined by his wife for a renewed effort at life together. At first this went quite well, but as they brought their four children back to them, the strains began to show. They had increasing difficulties with their medical practices (both were physicians); they again proved to be erratic parents; and there was a reversion to mutual drinking and brawling, and, on the patient's part, to drug abuse and promiscuous homosexuality. Though the psychoanalytic effort was continued doggedly and heroically, the patient's course from that point on was a progressively downhill one until his death. The Suspended Medical Student (see pp. 363–370) terminated his analysis with seemingly reasonably successful results—amelioration of all his symptoms, and a successful return to and graduation from medical school—only to unravel completely in the posttreatment period, when he tried to take on the ordinary pressures of a country general medical practice. In this endeavor he collapsed completely (and more than once), finally committing suicide 7 years after treatment termination.

On the other hand, there has clearly been the opposed and equally serious danger that the treatment requirements of Topeka would remove patients from the natural interactions of their ongoing life, to the severe detriment of both their lives and their treatments. The Divorced Nurse (see pp. 314–321) was a striking example of this. This patient, caught up in bitter neurotic struggles with her husband, came to the psychoanalytic treatment that she needed in Topeka (and could not obtain at home), at the cost of being removed for the duration of the treatment from her ongoing regular life with her husband and their children. This reality circumstance played a very significant role in the bitter rupture of her marriage, the attendant loss of custody of her children, and the fairly limited outcome of her analysis as well.

The issue is thus clearly not one-sided. The more usual situation in general (outpatient) practice in psychoanalysis and intensive psychotherapy is one of treating patients within the contexts of their usual and ongoing life situations. And this is appropriate, and benefits the treatment, in the majority of instances. Of course, however, there are instances where patients need to be hospitalized or otherwise disengaged from their usual life circumstances in order to give the treatment endeavor its maximal chance for success (the Bohemian Musician, the Housebound Phobic Woman, and Peter Pan have just been adduced, each in a different way, as illustrative cases of this). These patients are naturally in the minority among those in intensive therapy, but the needs of this minority group constitute precisely the central therapeutic *raison d'être* of clinical institutions with sanatorium bases, such as The Menninger Foundation. Patients who needed such "disengagement" therefore made up a very significant segment of the PRP population—actually, 9[2] among our 42, 3 men and 6 women, over 20% of our sample. The treatment of one patient, the Phobic Girl, is described here in order to highlight this particular perspective as an important element in many *supportive* psychotherapeutic efforts in a psychiatric sanatorium. (It is even important with many patients whose specific treatment within that sanatorium setting is psychoanalysis; 6 among our 9 were patients recommended for analysis. See my discussion of the role of adjunctive hospitalization in Section IV, Chapter 11, pp. 215–227, especially pp. 215–216).[3]

Therapy of the Phobic Girl

BACKGROUND AND PROGNOSIS

The 21-year-old Phobic Girl was referred to The Menninger Foundation for psychiatric hospitalization and treatment because of her crippling phobias and her regressed, infantile–dependent life. The patient's father, a dentist, was a willing and affable man at work, but fiercely irritable and impetuous at home. His severe temper outbursts were visited on all family members; at the frequent gatherings of the extended family, everything had to be arranged exactly as he wished, or he would be disagreeable and annoying to all. He tried to "let the wife bring up the kids." The mother was outwardly sweet and compliant toward her husband, but made no secret to the patient of her ability always to get around him. It was

2. The counting of 9 patients here for whom inpatient sanatorium care, "disengaged" from their usual life circumstances, was felt to be a significant element in their appropriate treatment planning is not identical with (but obviously mostly overlaps with) the earlier enumeration (see pp. 231–233) of 7 patients for whom proper treatment planning included "disengagement" from specific neurotic and neurotogenic interactions with important interpersonal objects (spouse or parents), whether or not they needed to be concomitantly hospitalized.

3. None of this gainsays two risks to some of the patients thus hospitalized, or otherwise removed or "disengaged" from their usual lives: the risk that, in an individual instance, the removal is dictated not by psychological need but by reality considerations of treatment availability, and may in fact be psychologically detrimental (as with the Divorced Nurse); or the risk that, whatever the beneficial effects upon treatment course of the removal, they will not endure when the patient inevitably returns to the exigencies of the life situation, however this situation is altered (as with the Alcoholic Doctor and the Suspended Medical Student).

her self-imposed task to "manage" him in such a way as to ward off his temper outbursts. The patient's brother, a medical student, analyzed the patient's illness (on the basis of his courses in psychiatry) as a matter of jealousy of himself and an inferiority complex about her obesity. When the question arose as to what the family, embarrassed about the social disgrace of the patient's illness, would tell people about where she was when she was hospitalized, the brother volunteered that he would tell them that she was in Mexico having a baby.

In her earliest life, the patient was described (by the mother) as having been a "darling child with no emotional problems." By the time she was 5, however, the patient's tendency to obesity had become a problem, and despite numerous diets, the involvement of several doctors, and her mother's constant nagging, her weight increased up to the time of admission (when she weighed 203 pounds). The patient was always very self-conscious about her size; she would play the buffoon to try to maintain her popularity, and was considered immature by her schoolmates and teachers. The patient's overt sex play had begun with children 5 to 6 years older when she was 6; this had included mutual undressing, fondling of genitals, and watching each other urinate. Her active sexual life had begun in junior high school, and after that she was quite promiscuous, often picking up men for transient encounters in taverns in the worst part of town. In intercourse, occasionally she "did not want to go all the way," and would ask her partner to withdraw so that she could watch him masturbate. On several occasions she persuaded her partner to beat her, and she received considerable pleasure from this.

The patient's fears and phobias had begun at age 10 when, following a tonsillectomy, she had become frightened of the dark and had many nightmares. Her mother would have to go to bed with her for up to 4 hours each night to reassure her and calm her. This continued fairly regularly for several years; even after the patient entered college, her mother would have to go to bed with her from time to time in order to comfort her. At about the same age, the patient had also developed a fear of being caught someplace where there was no toilet, and on one occasion she had refused to go on a museum trip with her class because of this. When she was 12, the patient had had her first panic outburst. She had been very frightened by the sight of a drunk in the street leaning unsteadily against a lamp post. She had become panic-stricken and telephoned her mother, who had come promptly to take her home. The patient subsequently suffered such attacks about twice a year, and each one necessitated her mother's coming to get her. During these attacks she would feel "as if my soul leaves my body." When the patient was 19, her father suffered a myocardial infarction; after that, the patient was cautioned very regularly by the mother not to distress him, lest he suffer another heart attack. The news of the father's illness was conveyed by the mother while they were driving home together for a vacation from college. It was a bright day, with the sun shining in the patient's eyes, and she became immediately fearful of the sunlight and spent most of her subsequent days at home lying around indoors. She would go out at nights, continuing her dating and promiscuity.

Because of her phobias, revealed in a college psychology course, the patient was recommended for and was in outpatient psychotherapy (with two therapists) over the next 2 years. Her daily life during this period consisted of staying home, sleeping, eating, staring at TV, and concerning herself and her parents with her widening phobias, which constricted both her and her mother's life more and more.

The mother had to take the patient to all her therapy hours, because the patient was fearful about driving the car herself that far from home. She thought of suicide and found and examined her father's gun, but she was unable to find a shell and carried the impulse no further. Yet, despite all this, her parents saw the patient as lazy and recalcitrant more than as ill. They regarded her obesity as her only real problem; her sexual adventures were, incidentally, quite well hidden from them.

The patient's therapist finally became convinced that the patient required psychiatric hospitalization and separation from her neurotogenic parents, especially from the intense symbiotic interdependency with the mother; he referred her to The Menninger Foundation. The patient was fearful to go that far from home, but the mother had an even harder time accepting the idea of separation than the patient did. She was not convinced that her daughter was ill enough to require it—obesity should be curable by proper diet and control. If the patient had to be hospitalized, the mother wanted to move into an apartment in Topeka in order to be near her. During the evaluation process, the patient would rock back and forth in her chair, often trembling. Every night before going to bed she would masturbate, "in order to feel more secure." She felt that she was very sick and wanted her doctors to make her well.

When initially hospitalized, the patient was very frightened, not wanting to leave her mother; the mother, for her part, had to be dissuaded from leaving her husband and moving to Topeka. But once settled into the hospital, the patient's contacts with her parents rapidly dwindled away. She intermittently pleaded to be sent home, but admitted that she felt extremely secure in this request because she knew it would not be allowed. She applied herself to a low-calorie diet and quickly lost some 15 pounds. In the course of the intensive casework with the parents, the father (much more than the mother) came to appreciate the extent of the patient's illness and her need for psychiatric hospitalization and treatment. He was worried about the adequacy of his financial resources; by using his savings he could afford possibly a year of hospital treatment, no more. As it worked out, the patient was hospitalized for a total of 8 months, at which time she moved into the day hospital and a foster home and began an intensive job hunt. Two months after she was out of the hospital, she started in formal psychotherapy.

Mainly because of the risks of a massive regression into a fixed infantile–dependent state (and also the severe neurotic involvement of the parents in the maintenance of the patient's pathological personality structure), the initial treatment recommendation was for an expressive psychotherapy, rather than psychoanalysis. It was thought, however, that this might lead to psychoanalysis after a time if all went maximally well.

COURSE OF THE THERAPY

At the time of "cutoff" Termination Study, the psychotherapy had been going on for 6 years (659 hours); because of the patient's precarious equilibrium and continued proneness to destructive acting out, she was neither seen nor tested at this time. The therapy all along had been more supportive and more directive than had been originally intended. In part, this stemmed from the patient's ever-present tendency to act out the transference in the form of grossly inappropriate and severely self-damaging social behaviors; she would "live out" her crude oral-dependent, masochistic, and perverse urges, sometimes to the point where the therapist often had to intervene decisively to protect the patient (and the treatment) directly from the consequences of her behaviors. In part, the more supportive–directive approach also stemmed from the reality of the family's limited finances and their inability to sustain the necessary supporting long-term concomitant hospital treatment.

Within this more reality-focused and behavior-controlling therapeutic program, the therapist directly encouraged the patient to get involved with less inappropriate and less disturbed men, and he encouraged her to work. Finally, he agreed to and implicitly encouraged her to go ahead with a marriage (which took place after 5½ years of therapy) that, though still strongly influenced by the patient's aggressively controlling needs, was certainly less hurtful and more suitable than any of her previous relationships with men. The subject matter focused on in the therapy was in accord with this same strategic stance. It revolved almost entirely around the patient's current life, with practically total exclusion of the past or the transference. The therapist held strictly to his managerial goals of helping the patient gradually to overcome her inhibiting symptoms (most particularly her phobias), and to make a reasonable life adjustment—that is, to be able to work satisfactorily, to get along socially with men and be able to marry, to live in peace with her family and friends, and generally to obtain her gratifications in socially acceptable ways.

The patient's life adjustment in therapy did show a slow but steady progression. She started in a foster home and full-time day hospital. Though she had helped select the home, she never got along well with the foster mother; she saw any involvement by the latter in her life as an expression of unwanted mother-type intrusiveness. After 5 months she moved into an apartment of her own, and managed her life about equally well. During her first months in the day hospital, the patient took business training courses, which she mismanaged sufficiently that she was not recommended for employment when she finished. She then turned to volunteer secretarial work in a welfare agency, which she handled passably enough that over time she could get into salaried secretarial employment. She finally secured and maintained a job as a secretary in a psychiatric agency. Though her provocative behaviors and tendency to buffoonery made for early difficulties on this job, by the time of the Termination Study the patient was serving efficiently and responsibly as secretary to the chief of the service.

Other aspects of her life showed similar slow progression. At intervals she took dieting seriously, but by the time of Termination Study (6 years) she had only lost 35 pounds; in part, this was a hostile provocation against the mother–therapist who would want her to reduce (to be the popular debutante). With her parents, the patient artfully manipulated their constant readiness to interfere to the detriment of her treatment. They never fully felt her illness or treatment need. They were ever ready to see her as lazy and spiteful, and The Menninger Foundation as heartlessly willing to have them spend all their money in this wasteful cause. For her part, the patient practiced her brinkmanship through constant financial mismanagement and extravagances, and through her seeming indifference to school and job failures; her behavior led to periodic pressures from the parents that the therapist "do something," or they would cut off the treatment and fetch their daughter home. Over the years, the parents had to be dealt with directly several times to quell crises of this sort, mutually engineered by the patient and themselves. And over the years, as the patient came to see her own initiating role in these episodes more clearly, she also came to do this less. Gradually the hostile interactions in the relationship with the parents subsided, to be replaced by a mutual forbearance. When the father died of his heart troubles (not unexpectedly) after the patient was in psychotherapy for 5 years, she responded with an appropriate if rather brief mourning period and thereafter undertook to pay her own way in treatment out of her earnings.

A similar evolution occurred in the patient's relationships with boyfriends. At first she was involved in a succession of degrading affairs with extremely disturbed, psychopathic, and quite sadistic young male patients. Her sexuality continued to be promiscuous and unsatisfying; she often provoked masochistic beatings. Gradually, under the pressures of interpretive clarification, she began to give up these liaisons one by one; she was ashamed of her hospital reputation as an "easy lay." At about the 4-year mark she met her future husband, a young businessman in town, an agreeable and quite passively compliant individual. This courtship was the most "normal" the patient had known. Shortly after her father's death, the patient married. The marriage was reasonably stable, and the husband was reasonably tolerant of the patient's obesity and continuing phobic restrictions (especially the persisting travel phobia). The husband was quite unfamiliar with psychotherapy, but if his wife wanted to spend her earnings from her job to pay for treatment he would enter no objection. Within the marriage, the patient's controlling aggressiveness and selfishness continued; she could always invoke her phobic restriction to proclaim her inability to do something that she didn't want to do. The patient said quite realistically of her marriage that it was not going to solve all her problems, but that it certainly gave her a more stable framework within which she could continue to work to solve her problems. And with the marriage, the patient's promiscuous and perverse sexuality dropped away.

The themes of the therapy reflected the patient's life vicissitudes accurately. They revolved around her destructive interpersonal interactions, her sadomasochistic relationship patterns with men, her hostile–dependent and provocative relationship with her family, her (mis)management of money matters, and her work difficulties. The ever-present reality of the limited available finances provided the patient with an important avenue for the acting out of her dependency and her anger toward her parents. For a long time the patient did not participate in defraying her treatment costs (and she could have), and was simultaneously an extravagant overspender (and need not have been). The transferences were successfully maintained in accord with the overall therapeutic intent: The patient was in the role of the dependent, nurture-seeking child, and the therapist met her transference demands in giving her constant support, attention, and advice, and in permitting her to act out her childish annoyances whenever she felt he was not complying adequately with her wishes. The transference was thus fostered at a level of continued positive attachment, and all the negative components (even the most conscious) were avoided.

And the whole interpretive work within the therapy was set within the limitations of this context. The therapist's wish to keep the peace was foremost. For example, in regard to the continuing obesity, the patient's position seemed to be that the therapist would either let her go on and be obese or try to do something about it, which would make him into the nagging mother (and for narcissistic reasons like the mother). This dilemma was posed as an ongoing provocation in the therapy, and the therapist left it uninterpreted, lest further upset and increased acting out be precipitated. The therapist did gently push in the direction of appropriate (i.e., healthy) life management and life change; there was always the patient's infantile disposition to see this only as a capitulation to a repetition of her mother's nagging. The improvements sustained within the therapy were all within this same framework: They were done to please the therapist (the transference cure), but in ways that preserved the underlying resentment and defiance— just as the patient had done things to please (and displease) the mother.

STATUS AT TERMINATION STUDY

At the time of "cutoff" Termination Study, the perceived changes were very real, but also very uneven, and far from consolidated. The patient could now work stably, enjoy a marriage and a home, take responsibility for her own psychotherapy, and enjoy an appropriate social life; she was also detached from the mutually disabling close union with her mother. But she was still very obese, still had a severe travel phobia and other residual phobias, and still had sexual difficulties and perverse fantasies. At this time treatment was still fully ongoing, and termination was not even being planned.

STATUS AT FOLLOW-UP

At the time of Follow-Up Study the patient was actually in the process of terminating her psychotherapy after 8½ years, and this time she was seen for research evaluation.

The patient had now been married 3 years, and the overall marital adjustment was experienced as a fairly good one. The patient was no longer working since the birth of a son (now 4 months old), and missed it; perhaps she would get back to work when her child was in school. The husband was away from home a good deal during the week, covering a rather large territory for his company. The patient was used to being alone, and anyway her husband was often very demanding when he was there. At times the patient's provocative behaviors would come to the fore, and she would needle and goad her husband and provoke him into attacks on her, just as she had done with her parents. The husband would be pushed into a passive, impotent role until he would explode angrily. He didn't like to talk, get analytical, or explore feelings. He was sure the patient's residual travel phobia would be cured if only she would "think positively."

The patient and her husband had established a sexual *modus operandi* that superficially "worked" for both partners. The patient never felt as strong a passion for him as she had for the other men with whom she had been sexually involved. She kept the history of her past sexual escapades a secret from her husband; in response to a direct query, she admitted that she had had sex once before. She professed surprise that she no longer even thought about other men. The patient's other symptoms showed a similar uneven pattern. Her phobias, she felt, had vastly receded; in contrast to her previous state, "I can do anything now." Mainly, she still had a moderate travel phobia. With the husband's support and urging, she had gradually widened her scope beyond the Topeka environs. By the time of Follow-Up Study she had taken three major trips across the country to visit family members. Each time the travel was handled with less discomfort. There had been some interpretive work done on the patient's need to hold the (internalized) mother image near her, as a check that she hadn't destroyed her through the enormity of her rage.

The patient's obesity was also still troublesome — in fact, essentially unaltered. Her weight, initially 203 pounds, and at one time down to 170, was now 195. It was her husband who made her weight a bone of contention between them; he would upbraid her for each failure to keep her diet. Other behaviors were much improved: "I'm no longer a clown, and I feel more respect for myself." Relationships were also improved; the hostile–dependent interactions with the mother had abated. About her father, she said, "I felt I had made my peace with him and we really liked each other before he died." Actually, she had felt "a little relieved" when he died. She had disappointed him so much in the past, and now she wouldn't be disappointing him any more. Her relationship with her child, the patient felt to be one of her real successes. She had wanted the pregnancy (more than the husband) from the beginning, but she felt she had started as a very anxious mother. She had been intolerant of the baby's crying and frightened of her own anger at those times; in the crying, she heard reproaches that she was not an adequate mother. All this she felt she had surmounted. She successfully breast-fed the baby.

Over the whole span of the therapy, the patient felt she had changed enormously. At the start she had been an infantile, demanding individual given to disorganizing depersonalization and estrangement states. She had changed to where "I can now live life instead of just struggling to survive until the next hour. . . . And I can now do anything[!] instead of feeling like it's impossible to do most things." The patient had very definite ideas as to how this had come about. She ascribed an important role to her initial period of hospitalization: "Much as I hate to be confined, what helped me was to be shut away from the world and really feel the world was locked out more than I felt I was locked in. . . . They give you a bath and take away your things and you feel you are starting over fresh." She approved of the very active management role of the hospital doctor. "The charting is important because you feel you are kind of mirrored back and it helps you think about what you are doing. . . . The hospital doctor made me work." The therapist's role was also very definite in the patient's mind. "He is very clever and has helped me deal with my daily life in a better way. . . . I felt unworthy, fat and a clown. He wouldn't tell me what to do, he would tell me I could do what I wanted to do, and that was the most important thing because I didn't think I could a lot of the time."

From the therapist's point of view, the marriage had provided a fortuitously more therapeutically useful framework. Now there were pressures in reality to take some external actions with respect to the patient's continuing travel inhibition (because of the travel requirements of the husband's job), and also to step up the pace of the work on the problems within the psychotherapy (because of their relatively modest financial circumstances). The patient and her husband intended to continue living in Topeka. And the patient could always call the therapist if need be. "But now I don't feel I need to hang onto him any more [he was now a more securely fastened introject?]. . . . And besides, my husband now does some of the same things for me the treatment has done."

There is additional follow-up information for some 16 years subsequent to this point (24½ years from the patient's initial presentation). The marriage has persisted and solidified, though there was a rocky period centering around an extramarital affair of the husband's. Under threat of marital breakup, he withdrew from that involvement. He is a successful businessman at a much higher managerial level; they live in another state. They are engaged together in active church work, as well as in other civic and social involvements. They have two sons, and at one point the patient sought psychiatric consultation in connection with a phobic development in one of the sons. The patient has had no further psychotherapy for herself, nor has she felt the need for any. She professes herself contented with her life and her outcome. The most recent follow-up information came from a social encounter with the original therapist on the occasion of a holiday visit by the patient and her husband to see old Topeka friends.

COMMENTS

The mutative elements in this overall story are clearly discernible and have much in common with many of the other successful outcomes with the supportive psychotherapeutic approaches: the nurturing of the positive dependent transference attachment to the benevolently guiding and directing therapist; the full complement of quite immediate transference gratifications within the therapeutic interaction; the compliant while still slightly defiant transference cure ("doing it for you"); and ultimately the transfer of the transference to a sufficiently willing, nurturant, and understanding husband within (at the therapy termination) the confines of Topeka, and with ready recourse, if need be, to the therapist. Those same elements have been delineated equally clearly in a number of the other case descriptions. Quite special to this case, and highlighted in this presentation, was the role of the treatment in disengaging the patient from a destructively neurotogenic reality situation: the removal from the home setting; the hospitalization (which, in the patient's words, "locked the world out" more than locking herself in); and the intensive work with the parents, especially the mother, to break the mutually hurtful hostile–dependent symbiotic tie. In this instance, the disengagement was accomplished very successfully, and all else that subsequently transpired in the direction of desired change then had a chance to take place.

Aside from the highlighting of this mechanism of disengagement, another aspect of this case warrants special mention—the efficacy of this kind of psychotherapeutic work in relation to gross obesity. The patient began her therapy at 203 pounds, and when she ended 8½ years later, with all the changes that had taken place, her weight was nonetheless essentially unaltered at 195 pounds. The Obese Woman, another grossly obese patient in the PRP sample, came to treatment (in her case, specifically *because* of the severe obesity and compulsive eating) weighing 238 pounds. She completed 5 years (1142 hours) of psychoanalysis moderately successfully, but her weight was also unchanged—in fact, it had reached an all-time high of 258 pounds. During the follow-up period it fluctuated between the high of 258 and a low of 176, and at the time of official Follow-Up Study was 200 pounds. Of the three most obese persons in our sample, only the Housebound Phobic Woman successfully overcame this major handicap through the course of her psychotherapy. In addition to her severe chronic barbiturate addiction and brain damage, she came to treatment weighing 180 pounds. In her first 2 months in the hospital she lost 28 pounds, down to 152; severe obesity was never a problem for her through the many years of her supportive–expressive psychotherapy (ostensibly psychoanalysis), nor is it in her current status as a "therapeutic lifer." Three severely obese patients constitute a very small sample, of course, and one should not try to generalize from it. Nonetheless, there is certainly no evidence that intensive psychoanalytic psychotherapy, geared broadly to the amelioration of psychological dysfunction, has the kind of specific therapeutic effect in relation to this particular disabling symptom that is claimed for the behavioral therapeutic approaches to such "target symptoms" as obesity (see Stunkard, 1976).

THE COLLUSIVE BARGAIN

Nature of the Concept

Robert Langs (1973, 1974) has popularized a concept that he calls the "antitherapeutic alliance," or, more felicitously, the "therapeutic misalliance." This he has defined as follows (within the context of an overall discussion of the therapeutic alliance and its role in the psychoanalytic psychotherapy process): "I will refer to alliances that are not based on mature and realistic wishes for symptom relief through inner change and do not foster the patient's resolutions of intrapsychic conflicts as 'antitherapeutic alliances' or 'therapeutic misalliances'" (1973, p. 82). He views these as unhappy treatment developments that arise out of the interplay of the patient's and the therapist's neurotic needs—that is, the interplay of transferences and countertransferences. He feels that "Usually both factors are involved" (1973, p. 82), or, in other words, that there is an active neurotic collusion. Later, however, he allows for another kind of determination, and, by inference at least, another kind of motivation: "Ultimately, in a sound therapeutic alliance, mature desires for help, and to be helpful, should predominate. Deviations and pathology in this area may be understood as ruptures in the therapeutic alliance, as the development of antitherapeutic misalliances. They may eventuate at the *conscious or unconscious* behest of either party, though both generally participate" (1974, p. 149, italics added).

    In thus posing the possibility of conscious *or* unconscious determination, Langs makes room for the *deliberate* fostering of such collusive agreements to leave particular arenas of psychopathology untouched, as a function of a planned therapeutic strategy by the therapist—not necessarily, therefore, always a reflection of interfering countertransferences that would limit the potential reach of the treatment. At least in this sense, collusion is allowable within the overall conceptualization of supportive psychotherapeutic approaches offered in this book, in which the fullest expressive exploration of intrapsychic conflict is not seen as the only (or even as the overriding and primary) therapeutic goal in all true psychodynamically based psychotherapeutic efforts. It is this mechanism of therapeutically *planned* collusion between therapist and patient, or what I have called the "collusive bargain"—a specific adaptation of Langs's concept—that I wish to pursue here, as seen in those psychotherapies within our PRP sample that were significantly marked by the active operation of such collusive purposes between therapist and patient.

To some degree, such a "collusion" — to make the therapeutic work and outcome look better than it indeed is, or to bypass major areas of conflict — is a clinical commonplace. It could be discerned in some measure with 14 of our patients (one-third of the sample), 7 men and 7 women, 8 in psychoanalysis and 6 in psychotherapy. At its mildest (and perhaps most trivial), this could be a bilateral viewing of the treatment effort through rose-colored glasses, like the degree of expressed mutual satisfaction with which the psychotherapy of the Bohemian Musician ended. Her therapist rode through the therapy (as did many of them) on the uninterpreted positive transference, with the negative feelings in this case all deflected off onto the hapless hospital doctor. The patient's gratitude for all the therapeutic good accomplished spilled over into the overcooperative attitude toward the research project, captured in her offer to "place myself completely at your disposal." Both therapist and patient were very impressed by the therapeutic result in this patient, who had come to treatment psychotically disorganized and depressed to the point where she received a course of ECT. Similarly, with two patients in long-term and originally very ambitious psychoanalytic treatment efforts — the Devoted Son and the Economist — there seemed to be some tacit consensus in each instance between analyst and patient that more had been analyzed, more intrapsychic conflict had been analytically worked through and resolved, and more analytic insights had been achieved than seemed evident to the research evaluators, who felt both these cases to have had sharply limited treatment results. The Devoted Son, as noted, was reluctantly "weaned" out of a seemingly insoluble (certainly a never really resolved) transference neurosis (see pp. 283–287), and the Economist was ultimately shifted into a supportive–expressive psychotherapy that has carried into the career of a "therapeutic lifer" (see pp. 336–343). With the Devoted Son, it even seemed clear that the tacit agreement between analyst and patient on how much had been analytically accomplished was being used as a way of helping to sustain the patient in trying to live up to this shared fantasy. (As subsequent events proved, the "weaning" from treatment did not hold; the patient ultimately returned to treatment and is also now a "therapeutic lifer.")

Clearly, this "viewing through rose-colored glasses" is both a somewhat commonplace and a "normal" enough event, hardly a problematic issue in relation to therapeutic course and outcome (unless in an individual case it produces a really skewed and quite self-deluding perspective). More in the direction of a truly "collusive" bargain, with real repercussions for treatment course and outcome, are those instances where the agreement (tacit or explicit) is to bypass major areas of evident psychic conflict and psychopathology, for whatever reasons. I have discussed a number of such instances in PRP already. For example, in the psychotherapy of the Manic–Depressive Physician, which was geared to the re-educational effort toward enhanced reality testing (see pp. 460–466), there seemed a clear "conspiracy" to avoid areas of undue anxiety and possible therapeutic clash, such as the patient's continuing sexual difficulties and covert self-medicating, and his apprehensions in relation to the possible pressures and temptations (renewed drinking, homosexual stirrings, authority problems, etc.) in the period of military service that he faced after treatment termination. By tacit mutual consent, none of all this was explored — and, therapeutically, this strategy paid off handsomely. Similarly, in the psychoanalysis of the Obese Woman, described as an instance of dealing with the defense transference and avoiding the potential "transference jam" (see pp. 288–293), it was clear that the constant analytic focus on the patient's Oedipal transferences was partly used as a defense against the feared analytic confrontation with the orally devouring and hateful pre-Oedipal mother transferences. This successful maneuver, described as a "transference switch" (see p. 292), in effect seemed to make possible a successful enough (but also limited) analytic resolution. On the other hand, a tragic instance where such a collusive arrangement worked to the severe detriment of the patient was the case of the Suspended Medical Student. The patient shared with his analyst the conviction that a reasonably successful analytic result had been accomplished, in the remission of his symptoms and his successful return to and graduation from medical school; the whole fabric then collapsed, with the return of total symptomatic expression of the same severe and unresolved internal conflicts, in the face of the ordinary pressures of the life in medical practice to which the patient went (and which had been his lifelong goal).

Here I describe two patients, both young adolescent women (the Actress and the Rebellious Coed), whose therapies seemed characterized by a very particular collusive bargain—the same in each instance: to avoid therapeutic scrutiny of the patient's homosexual propensities (and behaviors) as the price of a collaborative therapeutic work in relation to all other aspects of the patient's life functioning.

Therapy of the Actress

BACKGROUND AND PROGNOSIS

The Actress was brought to psychiatric evaluation following an unsuccessful first year at college, marked by alcohol excess, homosexual activity, and grossly disturbed relationships. The patient's father was an architect, alcoholic, referred to contemptuously by her as "a big little man" or "an old sot." She was likewise estranged from her aggressive mother, whom she blamed for her dislike of her father, stating that she would have been very fond of him if her mother hadn't kept always saying how "bad" he was.

In her early years the patient had been tractable, a good pupil but somewhat preoccupied and withdrawn. She had felt frequently criticized by her parents, who seemed to wish her always to behave like one or another of her friends. With the onset of puberty, the patient's quietness gave way to truculence. She became difficult to discipline, seeming "unconquered" by punishments like spanking. Under the pressure of increasing difficulties with her parents, the patient began to go out more with her age-mates, "in order to get away from home." The parents became more and more distraught because of her running around and their inability to control her. She often could play off one parent against the other. She had hysterical tantrums and histrionic dramatizations when she did not get her way; at school, appropriately enough, the patient was especially interested in dramatics. Both the patient and her parents came to feel that she was only real and expressing herself genuinely when she was angry. In her senior year of high school she became involved in promiscuous heterosexual behaviors, in which she could show her contempt for the (older) men she sought out through being cold and unresponsive.

In college, the patient's problems came to a head. She had scholastic difficulties from the start. She was interested only in dramatics, where she displayed real talent; in her theatrical roles, she seemed more genuinely involved and more real than in her day-to-day life. At this time her hair was dyed black, and, as already described, her dormitory room was also primarily in black—it was described as a "funeral vault" (see pp. 121–122). She had episodes of solitary drinking in her room, and moods alternating between hysterical excitement and silent withdrawal. She entered a homosexual life, including a brief but violent homosexual involvement with a senior student. When this partner rebuffed her and sought to break the relationship, the patient had a screaming hysterical episode in the dormitory, which brought her to the dean's attention. Rather than expel her, the dean took the patient out of the dormitory into her own home, where the patient suddenly became quiet, dutiful, and excessively neat and clean (with three baths daily and obsessive cleanliness rituals). The patient tried to make light of her homosexual relationship, alternately blandly denying it or boasting of it as "a phase of development." A referral for psychotherapy at the student health service did not work out.

When the patient arranged for her parents to learn of her homosexual life by leaving a letter to her former homosexual partner in plain view on her desk at home during the summer vacation, the shocked parents arranged for her immediate psychiatric hospitalization and evaluation at The Menninger Foundation. When she arrived, the patient was preoccupied with her desire to be an actress and could talk of little else. Most of her time in the hospital was spent in acting out "as-if" roles; she never seemed sure of what she really was or wanted to be—grown up and mature, or a confused child. In the hospital, episodes of drinking, homosexual crushes, and lying all continued. To the hospital doctor, the patient confessed a history of homosexual behaviors going back to grade school. After 10 months of hospitalization, the patient entered a first abortive psychotherapy, which lasted 20 hours over 2 months. As noted earlier (see pp. 141, 210), she disliked her "typical Babbitt" therapist intensely; after the 20 fruitless hours, he gave up. Shortly after that, the exhaustion of available money forced the patient's discharge to the day hospital plus apartment living, and soon thereafter she was again placed in psychotherapy, now on an outpatient basis.

COURSE OF THE THERAPY

The patient was in supportive–expressive psychotherapy for 4 years (318 hours, not counting the prior 20). Because the limited family finances now necessitated a totally outpatient psychotherapy effort, the patient fell readily into an unstructured, unsupervised living situation in which she lived out a Bohemian life—not working, carousing and drinking, and engaging in indiscriminate homosexual and heterosexual promiscuity when drunk. The therapist's efforts were necessarily directed supportively and controllingly toward helping the patient calm down and gain some controls over her life. He actively encouraged more adaptive behavior patterns, counseled a realistic approach to the theatre as a possible career, and suggested that work and social conformity would lead to realistic sources of enhanced self-esteem. Simultaneously, there was strong direct discouragement of sexual acting out and promiscuity, both heterosexual and homosexual. The patient eventually gave up all heterosexual activity, and also stopped frequenting homosexual hangouts, "cruising" when drunk, and the like; she settled into stable homosexual attachments. This "compromise" the therapist tolerated as long as a relationship with a partner was reasonably stable and reasonably free of exploitation either way. There was an implication that the homosexuality would be studied and understood sometime in the future. To the patient, this compromise "homosexual solution" was eminently satisfactory; it allowed open gratification of her oral needs, her sadomasochistic needs, and her directly sexual needs, while at the same time defending her against the anxieties related to heterosexuality. This is what I have called the tacit therapeutic "collusive bargain."

The subject matter of the therapy revolved almost wholly around the patient's current life activities: Her homosexual (and heterosexual) acting out, her drinking, and her generally disorganized life were overwhelming in immediacy and importance. Through all this, the patient was being moved to adopt as her own the therapist's vistas of more adaptive-appearing patterns in her social–sexual behaviors and in her work behaviors, so that she could pass for a more "normal"-behaving young woman. And the patient's life through treatment progressed in accord with these now jointly defined goals. She started, as noted, by leading a disorganized life marked by wild parties, drunkenness, promiscuity, indolence, and nonproductiveness. She made no move to work. The therapist's stance vis-à-vis this life could be paraphrased as "Look what you're doing to yourself. I don't understand how you can continue to hurt yourself that way." When a particular homosexual or heterosexual excess threatened to get too far out of hand, the therapist moved to proscribe it more directly.

Under these kind but firm pressures, the patient's behaviors gradually altered in progressively less disruptive directions. She gave up drinking and became somewhat prudish and quite phobic about alcohol. She took Dexedrine (in its place?), in part to help with her weight problem, in part "to give me energy." Her mild obesity melted away, and at the end of treatment she was "trying to stop" her drug use. All heterosexual contacts ceased permanently. The patient also gave up her transient, often brutal homosexual encounters. She had three major homosexual attachments, each almost a year in length, over the balance of her time in treatment. Each was a little less stormy and, for the patient, less sadomasochistically tinged than the preceding one. During the patient's first year in treatment, she made a visit home during which her father, now drinking more heavily, insisted on taking the patient to bars with him. He told her that he didn't care whether she wanted a man or woman in bed with her, but that her trouble was that she hadn't had a good man, and that was what she needed. He assured her that if she got pregnant he could help her take care of it. The patient was horrified and disgusted by this vulgar, thinly disguised incestuous behavior. It strengthened her in turning further away from men into homosexuality.

After about 1½ years of treatment, galvanized by the threat of her support money running out, the patient suddenly undertook to get a job. To do so, she totally transformed her appearance within a matter of days: She gave up her unkempt hair and men's jeans and shirts in favor of feminine clothes and a new, stylish hairdo. She became a quite attractive young lady, and thereafter remained that way. Her first job was a poorly paid clerical position; later she was a saleslady in a fashionable dress shop. At the same time, she became fanatical about keeping her apartment and her clothing in immaculate order. She cleaned her apartment ceaselessly and bathed several times each day. She lived by very rigid schedules that she made out. When the patient looked back at the changes in her life, she said, "I overacted terribly much; I had to get it out of my system. It was like there was something evil inside of me and it had to come out and I acted it all out. And then I could say I don't like myself and I pulled myself together. And this all happened through the treatment. It was just something about saying it out loud that does help because it tells something, how sordid it sounds, and how unhappy, and how unprideful, and it somehow fills you with a kind of disgust that gives you the determination and guts enough to stop it."

While all this was being talked of within the treatment, the patient was displaying one fixed transference attitude throughout—that of respectful friendliness to an interested, nonjudgmental, benevolent parent. The therapist felt the patient to be very resistive to transference interpretation, and he made no concerted effort to work with transference material. And he certainly avoided the negative transference manifestations, in their displacements into the acting out in the patient's hostile interactions and turbulent life outside the treatment. The treatment hours, in fact, were almost completely devoid of angry feelings or inappropriate behaviors; here the patient was a good little girl behaving herself for the kindly and patient father–therapist, the idealized, desexualized, and nurturant parent. Within this orally dependent and nourishing transference, the patient would modify her behaviors to please her therapist, and in return was allowed to perpetuate her homosexuality and the gratifications derived from it in her day-to-day living. She could have her cake and eat it too—getting what she wanted, giving not so much in return, and keeping a safe distance from emotional interactions centered around her deeper conflicts. The therapist, from his side, allowed and maintained this transference position, since he could use it as leverage to influence the patient "educationally" via suggestions and manipulations concerned to alter her behaviors. Thus, both their separate purposes were served by the tacit bargain that had been struck between them.

TERMINATION

By the time of termination there had been a major lessening of the patient's symptoms in all areas except for her homosexual proclivities, which had concomitantly gradually consolidated into a more ego-syntonic aspect of her total character functioning. Both the patient and the therapist seemed to agree that this acceptance of a stabilized homosexuality was the best solution that the patient was capable of at this time. And as the patient's homosexuality crystallized in this manner, all the other behaviors previously used to express conflict dropped away—the promiscuity, rebelliousness, lying, belligerence, alcohol excess, and so on. The patient could sustain a job, maintain friendships, and get along much better with her mother (though not with her increasingly alcoholic and philandering father). The patient was far from fully contented with this state of affairs. Of her homosexuality, she said in the research interview, "I never could find any experience in my childhood or anything that made this happen." And of the result achieved, she said, "I wished I had a normal interest in men and there wouldn't be all this other conflict but I just don't and it would be a lie for me to say so. . . . It's a very alone kind of thing to survive without the normalcy of a home and a husband and children." She felt that life among homosexuals would be very unsatisfying, because so many had severe personality problems, and so many were drifters who had no goals in life. "It's an awful limited life."

Termination came when the therapist agreed with the patient that they had reached a therapeutic plateau. There was no use going on except for "5 more years of deep analysis, and maybe I'm not the right kind of person for it, capable of it." The patient decided to strike out on her own and wanted to head for New York and the Broadway theatre (and the Greenwich Village life?). She was convinced by her therapist and family to try herself first in a medium-sized metropolitan area, where she could find department store employment and try to make her way into the local theatre. Her parents agreed to help underwrite this venture financially, and her mother undertook to accompany the patient and help her settle in the new city—an offer that the patient welcomed.

STATUS AT FOLLOW-UP

The patient was seen for Follow-Up Study 2½ years after her treatment termination. She still lived in the city to which she had gone to seek her livelihood when she left Topeka. Her mother had indeed been helpful in the transition process, leaving the patient settled in an apartment and hired as a saleslady in the local prestigious department store; at Follow-Up Study time she was firmly ensconced in the same job, in a routinized and somewhat monotonous way. She felt she was treated fairly at work, and she maintained a pleasant facade but also a cool distance with her coworkers. Her theatrical ambitions had dissipated completely, after some abortive and not very intensive efforts in this direction when she had first arrived. In her home, the patient was always doing things; she was caught up in rigidly compulsive housekeeping routines, with particular unvarying evenings set aside for washing and ironing, for cleaning the apartment, and so forth. She had a circle of actively homosexual friends, and through them she had gradually gotten to know the gay bars and the fringes of the gay world. She seemed completely accepting of a homosexual life; in fact, only in this area did she respond with real animation in the Follow-Up interview. From a confused and sexually amorphous adolescent at her treatment onset, the patient had by now become a grown homosexual young woman.

The patient's own homosexual attachments had been few and intense. Her first liaison was a very unsatisfying one with an unreliable, impecunious, exploitative, somewhat older woman. The patient sought in vain for a tactful way to disengage from their relationship and finally broke it up in a humiliating public rejection, when she flouted her by leaving a party to spend the night with another partner. At the time of Follow-Up Study the patient was finding herself drawn to a very attractive woman, who, however, had a reputation for brusquely breaking up relationships once she had her partner committed to her. The patient fantasized that she would beat this game by really hooking the other woman despite herself. She felt her own behavior to be very discreet, and she denied any drug taking or hard liquor. With her family, she was on a better footing. She was less entangled with her father, who was continuing his philandering and alcoholic behavior. At times he would phone the patient and ask that she come home to nurse him. When she would decline, he would berate her as a selfish bitch. She had accepted a gift of a car from him; he had pressed it upon her, declaring that it was not because he felt guilty toward her but because he loved her. The patient was supportive of her mother when she periodically agonized over the idea of seeking a divorce from her husband, but she did not urge her mother to take this step.

The patient's perspective on her psychotherapy was avowedly positive. She called her treatment "life-saving." Before it, her life had been completely disorganized, on a downhill gradient heading for suicide. She felt the treatment had stabilized her so that she had been able to come to terms with her personal needs and wishes, particularly in the area of sexuality. Though it was far from a joyous life, it at least offered a modicum of satisfaction and of steadiness that she would not otherwise have had. She spoke admiringly of her therapist, with full appreciation of all the help she felt she had received from him. But as for further treatment, she felt that there were people who could utilize a more intensive therapy, who were able "to go down deeper and come up dirtier," but that she wasn't one of them. She had never seriously thought about the possibility of further treatment for herself. All in all, the patient felt far better off than before—contentedly (or resignedly?) committed to a homosexual life, and part of a different world adhering to different values. The whole contact with her, however, was marked by an aloofness and a sparsity of feeling that strongly suggested a chronic depressive undercurrent.

Again, we have some further follow-up information. For the next several years, the patient continued an annual contact with her therapist by way of a Christmas card and an attached note. She continued satisfactorily in the same job, and also in the same quite discreet homosexual life. The therapist indicated that she "seemed to be getting along well," meaning the same. Then the Christmas card contacts ceased.

COMMENTS

Overall, this was another instance of a psychotherapy that basically rode on an uninterpreted positive dependent transference attachment to a benevolently controlling, succorant, and *permissive* parental figure. Whether by intent or unawareness, the therapist made no effort to penetrate the positive dependent defensive transference in order to link the sexual and aggressive acting out in the patient's life to the warded-off erotic and aggressive transferences. Within this maintained positive dependent tie, the patient gave up her flagrantly disturbed behaviors in exchange for permission to maintain a "benign" homosexuality. This "bargain" that was struck facilitated a homosexual adaptation as the characterological vehicle through which an adapted (or at least neurotically adjusted) pattern of impulse and defense balance was achieved.

Therapy of the Rebellious Coed

BACKGROUND AND PROGNOSIS

The Rebellious Coed's homosexual problems were less blatant at the start. She was referred for psychiatric evaluation because of a depressive reaction to her mother's death (of cancer) 6 months previously, set against a background of progressive difficulty in getting along with people, family members, fellow students, and teachers, of a good many years' duration. The patient felt that the mother was the only one who had loved her, and that she had been her natural ally against the father, but that she had also been strict and narrow in bringing her up. The father was an irascible man, very critical of the patient, and concerned with her chronic poor social adjustment. The parents had never gotten along well together, usually living in a kind of armed truce.

From the beginning, the patient had not gotten along well at home. "I have always been a rebellious person. I was never afraid of my parents and their discipline." She would be resentful when spanked, and would not change her ways. In contrast to her constant disciplinary problems at home, the patient had always enjoyed school and excelled academically. The family moved to a small hamlet just before she entered high school, and the patient felt that she underwent a major personality change with this unwanted move. She became resentful and aloof, and developed a "chip on the shoulder" attitude. She professed herself shocked by the uncouth farm people with their vile language and their open displays of sex. People got the impression that she felt she was better than they were; from her side, she was frightened and embarrassed, "razzed for being such a prude and a goody-goody." She would cry herself to sleep at night.

The patient was also intellectually bored and began to chase around with an older crowd. She would surreptitiously drink, smoke, or race around in cars at excess speeds. She had a boyfriend, "the prize catch," but she provoked him by being stubborn and unreasonable and by flirting with other boys in his presence; he got fed up and left her. The patient then had some other, less intense romances, and she had one heterosexual experience about a month before her mother's death while away on a summer job. The young man was engaged, and it was clear to the patient that "there was no possibility of anything coming of it."

The patient did not think of herself as ill until she had a frightening dissociative episode about 18 months before her psychiatric referral. She and another girl were driving a car that got off the shoulder of the road and slid into a ditch. A number of boys they knew came along in another car and teased them for their plight. The patient exploded into a fit of crying and rage that was so disturbing that the boys took her off to a doctor. The patient remembered nothing of the next 4 days. She was hospitalized, and was told later that she had been incoherent and wildly excited and had had to be sedated. The next year in college the patient was lonely and unaccountably depressed. She ran around with a crowd of girls who acquainted her with the facts of homosexuality. She warded off the advances of an older student, but then submitted to another who proclaimed her love and need to the patient and was fiercely possessive and jealous. The patient felt as if someone at last loved and appreciated her, and she was immensely grateful.

The next summer the patient was working in a distant city to earn money for the next school year, despite the family's protestations that her absence would hasten the mother's decline. In the middle of that summer, the patient received word that her mother was dying; she used up all her savings for a hurried airplane trip home. She felt very guilty about her mother's death, and also over her single heterosexual transgression, which had occurred a month earlier. When she returned to college with the same homosexual roommate, she also withdrew in disgust from this liaison, though they continued to share the same room and bed. During the fall semester, the patient's depression and apathy grew apace. She withdrew from her friends and failed to keep up with her schoolwork. She would get drunk episodically, and finally had another hysterical crying jag after a quarrel; this led to academic and disciplinary probation, and to a psychiatric referral suggested by the dean. The patient realized that if the dean had not thus interceded with her, she would have gone on to destroy her college career.

On evaluation, though her manner was initially angry and contemptuous, the patient readily evinced her great discomfort. She felt that she had always been the black sheep of her family. Her parents would have preferred a boy, and the patient had always felt unwanted and unappreciated. The father, who came with her for the evaluation, presented the patient's difficulties from the other side. She had always had people "wrapped around her little finger. When she was in high school, she snapped her fingers and everybody jumped. Now she snaps her finger and somebody snaps it right back in her face. It's a different psychology, but she doesn't seem to see that."

During the evaluation, the need for long-range intensive psychotherapy, possibly psychoanalysis, became clear. However, this would pose a serious financial problem, since the patient's father had a very modest income and the patient was already using up more than half of it in living expenses and going to college. The patient nonetheless constantly saw her father as stingily depriving. She was unwilling to secure a job in order to have more money for more intensive treatment, and it was agreed that she would enter an interim once-weekly psychotherapy (the cost of which her father would somehow manage to defray) while working out her motivation for (and the feasibility of) more definitive treatment.

COURSE OF THE THERAPY

This psychotherapy actually lasted only 14 months and comprised only 35 hours (it had become twice-monthly). The reduction of frequency had come when the father indicated that he could not continue to pay fully for the weekly sessions. The patient refused to bear any of the expense, and (it turned out later) felt angry at the therapist for not insisting that the father would need to continue to support weekly treatment.

From the beginning, the treatment mode was predominantly supportive. The patient was single-minded in what she wanted: to achieve relief from her depression and to get through college successfully. She was never really motivated for more than that, and the therapist soon abandoned the goal of preparing her for the choice of a more definitive therapy (psychoanalysis). Rather, he participated actively in helping the patient make decisions in regard to the various problems that arose in her life during treatment, and in helping her consciously to adjust to possibly disturbing circumstances, such as the father's remarriage in the middle of the treatment. He tried to get the patient to move away from the homosexual roommate who constantly presented temptations, to pay more diligent attention to her schoolwork, to keep concentrated on the goal of completing college successfully, and to curb her direct sexual impulses and behaviors.

Actually, in contrast to its previous storminess, the patient's life during treatment was calm and progressive. She began to make the college honor roll; she went on steadily to complete college successfully, without depression and without further difficulty with the authorities. At graduation she secured a coveted high school teaching position in a nearby city. She continued to visit her father over weekends through the treatment course; despite her initial upset, she accepted his remarriage with fair grace and got along tolerably well with the new stepmother. The father, incidentally, was involved in an occasional casework contact, which was helpful in smoothing the ongoing interaction from his side.

The patient's social life throughout treatment was much more ambiguous. She occasionally went out with boys and tried to convey the impression that she did this more often than she did. She continued her homosexual relationships clandestinely; there were two successive ones over this period. They seemed by tacit agreement to be undermentioned in the therapy. It was only after the father's remarriage that the patient confessed to an intensification of the homosexual activity that she half admitted had been going on all along. It was "driving her crazy" especially since the partner (and roommate) also had a boyfriend, whom she would bring around to their room, openly drinking and petting with him. Yet the patient professed herself unable to get out from under this relationship, and the therapist urged her to use the help of the dean's office to secure a room reassignment. He was led to believe that she had moved out and that she had succeeded in bringing her homosexual proclivities under control.

The themes that occupied the therapy were the patient's ongoing life conflicts, nothing more. The treatment relationship was marked by an early phase of truculent, stubborn silences; gradually the patient became more conversant, willing to engage in active discussion of her everyday problems. But the patient was frightened of closeness to a male figure and had to keep the therapist at a distance by reassuring him constantly about how well all was going, and by not telling him what was really going on with her. This was hinted at directly by the patient: "If I were to tell you some of the things in my mind, it would knock you off your chair." At these times, the therapist did not press. He knew no details of the patient's homosexual activities, nor even how overt her homosexual relations were.

TERMINATION

In her Termination Study interviews, the patient made clear that her homosexual liaisons had continued more actively than her therapist had been informed; that she had not fully moved out of her shared room, even when she had begun to sleep elsewhere; and that in her new job as a schoolteacher she was sharing an apartment with her first homosexual girlfriend, while the more recent one (from whose attentions she was trying to free herself) was taking an apartment nearby. Yet the patient had pushed for the termination, which came "logically" at the point of successful college graduation. Her symptoms had remitted, her homosexuality was more covert, her self-esteem was enhanced, and she was less rebellious and truculent in general. Because she was so busy with commencement events and her pending move to her new city of employment, the patient did not keep her final scheduled treatment hour, but excused herself by phone. She followed this up with a grateful letter to the therapist, thanking him for all his help and indicating that all was going extremely well during the summer. The therapist felt that he and the patient had agreed to see how things went with her life during the next years, keeping open the possibility of return to treatment should the support she had received up to this point prove insufficient to sustain her.

STATUS AT FOLLOW-UP

When contacted for Follow-Up Study, the patient sounded cheerful, indicating that she wanted very much to come, and had been "hoping to hear from you." In her letter of confirmation of the appointment schedule, the patient said, "Contrary to public opinion, I am looking forward to these days." When she was seen, it quickly became apparent that she saw herself as still very emotionally troubled and was seeking a return to therapeutic help. She now gave a very different perspective on her behaviors and her motivations. Her difficult behaviors she saw as ways of getting her family to take her troubles seriously and get help for her. Yet, once in treatment, she had not felt able to discuss the things that bothered her so much with her therapist: "If he had *made* me talk about them, I could have done it." She had ended her treatment disappointed that, despite the surface improvements, her psychological problems were essentially unaltered. Now she was back, feeling that "this is my last chance."

The patient's life during the follow-up period had been, on the surface, progressive and seemingly unruffled. Her teaching was very successful, and she had earned unexpected praise from her administrative superiors. She was productively busy at work, but she herself was not content with it. The patient's father had died during the interim, about 6 months following an automobile accident. During this illness period, his new wife's "true colors" had become manifest: She had not been anxious to nurse him in his declining months, and had practically deserted him. The patient was now engaged in a struggle (and potential litigation) to win her share of the modest estate, but she had taken these events without major upheaval. The patient's main difficulty had been and remained in the sphere of her interpersonal and sexual relationships. She now acknowledged that overt homosexual relationships had continued unabated all through her psychotherapy and for a year or so into the follow-up period. She had now struggled her way out of these and was trying to develop heterosexual involvements, but was having difficulty in finding a suitable man. She said, "Maybe my standards are too high." She had had one actual heterosexual relationship with a man she thought she loved, but it had unaccountably then soured. She realized that she was hampered by the holdover of childhood attitudes, identified with the mother, of the filthiness and forbiddenness of sexual unions with men. She thought it ironic that as part of her teaching, she had to explain about normal sexual functioning to her high school students.

COURSE OF RENEWED TREATMENT

The patient was clearly seeking a renewed trial of psychotherapy; simply curbing her overt homosexual behaviors by an exertion of will had not by itself quelled the homosexual strivings. The patient accepted a referral for psychotherapy, to a colleague in the city in which she worked. This second psychotherapy lasted about a year (74 hours). The new treatment did not go easily. The patient handled her treatment in ways that could seem spiteful or indifferent; she would often be late, or miss appointments, or threaten treatment rupture. At such times, the therapist's stance would be that the issue was not whether the patient had problems or whether she could use help—they both knew the answer to those questions—but whether she herself wanted at that point to work toward solving those problems.

Throughout the new treatment course, the patient continued a renewed active homosexual life with a variety of partners. In contrast to the previous treatment, this therapist tried to work actively and interpretively with these problems, as far as the patient would allow. And all along, despite the ever-present fright and mistrust, a growing transference closeness did evolve. Along with this, the patient began to develop very uncomfortable transference feelings, which she could only talk about most indirectly. This growing transference discomfort played its role in the dramatic and traumatic events of one weekend that heralded the termination of this second major attempt at psychotherapy. The patient's roommate called the therapist one evening to tell him that the patient had been drinking and was extremely agitated; she was babbling incoherently and stating how much she needed the therapist, as only he could help her. He saw the patient in an emergency night consultation and hospitalized her immediately, accompanying her to admission. The patient acted coquettish on the way; before he left her, she pulled off her blouse and said something about getting ready, since they might as well go to bed.

The next day the patient was in a black, depressed rage. She would not talk to the therapist, but only demanded immediate release from the "unnecessary" hospitalization. She was released, and the next night the therapist received another call. It was from another hospital, where the patient had been brought following an apparent "suicide attempt" with a sedative overdose. Again, when she calmed, she was released. In the next therapy hours, the events that had precipitated this upset period emerged. The patient had had a heterosexual date, and had first encouraged and then refused the man's advances. He had gone into a rage, and in an overtly sexualized assault had choked the patient. It was when she had succeeded in averting the assault that the patient fell apart and the therapist was called. Subsequent to these events, the psychotherapy never again seemed the same. The patient became fearful and withdrawn; she again began to miss appointments, and soon terminated.

Nine months later, the patient urgently sought an emergency appointment with the psychiatrist who had conducted the initial clinical evaluation when the patient had first sought therapy at The Menninger Foundation. Yet, when the patient came for the hour, she wasn't sure what she wanted to do with it. Though she still turned to psychiatry when she got upset, she also felt that she didn't believe in it any more. She was now deeply entrenched in her homosexuality, without even a facade of interest in men. She was involved in a homosexual love triangle at the time of this visit. She said that what had gone wrong in her second treatment effort was that she had found herself falling in love with the therapist, and these feelings had been, to her, unbearable. She had come to the initial examining psychiatrist now, rather than to either of her therapists, because with him she was not subject to complicated transference arousals. She knew she needed further treatment but could not see her way clear to accepting it. This was the last follow-up contact with this patient.

COMMENTS

This patient had, by this point, been in two very differently oriented psychotherapy efforts. The first therapist had been willing to see the patient's illness in terms of the (somewhat exaggerated) problems of a protracted adolescent upheaval; with her, he collusively underestimated the serious and potentially chronic character of the patient's homosexual propensities. By thus rarely challenging the patient's version of her life problems, by accepting manifest material as literal, the therapist (unwittingly?) encouraged the patient to paint a rosy picture of her life progression and discouraged her from talking about her homosexual conflicts (which at the same time he *knew* she had). This strategy, with the therapist playing out the comfortable and congenial supportive psychotherapeutic role, seemed at termination to have paid off.

Yet at Follow-Up Study it was clear that the patient had returned for a "last chance" to secure treatment for her homosexuality, which she now avowed she had originally come seeking and had been bitterly disappointed in never receiving. The new therapist to whom she was now referred did undertake the more ambitious goal of treatment of the patient's characterological problems and sexual symptoms. And yet the second therapy ended equally inconclusively and over the same issues. Whereas the first therapy had sought to effect desired life change through a tacit collusive agreement to leave the issues centering around homosexual strivings and behaviors untouched—and whereas this was ultimately unsuccessful, because this patient, unlike the Actress, was not willing to settle for this kind of compromise resolution—the second therapy undertook to deal with just these same issues of homosexuality directly, and it foundered over the patient's inability to tolerate the unfolding positive Oedipal transference attachments and Oedipal conflicts (which were centrally related to the patient's defensive homosexuality) and the therapist's inability to make this transference unfolding more bearable to her. Thus neither therapy could get to work effectively with the unfolding eroticized Oedipal transferences. The second therapist tried to and did not succeed; the first therapist had struck a collusive bargain not to, and for this patient (unlike the Actress), this also did not succeed. In this sense, the Rebellious Coed expressed herself as considerably less content with her treatment outcome than the Actress. Her homosexuality was not consolidated ego-syntonically in the same way.

"Rescue" by Factors Other than Psychotherapy

RESCUE BY REALITY CIRCUMSTANCES

The Role of Material Support

The role of the reality circumstances (the total, evolving life situation) of the patient as a critical set of codeterminants of therapeutic possibility, course, and outcome has been stated in a number of contexts as one of the guiding assumptions shaping the design and the data-gathering activities of PRP. This view of reality circumstances has been specified within the conceptualization of the Situational Variables as one of the interacting set of determinants (along with the Patient Variables and the Treatment Variables) of change in therapy (see Sargent *et al.*, 1958, especially pp. 151–155). I have discussed the importance of the Situational Variables a number of times (see pp. 15–18, 79–83), most recently in connection with the issue of disengagement from an unfavorable life situation (see pp. 466–468).

In the present discussion, I focus more narrowly on the issue of the available material supporting resources in relation to the therapeutic prospects. Like all other human enterprises, psychiatric treatment must be appropriately financed, whether through private resources, insurance coverage, or public support. With the kind of long-term treatments under study in PRP, this was always a significant consideration, and cases have already been described (e.g., the Bitter Spinster, pp. 349–353, and the Rebellious Coed, pp. 483–489) where for reasons of inadequate financial resources, the modality adjudged initially to be the treatment of choice (psychoanalysis, in those instances) could not be undertaken, and a less frequent (and more limited) psychotherapy had to be entered instead. With those patients who required psychiatric hospitalization of any length, this cost issue is of course compounded manyfold; again, cases have been described (e.g., the Phobic Girl, pp. 468–476, and the Actress, pp. 478–483) in which the treatment result was either actually or potentially impaired, or at least altered, by the family's inability to support the amount of concomitant hospitalization deemed ideal in the individual circumstance. For the most part, however, the PRP patients had sufficient financial resources for their projected treatment needs (see Section II, Chapter 5, pp. 66–68).

The issue of great wealth can be a very different one, however, both in its life impact and in its impact on treatment course and potential, than that of simply adequate financial resources as a necessary precondition to the possibilities for help via psychiatric treatment. I have already indicated (see p. 66) that, contrary to the public stereotype about The Menninger Foundation and its clientele, only 5 of our 42 patients (12% of the sample) came from families of great wealth. (A sixth, while a hospital patient, eloped with and married another hospital patient who was an extremely wealthy young man; see p. 68.) I have also already presented the details of the one case among these five, that of the Adolescent Grandson (see pp. 256–257), in which the great family wealth clearly played a significant role in affecting the treatment outcome adversely. The issue there was that of the interfering role of the very wealthy, very powerful, and very unsympathetic grandfather on whose financial support the treatment rested; when he indicated his unwillingness to support any further such a frivolous enterprise as psychotherapy, he was all too readily acceded to. Had he not been a man who had always gotten his way just because he was so used to manipulating his power and wealth, this treatment might not have been so prematurely disrupted.

Curiously, though, the case of the Adolescent Grandson was not only the chief instance where wealth and its manipulation served to wreck whatever chances for real success the treatment might have had; this same wealth also served subsequently (in the patient's hands) to stabilize his life in the face of his continuing totally unresolved psychiatric illness, just because the patient had the very large financial resources to create a sustaining enough life situation. That treatment course is therefore presented here as one characterized by "rescue by money."

Therapy of the Adolescent Grandson

BACKGROUND AND PROGNOSIS

This patient was the 17-year-old schoolboy who was brought to psychiatric treatment because of two bizarre (seemingly out-of-character) occurrences of cavorting nude on his grandfather's estate, set against a background of chronic unhappiness, isolation, and poor school adjustment of 7 or 8 years' duration (see pp. 131, 150, 165).

The patient's family constellation was quite special and quite skewed. The natural mother was an alcoholic, promiscuous, and grossly neglectful woman, who had permanently deserted her three children when the patient was only 2 years old. The father was a gentle, nonaggressive man, a cardiac invalid, who had remarried when the patient was 7 and enjoyed 2 idyllically happy marriage years before his death of heart disease. The stepmother was a nurturing woman, but she was always treated by the grandfather (the father's father) as the governess hired to care for his grandchildren, and she complained bitterly about this assigned role and lack of family support. The grandfather was a domineering, self-made industrial tycoon, brilliant and ruthless in his business dealings, aloof but totally controlling with his family. The patient and his stepmother were always kept at a distance, managed by the grandfather, and occasionally permitted to visit with him at one of his various estates. At such times, the patient always found his grandfather hard to talk to.

The patient's whole life was marked by a succession of traumata and deprivations. Because of the natural mother's neglect, the father had often taken the patient with him to his laboratory, keeping him there in a basket all day, and then had often also taken over feeding and bathing him at home in the evening. Following the mother's desertion, there had been a succession of unfortunately chosen housekeepers, neglectful and violent-tempered, and the father himself had often had to be away for extensive business trips. The stepmother was the first nurturant individual to remain in the patient's life for any length of time; in her own family she had always fulfilled a caretaking role. The father's death had occurred when the patient was 9. The day before, the father, for the only remembered time, had spanked the patient, and the patient remembered during their struggle consciously wishing his father dead. He had then been present the next day when the father suffered a cardiac episode, and felt that he had not "fetched his father's heart pills on time." His brother accused him of having been "lackadaisical" in going after them. The patient felt, with guilt undiminished over the years, that had he behaved differently, his father might still be alive.

After the father's death, the grandfather became the guardian of the children, controlled their trust inheritances, and undertook to make all the decisions about their education and subsequent careers. The stepmother, in her role as hired governess, had allowance money doled out to her; the grandfather was determined that she not share in the family fortune in any way. The stepmother and children could visit the big estate only on invitation—which came seldom. Occasionally the grandfather sent the children on visits to their "real mother," who let them run wild and filled them with tales of what an ineffectual failure their father had been, and how their stepmother had come into their lives as a marriage wrecker. The patient fled from these visits, bewildered and frightened. When he was 13, the patient accidentally wounded his stepmother with a shotgun. She said that "boys sometimes hate their mothers," which he guiltily took to be her reproach that he had tried to do this deliberately. Thereafter she locked her bedroom door each night.

From the time of his father's death, the patient never did well in school again, though he was shifted from school to school by his grandfather in a fruitless search for the environment that would motivate him to be a good scholar. The patient attributed his poor scholarship to his not being "a brain." His schoolmaster spoke of his wretched study habits, his cultivated poor memory, and his absorption in such diversionary pursuits as writing poetry (which was bitter, but not without talent). The patient grew up an inhibited, depressed adolescent, always brooding inside. He had no close friends. He was a regular churchgoer, being an acolyte in the Episcopal church. He enjoyed the ceremonies but had no deep religious conviction. Sexually, he was naive and inhibited. He was glad that he had less sexual feelings than other boys (his wild brothers were always held up to him as bad examples); he felt that masturbation and premarital sexual experiences were very "disgusting."

The events that led to his referral for psychiatric care have already been presented (see pp. 131, 150, 165). These were the episodes of scampering naked across his grandfather's estate "to give me a sense of freedom." When he was caught (on the second occasion), he was accused of public masturbation and exhibitionism, which he stoutly denied. He did acknowledge an episode years earlier of riding a horse naked over the estate. How the grandfather (through his private secretary) arranged for the patient's immediate hospitalization at The Menninger Foundation and shut the patient's stepmother totally out of participation in this process has already been detailed (see pp. 256–257). When the patient came, he expressed his bewilderment about all the fuss. He professed not to understand why he was being brought for treatment, since he had done very little wrong; he saw his behaviors only as incomprehensible "foolish actions." He was reserved and inhibited, except that with mention of his father, especially the father's death, he could dissolve into tears and express mixed feelings of guilt and deprivation. Underneath, one could discern as well the welling of anger against the stepmother, bound to him, he felt, only by the burdens of obligation, and the grandfather, who didn't really care.

The patient was hospitalized for 6 months and then discharged to day hospital care combined with foster home placement. Special care was taken with the foster home placement to ensure the patient the kind of normal home environment he had never had. When he began to complain that the father in the house was too often away and preoccupied with business affairs, a transfer was arranged to another home with a more companionable father. The supportive–expressive psychotherapy for which the patient was recommended was designed with two purposes: first, to provide in a specifically verbalized format what the total management and living program was intended to effect — the creation of a strong and stable object for attachment and identification, the concerned and caring parent who would provide the truly "corrective emotional experience"; and, second, to engage in specific uncovering and interpretation of the unsettled, unresolved complex surrounding the father's death — the patient's guilts, inhibitions, and impulse breakthroughs.

COURSE OF THE THERAPY

The psychotherapy lasted 2 years (224 hours). The appropriately very high treatment fee set in this case and the specific problems that it posed to the treatment, including the way it allowed the patient to feel exploited and the grandfather to feel justified in prematurely terminating his support of the treatment, have already been described (see pp. 195–196). The therapist engaged in many very specifically supportive interventions through the course of the treatment. He made suggestions in regard to the patient's manner of life, academic pursuits, study habits, dating behaviors, and the like; he made many time accommodations to the patient; he actively entered (along with the whole hospital staff) into the patient's total life planning; and (unfortunately) he had to divert energies into countering the grandfather's negative pressures upon the treatment. Through all this, the patient was for the most part passively in therapy, sent by his grandfather, and ready at any sign of (too much) involvement or discomfort to contemplate flight. The therapist was trying to help the patient bring some kind of order into his life, with reasonable school, work, and social adjustments.

When the psychotherapy started, the patient was in a foster home, attending the local high school and "getting along." He saw no purpose to this new involvement and kept asking why he was in therapy. He engaged in defensive flights into transitory attachments to mixed-up and unsuitable girls; when he succeeded in having a sexual experience (his first ever) with one who had quite a "loose reputation," he was abruptly turned upon and turned out by both the girl and her mother, and he fled in humiliation. He visited his family on every available holiday occasion, but came back from these visits feeling rejected and more alone than ever, since their reception of him was always most perfunctory and formal. At one point (7 months along in the therapy), a growing panic and an evening phone call precipitated an immediate emergency appointment with the therapist. The patient, comforted (and surprised) by the therapist's concern, suddenly sobbed out his great loneliness, his feelings of overwhelming humiliation and unlovableness— all linked to the rejection by the girlfriend, absences by the therapist, and the lifelong traumata of rejections at home (going back to the original desertion by the mother). The crisis calmed, and the patient was rehospitalized to restabilize his controls. (He remained in the hospital 3½ months.)

It was following this episode that the middle, most productive, phase of the therapy was ushered in. The patient could acknowledge that he was "a very lonely boy and that he never had anybody who had unequivocally cared for him." (His only mail was an occasional letter from his grandfather's secretary.) The therapist began to be able to interpret the growing transference attachment (hitherto always defensively denied), as well as the transference acting out with his succession of girlfriends (at times with a pathological, almost delusional, jealousy) and with his escape trips to his home. During this period the patient completed high school; he was pleased that at least his stepmother, if not his grandfather, could be induced to think the occasion important enough to attend. He took a summer job and planned on college enrollment in the fall. He identified awkwardly with his therapist by getting a similar crew cut, switching his brand of cigarettes, and planning self-consciously to be a premedical student.

Within the therapy, the patient was now also able to bring up much hitherto unavailable (or withheld) material. This revolved around his terrified reaction to the seductiveness he had always experienced in his relation with his stepmother— she had slept in his bed with him when he was already a good-sized boy. In response, he had violent sadistic fantasies of tearing, clawing, raping, and murdering her (were the primitive rages at his natural mother for her real desertion behind these?). When the patient had shot his stepmother at age 13, the action had been driven by these fantasies; the patient was both terrified and guilty that it should so readily have been ascribed to an accident, and that everyone should have been so sympathetic about this "accident." But this material, and the closer, trusting attachment to the therapist within which it came out, were more than the patient could be enabled to tolerate. He began to be more upset again, and to retreat to his old defenses of denial and avoidance. He kept making brief visits home that were neither indicated nor authorized, and each one presented him with renewed evidence that he had no real place in his family. His passionate and unrealistic involvements with new girls—either semidelinquent girls in town or the youngest of the sick adolescent girls in the hospital—continued. He backed away from the pressure to join a college fraternity, fearful of the homosexual temptations, and was anxious over his growing fondness for and increasing attachment to the therapist.

Under the impact of this burgeoning homosexual panic, the patient again became unreflective and uncommunicative in the therapy. His college work deteriorated, and his new foster parents (the third set), who were very fond of him and realistically very concerned for him, felt that his life was increasingly out of control and disorganized (the hours he kept, the company he kept, etc.). And within the therapy, the therapist, who rode therapeutically for quite a while on the positive transference attachment engendered by the events of the emergency consultation when the patient panicked, could not safeguard the continuation of the treatment from the disruptive effect of the uninterpreted, threatening, eroticized homosexual component in this "transference submission." (The patient did acknowledge from time to time considerable fantasizing about the therapist, but this was always used more abreactively than interpretively.) At the very end of the treatment, the patient "confessed" (to the hospital director) that his perverse exhibitionistic practices had not only been far more frequent and far more ego-syntonic than his initially presenting picture had indicated, but that they had continued throughout the treatment and that he had never been able to discuss this in the therapy. These practices consisted of public masturbation in full view of a young female neighbor, running nude in his foster parents' backyard, and similar behaviors.

TERMINATION

The specific treatment termination (and flight from the feared homosexual transference) was engineered by the patient on an Easter visit home. He was delighted to find that he could present himself to his grandfather in such a way that he appeared well, and the grandfather thus re-evoked all his own doubts about the need for therapy. How the grandfather blustered and browbeat the hospital doctor and therapist into acceding to the treatment disruption has already been described (see pp. 256–257). The therapist had never succeeded in dealing interpretively with the eroticized aspects of the positive transference tie, or with the latent negative transference feelings stemming from the patient's lifelong deprivations at the hands of putatively nurturant figures; therefore, he could not block the patient's frightened withdrawal. At the termination point, the patient loudly complained about the "inconsistency" of the therapist. At times the therapist had been stiff and formal, at other times warm and friendly. Mostly, he wouldn't talk about his private life, in contrast with the chatty hospital doctor, who would talk with the patient of his own adolescence. The patient said that he could work better with a doctor like that, who had once also been a mixed-up kid, living on "wine, women, and song," and yet had now achieved a solid position as a doctor.

STATUS AT FOLLOW-UP

When the patient was contacted for Follow-Up Study, he was living permanently in Topeka. Though he agreed to cooperate, he canceled at the last moment, but then came willingly and agreeably when contacted a year later. He offered no special explanation for his avoidance a year earlier. He had one day impulsively married his then-current girlfriend (a hospital inpatient awaiting assignment to psychotherapy), and the couple had taken off on a combined "vacation–honeymoon–runaway trip," from which they returned to Topeka after several months. They had bought a home next door to the patient's ex-foster parents (the third family, with whom he got along so well). The marriage had now endured almost 3 years. After the patient had been married about a year, his grandfather died suddenly (at 74) of a heart attack. The patient took this without severe response. He suddenly came into an inheritance of great wealth and position, and uneasily felt himself having the responsibilities of the "head of the family." Most of his actual fortune was tied up (against the possibility of dissipation) in a number of trusts; his lifetime income was very considerable, however.

The patient began to take stock of his situation in the wake of his grandfather's death and this sudden change in his fortune. He sought out psychiatric consultation (not with his former therapist) and wondered whether he "ought to get back into psychotherapy." He saw his problem now as becoming a man in his own right, not just living parasitically on his inheritance. He agreed in the abstract about his need for more treatment, but he felt reluctant to "start with a stranger" and agreed that he would rather not resume with the same therapist. Of treatment he said, "Sometimes I want treatment, and sometimes I don't. It's like if you have a backache, if it's really bad you want to see a doctor. When it's not so bad you don't want to see a doctor. And being able to stick to treatment when you're not feeling so bad is a problem with me."

And actually, overall, the patient was not feeling bad. He seemed in many ways contented. The marriage seemed reasonably stable and harmonious. They had (within 3 years) two small children, both sons. The patient spent much time happily playing with them. There were, however, quarrels in the marriage, centered around religion (the wife's ardent Catholicism). On one occasion the patient indicated to his ex-hospital doctor some unhappiness in the marriage; he felt that he had married "on the rebound" and now regretted it, but would stick with it for the babies' sake. In many other ways, the patient's life was still unsettled and unformed. He had finally dropped out of college altogether, feeling too restless and impulsive for that. He took many sudden and impulsive trips (e.g., to visit his brother). He called this one of his residual problems. "My impulsiveness isn't any better. In fact, it's worse because now I'm financially independent." He gave as an example the fact that he had bought and sold eight cars in less than 2 years before settling on one that he was determined to stick with. He felt it a good sign that he had stuck to his marriage for 3 years.

The patient occupied his time with a succession of business ventures. The biggest one had been a real estate leasing and developing enterprise, in which un-scrupulous partners had absconded with $200,000 of the patient's money. He felt himself now a sadder and wiser man. His stock market affairs were handled for him by his grandfather's personal secretary, who had full power of attorney. The patient regularly sent her money, and she made the investments. The patient was thinking again of investing in real estate and had recently been negotiating for a large piece of woodland and pastureland near Topeka where he would farm, raise cattle, grow Christmas trees, and perhaps ultimately live (it was about an hour out of town).

The patient's best relationship was with his ex-foster parents. They were the only people whom he felt he could trust to be unselfishly interested in him. He had been hurt and angry when they had taken another patient into their home in a foster placement, but this had subsided after he talked out his "jealousy and sense of rejection" in an interview with his hospital doctor. The foster parents were "grandparents to our children," and the foster father once told the patient that the only difference between him and their real son was the blood relation-ship. On their wedding anniversary the patient surprised them with the gift of the carpet they had long wanted. Beyond this, the patient had no close relation-ships. He was ashamed of how shabbily his grandfather had treated his stepmother, and he now tried to make amends by setting his stepmother up financially, buy-ing her a modest home, giving her a monthly income, and paying for her periodic visits to his home and children. But it was not a close relationship, and the pa-tient was bothered by the stepmother's religious fanaticism. He avoided most other people and community involvements, because he always felt people were after him because of his wealth and prominence. When he felt particularly at loose ends, he ate a lot; he was beginning to get obese. About his therapist, he revealed a ques-tion that had plagued him all during the treatment: Why wasn't the therapist mar-ried? "I never asked him—a good-looking guy like that with as much on the ball as he's got. I just figured he was more interested in his work." There is no fur-ther follow-up information on this patient.

COMMENTS

Clearly, though the Adolescent Grandson was essentially unimproved and drift-ing at the time of treatment termination—when he and his grandfather, each for their different reasons, conspired together to disrupt the treatment effort—he seemed stabilized and (considerably?) improved in functioning at Follow-Up Study, with no interim treatment. A number of factors seemed operative here. The first was the grandfather's death and the patient's coming into access to his family for-tune. He used this money, influence, and social status to set up ("to endow") a network of dependency gratifications (from the wife, the grandfather's personal secretary, and the stepmother), each catering to an aspect of his needs and wishes. And he could use his money to create a kind of reality, which concealed his basic incapacity for real autonomy: His wealth surrounded him with an artificially "meaningful" life concerned with business ventures, community involvements, and the like. In addition, he appeared to have outgrown his adolescence and its tur-moils, was married (seemingly contentedly), and had two small children to whom he appeared very devoted. Another very important factor was the stabilizing in-fluence of his third foster home, which gave the patient his first sustained and trusted experience of integrated and harmonious family living. The foster parents were continuing *in loco parentis* to him, and as very real grandparents to his children. And, lastly, there was the delayed positive impact of the therapist and of the formal psychotherapy itself. Clearly, the patient carried over the therapist's interest, concern, and willingness to help (the helpful side of the protective positive countertransference); all of this was the therapist's contribution to the patient's "corrective emotional experience." It was no doubt this element in the therapy, added to this same major component in the relationship with the foster parents, that gave the patient the capacity to try himself successfully in the marriage, to overcome his adolescent pressures, and to handle as well as he did the consequences of his grandfather's death and his inheritance.

Of course, not all wealthy patients are able to use their available money to rescue (or better) themselves after such an inconclusive and unsuccessful trial at psychotherapy. In fact, the fates of our own sample of rich patients varied sharply. The Alcoholic Heir was embarked on a downhill alcoholic course to his death, from which he was not deflected by intensive psychoanalytic treatment launched within the hospital setting, or by any other aid or support that money could buy (see pp. 345–349). On the other hand, the Sexual Masochist, probably the very sickest among all our project patients, was modestly stabilized at the time of Follow-Up Study (after a most unsuccessful treatment course) within the gratification of a properly diluted and properly disguised dependent transference, as a "therapeutic lifer" in "family therapy" with his wife; he has continued in treatment until the time of present writing, by now at a moderately improved level. His money and his freedom from the need for truly gainful employment did play a central role in making all this possible (see pp. 405–412), somewhat analogously to the role of personal wealth in the outcome with the Adolescent Grandson.

The Heiress started at a position much different from that of either the Alcoholic Heir or the Sexual Masochist: She was a functioning mother of four children beset by her disorganizing "turbulent periods" and caught in a destructive marriage. She seemed to do reasonably well in her prolonged psychoanalytic treatment, got out of the very bad marriage, and seemed to be stabilized in a much better marriage to a much nicer person. By the time of Follow-Up Study, however, there had been significant (though far from total) loss of the treatment gains, as the new husband had (in different ways) turned out to be also a difficult and unsuitable man (see pp. 421–426). Clearly, the patient's wealth had not protected her from another (almost equally) bad marriage choice. The treatment course of the fifth of the group of very wealthy patients, the Bohemian Prep School Boy, has not yet been presented, though he too had a treatment disrupted by the family (like that of the Adolescent Grandson). At the time of Follow-Up Study, his life was no different: He was still unsettled, still very young (20), and still living on his parents' largesse.

RESCUE BY ALTERNATIVE PSYCHOLOGICAL SUPPORTS

The patients in the PRP sample entered their psychiatric treatments in the decade of the 1950s (between 1952 and 1958), before the great rise of the alternative therapies — the encounter movement, the human potential movement, the various adaptations of Eastern religions, mysticism and meditation, and so on. Yet, even in the 1950s there were significant alternatives to mainstream or conventional treatment methods within a psychiatric framework. One has been Alcoholics Anonymous (AA), probably the first and certainly the most successful of all the mental health self-help movements (and one with a significant antimedical and antipsychiatric bias); another, totally out of and against the mainstream of the organized health care system, has been Christian Science. Within the PRP sample, we had two cases in which conventional psychiatric treatment turned out totally unsuccessfully, but the patients rescued themselves through alternative supports to some level of bettered functioning. In one case, this took place through recourse to AA; in the other, through recourse to Christian Science.

Treatment of the Alcoholic Raconteur

BACKGROUND AND PROGNOSIS

The Alcoholic Raconteur was the 1 patient among the 19 in our sample with a major alcohol problem (45% of our total of 42) with whom adherence to AA played a significant role at some point in the process of treatment and stabilization.[1] He was referred originally for psychiatric hospitalization because of his severe alcoholism and his deteriorated life; he was pretentiously intellectual and very disdainful of AA, seeking only psychoanalysis. This patient came from a devoutly Catholic family that, all through his difficulties, always exhorted him to turn for solace and help to his priest and to God. The father was a successful businessman, but insecure, self-deprecatory, and prudish, though a stern, compulsive martinet with the patient. By contrast, the mother was an indulgent woman, but she had been alcohol- and barbiturate-addicted for years (and intermittently a fervent member of AA); she was also subject to recurrent psychotic depressions. The parents had not slept in the same room for 20 years. The father said that the marriage had never been congenial; he had "often thought of murder, but never of divorce." The patient had largely been raised by a kindly nurse, a "second mother" who stayed with the family till he was 22. "If there was any serenity in the family she had it." She was indulgent like the mother—a practice to which the father roundly objected, feeling that the patient was always too infantilized.

The patient had had many childhood symptoms (teeth grinding, bed wetting, breath-holding spells to the point of unconsciousness, frightening nightmares). In his early school years, he had been a precocious student and an avid reader. By high school years, however, the patient's scholastic interests had flagged. He became much preoccupied with his physical health (he had intense fears of tuberculosis) and went in for weight lifting to develop his strength. He was very concerned with the lateness of his pubescent changes and his fear that his genitals were much below average in size. He had no close friends and seldom dated. His

---

1. As already described in full, there was one other patient, the Sexual Masochist (see pp. 405–412), whose long-term stabilization and improvement—up until the present writing, as a "therapeutic lifer"—has been in the context of an involvement with AA. In his case, however, it is clearly emphasized that this has become a therapeutic attachment to a quasi-professional couple devoting themselves to leadership in the local (Topeka) AA organization; it has not been a specific involvement with the AA ideology. How much this result with the Sexual Masochist, then, has reflected a sustaining beneficial *psychotherapy*, and how much is rather an AA commitment *instead of* formal psychotherapy, is certainly not clear.

"sexual problems" he blamed on his prudish upbringing, his shame over his late puberty, and his embarrassment with girls. He was preoccupied with struggles over masturbation; he made a number of abortive attempts at sexual relationships, which culminated finally in a completed sexual experience with a prostitute. He was concerned always with issues of impotence and sterility. He had some desultory adolescent homosexual encounters, but derived no satisfaction from them: "Homosexuality leaves me with a revolting moral hangover."

In high school years, the patient developed an implacable hostility toward his father, whom he felt to be a nagging, belittling man; he also had contempt for him as a weak man. In college, this intellectually gifted individual's scholarship was mediocre, and his behavior was marked by the onset of heavy drinking and sexual promiscuity. He never graduated, and his college career was marred by interruptions (e.g., he had to help hospitalize his mother for a psychotic depression, which horrified the patient). The only job of any duration the patient ever held was one his father secured for him in a stockbroker's office, at which he worked quite responsibly for 3 years. The patient, however, felt that he had a terrible time adjusting to the authority structure there, and he drank more and more. He carried on a rather prolonged affair with a young woman coworker, which he characterized as constant desperate effort to convince himself of his potency. The affair broke up over his drinking, and "I went completely to pieces."

After a period in the Army, where he also drank constantly and suffered a good deal of company punishment for it, the patient returned to his parents' home and went into an almost total withdrawal from society and retreat to his room, where he essentially stayed for 8 months. He brooded about his swelling sense of hurt and rage against his father. His day–night schedule was completely reversed; he slept all day and was out drinking at night. He would often pass out when drunk, and would be brought home by cab drivers and deposited at dawn on the front porch. Tensions with the father escalated: The patient would dramatically order the father out of the house, with threats to kill him if he stayed, and twice the patient physically assaulted his father. After the second beating, as noted earlier (see p. 125), the father moved out of the house and into his club downtown in the interests of family peace.

When the patient emerged from this period in his room, he decided to make a fresh start in a distant city. Actually, he never worked there, but lived on money that he received from his parents and carelessly squandered. He drank constantly and was frequently picked up by the police as a "skid row drunk." He finally sought psychiatric consultation (he would have no part of AA) and was referred for hospitalization at The Menninger Foundation, which his father agreed to support. The patient arrived for admission drunk and penniless, and the father, who met him at the airport, had to pay his final cab fare to the hospital.

On admission, the patient tried to convey an impression of sincerity and warmth. His language was pretentious, intellectualizing, and pseudoanalytic. He was preoccupied with his feeling that only psychoanalysis could hope to correct his profound illness. He spoke warmly of only one person, his mother; he was enormously hostile toward his father, paranoidly so. Gradually the patient felt better controlled within the hospital, and his full, compulsively scheduled activities regimen. He renewed his attachment to religion, saying, "In my life, the Catholic church is the most stringent yet wonderful limitation I have." He pleaded his motivation for psychoanalysis, but averred also the importance of faith: No therapy could be effective unless the patient had given himself up to God, and was in a state of grace to receive it.

The patient was hospitalized for 7 months before starting in formal therapy. He gradually succeeded in convincing the clinical evaluation team, which originally felt that psychoanalysis would be out of the question, to reconsider his suitability for a trial of psychoanalysis, starting of course in the hospital. This was one of those instances where the research group disagreed completely, feeling psychoanalysis to be completely contraindicated. The appropriate recommendation, it was thought, would have been for an essentially supportive therapy directed toward helping the patient gain enhanced controls; this would be done through "borrowed ego strength" from an identification with a therapist who would be a closer, more real, and less judgmental figure than God, with whom fear of sin and damnation was involved. If the effort at analysis were undertaken, the research group felt that the treatment would eventuate in either a disrupted therapeutic situation or a chronic, unbudgeable, stalemated one.

COURSE OF THE TREATMENT

The patient was taken into psychoanalysis. This treatment effort lasted not quite 3 years (546 hours), though the treatment was for different stretches (5 months in the middle and 2 months at the end) converted into a face-to-face psychotherapy aimed at more direct behavior control. The patient was out of the hospital after 6 months, claiming a false but plausible financial crisis, and for the rest of his treatment (except for a 3-day rehospitalization) was in the day hospital and in outpatient status (during the latter half of his treatment course with concomitant Antabuse). As much as possible throughout the treatment course, the effort was at classical analysis. Because the patient's drinking and frantic sexual promiscuity were never under effective control, the therapist undertook the periods of formal switch to psychotherapy, the returns to the day hospital, and the institution of concomitant Antabuse; each time, however, the patient exerted a relentless pressure to convince his analyst (through good behaviors and "working well") of his readiness to renew "full analysis," and each time the analyst ultimately acceded. Each time the patient agreed to regularize his life, control his impulses, and get and hold a job, but he never really fulfilled these conditions, living up to each of them fitfully at best.

Within the treatment, the patient at all times tried to make his past life and traumatic memories the main treatment themes—this was part of his drive to be in analysis rather than in therapy. His current life situation (with its constant emergencies and misbehaviors), in fact, only came up when pressed by the analyst under the impact of the patient's continued destructive acting out. This became a major focus during the period of formal psychotherapy, but as soon as the patient got back to analysis, he took fullest advantage of the analytic permissiveness of free association to wallow again in past life and memory while ignoring current chaos. To him, discussion of current activity was always unwanted. It was always begun at the behest of the analyst's effort to bring order into the treatment situation and control into the life outside; it was never seen by the patient as being in the service of any effort to alter current behaviors through understanding them.

As is already clear, the patient's life throughout the treatment course grew more and more disorganized, to the point of utter chaos and collapse—starting with his hospital release after the first 6 months of analysis. The ostensible financial crisis at that point was generated by the dramatic deaths of both parents, 10 days apart, each from a heart attack. Upon the patient's return from the funerals, during which time he hardly went through any overt mourning process, he claimed that the family monies were now all tied up in probate and that there were no more funds available to sustain continued hospitalization. The truth (which came out only much later) was that there was a substantial immediate inheritance that would have been available, but now it was the patient's own money and he was unwilling to spend "his own money" for hospitalization. Rather, he squandered this sum over the next 2 years in alcoholic and sexual exploits.

Over the course of the treatment, the patient held two salesman jobs, each of which he lost for poor performance and negligence. Throughout the entire treatment course, the patient had no sustained social relationships. He had a series of frenzied, brief sexual affairs, with disturbed partners who were masochistically willing to submit to him. He boasted of his prowess, thinking of himself as a "walking erection," but he was always fearful for his potency and would have to fortify his performance by alcohol. He was fearful also of potential homosexual attacks. Mostly he drank alone, holed up in his room, going into stupors and blackouts. When with others, he would get raucous and bellicose, and feared being thrown into jail with its dangers of homosexual assault. Over the course of treatment all pretense of religious observance dropped away, because he would have to go to confession and did not wish to. By the end of treatment, he was quite abandoned and alone. His sister would have nothing to do with him or his importuning for money. She said, "He's had his chance of treatment and not used it."

The themes of the treatment were, in a sense, as unorganized in sequence and pattern as was the patient's life outside. There was a constant intellectualized deployment of isolated "deep" dynamic contents in the service of manipulating the analyst into thinking that analytic progress was being made, while neutralizing the analyst's efforts to affect the patient's behaviors. At the same time, the patient lived out a primitive, oral-aggressive dependency within the treatment situation: He used the treatment hour to obtain the fullest possible dependency gratifications from the person he idealized as the perfect God-like helper, so long as the helper remained faithfully at his disposal as a noninterfering listener. The analyst, for his part, was finally driven in desperation to try to cope with the patient's enormous diffuse acting out by direct prohibition, without having succeeded in connecting the acting out consistently with the analytic situation itself. The transference consisted of one major paradigm—the enactment of a primitive, orally aggressive search for total dependency gratification, built around the regressive fantasy that the couch would be a better breast than the original one. Within the patient's projected narcissistic omnipotence, the analyst was the "most important person in the world." The analyst never got past this transference defense against the primitive paranoid projection of the patient's deep rages over infantile oral frustrations. With the lack of clear separation of the analyst as transference object from the narcissistic extension of the patient's own omnipotence fantasies, a more regressed (and never resolved), more psychotic transference state always threatened, though it never fully emerged.

DISRUPTION OF THE TREATMENT

The fact and timing of the termination were determined by the patient. When the analyst was finally convinced that the analytic effort was totally fruitless, he again converted the treatment to psychotherapy, this time with the statement that the change was irrevocable. To the patient, this was being forever deprived of "having the best"—the opportunity of endless indulgence in talking to a captive audience about his childhood deprivations, his current exploits, and his wishful fantasies. He declared that this shift was unacceptable and that his treatment had to be analysis or nothing; if he could not continue it at The Menninger Foundation, he would seek it elsewhere. He abruptly stopped coming to his hours, disappeared from his lodging, and left the analyst to close out the treatment alone.

It took 9 months of increasing search to locate the patient for Termination Study. He wandered from place to place, in and out of Topeka; he made brief sallies into sexual escapades, but mostly holed up in cheap hotels, drinking and living on handouts from acquaintances and hotel employees. Finally, as noted earlier (see p. 89), his hotel landlady wrote to The Menninger Foundation asking help for the patient, who was drunk, sick, and penniless. When he was asked to come for research evaluation at our expense, he responded eagerly, asking only for transportation and expense money in advance. Before arrival he had to ask for more money, and he arrived disheveled, disorganized, drunk, disoriented, and belligerent. He wanted to refuse hospitalization, but passed out drunk before he could do so. The next day he was subdued and remorseful. He called the research contact a Godsend. He had been down to his last 20 cents and fearful of being jailed as a vagrant.

During the course of his Termination Study, the patient revealed his real awareness of how he had misused his treatment, though, characteristically, he could not refrain from indicting the analyst as well. The patient said he knew that "treatment was there for me and I didn't accept it but it should have been obvious to them that I didn't accept it and they should have done something." Of the analyst, he said, "He wasn't forceful enough for my type of person. I should have had directive therapy." At the close of the study, the patient expressed his dismal prognosis: "I won't be alive in 2 years, or if I am alive, I'll be in some institution, correctional probably, unless I get some help and cooperate with the help. . . . I'm on the way out! [pause] I'm at the bottom, you know." He left planning to check in at the nearest VA hospital.

STATUS AT FOLLOW-UP

The patient's later whereabouts (back in his home city) were determined when he spontaneously wrote a brief follow-up letter to his previous hospital doctor almost 2 years later. He was working, and he was sober—on a day-to-day basis. He was doing this through the AA program, "with the accent on honesty." He said, "I do know that these consecutive 24-hour periods wouldn't be possible were it not for the work we did in Topeka." To the surprise of some researchers, after some delays, the patient came back willingly for Follow-Up Study. He was sober, neatly dressed, and well-groomed, exuding the general appearance of a young businessman. His story was as follows. He had never sought out the VA hospital, but after the Termination Study had continued his steady, solitary drinking, subsisting mainly on the handouts of drinking acquaintances, sympathetic ladies, and hotel employees. Finally, about 10 months before the present contact, he "really hit bottom"—ending up in police court, badly battered after a barroom brawl.

At that point, the patient presented himself to an AA-related home for alcoholic transients. He became a faithful AA member and claimed not to have had a drop to drink since. He had discovered that he was "really allergic" to alcohol; it was poison in his system. He had a job as an "assistant sales manager" in an export–import house, which he had secured through his AA connections. He worked long hours and pleased his boss; he had already had one raise. He described his boss both as a rather violent, impulsive man and also as a sympathetic, friendly man. The patient had been finally cut off completely by his sister, and he said he was glad to be free of her constant moralizing. He had met a young woman 15 years his junior, and they were involved in a stormy romance. They had met when his drinking was at its height; she was also an alcoholic, was depressed as well, and had made a few suicide gestures. She was also, however, very accepting and maternal toward the patient. When the patient joined AA, her drinking dwindled also. The patient soon became frightened of the press towards marriage and took up with an older woman ("for 13 years a benzedrine addict"); his girlfriend then made a dramatic suicide effort, following which they were tearfully reunited. They were now living together and were officially engaged. But the patient was at the same time still keeping up his active sexual contact with the older woman. The patient's problems with masturbation and potency "still bugged him." The latter, however, he attributed to his carrying on a simultaneous relationship with two women, plus the exhausting demands of his work. And, in any case, he professed less interest in his sexual life: "The mechanics of this thing, of any sex action, is boring." He wondered if he were getting older. He was still troubled by his fears of homosexuality, but not so insistently.

There was further follow-up information for another 9 years. The patient did marry very shortly after the Follow-Up interview and offered to come for another Follow-Up Study (he was the only patient in the entire series who did this). He wrote, "I'm beginning to learn what love can be like in marriage." He was sober, and things were continuing "generally upward": He held the same job, was doing well, and had had two further raises. Eighteen months after the Follow-Up interview, an announcement was received of the birth of a baby girl. The next (and last) follow-up contact was almost 8 years later, now 12 years after the treatment termination. The patient brought his wife for hospitalization at The Menninger Foundation because she had made a serious suicide attempt. A diagnosis of a schizophrenic reaction within a narcissistic personality was made, and the hospitalization lasted 10 months. The patient himself was still active as ever in AA, and professed to be doing very well economically as a major sales representative for a national firm. At the same time, he was poorly organized, alternately depressive and hyperactive, always insecure, suspicious of his wife, domineering, and yet also curiously indulgent. He was at times thinking of trying to commit his wife to an institution, or, alternatively, of divorcing her. He had taken no steps to do either. They had two children, a boy of 6 and a girl of 3 (their first child, a girl, had died at age 5). Overall, the patient was sustaining an equivocal and tenuous improvement at the 12-year mark, thanks, he felt, to AA.

COMMENTS

In overall perspective, it was evident that an inappropriate treatment effort (psychoanalysis) was embarked upon and persisted in, and brought this very ill (paranoid, borderline, and "preschizophrenic"—see p. 146) individual to the verge of psychotic decompensation. At the point when the patient ruptured his treatment by fleeing, his life was totally disorganized and alcohol-ridden, and his prognosis was very gloomy indeed. Surprisingly, by Follow-Up Study time, there had been a turnaround through (1) his turn to AA and the acceptance of its strictures, along with its daily supports, and (2) the nurture provided by a maternal and at the same time masochistically willing young woman. The patient continued from there in an effortful, tenuously controlled state; his deviant thinking and aberrant behaviors were held in check by the strong, conscious exertion of will maintained through AA, and by the new love relationship (but clearly AA was the much more powerful force of the two). AA probably helped him by means of the same mechanisms that the initial research evaluators felt would have been operative in a supportive–expressive psychotherapy. An interesting sidelight on this treatment was that this patient, who managed to rescue himself through AA (which he had initially scornfully rejected) after he had failed with the psychoanalysis that he had so ardently sought, had an alcoholic and psychotic mother who had likewise achieved a degree of help through an intermittent fervent devotion to AA.

Treatment of the Exhibitionistic Dancer

BACKGROUND AND PROGNOSIS

The Exhibitionistic Dancer was the patient whose turn to Christian Science played a role in the process of treatment and stabilization.[2] She was initially brought to psychiatric treatment by her troubled parents, who felt unable to cope with her immaturity, her rebelliousness, and her antisocial behaviors. She saw her troubles as centering around her "inconsistent parents." The parents, each in his or her own way, had always treated the patient as a narcissistic extension of themselves. The father was an achiever (in business), to whom ambition, accomplishment, and academic performance meant the most, and who set these high expectations for his children. He acknowledged that he was usually critical and nagging and not patient enough with them. The mother, a more flighty person with a variety of ill-sustained interests (which ranged through Christian Science, the arts, and Dr. Fosdick's writings), saw herself as a lifelong ugly duckling who could glory in the recognition her daughter received for her beauty and her talented performances at acting and dancing. The mother participated voyeuristically as a seductress in the patient's sex life as an adolescent. When the patient remonstrated at her mother's insistent probing into the details of her sexual behaviors, the mother

---

2. Only one other PRP patient had any involvement with Christian Science. This was the Housebound Phobic Woman, who spent much of her life trying to shake off what she felt to be the hurtful impact of her mother's fanatic Christian Science teaching (see p. 65); throughout her long career as a "therapeutic lifer" (25½ years of continuous contact by now), she has never evinced the slightest interest in Christian Science.

said, "You shouldn't object so to my questioning. Any mother has a right to live a little bit vicariously through her daughter."

The patient was said to have been "a beautiful baby whom everyone loved and everyone spoiled." As the only girl and the baby of the family, she was the center of attraction and a showpiece for her parents, who displayed her wherever possible. At 4, she had been "the queen of all she surveys." Not surprisingly, at an early age, the patient developed exhibitionistic tendencies, which were channeled into elocution, dancing, and singing lessons. When the patient was 11, she was seduced into sex play by a brother (which involved masturbating him and ultimately "everything short of intercourse"); this continued irregularly until she was 16. She was very mortified that her menarche was delayed until she was 15, thus putting her out of step with her peers. By high school years, the patient's academic record began to become less bright. She began to get sloppy and lazy, clashing more with her father and his ambitions, finally becoming openly rebellious. She was forced to go to the college of her father's choice, not her own; however, she only lasted there through three semesters, by which time she was asked to withdraw because of poor grades and disorganized behaviors.

The patient then went off to a big city to try to make it on her own. There she lived in a deplorable rooming house, did poorly at odd jobs, and worked most consistently at nude modeling for a photographer. The mother dragged her back home from this life. The next summer, in the camp where she was working, the patient got involved in two successive homosexual liaisons with older women; she gleefully strutted her homosexual leanings in front of her parents. The alarmed parents then pushed the patient toward her first abortive trial of psychotherapy. Subsequently, the patient went off to another big city to study ballet and acting. Her performance in the ballet and theatre schools was called mediocre despite some talent; she was said to have "only a romantic and social interest" in the art. But, again, the patient became involved with a Bohemian group of underdogs—psychologically disturbed, overt homosexuals. She also got involved with older men, either Jewish or black, and got into simulated intercourse and masturbatory experiences with them. Again, this became known to the parents, and this time they brought her to The Menninger Foundation. The parents played down the sexual behaviors and presented the patient as immature and lazy, with disorderly habits and "undesirable companions." They differed on how to control this: The father favored firmness and nagging, while the mother tried to guide through permissiveness.

At the evaluation, the patient was attractive and girlish, but also blatantly seductive and provocative. She alternated among a variety of postures—a truculent, misunderstood youngster bitterly assailing her parents; a suave young sophisticate engaged in pseudointellectual discussions of the arts; a helpless little girl overwhelmed by the pressures of impulses. As the evaluation progressed, the patient became more anxious and disorganized. One episode during this regressed period, has already been noted (see pp. 130–131, 140): While sitting in the motel lobby, the patient lifted her dress up over her hips. When the mother remonstrated with her, she replied, "But mother, you know that I am a whore." In the face of this regressive thrust, psychiatric hospitalization with a structured and controlled therapeutic environment was urgently recommended as an essential context for the planned formal psychotherapy.

Both the parents and the patient had to be convinced of the need for this recommendation. The parents had come seeing the patient's difficulties not as illness, but as adolescent turmoil and rebellion, which she could grow out of (the mother's view) or be forced out of (the father's view). The patient tried to rally to an identification with Christian Science as the means to help. She saw her difficulties in terms of her intolerable, misunderstanding parents and her own minor confusions over her career choices. Both the parents and the patient finally agreed to the treatment plan; the patient entered the hospital and started in a planned expressive psychotherapy.

COURSE OF THE TREATMENT

The psychotherapy lasted for 3½ years (441 hours), but the concomitant hospitalization lasted less than a year. At that point—after only 5 minutes of deliberation, and with no prior planning—the patient eloped from a hospital party with a delinquent and very rich boy 4 years her junior (another patient of the same therapist), with whom she had been carrying on a romance as best she could in the hospital; they drove off to a neighboring state to get married.

After the elopement, the newlyweds returned to Topeka to go on in treatment, which they felt they would now need more than ever (to help consolidate their marriage), but would of course have to have on an outpatient basis. The patient's family claimed to be gratified by their daughter's progress thus far, and they were pleased and proud of the marriage, which linked them with a famous family and great fortune. They strongly wanted the treatment continued. As already described (see p. 204), professional opinion within The Menninger Foundation was divided. Some staff members were on the side of discontinuing the treatments and referring the patients elsewhere (feeling that in Topeka the treatment prospects would be handicapped by both patients' needs to "prove" their marriage); others were on the side of continuing them on their terms (i.e., as outpatients), with one of them referred, however, to another therapist within the institution. The latter view finally prevailed. The patient remained with their (female) therapist, while the husband was referred to a very senior (male) analyst and went into a treatment that he insisted on calling "psychoanalysis."

The patient thus succeeded in using her elopement and marriage to coerce the continuance of psychotherapy in an outpatient status, at what, from the point of view of her inner psychological readiness, was a most inopportune time. She was precipitated from the sheltered and supervised hospital situation (within which she had struggled through constant management crises) to an irresponsible, chaotic outside living situation, with a husband even wilder and sicker than she, and with few controls. The relationship with the husband had started in the hospital as a romantic love affair; after the marriage, it continued for a brief honeymoon period in a tender, mutually supportive way. But this soon gave way to open hostility, mutual recrimination, provocation, and even overt assaults. The very unstable young husband began to stay away till late at night, drank heavily, surrounded himself with like-minded young hoodlums, started all kinds of unprofitable business ventures, and spun out grandiose schemes. At one point he brought a homosexual friend home to live with them, and was planning a summer vacation "honeymoon" with this friend. The patient ultimately threw the friend out of the house, and used this relationship to belittle and abuse her husband.

After 8 months of marriage the patient became pregnant. She was openly ambivalent about having a child in such "a mess of a marriage." When she brought her infant son home from the hospital, the husband was nowhere to be found; the patient, mortified, had to go home alone. The husband talked from the start of giving the baby up for adoption, calling it "the bastard," and constantly demanded that the patient park the baby with sitters in order to go out carousing with him. The patient's level of care for the child was always at least marginally adequate, and despite all her wild behaviors, the baby was never left unattended or grossly neglected. A year after the son was born, the patient became pregnant again, but had a miscarriage; a year after that, she was pregnant a third time. During this period, the patient began on occasion to drink to excess in order to keep up with her husband. At such times they might end with a violent fight, and in one of these the husband knocked out two of her front teeth. He was momentarily afraid and ashamed; he took her in his arms and said he was sorry and would never do it again. This apology gratified the patient. She said, "It was worth it."

The themes of the psychotherapy during this chaotic life course were simple and repetitive: the patient's manifold externalizations of responsibility for all of her recurrent difficulties. The therapist, for her part, focused mainly on the patient's role in all this—her provocativeness and the hostile retaliations that she constantly invited. The patient needled her husband mercilessly for his lack of masculinity, of intelligence, and of education. She had (it turned out) entered the marriage a frightened virgin, and she used her sexual favors aggressively with her husband, trying always to "force him to treat me decently." Once, when very angry at him and his family, she flushed an expensive diamond ring that his mother had given her down the toilet.

Within the transference there was an involvement, which grew. The patient felt very dependent; when under severe stress, she called at night, and occasionally obtained emergency appointments. The therapist was experienced mainly as a mother, and the relationship with the husband was the repetition of the sexual acting out with the brother (as noted, they had started in treatment with the same therapist). It was in a period of revived memories of the mother's jealousy at the patient's childhood relationship with the father that the patient eloped with a fellow patient of her therapist's. The patient's complaint in all this was of insufficient treatment gratification. She was always being held accountable, and this she felt to be unjust and harsh: "You never say that I don't mean it, or that it's my father or my brother or someone else who is responsible. You always say it's me." In contrast to her husband's therapist, who took the young couple and the husband's parents out to lunch when those parents were visiting, the patient's therapist never had lunch with *her* parents, or did anything active with her. Very little of this transference material could be, or was, interpreted at all effectively. And with the abrupt treatment termination, there was no transference resolution; the patient departed on a disillusioned note of not having had anything done for her.

TERMINATION

The treatment termination came soon after the episode of the patient's teeth being knocked out. She became disillusioned with her therapist and compared her increasingly unfavorably with the husband's therapist. His therapist related all such unhappy events to the unfortunate circumstances of his past; her therapist kept harping on her provocativeness and her accountability. The patient used a visit by her parents to impress them with the wretchedness of her life and her marriage, and, armed with their support, she announced her intention to stop her treatment. She wanted to prove "that I can live my own life," and she wanted to go ahead with divorce planning. Perhaps she also wanted to be out of treatment while her husband was still in, so that she could be in a better legal position in regard to a possible custody fight for the children.

When approached to participate in her research Termination Study, the patient refused. She claimed at first to be too busy. Then she said, "I would be thinking and talking about the treatment and that's the trouble. It's not good for me to think along those lines. I should stay away from it. . . . I don't want to go into my treatment again. It didn't turn out successfully. . . . I don't believe in treatment. I suppose it helps a lot of people but it didn't help me."

STATUS AT FOLLOW-UP

When contacted for Follow-Up Study, the patient was living in Topeka and was now willing, even eager, to participate, in contrast to her earlier reluctance. She had a frequent wish "just to talk to someone."

The patient's life after treatment termination was chaotic, inefficient, and disorganized. It was also essentially alone and lonely, despite her multiple frantic involvements with people. She had sued for divorce and had already received the final decree, including custody of the children and a very handsome financial settlement, assuring her and her children's futures. The patient's parents had been shocked by the total turn of events and were bitterly reproachful that The Menninger Foundation would not take steps to somehow reimpose proper treatment and control upon her. There were many facets to the patient's life's disorganization. She barely managed the minimal care of the children, who were often left haphazardly, with multiple baby sitters and for unpredictable periods. At times the patient felt happy with them, and at other times resentful. She knew that she didn't give them enough. They always had to take the "leftovers"; they were "always clamoring for more."

The patient did not work. She did participate enthusiastically in a Dale Carnegie course, to build up her self-confidence. She had decided to do all her own housework; otherwise, the situation was "too easy" for her. But there was never time enough, so she would periodically stay up all night and drive herself frantically, doing housework, rearranging the furniture, straightening out her checking account, catching up on reading, and "preparing for the next day." This all gave her a "sense of accomplishment." On the other hand, if she just went to sleep at night in the face of so much to do, she felt guilty. "It sounds wild to you, I know, but when I sleep all night I feel terrible." She called sleep "an escape from responsibility" and said that one "should not lie down and go to sleep."

The patient's interpersonal relationships were in equal turmoil. She felt her relationship with her parents to be improved, because they had learned that she was "no longer under their control. Now they let me alone." She fiercely rejected their plan to get her to move closer to them; on one of their visits, when she was out of the house, they packed up her belongings for shipment home, but she angrily unpacked them when she came back. Though lonely, the patient had a variety of frantic involvements, as noted. She called her friends an "odd group of acquaintances" and had a series of what she called "wild affairs" with some of her husband's hoodlum friends, with black intellectuals, and with fellow patients. Her attitude toward men was openly exploitative, and she had no qualms about hurting them or throwing them over when she tired of them. She saw her lack of contraceptive precautions as reflecting her general attitudes: "It's just like the other things I do, like not having car insurance for months, or getting about 10 speeding violations." She said, too, "A large part of me doesn't like men. I know that this is ugly to look at, but that is the way it seems to be." And she felt unable to hold a man: "One has to be more self-effacing to keep a man happy." Through it all, she was holding a torch for her ex-husband. He visited very sporadically to see the children, but somehow the patient kept hoping that things would change enough in each of them (in him, through his "analysis") that he would return and remarry her in the end, and they would "live happily ever after."

Christian Science was clearly the most active influence in the patient's life throughout this entire period. She had begun to see a Christian Science practitioner regularly during the last months of her psychotherapy, and it now became clear that a principal immediate cause of the treatment termination had been the strong advice by the practitioner that psychotherapy and the help available from Christian Science were incompatible. She continued to see the practitioner on a regular basis for another year after her psychotherapy stopped. She formally joined the church, worked actively in it, served on committees, and went to evening meetings "to make testimony." She said, "This is the biggest thing in my life. . . . I owe everything to that as far as getting along and sustaining myself as well as I have. It has shown me everything that is valuable. . . . It's completely important to me. I feel protection for myself. One of my problems is impulses and this kind of holds me in line."

The patient said that having a psychiatric background helped her to understand Christian Science, but that Christian Science was definitely more helpful. With the practitioner, "there was a more definite guidance. She encouraged me to do what I knew was right. . . . With the practitioner I could go ahead on the basis of what would seem more reasonable, you know, in the human situation." By contrast, psychotherapy was not directive enough. It was "unscientific" and "not founded on any principle." In psychotherapy, she felt, patients are indulged too much and not told what is right and wrong: "One pitfall of psychotherapy is that patients feel that they are victims of the subconscious instead of realizing that the conscious can control the subconscious." Though the patient was indeed aware of her unsatisfactory plight and her continued treatment needs, she specifically rejected further psychotherapy. "I feel I should be on the giving end, not the receiving end any more." The important thing was not psychotherapy, "but to believe you can do it and do it." In fact, with her staunch adherence to Christian Science, it seemed to the patient almost immoral to think of more psychotherapy. There has been no further follow-up information past this point.

COMMENTS

In overview, this very narcissistic patient, reared as the projected extension of her parents' narcissistic investments, was recommended for an intensive psychotherapeutic effort set within the needed constraints of concomitant active inpatient hospital management and program. Within a year, however, the patient was able to pry herself out of the hospital and out of that total treatment arrangement through her elopement and marriage to a youngster even sicker than herself. Trying to manage within that extraordinarily difficult marriage, while only in an outpatient psychotherapy, made for a treatment and life situation that the therapist and patient together could not cope with. Both the treatment and the patient's ongoing life deteriorated to the point where the patient switched her allegiance to the Christian Science church, while getting out of both her marriage and her psychotherapy. Whatever degree of minimal life stabilization the patient did subsequently effect, she felt she owed to her renewed faith in Christian Science and its capacity to bolster at least the illusion of satisfactory life controls and directions. Certainly, nothing in the overall treatment course made any aspect of the original treatment plan seem inappropriate. However, when the patient had succeeded in precipitating herself into a near-impossible reality situation in her marriage, the outpatient psychotherapy she was in provided neither enough support and control, nor enough gratification, to enable her to handle it. The patient did find this support and control in the ministrations of the Christian Science practitioner, and she thus used Christian Science to "rescue" herself from the failures of the therapy. The fact that there was a very adequate financial settlement from the very wealthy ex-husband, of course, also helped make the patient's degree of achieved stabilization possible. There is, too, an interesting parental parallel here: Like the just-described Alcoholic Raconteur who turned from a failed psychotherapy to AA, which had been help and solace to his mother in her alcohol excess, the Exhibitionistic Dancer turned from a failed psychotherapy to Christian Science, which had been a commitment of *her* mother's in her neurotic struggles. In both instances, of course, the patients played their very considerable role in the unsuccessful psychotherapeutic outcomes.

VII

The Treatment Courses and Outcomes

Overviews

PSYCHOANALYSIS VERSUS PSYCHOTHERAPY:
COMMENTS AND CAVEATS

PRP was conceived as a study of changes that come about and how they are brought about in psychoanalysis and in long-term and intensive psychoanalytic psychotherapies. It has already been emphasized (see p. 51) that PRP was not a comparative study of the efficacy, the reach, and the limitations of these two modalities, psychoanalysis and psychotherapy, against each other in relation to comparable patients. Our naturalistic design—the commitment to offer treatment to each prospective patient who wanted and could use it, and especially the commitment to offer each prospective patient that treatment modality deemed clinically most indicated for him or her in terms of the current extant knowledge in the field—meant that we were in a position only to study each kind of therapy against itself, against its own indications, in order to see how well it realized or fell short of the usual expectations for it.

Therefore, though we had 22 patients in psychoanalysis (at least started in psychoanalysis; as noted earlier, 6 of these were converted subsequently to psychotherapy) and 20 in varyingly expressive and supportive psychoanalytic psychotherapy from the start, the rough global judgments of how each patient did overall do not provide any information (even soft information) on the comparative efficacy of these two major approaches, though they do provide some (soft) information about the extent to which each of these approaches fulfilled its own promise with the patients deemed appropriate for it. As I indicate in this chapter and the next, the two major treatment modalities did about equally well for the patients who received them, both on a rough 4-point improvement scale (my judgments at this overview point of really good improvement, moderate improvement, equivocal improvement, and no change or treatment failure) and in scored changes on the 100-point anchored HSRS (see pp. 5, 79).

Of course, one must also bear in mind in all that follows, and especially in regard to any kind of comparative questions that come to mind concerning these groups, that what constitutes "improvement" (as reflected in placement on the global improvement scale, or in the degree of [corrected] change in HSRS status) often differs quite radically in psychoanalysis and psychotherapy. It depends first on the baseline functioning—the level of dysfunction and life disorganization at the point of initial evaluation and treatment onset. This is reflected, of course, in the initial HSRS level; qualitatively, it can be the difference between (at lower levels of functioning) a patient so disturbed and disorganized that he or she requires hospital care and control in order to manage both life and psychiatric treatment, and (at higher levels) a patient seeking treatment for relief of inner distress who is nonetheless (all through the treatment) living a complicated life of highly effective functioning in his or her life space. Clearly, more of the patients designated for psychotherapy started at the lower levels, and more of those designated for psychoanalysis started at the higher levels.

In addition to the baseline or starting point, there is also the issue of the goal set against which the therapeutic attainment is to be assessed. A goal of restored extramural functioning within the usual life context—and perhaps, in some instances, with the indefinite availability of or persistence in recurrent or continuing psychotherapeutic contact—may be a very appropriate and very satisfactory goal for some "sicker" patients (e.g., the Sexual Masochist or the Manic–Depressive Physician in PRP). On the other hand, with some of those recommended for psychoanalysis, conflict resolutions short of the most thoroughgoing (e.g., as with the Prince or the Adoptive Mother in PRP) may engender disappointments in the discrepancy between the actual and the potential achievement, no matter how contented (like the Adoptive Mother) or discontented (like the Prince) the patient feels that he or she has reason to be. To put this whole issue more dramatically, some of the PRP patients with the best achievements in psychotherapy (e.g., the Intellectual Fencer or the Bohemian Musician) were not functioning at the end of their eminently successful treatments as well as some of the psychoanalytic patients at the point when they came to therapy (e.g., the English Professor and the Devoted Son—patients who also ended their treatments significantly short of the initial expectations for them).

The last point to be made in this context (also previously discussed; see pp. 56–61) is that because of the nature of The Menninger Foundation's patient population, and because of the way the PRP sample was drawn and certain exclusion categories set up within that population, there has been an adverse loading of "sicker than usual" psychoanalytic patients in our research sample, some of whom were also in treatment with less experienced analysts. The issue of the nature of the patients who come or are sent to The Menninger Foundation for evaluation and possible treatment has already been discussed (see pp. 215–216) in relation to a number of factors: the concept of the psychoanalytic sanatorium; the drawing of many impulse-ridden, addicted, alcoholic, sexually disordered and/or potentially paranoid patients for trials at intensive psychoanalytic treatment within the protected sanatorium setting; the pioneering work of the Menningers and Knight in this treatment arena; and the theoretical commitment to explore empirically the actual outcomes of Glover's (1954) so-called "heroic indications" for analysis in that setting. The way in which the PRP sample was drawn and its exclusions set up—which skewed the results against the analytic cases' showing up as well as could normatively be expected, and in favor of the psychotherapy cases' getting the fullest benefits of the best opportunities for them—has likewise also already been discussed (see the special comments of John Benjamin in this regard, pp. 58–59).

THE GLOBAL OUTCOME RATINGS

Given these general cautions on interpreting the data at all comparatively, how do our global ratings of improvement group themselves? Of the 22 patients (10 men and 12 women) started in psychoanalysis, 8, or 36% (2 men and 6 women), showed really good improvement; 5, or 23% (2 men and 3 women), showed moderate improvement; 3, or 14% (2 men and 1 woman), showed equivocal improvement; and 6, or 27% (4 men and 2 women), were failed cases. Of the 20 patients (11 men and 9 women) started in psychotherapy, 9, or 45% (4 men and 5 women), showed really good improvement; 3, or 15% (2 men and 1 woman), showed moderate improvement; 3, or 15% (2 men and 1 woman), showed equivocal improvement; and 5, or 25% (3 men and 2 women), were failed cases. The total of 11 failed cases, of course, includes the 6 who died of mental-illness-related causes either during or subsequent to their treatments—4 of the 6 failed cases in psychoanalysis (this issue is discussed in Section IX of this book, in connection with the reconsideration of "heroic indications" for analysis) and 2 of the 5 failed cases in psychotherapy. I have put these data side by side in Table 1 to reveal more clearly that these major modalities were about equally effective with the patients chosen as appropriate for each of them (again, these were *not* comparable patients).

Table 2 shows the breakdown by sex within categories. Of interest here is that with the patients started in psychoanalysis, there seems a real trend (given these very small samples) for the women to have had more good outcomes and the men more poor outcomes; this sex differential is not suggested in the psychotherapy outcomes. An obvious explanation for this finding is the sexually differential clustering of the severely alcoholic patients (12 men and 3 women), severely drug-addicted patients (6 men and 2 women), and patients vulnerable to psychotic transference regressions (10 men and 4 women). These patients constitute the very group that was specifically recommended for analysis on the basis of "heroic indications": It was felt that their prospects with analysis might be poor, but that nothing else held out any hope for thorough conflict resolution and major life amelioration. (Again, these "heroic indications" are to be reconsidered in Section

TABLE 1.
Number and Percentage of PRP Patients in Each Global Improvement Category, by Treatment Mode

CATEGORY	PSYCHOANALYSIS		PSYCHOTHERAPY	
	NUMBER OF CASES	PERCENTAGE	NUMBER OF CASES	PERCENTAGE
Really good improvement	8	36	9	45
Moderate improvement	5	23	3	15
Equivocal improvement	3	14	3	15
Failure	6	27	5	25
Total	22	100	20	100

TABLE 2.
Number of PRP Patients in Each Global Improvement Category,
by Treatment Mode and Sex

	PSYCHOANALYSIS		PSYCHOTHERAPY	
CATEGORY	MALE	FEMALE	MALE	FEMALE
Really good improvement	2	6	4	5
Moderate improvement	2	3	2	1
Equivocal improvement	2	1	2	1
Failure	4	2	3	2
Total	10	12	11	9

IX, Chapter 36.) And the 4 treatment failures among the men in analysis (the Alcoholic Heir, the Alcoholic Doctor, the Suspended Medical Student, and the Masochistic Editor; 3 of those 4 were among the total of 6 who died) were all in that group with severe alcoholism (all 4 of them), severe drug addiction (2 of them), and psychotic transference reactions (all 4 of them).

It should be recalled that 6 patients started in psychoanalysis but were shifted to psychotherapy at some point, ranging from a tacit shift at almost the start of treatment with the Housebound Phobic Woman, to an explicit shift after 6 full years of psychoanalytic work with the Economist. If the first tabulation of overall psychoanalysis and psychotherapy results (without sex breakdown) is redone after placing these 6 in the "Psychotherapy" column rather than the "Psychoanalysis" column, we then have totals of 16 patients (7 men and 9 women) in psychoanalysis and 26 patients (14 men and 12 women) in psychotherapy. The retabulation is presented in Table 3.

Again, given the small numbers in each cell, there seems no real alteration of the kind of distribution of results within each modality, or in the assessment that these major modalities were about equally effective with the patients chosen as appropriate for each of them. Appendix 2 of this book lists each PRP patient with the assessed treatment outcome on this 4-point global improvement scale. (It should also be indicated here that, though this discussion precedes the explicit

TABLE 3.
Number and Percentage of PRP Patients in Each Global Improvement Category,
by Final Treatment Mode

	PSYCHOANALYSIS		PSYCHOTHERAPY	
CATEGORY	NUMBER OF CASES	PERCENTAGE	NUMBER OF CASES	PERCENTAGE
Really good improvement	6	38	11	42
Moderate improvement	4	25	4	16
Equivocal improvement	1	6	5	19
Failure	5	31	6	23
Total	16	100	26	100

treatment of the follow-up period and the Follow-Up Study in Section VIII, it nonetheless does encompass the overall outcomes for these patients, from the start of treatment through to the very latest follow-up information that we have obtained on each of them. See footnote 1, Chapter 1, pp. 6–7, for presentation of the various durations of available follow-up information.)

CONSTELLATIONS OF PATIENTS AND THEIR OVERALL RESULTS

Within the total sample of 42 patients in PRP, it has been apparent over the course of the individual case presentations that there have been varying clusters of patients with major attributes or overall configurations in common, despite the many individual differences that keep any two patients from ever being totally alike or fully comparable. It is helpful here to review what has been said about these different constellations from the point of view of their relation to the overall outcomes achieved. I also wish to put into the same context two other patient groups that were well represented in PRP and are of considerable clinical interest, but have not been discussed up to this point in terms of how they fared as a group: the patients with major crystallized phobic illnesses (the originally "classical" patients for psychoanalysis), and the adolescent patients (a group whose best psychotherapeutic management has always been the subject of widely discrepant viewpoints).

Hysterical Patients

One of the most striking findings within PRP has related to our cluster of hysterical patients. As described earlier (see Section V, Chapter 15), these were all women, who, with all their individual variation, shared a common core of symptoms—anxiety, depression, and phobic propensities of varying intensity, as well as varying intensities of both phallic-Oedipal and oral developmental fixation points and conflict structures. As a group, they were originally felt to be almost ideal patients for thoroughgoing symptom relief and character reorganization, with the very best of prognoses in psychoanalysis. They all achieved very good therapeutic results, to varying degrees, though they also shared to an unexpected extent significant limitations in the full analytic resolution of a common conflict area: the hostile identification with, and the hostile–dependent tie to, the malevolently perceived pre-Oedipal mother imago. The six patients most clearly in this category included the Phobic Woman, the Adoptive Mother, the Tantrum Woman, and the Snake Phobia Woman (who ended in our highest category, of really good improvement), and the Obese Woman and the Divorced Nurse (who ended in the second category, of moderate improvement). (There were six other patients, among them some men, who to some extent shared features of illness picture and personality organization with these six, but these additional six had other more salient personality characteristics that determined their grouping into other clusters.) The fact that this group of hysterical patients emerged in the topmost categorizations of *therapeutic* results achieved (and were varyingly content with these outcomes—the Adoptive Mother, for example, extremely so) does not in any way detract from the still unresolved issue of whether the characteristic limitation of such patients in achieving the fullest potential psychoanalytic conflict resolution can, on the basis of the PRP experience, be overcome through altered technical implementation of the analytic work. (For more discussion of this issue and the case description of the Adoptive Mother as the paradigmatic example of this limitation of outcome, see Chapter 15, pp. 295–302; the issue is also discussed further in Section IX.)

Patients with Evolved or Threatened Transference Psychoses

Another, even larger, and much less happy cluster of patients were those paranoid and/or borderline patients (many of them alcoholic and/or drug-addicted), often taken into psychoanalysis on the basis of "heroic indications," who either developed flagrant "transference psychoses" within their treatments or, like the Alcoholic Raconteur, succeeded in warding off such psychoses through disrupting their treatments. There were 12 patients in this cluster[1]—the large number, almost 30% of our total PRP sample, is in itself a reflection of the severe degree of illness in the patient population who came to The Menninger Foundation for intensive psychoanalytic treatment efforts. Of this group, 9 were taken into psychoanalysis and 3 into psychotherapy; 8 were men and 4 were women (the uneven sex distribution reflects the higher concentration of the alcoholic–addicted–paranoid symptom cluster among the men). In overall results, none placed in the category of very good improvement. Only 2 placed in the category of moderate improvement—the Economist and the Sexual Masochist, both of whom have reached the 28-year mark as "therapeutic lifers" at the time of this writing. Another 3 placed in the category of equivocal improvement (the Heiress, the Bohemian Prep School Boy, and the Alcoholic Raconteur), and no fewer than 7 were treatment failures (the Alcoholic Heir, the Alcoholic Doctor, the Suspended Medical Student, Peter Pan, the Masochistic Editor, the Bitter Spinster, and the Script Writer); the first 4 of these 7 were among the 6 PRP patients who died of mental-illness-related causes). Certainly this whole issue of so-called "heroic indications" for psychoanalysis in these very ill patients, even within the milieu of a psychoanalytic sanatorium, needs major reconsideration (see Section IX, Chapter 36). (For more discussion of this issue, see Section V, Chapter 17.)

Patients with Evolved or Threatened Insoluble Transference Neuroses

Another major potential difficulty for psychoanalytic treatment, apart from this psychotic regressive potential in certain categories of vulnerable individuals, is the potential for the development of an insoluble transference neurosis in another

---

1. Actually, I have twice (see pp. 143, 330) previously mentioned a 13th patient, the Fearful Loner, as one of the paranoid patients who was potentially vulnerable to a paranoid transference psychotic reaction. As I have noted, however, this never became an ongoing treatment concern with him. This was basically because of the skill of his third therapist in delicately titrating the intensity of the closeness in the therapeutic interaction, in order to keep it within bounds that were tolerable to the patient. At subsequent points in this book (pp. 562, 640), when I refer to the group for whom transference psychotic reactions developed or threatened, I therefore use the number 12, excluding the Fearful Loner.

category of vulnerable individuals—the unduly dependent and/or masochistic. (Of course, there will also be occasional overlap between these groups, with particular individuals open to either or both of these two unfavorable treatment turns.) Within the PRP sample, 16 patients (almost 40%) were regarded as at risk for the development of insoluble transference neuroses. With 6 of these, the treatment plan was deliberately tailored to avoid this untoward development through avoiding or minimizing supportive hospitalization concomitant with the psychotherapy; with at least 2 of these 6 (the Addicted Doctor and the Car Salesman), this decision was highly injurious to them and their treatments, in terms of laying them wide open to other treatment and life dangers. In the other 10 cases, the potential for an insoluble transference neurosis posed a serious treatment problem with 7 (4 men and 3 women). This problem was resolved varyingly. Three of the patients remain "therapeutic lifers" at the time of this writing (the Housebound Phobic Woman, the Economist, and the Sexual Masochist), and 4 were "weaned" out of treatment with varying difficulty (the Phobic Woman, the English Professor, the Bitter Spinster, and the Devoted Son; the last-named ultimately returned to treatment and became another "therapeutic lifer"). These 7 patients also had varyingly successful outcomes. Three had really good improvement (the English Professor, the Phobic Woman, and the Housebound Phobic Woman); 2 had moderate improvement (the Economist and the Sexual Masochist); 1 had equivocal improvement (the Devoted Son); and 1 was a failed case (the Bitter Spinster). (For more discussion of this issue, see Section V, Chapter 14, pp. 278–287.)

Patients Removed from Their Life Situations

A very complicated treatment issue arises with particular cogency in The Menninger Foundation setting, because so many of its patients are sent to it from out of their home settings around the country just because of its protective sanatorium setting (within which presumably sicker patients can be treated with intensive, psychoanalytically based therapies) and its remoteness from the patients' usual life surroundings. The issue is that of the relative balance between the advantages of (and sometimes the necessity for) disengagement by the patient from neurotogenic interactions in the home setting in order to maximize the patient's opportunity for treatment gain, as against the advantages of (and the necessity for) being treated within the usual life situation in ongoing interaction with the important life figures, lest the treatment-induced separation lead to irrevocable deterioration of the very life situation that the patient is seeking to ameliorate through therapy.

Just because there is this opposed balancing, with patients so often having advantages and needs in both directions, this problem is rarely overridingly onesided. Occasionally it is. For 3 patients within our sample (7%), it was clear that the vital need was for maintenance of the ongoing life situation, and in only one of these cases (the Snake Phobia Woman) was it, at least in part, maintained. She ended treatment with a very good improvement. With the other two, who remained in Topeka for their treatments and were totally removed from their families, the results were less good. The Divorced Nurse ended with moderate improvement; the Invalided Hypochondriac ended as a treatment failure.

By contrast, for 7 patients within our sample (17%), the vital need was for separation of the patient from the ongoing family interactions. The treatment outcomes of these 7 were sharply dichotomized. Three emerged in the first group of really good improvements—in fact, among the very best in the whole PRP sample (the Medical Scientist, the Tantrum Woman, and the Phobic Girl). Of the other 4, one had equivocal improvement (the Bohemian Prep School Boy); and the other 3 were not only total treatment failures, but were also among the 6 who died of mental-illness-related causes (the Alcoholic Heir, the Alcoholic Doctor, and Peter Pan). Clearly the removal of these patients from a pathological life situation, though deemed very necessary in these cases, was very far from sufficient to insure a good treatment outcome. (For more discussion of these issues, see Section V, Chapter 15, pp. 314–321, and Section VI, Chapter 21, pp. 466–476.)

Obese Patients

A perhaps more minor issue, at least in relation to the patients who come to intensive psychoanalytic treatments, is that of obesity. This is an area where behavior modification techniques have had an important development: They have been used effectively in dealing with the problems of the very obese patients who seek the cure of this single targeted symptom (Stunkard, 1976). Usually when severely obese patients come to psychodynamic psychotherapies, it is within the context of a far wider dissatisfaction with their overall life functioning; the obesity itself is but one of their distressing array of symptoms. In such cases, a broad-gauged therapeutic goal is geared to the totality of the life functioning, with the amelioration of the obesity one of the hoped-for concomitants of the desired improvement.

As has already been stated (see pp. 134–135), some degree of obesity was an issue with 11 or a quarter of our patients; as might be expected, they were predominantly female (8 women to 3 men). In only 3 (all women) was it one of the centrally presenting symptoms, however (see pp. 475–476). The Housebound Phobic Woman, though brought to treatment because of acute barbiturate intoxication superimposed on a barbiturate-induced chronic organic brain syndrome, also came to treatment weighing 180 pounds. She lost 28 pounds in the first 2 months of hospitalization, down to 152 pounds, and her weight was never an issue again through her very long treatment career (nor is it one now in her status as a "therapeutic lifer"). She ended in the most favorable group of really good improvements. The Phobic Girl was referred for treatment because of a regressed, infantile, and dependent life, and an array of crippling phobias; she also weighed 203 pounds. She ended the treatment very much improved in many areas, enough also to be put into the most favorable group of really good improvements. Her weight at the Follow-Up Study point, however, was essentially unaltered, at 195 pounds. She stated at that time that she didn't mind her weight, she so much enjoyed eating; it was only her husband who made the weight issue a bone of contention between them and would upbraid her for repeated failures to keep the various diets she periodically went on as gifts to him. The Obese Woman was the one patient in our sample who came to treatment centrally because of severe obesity and compulsive eating, though she also complained of a number of other symptoms and interpersonal difficulties; she weighed 238 pounds. Her overall treatment result was adjudged in the second group, of moderate improvement. Her weight, however, was not affected. She ended treatment (psychoanalysis) at an all-time high of 250 pounds, fluctuated during the follow-up period between 176 and 258 pounds, and was at 200 pounds when she returned for Follow-Up Study.

It is clear with these obese patients that, however beneficial on other counts, psychodynamic therapies by and large did not affect their weights favorably. The one least obese (the Housebound Phobic Woman), who was (and still is) in a long ostensible psychoanalysis, really a psychotherapy, did lose weight (and very early) as part of her overall favorable response. The two extremely obese, one in intensive psychotherapy (the Phobic Girl) and the other in psychoanalysis (the Obese Woman), were left at the end of otherwise quite good treatment courses with their weights unaltered.

Phobic Patients

A particular group of patients who commonly come to intensive psychotherapeutic help (more often than the obese), and who have also been a special focus of interest of the behavioral approaches (especially in their discretely monosymptomatic forms), is that of phobic individuals. Phobic propensities are in fact very widespread; a total of 18 of our 42 cases, or close to 45% (8 men and 10 women), evinced crystallized phobic attitudes and/or symptoms. The 5 whose multiple phobias were so dominant in the presenting clinical picture as to be reflected in the titles given to the patients (the Phobic Woman, the Snake Phobia Woman, the Housebound Phobic Woman, the Claustrophobic Man, and the Phobic Girl) have all already been described under a variety of headings. Of these 5, 3 were taken into psychoanalysis (tacitly converted in 1 case into a continuing psychotherapy), and 2 were taken into psychotherapy; 4 were women and 1 a man. All 5 of them ended in the group of those with really good improvements, despite the ramifying complexity of the numerous phobic complaints each one suffered (see pp. 122–124 for a description of this array), and also despite the complexity of their character problems and neurotic conflict structures. In different ways, they each did at the end have some residual phobic propensities or phobic constraints, but these were very different indeed from the severe dysfunctions with which they came to treatment. (For the individual details on each patient, see pp. 271–277 for the Phobic Woman; pp. 308–314 for the Snake Phobia Woman; pp. 391–398 for the Housebound Phobic Woman; pp. 398–403 for the Claustrophobic Man; and pp. 468–476 for the Phobic Girl.)

Adolescent Patients

GENERAL COMMENTS

The last "special" group to be singled out for mention here is that of the adolescent patients. As noted earlier (see pp. 57, 61–62), the original intent of PRP was to confine the sample to adults in the younger adult range between 20 and 45, in order to simplify a study of psychiatric illness and its treatment by eliminating the confounding effects of growth and development processes with younger patients and of physical and/or mental impairments and aging processes with older patients. Actually, as it worked out, there were two patients above this age range (the Claustrophobic Man at 47 and the Involutional Woman at 50), and four below it (the Bohemian Prep School Boy and the Adolescent Grandson, each 17, and Peter Pan and the Actress, each 19). The fact that four patients (almost 10% of the sample) were clearly young adolescents itself only reflects the fact that there has been a whole downward age trend among those hospitalized in psychodynamically guided psychiatric hospitals, as the inpatient population has shown over time a substantial shift from those with major psychotic episodes (and organic brain syndromes) to those with impulse and character disorders. In addition to the four patients actually under 20 in our project sample, there were five others who either were very close in age (four of them) or still had unresolved "adolescent problems" as central psychopathological issues, despite a chronologically considerably older age (one of them). These facts warrant placing these additional five together with the other four into a cluster of nine adolescent patients and/or patients with central adolescent issues. These other patients were the Rebellious Coed, aged 20; the Phobic Girl, and the Exhibitionistic Dancer, both aged 21; the Homesick Psychology Student, aged 23; and the Intellectual Fencer, the considerably older patient, aged 30.

The eight young patients of this group (I set the Intellectual Fencer aside for the moment), 3 males and 5 females, were all single, all still in school, and all in some combination of school and/or interpersonal difficulties. I recapitulate these briefly here. The Adolescent Grandson was brought to treatment because of his bizarre, seemingly out-of-character nude capers on his wealthy grandfather's estate, set in the context of chronic unhappiness and a poor school adjustment of 7 to 8 years' duration (see pp. 490–497). The Bohemian Prep School Boy was referred for psychiatric treatment by the headmaster of the private school he attended because of his increasingly bizarre school behaviors (his treatment course has not yet been described). Peter Pan, with severe alternating anorexia and bulimia, was referred for psychiatric treatment when she was caught stealing food from her college cafeteria (see pp. 426–432). The Actress was referred for psychiatric treatment by the dean of her college because of alcohol excess, homosexual activity, and grossly disturbed relationships and behaviors (see pp. 478–483). The Rebellious Coed was likewise referred for psychiatric treatment by her college dean because of an acute depression in the wake of her mother's death, on top of progressive school and interpersonal difficulties (see pp. 483–489). The Exhibitionistic Dancer was a drama and ballet student (who had previously failed as a college student), brought to psychiatric treatment because of her poor school record and grossly disturbed behaviors (see pp. 504–510). The Phobic Girl was referred to therapy because a college essay written for a psychology course revealed the ramifying complexity and crippling nature of her multiple phobias (see pp. 468–476). Finally, the Homesick Psychology Student was the graduate student who came to psychotherapy because of intense feelings of inadequacy and an unhappy school and social adjustment (see pp. 417–421).

In addition to these eight young patients, there was the Intellectual Fencer, also single, also a failed college student, now aged 30, who had spent the years after being asked to leave college because of "unacceptable social behaviors" in an unsuccessful work career and a progressive barbiturate addiction. Her age notwithstanding, her conflict structure still seemed that of an unresolved adolescent rebellion against dependent family ties. In her case, however, the conflicts were hardened, more "dug in," and perhaps more difficult of resolution (see pp. 439–445).

Of this whole group of nine patients, eight were taken into varyingly expressive–supportive psychotherapy — some as *the* appropriate treatment approach; some with an eye to ultimate transition to a more definitive psychoanalysis, when both material resources and psychological readiness would warrant such a shift. None of them actually did come to later psychoanalysis. Their overall outcomes were as follows: The Phobic Girl, the Actress, and the Intellectual Fencer ended in the group with really good improvement; the Rebellious Coed and the Homesick Psychology Student ended in the group with moderate improvement; and the Adolescent Grandson, the Bohemian Prep School Boy, and the Exhibitionistic Dancer ended in the group with equivocal improvement. Peter Pan, the only one of the nine taken into psychoanalysis, was the only totally failed treatment case in the group, going through an 11-year-long treatment effort with three therapists before her successful suicide jump off a bridge. She was also in many ways the very sickest in the group of nine, with her uncontrollable alternating anorexia and bulimia, her compulsive kleptomania, and her final progressive psychotic decompensation.

The overall group of adolescent patients, in the distributions of their outcomes, seemed to fare no differently from the PRP population at large. Perhaps in connection with the outcomes in this particular group, where it is again particularly pertinent, the point should once more be reiterated that the judgment of degree of improvement on the 4-point global scale is made in relation to the individual patient's initial level of functioning and the expectations for improvement held out for that patient when treated by the recommended treatment approach. This means that a patient judged to have an equivocal improvement (or, theoretically, even to have had a totally failed treatment) could be functioning at a better level than one adjudged to be much improved who started at a much more disorganized level. Only when this understanding is held firmly in mind will some of the designations and groupings make sense.

THERAPY OF THE BOHEMIAN PREP SCHOOL BOY

Of all the group of adolescent patients, the treatment course of one, the Bohemian Prep School Boy, has not yet been presented. It is one that raises an important differential diagnostic issue among sicker adolescents — the degree to which the behavioral, cognitive, and/or affective disorganization that may be evident reflects the more usual neurotic adolescent turmoils (in perhaps starker form), or, possibly, the onset of a more serious (psychotic) disorganizing process. His case history is presented here from this perspective.

Background and Prognosis. The patient was referred for psychiatric treatment, as just stated, by his school authorities, who were concerned with his increasingly bizarre behaviors. He had been brought up in a wildly eccentric and highly intellectualized home. The father, a Jewish immigrant, was a famous artist, a very passive man, but one who delighted in poking satirical fun at the world of conventional standards. The mother, an Episcopalian, an heiress to a great fortune, was a domineering person who abetted the father in his passive withdrawals from any active role in family affairs. The parents married in common rebellion against their families, and delighted in being intellectual and "different" together. The marriage was also a stormy one, however. In the face of the incessant conflict, the father would retreat to his room and lock the door, saying, "I'm an artist." The mother would then bang on the door with a hammer, demanding that he come out and stand up to the situation.

From the start, the patient was incredibly indulged and inconsistently handled. His mother would try to set some boundaries (e.g., the degree to which people would be allowed to indulge him when he was taken to cocktail parties as a 2-year-old), whereas the father opposed all limitations. From the beginning, the patient developed precociously; he was always a problem in school years, being bored, daydreaming, challenging the teachers. He also had a myriad of symptoms while growing up: recurrent severe headaches, enuresis till age 9, stomach aches, urticaria, asthma, and severe nailbiting (to the point of developing infected fingers). His first psychiatric referral was at age 6 for the unremitting headaches. At age 12, he was sent to a fashionable prep school, where he stayed for the next 5 years until he was finally asked to withdraw.

At school the patient always felt out of place and different, "neither a Christian nor a Jew." He fought more constantly and openly with his parents. His fears and complaints multiplied. He developed fears of smothering, of knives, of needles, of going crazy, and of having his eyes poked out. He was given to obsessive doubting, and he suffered frequent nightmares. When he was 16, the patient began to isolate himself periodically in his room, anxious and depressed, and to sleep for long periods. He felt that he was empty inside and that the world was unreal. The psychiatric consultant felt the patient to be hovering on the edge of an acute paranoid schizophrenic break and sent him off on a European vacation with his parents.

During the next semester at school, the patient's decline accelerated. He felt that the left side of his body was falling asleep, that he was a small presence in a big world, that people were always looking at him. He developed fears of disintegrating, of the dark, and of looking in the mirror lest he not see himself. As noted earlier (pp. 145–146), he brought some like-minded schoolmates together into a salon that met in a closet to debate existentialist philosophy, and he wrote a final examination in the form of an allegory about the behavior of bedbugs in a bathtub. At this point he was withdrawn from school at the request of the headmaster and referred to The Menninger Foundation for treatment.

Upon evaluation, the patient gave evidence of rich, vivid, and creative ideational activity, but it was all loose, without discipline or restraint. His chief interpersonal stock in trade was intellectualizing: It was his way of winning acceptance and respect, also his way of intimidating and alienating others. Of his task in treatment, he stated, "What I have to do is find out what kind of person I really am." Much of his "craziness" he saw as the consequence of having been brought up in such a "crazy" household—one in which there were not only pet dogs, but at various times a pet tarantula and a pet boa constrictor, which reputedly had the run of the house. Of the two parents, the patient's mother was more willing to see him as ill. In a recent argument he had tried to choke her, and her throat was still bruised. She feared he might be homosexual; once, when she found the patient in her husband's studio, she had accused her husband of "entertaining his paramour." On the European vacation, she had been afraid the patient would be attacked by homosexuals. The father, on the other hand, had suggested that the patient take advantage of the European trip to acquire some heterosexual experiences. He was unaware of how this advice had panicked the boy. The father was hard put to acknowledge any evidence of illness beyond "normal adolescent rebellion."

The initial diagnostic formulation was of an overideational preschizophrenic state, and the patient was recommended for a supportive–expressive psychotherapy. It was hoped that the therapist would be an important identification figure around whom the patient could correct his own impaired reality testing, institute working controls over impulse and affect, and organize himself in more compulsive and productive life directions.

Course of the Therapy. The psychotherapy lasted only 7 months (71 hours). The therapist's predominant effort was to conduct as expressive a therapy as possible within a climate of maximal permissiveness. He tried to make the patient more thoughtful and reflective and less impulsive, and, indeed, the patient did slow down and become quieter; in fact, he described that as the major change he experienced in himself.

Throughout its course, the patient's treatment was heavily impinged upon, both by events within his life in Topeka and by pressures emanating from his family. The patient's life was neither orderly nor stable. When he got out of the hospital into a foster home, he began to complain loudly that the home was an intellectual desert, peopled by bourgeois farmers with whom one could not exchange ideas. Actually, it was the home of a university professor whose wife was an artist and art patron; it happened to be a stable and stabilizing place that was beginning to get to the patient. After the patient pried himself out of the foster home, he moved into an apartment where he could lead an irregular life of continuous partying and very dilatory schoolwork. He also made some fitful job efforts, usually with an enthusiastic beginning and early resignation or dismissal, and threw himself as well into amateur theatricals. He always tried for shortcuts; in the theatre he would neither study his lines nor pay attention to the overall plan of the play, but would try to rely on his quick capacity for improvisations. In all these ways, the patient was the despair of his mentors. And he was characteristically irresponsible in handling money: His idea of saving money was to buy the large-economy-size bottles of champagne.

Meanwhile, things were not going well at home either. Parental discord deepened to the point of physical fights. The mother found it hard to tolerate the patient's absence from home; she became openly upset and began to behave strangely. The patient experienced this as pressure to leave treatment and return to his family. The father was talking of committing the mother to a mental hospital, while speaking wistfully of his own desire for a closer relationship with his son. They could only have a bantering relationship together, joining hands in poking fun at psychiatry.

As would be expected from the nature of the patient and his life, the major focus of the therapy was on the changing vicissitudes of this colorful and constantly crisis-ridden current life. The main themes were as follows:

1. The patient's impulsivity, with its counterphobic quality, as in his associating with open homosexuals in an effort to deny the temptation and danger he experienced in the association. The therapist characteristically responded to the impulsive behaviors with the injunction to "stop and think before you act."

2. His intellectualizing, philosophizing, and externalizing (blaming his parents for his personality and his plight).

3. His masochistic fantasies, as when he cut his arm once to "prove what real suffering is."

4. His constant quest for praise for his showmanship and his public successes, especially his theatrical activities.

5. His budding heterosexual strivings in an attachment to a woman 10 years his senior; he anxiously reassured the therapist that this was completely platonic.

6. All throughout the therapy, his fear of involvement in the treatment—fear because of the autistic preoccupations it might let loose within, and fear that it might get disrupted from without.

The major transference posture that emerged was the patient's effort to dazzle and overwhelm the therapist by his esoteric and facile knowledge. At the same time, much of this presumed greater knowledge was clearly pretense and fantasy. The patient was searching to have this challenged, to be helped to control his expansive ideation and his impulse-ridden life, and to be brought within the confines of a more mundane reality. And without direct transference interpretation, the patient's transference stance gradually altered as he came to experience the therapist as a consistently interested person, trying to be genuinely helpful.

Within this treatment course, there was considerable amelioration of some of the patient's flamboyant symptoms. The patient's controls tightened; he experienced this as being slowed down, quieted, constrained to delay and reflect. Resulting thinking and communicating became less overgeneral, pretentious, and intellectualized. The patient constantly expressed his need to "stop, look, and listen"—to curb his impulsivity. Yet, throughout this treatment, both the therapist and the patient were always aware of its continuing tentative nature. The patient constantly kept an eye toward expected adverse parental pressures, and the therapy ended when it did when these pressures ostensibly became irresistible.

Termination. The father, as noted, was dubious all along about his son's illness and treatment need. He saw much of the symptom picture as an unwillingness to assume appropriate responsibilities. He wrote (see p. 197) that he felt his son to be in a "*Magic Mountain* atmosphere," playing "the role of the misunderstood aesthete, wounded and unable to do an honest day's work, be it at school or on a job." The father felt that his money was being used unwisely and unwarrantedly, both by the treatment and by his son's extravagant living, which he felt was not sufficiently curbed. After several months of the patient's treatment, the father announced that the family was moving permanently to Europe and that he had purchased a boat ticket for the patient as well. The parents promised that the patient could continue psychotherapy in Europe if he really wanted it.

The patient felt caught in a conflict between his growing attachment to the treatment and its goals, and his loyalty to and dependence upon his parents. He doubted whether he could hold onto his tenuous identifications with the therapist, particularly in the face of the weakening of his denial mechanisms and the consequent anxieties being increasingly aroused within the treatment. He therefore felt he had to run to be with his parents, not to be left behind when they went to Europe. He said of this, "I probably should not be leaving." For their part, neither the therapist nor the hospital had taken the parental pressures seriously until the very end, because the parents had always been so inconsistent. Their difficulty in taking a consistent and firm position with this reluctant family also reflected a disagreement of diagnostic assessment. The therapist was in accord with the clinical evaluation team's formulation; he felt that the patient actually experienced schizophrenic-like episodes in his periods of panic, depersonalization, and acutely disordered thinking. The hospital staff thought in the more benign terms of "severe adjustment reaction of adolescence, in the precocious youngster, from an aberrant cultural milieu." Under such circumstances, the treatment terminated only 7 months after it began.

Status at Follow-Up. The patient returned readily for Follow-Up Study and expressed surprise that we were willing to pay his expenses; he said he would have come anyway. He had come back to Topeka once before (upon returning from Europe) to consult his ex-therapist about a return to therapy. He would work and his father would help support it, but the father had also said that the patient "would have to demonstrate more ability to do my share of the helping than I have done thus far." These plans for further treatment had not materialized. The patient had gone to Europe with his parents, but a year later had returned to the states to enroll in an academy for dramatic arts (after being turned down by a number of Ivy League colleges). The patient was most enthusiastic about his training as a mime and was attached in a hero-worshiping way to his teacher in that art form. He said of this, "The day I stop doing mime, I won't exist. This is the first time I've ever allowed myself to do well." Aside from this, he was leading the same kind of only semiorganized life. He shared an apartment with a succession of other aspiring actors and literati, where he maintained a salon-like atmosphere and gave pot and peyote parties. All this was wholly supported by his parents.

The patient's relations with his parents were now somewhat less strife-ridden and more distant. He also had a rather steady girlfriend; however, he called this romance "puppy love," and indicated that though the girl would willingly marry him, he couldn't invest that much of himself in the relationship. He thought of marriage only as something in the far distant future. If he did get married, he guessed he would be unfaithful to his wife. The patient saw his two major life problems at this point as (1) getting along with people (he could get "physically close but not emotionally; I start hating people if I get too close to them"); and (2) his sexual inhibitions and his homosexual fears and attractions (all the homosexuals seemed to make passes at him, and he was fearful of responding).

About his psychotherapy, the patient wistfully said that he had just not been able to use therapy at the time that he had it; he wished he was going into it now. At the time, the treatment had been "because of me . . . relatively superficial." But he felt that the therapist also should have handled him differently. "Instead of talking about what bothers you, about problems, about abstractions, establish yourself first, because you can't cut out the cancer until you find where the body is to cut it from. . . . I'm the type of person I can't respond to abstractions because I have very little faith in them. . . . I have to see blood before I will go to the doctor." In all his treatment, the patient felt that he had never discovered anything that he didn't already know. And he "always felt slightly insulted that I wasn't being analyzed." All in all, he felt that his treatment had been pretty much a waste of his parents' money. Nothing exciting had happened in it: The therapist should have tricked him, or hypnotized him, or somehow pulled his problems out against his will. He complained that only the "stupid ones" get well. "You psychiatrists have trouble with bright people. You can't surprise us. . . . You throw out the bright ones as hopeless." (Incidentally, during this follow-up period, the patient's one sibling, a younger brother, had been hospitalized with an acute schizophrenic break. This brother had put arsenic into the parents' food, had been the author of bomb scare notes that had led to evacuations of several local schools, and had confessed to the patient his many fantasies of killing all his enemies.) Those who saw the patient at Follow-Up Study had the impression that he was the "same old fellow" — putting a good face on things, magnifying his achievements and aspirations, parasitically sponging on people, and unwilling to face his obvious continued treatment needs honestly. There is no further follow-up information on this patient beyond the official Follow-Up Study.

Comments. Clearly, the total treatment course was insufficient to make a real difference in the functioning of this gifted but very disturbed and confused young man, with a wholly unconsolidated psychic organization and a most uncertain life ahead. At the Follow-Up Study point, things seemed much the same — still unresolved and unresolving. In part, the therapy was beset by an ongoing controversy in diagnostic understanding. Though conceptualized at the time of initial evaluation as a decompensating (overideational) preschizophrenic individual, the hospital staff took a less serious view of the patient's pathology, as noted. He was adjudged there as suffering with a more than usually intense "adjustment reaction of adolescence," aggravated by his unstable and deviant family background. The psychotherapist vacillated somewhat between these two views. He was aware of the regressive potential and disorganizing sweeps (and at one level concurred with the more ominous conceptualization), but he also stressed their uncrystallized and transitory nature. And, in his therapeutic work, the therapist tried as much as possible to conduct an expressive therapy as he would have done with a neurotic adult — a therapy in which the patient would have license to make his own mistakes and opportunity to discuss them in the therapy. Within this permissive climate, marked by minimal efforts at direct control, the therapist's main effort was to focus on the patient's ready impulsivity, to interpretively bring about a capacity for increased delay. The patient, when he was complaining about the ineffectiveness of his therapy during the Follow-Up Study, spoke glowingly by contrast about a single interview with one of the senior hospital doctors. "He was direct with me. . . . I remember he sat down and said, 'Well, let's see, now what's coming off here now.' . . . I liked that."

But at least equally implicated in determining the equivocal outcome of the total treatment effort was the limited impact of casework on the parents. Both of them, especially the father, early signaled their ambivalence about supporting the treatment. In the face of this, the casework proved inadequate — neither consistent enough, nor firm enough—to maintain a cooperative family attitude. And throughout the treatment, the father felt that his complaints about finances were not taken seriously. An arrangement was made for the father to send both living expense and treatment money to his son, who was to be "responsible" for keeping all his bills current; this was decided upon despite the father's insistence that it could not possibly work. All these factors played into the father's decision, with the planned long-term treatment program barely under way, to force a premature termination. The patient, not yet really "captured" by the therapy, was all too willing to fall back on being only a minor, who could neither fight for his father's support nor sustain the therapy without it. In Chapter 26, I discuss this more general issue of therapies that were disrupted under the impact of adverse family pressures.

Changes in HSRS Ratings and Changes in IQ

RESULTS ON THE HSRS

From the very start in the creation of PRP, one rating instrument—the 100-point HSRS, anchored by 34 clinical case descriptions covering the whole scale range—was incorporated into the project design as an assessment tool, and as a predictive as well as an adjudged outcome measure. This scale had actually already been created and was at hand for use when PRP was designed. It had, in fact, been created by a group of clinicians and clinical researchers who were the precursor group to PRP, and who had agreed upon the need for such an instrument as a tool for the kind of psychotherapy research that the group wanted to plan (see p. 5). The way in which the HSRS was planned to be used at the three points in time of PRP research study (Initial, Termination, and Follow-Up)—as a global assessment of current level of psychological functioning at all three points, as well as a predictive assessment at Initial Study of future functioning after treatment, and at Termination Study of functioning after the period of follow-up observation—was stated in the very first publication from PRP (Wallerstein *et al.*, 1956). (It is also presented in Section II of this book under the description of the organization of the research; see Chapter 6, pp. 79, 90, 99.) The scale itself, including the full definition of the range of scale points and the vignette case descriptions anchoring 34 scale points for detailed clinical comparison with patients being judged, as well as experiences in using the scale within PRP, has already been published (Luborsky, 1962a, 1975). A survey of 18 different experiences with the scale by a wide variety of psychotherapy research programs has also appeared (Luborsky & Bachrach, 1974).

Here, as part of the assessment of project results, I summarize some of the HSRS data from PRP. These data are used raw, without statistical correction for the fact that there is much more room to move within the 100-point scale when the initial position on it is a low one, so that movement in the lower ranges is easier and therefore signifies less than similar movement in the higher ranges. That is, increases in HSRS position made by an individual starting at a higher initial level should be given proportionately more weight than the increases of a patient who started with a very low initial level and has most of the range in which to move. The statistical manipulations involved in making proper allowance for this problem with our PRP data have been presented in detail by Coyne (unpublished manuscript). However, for my general overview purposes here, and for simplification and clarity of exposition, the raw figures are sufficiently useful and do not significantly distort the kind of information to be presented.

Initial Levels and Predictions

Initial Study HSRS levels ranged across the whole sample from 25 to 70, with an average of 46.5. There was no difference by sex; the 21 males ranged from 28 to 70, with an average of 47, and the 21 females ranged from 25 to 70, with an average of 46. The closest definitional statement to this "average" level patient starting treatment within this sample is for scale point 50, and it reads as follows: "Definitely needs treatment to continue work satisfactorily and has increasing difficulty in maintaining himself autonomously (even without expressed or recognized need for formal treatment). Patient may either be in a stable unsatisfactory adjustment (where most energy is bound in the conflicts) or an unstable adjustment from which he will likely regress" (Luborsky, 1975, p. 454). Patients at such a level were stated to include those with compensated psychoses, many character disorders, neurotic depressions, and severe neuroses (such as severe obsessive–compulsive disorders). Five paragraph-long case descriptions of the patients at levels 45, 45, 47, 50, and 50 illustrate the kinds of psychiatric disorders and psychological dysfunction characteristics of the "average patient" at PRP Initial Study time (Luborsky, 1975, pp. 462–464).

At the Termination Study point, 3 of the 42 patients in the PRP sample had their Initial Study HSRS assessments retrospectively lowered. This was done in each instance in the light of widened information now available about the patient's psychological conflict and disability—information that had been carefully concealed during the initial evaluation process. These 3 were the Obese Woman, who had concealed her long history of kleptomania and her sadomasochistic perverse sexual practices (lowered 10 points); the Suspended Medical Student, whose paranoid potential and gravely handicapped ego functioning, with its vulnerability to major fluctuations in level of consciousness and control, had been carefully concealed behind his original presentation of the episodes of unethical behavior that brought him to treatment as inexplicably out of character (lowered 20 points); and the Economist, who had concealed a severe sexual potency disturbance within a much broader symptom and character concealment—see p. 161 for details (lowered 15 points). The three together (lowered 45 points) retrospectively dropped the overall average initial HSRS level for the 42 patients by only 1 point. And it should be noted that, although 24 of our 42 patients (more than 55% of our population sample) concealed significant issues of major symptoms, behavior dispositions, and character trends at the time of initial evaluation (see pp. 158–162), in only 3 instances out of the 24 did this concealment operate to lower the Initial Study HSRS assessment when viewed retrospectively in the light of the total therapy revelations. Thus, such concealment led to serious misjudgments about overall functional level only in singular instances.

At Initial Study these HSRS levels of 25–70 (average 46.5) were predicted to go to a range of 28–90 (average 67) across the whole sample. There seemed to be a slight differential trend by sex in the predictions; the 21 males were predicted to go to a range of 35 to 90 (average 64), and the 21 females were predicted to go to a range of 48 to 85 (average 71). Again, as with other sex-linked differences, we can look for an explanation at the greater clustering of men in the group of severely alcoholic–addicted–paranoid–borderline individuals, with the liability (and, as it turned out, the actuality) of transference psychosis reactions and severe treatment outcome impairments.

Of interest also in the Initial Study predictions were the 11 instances where alternative predictions were clearly made, depending on which of the possible alternative treatment courses and outcomes actually did take place. For 2 patients, the clinical treatment recommendation was for psychoanalysis, and the research evaluators had a significantly different judgment—that psychoanalysis was in fact contraindicated, and that a direct and face-to-face psychotherapy geared not toward analytic conflict resolution but toward behavioral change and control would offer more effective therapeutic help. These patients were the Alcoholic Doctor and the Alcoholic Raconteur. For both of them, zero change from the initial point was predicted for their level of psychological functioning if they were treated in psychoanalysis, but very significant changes (reflected in overall HSRS gains of 22 points for the one and 20 points for the other) were predicted with a successful supportive–expressive psychotherapy, should the patients be (appropriately) shifted in this direction.

In 5 other instances, patients for whom psychoanalysis was felt to be the more indicated and definitive treatment were recommended initially for psychotherapy, either because psychoanalysis was not at the time feasible (for reasons of geography or financial limitation), or because the patients were not then psychologically ready for it or motivated for it. In each such instance, it was felt that a wider gain in level of functioning (reflected in HSRS outcome) could be achieved, should the patient come to subsequent psychoanalysis. For these 5 (the Phobic Girl, the Intellectual Fencer, the Rebellious Coed, the Homesick Psychology Student, and the Bitter Spinster), a gain of between 7 and 30 (average of 16) was predicted for them in psychotherapy, and a gain of between 22 and 50 (average of 31) was predicted if the treatment (through either conversion or a later treatment effort) were carried through ultimately to a completed psychoanalysis.[1] Actually, none of these patients were either converted to psychoanalysis or received subsequent psychoanalysis, and so this predictive set could not be tested. The issue does, however, reflect the initially far more ambitious goals set for the possibilities of change and cure by psychoanalysis (when feasible) for these same patients. This was, of course, one of the conditions under which the so-called "inadvertent controls" (see pp. 114, 199–205) set up within PRP were intended to operate.

---

1. In the 2 instances clinically recommended for psychoanalysis where the research team felt this to be contraindicated, a zero gain in level of functioning was predicted if the patient were taken into the treatment felt to be contraindicated, as noted above. By contrast, in each of these 5 instances, it was felt that the clinically recommended psychotherapy would be therapeutically helpful, and would therefore in each instance register a real treatment gain (the average predicted 16-point HSRS gain in assessed overall psychological functioning). However, it was not expected to be *as* helpful as psychoanalysis would prove to be if it could be gotten to (hence the larger expected HSRS gain there).

In addition to these 7 patients for whom sets of alternative predictions were generated, depending on whether they went into psychoanalysis or psychotherapy, there were 4 other patients who were felt to be recommended for the appropriate treatment modality for them, but for whom alternative outcomes were postulated, depending on how well the treatment went and coped with the problems deemed likely to arise within it. Three of these went into psychoanalysis (the Phobic Woman, the Housebound Phobic Woman, and the Masochistic Editor), and one into psychotherapy (the Actress). The predicted outcomes had a worst-case gain of between 0 and 25 (average 10) and a best-case gain of between 25 and 45 (average 32.5). In all, in the 11 instances of alternative predictions, there was an average spread of 19 HSRS points between the lower and higher postulated outcomes.[2]

Termination and Follow-Up Results

I turn now to the HSRS changes actually reached at the Termination Study and Follow-Up Study points in these therapies. The data are separated out between the 22 started in psychoanalysis and the 20 treated throughout in psychotherapy.

PATIENTS IN PSYCHOANALYSIS

Of the 22 patients started in psychoanalysis, the Initial Study HSRS range was 25–70, with an average of 48; 8 of the 22 were at the modal number, 50. The predicted Termination Study range for them, if psychoanalysis were indeed the treatment carried out (including the 2 for whom it was felt contraindicated), was 28–90, with an average of 74—up an average of 26 scale points over the initial levels. If the two who were predicted to achieve zero gain if treated in psychoanalysis (the Alcoholic Doctor, starting at 40, and the Alcoholic Raconteur, starting at 28) are removed from this tabulation, the predicted range at Termination Study is changed to 57.5–90,[3] but the average has only gained 3, up to 77.

In contrast to these ambitious (as usual) expectations for psychoanalysis, the actual range of Termination Study HSRS assessments was between 23 and 86.5, with an average of 62. This was, on the average, up 14 points over the initial average of 48, but significantly short of the predicted Termination Study average of 74 or 77. The termination figure in 2 instances of the 22 actually went *down*, and these were indeed the 2 for whom psychoanalysis was felt by the research group to be contraindicated. (With the Alcoholic Doctor, who dropped from a level of 40 to one of 24.5, the effort at psychoanalysis was persisted in over his entire 7-year treatment course until his death; with the Alcoholic Raconteur, who went from a level of 28 to one of 23, the patient disrupted the treatment at the point at which the analyst insisted on a definite and nonreversible conversion of

2. Here again, a worst-case scenario could be for no treatment gain at all if the indicated and selected treatment modality nonetheless foundered over expectable intratreatment difficulties (the Actress and the Masochistic Editor were in this category).

3. A predicted or adjudged HSRS rating can be other than a whole number, because these ratings are each averages of several judges.

the treatment to psychotherapy.) The other 20 all registered HSRS gains, ranging from 4 to 40 scale points; these of course included those instances of appropriate and successful conversions of the treatments to varyingly supportive–expressive psychotherapies. Overall, these numbers reflect in a condensed way the judgments that have emerged singly (and on different bases) in the individual case presentations: of significant limitations in the psychoanalytic results achieved, even in the most favorable cases (e.g., the phobic patients and those with hysterical character neuroses).

At the Follow-Up Study point, HSRS judgments were again rendered for each of the patients, in order to determine (among other things) how well treatment-induced gains had been sustained (or perhaps even further consolidated and built upon), or, by contrast, whether they had been wholly or in part lost during the period of follow-up observation. The actual Follow-Up Study range for the 22 patients started in psychoanalysis was 40–86.5, with an average of 65 — hardly up from the Termination average of 62. However, within the group, there were distinct movements. Within an overall sustaining of gains, 2 of the patients showed significant HSRS drops (of more than 5 points) between Termination and Follow-Up Studies. One of these was the Heiress, who dropped from a Termination judgment of 71 to a Follow-Up judgment of 60.5. This reflected the failure of her treatment gain, which was largely dependent on the successful "transfer of the transference" to her second husband, to hold in the follow-up period when the inadequacies of *this* husband and the neurotic nature of *this* marital relationship had clearly emerged (see pp. 421–426). The other was the Suspended Medical Student, whose Termination HSRS assessment of 82.5 plummeted 37.5 points to a Follow-Up assessment of only 45. This reflected the illusory nature of the patient's apparent psychoanalytic progression and change, which came rapidly apart when he left his treatment to take on the usual vicissitudes of his chosen professional life (see pp. 363–370). (For the same reasons, this patient also had his Initial Study HSRS assessment retrospectively lowered, as has already been indicated.)

Of the 2 patients who at Termination Study had a lower HSRS assessment than at Initial Study, one, the Alcoholic Doctor, was now dead. The other, the Alcoholic Raconteur, who had fled his treatment at the nadir of his illness, had subsequently rescued himself via his AA involvement (see pp. 498–504) and was at the Follow-Up Study point married, holding down a job, and not drinking. His HSRS rating consequently went up from an extremely disordered Termination level of 23 to a still not very healthily integrated Follow-Up level of 43.

In contrast to those who went down between Termination and Follow-Up Studies, 4 patients went up more than 5 HSRS scale points during that observation span. They included the Alcoholic Raconteur (just mentioned), as well as 3 of the patients who were among those with the more successful outcomes — the Adoptive Mother (see pp. 295–302), the Movie Lady (see pp. 413–417), and the Obese Woman (see pp. 288–293). All three of these were in the cluster of patients with more or less hysterical character formations, together with general phobic, depressive, and anxiety symptoms (see pp. 293–295 for the general discussion of this group and their psychoanalytic outcomes). These Follow-Up HSRS gains with these "hysterical" patients reflected the strengths in this group: They were able to take their treatment-achieved gains (however short they fell of the psychoanalytic ideals for them) and build further upon them in consolidating directions during the follow-up observation period, on the basis of different mechanisms as individually specified.

Overall, with 5 of these 22 patients started in psychoanalysis, the actual Follow-Up Study HSRS outcome was in the range between 5 scale points below and 5 above the predicted outcome. In only 4 cases was it more than 5 scale points above the predicted level. These included 2 of the very sickest patients, whose original outcome predictions were quite pessimistic (the Masochistic Editor and the Alcoholic Raconteur), and also the 2 with the very best psychoanalytic treatment outcomes, (the Medical Scientist and the Phobic Woman; see Chapter 13). By contrast, 13 of the 22 ended at an HSRS level more than 5 scale points below their predicted level, ranging down to 40 below it (the Suspended Medical Student). Again, overall, the psychoanalytic outcomes, as measured by achieved changes in the HSRS, fell significantly short of our original predictions for those cases. This phenomenon is discussed in a variety of contexts in Section IX of this book.

PATIENTS IN PSYCHOTHERAPIES

For the 20 patients started (and treated throughout) in varyingly supportive–expressive psychotherapies, the Initial Study HSRS range was 30–68. The one at 68, the Bitter Spinster, was felt to be one of those patients who ought to have been in psychoanalysis, but this more ideal treatment was precluded by lack of available financial resources. Leaving out the Bitter Spinster, the initial range was 30–62, with an average of 43; 6 of the total (of 19 or 20) were at the modal number, 35. The predicted Termination Study range for them was 35–75, with an average of 61 — up 18 scale points over the Initial Study average.

The actual range of Termination Study HSRS assessments for this group was between 30 and 80, with an average of 56.5. This was, on the average, up 13.5 points over the Initial Study average of 43, but it was also short of the predicted average of 61. The Termination Study figures included three instances of an HSRS drop between the Initial and Termination points. One was a 13-point drop from 68 to 55 for the Bitter Spinster, who, as just stated, was originally considered an almost ideal patient for psychoanalysis, but who ended as a totally failed treatment case (see pp. 349–353). In terms of the original expectations for her, she represented probably the single most disappointing and unexpected treatment outcome in the entire project, aside from some of the patients whose treatment careers ended in deaths from mental-illness-related causes and who likewise entered treatment with good expectations (e.g., Peter Pan, or the Suspended Medical Student). The other two were but small drops — from 35 to 30 and from 32 to 30 in two extremely ill patients who both ended as failed treatment cases, the Sociopath and the Addicted Doctor (their treatment courses have not yet been described). In addition, 3 other psychotherapy patients ended their treatments at the same HSRS level at which they started. With the Invalided Hypochondriac (whose course has also not yet been described), the level at both points was 30; this also reflected a treatment failure. With the Adolescent Grandson, who colluded with his grandfather in a treatment disruption, the level at both points was 50, and the outcome was an equivocal one (see pp. 490–497). And with the Fearful Loner, who was stabilized much more contentedly at a very circumscribed evenness of functioning, the level at both points was 55; in his case, this was considered a very good treatment outcome (see pp. 452–458). The other 14 patients had increases in HSRS levels ranging from 4.5 to 39 scale points.

At the Follow-Up Study point, the range of HSRS levels was now 25–74, with an average of 58 — hardly up from the Termination average of 56.5. However, again there were distinct movements within the overall group. Four of the patients showed noticeable HSRS drops (of more than 5 points) between Termination and Follow-Up, but two of these drops were barely more than that, and represented mainly a shaking down of some of the treatment-induced gains. One of these patients was the Claustrophobic Man, who lost 7 HSRS points of the 30 he had gained, reflecting some partial return of his phobic anxieties when away from the sustaining psychotherapy (see pp. 398–403). The other was the Homesick Psychology Student, who lost 6 HSRS points (most of the 9 he had gained); he had stabilized his functioning during the follow-up period through his marriage, but at the price of a very severe sexual inhibition and disability (see pp. 417–421).

The other two cases of this group who suffered HSRS losses between the Termination and Follow-Up Studies were of a more ominous nature. The Bitter Spinster, who was started in expressive psychotherapy with high hopes and at a high starting level of functioning (HSRS level of 68), was the psychotherapy patient who suffered the largest treatment decline; she terminated her failed therapy at 55, and went on to a further decline through the follow-up period to a Follow-Up Study level of 47. At Follow-Up Study, she was apathetically bogged down in a total life impasse. And the very alcoholic Car Salesman (treatment course not yet described), who had started very ill (HSRS level of 38) but had seemed to make some minimal stabilizing gains in treatment (Termination HSRS level of 42.5), had lost all this and had fallen into an even worse state than initially through his follow-up period, to the final level of 32 (a 10.5 point drop from Termination Study).

Of the three patients who had a lower HSRS assessment at Termination Study than at Initial Study, one, the Bitter Spinster, has just been mentioned as having dropped still further by the Follow-Up point. Another, the Addicted Doctor (treatment course not yet described), who had started very ill (HSRS level of 32), whose failed treatment terminated with his transfer to the state hospital (HSRS level of 30), was adjudged in the context of his further failing adjustment in the state hospital to be functioning at the Follow-Up point at the further lowered HSRS level of 25. The third in this group, the Sociopath (treatment course also not yet described), had reversed his 5-point loss at Termination and was adjudged at Follow-Up at a 5-point higher level than at Initial Study (final HSRS level of 40); this represented a very tenuous low-level life restabilization.

On the other side, 6 of the 20 patients in psychotherapy went up more than 5 HSRS scale points (ranging from 6.5 to 17 more) during the follow-up observation span. They were a mix of cases. Three of them were among the most successful cases within the project, and their further gains during follow-up (6.5, 17, and 10 points) were on top of already substantial treatment gains (5.5, 27, and 29 points). They were the Involutional Woman, the Bohemian Musician, and the Intellectual Fencer. Two others represented the stabilizations, with uncertain degrees of solidity, of two very ill patients, the Sexual Masochist and the Sociopath. One other, a more unsettled character, was the Adolescent Grandson, who seemed better stabilized through the deployment of his inherited monies, as well as through his marriage; however, the future course of his life as well as of his psychological difficulties was not at all yet clearly charted.

Overall, with 8 of these 20 patients treated by varyingly expressive and supportive psychotherapies, the actual HSRS outcome at Follow-Up Study was in the range between 5 scale points below and 5 above the predicted outcome. With another 5, it was more than 5 points above the predicted level, ranging up to 24 points higher (for the Bohemian Musician). Of these 5, 4 were in the group of best psychotherapy outcomes, some of them surprisingly so; these were the Bohemian Musician, the Manic–Depressive Physician, the Phobic Girl, and the Intellectual Fencer. The fifth one who did considerably better than expected was the very sickest patient in the whole sample, the Sexual Masochist, who did finally overcome his manifest severe sexual perversion and stabilize his life within a new marriage and as a "therapeutic lifer" (see pp. 405–412). At the other extreme, 7 patients ended at an HSRS level more than 5 scale points below their predicted level, down to 28 and 30 points below (the Bitter Spinster, who fell from an Initial level of 68 to a Follow-Up level of 47, in contrast to the predicted 75; and the Invalided Hypochondriac, who persisted throughout at the unchanged HSRS level of 30, in contrast to the predicted 60).

Overall HSRS Results

Table 4 displays some of the figures from the two groups side by side. The table shows clearly that the patients recommended for psychoanalysis started at a higher HSRS level than those recommended for psychotherapy as expected; there was a 5-point average difference between the two populations. The difference for the modal figure, of 15 points, reflects even more strongly the better starting point of patients deemed appropriate for psychoanalysis, in terms of overall psychological functioning. Even more, a more far-reaching treatment gain was predicted for

TABLE 4.
*Predicted and Actual HSRS Results for PRP Patients,
by Treatment Modality*

HSRS RATING	PSYCHOANALYSIS ($n = 22$)	PSYCHOTHERAPY ($n = 20$)
Initial average level	48	43
Initial modal level	50	35
Predicted average level	74	61
Predicted average gain	26	18
Termination average level	62	56.5
Termination average gain	14	13.5
Follow-Up average level	65	58
Follow-Up average gain	17	15
Gains higher than expected	4 of 22; 18%	5 of 20; 25%
Gains lower than expected	13 of 22; 59%	7 of 20; 35%

the patients in analysis—an average predicted gain of 26 as against 18 points, despite the higher starting point and the greater difficulty in moving within the higher scale ranges. If things had worked out in terms of these normative expectations for the two modalities, the final average HSRS spread between the two groups would have widened from 5 scale points to 13 scale points.

The actual outcomes were, of course, different. The average Termination Study HSRS gain for the patients started in psychoanalysis was 14 rather than the predicted 26; the patients started in psychotherapy had a similar average gain of 13.5, as against the predicted 18. In both groups the average gain was less than predicted, but the group in psychoanalysis fell more substantially short of the predictions for it (lived less well up to its own postulated potential and goals). In consequence of the two average gains' being equivalent, the 5-point spread in favor of those in psychoanalysis between the averages of the two groups at Initial Study remained the same (5.5 points) at Termination Study. And again at Follow-Up Study the two averages moved upward barely perceptibly; at the end, then, the psychoanalytic cases had gone up an average of 17 points and the psychotherapy cases an average of 15 points, with the initial 5-point disparity in favor of those recommended for psychoanalysis now an equivalent 7-point disparity. This relatively disappointing overall performance of the patients recommended for psychoanalysis, in terms of the expectations of the modality for *them*, is reflected in the fact that among those 22, only 4 (or 18%) ultimately did better than predicted, while 13 (or 59%) did less well. By comparison, among the 20 in psychotherapy from the start, 5 (or a roughly equivalent 25%) ultimately did better than expected, while the number who did less well than expected, 7 (or 35%), was a much smaller proportion than with psychoanalysis. At the properly conservative reading of these data, we suffered more disappointments (13 as against 7) with those entered into analysis. This is discussed in terms of plausible explanations in Section IX.

RESULTS ON THE TEST OF IQ

General Results

One of the surprising outcomes of PRP, which perhaps should not have been so surprising, was the favorable impact on the other readily available quantitative measurement with the project patients—the IQ as measured by the Wechsler–Bellevue, Form I. This test was a component of the psychological test battery administered to our patients at the three points in time, Initial, Termination, and Follow-Up.[4] It turned out that there was an upward trend in the IQ data over

---

4. Because of vagaries of oversight or incompleteness of data gathering at Initial Study, and because of noncooperation or nonavailability of some of the patients at Termination Study and/or Follow-Up Study, we did not have 42 IQ levels at each point in time. At Initial Study, 5 were missing; at Termination Study, 7 were missing; and at Follow-Up Study, 7 were missing. Of the 19 missing instances, 11 occurred on a single occasion for those patients; the other 8 occurred with 4 patients for each of whom the IQ data were missing twice and only available once. None were missed all three times, and for 27 patients the IQ data were obtained at all three points in time.

the course of psychoanalysis and psychotherapy and their follow-up periods. Among the 38 project patients for whom the IQ determination was made at least twice (27 were tested at all three times, 11 only twice, and 4 only once—see footnote 4), the IQ moved upward in 29 instances (from as few as 2 to as many as 23 points), downward in 7 instances (from 1 to 8 points), and was unchanged in 2 instances.

These IQ data and their possible interpretation have been discussed in detail in two articles by S. A. Appelbaum, Coyne, and Siegal (1969, 1970) and then summarized in the book by S. A. Appelbaum on the changes in the overall psychological test data (1977, pp. 192–202). Here therefore, I only abstract some of the observations and conclusions from these sources. The mean length of time between Initial and Termination testing was 57.4 months (almost 5 years), and that between Termination and Follow-Up testing was 26.2 months (more than 2 years); thus the interval between Initial and Follow-Up Studies was almost exactly 7 years (83.6 months). The mean age of the patient population at these three points in time was 31, 36, and 38. And the mean IQ figures rose from 124 at Initial Study to 128 at Termination and further to 131 at Follow-Up. The statistical analyses demonstrated significance for these changes at the .001 level for the Initial to Termination comparison of means, and at the .01 level for the Termination to Follow-Up comparison of means (S. A. Appelbaum, 1977, p. 194).

Striking Individual Changes

The three most striking individual changes were as follows. The Tantrum Woman, an individual with a basically hysterical character neurosis who came to treatment with an acute depression in the wake of her husband's sudden accidental death, actually had two extended periods of analysis with the same analyst before achieving her final very good improvement. Her initial IQ was measured at 112, which was thought to be too low and to reflect the probable impingement of her conflicts upon her innate intellectual capability. At the Termination testing this had risen 15 points to 127; this rise was felt to reflect the general freeing of her psychological functional capacities from the burden of active psychic turmoil. At the Follow-Up point, which was one of reactivated turmoil and returned symptoms in the wake of a stressful second marriage entered into during the follow-up period, the patient's IQ had risen further to 133, or 21 points over the initial level. It was as though a real hysterical pseudodebility had been overcome, even in the face of reactivated conflict and symptom formation. (This reactivation itself was what led to her second analysis, starting *after* the official Follow-Up Study, which finally brought the patient the enduring conflict resolution that she sought. For her treatment course, see pp. 302–307.)

A quite comparable IQ course was seen with the Bohemian Prep School Boy, who demonstrated the second largest increase. His IQ was measured at 127 initially, which seemed unexpectedly low in this extremely gifted young man; it was felt to reflect the disrupting impact of his intense anxiety and his struggles with impending psychotic disorganization. At Termination Study, it had risen to 142 (this was felt to be evidence of lessened inundation by disruptive fantasy), and it held stably at 141 at Follow-Up Study. The very major difference from the Tantrum Woman, however, was that this very ill young man had a very short and disrupted treatment course with no real change, and was in a totally unsettled psychological situation described as still unresolved and unresolving at the Follow-Up Study time. Yet his IQ showed an equally dramatic rise, and from a considerably higher starting position — 127 as compared with 112 for the Tantrum Woman. (For his treatment course, see pp. 523–529.)

The third patient with a striking individual change was the Sexual Masochist, who demonstrated a very different pattern. His Initial Study IQ level was 114, which was felt to be unremarkable for him; he had gotten through college and some graduate work, despite the grossest negligence of his schoolwork, but it was also unclear how dependent this was on the pervasive cheating. At Termination Study, after what seemed like a totally collapsed psychotherapy effort (with the sickest of patients), his IQ had declined to 101. His perceptual–motor performance, his attention, and his concentration all showed significant functional decompensation, paralleling the increased straining of ego-adaptive capacities. But by Follow-Up Study, when this patient was unexpectedly restabilized in a return to treatment (as a probable "therapeutic lifer," together with his new wife and ostensibly in "family therapy" with his original therapist), his IQ had now risen 20 points to 121; this made up the whole loss that had occurred during the treatment and forged ahead of the Initial Study level as well. Particularly involved, again, were the functions of concentration and attention: The patient could now concentrate, where before he had simply been unable to do so. (For his treatment course, see pp. 405–412.)

S. A. Appelbaum et al.'s Conclusions

A number of overall observations were made and conclusions were drawn by S. A. Appelbaum and his coworkers concerning this issue of the relationship of IQ change to psychoanalysis and psychotherapy in a younger adult population, which would not expectedly show such change over a 5- to 7-year span. First, they did feel that there was a successfully demonstrated upward change of IQ during psychoanalysis and psychotherapy; that this change was for the most part further consolidated and enhanced after the terminations of the treatments; and that all this had occurred despite the probable existence of some practice effects, which could becloud the specific extent of the change. They felt the change to be especially clearly demonstrated since the patient population was in the superior range of intelligence to begin with (they ranged initially from 111 to 141, with a mean of 124, despite evidence in numerous instances of being adversely affected by the ravages of decompensated mental illness), with consequent lesser room for improvement; they also bore in mind that the Wechsler–Bellevue has a curtailed upper range. There was (as expected) no difference in the IQ effect between men and women, and (perhaps less expected) no difference in the effect between patients in psychoanalysis and those in psychotherapy. Truly unexpected, however, was the fact that there was no difference in the effect on IQ between those with successful treatment outcomes and those with failed treatment outcomes. This has just been illustrated with the statements about the two patients who displayed the very largest favorable effects upon the IQ. The Tantrum Woman, with an overall rise in IQ of 21 points, was from the group with most successful treatment outcomes (although her needed second analysis — with the same analyst — did not come until after this total IQ gain was registered); by contrast, the Bohemian Prep School Boy, with an overall rise in IQ of 14–15 points (and starting from a considerably higher level than the Tantrum Woman), was from the group of unsuccessful and disrupted treatments. In his book, S. A. Appelbaum (1977) tries to link highly individualized routes to change in IQ to changes in varieties of other Patient Variables and varying configurations of Patient Variables.

Turning Points in Treatments

A particular bias that seems to run through the clinical case literature of psychoanalysis and psychotherapy is the highlighting of the concept of the dramatic "turning point" in treatment, though it is not usually explicitly referred to as such. However, many articles built around clinical case reports, whether they are trying to make a contribution to theory or to clinical practice, share a common format. The problem at issue is first presented, usually within the context of its historical unfolding. Then the illustrative case material is entered upon, in which a particular patient and a particular treatment course are presented up until some point of difficulty or impasse. At that point, some interaction or sequence of interactions is detailed (over whatever time span, but often brief), during which new clarifications emerge that both set the clinical course back on target and illuminate the theoretical conceptualization that the author is advancing. The overall effect is often to leave the reader with the impression of a pending treatment stalemate that got resolved and turned around at some turning point of understanding and clarification, which then served to make the overall theoretical point of the article.

What constitutes such a "turning point," and the extent to which one can discern one within a treatment process, depend of course both on one's criteria for the phenomenon and on one's sensitivity to it. Within our PRP sample of 42, there were 7 instances (one-sixth of our total) where, in terms of our research overview, such a conception could be applied. In 4 instances, the turning points led to an upward treatment course, and in 3 they led downward — and 1 of these 7 instances was indeed startlingly dramatic. How much these are discerned as such by the patient and the therapist within the treatment interaction, and the extent to which they agree on the assessment and the timing of the phenomenon, are of course matters of interest; the whole question of how much difference such turning points really do make to the therapeutic course and outcome is also important.

CHANGES FOR THE BETTER

The Tantrum Woman

To start with the most dramatic and most clearly fateful such turning point in a successful direction, I turn to the Tantrum Woman. She was the young widow with a hysterical character neurosis who came to psychoanalysis with the acute depression following her husband's abrupt and accidental death. From the beginning, her analysis was beset by increasingly unmanageable "affect storms." These were patterned after her childhood temper tantrums, in which, according to her informant aunt's report, "she would scream and slam doors and try to break objects or tear her clothes. With her tongue she did much to destroy the liking and respect of those who knew her best." In her analysis, as already described,[1] these were repeated episodes of torrential affective outpourings during the analytic hours, which inundated all reasonable processes in the patient, and which served less as abreactive discharge processes than as defensive barriers against hearing either herself or her analyst. When waiting them out seemed fruitless, and when interpretation of meaning alone was lost in the absence at such moments of adequately cooperating ego, the analyst began to intervene—not simply via a command to stop emoting, but with a firm and insistent reminder that he was present to listen to her: "Just a minute! There's no need to shout. I'm listening."

To the patient, this marked the turning point of her treatment, and she explicitly called it that. "For the first year and a half I didn't feel I was getting anywhere. At the time he started yelling back, that was the first big turning point. He said 'shut up.' I needed someone to shut me up. I needed it then. . . . Before that I was running wild and he was letting me. Now I felt there was someone who would help me and not let me run wild . . . someone was there who was interested." In this case, the analyst clearly concurred with the patient's assessment that this sequence of interactions did mark just such a major turning point in a previously undisciplined analytic situation. It is not that all went well (and easily) thereafter: The patient spent 3 further years in the analysis, and then, after a flare-up of her problems and her symptoms in the subsequent follow-up period, returned for yet another span of 4 years in a second analytic effort with the same analyst before finally achieving the point of very good improvement that she did reach (see pp. 302–307). It is just that the interactions that characterized the "turning point" made all the rest possible, including the subsequent very elaborate working out over time of the multiple meanings of the patient's affect storms.

The Obedient Husband

With the Obedient Husband, there was an almost equally dramatic turn for the better. He was the businessman who came to psychotherapy when he felt the peculiar neurotic equilibrium in his marriage to be seemingly inexplicably threatened by his wife's improvement in her psychotherapy. In the course of his 18-month psychotherapy (see pp. 434–439), a widening network of ramifying psychological problems and symptoms came into focus, including the patient's constant "escape" into excess drinking—a symptom that at the time of initial evaluation had been presented (to himself as well as to others) as nothing more than "social drinking." When the therapist (at a point 3 months before the end of the treatment) insisted that the patient would never know all the defensive and "escapist" meanings that

---

1. For expository purposes, because the "turning point" interactions in this case so clearly illustrate the phenomenon that is here being discussed, their description is being repeated at this point almost verbatim (actually expanded a little) from those given previously (see pp. 179, 303).

went into his drinking behavior unless he stopped, the patient took this as a *demand* to stop drinking and a kind of test that he had to pass if he wanted the therapist to be willing to go on with him. He promptly responded positively and quit his drinking. Both he and the therapist saw this interaction as the turning point of the treatment, after which the patient felt enabled to undertake a variety of other desired behavioral changes. He saw himself now for the first time as effectively working toward shared goals with the therapist—that he be more autonomous, more assertive, in effect, more manly. It was his exertion in giving up the drinking and making this stick that the patient felt paved the way for all the other changes he could then bring himself to make (disengaging himself from his attendance upon his wife, securing a self-respecting job, involving himself with friends and a wider social life, etc.). The therapy went on from there to a successful outcome.

The Medical Scientist

A much less dramatic, more "workaday" turning point came during the analysis of the Medical Scientist, the severely barbiturate- and alcohol-addicted physician who had several times holed up to withdraw himself in desperate self-help attempts, only to revert to his addictions. He was a very reticent individual, and, despite his high intelligence, was somewhat inarticulate—especially in regard to feeling states. In the transference, he initially behaved like the pupil with a stern teacher who must be appeased at all costs. He saw the analyst as someone always telling him in a harsh voice that he must do better and disdaining his efforts. As he gradually became convinced over time that the analyst was "really in his corner," neither the remote father nor the bossy mother, deeper transference positions came to the fore. The turning point in this regard came when the patient could confess homosexual feelings toward the analyst and was not driven out of the therapy in outrage. After that, he could accept the analyst's real concern and interest, and at the same time could begin to identify with the analyst's acceptance of his worth as a person whom it was worthwhile to try to cure. The patient went on to achieve probably the best psychoanalytic treatment result in the whole PRP population (see pp. 266–271).

The Adolescent Grandson

The fourth instance of a turn for the better in treatment was quite similar to this one, though unfortunately it was less enduring. It was with the young Adolescent Grandson, brought to psychotherapy when he was caught scampering nude across his wealthy grandfather's estate (see pp. 490–497). He had been outwardly a very reserved, inhibited, and even depressed youngster. He saw no special need or purpose to his psychotherapy and kept asking why he was in therapy. His manner over the first 7 months was distant and aloof. The turning point of the therapy (again, in both the patient's and the therapist's eyes) came after an episode when the patient was humiliated by his girlfriend and turned out by both her and her mother. He experienced rising anxiety over this, capped by an evening phone call to his therapist, who saw him immediately in an emergency appointment. The patient, comforted (and surprised) by the therapist's concern and willingness to see him, sobbed out for the first time his great loneliness, his feelings of overwhelming humiliation and unlovableness. The therapist felt that he was able to relate the feelings of rejection by the girl (to whom the patient had given himself in his first full expression of sexual love), and by the therapist (who had been away and canceled some sessions), to the lifelong traumata of the successive severe rejections in his life, going back to the original desertion by the mother.

The patient was rehospitalized for a short time, and the immediate crisis calmed. It was following this episode that the middle, most productive phase of the therapy was ushered in. The patient realized that he was "a very lonely boy and that he never had anybody who had unequivocally cared for him." He now felt closer to the therapist and was comfortable enough to confide his feelings, fears, and wishes to someone for the first time. Unfortunately, this period of productive work together could not be sustained over time: A burgeoning eroticized transference attachment unfolded and was not successfully coped with interpretively. The patient—in defensive flight—lent himself to his grandfather's blustering, premature disruption of the treatment, which the grandfather declared to be unnecessary, upsetting, and anyway too expensive. (Ironically, this may have been the wealthiest family in the entire PRP sample.)

CHANGES FOR THE WORSE

The Silent Woman

Of the three patients for whom the turning point had a negative impact upon the subsequent therapy, one was just like those described, except in reverse. This was in the case of the Silent Woman, a divorcée with the problems and burdens of two children to support, who sought psychiatric treatment because of increasing feelings of anxiety, depression, and indecisiveness. An encounter, only retrospectively viewed as such a crucial contributor to the subsequent difficulties in the treatment, took place at the very beginning, in the second psychoanalytic hour. The patient had to sit up to make a "confession" of a secret not yet divulged—that on a recent consultation at a famed medical center, her younger son (aged 6) had been diagnosed as suffering from "psychomotor epilepsy." She had many forebodings concerning the consequences for his future health and well-being, fears about her family members' possible unenlightened reactions should they find out, and guilt about starting in treatment separated from her son (who had stayed behind in her home town with her parents) under these circumstances. The analyst's response to this revelation was in terms of possible barriers to treatment becoming evident just at the start of the process, and the patient perceived this as accusatory. The analyst admitted later that, though "technically indicated," his reaction was "too scientific" and insufficiently empathetic with her plight. Whatever role this interaction played in the subsequent events, the analytic course was at all times difficult, beset by prolonged and painful silences (see pp. 445–451). The patient, after a year, broke up the treatment when the analyst insisted on treating analytically the patient's intent to take a week off from the analysis because of an anticipated increase in pressures on her job, and her desire also not to pay for that week. Despite the difficulties, however, the year of analytic work had been somewhat helpful to the patient in relieving her presenting symptoms and helping her to organize her life. The analyst felt the analysis to have always been a very hard job in which he could never feel relaxed.

The Exhibitionistic Dancer

The other two negative turning points discerned in the PRP population were of a different order from the five described thus far. Rather than being happenstances (for better or for worse) of treatment interactions, these two were occasions on which, in varieties of ways, the patients succeeded in manipulating their treatment and/or life arrangements, to the ultimate detriment of both their treatments and their lives. One of these was the Exhibitionistic Dancer, the young woman whose parents could no longer cope with her immaturity and rebelliousness, and her constant involvements with undesirable companions, antisocial behaviors, and bohemian life styles (see pp. 504–510). The diagnosis was of narcissistic character disorder, and the patient was recommended for an intensive psychotherapy with concomitant prolonged hospital care and control. The treatment began, as planned, in the hospital, and the patient understood that this would be a long-term venture. In the hospital, she quickly got into a romance with a delinquent (and very rich) boy 4 years her junior, who was in psychotherapy with the same therapist. After not quite a year, the patient and her boyfriend, with 5 minutes of deliberation and no prior planning, eloped from a hospital party and drove off to a neighboring state to get married.

The patient and her husband returned to Topeka after a week to resume their treatments, which they would now need more than ever—to help consolidate their marriage—but which of course they now wanted on an outpatient basis. As noted earlier (see p. 204), there was considerable controversy within the institution as to whether to continue to offer treatment to either or both of them, or to make a referral elsewhere at this point; there was also further discussion on the basis upon which continued treatment could be offered, should the decision be made to do so. The patient's family claimed to be very gratified by their daughter's progress up to that point, felt very pleased and proud of the marriage, and strongly maintained that The Menninger Foundation would be abdicating its responsibilities if treatment were discontinued in the light of the new circumstances.

Professional opinion on the side of discontinuing the treatment and referring elsewhere, as noted, was based on the conviction that the young couple had effectively destroyed the treatment programs planned for each. It was felt that accepting them now on the new basis would handicap their further treatment prospects, since they could have strong needs to "prove" their marriage, and thus might have to remain together even if they later came to feel an unwisdom in their marriage decision. Of course, on the other side was the feeling that professional guilt feelings over not having successfully forestalled the romance and marriage should not be translated into a response that could be construed as reflecting exasperation and a wish to punish. Treatment was then finally resumed in Topeka for both (as outpatients); the patient remained with the same therapist, and her new husband transferred to another (actually much more senior) therapist. With this resolution, the patient was precipitated from the sheltered and supervised hospital environment to an irresponsible, chaotic living situation, with a husband wilder and sicker than she, and with few controls. The psychotherapy never went well thereafter, and when the patient finally abruptly terminated it some 2½ years later, armed with her parents' support in that decision, her treatment gains had been very equivocal, with only very slight changes in symptom, behavior, or disposition.

The Sociopath and His Therapy

The other major manipulation of a treatment arose at the very start of the treatment of the Sociopath. His treatment course, which ended in failure, has not been described yet and is highlighted here from this particular perspective.

BACKGROUND AND PROGNOSIS

The patient was an attorney who came actually seeking psychoanalysis, propelled by complaints from many sources that he had an unbalanced personality, was a pathological liar, and was an embezzler who had recently escaped criminal prosecution by virtue of his lawyer father's undertaking to make full restitution for his depredations. I have previously described aspects of this patient and his difficulties at a variety of points. These have included (1) his shame over, and revolt against, his Eastern Orthodox heritage, and his bitter resentment and revengeful feelings toward all American "400 percenters" (see p. 64); (2) the extreme violence proneness that marked his personality, which led the testing psychologist to express concern (on the basis of the psychological test protocols) that this patient was a potential rapist or murderer (see p. 125); (3) the emergence of his violent propensities in his proud savaging of courtroom opponents, especially when they were hated "400 percenters," and in his fiercely predatory life style with women (see pp. 64, 130); (4) his many criminal activities (forging documents, embezzling, involvements with gangster elements, etc.), which finally led his appalled father to take responsibility for making restitution of all debts and bringing his son for psychiatric treatment (see p. 132); and (5) the extreme coercion that finally brought the patient to a willingness to accept treatment—he was fleeing both criminal prosecution and legal disbarment proceedings (see p. 171).

To fill out this picture of the patient's life and illness, I add the following. From the beginning of his life, the patient had experienced inordinate indulgence, particularly from the father. He had always had more toys than any of his friends, and he would often break them wantonly in temper outbursts. They would then be promptly replaced by duplicates. As a young man he was in wartime military service; alongside his glorying in the opportunity to take out his "hatred of the enemy" by pistol-whipping prisoners, he also relished doing so many things that were forbidden at home—running wild, carousing, drinking, and smoking. He returned from the war with a total disability pension, consequent to a machine-gun leg wound and a residual permanent disability because of nerve destruction. He came back pained by his disability, calling himself "a freak" and feeling that "the government now owed him a living." He said he liked law school because the law would help him be able to "push people around." His subsequent behavior as a lawyer, his profligate money schemes, and his involvements in criminal activities and with known racketeers have already been indicated. His behaviors with women were comparable, as also noted.

Yet in the midst of all this—with his law practice ruined, his enormous debts and his embezzlements finally public knowledge, and with his father heroically covering for him and saving him from disbarment—he nonetheless met and courted his wife. During the courtship they discussed mainly "family tensions," but not his outside troubles. His fiancée "knew that he prevaricated," but he was also "a convincing talker," and he talked her into marrying him 3 months *after* the public discovery of all his malfeasances. The marriage never did go well. When he finally agreed to come to The Menninger Foundation, his family, his creditors, the police, and the underworld were all after him; the psychiatric hospital was his only haven.

The patient came to The Menninger Foundation asking for outpatient psychoanalysis, which he wanted very much and which he would finance out of his own income (he had already found a job locally with a credit organization!), his wife's income, and his government pension. He wanted to stop his lying, cheating, and stealing, and to overcome his "hate complex," his pride, and his egotism. The patient made an impressive appearance, being expensively but conservatively dressed. He had an earnest, confiding manner, and was clearly intelligent and very engaging. He said that he had been overcome with the error of his ways and was now coming to analysis with the highest motivation, unbounded optimism, and the most sincere intentions. Beneath his suave exterior, however, his condescending manner was just short of being openly contemptuous. The patient's family all came for the evaluation. The wife saw him as a spoiled child requiring constant praise. She had unquelled suspicions of infidelity on his part, never knowing when he lied and when he told the truth; yet she wanted to give the marriage a chance. The father felt guilty for having advised the patient to enlist in the Army where he was later wounded. He felt the patient blamed him for being "just a half person." The mother was the most derogatory and complaining about him. It turned out that there were legal charges on file against the patient and pressure for his extradition in order to stand trial in his home state. Both the father and the district attorney (a friend of the father's) were hoping for some statement that the patient was psychotic and therefore not responsible and ought not to be brought to trial. The father was most disappointed when he was informed that such a statement could not properly be given.

The treatment plan recommended involved long-term hospitalization concomitant with psychotherapy. The patient rejected this out of hand: He could control himself on the outside, and besides, it was financially out of the question. He was told then to maintain himself in some trouble-free equilibrium on the outside for a year, and then, with that proof of his capacity to do so behind him, to return for outpatient psychotherapy. The patient and his family accepted this frustration reluctantly. A year later, to the exact day, the patient called, asking for his re-evaluation. He said that in that year he had resigned from the bar (in the face of pending charges); had continued working for the same loan company; had maintained his family; and had had only minor problems with money matters, truth telling, and so on. He still lied, but his lies were reduced 90% and now they were only "white lies." The patient's wife's account of the intervening year was a more flamboyant one. His lying, cheating, and depredations had continued, though on a diminished scale. So had his playing the big shot—buying a car they couldn't afford, showering her with unneeded gifts. When she had become pregnant a second time (they already had one child), she had insisted on an abortion, being fearful of increasing her ties to him. She suspected continued marital infidelities; she hoped the treatment now would salvage their marriage. At 23, she appeared aged and beaten.

The patient, for his part, very articulately now demanded that The Menninger Foundation's side of the bargain be kept, and that he start in his outpatient therapy, preferably psychoanalysis. He was accepted into once-weekly outpatient supportive psychotherapy. The stated rationale for this frequency, aside from the patient's limited financial resources, was the feared risk with more frequent contact of an overly intense involvement, with possible transference regression and an increased potential for destructive acting out. The research evaluators felt that long-term supporting hospitalization was really needed, but that if this were totally precluded, that then the supportive treatment should be minimally on a three-times-a-week basis. The psychotherapy would inevitably engender intense anxieties; only a more frequent therapeutic contact, properly conducted, could have the necessary continuous steadying effect, could effect adequate control, and could prevent the anxieties generated from spilling over between hours into constant crises, emergency situations, and destructive acting out. And even then, recourse to temporary hospitalization (in this case, it would be without cost to the patient at the affiliated VA hospital) would need to be available, to cope with treatment emergencies from time to time.

COURSE OF THE THERAPY

The outpatient psychotherapy lasted 2 years and 9 months (121 hours); it never went well. The description of the therapeutic course can be greatly condensed. Through it all, the patient's level of life functioning progressively declined (though this was not manifest at first, covered as it was by the patient's high capacity to dissemble). He lied all along about his earnings and how he was paying for his extravagances—a new car, a motorboat and trailer, a piano, a fur coat. Checks were being written in advance, and when that proved insufficient, check forgery (on his friends' accounts) was added. With creditors pressing in, the patient's whole past came to light; his company, which had been considering him for promotion, summarily fired him from the position he had held almost 3 years. He got another job, and the same troubles recurred and escalated. When the denouement came there and the dust settled, the patient was heavily in debt, plus having bad checks and illegal deals (e.g., selling property the he did not fully own). At this point the patient's wife left him, with the intention to secure a divorce. She could no longer take the lying, the illegalities, the financial pressures, and never knowing what would happen next. Surprisingly, she was not vindictive: She declared that she still loved the patient and would be glad to return to him whenever his therapist could assure her that her husband had overcome his difficulties. The patient's reaction to this loss was to be temporarily stunned (by the narcissistic blow), but then to bounce back optimistically, confident that he could win her back. He handled his financial and legal disasters by declaring bankruptcy. His creditors got about 15 cents on the dollar, but he declared that that served them right; they were fools for having gotten mixed up with him in the first place.

Therapy was effectively over at this point, but it dragged on a while longer. There was a brief time in jail on a bad check charge. There was another job selling insurance, with the patient living high and gleefully thumbing his nose at creditors. When he was fired from that job, he disappeared from town. At that point, the police were looking for him because of bad checks; the YMCA had impounded his few belongings; and his lawyer who had "been strung along with empty promises and lies," had completely given up—having no money to pay the patient's debts and bills (including his own bill), and being the daily recipient of many phone calls from creditors and holders of bad checks. His family sadly disclaimed all knowledge of his current whereabouts. He had indeed shown up at home, borrowed his mother's car, and simply disappeared with it.

What kind of therapy could be going on during such a life? Actually, the patient had started the therapy with a special expectation: He had kept his part of the bargain, and from now on he ought in return to receive special indulgence, protection, and rescue. Therapy was a place to be properly shielded from the hurtful consequences of his behaviors by the therapist, much as he had been shielded by his father earlier in his life. The themes within the therapy revolved around the patient's deepening life troubles and ways in which the therapist could apply leverage to try to halt the decline. About his problems, the patient was unreflective and unwilling. He would pace up and down shouting about his wife, the dumb people he had to work with, the vengeful creditors, the foolish neighbors, the yokels in Kansas. He called his explosiveness his volatile "Mediterranean temperament." With the therapist personally, he was voluble but always verbally compliant. When he felt reproached, he would instantly come to heel and make good resolutions about how he intended to overcome the difficulties that were pointed to. The patient at such times would be like a bad boy before a stern but just father, making shame-faced "confessions." The transference picture was just what had been anticipated—the patient's searching expectation for an indulgent, protecting, rescuing father. When the therapist couldn't fulfill this expectation, the patient simply gave up the search and abandoned the therapy. When the patient fled, it was in a state of transference disappointment. There was no transference understanding.

STATUS AT FOLLOW-UP

Surprisingly, the patient was reachable for Follow-Up Study through his parents, whom he visited regularly—for money. Both the patient and his mother were involved in the Follow-Up inquiry, and their two accounts of his life and functioning during the 2-year period were widely discrepant. According to the patient, he now had a responsible job in the legal department of a major bank, and was on his way to getting his law license restored. His biggest change was that he no longer lied. He felt that the best thing that had ever happened to him was his divorce from that "stupid, peasant wife . . . I just can't stand stupidity." He had little to do with his parents, seeing them only once or twice a month, since they aggravated his old unhappinesses. Nor did he see his old cronies and associates. He no longer did any "high-powered boozing." Instead he spent his time reading, enjoying fine music, and doing gourmet cooking. He acknowledged feeling still angry and revengeful with people whom he felt had hurt him. At his divorce trial proceedings, he had bullied his wife mercilessly and had "taught her a lesson. When I got through with her she never bothered me again." He said that "to this day the therapist doesn't know why I want revenge so much."

In contrast with this quite bland portrayal was the picture given by his mother. He was in the same old difficulties: He was working in spurts, interspersed with heavy drinking and jail episodes on bad check charges. The parents kept "hoping and hoping and hoping," and mostly they fully supported the patient. The patient simply asked for money as he wished it, which his father always gave him. "He would squander $1000 a week if we let him. He gets ferocious when we get after him about taking some responsibility. It simply does no good." Actually, the mother's relationship with the patient was always strained and quarreling; she thought he might "have a criminal mind." The father got along with him better, but if the flow of money were to cease, that friendship might also stop. Contact with the patient's ex-wife and his now two children had ceased. He was far in arrears on child support payments, and his ex-wife in turn was not allowing him visiting rights. He was not pressing the issue; according to his mother, he seemed to have forsaken his children completely. He was instead spending his time drinking with a new girlfriend. None of this picture of a restabilization of the patient's life at the most minimal level of extramural functioning, by way of this kind of parasitism upon and subtle blackmail of the parents, had emerged in the patient's interview account.

The patient did indicate during the Follow-Up interviews how he felt his treatment could have been improved. The therapist had tried to be helpful with the patient's troubled life, but that was "too much buddy-buddy stuff." Treatment should have been otherwise. "I should have been hospitalized. You have to check up on the patients or you have to lock them up. But you can't let lying go on because it destroys the treatment. . . . You have to watch them. You have to check on the smarties." But he also acknowledged that he would not have accepted such a treatment recommendation, no matter how imperatively it had been advanced. He was well aware of his self-created dilemma: He would accept nothing but outpatient treatment on his own terms, while clearly perceiving its total inability to contain and help him.

With this last statement, the patient was perhaps declaring himself untreatable. He was also, however, declaring his full awareness of the only conditions under which he could have had some chance in treatment. And he certainly did acknowledge that he had forced a bargain that created a totally inadequate treatment plan, doomed from the very start to complete failure, with the tenuous restabilization achieved at the Follow-Up Study point dependent on the father's continued reluctant largesse. Now that his parents were aging and the father ill, the patient's future (beyond where the parents could continue their coerced compliance) was bleak indeed.

The patient was only heard from once more. He called his former therapist some 3 years after the Follow-Up Study, indicating that he was "having some difficulties," and urgently asking to see him in consultation. The therapist said that he would be glad to, but that he first wanted the patient to make some arrangement to pay his back bill. The patient said that this would be "no problem," but then he was never heard from again.

COMMENTS

This patient was not the only one for whom a clearly totally inadequate treatment plan was set up from the very start, leading inevitably to treatment failure. The case of the Bohemian Prep School Boy, a very disorganized youngster allowed too uncontrolled an outpatient life and too uncontrolled a therapy, was another. (For his case description, see pp. 523–529.) Here I want rather to emphasize another point. As with the Exhibitionistic Dancer, who via her elopement and marriage succeeded in prying herself out of the hospital-supported psychotherapy that could have given her treatment a real chance, the Sociopath likewise forced a similar negative turning point in his treatment. In response to his adamant refusal of the same needed hospital-supported psychotherapy, the patient manipulated the promise of being allowed outpatient treatment if he could prove his capacity for it in a year's trouble-free living. After that, he succeeded (despite sufficient evidence to the contrary) in convincing the examiners that he had lived up to his end of the bargain, and in turn demanded that we at The Menninger Foundation live up to ours.[2] With both these patients (the Exhibitionistic Dancer and the Sociopath), things never went well in their treatments after these manipulations.

Treatment Disruption by External Pressures

INVOLVEMENT OF THE FAMILY IN TREATMENT

A hallmark of therapeutic work at The Menninger Foundation built into the conceptualization of total treatment strategies within a sanatorium setting has always been the involvement of the patient's family in the treatment structure. As has been described (see pp. 71–72), with the initial evaluation of the prospective patient, some significant relative (usually the spouse, a parent, or an adult child) is involved in the evaluation process from the very start—both as the provider of a comprehensive family and situational history, and as a participant, along with the patient, in the final conference where the overall findings and recommendations are conveyed to them and joint planning for the prospective treatment is engaged in. For those patients then taken into treatment at The Menninger Foundation, especially for those who are concomitantly hospitalized or have other life-managing involvements (day hospital, foster home, etc.), ongoing social casework involvement with the family is ordinarily set up. If the patient has come from Topeka or its environs (or is moving to Topeka along with his or her family), this is usually set up on a regularly scheduled basis. If the patient has come to Topeka for treatment while the family remains behind in a distant locale, the social work contact is via fairly frequent letters, supplemented as need be by phone calls, plus a regular schedule of periodic visits by the responsible or concerned family mem-

2. One can readily question the wisdom of such a therapeutic test (and bargain). It clearly permits a patient, by fulfilling his or her commitment (however marginally), to compel a countercommitment to an inappropriate treatment plan. Using this kind of waiting period as a therapeutic test can of course work out differently in other circumstances, but only where the countercommitment is to a clearly more feasible (and, one hopes, optimal) treatment strategy.

ber(s) to Topeka and to the patient. This in fact becomes a regular part of the cost of maintaining a patient in treatment in that setting.

Of course, there are categories of patients for whom such concomitant involvement of family members in the overall therapeutic strategy is clearly not part of the treatment plan. These are, as expected, the "usual patients" in outpatient psychoanalysis and psychotherapy. But it has been made abundantly clear by now that The Menninger Foundation tends, by nature of its facility and the circumstances under which patients come to it, to have very few such "usual patients" where some kind of concomitant casework with the families is either not indicated or not appropriate.[1] Furthermore, given the kinds of patients and the kinds of family patterns and family interactions I have been describing through this book, in a great many instances the spouses and/or other significant relatives are themselves also in psychiatric treatments in terms of their own therapeutic needs. (See Chapter 28 for further discussion of this point.)

Notwithstanding all of this planning with and work with relatives, however, it still is not always possible to keep families from interfering with ongoing treatments as a result of their own conflicted involvements — even to the point of precipitating premature disruptions of the treatments. When this occurs, of course, it is rarely a purely one-sided phenomenon. It usually clearly involves the collusive participation of the patient, who may be only too willing for his or her own reasons to see the therapy adversely affected by these evoked "outside" pressures. Actually, such pressures escalated to the point of treatment disruption with 6 of our patients (one-seventh of the sample of 42) — in all cases to their detriment, leaving treatments incomplete and mostly totally failed. In 4 of these instances, the pressures came from the spouses; with our two youngest adolescent patients (both 17 years old when they started), it was the grandfather and the father, respectively, who were the responsible parties. The 6 individual cases follow.

DISRUPTION BY PARENTAL FIGURES

The Adolescent Grandson

The Adolescent Grandson, who was growing very anxious over an increasingly intense transference involvement with unwelcome homosexual awakenings (see pp. 490–497), was delighted to find on a holiday visit home — after 1 year and 9 months of therapy — that he could present himself to his grandfather in such a way that he appeared quite well. As a result, the grandfather re-evoked all his own doubts about the need for therapy. He had never seen the need to spend all that money, since he had all along seen his grandson less as sick and more as just lacking in discipline. Furthermore, he was old and wanted to be left in peace; he wished to be rid of the whole mess of supporting a treatment that he could see only as an unnecessary and upsetting influence upon his grandson. With his domi-

---

1. This statement does not, of course, apply to the considerable number of patients in analysis or therapy who are themselves members of the professional community (staff colleagues, students, or spouses), in treatment for either training or therapeutic purposes. As restricted cases, such patients were categorically excluded from the PRP sample.

neering and blustering way of always getting what he wanted, the grandfather succeeded this time also, and the treatment was terminated at a point of most equivocal improvement. This outcome was abetted in this instance by the fact that the grandfather, who was indeed the responsible and controlling relative had always kept aloof from casework involvement with the patient's treatment; this had been relegated to his secretary. (And, of course, the patient's father was dead, and his stepmother was excluded by the grandfather from any responsibility for the patient's life.)

The Bohemian Prep School Boy

The Bohemian Prep School Boy, (see pp. 523–529) had an even shorter therapeutic course, only 7 months. Here the patient's instigating role in the disruption was far less; it was the father who was from the start very dubious about the nature of his son's illness and of his treatment need. The father saw most of the patient's symptom picture as just an unwillingness to assume appropriate responsibilities (the "*Magic Mountain* atmosphere" and "the wounded aesthete"). He felt that the treatment was an unwarranted expense and that his son's extravagant living was not sufficiently curbed. His ploy (at this early treatment point, with the patient not yet really attached to the therapy) was to announce the family's imminent move to Europe, with an offer to take the patient along and even allow him to continue psychotherapy there if he really wanted it. Caught in this loyalty struggle, the patient chose to leave with his parents for Europe; he said of this, "I probably should not be leaving." He did return to the United States for further schooling (in the dramatic arts) during the follow-up period, but he did not seek further therapy, either overseas or back in this country.

DISRUPTION BY SPOUSES

Peter Pan

With each of the other four patients, it was the spouse who exerted the hostile pressure upon the treatment. Of these, one, Peter Pan (see pp. 426–432), came to treatment as a young single woman; a treatment first undertaken in her home city had been undermined by the interference of her parents. While in her 3 years of outpatient psychoanalysis in Topeka, the patient met a fellow college student who passionately courted her and succeeded finally in marrying her. Actually, the patient wanted to marry when she "recovered" from her illness. The boyfriend, impatient, wanted a more immediate closure; he conceded that she had been ill and had been helped by treatment, but he wanted to break into what he feared was an inordinate continuing dependency upon the treatment. It was his decision upon college graduation to pursue his graduate studies at a distant university, and his pressure on the patient to follow him under the implicit threat of perhaps losing him, that led to her decision to terminate her analysis and to resume with another analyst in the new city. Actually, the patient only had another 6 months of analytic treatment. She then terminated so that she could feel free to marry her boyfriend (with whom she had been living up to then) and not have to continue the analytic scrutiny of the relationship. She was helped to this decision after being assured by her fiancé that in his eyes she was all right and didn't need further treatment. He was tragically wrong, as confirmed by the patient's subsequent progressive decompensation into a psychotic course, and finally by her suicide, 8 years later. (Toward the end of that interval, the patient was indeed back in an unavailing psychotherapy, and her husband had meanwhile separated from her.)

The Invalided Hypochondriac and Her Treatment

The other three cases that terminated under pressure from spouses were all (like that of Peter Pan) totally failed cases. They are among the four whose overall treatment courses have not been described to this point in connection with any of the various headings that I have used to characterize change mechanisms in psychotherapy and psychoanalysis, because these were patients who really showed no change; their treatment was insufficient, and it was in each instance disrupted by some combination of patient and spouse collusive pressure. The shortest of these treatments was that of the Invalided Hypochondriac, whose psychotherapy (and concomitant hospital treatment) lasted only 4 months (42 hours). She was certainly a malignantly ill woman, hypochondriacal to the point of psychotic decompensation, and perhaps untreatable under any circumstances.

BACKGROUND AND PROGNOSIS

The patient's somatic symptoms had started with her weaning, when she had begun to vomit severely. Her whole childhood upbringing had been filled with one childhood disease after another, often with some unusual debilitating complication. By the time she was an adult, the patient's various somatic afflictions had fused into a general state of chronic but still mild somatic distress, marked by weakness, fatigue, irritability, and nervousness. With her (reluctant) marriage, the tempo of the patient's complaints accelerated. Within a week she was talking annulment, and when angry she could give her husband "the old silent treatment" for days at a time. She began in the marriage to develop a full panoply of somatic ailments: gastrointestinal disturbances, bladder disturbances, menstrual disturbances, assorted allergies, sinus trouble, nose and throat trouble, and so on. Her life became, and remained, a constant parade of visits to doctors and clinics.

The patient's two pregnancies were each extremely difficult, and when the babies were born the patient became more incapacitated. She could for the most part only lie in bed and cry, while the husband cared for the infants. Eventually the patient totally abdicated all responsibility for husband, children, and home, and remained in bed practically all day—and the husband could be called home from his office to take care of things as many as five and six times in a working day. (See p. 133 for a description of the patient's lifelong hypochondriasis; p. 142 for the character infantilism within which this was embedded, and also for the impact of this on the husband; p. 138 for her obsessional fears; and p. 144 for her paranoid propensities.) At the same time, the patient always had the "amazing ability" (already mentioned) to pull herself together to go out to an evening cocktail party or bridge tournament. It was at a state of total functional breakdown, punctuated by explosive rages, crying spells, and uncontrolled barbiturate intake, that the patient was brought for psychiatric treatment. Upon initial consultation she collapsed completely, cried uncontrollably for the whole hour, and readily accepted immediate hospitalization.

COURSE OF THE TREATMENT AND ITS DISRUPTION

The patient was in psychotherapy and in the hospital only the 4 months already mentioned. Throughout its brief course, the therapy was stormy, tense, and out of control. It was flooded from the start by explosive affects, intense and wildly fluctuating transferences, dramatically voiced fears and melodramatic blocking, and a disorganized "wild" quality to the patient's ideational content ("crazy talk"). When voicing her somatic complaints and sensations, the patient was near-delusional; she talked of strange crawling feelings, color changes on her skin, sensations of her chest being pumped full of air. At times she said that she "had talked to God and He has forgiven me." In her panicky, depersonalized experiences, she "heard voices." She said, "You must understand, I had never heard voices before in my life." The voices said various things: "Your brain is dead," or "My body is psychotic but my mind is OK," or "My soul comes up to my mouth."

Meanwhile, in her hospital life, the patient for the most part played out the role of the "good little girl"; she was compulsively productive in a variety of tasks in her organized activities program. Her major symptoms (the somatic disorders, the infantile demandingness in all her interpersonal relationships) diminished in their overt expression. This was the thinnest sort of "flight into health," accompanied by verbal offerings like "I know what a mess of a human being I am and what I've done to my husband and children. I have a duty to return to them and to try to face up to my responsibilities that I've never faced up to before." To this pressure from the patient was added increasing pressure from the husband. From the start he complained about the expenses; within a few months, he was quite angry at the doctors for having thus far failed to cure his wife more completely. A number of times he threatened to take his wife out of the hospital, saying that if she needed this much hospitalization she could just as well go to a state hospital. He was readily enlisted alongside his wife when she began to clamor for discharge in order to make a renewed try at life with her family. Faced with this solid front of the patient and her husband, the hospital and the therapist capitulated and accepted her discharge from the hospital and the termination of her psychotherapy.

Thus, this was a totally unsuccessful and failed treatment attempt. This patient may indeed have been, in the end, untreatable under any circumstances; certainly much about her illness picture can support such a view. But in any case, the treatment never had a chance, and the husband's adverse pressures playing into the patient's own very thin "flight into health" insured that the treatment effort would be disrupted, totally prematurely.

THE FOLLOW-UP PERIOD

Though there were some pious plans for weekly "follow-up check-ins," these only endured for 10 additional sessions. Even for these the patient fought against coming, and on some of these return trips to Topeka the patient literally had to be restrained from throwing herself out the car door. Meanwhile all had collapsed again at home; the patient's somatic symptoms, major mood swings, temper tantrums, and extremely difficult relations with husband and children had all returned. And the patient was now expressing insistent suicidal and homicidal impulses.

Yet when rehospitalization was urged, the husband at first demurred. His expressed attitude was "No. You guys have had your chance with her in the hospital. Now I'll straighten her out—just do your part when I get her up here for her hour each week." Nonetheless, the husband was ultimately prevailed upon to allow temporary rehospitalization while more long-term arrangements were being worked out for the patient. On readmission, many sleeping pills were found sewn into the lining of the patient's coat or buried among her cosmetics. A razor blade that was missed at this time was later surrendered by her. This episode of hospitalization terminated with the patient's transfer to a state hospital in her nearby home state.

The patient spent the first 7 months of the follow-up period in the state hospital, where she worked as a typist and "general office flunky" and also participated, in a semiteaching way, in the occupational therapy program. She did not have formal individual psychotherapy. While she was still there, the husband filed for divorce; in the subsequent uncontested proceedings, he secured the divorce and custody of the children. The patient ever after angrily blamed what she called the total mismanagement of her case at The Menninger Foundation for the divorce, and for the changes in herself and in her ex-husband, including the husband's seeking the divorce. After all, "He loved me when he brought me up there, because no one would spend that kind of money for someone unless they loved them." What happened in the patient's life after the divorce never became clear. There was some contact of unspecified duration with a psychiatrist in her home town. There was little, if any, contact with the patient's ex-husband or children. The patient was living alone, on her alimony settlement (her husband was financially well off and was not vindictive), and would only say "I am not as active as I used to be." (What she used to be was almost totally confined to house and bed.) Overall, the patient was somehow hanging on outside an institution, without any overt worsening in her level of functioning, despite the vicissitudes of the divorce proceedings and the losses she suffered there.

This was the patient who was not urged to return to Topeka for formal Follow-Up Study. When she was contacted, she was continuing in this very tenuous equilibrium, querulously hypochondriacal and suspiciously paranoid. As noted earlier (see p. 144), she would only cooperate with a follow-up inquiry if she received explicit assurances in writing, but she was loath to say what assurances she required. It should come from "heart and soul" and not just be something dictated under pressure from her. Besides, her attorney would have to be present at any interviews in which she participated. Given this stance, and the very real possibility that, should she come back to Topeka for Follow-Up Study, the patient might again collapse totally in hypochondriacal decompensation on our doorstep (as she had when she was initially brought for evaluation), it was decided not to press the inquiry further. The patient ended the last long phone conversation by indicating that she had "given a lot" but had "withheld the essence." There has been no further follow-up contact with her beyond this point.

COMMENTS

Whether this malignantly hypochrondriacal woman would have been treatable at all within a psychotherapeutic framework was most questionable; she was one of those looked at as perhaps untreatable, whatever the treatment plan was and however diligently it could be carried out. When the husband's negative pressures upon the treatment were added to the patient's own disruptiveness, manipulativeness, and push into a precarious "flight into health," there was no way of warding off a total treatment failure. As a consequence, an outpatient treatment attempt failed; so did inpatient efforts, both at The Menninger Foundation and subsequently at a state hospital in the patient's home state. Each of these efforts was successfully nullified by this combination of adverse pressures.

The Script Writer and Her Treatment

BACKGROUND AND PROGNOSIS

The next shortest treatment of this group of patients whose treatments disrupted under the combined collusive pressures of the patient and the spouse was that of the Script Writer. Her try in psychoanalysis lasted only 8½ months (129 hours), at which point she terminated the treatment in order to return to her home and family, with the stated intention of continuing with an analyst in her home town. The patient had been referred for psychiatric treatment because of uncontrolled alcoholism (complicated by two suicide attempts) of 6 years' duration, dating from her younger son's crippling attack of poliomyelitis. The patient's family constellation has already been described (see p. 148). Through her growing-up years, the patient excelled academically; in college she was a chemistry major and went to work subsequently as a lab technician. While in college she met her husband, then a medical student. The courtship was fitful; the marriage finally only took place after the patient became pregnant, with both parties expressing open doubts and reluctance.

The early part of the marriage was devoted to the rapid building of the husband's practice and the couple's involvement with a socially prominent set, given to much entertainment and drinking. Here the patient felt quite inadequate over her more humble social and intellectual origins, and tried hard to compensate with university courses and with intellectual and civic activities. It was, however, in regard to the children that her emotional disturbances became clearly evident. She wanted girls rather than boys, but had two sons; she was especially unwilling to reconcile herself to the second one, who, after all, "should have been" a girl. When this second son was 3, he developed a crippling case of poliomyelitis, leaving him with a completely paralyzed right leg and a partially paralyzed left leg. There was a long rehabilitation struggle ahead, with a succession of necessary operations, in the effort to maximize the functional restitution.

The patient was completely unable to cope with this task. She was guilty and depressed about the illness; she began to drink often and heavily, and alone—up to then it had all been "social drinking." She found herself inappropriately impatient with her son, and unable to cooperate properly in carrying out his program of rehabilitation exercises. Her response was to drink more heavily and to insist on a move to a remote suburban area, already mentioned (see p. 148), which made her husband's practice more difficult and time-consuming. The drinking then intensified further; she now justified it partly as providing relief for her painful rheumatoid arthritis, and partly as assuaging her loneliness out in the country with the husband away for such long hours. Matters kept worsening. The patient and her husband fought constantly over the patient's drinking, her poor household management, and the high bills and debts all over town. When the husband tried physically to remove the alcohol from the home, the patient began to hide it all over the house in innocent-appearing bottles, so that she had some in every room.

For over a year before her hospitalization at The Menninger Foundation, the patient was drunk every day, and she suffered many mishaps. She would burn herself at the stove cooking; she had several minor car accidents; and she once flooded the house when she fell asleep in the bathtub with the water running. Once her crippled child fractured his ankle at play, and the patient was so "staggering drunk" that the neighbors had to call the husband from work in order to cope with the situation and hospitalize the son. On two occasions the patient made suicide attempts — once with codeine and once with aspirins, after scoldings by her husband and a neighbor, respectively. Nonetheless, through the worst of this illness, the patient kept up her work with a university radio program, on which she showed initiative and creative ability in script writing, and poise and tact before the radio audience. But the husband was running out of patience; over his wife's protests, he succeeded in pushing her to close out her radio program and come to The Menninger Foundation for psychiatric evaluation. He still professed to be very fond of the patient and to admire her abilities, but he was disconcerted over her avowed unhappiness, and unable any longer to take the never-ending drinking.

The patient was hospitalized for 7 months before entering formal psychotherapy. During this time, she flaunted a sexual courtship with another equally disturbed (and equally alcoholic) married patient; she also persisted in defiant illicit drinking in the hospital, with liquor smuggled in her underwear. Nonetheless, she was recommended for and started in psychoanalysis. This recommendation was based in part on the feeling of the need for so intensive a treatment if the necessary major life alterations were to be effected, and partly on the feeling that analysis was not precluded, since the patient had such actual life capacities and achievements, and had suffered lesser regression than is usually seen in such severe alcoholics. The patient's characterological aggressivity, phallic strivings, and active rebelliousness were all felt to contribute to the "better prognosis" with analysis in this case, as compared with that of "the usual severe alcoholic."

COURSE OF THE ANALYSIS

The patient's hospitalization lasted only another 2½ months after her analysis began. At that point she seemed so "improved," in the sense of seeming to handle manifest anxieties (including on a holiday visit home) without resort to drinking, that she won a move to day hospital status and an apartment of her own. She wondered why everyone was making such a fuss over so simple a move. At the same time, she played on her husband's anxieties over her treatment in Topeka, so far from home. Treatment expenses in Topeka were a serious financial drain.

More importantly, the husband felt the need to have the patient return home and take her place in the family; otherwise, he felt he might lose her to her new interests and new romantic involvement in Topeka. When the husband visited the patient in Topeka, she flaunted her interest in her lover, and succeeded in making the husband uneasy enough that he intensified his pressure to have the patient come home and go on with outpatient psychoanalysis there.

At the same time, within the analysis, the patient's alcoholism and domestic problems could never be wholly uncovered from a screen of denial and minimization. Drinking was consistently downgraded as a problem; she saw it as a response to a "more basic" source of distress, her goallessness and boredom. Guilt and depression seemed always less than what might be expected in connection with the patient's obvious hostile and destructive impact upon her environment. Especially startling was "her amazingly little uneasiness over her incompetent handling of the crippled child." The patient did focus on her lifelong fear and hostility in relation to her mother, who had always made life miserable for her, resulting in characteristic withdrawal and avoidance on the patient's part. This was clearly a major factor in the transference: The patient expressed at the start great apprehension over having a woman analyst (since she always "had so much more trouble getting along with women than with men"), and she had an "inexplicable" panic reaction in her first hour, when her associations led immediately to her bad relationship with her "bitchy mother." However, she also had to fight throughout against seeing this transference projection, saying, "If you ever would become a mother figure for me, I'd have to leave treatment immediately." Related to this transference fear was a reactive competitiveness with the successful woman psychoanalyst, as well as the struggle against awareness (over the course of the analytic effort) of a growing positive attachment—at once both a temptation and a fear.

TERMINATION

None of this work ever came to fruition in the treatment. The period of analysis was too brief, and the patient was too frightened (and her external life too uncontrolled). The threat of the conscious crystallization of transference feelings; the patient's inability to tolerate anxiety; her alloplastic proneness (what she called her "escapist pattern"); and her narcissistic protectiveness—all these factors converged toward her decision to flee the treatment. All efforts to work with the transference acting out in the extratreatment and extramarital romance were unsuccessful. The intratreatment pressure to terminate was supported by escalating external pressure in the same direction. The husband was insistently demanding: "I'm up there. I've been alone for 15 months. I'm at the end of my rope. I have two children to take care of. . . . The people she is in with are parasites, living off the land. . . . There's too much marital mixup there and if she stays any longer I'm going to lose out. . . . I've got friends there who are divorced. I don't want this to happen to us." And it was precisely these fears that the patient activated and manipulated. She kept her husband in a state of constant emotional turmoil by her flaunting of her romance, by the ups and downs of her drinking, and by her financial extravagances. Out of all this came a jointly rationalized plan for the patient to leave Topeka and to transfer to treatment in her home town. It was her need to return to her crippled child. It was a choice between remaining in treatment in Topeka and risking the fate of her marriage, as against going home and making her marriage work. That the analyst clearly saw this plan as "escapist and self-destructive" was insufficient to stop it. When the patient left treatment, there were some slight treatment-induced symptom and behavior changes, but it was considered doubtful how well any of these might hold up in the face of her return to the stresses at home.

STATUS AT FOLLOW-UP

The patient did return for Follow-Up Study 3 years later. Much had happened to her in the interim. Upon her return home, she had not gone into further analysis, but into a once-a-week "supportive psychotherapy combined with chemotherapy." The psychiatrist was a social friend, and, since she was a physician's wife, he had not charged her for the treatment. He saw the patient as suffering a severe character problem—immature, rebellious, dissatisfied. He had tried to persuade her to take Antabuse, but without success. The patient saw him as a friend who would give her medications as needed and countenance her "having a drink" to relieve emotional stresses. With the marriage ever deteriorating, an "amicable divorce" had been worked out.

Shortly thereafter, the patient had sought consultation again at The Menninger Foundation, but not with her former analyst. She was now going to leave her home town, because living there hadn't worked out. She couldn't get along with her ex-husband or her crippled son; her drinking, she said, was much less except when she was around them. She had written a play and submitted it for professional consideration for Broadway. She wanted to return to The Menninger Foundation for treatment, but as an outpatient only. She would willingly leave her children behind with their father (he had custody) "so as not to interrupt their schooling." When psychotherapy on an inpatient basis was urged instead, the patient angrily demurred, stating that we "were at cross purposes." The patient instead then entered psychotherapy with a local psychiatrist not on The Menninger Foundation's staff, and when her new lover left for another city, the patient went along and again found a new therapist (the third since leaving her analysis).

This third therapist reported in a Follow-Up interview on the patient's disorganized life. She had been drinking all along more than she would acknowledge. She was living in a mutually dependent relationship with a fearful, schizoid, much younger boyfriend, but not settling down toward a marriage: If she married him, she would lose her substantial alimony, on which she lived and partially supported him. They did share musical and intellectual interests. Meanwhile, the patient had still another man on the string—a wealthy, very dependent, also alcoholic individual, also a former patient from Topeka. As always, the patient was proud to be able to attract and keep two men interested. Other than with the men in her life, the patient was not doing much. She talked about the values to her of working and about exploring various jobs, but mostly had excuses about why she had replaced doing by talking about doing. That the patient's total treatment course had gotten nowhere and ended a failure was manifest as well in her comportment on the Follow-Up visit. She stated that she was no longer drinking except "socially in a conventional sense," and yet on the third day, she came to her early-morning interviews reeking of alcohol. She emphatically disclaimed the slightest interest in her lover from her treatment days in Topeka, and yet she sought him out and spent a good deal of time with him. As noted earlier, she was the only patient in the project who grossly overcharged her Follow-Up expenses, doing so in a clumsily flagrant manner. There is no further information on her beyond this official Follow-Up visit.

COMMENTS

Clearly, this overall treatment effort failed for many reasons. The patient's capacity to tolerate psychoanalytic treatment had been grossly overestimated; concomitantly, she had been allowed a premature discharge from hospitalization (on the basis of spurious "improvements"), which alone might have given the intensive psychoanalytic treatment a chance. But the husband's attitudes had also been incorrectly assessed. He had been viewed at the beginning as a devoted husband and a compliant person, willing to support fully any reasonable treatment plan. But the combination of the husband's dependent needs for the patient, his fear of losing her, and his concerns about his limited financial resources made his whole attitude toward the patient's (very expensive) treatment away from home much more negative than originally reckoned. More than that, his overtly negative attitudes made it easy for the patient to fan pressures in the husband, onto which she could externalize her own struggles against the treatment.

Thus, like the Invalided Hypochondriac, the Script Writer—though not as clearly "untreatable" as the Invalided Hypochondriac—was able both to manipulate herself into an infeasible treatment plan (basically outpatient psychoanalysis) and to ensure the husband's negative pressures that led to "unavoidable" premature treatment disruption. Both patients, as a result, were failed cases.

The Car Salesman

The last of these four treatments that terminated prematurely under adverse pressures from the spouse was that of the Car Salesman—the only instance of the four where the patient was a male and the spouse a female. His treatment went on the very longest of the four, 3½ years, and the adverse pressures, while real, were less consequential. The case is thus described more fully in the next chapter, within a discussion of intrinsically "untreatable cases" and failed cases.

GENERAL COMMENTS

Here, to summarize, it should be pointed out that the treatment outcomes for the six patients in this group were very bad. The four whose terminations were in response to negative pressures from their spouses (with whatever degree of collusive participation by the patients) were all treatment failures. Two of these cases ended in the patients' deaths: Peter Pan, with 3 years of psychoanalysis, finally committed direct suicide, though not till after a total of 11 years of unavailing therapeutic effort; and the Car Salesman, with 3½ years of psychotherapy, died by indirect suicide a year after the treatment termination. The other two of these four were also treatment failures, though not lethal failures-both patients ended in situations almost identical with those existing when they came to treatment. These were the Invalided Hypochondriac, whose therapy only lasted 4 months, and the Script Writer, whose analysis only lasted 8½ months. The two of the six whose treatments were disrupted by parental pressures—the Adolescent Grandson, whose grandfather halted the treatment after 1 year and 9 months, and the Bohemian Prep School Boy, whose father halted the treatment after 7 months— had equivocal outcomes, with some stabilization and some minimal betterment of their psychological functioning (without additional treatment) by the time of Follow-Up Study.

Not all treatments succumb, of course, to the interferences of family members. What have been recounted to this point are the six instances where such interference (in every case, colluded with to some varying but significant extent by the patients' own conflicted neurotic pressures) led, in conjunction with other unfavorable circumstances, to prematurely ruptured treatments and most unhappy treatment outcomes. Two other instances have been described with our population where adverse family pressures (by the husbands) existed, but did not significantly compromise the results ultimately achieved. One was the case of the Adoptive Mother, whose 3-year psychoanalysis terminated when it did ostensibly under pressure from her husband ("orders from headquarters"), who was insisting that they move to undertake his lifetime professional practice in their city of choice. It was also clear, however, that the patient had successfully resisted just such pressures at prior junctures, when she had been intent on her therapeutic need and therapeutic commitment. She allowed herself to be persuaded by her husband to leave the treatment only at the point where she felt content that she had achieved her desired therapeutic gain; she wanted to have reason to get out at this point and "quit while she was ahead," in order to ward off further analytic exploration and its highly disturbing potential. The situation was somewhat similar with the Snake Phobia Woman, who had the difficult "weekend marriage," being with her husband and family in her home town on weekends, and in Topeka for psychoanalysis all week. This patient too maintained her treatment for 2½ years when she was intent upon it, despite the difficult realities of the "weekend marriage" and the constant anti-treatment pressures of the husband. She let it be drawn to a close by these pressures only when she too had achieved her desired therapeutic gains and wanted to avoid further analytic explorations, for much the same reasons as the Adoptive Mother. Both these patients had reason to feel very substantially satisfied with their treatment achievements, despite the fact that each treatment terminated at a point sooner than the analyst felt optimal, and purportedly in response to strong pressures from the husband that the patient felt unwilling to counter.

Treatment Failures and "Untreatable" Patients

CHARACTERISTICS OF THE FAILED CASES

In the total PRP population of 42, 11 of the cases (just over 25%) were adjudged overall to be failed cases—6 of the 22 who started in psychoanalysis and 5 of the 20 who started in psychotherapy; 7 of the 21 men and 4 of the 21 women. As has been emphasized throughout this book, this finding must be viewed within the context of the "sicker than usual" patients taken into intensive psychotherapy and psychoanalysis at The Menninger Foundation, and of the "heroic indications" for such treatments, for which the psychoanalytic sanatorium has seemed to provide the logical locus of trial and of application. These 11 failed cases therefore included 8 of the 15 severely alcoholic PRP patients, 4 of the 8 severely drug-addicted patients, and 8 of the 14 significantly paranoid patients. This group of alcoholic, drug-addicted, and/or paranoid patients, as might be expected, clustered together among those who developed psychotic transference reactions; the 11 failed cases included 7 of the 12 who developed this psychotically regressive transference response (in 9 instances within psychoanalysis and in 3 instances within psychotherapy). In addition to the 7 whose treatment failures took place within the context of a psychotic transference unfolding, 3 others were in the group of 4 adjudged to be essentially untreatable within any available or known psychotherapeutic approach.[1] The 11th failure, who neither developed an unfolding transference psychosis nor was considered inherently untreatable, was the extraordinarily difficult Sociopath whose whole treatment plan (which he successfully manipulated) was totally inadequate to his treatment needs. Perhaps he should have been declared among the "untreatables."

DEATHS FROM MENTAL-ILLNESS-RELATED CAUSES

General Comments

Among these 11 treatment failures, it has been repeatedly mentioned that six (one-seventh of the entire sample of 42) died of mental-illness-related causes either while still in treatment at The Menninger Foundation, or afterward while still in the line of treatment (somewhere) or of struggle against treatment. Although these patients have been referred to in a variety of contexts, they are discussed here specifically in relation to their treatment failure and the precipitants of their deaths. The six were the Alcoholic Heir, the Alcoholic Doctor, the Suspended Medical Student, the Addicted Doctor, the Car Salesman, and Peter Pan. Five were men; the one woman, Peter Pan, was also the only younger adolescent patient in the group (she was 19 when she came for treatment). Four were taken into psychoanalysis (good examples of "heroic indications"), and two, the Addicted Doctor and the Car Salesman, were taken into psychotherapy. (The latter are the only two of the project patients whose treatment courses have not been described yet, and they are therefore described in detail under this heading.)

Three of the six—the Alcoholic Doctor, the Addicted Doctor, and the Suspended Medical Student—were physicians (a striking finding), and they were three of the five physician patients in the PRP population. Two of these three were among those in the alcoholic–addicted–paranoid group who were taken into psychoanal-

---

1. See pp. 405–412 for the description of the fourth so-called "untreatable patient," the Sexual Masochist. Seen in some ways as the sickest and the unlikeliest patient in the entire PRP population, he nonetheless was treated (surprisingly) to a point of moderate treatment gain and seeming stabilization, under the combined influence of a transfer of the transference (to his wife) and an established status as a "therapeutic lifer."

ysis; the Alcoholic Doctor developed a full-blown psychotic transference regression in the course of it, and the Suspended Medical Student mostly staved off such a regression while in the analysis, only to succumb after treatment to a progressive paranoid decompensation. The third of the physicians who died, the Addicted Doctor, also alcoholic and addicted, but not paranoid, was one of that cluster of probably untreatable patients. Curiously, the other two physicians in the project sample, who by contrast did very much better in their treatment courses, seemed comparably ill on initial presentation. One of these was the Manic–Depressive Physician, with a psychotic character structure and given to the most explosive violent outbursts, who nonetheless achieved very good improvement in the course of his supportive psychotherapy built around reality testing and re-educational components (see pp. 460–466). The other of these was the Medical Scientist, as severely alcoholic and addicted a patient as any in the project, but not paranoid, and with the prognostically favorable history of intense (though unsuccessful) self-cure efforts. He achieved probably the very best improvement of all the project cases in the course of his psychoanalysis (see pp. 266–271).

Also, in summary of the six who died, it should be noted that four were in the group who in their psychoanalyses developed or struggled against psychotic transference decompensation (the Alcoholic Heir, the Alcoholic Doctor, the Suspended Medical Student, and Peter Pan); the other two were among the total of four adjudged essentially untreatable, and were in psychotherapy, not analysis (the Addicted Doctor and the Car Salesman). Two of the six were among the six discussed in the preceding chapter in connection with treatment disruptions by external pressures. With Peter Pan, as noted, the fiancé's persistent negative pressures upon the treatment induced the patient to decide, first, to leave her analyst in Topeka, and then to leave her second analyst in order to marry him and opt for cure by love rather than by understanding. Unfortunately, this did not prevent the advancing psychotic decompensating process. With the Car Salesman, his wife's negative pressures, less insistent than in the case of Peter Pan, nonetheless played their role in the various decisions to leave treatment and move on that punctuated the patient's treatment career.

Here the circumstances leading to each patient's death are focused on in the order of length of overall treatment course.

The Alcoholic Heir

The Alcoholic Heir was in an unsuccessful effort at psychoanalysis for 1 year. He was the severe alcoholic patient whose alcoholic decline progressed as he advanced along his preordained path in the giant scientific–industrial enterprise of which his father had been a major executive (the case of the "success neurosis"), and who had an almost equally alcoholic wife ("We're just a pair of old drunks"). As described earlier (see pp. 345–349), the analysis took a grossly paranoid turn, both within the analysis itself and in relation to his wife (who he feared intended to use a "jeweled ice pick" or a purchased gun against him); the treatment was disrupted when the analyst took a firm stand that periods of outpatient treatment had grossly failed and that the analysis could only go on with the patient's commitment to concomitant full hospitalization.

The follow-up period (punctuated by only one 2-week period of rehospitalization for alcoholic collapse) lasted but 6 months. At that point, the drunk patient called a physician, complaining of feeling ill for a week with headache and backache. He had evidence of bilateral lower-lobe pneumonia and probable delirium tremens. Upon hospital admission, the patient sank rapidly into stupor, with meningismus and focal neurological signs. Lumbar puncture revealed an acute purulent pneumococcal meningitis. After massive antibiotic therapy, the patient's meningeal, pulmonary, and other signs all improved. Nonetheless, he never regained consciousness; he went steadily downhill and died after 4 days. With his massive uncontrolled alcoholism, his poor nutrition, the low ebb of his resistance, and a massive infection probably consequent to alcoholic exposure, the patient's death can be counted an indirect suicide.

The Addicted Doctor and His Treatment

BACKGROUND AND PROGNOSIS

The Addicted Doctor (one of the two whose treatment course has not yet been described) came to psychiatric treatment on referral by the state board of medical examiners, which had revoked his medical license because of severe and incapacitating chronic barbiturate addiction. The patient had grown up with an alcoholic, improvident father, and an often bedridden hypochondriacal mother. He married twice (with children of each marriage), but during both marriages he had ongoing affairs with other women, as well as periodic homosexual relationships. As an adult, he developed both grand mal epilepsy and migraine; once, in a seizure, he dislocated a shoulder and required three open reductions. The patient dated his drug addiction to the convalescent period following his surgery, when sedatives and narcotics were prescribed for pain. The second wife said that his intense drug taking predated the surgery by 2 years. Prior to coming to The Menninger Foundation, the patient had had several hospitalizations, including at the Federal Narcotics Center, for drug addiction; he was involved with a plethora of drugs (barbiturates, bromides, codeine, Demerol); and he was enveloped in intense marital strife, with cross-accusations of infidelity and threats of divorce. It was his colleagues in the local medical society who pushed the events that led to his licensure revocation and the referral to The Menninger Foundation.

COURSE OF THE THERAPY AT THE MENNINGER FOUNDATION

As noted earlier (see pp. 141–142), the patient seemed cheerful and contented with his hospitalization, where he could abdicate adult responsibilities and be his "real self"—a playful, self-centered youngster. He could play practical jokes, such as dropping lumps of ice into the blouses of female aides on a picnic. Meanwhile, his wife went back to work as a nurse to support the two children.

The patient was in his first treatment, supportive psychotherapy at The Menninger Foundation, for not quite a year (102 hours). For a variety of reasons—the desire not to entrench the patient's dependent gratifications further, and to enable him to secure financially necessary gainful employment as a pathologist in the protected state hospital setting—the patient was out of the hospital after only 2 months and in outpatient psychotherapy throughout. All through, the therapy was focused principally on the patient's immediate difficulties in the handling of day-to-day "reality problems" (giving up drugs, paying his bills, covering his checks, etc.). The patient was repeatedly encouraged to bring decisions and actions to the therapy for discussion before he embarked on them, and he sporadically did so. The patient said, "I'd come in screaming about wanting a divorce or leaving home and he'd say 'No! Let's settle down and wait.'" There was a good deal of this kind of direct advice giving: "Maybe it would be better if you paid more attention to the backlog of daily work that needs to be done, instead of to all those changes you want to make in the lab," or (often) "Why don't you just throw out those pills you have around the house?"

The patient's life throughout this treatment course was never under effective control. The patient carried on extramarital affairs alongside his marriage. He lived beyond his means, and when he could not afford the down payment on a house they had bought, he manipulated his wife into forcing her parents to come to the rescue by mortgaging their home in order to raise the down payment for this one. The patient's only regret about this was that his own father had not come through and put up the money; it had to be his wife's family. There were endless problems in his job: of paying for his treatment, of fending off loan sharks, of desisting from taking drugs, of keeping at work. The therapist tried heroically to keep in touch with (and on top of) each of these situations that could threaten to undermine the patient's treatment, his marriage, or his job. The patient constantly withheld and lied, but so clumsily that he would be discovered, to which he would respond with "Well, you caught me again." The drug taking continued throughout the treatment. On occasion, the patient came to hours so drug-intoxicated that he was almost incoherent, but he would stoutly deny any drug intake. Within the transference, the patient expected an admixture of rescue, control, and punishment. In turn, he tried to provoke each of these. Basically he felt justified in all his inordinate demandingness — in getting anything whatever that he could from the parent figure, by hook or by crook.

DISRUPTION OF THERAPY

This treatment ended with a grave suicide attempt. Over time, the patient was feeling increasingly pushed to the wall. His wife was more and more hostile to him, and he felt frozen out of his home, being made to sleep in the basement. He was in increasing arrears at his work; when he did not respond to several warnings, he was finally abruptly dismissed from his hospital job. In his therapy, the patient said he had quit and had taken another, better job in another hospital, which he talked about enthusiastically and in great detail. He regularly left home each morning to go to this "new job" and made false entries in his checkbook to indicate salary payments. When his wife inevitably uncovered the deception, there was a stormy argument. The day after the fight with his wife, at the precise time that he was due for his therapy hour, the patient took 40 Seconal pills and drove off in his car, expecting to fall unconscious, perhaps to hit someone. He said afterward, "It was either my life or the therapy and the two couldn't be together." The patient was found unconscious in his car and was rushed to a general hospital, where he remained in coma for 30 hours. An emergency tracheotomy and the use of an iron lung were necessary to save his life, but he then recovered without any discernible harmful physiological sequelae. As soon as it was safe to do so, the patient was transferred as an inpatient to the local affiliated state hospital, terminating his psychotherapy at The Menninger Foundation.

FURTHER TREATMENT, DECLINE, AND DEATH

The patient remained an inpatient at the state hospital up to the time of his death from the next (and this time successful) suicide attempt with a Nembutal overdose 2½ years later. For most of that period and up to the very end, he was in psychotherapy with a therapist at The Menninger Foundation who employed the "Aichhorn technique," placing himself on the patient's side in the face of a hostile world. The therapist as inquisitor was thus replaced by the therapist as ally and coconspirator. The various ways in which the patient manipulated his position as a doctor to win extra privileges, to be the buffer between patients and staff, to be covered for his delinquencies, to engage in a large-scale contraband drug traffic, and to have major drug caches stashed away in the hospital and in his home (about which his wife did nothing) have already been recounted in detail (see pp. 225–226, 259). Clearly, while he was a hospital inpatient, the patient's whole pattern of symptoms and (mis)behaviors continued almost as before; hospitalization hardly curbed them in the way it was intended to do. His drug taking, his extravagant spending of more money than he seemed able to afford, and his promiscuous romances all continued, hardly abated.

The patient's wife's posture in the face of all this had two opposed dimensions. On the one hand, she seemed to support the patient's efforts to flout all controls and to be at home from the hospital as much as possible. She needed him around the house, and she felt as critical as he of the doctors and their ineffectual efforts to help. She indicated that she didn't think they knew what they were doing; she would have used ECT which would have snapped him out of his illness. And she was very lackadaisical in handling the patient's drug storing and drug using. At the same time, her bitterness and disillusionment with the patient himself were growing. She had been shocked that a major source of medical income for the patient had been the many illegal abortions he had performed. She had been frightened that once, when she was visiting him when he had been working in the hospital as a pathologist, he had tried to have her detained and committed as a mental patient. She had thought and threatened divorce a number of times, but had withdrawn each time in the face of the patient's violent upset. Just a month before his suicide, she finally served him divorce papers.

Within the therapy—this time handled quite differently, and also now on an inpatient basis—the same cycle seen in the first effort repeated itself. This therapy too began in a flush of enthusiasm, only to be finally pervaded by a sense of helpless discouragement, and for much the same reasons. Things came to a head with the wife's divorce filing, coupled as well with the pending loss of the therapist, who was planning to leave the hospital staff. The patient's desperate response to the pressures of this double blow was to hand in his 10-day notice for release from the hospital. He was informed that he was in no position (or condition) for this step; that he needed to stay in the hospital and continue his therapy; and that his therapist's plans had altered and the therapist would not be leaving the hospital staff after all. But, for the patient, it was too late: He felt boxed in, having handed in his notice. He went to his last therapy hour, concealing that he had handed in the discharge notice, and seemed unusually cheerful. He then wrote three letters (one to his parents, one to his wife, one to the ward doctor—none to the therapist), indicating that life without his wife was unbearable. He took a large dose of Nembutal at bedtime and was found dead in his hospital bed in the morning; in contrast to the Alcoholic Heir's death this was a *direct* suicide. The patient's parents indicated to his wife that they did not wish his body returned for burial in the family cemetery plot; it was rather "her problem" to handle as she saw fit.

COMMENTS

Two intensive treatment efforts thus successively failed. The first therapist did not have the help of a concomitant behavior-controlling hospitalization to support the therapeutic activity. The second therapist was backed by hospitalization, but the patient manipulated the hospital control so that it was almost totally ineffective, while the therapist (as part of his technique) kept himself relatively isolated from the hospital context and avoided using its potential both for control and for information. And the wife, for her part, too often abetted the patient's dangerous and sick behaviors rather than posing a barrier to them. Given the depth of the patient's illness picture and his self-destructiveness, one can also feel that no treatment plan (no matter how well the ingredients might be put together and implemented) had much to offer him.

The Car Salesman and His Treatment

BACKGROUND AND PROGNOSIS

The Car Salesman (the last patient to be described in detail) was referred for psychiatric treatment after a serious suicide attempt with barbiturates, in the context of severe alcoholism and a progressively impaired work capacity over many years. The patient's father, a highly successful manager of an automobile agency, was a cold and withholding man. The alcoholic mother was possessively overprotective. The patient had grown up with a "sweet disposition"; he had been a "good boy" who avoided drinking, smoking, and sexual experiences. He said that this was because his father had offered him $1000 if he would not drink or smoke before he was 21. At 22, the patient began a life of heavy drinking, smoking, and callous sexual promiscuity. The marriage he entered was stormy from the start, with much talk of divorce, and one actual divorce followed by remarriage within a month. There were chronic financial difficulties, compounded by the patient's drinking and his wife's extravagances. Most of the patient's working life was spent in his father's employ, and this was beset by constant quarrels. Occasionally he would break away in anger and attempt to strike out independently in another job, but he could never retain these positions and would return contritely to his father. He went on periodic drinking sprees, spending large sums on liquor and expensive prostitutes, chartering planes for special flights across the country. These sprees would characteristically end with a remorseful call back to his wife, who would fetch him home and nurse him back to a state of well-being.

Over the years, the patient suffered many hypochondriacal complaints. He was preoccupied with his body sensations, often checked his pulse and temperature, and was given to self-medication. There were several hospitalizations for acute alcoholism as well, on one of which he was given ECT and insulin treatment. As his father was finally about to retire, the patient was concerned as to whether the company would allow him to succeed to the dealership. The company was reluctant to grant this, and the father, concerned about his son's irresponsibility and alcoholism, was reluctant to push it with the company. While this situation was coming to a head, the patient, when drunk, made a suicide attempt with all the barbiturates he found in the medicine cabinet (26 pills). He was unconscious for 24 hours; shortly after this episode, he was brought to The Menninger Foundation.

The treatment recommendation was for the patient and his family to move to Topeka to live and work, and for the patient to have outpatient supportive–expressive psychotherapy (for fear that hospitalization would unduly play into the patient's strong dependency strivings). These recommendations were followed willingly.

COURSE OF THE THERAPY AT THE MENNINGER FOUNDATION

The patient was in treatment at The Menninger Foundation (in three specific periods) over a span of 3½ years (249 hours).[2] The first treatment period, during which the therapist tried to combine an expressive, uncovering approach with an authoritative and direct effort to control the patient's impulses and behaviors, lasted a year. During this period the patient secured and then quit a job as a car salesman, secured and held a job as a liquor salesman, and finally felt emboldened enough to leave treatment at the 1-year mark in order to go out again to seek an auto dealership of his own. Within that same week the patient's father died; i.,stead of investing in a dealership, since "the situation didn't look good," the patient took his immediate inheritance and went off on a manic spree marked by extravagant spending and sexual adventures (but no drinking). Within 4 months he was back for therapy, severely depressed. This time the therapy lasted 8 months, with no recurrence of drinking, until the patient was again off, further away still, to try for another dealership. And this time he was back within 2 months, with resumed drinking, impulsive spending, marked depression, and four abortive suicidal efforts. The third treatment was a 10-month hospital stay, with a strongly supportive relationship with a hospital doctor and no formal psychotherapy. This treatment, too, the patient left precipitously—this time against the strong advice of his doctor, but urged on by the wife, who had not come to Topeka for the third treatment period.

Throughout these three treatment periods, the patient suffered conflicting family pressures. He often felt caught between the requirements of his therapy and the narcissistic demands of his wife. She often taunted him, quoting her uncle to the effect "that she was still a very attractive woman and certainly could win the affection of a man who could offer her considerably more than her husband seemed to be offering her." During this whole time, the mother was the financially respon-

---

2. Again, this was one of those instances where the research evaluation group felt that, despite the justified concerns of the clinical evaluators, the recommended psychotherapy should have started within the framework of a preparatory prolonged period of hospitalization if it were to have any significant chance of success.

sible relative paying all treatment expenses. She had no use for her daughter-in-law, feeling the wife to be largely responsible for the patient's troubles.

Material of the therapeutic sessions centered mainly around the patient's current external life, and also the events of the treatment hours. Major characterological patterns manifest in the therapy, such as the patient's compliant propensities and his boringly repetitive long-windedness, were focused on. The patient once quoted his child interrupting one of his recitals to ask, "Daddy, will this take very long?", and this quotation was seized upon and used by the therapist on a number of occasions as a way of sharply confronting this trait. The patient in the therapy said that he "wanted to get well without being responsible for anything." Major themes that emerged for clarifying discussion during the course of all the therapy included (1) the patient's characterological compliance, preparing for his "school assignments" in order to please the therapist; (2) his endless obsessional preoccupations, intellectualizing rationalizations, and (as noted) boring long-windedness; (3) his marital troubles and squabbles, albeit with his own resentments against his wife kept under careful wraps; (4) his depressive trends, linked (by the therapist) to upsurges of hostile impulses; (5) his low frustration tolerance and self-destructive acting out; (6) his recurrent somatic complaints, which he used to justify such actions as quitting his first job; and (7) the ever-recurring wish to run away and break off treatment.

The treatment began and ended with the same transference pattern, with no shift and no unfolding. The therapist was the powerful father, whom the patient tried to please, with whom he had to be on good behavior, with whom he grew angry when frustrated, and toward whom he was fearful of evincing his hostilities. The patient was caught between an intense yearning to be guided and controlled, and a childish form of reactive assertiveness that prompted him to defy all direction. He had come to therapy hoping for an ideal parent, whose advice would always be forthcoming and correct, and whose approval would be unlimited. What he felt he found was a replica of his cold and disapproving father. While the patient and the therapist both felt that he had acquired a range of insights into his need for approval, his horror of responsibility, his desire to play the big shot, his difficulty in expressing anger, and so forth, these sounded to the research team like well-drilled clichés, drummed into him by the therapy, but not integrated into his functioning in any useful way.

The treatment was constantly marked by the patient's threats to leave, always as demonstrations of his independence; as stated, it was actually terminated on three separate occasions. The first two times, the therapist convinced himself that it was a gamble worth taking—a shared overestimation of the termination state of affairs within the patient. The third time, however, the termination tone was a mutually more discouraged one, and to the patient this ending was more clearly driven by external pressures from his wife.

FURTHER TREATMENT, DECLINE, AND DEATH

The patient died 12 months after leaving treatment at The Menninger Foundation; it was his wife who subsequently came for the Follow-Up Study interviews. It became clear that she had played an even larger role in the patient's treatment termination than had been realized at the time. He had left the hospital out of his wife's discouragement with his total treatment progress. For a while the patient tried to work at some salesman jobs in his new locale, but he did poorly at them. He and his wife were living extravagantly, quite beyond their means. He had quit alcohol but was on numerous drugs, and he concealed the drug taking from the new therapist he was now seeing. Soon the patient quit work and began to seclude himself, drugged, in his room for hours and days. He felt completely dependent and a complete failure. He decided finally to retire to Mexico, where he felt he could live more cheaply on his inherited money. His wife strongly supported this move, despite her knowing how heavily the patient was on drugs, and how freely these drugs could be purchased in Mexico without prescription.

Through the patient's terminal 6 months (in Mexico), he was yet again with another psychiatrist in a supportive psychotherapy marked by assurance, suggestion, and persuasion. The therapist was struck by the patient's evasiveness, impulsivity, and infantilism. The patient was heavily on alcohol and drugs and was often stopped for his drunken driving. Once he drove his car over an embankment into a lake. The main life problem was the constantly worsening relationship with his wife. The patient was becoming ever more openly dependent on her, and she was increasingly tiring of this. He was spending more time secluded in his room, losing weight and physically going downhill. Clearly disaster was close at hand, but the wife, out of her hopelessness and anger, did not actively intervene to get the patient hospitalized, or even to inform his therapist. "When I returned home after an evening out I noted that he was breathing heavily, but decided not to bother him. In the morning I found him dead." An empty barbiturate bottle was found in the room. Six months after the patient's death, the wife was remarried—to a psychiatrist.

COMMENTS

Like the Addicted Doctor, the Car Salesman, also heavily alcoholic and addicted, had a succession of treatment efforts (five in his case, three at The Menninger Foundation and two others in the subsequent year), including one within a hospital setting. All, however, were inadequate to his needs and to the depth of his illness picture and self-destructiveness. Each treatment termination consisted of a precarious flight into an unrealistic business venture and a highly stressful marriage; each represented the acting out of a neurotic pseudoindependence. When his wife tired of supporting him, began to press negatively against his treatment (especially hospital treatment in Topeka), and then finally just gave up on him, the patient slid into a drug–alcohol overdose—it was totally unclear how deliberate this was. As with the Addicted Doctor, it was not clear that any treatment plan or combination could have had much to offer him.

The Alcoholic Doctor

The other three patients who died had considerably longer treatment (and other supportive) contact. The Alcoholic Doctor was in an ultimately totally unsuccessful effort at psychoanalysis (described on pp. 332–336) for almost 7 years, up until the time of his death. Like the Alcoholic Heir, the Alcoholic Doctor also had an almost equally alcoholic wife (a fellow physician), with whom he got into drunken brawls and who was at times as depressed and suicidal as he. This patient seemed to be doing well in treatment while he was hospitalized and even afterward, while living alone and working in Topeka. It was after his wife joined him and they tried to establish their medical practices and a home together, as well as to bring their four children to live with them, that their life functioning began again to unravel. In the last 2 years of the patient's treatment (and life), he was living in a room at the hospital where he worked; he was there all his free time (drinking and taking drugs), except for his daily analytic hour and weekend trips to his wife at home (30 miles away). He had one brief hospitalization during this period for a toxic encephalopathy, and was also becoming increasingly depressed. He came to every analytic hour with the statement, "I want to die."

His death came suddenly, as described earlier (see p. 336). He became ill at work with an apparent flu, aching and vomiting, and was sent home. In midafternoon he spoke by phone with his wife, who detected nothing unusual. When she came home in the evening to prepare supper and tried to rouse the patient, he was cyanotic and dying; vigorous resuscitation efforts were unavailing. At autopsy, it was determined that the patient had died from a massive, forceful aspiration of vomitus. It was not clear how depressed and drugged the patient was that day, and how much his generally debilitated state, together with the weakening by the viral infection, had so blocked his reflexes as to allow the aspiration. Again, this can be counted as indirect suicide; the analyst called it "an unconscious suicide."

Peter Pan

Peter Pan's overall course ran 11 years until her death (see pp. 426–432). She came to treatment as a 19-year-old adolescent suffering a severe anorexia nervosa with regularly recurring episodes of bulimia, anorexia with starvation, and kleptomania (stealing food). She was in analysis at The Menninger Foundation for 3 years. As described earlier, she left under pressure from her boyfriend that she follow him to another city or risk losing him; she continued in analysis another 6 months in the new city and again left when she felt forced to choose between the analysis and marriage to her boyfriend. She and her husband were both buoyant at this termination point, feeling that she was now recovered and no longer needed treatment.

The subsequent course revealed the tragic error of this judgment. She came to Follow-Up Study 3 years after treatment, with many recurring problems and symptoms; however, she tried to put on a brave façade, and expressed open ambivalence about more treatment just then—perhaps later when they were both more settled in their joint academic careers. Another 4 years later, the progressive return of the whole original presenting psychopathological picture precipitated a serious suicide attempt and a return to therapy in her new city. This therapy lasted 10 months, was punctuated by six brief hospitalizations, and consisted often of daily therapy sessions plus many telephone calls and emergency contacts. With it all, the symptom picture worsened uncontrollably: Repeat psychological testing during one of the hospital stays revealed the advancing encroachment of a disorganizing psychotic process. The patient and her husband had by now separated; after another serious suicide attempt with barbiturates, from which the patient was saved when her husband unexpectedly came by to see her and found her comatose, the patient talked increasingly about commitment to a mental institution.

Shortly after a last hospitalization for depression, the patient finally successfully committed suicide by jumping off a bridge. Just before doing so, she sent her husband and other relatives farewell snapshots. In their last phone conversation, the husband had assured her of his continuing love, and "she could now die happy." Like the death of the Addicted Doctor, this was a very deliberate suicide.

The Suspended Medical Student

The last in this group of patients who died was the Suspended Medical Student, whose death took place 11½ years after his treatment start (see pp. 363–370). He came to psychoanalysis after being suspended from medical school because of his unethical behaviors with surgical patients while he was in alcohol-precipitated fugue states. The analysis went on for 4½ years; it ended when the patient had returned to medical school and was at the point of successful graduation. Both the analyst and the patient were very content with the treatment achievement.

Once launched on his medical career, however, the patient could not make it. Each effort at medical practice (and there were several) led to increasingly incapacitating drug intake, dangerously reckless driving, and improper medical behaviors, ending each time in a withdrawal to his parents' farm with "nervous exhaustion." Through all this period, the patient did not return for psychiatric treatment, but was supported and stabilized as best as possible by his mentor—a long-time friend and his family doctor, who had encouraged him to pursue a medical career in the first place. The patient finally broke with this mentor, and, against his advice, made another disastrous effort at medical practice. After that, he had no further direct psychological help of any kind; shortly thereafter, his wife moved finally to divorce him as well. Toward the end, again trying himself in solo practice, he was in constant trouble, antagonizing patients, fellow physicians, tradespeople, and the police. His bad professional judgments created medical difficulties from which the other local physicians had to rescue him. He was not accepted by the county medical society or on the staff of the local hospital. His erstwhile mentor thought him now clearly schizophrenic, a danger to medicine and his patients, but no one wanted to make a move toward revoking his medical license; the local doctors were content to make good his mistakes. Everyone was relieved when he finally totally gave up his efforts at practice.

The final event took place 7 years after the treatment termination. The patient went out for a little air one evening. It was not unusual for him to "prowl about at night," so he was not immediately looked for when he did not return. He had not seemed depressed. When he was found the next day, his car was parked off the road, the windows were closed, and the engine was still idling; the patient was dead, slumped over the wheel. Although the coroner ruled it a death from "coronary thrombosis," this was also a deliberate suicide, like the deaths of Peter Pan and the Addicted Doctor.

NONLETHAL TREATMENT FAILURES

In addition to these six patients who died—three of direct suicide, three of indirect suicide, over time spans ranging from 1½ to 11½ years after the treatment onset— five other patients also had failed treatments, but in their cases these did not end lethally. Their treatment courses have all been described, and the five are only mentioned briefly here. Three of the five fell into, or fled from, psychotic transference episodes; these were the Masochistic Editor, the Script Writer, and the Bitter Spinster. The Masochistic Editor and the Script Writer were both from the severely alcoholic–paranoid cluster, and their treatment fates were not unexpected in the context of how that whole group fared overall. (The Script Writer, in addition, was one of the six whose spouses exerted a negative and disruptive pressure upon the treatment course.) The Bitter Spinster, on the contrary, had one of the most unexpectedly negative treatment courses and outcomes in the whole PRP population (along with Peter Pan and the Suspended Medical Student, whose treatment courses ended even more tragically — lethally). She was thought to be an excellent candidate for psychoanalysis, but for financial reasons she had to go into an expressive psychotherapy, which (it was felt) could also be very helpful to her. Her psychotherapy went on over 8 years, during which time her life functioning progressively deteriorated and a psychotic transference reaction developed. When the dug-in transference impasse could be resolved no other way, the therapist ultimately pried the patient out of treatment by sending her to another psychiatrist, basically for termination counseling. The patient ended the treatment with bitterness, and during the follow-up period her life functioning constricted and declined further. She had the largest drop in HSRS assessment from Initial Study to Follow-Up Study of any patient in the whole PRP sample. Her therapist, incidentally, was one of the most senior and skilled at The Menninger Foundation.

In addition to these three with transference psychotic reactions, there were two other nonlethally failed cases. One was the Invalided Hypochondriac, who was adjudged to be essentially untreatable, and whose interfering husband proved unwilling to support the prolonged concomitant hospitalization and psychotherapy that might alone have given her some treatment chance. And the last was the Sociopath, probably also quite untreatable, who ensured his treatment failure by manipulating a collusive bargain; by remaining away and somehow afloat for a year, he extracted in return the commitment to a totally inadequate outpatient treatment plan, which just could not contain so malignantly psychopathic a character structure.

The Patients' Marital Families: Problems, Changes, and Treatments

Through the course of the case descriptions in this book (and in this section in particular), it has been abundantly evident that a significant, and at times an overriding, part of the manifest psychopathology of many of the patients was expressed in extremely difficult and conflicted family interactions (mainly of course with spouses, occasionally also with children). In addition, it has also been evident that the spouses were themselves most neurotically troubled individuals — at times, also, official psychiatric patients as well.[1] In this chapter, I want to summarize the PRP

---

1. I am not talking here of conflicted interactions within parental families. Given the nature of personality development and of neurotic illness, it goes without saying that difficult and conflicted upbringings and growing-up periods were ubiquitous in this as in all populations of neurotic patients. For the most part, however, our PRP patients came to us as adults, many married and with children. The neurotic entanglements with their parents were part of their historical development, their past, and no longer — in reality — significant

data about the marital families: the nature of the spouses and of the marital inter-actions; the changes in the marital families (marriage, divorces, and remarriages); and the psychiatric helping relationships that the spouses were in or got into over the span of the patients' treatment courses and follow-ups.

As stated in the demographic description of the patient population when they came to treatment (see p. 62), 19 of the 42 patients were married at that time; 1 was very recently traumatically widowed (the Tantrum Woman); 7 were di-vorced; and 15 had never married. The 15 never married included, however, the 8 who were still adolescents and students, as well as the one older patient (the Intellectual Fencer, aged 30) seen as also still caught up in adolescent emancipa-tion struggles. Only 6 came as clearly adults and, for varying reasons, unmarried. Of the 19 who came to their treatments married, 8 divorced over the project's span of observation. Three of those who divorced were remarried (to new spouses); also, 14 of the total of 23 who came to treatment unmarried did marry over this same span of observation. Adding the 3 divorces and remarriages, and the 14 who came unmarried and did marry during that time, we had under observation a total of 17 new marriages.

NEUROTIC PROBLEMS IN SPOUSES AND MARRIAGES

Putting together the 19 who came married plus the 17 who had new marriages makes a total of 36 marriages and marital interactions, the nature and fates of which we could follow over the project time period. (Since there was a divorce from a first spouse and a remarriage to a second in 3 instances, these 36 mar-riages covered 33 of the total 42 PRP population.) The degree of neurotic character and neurotic illness in these spouses was striking. Of the 36 marriages, in only 8 cases could one say that there was no evident neurotic problem or character discerned in the spouses or in the marital interactions from the side of the spouses. With the other 28, there were varying degrees of manifest neurotic difficulty and/or neurotic involvement with the patients, and in most of those cases to the point of warranting a psychiatric diagnostic designation.

Passive or Masochistic Accommodation to Patient's Illnesses

With a good number of those 28, the neurotic character of the spouses was simply an unduly passive or masochistically compliant character structure. This passivity or masochism often served the patients well, by giving them a more tolerant cushion within which their own neurotic illnesses could unfold and play themselves out,

---

in the ongoing present. Even those who came as younger patients, still caught up in independence strug-gles and other issues with their parental families, for the most part got out from under such entanglements (as reality issues) during the course of their therapies. The one significant exception was the aptly named Devoted Son, who came to psychoanalysis as a 32-year-old single man still closely tied to his parents, with whom he was spending every weekend in their nearby town. He was in analysis for 5½ years; when seen at official Follow-Up Study 2½ years after that, he still had a totally constricted social life, and his parents were still the salient relationship in his life. Needless to say, this patient's treatment result was considered very equivocal.

and within which also their treatments could be supported. Severely phobic patients like the Phobic Woman could command near-total environmental compliance (in her case, first from her parents and then especially from her husband); such compliance was what made it possible for these individuals to manage at all, both in sickness and in the treatment for it. For most of the phobic patients, constriction of the lives of their spouses (and, at times, of other family members) was a major part of the illness expression. It was the much rarer phobic who, like the Movie Lady, tried to live life as fully as possible despite the phobic anxieties, and who took pains to keep the phobias' encroachments upon the life space of the spouse minimal.

At times, of course, such passive or masochistic compliance was a double-edged sword, also operating to keep a patient out of needed treatment through the totally gratifying accommodation by the spouse to the requirements of the patient's neurotic illness. As long as the husband of the Bohemian Musician was willing to work at his business at home, and to support his wife in her aesthetic and intellectual life with her romantic lover in the distant big city, a tenable conflicted equilibrium existed for the patient. It was only when the husband tired of this and demanded that the patient either return to him or be divorced that she did return home; shortly thereafter, she collapsed into the acute disorganization that brought her to psychiatric treatment. Similarly, the Phobic Woman might not have come to treatment at all, except that the passive and easygoing husband began to rebel against the relentlessly increasing constriction of his life, and finally came to the point of threatening divorce unless something was done quickly to alter his wife's symptoms and the controls she exerted upon him.

It was often amazing to find out how much spouses were willing to endure out of their own neurotic (call it masochistic) involvements. The Sociopath met and courted his wife during the period when his whole life—built on deception, check forging, embezzlements, and gangster involvements—was publicly unraveling; the two were married 3 months *after* the public discovery of all the patient's malfeasances. It was not enough explanation for the wife to say that she "knew that he prevaricated" but that he was also "a convincing talker." During the course of the patient's treatment fiasco, as noted (see p. 547), the wife finally left to sue for divorce because she could no longer take all the pressure and strain of living with him. Even then, however, she declared that she still loved the patient and would be glad to return to him if he could extricate himself from his financial and legal jams, and if the therapist could assure her that the patient had at last become stabilized.

Another extreme accommodation came in the marriage that the Homesick Psychology Student entered into during the follow-up period. He and his new wife felt that they had a good marriage; they enjoyed their friends, their outings, their mutual community involvements, and so forth. The one (and continuing) problem in the marriage was the patient's extreme sexual inhibition. He had confided all his fears to his wife before the marriage, but she had firmly stated her willingness to give it a try. The try was never successful, and the marriage was never consummated because of the patient's extreme premature ejaculations. Though they were both bitterly disappointed by this, the wife was "taking it well," without overt complaint. Each time they would "give it a try" and not succeed, she would dismiss it with some philosophical remark. The wife professed optimism that the patient would work this all out, not through more psychotherapy, but through gradually building his confidence (see p. 420). She saw herself as providing the corrective experience that would gradually overcome his difficulty.

And the last in this account of extreme accommodations within marriages to be described here came in the second marriage of the project's very sickest patient, the Sexual Masochist. His first wife had finally divorced him (prior to his psychotherapy) when she was no longer able to tolerate living with his alcoholism and participating in his perversions (e.g., at his request, urinating or defecating on his face). In the course of his psychotherapy, during which most of his sexual involvements were casual pickups, the patient met his second wife, who from the first very tenaciously wanted to marry him and would not be dissuaded by all his vacillation, his expressed psychopathology, or even his outright refusals. The patient set many humiliating conditions to the marriage (see p. 408 for details); she assented to all of them. When, under such pressures, the patient would finally agree to a tentative wedding date, he would usually at such times turn to his lapsed therapy, for rescue from "the trap." He finally did marry this woman, however, and both he and his wife declared the marriage to be happy and successful. (The patient was often sexually impotent, but the wife minimized this. Sexual activity was mainly mutual masturbation, accompanied at times by talk of the patient's perverse fantasies.)

Active Participation in a Complementary Neurosis

With some of the patients, the neurotic involvement of their spouses was more than an accommodation; it became more an active participation in a complementary neurotic interaction powered by the neurotic needs of the participants. For example, the Heiress had lived before her analytic treatment in a masochistically compliant marriage with an exploitative, quite unstable, and even somewhat sadistic husband who was improvident and a philanderer, but who had appealed to her as a kind of romantic adventurer fighting for progressive ideas against entrenched interests. During the height of the patient's illness (with her disorganizing "turbulent periods"), this husband was maintaining himself and their four children on the patient's money—aided by two foreign nursemaids, with both of whom he had sexual liaisons. During her long treatment the patient was able to see the "neurotic need" that had driven her into her sadomasochistic partnership and to disentangle herself from this husband (actually, the husband divorced her for another woman). The patient was then able to remarry someone who seemed warm and friendly—a talented but financially quite unsuccessful musician and composer. In fact, this second marriage turned out more like the first than the patient had consciously bargained for. The second husband proved rigid and narcissistically self-preoccupied; he was a food and health faddist, with peculiar ideas and with uninformed (but loudly proclaimed) opinions, which he imposed on the patient and their friends in the form of long soliloquies. In an attenuated form, the patient was again caught up in similar sadomasochistic interactions, and she found herself fighting as bitterly with this husband as with the first.

A similar sadomasochistic interaction—this one more reciprocal, and directly in the sexual sphere—took place between the Obese Woman and her husband (they were subsequently divorced). The marriage was marked by open fights; these would then be made up, and the reconciliation would be capped by sexual relations in which the patient had to be hurt sexually in order to atone for her guilt feelings and to be sexually aroused. She accused herself of being "masochistic." In the analysis, it turned out that there was a mutual sadomasochistic perversion between the patient and her husband. They played a sex game in which the loser would be tied to the bed with rope during intercourse; they each enjoyed being the one tied up. They rationalized this game as an expression of their uninhibited sexuality.

Concordant Illness Pictures

There were considerably more instances where the illness pictures of the spouses were concordant rather than complementary, as in the sadomasochistic relationships of the Heiress and the Obese Woman. For example, both the Alcoholic Heir and the Alcoholic Doctor have been frequently mentioned as having just about equally sick and equally alcoholic wives, with whom they caroused and brawled. In both instances, the wives had been strongly urged into treatment for themselves, and in both cases, they refused. The Alcoholic Doctor's wife, incidentally, was the one who suggested that her husband's potency problem might be a reflection of latent homosexuality. She encouraged him not only to try out homosexual partners, but to bring the partners to live with them in the house so that they could all be together more. By contrast, the much quieter illness of the Fearful Loner—a lonely, inhibited, schizoid individual—was matched by his marriage during treatment to a woman much like himself. Together, they fitted into a compatible married life that did not shake the patient's fearful equilibrium in any way.

MARRIAGE TO OTHER MENNINGER FOUNDATION PATIENTS

Four of the PRP patients were actually married to other Menninger Foundation patients, for better or for worse. One of the sample, the Obedient Husband, had actually come to treatment when his wife (who was the prior patient) seemed to be improving, and he paradoxically found himself getting depressed; he feared that as his wife improved, she might no longer need him in the same ways. The patient's treatment went on for 1½ years until its favorable termination. The wife is still in ongoing treatment as of this writing (25 years later), as a true "therapeutic lifer."

The other three in this group married patients that they met at The Menninger Foundation. The severely alcoholic Medical Scientist, who achieved probably the best psychoanalytic result of any of the project patients, divorced a first wife with whom he had had a difficult marriage, and then courted and married a fellow patient—also alcoholic, also disentangling herself from a bad marriage, and also achieving a very good result in her own treatment. This marriage was enduring and successful, as were the treatments of the two partners. Much more problematic was the marriage of the very drug-addicted and homosexually oriented Intellectual Fencer to a fellow patient, severely alcoholic and openly homosexual. They both seemed to be doing reasonably well in their treatments, and in their marriage each intended to *fully* cure the other. (After her first sexual experience with the husband-to-be, this patient said triumphantly, "I slept with him and he's not homosexual.") And in identifying with her husband in the marriage role, she was also proving that her own homosexual proclivities could be surmounted as well, without the help of the therapist. This was the marriage that I have called a "pseudoheterosexual accommodation," in which each partner overcame manifest homosexual proclivities, but nonetheless fully enacted them on the fantasy level: This powerfully phallic-competitive woman found a submissively dependent man reenacting his pre-Oedipal anaclitic attachment to a nurturant mother figure. This marriage did not work out over the long run. The couple had a child, and several years later they divorced reasonably amicably. The patient was at this point "making it" (without treatment), as a woman with a child, but without a husband.

Finally, the elopement and marriage of the Exhibitionistic Dancer and an even sicker delinquent and narcissistic young man have already been described in detail. This was the marriage that was used to coerce a totally unsuitable outpatient treatment plan for both these young people. The marriage had the very briefest honeymoon period and became shortly a chaotic, brawling life, ending finally in a divorce less than 3 years later. The patient was left with a handsome financial settlement (from her very wealthy husband's family) and two small children. Her therapy was unsuccessful, and she was maintaining her functioning at Follow-Up Study, under the aegis of her intense involvement with Christian Science and a Christian Science practitioner.

Adverse Spouse Pressure on Treatment Course

In Chapter 26, I have described the four instances in which spouses, out of both their realistic and their neurotic entanglements, exerted adverse pressures on the patients' treatment courses that played very substantial roles in the premature treatment terminations and unsuccessful outcomes in each case. The Invalided Hypochondriac thus left treatment after 4 months, the Script Writer after 8½ months, Peter Pan after 3 years, and the Car Salesman after 3½ years. And, in Chapter 27, I have described those two instances among the six patients who died where the wives were sufficiently aware of the lethal course their husbands' lives were on and did not intervene to prevent this course. The Addicted Doctor's large contraband drug traffic at the state hospital where he was an inpatient has already been described in detail. Important in this present context was the fact that the wife knew of drug caches of up to 1000 barbiturate pills in the rafters of their home, and yet she took no action to control this danger. This was perhaps the culmination of the wife's progressive disillusionment and despair with a marriage in which she had long very masochistically borne an inordinate burden of suffering and exploitation. The patient did commit suicide with a drug overdose in his hospital bed. The other, quite comparable instance was with the severely alcoholic Car Salesman, whose Menninger Foundation treatment(s) (three attempts) had finally been aborted under the pressure of his wife's growing disillusionment, and who was living in Mexico (where sedative drugs could be easily obtained without prescription) at the time of his death a year into the follow-up period. At that time he was heavily on alcohol and drugs, and his wife paid no attention at the point that a (heavier than usual?) combined dosage was carrying the patient to his death. It was not clear how directly suicidal the patient's death was.

CHANGES IN MARITAL STATUS

Through the course of their treatments and follow-up periods, there were, as already indicated, many changes in the marital status of the patients and their often equally ill spouses. I have already indicated that, of the 19 of the PRP patients who came to treatment married, 8 divorced during the period of observation. Of these, 3 remarried and 5 did not. However, these 5 "unremarrieds" were not all in similar situations by any means. For example, the Obese Woman, when seen at Follow-Up Study, had a steady boyfriend and fiancé—a school music teacher and night club piano entertainer, whom she was hoping to marry just as soon as he got his own neurotic problems straightened out in his psychotherapy (he was quite passive–dependent, hypochondriacal, and inhibited). By contrast, the Divorced Nurse remained unhappily unmarried, raising her children and coping with an aging mother over a 20-year follow-up observational span. This was the patient whose long-drawn-out divorce struggle and custody litigation was the central unhappy life event that clouded her whole analysis. She was also the patient whose analysis in a setting that removed her from her usual and ongoing life interactions with her husband could not help set the failing marriage aright, or reverse the husband's push to divorce, as the patient had come to treatment desperately hoping. Whether analysis conducted with the patient living at home with her husband would have had a different outcome, which would have included saving the marriage, is of course not at all certain; it could, however, have had a better chance to do so.

Counting the 3 patients who divorced during treatment and entered new marriages, plus the 14 of the 23 who came to treatment unmarried and then married during the span of treatment and official follow-up observation, there were 17 new marriages (40% of the population of 42) consequent to the treatment courses. But of the 17 new marriages, 3 in turn broke up during this same period. The Exhibitionistic Dancer, within 3 years, divorced the even sicker hospital patient with whom she had defiantly eloped from the hospital. The Intellectual Fencer also married a fellow patient in a mutual overcoming of addiction and homosexuality; this marriage held together some 5 years. Finally, the Suspended Medical Student was married (not to a patient) during his seemingly successful psychoanalytic treatment, and the marriage lasted 5 years across the period of the patient's progressive total collapse. When his wife, who was having more and more difficulty in coping with the patient's constant drug taking to the point of incoherence, his wildly reckless automobile driving, and his totally irresponsible behaviors, could take this situation no longer and finally left him, his mother nonetheless said of it that "out of the blue, with no warning whatsoever, his wife . . . walked out on him. Unbeknownst to any of us, she had started divorce proceedings. This was a terrific blow." Clearly, of these three treatment-linked marriages and divorces, the failures in the first two of them (but not the third) reflected the psychopathology of the spouses almost as much as that of the patients. Both the Exhibitionistic Dancer and her husband were hospital inpatients; both of them were behaviorally disturbed, delinquent, and narcissistic. Similarly, both the Intellectual Fencer and her husband were psychotherapy patients who had begun with long hospital stays. Both of them were severely addictive, and both were homosexual (the husband more blatantly than the patient).

Since 14 of the 17 new marriages endured, and since 11 of the 19 who came to treatment married remained that way, there were a total of 25 patients married at the end of the official follow-up periods, as compared with 19 at the start of treatment. The 17 now unmarried included 5 of the originally married patients who had divorced and had not remarried, the 3 from the new marriages that had broken up, and 9 patients who had come to treatment unmarried and remained that way. These 9 included 3 who had once been married but came to treatment divorced and 6 who had never been married; they included some who came quite urgently seeking to be able to get married (the Economist and the Silent Woman), and several who instead became confirmed homosexuals (the Actress, the Rebellious Coed, and the Masochistic Editor).

Finally, counting the 11 of the 19 who came to treatment married and remained that way, plus the 9 who came unmarried and remained that way, a total of 20 of the 42 (almost half) had *no* change in their marital status through the course of their treatments and their official follow-ups. The other 22 did change their marital status—some more than once—with a total of 17 marriages, 8 divorces, 3 remarriages following the 8 divorces, and 3 divorces of the new marriages. Thirteen of the patients had a total of 21 new children during and immediately after their treatment periods, 4 of them in their original marriages and 9 in their new marriages. Two of these were the adopted children of the Adoptive Mother, whose inability to keep an adopted child had been the central element in the patient's original coming to psychoanalysis. The successful adoption of the two children during and right after the follow-up period represented the cherished fulfillment of the wishes that had brought her to treatment, and were to her, the chief mark of the (to her) very successful analytic outcome.

TREATMENTS RECEIVED BY SPOUSES AND CHILDREN

Given that there was so much psychopathology in its own right within the spouses of the patients in the PRP population, and given as well the problems in living with these very sick patients that so many of the spouses had, it should be no surprise that among the 33 patients of the 42 who either were married when they came for treatment, or got married during the course of their treatment or in its immediate aftermath, in 15 of these 33 cases (45%) the spouses got into or were already in some kind of concomitant psychotherapeutic or intensive casework counseling helping situation. Because of the particular kind of "psychotherapeutic climate" that flourished in and around The Menninger Foundation psychiatric community, and the strong focus (mentioned at a number of points) on ongoing work with the families of patients, this figure is of course probably larger than it would be with the "usual" psychotherapeutic and psychoanalytic (outpatient) practice.

Casework and Joint Marital Counseling

The 16 spouses of the 15 patients who had such help (with one patient, the Medical Scientist, both the wife he divorced and the one he subsequently married received it) ranged across a whole spectrum in regard to intensity and focus of the help.

Some spouses (e.g., the wives of the Sociopath and the Addicted Doctor) specifically had intensive casework designed both to help them with their own constant problems within their very difficult marriages, and to help the patients' treatments by serving as an independent avenue of access to an accounting of their life activities.

With other spouses, the help they received was jointly attended marriage counseling, either apart from or as part of the patients' ongoing individual treatments. In the case of the Heiress and her second husband, this marriage counseling (during the follow-up period and with someone other than the patient's ex-analyst) was short-lived and unsuccessful. This marriage had become much more troubled as time went on. The husband, as noted (see p. 576), proved to be very rigid, suspicious, aloof, opinionated, unsuccessful in his music, and argumentative. The patient, for her part, was experiencing the return of anxiety, of drinking, and of intrusive masochistic sexual fantasies as she fought with this new husband over their relationship, over her children from the first marriage, and over their own new infant. Though divorce was unthinkable to the husband, to the patient "the idea of divorce is almost constantly in my mind." At the patient's insistence, and with the threat that otherwise she would institute divorce proceedings, they had gone jointly to a marriage counselor. Much of their time there centered around their struggles over the raising of the new baby. The husband finally broke it up, accusing the counselor of always siding with his wife because she paid the bills. At subsequent follow-up contact (5 years later), it turned out that this couple was still locked in a stormy marriage—once, when drunk, the patient had chased the husband with a knife and hammer—and that they were now seeing a marriage counselor regularly.

More positive was the case of the Sexual Masochist, considered among the group of "untreatable patients," who had terminated his seemingly utterly failed drug-ridden treatment by simply stopping coming, and who had gotten into his second marriage only because his new wife masochistically agreed to the most humiliating of marriage conditions. By Follow-Up Study, however, the patient, his life, and his marriage were all now restabilized at some level of equivocal improvement and marginal functioning by way of a joint return of the patient *and* his wife for conjoint family counseling and family therapy with the patient's original therapist. On the basis that this was jointly addressed to the problems of each with the other, and within the marriage, the therapy was acceptable to the patient. The overall situation was stabilized, albeit with the expectation that the couple, together, had now become "therapeutic lifers."

Therapy for Spouses' Own Problems

With some of the spouses, their psychological help was specifically in the form of psychotherapy entered into for their own problems, and not necessarily just in connection with the problems in the marriage. The husband of the Snake Phobia Woman was very unsympathetic toward her analysis while she was in it, constantly created financial pressures upon the treatment by being delinquent in meeting the treatment bills, and exerted an unremitting pressure to hasten the treatment termination. Nonetheless, during *her* follow-up period, he entered a once-a-week psychotherapy of his own, which lasted 1½ years and from which he felt he was much benefited. He had gone into it in part because of chronic and annoying marital problems, but just as much because of his own dissatisfactions in not achieving the business success and stability that he always seemed just short of. In his therapy, he worked both on his problems with a domineering father and on the discordant marriage relationship. He confessed that from his side, his treatment had "saved the marriage."

Others of the spouses, as noted earlier in this chapter, were Menninger Foundation patients in their own right. The sick, delinquent young husband of the Exhibitionistic Dancer, who joined her in the ill-fated elopement and marriage, was one such; the alcoholic and homosexual husband of the Intellectual Fencer, who joined her in the mutual endeavor to cure each other of like difficulties, was another; the recovering alcoholic second wife of the recovering alcoholic Medical Scientist, who went on with him toward two established cures and a highly successful marriage, was still another. All three of these were marriages entered into by individuals who met when they were Menninger Foundation patients—in two of the instances (the Exhibitionistic Dancer and the Medical Scientist), patients of the same therapist. In another case, (an extreme and probably the record in some respects), that of the Obedient Husband, it was the far sicker wife who was the patient initially; the husband only went into treatment because of his paradoxical anxiety and disturbance as his wife seemed to be improving and seemed to be needing his support and caretaking less. The patient's psychotherapy lasted only 18 months and terminated with a very substantial improvement. By contrast, at this writing, 23 years after his treatment termination, the wife, a chronically disabled individual, is still in her treatment at The Menninger Foundation, being seen regularly once a month. The couple has lived in Topeka all these years, and the husband has, by now, become indeed her chronic supporter and caretaker, since he is now retired and she has become wheelchair-bound with crippling arthritis.

Though so many spouses were receiving some form of psychiatric help, this was still far from as many as could have profited from it and for whom it was strongly recommended. No help was obtained in some instances where the need seemed the very greatest, from the point of view of the evident psychopathology of the spouses and/or the sickness of the patients, and the constant destructive pressures upon the marriages. There were 7 instances among the 18 patients whose spouses were not in an ongoing helping situation where help was strongly urged (usually both through the patients and in consultation sessions with the spouses), and where the recommendations were firmly declined. Two of these have been mentioned a number of times in different contexts—the almost equally sick and equally alcoholic wives of the Alcoholic Heir and the Alcoholic Doctor. In both instances, the husbands were among those who died of mental-illness-related causes, and their wives were subsequently lost to follow-up.

Children in Treatment

Lastly, in this connection, there should be mention of the number of children of these patients who entered psychotherapy, to the extent that we knew of it within the limited follow-up observation spans for so many of the patients. This number came to 8 children of 6 of the patients; no doubt, however, this is a considerable undercount that could be corrected if there were a truly comprehensive long-term follow-up (25–30 years) covering *all* of the patients. Two of these situations are used here to illustrate the issues.

With the young, recently widowed Tantrum Woman, at the time that her own affect storms were at their height in the analysis (and spilling over into uncontrolled angry outbursts at the children), her older child, a girl aged 3, developed temper tantrums, crying spells, and transitory conversion symptoms. The difficult relationship between the two of them was reminiscent to the patient of her own difficult childhood relationship to *her* mother. The child was brought to psychiatric evaluation and then entered into what became a long-continued psychotherapy. A few years later, the younger child, a boy, asthmatic and somewhat fearful, entered into a "companionship therapy" designed to introduce male figures into his life for him to relate to and identify with. The children seemed to do well in their treatments (just as their mother made continuous progress), and shortly after the mother ended treatment, they were able to end theirs. At that point, the patient's relationship with her children was much improved; she was more understanding and relaxed, and no longer readily provoked to angry outbursts. In the light of the patient's overall limited finances (as a self-supporting young widow), her fees had been systematically reduced when it became indicated to bring the children into treatment as well.

Six months after the onset of the psychotherapy of the Obedient Husband, his older son, aged 7, entered psychotherapy. The patient at first strenuously opposed this, "because I felt that his bad points would reflect back on me." The boy's symptoms were behavior outbursts and hyperactivity; he was felt to suffer from some organic brain damage, a mild cerebral palsy, and concomitant emotional disturbance. With simultaneous casework guidance for both parents (alongside the individual psychotherapy they were each in), the patient became both less harsh and inconstant in managing his son's behaviors, and began to spend more time with him and his activities (Cub Scouts, swim lessons, Sunday School, etc.). This psychotherapy for the son totaled 309 hours over 3½ years (as contrasted with 1½ years and only 124 hours for the father) and was just terminating at the time of the patient's Follow-Up Study. The mild cerebral palsy was very minimally limiting, and there had been considerable improvement in the passive–aggressive and angry destructive behaviors. It is the mother, the patient's wife, who (as has just been indicated) is still in continuing treatment more than two decades later.

VIII

The Follow-Up Courses and Outcomes

Overviews

Follow-Up in General: Observation Spans and Degree of Cooperation Obtained

THE SPANS OF OBSERVATION

PRP has been very fortunate, and perhaps unique among research studies of cohorts of patients whose therapies have been followed over their course and outcome, to have been able to secure comprehensive follow-up data at the specified time[1] on the entire sample, with zero attrition. Even more remarkable is that additional follow-up information has been obtained for a large majority of the patients (actually 32, just over 75% of the sample) for periods up to 24 years after the official Termination Study. That we could ensure so comprehensive a follow-up study reflected a combination of circumstances peculiar to The Menninger Foundation and to PRP, each of which has been indicated in various ways:

1. The positions and status of the typical Menninger patient population, which make many of them (and/or their families) highly visible individuals, and therefore readily traceable into prolonged follow-up contacts almost wherever they subsequently happen to live.

2. The setting up of exclusion criteria for PRP that eliminated from the sample selection categories of patients who might not be readily available for Follow-Up Study (e.g., patients from foreign countries other than Canada, personnel in military service, etc.; see p. 58).

3. The enlisting of the patients' cooperation at the time of Termination Study with PRP's intent to have them return to Topeka for follow-up. The inducement was held out to them of a return visit to Topeka several years later, together with their spouses, at our expense; apart from participating in the Follow-Up Study, they could have a holiday visit with old friends they had made while living in the Menninger and the general community over the span of their treatment years.

4. The particular ecology of the Menninger therapeutic community, where some treatments go on for many years (even into "therapeutic lifer" status); where some ex-patients remain permanently in Topeka after having lived and worked

---

1. I have earlier indicated (see pp. 6, 94) the funding and time constraints that made us set the official Follow-Up Study at the 2- to 3-year mark, rather than at 5 years (which we would have preferred, since 5-year Follow-Ups have become the customary time spans in cancer research).

there throughout the course of their own and/or their spouses' treatments; and where some ex-patients keep in touch for years—by letter, by phone, or even by an occasional visit—with former therapists, social workers, hospital doctors, or activities therapists, or with friends among patients still in treatment (who may then inform their therapists of this news of the ex-patients, which characteristically then travels around within the Menninger community).

Given these confluent circumstances, The Menninger Foundation was probably an unparalleled place in which both to conduct this kind of research study and to maximize the possibilities for official and unofficial follow-up, extending in several instances literally over lifetimes.

Observation Periods Prior to Entering PRP

With 17 of the 42 patients (40% of the sample), there was some period of preceding psychotherapy, hospitalization, or observation within Topeka prior to the patients' formally entering their psychoanalyses or their psychotherapies as members of the PRP population. This period extended to 4 years in the case of the English Professor, who was first hospitalized and treated over a 7-month period at the local VA hospital, which he had entered in the wake of his initial phobic decompensation. He was then evaluated at The Menninger Foundation. Because of a suspicion of an encapsulated paranoid state, he was taken into an expressive psychotherapy to be initially pursued cautiously, possibly leading to psychoanalysis over time, if later indicated. This therapy lasted 2½ years, following which he left Topeka to do free-lance writing in his home town (and to live with his mother, in fulfillment of his father's dying request that he take care of her). His mother drove him to distraction, and after 8 months the patient had had enough of living with her; his work had also gone badly, and he was also involved in a courtship with a new girlfriend, who was pressing for a firm commitment. All this was leading to a rising anxiety. The patient thus came back to Topeka and to the college faculty position he had held during his psychotherapy there. He was re-evaluated, this time entering psychoanalysis and becoming part of the PRP sample.

   Of course, in most instances, these periods of documented prior observation in Topeka and in treatment there were much shorter. For the 17 patients so observed, they averaged 1⅓ years.

Durations of Treatments While in PRP

The treatments the patients entered into were all intended as psychoanalyses or as comparably long-term psychotherapies (those recommended for briefer therapy were excluded; see p. 57). The actual range of the 38 treatments that were actually terminated at the time of Follow-Up Study was from 6 months (the Bohemian Prep School Boy, who responded to his father's ultimatum by leaving treatment and going with his family to their new home in Europe) to 9 years (the Masochistic Editor, who was in active treatment—first psychoanalysis, then psychotherapy—for 7 years; for a variety of reasons, the therapy was not being declared officially terminated till the 9-year mark), or 8½ years (the Phobic Girl, who at the time of Follow-Up Study was in the midst of actual termination; at "cutoff" Termination Study she had still been in active treatment, and thought to be a potential "therapeutic lifer"). The average treatment duration of these 38 patients was 4⅓ years. In an earlier discussion (see pp. 193–195), I have indicated that the patients started in psychoanalysis had average treatment durations longer by about 1⅓ years than those started in psychotherapy.[2]

The four who at the time of official Follow-Up Study were still in ongoing treatment and were then considered "therapeutic lifers" had, of course far longer treatment careers. As of this writing (spring 1982), the Housebound Phobic Woman is still in treatment at The Menninger Foundation—now being seen once a month, with only her fourth therapist—at a point 26 years after her start. (Her first therapist died, and each of the next two at some point left The Menninger Foundation.) It is now 16 years since the "cutoff" Follow-Up Study. The Fearful Loner remained in the same treatment—30 minutes weekly, most of it with his third therapist—for a total of 16 years, at which point he terminated in order to retire with his wife to a small farm they bought in his home state. This was 8 years after the "cutoff" Follow-Up Study, and there was further follow-up (an exchange of letters with the ex-therapist) for 3 years after that.

The other two apparent "lifers" at the time of "cutoff" Follow-Up Study were the Economist at the 11½-year mark and the Sexual Masochist at the 10½-year mark (plus, for the latter, 3 years of prior documented observation). They have also continued as "therapeutic lifers" up until the present writing, but not at The Menninger Foundation. The Economist has remained in continuous touch with his original therapist, who himself left Topeka for practice in a distant community. For a while the patient moved to that same community and was in regular face-to-face therapy with him there; currently the patient lives in another part of the country, but still keeps in regular touch with his therapist by phone or mail at least twice a month. The Sexual Masochist has remained in Topeka all this time, and he continued with his therapist until the latter left Topeka at the 17-year mark in the treatment. At that point the patient was transferred to the therapeutic couple who were leading the local AA group (not officially connected with The Menninger Foundation) and has remained with them ever since.

There is, however, a fifth patient who should be added to this group—the Devoted Son, who terminated his analysis at 5½ years after a reluctant "weaning" process designed by the therapist to forestall the unfolding of an insoluble transference neurosis and the transition to "therapeutic lifer" status. Actually, 13 years after his termination, this patient returned to his former analyst for a series of spaced consultations spread out over 2 years; these revolved around his concerns with his aging and declining father and his own somewhat reactivated depressed and hypochondriacal state. After 2 years, the analyst left The Menninger Foundation, and the patient settled down (7 years ago now—15 years after his terminated analysis) to a regular weekly 30-minute session with another therapist. He has thus now also become a "therapeutic lifer." The treatment spans of these

---

2. The actual numbers are not quite comparable, because the figures given at the earlier point include the treatments of the several "therapeutic lifers" in the averaging process. At this point, those 4 have been kept apart from the other 38. The *comparative* lengths of the psychoanalyses and the psychotherapies have not been altered by the inclusion or exclusion of the small group of "therapeutic lifers."

5 patients range thus far from 12½ to 28 years and average 22 years. With these 5 averaged in, the overall known average treatment duration for the whole population of 42 is over 6½ years.

Post-Follow-Up Information

The official Follow-Up Studies were intended to take place 2 to 2½ years after the Termination Studies, and this intention was held to with great uniformity. The post-follow-up information has, of course, been much more variable. In addition to the information about the 5 "therapeutic lifers," we have follow-up information beyond the official Follow-Up Study from a variety of sources (but mostly through continued contacts with the original therapists) on 23 more patients. With 10 of these, the information covers a period ranging from 12 to 24 years beyond their treatment terminations; 3 of those are covered right up to the time of present writing, and 2 others are covered up to the times of their deaths from non-mental-illness-related causes (the Medical Scientist of a heart attack 12 years after his treatment termination, and the Involutional Woman in a nursing home, invalided with arthritis, 15 years after her treatment termination). With 11 other patients, the follow-up information ranges from 4 to 6 years beyond the treatment termination and therefore covers just a few additional years after the official Follow-Up Study. Sometimes this has come out of renewed treatment with the same or a different therapist—the reanalysis of the Tantrum Woman with the same analyst, the psychotherapy of the Prince with his prior analyst, or the psychotherapy of the Rebellious Coed with another therapist. More often, this additional information has come from consultation visits, letters, telephone calls, or chance encounters. The other 2 patients for whom there has been additional information past the official Follow-Up Study are 2 of those who died of mental-illness-related causes: Peter Pan, who was back in psychotherapy with a new therapist in a distant city at the time of her death by suicide 7 years after her treatment termination; and the Suspended Medical Student, who was being followed in an avuncular way by his physician mentor at the time of his death by suicide 7 years after his treatment termination.

Of the 14 patients (only one-third of the sample) on whom we have no information past the official Follow-Up Study, 4 are patients who died of mental-illness-related causes either during the follow-up period (the Addicted Doctor, the Car Salesman and the Alcoholic Heir) or while still in the original treatment (the Alcoholic Doctor). Only 10 (less than one-quarter) are individuals whose careers after their official Follow-Up Studies are totally unknown. Six of these have simply not been heard from; the therapists of the other 4 have either died or are currently gravely ill, and so inquiry simply cannot be made.

Total Observation Spans

In terms of time spans of observation, if we count the 5 "therapeutic lifers" together with the 10 patients on whom we have follow-up information ranging from 12 to 24 years, and count from either the actual termination point or the "cutoff" Termination Study, the average length of follow-up information for these 15 patients (over 35% of the sample) is over 17 years. (This group of 15 also includes 2 followed until their deaths at points 12 and 15 years after their treatment terminations). If we then count the 11 patients on whom we have follow-up information for 4 to 6 years together with the 2 followed until their deaths from mental-illness-related causes (both 7 years after termination), the average length of follow-up information for these 13 patients (almost 30% of the sample) is 5 years and 9 months. This leaves, then, 14 (exactly one-third of the sample), including 4 who died of mental-illness-related causes during the follow-up or the treatment period, with no information beyond the official Follow-Up Study. These varying periods of average post-follow-up information in the three equal groups of patients (over 17 years; 5 years and 9 months; and none) need to be added to the average of pretreatment observation of 1⅓ years (for 17 patients), average treatment duration of 5½ years, and official follow-up observation period of 2 to 3 years.

COOPERATION WITH THE FOLLOW-UP STUDY

I have indicated at a number of points the uniqueness in psychotherapy outcome research of truly 100% follow-up information, as well as some of the special conditions of our study and special characteristics of our sample that made this result possible. This does not mean that we actually saw all of the patients at either the Termination Study or the Follow-Up Study point. In Section II (see Chapter 6, pp. 85–90 and 93–99), I have described the nature of the information we were able to obtain (and from whom), and the nature of the studies we were then able to do when, for whatever reason, a particular patient was not available for study at either the Termination or the Follow-Up Study point. Nor, of course, does it mean that all the patients who did participate in these studies did so equally willingly, or equally disinterestedly or altruistically on behalf of science and the accrual of knowledge about therapy. Again, the range of ways in which patients did or did not participate in these studies, and the range of attitudes and feelings that were expressed or discerned in connection with the studies, have been detailed in Chapter 6. Here these data are reviewed and grouped somewhat differently, considering the sequence of Termination and Follow-Up participation together.

Patients Seen at Both Termination and Follow-Up

WHERE AND HOW PATIENTS WERE SEEN

Of the 42 patients, 25 (60% of the sample) had both their Termination and their Follow-Up Studies in Topeka, in the "routine way"—with their full participation in all aspects of the information gathering, and with our having comprehensive access to all the other usual data sources (clinical records, interviews with the therapist and all other pertinent members of the therapy staff, and interviews with the relevant people in the patient's life). The one small exception to this totally comprehensive study in the 25 cases was with the Intellectual Fencer, who, as already indicated (see p. 88), would consent to interviewing but would not allow repeat psychological testing at Termination Study; she sensed rightly that her control over unwitting self-exposure could not be maintained as well in the testing situation. However, she did not raise this objection at all at Follow-Up Study, when she participated fully and willingly in everything, including testing. Of these 25 patients, 20 lived either in Topeka or close enough to it that coming for several hours of interview or testing contact could be done readily enough within a day's round trip. The other 5 were, of course, residing in Topeka at the time of Termination Study but had to return from distances across the whole country for Follow-Up Study; 1 of these 5 (the Manic–Depressive Physician) returned to Topeka for his Follow-Up Study at the point that he was returning from his overseas military assignment, was being discharged from the Army, and was about to take on his new (civilian) medical practice career.

In addition to these 25 patients for whom both Termination and Follow-Up Studies were done in Topeka, there were 5 other instances (making a total of 30, or over 70% of the sample) in which both studies were done, but, for one or another reason, one or both were done in the patients' home towns by a research team. This team consisted of at least one interviewing clinician and one psychologist tester who came from Topeka and conducted the study, usually in office space rented in a business hotel for that purpose. Of these 5 patients, 2 (the Actress and the Masochistic Editor) had had their Termination Studies in Topeka but claimed to be too busy (and were clearly unwilling) to come back to Topeka for the Follow-Up inquiry; however, they participated cooperatively when seen in their home cities, though one of them insisted that it had to be on the weekend. Another patient (the Adoptive Mother) was the only one who had left Topeka before she could be contacted for Termination Study; this was then done in her home city (in fact, in her home), and she was of course among those who came back to Topeka most eagerly for Follow-Up Study. Still another (the Heiress) had followed her analyst when he had left Topeka for another locale, and it just seemed more logical to see her at both Termination and Follow-Up Studies in her new city of residence, where she had already been living for several years when her treatment terminated. And the last in this group (the Movie Lady) was the one patient in the PRP population who had not been treated in Topeka (for the basis of her inclusion in the sample, see Chapter 6, footnote 8, p. 95). She was therefore seen by us for Termination Study in the city in which she was treated, and then for Follow-Up Study in the city to which she subsequently moved.

PATIENTS' REACTIONS

The range of reasons and feelings that the patients expressed concerning their participation in these studies has already been described in part. In most cases, they came willingly and even eagerly, and for a variety of reasons. Most striking in her motivation was the Adoptive Mother (see p. 97), who came for Follow-Up Study with her husband and also her 3-year-old adopted daughter, in order to show us how successful her treatment had been in achieving its desired objectives (to enable her to adopt successfully) and much more particularly to show her ex-analyst the "fruit of his labor"—the daughter. Quite differently, the Tantrum Woman came to Follow-Up Study equally eagerly, but with great anxiety: After this point, The Menninger Foundation's "official" interest in her would cease, and she felt that this would be her "last chance" to convince us of her need for more psychoanalytic treatment. (She did succeed in re-entering treatment with her former analyst within a month after the Follow-Up interviews.) A similar motivation to work out a return to treatment operated with the Rebellious Coed. And still differently, Peter Pan wanted to return with her husband for Follow-Up Study because they were now students in a distant university, and this would be a chance for a paid vacation visit back to the husband's family, who lived in Topeka (the patient had met her husband as a fellow-student at the local college).

Other situations were more complex (or ambivalent?). The Bitter Spinster, for example, expressed herself as half glad, half distressed about the Follow-Up contact. She said that she would like to come but it might not be a good time, and she querulously complained of some picayune discrepancies about the expected timing of the inquiry. Actually, she was fearful; her Termination Study interviews had been upsetting, and a number of aspects of the situation had bothered her, especially having more than one interviewer present at a time. When her requested rearrangement of conditions (and personnel) was agreed to, the patient's reluctance gave way, and she said she wanted to come because things had been so rough that it would be a good time to take stock. The patient then panicked and canceled her first appointments with a phone call just an hour ahead of time. When reached the next day, she said that she had immediately regretted her abrupt action of the day before. She knew that she ought to come in for this kind of stock taking, but then (characteristically depressively) thought that perhaps there was nothing to take stock of. She was willing to try again and kept the rest of her appointments, though with latenesses. She presented herself on interview with the statement, "I haven't done a thing in 2 years, really not a thing." The research interviews concurred with her gloomy self-assessment.

The Bohemian Musician was the patient who at Termination Study so gratefully offered to "place myself completely at your disposal." At Follow-Up Study she was equally eager to participate, but only under certain conditions—that it be over a particular group of days, when her new husband would be away on a business trip. As noted earlier (see pp. 385–386), it turned out that he knew nothing of her previous illness and treatment, and that the patient had her reasons (realistic enough and neurotic enough) to want to keep it that way. So she dissembled to her husband about the Topeka visit, telling him that she had been called in consultation by the rehabilitation center for the handicapped where she had worked, to help them with a research grant application they were planning. The Bohemian Prep School Boy was the one who expressed surprise that we would pay Follow-Up trip expenses, saying that he would have come anyway. (He was from one of the very wealthy families.) And even more "grateful" was the Alcoholic Raconteur, who had essentially disappeared after his disastrous treatment course and could only be located for Termination Study when he was drunk, down and out, ill, and penniless, and his landlady appealed to The Menninger Foundation for help (for details, see p. 89). He then came readily and sober at Follow-Up time (having been in the meanwhile rehabilitated via AA), and then spontaneously kept in touch with the research project, offering to come for study once again if wanted (the only patient in the entire series who did this, see p. 98).

By contrast to these patients, others came to Follow-Up Study with some sense of obligation, but definitely very reluctantly. The Divorced Nurse, as noted (see p. 318) was one such. She was afraid of showing that she hadn't done as well as she had hoped she would; she was afraid that she would be a disappointment to her analyst; and she didn't want to suffer any further blows to her self-confidence. She perhaps enjoyed, too, the little feeling of stubbornness and defiance in this. She clearly stated her view of her limited treatment achievements: "I feel I'm keeping my head above water because I had that treatment, but I want more out of life than that." For this she (properly) in part blamed the situation. "If only I had gone East for the analysis — before the divorce. . . . if my husband had given me one bit of encouragement I would have." Similarly, the Claustrophobic Man, who had suffered some regression into partial phobic and anxiety revivals during the follow-up period, came when asked, but expressed resentment about the feeling that he *had* to come for Follow-Up Study. He indicated that he was chronically more tense: "A lot of things irritate me that I could control before." Finally, the Adolescent Grandson's postponement of his Follow-Up Study for a whole year, and the Script Writer's negativistic comportment and gross overcharging for her expenses (alone of all the patients), have already been described (see pp. 97 and 98).

Patients Seen at Only One Time or Not at All

TERMINATION STUDY ONLY

The other 12 patients in the project (not quite 30% of the sample) were not seen at one or another of the two times, either Termination Study or Follow-Up Study. Of these 12, 3 were not seen at either one of the times (i.e., were not actually seen at all). Another 4 did have full Termination Studies with their participation, but not Follow-Up Studies. Three of these had died by the Follow-Up point (the Alcoholic Heir, the Addicted Doctor, and the Car Salesman), and in the fourth case the decision was made — largely on the basis of what transpired in the initiating telephone contacts with her — not to press her to come for Follow-Up (the Invalided Hypochondriac).

The circumstances with each of these 4 not seen at Follow-Up Study were different. The Alcoholic Heir, who disrupted his psychoanalysis after 1 year, had initially very paranoidly refused to participate in his Termination Study (see p. 89 for details), but changed his mind completely and cooperated fully when he sought readmission to The Menninger Hospital at a point of uncontrolled drunkenness 3 months after his treatment disruption. He came in afraid to be alone, and "fearful that he might have too much to drink and set fire to his clothes" (his alcoholic brother had died that way, and he himself had had his house burn down under identical circumstances, and had escaped that time with his life, with burns only on his hands). The patient would not allow further treatment at this time, however, and was discharged against medical advice after 2 weeks of drying out; 6 months later, he was dead of pneumococcal meningitis.

The Addicted Doctor and the Car Salesman were seen "willingly" enough at Termination Study. The Addicted Doctor was just being transferred from his failed outpatient psychotherapy at The Menninger Foundation to a successor psychotherapy within the inpatient setting of the local affiliated state hospital (because of a drastic and near-successful suicide attempt); the Car Salesman had broken up his third (unsuccessful) treatment effort at The Menninger Foundation, and under pressure from his wife had departed Topeka, participating in the Termination Study in his new city of residence. Both of these patients were also dead before Follow-Up Studies could be done—the Addicted Doctor committing suicide while still an inpatient in the state hospital, and the Car Salesman dying of an alcohol–drug overdose while living in Mexico. In both these instances, the widow was willing to come for the Follow-Up Study (in the case of the Car Salesman's widow, from a considerable distance).

The fourth patient of this group, the Invalided Hypochondriac, had had a regular Termination Study in Topeka at the point that she was being transferred at her husband's insistence to a state hospital in her home state (after only 4 months of psychotherapy at The Menninger Foundation). As noted, she was the one patient within the total sample whom the research group decided not to urge to come for Follow-Up Study. At the point that the patient was initially contacted for this purpose, she had been divorced by her husband and was somehow living extramurally and alone, with little contact with her ex-husband or her children. The patient's response to the follow-up inquiry was mistrustful and negative; it consisted of exchanges of letters and three lengthy (collect) phone calls that she was invited to make. She indicated her fear of being further harmed by the study and asked for explicit assurances to the contrary. She would not specify the kind of assurances she sought, since these would have to come, without prompting by her, from our "heart and soul." She further stipulated that if she did agree to participate, her attorney would of course need to be present. And she ended the first long conversation by indicating that though she had "given a lot" in this talk, she had nonetheless "withheld the essence." In view of the many paranoid reservations that she expressed, we wrote her that it seemed best to take her feelings seriously and not have her participate with us at this time. This did not close the matter, however, since the patient then followed with other long telephone calls expressing her distress that her conditions had not been met. This seemed like a breach of promise to her, perhaps because the research team members were not truly free agents but had to "abide by what the others have to say." Given not just the intensity of this paranoia, but the real risk that, should the patient return to Topeka, she might collapse just as helplessly as she had when she had come initially (and this time without the resources to support treatment at The Menninger Foundation), the research group stood firm and declined to let the patient come. We contented ourselves with all the information that she did convey during these calls and exchanges of letters, as well as the information obtained from those who had treated her during the follow-up interim, both in the state hospital and afterward.

FOLLOW-UP STUDY ONLY

Another five patients were not seen at the Termination Study point, but were seen at the time of Follow-Up Study. Three of these were from the group of 5 who had seemed to be "therapeutic lifers" and had had so-called "cutoff" Termination Studies. These were the Housebound Phobic Woman, the Economist, and the Phobic Girl. Their therapists had felt it not appropriate for them to participate in their Termination Studies, which thus had to proceed as "truncated studies." (However, for clinical reasons—namely, to assess the issue of chronic residual organic brain damage secondary to the long-standing barbiturate addiction—the therapist of the Housebound Phobic Woman felt that it was indicated to have the psychological test battery repeated at that point; this was done, and the findings from that were incorporated into the "cutoff" Termination Study assessment of the patient's functioning.) The same therapists felt that these patients could participate at the time of official Follow-Up Study 2 years later, though only one (the Phobic Girl) had in the meantime actually terminated her therapy. The Housebound Phobic Woman and the Economist had maintained their status as apparent "therapeutic lifers" and were still being seen regularly.

Of the other two who at the Termination point had seemed to be "lifers," one, the Fearful Loner, was among the three who were not seen at either Termination Study or Follow-Up Study. The other, the Involutional Woman, was seen anyway at Termination Study because her therapist felt that this could be done without adverse effect upon the treatment; she was seen again for Follow-Up Study, at which time it turned out that she had actually terminated her treatment. She was thus among the 30 seen at both those points in time.

The two other patients (aside from the three apparent "therapeutic lifers") who were not seen for Termination Study but were seen at Follow-Up Study included one of the two who had refused to participate at Termination time but was willing to cooperate at Follow-Up (the Exhibitionistic Dancer), and one who had disappeared at the time of Termination but could be located through his parents at the time of Follow-Up (the Sociopath). The angry, fearful, and also somewhat vindictive way in which the Exhibitionistic Dancer had refused to participate in her Termination Study has already been described (see p. 88). By contrast, when the patient was asked to come for Follow-Up Study, she was not only willing but even eager to come—so much so that there was some question whether the patient was intending, in view of her continuing unsatisfactory life, to make a bid for renewed therapy. This turned out not to be so. The patient felt strongly attached now to her Christian Science faith, and it seemed to her now almost immoral to think of more psychotherapy. She did, however, specifically acknowledge her continuing painful loneliness and the frequent intense wish "just to talk to someone." The Sociopath, who had disappeared from his treatment with his creditors, his landlord, his lawyer, the police, and his family all in full pursuit, was located through his parents at Follow-Up time; he readily assented to interviewing and testing, provided that it was over a weekend in a meeting place in his home city (he claimed that he was too tied to the demands of his job to get away).

NO CONTACT AT EITHER POINT

The remaining three patients were not seen at either Termination Study or Follow-Up Study, each for very different reasons. The Fearful Loner, as just noted, was a "therapeutic lifer" whose psychotherapy indeed did go on for an additional 8 years past the follow-up point. He was the one patient of the sample whose attachment to his therapy appeared so tenuous all along that his therapist deemed it inappropriate on clinical grounds to intrude with the research study inquiry at both the "cutoff" Termination and Follow-Up points. The research team concurred, and this patient was therefore not seen at either point.

The Suspended Medical Student was the one patient in the total sample who would not let himself be seen at either of the two points of inquiry. His overt attitude was different on the two occasions, as described earlier. At Termination Study time, when the patient was in the flush of a seemingly successfully completed analysis, graduation from medical school, and a seemingly stable new marriage, he professed great willingness to cooperate with the research inquiry, but stated that he simply felt that he could not work out an appropriate time, given the busyness of his new life (see pp. 88–89 for the details). At Follow-Up time, when it was plain that everything had collapsed in the patient's life, the patient was just evasively hiding (see p. 98). The quite complete information obtained about him came partly from his family and even more from the old-time friend, family physician, and mentor who had guided the patient's career and was a close witness to its sad decline.

The third patient of this group, the Alcoholic Doctor, was the one patient who had actually died (of the massive aspiration of vomitus while in a grossly debilitated and toxic state) while still in his original treatment at The Menninger Foundation. On that account, obviously, he was not available for any cooperative research study.

Summary

I now summarize the data under this heading. In various ways, and with varyingly expressed attitudes, we were able to secure the participation of 34 of the 42 patients (80%) in their Termination Studies. Of the 8 who did not participate in 4 instances (the Housebound Phobic Woman, the Economist, the Phobic Girl, and the Fearful Loner) clinical contraindications were expressed by the therapists and accepted by the research group (these were 4 of the 5 seeming "therapeutic lifers"); in 2 instances the patients refused (the Exhibitionistic Dancer and the Suspended Medical Student); in 1 instance the patient had simply disappeared and had ample reasons to make sure that he could not be traced (the Sociopath); and in 1 instance the patient had died while still in treatment (the Alcoholic Doctor).

At the Follow-Up Study point, we were able to secure the participation of 35 patients (not quite 85%) in the research study, including one of the two (the Exhibitionistic Dancer) who had refused at the Termination Study point. Of the 7 who did not participate, in 4 instances the patients were now dead (the Alcoholic Doctor, the Alcoholic Heir, the Addicted Doctor, and the Car Salesman)[3]; in 1 instance the therapist felt it clinically contraindicated (the Fearful Loner), though there were still several "therapeutic lifers"; in 1 instance the research team felt it contraindicated to try to bring the patient to Topeka for study, or even to try to see her in her home community (the Invalided Hypochondriac); and in 1 instance the patient refused (the Suspended Medical Student).

A commentary on the overall willingness of the patients is the fact that in the total sample of 42, we only encountered a single patient, the Suspended Medical Student, who would not let himself be seen at all in research study. Ironically,

---

3. The other two of the six patients known to have died of mental-illness-related causes did so (both by direct suicide) in their post-follow-up period of observation. The Suspended Medical Student asphyxiated himself in his car 4 years after the Follow-Up Study time (and 11½ years from the point of original contact with him). Peter Pan jumped off a bridge to her death 5 years after the Follow-Up Study time (and 11 years from the point of original contact with her).

he was the one who, during the Termination Study negotiations, proclaimed the value of medical research and its importance to future patients, as well as his sense of obligation — "I really do owe it to The Menninger Foundation, too." But, as has been indicated, he had his reasons to stay away, and adequate information about him and his doings could nonetheless be garnered from collateral family and medical sources.

The Impact of Follow-Up upon Treatment Termination and Resolution

One of the major conceptual barriers to planned follow-up studies in psychoanalysis — and, by extension (though not as strongly), in psychodynamic or psychoanalytic psychotherapies — has been the conception of the centrality to the proper termination process of the most thorough resolution possible of the complexity of transference ties and attachments, in all of their positive and negative affective colorations. It has been an implicit tenet of this perspective that planning in advance for contact after treatment termination could exert a powerful, unconscious delaying current upon the full acceptance of the actuality of the terminating treatment relationship; could impinge upon the proper termination mourning process for the closely intimate relationship being given up; and thus in various ways could delay, distort, or even (in extreme instances) preclude proper treatment termination. It is a reflection of such thinking that some of the earliest and best-known follow-up accounts in the psychoanalytic literature have been either instances where the follow-up data have come out of the continuing therapeutic observation of the same patient by successive analysts, as with Freud's famous Wolf Man (Gardiner, 1971), or happenstance instances of renewed contact with an ex-patient many years after the treatment termination (Deutsch, 1959). This whole issue has already been discussed in more detail in Section II (see Chapter 6, pp. 93–97). Here I want to present our data on two closely related aspects of this issue of both the place and the propriety of formal follow-up study of intensive psychoanalytic treatments. The first is that of the actual impact of such study in relation to possible delaying of psychological closure or "real termination." The second is that of the deliberate (or unconscious) use of the built-in follow-up inquiry as a face-saving mechanism for getting back into more treatment, or, if not fully that, for explicitly discussing the appropriateness of such an idea.

FOLLOW-UP AS A FACTOR DELAYING PSYCHOLOGICAL CLOSURE

Explicit Seeking of Further Treatment

For 6 patients (14% of the sample), there was definite evidence that the fact of follow-up served in some way to attenuate or to delay processes that would otherwise have led to psychological closure of the treatment process. With the Tantrum Woman, this was very strongly (and very explicitly) the case. This young recent widow had terminated her analysis quite successfully, she felt, though she was still unhappily unmarried. She had actually seen her analyst fairly regularly during the follow-up period—almost monthly, in fact—to complain about her unabated loneliness, her occasional transient anxiety or symptom recurrences, her troubles in establishing a social life and finding a suitor, and her depressive feelings. This contact was really a clear plea to resume intensive treatment, and the patient showed a real reactive anger when it became evident that her analyst did not think this advisable. During one intensive period of weekly sessions over a 6-week span, this whole interplay was vigorously interpreted as a clinging to the fantasy of "getting the father" and an unwillingness to try herself out in life, to turn her thoughts from the analyst to new objects "out there." The analyst added, "Who knows, your future husband might live in the very next block." Quite promptly after that, the patient reported that she had met a lonely widower living in the very next block (with three children); this quickly blossomed into an intense courtship and a marriage proposal, during which time the patient did not see her analyst for 3 months. After a good deal of indecision, the patient rallied from her anxieties and went into the marriage and new family with the combined total of five children (see p. 306 for more details). This was now close to the Follow-Up Study time.

When the patient was called for enlistment in the Follow-Up Study, her anxieties suddenly renewed. After the follow-up, The Menninger Foundation's "official" interest in her would cease, and she would be truly terminated. "It was as if this were the real end, the real separation, the real termination." As long as she was still a case under continuing study, her treatment was still continuing in fantasy, and true separation did not have to be faced. Besides, the new marriage had relighted some of the old problems of hostility and dependency in relation to mother figures—both her true mother and her husband. The analyst stated that these problems had not been sufficiently worked out in the nearly 5 years of analysis and could not be "until she got into a situation like a marriage which would bring them actively to the fore again." The Follow-Up Study thus led naturally into a renewed 4 years of reanalysis with the same analyst, to its final very good conclusion. (For the description of this whole treatment course, see pp. 302–307.)

The situation with the Rebellious Coed was quite similar. She had ended her treatment adjudged moderately improved, having returned to college, successfully graduated, and embarked on a career as a spinster schoolteacher. Her homosexuality was quite covert, and her self-esteem was clearly enhanced. Yet it was also abundantly clear at Follow-Up Study that the patient had ended her treatment disappointed that despite the surface improvement in her functioning, her underlying distress and psychological problems were largely unaltered. Her initial treatment goals for herself (which had included overcoming her homosexual proclivities) had not been realized. She had had only one contact with her ex-therapist during this interval—a letter ostensibly asking for vocational advice, which began, "This may seem rather strange to you, but I have become quite interested in psychology and psychiatry." The patient had come to the Follow-Study, which she had been consciously awaiting, with the explicit feeling that "this is my last chance." The Follow-Up interviews were then used to make a referral for a renewed attempt at psychotherapy with a colleague in the city in which the patient now worked.

This new therapy went on for another year, but unhappily ended no differently than the first. And when the patient was seen again in consultation at The Menninger Foundation a year after the second therapy ended, she said that though she still turned to psychiatry when she got upset, she also felt that she didn't believe in it any more. She was then deeply entrenched in her homosexuality without even a facade of interest in men. (For the description of this treatment course, see pp. 483–489.)

Clear Delays in Treatment Resolution

With two other patients, the planned follow-up observation period contributed to a clear delaying of treatment resolution, but without the same clear intent to utilize this occasion to find their way back to treatment. The Phobic Woman felt sad all through the Follow-Up interview process—as if undergoing a mourning process. Her treatment was finally over and she was mourning its loss. All during the 2½-year period, she had awaited the Follow-Up Study that was coming. In that sense, she had still felt herself in her treatment, which was finally undergoing its (delayed) resolution. She had occasionally thought of returning to her analyst, but she had acquiesced in her husband's feeling that she should be able to see this through on her own, or, if she needed to return to therapy, that it be other than analytic therapy. The husband was disenchanted with "depth therapies" ("He is not psychoanalytically oriented") and felt that she could get other, faster, and more effective treatment at their university counseling center.

The Devoted Son came to Follow-Up Study professing his status to be much the same as at treatment termination: "I have gone in the same grooves, wearing a little more deeply." He was half consciously hoping to use the Follow-Up interviews to achieve true treatment closure. If he could only use the Follow-Up Study to represent the final disenchantment that he could no longer expect dramatic and magical changes, then maybe he could apply himself to making more effective use of himself in his life. As it turned out, of course, he ultimately found his way back to renewed continuing psychotherapy 15 years after the termination of his analysis, and is now a "therapeutic lifer."

Mixed Effects on Treatment Resolution

The other two patients in this group of six came to Follow-Up Study with a much more mixed state of mind. The Adolescent Grandson had colluded with his grandfather's heavy-handed disruption of his totally unfinished treatment process. At Termination Study, the patient was clearly drifting and clearly upset that he would now have to get along without the psychotherapy, which he realized full well he needed as much as ever. Yet he acceded to the termination, fleeing the dangerously eroticized transference involvement with his therapist, and hoping in exchange to win himself back into his grandfather's good graces. In this, he failed; and subsequently he seemed to be half-looking for a face-saving way back to treatment, perhaps via the Follow-Up Study. But as it turned out, the patient used the Follow-Up inquiry to opt more decisively against more treatment.

The Bitter Spinster was similar. She was, as already mentioned, half glad and half distressed about the Follow-Up Study contact. She had spent 2 years fighting her "dependency and aggression" alone; maybe she needed more treatment, though it might be better not to give in to her dependency in this way. But then the patient failed to use the Follow-Up interviews either to effect a true closure of her treatment career or to get herself back into more treatment. Her ambivalences prevailed, and the patient ended her Follow-Up Study in the same kind of impasse with which it began.

Facilitation of Treatment Resolution

In contrast to these six patients who, to a greater or lesser extent, used the follow-up period and the planned return for official Follow-Up Study as a way of keeping their treatment relationship incompletely terminated (perhaps as an open channel back into more treatment), there were at least two who reacted in quite the opposite fashion. For example, the Involutional Woman was the one individual thought to be a "therapeutic lifer" at the time of planned "cutoff" Termination Study who the therapist agreed could be seen in evaluation at that time without risk of distorting or possibly hurtful impact on the ongoing therapy. It turned out that the impact of this research study may well have been in the direction of speeding up the process of treatment resolution. For at the time of presumed "cutoff" Follow-Up inquiry, it turned out that the patient had actually been able to terminate her treatment halfway through the follow-up period, though this was quite contrary to the predictions made at the time of "cutoff" Termination Study. It had then been predicted that the treatment would not terminate, but that the patient would keep using such stress situations as would continue to arise in her life to justify her need for going on in treatment without ever having to face the dependency that tied her to it. And, actually, there *was* a constant ongoing stress in her life—the ever-worsening arthritis, with its progressive reduction in the scope of the patient's activities and in her ability to work. It had therefore been felt at Termination Study that continued supportive treatment with this therapist (her second) would be needed to help maintain the patient's level of functioning or even perhaps to enhance it a little. And it had then been predicted (incorrectly) that should additional acute stresses be superimposed, or should the therapy not continue for some reason, the patient's functioning could be expected to worsen.

Quite similar in his response to research inquiry was the Homesick Psychology Student, who at Follow-Up Study was working and married, but with the massive compromise of severe sexual inhibition and a totally unconsummated marriage. Though the research examiners clearly sought to use the Follow-Up interviews to reopen the issue of a return to treatment for the patient, he dug in against the idea. He did occasionally think of recourse to outside help—even wistfully of psychoanalysis, which he could now afford, in contrast to his inability to support such a proposal at the time it had originally been discussed with him during his presenting evaluation before his psychotherapy. But then the patient thought even more of drugs and hormones, and of the magic of hypnosis, "maybe not for a cure but for whatever it might do." He ended by committing himself to working more with his wife on all the issues between them, such as the sexual disability. The wife reported, as hopeful evidence that this could work, that the awful nightmares the patient had suffered with in the beginning of the marriage seemed to have disappeared; the patient had never reported nightmares as a complaint, either in therapy or in research evaluation.

Resolution of Unsettled Life during Follow-Up Period

One last patient to be mentioned in connection with this issue of "delayed" treatment termination is the Bohemian Musician. In her case, it was not the research and the wait for Follow-Up Study that served to keep the treatment situation open, but rather the unsettled state of the patient's ongoing life at the termination point. She was the patient who had come back to Topeka to see her former therapist once during the follow-up period in order to consult with him about a possible marriage, bringing along a full dossier on all her fiancé's material assets. When she felt she had received license to go ahead, and had gotten married, she began to feel freer of her sense of dependence upon the actual therapist. Enough of him was now, in the patient, "transferred" to the husband that she could have the "psychological termination" of her therapy. The residual feeling toward the therapist was one of gratitude and admiration. Realistically, she saw him as someone who could and would help her further if she needed it, but at this point she did not feel the need for such help.

Overall Comments

Overall, there was no great evidence that the imposition of an ongoing research program, and its planned period of follow-up observation, acted importantly to delay or impair the treatment resolution process for the PRP patient population. In some cases, it did seem to do so, but in others it seemed to act differently and even oppositely. Furthermore, in those several instances where the Follow-Up inquiry did seem to act strongly in this delaying direction (as with the Tantrum Woman and the Rebellious Coed), it was in connection with a strong push by the patients to find their way back to renewed treatment, which they both felt they needed and wanted. A somewhat related (but different) point about treatment closure is made by Horwitz in his book from the project (1974, pp. 42–45). In talking about treatment termination, he refers to the common assumption that this is a very stressful period for most patients who have been in intensive therapy, and that this gets characteristically reflected in a "number of special termination phenomena: depression, exacerbation of character defenses or symptoms, as well as a clinging to the treatment relationship" (p. 43). He indicates that predictions of this kind were made for half the research subjects, and that a relatively large percentage of these particular predictions were disconfirmed. He then goes on to indicate why he feels it worked out that way—why the gratifying treatment dependency that it was anticipated patients would have great difficulty giving up was so often more than balanced by opposed feelings and fears which outweighed these dependent attachments. The point of correspondence between Horwitz's discussion and mine here has to do with the lesser concern suggested by the PRP data about difficult termination phenomena than is so often postulated in clinical thinking and teaching.

FOLLOW-UP AS A MECHANISM FOR SEEKING
ADDITIONAL TREATMENT

I go on now to the closely related question of patients in the PRP population coming to their Follow-Up Studies as a convenient and face-saving road to additional treatment, or at least to the consideration of it. This turned out to be the case with 10 patients (almost 25% of the sample); of course, it should be looked at as one of the specific *clinical* values to be derived by the patient from the *research* Follow-Up Study (or perhaps better put, provided to the patient by the research study).

Clear Desire for Further Treatment

In four cases, this intent to return to treatment via the Follow-Up Study process operated very powerfully. The Tantrum Woman and the Rebellious Coed, as just described, did each return to treatment—the Tantrum Woman for 4 more years of psychoanalysis with the same analyst and the Rebellious Coed for 1 more year of psychotherapy with a different therapist. Almost equally strong was the retreatment push at Follow-Up Study of the Prince and the English Professor. The Prince, for example, came to his Follow-Up Study feeling explicitly that he had terminated his analysis too soon, and that he had not gotten out of it what he could have and should have. At the same time, he felt dubious about going back for more, and he felt that perhaps a different treatment might be more effective for him than analysis. He expressed interest in "a more directive therapy. Most of what I want is a more natural sort of engagement, a more normal kind of movement, of give and take, between us. . . . I think I could express my feelings more directly if I have something to express them against, rather than nothing, or rather than someone just sitting there listening." And within a year after the Follow-Up Study, the patient was back in treatment—psychotherapy (once weekly) rather than psychoanalysis, and with his ex-analyst. The patient had returned because of "the same old problems," and the new treatment went on for about a year. The whole treatment and retreatment course of this patient has been described in Chapter 16.

The other patient in this group motivated to seek out more treatment was the English Professor. This patient not only came back for Follow-Up Study, but regularly, at about yearly intervals, sought out his former analyst at various points of decision and crisis in his life. The first time was a year after treatment termination, when his mother died suddenly of a stroke. Other visits were in connection with his new marriage, and with marital tensions in it. Once he returned to present a gift to his analyst—an inscribed copy of a book of literary criticism that he had just had published. Each time he stressed that there was no great joy in his life, and, in fact, that he still had many of the same complaints about it. However, when he would ask the analyst whether the latter thought he should come back for more treatment (which he would readily have done), the analyst would look quizzically at him in response; the patient would then back off from the intention, saying that he personally saw no need for it, since he was doing so well. (This was the same analyst, incidentally, who had also treated the Tantrum Woman and was willing to take *her* back into 4 additional years of reanalysis.)

Ambivalent Motivation for Further Treatment

Six other patients beyond these four were very ambivalently motivated to seek further treatment via the route of their Follow-Up Studies, or, alternatively, to use the research study to struggle against this longing. The situations of two of these, the Adolescent Grandson and the Bitter Spinster, have just been described (pp. 600–601). The others were similar to these two. The Bohemian Prep School Boy, in fact, returned to Topeka to see his former therapist even before the official Follow-Up Study. He told the therapist that, now that he was gone, he realized that he needed treatment and that he wanted it with him. He said he would come back for it; he would attend college locally and work to support himself. His father would support the college and therapy expenses. He emphatically did not wish to change therapists. Even his negative father was generally supportive of these plans. However, none of this planning for further treatment went any further, and at the official Follow-Up Study interviews the patient spoke very critically of the psychotherapy he had had (see pp. 527–528).

Peter Pan expressed herself very similarly (ambivalently). She "wanted" to see her ex-analyst on her Follow-Up Study visit to The Menninger Foundation, but failed to make an appointment. Her various ambivalent expressions concerning more treatment, and her husband's negative pressures, have all been previously detailed (see pp. 430–431). Her final statements were "I'm ambivalent about treatment in the past and treatment in the future, but all in all, I think treatment is a wonderful thing," and "If I really felt a year of treatment would help me an awful lot, then I would be very willing to do it, but I'm not that sure, and I'm not that willing to spend a lot of money finding out." Perhaps when her husband went overseas for a year for the final field work on his dissertation, she could stay behind and go into therapy while he was away—or maybe she could even do it with him present, after they were academically settled. "It's not inconceivable." (Of course, the patient did go back into treatment 4 years after that Follow-Up Study, in her new home city and with a new therapist, at the point when she had again completely decompensated in a progressively malignant direction. And this new therapy did not prevent the patient's death by suicide less than a year later.)

The Alcoholic Raconteur expressed no conscious desire to seek more treatment; at the Follow-Up point he was doing well, thanks to AA. But a year after the Follow-Up Study, he wrote to the research group offering to come for study again (as has been said, he was the only patient in the entire series to do this): "If you wish me to participate in your research program this year again, please do contact me." When it was indicated to him that there was no provision for such repetitive follow-up visits, he replied with a cordial letter of appreciation. He wrote, "Your letter was received with mixed emotions. I will now spend a week in more traditional vacation climes, yet last year it was like visiting home (and a pleasant one) when I went to Topeka." He then reported about his doings. In all of this, one can probably reasonably infer a covert intent to get back into a Menninger Foundation treatment—perhaps preferably with his ex-analyst, whom he described at Follow-Up Study as "a discerning chap," though he was a little off in his appreciation of the subtle nuances of modern jazz music.

The Script Writer, an equally alcoholic patient, expressed her desire to return for treatment at The Menninger Foundation very explicitly. But the patient indicated her terms. She did not want her former hospital doctor, and in fact, would not accept rehospitalization at all; she did want her former analyst, but for once-a-week outpatient psychotherapy, not psychoanalysis. Analysis was not for her; her recent psychotherapy during the follow-up interim and her recent voluminous reading on the subject all confirmed that feeling for her. It was somewhat unclear why she specifically wanted to return to Topeka for treatment, given these stipulations she was making. She indicated that she had, as a matter of fact, considered a variety of other places. But in Topeka she had old friends, she could live more cheaply and conveniently, and she could more readily combine treatment with a return to graduate university studies. She did make clear, however, that she would accept only her own treatment prescription. When it was indicated to the patient that from the Menninger Foundation's point of view renewed psychotherapy only made sense on an inpatient basis, the patient responded angrily that we "were at cross purposes." These recommendations were very different from what she had gotten at home, and she found them unacceptable. What she did then was to make her divorce final, move back to Topeka, and then go into outpatient psychotherapy with a local psychiatrist not on The Menninger Foundation staff.

Decisions against Further Treatment

Alongside these 10 patients whose return for Follow-Up Study carried important components of either seeking a direct road back to therapy or at least posing the issue, struggling with ambivalences about it, and/or laying down conditions for it, there were several other patients whose intent was to use the Follow-Up visit to close off any prospect of return for retreatment. As just discussed, the Bohemian Musician came to Follow-Up Study to complete the closure, the "psychological termination" of her therapy, now that she had a new husband to whom she could "transfer" her allegiance and her dependency. Another, the Intellectual Fencer, came to Follow-Up Study intent to affirm (and to have confirmed) that she had acted wisely in her marriage to an equally addictive and an even more homosexual patient, in which basically each partner could cure the other, and thereby do better than each of their therapists. She wanted to show the consolidation that she felt she had achieved in her life and her marriage during the follow-up period, by dint of so much effort. Unhappily, from the perspective of the research group, it had indeed been achieved by dint of much effort—much denial and dissimulation. There was a clear cautionary note that it might be too brittle to last under the impact of future life stress; it seemed based too much on a "counterneurotic" effort at mastery, and too little on adequate working through of underlying conflict.

A third patient with similar concerns who decided against more treatment was the Divorced Nurse. Though she had maintained an extremely intense and eager contact with her former analyst (by mail, to be described), her attitude toward the Follow-Up Study was quite reluctant. I have already described her fear of showing that she hadn't done as well in analysis as she had hoped she would, and that the research group in turn would urge her back into more treatment. This she felt she did not want, though she expressed fears of being alone and getting old, and knew that this feeling might grow worse as the years went on. When her sons grew up, she wouldn't have anything. The patient, incidentally, continued in sporadic contact with her ex-analyst over an 18-year span beyond the official

Follow-Up Study, all the while still living in Topeka. She went through the problems of caring for an aging, senile mother; her own menopause and fears of aging; severe back trouble (scoliosis and sciatica), leading to spinal fusion more than once; worry about her sons, one of them emotionally quite unstable, and another with seeming temporal lobe epilepsy and either some organic brain damage or a mild psychotic (schizophrenic?) process; and all the while the bleakness of her life alone. On these periodic follow-up visits with the ex-analyst, actually spaced years apart, the patient did not specifically request more treatment. She usually responded quite positively to the analyst's "friendly exhortations" to overcome her lethargy and "get going" with her life.

The fourth (and last) of the patients to be here mentioned as determined against further treatment was the Suspended Medical Student, who, as stated, was the only patient in our entire sample who refused to participate in the research study at either the Termination or the Follow-Up point. Unfortunately, his need for more treatment was probably greater than that of any other patient. This was clearly what he was specifically aware of and what he was so unwilling to have to face in our presence—either at Termination Study, when he seemed to be doing well enough (on the surface), or at Follow-Up Study, when everything in and around him had completely collapsed. The patient's physician mentor and long-time friend now was serving as the stabilizing and guiding influence in the patient's life, but this individual did not succeed in his numerous efforts to get the patient back into psychiatric consultation and treatment (even at some place other than The Menninger Foundation, which the patient wanted so desperately to avoid). The patient declined every possible arrangement. He refused to return to see his old friend, the dean, as well as a psychiatric consultant at his medical school hospital. A scheme was then worked out whereby the patient's father actually feigned illness and was hospitalized at the university hospital. When the patient came to visit his father there, the psychiatric consultant entered and tried to visit with him, but the patient "flew the coop." The final result was the patient's death by suicide some 7 years after his treatment termination, 4 years after the time of official Follow-Up Study. Clearly, the Termination and Follow-Up inquiries could be used by patients not only as open channels to more treatment that they might need and want, but equally as foci around which to organize themselves against any acknowledgment of such need, depending on their psychic positions.

Posttreatment Returns for Help: Psychotherapy and Other Therapy

A most striking finding from the observations of the PRP subjects at Follow-Up Study was the very large amount of posttreatment therapeutic contact that they engaged in—whether formal psychotherapy, or some other broadly "supportive" or "therapeutic" ingredient, or some combination of ingredients fashioned by the ex-patients in their interactions with the helping world. Of the entire sample of 42 patients, in only 3 instances do we have no record of one or another kind of posttreatment "therapeutic" involvement (the Medical Scientist, the Manic–Depressive Physician, and the Intellectual Fencer, all among those with very good results).

This evidence of such overwhelming return for continued help, support, and/or therapy is all the more impressive, since it is based on follow-up observation periods only 2–3 years in duration for 14 of the patients[1] (though, as already indicated, the span of additional contact and observation extended from a few posttreatment years for another 13 to 12–24 posttreatment years for a third group of 15). Of the 3 who did not seek additional help, the Medical Scientist, a truly cured severe alcoholic, functioned very well over a span of 12 years (until his rather sudden death of heart disease)—first as a member of the Menninger therapeutic community, where he was an internist in an affiliated teaching hospital and developed a psychotherapeutically oriented psychosomatic training program for general practitioners, which he called "barnyard psychiatry" (for fuller details of the nature of this identification with the analytic endeavor, see pp. 270–271). He and his wife also enjoyed a social relationship with the Menninger professional psychiatric community. This patient did later on move elsewhere for a career opportunity of wider scope.

The fact that most of the patients in PRP sought out and used continued psychotherapeutic help of various sorts to be specified—in some cases, making use of this help in a very regular and ongoing way—fits perhaps with a different perspective on the nature of the interpersonal helping model than the one that has derived quite understandably from psychoanalysis as a therapeutic endeavor addressed to the problems in living and the neuroses of very adequately and competently functioning individuals. Though Freud, in a famous passage in "Analysis Terminable and Interminable" (1937, p. 249), did speak about every analyst submitting himself "at intervals of five years or so" to periods of further analysis, this has been an admonition honored much more widely in the breach than in the observance. In any case, it was specifically intended to apply to those who are analysts by profession, not to all analysands. However, with the kind of "sicker" patients represented in the PRP sample (a consideration adduced in a variety of differing contexts in this book), perhaps a different therapeutic model does, or should, apply. This perspective would be one of a periodic, in-and-out, sustaining relationship to the psychological helping process, which is only initiated by the first formal coming into specific psychoanalysis or psychotherapy. The kinds of subsequent psychological help, however, can range widely, can be varyingly formal, and can be varyingly explicit. In that sense, this perspective represents an implicit widening of the concept of the "therapeutic lifer," which I have invoked to this point to cover those patients who have continued on past the official Follow-Up Study in a specific and formal psychotherapeutic endeavor that gave promise at that time to be continuing regularly and indefinitely (and, of course, we have had several such).

I now consider the varieties and combinations of Posttreatment psychotherapy and "other therapy" in the PRP sample. I exclude from this discussion the 3 just mentioned who to our knowledge had no such further help, and also of course the 4 who continued uninterruptedly in "therapeutic lifer" status from their original Menninger Foundation treatment, either up to the present time (the Housebound

---

1. The 14 are the 10 for whom we have no further information past the official Follow-Up Study at the 2- to 3-year mark, plus the 4 who were dead by that time (one of whom, of course, the Alcoholic Doctor, had died while still in his original psychoanalytic treatment).

Phobic Woman, the Sexual Masochist, and the Economist) or until retiring and moving away from Topeka (the Fearful Loner). I should also reiterate that this listing is an undercount and perhaps even a major undercount, because of the limitations already noted on follow-up observation spans for so many of the patients.

RETURNS TO FORMAL PSYCHOTHERAPY

Seven patients are known to have returned to formal psychotherapy comparable to what they had originally. The Tantrum Woman, as noted earlier, had 4 additional years of reanalysis with her original analyst; she entered into this as a consequence of the reactivation of old conflicts and symptoms in her new marriage, brought to explicit focus during the Follow-Up Study. Also as noted earlier, the Prince went back for a year of psychotherapy with his original analyst (starting about a year after the Follow-Up Study) for a recrudescence of "the same old problems." However, these were treated now with a more directly confronting and also suppressive approach, since the analyst by this time considered the patient "probably unanalyzable."

Other patients went to or were referred to new therapists in their own new communities. The Rebellious Coed, who, like the Tantrum Woman, came to Follow-Up Study intent on obtaining further therapy, and who had many dissatisfactions about where her first course of psychotherapy had left her, was referred for the new trial at psychotherapy to a psychiatric colleague in her home city. This lasted another year and unhappily left her no further improved than the original 2 years in Topeka did. The Car Salesman was the man who fled The Menninger Foundation (prodded by his wife) after three unsuccessful attempts at psychotherapy over a 3½-year span; he had two further unsuccessful efforts in two different cities in the following year before his death of a drug–alcohol overdose. Peter Pan, whose Menninger Foundation treatment was also incomplete, went on for another 6 months of analytic effort with a new analyst in her new city of residence (which was also terminated totally incomplete). Then, 6 years after leaving Topeka, she brought herself (in a now ominously decompensating state) for another attempt at intensive psychotherapy. This renewed therapy (buttressed by repeated emergency hospitalizations as needed) lasted another year before her death—in her case, suicide by jumping off a bridge. And the Masochistic Editor, who had had a long and failed treatment (a psychoanalysis converted finally to a supportive–expressive psychotherapy, spanning a total of 9 years), sought renewed psychotherapy when he went on to his home city with a local psychiatrist who had once been at The Menninger Foundation and in fact had been this patient's hospital doctor there. This therapeutic arrangement was supplemented by a regulatory arrangement the patient had set up to curb his improvident ways: He turned his entire paycheck over to an accountant, who paid his bills for him and gave him a regular allowance of spending money.

The most interesting treatment course in many ways of the seven patients known to have come back to formal psychotherapy is that of the Devoted Son. His psychoanalysis lasted 5½ years and had to be terminated through a "weaning" process, which the analyst deemed necessary in order to head off the danger of the treatment's settling into an insoluble transference neurosis. Thirteen years after the termination of this treatment, with its only equivocal outcome, the patient returned and then saw his ex-analyst sporadically over the following 2 years, in connection with his own still anhedonic life and his concerns for his aging and declining father. Two years later, at a point 15 years after his original treatment termination, the patient's ex-analyst left Topeka. The patient then switched to another senior clinician with whom he entered regular, once-weekly (30-minute) psychotherapy sessions. This relationship has continued ever since; it is now 7 years later, and the patient is now a true "therapeutic lifer" at a point now 22 years after the termination of his analysis and 27½ years after its start (having joined the other 3 patients who are still "therapeutic lifers").

OTHER "TREATMENT" ARRANGEMENTS

In addition to these 7 who entered a known period of formal psychotherapy at some time after the conclusion of their original analysis or therapy, another 19—the largest group, 45% of the sample—got into other "treatment" arrangements. These could be either single efforts or combinations, explicitly therapeutic or not, explicitly "psychological" or not. Because of the various combinations of approaches or modes of help employed by these patients, there were altogether at least 29 different such helping efforts in which the 19 patients involved themselves.

Self-Medication

Either alone or in combination with something else, 6 of the patients were essentially self-medicated on quite regular and quite substantial doses of psychoactive drugs. No doubt many other of the patients took these and related medications (sedatives, analgesics, stimulants, etc.)—in either larger or lesser doses; regularly or sporadically; self-medicated or prescribed; and either singly or in planned or unplanned conjunction with other, more psychological treatment approaches.

Involvement with Nonpsychiatric Physicians

Five of the patients had continuing involvements with nonpsychiatric physicians (internists or family practitioners) in some central or adjuvant relationship to their continuing psychological difficulties. For example, the Obese Woman had ended her analysis mostly moderately improved, but with her obesity essentially unaltered: She weighed 238 pounds when she came for treatment, and was still at 200 pounds at Follow-Up Study 8 years later. She now was having weekly medical checkups for the treatment of this same obesity, with her diet under close medical management and with sporadic adjuvant amphetamine as an appetite control; none of this, up to this point, was yet very effective. And the Sexual Masochist, whose life adjustment was now tenuously restabilized after a disastrous psychotherapy course, was back in "marriage counseling" with his new wife, as well as now continuously seeing his internist. This latter had begun about a year after his psychotherapy termination, when the seemingly inexorable downhill progression of his life brought him in a severely deteriorated state to his internist, with total exhaustion and all the signs of acute myocarditis. As noted earlier (see p. 410), this "serious heart attack" frightened the patient very much. At the urgent instigation of the internist, he promptly (and totally) gave up his heavy tranquilizer use and smoking. From there on, the patient had taken no more drugs, promptly gained weight and increased in physical well-being, and remained closely under the continued care of the internist (digitoxin for his heart). About this complete turnabout and its aftermath, the patient said, "I think I had enough. I had a bad scare and it was about time I grew up."

With the other three under medical care, the situations were psychologically still more complex. The Involutional Woman, who at the time of Termination Study looked like a "therapeutic lifer," had by Follow-Up Study terminated her psychotherapy, with a highly successful "transfer of the transference" to her internist ("one of the country's great internists"). She saw him constantly for her progressive arthritis. He was an enthusiastic medicine giver and trier of new approaches, and had the patient on a ceaseless, ever-changing round of drugs (antirheumatics, muscle relaxants, analgesics, sedatives, tranquilizers); all were offered with persistent optimism, and often procured for the patient prior to their official marketing. The patient, as noted (see p. 379), was wryly proud of her great capacity to absorb medications. This patient was also concomitantly seeing her minister for spiritual guidance and solace, and, between the ongoing ministrations of her internist and minister, was able to relinquish her psychotherapist and maintain her very good psychotherapeutic improvement.

The Adoptive Mother was the patient who went on to her permanent community of residence after the completion of her analysis, determined to try to "make good" in the arena of central significance to her — the question of adopting and successfully holding and raising a child. When she put her name on the adoption list at the social agency and her anxieties recurred, she did not seek additional formal analytic therapy in her new setting, which it had been predictively asserted by the research evaluators would have been unwise (see pp. 301–302 for the circumstances and the reasoning). Instead, she sought out her friendly family physician, who prescribed medications to help her cope with her anxieties and tensions; the priest, who admonished her to her Christian duties; and the social worker, who could understandingly listen to her full burden of worry. In this way the patient indeed put together the ingredients of a helpful supportive–expressive psychotherapy that enabled her to carry through the adoption, and what came after, very successfully indeed. It also served to preclude any more ambitious psychotherapeutic or psychoanalytic effort.

With the Suspended Medical Student, the role of the long-time family friend and physician mentor in his posttreatment life was a different one; more explicitly than with any of the others in this group, it was psychologically supportive. This physician was the individual who had inspired the patient to pursue his medical career in the first place. During the posttreatment period, when all the patient's seeming achievements from his completed analysis were crumbling into massive symptomatic and behavioral regression under the impact of his efforts to establish himself in a medical practice, the physician mentor devoted himself to trying to keep the patient psychologically afloat. He did this in part by trying to work out the patient's return for further psychiatric evaluation and treatment (as already described); in part by using his influence to try to shield the patient from the consequences of his malfeasances (threats to his medical license, his hospital practice, privileges, etc.); and in part through life counseling in the direction of stress reduction. Ultimately, of course, this was all totally unavailing. (Of course, with all five of these patients who were seeing nonpsychiatric physicians in the ways described, not just with the Suspended Medical Student, the physician—whatever else he was doing medically—also played a sustaining psychological role. It could be as unsuccessful as it was with the Suspended Medical Student, or as successful as it was with the Adoptive Mother or the Involutional Woman.)

Social Casework Relationships

In more traditional psychological helping terms, three of the patients were in very significant ongoing social casework relationships. With the Adoptive Mother, the social worker was one of the trio of helpers she put together to help her over the crisis of adoption. The Divorced Nurse was seeing a social worker in relation to the ongoing psychotherapy of her young son. She was fearful that she might lose his affections to his female therapist, who would prove a better mother and succeed where she had failed; the patient could use her casework help not only to alter her relationship with her son in a favorable direction, but also to help bridge the gap between her former intense involvement with her own analyst and her future on her own. Finally, the Obedient Husband, after his own therapy terminated, continued in casework guidance linked also to his son's psychotherapy. This shaded over then into a family counseling process, centering around the mutual give-and-take of intrafamily problem solving, which the patient was reluctant to carry on without sustaining help.

Marriage and Family Counseling

Similarly, three patients were in marriage and family counseling together with their spouses, as a successor to their terminated individual psychotherapies. These have all been mentioned. The Obedient Husband's family counseling grew out of the casework involvement around the son's therapy, but then went on as a joint endeavor. It was especially helpful to the patient in his relationship to the ongoing psychotherapy of his wife—a chronically psychotic character, "sicker" than he ever was, whose psychotherapy predated his and has long survived his. (In fact, *she* is still in the same treatment today, a "lifer" of by now over 25 years.) The Heiress, after finally terminating with her analyst and becoming caught up in a second marriage that was reminiscent of, rather than different from, the strongly sadomasochistic interactions of the first marriage, was in marriage counseling (with someone else than her analyst) centered around the couple's struggles over the raising of their baby. Unhappily, the husband broke the counseling up, accusing the counselor of always siding with his wife because she paid the bills. However, they returned to it several years after the Follow-Up Study, when the marital struggles had exploded to the point where the drunk patient finally chased her husband with a knife and hammer in a serious assault attempt. And the Sexual Masochist, described already as the very "sickest" patient in the whole PRP population, was able after his psychotherapy had ended disastrously to come back to treatment with his former therapist, under the guise of its being "family therapy" addressed to his and his wife's joint problems in the marriage. With his concomitant regular and intense medical care subsequent to his heart ailment, this patient was at official Follow-Up Study seemingly an entrenched "therapeutic lifer." This indeed proved to be the case.

Further Hospitalization

Even more comprehensive as a major management and psychotherapeutic intervention was continued hospitalization or rehospitalization for patients in our research sample. There were a fair number of instances of this, especially in brief "drying-out" spells with some of the continuing, unstable, still recurrently alcoholic PRP patients. With four of the patients, further hospitalization(s) played a more significant role. The Addicted Doctor was the individual transferred to the affiliated state mental hospital after a very serious suicide attempt terminated his outpatient psychotherapy at The Menninger Foundation. He then went on in a successor inpatient psychotherapy at the state hospital for the next 2½ years. I have already recounted how the patient made a shambles of the intended controls of the managed hospital environment, carried on a large-scale contraband drug traffic, and was in an easy position, when his psychic state was at an all-time low point, to end his life with a drug overdose in his hospital bed. The Invalided Hypochondriac likewise went on from an incompleted Menninger Foundation treatment (hospitalization and psychotherapy) to a successor hospitalization: Her husband removed her to a state hospital in her home state, where she stayed 7 months. Peter Pan was the patient whose psychotically decompensating course, 6 years after the official treatment termination (which had been strongly pressured by the husband and was very premature), could not be stayed by the most intensive and devoted year-long psychotherapeutic work punctuated by six emergency periods of hospitalization in three different hospitals. Like the Addicted Doctor, this patient also ended as a suicide, jumping off a bridge. And, last in this group, the Masochistic Editor had a 2-month Menninger Foundation hospitalization for treatment of his continuing chronic alcoholism, 17 years after the termination of his failed psychoanalysis which provided a vital window of contact upon the subsequent life and career of such a masochistically and self-destructively oriented individual. Therapeutically, this renewed hospitalization ended just as fruitlessly as had the prior long and intensive treatment effort.

Support from the Clergy

In addition to these many kinds of planned psychiatric and medical treatment interventions, ranging from hospitalizations and medications through formal psychotherapy, social casework guidance, and marriage and family counseling, other patients employed a variety of other kinds of helping modes, not explicitly psychotherapeutic. Two who sought help from the clergy have been mentioned. The Adoptive Mother found the priest to admonish her to her conjugal duties (supported by her own direct appeals to God, praying intensely and "storming heaven"), and he became part of her total package (physician, priest, and social worker). The Involutional Woman also obtained support and solace from her minister in bearing up under the pain and disability of her advancing arthritis; he became part of *her* total package, along with her enthusiastic and optimistic internist.

A third who belongs in this category is the Exhibitionistic Dancer, who had an essentially failed psychotherapy and a badly failed marriage (to an even sicker, more behaviorally disturbed fellow patient). She was the individual whose mother was a Christian Science devotee, and who, during her hardly helpful psychotherapy and her very unhelpful marriage, attached herself strongly to the Christian Science faith. She had begun this involvement unbeknownst to her therapist while still in her psychotherapy; in fact, it had been under the influence of the Christian Science practitioner's statements that the two approaches were incompatible that the patient had left the therapy and swung her allegiance and her hope for psychological stabilization to Christian Science. The details of this relationship have been previously given (see pp. 509–510). To this patient it became the sustaining relationship of her life, one that she felt rescued her to some achieved functional restabilization. Certainly the Pollyannaish denials fed by Christian Science became a major organizing part of the patient's patterning of defenses and ego organization, as discerned in the Follow-Up Study evaluation process. Her quite borderline functioning could seem to be maintained within the supportive confines marked out for her by her Christian Science precepts. And certainly to this patient, Christian Science provided a far greater sense of psychological nurture than psychotherapy itself ever had.

Support from Other Helpers

With other patients, it was not the clergy but others who fulfilled similar roles. The Sexual Masochist maintained as a vital part of his support system—along with his internist, and his psychotherapist now doing "family and marital therapy"—an intense relationship with his lawyer. During his psychotherapy, and at a time when his attendance at his scheduled therapy hours was quite sporadic, this patient had gotten into the custom of daily, hour-long sessions with his lawyer, who served as a combination of counselor, friend, legal advisor, business partner, and, not least, amateur therapist. These sessions were filled with endlessly repetitive questions concerning his stock market transactions of that day, the rules and regulations of his rental properties, and the like; the same question could be asked concerning each house in turn. For his daily interviews, the lawyer charged a regular fee. This same relationship continued into the follow-up period, both when the psychotherapy had dropped and after it was resumed as conjoint marital therapy. It only began to diminish some when the intensity of the patient's medical involvements with his internist began to replace it as a central guiding focus.

With the Alcoholic Heir, a chief source of psychological support both during and after his analytic therapy was his employer. He had originally found this employer when he asked for a job, stating that he had a drinking problem, that he did not need to work for a living, and that he had come to this office because of the reputation of the manager as a good teacher and supervisor. The manager took an interest in the patient and took a chance on him when no one else would—the patient had been turned down everywhere else he had tried. This employer felt that the patient had business talent and was "potentially very successful." Once involved, the employer "couldn't remain objective. I always get subjectively involved." He tried "to develop the man"; he deplored his problem with alcohol and tried to curb his drinking. He ended up spending an average of three evenings a week with the patient for the purpose of helping him stay sober and regain his confidence. Unfortunately, none of this prevailed against the patient's destructive course. At the employer's last contact, the patient seemed to be drinking somewhat less and was, with a fair degree of diligence, following through on some complex insurance schemes with a number of clients. It was only 4 days afterward that the patient called a physician, turned out to have pneumonia and pneumococcal meningitis, and, in his alcohol-weakened condition, went rapidly downhill to his death in another 4 days despite heroic medical measures.

Finally, the Bohemian Prep School Boy, who colluded with his father's disruption of his psychotherapy after only 7 months in order to follow the father's call to join the family in their move to Europe, was back in the United States within a year and enrolled in an academy for dramatic arts in a large city. There, he was most enthusiastic in his training as a mime and was attached in a hero-worshipping way to his teacher in that art form. This was clearly at the time the most central involvement and sustaining relationship in his life. "The day I stop doing mime I won't exist. This is the first time where I've ever allowed myself to do well." For the rest, he was leading the same kind of only semiorganized life as of yore.

Alcoholics Anonymous

Two other patients need to be mentioned here in this description of the array of psychological supports that they individually worked out in their posttreatment lives. The Alcoholic Raconteur was the patient who came demanding to be treated by psychoanalysis (to be buttressed by having given himself up to almighty God, so that he could be in a state of grace to receive the benefits of the analysis); he was scornful of AA, to which his alcoholic mother had been intermittently fervently attached. When the patient's 2 years and 9 months of psychoanalytic effort ended over his refusal to tolerate the conversion to a face-to-face supportive–expressive psychotherapy, which the analyst deemed essential in order to control the patient's wildly uncontrolled, alcoholic, and otherwise destructive behaviors more directly, the patient embarked on a downhill course of steady drinking. He subsisted on handouts and descended into a skid row life; after a year or so, he "really hit bottom," ending in police court badly battered after a barroom brawl. At this point, he presented himself at "Twelfth Step House," an AA home for alcoholic transients. He became a faithful AA member and claimed not to have had a drop to drink since. He attended AA meetings almost daily. He did not always get along well with his AA sponsors and seemed to exchange these rather frequently as he felt rising tides of hostile tensions with each of them successively. But this did not seem to matter; he had been saved by AA, not by individuals. (For the presentation of his whole treatment course, see pp. 498–504.)

A Combination

And last in this listing of the array of psychological supportive modes entered by these 19 patients is almost a side note to the eminently successful psychoanalytic outcome of the Phobic Woman. This patient still had accretions of phobic or social anxiety, for which at times she took minor tranquilizers; at times she also "lubricated" her social life with alcohol. Mostly, however, she liked to rely on the semihypnotic relaxation techniques that she had learned during one of her pregnancies and that she felt generalized very helpfully.

MAINTENANCE OF CONTACT
WITH EX-ANALYSTS AND
EX-THERAPISTS

A very large proportion of the PRP patients maintained some kind of personal contact with their ex-analysts or therapists, whether in the form of periodic consultations, sporadic or rare consultations, or simply "social visits" spaced over time to bring the therapists up to date on their doings. These included a good many of the 28 patients already mentioned up to this point in this chapter — the 3 who had no subsequent therapeutic contacts as far as we know; the 7 who returned to formal psychoanalysis or psychotherapy (either with the same or with a different therapist); and the 19 who had varieties of other treatment approaches (specifically psychotherapeutic or not), geared in some way toward psychological understanding and/or support.[2] But, in addition, ten of the 14 remaining PRP patients continued such consultations or visits as the main vehicle of posttreatment therapeutic contact.

A Single Personal Contact

The nature of these contacts varied widely. The Bohemian Musician made a single decisive return visit, when she came back to Topeka to seek her ex-therapist's counsel about her pending remarriage. Her fiancé was an executive in a major industry, the scion of a distinguished and aristocratic family, and someone who shared her serious interest in music. As noted earlier (see p. 386), she brought along a variety of papers covering the prospective husband's financial condition, income, family responsibilities, and work plans, and, after spreading them out all over the therapist's desk, wanted to know whether she was overlooking something. At the same time, she spoke of her fiancé in a genuinely affectionate manner. The therapist pointed out that, though she was asking advice about her choice, she had presented nothing that would weigh on the negative side. The patient knew

2. These figures actually add to 29, because one patient (Peter Pan) has been listed both among those who returned to formal therapy and among those who received other kinds of therapeutic supports (in her case, rehospitalizations).

this, and it became clear that what she came seeking was license to go ahead with what she had already decided upon. She also discussed how to sever her ties to her previous boyfriend (the handicapped man), whom she still saw periodically; following this session, she was able to withdraw from that relationship in a direct, yet kindly way. Thus fortified, the patient went into the new marriage a few months later. She did not seek further psychiatric counsel.

Repeated but Circumscribed Personal Contacts

By contrast, the English Professor, after his analysis, sought out his ex-analyst for periodic consultation at various significant points in his life. In part, his motive was to ask whether he should seek more treatment (see p. 603). In equal part, it was to touch base and to seek counsel concerning his marriage, his conflicts with his wife over the demands of her glamorous job, their conflicts about having children, and so forth. These contacts, about one a year, were kept very discrete and circumscribed.

With the Claustrophobic Man, the recovered cancer victim, a similar process was more intense. He had about a dozen contacts with his ex-therapist over a span of about 5 years posttreatment. There was a concentrated series of five interviews about a year into the follow-up period. His father was quite ill (heart disease, pneumonia, gall bladder attacks); however, though retired, he still kept an office at the business and was constantly interfering, prying, and critical. The patient had begun to note some return of his phobic symptoms and increasing difficulty in controlling his irritability with his father. During this series of interviews, which centered almost entirely around this difficult relationship, the patient was ultimately able to say that he "knew darn well that the thing that was causing him trouble was that every now and then he found himself thinking how much more pleasant life would be if his father died." After the 5 hours, the patient said to the therapist, "I no longer need you to act as a buffer between myself and my father." (See pp. 401–402 for more details on this.)

A year or so later (after the official Follow-Up Study), the patient contacted the research group to indicate that he had "cut the Gordian knot." He had sold out his share of the family business to his brother, and was planning a new business venture in a related area that would be all his own, and therefore less constrictive and confining. Two years later the patient saw his ex-therapist and also a neurologist when he developed some transient visual difficulties. An episodic cerebral anoxia due to carotid artery insufficiency (from postirradiation scarring) was diagnosed. The difficulty was minimal, and the patient was reassured. And again, 2½ years later, now semiretired, the patient came with his wife; they were concerned about their son, who was now divorced and running around irresponsibly with "a fast crowd." They were distressed that the son was warding off any acknowledgment of need for psychiatric help. All these contacts took place in the context of this patient's having terminated his own successful therapy with an intense positive glow and a powerful identification with his therapist, expressed through his taking on the role of popularizing psychiatry in his home town. Psychiatry became his new civic duty, as described earlier (see p. 401).

Very Long-Term Personal Contacts

And two of these ten patients are mentioned just in terms of the truly long time spans over which these posttreatment contacts could go on, without the patient's ever going back into treatment (though the patients might or might not be asking for it or asking about it). The Snake Phobia Woman's analysis itself spanned only 2½ years and seemed to be quite successful. Yet this patient continued in contact with her ex-analyst, fairly frequently during the immediate posttreatment period of follow-up observation, and then spaced more widely over a 22-year span. These contacts were usually consultation visits. Sometimes the patient was accompanied by her husband, who himself went into treatment for 1½ years early in this time (from his point of view, this "saved the marriage"). Occasionally there was contact by mail. (For the details of these follow-up contacts over this whole time span, see pp. 312–314.)

The other patient to be mentioned here is the Phobic Girl. She had married during her 8½-year-long psychotherapy (she was the patient who had looked like a "therapeutic lifer" during her Termination Study but actually terminated her treatment before the Follow-Up Study). The husband was the first nonpatient with whom the patient had gone out, and the courtship was the most "normal" such relationship the patient had known; the patient married with her parents' approval. From the start, the marriage was reasonably stable and the husband reasonably tolerant of the patient's obesity and her still continuing phobic constrictions. He was quite unfamiliar with psychotherapy, but if his wife wanted to spend the earnings from her job to pay for treatment, he would enter no objection. The actual treatment termination took place after the patient's return from her third and (to this point) most successful cross-country trip to visit her in-laws. The couple decided to continue living in Topeka. The patient could then always contact the therapist if need be, though "now I don't feel I need to hang on to him any more. . . . And besides, my husband now does some of the same things for me the treatment has done" (the seemingly ubiquitous concept of "transfer of the transference"). There was a further 16-year period of sporadic (and happenstance) follow-up contact with the therapist beyond that point, the content of which has been described on p. 475. It took place in visits a year later, 13 years later (at both of which times the patient was still living in Topeka), and 16 years later (on a return holiday visit by the patient in Topeka—this time in the context of a social encounter with the original therapist).

Exchanges of Correspondence

With the remaining patients, the chief contacts with the ex-therapists were by way of exchanges of correspondence. Again, these were not the only ones who used this modality of discourse, since many of the other patients as well (among those living away from Topeka) were involved in letter writing; this ranged from the annual Christmas card catching up to a much more intensive and much more deliberately therapeutic correspondence. Two instances are described here that represent the more intensive extreme of such correspondence. For the Movie Lady, the correspondence was her sole "therapeutic" contact; for the Divorced Nurse, there were other contacts (such as the concomitant social casework guidance in connection with her son's psychotherapy), but for a period the letter writing occupied a very central role indeed.

The Movie Lady, who had moved to her distant home city, exchanged letters with her therapist about three or four times a year. They were chatty, newsy letters as between old friends, with exchanges of personal information both ways (minor illnesses, family news, the doings of the respective children, etc.). On one occasion, when the therapist had not heard from the patient for a considerable interval, he called her; she apologized for being remiss in her correspondence. On another occasion, at the patient's suggestion, her husband made an appointment and called on the therapist when business travel took him back to that area. In one of the therapist's letters, he gave the patient the essence of the kinds of changes and improvements that the psychologist had seen in comparing the before-and-after psychological testing protocols. It was an optimistic portrayal. One letter (the very first) from the patient ended with a statement embodying her conception of her psychotherapeutic experience: "I hope you are enjoying your vacation and will be rested to face another year of comforting." Clearly, these exchanges were emotionally forthcoming in both directions. The therapist, for example, wrote in one of his letters that the patient was right; his daughter could wrap him around her little finger. The patient felt that the therapist had always wanted her to have warmer feelings toward him in the therapy, to feel toward him as one would towards a father. She indicated that he did seem like a father to her, and she worried about him as she would have about a father. The entire climate of the correspondence in this case must be set within the framework of a therapy originally planned as psychoanalysis, but altered within 6 months to an expressive-supportive psychotherapy, within which the therapist tried to give the patient "a corrective emotional experience" that a man could be trusted and could care; as part of this, he was willing to "honestly" discuss his own responses and his own problems (his heart illness) with the patient (see pp. 414–415, 239–240).

The Divorced Nurse was the patient whose husband divorced her during her analysis and whose bitterly contested divorce litigation ended in her losing custody of her children to her ex-husband. During the 2½-year period of follow-up observation, the patient continued her direct contacts with her analyst and The Menninger Foundation. During the 18 months when she lived in her old home town, she wrote 25 long and detailed letters to her ex-analyst—13 of them in 1 month when the turmoil over whether and to what extent to pursue the custody fight was at its height. The analyst responded to a number of these: "Stop running, take your time, don't make emergency decisions. . . . I'm glad that you feel free and able to 'talk' to me this way and to share with me so many of your feelings and thoughts. . . . I have lots of faith in you. I feel that things will work out." For more details on his advice to the patient concerning her litigation problems, her prospective move back to Topeka in order to get her son into treatment (which she did), and his interpretations concerning her continuing masochistic and guilt-ridden behaviors, see pp. 318–319. This patient has lived in Topeka ever since her return for her son's treatment. The flood of letters was replaced by periodic consultations with her ex-analyst over the years, but these became very widely spaced after the acute posttreatment and postdivorce turmoil had subsided. These occasional consultations (over another 18 years) concerned problems with her children, her aging mother, her own menopause, her severe back problems and surgery, and so forth. Her life continued bleak, and the ex-analyst's role in these consultations was predominantly exhortatory.

GENERAL COMMENTS

For the four remaining patients unaccounted for thus far under this heading, the issue of posttreatment return to treatment did not apply. One, the Alcoholic Doctor, died during the course of his original psychoanalytic treatment. The other three were the continuous "therapeutic lifers," who at the Follow-Up Study mark were still in their original treatments and seemed to be continuing indefinitely (the Housebound Phobic Woman, the Fearful Loner, and the Economist).

The issue of how "normal" or how "usual" this very widespread continuation of varieties of posttreatment therapeutic contacts is has already been discussed as a reflection in part of the "sicker" patients represented in the PRP sample (i.e., sicker than the usual patients in private practice outpatient psychoanalysis and intensive psychotherapy). It surely also reflects the particular ambience of The Menninger Foundation psychiatric community, and the close contact and clustering that seem to be characteristic for so many of those who have come within its therapeutic orbit. And, of course, there is the question already raised in Chapter 30 of how much the structuring of PRP—taking the patients into formal Termination Studies, and then preparing them for subsequent formal Follow-Up Studies, including paid return trips to Topeka with their spouses for that purpose—tended to powerfully reinforce the continuing attachment to the therapist, the institution, and the psychotherapeutic enterprise. The fact that we were collectively so interested in the continuing careers and lives of the patients could certainly play a role of undetermined scope in buttressing the patients' willingness and desire to maintain themselves in relation to the availability of psychological help and counsel. Finally, of course, there just are no real data on how much an "ordinary" population in comparably intensive analytic therapies in the more usual kind of setting (and without formal research and/or follow-up participation) also maintains posttreatment therapeutic contacts and/or comes to posttreatment therapies.

Stability at Follow-Up:
The Role of the Environment

"TRANSFERENCE" TO THE MENNINGER FOUNDATION

Nature of the Phenomenon

In a widely influential article, Reider (1953) first applied the concept of "transference to the institution" to the emotional valences established by certain kinds of patients to the institutional setting (hospital or clinic) in which they have their psychiatric treatment, quite apart from those they may have to the individual therapist who treats them. Such valences can be manifested in a variety of ways: The patients can accept a change of therapist without significant evidence of resentment or sense of loss; they may refer impersonally to their treatment ("I have an appointment at the clinic," rather than "with Dr. X."); they may actually come to the clinic at their usual appointed hours even when their therapists are on vacation, claiming momentarily to have forgotten, but being content then just to sit there in the waiting room visiting with the other patients they know who have the same appointment time; they may idealize the institution and accept every offered therapist as surely competent ("Oh, he must be good or he wouldn't be here"); and so forth. For obvious reasons, these kinds of observations were first made in the public hospital or clinic settings to which poor patients were used to coming for their varieties of physical and mental health problems. For the same reasons, such observations would not arise from the usual outpatient therapeutic practice setting, with the isolated office and waiting room, the rare and only chance contact with other patients, and all of the therapeutic transferences focused very clearly onto the person of the therapist (and the very personal extensions of the therapist—office decor, car in the parking lot, etc.).

In these senses, The Menninger Foundation has had a very special character. On the one hand, it has always (especially in the days before at least partial coverage for mental health benefits under comprehensive health insurance plans became widely available through government or business employment) catered to the segment of the community wealthy enough to mobilize the resources for such expensive and long-term care, which always costs much more than just being in outpatient analytic treatment in one's home community. On the other hand, these patients are clearly being referred or are coming to The Menninger Foundation for consultation and/or treatment; they very rarely come specifically to, or even have the name of, a particular staff member, no matter how nationally known and eminent that individual might be. And when seen in evaluation and then taken into treatment, each patient is assigned to a therapist in terms of the availability of time and the particular degree or kind of skill and training that is felt to be required by the nature of that particular patient's problems. Very explicitly, there is no relation between the fee charged and the prestige or seniority of the assigned therapist.[1] In these senses, then, a situation of "transference to the institution" usually exists (in some instances strongly) even before the patients come to The Menninger Foundation (as it does, for example, with the Mayo Clinic), and this tendency is clearly fostered by the nature of the institutional arrangements at The Menninger Foundation.

All this, of course, plays a very substantial role in the large extent to which these patients—drawn for the overwhelming part from across the country, and often from the very far reaches of the country—remain after their treatments (and

---

1. Prospective therapists, of course, have some degree of leeway in taking patients from the waiting list into treatment (in terms of personal preferences, considerations of overall balance in one's caseload, etc.), though, on his or her side, the director of the psychotherapy service has to make sure that every patient on the waiting list is somehow appropriately placed without undue delay, no matter what the foreseen difficulties or complexities of the case. And, from their side, the prospective patients have some degree of leeway in feeling that a particular treatment assignment will not be congenial or will not work out, and in asking for another assignment—which may, however, take a while.

often for their lifetimes) in close physical proximity to The Menninger Foundation. This naturally then becomes another aspect of their ready recourse to posttreatment therapeutic contact and counsel. And this ready establishment of the transference to this particular institution, combined with the resulting facilitation of the recourse to posttreatment psychological help, plays a very substantial role in helping determine the posttreatment and continuing psychological fate and stability of these patients. It becomes a major generally positive prognostic indicator, perhaps balancing off to some extent the generally worse prognostic outlook of these "sicker" patients.

Long-Term or Permanent Relocations

The PRP data on this kind of (quasi)-permanent settling in Topeka (and the reasons for it) are impressively extensive. Of the whole sample of 42, only 5 (12%) to begin with, were either residing in Topeka (just 1, the Devoted Son, a civil engineer in a local office) or within easy enough commuting distance (4 more) for their recommended outpatient treatments. And of the 4 who had to commute, only 1 (the Obese Woman) was in psychoanalysis and thus faced with a daily commute, which in her case was from a town 35 miles away. These 5 patients, as expected, went through their treatments and maintained their domiciles and ongoing lives intact through and after their treatment processes.

Another 15 patients (just over 35% of the sample) came or were sent to Topeka in order to have their treatment, remained for its durations (6 months to 9 years in their cases), and then returned to their home communities or moved to new home communities at the conclusion of the treatment—in other words, they followed what would be expected to be the usual course of events. In one kind of instance, the husband of the Adoptive Mother engineered his military assignment to be stationed at an installation right outside Topeka in order for his wife to be able to secure her needed psychoanalytic treatment easily. In another instance, Peter Pan, was referred for treatment at The Menninger Foundation because an effort at comparable inpatient treatment with psychotherapy in her home community had foundered over the therapist's inability to deal with the continuous interferences of the patient's parents. In most instances, the needed psychoanalytic treatment was just not available in the patients' home towns, or the patients needed concomitant hospitalization within a therapeutically geared sanatorium setting. Finally, 1 of these 15 (the Movie Lady) was the patient treated not in Topeka but in the city in which she was then residing; she then moved after the completion of her treatment to a new permanent city of residence with her husband. (For the circumstances of her inclusion in PRP, Chapter 6, footnote 8, p. 95). In the categorizing here, she seems best included among those patients who sought treatment and then returned to or went on to permanent cities of residence.

All the other patients in PRP—22, or just over half the sample—had their life courses permanently altered (or modified for a substantial continuing period of time) by virtue of their relationship to their treatments at The Menninger Foundation and their living and working in Topeka during their treatments. Of these 22, 13 (almost one-third of the total sample) settled in Topeka either for the rest of their lives or for very long periods indeed after their treatment terminations. They did this on various expressed bases and with widely varying subsequent life courses. The duration was as short as 6 months in one instance (the Alcoholic Heir, who was working in a local insurance office until his illness and death of pneumonia and meningitis); by contrast, several others are still known to be in Topeka as of this writing. In one of these cases, Topeka is now just a permanent home (the Divorced Nurse, after trying herself for 18 months in her home community, came back ostensibly for her son's psychotherapy and her own casework, and also for her own nearness to her former analyst). Another patient remains in Topeka because of continued treatment needs in the family (the Obedient Husband's own formal psychotherapy lasted only 18 months, but his wife, the chronic psychotic character, is still in her ongoing psychotherapy at The Menninger Foundation 25 years later).

With someone like the Silent Woman, who came to Topeka for an analysis that lasted only a year, settling in Topeka represented many "firsts" in her life. For the first time, she successfully established a home for herself away from the parental home; for the first time, she sought, secured, and maintained a job for herself (not selected by and protected by her father). Beyond these achievements, she prepared herself educationally for a job at a higher level of responsibility and interest, which she likewise obtained and maintained with ever-growing job performance, job satisfaction, and overall morale. Finally, for the first time, she could consolidate these achievements by bringing her two separated and quarreling sons together under one roof, her roof, and undertaking to be simultaneously a successful parent, homemaker, and breadwinner. Though the patient abruptly disrupted her painfully silent analytic treatment after only a year and with very modest analytic gains, she felt her life achievements to be considerable at this point. She also maintained a friendly contact with The Menninger Foundation and did come back for several consultations with the staff psychiatrist who had conducted her initial evaluation for treatment (not with her former analyst). These were spread over a span of 11 years and concerned such issues as her successful return to and completion of her college education with honors, her father's death, her decision on some recommended elective surgery, and even a brief romantic involvement with a very disturbed man who had been an old high school flame 30 years earlier.

The Tantrum Woman's story in this regard is quite similar. After graduating with a graduate clinical degree, she obtained full-time employment in Topeka and built herself a larger home than she had lived in during her analysis. ("By chance," it was in the immediate neighborhood of her ex-analyst.) She continued to see the ex-analyst in regular consultation; in the context of his "suggestion" about marriage, she met a lonely widower living in the very next block, shortly married him, and joined him in a business venture to make some income supplemental to their jobs. And, of course, she had her 4 years of reanalysis with her original analyst in Topeka.

Other cases were broadly similar, but individually diverse. The Phobic Woman settled into attendance as a student at a nearby university; the Medical Scientist obtained employment as a staff internist at the affiliated VA hospital, teaching psychosomatic medicine to medical residents and general practitioners. The English Professor gradually consolidated his position as a senior and admired professor in the local college, and felt his phobic propensities were enough under control so that he could fantasize about accepting the deanship some day, or perhaps even one of the offers he got from time to time from a larger, more prestigious university ("I wouldn't have to be too much less anxious in order to be able to be the dean"). Finally, different from the others, the Addicted Doctor remained in Topeka as a transfer patient to the local affiliated state hospital, where he continued in treatment with a Menninger-trained psychiatrist until his death by suicide.

In addition to the 13 who thus settled in Topeka more or less permanently after the completion of their psychiatric treatments, 2 others (the Heiress and the Bitter Spinster) followed their therapists to the therapists' new permanent cities of residence and resided in those cities after their treatments terminated (dynamically, this was a quite equivalent phenomenon). Three others stayed on in Topeka because they had become "lifers" (the Housebound Phobic Woman, the Sexual Masochist, and the Fearful Loner). The Housebound Phobic Woman is still in Topeka and still in treatment (now at the 26-year mark), as is the Sexual Masochist (now at the 28-year mark). The Fearful Loner remained in Topeka for another 11 years of treatment past the Follow-Up Study point, until his retirement, at which time he and his wife felt ready to leave in order to retire to a small isolated farm in the patient's home state and home area.

Of the remaining 4 patients not yet accounted for, 1 (the Economist), who was the other "therapeutic lifer," eventually moved to another state in connection with a university employment opportunity—at a point where the patient was finally convinced (after over 10 years together) that the therapist would be "instantly available" in any emergency, and so he could allow some loosening of his tenacious attachment. From this job, he would come back to Topeka for weekend visits every 6 weeks, with late Friday afternoon and early Saturday morning therapy hours. He has remained in continuous contact with his original analyst, who himself now lives in a distant state. For a time the patient moved to the therapist's new city of residence for regular psychotherapy; he now lives across the country from him, but is still in regular twice-monthly contact. Two others (the Alcoholic Raconteur and the equally alcoholic Script Writer) lived in Topeka or its environs for much briefer periods. The Alcoholic Raconteur did so in connection with his continued alcohol excess and his being where he could be rescued by The Menninger Foundation when he got down and out enough; the Script Writer remained in Topeka in order to defiantly enter outpatient psychotherapy locally with a psychiatrist *not* on The Menninger Foundation staff, when the urgent recommendation of The Menninger Foundation was for a renewed treatment effort only with concomitant hospitalization. The last patient, the Alcoholic Doctor, died of aspiration of vomitus during a debilitated period while still in his original analytic treatment at the 7-year mark.

NEW MARITAL RELATIONSHIPS

Another whole aspect of major change in a patient's life space and life surroundings that could play a most significant role in the stabilization of the patient's life in the posttreatment period would be, of course, altered marital status and family constellation. In Section VII (see Chapter 28), I have already described the marriages of the 19 PRP patients who came to their treatments married, as well as those of the 17 who married during or after the course of their treatments (14 of those who came unmarried, and 3 of those who came married, then divorced and married again). I have emphasized there the various ways in which these marriages operated helpfully or hurtfully in relation to the patients' psychological stability, both in those instances where spouses brought their own serious psychopathology to bear upon the marital interaction, and in those other instances that did not carry such an extra psychological burden. Part of Chapter 28 also describes those spouses whose psychopathology and/or interactions with the patients helped maintain or allow an accommodation to the patients' illnesses, often over long periods of time (with concomitant long delays in seeking treatments), as well as those that contributed to or conduced to psychological restoration and therefore facilitated the treatment. I do not go over that ground here again, except to underline a few of the instances in the 17 new marriages where the new marital relationships played a role similar to and often synergistic with that of the Menninger therapeutic community in helping stabilize the patients' post-therapeutic life functioning.

Highly Effective New Marriages

Most striking in its effectiveness was the second marriage of the Bohemian Musician. She was the woman who could not tolerate her first marriage to a well-to-do businessman and a good burgher, who just could not share the intellectual and artistic interests that she so sedulously cultivated (see pp. 141, 173, 382–383). Her interests were in music, the arts, and partying with her unconventional friends; the husband's interests were in home and gardening, hunting and fishing. The care of their house and their adopted son fell largely to the husband.

The patient, as described, then "resolved" her dilemma by picking up with an interesting, intellectual, artistic lover in a big city; the husband tolerated her living apart from him (and with her lover) for 5 years. When the husband finally presented the patient with the ultimatum that they either divorce or she return to him, the patient did forsake her lover and return home, only to collapse rapidly into the totally disorganized state that brought her to psychiatric hospitalization at The Menninger Foundation (see pp. 124, 145, 150). She had to receive a course of ECT before her deepening depression could be coped with and the patient rendered accessible to psychotherapy. This highly narcissistic woman was then in a supportive–expressive psychotherapy over a span of 3 years (see pp. 382–388 for the description of the treatment course). At its termination, the patient had been divorced by her husband in a bitterly litigated proceeding; surprisingly, she went back to her home town (ostensibly to be near her son), accompanied by a dependent, handicapped lover.

It was during the follow-up period that this patient made her return visit to her ex-therapist (see pp. 602, 615–616) to seek counsel about her pending remarriage, and came armed with such impressive financial documentation. It turned out that this man, a business executive from a very distinguished family, shared the patient's serious interest in music; he had a large record collection, was an avid concert goer, and played in a small recorder ensemble. He and the patient had both recently left incompatible marriages and were looking for someone to remarry. In the marriage, they regularly attended concerts and the theatre, and the patient became the director of the amateur recorder-playing group. A couple of evenings a week were spent listening to or playing music together. They had a rather wide circle of friends, some hers, some his, and found them all mutually congenial. The patient, of course, had "always had all kinds of feelings about the responsibilities associated with marriage, especially the domestic ones, but here it didn't seem to be a problem." She was an adequate housekeeper and a willing cook. About once a week they were invited out to dinner with friends, and once a week they gave dinner parties in return. At Follow-Up Study, the patient talked only enthusiastically about her happy marriage and their shared life.

As previously stated (see pp. 387–388), the overall consolidated psychological functioning of the patient evident at the Follow-Up Study point reflected an interacting facilitation between treatment and fortuitous life circumstance. The new husband constituted exactly the kind of culturally and intellectually appreciative and nurturant environment that fulfilled the patient's narcissistic requirements, and to which she could then (for the first time ever) return an emotional *quid pro quo*. The first marriage to an uncongenial husband, with its burdensome requirements of home, family, and son, was for the patient completely out of kilter; the second marriage, to a husband far more congenial to her interests, precisely altered this balance. The patient's psychotherapy had helped her to get out of the one and to secure the other.

Other new marriages evidenced the same phenomenon, but far less dramatically. For instance, the severely alcoholic and addicted Medical Scientist came to his analytic treatment in a seemingly stable marriage, even though at times when he was drunk he could be violently abusive to his wife. He said that "a man could kill a woman when drunk." The patient's relationship with his parents had always been dependent and agreeable. At the patient's initial evaluation for treatment, the parents had stressed that they had always been a "normal," average family, and were "hit like a ton of bricks" by the patient's illness. In the course of his successful psychoanalysis, however (see pp. 266–271), the mother figure emerged in the transference as sly and cold, sadistically scheming, always trying to keep the patient from other girls. When after his (secret) marriage, the patient had written an apologetic letter to his mother, he had said, "Very sorry. Will never do this to you again." In this context, the patient slowly came to understand his lifelong pattern of evading and betraying the threatening mother with another woman, and then in turn feeling threatened by the new woman in the same way he felt threatened by the mother (underlying his restless promiscuity).

And gradually, too, the patient saw his relationship with his wife as but an extension of that with his mother. As noted earlier, he had divided his life into two 20-year segments, the first of which was his mother's responsibility, and the second of which was his wife's; he had just been the innocent victim. He had entered the marriage impulsively and regretted it directly thereafter. He was episodically unfaithful in it, and would also periodically get drunk and tell his wife off, only to be guilty, depressed, and usually apologetic afterward. He was constantly angry at her, and only relatively happy during his years of wartime military service away. On vacations he had to take long hikes away alone; when home and working, he got out of the house before his wife arose and kept himself busy all day long. His wife was a sharp, competitive person, sarcastic, a "sadistic bitch," and sexually unresponsive. The patient became convinced that they were totally mismatched and decided on a divorce. One didn't have to be inextricably tied to a quarrelsome extension of one's mother.

The patient found it difficult to discuss this divorce decision with his analyst, because he felt that the latter, like his parents, would doubtless oppose it. But he went through with it. He then met and courted another patient, also a recovering alcoholic, also in analysis (with the same analyst), and also doing very well in her treatment. The patient moved smoothly into a second and much more gratifying marriage, marked by a mutuality and an interdependency he had not experienced before. Within a year they had a child. By the end of his analysis the patient was leading a contented married life with a multiply layered family—three children of his wife's, one of his own adopted children, and their new joint child. His own competitive relationship with his new wife's own three children (he had yearned to be her only dependent) had been transformed into an accepting and affectionate relationship.

At Follow-Up Study, the patient described his new marriage as very successful, and in a way that didn't just happen. "You have to work at it. You can't just take people for granted. . . . I like going home to her, I enjoy being with her, we have a lot of fun just talking together. . . . When I say work on it, I think I mean to bring my interests home with me, and to include her in my thinking and planning and worrying and everyday experiences." From the wife's point of view, she felt "up to my neck in children" (now seven—her own three, the patient's two adoptive children, and now two of their own) and often overwhelmed by their gang of adolescent girls, but the patient "came out and straightened it all out neatly. It took his presence. They just didn't try to get by with all this rebelliousness." She admired her husband's ability to work hard: "It's amazing, all he can take without taking it out on the family."

Effective but More Impaired New Marriages

With other patients, similar dynamics seemed operative, but at much more impaired levels of functioning. The Alcoholic Raconteur was the individual who came to treatment loudly demanding psychoanalysis and contemptuous of AA, to which his own alcoholic mother had fervently attached herself. After his failed psychoanalytic treatment and his subsequent decline into a skid row existence, this patient was "rescued" by his own turn to AA and his compulsive attendance within it. At the same time, he was pursuing a strange and stormy romance with a young woman. They had met when his drinking was at its height; she was also quite alcoholic and depressive and had made a few suicide gestures. But she was very accepting and mothering of the patient. "She met me when I was literally on the point of starvation and with every kind of love and help possible brought me around and gave me the confidence and stuck with me." They lived together; they fought (often brawling physically when both were drinking); and all the while she pressed the patient to stop drinking and to marry her. When he joined AA, her drinking too dwindled away. When an episode of philandering by the patient led her to an acutely disturbed state and a dramatic suicide effort, they were tearfully reunited. After that, the two were formally engaged and the patient was insisting that they would get married shortly, since this relationship was different from any he had previously known. The fiancée was converting to Catholicism.

The patient did marry a few months after the Follow-Up Study. As noted earlier, he was the one patient who offered to come back for still another follow-up evaluation; when he was informed that this was not possible, he kept writing letters. He reported that he was still sober and things were continuing "generally upward." He had now been married 8 months, "and I'm beginning to learn what love can be like in marriage." His wife had been pregnant already and had lost the baby, but was now pregnant again and doing well. Six months later came an announcement of the birth of a girl. There was further follow-up when, 12 years after his treatment termination, the patient returned in order to hospitalize his wife at The Menninger Foundation. She was diagnosed as having a narcissistic personality disorder and suffering a schizophrenic decompensation; she came to hospitalization at the point of a severe suicide attempt. This hospitalization lasted almost 2 years.

During this period, the patient had some contact with his ex-therapist. He was still with AA. He was employed steadily as a sales representative for a large firm and had a substantial income. He tried to be cheery and breezy, but he seemed also rather poorly organized, intermittently depressive and hyperactively manic, and actually quite domineering and insecure with his wife. But despite all these very major problems, the patient was holding up, and so was the (very strained) marriage. It would be hard to disentangle the interacting roles of the patient's AA involvement and his troubled yet enduring marriage in helping maintain the patient at a level of functioning that, however limited, was far more substantial than what he had predicted for himself at his Termination Study ("I won't be alive in 2 years, or if I am alive, I'll be in some institution"). (See pp. 498–504 for the description of the whole treatment course.)

A patient quite comparable to the Alcoholic Raconteur in many respects in these regards was the Sexual Masochist. He had come to his treatment divorced by his first wife, who would no longer tolerate his perverse sexual practices, his heavy alcoholism, and his total irresponsibility. His second marriage was entered into during the course of his 8-year-long psychotherapy and started under the most inauspicious of circumstances. The humiliating conditions that this patient set, and to which his wife-to-be agreed prior to the marriage, have already been detailed (see p. 408). Nonetheless, the patient still demurred and did not actually marry until the point when, chronically drugged and by now quite dilapidated, he was being pressured by his therapist toward immediate rehospitalization. The patient instead promptly married and disappeared from his therapy.

Yet, when seen for Termination Study interviews, both the patient and his wife attested to the happy and successful marriage, now 6 months old. They "looked well together." The wife cooked well; she was a nondemanding person who wanted, liked, and fully accepted the patient. She allowed him an almost total infantile dependency within the marriage, and tolerated the fact that he gave her little in return. They admitted to *small* problems within the marriage. The patient was very possessive of his wife's time and would resent the planned visits with her parents in a nearby city, though he would seem to enjoy them when they went. He was often sexually impotent, but his wife minimized this. It was not too important in the marriage except in terms of her wish ultimately to have children, which she might still have in the future. Sexual activity was mainly mutual masturbation, accompanied at times by talk of the patient's perverse fantasies.

At Follow-Up Study, the patient's psychological equilibrium was surprisingly at least holding steady, despite the Termination Study prognostication of a gradual downhill progression. In part, this prognosis had been based on the uncertainty as to whether the patient's wife would continue to abide his infantile dependency and his perverse impulses, since it was so unclear what motivated and held the wife to marriage (rescue satisfactions, pecuniary gain, etc.?). When they were seen at Follow-Up, much had happened in the interim, including the patient's physical collapse with an acute myocarditis, and his frightened turn to a total reliance on his sustaining physician (see pp. 410, 609–610). And the patient and his wife were now back in treatment—"family treatment" with the patient's ex-therapist.

The main focus of this "family treatment," as described earlier (see pp. 410–412), was the marriage and its problems. The patient saw one of these problems as his wife's inordinate dependence upon her parents, whom she felt that she wanted to (and ought to) visit with fair frequency and regularity. The wife saw his reaction to this as jealousy and possessiveness—inability to tolerate her divided attentions, or any signs of her parents' concern and affection for her. The patient constantly derogated the parents and tried to disrupt his wife's relationship with them, which she was then defensively driven to defend frantically. Beyond this source of conflict, the patient could come to acknowledge the severe continuing sexual problem, despite his evasiveness. The details of the massive sexual inhibition with almost total impotence that replaced the patient's former perverse practices and impulses have already been presented, as has the way in which he explained and rationalized his changed behaviors. In any case, the patient no longer approached his wife sexually or even tried to talk about his old perverse fantasies. Sex was dirty and evil, and could not be properly indulged with somebody he liked and respected. He said, "She understands this. . . . she understood this before we got married . . . although I know that it bothers her." It was the therapist who the patient felt was putting pressure on him to stay in treatment in order to work on the sexual problem. The therapist, on the other hand, indicated that in the therapy interviews the patient presented the pressure to solve the problem as his wife's, so that she could come to have a normal sexual life and children. From time to time, the patient would indicate his fear that his wife might leave him over her mounting sexual frustration and dissatisfactions. The wife, however, was sticking by the marriage: Things were better all the time, and she still hoped for improvements. As previously stated, she saw her role as that of mothering a disturbed, even a potentially dangerous, but a very appealing, son.

Failed or Unhelpful New Marriages

Clearly, every new marriage for the PRP patients did not help to maintain the psychological functioning of the patients at so impressive a level as with the Bohemian Musician or the Medical Scientist, or even at as much of a modicum of functioning as with the Alcoholic Raconteur and the Sexual Masochist. In fact, 3 of the 17 new marriages failed completely during our span of observation. These instances have each been described. The Exhibitionistic Dancer married a young delinquent hospital patient even sicker than she, and divorced him 4 years later after a chaotic life together; the Intellectual Fencer's defensive marriage and flight into heterosexuality with another equally addictive and even more blatantly homosexual patient lasted only 5 years, but ended more amicably, with some civilized arrangements over the care and raising of their one child; and the Suspended Medical Student had a marriage that seemed actually the best and most sustaining of the three, but that proved in many ways even less effective than the other two. I describe this last marriage in more detail now.

When the Suspended Medical Student came to analysis after being asked to withdraw from school because of his unethical behaviors during the alcohol-induced fugue states, his second close girlfriend was pressuring him to decide about marriage (a prior engagement with someone else had broken up over the patient's drinking). When he started his analysis, the patient's goals were to be able to return to medical school and to work things out with his second girlfriend so that he could, this time, marry her. After about 2 years of analytic work, the patient finally set the wedding date with his fiancée, who had been patiently standing by through these many vicissitudes; the patient experienced this setting as a rebellious act and feared punishment. But, following the wedding, things seemed to be turning out well. The patient's excess drinking and reckless driving finally dwindled away. The two had by now known each other a long while and seemed well suited to each other. The wife was a good, steady person, and it was only the patient's neurotic disability that had kept them apart so long. And yet, after the patient's successful return to and graduation from medical school, the termination of his analysis, and the embarking on the general medical practice that had been such a long-time goal, everything suddenly began to come apart and the patient proved totally unable to cope; in all of this, the wife's continuing support seemed to avail nothing. She tried in every way she could to counter the patient's renewed alcoholic states and reckless driving, even at times calling the highway patrol to stop her wildly driving husband and hold him in jail overnight. But when she finally pulled out of the marriage after 5 years, the patient's parents were quick to blame the wife for this "terrific blow," calling it "out of the blue" (see p. 579). (For details of this treatment course, see pp. 363–370.)

And even where the marriages did not break up, some were clearly not helpful, and some resulted in neurotically crippling psychological compromises. An example of the former type was the marriage of Peter Pan, and of the latter, that of the Homesick Psychology Student. Peter Pan was the patient whose husband, whom she met and married during her analysis while they were fellow college students, pressured her out of her analytic treatment on two occasions—the first time to follow him to a new university setting for their joint graduate studies, and the second time to marry him, attempting to trade a cure by love for a cure by analysis. Unfortunately, however well-intended, the husband's ministrations could not prevail against the patient's malignant illness and continuing decompensating trend. By the end, when the patient was back in a desperate psychotherapy trying to save her life against the onslaughts of the fully returned anorexia, kleptomania, and suicide thrust, the husband himself lost patience and separated from her. (Just before her suicide, however, he assured her of his continuing love for her. (For details of this treatment course, see pp. 426–432.)

The Homesick Psychology Student too had met a new girlfriend during his psychotherapy, and this relationship seemed sounder and more stable than any he had previously had. He thought she loved him and felt that he loved her. Yet when this girlfriend began to press marriage, the patient demurred, claiming his sexual disability (fear of impotence) as a barrier. When his girlfriend responded with "How do we know until we try?", the patient reacted with fright but also with contempt and disgust, asking in his therapy, "What kind of woman is she if she makes such a proposal?" When this psychotherapy ended after 4½ years with some modicum of improvement in order to plan for a more definitive psychoanalysis, the patient felt that the "demands" of double employment (in order to afford analytic fees) and the pending analysis required that he shelve for the time being any expectations he had for marriage or for further advancement toward his doctorate.

But after further consultation, the patient did not go into analysis; he took the consultant's statement that one could not really assess the nature of sexual difficulties in the absence of a reality situation that allowed a regular sexual relationship as a "command" to get married ahead of getting analyzed. Within 3 months the patient was married. As already discussed in detail, however (see p. 420), the marriage did not succeed sexually—in fact, it remained totally unconsummated, to the expressed disappointment of both. Yet both members of the couple felt the marriage to be harmonious in other particulars, and neither thought of changing their marital status. By being "accepting" and "understanding" of the patient's disability, the wife kept potential sources of overt tension to a minimum. She was also quite willing to cater to the patient's dependency urges. (For details of this treatment course, see pp. 417–421.)

GENERAL COMMENTS:
INTERPLAY OF THE SITUATIONAL VARIABLES

This overview of the stabilizing effects (or, in some cases, the unsettling effects) of major environmental influences—the permanent settling into the supportive Menninger and Topeka therapeutic world by so many of these patients who had come initially from homes and lives all over the United States, together with the working toward better and more supportive marriages—should be seen against the original PRP conceptualization of the Situational Variables. As detailed earlier (see pp. 79–83, 466–468, 489–490), the Situational Variables were conceived not as outcome criteria of changes induced by or consequent to psychotherapy, but as interacting sets of variables codetermining (along with the relevant Patient Variables and the Treatment Variables) the changes that come about during the course of therapy and the ways in which those changes are manifested, are sustained or even extended, and/or are diminished. In this sense, the roles of the particular supporting therapeutic milieu in Topeka, and of the individually supporting new (or renewed) marital relationships, are of signal importance as interacting determinants of the individual outcomes reached by these patients. In the preceding chapter, I have also discussed the return of so many patients to a specific psychotherapy, some other kind of explicit psychological helping, or some "other" helping relationship as part of the interplay of sustaining and equilibrating forces in the continuing lives of this patient population. And other influences, likewise played their role as major environmental support systems for patients for whom they had special valence, derived from the particularities of the patients' individual histories. These influences included employment (e.g., the Obedient Husband was very proud of the job he obtained in Topeka—the first he had ever secured for himself—as well as of his substantial chances for advancement in it, and of his assertiveness in being thus able to disentangle himself from being the maidservant to his wife's neurosis), as well as cultural and avocational interests (e.g., the Bohemian Musician sought always to arrange her life so as to maximize her musical involvements—playing, teaching, and listening). The patternings of these situational or environmental forces and configurations that can interactively play such an importantly stabilizing role in the posttreatment lives of patients are clearly as intricately varied as the diverse operative mechanisms within the treatment courses, which are usually more exclusively focused upon to account for the achieved changes consequent to those treatments.

The "Therapeutic Lifer"

THE ANALOGY TO CHRONIC MEDICAL ILLNESS

The concept of the "therapeutic lifer" has by now been well developed in the descriptions of the patients and their courses in therapy throughout this book. It has been counterposed, usually implicitly, but at times more explicitly, against the more usual model of psychiatric illness (at least with the usual outpatient, neurotic-range patients). In this model, illness is taken to represent a dysfunctional state that should be properly responsive to a single appropriately planned treatment course, which, whatever its open-endedness, and whatever its overall length, does have some natural termination point. In somatic illness, there has of course always been another model as well—that of chronic illness. At times, such illness is normally progressive (e.g., severe rheumatoid arthritis or osteoarthritis), and the therapeutic role is to ameliorate, as best as possible and for as long as possible, the advancing pain and disability. In other such illnesses (e.g., diabetes, pernicious anemia), there can be substantial hope, at least from certain perspectives, of staying any disease progression and working to ensure as close as possible a normal (symptom-free and complication-free) life course. With still others (e.g., various kinds of cardiac impairment), the prognosis in relation to the possibilities for effectively stabilizing the individuals' functioning may be intermediate. What all these afflictions share in common, however, is that they are chronic, and that good functional maintenance, rather than true illness cure, is the reasonable treatment goal. And a corollary to this, of course, is the concept of continued maintenance care by the treating physician that is regular and lifelong, however the actual visits to the physician are eventually spaced.

With the advent of the psychoactive medications, and the almost simultaneous spread of the community mental health center movement and its implementation by federal law and commitment, we have of course seen a counterpart phenomenon of chronic and lifelong outpatient maintenance care in the realm of mental illness. This is with the chronically psychotically ill who previously populated our state hospitals with long stays (often lifelong stays); now many are on maintenance psychoactive medication, and in the era of "deinstitutionalization" they are, with only a small percentage of exceptions, maintained in varieties of outpatient aftercare programs—mixtures of drug management, life counseling, and social and vocational skills training, which are intended to be indefinite over many years, if not lifelong.

Given these contexts, what I am proposing out of the experiences of PRP is the explicit recognition of a similar cadre of patients, drawn from the "sicker" elements of those who come to outpatient psychotherapy (and even, initially, to psychoanalysis). These patients, whether this is recognized at the onset of their treatment or not, turn out also to require lifelong therapeutic contact, maintenance care, and the like. The goal is not one of cure, in the sense of restoration to reasonably complete functional autonomy and well-being, but of life management with ongoing help and support at a significantly better functional level than would be possible to the patients on their own.

ORIGINAL EXPECTATIONS REGARDING "LIFERS" IN PRP

Based on the ongoing clinical work and experience of The Menninger Foundation at the time that PRP was created—with the usual population there of such "sicker" psychotherapy patients, and the prevailing conceptualization of supportive psychotherapies as being only ameliorative and not fully curative in intent—it was thought from the start that a certain limited number of the PRP patients might indeed turn out to be such "therapeutic lifers." Certainly within the whole cohort of several hundred ongoing psychotherapy cases at The Menninger Foundation at any given time, there were a certain number of such patients known to be in such treatment, and to intend to live permanently in Topeka, with the therapists and the patients committed to each other until death (or the vicissitudes of life) did them part. And there were always certain therapists within The Menninger Foundation staff group who had a particular predilection for working with these patients; they could work patiently and willingly over long periods of time, without the need for reinforcement by visible evidences of movement and change. These particular patients at issue would tend somehow to cluster with those therapists—sometimes through the initial selection process on the part of the therapists, sometimes by referral to them when the original treating therapists might transfer careers and move away from Topeka.

Of course, we had no way at the start of knowing with any certainty how many such "therapeutic lifers" would emerge in the PRP cohort and which patients they would turn out to be. We expected (wrongly, as it turned out) that by the nature of the kinds of personality and illness structure that were linked to particular therapeutic modalities as most appropriate and efficacious with them, the "lifers" would come primarily from the ranks of those in supportive psychotherapies, in relation to very refractory psychiatric illnesses not deemed amenable to insight-aiming (hence, more intendedly "definitive") approaches. Perhaps we did not count sufficiently, or explicitly enough, on the self-sustaining capacities of so many of even the chronically functionally bogged down, if concomitantly the proper array of supporting circumstances eventuated (or was, in some instances, deliberately brought into being). The concept of "transfer of the transference" is very germane here. Four particular instances of this, of varying degrees of success, are described under that rubric in Section VI, Chapter 20 (see pp. 413–432)—the Movie Lady, the Homesick Psychology Student, the Heiress, and

Peter Pan. Also, on the other side, perhaps we counted too much on forethought making one truly well enough forearmed concerning the risks of the development of an insoluble transference neurosis, in certain patients in psychoanalysis and even in some patients in very intensive long-term expressive psychotherapies. This issue has been closely discussed in Section V, Chapter 14 (see pp. 283–287), in connection with the analysis of the Devoted Son. It has also been discussed in Section VI, Chapter 20 (see pp. 391–412), in relation to the treatment courses of the Housebound Phobic Woman, originally recommended for psychoanalysis but tacitly shifted to psychotherapy; the Claustrophobic Man, in psychotherapy; and the Sexual Masochist, in psychotherapy.

"LIFER" RESULTS

In any case, to our surprise at the time of the official Termination Studies, it looked as though 5 patients were well on their way to becoming "therapeutic lifers," and 2 of these were from the 22 originally recommended for psychoanalysis. At the time of the official Follow-Up Studies, there seemed to be 4 patients in this group of "lifers," with 2 of the first 5 no longer with it, but a new one added; but the 2 who were originally in analysis were still among the 4. And, as of this writing, approximately 16–17 years after the official Follow-Up Studies were done, 2 of the original 42 patients are still in ongoing treatment at The Menninger Foundation, and both of these are patients who started in psychoanalysis. One of them has been in continuous treatment over all the intervening years, and the other, a once terminated psychoanalytic patient, came back 15 years later into what has become a seemingly permanent treatment situation. And 2 others are also still in treatment, though not at The Menninger Foundation: One is still in Topeka but in treatment via the local AA organization, and the other is no longer in Topeka, but still with his original analyst, who is himself now in a distant part of the country. This group of patients, all of whose case histories have already been described, are discussed in this chapter from this comparative perspective.

Apparent "Lifers" at Termination Study

The first determination of who turned out to be in the "lifer" group was a pragmatic one. The PRP Initial Studies were done over the years 1954–1958 on patients who entered their therapies, psychoanalysis or psychotherapy, during that time period and met the various inclusion and exclusion criteria that were set up (see Section II, Chapter 5, pp. 56–61). Because of the funding exigencies of this research program, as well as the issue of how long the research group could be maintained relatively intact over time, still working within that particular setting and still maintaining a commitment to the research enterprise, it was decided to do "cutoff" Termination Studies on the patients who had not yet terminated their treatments over the winter of 1963–1964. The five patients who were then still in treatment had treatment durations by that time of 6–9½ years.

The five apparent "therapeutic lifers" at "cutoff" Termination Study were the following:

1. The Economist, who had started in psychoanalysis, which was maintained as such for almost 6 years. At this point, the risks posed by an unfolding psychotic transference regression led to a formal change to a supportive–expressive psychotherapy. This, in turn, after now a total of 9½ years and 1601 treatment hours (the greatest number of hours at that point of any patient in the project), was still ongoing, although seemingly tapering off. (His full treatment course is described on pp. 336–343).

2. The Housebound Phobic Woman, who was recommended for psychoanalysis, but was very early (though never explicitly) converted to a supportive–expressive psychotherapy. After a total of over 7 years and 1210 treatment hours, this was still ongoing—with a second therapist, due to the first therapist's sudden death of heart disease. (Her full treatment course is described on pp. 391–398.)

3. The Fearful Loner, who was treated in a purely supportive psychotherapy explicitly geared to the provision of a "corrective" emotional experience," carried at a frequency of once a week (and after a while, only 30 minutes each time). After now 6½ years and 281 sessions, and with the third therapist (the patient had "fired" the first two), this was still fully ongoing. (His full treatment course is described on pp. 452–458.)

4. The Phobic Girl, who was treated in a supportive–expressive psychotherapy, three and then two times weekly. This, after now 6 years and 659 hours, was still ongoing. (Her full treatment course is described on pp. 468–476.)

5. The Involutional Woman, who was treated in a supportive–expressive psychotherapy, ranging from a frequency of three times weekly for 1 year to once weekly for the rest of the time. This, after now 6 years and 362 hours, was also still ongoing. (Her full treatment course is described on pp. 375–382.)

Because of the clinical contraindications expressed by the therapists, three of these patients were not seen or examined as part of their Termination Studies; "truncated" studies were accomplished on them, involving interviews with the therapist and with others involved therapeutically with the patient, study of the clinical records kept routinely on that case, and so forth. These were the Economist, the Fearful Loner, and the Phobic Girl. A typical concern was expressed by the therapist of the Phobic Girl, who felt that if the patient were asked, she would grudgingly agree to participate in the Termination Study, but would then subsequently express her ire and her hurt feelings by a major piece of self-destructive acting out. He did not want to "rock the boat" that seemed at last stabilizing. Another of the five, the Housebound Phobic Woman, though not interviewed, did have a repeat psychological projective test battery at the Termination Study point. As noted earlier, the therapist felt this to be clinically warranted and useful in relation to the ongoing clinical issue of the degree to which the patient's difficulties with the verbal and expressive psychotherapeutic process reflected an irreversible residue of organic brain damage consequent to the 14-year-long chronically barbiturate-addicted state with which she had come to treatment over 7 years earlier. Her "truncated" study actually then had the additional very rich data provided by the psychological retesting, along with what was otherwise available. And the fifth, the Involutional Woman, though still in ongoing treatment, was both interviewed and retested because the therapist felt that this could be appropriately done without any detriment to the ongoing therapeutic work. Indeed, a full Termination Study was done just as if the treatment had actually terminated rather than being still in process, and it seemed clearly to cause no discernible special perturbation.

"Lifers" at Follow-Up Study

By the time Follow-Up Studies were done, 2–3 years further on (these were in 1965–1966), there had been some shifts in alignments. One of these patients, the Involutional Woman, had actually terminated her therapy only a year into the follow-up period, and this had not been anticipated at the time of Termination Study. (As just noted, hers was the one case where we had direct termination interview access to the patient in this group of presumed "therapeutic lifers.") When seen for Follow-Up Study, she was contentedly in the hands of her internist, who was enthusiastically treating her progressive arthritis with various (mostly new) drugs; she was also on occasion seeing her minister. I have previously speculated on the possible role of the Termination Study stock-taking process in perhaps catalyzing the process of treatment resolution (see p. 601). The Phobic Girl was interviewed and tested for the first time at her Follow-Up Study, since it turned out that she was then in the process of actual termination of her treatment, and the therapist no longer felt it contraindicated that she participate with us. This patient consciously participated very willingly in the study, expressing a desire to contribute to research. In conjunction with these interviews, the patient had a dream of herself back in the hospital, on the pediatric ward, which she interpreted as a return to her previous childish state. This is a patient for whom we have additional, almost completely current follow-up information, for another 14 years beyond the Follow-Up Study point. Despite occasional phobic revivals, anxiety periods, and regressive reawakenings of her hostile interdependency with her mother, which brought her to occasional consultation return visits with her ex-therapist, she never did go back (or need to go back) into further therapy.

The other three "lifers" at Termination Study still seemed to be in the same category at the "cutoff" Follow-Up Study. Two of them, however, were now interviewed and tested with the full concurrence of their therapists. The Economist had "officially" terminated his ongoing therapy during the interim but this turned out to be an "administrative termination" (i.e., only an alteration in the patient's medical records status to that of a discharged patient being seen then only in regular "follow-up interviews"). The patient, however, did not know of the alteration in his official status, which in no way changed the frequency or the nature of his ongoing contact with his therapist. He now had a university appointment in a major, geographically somewhat distant state university; as noted (see p. 623), he was coming for treatment once every 6 weeks, over a long weekend, with late Friday afternoon and Saturday morning therapy hours. The therapist felt that this tapering off might reflect something of a terminating phase in the therapy. Nonetheless, he did not expect any actual alteration in the frequency of ongoing contact so long as the patient remained at the same university within weekend driving distance (750 miles round trip). The patient was certainly content with his work life; he was becoming a full professor, with a salary double what he had been earning but two years earlier in another setting. He felt his continuing (and improving) psychic equilibrium to be dependent in a very substantial way on his now assumed and accepted role as a "therapeutic lifer." This patient has persisted with this same therapist up to the time of present writing, now 28 years from his treatment start. The details have already been given (see pp. 342–343). Briefly, he continued to see his therapist on periodic weekend visits in Topeka as long as the therapist remained with The Menninger Foundation; the patient lived again briefly in Topeka at a subsequent period of emotional malaise and then moved to his therapist's new community in order to resume a regular psychotherapy with him. He now lives and works in another university town far removed from his therapist, with whom he nonetheless keeps in regular touch by phone or by mail, about twice a month.

The Housebound Phobic Woman was the other one from the group of three patients still in ongoing treatments at the time of "cutoff" Follow-Up Study who was interviewed and retested at this time. As with the Economist, her therapist felt that this could now be done without detriment to the treatment process. She was now at the 1356-hour mark, second only to the Economist. She came to the Follow-Up interviews expressing her gratitude for all that The Menninger Foundation had done for her, despite her far lesser satisfaction with her current therapist (the "pygmy") than with her therapist who had died (the "giant"). As noted earlier, she refused expense money, feeling amply repaid by all the help that The Menninger Foundation had been to her all those years. Neither she nor the therapist anticipated her terminating. She is the only patient in the whole cohort of 42 still in the same continuous treatment at The Menninger Foundation, which as of this writing had gone on for 25½ years. After the Follow-Up Study, the patient continued another 5 years with her second therapist until he left The Menninger Foundation staff; she went another 5 years beyond that with her third therapist until he in turn left The Menninger Foundation staff; and she has been now for 6 years with her fourth therapist, a social worker. This current treatment consists of one appointment per month. The patient, of course, still lives in Topeka and still has difficulty in traveling outside Topeka, but she has made airplane trips to visit relatives in various parts of the country. She has been working in a white-collar job and is now close to retirement, concerned with issues of retiring, aging, and the changes of friends as people leave Topeka, retire, or die. She has occasionally tried hypnosis, relaxation techniques, and self-prescriptions of Valium to help deal with increments of social or phobic anxiety. She is, of course, a "therapeutic lifer" in the purest sense; there is still no thought of treatment termination.

The remaining one of the three "lifers" still in ongoing treatment at "cutoff" Follow-Up Study was the Fearful Loner. He was the very lonely, very schizoid individual, tenuously tied to his ongoing 30-minutes-weekly supportive psychotherapy, whom it was felt still contraindicated to see. He was thus the only patient in the whole cohort who was never asked to participate formally in either the Termination or the Follow-Up Study, and therefore remained in fact the one patient in the sample who was never informed of the existence of PRP or of his inclusion in it. He was also the individual who, prior to the time of "cutoff" Termination Study, had "fired" two previous therapists for gross incompetence and malfeasance (as he saw it). He seemed, however, to be making it with his third therapist, who indeed held him for an additional 8 years beyond the point of Follow-Up Study for a total treatment span covering 16 years. At that point the patient retired from his job, and he and his wife moved to an isolated farm in the patient's home state and home area, where they could continue their same cloistered life and could grow their own natural and organic food (a passion of theirs). They had no children or other family, though they had thought on occasion of adopting.

Three years after the patient's retirement, the third therapist, with whom the relationship was always positive (it could never of course be described as close), received a very long and detailed letter from the patient's wife. Their life was continuing in the same manner and uneventfully. They had had some brief encounters with chiropractic and with orthomolecular therapy. The letter ended with the statement, "I have rambled long enough. I just thought I'd let you know we think of you often, and if you ever decide to come this way, look us up, and thanks again for all you did for us. Love, X. P.S. We hope you and your family are well and happy." The therapist in his brief response, ended with "If I am ever around your part of the country, please do not be surprised if you get a call from me, for I should like very much to see both of you, and I hope that if your travels ever bring you back around Topeka, you will get in touch with me." Needless to say, this patient is also in essence a "therapeutic lifer."

In addition to the three out of the five apparent "therapeutic lifers" from the Termination Studies who still seemed in that status at Follow-Up Study, one other, the Sexual Masochist, had now been added to this group. He had been in an 8-year (540-hour) unsuccessful psychotherapy, which had ended through a process of petering out. The patient would not give up his continuing drug intake and would only maintain his attendance in therapy if the therapist would at least condone (and preferably prescribe) his tranquilizer drug intake. His position was clear — that the drug calmed his nerves and made him content. He experienced the therapist's demand that he desist as unnatural and cruel. The therapist indicated that he could not take full medical responsibility under these circumstances. The patient's response was to refuse hospitalization, to marry instead, and then just to drop away from keeping his therapy appointments. The therapist was finally driven to write a letter "officially" terminating the therapy, to which the patient had by now entirely stopped coming. The patient and his wife were both willing to be seen for Termination Study and expressed some guarded optimism over their prospects, which the research team did not feel at all warranted. They were contentedly settled in Topeka, chosen because they felt it was a wonderful place in which a businessman with the patient's talents could increase his fortune. He was emphatic that The Menninger Foundation and the therapy had nothing to do with the choice.

To everyone's surprise, at the point of Follow-Up Study, the patient was now at least marginally stabilized. He had had the intervening "serious heart attack" and terrible fright that led him to renounce his heavy tranquilizer and cigarette use, and with his wife's full support (and pressure) and participation, was now back in "marriage and family counseling" on a regular weekly basis with his original therapist. This renewed treatment has already been described in detail (see pp. 410–412, 627–628). The patient implied that he was coming to the counseling only because of his wife's and the therapist's interest that he do so, but he came. And there seemed no thrust toward terminating. The improved adjustment at Follow-Up Study seemed clearly contingent upon the continuation of these profound dependency relationships upon the important personal figures in his life—the wife, the therapist, and the internist—also, to an indeterminate extent, upon the patient's continued (realistic?) fears for his bodily integrity in the face of his cardiac affliction. (His full treatment course is described on pp. 405–412.)

We have additional information about this patient for another 17 years beyond the Follow-Up Study point, and completely current as of this writing. The "marriage counseling" continued for another 6 years until the therapist left Topeka, and the patient and his wife came regularly for it. At that point, the therapist "transferred" the case to friends he had who were active within the AA organization in town, and the patient has continued with that ever since; he is less attached to AA per se than to the therapeutic couple. The patient has had no other formal therapy, nothing at The Menninger Foundation. The patient's life and his marriage have both continued reasonably well, and all the humiliating financial stipulations that the patient originally set to the marriage contract just dropped away with time. The couple have had two children, one handicapped, and have been very concerned with this handicapped child, whom they have intended to keep living with them. The patient has been mostly abstaining from alcohol; his perverse behaviors and expressed perverse impulses have apparently dropped away completely. He is permanently settled, a businessman in Topeka, with a variety of real estate holdings. There has been no known further cardiac problem, and the patient engages in vigorous physical exercise. With the 3 years of observation and contact with this patient before he entered his formal psychotherapy at The Menninger Foundation, his 16½-year total psychotherapy course, and the 11 years since his therapist left Topeka and he went to AA, the Sexual Masochist has been followed over the longest time span—over 30 years—of any patient in the research population. He has also been described a number of times as perhaps the "sickest" patient in the entire cohort, and classed among those considered probably untreatable. Reviewed now over the whole time span, his overall treatment result, which seemed to have been a total failure at the time of Termination Study, and to have been equivocal at best at the time of Follow-Up Study, should now be looked at as in the second group, those with moderate improvement.

A Post-Follow-Up "Lifer"

I have already indicated (see pp. 590–591) that we have further data beyond the official Follow-Up Studies on a total of 28 of the 42 patients, or two-thirds of the sample. There is an average of 5 years and 9 months of posttreatment follow-up information for 13 of them (range 4–7 years), and an average of over 17 years of posttreatment follow-up information for 15 of them (range 12–24 years). With 8 of them, our information is completely current as of this writing. My concern here is with 1 of those 8, because he became another "therapeutic lifer" in the post follow-up period. This is the Devoted Son, the only patient in the PRP sample who was actually a resident of Topeka when he came to treatment. This patient was in an analysis that spanned 5½ years (1030 hours). Because of the thrust toward a bogging down into an insoluble transference neurosis (i.e., a "cloying dependency" that the analyst felt could not be analytically resolved), he was terminated through a gradual and difficult weaning process; this involved first having the patient sit up, and then reducing the frequency and the duration of treatment sessions in stepwise fashion. The outcome of this analysis in relation to the expectations for it was equivocal. (The full treatment course is described on pp. 283–287.) At the Follow-Up Study, the patient expressed a reluctance to see his former analyst—perhaps because of temptation (see p. 286). There was no sign at the time of any further real treatment plan.

However, 13 years after the treatment termination, the patient, still living and working in Topeka, sought out his ex-analyst for a series of consultation visits that spanned the next 2 years. These were in connection with his concerns about his aging and declining father—the patient had continued his lifelong close devotion to and involvement with his parents. When his ex-analyst left Topeka at the end of those 2 years, the patient moved over into a regular weekly 30-minute psychotherapy session with another analyst; this arrangement still continues as of this writing, 7 years later, or 22 years after the original analytic termination by "weaning." The patient is still single, and is now alone, with both his parents dead. He still works in the same engineering firm, has a small circle of friends, is somewhat more adept socially, and occasionally resorts to Valium for his social anxiety. The current therapist sees his role as "helping the patient expand his life a little." There is no plan to terminate this therapy, though the patient is now not far from retirement.

Patients Who Could Have Become "Lifers" but Did Not

In addition to this recounting of the treatment careers of the group who turned out to be "therapeutic lifers," I should mention others who were expected to go in that direction but in fact did not. A good example was the Alcoholic Raconteur. This was the severely alcoholic patient who came to treatment demanding psychoanalysis and scornful of AA. His was also one of those instances where the research evaluators disagreed sharply with a recommendation of analysis, feeling that the patient required an essentially supportive and only potentially somewhat expressive psychotherapy, with concomitant prolonged hospitalization; all of this treatment, it was felt, should be geared in the first instance toward enhanced control over impulse and behavior. In the detailed research prognostication made at the point of Initial Study, it was felt that even such a treatment course might never be psychologically terminable. At its best, "The patient might then come to a permanent life in Topeka with the aura of the hospital therapeutic community and its fellowship providing the necessary supporting and gratifying fantasies of being protected and cared for, hopefully leaving the patient a considerable range of freedom within the Topeka area." Should the patient, on the contrary, be taken into the psychoanalysis that turned out to be clinically recommended, the prediction was for a psychotic transference regression and/or a precipitate treatment disruption.

Actually, the patient was taken into an effort at psychoanalysis; this lasted 2 years and 9 months, at which point the patient did abruptly break off his treatment when the analyst was finally persuaded that the treatment needed to be converted to a face-to-face psychotherapy together with renewed hospitalization. This the patient would not tolerate, and he left, ostensibly to try to make a fresh start in psychoanalysis elsewhere. His treatment course to that point was totally failed. It was within the follow-up period that the patient "really hit bottom" (skid row);

he turned to AA, and after that to a prospective marriage (actually getting married very shortly after the official Follow-Up Study). This was the patient who thus "rescued" himself via AA as his self-help substitute for the predicted "therapeutic lifer" career. Central to the AA ethos, of course, is that the struggle with the alcoholic illness is a never-ending one, requiring a lifetime AA commitment. (This patient's full treatment course is described on pp. 498–504.)

There were several patients, like the Alcoholic Raconteur, where the original research treatment plan and prognostication was for a prolonged supportive–expressive psychotherapy that would probably lead, at best, into "therapeutic lifer" status. There were also literally any number of others among the failed treatment cases (11 in number) and those with active or incipient transference psychotic reactions (12 in number)—with 7 instances of overlap between these categories—where it was clear that the patients would have been better off if the therapy could have gone in a sufficiently supportive and an explicitly function-stabilizing and maintaining direction; if ambitious psychoanalytic treatment efforts had not been undertaken with these patients (such ambitious uncovering efforts were undertaken with 8 of the 16 different patients in the two categories just stated); and if their treatments had then evolved into a sustaining "therapeutic lifer" status. It should be noted in this context, of course, that of the five patients who appeared to be becoming "therapeutic lifers" at the time of Termination Study, two (the Housebound Phobic Woman and the Economist) were from among those started in analysis. And of the four patients at this writing still in ongoing treatment, three (the Housebound Phobic Woman, the Economist, and the Devoted Son) were among those who started in analysis. Clearly, being taken into an intensive psychoanalytic treatment effort does not at all preclude the treatment's ultimately evolving into a maintained "therapeutic lifer" status, albeit no longer as psychoanalysis.

GENERAL COMMENTS

Those who did become "therapeutic lifers," not necessarily lifelong, have been grouped among those with better therapeutic outcomes. Counting five patients—four who seemed to be in "therapeutic lifer" status at the point of Follow-Up Study, and the one currently in treatment who came back after 15 years—two have had very good improvements (the Housebound Phobic Woman, with 25½ years of continuous treatment, and the Fearful Loner, with 16 years of now terminated treatment); two have had moderate improvement (the Sexual Masochist, with 16½ years of treatment until his transfer 11 years ago to the AA leadership couple for still-continuing treatment, and the Economist, with 28 years of continuous treatment); and only one has had overall equivocal improvement (the Devoted Son, with 5½ years of analysis originally, a 15-year hiatus, and now 7 years of once-weekly, 30-minute psychotherapy sessions). In addition, the two other patients who seemed like "therapeutic lifers" at the time of "cutoff" Termination Study but were both finished by the time of Follow-Up Study also had very good improvement (the Involutional Woman, with 7 years of treatment altogether, and the Phobic Girl, with 8 years altogether). Of course, with patients still in ongoing treatment at any point of assessment, part of that assessment of level and quality of achieved functioning encompasses the fact that it is within the context of the need for maintained therapeutic support; it is not really autonomous functioning. To put it another way, the fact of the ongoing therapy and the continuing need for it is itself part of the new functional life plateau.

It should also be reiterated here that the concept of the "therapeutic lifer" is not an all-or-none proposition. Between being seen in continuous and lifelong sustaining therapy on the one hand, and having a clear-cut, circumscribed therapeutic course with a natural evolution and a definite (and permanent) termination on the other hand, there are all the other varieties of circumstances considered under the various chapters in this section. These comprise such factors as linkage physically and/or psychologically to a sustaining therapeutic and caring community like the Menninger and Topeka psychiatric world; continued sporadic therapeutic contact, usually with the former therapist, by way of consultation, exchanges of letters, telephone calls, even "social visits"; other kinds of psychologically reinforcing health care from nonpsychiatric physicians; social work counseling, ostensibly concerning the problems of others (other family members in formal psychotherapy); marriage and family counseling, ostensibly concerning *joint* problems in living; pastoral counseling; legal, vocational, educational, and other types of counseling; prescribed (psychoactive) medication, as well as self-medication; self-help organizations; revivalist and evangelical commitments; and of course periodic returns for formal psychotherapy itself (whether with the same or a different therapist, etc.). The varieties are almost endless in today's "psychological society," and the degrees of seriousness and usefulness vary across a range from the explicitly psychotherapeutic in a sustaining way at one end to the almost dangerously cultist and potentially psychologically constricting or otherwise detrimental at the other end. What needs underlining is that fact that for the PRP patient population, once they entered into the psychotherapeutic helping orbit by way of formal intensive analysis and therapy, this new dimension became a more or less actively continuing part of their ongoing lives and tended to endure over a far longer time span than heretofore appreciated. The degree of generalization to the wider population of more usual patients in more usual outpatient psychoanalysis and psychotherapy is, of course, undetermined.

Termination and Follow-Up: Comparative Assessment

CHANGES IN FUNCTIONING BETWEEN TERMINATION AND FOLLOW-UP: QUESTIONS AND ISSUES

A central value of the formal follow-up study, whether in a research or in a straight clinical context, is in the light thrown on the issue of whether any favorable changes in life functioning that take place during the treatment process, and in the context of the ongoing therapeutic relationship, actually turn out to endure once the patient is removed from the intensity of the therapeutic interactional process, and is again living life in its more usual context. (I have, of course, just indicated at the end of the preceding chapter how, at least for the PRP patients, that more usual life context was now anchored within a wider psychological helping world or ambience than their pretreatment life context for the most part had been.) The central questions here are these: Are the changes that come about or have been brought about during treatment maintained? Or, contrariwise, is there some degree of regression, of loss of treatment gains? And does such regression go only part way back to the pretreatment starting point? Or are there instances of going all the way back, even of loss to impaired functional levels below those that characterized the patients at the start of treatment? And, to look at the opposite possibility, is there some degree of further consolidation of treatment gains—are there levels of functioning at the follow-up point that are significantly enhanced over those at termination? This last question, of course, relates to the issues of processes set in motion by the treatment period that continue to have a sustaining and enhancing effort in the ongoing life afterward. One such process, in psychoanalysis, is the self-analyzing functional capacity that, to a debatable degree, does or can develop during the course of an effective psychoanalytic treatment (see Grinberg de Ekboir & Lichtmann, 1982; Kramer, 1959; G. Ticho, 1967). Another consists of the environmental reinforcements and rewards for altered behaviors that can have positive feedback effects through the new gratifications that accrue; to quote Horwitz's (1974) paraphrase of an old proverb, "Adaptive behavior is its own reward" (p. 230).

The design of PRP was in effect ideal for throwing specific light on these particular questions. Its cross-sectional formal assessments of the functioning and the psychological organization of the patients at three points in time (before treatment, after treatment, and at a point of meaningful posttreatment follow-up) facilitated such inquiries, as did the counterpart assessments at the same points in time of the patients' environments and life spaces in their interactive interplay with the patients' functioning (all organized in terms of the 28 Patient Variables and 7 Situational Variables, assessed by as comparable criteria as possible at each of the points of inquiry).

CONSOLIDATION AND ENHANCEMENT
OF FUNCTIONING

Considered from this perspective of the side-by-side comparison of all the variables in the patients' psychological functioning and life situations, singly and in meaningful combinations, there was an actual consolidation and enhancement of functioning between the Termination and Follow-Up Studies in 18 of the 42 cases (the largest group, not quite 45% of the sample).[1] These cases, of course, clustered among those with the best treatment results, but these 18 were not only the successes of the project. Of the 18, 10 were from the 17 with very good improvement, 5 were from the 8 with moderate improvement, only 2 from the 6 with

---

1. In those instances (28 of the 42, or two-thirds of the sample) where we had additional happenstance follow-up information beyond our formal Follow-Up Studies—in some instances, completely current as of this writing—this information has been taken into consideration in making these groupings. However, more weight has been given to the immediate period of formal follow-up observation and less to what happened after, mostly because of the supervening over the longer time span of so many new and important life vicissitudes, less and less linked to the actual treatment process and its consequences.

equivocal improvement, and only 1 from the 11 failed outcomes. This last was the Sociopath, whose disastrous treatment ended in his flight and disappearance, with his creditors, the law, his landlady, his lawyer, and his family all in hot pursuit. At Follow-Up Study, however, the patient was at least visible and functioning—albeit marginally, and to a large extent on the bounty of his resigned but still somehow hopeful parents. This degree of tenuous stabilization could hardly be looked at as significantly related to the patient's psychotherapy, except insofar as it had helped the patient and his family to tolerate each other better and had diminished to some degree the ruthless exploitativeness that the patient had previously directed at everyone in his orbit, family members included. Now, at least with his father, the patient seemed to get along pretty well.

The other 17 in this group had more significant posttreatment enhancements— ones that could also, in most cases, be more clearly linked to the previous treatment processes. Some of the more striking as well as more unusual are used here by way of illustration.

Consolidation of Very Good Outcomes

The Adoptive Mother, for example, left her analysis for her new home in a distant city, in many ways very content with her therapeutic result, but still completely unclear as to whether she could actually make it in the arena that counted most—adopting successfully, and so being finally a successful wife and mother. During the follow-up period in her new home city, this patient put together the necessary supportive psychotherapeutic ingredients (the family physician who medicated her, the priest who admonished and exhorted her, and the social worker who consoled and "understood" her); with that help, she was able to adopt successfully, and to proudly rear her adoptive daughter. And shortly after the official Follow-Up Study point, the patient added to this achievement by adopting successfully a second time, and this time an infant boy. She perceived this as the ultimate test: It had been the attempt to adopt a boy and the patient's conflicts over being a mother of a boy that had triggered her original depressive collapse. In the patient's mind, all this was clearly linked to the work of the previous analysis. With all the overdetermined transference meanings evident in the phrase, the patient wanted to bring her daughter along on the Follow-Up visit in order to show her former analyst "the fruit of his labors."

Other patients consolidated their functioning in very different ways, and under the impact of a variety of life possibilities that had now become available as a result of their freeing by the psychotherapeutic work. The Medical Scientist could return to his previously shattered medical career in a teaching setting; by Follow-Up Study, he was an established member of the Topeka professional community with close friendship links among the psychiatric staff, and was purveying his brand of "barnyard psychiatry" to his psychosomatic fellow physicians and general practitioners in training. The Bohemian Musician, who had gotten out of an ill-suited and uncongenial marriage, was able, with the gentle concurrence of her ex-therapist (see pp. 602, 615–616), to get into a new marriage. The new relationship was much more compatible in the sharing of interests (and the sharing of character); the patient truly felt her needs to be met for the first time in her whole life, and could therefore function at a startlingly higher level than before treatment. With the

English Professor, the feedback reinforcements that the patient obtained from both job and marriage (his more confident, less phobic performance in his academic teaching position, and the marriage he could now bring himself finally to enter) all reflected and contributed to his now being "not one of the boys anymore," but someone who could get (and deserved) offers from larger, more prestigious universities. He could fantasize even being the college dean at some point.

Consolidation of More Equivocal Outcomes

Other patients managed to consolidate or enhance much more equivocal outcomes. The Alcoholic Raconteur, for example, was finally willing to swallow his pride and turn for succor to the once-despised AA, identified so much with his weak, psychotically depressed, and alcoholic mother. It was never clear how much this turn to AA at the point when the patient "really hit bottom" (skid row) was the kind of happening that would have occurred with him even without his previous therapy (in the way that so many alcoholics do come to AA), and how much the interactions of the analytic therapy had altered the patient's perspectives sufficiently to make the AA alternative at last acceptable.

With the Adolescent Grandson, prematurely pried out of his treatment by his bullying grandfather, the pivotal event was the more adventitious circumstance of the grandfather's sudden death (at 74) of a heart attack. This brought the patient very immediately an inheritance of great wealth and position, as well as the responsibilities (which he accepted rather uneasily) of the "head of the family." Again, it was unclear how much the previous treatment helped make it possible for the patient, now in this position, to stabilize his life in a contented marriage, actually able to enjoy his wife and two children. This new equilibrium was certainly aided by the normal maturational process (with the outgrowing of the special adolescent turmoils and drive pressures), and probably more so by the deployment of his money to set up a life style allowing a socially adaptive expression of his dependent needs via a number of figures (wife, grandfather's secretary, foster parents, stepmother, etc.). This "team" combined to take care of his interests and his life, but in ways that he could feel he moderated and controlled.

Actually most striking among all the posttreatment consolidations was the case of the "sickest" of the patients, the Sexual Masochist. When his 8-year-long psychotherapy had ended by simply petering out, it had seemed a thoroughly failed case. At the Follow-Up Study, things seemed equivocally improved out of the response to the "heart attack" scare, the marriage, and the return to therapy under the guise of marriage counseling. At our completely current follow-up information point, the patient has managed—over more than 30 years—a truly substantial improvement in functioning and capacity (see pp. 637–638) by dint of the long-continued "marriage counseling," succeeded by the attachment to the two AA group leaders.

NO CHANGE IN FUNCTIONING

In contrast to the expected clustering of the patients with the best treatment outcomes among those 18 who consolidated their level of functioning by the Follow-Up Study point (10 of the 17 with very good outcomes and only 1 of the 11 with failed outcomes), the 10 (not quite 25% of the sample) whose level of functioning was essentially unchanged between Termination and Follow-Up Studies were spread quite evenly over the four broad outcome categories: 3 from the group with very good improvement, 2 from the group with moderate improvement, 3 from the group with equivocal improvement, and 2 from the group of treatment failures. One from each of these groups is used in illustration.

No Change in a Very Good Improvement

The Phobic Woman had an apparent very good improvement of her intense phobic illness that before her analysis had totally constricted not only her own but also her husband's life, and had finally brought him to the point of threatening divorce unless something drastic were done promptly. The patient was in an analysis that ended generally successfully after 4 years and 9 months (1012 hours). During the 2½-year follow-up interim, the patient had had a moderate symptom relapse into her anxiety and phobic propensities, lasting over a year. This centered around the confluence of a number of factors. First, she had gotten pregnant with a third child, the first one conceived on her own without her analyst's benevolent encouragement. This was, to her, a significant "independent" step: "I could never have had any children if I hadn't been in analysis; it takes two to make a child and yet it sort of took three to make my children." Second, her husband was completing his doctorate, and this would also make him "independent" and the equal of the patient's father—"no longer a dependent child alongside of me." Finally, the patient had had a tense and stormy visit with her mother, who was frightened of aging and was hypochondriacally bogged down. The patient "finally had it out with Mother," belaboring her with whether she wanted to be considered a fun grandmother or an aging invalid. During this time period, the patient had been "ready to return to treatment." But she had weathered it, and at Follow-Up Study things were back to their "usual" state. She was still somewhat apprehensive when alone or when feeling especially burdened with the responsibilities of home and children. She felt better with people around, as protectors against phobic apprehensiveness, but could always arrange it so that others were not aware of her binding to them. She still had two residual specific phobias—riding in elevators alone, and driving on the highway alone (she came to the Follow-Up interviews from her nearby city of residence accompanied by her husband). But the patient felt all of this to be clearly containable within the bounds of relatively innocuous protective maneuvers, and she felt that she was sustaining her treatment achievements, even though she felt that she had terminated her analysis under some pressure from her analyst and at a point when she was not yet fully ready.

No Change in a Moderate Improvement

The Homesick Psychology Student was from the group with moderate improvement at the termination of his 4½ years of psychotherapy. The patient had detached himself from his very close dependent relationship with his parents (the showering with gifts had stopped, he had stopped his parents' buying his clothing for him, the visits and mail had diminished in frequency and urgency, he could return from visits home without mutual tearful separations, etc.). He had made some steady work and educational progress. He had established with a new girl-friend a sounder and more stable relationship than any he had previously had; he thought she loved him and felt that he loved her, but demurred still at her pressures toward marriage, claiming his sexual disability (fear of impotence) as a barrier. During the follow-up period, the patient obtained better and far more suitable employment (also doubling his income), and his visits to his parents were now only about once a month. Mostly, he had gotten married (on "command"), but this was the marriage that was still unconsummated after 2 years. The patient and his wife seemed reconciled (he much more than she) to a socially congenial marriage, with great mutual protestations of love, but at the price of a still total sexual inhibition. The patient's wife was expressing herself as hopeful that she could still help the patient work this out. Clearly, there had been no alteration in the functional status achieved by the termination point, since the patient was still left with such a major life limitation.

No Change in an Equivocal Improvement

The Devoted Son was the individual who ended his analysis quite unwillingly after 5½ years (1030 hours), under the "weaning" efforts of the analyst, who was working against the patient's "cloying dependency" and the spectre of bogging down into an insoluble transference neurosis. In view of the intensity of his treatment, the patient's achieved changes had been unsubstantial. He could get along better with his co-workers, with some diminishment in social anxiety; he could be more comfortable with his parents; he could be less obsessive in his work and accept suggestions and criticisms from colleagues with better grace; he could now use public swimming pools without the same horror of people seeing his awful physique. But despite all this, there was an overall substantial sameness to his life, which was no different at Follow-Up Study. "I have gone in the same grooves, wearing a little more deeply." And he was the patient, who in the context of this sameness, brought himself back to therapy 15 years after his treatment termination; he is now a "therapeutic lifer," with the therapist trying to "help expand his life a little."

No Change in a Failed Outcome

The Invalided Hypochondriac was the patient who went from a failed combined hospitalization and psychotherapy at The Menninger Foundation, where she came in a state of total life collapse in the context of a prolonged and progressive malignant hypochondriasis, to a failed combined hospitalization and psychotherapy in a state hospital in her home state, from which she emerged somewhat less hypochondriacal and somewhat more paranoid. At the Follow-Up Study point, the patient was somehow just managing extramurally, and in that sense was perhaps marginally better off than at termination. However, her equilibrium was adjudged so tenuous that it was felt to be an unwarranted risk to try to persuade her to return to Topeka for the Follow-Up Study and to chance having her collapse completely on the premises, in the way that she had when she was first brought for evaluation.

REGRESSION IN FUNCTIONING

In contrast to the clusterings both among the 18 patients who consolidated their functioning in the follow-up interim (mostly among the substantially improved patients), and among the 10 whose level of functioning remained essentially unchanged (spread quite evenly among the four improvement categories), were the 10 patients (again, not quite 25% of the sample) who showed regression in psychological functioning during this period. Those 10 clustered heavily among the failed cases. In fact, of the 10 in this category, 2 were from the group with very good improvement, none from the group with moderate improvement, 1 from the group with equivocal improvement, and 7 from the group with failed outcomes. These 7 were from the total of 11 with failed outcomes in the whole sample.

Regression in Failed Outcomes

Three of these failed cases were from the group of alcoholic–addicted–paranoid patients who did very poorly during their treatments and went on to die of mental-illness-related causes during the follow-up period—in the context either of continuing treatment in a Menninger-affiliated setting (the Addicted Doctor in the local state hospital), or of a new psychotherapy in another setting to which he moved (the Car Salesman), or of trying to manage without therapy from which he had fled (the Alcoholic Heir).

Two others were patients who had seemed to do well enough in their psychoanalytic treatments, but who collapsed afterward under the press of the usual exigencies of their posttreatment lives and died by suicide some years after their treatment terminations. With the Suspended Medical Student, who avoided coming for both Termination and Follow-Up Studies, it was crystal-clear at the time of the Follow-Up Study (when the patient's family and his physician mentor were contacted) that his posttreatment life had collapsed in total disarray with a massive symptomatic return, and that much of the apparent treatment improvement had been a facade. His death came 4 years after the Follow-Up Study. Peter Pan, by contrast, was trying to still put a good face on things at the time of Follow-Up Study. It was apparent, however, that though her level of functioning seemed unchanged between Termination and Follow-Up Studies, it was far less secure at Follow-Up Study—more liable to loosen into renewed decompensation, unless the husband's emotional accommodations kept escalating beyond what would be usually expectable in a marital relationship. Even then, it might be problematic unless the patient returned at some time for a further treatment effort. Four years later, the now desperate patient, with a full return of her now psychotically progressive illness, and with all the symptoms of anorexia, kleptomania, and depression back in full force, did return to a very intensive psychotherapy (with hospitalizations) in a new setting. It was to no avail; her death came 5 years after the Follow-Up Study.

Regression in Very Good Improvements

A much less expected finding among this group of 10 who showed some regression in overall psychological functioning between Termination and Follow-Up

Studies is that it only included 2 of the 17 patients who had very good treatment results. The concern (often the charge) in the mental health field—that the results achievable in psychoanalysis and in very intensive and equally long-term dynamic psychotherapies are not only often insubstantial, and obtained at great cost in time, money, and emotional investment, but often also are not enduring and are subject to ready relapse once the protective and supportive presence of the analyst or therapist is removed from the picture—is simply not in accord with our experience with this particular patient population.

The two who did show at least partial regression from very good treatment results are of interest. One was the Tantrum Woman, the young recent widow who ended her 4⅔ year analysis having overcome her regressive and depressive illness, her hostile affect outbursts, her school and work difficulties, and her problems in relating to and rearing her children. At that point, though, her social life was still the least satisfying part of her life adjustment: She was still unhappily unmarried, had few friends, and felt her emotional investments revolving too much around her analyst. It was during the follow-up period, that, instigated by a "suggestion" from her ex-analyst (whom she was consulting quite regularly), the patient met a receptive and equally lonely widower, was courted, and was soon married. It was the effort at the adjustment within this marriage, with its revival of issues unresolved in her previous analysis (e.g., her guilt over the "Oedipal triumph") and renewed symptoms (e.g., anxiety attacks, leading into panic episodes), that brought the patient to her Follow-Up Study determined to win her way back into treatment. And at this point, the ex-analyst was willing to state that the patient's problems had not been sufficiently worked out in the analysis and could not be "until she got into a situation like a marriage which would bring them actively to the fore again." The patient went back into 4 more years of reanalysis, and emerged this time with a much better consolidated result. (This whole double treatment course has been described on pp. 302–307.)

The other patient who showed some posttreatment relapse from a very good treatment outcome was the Claustrophobic Man—the individual who came to psychotherapy with no anxiety in connection with his several operations for recurrent cancer of the thyroid, but intensely phobic crippling anxiety about nonexistent heart disease. The psychotherapy turned out to be less expressive than originally anticipated, and the patient's main defensive position, the denial, was essentially untouched. Nonetheless, he achieved a very good symptom remission within the context of a very positive attachment to the therapist (a "transference cure"), marked by a reconstitution of the patient's premorbid defenses, especially his counterphobic capacities and his reaction formations. All this, incidentally, was aided by a very favorable life turn—the nonrecurrence of his malignancy over a 5-year period. During the follow-up period, however, there was a symptom relapse in the context of continuing life difficulties, business burdens, the patient's still-troubled relationship with his father, and also now his relationship with his adult son. This relapse led basically to renewed contacts with the ex-therapist spaced over the next several years, during which the patient worked out a number of major life changes (e.g., selling out from under his family business and entering a new business venture more his own, taking an enlarged civic and philanthropic role in the community, arranging much more travel and vacation time with his wife, etc.). These contacts, over the span of time, helped consolidate the patient's functioning at the new (still very acceptable) level, though not quite at the euphoric high achieved in the first flush of his enthusiastic treatment response. (The whole treatment course is described on pp. 398–403.) This treatment story bears clearly on the issue of how sustained changes based on such clear-cut transference cures can be over time. The Claustrophobic Man seemed to be the one such patient in the whole PRP sample who evidenced partial regression in the treatment achievements when the formal therapeutic contact officially ended.

Regression in an Equivocal Improvement

The one other, not quite comparable, patient who also showed some posttreatment regression was the Heiress. Her therapeutic course and improvement (see pp. 421–426) has been conceptualized under the rubric of a transference cure, supplemented by a "transfer of the transference" onto the new (presumably far less neurotically conflicted) marriage into which the patient entered after disentangling herself from the very destructive and sadomasochistic marital interaction in which she was caught when she came to treatment. What went awry there, and was linked to the partial loss of the treatment-achieved gains during the follow-up interim, was the fact that the second marriage turned out to be far more like than unlike the first marriage (at least in some salient aspects). The problems within it were associated directly with the patient's partial symptom returns.

CONCEPT OF CHANGE IN FUNCTIONING NOT APPLICABLE

There are still 4 patients unaccounted for in this tabulation of the 18 who showed enhancement and further consolidation between Termination and Follow-Up Studies, the 10 who showed no significant change, and the 10 who showed regression (either partial regression from results achieved in successful treatments, or further regression from the outcomes of unsuccessful treatments). Of these last 4, 1 is of course the Alcoholic Doctor, the one project patient who died while still in his original treatment course. The other 3 are the Housebound Phobic Woman, the Fearful Loner, and the Economist, who remained in their original ongoing treatments past the point of "cutoff" Follow-Up Study (i.e., the 3 who were "therapeutic lifers" at the time of Termination Study and were still in that status at the time of Follow-Up Study). These 3 were actually each in stabilized maintenance psychotherapies at this time (although the Housebound Phobic Woman and the Economist had started out as psychoanalytic cases); from that point of view, they could be considered to be numbered with the patients who were unchanged over the follow-up period of observation.

We, of course, know the subsequent careers of all three. The Housebound Phobic Woman is still in treatment as of this writing (by now for 25½ years), and has had a stable and effective, albeit circumscribed, life functioning all along. With her ongoing treatment (only 1 hour monthly now) as a regular part of her life, she does indeed have a very good improvement over the chronic and acute drug-intoxicated state with which she had been originally brought to treatment.

The Economist is also still in treatment as of this writing (by now for 28 years) and has stabilized his life at the same moderate degree of improvement achieved by the time of the "cutoff" studies; that is, he is occupationally consolidated in his academic career, financially very successful (in his stock market dealings), still single and alone, and given to occasional mildly depressive periods. And, of course, the Fearful Loner, whose treatment lasted a total of 16 years until his retirement and move from Topeka, has seemed to maintain permanently the absolute sameness of his life at the level of (for him) very good improvement achieved with his third therapist—that he could marry and live contentedly and congenially in that marriage. All three of these "therapeutic lifers" should therefore, in truth, be classed with the 10 whose level of functioning was adjudged to remain essentially unchanged between termination and (in their case, very long-term) follow-up.

IX

What Have We Learned from These Cases?

Second-Guessing: Misdiagnoses and Wrong Treatments?

> Human beings must learn to accept their imperfection. We should do all we possibly can to avoid errors, but recognize that the limitations of our nature are also the limitations of our duty. Nobody can be expected to do more than his best. I may add that instead of being deterred by the possibility of error, I am rather encouraged by it. If I were certain of knowing the truth, the whole truth, I would not dare to criticize anything, because my judgment would be final and inexorable. (Sarton, 1960, p. 1186)

Second-guessing is a commonplace game in the human enterprise. It has been particularly enshrined within the psychological/clinical helping professions, in which so much of the teaching and the transfer of knowledge, skill, and experience is via the apprenticeship (tutorial) system of supervision, introduced by psychoanalysis, and via the derivative of individual supervision, the clinical case conference. In these settings, the data of the clinical consulting room are conveyed—usually verbally, at times in writing—to the teacher (supervisor) or the case conference participants. The presentation is then supplemented by questions directed toward the presenter (and, quite exceptionally, supplemented by first-hand interview contact with the primary data source, the patient). Comprehensive assessments, judgments, diagnostic formulations, treatment plans, and prognostications are arrived at; these may be long-term or short-term, detailed or general, explicit or at least in part implicit, and so forth. As this process is repeated with the same supervisor and/or conference leader over time, or with different experts independently, and also at varying points in time, there is often a significant degree of reformulating or second-guessing—often with all the benefits of hindsight and of retrospection in the light of unfolding circumstances, as viewed over an extended time frame or from a more productive or objective vantage point.

POSSIBILITIES FOR SECOND-GUESSING IN PRP

By the nature of its structure, PRP enjoyed, in a multiplied manner, all the possibilities as well as the pitfalls of second-guessing. The comprehensive Initial Studies on which the rest of the predictive and observational enterprise was built were done by two psychoanalyst clinician–researchers (Robbins and myself) at some remove from the primary data. In order to fulfill the commitment to a naturalistic research design, in which the psychoanalysis and psychotherapy would

653

be studied without the involvement or even knowledge of either participant in the therapeutic process (see pp. 50–51, 71–85 for the details of this conception and its implementation in the research operation), each Initial Study formulation was derived *only* from the clinical record of the comprehensive psychiatric evaluation done on the prospective therapy patient. The patient was not seen directly; the research investigators were removed in space and time from the direct evaluation process. The formulations of the psychiatric evaluation team (diagnosis, treatment plan and recommendations, prognosis) were all available for research scrutiny—and, of course, for second-guessing. And there were of course instances, described earlier as one type of "inadvertent control" (see p. 114), where the judgments of the research team, whether about diagnostic formulations or treatment recommendations (more often the latter), differed from those arrived at by the examining clinicians. These instances led then to alternative predictions, depending on which of the two projected treatment plans the treating clinician happened to follow—whether that recommended by the clinical evaluation team (which was, of course, available to the intended therapist), or that recommended by the research evaluation team (which was not available). The cases of the Alcoholic Raconteur and the Alcoholic Doctor are good examples of wide discrepancies in judgments and recommended treatment plans between the clinical and research evaluators, with, therefore, alternative sets of predictions for the different possible treatment plans.

And this same possibility for second-guessing existed at the points of inquiry (now with access to the patients as well) further along the line, the Termination and Follow-Up Study points. In fact, these possibilities were even greater at the later points in time, just because of both the retrospective viewing that they afforded, as well as the large-sweep overview that was available at Termination or Follow-Up of a whole treatment course culminating in a particular outcome. Given these various "advantages" of the contemplative research perspective, and its possibilities for overview and review, over the hurly-burly of the front-line clinical encounter, what can we say here about issues of differing judgments over treatment course and outcome between treating clinicians and researchers?

Clearly, this begins with issues of diagnosis (not in the DSM sense; see pp. 34–35)—a better term might be "diagnostic case formulation." I have already described in detail the astonishingly widespread concealment of major elements of psychopathology, which then clearly emerged during the course of the subsequent therapy, by our PRP patients during the initial diagnostic evaluation process: Such concealment took place in 24 instances out of the 42, or more than 55% of the whole sample (see pp. 158–163). The astonishment is related, of course, to the perhaps naive expectation that such a degree of concealment could hardly be possible, given the quite unparalleled comprehensiveness of the psychiatric evaluation process at The Menninger Foundation—truly as comprehensive as such a process could (practically) be or should (conceptually) be. This sort of concealment of course has obvious implications for (though not at all complete correlation with) issues of misdiagnosis. These issues have also already been described in detail (see pp. 164–167). I have described there, in all, 18 instances (not quite 45%) of substantial misdiagnosis; in every instance, it was in the direction of underestimation of pathology. The majority of the 18 were male (11 to 7), and this is in accord with the fact that such underdiagnosis of the degree of pathology, in the direction of ego weakness and ego distortion, clustered heavily within the predominantly male alcoholic–addicted and paranoid–borderline groups (themselves categories that overlapped significantly). Actually, among the 24 "concealers" of *major* psychopathology, the concealment played a very significant role in the underdiagnosing process in 14 instances. With the other 10 "concealers," the issues withheld did not make a significant difference to the overall diagnostic conceptualization. However, in addition to the 14 for whom the concealment made such a difference, there were 4 other patients (the Alcoholic Raconteur, the Sexual Masochist, the Housebound Phobic Woman, and the Car Salesman) who withheld or concealed nothing substantial of the presenting symptoms or problems, and still there was a serious underestimation of the true breadth and depth of the psychopathology.

APPROPRIATENESS OF RECOMMENDED TREATMENTS

Given this starting base, it is no wonder that in retrospect one can have serious doubts about the ultimate appropriateness of the recommended (and, for the most part, implemented) treatment courses. With the constant direction of the "misdiagnosis"[1] being that of underestimation of pathology, the counterpart undue treatment recommendation would be in the direction of more extensive, ambitious, and thoroughly reconstructive treatment efforts than would turn out to have been warranted—that is, the recommendation of more cases for psychoanalysis than could really use it to maximal advantage.

Psychoanalysis

ANALYSIS CLEARLY APPROPRIATE

Of the 22 patients recommended for and at least started in psychoanalysis, for 12 (2 men and 10 women) it seems at this retrospective overview point, and to the research judges, to have been clearly the most appropriate treatment choice.

---

1. It should be borne firmly in mind that what is being dealt with here is not a simple matter of "misdiagnosis" based on insufficient clinical understanding, skill, or experience. Certainly issues of concealment and withholding played some role in this overall process by leading to insufficient and therefore improper understanding. But this is indeed only part of the story. As already stated, the diagnostic process at The Menninger Foundation is as well developed and comprehensive as that anywhere in the world, and it is quite uniformly carried out with high levels of devotion, diligence, and skill. And the clinician–researchers in PRP were drawn from the ranks of senior, skilled, and experienced psychoanalyst–clinicians. An additional factor involved here is discussed at the very outset of this book (see pp. 20–21) in regard to the predilection of treating clinicians and clinical researchers alike to think and to prognosticate in terms of a "best-case scenario." That is, for each patient and each prospective treatment course, the tendency was to think in terms of the most that could be accomplished, given the utmost potential reach of the proffered treatment plan. This was in accord with the operating dictum in the Menninger clinical community that in any given psychotherapeutic situation one should be "as expressive as one can be, and as supportive as one has to be" (i.e., should push as much in the direction of analytic work, of psychoanalysis proper, as the patient can go or can be brought). This dictum, of course, rests on the *a priori* value judgment that expressive approaches are "better" than supportive ones in terms of their ultimate promise to the patient— an issue that is discussed in more detail in Chapter 37. All of this does relate in a major way, though, to the issues of diagnostic conceptualization, treatment planning, and treatment prognostication that are being considered here, and are also considered in more detail in the next chapter.

This does not mean that these 12 represented all the best outcomes, or that they had no disappointing outcomes among them. Nor does it mean that in every case the analysis was carried out in a way adjudged to have been maximally effective. Of the 12, 7 actually had very good outcomes, 3 had moderately good outcomes, 1 had a very equivocal outcome, and one was a completely failed case.

Limitations on Good Outcomes. It should be clear, of course, from the reading of the case descriptions that even among the best of these outcomes, with hardly an exception, there were significant elements of insufficient and incomplete analytic work and outcome—at least against our (no doubt idealized) psychoanalytic standards. For example, the Adoptive Mother was the patient whose analysis was specifically modified (under the aegis of the supervisor) in the direction of a "defense analysis," with major interpretive focus on the formal (defensive and resistant) aspects of the analytic process at the expense of the specific interpretation of content meaning. Her case has been presented as the paradigm instance (there were a fair number of others as well) of specific limitations in the resolution of intrapsychic conflict, in the area of the unconscious hostile identification with, and the infantile–dependent relationship to, the malevolent pre-Oedipal mother imago. The possible role played by the maintained "defense-analytic" approach in the limitation of outcome, as against the operation of other factors in the patient and in the treatment, has been discussed in detail in the description of that treatment (see pp. 295–302).

The Tantrum Woman was the patient whose first 4 years of analysis, albeit terminated at a point of substantial improvement, left enough unconscious conflict unresolved that it was reactivated to symptomatic degree by the stresses of a new marriage; she felt it necessary (shortly after the Follow-Up Study) to enter upon another 4 years of analysis, with the same analyst, in order to come to a better and more enduring analytic resolution (see pp. 302–307). The Snake Phobia Woman was the patient whose terminated analysis left her seemingly dissatisfied enough and with enough continuing marital friction that she maintained a regular pattern of periodic consultation visits to her ex-analyst, sometimes with her husband (as a result of which he went into a psychotherapy that he found very helpful for himself and for the marriage). This pattern finally led into an exchange of letters that over a 22-year follow-up span brought the patient adequate fruits (for herself and for the marriage) of the original analytic work (see pp. 308–314). And the Divorced Nurse was the patient whose analytic outcome was clouded to a significant degree by the very unfavorable life circumstances in which it seemed that the analytic work had to be carried out: She was in Topeka being analyzed, while the husband and children remained in their home city, and the two of them became locked into a bitter divorce litigation that made for many analytic interruptions and hurried trips home. This patient was quite convinced (perhaps very correctly) that she would have had a much better chance to salvage her marriage if the analysis could have been carried out in the context of her living at home, in ongoing living interaction in the troubled marriage (see pp. 314–321). Of these 4 patients, 3 of them were nonetheless adjudged to be in the group with very good treatment results; only one (the Divorced Nurse) finished in a troubled enough state to be considered only moderately improved.

More Problematic Outcomes. As against these good enough analytic results, there was a different group in terms of the nature of the problems and outcomes among the 12 for whom analysis was felt to be the appropriate treatment modality. One, for example, was the Silent Woman; her psychoanalysis, right treatment though it was, foundered after 1 year over a transference–countertransference impasse centering around the handling of the lengthy, stubborn, and painful silences that were the hallmark of this analysis. Despite this, the patient achieved (and maintained over 14 years of follow-up observation) a moderately good improvement in her life functioning and in symptom relief by the mechanism I have called the "antitransference cure." However, she paid a price for this failure of proper analytic resolution in her subsequent quite anhedonic life, without sexual or marital fulfillment. There was nothing in the evolution of the treatment that should have altered the initial conception of psychoanalysis as the appropriate treatment of choice; the problem rested throughout in the handling of its technical (transference–countertransference) difficulties (see pp. 445–451).

The case of Peter Pan was perhaps somewhat more perplexing. She came to psychoanalysis with a flagrant, severe anorexia nervosa and a hidden severe kleptomania. She seemed, however, to have the requisite ego resources, and psychoanalysis seemed clearly the treatment of choice. The patient's analysis was, however, terminated prematurely (after 3 years) under pressure from her fiancé, who was moving to another city to pursue his university studies and confronted her with an ultimatum to choose between the analysis and following him. She did try to resume the analysis in the other city, but this renewed effort was closed out after only 6 months—this time by confrontation within the analysis, combined again with pressure from the fiancé, leading the patient to feel that she had to choose between the analysis and marriage. Nonetheless, between the degree of psychoanalytic work that was accomplished, and the labored effort at a transfer of the transference (with the promise of a cure by love held out by the husband), the patient did maintain her functioning over a total 10-year course before she returned to treatment. This time it was a very intensive psychotherapy (not analysis), in the throes of full symptomatic relapse just about to the originally presenting state, as well as an inexorably unfolding psychotic decompensating process. Clearly at this point psychoanalysis was no longer indicated; but neither could the psychotherapy, devoted and skilled as it was, and combined with periodic hospitalizations as it was, stay the downhill course to the patient's death after 1 year in that treatment.

Even in full retrospect, however, the original recommendation for psychoanalysis still seems to have marked the only course that could have truly resolved the deep and intensely driven intrapsychic conflicts and destructive symptoms of this patient—if only it could have been held to, against the external pressures upon it, and with perhaps more effective adjuvant life management and control. The complex diagnostic problem in this case has been previously discussed (see p. 167). The conclusion was reached, as noted, that the diagnostic issue was not that of initial underdiagnosis of ego pathology (which would have made psychoanalysis an inappropriate treatment) so much as a sequential decade-long unfolding of a progressively decompensating course that the original analysis was insufficient to prevent. (For the full treatment course, see pp. 426–432.)

Conversions to Therapy Judged Inappropriate. Two others of this group that should be noted here are 2 patients among the 6 whose analyses were converted after some time to psychotherapies, varyingly expressive and supportive. It is the overall research team judgment for these 2 patients that the original recommendation for analysis was still the appropriate one and could have in the end provided the patients with a fuller outcome if it had been held to. The two sets of circumstances were somewhat different.

One of these patients was the Movie Lady (see pp. 413–417). Her analyst decided to shift her explicitly to a supportive–expressive psychotherapy within the first 6 months of the treatment, because he felt (with not substantial enough evidence) that he was dealing with a much sicker individual (paranoid, borderline, psychotic) than had been originally anticipated. She was the one patient not treated in Topeka, but selected for the PRP sample because of the rare opportunity to do our kind of study in relation to the research data that would be simultaneously gathered from a very intensive study (by a whole team of investigators) of the daily verbatim transcript and movie viewing of the first psychoanalysis ever to be filmed from start to finish. The analyst was well known to the PRP members because he had earlier worked at The Menninger Foundation; in fact, he was one of the founders of the forerunner group in Topeka that fashioned some of the preconceptions of PRP back in 1948 (see p. 5). Unfortunately from our perspective, he had also come to have serious reservations about the efficacy of classical analysis. He had experimented over the years with a variety of briefer substitutive therapeutic approaches, and was more than willing to make analysis into the kind of psychotherapy that this treatment became—an effort at a "corrective emotional experience" linked to a mutuality of personal interchanges with the patient, with auxiliary "homework," relaxation exercises, and the like, all designed to do at least as much good for the very same problems. It is a very reasonable expectation that other analysts, in the same (research) circumstance and dealing with the same patient, would have adhered more firmly to a classical psychoanalytic approach. This patient did have a very good improvement in the treatment received; it seemed sustained afterward with the help of continued interchanges of very personal correspondence (in both directions) with the therapist, as well as a very gratifying transfer of the transference onto the husband. How much "better" a result could have been achieved with classical analysis cannot of course be positively stated.

The other patient, the Heiress, was converted to psychotherapy under very different circumstances (see pp. 421–426). She was a very rich woman who had been raised under emotionally extraordinarily deprived circumstances, albeit surrounded with lavish material advantages. Within her psychoanalysis a stalemate gradually developed around her transferences to the "cardboard analyst"; this was resolved after 2½ years by her transfer to a much more senior analyst, who then felt that the transference impasse could only be reversed by systematically altering the analysis (without ever making this explicit) into a sustaining psychotherapy. He introduced a variety of specific parameters, all in the direction of presenting himself as a real figure, steadily present and benevolently interested, the first good and willing father figure in her life. This "analysis" went on for 4½ years more, during the overall course of which the patient got out of a destructive sadomasochistic marriage and into a seemingly much better second marriage; the ultimate termination of the treatment then came with a transfer of the transference onto the husband and into the new marriage. Unfortunately, the second marriage was not as different in the character of the marital interactions as had initially seemed to be the case, and the patient's life and marriage bogged down into an unhappy (albeit somewhat attentuated) reprise of the first marriage, with a significant return of symptoms as well. The overall result was quite equivocal. Had the first analytic effort not gotten bogged down in such a transference impasse, and had no need been felt therefore to counter this somewhat drastically by such systematic modification of the treatment in a psychotherapeutic direction, again a greater and a more enduring treatment result could perhaps have been achieved psychoanalytically. Here, as with the Silent Woman, the problem originated in the handling of technical (transference–countertransference) difficulties, rather than in the appropriateness of psychoanalysis as the treatment of choice.

ANALYSIS CLEARLY INAPPROPRIATE

As against the 12 patients (of the 22 started in analysis), 2 men and 10 women, for whom psychoanalysis seems retrospectively to have still been clearly the treatment of choice, there were 6 others for whom it oppositely proved to be very much an untenable treatment. Here the sex ratio was exactly reversed—5 men and 1 woman. These 6 were drawn clearly from the ranks of the sicker patients, the alcoholic–addicted and the paranoid–borderline. All 6 were heavily alcoholic, 2 were drug-addicted, 4 had very major pathology of sexual functioning, all 6 were paranoid, and 4 of them clearly had borderline ego functioning. They were all taken into psychoanalysis on the basis of "heroic indications." These have been discussed in this book as part of the conceptualization of the particular kind of treatment role that could be played by a psychoanalytic sanatorium setting like The Menninger Foundation—committed, by its ethos, its history, and its practice, to intensive psychoanalytic treatment for precisely that wider range of patients who might be amenable to it under the special protective and supportive sanatorium circumstances.

These six patients, however, who are discussed as a group in more detail in the next chapter, all got into major unresolvable problems in their analyses: four in the direction of an evolving psychotic transference reaction, another over a masochistic need to fail and a profound negative therapeutic reaction, and one over an incapacity or unwillingness to confront the requirements of analytic work in the first instance. Two of them disrupted their analyses quite early, within a year; one disrupted treatment at a later point when the analyst insisted on a permanent conversion to an explicit psychotherapy; one was converted, after more than 4 years of analytic effort (and then only when the father felt he could no longer carry this very expensive burden), to an explicit psychotherapy for almost another 3 years—with no better success, however; one terminated his analysis with (at that time) a seemingly satisfactory result, which subsequently fell apart disastrously; and one went on in a continuing analysis until his death at the 7-year mark. Incidentally, two of these individuals were felt by the research evaluators from the very start to be misplaced in analysis, even in the context of the general institutional commitment to extended "heroic indications"; they were thought instead to require a supportive–expressive psychotherapeutic approach. They were among the instances of "inadvertent controls" where alternative predictions were made for the outcomes of the two different treatment approaches that were posed.

The final results with this group of six were dismal. Five were total treatment failures, including three of the six deaths from mental-illness-related causes in the project; the sixth was the one who rescued himself by his conversion to AA, which sustained him in an equivocal treatment result. This group of clearly (to us) wrong selections for analysis is not considered further at this point, but is discussed in the next chapter.

WAS THIS TRIP NECESSARY?

In addition to the 12 patients (2 men and 10 women) for whom we feel analysis to have been thoroughly justified as the treatment of choice, and the 6 (5 men and 1 woman) for whom it turned out not to be, there were 4 other patients taken into analysis (3 men and 1 woman) who had widely varying results (though none of them were failed cases)—clustered neither toward the successes (like the indicated cases) nor toward the failures (like the contraindicated cases). These were individuals whose achievements in their treatments have been described in relation to the World War II question emblazoned so widely in national advertising: "Was this trip necessary?" To put it more precisely, did it take all that intensive psychoanalytic treatment, with such enormous investments of time, money, and emotional commitment, to achieve the results that were reached? Or could that gain have been arrived at with some lesser effort in intensity and/or duration? This is clearly a salient question in the field. It has been the impetus for so many of the efforts to shorten the psychotherapeutic task, arising either from psychoanalysis centrally (going back to the innovations of Ferenczi and Rank and brought to a major focus by Alexander and French [1946] and their coworkers); from approaches very much based on or influenced by analysis, such as dynamic brief therapy (Malan, 1963; Mann, 1973; Sifneos, 1972; and others) or of course from orientations totally outside analysis, such as the behavioral approaches and the so-called "existentialist–humanistic" approaches (Marks, 1981; Rogers, 1951; and many, many others). And it is an equally salient question to the health policy planners, both in government and in the private sector (the insurers of health care), who are faced with the issue of the kind of mental health benefits that should be provided to their beneficiaries. It is therefore incumbent to look at this question of appropriateness of treatment or warrant for treatment as carefully as possible at this point, in relation to the treatment courses of the four patients taken into psychoanalysis within PRP about whom this issue has been raised.

Pure Analytic Cases. Two of these four patients were maintained in psychoanalysis throughout. The issues in the two instances were quite different. One was the Prince, the individual with the intensely narcissistic character neurosis whose analysis lasted 4½ years and ended with moderate improvement (see Chapter 16). A variety of circumstances converged at the termination point: on the one hand, an analytic pressure to deepen the analytic work, and on the other, the reality pressure of the patient's fiancée's pregnancy and their marriage. (Contributing countertransference propensities of the analyst also played their role in the termination in the state in which it occurred; see p. 238.) At the termination, which came at a point significantly short of the original expectation, the patient said, "I'm very aware that my analysis is not completed." He did subsequently come back for a year more of once-weekly psychotherapy with his analyst. At this point, the analyst considered the patient "probably unanalyzable." This second treatment of 43 additional hours over 1 year did seem in one sense equally efficacious as the previous 950 hours, although, to be fair, it did indeed come after and on top of all the previous intensive analytic work.

Yet a question does arise about the nature of this treatment result, but complexly, from two sides. On the one hand, need such a maximum treatment effort have been mounted to achieve this much less than (potentially) maximum gain? From the available evidence, the most reasonable answer is probably not. Much the same amount and kind of gain could probably have come from a much less intensive psychotherapy (say, twice weekly); this could perhaps have been pursued in a more vigorously confrontative way in relation to the patient's avoidant defenses, which safeguarded his narcissistic integrity so well, and perhaps could also have led to his being able to terminate over a (considerably?) shorter time span. However, there is an opposite vantage point in this case. I have posed this earlier as follows: "Could more attention specifically to the grandiose and idealizing selfobject transferences, and more focused awareness of the countertransferences that they in turn successfully played upon and/or evoked . . . have enabled the patient and the analyst to come jointly to a more successfully accomplished analytic resolution?" (p. 328).[2] In other words, in at least this one case, we are caught in a dilemma between two opposed prescriptive remedies—either less analysis, or, rather, less treatment (psychotherapy of lesser intensity and duration), to reach at least the same treatment result; or an equal or maybe even longer analysis, albeit focused more sharply on the world of selfobject transferences, to try to achieve a much more thorough and ambitious character reorganization. Clearly, different analytic therapists might choose differently between these alternatives. The patient, though, would probably have preferred the more ambitious effort at the original starting point.

The other patient in this group who was maintained in analysis throughout was the Devoted Son (see pp. 283–287). He was the patient with the extremely inhibited and dependent (and rigidly defended) obsessive–compulsive character structure who came to analysis with no specific focused symptoms ("I know I am not getting what I want out of life"). He was in analysis for 5½ years, and terminated with very limited changes under the pressure of the analyst (via the "weaning" process), who was fearful of the patient's "cloying dependency" and the risks of the insoluble transference neurosis. This patient was unchanged at Follow-Up Study ("I have gone in the same grooves, wearing a little more deeply"), and kept going that way until the point at which he renewed his contacts with his ex-analyst 13 years after treatment termination (for the *same* problems in living). When his analyst left Topeka 2 years later, he was transferred to another therapist, who has seen him continuously ever since (at 30 minutes each week) for 7 years now; the patient at this point is a true "therapeutic lifer." With this patient (unlike the Prince), there was no question of an alternative, more thoroughgoing psychoanalytic approach. There is only the very real question that perhaps the kind of treatment approach carried out in the actively supportive and insistently pressuring

---

2. During the time span of this particular analysis (1954–1959), Kohut's major books (1971, 1977) were still two decades in the future.

termination phase of the original analysis (its final 8 months) might well have by itself, and perhaps over a not much longer time span, accomplished practically all of the limited therapeutic change that was achieved in the whole treatment. The limitation here may well have been in the actual limited applicability of psychoanalysis as a thoroughly reconstructive effort in the face of this overwhelming an obsessive–compulsive character rigidity—the most entrenched in the whole PRP population (along with perhaps that of the English Professor), just as the Prince had the most entrenched narcissistic character neurosis.

Analysis Converted to Therapy. The other two patients about whom this question about analysis, "Was this trip necessary?", has been raised were among the six patients who indeed were converted from psychoanalysis to psychotherapy—each, again, under different circumstances.[3] One was the Housebound Phobic Woman, the patient who had chronic cerebral damage underlying the acute and flagrant drug-intoxicated state with which she came for treatment, and who thus never proved really able to handle the introspective requirements of the psychoanalytic process (see pp. 391–398). Her first analyst sensed this almost from the start, and very rapidly converted her treatment into a psychotherapy marked by a very directive and supportive handling. It is one of the treatments in the PRP population that has gone on uninterruptedly for the entire time (25½ years) since its start until this writing (now with the fourth therapist). However, the conversion to psychotherapy was not made explicit for a long time; the first analyst, for example, kept the treatment frequency at 4 hours weekly until his sudden death of heart disease at the 6-year mark. It was only the second analyst who undertook to reduce the treatment frequency, at first just to 3 hours weekly (ostensibly in response to the patient's financial stringencies)—and the patient reacted very angrily at first to this "realistic deprivation." By now, the treatment frequency is (very properly) only 1 hour a month.

This does seem to be one of those unusual instances where such lifelong continuing therapeutic contact and support may well be a vital element in maintaining the patient at a satisfying level of functioning. And, in that context, and considering where she started, this patient is one who overall has achieved a very good treatment result. But this whole intensive psychoanalytic trip was probably not necessary, certainly not over the time span for which it was sustained. A more supportive–expressive psychotherapy from the start, less ambitious in its reach, and much less intensive in its application and in its requirements, could very probably have served this patient equally well.

---

3. Of the 6 who were converted to psychotherapy explicitly or implicitly from among the 22 who were recommended for and started in psychoanalysis, 2 (the Movie Lady and the Heiress) were among the 12 who the research group felt were very appropriately recommended for analysis (and who we felt could have profited even more from their treatments if the recommendation for classical analysis could have been more properly adhered to). Another 2 (the Alcoholic Raconteur and the Masochistic Editor) were among the 6 who the research group felt (in one case from the very start and in the other case certainly in retrospect after studying his treatment course over time) turned out to be in the wrong treatment and might have had a better chance in a more direct supportive–expressive psychotherapy (combined with hospitalization). One of these two, the Alcoholic Raconteur, would not tolerate the conversion and fled the treatment, thereby never allowing the question a test. The other, the Masochistic Editor, did go on in psychotherapy after his family would simply no longer bear the cost of analysis, but in his case it was (by then anyway) to equally little avail.

The other converted patient in this group was the Economist, who came to analysis with what looked like a typically neurotic character structure (moderately obsessive–compulsive), and with a symptom problem, a repetitive difficulty in working out a meaningful and durable heterosexual involvement and marriage; all of this seemed to make him highly amenable to the recommended psychoanalytic treatment (see pp. 336–343). As it turned out, the patient was in a still continuing though seemingly tapering therapeutic contact 11½ years later, at the "cutoff" Follow-Up Study point, and was classified among the "therapeutic lifers." The psychoanalysis had been maintained as such for almost 6 years and was only converted explicitly into a supportive–expressive psychotherapy at a point when the treatment, which had the potential all along for the development of a very oral-dependent insoluble transference neurosis, evolved (under the impact of the analytic work) into an unfolding psychotic transference reaction. The explicitly very supportive psychotherapy that followed has remained that way for the balance of the treatment, which, like that of the Housebound Phobic Woman, still continues at the time of this writing. At the point of "cutoff" Follow-Up Study, the patient was now in a much better academic position in a distant university, but was still coming back for regular intensive weekend sessions every 6 weeks. He had a moderately good improvement in his prolonged treatment, but again with this patient, the question can be asked: Did he need all that analytic treatment to achieve that much? (At the "cutoff" Termination Study point, he already had 1601 hours, the most of any patient in the research sample.) In retrospect, again, it seems quite likely that a less intensive and ambitious treatment could have served this patient equally well. But though there was some fateful evidence of proneness to ego weakness from the start (e.g., his bizarre conviction that he could classify people and tell their sincerity by the shape of their fingers and of their gums), the patient did look at the start like such a typically neurotic character—and the risks of the later-developing insoluble transference neurosis and unmanageable psychotic transference regression seemed so remote—that the initial recommendation for analysis was at the time very plausible indeed.

In fact, in summarizing the four patients[4] for whom the question of "Was this trip necessary?" has been raised, in only the case of the Housebound Phobic Woman was it really clear from the start that a less intensive supportive–expressive psychotherapy would have been the modality of choice. In addition, with the Prince, there is the unresolved issue of his greater amenability to an intensive psychoanalytic approach focused more specifically on the grandiose and idealizing selfobject transferences. With only two, the Devoted Son and the Economist, does it seem that the truly limited efficacy of psychoanalysis in their cases (given the intensity of the psychoanalytic effort involved) only became really clear during the therapeutic trial at analysis—and that that trial was therefore indeed warranted.

---

4. There is 1 other patient of the 22 recommended for psychoanalysis for whom this question has been raised—the Masochistic Editor. For him, however, this question is raised alongside the more pertinent issue of "Was it (in conception) the wrong trip altogether?" (see p. 362). That is, this patient was one of those in the group of sicker alcoholic–addicted and paranoid–borderline individuals for whom psychoanalysis was undertaken on the basis of "heroic indications," which our PRP experience calls into severe question. It was not a treatment that may have been too much (i.e., too intensive) in relation to the objectives achieved, as was more the case with the other four patients grouped together here.

Psychotherapy

THERAPY CLEARLY APPROPRIATE

I turn now to the 20 patients (11 men and 9 women) who were recommended for varyingly expressive and supportive psychotherapy. For 12 of these (5 men and 7 women), the psychotherapy seems to have been clearly appropriately selected and implemented, with, for the most part, the requisite amount of concomitant hospitalization. This does not mean that the treatment was completely uniformly successful with this group, though all the better outcomes did cluster there—all 9 of the very good improvements among them, 2 of the 3 moderate improvements, and only 1 failed case. The 1 failed case in this group was the Invalided Hypochondriac, who was in an appropriate treatment plan (supportive psychotherapy with concomitant hospital care and management); her treatment, however, was broken up very prematurely after only 4 months, out of the combined disruptive and manipulative pressures of the patient (she had been converted to a new light— she had "talked to God" and He had "forgiven" her) and the husband (he felt that his wife could be treated just as well, and without expense, at the state hospital in their home state). Faced with this solid front of the patient and her husband, the hospital and the therapist capitulated, and accepted her discharge from the hospital and the termination of her psychotherapy (see pp. 553–556).

With the other 11 in this group who did well or well enough, as with their counterparts in psychoanalysis, one can wonder whether some could have done even better. For example, the Involutional Woman, whose lifelong throttled resentments were focused around her husband, and who came to treatment with a severe involutional depression set in the context of a rigidly conforming character structure, ended her successful psychotherapy tied now to the internist who was caring for her progressive arthritis (rather than to the therapist, whom she could relinquish). The question nonetheless remained of whether a more fully expressive psychotherapy could have resolved more fully the neurotic problems within the marriage, related to the patient's chronic repressed hostility, competitiveness, and envy. The overall result could therefore perhaps have relied less on the transference cure, and on the shift from the despairing sense of unfulfilled (oral and narcissistic) needs to a sense, at last, of therapeutically fulfilled needs (see pp. 375–382). And, similarly, the Claustrophobic Man, whose intense phobic illness centered around the fear of nonexistent heart disease (displaced from the real threat of cancer recurrence), all set into a very passive–dependent character structure, had a very good outcome. The comparable question nonetheless remained of whether a more fully expressive psychotherapy could have better resolved the fabric of denials on which the patient's whole symptom picture rested. Again, the treatment result rested on the transference cure that fostered the reconstitution of the premorbid defensive structure; the cure in this case was buttressed, of course, by the powerful reinforcement of the silent passage of time (past the magical 5-year mark), with its increasing reassurance against cancer recurrence. This was, by the way, one of the good treatment outcomes where there *was* some partial regressive symptom return in the follow-up interim, when the sustaining contact with the therapist was no longer regularly present (see pp. 398–403).

And within this same group of 12 patients were the 2, the Actress and the

Rebellious Coed, for whom a goodly part of the treatment result achieved was by way of the collusive bargain struck in both instances—to avoid therapeutic scrutiny of the patients' homosexual propensities and activities, in return for a collaborative therapeutic working together in relation to all the other aspects of the patients' life functioning. This bargain got the Actress exactly where she wanted to be; she ended treatment as a successful young career woman, with her troubling interpersonal behaviors as well as her depressive symptoms all remitted, and her sexual life stabilized into an ego-syntonic homosexuality (see pp. 478–483). By contrast, it left the Rebellious Coed grossly dissatisfied—enough so that she went on into another effort at psychotherapy elsewhere for another year, this time trying to deal with her conflicts over homosexuality directly. This second treatment effort foundered over the patient's inability to tolerate the unfolding Oedipal transference attachments that were so centrally related to her defensive homosexuality. In the end, both psychotherapies (the one that colluded to ignore the homosexual problems and the one that sought to resolve them) failed to bring about changes in this area; they left the patient at the finish, like the Actress, a spinster career woman entrenched in a homosexual life, but less ego-syntonically so (see pp. 483–489).

The last patient who should be just mentioned from this dozen who were appropriately in various psychotherapies is the Fearful Loner. His treatment in the end worked out very well—over its 16-year course till his retirement and move from Topeka—but not till after he "fired" two therapists, a male psychiatrist and a female social worker, with whom (each for different reasons) he felt he could not get along. He was truly a patient with a strong "transference to the institution"; he felt it his prerogative each time to require the director of psychotherapy at The Menninger Foundation to try to do better by him and furnish him another therapist "on approval," until he finally got the one he was satisfied with (see pp. 452–458).

THERAPY INSUFFICIENT FOR VARIOUS REASONS

Of the other 8 patients among the 20 recommended for psychotherapy, 6 of them (5 men and 1 woman), though indeed in psychotherapy, had treatments that proved insufficient—either because they were not explicitly supportive enough, or had insufficient concomitant hospitalization, or had insufficient adjunctive support (casework with the family), or suffered from some combination of all these insufficiencies. Not surprisingly, there were 3 cases with equivocal results and 3 failed cases among these 6.

Hospitalization Not Part of Treatment Plan. The Addicted Doctor and the Car Salesman were two very addicted, very alcoholic patients who were recommended for an essentially supportive psychotherapy; in each instance, however, because of the fear of unduly playing into the patients' powerful dependency strivings, it was offered on an outpatient basis. In neither instance did this work out, and both treatments ended disastrously. The Addicted Doctor was finally transferred after a near-lethal suicide attempt to an effort at continued psychotherapy on an inpatient basis at the Menninger-affiliated local state hospital (see pp. 564–567); and the Car Salesman took flight to seek treatment elsewhere when three successive efforts at The Menninger Foundation (the third of which *was* a 10-month-long hospital stay, with a strongly supportive relationship with a hospital doctor and no formal psychotherapy this time) did not avail (see pp. 567–570). With both these patients, the inpatient treatments that they finally came to proved no more helpful than the outpatient therapy, and it is not clear that any combination of ingredients could have made any difference to these two very ill individuals with such infantile character structures and such overwhelmingly self-destructive symptom pictures.

Hospitalization Evaded by Patients. Two others of these six were originally recommended for psychotherapy combined with a properly managed hospitalization but found ways to evade this recommendation. The Exhibitionistic Dancer actually started her psychotherapy within the hospital, but after her impulsive elopement from the hospital with another young inpatient and their quick drive to a neighboring state to get married, returned to Topeka within a week; she clamored to be taken back into the treatment that, now that she was married, she needed all the more (to help stabilize the marriage), but in her newly wedded state, would necessarily have to have on an outpatient basis. The circumstances under which this treatment plan was acceded to and the grievous consequences of this shift have been described in detail (see pp. 504–510). The Sociopath was able to keep from being hospitalized at all by managing to get the original evaluation team to commit itself to recommending him for outpatient psychotherapy if he could, from his side, demonstrate his capacity to maintain himself in a reasonably trouble-free equilibrium on the outside for a year. The patient lived up to his end of this bargain in the most marginal way, but he extracted a full compliance from the other end, and entered what then became his ill-starred psychotherapy (see pp. 545–550). The Sociopath could have been speaking for this whole group of patients when, in retrospect, he said of his own failed treatment, "I should have been hospitalized. You have to check up on the patients or you have to lock them up. . . . You have to watch them. You have to check on the smarties."

Inadequate Casework with Families. The other two of the patients with insufficient overall treatment plans were the Bohemian Prep School Boy and the Adolescent Grandson, both 17-year-olds, for whom the problem lay in the totally inadequate social casework with their families. In each instance, this culminated in a treatment disruption pressured by the family. The Bohemian Prep School Boy's father felt dubious about his son's treatment all along, seeing it as an unwarranted financial drain; he pushed within 7 months to confront the patient with a planned family move to Europe, leaving him to choose whether to come with them or remain behind. He did go with them and thus disrupted a treatment that had never really gotten under way (see pp. 523–529). The Adolescent Grandson lasted longer in psychotherapy (almost 2 years) before he too managed to re-evoke his grandfather's never-dormant doubts about the treatment; the issue of financial drain was involved, as well as the grandfather's conviction that his grandson suffered mostly from lack of discipline rather than legitimate emotional illness. Here too pressure was placed on the treatment (and acceded to by the patient), resulting in its premature termination (see pp. 490–497). Incidentally, both of these patients whose families made such a fuss about the great financial expense of the treatment came from the small handful of the very wealthiest families in the project. In both instances, however, the social casework was never adequate to the task of maintaining a good treatment-supporting alliance with the family. (With the Adolescent Grandson's grandfather, who delegated everything to his secretary and kept himself aloof from the whole treatment and treatment-supporting process, this was admittedly an inordinately difficult task.)

ANALYSIS RATHER THAN THERAPY APPROPRIATE

For two further patients recommended clinically for psychotherapy, a different issue of treatment appropriateness can be raised. Just as there was a whole large group of patients recommended for and started in psychoanalysis, either for whom an expressive–supportive psychotherapy would have been a far safer recommendation (the six for whom psychoanalysis was recommended on the basis of "heroic indications") or about whom one could ask whether a far less intensive expressive–supportive psychotherapy could not more expeditiously have arrived at the same goals (the four for whom the question "Was this trip necessary?" has been raised), so there were two patients in psychotherapy for whom the more appropriate treatment choice might have been psychoanalysis.

One of these instances, the case of the Homesick Psychology Student, was the more clear-cut. The patient was originally recommended for a once-a-week psychotherapy, which was all he could afford at that time. If the rather slight suspicion of an autistic trend were allayed in this therapy (as expected), it was hoped that, beyond the consolidation of the separation process from his parents, the patient would want a more thoroughgoing working through of the neurotic character configurations that had so markedly hampered his fullest adaptive (and creative) unfolding. It was also hoped that, by then, analysis would have become a more viable treatment plan financially. As it worked out, the treatment never evolved into anything more than a once-weekly psychotherapy, and though there was moderate improvement in many areas of his life functioning (and symptom relief as well), the patient paid a significant price in the total sexual inhibition and unconsummated marriage with which he emerged from the treatment (see pp. 417–421).

With the Bitter Spinster, this same issue can be raised. She was felt to be suffering from a hysterical character neurosis, in the symptomatic form of a "success neurosis." In this sense, she was felt to be almost an ideal patient for psychoanalysis, as the only treatment that could promise real resolution of the deep-seated character problems manifest in her recurrent life difficulties and in her dissatisfactions on both the vocational and the social–sexual levels. For practical reasons (she could not afford analysis), the patient was recommended for a fully expressive psychotherapy, which, if all went well, it was hoped might evolve into a full-blown psychoanalysis. Again, this never happened. The psychotherapy went on for 8 years; instead of improving in any particular, the patient's life functioning progressively worsened, and she began moving toward a paranoid transference regression. At the end this patient was worse off than when she started, and at Follow-Up Study she had regressed still further, into an embittered, depressed, and altogether lonely state. At the time of the Follow-Up Study, it was not completely clear whether this patient was indeed too ill (with her ego weakness and proneness to regression) to tolerate any expressive therapeutic course (let alone psychoanalysis), or, conversely, whether she could perhaps have been helped if a really full and comprehensive *analytic* effort could have been originally undertaken with the requisite resources for it. Both sides of this issue have been developed at the end of the case description (see pp. 349–353).

"Heroic Indications" for Psychoanalysis Reconsidered

THE NATURE OF "HEROIC INDICATIONS"

The concept of "heroic indications" for psychoanalysis was most clearly articulated (though not by that name) in Glover's 1954 article "The Indications for Psychoanalysis." After delineating very simply (and elegantly) the definitional parameters of psychoanalysis as a treatment, and then sketching out a developmental approach to the classification, diagnosis, and prognosis for mental disorders, Glover approached the indications for analysis in terms of three main groupings: those prospective patients accessible to that treatment, those only moderately accessible, and those called alternately "only slightly accessible" or "intractable" (p. 399). The third or intractable group, Glover said, "includes cases which would ordinarily come in the earlier groups but for evidence of deeper or wider ego disorder" (pp. 399–400). Among these, he listed certain types of alcoholics (who "cover either an endogenous depression or a paranoid predisposition"), patients with anxiety hysteria with a "psychotic sub-structure," those with severe monosymptomatic phobias, those with pure psychoses, those with psychotic characters, those with severe cases of psychopathy, and those with "sexual perversions and inhibitions of an equivalent order" (all on p. 400). Quite aside from the fact that Glover has thrown this net of possibilities too widely for most of us (few would include patients with "pure psychoses" unless Glover meant something else by this category than is usually understood), few would disagree with his careful cautionary statement:

> In the third group certainty of cure or even of major improvement cannot be expected and should never be promised. It is true that well-selected cases taken from this third group may from time to time give surprisingly good results, but it would be absurd to pretend that on the average more than a mild degree of betterment can be expected. No organic physician would refuse to treat a case of rheumatism because it was chronic, intractable and promised at best only a mild degree of improvement. . . . Particularly in the psychoses, psychotic characters and severe sexual disorders therapeutic failure is an honorable failure which may in course of time lead to an improvement of the therapeutic instrument. (pp. 400–401)

This same ground was covered in a far more comprehensive and wide-ranging, albeit less precisely delineated, way by Stone in a better-known and more widely influential article published in the very same year, 1954. Stone's descriptive framework was set in his title, "The Widening Scope of Indications for Psychoanalysis." He presented, from both a historical and a metapsychological perspective, the gradual expansion of psychoanalytic endeavor from the classical symptomatic psychoneuroses (the original transference neuroses, around which the theory and method of psychoanalysis were created by Freud and where its applicability is still most manifest and least challenged) into the gradually evolving and widening spectrum of the delinquencies, the addictions, the psychosomatic disorders, the character neuroses, the impulse neuroses, the narcissistic and borderline disorders, even the incipient psychoses or schizophrenias.[1] Stone's overall judgment about this gradual development was stated in conclusion in a form characteristically tempered, subtle, and elusively unprecise:

> Now a few words in brief conclusion: the scope of psychoanalytic therapy has widened from the transference psychoneurosis, to include practically all psychogenic nosologic categories. The transference neuroses and character disorders of equivalent degree of psychopathology remain the optimum general indications for the classical method. While the difficulties increase and the expectations of success diminish in a general way as the nosological periphery is approached, there is no absolute barrier; and it is to be borne in mind that both extranosological factors and the therapist's personal tendencies may profoundly influence the indications and prognosis. (p. 593)

A little further on, Stone declared his uttermost: "[P]sychoanalysis may legitimately be invoked, and indeed *should* be invoked, for many very ill people, of good personality resources, who are probably inaccessible to cure by other methods, who are willing to accept the long travail of analysis, without guarantees of success" (pp. 593–594).

"HEROIC INDICATIONS" IN PRP: THE AVAILABILITY OF THE SANATORIUM SETTING

But clearly reference has been made to "the therapist's personal tendencies," and Stone elaborated this element of judgment and preference at an earlier point in his article: "The important clinical issue in these cases is that, according to the individual therapist's prognostic point of view — and according to individual severity — they may be judged unanalyzable, or possibly liable to psychosis under treatment, or liable to become generally worse under treatment, or to occasion interminable analyses, or perhaps to require very long, especially skillful analyses,

---

1. Stone made it clear that he was not advocating a tendency he gently decried — that there is a "section of the informed public which is devoted to psychoanalysis . . . for whom scarcely any human problem admits of solution other than psychoanalysis. . . . Hopeless or grave reality situations, lack of talent or ability (usually regarded as 'inhibition'), lack of an adequate philosophy of life, and almost any chronic physical illness may be brought to psychoanalysis for cure" (p. 568). And he also made it clear that he was not advocating what he called a "spurious increase of psychoanalytic indications. There is sometimes a loss of sense of proportion about the human condition, a forgetting or denial of the fact that few human beings are without some troubles, and that many must be met, if at all, by 'old fashioned' methods: courage, or wisdom, or struggle, for instance" (p. 569). These phenomena of course represent the "widening scope" in the direction of the too trivial, the not *psychologically* ill enough, or those improperly thought to be psychologically ill. Most of Stone's article covered the issue being discussed here in relation to the PRP sample — the opposite "widening scope," toward the sicker and sicker, with the question of where the line is that separates off the too sick (i.e., too sick to tolerate and profit from the analytic experience).

with eventual minimal improvement" (p. 582). Within the PRP context, where each of these possible untoward outcomes was under ever-present consideration, and where each actually occurred more than once within the sample, the major additional element (not specifically considered either by Stone or by Glover, both of whose accountings were geared to the vicissitudes of outpatient psychoanalytic practice) was that of the availability of the specific sanatorium setting of The Menninger Foundation. Within this sanatorium setting, the question became one of how far the reach of psychoanalytic treatment could be extended—either in classical form, or modified (with reducible parameters; see Eissler, 1953) in the direction of Stone's "widening scope" toward "the nosological periphery" or toward Glover's third group of "only slightly accessible" or "intractable" patients—even in the (relative) absence of what Stone called "good personality resources." It is this issue of the validity or worthwhileness of the "heroic indications" for analysis (in the language of PRP), given the availability of psychoanalytically informed and guided hospital support and protection, that was put to empirical scrutiny in the PRP experience. Concomitantly, another question was at research issue—the belief that, if possible, these patients (or rather, many of them) should be *analytically* treated because no other available therapy can offer them comparable help.

Of course, the rationale of the psychoanalytic sanatorium, pioneered in the United States with the establishment of The Menninger Clinic in 1925, has been from the very start that these "only slightly accessible" or "intractable" cases, could be rendered amenable to psychoanalysis if they could be treated within a supportive and protective sanatorium (hospital) environment, guided in its management by a focused psychoanalytic understanding of the specific treatment needs of each particular patient. This rationale had been detailed in my discussion of the role of adjunctive hospitalization in relation to the PRP population (see pp. 215–227, especially 215–216), including reference to Knight's early papers (1937a, 1937b, 1938) on the psychodynamics of severe alcohol addiction and his experiences with its psychoanalytic treatment within such a sanatorium setting. The counterpart, of course, to the conviction that this kind of managed life setting could make more possible the psychoanalytic treatment of such severely ill patients has been the concomitant conviction, just stated, that those particular patients also require a treatment as thoroughgoingly reconstructive as psychoanalysis in order to have the optimum chance at significant and enduring treatment amelioration.

It was then this *double* set of convictions that PRP was in an excellent position to try to put to empirical test. There were many just such very sick patients coming to therapy at The Menninger Foundation and its hospital—the large group of the severely alcoholic–addicted and sexually disordered, often overlapping with the severely paranoid–borderline, yet not flagrantly psychotic, and with many seeming resources of superior intellectual capacity, (variable) motivation, rich material and family support, and the like. In keeping with just this kind of treatment ethos being elaborated here, which was part of the whole clinical mores of The Menninger Foundation, these patients were typically recommended for psychoanalysis whenever it seemed that some likelihood or some justification could be advanced for it (usually, of course, with the stipulation that there be an ongoing concomitant hospitalization as long as clinically indicated and useful). It is this particular group within the PRP sample, treated psychoanalytically in accord with these so-called "heroic indications," whose treatment careers in that psychoanalytic treatment I want to review here.

"HEROIC INDICATIONS" PATIENTS

Outcomes

Actually, within our PRP population of 42, there were a large number who met these specifications. There were, for example, 15 patients (35% of the sample) who were severely alcoholic; 8 (20%) who were severely drug-addicted; 18 (not quite 45%) with severe sexual disabilities beyond just potency and orgastic disturbances; 14 (33%) with strongly paranoid character trends; and 20 (just under half) with "weak," borderline, or otherwise brittle and precarious ego organizations. There were also, as might be expected, multiple overlappings on these lists. If we take those 11 who appeared in at least three of these five listings, we would clearly have a group of extremely ill patients for whom psychoanalysis would indeed be a heroic treatment choice. Of those 11, 6 were recommended for psychoanalysis: the Alcoholic Doctor, the Alcoholic Heir, the Suspended Medical Student, the Alcoholic Raconteur, the Masochistic Editor, and the Housebound Phobic Woman. Of these 6, 3 were among the 6 patients in the PRP sample who ultimately died of mental-illness-related causes. The Alcoholic Doctor died of a massive aspiration of vomitus while ill in a chronic drug-weakened condition, and while still in his lengthy psychoanalytic treatment; the Alcoholic Heir died of pneumococcal pneumonia and meningitis while in a chronic alcohol-weakened condition, barely 6 months after he disrupted his analysis at the 1-year mark; and the Suspended Medical Student committed suicide by asphyxiation in his car a full 7 years after his treatment termination, during all of which period the patient's life had gone progressively downhill.

The other 3 in this group in analysis, whose illness courses did not end fatally, were all converted (or converted themselves) out of psychoanalysis. The Alcoholic Raconteur fled his analysis after 2¾ years because he felt unable to accept the permanent conversion to an explicit supportive–expressive psychotherapy that his analyst was now insisting upon; he "rescued" himself to a marginal degree of improvement via his turn to AA. The Masochistic Editor's analysis was pursued for 4⅓ years, until his father declared himself unable to support it any longer; he was then switched to psychotherapy, which lasted another 2⅔ years. It was 7 years all told before the treatment, which had gotten nowhere with either modality, petered out through gradually missed hours, then longer absences, and finally complete cessation of contact. Finally, the Housebound Phobic Woman was the one patient in this group who had a very good treatment outcome—this in the context of a conversion to a supportive–expressive psychotherapy almost from the very start, when it seemed clear that this organically damaged woman could not accommodate to a truly psychoanalytic effort. This, of course, is the patient who has continued uninterruptedly in "therapeutic lifer" status for 25½ years, up to the time of the present writing.

Of these 6 patients, 5 were in the group of 6 psychoanalytic patients referred to in the preceding chapter (see pp. 659–660) for whom psychoanalysis proved to be an untenable treatment, tried on the basis of "heroic indications" that ultimately failed. The Housebound Phobic Woman was not in the group referred to there, precisely because her total misfit with the requirements of analysis was recognized by her analyst almost from the start; she was at that early point converted (though not explicitly) into a long-term sustaining, directing, controlling, mostly supportive psychotherapy. Within the context of a lifelong treatment and a life-long restriction pretty much to Topeka and its environs (with occasional trips across country to visit relatives), hers has been indeed a successful treatment course, as measured against her starting point (14 years of unremitting drug addiction and a totally housebound phobic state). The issue with her, rather than being one of "heroic indications" for analysis (since she was never really in analysis), was the question of "Was this trip necessary?" This question has been discussed in the preceding chapter (see p. 662).

Reasons for Treatment Failures

Here I want to discuss, from the point of view of the issues over which the intensive psychoanalytic effort foundered, the other five patients in this group taken into analysis on the basis of "heroic indications," together with the one other (the Script Writer) who was also in the group of six mentioned in the preceding chapter as having proved to be totally unsuitable for analysis. The Script Writer, the one woman among these six, was also severely alcoholic and strongly paranoid, but she only appeared on two of the five listings in which these patients clustered (alcoholic, addicted, sexually disordered, paranoid, borderline), rather than three or more as did the other five in the group.

EMERGENCE OF PSYCHOTIC TRANSFERENCE REACTIONS

With four of these six, the central salient issue proved to be the (not unexpected) emergence of a psychotic transference reaction that threatened to be totally unmanageable. In two cases these reactions were flagrant, and these two are redescribed briefly for emphasis here.

The Alcoholic Doctor. With the Alcoholic Doctor, there turned out to have been regressive forerunners. During his most severe illness period—at the height of the pretreatment collapse, when there was much homosexuality and drug taking—the patient had experienced actual psychotic episodes in which he had been even seemingly delusional and hallucinated. He would run out of the home nude; on one occasion he had barricaded himself in the basement of his home against the people who were out to get him. Within his analysis (described fully on pp. 332–336), much of the initial analytic work centered around the transference fears relating to his image of his violent and cruel father. The patient once had to get up from the couch in order to look for a knife he was sure the analyst had concealed in the stand next to the chair. (When he was 5 years old, the patient's physician father had had him circumcised by an uncle, while he, the father, assisted; the patient was ever troubled that they "had cut off too much.")

But the main thrust of the analytic material shifted to the mother-transference and remained there. Sedatives and alcohol were mother's milk, vital to his survival. His many vagina dentata dreams and his homosexual activities were all ways of denying his direct sexual interest in his mother. As he came to feel more helpless and infantile, the patient began to take on all the mother's abdominal symptoms and to take the identical catalogue of medications. He was frightened of his symbiotic union fantasies; if she were to die, he would have to die. And his murderous hostilities against the mother were concomitantly evoked. He wanted to tear his mother out of his stomach, where she gave him his pains (his symptomatic hiatus hernia); he purchased a gun to shoot himself in the stomach and get rid of the mother and her pain once and for all. The vanishing of his observing ego and the inability to distinguish transference fantasy from reality led to his once crawling over to the analyst to be petted, or to his voicing his heartfelt wish that the analyst be a kangaroo with a pouch carrying the patient around close inside him. The patient initiated periods of sitting up. "He wouldn't know who I was and he would have to look at me to see that I was his therapist." His drug taking often seemed to be an effort to blunt the edge of the psychotic regressions.

And apart from this long psychotic transference episode coursing through the treatment, this analytic effort was also beset by constant uncontrolled drinking, drug taking, depressive plunges, and family turmoil. The patient became ever more demanding, more dependent on the analyst and on the environment for his survival. The one bright spot (perhaps this is what kept the analyst working with some hope) through the 7-year analytic course and up to the patient's death was that he functioned reasonably effectively and competently in his various jobs as a physician, which prior to his treatment he had given up.

The Alcoholic Heir. The other blatant psychotic transference reaction to be redescribed here (more briefly) was that of the Alcoholic Heir. This patient's paranoia first emerged in his drunken, brawling relationship with his wife. He would accuse her of trying to drive him to drink. To his analyst, the patient insisted that there could be but two explanations: Either his wife was an alcoholic, or she was identified with the Communists in trying to drive him to alcoholic ruin and thus to revenge herself upon his wealthy family and what they represented. Toward the end of the patient's 1 treatment year (at which point he bolted), the patient rummaged in some attic trunks and found "a jeweled ice pick"; he brought this to his analyst for safekeeping, fearful that his wife intended to use it on him. On another occasion he asked the analyst for permission to hire a detective agency to investigate whether his wife had purchased a gun to use against him. This same paranoia of course colored the patient's other life relationships as well. The patient was trying to work all during this treatment year in estate planning with a local insurance firm, but since his work was all on commission, he never made much because of his many absences due to strife and drinking. (Somehow, he, like the Alcoholic Doctor, could nevertheless impress people at work: According to the insurance company general agent who took him on, the patient had talent and knowledge in this area, and was "worth working with.") This whole treatment effort ended abruptly when the patient refused to accept the analyst's insistence that inpatient hospital care would be an essential precondition to the continuation of the analysis. He was dead 6 months later. (For the description of the full treatment course, see pp. 345–349.)

Other Psychotic Transference Reactions. There were two other analytic treatments that foundered (but in different and more covert ways) over this same issue of the psychotic potential set into motion by the psychoanalytic treatment effort. With the Suspended Medical Student, it was clear in retrospect that the entire 4½ years of seemingly reasonably successful analysis was but an elaborate facade.

The patient made many improved life adjustments (returning to medical school and graduating successfully, getting married, etc.), while all the while keeping his underlying psychotic potential uneasily throttled. The glimpse that was had of this was in the peculiarly fearful and suspicious way that the patient evaded every effort and every plan to bring him to participate in his Termination Study, despite all his disavowals of such evasive intent and his protestations regarding the high scientific value of such research study. It was only when the patient essayed himself in medical practice after the termination of his analysis that the progressive psychotic decompensating state unfolded so grimly and inexorably. Toward the very end (the patient lived for 7 years past the treatment termination), the patient's physician mentor sadly averred that the patient was "clearly schizophrenic" and that all of the patient's hostility and persecutory fear had by then come to focus on him. Here too, the patient's life was beset by severe drug taking, wildly reckless driving, violent outbursts, and a totally irresponsible carrying out of his medical practice, to the point where he endangerd his patients and had to be constantly rescued by his fellow practitioners.

The Alcoholic Raconteur, by contrast, was not able to get through an entire analytic course while throttling the underlying psychotic potential. In his case, at the point of crisis, he was faced by his analyst with the requirement of more control (rehospitalization and a conversion to an explicitly supportive–expressive psychotherapy); he was frightened as well of his awareness within the treatment of his increasing difficulty in keeping the analyst as a transference object separate from the narcissistic extension of his own omnipotence fantasies. The patient disrupted his treatment, claiming that he would make a fresh start in psychoanalysis elsewhere. His analytic course too (which lasted 2¾ years) was marked by alcoholic binges, wild sexual adventures, brawling, lost jobs, and in general, disorganization to the point of utter chaos and collapse.

OTHER REASONS FOR TREATMENT FAILURE

The psychotic transference response was not the only basis on which these six "heroic" analyses came to grief. With the Masochistic Editor, the issue was that of an unswervingly self-destructive course, marked in his life by an intense constant alcoholism and a dangerous and degrading homosexual prowling after pickups, and in his treatment by a constantly evident "negative therapeutic reaction"— the reflection of a pervasive masochistic need to undo any accomplishment and to fail at every turn. And with the very alcoholic and quite paranoid Script Writer, the only woman in this group, it was more a total unwillingness (or incapacity?) to submit herself to the rigors of analytic inquiry that made her so apprehensive from the start, and so ready to call on what she called her "escapist pattern" to break out of her treatment after only 8 months. She rationalized this with the plan that she could resume analysis in her home city (which she did not do) and reclaim her marriage (which anyway ended in divorce).

Analysis and the Potential for Psychotic Transference Reactions

This bringing together of these six patients where psychoanalysis undertaken on the basis of "heroic indications" all failed—five totally failed cases (three of which ended in mental-illness-related deaths), and the sixth, the Alcoholic Raconteur, able by dint of his turn to AA to achieve a marginal life stabilization—has not been an attempt to assert that the potential for a psychotic transference reaction should be in itself an absolute barrier to a psychoanalytic treatment effort. There is indeed a literature to the contrary (see Wallerstein, 1967, as well as the references cited there). And within PRP there were other, quite adequate, psychoanalytic outcomes in which a flagrant psychotic transference reaction had erupted during the long course of the analysis. The Economist was perhaps the outstanding example of this. He was thought to be well suited to a "usual" psychoanalytic expectation and treatment course; he seemed to have a moderate obsessive–compulsive personality structure, a successful work career, and a recurring neurotic difficulty in being unable to establish an effective and enduring relationship with a woman. His very long-drawn-out analytic treatment, which was converted to an explicitly supportive–expressive psychotherapy at the 6-year mark because of an unfolding transference psychosis, was still in an ongoing status (though "tapering") after 11½ years at the "cutoff" Follow-Up Study point (he had logged 1601 hours by the Termination Study point, the largest total in the project). And this treatment is still going on with the same therapist (currently with only a twice-monthly contact) at the 28-year mark.

As the overall case description makes clear (see pp. 336–343), a great variety of the issues that have been discussed throughout this book were salient to this patient's treatment: (1) the issues of concealment and possible misdiagnosis; (2) the issue of transference psychosis, which flowered in this case, including delusional accusations directed toward a presumed illicit affair between the analyst and the patient's mother; (3) the issue of insoluble transference neurosis; (4) the issue of conversion of psychoanalysis to psychotherapy; (5) the issue of transference cure and transference gratification; (6) the issue of the "therapeutic lifer"; and (7) the question "Was this trip necessary?" Central here, given all these complications and the overall complexity of the case, is the fact that the unfolding transference psychosis was indeed coped with, within a modified treatment strategy, and that this patient ultimately succeeded to a moderately good treatment outcome. A significant consideration, of course, is that the Economist—though indeed he had a paranoid potential, a clinging dependent propensity, and even a vulnerability to ego-weakening pressures—did not have the disordered life and the severe symptom excess (alcoholism, addiction, violent behaviors, sexual disorders, etc.) that marked the presenting histories of all the failed "heroic indications" cases.

SEVERELY DISTURBED PATIENTS IN PSYCHOTHERAPY

Outcomes

Nor does it follow that simply withholding psychoanalysis per se, and from the beginning constructing a controlling and protective supportive–expressive psychotherapy, would ensure a better overall treatment outcome with these very disturbed patients. Actually, though 6 of the 11 patients who appeared in at least three of the five groupings of severely behaviorally disturbed patients (alcoholic, addicted, sexually disordered, paranoid, and borderline) were taken into psychoanalysis, 5 were not; these 5 did not, as a group, fare any better in their treatment courses.

Of course, the two groups are not directly comparable: The 6 selected for trials at psychoanalysis (however "heroic" the indications) were at least deemed in some context to warrant so thoroughgoing and so ambitious a treatment effort, while the other 5 for the most part were denied it precisely because it was felt that they could not tolerate a psychoanalytic effort (i.e., they were deemed "too sick" for it).

Yet those 5 (the Addicted Doctor, the Car Salesman, the Sociopath, the Sexual Masochist, and the Bitter Spinster) included 4 total treatment failures, including 2 deaths from mental-illness-related causes. Only 1 (the Sexual Masochist), by dint of now close to 30 years of almost continuous treatment effort of one sort or another, has now been able to climb to some degree of moderate improvement; this is all the more impressive, because he was the patient who has been referred to several times as probably the very "sickest" patient in the entire sample.

Reasons for Treatment Failures

HOSPITALIZATION NOT PART OF TREATMENT PLAN

The other four in this group explicitly in psychotherapies geared to being more supportive than expressive nonetheless had treatment results as dismal as those "heroically" being tried in formal psychoanalysis. With the Car Salesman and the Addicted Doctor—both severely alcoholic, addictive, and weak in ego controls—the basis for this failed outcome seemed the same. In both instances, the patients were felt (very properly, according to the research evaluators) to be too ill to tolerate the psychoanalytic experience, even on the basis of so-called "heroic indications." With the Car Salesman, this was put as follows: "These limited recommendations were predicated on the grounds that the patient's anxiety tolerance was limited, his ego controls weak, *his achievements in life nil*, his conflicts many, his fixations relatively primitive, his chief defenses externalizing and alloplastic in impact, and that he revealed no special capacity for psychological-mindedness, nor any useful insight" (italics now added). With the Addicted Doctor, this was put even more starkly: "The goal [of treatment] was that of trying to stop a destructive regressive process, to hold things at some tolerable level of functioning without further disintegration in terms of the patient's personality and life situation." In effect, these were two individuals with profound symptoms and character deformations, and minimal achievements in life to balance these out.

For both these patients, therefore, the proposed treatment plan was a stabilizing and protective supportive–expressive psychotherapy. But then, as noted in the preceding chapter (see pp. 665–666), there was a strong concern that concomitant hospitalization, especially if (adequately) prolonged, would unduly deepen the dependent gratifications of these two excessively dependent characters and make the subsequent route to achieved self-sufficiency all the harder. This concern led in both instances to the fateful decision to conduct these treatments on an outpatient basis, with the psychotherapy itself then having to bear the burden of the patients' life management and control. The consequences were of course disastrous, and both of these patients were among the six who died of mental-illness-related causes.

In retrospect, it is quite clear that, though the risk of unduly accentuating dependency gratifications can be a real one, and though the development of the insoluble transference neurosis is a real issue with some patients, these possibilities nonetheless can usually be dealt with within the confines of the treatment situation. In various instances in PRP, it was dealt with through successful enough treatment resolution (the Phobic Woman); through some kind of "weaning" (more successfully with the English Professor and less successfully with the Devoted Son); or through transition into the status of a "therapeutic lifer" (the Housebound Phobic Woman, the Economist, the Sexual Masochist, and, in the end, the Devoted Son as well). For someone like the Housebound Phobic Woman, this outcome has been an eminently successful one, given that she came to treatment in a state completely comparable to that of the Car Salesman and the Addicted Doctor, and with the added handicap of her superimposed chronic brain damage consequent to her prolonged chronically drug-addicted state. With the Sexual Masochist, our very "sickest" patient, the long-term result has been almost comparably successful, again given the degree of illness and ego disorganization with which he came to treatment.

HOSPITALIZATION EVADED

The determining circumstances of the Sociopath's treatment failure were different. He was clearly the most alloplastically oriented patient in the whole research sample: His pretreatment career included pathological lying, cheating, embezzling, involvement with gangster elements, promiscuity directed as revenge upon "400 percenters," severe drinking and abuse of his wife, and vicious exploitation of people in his work career. Though he came to treatment clamoring for psychoanalysis (the only treatment in keeping with his pride and his inflated self-image), the clear recommendation was very properly made for long-term hospitalization undergirding and supporting a rehabilitative psychotherapy. The patient rejected this out of hand, and his successful maneuvering to trade a year of proven self-maintenance in some reasonably trouble-free equilibrium for a promise of outpatient treatment has already been described. With this plan, he outwitted both his examiners and himself and helped insure his subsequent totally unsuccessful treatment course. It was clearly felt (and underlined by the subsequent treatment course) that this patient could have had a considerably better treatment chance, had the originally stipulated treatment plan been adhered to. Of course, successfully treating so antisocially embedded a character structure within any psychotherapeutic context, however protective and supportive, would have been inordinately difficult.

ANALYSIS RATHER THAN THERAPY INDICATED?

The last in this group, the Bitter Spinster, was in many ways the most puzzling patient in the whole research sample. As has been stated several times, she seemed to have so properly neurotic a character structure and problems that she was initially deemed ideally suited for psychoanalysis (with a good prognosis); when this ideal treatment was precluded by lack of financial resources, she was deemed someone who could profit equally well—though probably in a more limited way— from as expressive a psychotherapy as could be carried out on a twice-a-week basis. She was the only patient whose placement among three of the five clusters of "sicker" patients (the sexually disordered, paranoid, and even borderline) was an after-the-fact judgment, in the light of what gradually unfolded within her 8-year psychotherapeutic course. She clearly was not helped by the psychotherapy, within which her functional state even worsened. And hospitalization was never really an issue with her, even though the regressive trends set into motion during the therapy precipitated episodic destructive acting out, which impelled the therapist to more reality-confronting pressures and re-educational measures. As the therapist said, "At times when there was little acting out, it was close to analysis; at other times when a lot of acting out was occurring, a different approach was necessary, and was used." Whether in retrospective view this patient could have been helped if she had been able to be in a full psychoanalytic treatment, as originally proposed, has been at least raised as a question for consideration in the conclusion of the description of her treatment course (see pp. 352–353).

GENERAL PERSPECTIVES ON SICKER PATIENTS

Limitations of Psychoanalysis

The anomalous case of the Bitter Spinster temporarily aside, some general perspectives do emerge from this overview of this group of 11 sicker patients in the PRP population. Of these 11, 6 were recommended for an effort at psychoanalysis on the basis of "heroic indications": It was felt that though the patients might be only in the "slightly accessible" or "intractable" group, they should nonetheless have a trial of the only treatment that (presumably) might offer them some prospect of significant help for their very refractory and deep-seated personality problems. In every case but 1 of those 6 the outcome was totally unsatisfactory, and 3 of the 6 died finally of mental-illness-related causes. The only exception was the Housebound Phobic Woman, who, though initially recommended for psychoanalysis along with the others, had her treatment course altered almost from the very start into the sustaining supportive–expressive psychotherapy accompanied by a sufficient period of hospitalization that has now consolidated a very substantial improvement in an ongoing "therapeutic lifer" status. Clearly, even with all of the availability of hospitalization within a psychoanalytically oriented sanatorium setting, and all of the historical clinical precedents for this course within the specific Menninger Foundation setting, psychoanalysis on the basis of these "heroic indications" has been found tragically wanting as a treatment course.

With all of the expansion of psychoanalytic or "modified" psychoanalytic treatment to widened categories of patients over the past decades (the "deeper or wider ego disorders" of Glover, the "widening scope" of Stone), as well as the strong reinforcement given to this direction by the writings of Kernberg on the borderline personality (1975, 1976, 1980) and Kohut on the narcissistic personality (1971, 1977) over the past decade, it is also well to remember that there has always been a countercurrent (cf. Anna Freud, 1954, p. 610) of concern with focusing or even "narrowing scope" of indications for analysis—back toward those kinds of patients around whom psychoanalysis was created and with whom it has always had its greatest degrees of success. Concerning such issues, there are always elements of fashion and of excessive swings of the pendulum in the one direction or the other. Here our PRP experience leads us in that same direction of "narrowing scope" and of retreat from "heroic indications."

The Role of Hospitalization

What should then emerge in the place of psychoanalysis as a more appropriate (in the sense of more promising) treatment plan for these patients under discussion? Here our data are less compelling. Certainly where varyingly supportive–expressive psychotherapy has been chosen as the direction of choice for such very sick patients, it has also failed in those instances where, for however plausible reasons, it has been tried on an outpatient basis. When the psychotherapy alone has had to bear the burden of carrying the controlling, protecting, and the supporting functions for these particular patients, they have quite conclusively demonstrated their (at least temporary) inability to maintain themselves autonomously. The overall results for the 11 PRP patients drawn from these sicker categories— with 6 going into psychoanalysis on the basis of "heroic indications," and 5 going into psychotherapy, but in almost all the instances without the (necessary) concomitant hospitalization—are disheartening. Of these 11, 9 were failed treatment cases, and 5 were among the 6 who died of mental-illness-related causes. These were also, of course, the kinds of patients often either given up on in their home settings, or never taken into intensive psychological treatment at all, but sent to an institution like The Menninger Foundation as an act of last resort and with the feeling that therapy within a sanatorium setting might give these patients their needed chance at significant help. Unfortunately, in most of these instances, the hospital and all its controlling and supporting functions, though always available, was (for differing reasons) insufficiently used.

Sicker Patients Who Did Well: Psychotherapy and Hospitalization

There were, of course, 2 patients in this group of 11 who did well in their treatment courses (and have been followed now for 25½ and 28 years, respectively)— the Housebound Phobic Woman and the Sexual Masochist. They were certainly as sick as any of the others, even more so. The Housebound Phobic Woman's 14 years of unremitting barbiturate addiction and alcoholism, permanently organically brain-damaged state, and total constriction of her life to the dimensions of her house have been well described, as have the Sexual Masochist's bizarre masochistic sexual perversion, heavy alcoholism and drug addiction, and intolerable panic states. What they each had, however, was an appropriately supportive–expressive psychotherapy (though with the Housebound Phobic Woman this required the assigned analyst's prompt reversal of the inappropriate initial recommendation for psychoanalysis). They also both had rather long periods of concomitant hospitalization; with the Housebound Phobic Woman this period was certainly long enough, but with the Sexual Masochist it was not really long enough (this related clearly to the hiatus where his treatment petered out seemingly unsuccessfully and was only rescued and gotten back on therapeutic course by the intervening events). It is the path pursued by these two individuals that I feel does hold out the prospect of truly significant improvement in these sickest patients: a supportive–expressive psychotherapy for however long needed (lifelong if need be), intimately conjoined with a psychodynamically guided hospitalization for however long needed, and both combined with whatever other supporting life modifications are required, such as permanent settling into a supportive psychotherapeutic community like the Menninger–Topeka world (which both these patients have done).

Conclusions from Other PRP Publications

This is one issue around which there has been some coming together of the findings and conclusions of the three books and one monograph already written on the different aspects of PRP. Horwitz (1974), who has written up the Prediction Study (the detailed tracing of the network of individual predictions to expected treatment courses and outcomes, with the study then of the correspondence of actual outcomes to the predictions, and an effort at explicating how and why predictions did or did not come true in various areas and among the different patients), has been most explicit on this particular issue. A series of brief quotations makes this clear. First, Horwitz states the general predictive position: "In addition to controlling destructive symptoms and contributing to a therapeutic alliance, the hospital was seen by the predictors as making it possible for some patients to be treated more expressively in their psychotherapy than would otherwise be possible" (p. 150). Then he makes a more specific statement about psychoanalysis: "Many of the patients in our population would more than likely not have been recommended for analysis had hospitalization not been available to provide the support they clearly needed. Among the analytic cases there were nine patients whom the predictors believed required some hospitalization during at least the beginning phases of treatment in order to achieve treatment goals" (p. 151). He then states the finding: "They were all hospitalized but the termination team considered seven of them as having been unanalyzable, whether hospitalized or not" (p. 151). (The other two who proved eminently analyzable, and had very good outcomes indeed, were the Medical Scientist and the Phobic Woman.) Finally, Horwitz concludes:

> Thus, the majority of the cases seen by the predictors as analyzable, provided they began their analysis in the hospital, actually proved to be incapable of tolerating analysis. Four of these cases [Horwitz's count] were of the so-called "heroic variety" where the chances of success were considered low, but the predictors felt nothing short of analysis could produce the necessary change. It is instructive that every one of these "heroic" cases failed in treatment and at termination were considered unanalyzable. One must seriously question the validity of the "heroic" indication. (p. 152)

The books by Voth and Orth (1973) and S. A. Appelbaum (1977) relate to this issue more indirectly. Voth and Orth, who have written up the Situational Variables study (the detailed demonstration of the often significant role played by the evolving and interacting environment or external life situation of the patients in either facilitating or limiting the conditions and possibilities for change), have taken the fact that they perceive so little evidence of real insightful conflict resolution — the presumed central mechanism of expressive psychotherapeutic and certainly of psychoanalytical treatment change — as one basis (much overemphasized, I feel) for the salient role of environmental pressure or its mitigation in determining the kind of treatment course and outcome achieved. This is of course congruent with the perception by Horwitz in his book, and myself in this book, that the patients who were in psychoanalysis on the basis of more extreme or "heroic" indications certainly showed no significant evidence of any internal change or ameliorative processes.

S. A. Appelbaum, who has written up the projective psychological test data (comparatively studied over the three points in time), has strongly emphasized in regard to predictive power that the research psychologists judging from test data alone were significantly more often in agreement with the criterion statements on issues of diagnosis, treatment recommendation, and predicted outcome than were the research psychiatrists judging from the total available clinical data. He stresses further that in just about every instance, the discrepancy was between a research psychologist's predicting a lesser achieved change (based on a more solidly emphasized statement of difficulty and limitation), and a research psychiatrist's predicting a more extensive range of achieved change (based on perceived potentialities within the presenting illness picture and the possibilities of the recommended therapeutic approach). Whatever the reasons for the research psychiatrists' characteristically predicting the potential reach of each treatment more optimistically (see my discussion, pp. 20–21), this clearly played its role in both the research and the clinical recommendations for trials at psychoanalysis on the basis of "heroic indications" that in practice went totally unfulfilled. The research psychologists predicted less capacity to change and less achieved change in these instances, and they were more often correct in that assessment.

The monograph by Kernberg *et al.* (1972) on the study of the (semi)quantitative data of PRP is the only one that has touched inconclusively on this issue of "heroic indications." In a summary statement, they say,

> [T]here were some patients who were known to have low ego strength where psychoanalysis was still indicated as a "heroic indication for treatment", with the rationale that even if they had little chance with psychoanalysis, they might have had no chance at all with other forms of treatment. Indeed, clinical experience does indicate there are some "heroic indications" for psychoanalysis. There were an insufficient number of these cases in our research project to conclude whether these "heroic" efforts are justified or not. (p. 178)

I would account for this discordance of conclusion in two perhaps additive ways, one methodological and one conceptual. The issue of method is that the Kernberg *et al.* monograph deals with the statistical as well as a kind of nonstatistical, mathematical (facet theory) handling of the data; the small number of cases that are at issue do not emerge with any kind of statistical significance when their treatment fates are set off against other equally small clusters. The issue of concept is that of Kernberg *et al.*'s commitment—derived in significant part from Kernberg's own experiences within PRP and his perceptions of the treatment careers of the project sample—to a particular conceptualization of the treatment needs of the "sicker," borderline patients in terms of a more rather than a less expressive (i.e., a "more psychoanalytic") approach than is customarily taken with them. His push in that sense is for a more expressive psychotherapeutic approach, especially within the framework of concomitant supporting and controlling hospitalization. My own alternative perspective on this issue of just what is expressive and what is supportive in Kernberg's conceptualization of the proper therapeutic approach to this particular segment of the patient population has been in part already stated (see pp. 26–27) and is developed more fully in the next chapter.

The Expressive–Supportive Dichotomy Reconsidered

THE SPECTRUM OF PSYCHOTHERAPEUTIC MODALITIES: PRP's ORIGINAL CONCEPTUALIZATIONS

In the original conceptualization of PRP, predictions about projected therapeutic courses and outcomes were to be made against the indications for an array of psychotherapeutic modalities, conceived within the framework of psychoanalytic theory and in current use in the ongoing clinical operations of the Menninger Foundation. These were described in terms of definitional parameters and the usual indications for their use, along the conventional spectrum from the most supportive to the most quintessentially expressive, psychoanalysis, in the first publication from the project (Wallerstein & Robbins, 1956, pp. 252–257). They included the following:

1. Psychotherapeutic counseling. This was conceived of as a process of educational clarification within an emotionally interactive engagement focused on the life-situational difficulties of the patient, and appropriate in cases of situational maladjustment, occupational misplacement, some marital problems, and the like.

2. Supportive psychotherapy. This was conceived of as a process of "strengthening the defenses" in ways that would restore a disrupted equilibrium between drive and reality pressures and the defensive and adaptive capacities to cope with them, which under disequilibrating pressures had generated symptoms and disturbed behaviors. It was felt that this therapeutic approach would be appropriate with either (*a*) basically healthy individuals overwhelmed by an acute reactive state, such as some acute depressive reactions, some traumatic neuroses, combat fatigue states, or panic states; or (*b*) patients with chronic severe personality disturbances or major "ego defects" of several varieties, such as character disorders with severe alloplastic symptoms, many impulse neuroses (addictions and perversions), borderline states, or even some mild overt psychoses.

3. Expressive psychotherapy. This would be designed to analyze defenses and uncover conflicts as projected against the transference screen, but within limited sectors of the personality functioning and without the genetic unfolding and recreation of the infantile prototype behind the childhood amnesia. It was felt that this approach would be appropriate to some patients with symptom neuroses and character neuroses where the illness picture could be undone and the personality functioning could be reintegrated just by working at the "level" of the patients' capacity to assume responsibility for their psychological functioning and its modification in relation to current conflict pressures (those neurotic conflicts that were relatively autonomous in the sense of being "detached enough" from their linkages to their prototypes in the infantile neurosis).

4. Psychoanalysis as classically conceptualized. It was felt that this would be appropriate for those patients—chiefly those with symptom neuroses and character neuroses—where the requisite ego capacities were present, and where the neurotic conflict was sufficiently intense, pervasive, and linked to its infantile prototype, that a satisfactory outcome could only come about through the unfolding of the regressive transference neurosis, the recreation of the repressed infantile neurosis, and their combined interpretive resolution. To take a distinction stated by Gill (1954), expressive psychotherapy was thought to be focused on the exploration of presenting symptoms and presenting problems, whereas psychoanalysis was seen as an open-ended compact to explore the unconscious together, out of which would come, among other things, relief of current symptoms and resolution of current conflicts.

The theoretical delineations that provided the context for these particular categorizations just presented from our initial PRP formulations were sharpened in a series of major psychoanalytic panels considering such issues as the nature of psychoanalysis as a therapeutic technique; the limits of its applicability and its reach; and the relationship, by comparison and contrast, between psychoanalysis and dynamic psychotherapy (i.e., psychoanalytically oriented, guided, or informed psychotherapy). The results of three such panels over the years 1952–1954 were brought together for publication in one issue of the *Journal of the American Psychoanalytic Association* in 1954 (Vol. 2, pp. 565–797). These panels were "The Widening Scope of Indications for Psychoanalysis," sponsored by the New York Psychoanalytic Society, at Arden House, New York (pp. 567–620); "The Traditional Psychoanalytic Technique and its Variations," sponsored by the American Psychoanalytic Association, in New York City (pp. 621–710); and "Psychoanalysis and Dynamic Psychotherapy—Similarities and Differences," also sponsored by the American Psychoanalytic Association, in Los Angeles (pp. 711–797). Among the papers published in that issue of the *Journal*, the ones most influential at that time in formulating our own conceptions, criteria, distinctions, and indications were those of Bibring (1954), Gill (1954), and Stone (1954); these have been referred to throughout the course of this book. Equally formative to us were such immediately preceding or contemporary papers as those of Gill (1951), Glover (1954), Macalpine (1950), and Stone (1951). Also very supportive to these formulations was the book subsequently published by Dewald (1964), *Psychotherapy: A Dynamic Approach*, with its extremely detailed spelling out (in ways completely comparable to our PRP thinking) of counterposed expressive and supportive therapeutic approaches—within a specific psychoanalytic theoretical framework—to all the relevant dimensions of the psychotherapeutic process. And in 1969, 15 years after the major series of American publications on the relationship between psychoanalysis and dynamic psychotherapy, the International Psychoanalytic Association held its first worldwide panel on these same issues. In the introductory presentation of that panel in Rome (Wallerstein, 1969), I spelled out the then-current various theoretical and technical issues and questions concerning the nature of that relationship, in much the same terms as had prevailed in the debates 15 years earlier. The issues, their problems, and their possible resolutions all seemed the same.

From the start, however, in the pragmatics of implementation in PRP, these initial conceptualizations and distinctions did not (and could not) work out so neatly. First, understandably, the category of "psychotherapeutic counseling" was never used. Patients for whom such a relatively uncomplicated and usually rather brief kind of intervention would have sufficed usually did not come for help to The Menninger Foundation (unless they were local Topekans); if they did, they were excluded in any case by our selection criteria, designed to eliminate brief therapeutic approaches. For the same reason, we did not employ that subcategory of supportive psychotherapeutic approaches geared to "basically healthy individuals" momentarily overwhelmed by acute reactive disorders (depressions, panics), who could expectedly, with a brief period of help, be assisted over the crisis and back toward a restored *status quo ante*. We were thus left essentially with three major usable "widely-spaced categories" (Schlesinger, 1969, p. 269), each encompassing some broad clinical consensus on meaning and usage. This consensus was specified most explicitly in the case of psychoanalysis, but much less so with expressive and with supportive psychotherapy; however, we were reasonably confident that, from our starting point in our stated conceptualizations—anchored as they were in the theoretical thinking of the 1950s that has been referred to—we would in the course of our detailed clinical study of the PRP experience arrive at increasingly refined and precise clarifications and delineations of these distinctions, as well as of the different mechanisms involved in working toward different goals.

MODIFICATIONS OF PSYCHOANALYSIS

Conversion to Psychotherapy

The problems of description and conceptualization that inevitably emerged were in the enormous complexity of the therapeutic process, even with an ostensibly homogeneous approach like psychoanalysis, in theory the "purest" of the deployed therapeutic modalities. Of the 42 project patients, 22 were recommended for and entered psychoanalysis; of course, a number were at some point, on the bases of clinical indications, converted to varyingly expressive and supportive psychotherapy. Where such conversions were explicit, including such changes as diminishing the frequency of sessions, having the patient sit up, and making other alterations in approach, ambience, expectation, and content, the distinction between the periods that were carried as analysis and as psychotherapy was indeed clear and easily enough characterized. The cases of the Economist and the Masochistic Editor were good examples of this. However, where the conversion was tacit and implicit and was never made a specific issue with the patient (as with the Housebound Phobic Woman, where this alteration was effected almost from the start, but where the patient continued to use the couch, maintained the same treatment frequency, and never clearly understood that she was no longer considered to be "in analysis"), this was a matter of judgment about the characteristics of the treatment process (in this instance, the judgments of the research evaluators and the therapist concurred completely). In many instances of presumed analysis, there were important judgment calls on which all observers did not necessarily agree, as to when (in terms of systematic modifications or parameters, temporary or longer-term) one should no longer call a treatment "just" analysis but rather a "modified analysis," and when again a modified analysis no longer properly deserved that name, but should rather be conceptualized as some variant of expressive–supportive psychotherapy.

Hospitalizations

It turned out, of course, that not a single patient in our sample could be said to represent the most "classical" interpretation of the nature of the psychoanalytic process in pure form—without some significant admixture of unanalytic, albeit certainly psychotherapeutic, maneuvers. (See, in this connection, the descriptions of the treatment courses of the Medical Scientist and the Phobic Woman in Chapter 13.) Certainly this reflects the fact that has been stated a number of times: The patient population at The Menninger Foundation, in psychoanalysis and all other modalities, is a sicker population than the usual psychoanalytic population treated in the customary outpatient setting. The fact that 10 of the 22 patients in analysis (45%) were hospitalized—either just for some initial period, or initially and with readmissions as indicated, and for varying time periods ranging up to 18 months, with all of the dimensions of hospital control and care as exerted by the hospital doctor and the total hospital staff—attests to the difference of the PRP sample from the usual psychoanalytic patient population, as well as the substantial modification of the usual understanding of the analytic process as something focused exclusively in the private transference–countertransference interplay between two people. (Incidentally, of those never hospitalized, it is quite clear that, for example, the Suspended Medical Student might well have profited from concomitant hospitalization. Perhaps it would have permitted enough relaxation of his repressive controls over feared ego-disrupting inner conflict pressures that he might have come to a better psychoanalytic resolution and a more benign subsequent fate.)

Other Modifications

But beyond something so gross as concomitant hospitalization (once or more than once), there were many other modifications: episodic or more prolonged sitting up; termination by what could become a rather long "weaning" process; extra contacts, either by phone or in ad hoc additional hours, in relation to the emergencies that so often arose with many of the patients (remember that there were a fair number of alcoholic–addicted and paranoid–borderline patients in analysis on the basis of "heroic indications"); and all the other ways in which analysts felt called upon to intervene to help these patients manage their lives or to protect them against the consequences of their destructive behaviors. A good example (among so many) of these last were the numerous extra-analytic interventions by Peter Pan's analyst aimed at her protection, such as going to check on her at her apartment when he thought her to be seriously suicidal, or wrapping her in blankets when she came to her analytic hour by bicycle drenched by a pouring rain. (See p. 188 for more such examples just in relation to Peter Pan.)

Final Classifications

In all, we ended by somewhat arbitrarily designating 10 of these patients as having treatments that adhered well enough to the model of classical analysis; there were some departures in each case, but these were "minimal" within the context of this group of quite sick patients, treated within the traditions and expectations of The Menninger Foundation. (In other settings, and with more "usual" psychoanalytic patients, even these so-called minimal changes might well be regarded as much more consequential—enough to get them designated as substantially "modified" psychoanalyses.) With another 6 of the patients, the analyses were more significantly "modified" (along various parameters, some of them being quantitative dimensions of how often or how intensely, etc.), but were still adjudged to be essentially psychoanalyses, albeit with modifications. And, of course, with 6, there was either a modification substantial enough to be adjudged a "conversion" to psychotherapy (a matter of clinical judgment) or an explicit conversion, clearly presented and acknowledged. The details of the individual modifications and conversions for *all* 22 patients started in psychoanalysis have been presented in Section IV (see Chapter 10, pp. 185–191, and Chapter 11, pp. 215–227), as well as in all the individual case descriptions. Clearly, with all of this, there has been a marked blurring of the interface zone between psychoanalysis proper and intensive psychoanalytic psychotherapy.

PSYCHOTHERAPY: BLURRING OF THE "EXPRESSIVE–SUPPORTIVE" INTERFACE

An equal problem existed—in fact, an even greater problem—among the 20 patients recommended for psychotherapy along the expressive–supportive dimension. Even to begin with, making the distinction between "expressive" and "supportive" was difficult. There were very few patients recommended initially for a "purely" expressive psychotherapy: The Bitter Spinster, who was originally not recommended for psychoanalysis (for which she was initially thought to be almost ideally suited) purely because of lack of financial resources, was one who readily comes to mind. And perhaps even fewer recommended for a "purely" supportive psychotherapy: The Addicted Doctor, for whom the only possible goal appeared to be that of trying to stop a destructive regressive process, and to hold things at some tolerable level of functioning without further disintegration in terms of the patient's personality and life situation, is probably the best example. In the great majority of the 20 cases in psychotherapy, however, plus in those patients converted from psychoanalysis to psychotherapy, the issue was one of the varying admixture of supportive and expressive techniques that would properly serve the particular clinical needs and clinical treatment goals of the specific patient. As I have stated earlier in this book (see pp. 191–192), and as has surely become evident in the descriptions of the individual case histories (and the varying identified mechanisms of change, and the technical means employed toward the specific implementation of those changes), any effort to distinguish more categorically among the more purely expressive, the truly mixed, and the more purely supportive treatment approaches would not emerge as a particularly clarifying or useful endeavor—either in realistic planning and prognostication, or in the assessment of course and outcome.

In one sense, in terms of our conceptual starting point, there is some surprise to this finding. After all, we began with a seemingly fundamental distinction between supportive and expressive techniques, adduced with great clarity by Gill (1951, pp. 62, 63, 65) and restated by us (Wallerstein & Robbins, 1956, pp. 253–255). The expressive (uncovering, interpretive, insight-aiming, etc.) techniques—including here expressive psychotherapy and psychoanalysis *together*—were seen as those directed toward *analyzing* the defenses (resistances, transferences) as the essential intervening step toward an eventual reintegration; expressive psychotherapy and psychoanalysis were seen as varying only in the breadth of the effort across the personality structure, and the depth of probe into its developmental history. By contrast, the supportive (ego-maintaining or ego-building) techniques were those polar-opposite approaches directed toward *strengthening* the defenses in order to make the repression of conflict more effective—that is, to effect the reduction of inner conflict pressures that had erupted into symptoms and disturbed behaviors. Much of Gill's (1951) article (see especially pp. 65–67) was actually devoted to an effort at elucidating the less well theoretically understood part of this polarity, the nature of those "strengthening" operations; he spelled out three kinds of technical maneuvers toward that end (summarized in this book, pp. 389–390). The underlying assumption in all this, never quite made explicit, was that the more fundamental demarcation line was between the supportive psychotherap*ies* and the expressive psychotherap*ies* (including psychoanalysis), rather than between the range of psychoanalytically oriented psychotherapies and psychoanalysis proper.

The (therefore expectable?) blurring of the interface zone between psychoanalysis and intensive psychoanalytic psychotherapy did indeed emerge in our findings and has been well enough demonstrated in the individual case histories of the PRP patients. However, it is equally clear in looking at the case histories of just those PRP patients in psychotherapy (the 20 who were in therapy from the start, or the additional 6 who were converted from psychoanalysis) that a similar blurring of the interface between the expressive and the supportive psychotherapeutic modes has also existed from the start in our observed data, and in our resulting conceptualizations about these treatment careers as well. This is the main point of the article by Schlesinger (1969), written from within The Menninger Foundation context by a practicing clinician in it who shared in its clinical experience and interchange, but was not a member of the PRP group and did not have study access to the particular PRP research sample. Schlesinger's views have already been quoted (see pp. 373–374): Basically, he has noted that all therapies, even psychoanalysis, are supportive in necessarily major ways (the open-ended time commitment to the understanding and unraveling of the psychological turmoils of a single individual is a powerful example), and all are necessarily expressive in major ways ("A psychotherapy in which the patient is not helped to express something of the depth of himself would be quite unthinkable"—p. 274). Schlesinger concludes that what we really have are "widely-spaced categories" (p. 269) that "have come to be misapplied and as used, no longer capture with any precision the distinctions they were coined to preserve" (p. 270).

I am in full agreement with this conceptualization. It will have been noted that throughout this book, and especially in its individual case histories, I have almost always used the descriptive phrase "expressive–supportive psychotherapy" or "supportive–expressive psychotherapy," depending on which side of this ad-mixed spectrum I have wanted to emphasize in characterizing a particular treat-ment course. In this, I have been mindful (and sometimes critical) of the clinical operating maxim that has guided so many of the actual choices in Menninger Foun-dation clinical practice—"be as expressive as you can be, and as supportive as you have to be."[1]

Kernberg *et al.* (1972), incidentally, in their statistical approach to the (semi)quantitative data of the project (see pp. 108–111 for a summary of their methods), have come to a conclusion comparable to Schlesinger's and mine about the operational distinctnesses of the treatment modality categories with which we undertook our work in PRP. They state in a summary section:

> When conceptualizing the Patient Variables, we discarded diagnostic categories in favor of descriptions of organizations of psychic structures, functions and attributes. A similar principle was applied to the Treatment Variables. When conceptualizing the treatment process, we discarded treatment modalities in favor of descriptions of the process in terms of the techniques used and the contents focused upon during the hours. As a consequence of this approach . . . we ended up with a group of variables [the specific Treatment Variables used in the quantitative statistical studies of the paired comparisons data] which defined only two modalities of Treatment: expressive psy-chotherapy and supportive psychotherapy. The full range of treatment offered to the patients included psychoanalysis, expressive psychotherapy, supportive–expressive psychotherapy, and supportive therapy. The variables we used to describe the treat-ment process were, therefore, insufficient to represent the differences among the [four] treatment modalities. This limitation had far-reaching implications for the testing of hypotheses, since one of our aims was to explore how treatment modalities combined with the psychic organization of the patients bring about improvement. (p. 63)

In other words, where they had expected (or hoped) that the individually designated Treatment Variables could be used to distinguish four main treatment approaches, they found the project data supporting only a twofold distinction. From the detailed case studies of this book, I think I have demonstrated that even this apparently most fundamental distinction, while it may define two broad directions of thera-peutic activity, has in actual practice often given way to complexly interacting and varying admixtures of approaches, with an equally broad blurring in the in-terface zone.

Where do such overall considerations leave us? We decided in the initial PRP conceptualization of the Patient Variables to use discrete psychic structures, func-

---

1. In Chapter 39, in the context of further discussion still to come on issues of insight, structural change, and the stability and durability of change achieved via more supportive versus more expressive change mechanisms, I come back to the value judgment inherent in the dictum that where possible, and to whatever extent possible, to be expressive is better than to be supportive. (A less boldly stated version of the dictum might be that change through expressive methods that lead to the insightful resolution of inner conflict will be more extensive, will last longer, and will be more proof against future environmental vicissitude and pressure than those changes brought about through "only" supportive methods.) This is a major "recon-sideration" in this final section on reconsiderations.

tions, and attributes, but not overall diagnostic formulations, as a basis for planning treatment and predicting treatment course and outcome (Kernberg *et al.* refer to this decision in the quotation above). Similarly, the data of the treatment courses and outcomes convinced us that individual specification in as detailed a way as possible of the kinds of interventions and technical maneuvers that characterized each individual treatment (in their specific interplay and varying over time) would be far more fruitful in illuminating the relationship between the psychological organization and psychological problems of the patients and the particular treatment courses and outcomes they came to than would any grouping by these "widely-spaced categories," useful as the latter perhaps are for orienting purposes and for initial coarse assessments.

THE NATURE OF "SUPPORTIVE" THERAPY

There is of course a voluminous literature on what makes therapies "expressive," and even more on what makes them "analytic." This literature has been referred to throughout this book in relation to the guiding conceptualizations of PRP, as well as illustrated in detail in relation to almost all of the treatment courses — those of the patients in psychoanalysis, as well as those of the patients in analytic psychotherapy. The question has to do with all the issues (problematic as they are in ways already partly discussed in this book, and to be discussed further in the next chapter) of interpretation, of insight, of working through, of uncovering (or analyzing) unconscious intrapsychic conflict, and so forth. What has always been much less clearly specified, both in the theoretical literature and in clinical case illustration, is what makes therapies "supportive." It is in the use of the PRP experience and its rich case material, followed over such long treatment and follow-up spans, that I trust more detailed specification can be given (and clinically documented) about the constituent elements of the supportive psychotherapeutic approaches.

Two articles, very divergent in their thrusts — that by Gill (1951) and that by Schlesinger (1969) — form a useful framework for this task. Gill was writing in the era (the early 1950s) of clarifying through sharpening the distinctions between psychoanalysis and (broadly speaking) psychotherapy, and between the opposed polar trends of expressive therapy ("analyzing the defenses") and supportive therapy ("strengthening the defenses"). His intent was to begin to specify the operative mechanisms that serve these opposed approaches and work toward "analyzing" (as a first vital step toward ultimate reintegration), as against those that work toward "strengthening" and could thus be said to characterize and to distinguish supportive psychotherapeutic modes. I have earlier referred to the three such operative supportive mechanisms that Gill described in his article (see pp. 389–390). Schlesinger's intent, almost two decades later, was quite different. He has spoken of the "artificial" nature of such a (perhaps pedagogically justifiable) dichotomy: All proper therapy is always both expressive and supportive (in different ways), and the question at issue at all points in every therapy should be that of expressing *how* and *when*, and supporting *how* and *when*. It is this latter spirit that has come to represent best the findings and the conclusions of PRP.

The Positive Dependent Transference

This effort to elucidate the how and the when of support is the conceptual under-pinning of Section VI of this book. We had actually begun in PRP with an array of six different (or at least differently named and conceptualized) operating mechanisms that had been variously said to be characteristic of supportive approaches; these are outlined on p. 54. It became clear, though, in the actual consideration of the treatment courses of our patients—not only those whose therapy was intended to be largely supportive, but to some degree those whose therapy was intended to be more expressive, even at times those explicitly in psychoanalysis—that a major common operative mechanism (whether explicitly intended and fostered or not) was the evocation and the firm establishment of a positive depend-ent transference attachment (wholly or at least significantly uninterpreted and "unanalyzed"), within which varieties of conflicted transference needs and wishes achieved varying degrees of (conscious or unconscious) gratification. Such an at-tachment almost always seemed to evolve in clearly visible form in those therapies that went well and were "supportive" in operation, and it also seemed to be an essential precondition to the operation of various other mechanisms that were admixed with it in different cases.

THE "TRANSFERENCE CURE"

The positive dependent transference is the basis of the so-called "transference cure"—the willingness and the *capacity* of the patient to reach therapeutic goals, to make changes in behaviors, symptoms, and modes of living, as something be-ing done "for the therapist." The changes become the *quid pro quo* for the transference gratifications received within the positive dependent transference at-tachment. It is in effect a "transference trade": "I do it—make the agreed-upon, desired changes—for you, the therapist, in order to merit thereby, to earn and/or maintain your support, your esteem, your love." That this mechanism operated as clearly and as pervasively as it did in so many of our cases (the putatively sup-portive and expressive alike) was no great surprise. What was surprising, however, was how stable and durable such achieved changes could turn out to be, in the many different ways that I have tried to delineate in the individual case descrip-tions. In Chapter 20 (see pp. 391–403), I have used two case descriptions as ex-amples almost in pure culture of this operative mechanism with minimal admix-ture of other factors: the Housebound Phobic Woman, originally recommended for psychoanalysis, and the Claustrophobic Man, originally recommended for psychotherapy.

THE CONTINUING POSITIVE DEPENDENT TRANSFERENCE AND THE "THERAPEUTIC LIFER"

On this base, then, an array of supporting and supplementary maneuvers were built in the various cases studied. These were designed in each instance to insure that the changes achieved on this basis of "transference cure" would indeed be stable, durable, and reasonably proof against adverse environmental vicissitudes. Where the need for the continuing transference gratifications within the established positive dependent transference attachment could not be otherwise transferred, attenuated, or internalized into new intrapsychic alignments, based on a consolidated introjection of the therapeutic relationship and the therapeutic gratifications, this benevolent dependent transference within the therapy could become maintained in the unending therapy of the "therapeutic lifer." Alexander and his coworkers (Alexander & French, 1946) saw this as the risk of the "insoluble transference neurosis"; they perceived it as a major therapeutic dilemma in many analyses, especially with severely dependent and masochistic individuals, and devoted much therapeutic effort to counteracting it, in order to bring those analyses to a speedier and more effective resolution. In PRP rather, it became the vehicle of continued maintenance of the therapeutically improved psychological functioning.

Given again, the degree of illness and ego deformation in the PRP research population, it is not surprising that in effect five patients in the total population, became more or less therapeutic lifers. The Housebound Phobic Woman is actually still in an uninterrupted continuous psychotherapy (with now her fourth successive therapist) that has gone on over a 25½-year span, originally on a daily basis, now an hour once monthly. The Sexual Masochist, with almost continuous and still ongoing treatment over 28 years, originally had an individual psychotherapy that did terminate after 8 years by a petering-out process (and a short hiatus); this was followed by a resumption of work with the same therapist as conjoint family counseling. He was ultimately transferred to the personal therapeutic care of a couple who were the leaders of the local AA chapter. The Economist started in formal psychoanalysis and was still continuing in psychotherapy at the 11½-year mark, though at that point at the level of intensive weekend visits every 5–6 weeks for which he traveled a long distance. He is still continuing at the 28-year mark, with the same therapist, through long-distance contacts (by phone or mail) twice a month. The Fearful Loner continued over 16 years (and three therapists) in a 30-minutes-weekly psychotherapy until his retirement and his move with his wife to an isolated farm in his home state. Finally, the Devoted Son seemed to have been able to terminate his 5½-year analysis (albeit by a "weaning" process), but surprisingly returned to treatment 13 years after that and has at this writing been in continuing treatment for 9 additional years, at 30 minutes a week.

Those patients with comparable dependent tendencies (needs?) but with stronger inner psychological resources—a greater capacity to relate helpfully to a consolidated introject of the therapist ego-ideal—were able to terminate treatments that perhaps could have become interminable, through just the kind of pressured tapering and "weaning" process advocated by Alexander in such circumstances. This weaning was accomplished very successfully with the Phobic Woman and the English Professor, both of them "good" psychoanalytic cases; successfully enough with the Bitter Spinster as a way of terminating her unsuccessful treatment; and only seemingly successfully so with the Devoted Son, who, as just indicated, had to find his way back to renewed supporting treatment 13 years after his psychoanalysis ended. With these instances of successful weaning and continued maintenance of the achieved level of psychological functioning, there was clear evidence of a reasonably consolidated identification with the therapist (or analyst) and the therapist's way of approaching and mastering conflict pressure.

TRANSFER OF THE TRANSFERENCE

Intermediate between those capable of being helped to psychological autonomy via such mechanisms of introjection and identification, and those for whom continued therapeutic contact (possibly lifelong) is necessary to a maintained level of adequate psychological functioning (in a manner quite akin to the continuing maintenance on physical regimens of diabetic patients, cardiac patients, etc.), are those patients with whom the transference attachments and the transference gratifications can be "transferred"—the successful so-called "transfer of the transference"—to the patients' now improved life situations, usually of course to their spouses. How successful this maneuver turns out to be in any particular case depends not only on the effectiveness and self-consciousness of the therapeutic work within the ongoing treatment, but also of course on the capacity and willingness of the other (the spouse) to carry this transferred transference burden indefinitely. The four patients whose treatments are described under this heading in Chapter 20—the Movie Lady, the Homesick Psychology Student, the Heiress, and Peter Pan—illustrate the full range from an effective result, through a limited or impaired result with significant compromise in terms of psychic inhibition or tolerance of an "acceptable" level of continued turmoil and/or symptom expression, through a total failure because of the ultimate refusal of the spouse (of Peter Pan) to continue to play the assigned transference role. I have earlier in this book (see pp. 412–413) stressed that the existence of this capacity in a patient, combined of course with the available favorable life circumstances, is an important favorable prognostic indicator. Contrariwise, the weakness of this kind of resolution of a supportive therapy is precisely at this point of its dependence on a continuing benign and fully supportive life context, in which some patients are more fortunate than others.

DISPLACEMENT OF THE NEUROSIS INTO THE TRANSFERENCE

Another very specific curative mechanism within the supportive psychotherapeutic mode, and one often operative alongside any of the other mechanisms being here described, is that of fostering the displacement (or transfer) of the neurosis into the treatment situation (into the transference), with the alleviation then of the external manifestations of the impaired functioning and/or the symptoms. The paradigm instance here (though it is not the only kind) is of the conversion of the unduly dependent and submissive individual into more satisfying and assertive life behaviors outside the treatment, on the basis of a (covert) new submissiveness to the therapist, experienced as requiring the altered external behaviors as the price of the continuation of the dependent gratifications within the treatment. That is, the new assertiveness in outer behaviors is not on the basis of having analyzed the roots of the submissiveness so that it is no longer needed as a neurotic compromise, but on the basis of transferring it into the safer arena of the therapy, and paying the price in return of chancing an obedient assertiveness in the outer world. I have described two patients in Chapter 20—the Involutional Woman (see pp. 375–382) and the Obedient Husband (see pp. 434–439)—for whom this mechanism could be seen with especial clarity. Its ultimate success again depends, of course, upon life circumstances: the reinforcing positive feedback and enhanced self-esteem when the new behaviors bring not neurotically feared disaster but real reward and gratification. Under such circumstances, and abetted by varying degrees of "transfer of the transference" as well, the specific tie to the therapist in person can be gradually relinquished.

THE ANTITRANSFERENCE CURE

Quite opposite to the transference cure and these varieties of maintained or transferred transferences on the behavioral level, though very comparable on the dynamic level, is the mechanism of change by way of the antitransference cure. These are the cures that result from negative transference struggles, from defiance and acting out against the therapist; in effect, the patient changes on the basis of or in the face of perceived contrary expectations by the therapist, usually as an act of triumph over the therapist in the overt or covert transference struggle. By their nature, such cures are far less frequent than the so-called "transference cures" and have to be buttressed in some way against their potential instability. The treatment courses of two such patients have been described in Chapter 20 (see pp. 439–451), the Intellectual Fencer and the Silent Woman. In those case descriptions can be discerned the reinforcements from a stabilizing life situation (even a neurotically constructed one, like the "pseudoheterosexual" marriage of the Intellectual Fencer) or from the positive environmental feedback from enhanced life functioning (as with the Silent Woman).

The Corrective Emotional Experience

A particular concept given much currency by Alexander and French (1946) is that of the "corrective emotional experience." For them, it was almost an all-explanatory construct invoked to elucidate the mechanisms of the supportive psychotherapeutic approaches, in almost the counterpart role to interpretation leading to insight as the central mechanism in the expressive psychotherapeutic approaches. The concept is of course an elastic one and can in fact be used to cover the whole range of supportive therapeutic maneuvers, since by its nature everything that goes on in a psychotherapeutic context is indeed intended to be a corrective emotional experience. And although Alexander developed the concept as the basis for recommending alterations and shortenings in the psychoanalytic process (his ideas were sharply criticized, as leading to a fundamental alteration of the analytic method so that a true analytic process would in fact be precluded), Gill (1954) advanced a different conception—one of the truly corrective emotional experience that classical (and unaltered) psychoanalysis does provide via its steadily concerned therapeutic stance, which remains equidistant from, and therefore neutral in relation to, the contending intrapsychic forces within the patient.

In this book, I have used the concept in a much more constricted way—in relation to treatments that provide a kindly, understanding, reality-oriented figure (the therapist), who, in Gill's words, is able "to meet the patient's transference behavior with neutrality . . . and therefore to give him a corrective emotional experience without the risks attendant on taking a role opposite to that which he expects, as Alexander suggests" (p. 782). The trick here is to be able to do this in a steadily effective way, without falling victim as others have to the transference–countertransference interactions by which the patient has been driven to maintain his or her neurotic suffering in the pretreatment life experience. The treatment course of the Fearful Loner (see pp. 452–458) has been described as an example of the kind of success that can be achieved through the deployment of this mechanism in almost pure form, even in the face of an extremely refractory character structure and neurotic outlook.

Reality Testing and Re-Education

Actually, only subtly different from such a corrective emotional experience is the operative mechanism I have called "reality testing and re-education" and illustrated with the case of the Manic–Depressive Physician (see pp. 460–466). Here again, reality testing and re-education can be conceived broadly as part of the therapeutic activity in every psychotherapy, whether supportive therapy at one end of the spectrum, or psychoanalysis at the other end (cf. the various quotations from Freud's writings on psychoanalysis as an "after-education" on pp. 458–460). However, again I am here using the term in a narrower sense: I am speaking of directly educational activities as part of the content focus in a supportive treatment, where the therapist plays a directly educational role in the transmission of advice, information, and education to normative and societal behavioral standards and expectations. Again, at issue is the therapist's capacity to play this role in a way that the patient perceives as nonjudgmental, and, if at all coercive, as guided solely by the patient's well-being and best interests. Clearly, the distinction between such activities (with which many of the treatments described in this PRP sample have been replete) and the steady provision of a corrective emotional experience cannot be and should not be a clear one. With both these technical strategies, the patient is both supported and educated toward reality-oriented problem solving and reality-corrected emotional responses on the basis of the "borrowed ego strength" that comes from the identification with the therapist in the role of helper and healer. And, again, the continued maintenance of changes achieved on this basis in the posttreatment life of the patient is dependent on some appropriate feedback reinforcement from a fulfilling environment, admixed with some transfer of the transference to significant other(s).

Disengagement from Unfavorable Life Situations

A different type of supportive mechanism is the kind of life manipulation that was so often involved with the PRP patients (even those in psychoanalysis), and that is in fact so much part of the rationale of the hospital or sanatorium treatment setting: the planned disengagement (temporarily or even, at times, permanently) from unfavorable and noxious life situations. This mechanism was, inevitably, so much a commonplace with our patients that it was emphasized (I feel, strongly overemphasized) as a main basis for symptomatic and behavioral improvement in our patients in the Voth and Orth (1973) book from PRP on the role of the environment in relation to change in psychotherapy. This overemphasis aside, this mechanism was indeed a pervasive supporting aspect of so many of the PRP treatments, supportive and expressive, psychotherapeutic and psychoanalytic. It became a very central and essential mechanism indeed with some, like with the

Phobic Girl, whose treatment course has been described from this perspective (see pp. 468–476).

Of course, the counterposed position should be kept in mind — that for other patients, it is critical to their best chances for treatment success that their therapy be conducted against the backdrop of an ongoing maintained interaction in their usual life situations. If this cannot be properly maintained, for whatever reason, their chances for an optimal result diminish, sometimes sharply. The treatment course of the Divorced Nurse is a good example of this (see pp. 314–321). Clearly, also, in the more usual patient population treated maximally expressively in the customary outpatient practice setting, a greater preponderance of the patients need maximal involvement in and commitment to their usual life situations; there is a much lesser requirement in specific instances and specific situations for therapeutically planned and guided disengagements.

The Collusive Bargain

And still another and different helping mechanism (hardly curative) is what I have called the "collusive bargain." It is perhaps quite common in tacit and in minor ways; at times, though, it can be quite explicit and can play a major treatment role, as illustrated in Chapter 21 (see pp. 478–489) in the case descriptions of two patients, the Actress and the Rebellious Coed. At issue here is the agreement, however tacitly or explicitly arrived at, to exclude particular areas of personality functioning and/or problems or symptoms from therapeutic scrutiny — leaving more or less consequential islands of maintained psychopathology — in return for the patient's willingness to make agreed-upon and substantial enough changes in (all) other areas of personality functioning and/or problems or symptoms. This is actually dynamically quite akin to the basis of the transference cure: After all, the patient is here making changes "for the therapist" in return for a very specific reward within the transference, the shielding from therapeutic probing of a particularly tenacious or rewarding symptom or behavior of the patient's. The success of such a maneuver obviously depends on the secondary and primary value of such a symptom or behavior to the patient — in the two cases just referred to, it was a settling into a homosexual life style — as well as the capacity of the patient to sufficiently detach the symptom or behavior at issue from the other aspects of life functioning, which the patient and the therapist can then commit themselves to trying to change. Since the symptom or behavior "allowed" to the patient in this compromise solution is experienced as at least in some ways rewarding or gratifying, these particular therapeutic outcomes have a built-in stability. This built-in stability, in fact, makes subsequent efforts at renewed therapy even more difficult (recall the course of the Rebellious Coed's two successive therapeutic efforts), but it is no guard against recurring disappointments with the results achieved.

"Rescue" by Other Factors

And last in this detailing of supportive therapeutic mechanisms is another kind of transfer of the transference, which I have called "rescue" by factors outside the therapy. One such factor can be fortunate life circumstances; in our research sample, wealth and other material resources could play this role with several of our patients. This type of "rescue" was epitomized in the treatment course and its aftermath of the Adolescent Grandson (see pp. 490–497), who upon his grandfather's death fell heir to a great family fortune. Another such factor could be alternative psychological supports selected by the patients, often in opposition to their therapies and therapists. The Alcoholic Raconteur, for example, turned finally to AA in identification with his mother, as against his therapist (see pp. 498–504); likewise, the Exhibitionistic Dancer turned to Christian Science in identification with her mother, as against her therapist (see pp. 504–510). In these various turnings by the patients to outside resources for the essential continuing transference dependencies and gratifications, the patients themselves "rescued" therapies that otherwise seemed unprogressive or even failing, and converted them at least to stabilizations if not always to enhancements of levels of psychological functioning.

General Comments

It is clear from all of this that there are a great variety of different and clearly specifiable ways in which psychotherapies (however expressive and analytic they can also be) can be supportive of improved psychological functioning. It is also clear that there are indeed ways to maintain such improvement in stable and enduring fashion over decades of follow-up (with whatever built-in acceptable limitations in degree or kind of achieved change), beyond what the conventional wisdom in the psychodynamic psychotherapy enterprise allows for. Obviously, these various mechanisms interact in uniquely distinctive configurations in particular therapeutic courses. There can be varying combinations of transference demands and expectations that are met; agreed-upon transference trades; specific substitutions of more adaptive impulse–defense configurations for less adaptive (more symptomatic) ones; specific agreements and decisions about what to talk about and explore in what directions, and also what not to talk about; various manipulations in relation to the patient's life situation; various kinds of transfers of the transference; specific engagements with and disengagements from ongoing life context; and ways of managing the positive feedback reinforcements that result in enhanced self-esteem from behaviors and relationships altered in desired directions.

In terms of the view adduced by Gill—of supportive techniques as ways of shoring up faltering defenses that have allowed overt conflict and symptom eruption—again our PRP data have encompassed diverse instances. One example was the effort to help reinstitute working compulsive defenses in an individual decompensated in obsessional and depressive directions, the Involutional Woman; with her, there was a planned return to schooling as part of the overall treatment design, including a refresher auditing of law school classes and learning typing and stenography was a step toward a reopened legal or paralegal work career. Another instance was the strengthening of the Bohemian Musician's intellectualizing propensities by giving her formulas that could be used in the continued service of self-mastery; for example, she would work to unravel and dissipate recurring depressed feelings with the learned model that depressed feelings represented anger that was being kept out of awareness. Still another instance was the buttressing of repression of conflicts around sex and gender identity through the collusive bargain struck with both the Actress and the Rebellious Coed to avoid probing issues of sexuality in return for willingnesses to explore and to change in all other problematic areas.

In all, the operative mechanisms and implementing techniques for the supportive psychotherapeutic approaches represent a technical armamentarium of great diversity. The unifying psychoanalytic theoretical conceptualization must be the particular patient's personality structure, illness picture, and treatment needs; out of the armamentarium, the therapist must needs select the particular technical approach(es) that will best implement the supportive mechanism(s) felt to offer that individual patient the best ameliorative/curative possibility. The proper conduct of such psychoanalytically informed and psychoanalytically based supportive psychotherapy is widely viewed as often being technically more difficult and requiring even more experience and skill than the application of a more properly expressive (interpretive, uncovering, insight-aiming) approach. Such a view reflects this greater diversity of technical implementing possibilities from which the therapist must try to choose appropriately; it also reflects the fact that, in contrast to the expressive approaches (which yield increasing knowledge of the ramifying complexity of the personality development and character organization, leading to more and more precisely informed intervention), the supportive approaches are based to a great extent on covering up, not on uncovering. The individual knowledge base out of which intervention decisions must be made is often much more inferential and less interactively (and consensually) arrived at.

CONCLUSIONS FROM OTHER PRP PUBLICATIONS

Horwitz and the Role of the Therapeutic Alliance

This overall reconsideration of the expressive–supportive dichotomy—in relation to the issue of sharpening versus blurring the conceptual distinctions across the interfaces of the range from psychoanalysis to expressive therapy to expressive–supportive therapy to supportive therapy, as well as in the use of the PRP data to move toward a more differentiated specification of the varieties of supportive psychotherapeutic mechanisms and approaches—is, in one major sense, in full accord with the very strong consideration of just these same issues in the Horwitz (1974) book from PRP and, in another sense, diverges sharply from it. The accord is in our strongly shared conceptualization concerning the place of and the effectiveness of supportive as against expressive mechanisms of change in our patient population. We fully agree that, at least in this particular research population, more of the treatment-related changes across the board (though of course more strongly so with the avowedly psychotherapy cases and a good deal less so with the psychoanalytic cases) were based on supportive techniques and mechanisms than we had anticipated in the original process of case formulation, treatment planning, and treatment prognostication. We also agree that these supportively based changes turned out to be more stable, more enduring, and more proof against future environmental vicissitude than we had anticipated. These are indeed major conclusions of the Horwitz volume, as they are of this one.

The divergence is over the conceptual umbrella that Horwitz essays to devise, in order to give a unifying structure to the supportive approach that is comparable to the centrality of the interpretive, uncovering, insight-aiming process in the expressive approach. The unifying umbrella that Horwitz offers is that of the "therapeutic alliance." I have quoted at the beginning of this volume (see pp. 23–24) his view that it is the therapeutic alliance that is the major vehicle, and so often the sufficient vehicle, for the desired therapeutic change to be brought about. This view is linked then to a particular and quite idiosyncratic usage of the "therapeutic alliance" concept: It represents a consolidated positive transference based on the capacity to exclude (repress or split off) negative transference elements. Quite aside from the fact that this definition of "therapeutic alliance" is at sharp variance with the original conceptualization by Zetzel (1956b), which has now come to be the widely accepted usage, and that therefore such an altered conceptualization risks new conceptual blurrings in our explanatory endeavors, I feel that at our present stage of theoretical development such a generalization represents a premature and oversimplified conceptual closure. Certainly what Horwitz calls the "therapeutic alliance" (the strong positive transference with its negative components unanalyzed) is very much akin to what I have called the evoked "positive dependent transference attachment"—the essential underpinning for the "transference trade" and "transference cure" that I have seen as a common element in (almost) all supportive psychotherapeutic approaches, but that I have also seen as being combined with a whole variety of other techniques, interventions, and manipulations, in individually very distinctive configurations, in the patients whose treatment careers I have traced. Where Horwitz emphasizes the unifying underpinning, I feel it more fruitful to try at this point just to spell out the various distinct mechanisms that can be delineated across the supportive approaches.

Kernberg et al. *and the "Modified Analytic" Approach*

A more complex issue in conceptual reconciliation is that between the views concerning the nature of supportive psychotherapeutic approaches that I have developed throughout this volume and summarized in this chapter, a broadly diversified and somewhat untidy array, with the narrower perspectives on the nature of supportive mechanisms within which Kernberg has viewed the PRP data. These have led to his developing, in his far-ranging theoretical writings on borderline and narcissistic disorders as gathered together in his three books (1975, 1976, 1980), a treatment approach to these patients that he has called "modified analytic" and that he specifically has declared not to be supportive therapy, since the latter would not be efficacious. Kernberg's argument in this regard has been presented in the first section of this book (see Chapter 2, pp. 24–27). The patients at issue, of course, are the many in our project among the "sicker" ones, clustering among the alcoholic–addicted and the paranoid–borderline. Some of these were taken into efforts at psychoanalysis on the basis of "heroic indications," which ended in treatment failure; others were taken into varyingly expressive–supportive psychotherapies, which seemed almost equally to have failed, usually linked to totally inadequate programs of concomitant hospitalization and life management; and a few of them ended up doing marginally (or even moderately or very) well on the basis of appropriately worked-out treatment plans and implementation in varying combinations of expressive and supportive therapeutic approaches and concomitant life management.

Briefly, Kernberg's thesis can be summarized as follows: First, supportive approaches, since they do not analyze negative transference components, are doomed to fail, because then the patients inevitably "are prevented from accepting the supportive aspects of psychotherapy" (Kernberg *et al.*, 1972, p. 184). Therefore, a "modified analytic procedure" (p. 173), built around the consistent interpretation of the negative transference and of "the 'here and now' of the pathological defenses of these patients" (p. 174), is vital to the hopes for treatment success. Kernberg *et al.* call this procedure "an expressive approach with relatively little structuralization in the treatment hours" (p. 168), but of course with concomitant hospitalization and the very supportive management burden that it carries. They conclude that for these patients "expressive psychotherapy is generally preferable to supportive psychotherapy" (p. 169) (ignoring the vital supportive role of the concomitant hospitalization), and that "Supportive psychotherapy frequently fails" (p. 184) with such patients. It should be clear that, within the far broader and far more diversified portrayal of the modes and methods of the supportive approaches (and of the expressive approaches as well) developed throughout this volume, I conceptualize Kernberg *et al.*'s technical recommendations for these particular patients as a complex conglomerate of intimately admixed expressive *and* supportive elements (and interplay between the formal psychotherapeutic and hospital management elements). This conglomerate is a proper response to the clinical questions of "Express what, how, and when?" and "Support what, how, and when?"; it is indeed a real and major contribution to the understanding of the particular treatment needs of these specific patients. To call it only "expressive–analytic" (or "modified analytic"), however, and not "supportive," is to attempt a sharpened conceptual distinction and a clear dichotomization, which I hope I have demonstrated are just not supported by the detailed case material. Such an attempt can lead to an improper denigration of the value of the equally vital supportive components in the overall therapeutic approach, and an undue emphasis on the expressive–analytic components. In the quotation in Chapter 2 (see pp. 26–27) from a discussion that I gave (Wallerstein, 1977a) of a presentation of Kernberg's views on this issue, I tried to recast Kernberg's counterposing of supportive psychotherapy, which would fail, as against his new approach built on incisive interpretations (encompassing the negative transference dispositions) of primitive conflictual units of self and object representations together with a holding structuring of the patient's life (concomitant hospitalization), which could succeed. I presented it as really the difference between *bad* (i.e., planless and conceptually unfocused) supportive psychotherapy and *good* (i.e., properly detailed and specified) supportive (or, better, supportive–expressive) psychotherapy — that is, a combining of specifically required, integrating, interpretive work with the equally specific structuring of a supporting and controlling environment (hospitalization *and* psychotherapy), within which the expressive interpretive work could be received and sustained. I trust that the kind of considerations adduced here will help toward the ultimate disentangling of these kinds of seeming conceptual and semantic unclarities, which still becloud theoretical formulations in psychoanalytic psychotherapy and in psychotherapy research.

Insight, Structural Change, and
Their Relationship Reconsidered

Central to conceptualizations of the theory of psychoanalytic therapy has always been the idea that properly mutative interpretations leading to insight into hitherto repressed unconscious conflicts constitute the basis of "real" structural change in the personality, and thus are the foundation for stable and enduring amelioration of symptoms and for alterations of attitudes and behaviors in desired directions. It has always been less clear that every component aspect of this formulation has all along been more or less admittedly problematic, both empirically and conceptually, and that the various controversies surrounding each of these issues have not to this point been satisfactorily enough resolved in the crucible of accumulating clinical experience and data-based theorizing.

THE NATURE OF INTERPRETATION AND
ITS RELATIONSHIP TO CHANGE

There is indeed a whole theoretical literature centering around each of these issues. Freud, of course, wrote a good deal in various places about the nature of interpretation, the first issue mentioned; see especially his 1911–1915 series of "Papers on Technique" (Freud, *Standard Edition*, Vol. 12, pp. 83–173). Major controversy was generated by James Strachey's 1934 paper "The Nature of the Therapeutic Action of Psycho-Analysis," in which he forcefully propounded the concept that the transference interpretation is the only properly mutative interpretation and that all other interpretive endeavor is only useful to the extent that it builds toward the salient transference interpretation. This particular controversy has been given renewed vitality by Gill, with his reiteration in a series of papers (Gill, 1979; Gill & Muslin, 1976, and others since) that the early and continuing vigorous interpretation of the transference in the "here and now" is not only *the* critically important element, but also an often quite neglected area of analytic work and thus deserving of intensified emphasis. Stone (1981) has responded extensively to these assertions, reaffirming the tripartite model of the overall interpretive activity directed in planned oscillation toward the transference, the current life dispositions, and the buried past, all in dynamic interplay. Stone does acknowledge at the same time all that is usefully emphasized in Gill's and Strachey's approach, and he also quite evenhandedly indicates the variety of ways in which recourse to the past at the expense of the current transference flow can be both diversionary and ineffective. In this regard, he cites Freud's "sarcastically trenchant remarks" directed at Rank's belief that just uncovering the primal birth trauma would undo the whole subsequent neurotic structure: "Freud compared [this] to a fire brigade, called to a house on fire, removing the overturned lamp from the room in which the blaze had started and regarding its work as finished" (Stone, 1981, p. 712).[1]

---

1. See footnote 1, p. 299, for a more detailed quotation (in a somewhat different context) of Stone's (1981) views concerning this renewed issue of the primacy accorded by Gill to the "here and now" in the mutative interpretive process.

The role of the insights achieved via (whatever) interpretive work, in relation to change—or, rather, so-called "structural change"—has been at least equally problematic in our literature. In our initial publication from PRP (Wallerstein & Robbins, 1956), we extensively discussed the question "as to whether insight is a precondition of change or a result of change, or an accompaniment of change, with either crucial or only incidental value" (p. 259), as well as "the horns of the other familiar dilemma, the distinction between 'intellectual insight' and 'emotional' or 'true' insight" (p. 259). The position taken on insight as part of our guiding PRP conceptualizations was this:

> Rather than being either a precondition of change or a direct consequence of change in the ego, we prefer to view it as the *ideational representation* of the change in ego functioning. That is, change which comes about through expressive psychotherapy and which is seen in altered behavior, patterns of defenses and trait configurations is reflected in the inner psychological life of the patient by an awareness that we call insight. This may be clearly articulated by some; only with difficulty by others. (p. 259)

Again, these same debates have been restated in almost the same form a quarter of a century later, in a sequence of four articles on the role of insight in a special 1979 issue on problems of technique in the *Journal of the American Psychoanalytic Association* (see especially Blum, 1979, and Neubauer, 1979). In an extended discussion of these same issues concerning insight (reflecting the PRP experience and foreshadowing this writing), I (Wallerstein, 1983b) have counterposed, among other things, the view of insight as the essential vehicle carrying the psychoanalytic change process, as against the view of what I condense into the phrase "the analytic relationship" as being of coordinate importance in inducing or promoting change— either alongside of insight, or in intimate interaction with it, or as the necessary base or framework that renders useful insight possible and achievable. In that connection, I have cited Alexander's efforts (Alexander & French, 1946) to downgrade the central role assigned to insight in relation to the process of change, in favor of the "corrective emotional experience," as he and his coworkers conceptualized it. I have also cited, within a more classical psychoanalytic position, the seminal paper by Loewald (1960) on the "integrative experience" (p. 25), in which the analyst as "co-actor on the analytic stage . . . makes himself available for the development of a new 'object-relationship' between the patient and the analyst" (p. 17); I have further cited the related literature on the therapeutic alliance (Zetzel, 1956b), the working alliance (Greenson, 1967), and the "real relationship" in analysis (Stone, 1961). All this, of course, can be viewed in relation to the whole discussion in the preceding chapter of the degree of supportive admixture in the most expressive of therapeutic approaches, even in classical psychoanalysis.

THE MEANING OF "STRUCTURE" AND "STRUCTURAL CHANGE"

Within this group of issues being here considered, the meaning of "structure" and "structural change," the next component of the statement with which this chapter begins, has probably achieved the least consensual agreement in the theoretical literature. Rapaport's statements in his 1960 monograph, *The Structure of Psychoanalytic Theory: A Systematizing Attempt*, have been widely regarded as both the most succinct and the most comprehensive. He stated that, "Controls and defenses are conceptualized as structures: their rates of change are slow in comparison with those of drive-energy accumulations and drive-discharge processes" (pp. 28–29). Furthermore, "The dominant level of analysis [with the development of ego psychology] is . . . the intrapsychic one, in terms of drives vs. structures" (p. 19). And, lastly, "In contrast to the drive processes, whose rate of change is fast and whose course is paroxysmal, the factors which conflict with them and co-determine behavior appeared to be invariant or at least of a slower rate of change. The observation of these relatively abiding determiners of behavior and symptom seems to have been the foundation on which the concept of structure was built" (p. 53).

And yet, despite the seeming simplicity, clarity, and coherence of this formulation of psychic structures as processes or attributes that are invariant or change very slowly, Schwartz (1981) has recently pointed out very convincingly that Rapaport, thinking (like Freud) in terms of dualities, approached the problem of structure within this monograph along at least four different such dualities, "some of which are highly problematical" (p. 61). Schwartz has enumerated them as (1) structure versus process (structure as a process of slow rate of change); (2) structure versus energy (structure as bound energy); (3) the role of environment (outside) versus biological endowment (inside) in the formation of structure; and (4) the specificity versus the generality of psychic structure. The last of these four counterposed dualities is most germane to my purposes here. Schwartz has elaborated as follows:

> The issue is clarified by noting that people acquire specific contents (words, ideas, images, etc.) but also learn how to learn, i.e., learn how to attend, concentrate, anticipate the future and organize experience. In this context, people also learn how not to learn, i.e., they learn to employ a set of defensive operations that restrict experience. . . . At issue is whether specific contents, general abstractions, global frames of reference (such as the distinction between reality and imagination) and generalized defensive and controlling structures can all be subsumed under the rubric of psychic structure. A good theory has a wide range of application. Nevertheless, a good theory also has limits. . . . Applying the term structure to cognitive skills, defensive operations and specific contents may be good theory or the use of the term structure in a loose or even metaphoric sense. (p. 62)

Given these issues concerning the concept and usage of "structure," it is no wonder that the ambiguity intensifies around the issue of what constitutes true structural change (as brought about by interpretation leading to insight followed by working through, as, for example, in psychoanalysis), as distinct from "only" adaptive or behavioral change (which can presumably occur without insight, on other bases, as in "purely" supportive psychotherapy, or even in the absence of therapy). Do we speak of "real" structural change when manic behavior gives way to depressed behavior, for example? Or, again, when the masochistic sufferer behaves sadistically? Or when the confirmed thief becomes an honest man, as in the conversion experience of Jean Valjean with the bishop in Victor Hugo's *Les Misérables*?

Rapaport (1960) had little to say about the process of structure formation or structural change. For example, "The problem of learning—how a process turns into a structure, or in other words, the long-term survival and availability of experience—has not been solved by psychoanalysis either" (p. 35). In an article on the goals of psychoanalysis (Wallerstein, 1965), I discussed at some length, among other issues, the controversy over the expectable outcome changes or structural changes in the successfully completed psychoanalysis. On the one side was the position advanced by Bibring (1937) at the Marienbad Symposium on the theory of the therapeutic results of psychoanalysis, where he spelled out in comprehensive detail the expectable changes in each of the three agencies of the mind, the id, the superego, and the ego. Overall, these changes were then "described as a change in the reciprocal relations between the various institutions of the mind. This alteration includes a change *within* these institutions, i.e., within the id, the super-ego, and most especially and decisively within the ego" (Bibring, 1937, p. 171). And among the changes within the id could be "the *demolition* of an instinct" (p. 178). Against this view, I counterposed Pfeffer's position, elaborated out of his series of careful follow-up studies of psychoanalyses adjudged to have been *satisfactorily* completed (1959, 1961, 1963). Pfeffer spoke not of the shattering or the obliteration of conflict (as did Bibring), but rather of the loss of poignancy of old conflicts; these had found new solutions in the cases he studied, but they were nonetheless still clearly discernible in the analytic follow-up interviewing procedure.[2] This distinction is, of course, crucial to the question of what we mean when we say that a goal of psychoanalysis is "real" structural change with the *resolution* of intrapsychic conflict.

And Freud at various times espoused both viewpoints—that of Bibring, and that of Pfeffer. In "The Dissolution of the Oedipus Complex" (1924a), he talked of the ideal outcome as a "destruction and an abolition of the complex" (p. 77). In "Analysis Terminable and Interminable" (1937), he talked only of "a 'taming' of the instinct" (p. 225), specifically stating, "To avoid misunderstanding it is not unnecessary perhaps, to explain more exactly what is meant by 'permanently disposing of an instinctual demand.' Certainly not 'causing the demand to disappear so that nothing more is ever heard from it again.' This is in general impossible" (pp. 224–225).

Finally, the view that only such major processes of personality unraveling and reconstruction as psychoanalysis engages in are able to lead to the kind of changes

---

2. Pfeffer, in his consultation visit to PRP in 1959, elaborated his view of "structural change in the ego" primarily in terms of economic considerations—that is, quantitative shifts in the intensity of impulse pressures, in the extent to which maladaptive defensive maneuvers are called upon, and so forth. In his words, it is not that intrapsychic conflicts are "shattered," but that they are made more manageable. Their poignancy is reduced; they are not only reduced in intensity, but are lifted into more conscious awareness so that as conflict-instigating situations arise, the individual is more immediately alerted and can take more appropriate coping steps in reality. However, under the impact of particularly traumatic circumstances or of circumstances that in some way re-evoke the original pathogenic situations (e.g., analytic follow-up interviews, with the memories and transference residues to which they give rise), these same conflicts can be reactivated. The quantitative shifts can backtrack, and we can see flare-ups of the original intrapsychic conflicts and even the original neurotic solutions (the presenting symptomatology). Nevertheless, if the treatment-achieved quantitative shifts are substantial enough, if the regressive moves occur only under the impact of sufficient provocation, and if they can now be more efficiently and more realistically coped with, then we can speak of "structural change in the ego" (and superego).

that are truly stable, enduring, and reasonably proof against subsequent environmental vicissitude is one that has already been discussed in detail through the case descriptions of this book and then summarized in the preceding chapter. It is especially significant in relation to our broad finding that treatment changes brought about by way of supportive techniques (and presumably without full intrapsychic "conflict resolution" and concomitant achieved insight) often turned out to be substantially more stable and enduring over prolonged time spans than anticipated. This issue is further discussed in the next chapter, after the detailed discussion here of the issue of insights sought and reached in our PRP population in relation to the structural changes achieved in their treatments.

THE RELATIONSHIP OF ACHIEVED INSIGHTS TO STRUCTURAL CHANGES IN PRP

Cases Where Changes Outstripped Insights

With a total of 19 (or 45%) of the research population of 42, 9 of them men and 10 women, the achieved changes in their treatments substantially outstripped their developing insights. This should come as no surprise, since I have described in detail the many ways (the various supportive mechanisms and techniques) through which substantial change was reached by many of the patients without a concomitant interpretive–expressive working through of conflict—in fact, often specifically with the avoidance of it. Of these 19, 7 of them were among the 22 started in psychoanalysis, while 12 were among the 20 started in psychotherapy.

PATIENTS IN PSYCHOANALYSIS

Analytic Patients Converted to Psychotherapy. Of the seven psychoanalytic patients in this category, it turns out, as might be expected, that four of them (the Housebound Phobic Woman, the Movie Lady, the Heiress, and the Economist) were among the six psychoanalytic patients explicitly converted to varyingly expressive–supportive psychotherapies. In fact, in each instance they were converted to psychotherapy just because it was concluded at some point during their treatment course that they could not tolerate and/or maximally profit from the interpretive, uncovering, and insight-aiming psychoanalytic process. With the Housebound Phobic Woman, that decision was made (tacitly) almost from the start, and it clearly related to the patient's very limited psychological-mindedness and reflective capacity—probably consequent to the chronic organic brain damage that (it gradually emerged) had resulted from her 14 years of constant severe barbiturate addiction.

The Movie Lady was the patient converted to psychotherapy after 6 months of analytic effort because the analyst came to see her as a substantially sicker individual than had been originally anticipated—someone who clung anxiously to a "culturally approved *average* pattern," and who would think paranoidly whenever she dared deviate from that limited pattern. Through the total 4½-year treatment, there were only slight gains in acquired insights. The patient's externalizing tendencies did turn out to be stronger than originally thought. Her intellectual functioning was superior, but it was employed very contentiously and exhibitionistically throughout. She battled it out with the therapist on the ground of psychological causation; in trying to defeat him there, she tried to show him to be an ineffectual, disappointing person (like her father), who couldn't do for her what he had promised treatment would do—give her an understanding of herself. She did have a good overall treatment result (the full course is described on pp. 413–417), and her view of how this was achieved was embodied in her first posttreatment letter to her therapist, which ended with the statement, "I hope you are enjoying your vacation and will be rested to face another year of comforting."

The 7-year treatment of the Heiress was converted to an expressive–supportive psychotherapy after the switch from the first, "cardboard analyst" (with whom she was locked into an unbudgeable transference jam) to the second analyst, who felt it necessary to provide a "corrective emotional experience" in order to break the transference deadlock. He did this by way of a variety of parameters of technique that he systematically introduced (the full treatment course is described on pp. 421–426). In a treatment significantly built around the transference gratifications gained within an established positive dependent transference attachment, with a subsequent effort to "transfer the transference" onto the new husband and the supporting material surroundings, there were significant "structural ego shifts." There was an introjection of the attributes of the new, benevolent father figure, with a modulation of the once excessively harsh superego; there was an amelioration of the intense fears of disorganization, abandonment, and helplessness, with a corresponding growth in the patient's capacity to experience and utilize anxiety as a signal. These changes were accompanied by a range of only partial and mostly intellectual insights into the sources of the patient's behavior difficulties: the destructive acting out of revengeful impulses with men, and aspects of her conflicts with the parents and the conflicted interactions with her children (especially the eldest daughter, with whom she had projectively identified, doing unto the daughter as she had unhappily had done to her—experiences of rejection, indifference, inconstancy). Insights were never fully accrued into the reactivation of all these past conflicts within the complex range of feelings in the transference. With all that was accomplished, communication was never free in the analytic work. The block and the withholding were never overcome with the first analyst; after the changes of technique by the second analyst, the withholding became less and the haughty, distant, and intellectualizing cover lessened. However, to the end of treatment, the patient could only pour out the acutely painful transference affects (the frustration of the love feelings) when drinking and in the safety of telephone distance. She would flatly discount them or even forget them the next day.

With the Economist, the fourth of these psychoanalytic patients converted to psychotherapy, the shift took place after almost 6 years of intensive psychoanalytic work, at the point of a widening, nonreversing paranoid psychotic decompensating process that unfolded under the interpretive pressures directed at the Oedipal dynamics. Thereafter, the treatment continued as a supportive–expressive psychotherapy and went on into "therapeutic lifer" status (the full course is described on pp. 336–343). The insights discerned at the point of "cutoff" Termination Study were a curious mixture. There seemed to be (and probably was) some range of insight into the dynamic structure of the patient's conflicts, from the long analytic phase of the treatment. However, this was admixed with rather primitive primary process thinking—a regressed indulging of the patient's inner fantasy world. The patient's inability to grasp the reality-distorted nature of so much of his transference fantasy and behavior indicated the low level of usable, real insight. Externalization had been much more prominent than initially thought; an example was the rages at women that accompanied the patient's revelation of his impotence—it was all their doing. The therapist was impressed by the patient's range of achieved insights into his psychodynamics and psychopathology, and saw the problem in the patient's inability to put these insights to effective use in the service of change. The research evaluators, however, were impressed that so much of the presumed insight reflected the patient's free access to his primitive, primary-process-like inner fantasy life (e.g., his assertion that he could have intercourse with his mother if he wanted and that no one should stop him, or his declaration to the analyst, "I'll kill you and marry your wife").

Of these four patients who started in psychoanalyses that were sooner or later modified into varyingly expressive–supportive psychotherapies, and who on a variety of bases effected changes that were beyond the concomitant achieved insights, two had very good outcomes, one had a moderately good outcome, and one had an equivocal outcome (the Heiress, whose transfer of the transference failed because of the unforeseen inadequacies and psychopathology of the second husband). The other two patients whose analyses were converted to psychotherapy with the same intent had less happy outcomes. The Masochistic Editor, who under both treatment regimens neither really changed nor achieved useful insights (though he, too, had primary-process eruptions in the form of aggressively tinged "awarenesses"), ended up as a failed case; and the Alcoholic Raconteur, who fled treatment at the point of the planned conversion to psychotherapy, was unhelped and without insights, and subsequently rescued himself to a most precarious outcome via his recourse to AA.

Other Analytic Patients. The other three psychoanalytic patients whose achieved changes outstripped the insights included two who subsequent to their treatments collapsed totally (Peter Pan and the Suspended Medical Student) and came to mental-illness-related deaths, 8 and 7 years after their treatment terminations, respectively. With Peter Pan, the situation was complex. Her analysis, with its wildly destructive behaviors and symptoms that the analyst was trying heroically to control (the full course is described on pp. 426–432), was also marked by many extraordinarily deep interpretations, some of which the therapist offered without gauging their appropriateness or their timing adequately. The interpretations related the patient's pathological eating behavior to fantasies of cannibalistic incorporation and destruction, devouring the father's penis and the mother's breast. The analyst felt that the patient's improvement stemmed from the period of working with this material; the patient, by contrast, said that many of the analyst's interpretations were not of real use to her and only upset her. On the other hand, transference interpretations were worked with less fully: The patient could never quite understand why she couldn't move into her analyst's home, or become his wife or daughter, and what the transference meanings of all this were. At Termination Study, the patient's major achieved insights were in some heightened awareness of the nature of her relationship with her parents. She could experience the meaning of autonomy and separateness from her parents, with some real understanding of why this had been such a complicated separation. This enabled some altered pattern of relationship with them, and, derivatively, with the husband-to-be. But as an example on the other side, the patient revealed no insight into her almost delusional belief about the urgent necessity to maintain a particular weight. The analyst had made a considerable interpretive effort in regard to the aggressive meanings in the patient's symptoms (her stealing and her wildly distorted eating pattern). The patient felt that she could not quite understand or really use these; nevertheless, the implicated behaviors did come under substantial control. But the analysis was incomplete, and the planned continuation in the new city to which the patient followed her fiancé did not work out. Though things appeared to be holding (shakily) for several years (including at Follow-Up Study at the 3-year-mark), the patient did come to subsequent therapy 7 years after treatment termination with a total and florid relapse of her illness, and this time the ultimately lethal course could not be stayed.

Quite comparable to Peter Pan, the Suspended Medical Student was another psychoanalytic patient who seemed to be doing well during his treatment course; however, his changes also outweighed the accrued insights, and he also had a subsequent downhill course to a lethal end. A series of seeming insights did develop, centered mainly around the patient's temptations and fears in regard to both destructive competition with and submission to his father and father surrogates. He could understand some of the ways in which these conflicts had pervaded and had limited his personality functioning. There was, however, almost no insight into the complexity of his relationship with his mother, who remained a more shadowy figure throughout, and the insights seemed always at the level of the least possible amount. The patient was neither particularly intellectually curious nor particularly articulate. Even at the end of his analytic treatment, he did not tend to think very much in terms of psychological causation in himself or in others. The fact that the judge exonerated him of official culpability in regard to a major automobile accident allowed him to dismiss thoughts about the accident's psychological determinants and meanings. This very limited development in psychological thinking complicated the entire treatment effort, and this patient's post-treatment collapse came much more promptly than did that of Peter Pan. (The full treatment course is described on pp. 363–370.)

The seventh (and last) of the patients started in analysis whose treatment changes surpassed the achieved insights (albeit with Peter Pan and the Suspended Medical Student we can say that the so-called treatment gains were more apparent than real, and subsequently collapsed even below whatever level of insight had been gained) was the Silent Woman. She was in an entirely different category. She seemed an excellent candidate for psychoanalysis, but, after a year of stubborn transference battle beset by prolonged painful silences, she disrupted her analysis (and, incidentally, went on from there without further treatment for the 14 subsequent years of our follow-up knowledge). During her year of analysis, there seemed no evidence of significant acquisition of insight. The patient said, "I never did get the drift of the treatment at all. . . . I always felt that something was going on that I wasn't getting. . . . There was confusion about the treatment. No light dawned. I still don't think I understand it [her illness]. . . . I was in a quandary right from the first about what it was I was supposed to be doing and

I don't think I ever found out." Nonetheless, despite this failed(?) insight-aiming psychoanalytic treatment, this patient still came to a moderate improvement in life functioning and in several (though not all) areas of involvement and feeling, on the basis of a transference triumph and a behavioral "resolution" of her conflicted tendencies that I have called the "antitransference cure." (The full description of how this came about and could be sustained appears on pp. 445–451.)

PATIENTS IN PSYCHOTHERAPY

With the 12 of the 20 patients started in psychotherapy who showed significant and sustained changes that far exceeded achieved insights, in most cases their treatments were planned that way; this result represented the appropriate (and mostly successful) kind of mostly supportive treatment outcome on the expected (and appropriately technically implemented) basis. Of these 12, 8 were in the group with very good improvements, 2 had moderate improvements, 2 had equivocal improvements, and none were failed cases. Three of them are of special interest and are individually noted here.

The Intellectual Fencer. With the Intellectual Fencer (who had a very good outcome), the original treatment recommendation was for a purely expressive psychotherapy (supported as long as need be by concomitant hospitalization); the excessive development of intellectual insights in this very intellectualizing and aggressively competitive individual was seen as a potentially serious technical problem for the treatment. This development would arise out of (1) the great importance to this patient of the intellectualizing defenses that would demonstrate her superiority and maintain her self-esteem; (2) the painfulness of the underlying warded-off affects; and (3) the usefulness of the hostile intellectual competitiveness with the therapist as a major transference weapon. Yet things never worked out that way. This is the other patient (in addition to the Silent Woman) who has been described under the rubric of the "antitransference cure." In triumph over her therapist, she surmounted her drug addiction and her homosexual proclivities by means of the "pseudoheterosexual" marriage she entered into, through which she also cured her alcoholic and homosexual husband—thus proving herself a better therapist than both her own and her husband's therapists. (The full treatment course is described on pp. 439–445.)

Given this kind of outcome, the insights acquired through the course of the therapy were most unimpressive and very much less than initially anticipated. For example, she saw herself as having been ill and now as recovered, but even this simple awareness was clouded by her vivid resentment of the way her parents had handled her in getting her to treatment; she seemingly had no awareness that her behaviors at the time had hardly left them any other choice (she had come with a chronic barbiturate addiction and in a superimposed acutely intoxicated confusional state). Actually, from the point of view of the kind of treatment course and outcome the patient had—with a good result sustained through 6 years of follow-up knowledge—this lack of insight was to the good, since the whole stability and sense of security about this outcome rested on the absence of insight into its mechanism. At Termination Study, the patient stoutly maintained that now her father, her husband, and her therapist all loved her dearly.

The Homesick Psychology Student. The Homesick Psychology Student, like the Intellectual Fencer, was seen initially as a very intellectual person, and was placed in an expressive psychotherapy that could lead into psychoanalysis if all went well. The treatment results, however (this case was in the moderately improved category), were achieved on the basis of the established benevolent transference attachment, carried over into a transfer of the transference into the marriage that the patient did achieve—though at the major price of a total sexual inhibition. (The full treatment course is described on pp. 417–421.) The concomitant insights achieved were most minimal. Certain relationships were minimally clarified: The patient felt his sexual inhibition to be linked to unresolved aspects of his relationship with his parents. But this perception went little further than this point, and was of no use in effecting change. The patient, curiously, felt that what most came to mind in assessing his therapeutic gains was that his longstanding very poor appetite had been overcome and he had gained some 15–20 pounds. This was important to him because he could now buy his trousers in the men's department and no longer had to go to boys' wear.

The Phobic Girl. The situation with the Phobic Girl was noteworthy in a very different way. She had a long but successful psychotherapy course. She was not seen at the "cutoff" Termination Study point, because her therapy was still ongoing and there were concerns over possible adverse reactions; however, she was seen and tested for the Follow-Up Study (now at 8½ years from the start), at which point her treatment happened to be actually terminating. In her case, there was a significant discrepancy (the only such instance clearly evident in our sample) between the clinical and the psychological test perception of the patient's achieved insights. On clinical interview, very little seemed available. The patient was indeed aware of all the changes in her behaviors, feelings, and thoughts, and knew that these related directly to the effects of the psychotherapy; she seemed to find it hard, however, to express precisely what in the psychotherapy had brought about specific changes, or precisely what kinds of knowledge she had obtained about herself in the therapy. The psychological testing portrayed a different picture: Here she revealed quite a bit of insight into the nature of the helping process, her feelings about the therapist and their source, the nature of her identifications with her mother, her own aspirations and limitations, her rebelliousness and how it had destructively pervaded her life, and the like. In fact, the range and kind of insights revealed in the psychological testing picture were close to what would seem the appropriate concomitants of a more expressive therapeutic experience than the patient in fact had. Why this particular kind of discrepancy in perspective occurred in this instance was not completely clear. The patient was not a particularly reticent or inarticulate person. Perhaps this is one of those instances where the patient (for whatever reasons) could allow freer access to her mental processes when shielded behind an array of test responses (responses to fixed stimuli) than she could when responding to clearly personal questions. In any case, these additional data reflected a significant strand of insightful working through as one of the mechanisms of the successful therapeutic result. Others included the disengagement from a very pathogenic life situation, the nurturing of the positive dependent transference attachment to the therapist, the ultimate transfer of the transference to a willing and understanding husband, and the patient and her husband's decision to settle in Topeka, which have all been previously described. The good result in this case has been maintained 18 years after termination, and the patient and her husband have by now moved out of the Topeka orbit. (The full treatment course is described on pp. 468–476.)

Altogether, of the 19 patients (7 started in analysis, 12 in psychotherapy) whose achieved changes systematically exceeded their acquired insights and were clearly based on other factors than the insightful resolution of conflict in response to interpretive uncovering, there were 10 with very good improvement, 4 with moderate improvement, 3 with equivocal improvement, and 2 who subsequently failed.

Cases Where Insights Appeared Commensurate with Changes

There were another 10 of the patients (not quite 25%) whose achieved insights seemed coordinate with and completely proportional to the changes reached. As might be expected, 9 of these 10 were in psychoanalyses that were maintained as analyses throughout, and one—a special instance, the Bohemian Musician— was in a supportive–expressive psychotherapy that was started after a course of ECT given in response to a presenting psychotic disorganization and deepening depression. Three of these 10 were men, and 7 were women.

THE CLUSTER WITH A HYSTERICAL CHARACTER STRUCTURE

Of these 10 patients, 6 of them, all women, were the very same cluster of 6 patients earlier identified (see pp. 293–295) as the group of patients (the Adoptive Mother, the Tantrum Woman, the Snake Phobia Woman, the Divorced Nurse, the Phobic Woman, and the Obese Woman) with a hysterical character structure; with various combinations of depression, anxiety, and phobic symptoms; and with a presumed excellent prognosis for thoroughgoing neurotic conflict resolution with psychoanalytic treatment. To our surprise, as a group, they then achieved psychoanalytic outcomes that fell varying short of the ambitious goals originally posited for them. Though 4 emerged in the group with very good treatment results (certainly so by their lights), and 2 ended in the next group with moderate improvement, all 6 of them fell short of a full psychoanalytic treatment result in a very similar way—in the inadequate working through of the pre-Oedipal negative mother-transference, and of the patient's unconscious hostile identification with this malevolent, feared, and hateful mother imago. Each in somewhat different ways was able to work around this major area of unresolved conflict, to come to very good therapeutic gains, to draw the analytic work to a close "while she was still ahead," and to maintain to the end an incompletely resolved positive attachment and sustained good feeling toward the analyst. Each successfully avoided the deeper analytic exploration of the earliest ties to the mother, so fraught with painful and hateful affect.

The treatment course of the Adoptive Mother (see pp. 295–302) has been described as the paradigm instance of this group. I have indicated in detail the counterphobic maneuvers and the external pressures that the patient successfully used to terminate her analytic treatment when she had achieved *her* goals; I have also described the various expressive and supportive therapeutic helps that she put together successfully in her posttreatment life in the face of renewed conflict pressures and symptom threat when she went ahead with the planned decision to adopt. This decision necessarily awakened unresolved aspects of the patient's relationship to her own mother, juxtaposed against what being a mother could bring out (in her unresolved hostile identification with her own mother). In the description of that treatment course, I have drawn specific attention via dream and associative material (see pp. 297–298) to these unresolved conflicts with the mother and about being a mother, together with clear evidence of the failures of insightful mastery in relation to them. What is clear about these 6 patients is that they all had good outcomes; however, they also all had psychoanalytically incomplete outcomes, and they had deficiencies in insightful mastery in precisely the area of analytic incompleteness. In that sense, there was a maintained proportionality between the degree and range of conflict resolution and achieved insight, and the character and symptom change that then ensued.

MEN IN ANALYSIS

The other 4 patients with the same proportionality between the degree of achieved insight and change included 3 men in psychoanalysis—each, however, in a quite different situation. The Medical Scientist was the one among the severely alcoholic–addicted patients who achieved a very successful and enduring result in his psychoanalytic treatment. He was also the one who had made such strenuous, though unsuccessful, self-help efforts to break his own addictions through self-willed withdrawals, prior to turning to others for help. On initial presentation he was seen as a reticent and even somewhat taciturn individual, socially awkward and relatively inarticulate despite his very high intellectual endowment. There seemed no evidence of any psychological-mindedness; in fact, his own efforts to cope with his illness had all been in the direction of trying to overcome it through the exertion of willpower, rather than making any attempt to think it through and come to understand it. Nonetheless, in his eminently successful 7-year analysis (the full treatment course is described on pp. 266–271), this patient developed probably the fullest range of concomitant and appropriate analytic insights of any of the patients in the whole PRP sample; these have been stated in detail on p. 176. They ranged over the dynamics of the development of his symptoms, his relationships with parental figures and their impact on him, his homosexual conflicts and submissive strivings, and his relationships with women (his two wives). Much more than most patients (even in analysis), he could verbalize his increased awarenesses of himself and connect them with real changes in his life and in his behavior, and he could talk insightfully about the process of treatment itself and the irrational aspects of transference (which, as they were interpreted to him, could be used to work out altered feeling and behavior dispositions). The relative inarticulateness and lack of psychological-mindedness at presentation, which had originally been seen as posing a specific treatment difficulty that might limit the extent of verbalizable insight actually achieved, had simply disappeared. The patient was now interested in what makes people tick, and was more able to sense and understand what others were experiencing, with all the important implications of this for his interpersonal relationships. He was now interested in psychological medicine. If there was a limitation in all of this, it was discerned at Follow-

Up Study in the tendency toward a somewhat pretentious psychologizing in his teaching his brand of "barnyard psychiatry," with its elements of idealization and of unresolved (and still somewhat ambivalent) relationship with his ex-analyst.

The situation with the Devoted Son was very different. In his 5½ years of analysis, he achieved only equivocal change—he was one of the patients concerning whose treatment course the whole issue of "Was this trip necessary?" has been most insistently raised—and concomitantly achieved only parallel and limited insights. The patient became more aware of the dimensions of his sharply inhibited personality functioning, but without genetic depth and unfolding; at the same time, he became somewhat more accepting of himself and at ease with himself, though he also felt painfully unable to change himself. The inordinate strength of the maintained dependent childhood relationship to the parents, recreated in the transference, came into clear view—but, again, without much dynamic and genetic enlargement. The patient did reach some range of insight into the nature of his dependency, his passive, infantile relationship to the mother figure. There was much less insight into the relationship with the father, and the whole constellation of Oedipal competition; hostility, especially directly between men, had been assiduously avoided. This was the patient who had to be unhappily "weaned" out of his analytic dependency, but who then 15 years later found his way back to renewed treatment. He is currently in "therapeutic lifer" status, now 27 years after his initial turn to analytic treatment (the full treatment course is described on pp. 283–287).

And the situation with the third in this group, the Prince, was different still. He was the narcissistically entrenched individual whose 4⅓ years of analysis brought only moderate change. Much of the core of his narcissism and the organization of his defenses to avoid narcissistic injury persisted. The patient still felt the same, but also felt that he knew more: He felt better able to recognize potential dangers, to mitigate situations in which he would feel immediate needs for the fulfillment of narcissistic wishes. He was aware of the strength of his need to compete and win, but he had more control over it. He could stop himself on the verge of an argument with his father, or he could now apologize to his wife after getting into an argument with her. He became more aware of how he had always thoughtlessly hurt people—not usually by intent, but rather by lack of sensitivity to them and of interest in what happened to them. His narcissistic preoccupations had always depleted his capacity for this kind of empathy. He could by the end of treatment thus get along much better on the job, with his wife, with his parents, and with his friends and coworkers. In effect, in keeping with the limitations in the actual psychoanalytic outcome (the full treatment course is described in Chapter 16), the Prince had acquired an array of intellectual insights that he had been able to turn usefully into behavior control mechanisms.

THE BOHEMIAN MUSICIAN

The remaining patient in this group with insights proportional to changes was the only 1 of the 10 in psychotherapy, the Bohemian Musician. Her treatment course began very gravely, with ECT having to be used to counteract her presenting psychotic depression. This patient then had a very good result from her 3 years of supportive–expressive psychotherapy; she developed "insights" in the course of it that were used and useful in ways quite comparable to those just described with the Prince, though they were more sharply limited. The treatment mechanisms were quite various (the full course is described on pp. 382–388), but interpretive endeavor was never a major component. The therapist, by and large, did not focus on intrapsychic conflict; he did not relate the present to the unconscious past to any great extent. And he avoided transference battles by riding throughout the therapy on the basically uninterpreted positive transference affects. Transference responses to himself were minimally interpreted, and he was usually rebuffed when such interpretations were sporadically offered; the triangular relationship of therapist–patient–hospital doctor was allowed to be a vehicle for splitting the transference and draining off all its negative components upon the hospital doctor. What then instead developed for insights were intellectualized formulas: For example, the patient could use the maxim that depressed feelings represented anger out of awareness to search out what she was really *angry* about. Usually this would succeed, the depressed feelings would lift, and the patient's mood would be again under stabilized control. These insights—really clichés—seemed useful, in the sense of appropriate to the patient's needs and the continued stability of her psychological functioning.

In all, the 10 patients in this category of insights proportionate to changes included 6 with very good improvement, 3 with moderate improvement, 1 with only equivocal improvement (the Devoted Son), and no failed cases.

Cases Where Insights Outstripped Changes

On the other end of the spectrum, there were just three cases (only 7%) where the attained insights considerably outstripped the discerned changes, and these three were a very mixed bag.

THE ENGLISH PROFESSOR

One of these was the English Professor, who, in many ways, was felt to have a very good result from his 6 years of psychoanalysis. There were very substantial shifts in manifest behavior patterns and a substantial reduction in symptom intensity. But the analyst felt, as did the research team, that these reflected much smaller intrapsychic shifts. The patient's deeply entrenched obsessive–compulsive and compliant character structure appeared essentially unaltered, despite a deceptive range of insights that the patient had achieved. These ranged over (1) the nature of the patient's struggles against commitment, his need to remain suspended, procrastinating; (2) the nature of his phobic symptoms, with his struggle against fusion, loss of self, and loss of identity; (3) his yearnings for dependency, with at the same time an effort at acceptance of himself as someone grown, who must stand on his own, must give up the hope that there would be others who would permanently take over for him or change things for him; and (4) his sexual difficulties ("I can't be comfortable in bed with her. The analyst and I have worked over it and I know exactly why, but I still feel uncomfortable and I can't go to sleep with her"). Of the sexual problems (and, by extension, other areas as well), he said, "I have real bitterness therefore because of this. I'm kind of filled with a vast quantity of know-how acquired over 6 years and I'm unable to do anything with it." He was referring, of course, to a large residue of psychologically undigested intellectual insights. (His full treatment course is described on pp. 279–283.)

THE ALCOHOLIC DOCTOR

The other two with much more insight than change were among the failed cases, as might be expected. One, the Alcoholic Doctor, was in a 7-year analysis that ended with his death from aspiration pneumonia, called by his analyst "an unconscious suicide." (The full treatment course is described on pp. 332–336.) During the long course of this patient's analysis, and over the span of the psychotic transference reaction that developed within it, the interpretive work was intense and a far-ranging array of insights was developed. Yet much of this work was ineffective. As already noted in more detail (see p. 336), the patient often responded with "I see this clearly, I understand what it is all about, but it doesn't make a goddamned bit of difference to me." And because of the ever-threatening, or present, psychotic regressive states in the transference, the analyst so often also felt that interpretations got nowhere, even though "the material was all there. I had everything in the case except I didn't get him well." However far-ranging the insights into the many aspects of the patient's interpersonal difficulties, especially the many facets of his relationship with his mother, they could not be used in the service of mastery or the enlargement of behavioral controls. And, concomitantly, the patient's externalizations actually intensified. He held his wife responsible for his open homosexuality, his parents for his lifetime deprivations, and his analyst for his current frustrations. And as things crumbled more and more about him, the patient more openly blamed all the others for their malevolent attitudes toward him.

The cases of the Alcoholic Doctor and the English Professor turned out to be the only instances in our whole research population of a phenomenon popularly imputed to psychoanalysis: For them, analysis was an uncovering therapy that led to much more insight than to behavioral change (and in the extreme case of the Alcoholic Doctor, to a great deal of insight and almost no change at all). And the Alcoholic Doctor's case, of course, was in the context of an unfolding, prolonged psychotic transference regression, which itself so weakened the ego's integrative resources as to put meaningful translation of insight into change effectively beyond the patient's capacities.

THE BITTER SPINSTER

The other patient in this group, the Bitter Spinster, was quite comparable as a failed case (though it did not end lethally) where acquired insights far surpassed worthwhile changes; however, she was in psychotherapy, not psychoanalysis. The patient was in an intended expressive psychotherapy for 8 years (she was not in psychoanalysis only because of financial limitations), which ended totally unsuccessfully. (The full treatment course is described on pp. 349–353.) During all this prolonged expressive psychotherapeutic course, meaningful insights, in the sense of combinations of intellectual and emotional awarenesses of intrapsychic conflict with appropriate concern and an impetus to change, simply did not develop. Instead, there was a widening array of intellectual understandings, which were often followed by bland indifference or blatant denial, and all put to purposes of defensive reinforcement. There was some occasional more concerned understanding of the patient's extremely hostile and inappropriate attitudes, but again these were disassociated from the rest of her psychological functioning and were not used to effect change.

Cases Where Little Change or Insight Was Achieved

In addition to these three gross categorizations—of patients with acquired insights less than changes (19, or 45% of the sample, mostly psychotherapy cases), insights commensurate with changes (10, or not quite 25%, mostly in psychoanalysis), and insights exceeding changes (only 3, or 7%)—there was a group of 10 (again, not quite 25%) where essentially there was little meaningful insight and little effective change on any basis. In effect, this was a clustering of failed cases. These 10 comprised 7 men and 3 women, 4 in psychoanalysis and 6 in psychotherapy (though of the 4 in analysis, 2 were among the 6 converted at some point to psychotherapy). Of these 10, 7 were treatment failures (including 3 of the 6 who died of mental-illness-related causes), and 2 had most equivocal results (the Alcoholic Raconteur, who rescued himself from total treatment failure by his turn to AA, and the Exhibitionistic Dancer, who rescued herself from total treatment failure by her turn to Christian Science). Only 1 (the Sexual Masochist) has managed by dint of a total treatment effort spanning now 28 years and still ongoing, to achieve a moderate overall treatment result despite his initial seeming total treatment failure. For him, this represents a tremendous improvement over his starting point as probably the sickest patient in the entire sample.

USE OF "PSEUDOINSIGHTS"

In regard to the role of insight and its development in relation to these 10 treatment courses, only two special points need be made. The first has to do with a variety of quite glib pseudoinsights that marked the treatment courses of three of them, all in psychotherapy (the Sociopath, the Car Salesman, and the Addicted Doctor), but that in no wise could be put to use in the service of change for the better, or even of staying the failing treatment course. The Sociopath, for example, could psychologize and try to "con" the therapist with glib statements that his lying, cheating, and other "undesirable traits" (his "hate complex," his pride and arrogance) were problems to him, and that he felt them to be expressions of his efforts to overcompensate for deeply ingrained feelings of inferiority. But this was talk, and not insight. The patient's externalizations were unchanged throughout: They were total, and ever more flamboyantly and destructively expressed.

The Car Salesman, whose three periods of psychotherapy all ended unsuccessfully, nonetheless could express certain "insights" that he felt accrued during his treatment. These included his overwhelming need for approval by authority figures, his desire to get well without being responsible for anything, his (now presumably renounced) desire always to be the big shot. He "learned" that when he was depressed he was really mad, and that he had difficulty expressing himself (especially his angry feelings) with his wife and also with his therapist; he felt that he could now do this more directly and honestly. The therapist, trying to be as optimistic as possible, felt that perhaps the patient had developed some insights into his neurotic ways of handling his aggressions, and that, concomitant with this, the depressive trends had diminished. To the research team, these insights sounded like clichés, repetitions of what the therapy had drummed into him; they appeared neither integrated nor useful in any way. The patient said that in his first two periods of (formal) psychotherapy he had talked mainly about his relationship with his father, but that in his third period, with the hospital doctor, he had talked mainly about his relationship with his mother, because the latter had told him "that by now I knew enough about Dad." This patient did go on into further, equally unsuccessful therapy elsewhere, and within a year was dead of a drug–alcohol overdose.

The "insights" of the Addicted Doctor were of a similar kind. There was perhaps some enhanced recognition, repeated in a cliché-ridden way, of the scope of his difficulties and the need for treatment. But for the most part he was content with a series of rationalizations that enabled him to find people to blame for his difficulties. This defensive displacement to objects outside himself seemed so integral to his whole narcissistic adjustment that it was doubtful whether it could be at all modified. The externalizations continued full force, and the people to blame were many: his colleagues, his therapist, his wife, and so on (the "so on" going back to what his parents did to him in his early years). This patient too went on in therapy during the follow-up period—as an inpatient in the local affiliated state hospital for the next 2½ years, at which point he committed suicide with a barbiturate overdose.

SPECIAL CIRCUMSTANCES:
THE SEXUAL MASOCHIST

The other special point to be made in relation to these 10 patients is the category of little meaningful insight and little effective change has to do with the special circumstances surrounding the long-term (and ongoing) treatment career of the Sexual Masochist. His long formal period of supportive–expressive psychotherapy ended by a petering-out process after 8 years, essentially as a failure. At that point there seemed to be no discernible insights of any kind—not even at the level of recognizing the seriousness of the continuing illness manifestations, the massive drug intake, and the severe sexual aberration. And in fact, though there seemed to be some facade of "normal-looking" improved functioning in the management of the patient's business life and in the appearances of his marriage, there was at the same time deepening evidence of underlying thought disorganization, with looser, more bizarre, more paranoid thinking and an even greater straining of reality.

By the time of Follow-Up Study, however, as described earlier, the patient had had an intervening "serious heart attack" and attendant great fright. He had abruptly stopped his enormous drug intake; had put himself under the close care of a very concerned internist; and, together with his wife, had found his way back to conjoint marital therapy with his former therapist—a therapy that has continued (with transfer to successors when his therapist finally left Topeka) uninterruptedly ever since, for a total therapeutic span of 28 years. At the Follow-Up Study point the paranoid ideation in the transference was now in abeyance, under the surface, and the whole treatment climate was correspondingly now different. And there were some "educational insights" in the area of reality testing. The patient could now better distinguish (with the therapist's help) what was real and what was not, and therefore could better see what was appropriate in his feelings and behaviors and what was not. On this basis, the patient—over this span of years—has been able to go on to a moderate improvement level.

OVERVIEW OF CHANGES AND THEIR MECHANISMS IN THE PRP SAMPLE

Relationship of Change–Insight Ratio to Therapeutic Modes Employed

In this chapter to this point, I have reviewed in detail the issue of the relationship of insight to change—that is, the relationship of the extent and range of the insights acquired during the course of the therapy, and the concomitant changes that eventuated (across the array of indicators, symptoms, manifest behavior patterns, attitudes and dispositions, inferred intrapsychic states, changes of impulse–defense configurations, etc.). For 19 patients in PRP (the largest subgroup), the changes were substantially in excess of the insights, and were thus presumably based on other factors than the interpretation of unconscious conflict leading to conflict resolution and concomitant insight. And in keeping with the difference in underlying operative mechanisms between psychoanalysis (where the designedly supportive elements would be less and the expressive, insight-aiming elements much more) and psychotherapy (where, especially in our sample, this ratio would be substantially reversed and a far greater part of the accrued changes would be on the basis of the variety of supportive and non-insight-aiming mechanisms), these 19 included 12 in psychotherapy, 4 of the 6 converted from psychoanalysis to psychotherapy, 2 of those in analysis whose changes turned out to be only a facade of change and who collapsed in the posttreatment period (Peter Pan and the Suspended Medical Student), and 1 who disrupted her analysis after only a year and represented an antitransference cure (the Silent Woman). None of them, therefore, were patients with "good" analyses and good analytic outcomes. They were overwhelmingly (16 of the 19) in psychotherapy (4 by conversion from psychoanalysis); the fact that they showed changes substantially in excess of insights was therefore what might have been expected of them as a group.

Next, there was the group of 10 patients where, by the same criteria, the insights and the changes seemed coordinate and proportional. Of these 10, 9 were in psychoanalysis (8 of them were "good" analyses with good outcomes); only 1 (the Bohemian Musician) was in psychotherapy, and the particular circumstances of her case have been recounted. Thus, again, the results were in line with what would be expected, from the theory of psychoanalytic therapy, for change in analytic or expressive endeavors. With both these change–insight categories, therefore, our data did conform to our expectations. With the patients in psychotherapy, where supportive elements were so substantial, changes exceeded insights and clearly came via other than insight-creating processes; with the patients in psychoanalysis where supportive elements were far less evident, changes and insights were directly proportional—or, to put it differently, the greatest bulk of the discerned changes could be appropriately related to counterpart insights into intrapsychic conflicts acquired by the process of insight-aiming interpretation.

Relationship of Degree of Achieved Insight to "True Structural Changes": S. A. Appelbaum's Analysis

However, this does not speak yet to the issue of whether, apart from the degree and proportionality of concomitant achieved insight, the changes arrived at by the two kinds of mechanisms—largely supportive and largely expressive—differed in the degree to which they were "true structural changes."[3] The data as elucidated to this point in this book are not set up to throw specific light on this particular issue, in the absence of independent criteria for "structural change." Fortunately, however, this particular issue has been specifically addressed in the book by S. A. Appelbaum (1977) on the specific findings in the comparative study of the projective psychological test battery data at the three points in time. In Appelbaum's book, there is a specific focus on a variable-by-variable comparison of the Patient Variables across those three points in time. "Structural change" is defined in terms of adjudged changes on a 3-point-scale in specific intrapsychic configurations, or Patient Variables, assessed by way of the projective psychological test data. These particular Patient Variables are Patterning of Defenses, Thought Organization, Affect Organization, Anxiety Tolerance, and Ego Strength (see S. A. Appelbaum, 1977, p. 206). (Parenthetically, these particular variables can be assessed with special clarity in projective test data, and often much more clearly than in overall clinical psychiatric assessment procedures.) In this independent assessment, structural change has been related (by chi-square analysis) to "conflict resolution"; this term means there, just as I have used it in this volume, change achieved "through classical expressive means" (p. 206). It has also been related to change by "miscellaneous means" (p. 206), which refers to change achieved "in neurotic conflicts by various means other than conflict resolution" (pp. 206–207)—that is, change by the variety of supportive mechanisms adduced throughout this book.

This analysis by S. A. Appelbaum (1977, table on p. 207) shows "a clear positive relationship between conflict resolution and structural change—the more conflict resolution, the more structural change. This relationship is statistically significant ($p < .025$), yet there are exceptions. Seven of 16 patients without conflict resolution did show structural change. "Thus, both points of view, that structural change is associated with resolution of conflict and that structural change can come about in the absence of conflict resolution, receive support from this analysis" (p. 207). Stated in fuller detail, of 27 of our 42 patients for whom full projective psychological test battery data were available for comparative assessment across the three points in time, conflict resolution was seen in 11, and there was concomitant structural change in 10 of those. With the other 16 patients for

---

3. The other two groupings discussed under this heading are not germane to this particular discussion of change and structural change. They are (1) the 3 patients for whom insights substantially exceeded changes and (2) the 10 patients—essentially the failed cases—for whom there were neither significant changes nor significant insights.

whom changes in their functioning, behaviors, and symptoms were adjudged to have come about by "various means other than conflict resolution" (p. 207), structural change—as independently defined by Appelbaum in the way specified—was still seen in 7, or almost half. S. A. Appelbaum summarizes these results as follows:

> The more that conflicts are resolved through expressive means, the more structural change is liable to come about. Yet a substantial number of patients showed structural change even in the absence of resolution of conflict through expressive means. This suggests that fundamental changes can be brought about in people even though they are unable to develop much insight. This is, therefore, an encouragement to supportive treatment. (p. 214)

This finding, of course, is fully in keeping with the perspectives I have been developing in this book. With the patients treated via primarily supportive modes (of all the varieties specified), changes have been substantially in excess of concomitant achieved insights; furthermore, they have seemed over the course of follow-up observation to be just as stable, as enduring, as proof against subsequent environmental vicissitudes, and as free (or not free) from the requirement for supplemental posttreatment contact, support, or further therapeutic help as the changes in those patients treated via a centrally expressive mode (psychoanalysis). Moreover, in the arena of clinical assessment at follow-up contact, when changes in psychological functioning and well-being were being assessed, it was by no means necessarily clear whether the adjudged structural changes reflected underlying conflict resolution or not. Certainly, from all the data, "conflict resolution cannot be considered essential to structural change and may be independent of it in some instances" (S. A. Appelbaum, 1977, p. 208); that is, structural change appears to occur independently of (without) conflict resolution in those instances.

Stability of Achieved Changes: Horwitz's Findings

Fully comparable findings have emerged as well from the Horwitz (1974) book based on the Prediction Study data. Horwitz has developed his findings around the study of stability of change with supportive treatment. Very briefly (since his findings are more directly equivalent to mine in this book), patients who improved with supportive psychotherapeutic modes could maintain and even consolidate their functioning through the period of follow-up observation. Furthermore, they could do so just as often without the significant continuing contact that had initially been presumed to be required, since such supportively based changes had been expected to be less stable, less able to weather the stresses of subsequent life. Horwitz feels that three major factors could be contributory to such relatively enduring treatment gains in supportive psychotherapies (see Horwitz, 1974, pp. 229–230): (1) continuing supportive environmental factors, such as the more appropriate marriages that some of these patients had by now entered into (the therapeutic process had helped these patients to understand better the nature of their needs, and thus influenced them to make wiser choices); (2) the positive feedback reinforcement from new, more adaptive behaviors, into which the therapists had implicitly or explicitly encouraged these patients; and (3) a continuing and durable positive feeling toward the therapists, seen as the conscious manifestation of significant shifts in the patients' inner world of object relationships and self and object representations. Again, clearly, these are all in accord with the very comparable conceptualizations developed in this book concerning the mechanisms for changing and for maintaining the changes in supportive psychotherapeutic modes.

Overall Results — and Their Bases

The discussions in the various chapters of this section can be brought together at this point under an array of sequential propositions regarding the appropriateness, the efficacy, the reach, and the limitations of psychoanalysis (varyingly "classical" and modified) and psychoanalytic psychotherapy or psychotherapies (varyingly expressive and supportive) — always, of course, as discerned within this particular patient population, those (usually sicker) individuals who were brought to or sought out their treatment within this psychoanalytic sanatorium setting.

"STRUCTURAL CHANGE" VERSUS "BEHAVIORAL CHANGE": A QUESTIONABLE DISTINCTION

The first proposition has to do with the distinction so regularly made in the psychodynamic literature between "structural change" and "behavioral change." Presumably, the interpretive exposure and resolution of unconscious intrapsychic conflicts result in varieties of *underlying* "structural changes" (or "real changes") in the ego and in the other psychic entities as well (cf. Bibring, 1937, pp. 171–189), such as the particular changes adduced by S. A. Appelbaum (1977) in specific Patient Variables. On the other hand, "behavioral changes" or changes in "manifest behavior patterns" are (invidiously) considered "just altered techniques of adjustment" and presumably are all that can come out of all other nonexpressive, noninterpretive, non-insight-aiming change mechanisms (i.e., all the varieties of supportive psychotherapeutic techniques and implementations presented throughout this book). Intrinsic to this way of dichotomizing between kinds of change has always been the easy assumption that only "structural change" or "real change," as brought about through conflict resolution marked by appropriate insight, can have some guarantee of inherent stability, durability, and capacity to weather at least ordinary future environmental vicissitudes. It goes without saying that the commonplace value distinction automatically follows — that change brought about by expressive means is "better." This is of course the basis for the operating clinical maxim, already quoted in this section, that has pervaded Menninger Foundation practice: "Be as expressive as you can be, and as supportive as you have to be" (i.e., in terms of the "weaknesses" of the patient, the inability to encompass and tolerate the rigorous intrapsychic requirements of the expressive–analytic approach).

It is clear from the experiences documented throughout this book that I question strongly the continued usefulness of this effort to link the *kind* of change achieved ("real" change, "better" change) with the intervention modes by which it is brought about (the more expressive, the better). If we accept the Rapaport (1960) conception of structure as being a process of slow rate of change, and the observations from the study of the PRP cases that the changes reached in our more supportive therapies and via supportive modes seemed just as frequently stable and enduring, just as able to cope with life's subsequent happenstances, and just as able (or as unable) to endure independent of further support as the changes reached in our more expressive–analytic cases, then we must accept that the interpretive, uncovering mode does not have an exclusive corner on inducing structural change. Certainly the data just quoted from S. A. Appelbaum's book (1977) — the psychological test assessments of changes in particular Patient Variables as the independent indicators of structural change — indicate that analytic results are more regularly accompanied by concomitant structural changes; however, they also indicate that supportively achieved results are also accompanied by indistinguishable structural changes in a very substantial proportion of the cases. And certainly my own detailed case histories of these treatment courses and of their long-term follow-ups are in full accord with this position.

Incidentally, the careers of the four patients known still to be in continuing posttreatment therapeutic contact and care provide an interesting perspective on the relationship (if any) between mode of intervention and type of change. One, the Sexual Masochist, was an extremely difficult (our "sickest") patient, with an ambulatory psychotic character structure, severe addictions, and bizarre perversions; he was felt from the beginning to require a supportive and counseling psychotherapy. Another, the Housebound Phobic Woman, severely addicted and totally phobically constricted, was at least at the beginning seen as a potential candidate for psychoanalysis, though shortly converted into an enduring supportive–expressive psychotherapy. Still another, the Economist, a manifestly obsessive–compulsive individual with an underlying psychotic potential that was ultimately mobilized in the course of his prolonged psychoanalysis, was converted at the 6-year mark to the supportive–expressive psychotherapy in which the erupting psychotic regression firmly receded and the patient fully stabilized (and consolidated). Finally, the Devoted Son, a neurotically very inhibited individual, was viewed from the start as very well suited for a classical psychoanalysis, and was treated by an adequately long, essentially unmodified analytic approach. These four who have ended as the literal "therapeutic lifers" (of course in psychotherapy, not psychoanalysis) in the PRP population thus have covered the full gamut of illness pictures and therapeutic approaches. All four seem equally dependent, as of this writing, on continuing therapeutic contact.

THE PROPORTIONALITY OF THERAPEUTIC CHANGE TO CONFLICT RESOLUTION AND TO ATTAINED INSIGHT

The second proposition has to do with the argument, discussed at some length in the book by Horwitz (1974, pp. 115–129), that therapeutic change will be at least proportional to the degree of conflict resolution. Put this way this proposition is almost unexceptionable. It is clear that there can be significantly more change than there is true intrapsychic conflict resolution, on all the varying (supportive) bases through which change is brought about; there can also be properly proportionate change, where the change is all or "purely" on the basis of conflict resolution with accompanying insight—if such an ideal type ever actually exists in practice. However, it would be hard to imagine real conflict resolution (and accompanying insight) without at least concomitant change in behaviors, dispositions, attitudes, and symptoms.

Horwitz (1974) adduces one possible exception from our PRP sample, the case of the Divorced Nurse. His summary of this is as follows:

> [This patient] had achieved a considerable modification intrapsychically in her need to depreciate men but was unable to establish a gratifying relationship with a man at the conclusion of treatment. Reality factors, like her age and having a small child, may have been contributing factors. But even more significant was a sense of guilt and self-depreciation, a feeling that she had "nothing to offer" a man, which prevented her from actively trying to form such a relationship. These feelings were apparently based upon the actual suffering she had inflicted upon her ex-husband and children, and were related to her loss of custody of the children. These life experiences seemed to have left a strong enough impression to handicap her future relationships with men, despite the resolution of her conflicts. (pp. 128–129)

My own write-up of this case and its treatment course (see pp. 314–321) has emphasized the various sharp limitations of the analytic treatment outcome—those residing in the analyst, in the analytic effort, and in carrying out the analysis within the context of so unfavorable a life situation, as well as those residing in the patient (the inner thrust toward termination at the level of an established "defense transference neurosis," and the avoidance of deeper penetration of the hostile and dependent pre-Oedipal attachments). One could, on this combined basis, at least question whether there was indeed sufficient "resolution and abatement of the phallic conflict" to "be sufficient to permit her to actively seek out new relationships with men to replace the one she had lost," in the face of the persisting withdrawal, depression, and guilt linked to her "unresolved oral dependency and oral demandingness" (all quotes from Horwitz, 1974, p. 124). That is, I am questioning whether the case of the Divorced Nurse represents the possible exception under this heading that Horwitz thinks she does.

In the closely related arena of the proportionality of therapeutic change to the degree of attained insight (as distinct from conflict resolution), discussed in the preceding chapter, three instances have been described (the English Professor, the Alcoholic Doctor, and the Bitter Spinster) of achieved insight in excess of change. This, of course, is a common enough problem and a frequent complaint both within and about psychoanalytic treatment, and has been the subject of considerable discussion in the analytic literature (e.g., see the seminal article by Wheelis, 1950). In the three cases described in Chapter 38, such concepts as "undigested intellectual insights" or "insights within an ego-weakened or psychotic transference state" have been invoked. What are meant, of course, are insights that for varying reasons are not consequent to true conflict resolution and do not reflect it.

CONFLICT RESOLUTION:
A NECESSARY CONDITION FOR CHANGE?

The third proposition—often linked to the proportionality argument, but in the light of our findings much more debatable, and to be clearly separated from it—is the necessity argument. This assumption is put by Horwitz (1974) as the proposition that "conflict resolution is a necessary condition for certain kinds of change" (p. 129). The form of this proposition is such that it readily lent itself to repeated precise testing within the structure of the formal, tripartite, "if–then–because" logical model of our PRP Prediction Study. In the light of all that has been presented in this book to this point, and the summarization in this final section, it should come as no surprise that Horwitz reports that this proposition was negated in half the instances within the PRP sample.

To put this more positively, it is clear, based on the case write-ups of this book, that an overall finding (almost an overriding one) has been the repeated demonstration that a substantial number and range of changes—in symptoms, in character traits, in personality functioning and in life styles rooted in lifelong and repressed intrapsychic conflicts—have been brought about via the more supportive therapeutic modes and techniques, cutting across the gamut of supportive *and* expressive (even analytic) therapies. It is also clear that in terms of the usual criteria—slowness to change (i.e., stability, durability), capacity to withstand external or internal disruptive pressures, and the like—these changes have in many instances been quite indistinguishable from the changes brought about by typically expressive–analytic (interpretive, insight-producing) means. In other words, these changes have often been as much "real" changes or "structural" changes (in the ego, or, more broadly, in the total character organization) as those customarily defined as "real" or "structural."

What this adds up to has been, again in overall perspective, a tendency to overestimate the necessity of the expressive–analytic treatment mode, and of its central operation via conflict resolution based on interpretation, insight, and working through, to achieve therapeutically desired change. Many examples of this overestimation have been given throughout this book, but, for purposes of ready comparability of methods and findings, I illustrate it here with the same three examples presented by Horwitz (1974, pp. 208–215).

The first example is the Adoptive Mother, the young woman troubled that she could not bear a child and be thereby a proper Catholic wife and mother, and plunged into a severe depression when her mounting distress with an adopted child caused her to return the baby to the adoption agency. This patient came to psychoanalysis trusting to resolve her psychological problems so that ideally she could conceive and become pregnant, or, if not that, at least could adopt and successfully manage the upbringing of the adopted child. On psychiatric evaluation, her symptom and behavior difficulties were (as might be expected) linked to unresolved neurotic conflicts centering around her femininity, around what it meant to be a mother, and around her relationship to her own mother. The patient was felt to be an appropriate candidate for a classical and unmodified psychoanalysis, on the grounds that only the full resolution of her underlying neurotic infantile conflicts via the psychoanalytic process could promise her the real change in psychological functioning (as well as symptom alleviation) that would enable her to successfully *be* a mother—through having thoroughly enough resolved her problems *with* her mother.

The description of the psychoanalytic treatment course (see pp. 295–302) has detailed the kinds of changes in symptoms and manifest behavior patterns that the patient did achieve, the kinds and degrees of conflict resolution that these changes were linked to, and the precise areas where conflict resolution was not achieved (especially the very area of the pre-Oedipal relationship and hostile identification with the malevolent and feared mother imago). Nonetheless, for the various reasons adduced in the case write-up, the patient pressed for termination; she was sad but resigned that she had not become pregnant and perhaps never would, but was determined (though very apprehensive) to go ahead now with a decision to adopt, in the permanent place of residence to which she and her husband were moving. The patient did then subsequently adopt successfully (twice, first a girl and then a boy), albeit not without some symptom recrudescence, and not without the supportive psychological therapy that the patient fashioned through her combined contacts with her family physician, her priest, and the adoption agency social worker. From the patient's point of view, she had finally an outstandingly successful treatment result, having achieved fully her treatment goal and life ambition to be a proper Catholic wife and mother. From the point of view of analytic process and analytic resolution, this was a very successful psychotherapeutic outcome but only a limited psychoanalytic outcome, with deficiencies in the area of the full analysis of the pre-Oedipal fixations and conflicts. From the standpoint of the necessity hypothesis, changes that had been expected to come about only in consequence of the fullest psychoanalytic working through and resolution (i.e., the ability to be a successful adoptive mother) had come about in the absence of that full resolution (the still unresolved conflicts of the hostile-dependent pre-Oedipal mother attachment). The thesis that this change might have been carried through with less symptom recurrence and less need for supplemental therapeutic support if there had been fuller concomitant analytic conflict resolution is plausible, but by no means necessarily true, and is certainly not established by these data.

The next, similar example is that of the Prince, who came to analysis with an awareness of his narcissistic needs to be treated like a prince, and of the great uneasiness these caused him in the mutual give-and-take demands of an intimate relationship with a woman. These needs had already cost him one marriage, and he was apprehensive that his history would doubtless repeat itself if these personal characteristics and the underlying problems they reflected were not resolved by treatment. Again, this patient was thought to be eminently suited for analysis. On the one hand, his narcissistic disorder did not seem to represent the more severe infantile kind of oral-narcissistic character fixations, but rather a more defensive envelopment, the denials of essentially phallic-level conflicts and hysterical character traits. On the other hand, with the patient's very deep-seated (albeit clearly neurotic) character problems, with no focal neurotic symptoms per se, there seemed to be no useful place for—or even any special palliative indications for—any other kind of treatment that would be less reconstructively ambitious in its scope.

Again, the description of the treatment course (see Chapter 16) has indicated the many very substantial life changes that the patient was able to effect. He got along much better at work, with his parents, and with his friends and coworkers; primarily, of course, he was able to court, to marry, and to work out a seemingly successful marriage and family (with a child). Again, however, the supposedly necessary concomitant analytic working through was only very partial, and the patient was able basically to use the analytic interactions to protect, rather than to penetrate, his narcissistic integrity. What had been initially assumed to be a narcissistic defensiveness in fact turned out to be a deeper and more pervasive oral-narcissistic character structure, which constituted an unsurmounted barrier in this analytic process. However, on bases other than the assumed essential full analytic conflict resolution, the patient married, found gratification in this relationship, and, even more importantly, was able to afford satisfaction to his wife. From a psychoanalytic perspective, the analysis was again incomplete, and in this instance (unlike that of the Adoptive Mother) the patient shared in the judgment of incompleteness and in the disappointment. However, he was now able, as he had not been before, to limit the more destructive and self-destructive aspects of his narcissism.

The third example—again from a psychoanalytic case, but one with a far less successful outcome than either the Adoptive Mother or the Prince—is that of the Heiress. She was a more disturbed individual, who came to treatment with severe symptom distress as well as disorganized "turbulent periods" of increasing severity. She too, however, was felt appropriate for an effort at psychoanalytic treatment, in large part because it was again felt that because of the deep-seated nature of her characterological problems, effective enough resolution could only come through a thoroughgoing psychoanalytic procedure. This was the psychoanalytic course (see pp. 421–426) that bogged down into a transference impasse with the "cardboard analyst," and that was then switched to another analyst, who soon converted it into a sustaining supportive–expressive psychotherapy. The patient's underlying conflicts were not resolved analytically through this whole treatment course. Again, though, this patient was able to make effective progress in certain areas of life functioning—primarily in becoming a more nurturant, maternal, and feminine individual, as seen very substantially in her improved relationship with her children. And, again, these were the kinds of changes that it had been predicted could only come in her case out of psychoanalytic conflict resolutions.

GREATER-THAN-EXPECTED SUCCESS OF SUPPORTIVE PSYCHOTHERAPEUTIC APPROACHES

The counterpart to the tendency to overestimate the necessity of the expressive–analytic treatment mode, and of its operation via interpretive conflict resolution, to effect therapeutically desired changes has been the happy finding that supportive psychotherapeutic approaches, mechanisms, and techniques so often achieved far more than were expected of them. In fact, they often reached the kinds and degrees of change expected to depend on more expressive and insightful conflict resolutions, and they often did so in ways that represented indistinguishably "structural" changes, in terms of the usual indicators of this state. Proportionately, within their own category, the psychotherapy cases did as well as the psychoanalytic ones: 12 of the 20 (or 60%) of the psychotherapy cases had very good or moderately good treatment results, as did 12 of the 22 (or 55%) of the psychoanalytic cases.

Of course, as has been emphasized throughout this book, these are not meant to be comparisons across modalities (since the patients were not randomly assigned but were systematically different in the two modalities, being in each case selected in terms of presumed suitability for that modality); they are assessments within each modality. More to the point, the good results in the one modality were not overall less stable, less enduring, or less proof against subsequent environmental vicissitude than the good results in the other.

An important aspect of the finding for supportive psychotherapy is that the changes predicted for the 20 patients in psychotherapy, though more often predicated to be based on the more expressive mechanisms and techniques, in fact were more often actually achieved on the basis of the more supportive mechanisms and techniques. Another significant fact is that, within the group of 22 in psychoanalysis, in almost every case there were modifications, parameters, and the like—some analytically resolved but mostly not; some (often) as gross as concomitant inpatient hospital care and protection; and all of them, of course, in the direction of more supportive modes and aspects. Even by our PRP liberal criteria, therefore, only 10 (not quite half) of the psychoanalytic cases were in overall retrospect viewed as having been essentially in unaltered analysis; 6 were felt to be in analyses substantially modified in supportive directions; and 6 were considered really converted to varyingly supportive–expressive psychotherapies. By the usual stricter criteria of customary outpatient psychoanalytic and psychotherapy practice, just about every single one of our PRP psychoanalytic cases would be considered substantially altered in varyingly supportive directions. To put this into overall perspective, more of the patients (psychotherapeutic and psychoanalytic alike) changed on the basis of designedly supportive interventions and mechanisms than had been expected or predicted beforehand, on the basis of either our clinical experience or our theoretical positions.

Such considerations do raise a variety of issues for us. One is the difficult-to-relinquish spectre of laying the way open for continuing treatments and treatment dependency if the goal of the fullest interpretive conflict resolution is at all abandoned, or even at all weakened. Actually, as I have just pointed out (see p. 721), the 4 patients of the 42 in the PRP population who are still in known ongoing treatment at this current writing, so many years after their treatment starts at The Menninger Foundation, came in a divided way from the ranks of psychotherapy (the Sexual Masochist), psychoanalysis converted to psychotherapy (the Housebound Phobic Woman and the Economist), and psychoanalysis (the Devoted Son).

A more difficult issue on which to get some conceptual handle from the PRP experience is the question of "What if?" What if the patients deemed appropriate for expressive psychotherapy and for psychoanalysis could actually have been held more unswervingly to the planned expressive and analytic courses? Would the same predicted outcomes (varyingly good or not) have been achieved? Would they have been achieved with less of the subsequent price in terms of symptom relapse and need for more therapeutic assistance, which, for example, characterized the Adoptive Mother's final achievement of her treatment goals and life strivings? Could even more have been achieved—"fuller" or at least different internal change (conflict resolution)—and could this have been reflected in even more substantial treatment achievements in terms of psychological functioning, life management, and life fulfillment? Other cases than the Adoptive Mother come to mind in this regard. For example, the Intellectual Fencer's actual psychotherapy was far less interpretive than initially intended; she ended much improved, to be sure, but with the somewhat precarious compromise of the antitransference cure — the cure by triumph and defiance in the transference, marked by the "pseudoheterosexual" marital choice in her life. Similarly, the Actress's actual psychotherapy was again far less interpretive than initially intended; she also ended much improved, but with the collusive bargain to place her homosexual behaviors and conflicts beyond the bounds of therapeutic scrutiny. The "What if?" question, of course, cannot be answered except speculatively on the basis of the PRP experience, but it is a central one to be addressed in the next (and last) chapter in this final section of the book.

LESSER-THAN-EXPECTED SUCCESS OF PSYCHOANALYTIC APPROACHES

I now reverse the field and consider these PRP treatment courses from the point of view of psychoanalysis as a treatment modality. Just as more was accomplished than expected (and more stably, and more enduringly) with psychotherapy, especially in its more supportive modes, so psychoanalysis, as the quintessentially expressive therapeutic mode, was more limited in the outcomes achieved than had been predicted or anticipated — *with these patients*. This also, of course, was a function of a variety of factors pointed out in general discussions through this book, as well as in the individual case descriptions of the 22 psychoanalytic treatment courses. One such factor was the whole ethos of the psychoanalytic sanatorium and the psychoanalytic treatment opportunities it makes possible, as first developed by Simmel (1929) at Der Tegel outside Berlin and established in America by the Menningers and others in the 1930s. This ethos was given powerful impetus by such persuasive writings as those of Robert Knight from The Menninger Foundation (1937a, 1937b, 1938) on the psychoanalytic treatment of the addictive disorders, and of Frieda Fromm-Reichmann from the Chestnut Lodge Sanatorium (1950) on the psychoanalytic treatment of the psychotic disorders, within the protective confines of such sanatorium settings. The dominant theme was that the concept of the psychoanalytically informed and guided sanatorium, with its possibilities for protection, care, and life management of (temporarily) behaviorally disorganized and incompetent individuals, could make possible the intensive psychoanalytic treatment and cure of patients who could not be helped to resolve their deep-seated personality difficulties satisfactorily enough with any other or lesser ("lesser" in the sense of less intensive, less thoroughgoingly reconstructive) treatment approach than psychoanalysis, but who also could not tolerate the rigors of the regressive psychoanalytic treatment process within the usual outpatient private practice setting.

This line of reasoning, of course, was what led by natural extension to the concept of psychoanalysis on the basis of so-called "heroic indications," which, by the nature of the kinds of patients brought to The Menninger Foundation sanatorium setting, necessarily comprised such a substantial segment of our research psychoanalytic population. In our PRP experience, however, the central tenets of this proposition were found wanting. These particular patients characteristically did very poorly with the psychoanalytic treatment method, however it was modified by parameters, and however buttressed with concomitant hospitalization; in fact, they comprised the great bulk of the failed psychoanalytic treatment cases. The Medical Specialist, who had very special demonstrated capacities of will, stands out as perhaps the single exception in the experience with this group. On the other hand, though many of the same kind of patients (actually, of course, even sicker, with demonstrably even weaker ego organizations and fewer countervailing resources or accomplishments) also were failed cases in their varyingly supportive–expressive psychotherapies, these failures usually occured in the context of grossly inadequate hospitalization and life control. There were certainly enough instances of very good outcomes among the very ill and disordered in supportive–expressive psychotherapies—for example, the Manic–Depressive Physician, the Bohemian Musician, the Intellectual Fencer, and even the Sexual Masochist—that we can feel that the whole broad spectrum of "sicker" patients being discussed here can indeed do much better in an appropriately arranged and modulated supportive–expressive psychotherapy, if the ingredients are put together skillfully and imaginatively enough, and if one can ensure truly sufficient concomitant hospital care and management. This last stipulation, concerning the need for adequate (prolonged enough) hospitalization and life management, is of course one of the central keys to the success of the treatment recommendations being here proposed; by that token, it reaffirms a proper role for the psychoanalytic sanatorium. The difference is in the departure from the effort at psychoanalysis per se (even modified psychoanalysis) as the treatment of choice for these "sicker" patients in that setting.[1] On this basis, I have spoken of the failure (in the PRP experience) of the so-called "heroic indications" for psychoanalysis, and am instead inviting a repositioning of the pendulum in its swings over time on this issue—more in the direction of "narrowing indications" for psychoanalysis proper, along the lines marked out by Anna Freud (1954).[2]

1. I have earlier in this section (see Chapter 37, pp. 698–699), as well as at the beginning of the book (see Chapter 2, pp. 26–27), indicated how I reconcile these statements with Kernberg's conceptualizations, built originally on the experience with this same PRP population sample, that these particular (he calls them mostly "borderline") patients require what he describes as a "modified analytic" (as *against* a supportive) treatment approach. This approach, he says should be built around particular kinds of interpretive activities directed to the negative transference components, and to the "here and now" of the pathological defense and resistance phenomena, with the needed support (he calls it "structuralization") delegated to the concomitant hospital management. Briefly, my thesis, presented earlier, is that we have essentially a semantic and not a conceptual difference; we are indeed talking about the same thing, the same patients. In my view, he (over) emphasizes the expressive component of the supportive–expressive psychotherapy, and I try (more evenly) to present both aspects. See my prior discussions for my fuller specification of the distinction I make between *bad* (formless) and *good* (conceptually sound) supportive–expressive psychotherapy.

2. See the discussion by Anna Freud (1954) on p. 610 of her article on this subject, from which I quote here but two salient sentences. The first is as follows: "For years now, our most experienced and finest analysts have concentrated their efforts on opening up new fields for the application of analysis by making the psychotic disorders, the severe depressions, the borderline cases, addictions, perversions, delinquency, etc. amenable to treatment." And the second sentence is this: "If all the skill, knowledge, and pioneering effort which was spent on widening the scope of application of psychoanalysis had been employed instead on intensifying and improving our technique in the original field [hysteric, phobic, and compulsive disorders], I cannot help but feel that, by now, we would find the treatment of the common neuroses child's play, instead of struggling with their technical problems as we have continued to do."

Of course, another major influence also contributed across the board, not just with the sicker patients treated on the basis of "heroic indications," to the overall finding of more limited psychoanalytic outcomes than originally predicted. This was the parallel tendency — resulting from the value commitment to the most intensive and the most thoroughgoingly reconstructive treatment (i.e., psychoanalysis) as the "best" — to estimate as highly as possible the strengths, assets, and islands of health of prospective or potential psychoanalytic treatment cases, and then to predict the optimal achievement and the maximal reach of psychoanalysis as a therapy, rather than perhaps more realistically expectable treatment outcomes. This predictive tendency was based not so much on any underestimation of the scope and severity of the psychopathology presented by the patients, which was quite evident in the comprehensive psychiatric evaluation process. Rather, it was based on the search for compensating factors in the whole array of available Patient and/or Treatment and/or Situational Variables that could together overcome the treatment handicaps resulting from all the discerned telltale evidences of major ego weaknesses, or lack of requisite ego resources, in these severely ill individuals. I have already discussed in detail (e.g., see, pp. 20–21) the ways in which this disposition to predict optimal rather than realistic psychoanalytic treatment outcomes, and to see the extent then to which the analysis would in each instance fully realize its promise, or, alternatively, fall in some way short of it, led in turn to treatment predictions and planning somewhat more optimistic than the predictions and planning engaged in by the psychological testing team on the basis of the psychological projective test protocol data alone (with their more "realistic" assessments of possibilities and limitations).

In other words, then, the predictions made for prospective therapeutic courses and outcomes tended to be for more substantial and more permanent changes (i.e., more "structural changes") in cases where the treatment plans and implementations were to be more expressive–analytic, and where these changes were expected to be more based on thoroughgoing intrapsychic conflict resolution through processes of interpretation, insight, and working through. *Pari passu*, and again in terms of the conventional psychodynamic wisdom concerning the mutative power and reach of the more strictly supportive psychotherapeutic modes, the more supportive the treatment was intended to be (or had to be), the more limited and inherently unstable the anticipated changes were predicted to be. As we have seen in the documentation of the 42 case reports in this book, these predictions were (again, overall) consistently tempered and altered in the actual implementation in the treatment courses. The psychoanalyses as a whole, as well as the psychotherapies as a whole, were systematically modified in the direction of introducing more supportive components in widely varying ways, even though in some instances — with the treatment failures among the so-called "heroic indications" cases in psychoanalysis, for example — one can feel that those particular treatments were not modified far enough in supportive directions (i.e., into actual conversions to explicitly expressive–supportive psychotherapies).

Given these various considerations outlined here, and in terms of the overall outcomes most broadly considered, it is clear that the psychoanalyses as they were carried out with this (overall sicker) Menninger Foundation patient population — that is, modified to the extent that they were with various supportive parameters — accomplished more limited outcomes than predicted and hoped. Moreover, as indicated, a varying amount of the success that *was* achieved was accomplished by nonanalytic (i.e., supportive) means. By contrast the psychotherapies, equally broadly considered, often accomplished a fair amount more (in several of the more spectacular cases, such as those of the Manic–Depressive Physician, the Bohemian Musician, and the Phobic Girl, a great deal more) than initially expected and promised. And with these cases as well, no matter how the admixture of techniques was originally projected, many of the changes took place on the basis of more supportive modes than anticipated.

PSYCHOANALYSIS AND PSYCHOTHERAPY: GENERAL SUMMARY AND DISCUSSION OF RESULTS

Put all together, these treatment outcomes can be summarized in the following broad ways:

1. The treatment results, with patients selected either as suitable for trials at psychoanalysis or as appropriate for varying mixes of expressive–supportive psychotherapeutic approaches, tended with this population sample to converge rather than to diverge in outcome.

2. Across the whole spectrum of treatment courses in the 42 patients — ranging from the most analytic–expressive through the inextricably blended to the most singlemindedly supportive — in almost every instance (the psychoanalyses included), the treatment carried more supportive elements than originally intended, and these supportive elements accounted for more of the changes achieved than had been originally anticipated.

3. The nature of supportive therapy — or, better, the supportive aspects of all psychotherapy, as conceptualized within a psychoanalytic theoretical framework — deserves far more respectful specification in all its forms and variants than has usually been accorded in the psychodynamic literature. This entire volume reporting the PRP experience can be read in one way as an effort to spell out some of these forms and variants in more detail, in relation to cases and case reports considered from various angles.

4. The kinds of changes reached by this cohort of patients — those reached primarily on an uncovering, insight-aiming basis, and those reached primarily on the basis of the opposed covering-up varieties of supportive techniques — often seemed quite indistinguishable from each other in terms of being so-called "real" or "structural" changes in personality functioning, at least by the usually deployed indicators.

How surprising should we take these overall findings to be? It is well known that Freud himself several times expressed reservations about the efficacy of psychoanalysis as a specific therapy for psychic disorders. It is less well known that he expressed the viewpoint consistently over the entire span of his psychoanalytic career. He ended his first specifically psychoanalytic publication, "Studies on Hysteria," written with Breuer (1895), with a direct statement to the expectable limitations of his new method: "But you will be able to convince yourself that much will be gained if we succeed in transforming your hysterical misery into common unhappiness. With a mental life that has been restored to health you will be better armed against that unhappiness" (p. 305). These same limitations on the reach of psychoanalysis *qua* therapy are the central theme of Freud's late great paper, "Analysis Terminable and Interminable" (1937). There, he said that "one ought not to be surprised if it should turn out in the end that the difference between a person who has not been analysed and the behavior of a person after he has been analysed is not so thorough-going as we aim at making it and as we expect and maintain it to be" (p. 228). He continued in the same paper, "Our aim will not be to rub off every peculiarity of human character for the sake of a schematic 'normality', nor yet to demand that the person who has been 'thoroughly analysed' shall feel no passions and develop no internal conflicts. The business of the analysis is to secure the best possible psychological conditions for the functions of the ego; with that it has discharged its task" (p. 250).

In between these two publications, at the height of Freud's synthesizing efforts, he made this same issue the subject of a whole section of one of the "New Introductory Lectures on Psycho-Analysis" (Freud, 1933, pp. 151–157). He began this section by saying that he wanted today to "inquire how much it achieves" (p. 151). In his carefully measured way, he then stated, "Psycho-analysis is really a method of treatment like others. It has its triumphs and its defeats, its difficulties, its limitations, its indications. . . . Its therapeutic successes give grounds neither for boasting nor for being ashamed" (p. 152). And he went on to note that "The expectation that every neurotic phenomenon can be cured may, I suspect, be derived from the layman's belief that the neuroses are something quite unnecessary which have no right whatever to exist" (p. 153). After discussing here, as in "Analysis Terminable and Interminable," a variety of factors that operate to limit the potential efficacy of psychoanalytic therapy, Freud ended this section with a paragraph beginning as follows: "I have told you that psycho-analysis began as a method of treatment; but I did not want to commend it to your interest as a method of treatment but on account of the truths it contains, on account of the information it gives us about what concerns human beings most of all—their own nature" (pp. 156–157).

Since Freud, a very significant analytical literature has accumulated around all these issues: the efficacy, differential indications, goals, relationship of psychoanalysis to psychotherapy, theory of technique and theory of results in analytic therapy, and so forth. A number of key articles, panels, and symposia in this accumulation have been referred to at various points through this book. None of that is repeated here. Rather, I wish first to call attention, just because of its challenging posture, to one characteristically terse and acerbic statement by Glover (1954), part of the round of contributions in the early 1950s. I then quote at greater length from a very contemporary statement by Rangell (1981), one of the central participants both in the series of discussions on this congeries of topics in the early 1950s and in the revived cluster of discussions 25 years later in the late 1970s. Glover (1954), referring to the natural protective reactions of psychoanalysts, pointed out that they so often buttress their own therapeutic claims by at times, "if only by implication, casting doubt on the depth and permanence of the results obtained by non-analytical treatment" (p. 393). He then made this criticism:

> To which it may be added that within their own walls, they gave short shrift to any followers who might be tempted to dally with short-term methods of treatment. This was an unfortunate policy; for like most psychotherapeutists, the psycho-analyst is

a reluctant and inexpert statistician. No accurate records or after-histories of psycho-analytical treatment exist: such rough figures as can be obtained do not suggest that psycho-analysis is notably more successful than other forms of therapy: and in any case none of the figures is corrected for spontaneous remission or resolution of symptoms. (p. 393)

Rangell's (1981) presentation—originally part of a 1979 symposium reconsideration of the similarities and differences between psychoanalysis and dynamic psychotherapy (presented together with talks by two other of the protagonists in the 1954 discussions, Gill and Stone)—has been made from a centrally clinical–theoretical experiential ground. He has put this at the beginning:

> My vantage point in this presentation is experiential: How I have actually conducted psychoanalyses and psychotherapy, as well as the theories which have guided them and which derive from them in turn. . . . In my opinion, we do not look enough to our experience to check new paradigms of theory and excited claims of breakthroughs repetitively embraced by large groups of people. . . . I will present as the background of this twenty-five-year survey a general view of my entire practice. This stands now on some four decades, beginning years before 1954 and extending to the present. In addition to my own amassed clinical material, I would like my readers to consider their clinical experiences. (p. 666)

From this perspective, Rangell has come to conclude that, as compared with the comparison of 1954, the outcomes achievable (and achieved) in psychoanalysis and psychotherapy are closer than previously thought.

> Since the comparisons of 1954, increasing experience and precision of technique have led to a lessening of the differences between the two. Structural change of time-enduring quality, also thought previously to characterize mainly psychoanalysis, can be achieved in analytic therapy carefully chosen and performed. . . . I have been able to reach convincing elements of patients' infantile neuroses in consistent analytic psychotherapy, with results comparable to what I have come to expect in psychoanalysis. An example was the uncovering of a patient's cognitive misperceptions and pathological affects from the circumstances of her birth, her father having committed suicide during her mother's pregnancy with her. (pp. 679–680)

And, further, Rangell has said that there seem also to be fewer clear-cut distinctions between the methods, techniques, and operating mechanisms of psychoanalysis and analytic psychotherapy than has been customarily thought.

> Empirically, it is not uncommon in practice for there to be a gap between the trains of free associations and the infantile experiences to which we believe they lead. While it might be assumed to be a distinguishing mark between psychotherapy and psychoanalysis that such a gap between data and interpretation exists only in psychotherapy, I would like to point out that this also occurs regularly in psychoanalysis and that this point is not sufficiently appreciated. Even in psychoanalysis proper we do not often come to the origin or even later experience of a castration fantasy with its accompanying anxiety, let alone to any such actual castration threat. We approach this formulation from a myriad of directions, from dreams, associations, memories, anxieties, behavior. But the link from current associations or behavior to castration

anxiety is not typically made without what one of my patients described as "the creative leap" which he felt necessary from the analyst to him. (p. 680)

Rangell does not (nor is it the intent of this book to) thereby obliterate all the distinctions between psychoanalysis and even the closest (expressive) psychotherapy. On this, he has said,

> While I have been largely discussing overlapping areas, there are also lines of demarcation between the two fields today as there were in 1954. I said then that there is day and night, although there is dusk (Rangell, 1954). There are still differences in quality and quantity, in consistency and goals, in the uniformity and relentlessness of the method of approach. The distances between the observational data and the genetic mysteries to which they open doors are generally less in psychoanalysis than in dynamic psychotherapy. Again a disclaimer: it is possible in an individual case to bridge this synapse effectively in psychotherapy while this distance may remain wide and the links over it sterile and theoretical even in a well-conducted analysis. (p. 682)

The overall message is that though the differences are real, they are also less (and less clear-cut) than previously felt. Rangell has put it this way:

> As a long-range observation over the years, empirically there is in numbers a large borderland in which therapeutic procedures are practical in a gray area between "psychoanalysis with parameters" and steady intensive psychotherapy which is not quite psychoanalysis. My belief today is that it is still possible to draw a line between the two, although it is also true that in many cases this line is difficult to define. I believe that Gill, Stone, and I are in agreement on the increased effectiveness of deep analytic work in psychoanalytic psychotherapy since our symposium of twenty-five years ago. There is also concurrence that the theory of technique is applied more commonly in both procedures than each of us emphasized in 1954. Beyond that, a sharp divergence has come about as to the direction in which this theory of therapy has developed which is then applied more equally to both. (pp. 682–683)

Given all this, Rangell's concluding statement and caveat perhaps could have been taken for granted:

> The neuroses or borderline states treated by either are explained by one theory. Freud (1933, Lecture XXXIV) pointed out that while there can be many treatments, there is only one understanding. The general theory of neurosogenesis and its derivative theory of technique, which for me has filtered through these twenty-five years, and which serves as the umbrella for the variety of therapies extant today, is what is called, with a multitude of meanings and tones, classical psychoanalytic theory, as this has been modified and expanded during this fertile period. (p. 684)

Clearly, I have quoted at such length from Rangell's recent "state-of-the-art" statement (as he sees it) because of its essential agreement with the thrust and the conclusions of this book based on the PRP experience at The Menninger Foundation. Just as strongly as presented by Rangell, we have operated theoretically and heuristically within the conception of one theoretical psychological explanatory system—psychoanalysis—within which a variety of psychotherapeutic approaches have been developed (psychoanalysis *qua* therapy in the first instance), in relation to the expanding varieties of psychopathology with which we have come over time to deal.

Just because of this established position of psychoanalysis as a theory of human development and personality organization, it will retain a very vital position as a therapy in its most classical (and unaltered form). First, it will remain, as a research instrument, an unparalleled avenue of access to the dynamic and temporal depths of human mental functioning. Closely linked to this, it will still be an unquestioned central aspect of the educational and training process by which individuals become proficient theoretically and clinically, so that they will (aside from their own investigative and teaching proclivities) be able to knowledgeably deploy the whole range of psychoanalytically conceptualized therapeutic approaches — from psychoanalysis proper through the whole spectrum of psychoanalytic expressive and supportive therapies — in relation to the patients differentially suited to them.

Beyond these aspects, the spirit here presented for psychoanalysis as a specific therapy is that of "narrowed indications" — a more circumscribed role for it, and more modest expectations for it in terms of therapeutic goals, than were the case just a few decades back. (See, in this regard, from within the guiding PRP conceptualizations, my 1965 paper, "The Goals of Psychoanalysis.") The counterpart position presented is, of course, that of both the "expanded scope" of psychoanalytic psychotherapy (expressive and supportive), and the enhanced therapeutic, heuristic, and also conceptual dignity to be accorded the supportive psychotherapeutic mode, psychoanalytically formulated. This book has turned out to be a substantial effort in that direction. At this point, I should reiterate a point repeatedly made: The spectrum of retrospectively altered therapeutic indications based on the PRP outcomes, and the observationally recorded technical alterations of so many of these treatment courses into more supportive directions than initially anticipated, all need to be measured against the nature of these patients and their range of presenting psychopathology, as presented in Section III of this book. The application of my conclusions here to the kinds of patients customarily seen within the range of usual outpatient psychoanalytic and psychotherapeutic practice would indeed need to bear that distinction in mind.

Tasks for the Future: Psychotherapy Research

THE IMPOSSIBILITY OF REPLICATING PRP

Difficulty of Obtaining Therapists' Cooperation

However much we may have learned from PRP, it was, as I have called it elsewhere, but "one paradigm" (Wallerstein, 1977b) of psychotherapy research, and one that can probably never be repeated again in comparable form and design. The problems in trying to do so would be many. First, any replication would involve the complete cooperation of a large group of well-trained psychoanalytic therapists who regularly keep detailed case records on their patients in intensive, long-term therapies, and who would uniformly make these records available to this kind of detailed research scrutiny in every single instance, except where a clear-cut contraindication in terms of a patient's clinical state at that time could be established to the satisfaction of a research group. This did, of course, occur in a number of instances in PRP, and was uniformly honored; however, even in such instances the PRP design called for the therapists' participation, *without exception*, in the research assessment of their patients whom *they* had *not* selected for participation in this study. Put this way, it is clear that such conditions simply cannot be met in the private practice arena, where it would depend totally on complete and unswerving voluntary participation of a community of engaged psychotherapists, and over a truly prolonged time. A moment's reflection should make clear that the logistical problems of organization would be too great, and the falling away of a significant segment of the cooperating therapeutic community over time would be inevitable. (Furthermore, it is hard, if not impossible, to imagine how Initial Studies of comparable scope and intensity to PRP's could be accomplished on prospective patients without the knowledge of the therapists-to-be, within the mechanics of the private practice market.)

Lack of Suitable Institutional Settings

These are, of course, all the reasons why such a project as PRP could only come into being in an organized institutional setting in the first place. It is, however, a little less obvious that the overwhelming majority of the major psychiatric institutional settings, including those most logical in many ways for organized research purposes—namely, the university medical centers and their affiliated teaching hospitals—would be almost equally unsuitable. They characteristically (I can almost say universally) do not have a large population of patients in their clinical settings who are seeking and suitable for the most long-term and intensive psychotherapies (including psychoanalysis), nor do any of them have on salaried staff and faculty a large enough corps of appropriately trained and sufficiently experienced therapists to mount any such research effort as PRP. Furthermore, their clinical service commitments are usually to the mental health treatment needs of the immediate communities that they serve (often in formal relationship to organized community mental health centers, with their own very sharp restrictions on the kind of individual therapy—usually very short-term by PRP standards—that they will support). Yet another consideration is that the university training mission necessitates having most treatment in the hands of trainees under supervision (psychiatric residents, psychology and social work students, etc.). In short, very different treatment settings and circumstances prevail in most university centers, and it would be extraordinarily difficult to introduce a PRP-like enterprise into such centers on any scale.

All of this brings the possibilities for the mounting of this kind of research enterprise (and remember that although PRP engaged the participation of as many as 20 investigators at any time, and kept going in its data-gathering phases over a dozen years, it only comprised a sample of 42 patients) down to the handful of psychoanalytically guided private hospitals and sanatoria where patients come and stay for long-term intensive analytic treatments in relation to the available care and management facilities. Even among that small number, several (like Chest-

nut Lodge) specialize more in the intensive therapy of the openly psychotic patients who were excluded from the particular PRP design. The Menninger Foundation may not be the only one of its kind, but there would be hardly any other
institution in which a project of this particular nature could have been conceived
and carried out even when it was.

Present Costs of Such a Project

Another factor that must be borne in mind is that PRP was initiated in the early
1950s, and the large direct costs (about $100,000 per year at the salary levels
of that time) could be raised at that time via private and governmental funding
agencies, Foundations' Fund for Research in Psychiatry, the Ford Foundation, and
the National Institute of Mental Health, as well as being necessarily supplemented
by direct Menninger Foundation institutional support. Today (three decades later),
the costs would be vastly greater and the likelihood of raising the necessary funds
much less, in view of the sharply altered scientific and political climate in relation to supporting any investigation of the mechanisms and the effectiveness of
long-term intensive individual therapy of the neurotically ill.

Changes in Ethical Guidelines for Research

To complete this recounting, the ethical guidelines for the research enterprise have
changed very substantially in these three decades, in ways that would preclude
the repetition today of anything like the PRP design. This issue has already been
discussed in Section I (see Chapter 3, pp. 35–42). At the time that PRP was being created, the climate was one in which the right of scientific institutions to engage
in scientific research was not seriously questioned, as long as the scientists acted
in ways that properly safeguarded the interests of the research subjects (as they,
the scientists, construed them). The requirement of the prior informed consent
of every prospective research subject was not then a regular research stipulation,
nor did Institutional Review Boards exist to monitor research. And in the organization of PRP, we did indeed make every effort to be totally scrupulous about our
ethical obligations as then understood. For example, we created a design that
avoided introducing any systematic intrusion—be it audiotape recording, or the
periodic use of questionnaires, or the like—with the therapists or the patients.
We did this on a variety of grounds, including political ones (see pp. 35–36,
50–51); ethical scientific issues were also involved, however, since *at that time*
we felt that it had not been established satisfactorily that the therapeutic enterprise could be carried out without significant detriment to the patients in the face
of such systematic invasion (albeit ethically controlled) of the privacy of the therapeutic setting. We also did honor those clinical instances where a therapist could
offer persuasive evidence that a patient's clinical situation at the time was such
that research involvement might be disequilibrating. There were several such instances—for example, the Economist, the Phobic Girl, the Housebound Phobic
Woman, and the Fearful Loner at Termination Study, and the Fearful Loner again
at Follow-Up Study.

    With all these considerations in mind, we created the project and its design under the administrative and scientific responsibilities of The Menninger Foundation's Departments of Research and of Adult Psychiatry; we planned the involvement of the therapists and their patients, without their foreknowledge, as a vital element of the design, relying only on our own internal ethical guidelines to ensure the proper protection of all the parties concerned. We took it for granted that there would be no serious scientific or ethical issues raised about this by either the participating therapists or the patients, and throughout the entire period of active data gathering from then (spanning roughly a dozen years until 1966) there were none. Clearly, not everyone was happy about being an involuntary participant in a research study examining the course and outcome of the therapeutic process, and (from the point of view of the therapists) inevitably subjecting the adequacy of their therapeutic work to research exposure. Nobody at that time, however, questioned the right of the institution to conduct the research as it did, and no one refused to participate on such a basis. The therapists and the patients were all of course assured that their anonymity would be preserved, and even those patients who refused to cooperate at one or another of the study times—the Suspended Medical Student at both Termination Study and Follow-Up Study, and the Exhibitionistic Dancer at Termination Study—never questioned the propriety of the research effort. In fact, the Suspended Medical Student always coupled his evasiveness about setting a research appointment schedule with strong protestations about the vital importance of this kind of scientific research. Nor did any one among the patients question the planned follow-up procedures, though one of them, the Bohemian Musician, who had entered into a new marriage during the follow-up period, wanted to keep her previous treatment and her return for the Follow-Up Study visit secret from her husband. She therefore returned to Topeka over a weekend on which he was to be occupied with his business affairs, and she indicated that the visit was for invited consultation services to the rehabilitation center for the handicapped where she had previously worked. And no one among the therapists or the patients questioned our right to bring our findings and conclusions to appropriate scientific publication. To this point, there have been 68 prior publications from PRP, 4 of them concluding books and monographs (see Appendix 4).

In the totally transformed research climate of today, a design like that of PRP, dependent as it was on the participants' not knowing that they would be subject to study until after the fact of the therapy, would be totally counter to the requirement for properly informed consent in advance. Moreover, this would not be the only such design difficulty.

PROBLEMS HIGHLIGHTED BY PRP: TWO POSSIBLE RESEARCH PROJECTS

Given, then, that a project with PRP's method and design cannot now (on both logistical and ethical grounds) be duplicated or replicated anywhere, the next question in any case would be "should it?". Actually, the expenditure of time, effort, and money over the course of PRP was vast (and would today be astronomical). Worthwhile as we (collectively in PRP) felt it to be, in terms of the findings, conclusions, and future directions discernible in it, its scientific successors can well be — in fact, should be — differently constituted. Indeed, it was our original intent that in its organization PRP would be a hypothesis-seeking and hypothesis-creating, and even a method-seeking and method-creating, enterprise. We felt that, if successful, it could lead to the specific delineation of more precise hypotheses (and concomitant methods) that could be subjected in successor projects to more definitive tests, probably by quite different research designs. (See pp. 51–53 for the initial discussion of this issue.)

In fulfillment of that intent, I would like at this point to sketch out two problems (or sets of hypotheses) that have emerged from PRP and are susceptible, in the light of the PRP endeavors, to more precise testing. The one concerns a group of patients with essentially good psychoanalytic outcomes — the cluster of patients with hysterical character neuroses and varying combinations of anxiety, depressive, and phobic symptoms. The other concerns a group of patients with essentially failed psychoanalytic outcomes — the cluster with alcoholic–addictive and paranoid–borderline features.

A Project with Hysterical Patients

There were six patients in PRP for whom hysterical character neuroses were the central dynamic (I do not consider here the six others who to a lesser extent shared the features of this illness picture and personality organization). The central findings that emerged more or less with all of the group have been most clearly described in the case write-up of the Adoptive Mother, who was considered paradigmatic in relation to these phenomena (see pp. 295–302). To recapitulate briefly, these were all patients with clearly neurotic illness and character structure of the kind that seemed to be ideally suited for psychoanalysis; they were thought to have the best prognosis for thoroughgoing resolution of the core neurotic conflicts, maximum enhancement of psychological functioning, and full symptom relief.

To our surprise, these analyses characteristically ended with very good psychotherapeutic results, but with limitation in the psychoanalytic results in terms of conflict resolution and maximal change in manifest behavior patterns. Of even more interest was the fact that the psychoanalytic limitation was regularly in the *same area* of intrapsychic conflict and of psychological functioning (in which it was, of course, varyingly reflected). This was the area of the hostile–dependent pre-Oedipal tie to a malevolent and feared mother imago, and of the hostile identification with her (these six patients happened to be all women). The reasons seemed to vary in the different instances. At times, the ending of the analysis before the time of optimal conflict resolution seemed to come in response to external situational pressures in the patient's life; at other times, it seemed to come in response to an inner dynamic in the patient to "quit while she was ahead," as put in the case of the Adoptive Mother. The result was in every case the same — an unexpectedly limited *analytic* outcome. The case write-up of the Adoptive Mother has delineated with especial clarity the forces that converged to bring about the premature analytic termination: (1) those within the patient, in her mounting inner anxiety as the analytic material threatened to approach the (for her) very disequilibrating press of the pre-Oedipal transference material; (2) those within the treatment, in the technical handling of the case; and (3) those within the life situation, in the husband's mounting pressures to terminate the treatment so that they could move to their permanent city of residence.

The scientific issue that now remains, in the light of these consistent findings in the psychoanalytic treatment of this cluster of cases, is whether this limited psychoanalytic outcome (albeit, from the point of view of most of these patients, an eminently satisfactory therapeutic outcome) represents a regrettable limitation of the analytic method with this group of hysterical patients at this state of the development of the art, a limitation that may not heretofore have been recognized so clearly; or whether, armed with the foreknowledge that such characteristic pressures tend to arise and to push toward premature analytic closures, these pressures can be resolved so that a "fuller" psychoanalytic treatment resolution can be brought about. And, of course, an effort to "hold" the analytic treatment course in the face of these typical pressures toward earlier termination would in turn raise other issues: (1) How disruptive or hurtful might it be to such a patient to try to carry her through the negative pre-Oedipal mother-transferences hitherto so fearfully warded off? (2) If such an endeavor were to prove successful, would the more complete analytic outcome give the patient overall, and over time, a better therapeutic result in terms of more consolidated structural change, less vulnerability to symptom return, and less need for future psychotherapeutic help of any kind?

A more precise test of such ideas would be in the design of another project, an outgrowth of PRP, focused specifically on this kind of patient with a hysterical character neurosis and some combination of anxiety, depressive, and phobic symptoms. Since the clear-cut instances of this constellation numbered 6 of the 42 patients in the total PRP sample, and, even more importantly, 6 of the 12 women taken into analysis (half of that subsample), such a group of patients should not be hard to gather in a variety of settings (including low-cost treatment clinics run by psychoanalytic institutes) where significant numbers of patients are being carefully evaluated for and taken into psychoanalytic treatment. The research design would encompass a randomized division of the patients into two groups. One group would be treated "as is"—that is, as patients of this kind have been customarily treated analytically, including as in the original PRP sample itself. The other group would be treated by an "augmented" analysis, in which the analysts would be prepared with foreknowledge of the hypothesis being tested and of the special factors discerned upon initial examination within the patients and their life situations that would represent in their cases special risks of vulnerability to pressures toward early closure. (Such factors were indeed actually precisely foretold in the initial predictions with the Adoptive Mother.) Of course, the usual research design precautions would need to be taken to ensure that comparable psychoanalytic skill and experience would be brought to bear in the treatments of the patients in both halves of the sample; that the research evaluators (at whatever point or in whatever manner of assessment chosen) would be "blind" in regard to specific issues where that both would be possible and would strengthen the credibility of the findings; and so forth. My purpose here is obviously not even to sketch out the details of the design, so much as to indicate the kind of successor project that could be readily set up both to test and to extend the PRP findings with a particular important group of patients in psychoanalysis.

A Project with Alcoholic–Addictive–Paranoid Patients

The other such illustrative problem to be presented here is that of another and quite different group of analytic cases—the cluster of essentially failed outcomes, the alcoholic–addictive and paranoid–borderline cases who were taken into analysis on the rationale of "heroic indications." Actually, no fewer than 11 of the 42 PRP patients (more than 25%) qualified for this sickest group (see p. 671 for the discussion of the inclusion criteria), and 6 of these 11 were actually recommended for analysis. The reasons why The Menninger Foundation would tend to have so many patients of this kind in its customary patient mix have already been amply discussed (e.g., see, pp. 215–216, 669–670). And the 6, as has been described, did very badly as a group in their psychoanalytic treatments; in fact, 3 of the 6 were among the 6 patients in the PRP population who died of mental-illness-related causes. Only the Housebound Phobic Woman (the only woman among the six) did well in her treatment course, and this has been related to a very prompt conversion of the recommended psychoanalysis to a sustaining supportive–expressive psychotherapy (which is still ongoing).

However, the other 5 of these 11 "sickest" patients, who were recommended for varyingly supportive–expressive psychotherapy rather than psychoanalysis, did not achieve better treatment outcomes: They too contained 4 treatment failures out of the 5, including 2 more of the project deaths. It has been pointed out (see p. 676) that the 5 designated for psychotherapy were collectively even sicker, with even weaker ego organizations and even fewer countervailing strengths and capacities, than those designated for psychoanalysis (which was why the recommendation for psychotherapy instead was made in the first place). More to the point here, however, their treatment failures almost all occurred in the context of grossly inadequate hospitalization and life control (only in the case of the Bitter Spinster was insufficient hospitalization not an issue central to the treatment failure). And it is very clear that there were some striking instances of very good outcomes among the very ill and disordered in expressive–supportive psychotherapies that *were* buttressed by adequate hospital protection and care (four such are cited on p. 728). Collectively, these patients were just as sick in terms of ego impairment, and destructiveness of life behaviors and symptoms, as the patients sent into psychoanalysis on the basis of "heroic indications." In short, it is evident that a recommendation for altered treatment planning in these directions for these alcoholic–addictive and paranoid–borderline patients is very much in order on the basis of the PRP experience.

The successor project here, unlike that with the hysterical character neuroses just mentioned, could not be carried out in an outpatient setting. It would require a psychoanalytic sanatorium setting like The Menninger Foundation, where of course such patients will continue to cluster (witness the 11 out of 42 within the PRP sample). In this project, the split into two groups would not be necessary; in fact, if we took the uniformly dismal PRP experience with the analysis at all seriously, taking a successor group into psychoanalysis under similar circumstances could be regarded as quite improper. Rather, a commitment would need to be made to take such a group of patients into a carefully crafted and managed expressive–supportive psychotherapy, combined with a guaranteed willingness on the part of each patient (and capacity on the part of the family) to maintain an adequate and sufficiently prolonged period of concomitant hospital care and life management. The research evaluation methods, controls for observations, and the like would of course have to be built into this research design, just as for the project for the hysterical character neurosis patients. The payoff in this case would be a systematic long-term improvement in life functioning in some significant number of these patients—enough to contrast sharply with flatly unsuccessful outcomes with the so-called "heroic" psychoanalyses.

It goes without saying that though both of the projects I have proposed here would be created to test the hypotheses generated by the original Menninger Foundation PRP, they could be expected to lead to fuller understandings of how psychological change (broadly conceptualized) is brought about; thus, they would necessarily lead to still further hypotheses for additional testing. What I am saying is that, properly, research vistas in psychoanalytic psychotherapy research will be as vast as in any other field of lively scientific activity.

DIRECTIONS IN WHICH PRP DOES NOT LEAD

However, I should also point out the directions, widely discussed as possibilities in the research–academic and the political–government worlds, in which in my opinion this kind of PRP research does not lead. I feel that the field is either not yet ready for these approaches or will not be able to grow toward them.

The Clinical Trials Approach

The first of these approaches stems from the debate, as much political–economic as research–clinical, over the safety and efficacy of long-term intensive individual psychotherapy (including but by no means limited to psychoanalysis) in relation to the appropriate indications for inclusion of such treatments under both private and governmental health care or health insurance plans. The call here, as already stated at the beginning of this book, is for the so-called "Clinical Trials" approach (see p. 30) for each of the major extant or proposed psychiatric treatment modes—psychotherapy (each of the specifically delineated treatment approaches or theoretical frameworks, as well as all the varieties of individual, family and group therapy, crisis-oriented therapy, brief and long-term therapy, etc.) and psychopharmacology (in all its varieties), both singly and in any plausible or advocated combinations. Each of these forms of treatment is proposed to be examined in relation to all the members of the array of mental illness categories (DSM-III?) with which that treatment plan or combination has a presumed or claimed application and efficacy.

In the Clinical Trials approach, on the basis of the model employed in somatic medicine, there would be all the problems of large enough groups in order to yield worthwhile statistical inferences, proper (untreated?) controls, and "double blindness" to the extent possible; there would also be issues of proper reliability and homogeneity of patient categories, treatment methods, improvement criteria, and so forth. As already stated (see p. 30), NIMH has responded to these pressures by mounting just such a study of depression (narrowly defined), treated by three supposedly very clearly defined and circumscribed specific psychotherapeutic approaches. This study of but one kind of difficulty treated by a narrow band of treatment approaches is currently under way at great expense, over a projected considerable time span, across a multiinstitutional cooperating clinical base; despite all this, there is a growing question whether it will properly be able to answer even the narrow range of questions to which it has been addressed. If we extrapolate from the Clinical Trials study of depression across the whole of psychiatric nosology, and then across the whole array of extant therapeutic approaches (psychosocial and psychopharmacological) that would clamor for inclusion as worthy of public trial and public support, we can readily see the inherent cumbersome unworkability of this approach to the scientific problems of psychotherapy research (the what, how, and why of induced psychological change) on just a logistical basis. There would also be innumerable thorny method and design issues involved in trying to transplant the methodology of the double-blind approach in the drug arena (where placebo pills are such a methodological savior) to the arena of psychological interventions, where one could wonder what being "blind" to the nature of the presumed actively mutative or curative agents would mean. And, of course, I have not looked at the Clinical Trials concept from within the framework of the PRP approach. All of the complexity (not to speak of expense, long-range time commitment, etc.) that is involved in an effort at comprehensive understanding of the internal events of this kind of (and probably every other kind of) intensive psychotherapeutic process, as demonstrated throughout this book, would become truly staggering if two or more processes were to be compared as the Clinical Trials approach demands.

A last side comment, more political than scientific, seems called for in response to the cry that the field of mental health and illness should subject itself to the Clinical Trials approach. Though it is far easier to apply this approach in somatic medicine, where issues of illness categories and of differential therapeutic approaches are far more crystallized, circumscribed, and defined, even there it is not as if the approach has been widely employed and has successfully sifted out the more efficacious treatment approaches from the less, in relation to increasingly precise indications and contraindications. In fact, only a small percentage (some estimate only 10% at most) of established and common medical and surgical regimens have met anywhere near such stringent Clinical Trials criteria. The other 90% or more include, of course, the vast majority of treatments carried out in all aspects of medical and surgical practice, including many of the most drastic and riskiest. And all these treatments are equally routinely, and unquestioningly, included for reimbursement in all the health care and health insurance plans.[1]

---

1. In a recent authoritative review, Parloff (1979), a policy maker in governmental mental health research, addressed the entire range and complexity of issues that beset this intersection of research–clinical and social–political considerations in regard to research into the effectiveness of the various kinds of psychotherapy and the related social policy issues of insurance reimbursement for it. Though the main thrust of the article was to point out that public policy decisions in this arena would be made only in part on the basis of advances in scientific research, and in part on social value judgments regarding need and technical and political feasibility, Parloff did make a number of statements very directly addressed to the issues I am here discussing. On Clinical Trials research, he said,

I have laid heavy emphasis in one of my earlier recommendations on the conduct of clinical trials research, but I do not wish to give the impression that I am unaware of its complexities and

Comparative Assessment of Major Therapeutic Approaches

There is another, and more specifically research–scientific, issue that I wish to discuss here. It has been the subject of lively debate in the field of psychotherapy research long before the surfacing of the Clinical Trials demand, and this debate has been maintained for years in a state of ongoing nonresolution. The issue is that of the strong need (and the question of the corresponding readiness of the field of psychotherapy research) for an overall comparative assessment of various major therapeutic approaches, such as the psychodynamic (psychoanalytic), the behavioral, and the humanistic–existentialist (linked to what had previously been called client-centered). Such an assessment would examine the effectiveness of these approaches with at least the major standard mental and emotional disabilities, and would employ some agreed-upon, standardized criteria for diagnosis, change indicators, outcome criteria, intervention specification, and so on. This, in some ways, does sound similar to the Clinical Trials demand, though it is in fact far from it in scope, in design requirement, or in precision of findings (in relation to strictly economic cost–benefit terms). Rather, it is a plea to try now (in terms of currently available knowledge of illness categories, treatment modalities, and instruments and designs in current use) to get established psychotherapy researchers, working within varying theoretical perspectives on shared protocols, to study therapy processes—with specification and definition to the point of mutual agreement on all of the relevant categories, criteria, instruments, and methods. This intent has actually been a preoccupation in the publications, already discussed, by Strupp and Bergin (Bergin & Strupp, 1972; Strupp & Bergin, 1969a, 1969b) and by Waskow and Parloff (1975). It was also a latent theme, occasionally brought to

---

its dangers. More particularly, I wish to urge that such studies not be designed simply as "horse races" to see which therapy wins. . . . Clinical trials research will be useful to the degree that it permits the study of interactions among patients, therapists, and therapies, and the identification of relevant process variables. (p. 305)

Of the process of getting to that point, Parloff, at an earlier point in the article, stated,

The support of such research [clinical trials research] should in no way deflect from the continued support [by NIMH] of independently initiated, high-quality research on the mechanisms of psychological interventions, nor should it reduce the support for the development and preliminary testing of new and established treatment forms. Such continued independent research is prerequisite to the more definitive clinical trials program. . . . Careful long-term research is required to produce answers to complex research questions. A crash program cannot be expected to yield definitive answers. (p. 303)

And last to be quoted in this series of statements is Parloff's sad commentary,

It is specifically recommended that the researcher attempt to study psychotherapy as it is practiced within community facilities and in private practice. . . . This recommendation grows partly out of the observation that there appears to be a remarkable disparity between the amount of research conducted on behavior therapy and on psychotherapy. This may be due to the fact that behavior therapies are more amenable to rigorous study than are the psychotherapies. In any event, there appears to be an *inverse relationship* between the frequency with which a treatment form is actually used by practitioners and the frequency with which that treatment is studied. (p. 304, italics added)

It should be clear, of course, that I do not concur with Parloff in one particular: I am far less sanguine than he about the (ultimate) possibilities of the Clinical Trials approach in the realm of psychotherapy research.

the surface, in the succession of Conferences on Research in Psychotherapy sponsored by the American Psychological Association (Rubinstein & Parloff, 1959; Shlien, 1968; Strupp & Luborsky, 1962); in fact, a deliberate and successful effort was made to have representatives at each Conference from each of the major therapeutic and research "schools." (See pp. 28–32 for the discussion of this literature.)

Another way to put the whole issue of this particular scientific debate is in terms of the distinction made for PRP by John Benjamin in one of his earliest consultation visits (see pp. 55–56): between pitching the level of inquiry, both conceptually and methodologically, at the level of questions of the theory of *psychoanalytic* therapy or that of the psychoanalytic theory of *all* therapy, whether designedly psychoanalytic in conception or not. We have been operating (clinically in our individual lives as therapists, and as organized psychotherapy researchers in PRP) within the framework of psychoanalytic theory—that is, within the first-specified level of the theory of psychoanalytic therapy. This has been in line with Rapaport's observation that, however comprehensive and well-articulated psychoanalysis can claim to be as a theory of the mind and of personality development, and even of psychopathology (the disorders of the mind), it has nonetheless remained in a much more rudimentary and ad hoc state ("rules of thumb"; see Rapaport, 1960, p. 17) as a theory of therapy. The intent of PRP—along with much of the *psychoanalytic* literature in the field of psychotherapy research—has been to better delineate and articulate a logical and meaningful fabric of the nature of the theory (and technique) of psychoanalytic therapy, and to describe the what, the how, and the why of changes induced by the range of psychoanalytically conceptualized psychotherapeutic approaches (from the most expressive, psychoanalysis, to the most supportive). All of PRP has been carried out within this intent.

By the same token, we have been mindful of comparable efforts being made by research workers within other theoretical traditions (client-centered, behavioral) to study the effectiveness, the reach, and the limitations of their own therapeutic approaches to the mentally and emotionally disturbed, employing their own theoretical framework, their own definitions, their own instruments, and their own criteria for illness and for improvement. The three sequential Conferences on Research in Psychotherapy sponsored by the American Psychological Association, beginning a quarter century ago, were (as just noted) the first major effort to bring together researchers operating within differing theoretical systems, but in relation to presumed common problems of mental illness and change or improvement. The intent was for them to compare notes; to learn from and teach each other; and perhaps to work toward converging methods, designs, definitions, and criteria.

Our own reaction to this effort from within PRP (as investigators who were invited to and made presentation at all three of these Conferences) was that the field as a whole simply was not then, and still is not, truly ready for this kind of broad comparative and synthesizing effort across differing conceptual frameworks. We have felt that we are *all* best off pursuing our research endeavors within our own theoretical frameworks—our own conceptualizations of how the mind hangs together, how it can come to malfunction, and how and to what extent the variety of its possible malfunctions can be ameliorated. In such efforts we can all, within our own perspectives, come to increasing specification and definition of hypotheses and to increasingly precise tests of them, just as I have hoped to demonstrate in this final overview book on the large-scale and long-term labors of PRP. At the present, I feel that with the very incomplete state of knowledge concerning just these issues within each of our perspectives, we can each help to advance the frontiers of knowledge best by such systematic and continued application within our own theoretical frameworks.

Pursuing research within our own perspectives in this manner, of course, would be in fulfillment of the intent marked out in Section II of this book (see Chapter 4, pp. 50–56), where I have discussed those of the basic premises of the project that had to do with the extent of hypothesis-testing as against hypothesis-seeking (or hypothesis-creating) project goals. To this, I have just added my views on the extent to which I feel that we are ready, on the basis of the PRP experience, to advance beyond the level of hypothesis seeking or creating toward more definitive hypothesis testing. In Chapter 4, I have also discussed the relationships of the project aims and activities to the psychoanalytic theoretical framework within which it was constructed; I trust, again, that the PRP experience has added enough evidence and enough delineation and refinement of the operating assumptions of psychoanalytic therapy to carry our conceptualizations of the theory of psychoanalytic therapy some steps beyond the stage characterized by Rapaport as consisting essentially of "rules of thumb" (1960, p. 17).[2] The discussion in Chapter 4 contains a quotation from an article by Gill (1979), which, as I state there, could be taken as a credo for the PRP as a whole and for this book. It is a plea for "systematic and controlled research in the psychoanalytic situation" (p. 286), which is necessary to the solid transition from conceptual advances that are subject to endlessly nonconclusive debate toward solid and secure knowledge upon which successive workers can incrementally build. Here, at the end of the book, I can quote from a similar (if implicit) plea made very recently by Arlow (1981), who speaks not as a formal systematic researcher in psychoanalysis, but as a thoughtful and concerned theoretician and clinician. He has said, "It is no revelation to assert that in the literature of psychoanalysis the production of theory far outstrips the supply of pertinent observational data" (p. 492). It is just this imbalance that this book tries to help correct.

The continued pursuit of this task is, of course, enough of a goal for psychoanalytic psychotherapy research. However, I do want also, in looking beyond it, to talk about the larger element in John Benjamin's distinction—a psychoanalytic theory of therapy, of *all* therapy. At some point, the overall field of psychotherapy research has to be ready for that next major step: the true comparative study of methods and results across theoretical frameworks and across "schools," using the kinds of mutually agreed-upon definitions, instruments, methods, and criteria that will make such comparisons meaningful.

To put this larger problem properly, if psychoanalysis truly provides a more

---

2. In this connection, see also Appendices 1 and 2 (pp. 277–348) in the book by Horwitz (1974) on the Prediction Study, where he outlines the overall Assumptive Tree (and also the detailed individual assumptions) that comprised our guiding conceptualizations about the theory of psychoanalytic therapy as actually employed predictively in PRP. These were subject to testing in accord with the tripartite, logical, if–then–because predictive model, and were then postdictively revised on the basis of our Prediction Study findings into a better-articulated assumptive network, more in accord with the actualities of the PRP clinical experience.

encompassing psychological explanatory framework, then its conceptualizations should be able to explain adequately not only what goes on and how changes come about within psychoanalytically guided therapies (i.e., the more specific theory of psychoanalytic therapy that I have been talking about), but should also be able to explain as well what goes on in other kinds of psychotherapies in which changes and improvements in psychological functioning can be brought about—regardless of the theoretical frameworks within which they have been conceived, have been carried out, and are explained by their proponents. That is, the burden on psychoanalysis as theory then would be to explain in terms of the psychoanalytic theory of therapy how change is brought about by other techniques (e.g., behavioral techniques) in psychoanalytically meaningful terms.

Of course, by the same token, if behavioral theory, or humanistic–existentialist theory, essays to provide a more encompassing psychological explanatory framework (assuming always that our minds operate in unitary ways—not with one kind of conceptualization of psychological mechanisms operative in relation to one arena of intrapsychic and interpersonal functions, and another kind operative in another arena), each of those theoretical systems would have to bear the same burden. Not only would it have to explain satisfactorily the results (changes) it achieves when its own methods are applied to segments of the mentally ill, but it would also have to explain the kinds of results achieved by other theoretical systems (e.g., psychoanalysis and its theory of therapy) when these are applied to the problems of mental illness that it addresses. The ultimate challenge will belong to all of us—to all workers in psychotherapy research, and all workers in research that relates to ("spontaneous" or induced) change in psychological functioning, across all our different theoretical allegiances—at some point. My feeling, of course, already amply expressed, is that we are not at that point yet and that we have more than enough prior tasks still to undertake of the kind I have outlined in this last chapter. The PRP experience, here reported in its final form, is but the beginning of a long journey ahead.

APPENDIX I

The Patient Code

The patients are numbered here in the sequence in which they are designated in the book *Psychotherapy and the Role of the Environment* by Voth and Orth (1973). They are named in accord with the designations in the present book, most of which were devised by Horwitz for his book *Clinical Prediction in Psychotherapy* (1974). Where my designation has been altered—in ways that I feel have even more felicitously captured a salient identifying feature of a patient's personality functioning—from that used by Horwitz, the original designation by Horwitz is set in parentheses. The keying here permits accurate comparison of the same patients as considered in these three books.

1. *Silent Woman*
2. *Car Salesman* (Salesman)
3. *Addicted Doctor*
4. *Claustrophobic Man*
5. *Adoptive Mother*
6. *Snake Phobia Woman*
7. *Script Writer*
8. *Invalided Hypochondriac* (Hypochondriac)
9. *Bohemian Musician* (Bohemian)
10. *Intellectual Fencer* (Fencer)
11. *Divorced Nurse* (Divorced Teacher)
12. *Tantrum Woman*
13. *Bohemian Prep School Boy* (Prep School Boy)
14. *Rebellious Coed* (Rebel Coed)
15. *English Professor*
16. *Alcoholic Heir*
17. *Obedient Husband*
18. *Prince*
19. *Exhibitionistic Dancer* (Dancer)
20. *Suspended Medical Student* (Suspended Student)
21. *Homesick Psychology Student* (Passive Student)
22. *Sociopath*
23. *Peter Pan*
24. *Devoted Son* (Good Son)
25. *Adolescent Grandson* (Grandson)
26. *Medical Scientist* (Medical Specialist)
27. *Alcoholic Raconteur* (Raconteur)
28. *Obese Woman*
29. *Actress* (Thespian)
30. *Manic-Depressive Physician* (Playboy)
31. *Heiress*
32. *Phobic Woman*
33. *Alcoholic Doctor*
34. *Bitter Spinster* (Spinster)

35. *Movie Lady*
36. *Sexual Masochist* (Covert Addict)
37. *Fearful Loner* (Loner)
38. *Phobic Girl*
39. *Masochistic Editor* (Editor)

40. *Economist* (Historian)
41. *Housebound Phobic Woman*
    (Travel Phobia Woman)
42. *Involutional Woman*

APPENDIX II

The Patient Outcomes

Psychoanalysis — Not Modified (10)

	VERY GOOD	MODERATE	EQUIVOCAL	FAILED
Snake Phobia Woman	X			
Tantrum Woman	X			
Silent Woman		X		
Divorced Nurse		X		
Prince		X		
Obese Woman		X		
Devoted Son			X	
Script Writer				X
Alcoholic Heir				X
Suspended Medical Student				X

Psychoanalysis — Modified (6)

	VERY GOOD	MODERATE	EQUIVOCAL	FAILED
Adoptive Mother	X			
English Professor	X			
Medical Scientist	X			
Phobic Woman	X			
Peter Pan				X
Alcoholic Doctor				X

Psychoanalysis — Converted to Psychotherapy (6)

	VERY GOOD	MODERATE	EQUIVOCAL	FAILED
Movie Lady	X			
Housebound Phobic Woman	X			
Economist		X		
Alcoholic Raconteur			X	
Heiress			X	
Masochistic Editor				X

Psychotherapy (Expressive and Supportive) (20)

Claustrophobic Man	X			
Bohemian Musician	X			
Intellectual Fencer	X			
Obedient Husband	X			
Actress	X			
Manic-Depressive Physician	X			
Fearful Loner	X			
Phobic Girl	X			
Involutional Woman	X			
Rebellious Coed		X		
Homesick Psychology Student		X		
Sexual Masochist		X		
Bohemian Prep School Boy			X	
Exhibitionistic Dancer			X	
Adolescent Grandson			X	
Car Salesman				X
Addicted Doctor				X
Invalided Hypochondriac				X
Sociopath				X
Bitter Spinster				X

Note. A number of cautions, all discussed within the text of the book itself, should be kept in mind in reading this table. First, the fourfold categorization of outcomes—"very good," "moderate," "equivocal," and "failed"—is quite coarse, and in a fair number of instances the placements are very arbitrary. However, I do not feel that there is any systematic bias in these placements, and the overall distribution among categories seems to be a good approximation of the actual overall results. Second, and similarly, the groupings within the psychoanalytic cases—"not modified," "modified," and "converted" analyses—are again quite coarse, especially since with almost every one of these patients there was some significant modification or introduction of "parameters." These were all quantitative shadings and arbitrary dividing lines in the first place, and relative distinctions in the second place; that is, as compared with psychoanalytic patients in usual outpatient practice, almost all of these patients had more "modifications" introduced.

Also, of course, the individual case write-ups should be consulted (see Appendix 3 for the page references) in order to understand not only why particular outcomes were adjudged to be in the particular categories here assigned, but also what the judgments mean. Here are two examples of the kind of errors of understanding that can result from using the data in this table without reference to the case write-ups: (1) The Silent Woman is listed here as having been in an unmodified analysis and as having a moderately good result. However, she was in analysis (relatively unmodified, to be sure) for only a year, and her moderate improvement was against rather than because of the analytic work; she is described in Chapter 20 in connection with the antitransference cure. (2) The Alcoholic Reconteur is listed here in the group whose analyses were converted to psychotherapy. The case write-up makes clear that he disrupted his analytic treatment at the point that the analyst was finally insisting on an irreversible conversion of the analysis to a supportive–expressive therapy as the only strategy that might give promise of rescuing a failing therapeutic situation; he therefore was never actually *in* a sustained psychotherapy other than analysis.

APPENDIX III

The Concordance of the Patients

The patients are listed here by number and designation as per Appendix 1. Immediately after each designation, in italics, are listed the pages in which the patient's full case description is given. This is followed by the listing then, in order of appearance, of every page on which reference is made to that patient (which in some instances carries over then to the following page(s).

1. Silent Woman: *445–451*, 70, 85, 138, 178, 180, 217, 243, 288, 293, 439, 543, 580, 622, 657, 659, 693, 707, 708, 717, 750.
2. Car Salesman: *567–570*, 38, 67, 70, 98, 122, 125, 126, 128, 129, 143, 170, 173, 177, 180, 196, 201, 210, 217, 218, 223, 242, 252, 253, 278, 345, 362, 405, 519, 535, 560, 562, 563, 578, 590, 594, 595, 597, 608, 647, 655, 665, 676, 677, 715.
3. Addicted Doctor: *564–567*, 38, 70, 85, 98, 121, 127, 130, 141, 155, 170, 173, 177, 180, 193, 195, 197, 201, 210, 211, 218, 221, 223, 225, 230, 241, 252, 253, 257, 259, 278, 362, 363, 405, 519, 534, 535, 562, 563, 570, 572, 578, 581, 590, 594, 595, 597, 612, 623, 647, 665, 676, 677, 686, 715, 716, 722.
4. Claustrophobic Man: *398–403*, 28, 62, 122, 123, 134, 137, 149, 153, 170, 180, 211, 229, 239, 391, 398, 413, 521, 522, 535, 594, 616, 633, 648, 649, 664, 690.
5. Adoptive Mother: *295–302*, 28, 62, 65, 71, 97, 110, 124, 129, 134, 136, 148, 156, 160, 170, 180, 187, 203, 213, 229, 238, 258, 294, 295, 302, 305, 310, 514, 517, 518, 533, 561, 580, 592, 610, 611, 612, 621, 643, 656, 710, 723, 725, 726, 727, 738, 739.
6. Snake Phobia Woman: *308–314*, 27, 39, 62, 63, 65, 71, 122, 136, 150, 157, 169, 172, 179, 180, 186, 207, 208, 213, 230, 231, 234, 247, 294, 308, 314, 517, 519, 521, 561, 581, 617, 656, 710.
7. Script Writer: *556–560*, 62, 85, 98, 122, 126, 148, 157, 160, 166, 180, 185, 213, 216, 221, 238, 244, 245, 248, 258, 260, 330, 343, 518, 561, 573, 578, 594, 604, 623, 672, 674.
8. Invalided Hypochondriac: *553–556*, 38, 85, 98, 129, 133, 138, 142, 144, 148, 170, 174, 180, 204, 223, 231, 234, 237, 242, 252, 344, 405, 519, 534, 536, 560, 561, 573, 578, 594, 595, 597, 612, 646, 664.

9. Bohemian Musician: *382–388*, 28, 40, 62, 89, 106, 124, 134, 141, 145, 148, 150, 153, 173, 180, 217, 220, 224, 328, 375, 413, 467, 468, 477, 514, 535, 536, 575, 593, 602, 605, 615, 624, 628, 631, 643, 696, 710, 712, 717, 728, 730, 737.

10. Intellectual Fencer: *439–445*, 28, 36, 38, 63, 65, 88, 89, 122, 127, 161, 177, 180, 192, 222, 238, 439, 445, 446, 514, 522, 523, 531, 535, 536, 574, 577, 579, 582, 591, 605, 606, 628, 693, 708, 709, 727, 728.

11. Divorced Nurse: *314–321*, 124, 133, 136, 139, 144, 156, 171, 179, 180, 186, 207, 208, 213, 231, 235, 238, 258, 294, 308, 354, 362, 467, 468, 517, 519, 579, 593, 605, 611, 618, 622, 656, 695, 710, 722.

12. Tantrum Woman: *302–307*, 62, 68, 122, 124, 134, 136, 147, 148, 156, 162, 169, 179, 180, 186, 196, 231, 294, 310, 517, 520, 538, 539, 540, 574, 583, 590, 592, 599, 602, 603, 608, 622, 648, 656, 710.

13. Bohemian Prep School Boy: *523–529*, 62, 65, 66, 67, 69, 70, 85, 97, 127, 133, 141, 145, 149, 167, 170, 177, 180, 197, 225, 232, 233, 255, 256, 328, 331, 343, 497, 518, 520, 522, 523, 538, 540, 550, 552, 561, 588, 593, 604, 614, 666.

14. Rebellious Coed: *483–489*, 63, 85, 130, 149, 163, 170, 173, 180, 202, 203, 240, 248, 253, 255, 478, 490, 522, 523, 531, 580, 590, 593, 599, 602, 603, 608, 665, 695, 697.

15. English Professor: *279–283*, 69, 124, 129, 133, 137, 143, 169, 177, 180, 187, 229, 286, 329, 344, 404, 412, 514, 519, 588, 603, 616, 622, 644, 662, 677, 691, 713, 714, 722.

16. Alcoholic Heir: *345–349*, 38, 63, 66, 67, 70, 85, 89, 98, 125, 126, 128, 147, 151, 154, 155, 160, 165, 171, 180, 186, 196, 213, 217, 223, 230, 231, 232, 239, 256, 330, 343, 344, 345, 349, 350, 351, 352, 354, 362, 497, 516, 518, 520, 562, 563, 570, 577, 582, 590, 594, 597, 613, 622, 647, 671, 673.

17. Obedient Husband: *434–439*, 70, 121, 139, 160, 169, 172, 177, 180, 227, 230, 246, 247, 354, 541, 577, 582, 583, 611, 622, 630, 692.

18. Prince: *322–329*, 33, 121, 131, 140, 169, 180, 209, 229, 238, 343, 514, 590, 603, 608, 660, 662, 663, 712, 713, 724, 725.

19. Exhibitionistic Dancer: *504–510*, 36, 38, 65, 68, 88, 130, 140, 171, 180, 204, 210, 217, 224, 238, 244, 245, 248, 255, 256, 328, 522, 523, 544, 550, 578, 579, 582, 596, 597, 613, 628, 666, 696, 715, 737.

20. Suspended Medical Student: *363–370*, 36, 38, 39, 88, 98, 124, 126, 144, 150, 165, 170, 175, 176, 180, 186, 197, 213, 219, 243, 257, 258, 259, 330, 343, 467, 468, 478, 516, 518, 530, 533, 534, 562, 563, 572, 573, 579, 590, 596, 597, 606, 610, 611, 629, 647, 671, 673, 685, 706, 707, 717, 737.

21. Homesick Psychology Student: *417–421*, 129, 130, 135, 139, 162, 180, 192, 229, 243, 255, 354, 413, 522, 523, 531, 535, 575, 601, 629, 632, 645, 667, 692, 709.

22. Sociopath: *545–550*, 38, 64, 68, 88, 89, 121, 125, 130, 132, 138, 143, 151, 154, 158, 171, 174, 180, 194, 197, 201, 202, 203, 204, 219, 224, 227, 241, 344, 534, 535, 536, 562, 573, 575, 581, 596, 597, 643, 666, 676, 677, 715.

23. Peter Pan: *426–432*, 28, 39, 62, 65, 98, 129, 135, 138, 146, 151, 161, 167, 169, 180, 188, 209, 214, 218, 220, 221, 232, 238, 247, 253, 255, 256, 331, 343, 413, 467, 468, 518, 520, 522, 523, 534, 552, 553, 560, 562, 563, 571, 572, 573, 578, 590, 593, 597, 604, 608, 612, 621, 629, 633, 647, 657, 685, 692, 706, 707, 717.

24. Devoted Son: *283–287*, 135, 137, 178, 180, 186, 187, 194, 196, 212, 240, 308, 328, 329, 343, 404, 477, 514, 519, 574, 589, 600, 608, 621, 633, 638, 640, 646, 661, 663, 677, 691, 712, 713, 721, 726.

25. Adolescent Grandson: *490–497*, 62, 66, 67, 97, 131, 133, 149, 150, 154, 165, 170, 172, 180, 192, 195, 222, 241, 248, 255, 256, 490, 522, 523, 534, 536, 542, 551, 561, 594, 600, 604, 644, 666, 667, 696.

26. Medical Scientist: *266–271*, 42, 60, 71, 122, 126, 127, 132, 137, 152, 161, 170, 172, 175, 176, 180, 187, 198, 212, 216, 220, 221, 231, 257, 258, 266, 520, 534,

542, 563, 577, 582, 590, 606, 607, 622, 625, 628, 643, 680, 685, 711, 728.

27. Alcoholic Raconteur: *498–504*, 64, 67, 77, 89, 98, 121, 125, 126, 134, 143, 146, 166, 169, 173, 174, 181, 191, 193, 200, 201, 206, 207, 212, 266, 330, 343, 510, 518, 531, 532, 533, 534, 593, 604, 614, 623, 626, 627, 628, 639, 644, 654, 655, 662, 671, 674, 696, 706, 715, 750.

28. Obese Woman: *288–293*, 19, 28, 121, 131, 135, 136, 138, 147, 151, 155, 161, 164, 169, 181, 242, 248, 288, 294, 295, 475, 478, 517, 520, 521, 530, 533, 577, 579, 609, 621, 710.

29. Actress: *478–483*, 62, 66, 121, 130, 138, 140, 149, 170, 181, 192, 203, 210, 222, 237, 240, 241, 248, 252, 255, 328, 478, 489, 490, 522, 523, 532, 580, 592, 664, 665, 695, 697, 727.

30. Manic–Depressive Physician: *460–466*, 28, 69, 70, 121, 125, 138, 145, 181, 217, 241, 257, 258, 267, 460, 477, 514, 536, 563, 592, 606, 694, 728, 730.

31. Heiress: *421–426*, 28, 63, 66, 67, 68, 70, 96, 124, 133, 138, 160, 181, 190, 206, 207, 212, 213, 230, 237, 238, 251, 256, 266, 331, 343, 413, 426, 497, 518, 533, 576, 577, 581, 592, 611, 623, 632, 649, 658, 662, 692, 704, 705, 706, 725.

32. Phobic Woman: *271–277*, 69, 123, 127, 132, 136, 142, 148, 171, 172, 175, 181, 188, 220, 222, 230, 243, 266, 278, 294, 295, 308, 404, 412, 517, 519, 521, 532, 534, 575, 600, 615, 622, 645, 677, 680, 685, 691, 710.

33. Alcoholic Doctor: *332–336*, 38, 62, 88, 89, 98, 122, 126, 128, 130, 147, 161, 164, 170, 173, 181, 188, 193, 200, 213, 217, 221, 230, 231, 232, 239, 257, 258, 259, 330, 332, 343, 347, 351, 354, 362, 467, 468, 516, 518, 520, 531, 532, 562, 563, 570, 577, 582, 590, 597, 607, 619, 623, 649, 654, 671, 672, 673, 714.

34. Bitter Spinster: *349–353*, 127, 152, 181, 192, 197, 202, 203, 214, 229, 239, 254, 258, 260, 278, 330, 343, 344, 345, 362, 374, 404, 490, 518, 519, 531, 534, 535, 536, 573, 593, 600, 604, 623, 676, 677, 678, 686, 691, 714, 722, 740.

35. Movie Lady: *413–417*, 95, 122, 123, 133, 134, 153, 156, 168, 179, 181, 189, 196, 206, 212, 229, 239, 258, 266, 329, 344, 354, 362, 413, 451, 533, 575, 592, 617, 618, 621, 632, 658, 662, 692, 704.

36. Sexual Masochist: *405–412*, 28, 66, 67, 68, 69, 70, 126, 128, 131, 137, 138, 146, 148, 154, 155, 171, 173, 181, 193, 194, 197, 211, 225, 238, 256, 278, 330, 343, 405, 412, 413, 497, 498, 514, 518, 519, 536, 539, 562, 576, 581, 589, 608, 609, 611, 613, 623, 627, 628, 633, 637, 638, 640, 644, 655, 676, 677, 679, 691, 715, 716, 721, 726, 728.

37. Fearful Loner: *452–458*, 36, 38, 70, 85, 88, 99, 122, 133, 137, 143, 153, 162, 181, 194, 198, 227, 239, 246, 250, 330, 343, 404, 405, 518, 535, 577, 589, 596, 597, 608, 619, 623, 634, 636, 640, 649, 650, 665, 691, 694, 736.

38. Phobic Girl: *468–476*, 38, 85, 88, 99, 123, 131, 134, 137, 138, 170, 181, 210, 232, 255, 404, 413, 468, 490, 520, 521, 522, 523, 531, 536, 588, 595, 596, 597, 617, 634, 635, 640, 695, 709, 730, 736.

39. Masochistic Editor: *354–362*, 63, 64, 70, 96, 125, 128, 130, 139, 149, 155, 169, 173, 177, 178, 181, 190, 206, 207, 212, 217, 221, 242, 266, 330, 343, 354, 363, 516, 518, 532, 534, 573, 580, 588, 592, 608, 612, 662, 663, 671, 674, 684, 706.

40. Economist: *336–343*, 38, 85, 88, 99, 125, 128, 137, 143, 151, 161, 166, 168, 181, 190, 193, 206, 207, 212, 229, 230, 266, 278, 308, 330, 332, 343, 351, 398, 404, 405, 412, 477, 516, 518, 519, 530, 580, 589, 595, 596, 597, 608, 619, 623, 634, 635, 636, 640, 649, 650, 663, 675, 677, 684, 691, 704, 705, 721, 726, 736.

41. Housebound Phobic Woman: *391–398*, 38, 65, 68, 69, 70, 85, 88, 97, 99, 123, 127, 131, 134, 136, 142, 165, 170, 177, 181, 191, 193, 206, 207, 212, 213, 237, 238, 249, 266, 278, 308, 391, 404, 405, 412, 451, 467, 468, 475, 504, 516, 519, 520, 521, 532, 589, 595, 596, 597, 607, 619, 623, 633, 634, 636, 640, 649, 655, 662, 663, 671, 677, 678, 679, 684, 690, 691, 704, 721, 726, 736, 740.

42. Involutional Woman: *375–382*, 62, 70, 85, 88, 99, 121, 129, 137, 146, 147, 181, 217, 220, 226, 229, 237, 243, 250, 375, 387, 404, 413, 434, 522, 535, 590, 596, 601, 610, 611, 613, 634, 635, 640, 664, 692, 696.

Bibliography of the Psychotherapy Research Project

1–5. Wallerstein, Robert S., Robbins, Lewis L., Sargent, Helen D., and Luborsky, Lester. (1956). The Psychotherapy Research Project of The Menninger Foundation: Rationale, Method and Sample Use. First Report. *Bulletin of The Menninger Clinic*, 20:221–278.

  I. Orientation. Lewis L. Robbins and Robert S. Wallerstein, pp. 223–225.
  II. Rationale. Helen D. Sargent, pp. 226–233.
  III. Design. Helen D. Sargent, pp. 234–238.
  IV. Concepts. Robert S. Wallerstein and Lewis L. Robbins, pp. 239–262.
  V. Sample Use of Method. Lester Luborsky and Helen D. Sargent, pp. 262–276.

6–8. The Psychotherapy Research Project of The Menninger Foundation: Second Report. (1958). *Bulletin of The Menninger Clinic*, 22:115–166.

  I. Further Notes on Design and Concepts. Robert S. Wallerstein and Lewis L. Robbins, pp. 117–125.
  II. Treatment Variables. Lester Luborsky, Michalina Fabian, Bernard H. Hall, Ernst Ticho, and Gertrude R. Ticho, pp. 126–147.
  III. Situational Variables. Helen D. Sargent, Herbert C. Modlin, Mildred T. Faris, and Harold M. Voth, pp. 148–166.

9. Robbins, Lewis L., and Wallerstein, Robert S. (1959). The Research Strategy and Tactics of the Psychotherapy Research Project of The Menninger Foundation and the Problem of Controls. In *Research in Psychotherapy, Vol. 1*, Rubinstein, Eli A., and Parloff, Morris B. (eds.), pp. 27–43, American Psychological Association, Washington, D.C.

10–12. The Psychotherapy Research Project of The Menninger Foundation: Third Report. (1960). *Bulletin of The Menninger Clinic*, 24:157–216.

  I. Helen D. Sargent and the Psychotherapy Research Project. Robert S. Wallerstein, pp. 159–163.
  II. Operational Problems of Psychotherapy Research: I. Initial Studies. Robert S. Wallerstein and Lewis L. Robbins, pp. 164–189.
  III. Operational Problems of Psychotherapy Research: II. Termination Studies. Bernard H. Hall and Robert S. Wallerstein, pp. 190–214.

13. Sargent, Helen D. (1960). Methodological Problems of Follow-Up Studies in Psychotherapy Research. *American Journal of Orthopsychiatry, 30*:495–506.

14. Mayman, Martin, and Faris, Mildred. (1960). Early Memories as Expressions of Relationship Paradigms. *American Journal of Orthopsychiatry, 30*:507–520.

15. Sargent, Helen D. (1961). Intrapsychic Change: Methodological Problems in Psychotherapy Research. *Psychiatry, 24*:93–108.

16. Wallerstein, Robert S. (1961). Report of the Psychotherapy Research Project of The Menninger Foundation: January 1954–July 1961. *International Mental Health Research Newsletter, 3*:12–15.

17. Voth, Harold M., Modlin, Herbert C., and Orth, Marjorie H. (1962). Situational Variables in the Assessment of Psychotherapeutic Results. *Bulletin of The Menninger Clinic, 26*:73–81.

18. Siegal, Richard S., and Ehrenreich, Gerald A. (1962). Inferring Repression from Psychological Tests. *Bulletin of The Menninger Clinic, 26*:82–91.

19. Siegal, Richard S., Rosen, Irwin C., and Ehrenreich, Gerald A. (1962). The Natural History of an Outcome Prediction. *Journal of Projective Techniques, 26*:112–116.

20. Luborsky, Lester. (1962). Clinicians' Judgments of Mental Health: A Proposed Scale. *Archives of General Psychiatry, 7*:407–417.

21. Luborsky, Lester. (1962). The Patient's Personality and Psychotherapeutic Change. In *Research in Psychotherapy, Vol. 2*, Strupp, Hans H., and Luborsky, Lester (eds.), pp. 115–133, American Psychological Association, Washington, D.C.

22. Siegal, Richard S., and Rosen, Irwin C. (1962). Character Style and Anxiety Tolerance: A Study in Intrapsychic Change. In *Research in Psychotherapy, Vol. 2*, Strupp, Hans H., and Luborsky, Lester (eds.), pp. 206–217, American Psychological Association, Washington, D.C.

23. Wallerstein, Robert S. (1963). The Problem of the Assessment of Change in Psychotherapy. *International Journal of Psycho-Analysis, 44*:31–41.

24. Wallerstein, Robert S. (1964). The Role of Prediction in Theory Building in Psychoanalysis. *Journal of the American Psychoanalytic Association, 12*:675–691.

25. Rosen, Irwin C. (1965). Choices in Psychotherapy Research. *British Journal of Medical Psychology, 38*:253–260.

26. Wallerstein, Robert S. (1965). The Goals of Psychoanalysis: A Survey of Analytic Viewpoints. *Journal of the American Psychoanalytic Association, 13*:748–770.

27. Wallerstein, Robert S. (1966). The Psychotherapy Research Project of The Menninger Foundation: An Overview at the Midway Point. In *Methods of Research in Psychotherapy*, Gottschalk, Louis A., and Auerbach, Arthur H. (eds.), pp. 500–516, Appleton-Century-Crofts, New York.

28. Kernberg, Otto. (1965). Three Methods of Research on Psychoanalytic Treatment. *International Mental Health Research Newsletter, 7*:11–13.

29. Wallerstein, Robert S. (1966). The Current State of Psychotherapy: Theory, Practice, Research. *Journal of the American Psychoanalytic Association, 14*:183–225. (Spanish translation: Las Nuevas Direcciones de la Psicoterapia: Teoría, Práctica, Investigación. Paidos, Buenos Aires, 1972, 92 pp.)

30. Horwitz, Leonard, and Appelbaum, Ann. (1966). A Hierarchical Ordering of Assumptions about Psychotherapy. *Psychotherapy, 3*:71–80.

31. Sargent, Helen D., Coyne, Lolafaye, Wallerstein, Robert S., and Holtzman, Wayne H. (1967). An Approach to the Quantitative Problems of Psychoanalytic Research. *Journal of Clinical Psychology, 23*:243–291.

32. Siegal, Richard S. (1967). A Psychological Test Study of Personality Change: The Psychotherapy Research Project of The Menninger Foundation. *International Mental Health Research Newsletter, 9*:2, 6, 7.

33. Mayman, Martin. (1967). Object-Representations and Object-Relationships in Rorschach Responses. *Journal of Projective Techniques, 31*:17–24.

34. Kernberg, Otto. (1967). Borderline Personality Organization. *Journal of the American Psychoanalytic Association, 15*:641–685.

35. Wallerstein, Robert S. (1968). A Talk about the Psychotherapy Research Project of The Menninger Foundation. *Nederlands Tijdschrift voor de Psychologie en haar Grensgebieden, 23*:137–164.

36. Wallerstein, Robert S. (1968). The Psychotherapy Research Project of The Menninger Foundation: A Semi-Final View. In *Research in Psychotherapy, Vol. 3*, Shlien, John M. (ed.), pp. 584–605, American Psychological Association, Washington, D.C.

37. Sargent, Helen D., Horwitz, Leonard, Wallerstein, Robert S., and Appelbaum, Ann. (1968). *Prediction in Psychotherapy Research: A Method for the Transformation of Clinical Judgments into Testable Hypotheses* (Psychological Issues 6: Monograph 21). International Universities Press, New York, 146 pp.

38. Kernberg, Otto. (1968). The Treatment of Patients with Borderline Personality Organization. *International Journal of Psycho-Analysis, 49*:600–619.

39. Mayman, Martin. (1968). Early Memories and Character Structure. *Journal of Projective Techniques, 32*:303–316.

40. Appelbaum, Stephen A., Coyne, Lolafaye, and Siegal, Richard S. (1969). Change in IQ during and after Long-Term Psychotherapy. *Journal of Projective Techniques, 33*:290–297.

41. Siegal, Richard S. (1969). What Are Defense Mechanisms? *Journal of the American Psychoanalytic Association, 17*:785–807.

42. Siegal, Richard S. (1969). Quantifications and Psychoanalytic Research. *Bulletin of The Menninger Clinic, 33*:146–153.

43. Robbins, Lewis L. (1969). Traditional reductionism Is Unsatisfactory. *International Journal of Psychiatry, 7*:153–156.

44. Wallerstein, Robert S. (1969). Introduction to Panel on Psychoanalysis and Psychotherapy: The Relationship of Psychoanalysis to Psychotherapy—Current Issues. *International Journal of Psycho-Analysis, 50*:117–126.

45. Kernberg, Otto. (1970). Factors in the Psychoanalytic Treatment of Narcissistic Personalities. *Journal of the American Psychoanalytic Association, 18*:51–85.

46. Kernberg, Otto. (1970). A Psychoanalytic Classification of Character Pathology. *Journal of the American Psychoanalytic Association, 18*:800–822.

47. Appelbaum, Stephen A., Coyne, Lolafaye, and Siegal, Richard S. (1970). Routes to Change in IQ during and after Long-Term Psychotherapy. *Journal of Nervous and Mental Disease, 151*:310–315.

48. Kernberg, Otto. (1971). Prognostic Considerations Regarding Borderline Personality Organization. *Journal of the American Psychoanalytic Association, 19*:595–635.

49. Wallerstein, Robert S., and Sampson, Harold. (1971). Issues in Research in the Psychoanalytic Process. *International Journal of Psycho-Analysis, 52*:11–50. (Condensation in *Currents in Psychoanalysis*, Marcus, Irwin M. [ed.], pp. 265–302, International Universities Press, New York, 1971.)

50. Kernberg, Otto F., Burstein, Esther D., Coyne, Lolafaye, Appelbaum, Ann, Horwitz, Leonard, and Voth, Harold. (1972). Psychotherapy and Psychoanalysis: Final Report of The Menninger Foundation's Psychotherapy Research Project. *Bulletin of The Menninger Clinic, 36*:1–275.

51. Appelbaum, Ann. (1972). A Critical Re-Examination of the Concept 'Motivation for Change' in Psychoanalytic Treatment. *International Journal of Psycho-Analysis, 53*: 51–59.

52. Voth, Harold M., and Orth, Marjorie H. (1973). *Psychotherapy and the Role of the Environment.* Behavioral Publications, New York, 354 pp.

53. Appelbaum, Stephen A. (1973). Psychological-Mindedness: Word, Concept and Essence. *International Journal of Psycho-Analysis, 54*:35–46.

54. Kernberg, Otto. (1973). Summary and Conclusions of "Psychotherapy and Psychoanalysis: Final Report of The Menninger Foundation's Psychotherapy Research Project." *International Journal of Psychiatry, 11*:62–77.

55. Horwitz, Leonard. (1974). *Clinical Prediction in Psychotherapy.* Jason Aronson, New York, 372 pp.

56. Luborsky, Lester, and Bachrach, Henry. (1974). Factors Influencing Clinicians' Judgments of Mental Health: Eighteen Experiences with the Health–Sickness Rating Scale. *Archives of General Psychiatry, 31*:292–299.

57. Luborsky, Lester. (1975). Clinicians' Judgments of Mental Health: Specimen Case Descriptions and Forms for the Health–Sickness Rating Scale. *Bulletin of The Menninger Clinic, 39*:448–480.

58. Appelbaum, Stephen A. (1975). The Idealization of Insight. *International Journal of Psychoanalytic Psychotherapy,* 4:272–303.

59. Appelbaum, Stephen A. (1975). Questioning the Question: The Effectiveness of Psychotherapy. *Interamerican Journal of Psychology,* 1–2:213–225.

60. Kernberg, Otto. (1976). Some Methodological and Strategic Issues in Psychotherapy Research: Research Implications of The Menninger Foundation's Psychotherapy Research Project. In *Evaluation of Psychological Therapies,* Spitzer, Robert L., and Klein, Donald F. (eds.), pp. 23–38, Johns Hopkins University Press, Baltimore.

61. Robbins, Lewis L. (1976). The Specificity of Psychoanalytic Concepts for Understanding Psychotherapy. In *Evaluation of Psychological Therapies,* Spitzer, Robert L., and Klein, Donald F. (eds.), pp. 39–46, Johns Hopkins University Press, Baltimore.

62. Harty, Michael, and Horwitz, Leonard. (1976). Therapeutic Outcome as Rated by Patients, Therapists, and Judges. *Archives of General Psychiatry,* 33:957–961.

63. Appelbaum, Stephen A. (1976). The Dangerous Edge of Insight. *Psychotherapy, 13*: 202–206.

64. Appelbaum, Stephen A. (1977). *The Anatomy of Change.* Plenum Press, New York, 308 pp.

65. Wallerstein, Robert S. (1977). Psychotherapy Research: One Paradigm. In *Communication and Social Interaction,* Ostwald, Peter (ed.), pp. 189–202, Grune & Stratton, New York.

66. Colson, Donald, Lewis, Lisa, and Horwitz, Leonard. (in press). Negative Effects in Psychotherapy and Psychoanalysis. In *Above All Do No Harm: Negative Outcome in Psychotherapy,* Mays, D., and Franks, C. (eds.)

67. Coyne, Lolafaye. (unpublished manuscript). *The Quantitative Measurement of Change.* The Menninger Foundation, Topeka, Kansas, 19 pp.

68. Horwitz, Leonard. (unpublished manuscript). *Therapist's Personality and Levels of Competence.* The Menninger Foundation, Topeka, Kansas, 18 pp.

APPENDIX V

References

Alexander, Franz, and French, Thomas Morton. (1946). *Psychoanalytic Therapy: Principles and Application*. Ronald Press, New York, 353 pp.

Allport, Gordon. (1937). *Personality: A Psychological Interpretation*. Holt, New York, 588 pp.

American Psychiatric Association. (1952, 1968). *Diagnostic and Statistical Manual of Mental Disorders, 2nd ed*. American Psychiatric Association, Washington, D.C., 134 pp.

American Psychiatric Association. (1980). *Diagnostic and Statistical Manual of Mental Disorders, 3rd ed*. American Psychiatric Association, Washington, D.C., 494 pp.

Appelbaum, Ann. (1972). A Critical Re-Examination of the Concept "Motivation for Change" in Psychoanalytic Treatment. *International Journal of Psycho-Analysis, 53*:51–59.

Appelbaum, Stephen A. (1973). Psychological-Mindedness: Word, Concept and Essence. *International Journal of Psycho-Analysis, 54*:35–46.

Appelbaum, Stephen A. (1975). The Idealization of Insight. *International Journal of Psychoanalytic Psychotherapy, 4*:272–303.

Appelbaum, Stephen A. (1976). The Dangerous Edge of Insight. *Psychotherapy, 13*:202–206.

Appelbaum, Stephen A. (1977). *The Anatomy of Change*. Plenum Press, New York, 308 pp.

Appelbaum, Stephen A., Coyne, Lolafaye, and Siegal, Richard S. (1969). Change in IQ during and after Long-Term Psychotherapy. *Journal of Projective Techniques, 33*:290–297.

Appelbaum, Stephen A., Coyne, Lolafaye, and Siegal, Richard S. (1970). Routes to Change in IQ during and after Long-Term Psychotherapy. *Journal of Nervous and Mental Disease, 151*:310–315.

Arlow, Jacob A. (1981). Theories of Pathogenesis. *Psychoanalytic Quarterly, 50*:488–514.

Bachrach, Henry M. (1980). Analyzability: A Clinical-Research Perspective. *Psychoanalysis and Contemporary Thought, 3*:85–116.

Bachrach, Henry M., and Leaff, Louis A. (1978). "Analyzability": A Systematic Review of the Clinical and Quantitative Literature. *Journal of the American Psychoanalytic Association, 26*:881–920.

Bergin, Allen E., and Strupp, Hans H. (1972). *Changing Frontiers in the Science of Psychotherapy*. Aldine-Atherton, Chicago and New York, 468 pp.

Bibring, Edward. (1937). Symposium on the Theory of the Therapeutic Results of Psycho-Analysis. *International Journal of Psycho-Analysis, 18*:170–189.

Bibring, Edward. (1954). Psychoanalysis and the Dynamic Psychotherapies. *Journal of the American Psychoanalytic Association, 2*:745–770.

Blum, Harold. (1979). The Curative and Creative Aspects of Insight. *Journal of the American Psychoanalytic Association, 27* (Suppl.):41–69.

The Changing Scene in Clinical Trials. (1980). *Triangle, Sandoz Journal of Medical Science, 19*:75–118.

Coyne, Lolafaye. (unpublished manuscript). *The Quantitative Measurement of Change.* The Menninger Foundation, Topeka, Kansas, 19 pp.

Cross, Alan W., and Churchill, Larry R. (1982). Ethical and Cultural Dimensions of Informed Consent: A Case Study and Analysis. *Annals of Internal Medicine, 96*:110–113.

Deutsch, Helene. (1959). Psychoanalytic Therapy in the Light of Follow-Up. *Journal of the American Psychoanalytic Association, 7*:445–458.

Dewald, Paul A. (1964). *Psychotherapy: A Dynamic Approach.* Basic Books, New York, 307 pp.

Eissler, Kurt R. (1953). The Effect of the Structure of the Ego on Psychoanalytic Technique. *Journal of the American Psychoanalytic Association, 1*:104–141.

Epstein, Nathan B., and Vlok, Louis A. (1981). Research on the Results of Psychotherapy: A Summary of Evidence. *American Journal of Psychiatry, 138*:1027–1035.

Erikson, Erik H. (1958). The Nature of Clinical Evidence. *Daedalus, 87*:65–87.

Fairbairn, W. Ronald D. (1954). *An Object-Relations Theory of the Personality.* Basic Books, New York, 312 pp.

Fenichel, Otto. (1941). *Problems of Psychoanalytic Technique. Psychoanalytic Quarterly,* Albany, N.Y., 130 pp.

Frank, Jerome D. (1959). Problems of Controls in Psychotherapy as Exemplified by the Psychotherapy Research Project of the Phipps Psychiatric Clinic. In *Research in Psychotherapy, Vol. 1,* Rubinstein, Eli A., and Parloff, Morris B. (eds.), pp. 10–26, American Psychological Association, Washington, D.C.

Freud, Anna. (1954). The Widening Scope of Indications for Psychoanalysis: Discussion. *Journal of the American Psychoanalytic Association, 2*:607–620.

Freud, Sigmund, with Breuer, Josef. (1895). Studies on Hysteria. *Standard Edition, 2*:1–305.

Freud, Sigmund. (1905). On Psychotherapy. *Standard Edition, 7*:255–268, 1953.

Freud, Sigmund. (1911–1915). Papers on Technique. *Standard Edition, 12*:83–173, 1958.

Freud, Sigmund. (1912). The Dynamics of Transference. *Standard Edition, 12*:97–108, 1958.

Freud, Sigmund. (1913). Introduction to Pfister's *The Psychoanalytic Method. Standard Edition, 12*:327–331, 1958.

Freud, Sigmund. (1914). On Narcissism: An Introduction. *Standard Edition, 14*:67–102, 1957.

Freud, Sigmund. (1916). Some Character-Types Met with in Psychoanalytic Work. *Standard Edition, 14*:309–333, 1957.

Frued, Sigmund. (1917). Introductory Lectures on Psychoanalysis, Part III. *Standard Edition, 16*:241–496, 1963.

Freud, Sigmund. (1918). From the History of an Infantile Neurosis. *Standard Edition, 17*:1–122, 1955.

Freud, Sigmund. (1923). The Ego and the Id. *Standard Edition, 19*:1–66, 1961.

Freud, Sigmund. (1924a). The Dissolution of the Oedipus Complex. *Standard Edition, 19*:171–179, 1961.

Freud, Sigmund. (1924b). The Economic Problem of Masochism. *Standard Edition, 19*:155–170, 1961.

Freud, Sigmund. (1925). Preface to Aichhorn's *Wayward Youth. Standard Edition, 19*:271–275, 1961.

Freud, Sigmund. (1933). New Introductory Lectures on Psycho-Analysis. *Standard Edition, 22*:1–182, 1964.

Freud, Sigmund. (1937). Analysis Terminable and Interminable. *Standard Edition, 23*:209–253, 1964.

Freud, Sigmund. (1940). An Outline of Psycho-Analysis. *Standard Edition, 23*:139–207, 1964.

Fromm-Reichmann, Frieda. (1950). *Principles of Intensive Psychotherapy.* University of Chicago Press, Chicago, 246 pp.

Gardiner, Muriel. (ed.) (1971). *The Wolf Man by the Wolf Man.* Basic Books, New York, 370 pp.

Gill, Merton M. (1951). Ego Psychology and Psychotherapy. *Psychoanalytic Quarterly, 20*: 62–71.

Gill, Merton M. (1954). Psychoanalysis and Exploratory Psychotherapy. *Journal of the American Psychoanalytic Association, 2*:771–797.

Gill, Merton M. (1979). The Analysis of the Transference. *Journal of the American Psychoanalytic Association, 27*:263–288.

Gill, Merton M., and Muslin, Hyman L. (1976). Early Interpretation of Transference. *Journal of the American Psychoanalytic Association, 24*:779–794.

Glover, Edward. (1931). The Therapeutic Effect of Inexact Interpretation. *International Journal of Psycho-Analysis, 12*:397–411.

Glover, Edward. (1954). The Indications for Psychoanalysis. *Journal of Mental Science, 100*: 393–401.

Greenson, Ralph R. (1967). *The Technique and Practice of Psychoanalysis, Vol. 1.* International Universities Press, New York, 452 pp.

Grinberg de Ekboir, Julia, and Lichtmann, Ana. (1982). Genuine Self-Analysis Is Impossible. *International Review of Psycho-Analysis, 9*:75–83.

Guntrip, Harry. (1961). *Personality Structure and Human Interaction.* Hogarth Press, London, 456 pp.

Hall, Bernard H., and Wallerstein, Robert S. (1960). Operational Problems of Psychotherapy Research: II. Termination Studies. *Bulletin of The Menninger Clinic, 24*:190–214.

Hammett, Van Buren O. (1961). Delusional Transference. *American Journal of Psychotherapy, 15*:574–581.

Horwitz, Leonard. (1974). *Clinical Prediction in Psychotherapy.* Jason Aronson, New York, 372 pp.

Horwitz, Leonard, and Appelbaum, Ann. (1966). A Hierarchical Ordering of Assumptions about Psychotherapy. *Psychotherapy, 3*:71–80.

Huxster, Howard, Lower, Richard, and Escoll, Philip. (1975). Some Pitfalls in the Assessment of Analyzability in a Psychoanalytic Clinic. *Journal of the American Psychoanalytic Association, 23*:90–106.

Jacobson, Edith. (1964). *The Self and the Object World.* International Universities Press, New York, 250 pp.

Jahoda, Marie. (1958). *Current Concepts of Positive Mental Health* (Joint Commission on Mental Illness and Health Monograph Series, No. 1). Basic Books, New York, 136 pp.

Kernberg, Otto. (1975). *Borderline Conditions and Pathological Narcissism.* Jason Aronson, New York, 361 pp.

Kernberg, Otto. (1976). *Object Relations Theory and Clinical Psychoanalysis.* Jason Aronson, New York, 299 pp.

Kernberg, Otto. (1980). *Internal World and External Reality: Object Relations Theory Applied.* Jason Aronson, New York, 359 pp.

Kernberg, Otto F., Burstein, Esther D., Coyne, Lolafaye, Appelbaum, Ann, Horwitz, Leonard, and Voth, Harold. (1972). Psychotherapy and Psychoanalysis: Final Report of the Menninger Foundation's Psychotherapy Research Project. *Bulletin of The Menninger Clinic, 36*:1–275.

Knight, Robert P. (1937a). The Dynamics and Treatment of Chronic Alcohol Addiction. *Bulletin of The Menninger Clinic, 1*:233–250.

Knight, Robert P. (1937b). The Dynamics of Chronic Alcoholism. *Journal of Nervous and Mental Disease, 86*:538–548.

Knight, Robert P. (1938). The Psychoanalytic Treatment in a Sanatorium of Chronic Addiction to Alcohol. *Journal of the American Medical Association, 111*:1443–1448.

Knight, Robert P. (1953). Borderline States. *Bulletin of The Menninger Clinic, 17*:1–12.

Kohut, Heinz. (1971). *The Analysis of the Self: A Systematic Approach to the Psychoanalytic*

Treatment of Narcissistic Personality Disorders. International Universities Press, New York, 368 pp.

Kohut, Heinz. (1977). *The Restoration of the Self.* International Universities Press, New York, 345 pp.

Kramer, Maria K. (1959). On the Continuation of the Analytic Process after Psychoanalysis (a Self-Observation). *International Journal of Psycho-Analysis, 40*:17–25.

Kris, Ernst. (1956). On Some Vicissitudes of Insight in Psychoanalysis. *International Journal of Psycho-Analysis, 37*:445–455.

Langs, Robert. (1973). *The Technique of Psychoanalytic Psychotherapy, Vol. 1.* Jason Aronson, New York, 659 pp.

Langs, Robert. (1974). *The Technique of Psychoanalytic Psychotherapy, Vol. 2.* Jason Aronson, New York, 552 pp.

Lewin, Kurt. (1935). *A Dynamic Theory of Personality: Selected Papers.* McGraw-Hill, New York, 286 pp.

Lewy, Ernst. (1941). The Return of the Repression. *Bulletin of The Menninger Clinic, 5*:47–55.

Loewald, Hans W. (1960). On the Therapeutic Action of Psycho-Analysis. *International Journal of Psycho-Analysis, 41*:16–33.

Loftus, Elizabeth F., and Fries, James F. (1979). Editorial: Informed Consent May Be Hazardous to Health. *Science, 204*:11.

Lower, Richard, Escoll, Philip, and Huxster, Howard. (1972). Bases for Judgments of Analyzability. *Journal of the American Psychoanalytic Association, 20*:610–621.

Luborsky, Lester. (1962a). Clinicians' Judgments of Mental Health: A Proposed Scale. *Archives of General Psychiatry, 7*:407–417.

Luborsky, Lester. (1962b). The Patient's Personality and Psychotherapeutic Change. In *Research in Psychotherapy, Vol. 2,* Strupp, Hans H., and Luborsky, Lester (eds.), pp. 115–133, American Psychological Association, Washington, D.C.

Luborsky, Lester. (1975). Clinicians' Judgments of Mental Health: Specimen Case Descriptions and Forms for the Health–Sickness Rating Scale. *Bulletin of The Menninger Clinic, 39*:448–480.

Luborsky, Lester, and Bachrach, Henry. (1974). Factors Influencing Clinicians' Judgments of Mental Health: Eighteen Experiences with the Health–Sickness Rating Scale. *Archives of General Psychiatry, 31*:292–299.

Luborsky, Lester, Fabian, Michalina, Hall, Bernard H., Ticho, Ernst, and Ticho, Gertrude R. (1958). Treatment Variables. *Bulletin of The Menninger Clinic, 22*:126–147.

Luborsky, Lester, and Sargent, Helen D. (1956). Sample Use of Method. *Bulletin of The Menninger Clinic, 20*:262–276.

Macalpine, Ida. (1950). The Development of the Transference. *Psychoanalytic Quarterly, 19*:501–539.

Mahler, Margaret S. (1952). On Child Psychosis and Schizophrenia: Autistic and Symbiotic Infantile Psychoses. *Psychoanalytic Study of the Child, 7*:286–305.

Mahler, Margaret S., in collaboration with Furer, Manuel. (1968). *On Human Symbiosis and the Vicissitudes of Individuation, Vol. 1, Infantile Psychosis.* International Universities Press, New York, 271 pp.

Mahler, Margaret S., Pine, Fred, and Bergman, Anni. (1975). *The Psychological Birth of the Human Infant: Symbiosis and Individuation.* Basic Books, New York, 308 pp.

Malan, David H. (1963). *A Study of Brief Psychotherapy.* Tavistock, London, 312 pp.

Mann, James. (1973). *Time-Limited Psychotherapy.* Harvard University Press, Cambridge, Mass., 202 pp.

Marks, Isaac. (1981). *Cure and Care of Neuroses: Theory and Practice of Behavioral Psychotherapy.* Wiley, New York, 331 pp.

Marmor, Judd. (1953). Orality in the Hysterical Personality. *Journal of the American Psychoanalytic Association, 1*:656–671.

Mayman, Martin, and Sells, Saul B. (1960). Helen Durham Sargent. *Journal of Projective Techniques,* 24:119–123.

McLaughlin, James T. (1981). Transference, Psychic Reality, and Countertransference. *Psychoanalytic Quarterly,* 50:639–664.

Neubauer, Peter. (1979). The Role of Insight in Psychoanalysis. *Journal of the American Psychoanalytic Association,* 27 (Suppl.):29–40.

Norman, Haskell F., Blacker, Kay H., Oremland, Jerome D., and Barrett, William G. (1976). The Fate of the Transference Neurosis after Termination of a Satisfactory Analysis. *Journal of the American Psychoanalytic Association,* 24:471–498.

Oremland, Jerome D., Blacker, Kay H. and Norman, Haskell F. (1975). Incompleteness in "Successful" Psychoanalyses: A Follow-Up Study. *Journal of the American Psychoanalytic Association,* 23:819–844.

Parloff, Morris B. (1979). Can Psychotherapy Research Guide the Policy Maker?: A Little Knowledge May Be a Dangerous Thing. *American Psychologist,* 34:296–306.

Pfeffer, Arnold Z. (1959). A Procedure for Evaluating the Results of Psychoanalysis: A Preliminary Report. *Journal of the American Psychoanalytic Association,* 7:418–444.

Pfeffer, Arnold Z. (1961). Follow-Up Study of a Satisfactory Analysis. *Journal of the American Psychoanalytic Association,* 9:698–718.

Pfeffer, Arnold Z. (1963). The Meaning of the Analyst after Analysis: A Contribution to the Theory of Therapeutic Results. *Journal of the American Psychoanalytic Association,* 11:229–244.

Rangell, Leo. (1954). Similarities and Differences between Psychoanalysis and Dynamic Psychotherapy. *Journal of the American Psychoanalytic Association,* 2:734–744.

Rangell, Leo. (1981). Psychoanalysis and Dynamic Psychotherapy: Similarities and Differences Twenty-Five Years Later. *Psychoanalytic Quarterly,* 50:665–693.

Rapaport, David. (1945). *Diagnostic Psychological Testing, Vol. 1.* Year Book Medical Publishers, Chicago, 573 pp.

Rapaport, David. (1946). *Diagnostic Psychological Testing, Vol. 2.* Year Book Medical Publishers, Chicago, 516 pp.

Rapaport, David. (1960). *The Structure of Psychoanalytic Theory: A Systematizing Attempt* (Psychological Issues 2: Monograph 6). International Universities Press, New York, 158 pp.

Reich, Annie. (1950). In Symposia on the Termination of Psycho-Analytical Treatment and on the Criteria for the Termination of an Analysis. *International Journal of Psycho-Analysis,* 31:78–80.

Reider, Norman. (1953). A Type of Transference to Institutions. *Bulletin of The Menninger Clinic,* 17:58–63.

Reider, Norman. (1957). Transference Psychosis. *Journal of the Hillside Hospital,* 6:131–149.

Robbins, Lewis L., and Wallerstein, Robert S. (1956). Orientation. *Bulletin of The Menninger Clinic,* 20:223–225.

Robbins, Lewis L., and Wallerstein, Robert S. (1959). The Research Strategy and Tactics of the Psychotherapy Research Project of The Menninger Foundation and the Problem of Controls. In *Research in Psychotherapy, Vol. 1,* Rubinstein, Eli A., and Parloff, Morris B. (eds.), pp. 27–43, American Psychological Association, Washington, D.C.

Rogers, Carl R. (1951). *Client-Centered Therapy: Its Current Practice, Implications and Theory.* Houghton Mifflin, Boston, 560 pp.

Rogers, Carl R., and Dymond, Rosalind F. (eds.) (1954). *Psychotherapy and Personality Change: Co-Ordinated Research Studies in the Client-Centered Approach.* University of Chicago Press, Chicago, 447 pp.

Rubinstein, Eli A., and Parloff, Morris B. (eds.) (1959). *Research in Psychotherapy, Vol. 1.* American Psychological Association, Washington, D.C., 293 pp.

Sargent, Helen D. (1956a). Design. *Bulletin of The Menninger Clinic,* 20:234–238.

Sargent, Helen D. (1956b). Rationale. *Bulletin of The Menninger Clinic,* 20:226–233.

Sargent, Helen D. (1960). Methodological Problems of Follow-Up Studies in Psychotherapy Research. *American Journal of Orthopsychiatry, 30*:495–506.

Sargent, Helen D. (1961). Intrapsychic Change: Methodological Problems in Psychotherapy Research. *Psychiatry, 24*:93–108.

Sargent, Helen D., Coyne, Lolafaye, Wallerstein, Robert S., and Holtzman, Wayne H. (1967). An Approach to the Quantitative Problems of Psychoanalytic Research. *Journal of Clinical Psychology, 23*:243–291.

Sargent, Helen D., Horwitz, Leonard, Wallerstein, Robert S., and Appelbaum, Ann. (1968). *Prediction in Psychotherapy Research: A Method for the Transformation of Clinical Judgments into Testable Hypotheses* (Psychological Issues 6: Monograph 21). International Universities Press, New York, 146 pp.

Sargent, Helen D., Modlin, Herbert C., Faris, Mildred T., and Voth, Harold M. (1958). Situational Variables. *Bulletin of The Menninger Clinic, 22*:148–166.

Sarton, George. (1960). Notes on the Reviewing of Learned Books. *Science, 131*:1182–1186.

Schlesinger, Herbert J. (1969). Diagnosis and Prescription for Psychotherapy. *Bulletin of The Menninger Clinic, 33*:269–278.

Schlessinger, Nathan, and Robbins, Fred. (1974). Assessment and Follow-Up in Psychoanalysis. *Journal of the American Psychoanalytic Association, 22*:542–567.

Schlessinger, Nathan, and Robbins, Fred. (1975). The Psychoanalytic Process: Recurrent Patterns of Conflict and Changes in Ego Function. *Journal of the American Psychoanalytic Association, 23*:761–782.

Schwartz, Fred. (1981). Psychic Structure. *International Journal of Psycho-Analysis, 62*:61–72.

Shlien, John M. (ed.) (1968). *Research in Psychotherapy, Vol. 3*. American Psychological Association, Washington, D.C., 618 pp.

Siegal, Richard S., and Rosen, Irwin C. (1962). Character Style and Anxiety Tolerance: A Study in Intrapsychic Change. In *Research in Psychotherapy, Vol. 2*, Strupp, Hans H., and Luborsky, Lester (eds.), pp. 206–217, American Psychological Association, Washington, D.C.

Sifneos, Peter E. (1972). *Short-Term Psychotherapy and Emotional Crisis*. Harvard University Press, Cambridge, Mass., 299 pp.

Simmel, Ernst. (1929). Psycho-Analytic Treatment in a Sanatorium. *International Journal of Psycho-Analysis, 10*:70–89.

Smith, Mary Lee, Glass, Gene V., and Miller, Thomas I. (1980). *The Benefits of Psychotherapy*. Johns Hopkins University Press, Baltimore, 269 pp.

Spitzer, Robert L., and Klein, Donald F. (eds.) (1976). *Evaluation of Psychological Therapies*. Johns Hopkins University Press, Baltimore, 312 pp.

Stone, Leo. (1951). Psychoanalysis and Brief Psychotherapy. *Psychoanalytic Quarterly, 20*: 215–236.

Stone, Leo. (1954). The Widening Scope of Indications for Psychoanalysis. *Journal of the American Psychoanalytic Association, 2*:567–594.

Stone, Leo. (1961). *The Psychoanalytic Situation: An Examination of its Development and Essential Nature*. International Universities Press, New York, 160 pp.

Stone, Leo. (1981). Some Thoughts on the "Here and Now" in Psychoanalytic Technique and Process. *Psychoanalytic Quarterly, 50*:709–733.

Strachey, James. (1934). The Nature of the Therapeutic Action of Psycho-Analysis. *International Journal of Psycho-Analysis, 15*:127–159.

Strupp, Hans H. (1960). Some Comments on the Future of Research in Psychotherapy. *Behavioral Science, 5*:60–71.

Strupp, Hans H. (1964). *A Bibliography of Research in Psychotherapy*. Psychotherapy Research Project, Department of Psychiatry, University of North Carolina School of Medicine, Chapel Hill, 105 pp.

Strupp, Hans H., & Bergin, Allen E. (1968). *Research in Individual Psychotherapy: A Bibliography* (Publication of the National Clearinghouse for Mental Health Information). National Institute of Mental Health, Chevy Chase, Md., 167 pp.

Strupp, Hans H., and Bergin, Allen E. (1969a). Critical Evaluation of "Some Empirical and Conceptual Bases for Coordinated Research in Psychotherapy." *International Journal of Psychiatry*, 7:113–168.

Strupp, Hans H., and Bergin, Allen E. (1969b). Some Empirical and Conceptual Bases for Coordinated Research in Psychotherapy: A Critical Review of Issues, Trends, and Evidence. *International Journal of Psychiatry*, 7:17–90.

Strupp, Hans H., and Luborsky, Lester. (eds.) (1962). *Research in Psychotherapy, Vol. 2*. American Psychological Association, Washington, D.C., 342 pp.

Stunkard, Albert J. (1976). *The Pain of Obesity*. Bull, Palo Alto, Calif., 236 pp.

Ticho, Gertrude R. (1967). On Self-Analysis. *International Journal of Psycho-Analysis*, 48:308–318.

van der Waals, Hermann G. (1965). Problems of Narcissism. *Bulletin of The Menninger Clinic*, 29:293–311.

Voth, Harold M., Modlin, Herbert C., and Orth, Marjorie H. (1962). Situational Variables in the Assessment of Psychotherapeutic Results. *Bulletin of The Menninger Clinic, 26*: 73–81.

Voth, Harold M., and Orth, Marjorie H. (1973). *Psychotherapy and the Role of the Environment*. Behavioral Publications, New York, 354 pp.

Waelder, Robert. (1962). Psychoanalysis, Scientific Method and Philosophy. *Journal of the American Psychoanalytic Association*, 10:617–637.

Wallerstein, Robert S. (1960). Helen D. Sargent and the Psychotherapy Research Project. *Bulletin of The Menninger Clinic*, 24:159–163.

Wallerstein, Robert S. (1961). Report of the Psychotherapy Research Project of The Menninger Foundation: January 1954–July 1961. *International Mental Health Research Newsletter*, 3:12–15.

Wallerstein, Robert S. (1963). The Problem of the Assessment of Change in Psychotherapy. *International Journal of Psycho-Analysis*, 44:31–41.

Wallerstein, Robert S. (1964). The Role of Prediction in Theory Building in Psychoanalysis. *Journal of the American Psychoanalytic Association*, 12:675–691.

Wallerstein, Robert S. (1965). The Goals of Psychoanalysis: A Survey of Analytic Viewpoints. *Journal of the American Psychoanalytic Association*, 13:748–770.

Wallerstein, Robert S. (1966). The Psychotherapy Research Project of The Menninger Foundation: An Overview at the Midway Point. In *Methods in Research in Psychotherapy*, Gottschalk, Louis A., and Auerbach, Arthur H. (eds.), pp. 500–516, Appleton-Century-Crofts, New York.

Wallerstein, Robert S. (1967). Reconstruction and Mastery in the Transference Psychosis. *Journal of the American Psychoanalytic Association*, 15:551–583.

Wallerstein, Robert S. (1968). The Psychotherapy Research Project of The Menninger Foundation: A Semi-Final View. In *Research in Psychotherapy, Vol. 3*, Shlien, John M. (ed.), pp. 584–605, American Psychological Association, Washington, D.C.

Wallerstein, Robert S. (1969). Introduction to Panel on Psychoanalysis and Psychotherapy: The Relationship of Psychoanalysis to Psychotherapy — Current Issues. *International Journal of Psycho-Analysis*, 50:117–126.

Wallerstein, Robert S. (1973). Psychoanalytic Perspectives on the Problem of Reality. *Journal of the American Psychoanalytic Association*, 21:5–33.

Wallerstein, Robert S. (1977a). Discussion of Otto Kernberg's Presentation, "Developments in the Theory of Psychoanalytic Psychotherapy," University of California San Francisco.

Wallerstein, Robert S. (1977b). Psychotherapy Research: One Paradigm. In *Communication and Social Interaction*, Ostwald, Peter (ed.), pp. 189–202, Grune & Stratton, New York.

Wallerstein, Robert S. (1980–1981). Diagnosis Revisited (and Revisited): The Case of Hysteria

and the Hysterical Personality. *International Journal of Psychoanalytic Psychotherapy,*
8:533–547.

Wallerstein, Robert S. (1981). The Bipolar Self: Discussion of Alternative Perspectives. *Journal
of the American Psychoanalytic Association, 29*:377–394.

Wallerstein, Robert S. (1983a). Self Psychology and "Classical" Psychoanalytic Psychology:
The Nature of their Relationship. In *The Future of Psychoanalysis*, Goldberg, Arnold (ed.),
pp. 19–63, International Universities Press, New York. (Reprinted in *Psychoanalysis and
Contemporary Thought, 6*:553–595, 1983; printed in condensed form in *Reflections on
Self Psychology*, Lichtenberg, Joseph D., and Kaplan, Samuel [eds.], pp. 313–337, Analytic
Press, Hillsdale, N.J., 1983.)

Wallerstein, Robert S. (1983b). Some Thoughts about Insight and Psychoanalysis. *Israel Journal
of Psychiatry and Allied Professions, 20*:33–43.

Wallerstein, Robert S., and Robbins, Lewis L. (1956). Concepts. *Bulletin of The Menninger
Clinic, 20*:239–262.

Wallerstein, Robert S., and Robbins, Lewis L. (1958). Further Notes on Design and Concepts.
Bulletin of The Menninger Clinic, 22:117–125.

Wallerstein, Robert S., and Robbins, Lewis L. (1960). Operational Problems of Psychotherapy
Research: I. Initial Studies. *Bulletin of The Menninger Clinic, 24*:164–189.

Wallerstein, Robert S., Robbins, Lewis L., Sargent, Helen D., and Luborsky, Lester. (1956).
The Psychotherapy Research Project of The Menninger Foundation: Rationale, Method
and Sample Use. First Report. *Bulletin of The Menninger Clinic, 20*:221–278.

Wallerstein, Robert S., and Sampson, Harold. (1971). Issues in Research in the Psychoanalytic
Process. *International Journal of Psycho-Analysis, 52*:11–50.

Ward, Joe H., Jr. (1963). Hierarchical Grouping to Optimize an Objective Function. *Journal
of the American Statistical Association, 58*:236–244.

Waskow, Irene E., and Parloff, Morris B. (eds.) (1975). *Psychotherapy Change Measures.*
National Institute of Mental Health, Rockville, Md., 327 pp.

Watterson, Donald J. (1954). Problems in the Evaluation of Psychotherapy. *Bulletin of The
Menninger Clinic, 18*:232–241.

Wheelis, Allen. (1950). The Place of Action in Personality Change. *Psychiatry, 13*:135–148.

Zetzel, Elizabeth R. (1956a). An Approach to the Relation between Concept and Content in
Psychoanalytic Theory (with Special Reference to the Work of Melanie Klein and Her Followers). *Psychoanalytic Study of the Child, 11*:99–121.

Zetzel, Elizabeth R. (1956b). Current Concepts of Transference. *International Journal of
Psycho-Analysis, 37*:369–376.

Zetzel, Elizabeth R. (1968). The So-Called Good Hysteric. *International Journal of Psycho-
Analysis, 49*:256–260.

Name Index

Subject Index

Acting out, 131, 132
  transference, 428–432, 470, 471, 629
Addictions, patient group demographics, 70, 71 (*see also* Alcoholism/alcohol abuse; Drug abuse/addiction)
Adolescence, 255, 256
  adjustment reaction to, versus preschizophrenia, 167
  anorexia nervosa, 256
  downward age trend in hospitalization, 522
  overall treatment results, 521–529
    impulse and character, cf. psychotic disorder, 522, 523
  separation from family, beneficial effects, 233
  suicide, 523
Affect-inhibition, Heiress, 423
After-education, supportive psychotherapy, 459
Age, patient group demographics, 56, 57, 61, 62 (*see also* Adolescence)
Aggression and hostility
  toward analyst, Medical Scientist, 269
  attempt on husband's life, Heiress, 425
  toward baby, Adoptive Mother, 124, 148, 149, 295, 296, 301, 302
  as central complaint, 124, 125
    warding off depression, 124
  covert, 124
  predatory lifestyle, Sociopath, 545, 547, 548
  primitive rage against mother, Obese Woman, 290–292
  temper outbursts, Snake Phobia Woman, 308, 311
  therapist intolerance of, 242, 243
  violence against wife, Manic Depressive Physician, 139
  and wife's lover, 461
  withholding of sex, Involutional Woman, 378–380
Aichhorn technique, 193, 225, 241, 252, 566
Alcoholics Anonymous, 169, 498, 502–504, 614, 626, 638–640, 671, 691
Alcoholism/alcohol abuse, 121, 125–128, 131, 138, 146
  Actress, 478–480, 482
  and appropriateness of psychoanalysis, 659, 663n.
  Car Salesman, 567, 568
  concealment, 160, 161
  dissociative states, 150
  fatal fire caused by, 126
  fugue states, unauthorized pelvic exams, 126
  Heiress, 423–425
  and heroic indications for psychoanalysis, 348, 670–676, 679
  high-speed driving, 124, 125

hospitalization, 221
infantile character, 141, 142
marriage disturbances, 147, 148
Masochistic Editor, 355–357, 359–361
Medical Scientist, 266, 267, 270
and motivation for treatment, secondary gain, 172–174
parents, 406, 421, 478, 481, 482
patient group demographics, 56, 64, 66, 67, 70
-related deaths, 126, 562–567
  unconscious suicide, 570, 571
Script Writer, 556–559
spouse's, 232, 347
and success neurosis, 152
  cf. psychosis, 345, 347
supportive psychotherapy
  Housebound Phobic Woman, 392, 393, 395
  Sexual Masochist, 405, 406, 408–410
  Suspended Medical Student, 363–365, 368
  underdiagnosis, 164, 165
Alloplastic cf. autoplastic patients, 131, 132
Alterations of treatment, 205–215 (*see also* Psychoanalysis, conversion to psychotherapy; Psychoanalysis, modified)
  inappropriate therapy outside Menninger Foundation, 207, 208
  procedural alterations
    psychoanalysis, 212–214
    psychotherapy, 214
  during psychotherapy, 209–212
    expressive versus supportive, 211, 212
    hospitalization, 210
    retreatment, 208, 209
    underdiagnosis, 214
American Psychological Association, 744
  Conferences on Research in Psychotherapy, 29
"Analysis Terminable and Interminable" (Freud), 607, 703, 731
Anatomy of Change, The (Appelbaum), 18–21, 26
Anorexia, 133, 135, 136, 146, 256, 426–428, 430–432 (*see also* Bulimia)
  misdiagnosis, 167
Antabuse, 500
Antitransference cure, psychotherapy, 439–451, 708
  and appropriateness of psychoanalysis, 657
  Intellectual Fencer, 439–445
  inverse of positive dependent transference, 439
  Silent Woman, 445–451
  supportive therapy, 693

771